Collins Complete DIY Manual

Collins complete DIY manual

Albert Jackson and David Day

Collins Complete DIY Manual
was originally created for HarperCollins Publishers by Inklink/Jackson Day Jennings

This new edition first published in 2007 by

Collins, an imprint of
HarperCollinsPublishers
77-85 Fulham Palace Road
Hammersmith
London W6 8JB

Collins is a registered trademark of HarperCollins Publishers Ltd

13 12 11 10 09 08 07
7 6 5 4 3 2 1

A catalogue record for this book is available from The British Library

ISBN 978 000 725260 2

Colour reproduction by Colourscan, Singapore
Printed and bound by Rotolito Lombarda, Italy

PLEASE NOTE
Great care has been taken to ensure that the information contained in the Collins Complete DIY Manual is accurate. However, the law concerning Building Regulations, planning, local bylaws and related matters is neither static nor simple. A book of this nature cannot replace specialist advice in appropriate cases and therefore no responsibility can be accepted by the publishers or by the authors for any loss or damage caused by reliance upon the accuracy of such information.

If you live outside Britain, your local conditions may mean that some of this information is not appropriate. If in doubt, always consult a qualified electrician, plumber or surveyor.

Authors
Albert Jackson and David Day

Contributors
Mike Lawrence (Repairs & Improvements, Storage)
David Bridle (Plumbing and Heating)
George Baxter (Planning Ahead)

Photographers
Airedale/David Murphy
Colin Bowling
Focus Publishing
Paul Chave
Ben Jennings
Neil Waving

(see page 551 for full details of photography)

Set Building/Projects for Photography
Airedale
David Bridle
Bill Brooker
Focus Publishing

Consultants
Roger Bisby (Plumbing and Heating)
John Dees (Electricity)

Design
Elizabeth Standley
Keith Miller

New Illustrations
Graham White

Illustrations
Robin Harris
John Pinder

Editors
Peter Leek
Barbara Dixon

Proofreader and Indexer
Mary Morton

How to use this book

Today's home improver enjoys the benefits of a highly sophisticated market that reflects the way 'do it yourself' has developed over the years. He or she has become used to a ready supply of well-designed products and materials, which produce first-class results that many a professional would be proud of.

Any work of reference for this generation of home improvers must reflect the same high standards in its presentation, depth of information and simplicity of use. No-one reads a book of this kind from start to finish in the hope of absorbing all the information in one go. Instead, every reader wants to read about his or her area of special interest or refer to a particular problem without having to extract it from page after page of continuous text. This book has been written and designed to make the location of specific information as straightforward as possible by dividing the subject matter into clearly defined, colour-coded chapters. And then every page is designed to present that information in easily digestible sections.

There is a detailed index for easy reference, but to guide you quickly from chapter to chapter or from one section to another, each page contains cross-references that refer you to other information related to the task in hand.

Main headings
Black headings introduce the main topic dealt with in a particular section of a chapter. Subsequent pages within the same section have main headings in grey.

Running heads
As a guide to the number of pages devoted to a particular subject, a running head identifies the broad outline of subject matter to be found on each page.

Sub headings
The main text is divided by easily identifiable sub headings so that you can locate a particular task or even a single stage in the work. It is a useful feature when you want to refresh your memory without having to reread the whole page.

Feature boxes
Clearly defined boxes isolate important information, such as safety tips and special tools or techniques.

Colour-coding
Colour-coded bars designate the extent of each chapter for easy identification.

462 PATHS, DRIVES AND PATIOS PAVING SLABS

Paving slabs

Paving slabs are made either by hydraulic pressing or by casting in moulds to create the desired finish. Pigments and selected aggregates added to the concrete mix are used to create the illusion of a range of muted colours or natural stone. Combining two or more colours or textures within the same area of paving can be very striking.

Regular or informal paving
Constructing a simple grid from square slabs (left) is relatively easy. Although mixed paving (below) is more difficult to lay, it is richer in texture, colour and shape.

Shapes and sizes

Although some manufacturers offer a wider choice than others, there's a fairly standard range of shapes and modular sizes. It is usually possible to carry the largest slabs without help, but it's a good idea to get an assistant to help manoeuvre them carefully into place.

Square and rectangular
A single size and shape can be employed to make grid-like patterns or, when staggered, to create a bonded-brickwork effect. Use rectangular slabs to form a basket-weave or herringbone pattern. Alternatively, combine different sizes so as to create the impression of random paving, or mix slabs with a different type of paving to create a colourful contrast. Mixing slabs in this way requires a degree of restraint to prevent a paved area looking uncoordinated – but if you get it right, the result can be a feast for the eye.

Hexagonal slabs
Hexagonal slabs form honeycomb patterns. You can use half slabs to edge areas that are paved in straight lines.

Half-hexagonal slabs

Honeycomb pattern

Tapered slabs
Use tapered slabs to edge ponds and for encircling trees or making curved steps. Progressively larger slabs can be used for laying circular areas of paving.

Circular slabs
Circular slabs make perfect individual stepping stones across a lawn or flower bed, but for a wide area fill the spaces between with cobbles or gravel.

Butted circular slabs

SEE ALSO > Brick pavers 467

PATHS, DRIVES AND PATIOS PAVING SLABS 463

Laying paving slabs

Although laying paving slabs involves a good deal of physical labour, in terms of technique it's no more complicated than tiling a wall. Accurate setting out and careful laying, especially during the early stages, will help you achieve perfect results.

Setting out the area of paving

Wherever feasible, plan an area of paving so that it can be laid with whole slabs only. This eliminates the arduous task of cutting units to fit. Use pegs and string to mark out the perimeter of the paved area, and check the measurements before you excavate.

You can use a straight wall as a datum line and measure away from the wall. Or if the location dictates that you have to lay slabs near the house, allow for a 100 to 150mm (4 to 6in) margin of gravel between the paving and wall. A gravel margin not only saves time and money by using fewer slabs, but also provides an area for planting climbers and for adequate drainage to keep the wall dry.

Even so, establish a slope of 16mm per metre (⅝in per yard) across the paving, so that most of the surface water will drain into the garden. Any paving must be 150mm (6in) below a damp-proof course, in order to protect the building.

As paving slabs are made to fairly precise dimensions, marking out an area simply involves accurate measurement, allowing for a 6 to 10mm (¼ to ⅜in) gap between the slabs. Some slabs are cast with sloping edges to provide a tapered joint and should be butted edge to edge.

Preparing a base for the paving
Paving slabs must be laid upon a firm, level base, but the depth and substance of that base depend on the type of soil and the proposed use of the paving.

For straightforward patios and paths, remove vegetable matter and topsoil to allow for the thickness of the slabs, plus a 35mm (1½in) layer of sharp sand and an extra 18mm (¾in) – so the paving will be below the level of surrounding turf, in order to prevent damage to your lawn mower. Compact the soil with a garden roller, and then spread the sand with a rake and level it by scraping and tamping with a length of timber.

To support heavier loads, or if the soil is composed of clay or peat, lay a subbase of firmly compacted hardcore – broken bricks or crushed stone – to a depth of 75 to 100mm (3 to 4in) before spreading the sand to level the surface. If you plan to park vehicles on the paving, increase the depth of hardcore to 150mm (6in).

Cutting paving slabs

It is often necessary to trim concrete paving slabs to size in order to fit narrow margins.

Mark a line across a slab with chalk or a soft pencil. Place the slab on a bed of sand and, wearing plastic goggles, use a bolster and hammer to chisel a groove about 3mm (⅛in) deep along the line.

Turn the slab face down and, with the hammer, tap firmly along the groove until the slab splits. If need be, clean up the edge with a bolster.

To obtain a perfect cut, hire an angle grinder fitted with a stone-cutting disc.

Using an angle grinder
An angle grinder makes short work of a concrete paving slab. Wear protective gloves, goggles and a face mask.

Level the sand base with a piece of wood

Laying and levelling the slabs

1 Lay five blobs of mortar under each slab

3 Check the fall with a spirit level

2 Level the slab with a block and hammer

4 Fill the joints with a dry mortar mix

Lay the edging slabs on the sand, working in both directions from a corner. When you are satisfied with their positions, lift the slabs one at a time, so you can set them on a bed of mortar (1 part cement : 4 parts sand). Lay a large blob of mortar under each corner, and one more to support the centre of the slab (**1**). If you intend to drive vehicles across the slabs, lay a continuous bed of mortar about 50mm (2in) thick. Wet the back of each slab just before you lay it on top of the mortar. Level each slab by tapping with a heavy hammer, using a block of wood to protect the surface (**2**). Add mortar to fill flush any gaps under the the slabs.

Lay three slabs at a time, inserting spacers between, then check the alignment. To gauge the slope across the paving, drive datum pegs along the high side, with the top of each peg corresponding to the finished surface of the paving, and then use a straightedge with a packing piece under one end to check the fall on the slabs (**3**). Lay the other slabs, each time working outwards from the corner in order to keep the joints square. Remove the spacers before the mortar sets, but don't walk on the paving for 2 to 3 days.

To fill the gaps between the paving slabs, brush a dry mortar mix of 1 part cement : 3 parts sand into the open joints (**4**), then sprinkle the area with a very fine spray of water to consolidate the mortar.

SEE ALSO > Mixing mortar 441, Crossfall 456, Subbase 457, 459

Dimensions
Although most trade suppliers use the metric system, some people are more familiar with imperial measurements. In this book, exact dimensions are given in metric followed by an approximate conversion to imperial for comparison. Make sure you don't mix imperial and metric dimensions when making calculations.

Cross-references
There are few DIY projects that do not require a combination of skills. Laying paving slabs, for example, will require additional information on mixing mortar, draining the site and laying a subbase for the paving. As a result, you might have to refer to more than one section of this book. The list of cross-references at the foot of each page will help you locate relevant sections or specific information that relate to the job in hand.

Numbers in text
Bold numbers in the text draw your attention to illustrations that will help to clarify the instructions at important stages in a sequence.

Contents

Planning Ahead

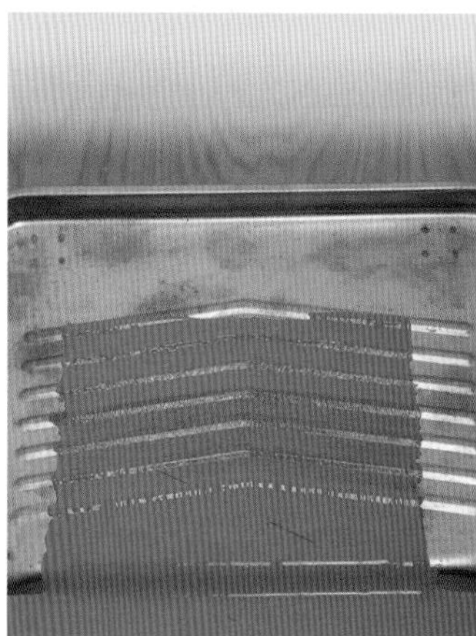

Decorating

Repairs and Improvements

Storage

Home Security

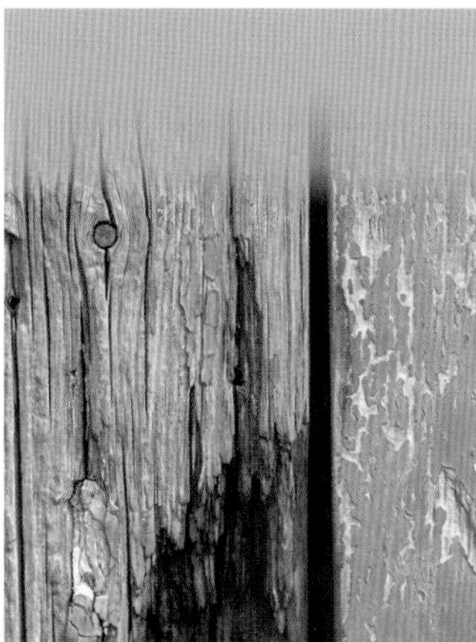

Infestation, Rot and Damp

Insulation and Ventilation

Electricity

Plumbing

Heating

Working Outdoors

Tools and Skills

Reference and Index

Planning Ahead

Forward planning: check lists

Carrying out substantial home improvements can be either an enjoyable and stimulating experience or a nightmare. If you plan each step carefully before you begin work, you are more likely to make real improvements that will benefit your family and add to the value of your property. On the other hand, if you buy a property that is unsuitable for your needs, or launch into an ambitious project without thinking through the consequences, you could waste time and money.

• **Public services**
Consider your new home's location in relation to public transport. Will you be affected by parking restrictions, road tolls or congestion charges, which could mean having to rely on public transport? You should also check the availability of other public amenities, such as schools and hospitals.

Buying a house or flat is an exciting event – when you find one that seems to be what you've been searching for, it can be a heady moment and it's easy to get carried away and fail to check the essentials. First impressions can be misleading and the shortcomings of what seemed to be your dream home may only begin to emerge after you have moved in. Consequently, it's a good idea to arm yourself with a check list of salient points when looking at a prospective house, so you are less likely to discover later that it's going to cost a great deal to bring the building up to the required standard.

In some ways, assessing the potential of your present home can be even more difficult. Everything fits like an old glove, and it's hard to be objective about possible improvements. Try to step back and take a fresh look at it by using the same sort of check list you would use when considering the purchase of a new house.

Structural condition

Before you decide to buy a house or flat, the building should be inspected by a professional surveyor to make sure it is structurally sound – but make some spot checks yourself before spending money on a survey. A pair of binoculars will help you inspect the building from ground level.

Look for cracks in walls, both inside and out. Cracked plaster may simply be the result of shrinkage, but if the fault is visible on the outside it may indicate deformation of the foundations.

Inspect chimney stacks for faults. A loose stack could cause considerable damage if it were to collapse.

Check the condition of the roof. A few loose slates can be repaired easily, but if a whole section appears to be misplaced that could mean a new roof.

Ask if the house has been inspected or treated for rot or insect infestation. If so, is there a guarantee? Don't rely upon your own inspection – but if the skirting boards look distorted or a floor feels unduly springy, expect trouble.

Look for signs of damp. In hot weather the worst effects may have disappeared, but stained wallpaper or even poor pointing of the brickwork should make you suspicious.

Insulation

Ask what form of insulation, if any, has been installed. Try to establish the level of insulation in the walls, roof and floors. External-wall insulation should carry a guarantee. Study your surveyor's report to check that the insulation is adequate by current standards.

Home Information Packs supplied to potential buyers should contain an Energy Performance Certificate (EPC). This will give a guide to the energy efficiency of the house or flat you are considering, rating it from A to G – excellent to poor, the level of insulation being one of the most important factors. Currently, this assessment is aimed primarily at newly built homes, but there is a possibility that the scheme will be extended to cover older properties.

As well as thermal insulation, consider the acoustic properties of the new home you are buying. Is noise travelling through walls or floors from adjacent properties likely to be a problem?

Decorative condition

Is the house decorated to a sufficiently high standard inside and out, both to protect the structure and enhance the appearance of the building?

The decorative condition of the house may be reflected in the price, but the chances are you will be expected to pay the same whether the work is up to a good professional standard or shoddily applied. It is up to you to point out the difference to the vendor.

Improvements

Make up your own mind whether 'improvements' have been carried out tastefully. Ask yourself if you're happy to live in a house where the original doors and windows have been replaced with alternatives at odds with the style of the architecture. The advantages sometimes claimed for certain types of stone cladding are very dubious, and stripping painted brickwork can be both time-consuming and costly. The neighbouring houses will probably give you an idea of the original appearance of the one you are considering.

Construction work usually requires Building Regulations approval, and possibly also planning permission from the local authority. Ask to see relevant documents relating to any approvals for Building Regulations and planning permission.

SEE ALSO > Decorating 32–116, Repairs and improvements 118–220, Insulation and ventilation 256–80

Services

An estate agent's written details of the property may briefly describe recent rewiring - but in the absence of such an assurance, try to determine the likely condition of the installation.

The presence of old-fashioned sockets and light switches may indicate out-of-date wiring - but new equipment is no guarantee at all that the cables themselves have been replaced. The age of the wiring around the consumer unit will be your best indication. Check that there are enough sockets in every room. Is the lighting well planned? In particular, see if there's adequate lighting on the stairs.

For your own property, ask a qualified electrician to test the whole system for you. It is recommended that this type of testing be carried out at least every ten years.

Is the plumbing of an age and type that can be extended easily to take new fittings? Take note of the size of the hot-water cylinder, to make sure it can supply enough hot water, and check that it is insulated. If the house is only partly centrally heated, check that the boiler is large enough to cope with extra radiators - or you may find yourself faced with the expense of buying a new one. Is the heating system fitted with proper thermostatic controls to keep costs down? Ask whether flues and fireplaces are in working order.

It is worth getting a plumber registered with Corgi (Council for Registered Gas Installers) to check your gas installation. If you have oil-fired appliances, go to a plumber who is registered with OFTEC (Oil Firing Technical Association) .

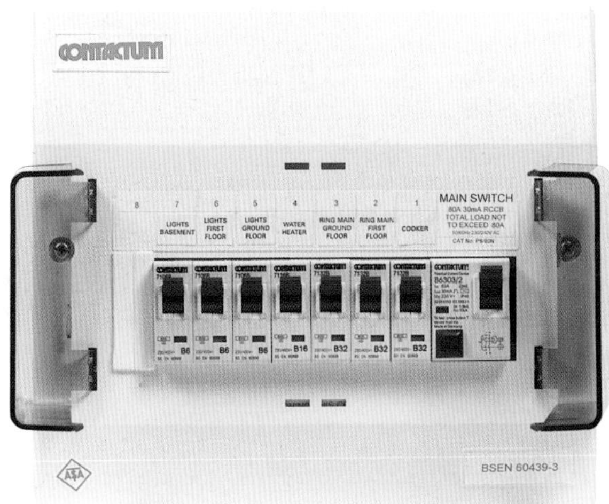

Home security

Check whether all doors and windows are secured with good-quality locks and catches. You will probably want to change the front-door lock, anyway. A burglar alarm is an advantage only if it is reliable and intelligently installed.

Make sure there is adequate provision for escape in the event of fire, especially in a block of flats where access routes are shared. Are smoke detectors fitted? If they are part of a professionally installed system, ask for documentation on its installation.

Garage and workshop

Is the garage or parking space large enough for your car, or cars? And will you be able to manoeuvre safely in and out of the property?

If there isn't enough space for the garage to double as a workshop, it may be possible to fit out a cellar, provided there is storage space for materials and you can deliver them without disruption or damaging decorations and furniture.

Erecting a new shed or outbuilding is another solution, provided there is room in the garden or beside the house and a utilitarian building will not spoil the outlook of the property.

Long-term storage is a perennial problem. Every household accumulates bulky items like camping or sports equipment that have to be stored for much of the year. Once again, a garage or outbuilding is ideal - but if necessary, can you use the loft for storage? Check the size of the hatchway, and consider whether you might need to board over the joists or reposition insulation.

Attached garages may give you the opportunity in the future for extending the house, at both ground and first-floor level.

Buying a flat

If you're buying a flat, make additional checks on the condition of the access, whether it is by stairs or lift. Ask about shared facilities such as laundry and waste disposal, and joint responsibilities such as maintenance of public areas and drains. In buildings that have been converted to flats, check adequacy of fire-escape routes and confirm with the local authority that all necessary permissions have been granted for the conversion. Also check whether sound insulation has been installed.

Is it a concrete-frame building, built between the 1950s and the early 1970s? These were sometimes constructed using high-alumina cement, which can lead to structural problems. Have the structure checked by a structural engineer.

The garden

Unless you're a keen gardener, you may not want a large garden requiring a lot of attention. If you are, does the garden receive enough sunlight for the type of plants you want to grow? Check the orientation of the garden in relation to the passage of the sun. Can you sit and enjoy the sun's warmth for a good part of the day?

Check the outlook. When climbers, trees and shrubs are bare of foliage, will you be confronted by an eyesore that is screened only during summer months? Check the position of trees near to the house. If a tree's too close, it could cause foundation problems; if it's too large, it is likely to block out daylight. Enquire if the tree has a preservation order on it, in case you need to have it removed.

Satisfy yourself that fences or walls are high enough to provide privacy. Check their condition, and whether you or your neighbours are responsible for their maintenance. If you view a house at the weekend, ask whether there are any factories, workshops, schools or playgrounds nearby that may disturb your peace and quiet during the week.

It is an advantage if the garden has access for building and gardening materials and equipment - otherwise, they will need to be carried through the house.

Will children be able to play safely in the garden without supervision? Make sure gates are secure, and high enough to prevent them wandering out of the garden and out of sight. Also, are there any water features that could pose a risk for small children?

SEE ALSO > Home security 232–40, Electricity 282–344, Plumbing 346–94, Heating 396–420, Working outdoors 422–78

Assessing potential

Assuming the structural condition of the house is such that you are willing to take on the work involved, check out the kind of points that a survey won't highlight. Is it the right home for you and your family? It takes a bit of imagination to see how a room might look when it has been divided in two or when a wall has been removed, and it's even more difficult to predict what your lifestyle might be in 5 or 10 years' time. Unless you are planning to live in the house for only a couple of years before moving on, try to assess whether it will be able to evolve with you.

Getting inspired

• **Websites**
Useful websites include:
www.homebuilding.co.uk
www.idealhomemagazine.co.uk
www.idealhomeshow.co.uk
www.periodliving.co.uk

Perhaps, like most people, you need some inspiration to help you recognize the potential of a future home or to engender some fresh ideas that would improve the house or flat where you live at the moment. There are a great many sources of inspiration that will help to kick-start your imagination.

Magazines

For a long time now, home and garden magazines have provided an array of innovative design schemes, as well as information on new products. It's a good idea to buy or subscribe to two or three magazines on a regular basis. Many home-design magazines illustrate newly built luxury homes, but they also feature alterations or extensions to more modest houses. These magazines often list useful contacts and provide information on building costs, too.

Television

Television series on home improvements and make-overs are enormously popular and provide not only good entertainment but also design ideas and information that you can record on a DVD or video tape. However, don't fall into the trap of thinking that arbitrary deadlines help to induce clear decision-making or favour good workmanship.

The Internet

The Internet is one of the most useful sources of information. Most magazine articles include website references providing links to products and relevant professional services.

Exhibitions

A visit to an interior-design exhibition is essential if you are considering a new home or extension or substantial alterations. Most of the major manufacturers of building materials, design products and services are present at these exhibitions and are anxious to sell their products and services direct to home owners. At the bigger exhibitions, you may have an opportunity to visit a number of show houses, where you can make notes of design features, colours and finishes.

Visiting friends

Don't underestimate the value of comparing what friends and family have done with their houses, especially your neighbours who may have had to tackle problems identical to your own. You will find that most people are only too happy to talk about how they came to a decision on a particular decorative scheme, or perhaps the design for their new extension. Ask how they get on with a particular layout, for example, and then consider whether the solution they have come up with would suit your own requirements.

SEE ALSO > Colour schemes 32–9

Measuring a room

If you think you might want to change the shape of a room or suspect there may be a problem with fitting certain items of furniture into it, measure the floor area and ceiling height, so that you can make a scale drawing later to clarify your thoughts.

Jot down the main dimensions, not forgetting chimney breast, alcoves, and so on. Make a note of which way the doors swing; and the positions of windows, radiators, electrical sockets and fixed furniture. Later, transfer the measurements and details to graph paper, drawing them to scale.

Having drawn your plan of the room, cut pieces of paper to represent your furniture, using the same scale, and rearrange them until you find a satisfactory solution.

Keeping a record

You can learn a great deal from other people's experiences – both good and bad – but remember, ideas and suggestions can easily be forgotten unless you write them down. It is worth maintaining a scrapbook or having a folder where photographs, notes, magazine articles and snippets of information can be kept.

Planning for people

Try to give function, comfort and appearance equal priority when you are planning your home. The best designers build their concepts around the human frame, using statistics from research into the way people use their domestic and working environments.

Anthropometrics

Although human stature varies a great deal, the study of anthropometrics has determined the optimum dimensions of furniture and spaces around it that are required to accommodate people of average build. These conclusions have been adopted by both designers and manufacturers, so that most shop-bought fittings for kitchens, bathrooms and living and dining areas are now built to standardized dimensions.

This is especially true of kitchen units, which are designed for compatibility with appliances such as cookers and fridges to make a scheme that fits together as an integrated, functional whole. The standard worktop height allows fridges, dishwashers and washing machines to fit beneath it, while hobs are designed to be let into the counter top and stand-alone cookers match the height of kitchen base units. Designers adopt the same criteria for other items of furniture: standard-size chairs, tables and desks allow most people to work and eat comfortably.

An appreciation of anthropometrics cuts down on accidents – for instance, correctly positioned shelves and worktops in the kitchen preclude climbing onto a chair to reach the top shelf. It also helps you to choose appropriate furniture around the home, avoiding low-level easy chairs and soft beds that offer no support for your back.

Using available space

As well as the size and function of the furniture itself, its positioning within the room falls within the province of anthropometrics. An efficient use of floor area is an essential ingredient of good planning, providing people with freedom of action and sufficient room to make use of furniture and appliances with ease.

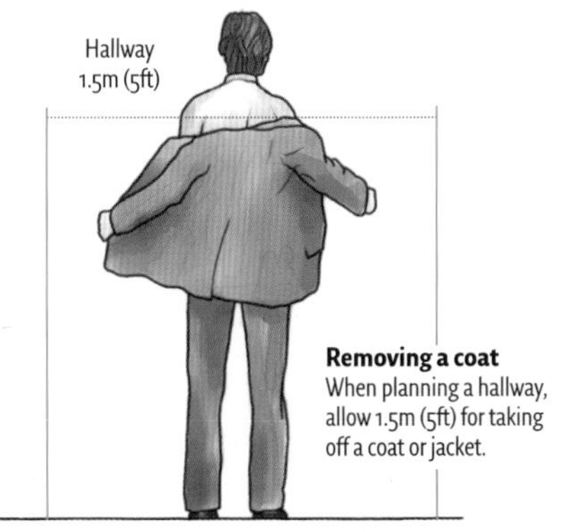

Removing a coat
When planning a hallway, allow 1.5m (5ft) for taking off a coat or jacket.

The hallway

When you are invited into the house, you will be able to gauge whether the entrance hall is large enough to receive visitors comfortably. Will there be room to store coats, hats, umbrellas and so on? Is the staircase wide enough to allow you to carry large pieces of furniture to the bedrooms?

If all the family tend to be out in the daytime, it is an advantage if there's some facility for deliveries to be stored safely under cover outside.

Check also whether you will be able to identify visitors before you open the door.

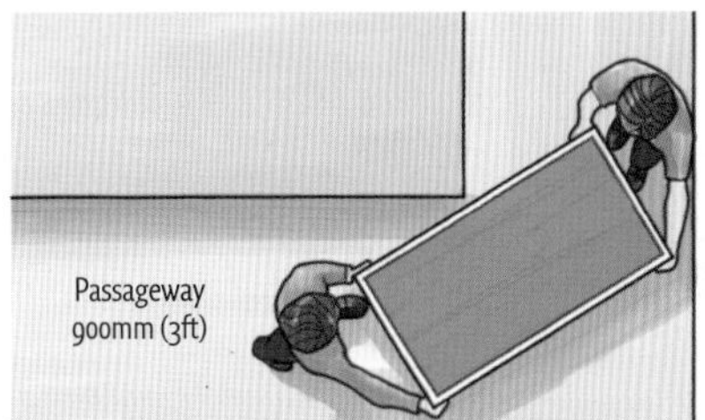

Staircase headroom
A headroom of 2m (6ft 6in) above a staircase will allow you to carry a wardrobe up to the next floor.

Negotiating a bend
You can turn a large piece of furniture around a bend in a 900mm (3ft) wide passageway.

SEE ALSO > Moving a door 141–3, Removing walls 142–9, Dividing rooms 150–5

Bathrooms

If the bathroom does not provide the amenities you require, estimate whether there is space for extra appliances, even if this means rearranging the existing layout or perhaps incorporating an adjacent toilet. Is there a separate toilet for use when the bathroom is occupied? Can a ground-floor toilet be installed for the disabled or elderly?

If the bathroom isn't accessible to all the bedrooms, it's worth investigating the possibility of installing a second bathroom, wet room or shower cubicle elsewhere. Alternatively, consider plumbing a basin in some bedrooms.

Make a note of electrical installations in the bathroom. If they do not comply with accepted recommendations, they must be replaced with new units.

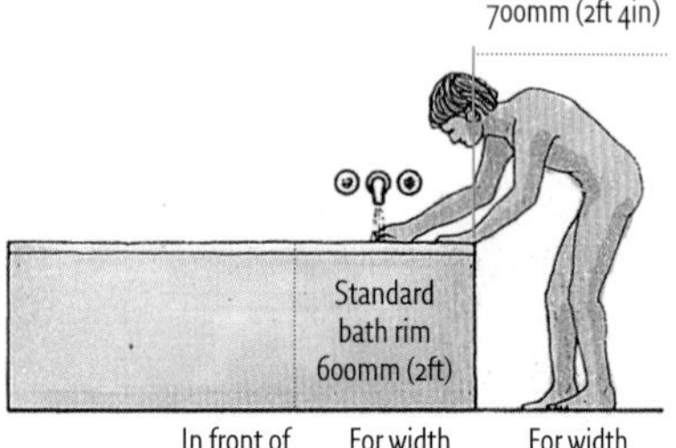

Between bath and wall
Allow sufficient room between the bath and the wall to dry yourself with a towel. The same amount of space will allow you to bend to clean the bath.

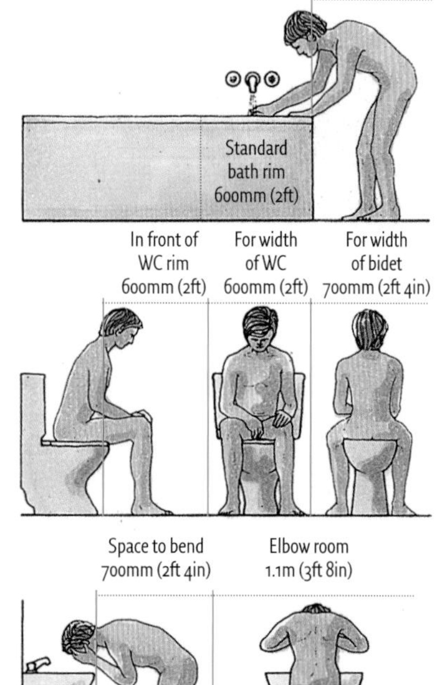

WC and bidet
Allow at least 600mm (2ft) space in front of a WC or bidet. For the width of a WC, allow 600mm (2ft): for a bidet allow 700mm (2ft 4in) to provide enough leg room.

Using a basin
Allow generous space, so you can bend over the basin and also have plenty of elbow room when washing hair. The same space will give you room to wash a child.

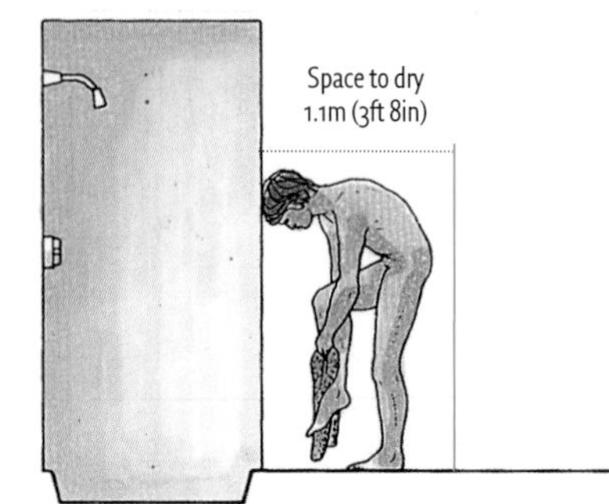

Drying after a shower
This is the minimum space required to dry yourself in front of an open cubicle. If the cubicle is screened, allow an extra 300mm (1ft) clearance.

Living rooms

How many reception rooms are there in the house? More than one living room will make it possible for members of the family to engage in different pursuits without inconveniencing each other. If there is only one living room, make sure there are facilities elsewhere for private study, music practice or hobbies that take up a lot of space or make intrusive noise.

Is the living room large enough to accommodate the seating arrangement you have in mind? Or will you have to remove a wall to incorporate extra space? If you do, it is worth considering sliding or folding doors, so you can divide the area when it suits you.

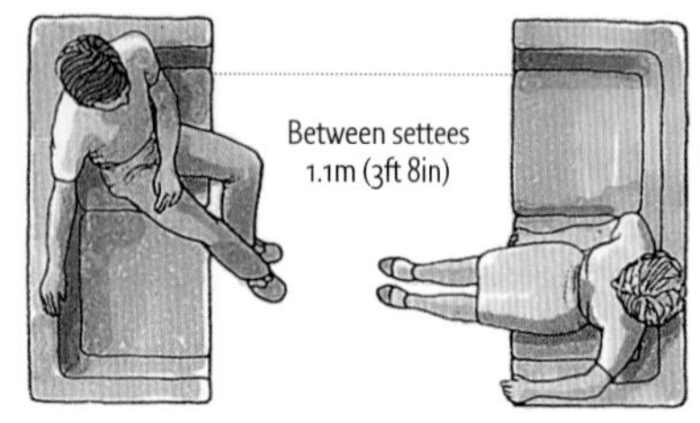

Arranging two settees
Allow a minimum of 1.1m (3ft 8in) between two settees facing each other.

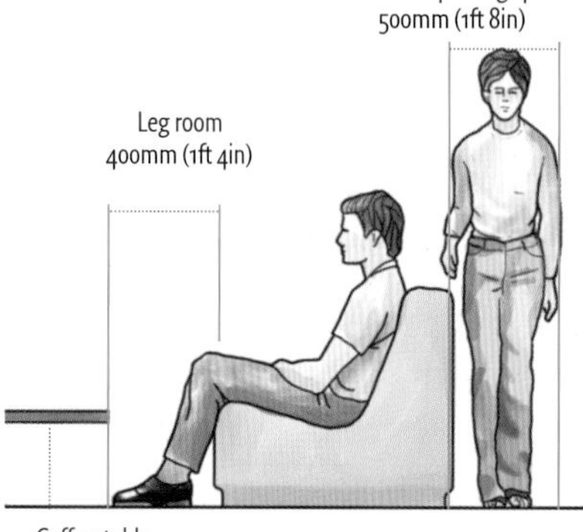

Low seating

The density of upholstery and the dimensions of the seat and back vary so much that it is impossible to suggest a standard, but make certain your back is supported properly and that you can get out of a chair without help. If you place a coffee table in front of a settee, try to position the table so that people can reach it from each end in order to avoid treading on the toes of someone seated.

Allow sufficient passing space around furniture, particularly if a member of the family is a wheelchair user – in which case, allow a clearance of 900mm (3ft).

Bedrooms

The number of rooms may be adequate for your present needs, but what about the future? There may be additions to the family – and although young children can share a room for a while, individual accommodation will be required eventually. You may want to put up a guest from time to time or have elderly relatives to stay for extended periods. In which case, will they be able to cope with stairs? It might be possible to divide a large room with a simple partition, or perhaps a room on the ground floor can double as a bedroom. As a long-term solution, you could plan for an extension or loft conversion.

Are all the bedrooms of an adequate size? As well as a bed or bunks, a bedroom must accommodate storage for clothes; and maybe for books and toys, plus facilities for homework or pastimes. A guest room may have to function as a private sitting room, possibly with provision for preparing snacks and hot drinks. You could dismantle or move a dividing wall, or possibly incorporate part of a large landing, provided it does not interfere with access to other rooms or obstruct an escape route in case of fire.

Try not to rely on using a bedroom that only has access via another room. Such an arrangement is fine when you want to be close to a young child, but a connected room might otherwise only be suitable as a dressing room or an *en suite* bathroom.

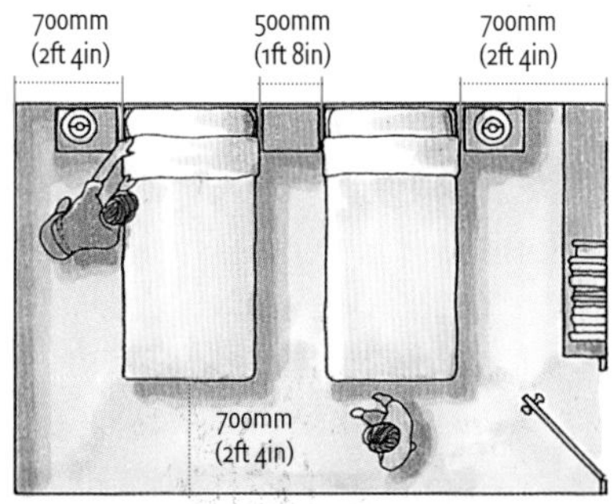

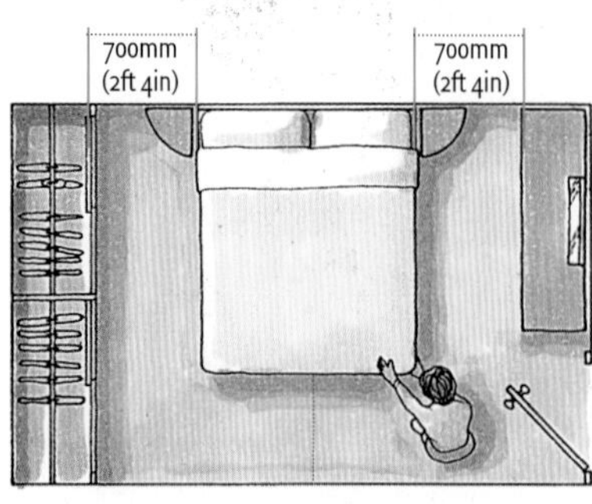

Circulating space in bedrooms

SEE ALSO > Moving a door 141–3, Dividing rooms 150–5, Plumbing 346–94

Dining room

Is there a separate dining room for entertaining? Estimate whether there will be sufficient space for guests to circulate freely once your table and chairs are in the room.

A dining room should be positioned close to the kitchen, so that meals are still warm when they get to the table.

If the dining area is part of the kitchen, efficient ventilation will be necessary to extract cooking odours. Some people prefer a kitchen that is screened from visitors. Are the present arrangements suitable for your needs?

Sitting at a table

The same area is needed for sitting at a dining table, dressing table or writing desk. Ideally a computer keyboard should be slightly lower.

Arrange your dining furniture so people are able to sit down or move a chair out from the table without difficulty – and if possible, leave enough room for a trolley to be pushed past.

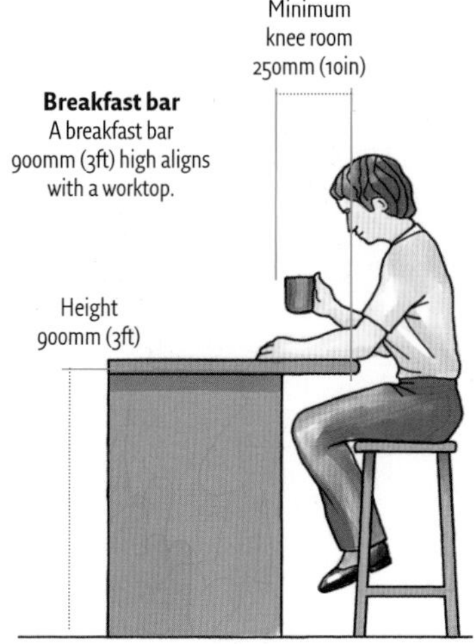

Breakfast bar
A breakfast bar 900mm (3ft) high aligns with a worktop.

Kitchen

The quality of kitchen furniture and fittings varies enormously – but every well-designed kitchen should incorporate the following features.

A labour-saving layout

Preparing meals can become a chore unless the facilities for food preparation, cooking and washing up are arranged within easy reach of each other – in order to avoid unnecessary movement – so the layout of the kitchen forms an efficient 'work triangle'. Ideally, the combined length of the sides of the triangle should not exceed 6 to 7m (20 to 22ft).

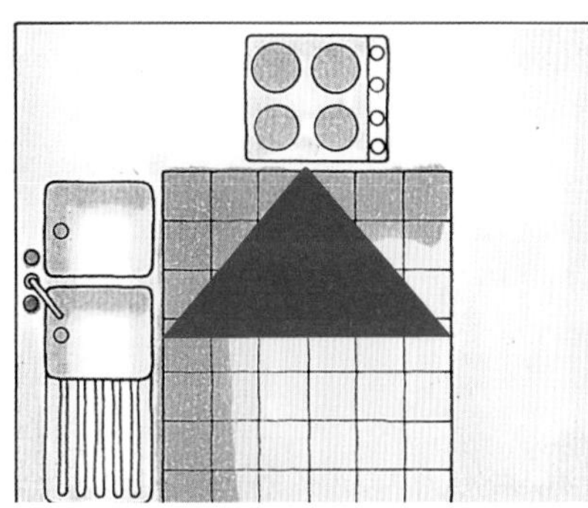

Work triangle
A typical work triangle links preparation, cooking and washing-up areas.

Storage and appliances

If the work triangle is to be effective, a kitchen must incorporate enough storage space in each area. The fridge and foodstuffs should be close to where the meals are prepared; also, adequate work surfaces need to be provided in appropriate locations. You may be able to find a place for a freezer elsewhere – although it needs to be somewhere conveniently close to the kitchen.

The hob and oven should be grouped together, with heat-proof surfaces nearby to take hot dishes. Cooking equipment should be within easy reach.

Appliances that require plumbing are best grouped, together with the sink, on an outside wall. In a small house the kitchen area may contain a dishwasher, washing machine and tumble dryer, although a separate laundry room is really the ideal solution.

Kitchen storage
Plan your kitchen storage carefully, to provide safe and efficient access.

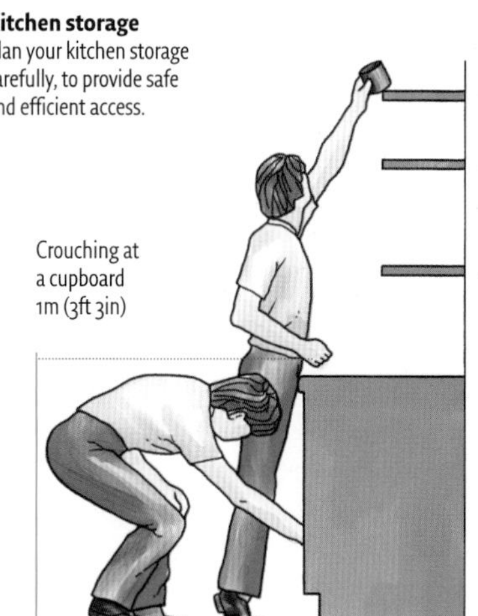

Access to drawers
Crouching at a drawer unit 1.25m (4ft 2in)

KITCHEN SAFETY

- Check the layout of the kitchen with a view to safety. A cramped kitchen can lead to accidents, so make sure that more than one person at a time can circulate in safety.
- Make sure children cannot reach the hob, and construct a barrier that will keep small children outside the work triangle. Cupboard-door clamps prevent young children opening cupboards containing dangerous chemicals and cleaning fluids.
- If possible, avoid an arrangement that encourages people to use the working part of the kitchen as a through passage to other parts of the house or the garden.
- Placing a hob or cooker in a corner or at the end of a run of cupboards is not ideal. Try to plan for a clear worktop on each side. Don't place a hob under a window, either – a draught could extinguish a gas pilot light, and someone will eventually get burned trying to open the window.

SEE ALSO > Shelving 222–7, Ventilation 273–80, Wiring appliances 310–17, Plumbing a sink 386–7, Plumbing appliances 288–9

Using professionals

Why pay someone to do a job when you can do it perfectly well yourself? There are plenty of skilled amateurs who can tackle just about any job to a high standard. However, an amateur usually takes longer than a professional to complete the work – and, for most of us, time is at a premium.

There are certain jobs it is worth paying to have done quickly and efficiently – ones that are holding up a series of other projects, for example, or that call for techniques with which you do not feel sufficiently confident. You may prefer to ask an electrician to do major wiring or a plumber to install a new bathroom, although you plan to carry out all the peripheral labouring and finishing yourself.

Then there are certain skills that require time and practice before you can become really proficient at them. In a house of average size you might develop the knack of plastering as the work is coming to an end – but you probably won't need to plaster another wall until you buy your next house.

Professional advice

In most cases you will need to seek professional advice in order to obtain planning permission and Building Regulations approval; and if you apply for a mortgage, the bank or building society will insist on the building being professionally surveyed. If the surveyor's report highlights a serious defect, the mortgage company will want the fault rectified by a specialist firm who will guarantee the work.

Royal Institution of Chartered Surveyors
12 Great George Street,
London SW1P 3AD
Telephone: 0207 222 7000
www.rics.org

Institution of Structural Engineers
11 Upper Belgrave Street
London SW1X 8BH
Telephone: 0207 235 4535
www.istructe.org

Surveyor

When you apply for a mortgage, the bank or building society will appoint a surveyor who is trained to evaluate the property in order to protect the mortgage company's investment. His or her job is to check that the building is structurally sound and to pinpoint anything that needs attention. You will have to pay for this service, but the surveyor will report directly to the mortgage company. There was a time when the bank or building society was not obliged to show you the report, but simply told you what work had to be carried out in order to secure your mortgage. Mortgage companies are now more compliant, however, and will give you a copy of the surveyor's report.

A survey can take the form of a basic evaluation (often used by by mortgage companies) or a more elaborate and detailed home buyer's report. A home buyer's report usually consists of comments entered under standard headings, though sometimes a more detailed survey is prepared including a lot more information. Alternatively, you can have a full structural report carried out by a structural engineer. For complete peace of mind, it's best to obtain the latter. Unless you are buying a fairly new property, this type of report makes depressing reading: if the surveyor has done a thorough job, it will list everything that needs attention, from peeling paintwork to dry rot. No surveyor will take responsibility for guaranteeing the condition of areas of the house that are inaccessible at the time of inspection. For example, if the house is occupied, fitted carpets make it difficult to examine the condition of the floors. The report will therefore point out that these areas cannot be guaranteed as sound – but that doesn't necessarily imply that there is likely to be a problem.

Study the report for specific references to serious faults that may be expensive to put right, such as damage to the foundations, dry or wet rot, woodworm, severe damp, or a badly deteriorating roof. Also take note of points that could lead to trouble in the future. For example, if the survey refers to leaking guttering that is soaking a wall, an urgent repair will be required to avoid penetrating damp.

If you are not satisfied with the mortgage company's report, commission your own survey before you finally commit yourself. Ideally use a surveyor who has been recommended to you for thoroughness; otherwise, contact the Royal Institution of Chartered Surveyors or the Institution of Structural Engineers.

Full structural survey
Very detailed report, concentrating on the structural condition of the property.

Home buyer's report
This type of survey follows a standard format set out by the Royal Institute of Chartered Surveyors. It is suitable for properties that are in reasonable condition and no more than 150 years old.

Basic valuation report
Often used by mortgage companies, in order to ascertain the value of the property.

SEE ALSO > Employing a builder 18, Seeking official approval 20–27

Architect

If you are planning ambitious home improvements, especially ones that will involve major structural alterations or extensions, you should consult an architect. He or she is trained to design buildings and interiors that are not only structurally sound but aesthetically pleasing. An architect will prepare scale drawings of the development for submission to the authorities for planning permission and Building Regulations approval. You can even employ the same architect to supervise the building construction, to ensure that it meets the required specifications. You and your architect must work as a partnership. Brief him or her by discussing the type of development you have in mind, how you plan to use it, how much you want to spend, and so on.

You can contact the Royal Institute of British Architects (RIBA) for a list of professionals working in your area, but a personal recommendation from a friend or colleague is far more valuable. Before entering into any kind of commitment, meet the architect and arrange to see some of his or her recent work.

See a Client's Guide to Engaging an Architect on RIBA's website, **www.architecture.com.**

Quantity surveyor

A quantity surveyor (QS) advises you on building costs, and will help monitor additional costs and savings through the construction stage of the project. You may not want to employ a quantity surveyor for smaller projects, but you will almost certainly benefit from the involvement of one in a more complex home-design project. Fees are usually based on a percentage of construction cost; guidance is given by the Royal Institution of Chartered Surveyors (RICS) on their website, **www.rics.org**. Most surveyors are happy to work on an hourly basis.

Party-wall surveyor

You are likely to need the services of a party-wall surveyor if your proposed extension will come close to a boundary, especially when there's another building close by. This type of surveyor has specialized knowledge of the Party Wall Act (see **www.communities.gov.uk**). To find a party-wall surveyor, go to **www.partywallact.info**.

Structural engineer

A structural engineer is responsible for the design of the structural elements of buildings, extensions and major alterations, including any foundations that are required. A structural engineer can also analyse soil conditions taken from trial holes on the site. You will need to consult a structural engineer for most major projects, and employing one is a requirement of most local authority Building Control Departments.

Fees can be charged hourly or can be agreed as a percentage of the overall construction cost. Contact the Institution of Structural Engineers (IStructE), via **www.istructe.org**.

Planning consultant

Don't underestimate how valuable a good planning consultant can be - not only in terms of helping to obtain planning permission for your extension or alteration but also in getting over difficult planning conditions imposed by a Planning Authority. Advice is usually charged for on an hourly rate. Information can be obtained from the Royal Town Planning Institute (RTPI) website, **www.rtpi.org.uk**.

Scheduling a major project

When scheduling a straightforward DIY project there is usually nothing but your own time to consider - the more hours you put in the faster the job is completed. But it's not quite so simple when you have to employ professionals. Their work has to be coordinated, and quite often a project cannot move forward until a particular specialist has been consulted or the relevant authority has given consent.

Each design and building project is different, and tricky planning problems can add weeks to a schedule, so it's impossible to be precise about how long it should take for each stage of the process to be completed.

- First, there is your own decision process, which you shouldn't rush under any circumstances. You need to do your research thoroughly before you can brief your architect.
- Once the design process is under way, there is bound to be a number of meetings with the architect, who will explain the results of any preliminary surveys undertaken and discuss with you his or her ideas for your building project. You must allow plenty of time for this process - everything that follows hinges on the design being right.
- Then the process to obtain planning permission and Building Regulations approval begins. At the same time, you need to ask suitable builders to submit tenders.
- Once you have official approval to proceed and you have appraised and accepted the best tender, the builder may need time to engage other contractors before the actual work on site can begin.
- From commissioning your architect to design a typical extension to the first day on site is going to take at least 4 to 5 months. Anything more ambitious is going to take considerably longer. What happens after the builder goes on site is difficult to predict.

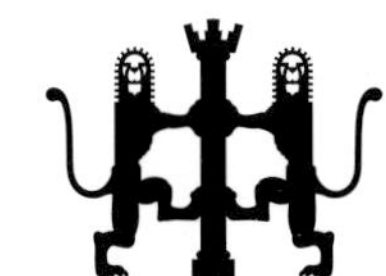

Royal Institute of British Architects
66 Portland Place,
London W1B 1AD
Telephone: 0207 580 5533
www.architecture.com

Royal Town Planning Institute
41 Botolph Lane,
London EC3R 8DL
Telephone: 0207 929 9494
www.rtpi.org.uk

SEE ALSO > Employing a builder 18, Seeking official approval 20–27, Party Wall Act 27

Employing a builder

Within the scope of home improvements, a builder is perhaps the one professional that all of us need to employ from time to time, and the search for a builder who is both proficient and reliable can be frustrating. You will hear plenty of stories of clients being overcharged for shoddy work or being left with a half-completed job for months on end. It's not that good builders do not exist, but there is an abundance of careless and inefficient ones who give the entire industry a bad name.

Federation of Master Builders
14 Great James Street,
London WC1N 3DP
Telephone: 020 7242 7583
www.fmb.org.uk

• **Recommendations**
The following sources may be able to recommend a good reliable builder:
Local Authority Building Control Office
Builders' merchant
Your architect

Recommendation is the best way to find a builder. If someone whose opinion you respect has found a professional who is skilful, reliable and easy to communicate with, then the chances are you will enjoy the same experience. Even so, you should inspect the builder's work yourself before you make up your mind. If a recommendation is hard to come by, choose a builder who is a member of a reputable association, such as the Federation of Master Builders. To be represented by the Federation, a builder must have a good reputation and supply bank and insurance references.

A good builder will be booked up for months ahead, so allow plenty of time to find someone who will be free when you need him or her to start work. If a builder is highly recommended, you may feel you do not want to look elsewhere – but, unless you get two or three estimates for the same job, you won't know whether the price is fair. A builder who is in demand may quote a high price because he doesn't need the work; on the other hand, an inexperienced builder may submit a price that seems tempting, but then cut corners or ask for more money at a later date.

Subcontractors

Most builders have to employ independent subcontractors, such as electricians, plumbers and plasterers. The builder is responsible for the quality of subcontracted work unless you agree beforehand that you will appoint the specialists yourself. Discuss anything relating to the subcontracted work with the builder – not directly with the tradesmen or tradeswomen concerned.

Writing a specification

Many of the disagreements that arise between builder and client are a result of insufficient briefing before work commences. Don't give a builder vague instructions: he may do his best to provide the kind of work he thinks you want, but his guesses might turn out to be wide of the mark. Also, he can't possibly quote an accurate price unless he knows exactly what you require.

A specification should be a methodical list of the work that the builder is required to carry out. It usually starts with the preliminaries, such as the starting and completion dates, insurance details (see opposite), payment issues and the type of contract. The specification should then go on to describe in detail the work required and the materials to be used. If the work is complicated, you should employ an architect to write a specification for you.

A specification needs to include a date for starting the work and an estimate of how long it will take to complete. You will have to obtain that information from the builder when he submits his estimate – but make sure it is added to the specification before you agree to the terms and price. There may be legitimate reasons why a job does not start and finish on time, but at least the builder will be left in no doubt that you expect him to behave in a professional manner.

Getting an estimate

When you ask builders to tender for work, what they give you is only an estimate of the costs. These will be based on current prices and the amount of information you have supplied at the time.

Before you engage a builder, always obtain a firm quotation with a detailed breakdown of costs. If you still have not decided on certain items, then you can both agree on a provisional sum to cover them – but make it clear that you are to be consulted before that money is spent. Also, a builder may have to employ a specialist for some of the work, and that fee might be estimated. If so, try to get the builder to firm up on the price before the work begins.

Agree how payment is to be made. Many builders are willing to complete the work before any money changes hands; others ask for stage payments to cover their costs. If you agree to stage payments, it should be on the understanding that you will only pay for work completed, or at least that the materials will have been delivered to the site. Never agree to an advance payment.

Provided you make it clear to the builder before he accepts the contract, you can retain a figure for an agreed period after the work is completed to cover the cost of faulty workmanship. Between 5 and 10 per cent of the overall cost is a reasonable sum.

If something unexpected occurs that will affect the price for the job, ask the builder for an estimate of costs before you decide what course of action to take. Similarly, if you change your mind or ask for work that is extra to the specification, you must expect to pay for any resulting increase in costs.

Working with your builder

Most people find they get a better job from a builder if they create a friendly working atmosphere. You will have to provide access to electricity and water if necessary for the job; and the workmen will need somewhere to store materials and tools. Unless you have an architect to supervise the job, at the end of each day, once the workers have left, inspect what they have done, to satisfy yourself of the standard of workmanship and that the builder is keeping to schedule.

SEE ALSO > Using professionals 16–17

Building contracts and insurance

A standard building contract covers a number of important issues, including costs, method of payment, insurance, and what will happen if something goes wrong. You can rely on your professional advisors, especially your architect, for advice on an appropriate contract for your particular project. There are different types of contract to suit the size, value and complexity of the job.

Standard contracts

The most commonly used contracts are those produced by the Joint Contract Tribunal (JCT), which is a collection of various bodies involved in building construction; some are professional advisors and others are construction contractors. The JCT produces three types of contract, starting with the simplest JCT Home Owner's Contract, which is really designed to cover alterations and extensions rather than houses built from scratch. Then there is the JCT Minor Works Form of Contract, which is good for simple projects involving few, if any, specialist suppliers and the minimum of complicated architectural detail. The JCT also produce an Intermediate Form of Contract more suited to the complex, higher-value home design. To get more information on any of these standard contracts, go to the JCT website, **jctltd.co.uk**.

Insurance policies

A good building contract will include provisions to cover the likelihood of something going wrong. Even though every effort may be made to avoid errors, you may need to have work redone or be in a position to recover your losses if the worst should happen. Appropriate insurance eliminates or at least reduces the risks involved when the professionals you have employed make a mistake. So what are the risks and what types of insurance policies are available?

Professional indemnity insurance

Errors made by any of your professional advisors can have serious consequences. For example, if your structural engineer designs the wrong type of foundation, movement may occur in the future and cracks could appear in the structure. Similarly, if your architect specifies the wrong floor tiles, they may crack or break up under load.

To cover such eventualities, professionals carry what is termed professional indemnity insurance. It is important that you, as the home owner, make sure your professional advisors have this type of insurance. It may be a little embarrassing to have to raise this subject with someone you hope to engage, but at some stage simply write a letter asking him or her to confirm that they have valid insurance that is sufficient to cover the value of the project. Some insurers prevent their names being disclosed to third parties, as this could at some future date prejudice the insurance. If this is the case, by writing a letter you are giving the professional's insurers the opportunity to consider your request and provide the appropriate information.

Contractor's All Risks insurance

This type of insurance covers a builder against any injury he might cause to individuals or to property. The same policy usually covers loss or damage to equipment. This may include any unfixed materials stored on site, which belong to the contractor.

As the home owner employing professionals to undertake the work, you need to make sure the contractor indemnifies you against an injured third party bringing an action against you, the employer. It's important to make sure there are adequate resources to meet this type of claim. For this reason, any contract you take out with a builder should require him or her to be appropriately insured to cover such eventualities.

Insuring the work

Most building contracts contain provisions for the insurance of the actual work that is to be carried out, and also some provision for the existing structure if you are building an extension onto it. If your builder has an existing policy, make sure your name, as the employer, is added to that policy. If you take out insurance, ask for the builder to be included. Once insurance has been obtained, check the policy to make sure it is appropriate and valid for the period required.

Insuring other people's property

Other types of insurance protect both you, the employer, and the contractor against damage that may be caused to adjacent properties as a result of your building work. This is probably more appropriate to an urban site where your new extension, garage or workshop will be close to another person's property. Consult your professional advisor about this type of insurance.

SEE ALSO > Using professionals 16–17

Seeking official approval

Before you undertake certain alterations to your property, you are obliged to obtain the approval of local-government authorities. Many house owners are reluctant to cooperate, fearing that the authorities are likely to be obstructive – but in fact their purpose is to protect all of us from irresponsible builders and developers, and they are most sympathetic and helpful to any householder who seeks their advice in order to comply with the statutory requirements.

People often confuse the two main types of control that exist: planning permission and Building Regulations approval. Receiving planning permission doesn't automatically confer Building Regulations approval, or vice versa, and you may need both before you can proceed. There is some degree of variation in planning requirements, and also in the Building Regulations, from one area of the country to another. Consequently, the information given on the following pages should be considered as no more than a guide, and not as an authoritative statement of the law. If you live in a listed building of historical or architectural interest, or your house is in a conservation area, seek advice before considering any alterations.

Planning permission

What might seem to be a minor alteration in itself could have far-reaching implications you have not considered. A structure that obscures drivers' vision near a junction, for instance, might constitute a danger to traffic. Equally, a local authority may refuse planning permission on the grounds that a proposed scheme does not blend sympathetically with its surroundings.

The actual details of planning requirements are complex; but in broad terms, with regard to domestic developments the planning authority is concerned with construction work – such as an extension to the house or the provision of new outbuildings.

Structures like garden walls and fences fall into the same category, because their height or siting might infringe the rights of other members of the community. Similarly, planning consultation is intended to protect the interests of neighbours who have a right to privacy and access to their property, which could be affected directly by your proposals.

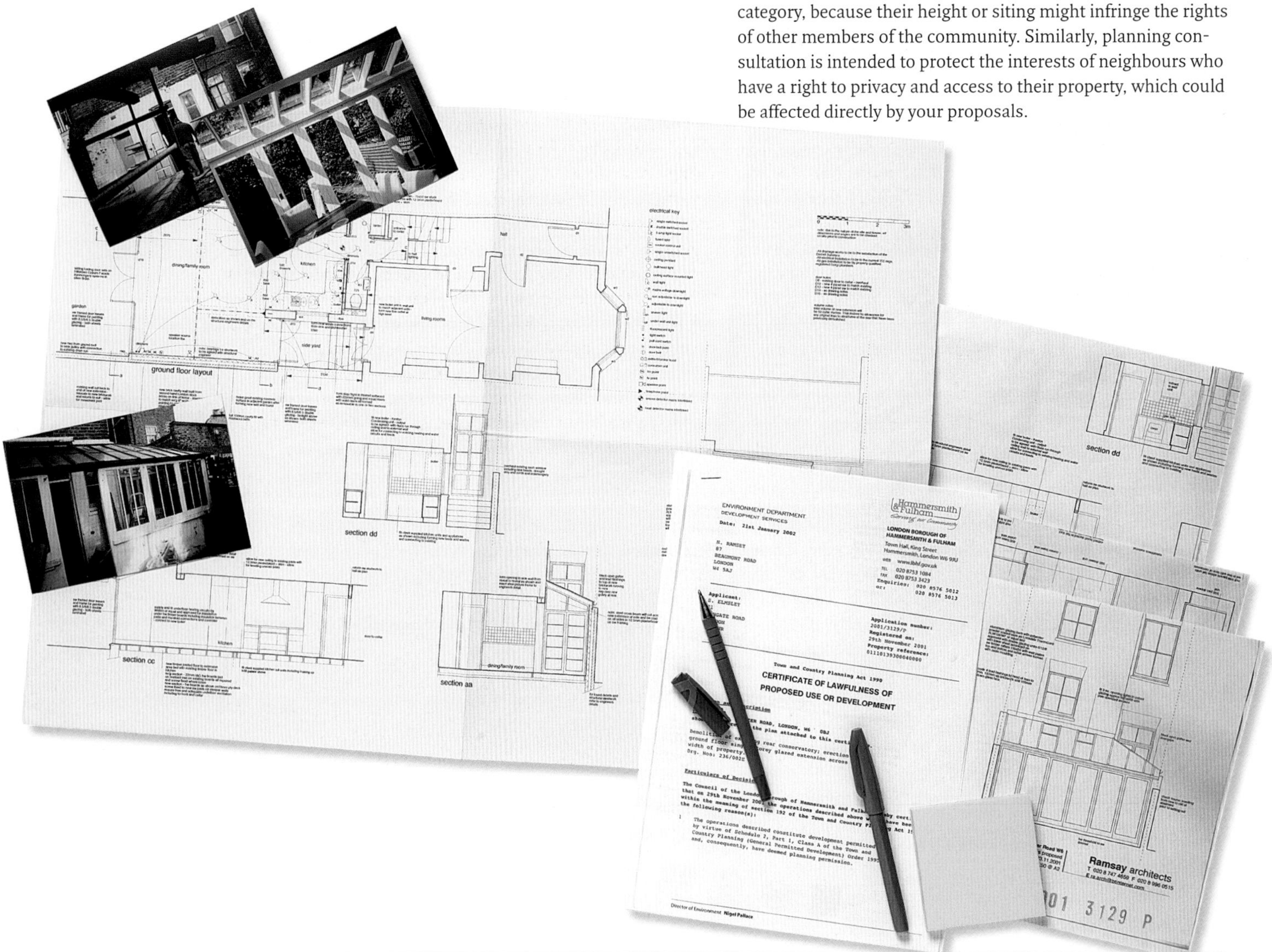

SEE ALSO > Building Regulations 22, When do you need official approval? 23–27, 30

The local authority must also approve any change of use, such as the conversion of a house into flats, or plans to run a business from premises previously occupied as a dwelling. However, planning policies are not intended to cover strictly private matters such as who lives in a house, the number of bedrooms or bathrooms it contains, the size of the rooms or what the rooms might be used for.

Your property and what you do with it may also be affected by legal restrictions such as a right of way, which could prejudice planning permission. Examine the deeds of your house, or consult a solicitor.

Applying for planning permission

The necessary application form is obtainable from the planning department of your local council. It is laid out simply, and there are guidance notes to help you fill it in. If the planning authority at your local council is willing to discuss your proposal in principle prior to making an actual application, that could save you a great deal of wasted time and effort.

Normally you will have to pay a fee in order to seek planning permission, though there are exceptions. The planning department will be able to advise you.

Getting professional help

Alternatively, you could ask an experienced builder or an architect to apply on your behalf. Asking a professional to make the planning application is sensible if the work you are planning is at all complicated, as you will have to include drawings that include accurate measurements with the application form. In all probability, you will have to prepare a plan showing the position of the site in question (called the site plan or location plan), so the authority can determine exactly where the building is located. You must submit another, larger-scale, plan to show the relationship of the building to other premises and highways (called the block plan). In addition, you will need to supply drawings that give a clear idea of what the new proposal will look like, together with details of both the colour and the type of materials you intend to use. You may prepare the drawings yourself, provided you are able to make them accurate.

DESIGN AND ACCESS STATEMENT

TOWN AND COUNTRY PLANNING ACT 1990

FORM ONE

APPLICATION FOR PLANNING PERMISSION

DISTRICT COUNCIL

You also need to include a design and access statement, giving information about building design, layout and landscaping, access, pedestrian safety and transport, all of which will be considered carefully as part of the assessment of your application. With increasing concerns regarding building in a sustainable manner, any information you can include on materials used, energy conservation and recycling of building materials can only help your chances of securing planning approval.

Outline application

Once you have applied formally for planning permission, there are few opportunities to modify what has been submitted. Consequently, your professional adviser may suggest making an outline application before preparing detailed plans. However, few local authorities are prepared to consider outline applications. Assuming outline permission is granted, you will then have to submit a further application in greater detail. In the main this procedure is applicable to large-scale projects only, and you will be better off making a full application in the first place.

Planning meeting

Having considered your submission in detail, planning officers prepare a report, with recommendations for refusal or approval of the application. This report is presented to local councillors at a planning meeting. In many cases, you or your agent will have an opportunity to speak at this meeting. There are cases where an application is recommended for approval but is then rejected by members of the local authority on the night - so being there to defend your case personally could make a difference.

Planning decision

Planning permission is normally granted unless there are very sound reasons for refusal - in which case the authority is obliged to explain the decision, so you can amend your plans and resubmit them for further consideration. A second application is normally exempt from a fee.

As a last resort, you have the right to appeal against a decision to the Secretary of State for the Environment within 6 months of the date of the decision notice. The planning authority will supply you with the necessary appeal forms. You can expect to receive a decision from the planning department within 8 weeks.

A planning decision is usually accompanied by a number of conditions, and these need reading carefully. Once granted, planning permission is valid for 5 years. If the work is not begun within that time, then you will have to apply for planning permission again.

What if I break the rules?

There is nothing to be gained by flouting the rules, and there could be a heavy cost if you are found out. If, for example, you build an extension or a high boundary wall without planning permission, the local council may decide to take enforcement action. In the first place you will be asked to make a formal application. If this is subsequently refused, you would still have the right to appeal to the Secretary of State for the Environment, who will then send an inspector from outside the area to assess the facts and make a decision. This decision is final - and if it goes against you, the building or structure will have to be demolished.

SEE ALSO > Building Regulations 22, When do you need official approval? 23–27, 30

Building Regulations

Even when planning permission is not required, most building works, including alterations to existing structures, are subject to minimum standards of construction to safeguard public health and safety. The Building Regulations are designed to ensure structural stability and to promote the use of suitable materials to provide adequate durability, fire and weather resistance, energy conservation, and the prevention of damp. The regulations also stipulate the minimum amount of ventilation and natural light to be provided for habitable rooms; and cover matters concerning drainage and sanitary installations.

Building standards are enforced by your local Building Control Officer (BCO), who is usually under the control of the local planning authority, although this varies from area to area. There are also approved independent inspectors who do the same job as Building Control Officers but are not employees of the local authority.

Obtaining approval

You, as the builder, are required to complete an application form called a building notice and to return it, along with basic drawings and all relevant information, to the Building Control Office at least 2 days before work commences. A building notice does not have to be accompanied by plans, but the authority may require information such as structural calculations as the work proceeds. This method may not be used where a building is to be erected or underpinned and is within 3m (9ft 9in) of a public sewer.

Your other alternative is to submit fully detailed drawings for approval before work starts. These drawings must include plans, section and elevations of the building, plus a site plan. All such drawings will be examined for compliance with the Building Regulations.

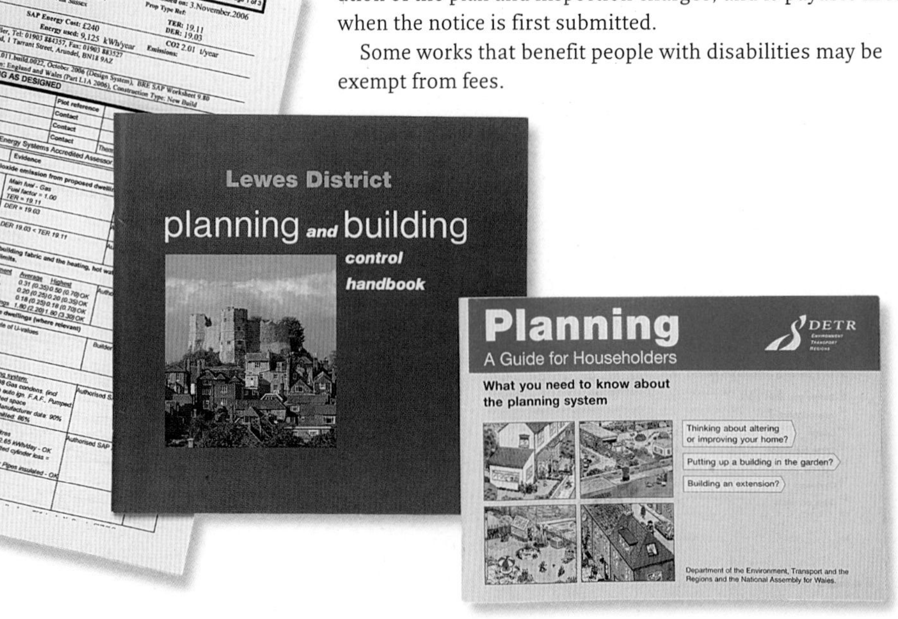

Consultation

Whichever method you opt for, it may save time and trouble if you make an appointment to discuss your scheme with the Building Control Officer well before you intend to carry out the work. He or she will be happy to discuss your plans – including proposed structural details and dimensions and the list of materials you intend to use – and to point out any obvious contraventions of the regulations before you make an official application. At the same time, he or she can advise whether it is necessary to approach other authorities to discuss planning, sanitation, fire escapes, and so on.

To make sure the work is carried out according to your original specification, the Building Control Officer will ask you to inform the office when crucial stages of the work are ready for inspection by a surveyor. Should the surveyor be dissatisfied with any aspect of the work, he or she may suggest ways to remedy the situation. You will be expected to pay certain fees to the local council for the services of the surveyor, which you can establish in advance.

Professional assistance

If you wish, you can appoint a builder or, preferably, an architect to handle everything for you. But don't be talked into ignoring a request from the Building Control Office's surveyor to inspect the site, or you could incur the cost and inconvenience of exposing covered work at a later stage. As well as losing you time, failure to submit an application form or detailed plans can result in a substantial fine.

When the building is finished, you must notify the council. At the same time, it would be to your advantage to ask for written confirmation that the work is satisfactory, as this will help to reassure a prospective buyer when you come to sell the property.

Charges for Building Regulations approval

Your local council is required to charge for Building Regulation services. The framework for these charges is laid down by the government, but the actual amounts are determined by the council. Where a full-plans application is made, the charge must be paid when the plans are deposited with the council. An inspection charge is payable after commencement of the work.

The charge made for a Building Notice represents a combination of the plan and inspection charges, and is payable in full when the notice is first submitted.

Some works that benefit people with disabilities may be exempt from fees.

SEE ALSO > Planning permission 20–21

When do you need official approval?

If you live in a single-family house, you may undertake certain developments without official approval. The information on the next few pages is intended to help you decide whether you need to seek planning permission or Building Regulations approval before starting work – but, since requirements change frequently, you should always write to the local authority, explaining what you propose to do, and ask for confirmation in writing whether or not official approval is required.

Loft conversion
(left)
No planning permission is required provided the volume of the house is unchanged and the highest part of the roof is not raised. Permission will be required for new front-elevation dormer windows and also for rear or side ones over a certain size. Permission is also required if the building is listed or in a conservation area.

Extensions
(below)
There's a strong possibility that you will need planning permission in order to build an extension to your home.

Repairs and decoration
Unless your home is listed, you don't need Building Regulations approval or planning permission for decoration or repairs. If you are renting or are a leaseholder, check with the landlord or freeholder.

Felling or lopping trees
Planning permission is not required unless the trees are protected or you live in a conservation area. But bear in mind that retaining trees may have practical advantages as well as aesthetic ones – they provide privacy, sound screening and shade.

SEE ALSO > Planning permission 20–21, Loft conversion 25, Building an extension 26

TYPE OF WORK	PLANNING PERMISSION		BUILDING REG. APPROVAL	
Decoration or repairs inside and outside	NO	Unless it is a listed building or, in some cases, within a conservation area.	NO	
Replacing windows and doors	NO	Unless they project beyond the foremost wall of the house facing a highway. Or the building is listed or is in a conservation area.	POSSIBLY	**No** for repairs and like-for-like replacement, but check with the BCO if you plan to make any changes to size or design. **Yes** if you plan to replace all windows with double-glazed units. Use only FENSA approved installers and get them to contact the Building Control Department on your behalf.
Installing additional insulation	NO		POSSIBLY	**No** for topping up loft and floor insulation. **Yes** for cavity insulation, which must be installed by a competent contractor.
Replacing roof coverings	POSSIBLY	If your house is listed or in a conservation area, contact your Development Control Officer.	POSSIBLY	**No** for repairs. **Yes** for complete roof-covering replacement.
Wall cladding	YES	On a listed building, or in a conservation area or an area of outstanding natural beauty.	YES	
Electrical work	NO		POSSIBLY	**Yes** for certain notifiable work. All work must also comply with IEE Wiring Regulations.
Plumbing	NO		POSSIBLY	**No** for replacements, but consult the BCO for any installation that alters present internal or external drainage. **Yes** for unvented hot-water system.
Central heating	NO		NO	Except for boiler replacement.
Installing a new boiler	NO		YES	
Installation of solar panels	POSSIBLY	It depends on how far they project above the roof plane.	NO	
Installation of wind generator	YES		YES	Mostly in terms of health-and-safety considerations.

SEE ALSO > Decorating 32–116, Roof coverings 123–5, Insulation and ventilation 256–80, Electricity 282–344, Plumbing 346–94, Heating 396–420

TYPE OF WORK	PLANNING PERMISSION		BUILDING REG. APPROVAL
Oil-storage tank	**NO**	Provided it is in the garden and has a capacity of not more than 3,500 litres (778 gallons) and that no point is more than 3m (9ft 9in) high and no part projects beyond the foremost wall of the house facing a highway - unless there will be at least 20m (65ft) between the tank and the highway.	**NO**
Structural alterations inside	**POSSIBLY**	**No**, so long as the house's use is unchanged. **Yes** if the building is listed, in which case you require listed-building consent (as opposed to planning permission).	**YES**
Loft conversion	**POSSIBLY**	**No**, provided the volume of the house is unchanged and the highest part of the roof is not raised. **Yes** for front-elevation dormer windows and for rear or side dormers over a certain size. **Yes** if the building is listed or in a conservation area.	**YES**
Building a garden wall or fence	**YES**	If it is more than 1m (3ft 3in) high and is a boundary enclosure adjoining a highway; or if it is more than 2m (6ft 6in) high elsewhere, or if your house is listed.	**NO**
Planting a hedge	**NO**	Unless it obscures the view of traffic at a junction or access to a main road.	**NO**
Laying a path or driveway	**NO**	Unless it provides access to a main road.	**NO**
Felling or lopping of trees	**NO**	Unless the trees are protected or you live in a conservation area.	**NO**
Installing a satellite TV dish	**NO**	Unless it's over 600mm (2ft) in size on a chimney or 1m (3ft 3in) elsewhere; or fixed above the highest part of the chimney or roof; or there's an antenna installed already; or the house is listed or in a conservation area.	**NO**

SEE ALSO > Repairs and improvements 118–220, Fences 426–33, Building walls 441–51, Laying pathways 460–63, 468–9

TYPE OF WORK	PLANNING PERMISSION		BUILDING REG. APPROVAL	
Building a porch	**NO**	Unless the floor exceeds 3sq m (3.6sq yd) or any part is more than 3m (9ft 9in) high or any part is less than 2m (6ft 6in) from a boundary adjoining a highway or public footpath.	**NO**	Provided it is under 30sq m (35.9sq yd) in area.
Building a conservatory	**POSSIBLY**	Treat as an extension.	**NO**	If it is under 30sq m (35.9sq yd) in area.
Building a garage	**POSSIBLY**	If it is within 5m (16ft 4in) of the house or over 10cu m (13.8cu yd) in volume, treat as an extension. Otherwise treat as an outbuilding.	**POSSIBLY**	Consult your BCO.
Hardstanding for a car	**NO**	Provided it is within your boundary and is not used for a commercial vehicle or vehicles.	**NO**	
Building an extension	**POSSIBLY**	You can extend your house up to certain limits without planning permission (see below). However, if the total volume of previous and new extensions exceeds the permitted limit, permission is required. The volume allowance will also be affected by existing buildings, including garages and sheds within 5m (16ft 4in) of the original building. See also OUTBUILDINGS (opposite).	**YES**	

EXTENSIONS

Planning permission is required if:

Volume: The extension results in an increase in volume of the original house by whichever is the greater of the following amounts.
For terraced houses: 50cu m (65.5cu yd) or 10 per cent, up to a maximum of 115cu m (150.4cu yd).
Other houses: 70cu m (91.5cu yd) or 15 per cent, up to a maximum of 115cu m (150.4cu yd).
In Scotland: General category, 24sq m (28.7sq yd) or 20 per cent.

Height: Any part will be higher than the highest part of the house roof.

Projections: Any part will project beyond the foremost wall of the house facing a highway or be less than 20m (65ft) from a highway.

Boundary: Any part within 2m (6ft 6in) of a boundary will be more than 4m (13ft) high.

Area: It will cover more than half the original area of the garden.

Dwelling: It is to be an independent dwelling.

Conservation area: It is in a conservation area or in an area of outstanding natural beauty.

Listed building: It needs listed-building consent.

SEE ALSO > Concrete 454–61, Paving 467–9

DEMOLITION

If you intend to partially demolish a building, you are required to give notice to the Building Control Office. A counter notice may be served on you requiring you to carry out work to services and adjoining buildings. Only when a period of 6 weeks has elapsed without a counter notice being served - or once you have received such a notice - can you proceed with the demolition. A Building Control Officer will visit the site and discuss with you the way in which the demolition is to be carried out. If a building is listed, or within a conservation area, planning permission will be required.

OUTBUILDINGS

An outbuilding can cover up to half the area of the garden without planning permission, so long as it is not closer to a highway than 20m (65ft 6in) and the height will nor exceed 3m (9ft 9in) or 4m (13ft) if it has a ridged roof. In a conservation area or in the curtilage of a listed building, you will need planning permission for any structure or building that exceeds 10cu m (13.08cu yd) in volume.

However, in terms of planning permission, an outbuilding is regarded as an extension if it is within 5m (16ft 6in) of the house and more than 10cu m (13.08cu yd) in volume.

TYPE OF WORK	PLANNING PERMISSION		BUILDING REG. APPROVAL	
Demolition	**POSSIBLY**	Consent is required if the building is listed or in a conservation area. You may need approval for substantial demolition anywhere - seek advice.	**POSSIBLY**	**No** for a complete, detached house. **Yes** for a partial demolition - to ensure that the remaining parts of adjoining buildings are structurally sound (see box headed DEMOLITION above).
Converting a house to flats or business premises	**YES**	Including conversion to bedsitters or to partial use for business or commercial purposes.	**YES**	If the alterations are structural; and for conversion to flats, even where constructional work is not intended.
Dividing off part of your home for commercial or business use	**POSSIBLY**	Depending on how much of the house is divided off for commercial or business use.	**POSSIBLY**	Check with your BCO.
Work affecting an existing means of escape	**NO**		**YES**	
Work to listed buildings	**POSSIBLY**	Listed-building consent is required.	**YES**	

• **Building work that affects wildlife**
Check the Wildlife and Countryside Act and EU legislation to make sure you are not affecting protected species through carrying out the work you propose.

• **Breach of planning conditions**
Always check that you would not be in breach of any existing planning conditions that could affect your decision to proceed.

PARTY WALL ACT 1996

The Act came into force on 1 July 1997 and provides a framework for preventing and resolving disputes between neighbours when work to a party wall is proposed or excavations are to be made within 6 metres (6ft 6in) of another building.

The Act requires you to give your neighbour notice of your intentions and gives him or her the right to agree or disagree with your proposals. It is best to engage the services of a chartered surveyor who specializes in work concerning party walls. He or she will make an assessment of the condition of the party wall before the work starts so that any future disputes over the way the work is carried out can be resolved and any damage caused as a result of the work can be repaired.

Failure to observe the conditions of the Act can result in an injunction being served on you by your neighbour, preventing work from proceeding until agreement has been reached.

There are usually guidance booklets available free at your local council offices. Further information can be obtained from the government website **www.communities.gov.uk**.

SEE ALSO > Using professionals 16–18

Saving energy

There is considerable pressure from the media and informed authorities on the urgency to reduce our use of energy to combat the effects of global warming. Most concerned consumers want to know what they can realistically do in the short term to reduce wastage and also how to design new homes and extensions that will conserve energy and take advantage of natural light and heat.

New building work

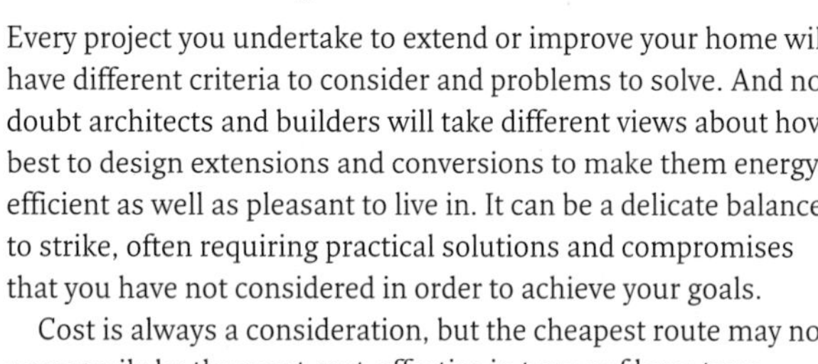

Every project you undertake to extend or improve your home will have different criteria to consider and problems to solve. And no doubt architects and builders will take different views about how best to design extensions and conversions to make them energy-efficient as well as pleasant to live in. It can be a delicate balance to strike, often requiring practical solutions and compromises that you have not considered in order to achieve your goals.

Cost is always a consideration, but the cheapest route may not necessarily be the most cost-effective in terms of long-term energy efficiency. These are aspects you need to discuss in detail with your professional advisors.

The following suggestions are intended as pointers to the way you approach the design and build for the future.

Websites
Useful websites include:

www.rainharvesting.co.uk
(rainwater harvesting)

www.greengardener.co.uk/wormeries.htm
(tiger-worm composting)

www.nef.org.uk
www.est.org.uk
(solar power for heating and hot water)

www.bwea.com
(wind turbines)

Siting a new extension

If possible, locate a new extension on the side of the house where it can gain most from the effect of sunlight – often referred to as passive solar energy. Try to incorporate ground-floor south-facing windows, and think about their height and proportion to maximize the winter sun's deeper penetration into your home, thereby reducing the need for electric illumination during the hours of daylight. A good rule of thumb is large windows to the south but smaller windows facing north. Similarly, grouping wall storage on the north, east and west walls provides additional insulation, helping to reduce heat loss.

Proportions

Consider the overall shape, size and layout of your extension or conversion. This can have a significant effect on thermal performance and building costs. For example, a simple cube may be cheaper to construct than a long, thin rectangular shape. However, the latter could, in the right circumstances, provide a longer south-facing surface, which offers more scope for passive solar energy in the form of free sunlight and heat.

Within your design, think about having an open-plan layout, with the minimum number of door openings. One room or living space is easier to heat than several individual rooms.

Roof construction

When designing the roof covering a new extension or loft conversion, try to construct what is known as a warm-roof system, whereby the insulation is contained within the sloping roof. This allows spaces within the roof void to be kept warm and used as habitable space. It also avoids having to ventilate the roof void above an insulated ceiling, thus reducing draughts and heat loss.

Buffer zones

Consider introducing buffer zones as part of the overall design. A porch, for example, serves as an airlock, reducing heat loss and providing extra insulation against draughts and cold.

A glazed conservatory on the west wall of the house can harvest solar energy in the late afternoon, and provide useful space for drying clothes. A similar conservatory helps to delay night-time cooling of the interior.

Build tight, ventilate right

Take measures to reduce losses from draughts and air movement through the external fabric of your home. The aim is to make the building envelope as airtight as possible and then provide controllable ventilation. Good ventilation helps provide a comfortable and healthy environment by diluting or extracting moisture and pollutants – such as nitrogen oxides, carbon dioxide, tobacco smoke and house-dust mites – from within your home. The worst pollutant, moisture vapour, should be extracted from bathrooms and kitchens, which are its prime source.

Insulation

Installing adequate insulation is perhaps the most important measure you can take to minimize your energy requirements. There are a number of materials you can use, including glass fibre, mineral wool, polystyrene and cellulose (recycled paper insulation). In the near future there will be other natural materials to choose from, such as straw, hemp and wool. One advantage in using these materials is that they are produced locally and do not have to be imported. Plan ahead and build for the future by incorporating high levels of insulation.

Minimize the potential for 'thermal bridges' – vulnerable areas in the external fabric where heat can travel easily to the outside. Make sure that insulation is continuous, eliminating cold spots where condensation could occur.

Building materials

Where practicable, use timber as your prime building material. This is without doubt the 'greenest' structural material available, provided you can ensure the wood comes from certifiable sustained managed sources. It also has the advantage of being a beautiful material that is relatively easy to work.

In addition, consider using second-hand materials, such as used bricks and recycled steel. And look for building blocks made with a high content of granulated blast-furnace slag (check manufacturers' descriptions for details).

Rammed-earth construction is now a recognized means of building walls, though you would need a professional to check that the soil is suitable in the area where the building is to be constructed.

SEE ALSO > Insulation and ventilation 256–80

Is your present home energy-efficient?

When working on your present home, try to build in programmes of energy efficiency as part of your overall scheme. Our expectations of comfort and convenience are such that we all require central heating, electric lighting and power to run our modern appliances. No one is suggesting we should do away with these modern conveniences, but it makes sense to protect the environment and reduce our personal expenses at the same time.

Reducing energy wastage is particularly difficult if you live in an older property. Not only will it be built without modern levels of insulation, but it may also be more difficult to bring it up to standard without compromising the essential character of your home.

Fitting draught excluders

Draughtproofing doors and windows is a relatively inexpensive yet highly effective way to reduce heat lost to the outside. And you may be surprised to discover that draughts can enter through power points, the junctions between skirting boards and floors, gaps in the floorboards, gaps between ceilings and walls, and around loft hatches. The aim should be to seal as many gaps as possible, but the degree of airtightness achievable will depend on the type of wall construction and finish, how well services have been installed, and the age and condition of windows and doors.

Reducing your use of electrical energy

One of the simplest ways to use less electricity is to replace at least some of your ordinary tungsten-filament light bulbs with low-energy compact fluorescent versions. These so-called long-life bulbs are relatively expensive to buy, but reduce costs in the long run. The Building Regulations now require you to take into consideration the use of low-energy lighting when designing conversions and extensions.

Many electrical appliances such as TV sets and music systems can be left on 'stand-by' so they can be reactivated, using a remote controller. The small lamp that indicates an appliance is in stand-by mode consumes an insignificant amount of electricity, but the cumulative effect represents wastage on a colossal scale. Try to remember to turn off these appliances when they are not in use.

When planning your kitchen, pay particular attention to the design of freezers and refrigerators, and monitor how they are working. Their thermostats have a habit of failing, often causing such appliances to run continuously. If you place your fridge freezer close to a source of heat, such as a cooker, it will have to work harder to maintain the required temperature inside the cabinet.

When planning extensions and conversions, consider the use of light pipes (highly reflective metal tubes) that can flood the interior with natural light, reducing the need for electric lighting during the daytime.

Thermostats and time switches

These are important for regulating heating appliances. Thermostats prevent appliances from getting hotter than necessary, and time switches can be used to make sure the appliances are running only during specified periods.

Fit thermostatic radiator valves to your existing radiators. This allows you to control the temperature of each individual radiator to suit the particular conditions in the part of the house where it is situated. A thermostatic radiator valve will shut down a radiator as soon as it reaches the required temperature, thereby preventing heat being wasted in areas of the home where it is not required. These valves are relatively inexpensive and easy to fit.

Boilers and hot-water cylinders

Water is a highly efficient, inexpensive and versatile medium in which to store energy, since you can move it around easily by pumping it through a central-heating system. In this respect, it is a much better material than bricks or blocks (as in storage heaters). At the moment, gas-fired central-heating systems are probably the most effective and efficient available, but this may change with fluctuations in the ever-volatile fuel markets.

The past few years have seen significant advances in efficient boilers and controls, so much so that the expense of replacing old worn-out equipment can often be recouped quickly in fuel savings. If you are replacing a boiler, choose an energy-efficient condensing boiler and make sure it is part of a well-designed heating system that allows the boiler to work in condensing mode most of the time.

Most hot-water storage cylinders are now supplied preinsulated, having a layer of foam sprayed on the outside. However, a lot of houses are still plumbed with older uninsulated copper cylinders that waste considerable amounts of heat. Wrapping a proprietary insulating jacket around the cylinder will start to reduce your heating bills within just a few months.

Similarly, wrapping exposed hot-water pipes in foamed-plastic tubing is an inexpensive energy-saving measure. Look especially for pipes running through unheated areas of the house, such as the cellar and roof space.

Loft insulation

Wherever possible, increase the insulation in your roof space. This is where the majority of heat is lost. Remember that increased insulation may require better ventilation in order to prevent condensation forming in the roof timbers.

It is worth thinking about installing a warm-roof system (see opposite) so that you can use the roof space for storage, if not for extra living space.

Reducing your household water consumption

There are some very simple ways to reduce your water consumption, such as installing spray taps, self-closing taps and electronic-sensor taps, all of which reduce the amount of hot and cold water that is poured away needlessly.

It is perfectly feasible to collect rainwater and use it for watering the garden, or it can be filtered then stored for household use. Some households recycle their waste 'grey water' by processing it naturally, using reed beds.

Reducing heat lost through doors and windows

When necessary, have replacement windows and doors made to a high standard. In terms of heat loss, the most efficient windows are large plain units without glazing bars (with every additional glazing bar there is more potential for heat loss). Similarly, the design of the window surround must be considered to maximize heat retention. Double-glazed units with large edge details transfer more heat than ones that utilize smaller sections. Most energy-efficient double-glazed units have an air gap of around 16mm (5/8in) filled with argon gas and are made from low-emissivity glass. If you are replacing windows on the north or east elevations of your house, it is worth considering triple glazing.

SEE ALSO > Insulation and ventilation 256–80, Reducing electricity bills 282–83, Plumbing 346–94, Heating 396–420

Energy conservation and older buildings

Energy efficiency comes within the scope of the Building Regulations, which are divided into various parts, each designated by a letter. Energy conservation is referred to as Part L, Conservation of Fuel and Power. The regulations apply to new buildings and to existing houses when they are altered, extended or subjected to a new use. However, Part L makes it clear that the special characteristics of a historic building must be recognized. The aim of this revised part of the Building Regulations is to improve energy efficiency where it is practical to do so.

For existing buildings, Part L (2002) generally requires energy-conservation upgrading only for elements that are to be 'substantially replaced' as part of the work. The requirements do not apply to general repairs or to elements that don't need replacing.

Where proposed alterations or replacements could trigger Part L of the Building Regulations, care must be exercised in deciding whether or not such work will affect the building's character. If your house is listed, listed-building consent may be required. In some instances, a historic building may be in an almost totally original state and like-for-like replacement will be the only appropriate solution. In many cases, however, some thermal upgrading may be practicable - for example, between the joists within roof spaces and under suspended floors – provided it doesn't pose technical problems, such as inhibiting ventilation. It may even be reasonable for this insulation to exceed the recommendations in Part L, in order to help make up for shortcomings elsewhere.

In terms of ventilation and moisture control, old houses can have quite different requirements from newer buildings. Houses built with solid walls without a damp-proof course and from permeable materials function differently from buildings constructed using modern standards and practices. As a result, these older buildings may require comparatively more ventilation to ensure their wellbeing. Nevertheless, a new extension to an old house will normally be expected to have a higher degree of thermal performance than the original building to which it is attached.

Energy Performance Certificates

Home Information Packs (HIPS) are intended to give potential buyers important information about a house they are thinking of purchasing, and contain an Energy Performance Certificate (EPC). This certificate rates a particular house or flat in terms of energy efficiency. In theory, it could affect the value of the property. Although they are intended initially to be applicable to new homes only, it is likely that, in time, such certificates will be issued to cover older homes too.

The aim is to increase public awareness of issues that may not be obvious from casual inspection. Generally, we know whether we like the appearance of a house, its size, layout and location, but now we are also being offered information about things like energy consumption and potential fuel bills. It is hoped that this measure will increase public demand for energy-efficient buildings and encourage home owners and builders to invest in low-carbon measures.

In practice, vendors, through estate agents, need to employ a competent person to produce a certificate that rates the energy performance of their home from A to G, very much like the ratings you see on appliances such as fridges or washing machines. The certificate outlines the running costs and the effects on carbon emissions of space heating, hot water and lighting. It also gives practical advice on how to cut these costs and reduce emissions. The EPC forms part of the Home Information Pack, which also includes searches and other legal documents. The entire system is designed to tackle the uncertainty and lack of transparency in buying a house, and will hopefully lead to fewer failed transactions.

For more detailed information, visit **homeinformationpacks.gov.uk**.

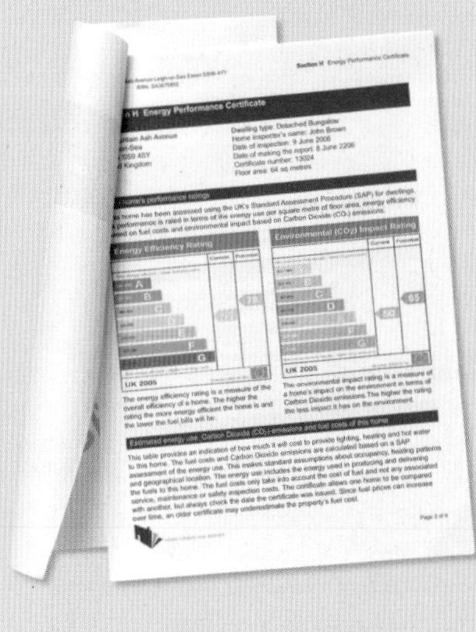

SEE ALSO > Building Regulations 22, Insulation and ventilation 256–80

Decorating

A basis for selecting colour

Developing a sense of the 'right' colour isn't the same as learning to paint a door or hang wallpaper. There are no 'rules' as such, but there are guide lines that will help. In magazine articles on interior design and colour selection, you will find terms such as 'harmony' and 'contrast'; colours are described as tints or shades, and as cool or warm. These terms form a basis for developing a colour scheme. By considering colours as the spokes of a wheel, you will see how they relate to each other – and how such relationships create a particular mood.

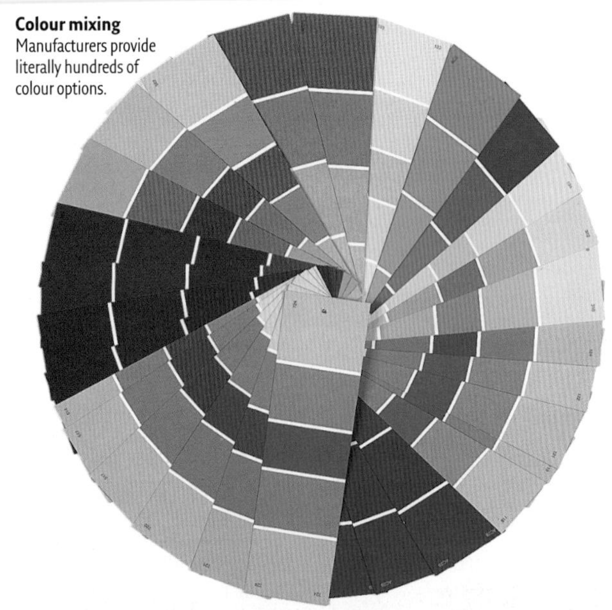

Colour mixing
Manufacturers provide literally hundreds of colour options.

Primary colours

All colours are derived from three basic 'pure' colours – red, blue and yellow. These are known as the primary colours.

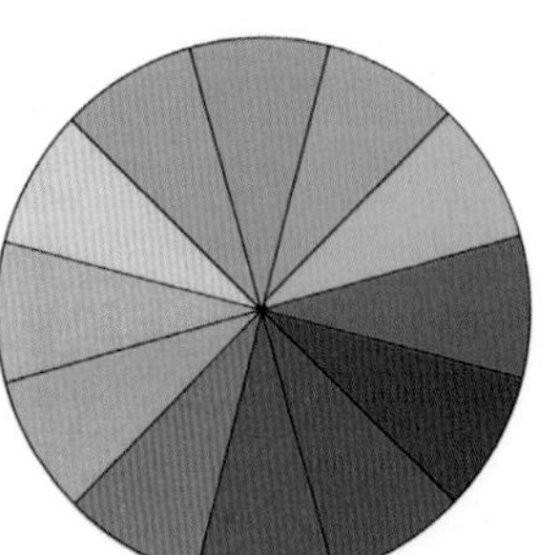

Basic colour wheel
A colour wheel shows the relationship of primary, secondary and tertiary colours. Warm and cool colours are grouped on opposite sides of the wheel.

Secondary colours

When you mix two primary colours in equal proportions, a secondary colour is produced. Red and blue make violet; blue and yellow make green; and red and yellow make orange. When a secondary colour is placed between its constituents on the wheel, it sits opposite its complementary colour – the one primary not used in its make-up. Complementary colours are the most contrasting colours in the spectrum and are used for dramatic effects.

Tertiary colours

When a primary is mixed equally with one of its neighbouring secondaries, it produces a tertiary colour. The complete wheel illustrates a simplified version of all colour groupings. Colours on opposite sides are used in combination in order to produce vibrant contrasting schemes, while those grouped on one side of the wheel form the basis of a harmonious scheme.

Warm and cool colours

The wheel also groups colours with similar characteristics, which we are able to use on a practical level when decorating our homes. On one side are the warm red and yellow combinations, colours we associate with fire and sunlight. A room decorated with warm colours feels cosy or exciting, depending on the intensity of the colours used. Cool colours are grouped on the opposite side of the wheel. Blues and greens suggest vegetation, water and sky, and create a relaxed airy feeling when used together.

Secondary colours

Tertiary colours

Primary colours
The three colours from which all other colours are derived.

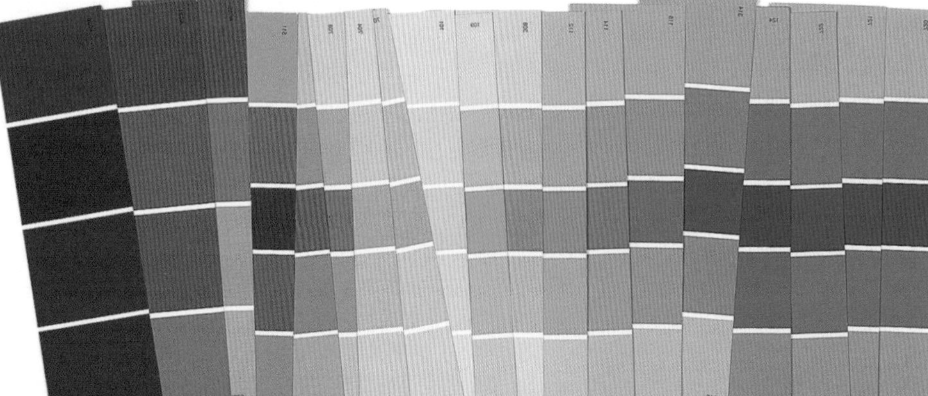

Warm and cool colours

SEE ALSO > Tone 34–5, Texture 36, Pattern 37, Manipulating space 38–9

Vibrant colour
(left)
There's nothing tame or safe about this colour scheme – a striking interior created by juxtaposing bold areas of blue, green and yellow.

Cool but comfortable
(below left)
A cool colour scheme that is fresh and light – but also welcoming, thanks to careful use of soft furnishings and fabrics.

Warm and cosy
(below right)
A welcoming and cosy bathroom created by warm yellows and natural materials.

SEE ALSO > Tone 34–5, Texture 36, Pattern 37, Manipulating space 38–9

Using tone for subtlety

Pure colours can be used to great effect for both exterior and interior colour schemes, but a more subtle combination of colours is called for in most situations. Subtle colours are made by mixing different percentages of pure colour, or simply by changing the tone of a colour by adding a neutral.

Neutrals

The purest forms of neutral are black and white, from which colour is entirely absent. The range of neutrals can be extended by mixing the two together to produce varying tones of grey. Neutrals are used extensively by decorators because they do not clash with any other colour, but in their simplest forms they can be either stark or rather bland. Consequently, a touch of colour is normally added to a grey to give it a warm or cool bias, so that it can pick up the character of another colour with which it harmonizes, or provide an almost imperceptible contrast with a range of colours.

Tints

Changing the tone of pure colours by adding white creates pastel colours or tints. Used in combination, tints are safe colours – it is difficult to produce anything but a harmonious scheme, whatever colours you use together. The effect can be very different, however, if a pale tint is contrasted with dark tones to produce a dramatic result.

Shades

The shades of a colour are produced by adding black to it. Shades are rich, dramatic colours, used for bold yet sophisticated schemes. It is within this range of colours that browns appear – the interior designer's stock-in-trade. Brown blends so harmoniously into almost any colour scheme that it is tantamount to a neutral.

Neutrals
A range of neutral tones introduces all manner of subtle colours.

SEE ALSO > Colour theory 32–3, Texture 36, Pattern 37, Manipulating space 38–9

Coordinated harmony
Pale colours are often used when a safe harmonious scheme is required. Darker shades from the same range of colours provide the necessary tonal contrast. With this approach, it is almost impossible to go wrong.

Tints
(above)
A composition of pale tints is always harmonious and attractive.

Shades
(right)
Use darker tones, or shades, for rich, dramatic effects.

Resolutely neutral
(left)
A room that is totally uncompromising in its use of neutral grey tiles, white paint and glass bricks. If required, the balance of the scheme can be shifted at any time by introducing different accessories that add small accents of colour.

SEE ALSO > Tone 34–5, Texture 36, Pattern 37, Manipulating space 38–9

Taking texture into account

We are much more aware of the colour of a surface than of the surface's texture, which we almost take for granted – but texture is a vital ingredient of any decorative scheme and merits careful thought.

The visual effect of texture is created by the strength and direction of the light that falls on it. A smooth surface reflects more light than one that is rough. Coarse textures absorb light, even creating shadows if the light falls at a shallow angle. Consequently, a colour will look different according to whether it is applied to a smooth surface or a textured one.

Even without applied colour, texture adds interest to a scheme. You can contrast bare brickwork with smooth paintwork, for instance, or use the reflective qualities of glass, metal or glazed ceramics to produce some stunning decorative effects.

Like colour, texture can be employed to make an impression on our senses. Cork, wood, coarsely woven fabrics and rugs add warmth, even a sense of luxury, to an interior. Smooth or reflective materials, such as polished stone, stainless steel, ceramic tiles, vinyl, or even a black-lacquered surface, give a clean, almost clinical, feeling to a room.

Sleek and modern
(below left)
A stunning combination of stainless steel and marble mounted against a high-gloss reflective background is made richer still by the use of bold colour.

Natural materials
(below right)
A wealth of textures – exposed stonework, flagstones, varnished and painted wood – fuse into an interior that is both warm and inviting.

SEE ALSO > Colour theory 32–3, Tone 34–5, Pattern 37, Manipulating space 38–9

Using pattern for effect

Fashionable purist approaches to design have made us afraid to use pattern boldly – whereas our less inhibited forefathers felt free to cover their homes with pattern and applied decoration, with spectacular results, creating a sense of gaiety and excitement that is difficult to evoke in any other way.

A well-designed patterned wallpaper, fabric or rug can provide the basis for an entire colour scheme, and a professional designer will have chosen the colours to form a pleasing combination. There is no reason why the same colours should not look equally attractive when applied to the other surfaces of a room, but perhaps the safest way to incorporate a pattern is to use it on one surface only, to contrast with plain colours elsewhere.

Combining different patterns can be tricky, but a small, regular pattern normally works well with large, bold decoration. Also, different patterns with a similar dominating colour can coordinate well, even if you experiment with contrasting tones. Another approach is to use the same pattern in different colourways. When selecting patterns, bear in mind the kind of atmosphere you want to create.

Geometric patterns
(below left)
An eclectic mixture of styles and influences, but the predominance of geometric shapes and patterns draws them into a cohesive whole.

Exotic bedroom
(below right)
Simply by juxtaposing brightly coloured fabrics in bold patterns, you can create a luxurious yet totally modern ambience.

SEE ALSO > Colour theory 32–3, Tone 34–5, Texture 36, Manipulating space 38–9

Manipulating space

There are nearly always areas of a house that feel uncomfortably small or, conversely, so spacious that one feels isolated, almost vulnerable.

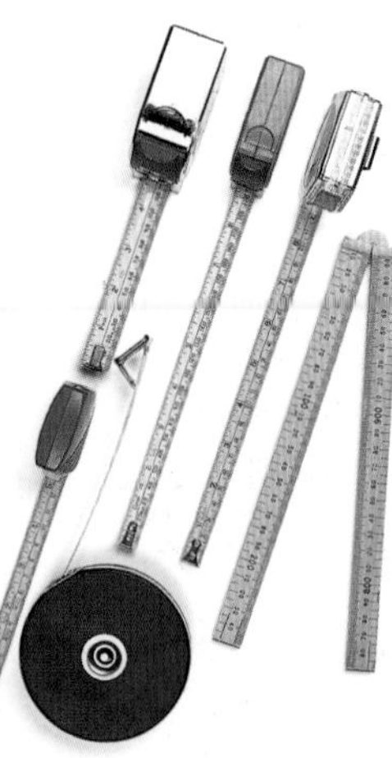

Your first reaction may be to consider structural alterations such as knocking down a wall or installing a false ceiling. In some cases, measures of this kind will prove to be the most effective solution - but they will inevitably be more expensive and disruptive than manipulating space by using colour, tone and pattern. Our eyes perceive colours and tones in such a way that it is possible to create optical illusions that apparently change the dimensions of a room. Warm colours appear to advance - so a room painted brown, red or orange will give the impression of being smaller than the same room decorated in cool colours, such as blues and greens, which have a tendency to recede.

Tone can be used to modify or reinforce the required illusion. Dark tones - even when you are using cool colours - will advance, while pale tones will open up a space visually.

The same qualities of colour and tone will change the proportions of a space. Adjusting the height of a ceiling is an obvious example. If you paint a ceiling a darker tone than the walls, it will appear lower. If you treat the floor in a similar way, you can almost make the room seem squeezed between the ceiling and the floor. A long, narrow passageway will feel less claustrophobic if you push out the walls by decorating them with pale, cool colours - which will, incidentally, reflect more light as well.

Using linear pattern is yet another way to alter the perception of space. Vertically striped wallpaper or wood-strip panelling on the walls will counteract the effect of a low ceiling. Venetian blinds make windows seem wider, and stripped wooden floors are stretched in the direction of the boards. Any large-scale pattern draws attention to itself and - in the same way as warm, dark colours - will advance, while from a distance small patterns appear as an overall texture and so have less effect.

Practical experiments
A model can help determine whether an optical illusion will have the desired effect.

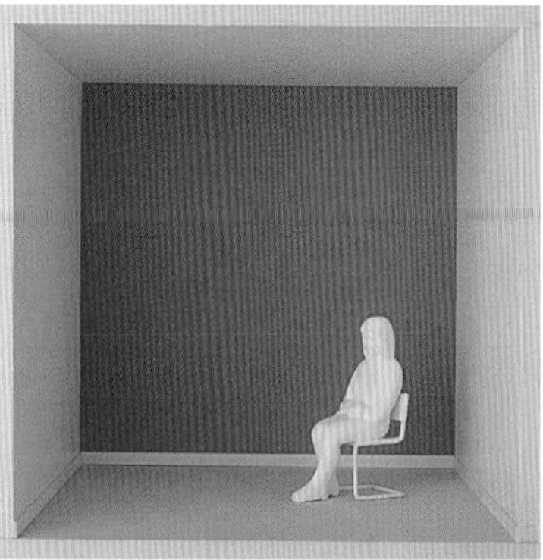

Warm colours appear to advance

A cool colour or pale tone will recede

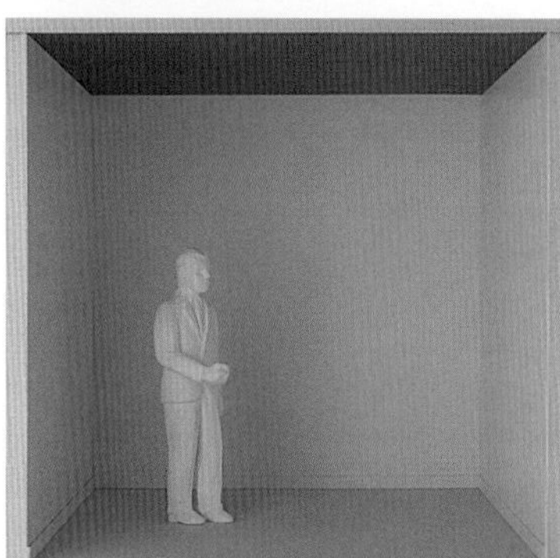

A dark ceiling will appear lower

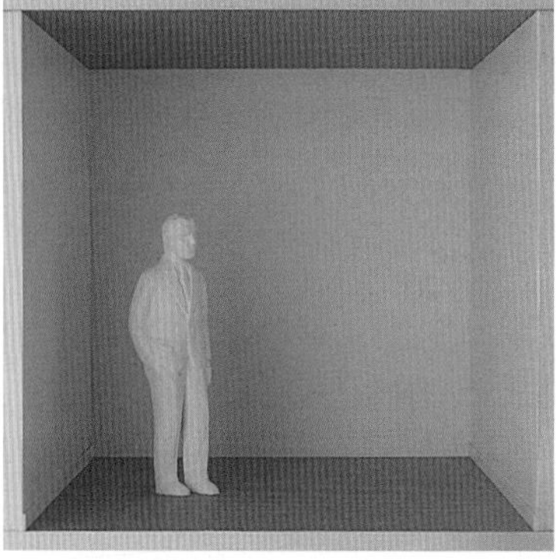

A dark floor and ceiling make a room feel smaller

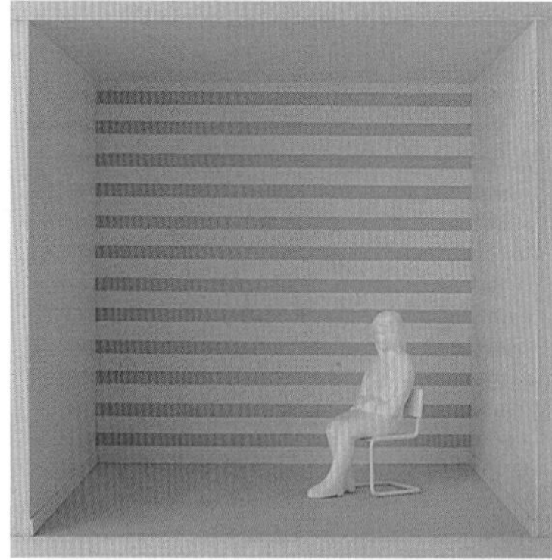

Horizontal stripes make a wall seem wider

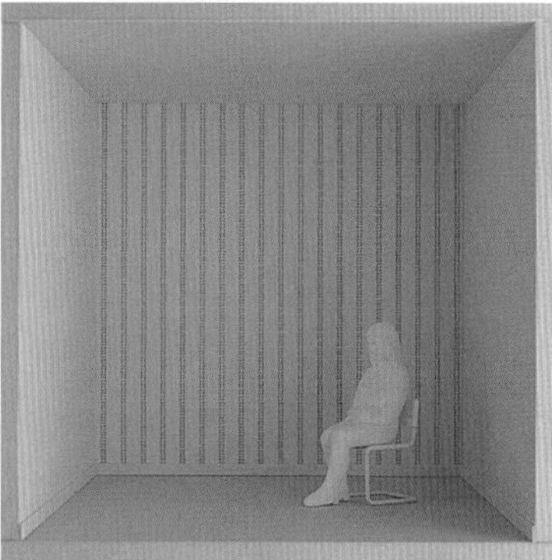

Vertical stripes increase the height

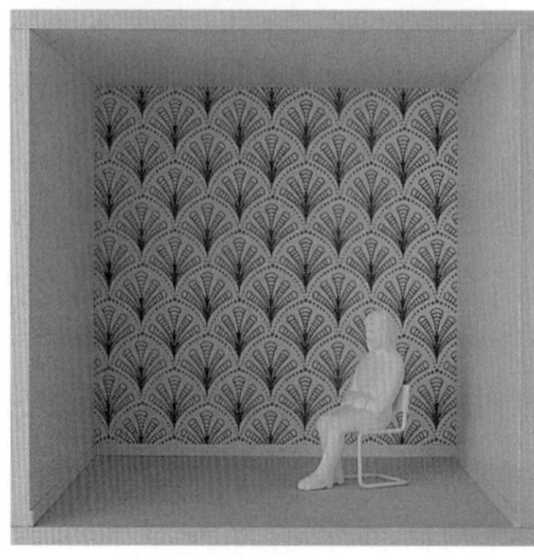

Large-scale patterns advance

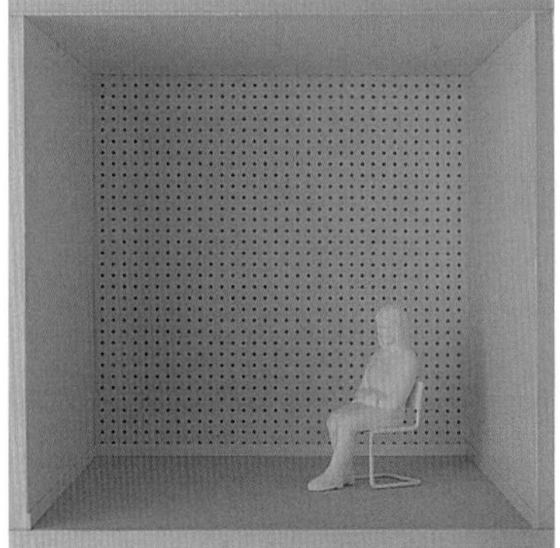

A small, regular pattern recedes

SEE ALSO > Colour theory 32–3, Tone 34–5, Texture 36, Pattern 37

Verifying your scheme

Before you spend money on paint, carpet or wallcoverings, collect samples of the materials you propose to use, in order to gauge the effect of one colour or texture on another.

Collecting samples

Make your first selection from the more limited choice of furniture fabrics or carpets. Collect offcuts of the other materials that you are considering, or borrow sample books or display samples from suppliers, so you can compare them at home. Because paint charts are printed, you can never be absolutely confident they will match the actual paint. Consequently, some manufacturers produce small sample pots of paint so that you can make test patches on the wall or woodwork.

Making a sample board

Professional designers make sample boards to check the relative proportions of materials as they will appear in a room. Usually a patch of carpet or wallcovering will be the largest dominating area of colour; painted woodwork will be proportionally smaller; and accessories might be represented by small spots of colour. Make your own board by gluing your assembly of materials to stiff card, butting one piece against another to avoid leaving a white border around each sample, which would change the combined effect.

Incorporating existing features

Most schemes will have to incorporate existing features, such as a bathroom suite or kitchen units. Use these items as starting points, building the colour scheme around them. Cut a hole in your sample board to use as a window for viewing existing materials or borrowed examples against those on the card.

Checking your colour selection
View your samples in natural and artificial light to check your colour selection.

Not an inch to spare
(left)
A tiny but exquisitely planned shower room makes the most of every inch of space. The use of pale neutrals, relieved by simple geometric tiling, keeps the room from feeling claustrophobic.

Optical illusions
(below)
A cramped space can feel like a dungeon, but in this case pale tints with a slightly warm bias are used to push out the walls, and the vertical stripes help lift the ceiling. The room, which is 'doubled' by floor-to-ceiling mirrors in the kitchen alcove, is flooded with natural light from the raised clerestory above.

SEE ALSO > Colour theory 32–3, Tone 34–5, Texture 36, Pattern 37

Preparation and priming

Thorough preparation of all surfaces is a vital first step in redecorating. If you neglect this stage, subsequent finishes may be rejected. Preparation means removing dirt, grease and loose or flaking finishes, as well as repairing serious deterioration such as cracks, holes, corrosion and decay. It is not only old surfaces that need attention. New timber must be sealed for protection, and priming is necessary to ensure a surface is in a suitable condition to accept its finish.

Seal absorbent MDF with special primer

Seal bare porous concrete

Coat new plaster with alkali-resistant primer

Listed here are the primers and sealers for all the materials and surfaces you are likely to encounter when decorating in and around your home. The same substrates and coatings are examined in detail throughout this chapter.

Primers for wood and man-made boards

Standard wood primer

The traditional solvent-based wood primer prevents subsequent coats of paint soaking into bare timber. White primer is used mostly on softwoods, while a pink primer is available for darker timbers. This type of primer can be used both outside the house and for interior decoration.

Acrylic wood primer

Water-based acrylic primers do not have the strong smell associated with solvent-based finishes and tend to dry faster. Another advantage is that you are able to wash brushes and pads in water. An acrylic primer is suitable for most timbers and boards, and some can be used as a primer and as an undercoat.

Aluminium wood primer

This primer is formulated to cover resinous softwoods and oily hardwoods such as teak and afrormosia. The same primer can be used to seal timber that has been treated with a timber preservative, preventing it bleeding through subsequent coats of paint.

MDF primer and clear sealer

Medium-density fibreboard (MDF) is particularly absorbent and can be difficult to seal satisfactorily, especially with solvent-based primers. Consequently, many paint manufacturers now offer a water-based white primer specially formulated for MDF. If you want to apply a coloured varnish stain, there is a clear sealer for MDF.

Primer/sealers for masonry

Alkali-resistant primer

Prevents the alkali content (salts) of building materials, such as mortar and plaster, from attacking decorative finishes. Once it is dry, the primer can be overcoated with emulsion and gloss paint, and also forms a suitable surface for wallcoverings.

Stabilizing solution/primer

Used to bind powdery or flaky materials, and to control suction on new plaster surfaces. It comes as a clear liquid or as a white primer. Use stabilizing solution as a primer to prevent traditional finishes such as distemper and limewash from shedding subsequent coats of emulsion or masonry paint.

Concrete sealer

This is ideal for sealing bare porous concrete, especially before applying a compatible floor paint. It is usually applied with a roller on a long extended handle.

Water repellent

This liquid is used for sealing porous masonry against water penetration. Although it contains a fugitive dye to help you apply it evenly, it dries colourless.

Dirt repellent

Applied over masonry paints, a clear dirt repellent minimizes dirt retention by inducing rainwater to disperse evenly over the surface, avoiding those unsightly dirt-carrying runs.

Quick-drying spirit-thinned primer

A useful white primer for obliterating troublesome stains on painted masonry, preventing them bleeding through a fresh coating. It is also one of the few materials that will successfully seal creosoted timber, tar and bitumen. Methylated spirit is the thinner for this primer, which is touch-dry in 10 minutes and can be overpainted after 30 minutes.

SEE ALSO > Priming brick 44, Waterproofing masonry 44, Repairing render 45, Flaking paint 46, Priming plaster 48, Preparing wood 52–6

Metal primers

Red-oxide primer
For decades red-oxide primer has been used as a protective coating to protect iron and steel from rust. One coat of this dark-coloured primer is sufficient as a base for decorative finishes.

Water-based metal primer
A quick-drying primer for most metals, both inside and outside the house. It will protect well-prepared ferrous metals, provided it is applied within the same working day. It is not a suitable primer for untreated galvanized metal.

Rust-inhibitive primer
This primer can be used directly over rusty iron and steel, provided all loose material has been removed previously with a wire brush or abrasive paper. This is an ideal primer to prevent further corrosion of garden furniture, gates and railings.

Zinc-phosphate primer
This versatile primer can be used on a wide variety of ferrous and non-ferrous metals, including galvanized metal and aluminium. It is suitable for interior and exterior locations.

Galvanized-metal primer
Galvanized metal tends to shed the majority of paints unless it is adequately sealed. Consequently, many manufacturers now offer a special primer for this extraordinarily difficult substrate. Use this primer as a protective coating on corrugated iron and new galvanized garage doors.

Radiator primer
This can be used on bare metal, and it can be used as additional protection on factory-primed and previously painted radiators. It dries within an hour and can be overpainted with any radiator enamel.

Prime melamine surfaces before painting

Specialized primer/sealers

UPVC primer
An essential primer for refurbishing exterior UPVC windows and doors. It provides superior adhesion for top coats.

Ceramic-tile primer
For use on interior wall tiles prior to coating with special tile paint. Without this primer, the paint would quickly peel from the glossy surface of glazed tiles.

Melamine primer
Specially formulated to enable you to brighten up dowdy melamine kitchen doors and drawer fronts. It can be used as a base for any good-quality gloss or satin paint. Brushes can be washed in water.

Stain sealer
Permanently seals problem stains such as nicotine, soot, crayon and ballpoint pen. It is most useful for masking disfiguring water stains caused by a leaking roof or plumbing, and is often the only way to cover up painted graffiti. Stain sealer can be brushed onto the surface, but it is also available in aerosols for spraying over small areas. Once it is dry, you can overcoat the sealer with emulsion or solvent-based paints.

Damp sealers
Formulated to prevent damp stains spoiling interior decorations. It does not eradicate the causes of rising or penetrating damp, which should be tackled prior to decorating.

Prevent damp stains spoiling new paintwork

Lead in paint

Lead – which is highly poisonous – was widely used in the past as a dryer in solvent-based paints, including primers. (Acrylic paints and emulsions are water-based and have never contained lead.) Most solvent-based paints are now made without added lead.

If possible, choose paints that are labelled 'no lead added' or similar. Never let young children chew old painted surfaces in case they have a high lead content.

Universal primers

General-purpose primers and multi-surface primers are convenient when you need to prepare newly built or refurbished rooms for decorating. You can prime plastered walls, architraves, skirting boards and other woodwork all at the same time, using the same primer.

Cover difficult marks with a stain sealer

SEE ALSO > Flaking paint 46, Priming plaster 48, Preparing wood 52–6, Priming metal 60–1

Brick and stone

Before you start to decorate, check the condition of the brick and stonework and carry out any necessary repairs. Unless you live in an area of the country where there is a tradition of painting brick and stonework, you may want to restore painted masonry to its original condition. Although some paint strippers cannot cope with textured surfaces, there are thick-paste paint removers that will peel away layers of old paint from masonry.

Treating new masonry

New brickwork or stonework should be left for about 3 months, until completely dry, before any further treatment is considered.

White powdery deposits – called efflorescence – may come to the surface over this period, but you can simply brush them off with a stiff-bristle brush or a piece of dry sacking (see right). New masonry should be weatherproof and so should require no further treatment, except that in some areas of the country you may wish to apply paint.

Cleaning off unsightly mould

Paint-stained brickwork

Organic growth

Efflorescence

Colourful lichens growing on garden walls can be very attractive. Indeed, some people actively encourage their growth. However, since the spread of moulds and lichens depends on damp conditions, it is not a good sign when they occur naturally on the walls of your house.

Try to identify the source of the problem before treating the growth. For example, if one side of the house never receives any sun, it will have little chance of drying out. Relieve the situation by cutting back overhanging trees or adjacent shrubs to increase ventilation to the wall.

Make sure the damp-proof course (DPC) is working adequately and is not being bridged by piled earth or debris.

Cracked or corroded rainwater pipes leaking onto the wall are another common cause of organic growth. Feel behind the pipe with your fingers, or slip a hand mirror behind it to see if there's a leak.

Neutralizing the growth

Scrape organic growth from the bricks, using a non-metallic spatula, then brush the masonry vigorously with a stiff-bristle brush. This can be a dusty job, so wear a face mask. Brush away from you to avoid debris being flicked into your eyes.

Starting at the top of the wall, use a nylon brush to paint on a fungicidal solution, diluted according to the manufacturer's instructions. Apply the fungicide liberally and leave the wall to dry for 24 hours, then rinse the masonry thoroughly with clean water. In extreme cases, give the wall two washes of fungicide, allowing 24 hours between applications and a further 24 hours before washing it down with water.

Removing efflorescence

Soluble salts within building materials such as cement, brick and stone gradually migrate to the surface, along with the moisture, as a wall dries out. The result is the white crystalline deposit known as efflorescence.

The same condition can occur on old masonry if it is subjected to more than average moisture. Efflorescence itself is not harmful, but the source of the damp must be identified and cured.

Brush the deposit from the wall regularly, with a dry stiff-bristle brush or coarse sacking, until the crystals cease to form. Don't attempt to wash off the crystals – they will merely dissolve in the water and soak back into the wall. Above all, don't decorate a wall that is still efflorescing, as this is a sign that it is still damp.

Masonry paints and clear sealants that let the wall breathe are not affected by the alkali content of the masonry, so can be used without applying a primer. If you plan to use solvent-based (oil) paint, coat the wall first with an alkali-resistant primer.

Curing efflorescence
Brush the white deposit from the wall with a stiff-bristle brush or a piece of coarse sacking until the crystals cease to form.

SEE ALSO > Stripping painted masonry 46, Painting exterior masonry 64–6, Masonry paints 650, Curing damp 247–54

Cleaning masonry

You can often spruce up old masonry by washing off surface grime with water. Strong solvents will harm certain types of stone - so seek the advice of an experienced local builder before applying anything other than water.

Washing the wall

Starting at the top of the wall, play a hose gently onto the masonry while you scrub it with a stiff-bristle brush. Scrub heavy deposits with half a cup of ammonia added to a bucketful of water, then rinse again. Avoid soaking brick or stone when a frost is forecast.

Removing unsightly stains

Soften tar, grease and oil stains by applying a poultice made from fuller's earth soaked in white spirit or in a proprietary grease solvent (check the manufacturer's instructions first).

Wearing protective gloves, dampen the stain with solvent then spread on a layer of poultice 12mm (½in) thick. Tape a sheet of plastic over the poultice, and leave it to dry out. Scrape off the dry poultice with a wooden or plastic spatula, then scrub the wall with water.

Remove dirt and dust by washing

Stripping spilled paint

To remove a patch of spilled paint, use a water-based paint stripper. Follow the manufacturer's recommendations, and wear old clothes, gloves and goggles.

Stipple the stripper onto the rough texture. Once the paint has softened, remove it with a scraper. Gently scrub the residue out of deeper crevices with a stiff-bristle brush and water. Then rinse the wall with clean water.

Stipple paint stripper onto spilled paint

Repointing masonry

A combination of frost action and erosion tends to break down the mortar pointing of brickwork and stonework. The mortar eventually falls out, exposing the open joints to wind and rain, which drive dampness through the wall to the inside. Cracked joints may also be caused by using a hard, inflexible mortar. Replace defective pointing, using a ready-mixed mortar or your own mix.

Applying the mortar

• **Mortar dyes**
Liquid or powder additives are available for changing the colour of mortar to match existing pointing. Colour matching is difficult, and smears can stain the bricks permanently.

Rake out the old pointing with a thin wooden lath to a depth of about 12mm (½in). Use a cold chisel, or a special plugging chisel, and a club hammer to dislodge sections that are firmly embedded, then brush out the joints with a stiff-bristle brush.

Spray the wall with water, to make sure the bricks or stones will not absorb too much moisture from the fresh mortar. Mix some mortar in a bucket and transfer it to a hawk. If you are mixing your own mortar, use the proportions 1 part cement : 1 part lime : 6 parts builder's sand.

Pick up a small sausage of mortar on the back of a pointing trowel and push it firmly into the upright joints. This can be difficult to do without the mortar dropping off, so hold the hawk under each joint to catch it. Try not to smear the face of the bricks with mortar, as it will stain. Use the same method for the horizontal joints. The actual shape of the pointing is not vital at this stage.

Once the mortar is firm enough to retain a thumbprint, it is ready for shaping. Because it is important that you shape the joints at exactly the right moment, you may have to point the work in stages in order to complete the wall. Shape the joints to match existing brickwork (see below), or choose a profile suitable for the prevailing weather conditions in your area.

Once you have shaped the joints, wait until the pointing has almost hardened, then brush the wall to remove traces of surplus mortar from the surface of the masonry.

Shaping the mortar joints

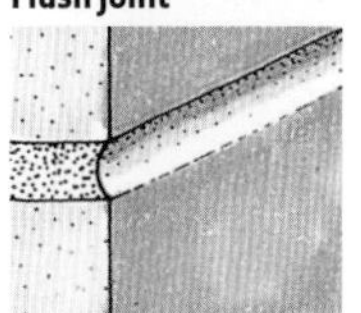

Flush joint

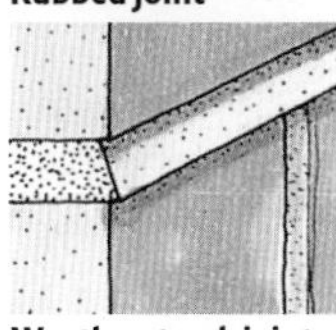

Rubbed joint

Weatherstruck joint

The joints shown here are commonly used for brickwork. Flush or rubbed joints are best for most stonework. Leave the pointing of dressed-stone ashlar blocks to an expert.

Flush joints

This is the easiest profile to produce. Scrape the mortar flush, using the edge of your trowel, then stipple the joints with a stiff-bristle brush to expose the sand aggregate.

Rubbed (concave) joints

This joint is ideal for an old wall with bricks that are not of sufficiently good quality to take a crisp joint. To make a rubbed joint, use a jointer - a tool shaped like a sled runner with a handle (the semicircular blade is run along the joints).

Flush the mortar first, then drag the jointer along the joints. Finish the vertical joints, then shape the horizontal ones. Having shaped the joints, stipple them with a brush so that they look like weathered pointing.

Weatherstruck joints

The sloping profile sheds rainwater from the wall. Shape the mortar with the edge of a pointing trowel, starting with the vertical joints. Then shape the horizontal joints, allowing the mortar to spill out at the base of each joint. Finish the joint by cutting off the excess mortar with a Frenchman, a tool that has a narrow blade with the tip bent at 90 degrees. Use a wooden batten to guide the tool along the joints. Nail scraps of wood at each end of the batten to hold it off the wall. Align the batten with the bottom of the joints, then draw the tool along it to trim off the excess mortar.

Use a Frenchman to trim weatherstruck joints

SEE ALSO > Paint stripper 59, Penetrating damp 247–9, Jointer 510

Repairing masonry

Cracked masonry may simply be the result of cement-rich mortar being unable to absorb slight movements within the building. However, it could also be a sign of a more serious problem – subsiding foundations, for example. Don't just ignore the symptoms, but investigate immediately and put the necessary repairs in hand.

Filling cracked masonry

If a brick or stone wall has substantial cracks, consult a builder or your local Building Control Officer to ascertain the cause. If a crack proves to be stable, you can carry out some repairs yourself.

Cracked mortar can be removed and repointed in the normal way, but a crack that splits the bricks cannot be repaired neatly, and the damaged masonry should be replaced by a builder.

Cracks across a painted wall can be filled with mortar that has been mixed with a little PVA bonding agent to help it stick. Before you effect the repair, wet the damaged masonry with a hose to encourage the mortar to flow deeply into the crack.

Cracks may follow pointing only

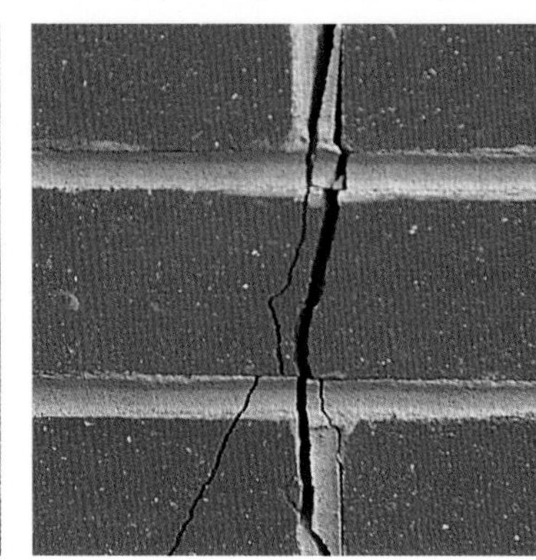

Cracked bricks could signify serious faults

Priming brickwork for painting

Brickwork will only need to be primed if it is showing signs of efflorescence or spalling. An alkali-resistant primer will guard against the former. A stabilizing solution will bind crumbling masonry and also help to seal it.

When you are painting a wall for the first time with masonry paint, you may find that the first coat is difficult to apply due to the suction of the dry porous brick. Try thinning the first coat slightly with water or solvent.

Waterproofing masonry

Colourless water-repellent fluids are intended to make masonry impervious to water without colouring it or stopping it from breathing – which is important in order to allow moisture within the walls to dry out.

Prepare the surface before applying the fluid: make good any cracks in bricks or pointing and remove organic growth, then allow the wall to dry out thoroughly. Cover adjacent plants.

The fumes from water-repellent fluid can be dangerous if inhaled, so be sure to wear a proper respirator as recommended by the manufacturer. Also, wear eye protectors. Apply the fluid generously with a large paintbrush, from the bottom up, and stipple it into the joints. Apply a second coat as soon as the first has been absorbed, to ensure there are no bare patches where water could seep in. So that you can be sure you are covering the wall properly, use a sealant containing a fugitive dye, which disappears after a specified period of time.

Carefully paint up to surrounding woodwork. If you accidentally splash sealant onto it, wash it down immediately with a cloth dampened with white spirit. If you need to treat a whole house, it may be worth hiring a company that can spray the sealant. Make sure the workmen rig up plastic-sheet screens to prevent overspray drifting across to your neighbours' property.

Spalled masonry

Moisture that has penetrated soft masonry will expand in icy weather, flaking off the outer face of brickwork and stonework. The result, known as spalling, is unattractive and admits more moisture.

If spalling is localized, cut out the bricks or stones and replace them with matching ones. The sequence below describes how to repair spalled brickwork, but the process is similar for a stone wall.

Where spalling is extensive, the only practical solution is to accept its less-than-perfect appearance, repoint the masonry, and apply a clear water repellent (see bottom left).

Spalled bricks caused by frost damage

Replacing a spalled brick

Use a cold chisel and club hammer to rake out the pointing around the brick, then chop out the brick itself.

To fit the replacement brick, first dampen the opening and spread mortar on the base and one side. Then dampen the replacement brick, butter the top and one end with mortar, and slot the brick into the hole. Shape the pointing to match the surrounding brickwork.

If you can't find a replacement brick of a suitable colour, remove the spalled brick carefully, turn it round to reveal its undamaged face, and reinsert it.

Replacing a spalled brick

SEE ALSO > Primers 40–41, Efflorescence 42, Organic growth 42, Repointing 43, Masonry paints 65, Penetrating damp 247–9

Repairing render

Brickwork is sometimes clad with a smooth or roughcast cement-based render, both for improved weatherproofing and to provide a decorative finish. Render is susceptible to the effects of damp and frost, which can cause cracking, bulging and staining. Before you redecorate a rendered wall, make good any damage and clean off surface dirt, mould growth and flaky material in order to achieve a long-lasting finish.

Repairing cracks

Cracked render allows moisture to penetrate

You can usually ignore fine hairline cracks in a rendered wall if you intend to paint the the surface with a reinforced masonry paint, but rake out larger cracks with a cold chisel. Dampen them with water and fill flush with a cement-based exterior filler. Fill any major cracks with a render made of 1 part cement, 2 parts lime and 9 parts builder's sand, plus a little PVA bonding agent to help it stick to the wall.

Reinforcing a crack

To prevent a crack in render opening up again, you can reinforce the repair with a polyester membrane embedded in a special primer that is sold specifically for use with the membrane. However, you will need to redecorate the wall with textured paint or a textured coating in order to disguise the repair.

Rake out the crack to remove loose material, then wet it. Fill just proud of the surface with a mortar mix of 1 part cement to 4 parts builder's sand. When this has stiffened, scrape it flush. When the mortar has hardened, brush on a generous coat of the primer, making sure it extends at least 100mm (4in) on both sides of the crack. Embed strips of polyester membrane into the coating, using a stippling and brushing action (**1**). While it is still wet, feather the edges of the primer with a foam roller (**2**), bedding the scrim into it. After 24 hours, apply a second coat of primer and feather with the roller. When the primer is dry, apply the textured paint or coating.

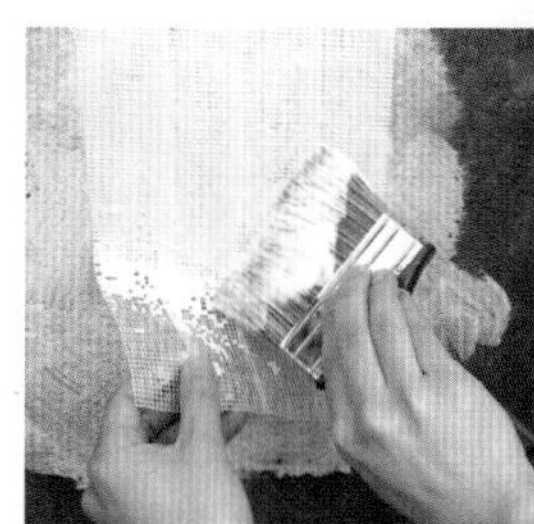

1 Embed the scrim

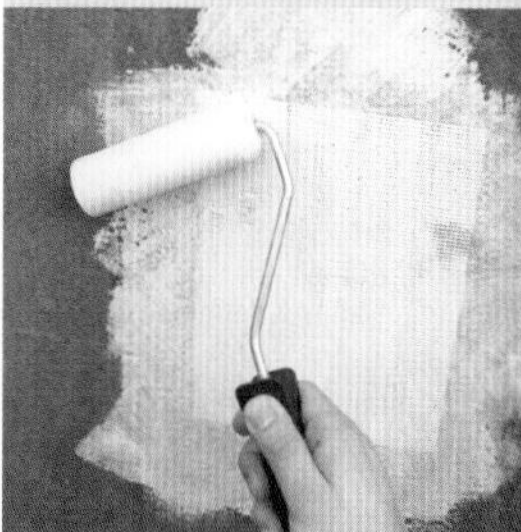

2 Feather with a roller

Blown pebbledash eventually falls off the wall

Patching render

Bulges in render normally indicate that the cladding has parted from the masonry. Tap the wall gently with a wooden mallet to find the extent of these hollow areas, then hack off the material to sound edges. Use a club hammer and bolster chisel to undercut the perimeter of each hole except for the bottom edge - which should be left square, so that is does not collect water.

Brush out the debris, then apply a coat of PVA bonding agent. When it becomes tacky, trowel on a layer of 1 : 2 : 9 render, 12mm (½in) thick, using plasterer's sand. Leave the render to set firm but not hard, then scratch it with a criss-cross pattern to form a key (**1**) for the finishing coat of render.

Next day, fill flush with a weaker mix (1 : 3 : 12) and scrape it level, using a straight wooden batten that is wide enough to span the repaired patch. Starting at the bottom, work your way upward, using a zigzag motion to scrape off excess render (**2**). Smooth the surface with a wooden float, using circular strokes.

1 Key the surface

2 Scrape the render level

Patching pebbledash

Throw chippings onto the wet render

For additional weatherproofing, small stone chippings are stuck to a thin coat of render over a thicker base coat, a process known as 'pebbledashing'. If water gets behind pebbledashing, one or both layers may separate. Hack off any loose render to a sound base, then seal it with stabilizer. If necessary, repair the underlying scratchcoat of render (see above).

It is rarely possible to match the colour of the original chippings, so it is usually best to paint a repaired wall.

Reclaim the chippings that inevitably fall to the ground by spreading a sheet of polythene at the foot of the wall before you start work.

Mix up the top coat of render, adding a little PVA bonding agent. Apply this coat as described above and, while it is still wet, fling washed chippings onto the surface from a dustpan. You may have to repeat the process until the coverage is even, then level the chippings by tamping them lightly with a wooden float.

SEE ALSO > Masonry paints 65

Painted masonry

Painted masonry inside the house is usually in fairly good order and, apart from a good wash-down to remove dust and grease and a light sanding to give a key for the new finish, there is little else you need to do. Outside, however, it's a different matter. Exterior surfaces, subjected to extremes of heat, cold and rain, are likely to be affected to some degree by stains, flaking and chalkiness.

Curing a chalky surface

Rub the palm of your hand lightly over the surface of the wall to see if it is chalky. If the paint rubs off as a powdery deposit, treat the wall before you redecorate.

Brush the surface with a stiff-bristle brush, then paint the whole wall liberally with a stabilizing primer, which will bind the chalky surface so that paint will adhere to it. Use a white stabilizing primer, which can also serve as an undercoat. Clean splashes of the fluid from surrounding woodwork with white spirit.

If the wall is very dusty, apply a second coat of stabilizer after about 16 hours, then wait a further 16 hours before applying paint to the wall.

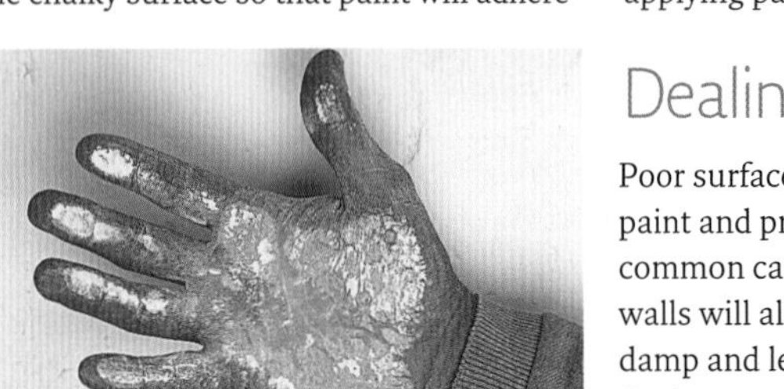

A chalky surface needs stabilizing

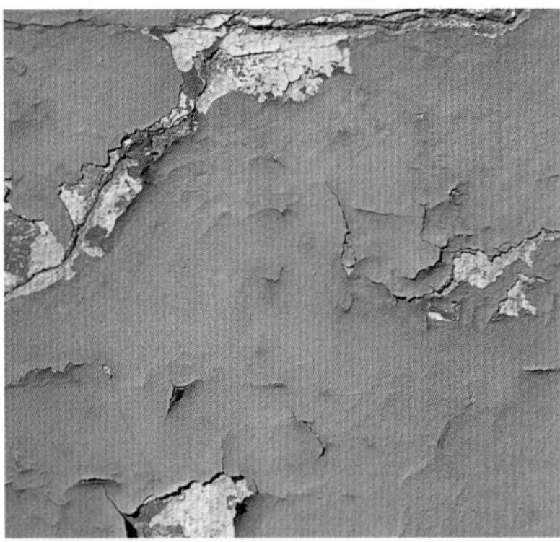

Strip flaky paintwork to a sound surface

Chimney stained by tar deposits from the flue

Dealing with flaky paint

Poor surface preparation or incompatible paint and preparatory treatments are common causes of flaky paintwork. Damp walls will also cause flaking, so cure the damp and let the wall dry out before further treatment. A new coat of paint will not bind to a flaky surface, so this needs to be remedied before you start painting. Use a paint scraper and stiff-bristle brush to remove all loose material. Coarse glasspaper should finish the job, or at least feather the edges of any stubborn patches. Stabilize the surface as for chalky walls.

Treating a stained chimney

If the outlines of brick courses show up as brown staining on a painted chimney stack, you can be certain it is caused by a breakdown of the internal rendering, or 'pargeting', of the chimney. Defective pargeting allows tar deposits to migrate through the mortar joints to the outer paintwork. To solve the problem, first fit a flue liner in the chimney, then treat the brown stains with a quick-drying thinned primer before applying a fresh coat of paint.

Stripping paint

In the past even sound brickwork was often painted, simply to 'brighten up' a house. In some areas of the country where painted masonry is traditional, there is every reason to continue with the practice. Indeed, houses with soft, inferior brickwork were frequently painted when they were built in order to protect them from the weather – and to strip them now could have serious consequences. However, one painted house in an otherwise natural-brick terrace tends to spoil the whole row; and painting one half of a pair of semi-detached houses may have an equally undesirable effect.

Restoring painted brickwork to its natural condition is not an easy task. It is generally a messy business, involving the use of toxic materials that have to be handled with care and disposed of safely. Extensive scaffolding may be required and, most importantly, getting the masonry entirely clean demands considerable experience. For all these reasons, it is advisable to hire professionals to do the work for you.

To determine whether the outcome is likely to be successful, ask the company you are thinking of hiring to strip an inconspicuous patch of masonry, using the chemicals they recommend for the job. The results may indicate that it is better to repaint – in which case, choose a good-quality masonry paint that will let moisture within the walls evaporate.

SEE ALSO > Primers 40–41, Spalled masonry 44. Curing damp 247–54, Flue liners 402

Repairing concrete

In common with other building materials, concrete suffers from the effects of damp – spalling and efflorescence – and related defects, such as cracking and crumbling. Repairs can usually be made in much the same way as for brickwork and render, although there are some special considerations you should be aware of. If the damage is widespread, resurface the concrete before decorating.

Sealing concrete

New concrete has a high alkali content. Efflorescence can therefore develop on the surface as it dries out. Use only water-thinnable paint until the concrete is completely dry. When treating efflorescence on concrete, follow the procedure recommended for brickwork. A porous concrete wall should be waterproofed with a clear sealant on the exterior.

Cleaning dirty concrete

You can scrub dirty concrete with water (as described for brickwork); but when a concrete drive or garage floor is stained with patches of oil or grease, you will need to apply a proprietary oil-and-grease remover. This is a detergent that is normally diluted with an equal amount of water, but can be used neat on heavy staining. Brush on the solution liberally, then scrub the surface with a stiff-bristle brush. Rinse off with clean water. It is advisable to wear eye protection. Keep all windows and doors open when working indoors.

It is worth soaking up fresh oil spillages immediately with dry sand or sawdust, to prevent them becoming permanent stains.

Repairing cracks and holes

Rake out and brush away loose debris from cracks and holes in concrete. If the crack is less than 6mm (¼in) wide, open it up a little with a cold chisel so it will accept a filling (see below). Undercut the edges to form a lip, so that the filler will grip. To fill a hole in concrete, add a fine aggregate such as gravel to a sand-and-cement mix. Make sure the fresh concrete sticks in shallow depressions by priming the damaged surface with 3 parts bonding agent : 1 part water. When the primed surface is tacky, trowel in the concrete and smooth it.

Undercut the edges of a crack

Cement-based exterior fillers

As an alternative to making up your own sand-and-cement mix, you can use a proprietary cement-based exterior filler for patching holes in concrete and rebuilding chipped or broken corners. When mixed with water, the filler remains workable for 10 to 20 minutes. Just before it sets hard, smooth or scrape the filler level.

Binding dusty concrete

Concrete is trowelled when it is laid, to give it a flat finish. If the trowelling is overdone, cement is brought to the surface; and when the concrete dries out, this thin layer begins to break up, producing a loose, dusty surface. Though not always applicable, it is generally recommended that you paint on a concrete-floor sealer before applying decorative finishes. Treat a dusty concrete wall with stabilizing primer.

Levelling concrete floors

An uneven or pitted concrete floor must be made level before you apply any form of floorcovering. You can do this fairly easily yourself using a proprietary self-levelling compound, but ensure the surface is dry before proceeding.

Testing for damp

If you suspect a concrete floor is damp, make a simple test by laying a small piece of polythene on the concrete and sealing it all round with self-adhesive parcel tape. After one or two days, inspect it for any traces of moisture on the underside.

If the test indicates that treatment is required, apply three coats of heavy-duty moisture-cured polyurethane sealant. No longer than 4 hours should elapse between coats. The floor should be as dry as possible, so that it is porous enough for the first coat to penetrate. If necessary, use a fan heater to help dry the floor.

Before applying a self-levelling compound, lightly scatter dry sand over the last coat of sealant while it is still wet. Allow it to harden for three days, then brush off loose residual sand.

Applying a self-levelling compound

Self-levelling compound is supplied as a powder that you mix with water. Having made sure the floor is clean and free from damp (see above), pour some of the compound in the corner that is furthest away from the door. Spread the compound with a trowel until it is about 3mm (⅛in) thick, then leave it to seek its own level. Continue across the floor, joining the areas of compound until the entire surface is covered. You can walk on the floor after an hour or so without damaging it, but leave the compound to harden for a few days before laying a permanent floorcovering.

Spread a self-levelling compound with a trowel

Treating spalled concrete
When concrete breaks up, or spalls, due to the action of frost, the process is accelerated as steel reinforcement is exposed and begins to corrode. Paint the metal with a rust-inhibitive primer before you patch the concrete with sand and cement mixed with a fine aggregate.

SEE ALSO > Primers 40–41, Efflorescence 42, Priming metal 60–61, Masonry paints 65, Damp-proof membrane 176–7, Curing damp floors 254, Mixing concrete 455

Repairing plasterwork

Solid masonry walls are usually covered with two coats of plaster: a thicker backing coat and a smooth finish coat. In older houses, ceilings and some internal walls are clad with slim strips of wood known as laths, which serve as a base for the plaster. In modern houses, plasterboard is generally used instead. Whatever you intend to use as a decorative finish, the plastered wall or ceiling must be made good by filling cracks and holes.

Preparing plasterwork

Even when your plasterwork looks in good condition, check carefully to make sure it is bonded soundly to the wall behind and that it is not decorated with a coating that would be incompatible with the paint you want to use.

Smooth finish
Smooth the surface of small repairs with a wet brush or knife in order to reduce the amount of sanding required.

New plasterwork

Before you decorate new plaster, wait to see if any efflorescence forms on the surface. Keep wiping it off with dry sacking until it ceases to appear.

Once fresh plaster is dry, you can stick ceramic tiles on the wall - but always leave it for about 6 months before decorating with wallpaper or any paint other than new-plaster emulsion. Even then, you should use an alkali-resistant primer first if you are applying solvent-based paints.

Size new absorbent plaster before hanging wallpaper, or the water will be sucked too quickly from the paste, and the paper will simply peel off the wall. If you are hanging a vinyl wallcovering, make sure the size contains fungicide.

Mix the size with water, according to the manufacturer's instructions, then brush it evenly across the walls and ceiling. If you splash size onto painted woodwork, wipe it off with a damp sponge before it dries.

Preparing old plaster

Apart from filling minor defects (see opposite) and dusting down, old dry plaster in good condition needs no further preparation. If the wall is patchy, apply a general-purpose primer. If the surface is friable, apply a stabilizing solution before decorating. Don't try to decorate damp plaster. Cure the cause of the damp, then let the plaster dry out.

Preparing painted plaster

Wash sound paintwork with sugar soap. Use medium-grade wet-and-dry abrasive paper, with water, to key the surface of gloss paint, particularly if you are going to paint over it with emulsion.

If the ceiling is stained by smoke and nicotine, prime it with a proprietary stain sealer. Sealers are sold in aerosol cans for treating isolated stains. You can use the stain sealer as the final coat or paint over it with solvent-based paints or emulsions. If you want to hang wallcoverings on oil paint, key then size the wall. Cross-line the wall with lining paper before hanging a heavy embossed wallpaper.

Remove flaking paint with a scraper or stiff-bristle brush. Feather off the edges of the paintwork with wet-and-dry abrasive paper, then treat the bare plaster patches with a general-purpose primer. If the edges of the old paintwork continue to show, prime those areas again, rubbing down afterwards. Apply stabilizing primer if the paint is friable.

You can apply ceramic tiles over sound paintwork. If there is any loose material, remove it first.

Plaster fillers

There is an extensive range of materials made specially for filling anything from cracks to deep holes in solid plaster and plasterboard.

Interior filler

General-purpose cellulose filler comes ready-mixed in tubs or as a powder for mixing to a stiff paste with water.

Deep-repair filler

Ready-mixed lightweight fillers can be used to fill holes and gaps up to 20mm (3/4in) deep without slumping. They are ideal for ceiling repairs.

Fast-setting filler

Sold in tube dispensers, fast-setting fillers are perfect for minor repairs. They set firm in 10 to 20 minutes.

Flexible acrylic fillers

Good for filling gaps between plaster and woodwork. When smoothed with a damp cloth, these gun-applied fillers can be overpainted in an hour. No sanding is required.

Expanding foam

Fill large irregular gaps and cavities with expanding polyurethane foam from an aerosol. Finish the job with cellulose or deep-repair fillers.

Repair plasters

Make more extensive repairs with easy-to-use, slow-drying repair plasters.

Dealing with distemper

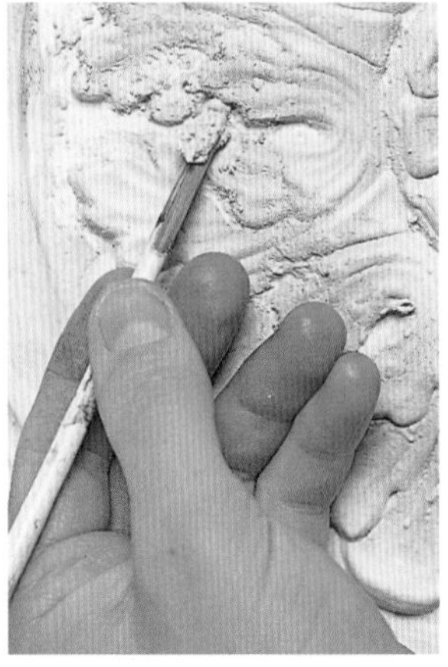

Most paints and papers will not adhere to a distempered surface, so brush away all loose material and apply a stabilizing primer to bind any traces left on the surface. You may find that delicate plaster mouldings have been obliterated by successive coats of distemper. Although it's a laborious task, you can wash off the distemper with water and a toothbrush, cleaning out clogged detail with a stick. Alternatively, hire a specialist to strip distemper with steam.

SEE ALSO > Primers 40–41, Efflorescence 42, New-plaster emulsion 67, Lining paper 84, 88, Filling plasterboard joints 168

Filling cracks and holes

Special flexible emulsions and textured paints are designed to cover hairline cracks - but larger cracks, dents and holes will reappear in a relatively short time if they are not filled adequately.

Rake loose material from a crack, using a wallpaper scraper. Undercut the edges of larger cracks in order to provide a key for the filling.

Use a paintbrush to dampen the crack, then press in cellulose filler with a filling knife. Drag the blade across the crack to force the filler in, then draw it along the crack to smooth the filler. Leave the filler standing slightly proud of the surface, ready for rubbing down smooth and flush with abrasive paper.

Fill shallow cracks in one go. But in deep cracks build up the filler in stages, letting each application set before adding more. Alternatively, switch to a deep-repair filler.

Fill and rub down small holes and dents the same way.

Press the filler into the crack, using a flexible knife

Gaps behind skirtings

Large gaps can open up between skirting boards and the wall plaster. Cellulose fillers simply fall into the cavity behind, so bridge the gap with a flexible acrylic filler or inject expanding polyurethane foam.

You can fill large gaps with expanding foam

Repairing damaged corners

Cracks sometimes appear in the corner between walls or between a wall and ceiling. Fill these by running your finger dipped in filler along the crack. When the filler has hardened, rub it down with medium-grade abrasive paper.

To build up a chipped external corner, dampen the plaster and then use a filling knife to scrape the filler onto to the damaged edge, working from both sides of the corner (1). Let the filler stiffen, then shape it with a wet finger until it closely resembles the original profile (2). When the filler is dry, smooth it with abrasive paper.

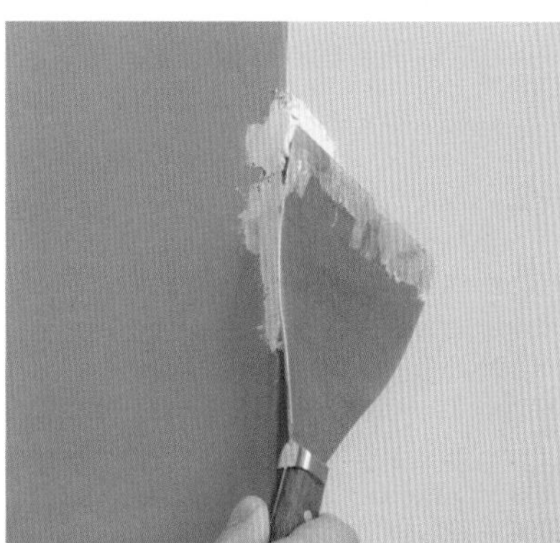

1 Build up the corner, using a filling knife

2 Shape the filler with the tip of your finger

Smoothing textured ceilings and walls
Textured coatings can be smoothed over with a lightweight non-drip repair plaster applied with a wide bladed filling knife supplied with the material.

Patching a lath-and-plaster wall

If the laths are intact, just fill any holes in the plaster with cellulose filler or repair plaster. If some laths are broken, reinforce the repair with a piece of fine expanded-metal mesh.

Rake out loose plaster, and undercut the edge of the hole with a bolster chisel. Use tinsnips to cut the metal mesh to the shape of the hole, but a little larger (1). The mesh is flexible, so you can easily bend it in order to tuck the edge behind the sound plaster all round (2). Flatten the mesh against the laths with light taps from a hammer; if possible, staple the mesh to a wall stud to hold it in place (3). For papering and tiling, patch the hole with one-coat repair plaster (4).

If you want a smoother surface for painting, finish the surface with a thin coat of skimming repair plaster.

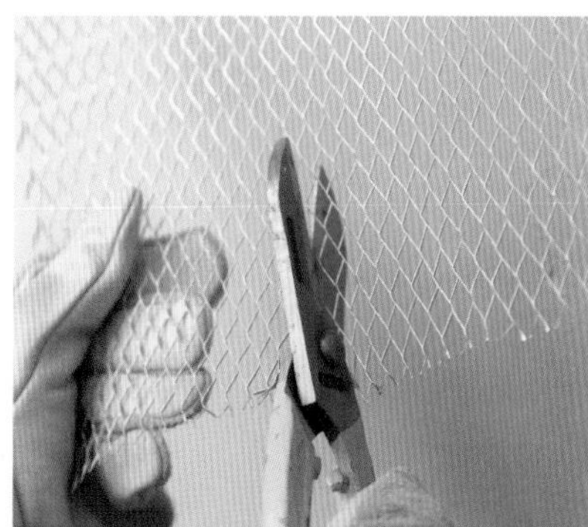

1 Cut the mesh to size, using tinsnips

2 Tuck the mesh into the hole

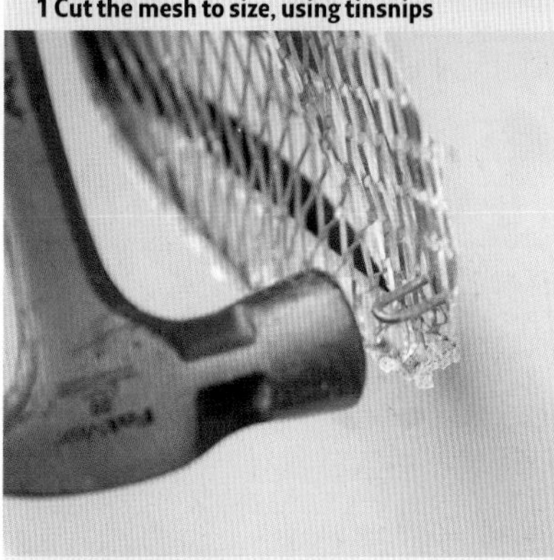

3 Staple the mesh to a wall stud

4 Patch the hole with one-coat plaster

Patching lath-and-plaster ceilings
If the laths are sound, fill flush, using a deep-repair filler or repair plaster. If the laths are broken, cut them back to the nearest joist and secure with galvanized nails. Fit a panel of plasterboard, and then spread on a coat of skimming repair plaster.

SEE ALSO > Primers 40–41, One-coat plasters 156, Plastering 158–9, Plasterboard joints 164, 168

Repairing damaged plasterboard

Unless there has been a mishap such as a serious plumbing leak, it is rare to find plasterboard in the poor condition often associated with older walls covered with lath and plaster. However, you will occasionally have to patch up damage caused by something like a piece of heavy furniture being knocked or scraped against a wall as it is being carried from room to room, or to fill a hole left by moving an electrical socket or switch.

Preparing plasterboard

Fill all joints between newly fixed plasterboards and then, whether you are painting or papering, daub all the nailheads with zinc-phosphate primer.

Before you paint plasterboard with a solvent-based paint, prime the surface with one coat of general-purpose primer. When using emulsion, you may need to paint an absorbent board with a coat of thinned paint before proceeding to apply the normal full-strength coats.

Prior to hanging wallcoverings, seal plasterboard with a general-purpose primer thinned with white spirit. After 48 hours, apply a coat of size. This will allow you in the future to strip the wallcovering without disturbing the board's paper facing.

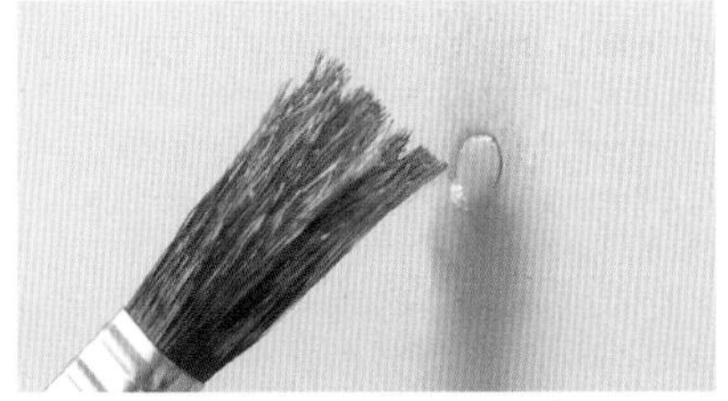

Prime plasterboard nails before filling

Filling holes in plasterboard

Use plasterer's glass-fibre patching tape to cover holes up to 75mm (3in) across, then apply cellulose filler and feather the edges. Stick several self-adhesive strips in a star shape over a large hole.

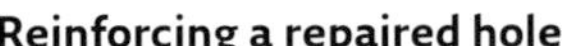

Reinforcing a repaired hole

Alternatively, use an offcut of plasterboard just larger than the hole yet narrow enough to slot through it. Bore a hole in the middle, thread a length of string through, and tie a nail to one end of the string (1). Butter the ends of the offcut with filler, then feed it into the hole (2). Pull on the string to force it against the back of the cladding (3), then press filler into the hole so that it is not quite flush with the surface (4). When the filler is hard, cut off the string and apply a thin coat of filler for a flush finish.

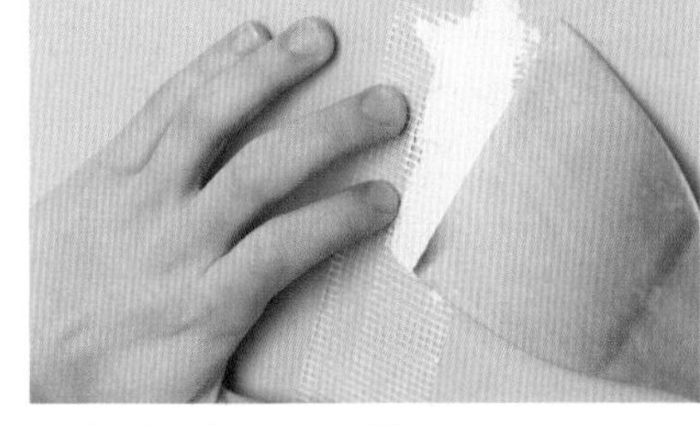

Feather the edge over patching tape

1 Attach a length of string to an offcut

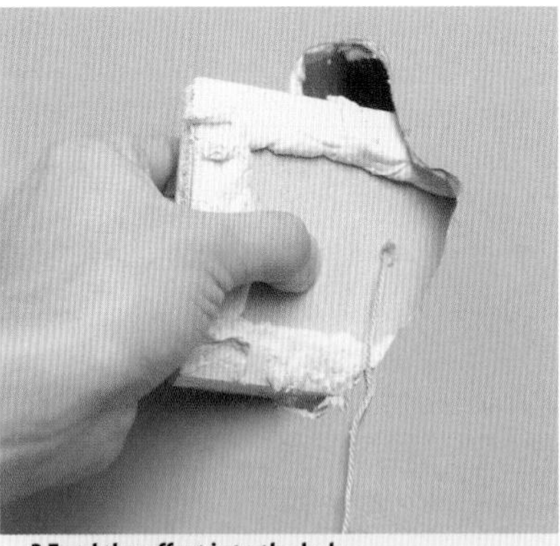

2 Feed the offcut into the hole

3 Pull on the string to hold the offcut in place

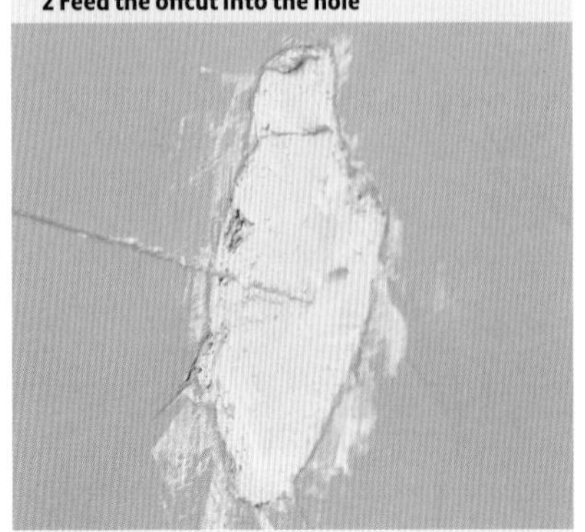

4 Press filler into the hole

Patching large holes

A large hole punched through a plasterboard wall or ceiling cannot be patched with wet plaster only. Using a sharp craft knife and a straightedge, cut back the damaged board to the nearest studs or joists at each side of the hole.

Cut a new panel of plasterboard to fit snugly within the hole and nail it to the studs, using plasterboard nails. Brush on a coat of skimming repair plaster and smooth it with a steel plasterer's trowel.

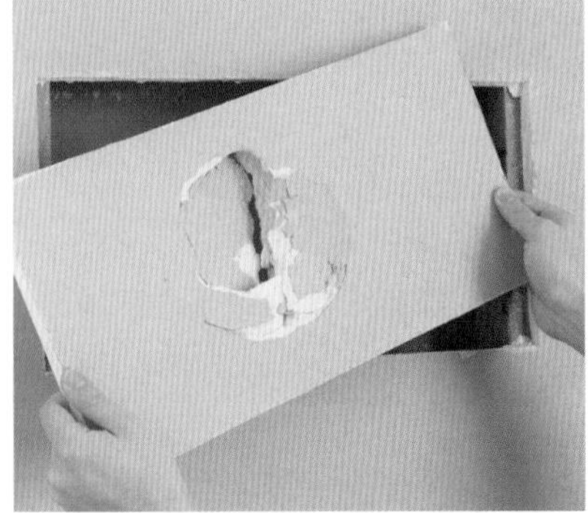

Cut back the damaged panel to nearest supports

SEE ALSO > Primers 40–41, One-coat plasters 156, Plastering 158–9, Plasterboard joints 164, 168

Stripping wallcoverings

It's always preferable to strip a previously papered surface before hanging a new wallcovering. However, if the paper is perfectly sound, you can paint it with emulsion or solvent-based paints, but painted papers can be difficult to remove in the future.

Don't attempt to paint vinyl wallcoverings, except for blown vinyl. If you opt for stripping off the old covering, the method you use will depend on the material and its condition.

Stripping conventional wallpaper

To soften the old wallpaper paste, soak the paper with warm water and a little washing-up liquid, or use a proprietary stripping powder or liquid. Apply the solution with a sponge or house-plant sprayer. Repeat and leave the water to penetrate for 15 to 20 minutes.

Use a wide metal-bladed scraper to lift the softened paper, starting at the seams. Take care not to dig the points of the blade into the plaster. Resoak stubborn areas of paper and leave them for a few minutes before stripping.

Electricity and water are a lethal combination: where possible, dry-strip around switches and sockets. If the paper cannot be stripped dry, switch off the power at the consumer unit before stripping around electrical fittings and unscrew the faceplates, so you can get at the paper trapped behind.

Collect the stripped paper in plastic sacks, then wash the wall with warm water containing a little detergent.

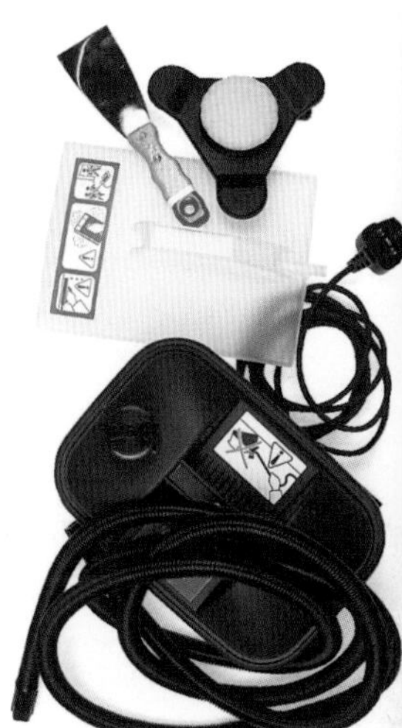

Steam stripper
Hire or buy a lightweight steam stripper to soften stubborn wallcoverings.

Scoring washable wallpaper

Washable wallpaper has an impervious surface film, which you must break through to allow the water to penetrate to the adhesive. Use a wire brush or a wallpaper scorer to puncture the surface, then soak it with warm water and stripper. It may take several applications before the paper begins to lift.

Scoring wallpaper
Running a wallpaper scorer across the wall punches minute holes through impervious wallcoverings.

Using a steam stripper

Wallcoverings that have been painted can be difficult to remove. If the paper is sound, simply prepare it in the same way as painted plaster and decorate over it. To strip it, use a wire brush or a proprietary scorer to puncture the surface, then soak the paper with warm water containing paper stripper.

Painted papers (and washables) can easily be stripped, using a steam stripper. Hold the stripper's sole plate against the paper until the steam penetrates, then remove the soaked paper with a wide-bladed scraper. Having removed the paper, wash the wall to remove traces of paste.

Steam stripping
Soften the wallcovering, using the sole plate, then lift the paper off the wall with a wide-bladed scraper.

Peeling vinyl wallcoverings

Vinyl wallcovering consists of a thin layer of vinyl fused with a paper backing. To remove the vinyl, lift both bottom corners of the top layer of the wallcovering then pull firmly and steadily away from the wall. Either soak and scrape off the backing paper or, if you want to leave it as a lining paper, smooth the seams with medium-grade abrasive paper, using very light pressure to avoid wearing a hole.

Eradicating mould

In damp conditions mould can develop, usually in the form of black specks. It is important to remedy the cause of the damp before you begin to redecorate the walls or ceiling.

If the mould is growing on wallpaper, soak the area in a solution made of 1 part household bleach : 16 parts water, then scrape off the contaminated paper and burn it outside. Wash the wall with a fresh bleach solution to remove paste residue from the plaster.

Apply a liberal wash of similar solution to sterilize the wall and leave it for at least 3 days – preferably a week – to make sure no further growth develops. When the wall is completely dry, apply a stabilizing primer thinned with white spirit, followed by a coat of size containing a fungicide solution if you are planning to repaper the wall. Alternatively, paint the wall with an emulsion that contains a fungicide.

If mould growth is affecting a bare-plaster or painted wall or ceiling, apply a liberal wash of the bleach solution. Wait for at least 4 hours and then carefully scrape off the mould, wipe it onto newspaper, and burn it outside. Wash the wall again with the solution, then leave it for 3 days in order to sterilize the wall completely before redecorating as described above.

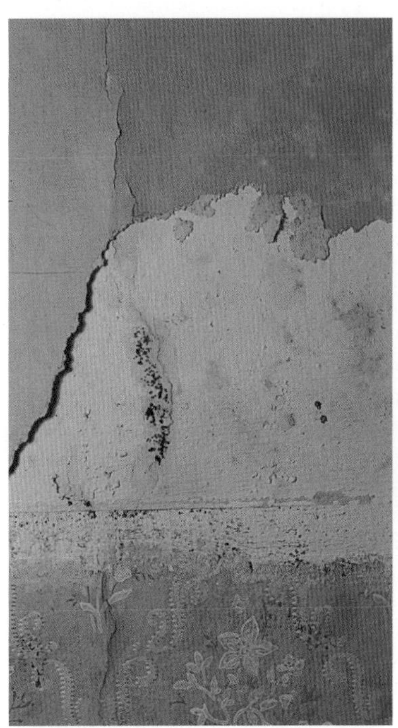

Mould growth
Mould, typified by black specks, will grow on damp plaster or wallpaper.

SEE ALSO > Primers 40–41, Anti-mould emulsion 67, Blown vinyl 84, Wallcoverings 84–5, Damp 247–54, Consumer unit 296

Preparing woodwork

The wooden joinery often needs redecorating long before any other part of the house – particularly bargeboards and fascias and the exterior of windows and doors. The main cause is that wood tends to swell when it becomes moist and then shrinks again when the sun or central heating dries it out. Paint won't adhere for long under these conditions, nor will any other finish.

Sealing gaps with flexible acrylic filler
Before painting inside or outside, fill large gaps around joinery, using acrylic filler.

Preparing new joinery for painting

New joinery is often primed at the factory, but before you start work it is worth checking that the primer is in good condition. If the primer is satisfactory, rub it down lightly with fine-grade abrasive paper and dust it off, then apply a second coat of wood primer to areas that will be inaccessible after installation. Don't leave the timber uncovered outside, as primer is not sufficient protection against prolonged exposure to the weather.

Make sure unprimed timber is dry, then sand the surface in the direction of the grain, using fine-grade sandpaper. Wrap it round a wood block for flat surfaces, and round a piece of dowel or a pencil for moulded sections.

Once you have removed all raised grain and lightly rounded any sharp edges, dust the wood down.

Finally, rub it over with a tack rag (an impregnated cloth to which dust will stick), or with a rag moistened with white spirit.

Paint bare softwood with a solvent-based wood primer or a quick-drying water-thinned acrylic primer. Apply either primer liberally, taking care to work it well into the joints and, particularly, into the end grain – which will require at least two coats to give it adequate protection.

Wash oily hardwoods with white spirit immediately prior to priming with an aluminium wood primer. Use standard wood primers for other hardwoods, thinning them slightly to encourage penetration into the grain.

When the primer is dry, fill open-grained timber with a fine surface filler. Use a piece of coarse cloth to rub it well into the wood, making circular strokes followed by parallel strokes in the direction of the grain. When the filler is dry, rub it down with fine abrasive paper to a smooth finish.

Fill larger holes, open joints and cracks with flexible interior or exterior wood filler. Press the filler into the holes with a filling knife, leaving it slightly proud of the surface so that it can be sanded flush with fine-grade abrasive paper once it has set. Dust down ready for painting.

If, just before starting to apply the undercoat, you find a hole that you've missed, fill it with fast-setting filler.

Sealing knots

Knots and other resinous areas of the wood must be treated to prevent them staining subsequent layers of paint.

Pick off any hardened resin, then seal the knots by painting them with two coats of shellac knotting. If you are going to paint with relatively dark colours, you can seal the knots and prime the timber in one operation, using aluminium wood primer.

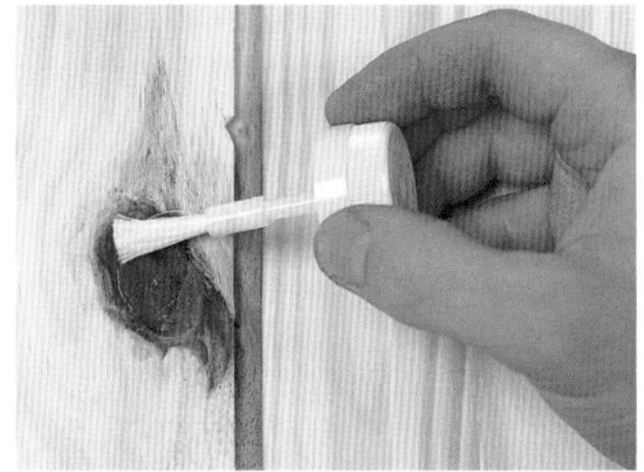

Seal resinous knots with shellac knotting

Using grain filler

If you plan to finish an open-grained timber with clear varnish, apply a proprietary grain filler after sanding. Use a natural filler for pale timbers; for darker wood, buy a filler that matches the timber. Rub the filler across the grain with a coarse rag and leave to harden for several hours, then rub off the excess along the grain with a clean coarse rag. Alternatively, apply successive coats of the clear finish and rub it down between coats until the pores are filled flush.

Clear finishes

There is usually no need to apply knotting when you intend to finish the timber with a clear varnish or lacquer. However, for very resinous timbers apply white knotting.

Sand the wood in the direction of the grain using progressively finer grades of abrasive paper, then seal it with a slightly thinned coat of the intended finish.

If the wood is in contact with the ground or in proximity to previous outbreaks of dry rot, treat it first with a liberal wash of clear timber preserver – but make sure the preserver is compatible with the finish.

Cellulose filler would show through a clear finish, so use a proprietary stopper to fill imperfections. Stoppers are thick pastes made in a range of colours to suit the type of timber. You can adjust the colour further by mixing a stopper with wood dyes. As stoppers can be either oil-based or water-based, make sure you use a similar-based dye. Where possible, use an oil-based stopper outside. Stoppers are generally harder than cellulose fillers, so don't overfill blemishes or you will spend an inordinate amount of time rubbing down.

Sand along the grain with abrasive paper

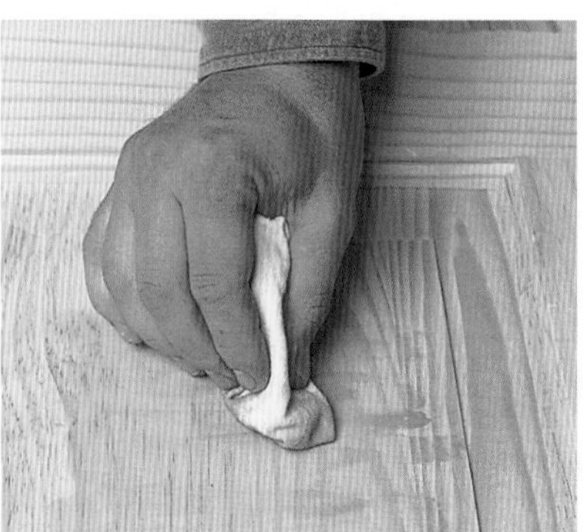

Apply grain filler with a coarse rag

SEE ALSO > Primers 40–41, Finishing wood 70–81, Wood dyes 74–5, Timber preservers 246

Man-made boards

Versatile and relatively inexpensive, man-made boards are used extensively in the home – most typically for shelving, levelling floors and building units for the kitchen or bedroom.

Preparing man-made boards for decoration

Wallboards such as plywood, medium-density fibreboard (MDF), chipboard, blockboard, hardboard and softboard are all made from wood but must be prepared differently from natural timber. Their finish varies according to the quality of the board: some are compact and smooth, and may even be presealed ready for painting; others must be filled and sanded before you can get a really smooth finish.

As a rough guide, no primer will be required when using acrylic paints, other than a sealing coat of the paint itself, slightly thinned with water. However, any nail or screw heads must be driven below the surface and coated with zinc-phosphate primer to prevent rust stains.

If you are using solvent-based paint, prime the boards first with a general-purpose primer or, for porous softboard, a stabilizing primer. Special primers are available for MDF.

Where possible, you should prime both sides of the board. If the boards are presealed, you can apply undercoat directly to the surface.

1 Plywood
2 Blockboard
3 Medium-density fibreboard (MDF)
4 Chipboard
5 Hardboard back
6 Hardboard face
7 Soft fibreboard

Bleaching wood

Unevenly coloured or stained board and timber can be bleached before the application of wood dyes and polishes. To avoid a light patch in place of the discoloration, if possible bleach the entire area rather than isolated spots.

Using two-part bleach

To use a proprietary two-part wood bleach, brush one part onto the wood and apply the second part over the first, 5 to 10 minutes later. When the bleach is dry, or as soon as the wood is the required colour, neutralize the bleach with a weak acetic-acid solution consisting of a teaspoon of white vinegar in a pint of water.

Put the wood aside for about 3 days, then sand down the raised grain.

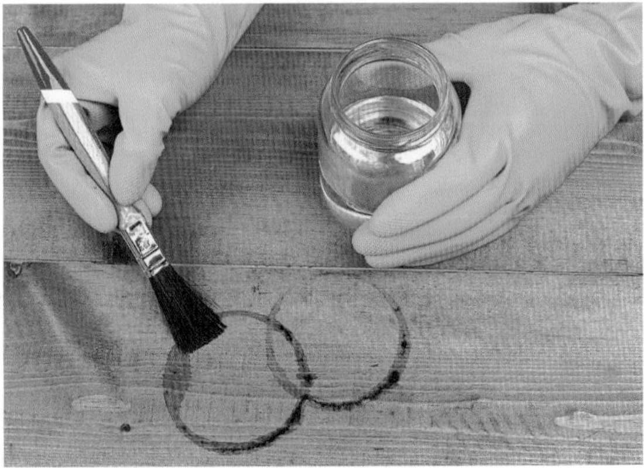

Bleaching timber
Use a paintbrush to apply two-part bleach to stained wood. Leave it until the discoloration has disappeared, then wash off with diluted vinegar.

SAFETY PRECAUTIONS

Wood bleach is a dangerous substance that must be handled with care and stored in the dark, out of the reach of children.

- Wear protective gloves, goggles and an apron.
- Wear a face mask when sanding bleached wood.
- Ensure that ventilation is adequate, or work outside.
- Have a supply of water handy, so you can rinse your skin immediately if you splash yourself with bleach.
- If you get bleach in your eyes, rinse them thoroughly with running water and see a doctor.
- Never mix both parts of the bleach except on the wood, and always apply them with separate white-fibre or nylon brushes.
- Discard unused bleach.

SEE ALSO > Primers 40–41, Stripping wallcoverings 00, Wallcoverings 51, Taping joints, 168, Panelling 219–20

Sanding a wooden floor

You can turn an unsightly stained and dirty wood floor into an attractive feature by sanding it smooth and clean with hired equipment. Although straightforward, the job is laborious, dusty and noisy.

Drum sander
An upright drum sander is used for sanding the main floor area with coarse, then medium and finally fine-grade abrasive paper to achieve a smooth finish.

Orbital sander
An orbital sander is comparatively gentle, and leaves a smooth finish free from swirls and scratches.

Choosing a sander

The area of a floor is far too large to contemplate sanding with anything but industrial sanding machines. You can obtain the equipment from the usual tool-hire outlets, which will also supply the abrasive papers. You will need three grades of paper: coarse, to level the boards initially, followed by medium and fine to achieve a smooth finish.

It is best to hire a large upright drum sander for the main floor area, and a smaller disc sander for tackling the edges. You can sand smaller rooms, such as bathrooms and WCs, using an edging sander only.

Hire an upright orbital sander for finishing parquet and other delicate flooring that would be ruined by drum sanding.

Some companies also supply a scraper for cleaning out inaccessible corners. If so, make sure it is fitted with a new blade when you hire it.

Edging sander
A small disc sander is used for sanding in corners and along edges that the drum sander cannot tackle.

Repairing floorboards prior to sanding

Before you start sanding, examine your floorboards carefully for signs of woodworm infestation. If necessary, have the boards and the joists below treated with a woodworm fluid.

Replace any boards that have more than a few holes in them - beneath the surface there may well be a honeycomb of tunnels made by the woodworm, and vigorous sanding will reveal these tunnels on the surface of the boards.

If you discover dry or wet rot when you lift up a floorboard, have it treated straightaway.

Look for boards that have been lifted previously by electricians and plumbers. Replace any that are split, too short or badly jointed. Try to find second-hand boards to match the rest of the floor; if you have to use new wood, stain or bleach it after the floor has been sanded to match the colour of the old boards.

A raised nail head will rip the paper on the sander's drum, so drive all the nail heads below the surface.

Sink nail heads below the surface

Filling gaps between the floorboards

What you do about gaps between boards depends on how much they bother you. Many people simply ignore them; but you will end up with a more attractive floor, as well as improved draughtproofing, if you make the effort to fill the gaps or close them up.

Filling with papier mâché

If there are only a few gaps, make up a stiff papier-mâché paste with white newsprint and wallpaper paste, plus a little water-based wood dye to colour the paste to match the sanded floor. Scrape out dirt and wax from between the boards, and press the paste into the gap with a filling knife. Press it well below the level likely to be reached by the sander and fill flush with the floor surface, smoothing the exposed surface with the filling knife.

Inserting a wooden lath

Large gaps can be filled with a thin wooden lath planed to fit tightly between the boards. Apply a little PVA adhesive to the gap and tap the lath in place with a hammer until the wood is flush with the surface. If necessary, skim with a plane.

Don't bother to fill several gaps this way - it is easier to close up the boards and fill one larger gap with a new floorboard.

Closing up

Over a large area, the most satisfactory solution is to lift the boards a few at a time and re-lay them butted side by side, filling in the final gap with a new board.

Fill narrow gaps with papier-mâché paste

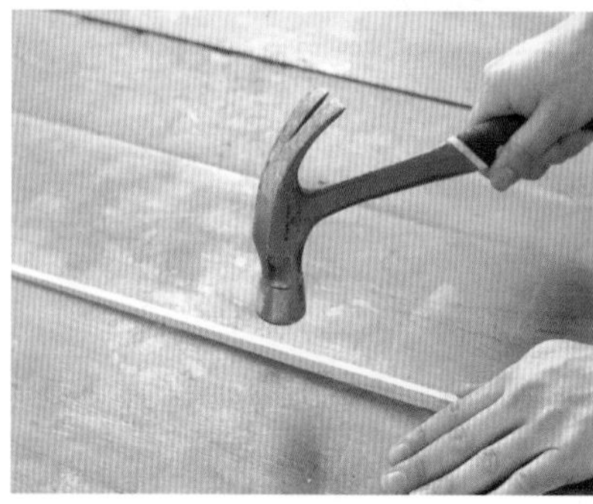

Wedge a wooden lath into a wide gap

SEE ALSO > Wood dyes 74–5, Replacing floorboards 179, Woodworm 242–3, Rot 245

Fitting abrasive paper to sanders

Precise instructions for fitting abrasive paper to sanding machines should be supplied with a hired kit. If they are not included, ask the hirer to demonstrate what you need to do. Never attempt to change abrasive papers while a machine is plugged into a socket.

With most drum sanders, the paper is wrapped round the drum then secured in place with a screw-down bar. Ensure that the paper is wrapped tightly round the drum: if it is slack, it may slip from its clamp and will be torn to pieces.

Edging sanders take a disc of abrasive, usually clamped to the sole plate by a central nut.

Drum sander
Tighten the bar clamp to hold the paper securely.

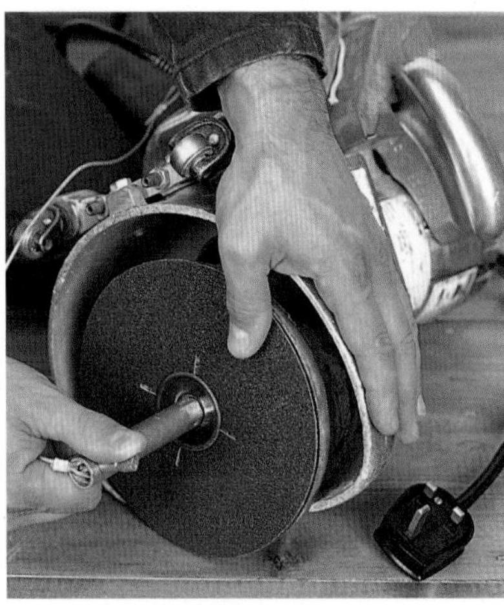

Clamp an abrasive disk to an edging sander
Use the box spanner supplied with the sander.

An alternative to sanding

Nicely finished bare-wood floors are very popular and can add a light airy feeling to a room. However, think carefully before sanding a floor in a characterful old house. Removing a mellow aged patina may not be the wisest course of action. Instead of sanding, you could remove surface dirt and old finishes with a plastic scouring pad dipped in a proprietary agent used for cleaning antique furniture. This leaves the floor almost intact, retaining the scars and patina that the wood has acquired over a long period.

Beautifully mellowed sealed and waxed pine board floor

Operating an upright drum sander

At the beginning of a run, stand with the drum sander tilted back so that the drum itself is clear of the floor. Drape the electrical flex over one shoulder to make sure it cannot become caught in the sander.

Switch on the machine, then gently lower the drum onto the floor. There is no need to push a drum sander: it will move forward under its own power. Hold the machine in check, so that it proceeds at a slow but steady walking pace along a straight line. Don't hold it still for even a brief period, or it will rapidly sand a deep hollow in the floorboards. Take care you don't let go of it, either, or it will run across the room on its own, probably damaging the floorboards in the process.

When you reach the other side of the room, tilt the machine back, switch off, and wait for it to stop before lowering it to the floor.

If the abrasive paper rips, tilt the machine onto its back castors and switch off. Wait for the drum to stop revolving, disconnect the power, and then change the paper.

Drum sanding
Hold the drum sander in check as you proceed at a steady pace across the floor.

Using an edging sander

Hold the handles on top of the machine and drape the flex over your shoulder. Tilt the sander onto its back castors to lift the disc off the floor. Switch on and lower the machine. As soon as you make contact with the boards, sweep the machine in any direction but keep it moving – as soon as it comes to rest, the disc will score deep, scorched swirl marks in the wood, which are difficult to remove. There's no need to press down on the machine. When you have finished, tilt back the machine, then switch off and let the motor run down.

Edging sanding
It is important to keep the sander moving, and make sure you tilt the machine onto its back wheels before switching off.

SEE ALSO > Sanding the floor 56

Sanding the floor

A great deal of dust is produced by sanding a floor – so before you begin, empty the room of furniture and take down curtains, lampshades and pictures.

Sanding in stages

Sweep the floor to remove grit and other debris. Stuff folded newspaper under the door, and seal around it with masking tape. Open all the windows. Wear old clothes, a dust mask, goggles and ear protectors.

Old floorboards will most likely be 'cupped' (curved across their width), so the first task is to level the floor across its entire area. With coarse abrasive paper fitted to the drum sander, sand diagonally across the room (1). At the end of the run, tilt the machine, pull it back, and make a second run parallel to the first. Allow each pass to overlap the last slightly. When you have covered the floor once, sweep up the sawdust.

Health and safety
Wear a dust mask, goggles and ear protection when sanding floors.

Now sand the floor again in the same way – but this time across the opposite diagonal of the room (2). Switch off and sweep the dust from the floor.

Once the floor is flat and clean all over, change to a medium-grade paper and sand parallel to the boards (3), overlapping each pass as before. Finally, switch to fine-grade paper in order to remove all obvious scratches, working parallel to the boards and overlapping each pass again. Each time you change the grade of paper on the drum sander, put the same grade on the edging sander and sand the edges of the room so that they are finished to the same standard as the main area (4).

Even the powered edging sander cannot clean right up to the skirting or into the corners of the room. Finish these small areas with a scraper (see below right), or fit a flexible abrasive disc in a power drill.

Vacuum the floor and wipe it over with a cloth dampened with white spirit, ready for finishing.

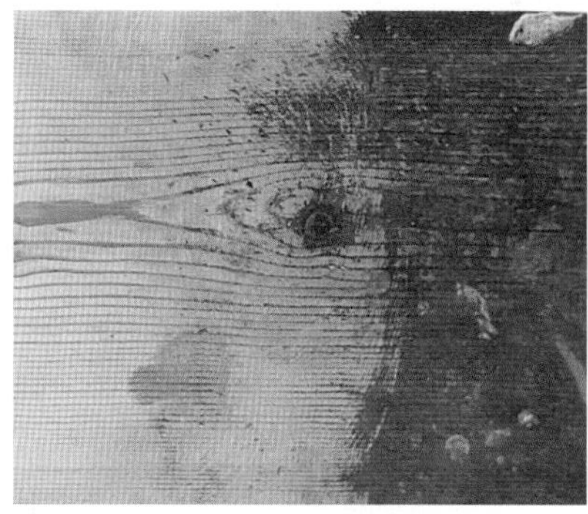
Sanding cleans and rejuvenates wooden floors

1 Sand diagonally across the floorboards

2 Sand across the opposite diagonal

3 Sand parallel to the floorboards

4 Finish the edges with a disc sander

Hook scraper

Use a small hook scraper for removing paint spots from the floor, and for reaching into spaces that are inaccessible to the disc sander. The tool cuts on the backward stroke. Various sizes and blade shapes are available to deal with most situations.

A hook scraper will only work well if the blade is sharp

SEE ALSO > Repairing floorboards 54, Sanding machines 54, Varnish and lacquer 76–9

Levelling a wooden floor

Tiles, sheet vinyl or carpet should not be laid directly onto an uneven suspended timber floor; the undulations would cause the tiles or covering to lift or even crack. The solution is to panel over the floorboards with hardboard 3mm (1/8in) thick or, preferably, with 6mm (1/4in) plywood. Whichever board you use, the method is the same.

Conditioning boards

Before you seal the floor with plywood or hardboard, make sure the underfloor ventilation is efficient, in order to prevent damp and dry rot. Bear in mind, too, that once the floor is sealed you will not have ready access to underfloor pipes and cables, so make sure these are in good order.

Match the moisture content of the board and the humidity of the room, or the board will buckle after it has been laid. If the house is not heated regularly, wet the textured back of hardboard or both sides of plywood with warm water and leave the sheets stacked back-to-back in the room for 24 hours. If you have been using central heating, there's no need to dampen the boards: just stack the sheets on edge for 48 hours, so they can adjust to the room.

Laying a base for ceramic tiles

A concrete platform is the most suitable base for ceramic floor tiles, but you can lay them on a suspended wooden floor provided the joists are perfectly rigid, so the floor cannot flex. The space below the floor must be adequately ventilated with air bricks, to prevent dry rot developing. Level the floor using 15mm (5/8in) marine plywood, screwed down to the joists at 300mm (1ft) intervals.

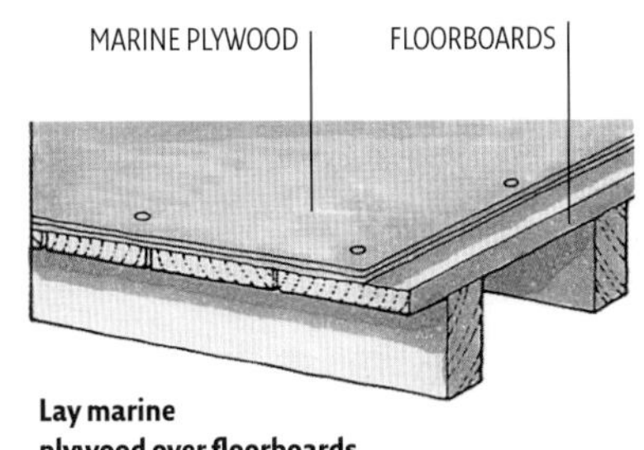

Lay marine plywood over floorboards

1
1
3
3
3
2
3
3
3

Laying hardboard
1 Snap centre lines. Cut boards into 1200 x 600mm (4ft x 2ft) rectangles.
2 Centre first board and secure it with nails from the centre outwards.
3 Butt other boards, staggering the joins. Work round central board.

Laying the boards

Cut the boards into 1200 x 600mm (4ft x 2ft) rectangles. Nail down loose floorboards and sink the nail heads.

Use chalked string to snap two centre lines across the room, crossing at right angles. Lay the first board on the centre, adjusting it so that its edges do not align with the gaps between the floorboards. Unless the flooring maker's instructions state otherwise, lay hardboard rough side up, as a key for the adhesive. Loose-lay the boards in both directions: if the margins will be narrow, reposition the boards.

Nail the first board to the floor with 20mm (3/4in) hardboard pins. Start near the centre of the board and fix it every 150mm (6in) until you get within 25mm (1in) of the edge, then nail around the edge every 100mm (4in). Nail other boards butted up to the first (see above).

To cut edge strips to fit the margin, lay the board on the floor touching the skirting but square to the edges of the nailed boards (**1**). Hold the board firmly, and use a block of softwood to scribe along it to fit the skirting (**2**). Cut the scribed line and butt it up to the skirting, then mark the position of the nailed boards on both sides of the edge strip. Join the marks, then cut along this line. Nail the board to the floor (**3**).

To fit into a doorway, butt a board up to the frame and measure to the doorstop. Cut a block of softwood to this size and scribe to the skirting (**4**). Use the same block to trace the shape of the architrave (**5**), and cut the shape with a coping saw or jigsaw. Slide the board into the doorway, mark and cut the other edge that butts up against the nailed boards, and then nail the board to the floor (**6**).

1 Butt board against the skirting

2 Scribe the board to fit

3 Nail the cut board to the floor

4 Scribe to the skirting

5 Then trace around the frame

6 Cut the board to fit and nail it

SEE ALSO > Laying floor tiles 104–7, Wood flooring 108–11, Laying carpet 114, Laying sheet vinyl 116, Ventilation below floors 274

Painted and varnished woodwork

Most of the joinery in and around your house will have been painted or varnished at some time; and provided it is in good condition, it will form a sound base for new paintwork. However, when too many coats of paint have been applied, the mouldings around doorframes and window frames begin to look poorly defined and the paintwork has a lumpy and unattractive appearance. In these cases, it is best to strip off all the old paint down to bare wood and start again. Stripping is also essential where the paintwork has deteriorated and is blistering, crazing or flaking.

Liquid sander
You can prepare sound paintwork with a liquid sander. Wipe it onto the surface with a cloth or sponge and leave it to soften the top paint layer slightly, creating a matt finish. It's a perfect surface on which to apply the new top coat of paint. The chemical cleans and degreases the paintwork, too.

• **Flexible acrylic filler**
An acrylic filler is ideal for filling large cracks or gaps in painted woodwork. It is squeezed into the gap from a cartridge gun and smoothed with a damp cloth. No sanding is required. You can overpaint it an hour later.

Sound paintwork

Wash the paintwork, from the bottom upwards, with a solution of warm water and sugar soap or detergent. Pay particular attention to the areas around the door handles and window catches, where dirt and grease will be heaviest. Rinse with fresh water - from bottom to top, to prevent runs of dirty liquid staining the surface.

Rub down gloss paintwork with fine-grade wet-and-dry abrasive paper, dipped in water, in order to provide a key for the new finish coat and to remove any blemishes.

Fill open joints or holes with a flexible filler and rub down when set. Renew crumbling putty, and seal around window frames and doorframes with flexible acrylic filler or mastic.

Preparing weathered paintwork or varnish

Unsound paintwork or varnish - such as the examples pictured below - must be stripped to bare wood. There are several methods you can use, but always scrape off loose material first.

In some cases, where the paint is particularly flaky, dry scraping may be all that is required, using a proprietary hook scraper and finishing with a light rub down with abrasive paper. Where most of the paint is stuck firmly, you will need to strip it down to the bare woodwork.

Stripping paint and varnish with a blowtorch

The traditional method for stripping old paint is to burn it off with a blowtorch fuelled with liquid gas from a pressurized canister, but you can obtain more sophisticated blowtorches that are connected by a hose to a metal gas bottle of the type used for camping or in caravans. This type of gas torch is finely adjustable, so is also useful for jobs such as brazing and soldering.

To reduce the risk of fire, take down curtains and pelmets; outside, rake out old birds' nests from behind your fascia board and soffit. Never burn off old (pre-1960s) paint that you suspect may contain lead.

It is only necessary to soften the paint with the flame in order to scrape it off - but it is all too easy to heat the paint so that it is actually burning. Deposit scrapings in a metal paint kettle or bucket as you remove them.

Start by stripping mouldings from the bottom upwards. Never direct the flame at one spot, but keep it moving all the time so that you don't scorch the wood. As soon as the paint has softened, use a shavehook to scrape it off. If it is sticky or hard, heat it a little more and try scraping again.

Having dealt with the mouldings, strip flat areas of woodwork, using a wide-bladed stripping knife. When you have finished stripping, sand the wood with medium-grade abrasive paper to remove hardened specks of paint and any accidental light scorching.

Strip mouldings with a shavehook

Use a scraper to strip flat surfaces

You may find that it is impossible to sand away heavy scorching without removing too much wood. Sand or scrape off loose blackened wood fibres, then fill any hollows and repaint the woodwork, having primed the scorched areas with an aluminium wood primer.

Dry, flaky paintwork

Heavily overpainted woodwork

Badly weathered varnish

SEE ALSO > Primers 40–41, Painting wood 71–3, Sealing frames 249

Using chemical strippers

An old finish can be removed using a stripper that reacts chemically with paint or varnish. There are general-purpose strippers that will soften both solvent-based and water-based finishes, including emulsions and cellulose paints, as well as strippers that are formulated to react with a specific type of finish, such as varnish or textured paint. Dedicated strippers achieve the desired result more efficiently than general-purpose ones – but at the cost of you having to acquire a whole range of specialist products.

Traditionally, strippers have been made from highly potent chemicals that have to be handled with care. Working with this type of stripper means having to wear protective gloves and safety glasses, and possibly a respirator, too. The newer generation of so-called 'green' strippers do not burn your skin, nor do they exude harmful fumes. However, removing paint with these milder strippers is a relatively slow process.

Whichever type of stripper you decide to use, always follow the manufacturer's health-and-safety recommendations – and if in doubt, err on the side of caution.

Before you opt for a particular stripper, you should also consider the nature of the surface you intend to strip. The thick gel-like paint removers that will cling to vertical surfaces, such as doors and wall panelling, are perfect for all general household joinery. Strippers manufactured to a thinner consistency are perhaps best employed on delicately carved work. For good-quality furniture, especially if it is veneered, make sure you use a stripper that can be washed off with white spirit, as water will raise the grain and may soften old glue.

Working with chemical strippers

Lay polythene sheets or plenty of newspaper on the floor, then apply a liberal coat of stripper to the paintwork, stippling it well into any mouldings. Leave it for 10 to 15 minutes, then try scraping a patch to see if the paint has softened through to the wood. (You might have to leave one of the milder strippers in contact with the paint for 45 minutes or longer.) Don't waste your time removing the top coats of paint only, but apply more stripper and stipple the partially softened finish back down with a brush, so the stripper will soak through to the wood. Leave it for another 5 to 10 minutes.

Once the chemicals have completed their work, use a scraper to remove the softened paint from flat surfaces, and a shavehook to scrape it from mouldings. Wipe the paint from deep carvings with fine wire wool – but when stripping oak, use a nylon-fibre pad impregnated with abrasive material, since oak can be stained by particles of steel wool.

Having removed the bulk of the paint, clean off residual patches with a wad of wire wool – or, in the case of oak, a nylon pad – dipped in fresh stripper. Rub with the grain, turning the wad inside out to present a clean face as it becomes clogged.

Neutralize the paint stripper by washing the wood with white spirit or water, depending on the manufacturer's recommendations. Let the wood dry out thoroughly, then prepare it the same way as new timber.

Industrial stripping

Any portable woodwork can be taken to a professional stripper, who will immerse the whole thing in a tank of hot caustic-soda stripping solution that must then be washed out of the wood by hosing down with water. It is an efficient process (which incidentally kills woodworm at the same time), but it risks splitting panels, warping the wood and opening up joints. At best, you can expect a reasonable amount of raised grain, which you will have to sand before refinishing.

Some industrial-stripping companies use a cold chemical dip, which does little harm to solid timber and raises the grain less. However, this treatment is likely to prove more expensive than the caustic-soda process.

Some strippers will dip pieces for a few minutes only in a warm alkali solution. If carefully controlled, this is safe for man-made boards, including plywood.

Most stripping companies are willing to collect items from your house. Many will rehang a door for you; and some offer a finishing service, too.

Never submit veneered items to industrial treatment unless the company will guarantee their safety. It is safest to strip veneered items yourself, using a chemical stripper, and finish off by wiping them with white spirit.

Hot-air strippers

Electrically heated guns do the work almost as quickly as a blowtorch, but with less risk of scorching or fire. They operate at an extremely high temperature: under no circumstances test the stripper by holding your hand over the nozzle. Some guns come with variable heat settings and a selection of nozzles for various uses.

Using a hot-air stripper

Hold the gun about 50mm (2in) from the surface of the paintwork, and move it slowly backwards and forwards until the paint blisters and bubbles. Remove the paint immediately, using a scraper or shavehook. Aim to heat the paint just ahead of either tool, so you develop a continuous work action.

Fit a shaped nozzle onto the gun when stripping glazing bars, in order to deflect the jet of hot air and reduce the risk of cracking the glass.

Old primer is sometimes difficult to remove with a hot-air stripper. This is not a problem if you are repainting the timber: just rub the surface down with abrasive paper. For a clear finish, remove residues of paint from the grain with wads of wire wool dipped in chemical stripper (see left).

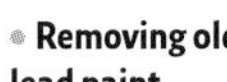

• Removing old lead paint
Wood and metal surfaces in many pre-1960s homes were decorated with paint containing lead pigments. Removing these paints can be hazardous. Never burn off old lead paint, and don't rub it down with dry abrasives – power sanding is especially dangerous. An ordinary domestic vacuum cleaner is not fitted with filters fine enough to capture lead particles, so hire an industrial vacuum cleaner designed for the job. Wash your hands thoroughly after work.

Nozzles for hot-air guns
Hot-air guns usually come with a range of attachments: typically, a flared nozzle to spread the heat (**1**); a nozzle that protects the glass when you strip glazing bars (**2**); a push-on nozzle with an integral scraper (**3**); and a conical nozzle to concentrate the heat on a small area (**4**).

1 2 3 4

With a hot-air gun there is less risk of scorching

SEE ALSO > Primers 40–41, Preparing woodwork 52–9, Finishing wood 70–81

Preparing metals

Metals are used extensively for window frames, railings, gutters, pipework, radiators and door furniture in both modern and period homes. Metals that are exposed to the elements or in close proximity to water are prone to corrosion. On their own many paints do not afford sufficient protection against corrosion, so special treatments and coatings are often required to prolong the life of the metal.

Dealing with rust

Removing rust
Remove heavy rust deposits from pitted metal, using a wire brush.

Rust is a form of corrosion that affects ferrous metals – notably iron and steel. Although most paints slow down the rate at which moisture penetrates, they do not keep it out altogether. A good-quality primer is therefore needed to complete the protection. The type you use depends on the condition of the metal and how you plan to decorate it. Make your preparation thorough, or the job could be ruined.

Treating bare metal

Remove light deposits of rust by rubbing with wire wool or wet-and-dry abrasive paper, dipping them in white spirit. If the rust is heavy and the surface of the metal pitted, use a wire brush or, for extensive corrosion, a wire wheel or cup brush in a power drill. Wear goggles while you are wire-brushing, to protect your eyes from flying particles.

Use a zinc-phosphate primer to protect metal inside the house. You can use the same primer outdoors – but if you are painting previously rusted metal, especially if it is in a very exposed location, you will need to use a high-performance rust-inhibitive primer.

Work primers into crevices and fixings, and make sure sharp edges and corners are coated generously.

Preparing previously painted metal

If the paint is perfectly sound, wash it with sugar soap or with a detergent solution, then rinse and dry it. Rub down gloss paint with fine wet-and-dry abrasive paper, to provide a key.

If the paint film is blistered or flaking – where water has penetrated and corrosion has set in – remove all loose paint and rust with a wire brush or with a wire wheel or cup brush in a power drill. Apply rust-inhibitive primer to any bare patches, working it well into joints, bolt heads and other fixings. Prime bare metal immediately, as rust can re-form very rapidly. When you are preparing cast-iron guttering, brush out dead leaves and other debris, then wash it clean. Coat the inside with a bitumen paint. If you want to paint over old bitumen paint, use an aluminium primer first, to prevent it bleeding to the surface.

Stripping painted iron and steel

Delicately moulded sections – on fire surrounds, garden furniture and other cast or wrought ironwork – will often benefit from stripping off old paint and rust masking fine detail. They cannot easily be rubbed down with a wire brush; and a hot-air stripper won't do the job, as the metal would dissipate the heat too quickly for the paint to soften. A gas blowtorch can be used to strip wrought ironwork, but cast iron may crack if it becomes distorted by localized heating.

Chemical stripping is the safest method – but before you begin, check that what appears to be a metal fire surround is not in fact made from plaster mouldings on a wooden background (the stripping process would play havoc with soft plasterwork). Tap the surround to see if it's metallic, or scrape an inconspicuous section.

Paint the bare metal with a rust-inhibitive primer or, alternatively, with a proprietary rust-killing jelly or liquid that will remove and neutralize rust. Usually based on phosphoric acid, these combine with the rust to leave it quite inert, in the form of iron phosphate. Some rust killers will deal with minute particles invisible to the naked eye and are self-priming, so that there is no need to apply an additional primer.

Alternatively, if the metalwork is portable, you may want to take it to a sandblaster or to an industrial stripper. None of the disadvantages of industrial stripping apply to metal. Clean the stripped metal with a wire brush, then wash it with white spirit before applying a finish.

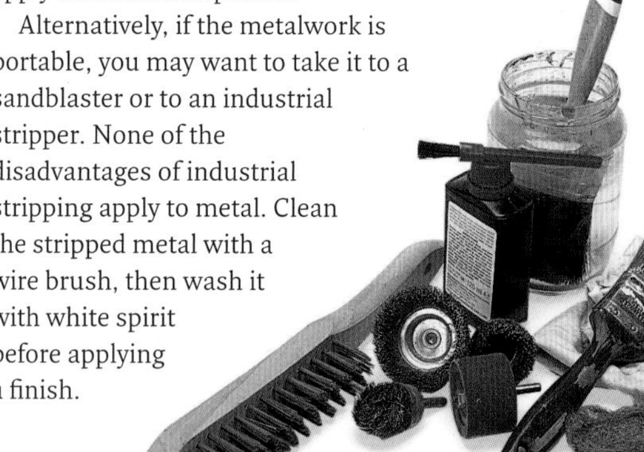

Cast-iron railings deeply pitted with rust

A rusty casement window sheds its paint

Corroded cast-iron drainpipe

SEE ALSO > Primers 40–41, Industrial stripping 59, Finishing metal 82–3

Corrosion in aluminium

Aluminium does not corrode as readily as ferrous metals. Indeed, modern aluminium-alloy window frames and doorframes are designed to withstand weathering without a coat of protective paint. Nevertheless, exposed to adverse conditions aluminium may corrode to a dull grey and even produce white crystals on the surface.

To remove corrosion of this kind, rub the aluminium with a fine wet-and-dry abrasive paper, using white spirit as a lubricant, until you get back to bright (but not gleaming) metal. Wipe the metal with a cloth dampened with white spirit, to remove metal particles and traces of grease. When it is dry, prime the surface with a zinc-phosphate primer.

Never use a primer containing lead on aluminium, as there is likely to be an adverse chemical reaction between the metals in the presence of moisture.

Painting galvanized metal

Galvanized iron and steel have a coating of zinc applied by hot dipping. When new, this provides a poor key for most paints. Leaving the metal to weather for six months will remedy this – but in many cases the manufacturer of galvanized metalwork will have treated it chemically for instant priming. Check when you purchase it.

Priming galvanized metal

If you need to paint galvanized metal before it has had time to weather, protect it first with a special galvanized-metal primer or two coats of fast-drying acrylic primer formulated for use on non-ferrous metals.

Treating chipped galvanizing

Any small rust spots resulting from accidental chipping of the zinc coating should be removed by gentle abrasion with wire wool, taking care not to damage the surrounding coating. Wash the area with white spirit, then allow the surface to dry. Prime with zinc-phosphate primer.

Maintaining brass and copper

Ornamental brassware – such as door knobs, fingerplates and other door furniture – should not be painted, especially as there are clear lacquers available that will protect it from the elements. Strip painted brass with a chemical stripper. Deal with corroded brass as described right.

Copper – mainly plumbing pipework – does not require painting for protection, but visible pipe runs can be painted to blend in with the room decor. Degrease and key the copper first with fine wire wool lubricated with white spirit. Wipe away any metal particles with a cloth dampened with white spirit. Prime the pipes and surrounding surfaces with a general-purpose primer.

Preparing lead pipes and windows

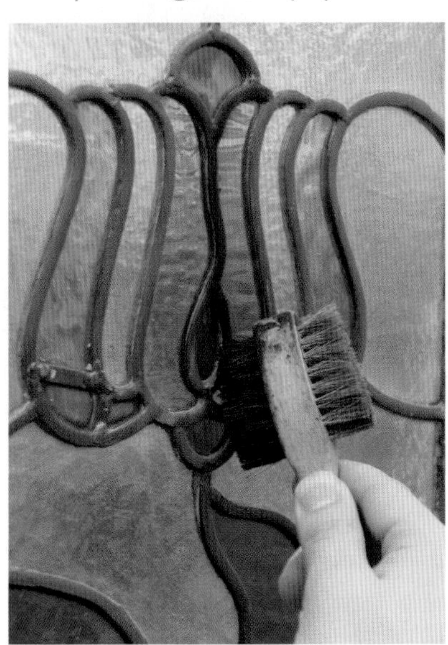
Darken lead cames with a touch of grate polish

Before proceeding to paint old lead pipework, scour the surface with wire wool dipped in white spirit. No further preparation is required before applying the paint, but you could start with a good-quality universal primer.

Advanced lead corrosion

The cames (grooved retaining strips) of stained-glass windows and leaded lights can become corroded, producing white stains. Unless the glass is etched or sandblasted, clean the lead carefully with a soap-filled wire-wool pad. Wipe the lead clean, then wash the glass with warm soapy water.

Darken the cleaned lead with a touch of black grate polish on a shoe brush. Brush across the cames, not along them. The grate polish will not adhere to clean glass, even if it is painted.

Cleaning brass

Brass weathers to a dull-brown colour, but it is usually simple enough to buff up dirty fittings with a metal polish. However, if exterior door fittings have been left unprotected, you may have to use a solution of salt and vinegar to soften heavy corrosion before you can start polishing.

Mix 1 level tablespoonful each of salt and vinegar in 275ml (½ pint) of hot water. Use a ball of very fine wire wool to apply liberal washes of the solution to the brass, then wash the metal in hot water containing a little detergent. Rinse and dry the fittings, before polishing them with a soft cloth.

Clean brass with salt-and-vinegar solution

Getting rid of verdigris

Badly weathered brass can develop green deposits called verdigris. This heavy corrosion may leave the metal pitted, so clean it off as soon as possible.

Line a plastic bowl with ordinary aluminium cooking foil. Attach a piece of string to each item of brassware, then place it in the bowl on top of the foil. Dissolve a cup of washing soda in 2.2 litres (4 pints) of hot water, and pour it into the bowl to cover the metalware.

Leave the solution to fizz and bubble for a couple of minutes, then use the string to lift out the fittings. Put any that are still corroded back into the solution. If necessary, repeat the process with fresh solution and new foil.

Rinse the brass with hot water, dry it with a soft cloth, and then polish.

Remove verdigris with a washing-soda dip

SEE ALSO > Primers 40–41, Finishing metal 82–3

Preparing tiled surfaces

Used for cladding walls, floors and ceilings, tiles are made in a variety of materials – ranging from ceramic to cork, vinyl and polystyrene – and in a number of different surface textures and finishes. If they become shabby, it's possible to either revive their existing finish or decorate them with paint or wallcoverings. With some kinds, it is even feasible to stick new tiles on top for a completely new look.

Removing ceramic tiles
To remove old tiles, first chop out at least one of them with a cold chisel, then prise the others off the surface by driving a bolster chisel behind them. Chop away any remaining tile adhesive or mortar with the bolster. Wear goggles to protect your eyes.

Ceramic wall and floor tiles

Ceramic tiles are stuck to the wall or floor with a special adhesive or, in some cases, with mortar. Removing them in their entirety in order to redecorate a wall is messy and time-consuming, but it is often the most satisfactory solution.

Provided a ceramic-tiled wall is sound, you can paint it with a special-purpose primer and compatible gloss paint. Wash the surface thoroughly with sugar-soap or detergent solution, then apply the primer with a synthetic brush. Leave it to harden in a dry steam-free environment for a full 16 hours, then use a natural-bristle brush to apply the gloss.

You can lay new tiles directly over old ones, but make sure the surface is perfectly flat – check by holding a long spirit level or straightedge across the surface. Tap the tiles to locate any loose ones and either glue them firmly in place or chop them out with a cold chisel and club hammer, then fill the space with mortar. Wash the wall to remove grease and dirt.

It is also possible to tile over old quarry or ceramic floor tiles in the same way. Treat an uneven floor with a self-levelling compound.

It is not practicable to paper over old ceramic wall tiles, as the adhesive cannot grip on the shiny surface.

Polystyrene ceiling tiles

You will find that old polystyrene tiles are stuck directly onto the surface with an adhesive that is often difficult to remove. In the past, adhesive was commonly applied in five small dabs – a method that is no longer approved due to the risk of fire. Nowadays, tile manufacturers normally recommend that a complete bed of non-flammable adhesive be used.

Remove old tiles by prising them off with a wide-bladed scraper, and then prise off the dabs of adhesive. Try to soften stubborn patches of adhesive with warm water or wallpaper stripper. Wear goggles and PVC gloves, as it's difficult to avoid splashes.

One way to give old ceiling tiles a face-lift is to paint them – but never be tempted to use a solvent-based paint, as it would increase the risk of fire spreading across the tiles. Instead, brush the tiles to remove dust, and then apply emulsion paint.

Cleaning a quarry-tile floor

Old quarry tiles are absorbent, so the floor becomes ingrained with dirt and grease. If normal washing with detergent fails to revitalize their colour and finish, try one of the industrial preparations available to cleaning and maintenance companies. Suppliers of industrial tile-cleaning materials are listed in the telephone directory. Describe the type and condition of the tiles to the supplier, who will be able to suggest the appropriate cleaner.

Loosen stubborn grimy patches by scrubbing with a plastic scouring pad.

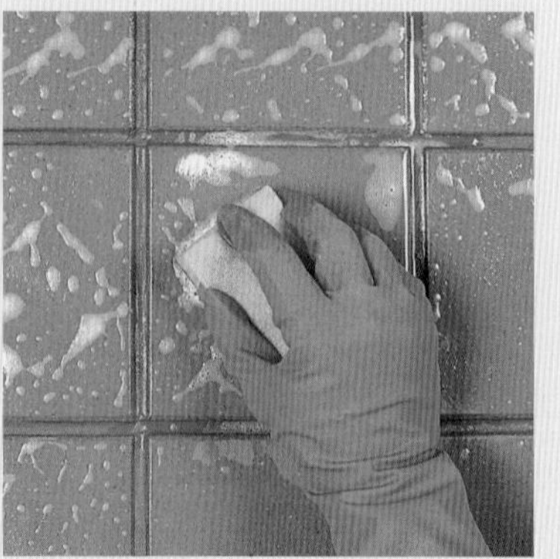

Removing ingrained dirt
Scrub stubborn patches of grime with a plastic scouring pad.

Vinyl floor tiles

To take up vinyl floor tiles, soften the tiles and their adhesive with a thermostatically controlled hot-air gun on a low setting, and use a scraper to prise them up. Remove traces of old adhesive by applying a solution of half a cup of household ammonia and a drop of liquid detergent stirred into a bucket of cold water. When the floor is clean, rinse it with water.

If vinyl tiles are firmly glued to the floor, you can change the colour with a flexible special-purpose vinyl paint. The floor must be cleaned scrupulously, and any silicone-based polish removed with a suitable cleaner. Apply a coat of paint, using a high-density foam roller. Let it dry for 4 hours, then apply another coat. You can walk on the floor 6 to 8 hours later.

Cork wall tiles

Dense prefinished cork wall tiles can be painted directly, provided they are clean and firmly attached to the wall. Prime very absorbent cork with a general-purpose primer first or, when using emulsion or water-based acrylic paint, thin the first coat in order to reduce absorption.

Unless the tiles are textured or pierced, they can be papered over – but size the surface with commercial size or heavy-duty wallpaper paste and then apply lining paper to prevent joins showing through.

Mineral-fibre ceiling tiles

Acoustic-fibre tiles can be painted with water-based acrylic or emulsion paint. Wash them with a mild detergent – but don't soak the tiles, as they are quite absorbent. Conceal stains with an acrylic undercoat before decorating.

SEE ALSO > Self-levelling compound 47, Lining paper 84, 88, Tiling 98–107

Applying decorative finishes

In decorating terms, a finish means a liquid or semi-liquid substance that sets, dries or cures to protect, and sometimes colour, materials such as wood or masonry. Finishes for wood include stains, varnishes, oil and wax – all of which are used to display the grain of the timber for its natural beauty – but paint in its various forms is probably the most widely used decorative finish for masonry and woodwork.

Common paint finishes and additives

Paint is made from solid particles of pigment suspended in a liquid binder or medium. The pigment provides the colour and body of the paint, while the medium allows the material to be brushed, rolled or sprayed; once applied, it forms a solid film binding the pigment together. Binder and pigment vary from paint to paint, but the two most common types of paint are solvent-based (sometimes known as oil-based) and water-based.The type of paint you choose depends largely on the material you are decorating and also whether you want a gloss or matt finish.

Solvent-based paints (oil paints)

The medium for solvent-based paints (commonly called oil paints) is a mixture of oils and resin. A paint made from a natural resin is slow-drying, but modern paints contain a synthetic resin – such as alkyd – that makes for a faster-drying finish. Various pigments determine the colour of the paint.

Water-based paints

Emulsion is perhaps the most familiar type of water-based paint. It too is manufactured with a synthetic resin – usually vinyl – which is dispersed in a solution of water.Water-based acrylic paints are primarily intended for finishing interior or exterior woodwork. They tend to dry with a semi-matt sheen, rather than a full gloss.

Paint additives

No paint is made simply from binder and pigment: certain additives are included during manufacture to give the paint qualities such as high gloss, faster drying time, easy flow and longer pot life, or to make it non-drip.

- Thixotropic paints are the typical non-drip types. They are thick – almost jelly-like in the can – enabling you to pick up a brushload without it dripping.
- Extenders are added as fillers to strengthen the paint film. Cheap paints often contain too much filler, which reduces their covering power.

Paint thinners

If a paint is too thick, it cannot be applied properly and must be thinned before it is used. Some finishes may require special thinners provided by the manufacturer, but most solvent-based paints (oil paints) can be thinned with white spirit; and emulsions and acrylic paints with water. Turpentine will thin oil paint, but it has no advantages over white spirit for household paints and is much more expensive.

Gloss or matt finish?

The proportion of pigment to resin affects the way the paint sets. A gloss (shiny) paint contains approximately equal amounts of resin and pigment, whereas a higher proportion of pigment produces a matt (non-shiny) paint. By adjusting the proportions, it is possible to make satin or eggshell paints. Matt paints tend to cover best, due to their high pigment content, while the greater proportion of resin in gloss paints is responsible for their strength.

Protective paint systems

Unless you are using a one-coat finish, it is necessary to apply successive layers, in order to build up a protective paint system.

- Painting walls requires a simple system, comprising two or three coats of the same paint.
- Painting woodwork and metalwork usually involves a more complex system, using paints with different qualities. A typical paint system for woodwork is illustrated below.

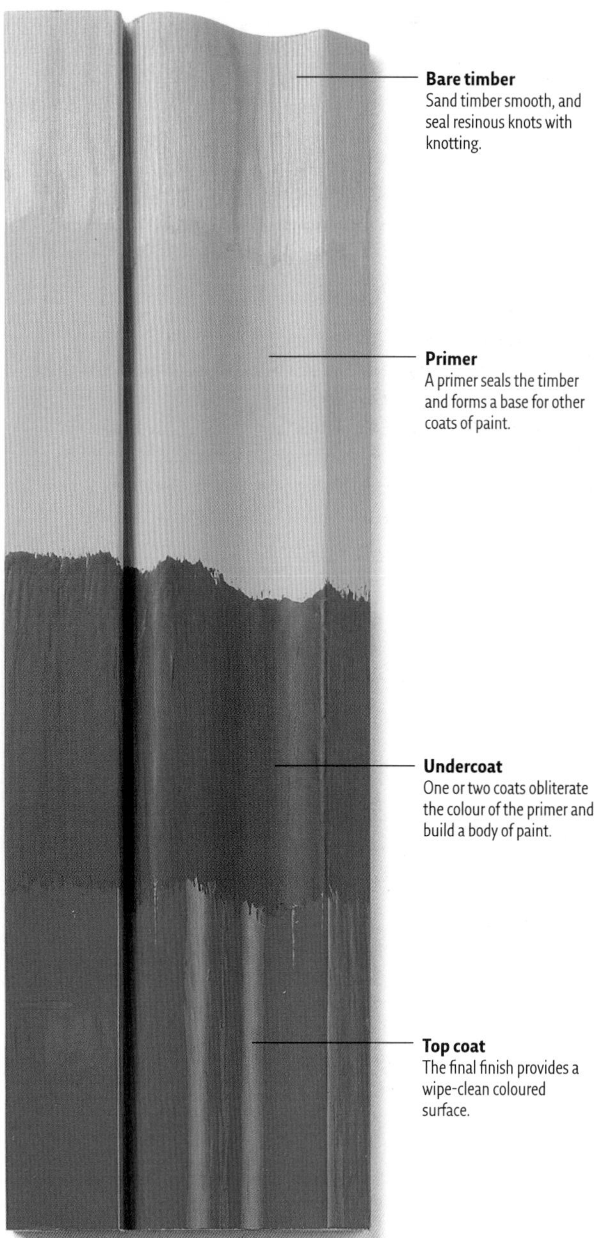

A paint system for woodwork
Different types of paint are required to build a protective system for woodwork.

SEE ALSO > Choosing colours 32–3, Primers 40–41, Lead in paint 41, Preparing paint 64

Safety when painting

The solvents in paint (Volatile Organic Compounds – VOCs) contribute to atmospheric pollution and can exacerbate conditions such as asthma. Whenever possible, it's therefore preferable to use paints and varnishes that have low VOC emissions. Most manufacturers label their products to indicate the level of VOCs.

Take sensible precautions when using solvent-based paints:

- Ensure good ventilation indoors while applying a finish and when it is drying. Wear a respirator if you suffer from breathing disorders.
- Don't smoke while painting or in the vicinity of drying paint.
- Contain paint spillages outside with sand or earth, and don't allow any paint to enter a drain.
- If you splash paint in your eyes, flush them with copious amounts of water, with your lids held open. If symptoms persist, visit a doctor.
- Always wear barrier cream or gloves if you have sensitive skin. Use a proprietary skin cleanser to remove paint from your skin, or wash it off with warm soapy water. Don't use paint thinners to clean your skin.
- Keep all finishes and thinners out of reach of children. If a child swallows a substance, don't make any attempt to induce him or her to vomit – seek medical treatment, instead.

Preparing paint

Whether you are using paint you've just bought or some left over from a previous job, there are a few basic rules to observe before you apply it.

- Wipe dust from the paint can, then prise off the lid with the side of a strong knife blade. Don't use a screwdriver: it will only buckle the edge of a metal lid, preventing an airtight seal and making subsequent removal difficult.
- Stir liquid paints with a wooden stick to blend the pigment and medium. There's no need to stir thixotropic paint unless the medium has separated; if you have to stir it, leave it to gel again before using.
- If a skin has formed on paint, cut round the edge with a knife and lift it out in one piece with a stick. It's a good idea to store the can upside down, so a skin cannot form on top of the paint.

Painting exterior masonry

The outside walls of houses are painted for two main reasons: to give a bright, clean appearance and to protect the surface from the weather. What you use as a finish and how you apply it depends on what the walls are made from, their condition, and the degree of protection they need.

Bricks are traditionally left bare, but may require a coat of paint if previous attempts to decorate have resulted in a poor finish. Rendered walls are often painted to brighten the naturally dull grey colour of the cement; pebbledashed surfaces may need a colourful coat to disguise unsightly patches. Or you may, of course, simply want to change the present colour of your walls for a fresh appearance.

Working to a timetable

Before you embark upon painting the outside walls of your house, plan your time carefully. Depending on the amount of preparation that is required, even a small house will take a few weeks to complete.

It's not necessary to tackle the whole job at once – although it is preferable, since the weather may change to the detriment of your timetable.

You can split the work into separate stages with days (or even weeks) in between, provided you divide the walls into manageable sections. Use window frames and doorframes, bays, downpipes and corners of walls to form break lines that will disguise joins.

Start at the top of the house – working from right to left, if you are right-handed.

Paint in manageable sections
You can't hope to paint an entire house in one session, so divide each elevation into manageable sections to disguise the joins. The horizontal moulding divides the front of this house neatly into two sections, and the raised door and window surrounds form convenient break lines.

SEE ALSO > Primers 40–41, Preparing masonry 42–6, Ladders and scaffolding 514–16

Paints for masonry

Various grades of paint are suitable for decorating and protecting exterior masonry, which take into account economy, standard of finish, durability and coverage.

Masonry paints

When buying weather-resistant exterior-masonry paints, you have a choice between a smooth matt finish or a fine granular texture.

Water-based masonry paint

Most masonry paints are water-based, being in effect exterior-grade emulsions with additives that prevent mould growth. Although they are supplied ready for use, on porous walls it pays to thin the first coat with 20 per cent water – then follow up with one or two full-strength coats, depending on the colour of the paint.

Water-based masonry paints must be applied during fairly good weather. Damp or humid conditions and low temperatures may prevent the paint drying properly.

Solvent-based masonry paints

Some masonry paints are thinned with white spirit or with a special solvent – but unlike most oil paints they are moisture-vapour permeable, so that the wall is able to breathe. It is often advisable to thin the first coat with 15 per cent white spirit, but check the manufacturer's recommendations.

Solvent-based paints can be applied in practically any weather conditions, provided it is not actually raining.

Reinforced masonry paint

Masonry paint that has powdered mica or a similar fine aggregate added to it dries with a textured finish that is extremely weatherproof. Reinforced masonry paints are especially suitable in coastal districts and in industrial areas – where dark colours are also an advantage, in that dirt will not show up as clearly as on a pale background. Although large cracks and holes must be filled prior to painting, reinforced masonry paint will cover hairline cracks and crazing.

FINISHES FOR MASONRY

● Black dot denotes compatibility. All surfaces must be clean, sound, dry, and free from organic growth.

	Cement paint	Water-based masonry paint	Reinforced masonry paint	Solvent-based masonry paint	Floor paint
Suitable to cover					
Brick	●	●	●	●	●
Stone	●	●	●	●	●
Concrete	●	●	●	●	●
Cement rendering	●	●	●	●	●
Pebbledash	●	●	●	●	●
Emulsion paint		●	●	●	●
Solvent-based paint		●	●	●	●
Cement paint	●	●	●	●	●
Drying time in hours					
Touch dry	1–2	1–2	2–3	4–6	2–3
Recoatable	24	4–6	24	16	3–16
Thinners					
Water	●	●	●		●
White spirit			●	●	●
Number of coats					
Normal conditions	2	2	1–2	2	1–2
Coverage, depending on wall texture					
Sq metres per litre		4–10	3–6.5	6–16	5–10
Sq metres per kg	1–6				

Cement paint

Cement paint is supplied as a dry powder, to which water is added. It is based on white cement, but pigments are added to produce a range of colours. Cement paint is one of the cheaper paints suitable for exterior use. Spray new or porous surfaces with water, then apply two coats.

Mixing cement paint

Shake or roll the container to loosen the powder, then add 2 parts of powder to 1 of water in a clean bucket. Stir it to a smooth paste, then add a little more water until you achieve a full-bodied creamy consistency. Mix no more than you can use in an hour, or it will start to dry.

Adding an aggregate

When you're painting a dense wall, or one treated with a stabilizing solution so its porosity is substantially reduced, it is advisable to add clean sand to the mix to give it body. This also provides added protection for an exposed wall and helps to cover dark colours. If the sand changes the colour of the paint, add it to the first coat only. Use 1 part sand to 4 parts powder, stirring it in when the paint is still in its paste-like consistency.

Leave a new floor to dry out
A new floor, which must incorporate a damp-proof membrane, should be left to dry out for 6 months before any impermeable covering, such as sheet vinyl or tiles, is laid.

Concrete floor paint

Floor paints are formulated to withstand hard wear. They are especially suitable for concrete garage or workshop floors, but they are also used for stone paving, steps and other concrete structures. They can be used inside for playroom floors.

The floor must be clean, dry and free from oil or grease. If the concrete is freshly laid, allow it to mature for at least a month before painting. In most cases it is advisable to prime powdery or porous floors with a proprietary concrete sealer, but check the manufacturer's recommendations first.

The best way to paint a large area is to use a paintbrush around the edges, then fit an extension to a paint roller for the bulk of the floor.

Apply paint with a roller on an extension

SEE ALSO > Primers 40–41, Preparing masonry 42–6

Techniques for painting masonry

Painting smooth masonry surfaces presents few problems, but in order to cover heavily textured walls evenly you need to adopt a few simple techniques.

Using paintbrushes

Using a banister brush
Tackle deeply textured wall surfaces with a banister brush.

Choose a brush 100 to 150mm (4 to 6in) wide for painting walls; larger ones are heavy and tiring to use. A good-quality brush with coarse bristles will last longer on rough walls. For effective coverage, apply the paint with vertical strokes, crisscrossed with horizontal ones. You will find it necessary to stipple paint into textured surfaces.

Cutting in

Painting up to a feature such as a doorframe or window frame is known as cutting in. On a smooth surface, you should be able to paint a reasonably straight edge following the line of the feature – but it's difficult to apply the paint to a heavily textured wall with a normal brushstroke. Don't just apply more paint in the hope of overcoming the problem; instead, touch the tip of the brush only to the wall, using a gentle scrubbing action, then brush out from the edge to spread excess paint once the texture is filled.

Wipe splashed paint from window frames and doorframes with a cloth dampened with the appropriate thinner.

Painting behind pipes

To protect rainwater downpipes, tape a roll of newspaper around them. Stipple behind the pipe with a brush, then slide the paper tube down the pipe to mask the next section.

Painting with a banister brush

Use a banister brush to paint deep textures such as pebbledash. Pour some paint into a roller tray, and dip the brush in to load the bristles. Scrub the paint onto the wall, using circular strokes to work it into the uneven surface.

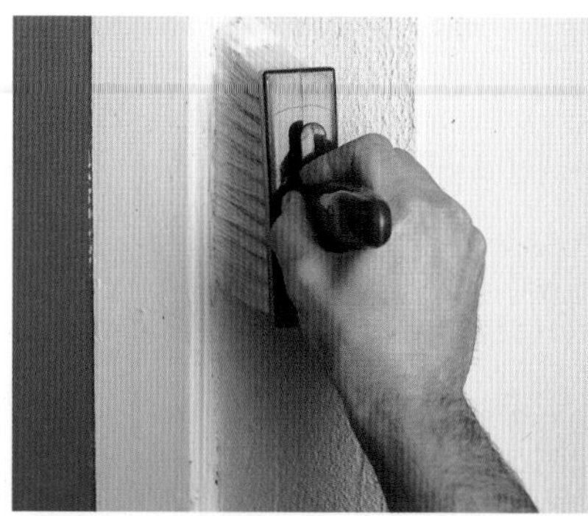

Cut in with a gentle scrubbing motion

Protect downpipes with newspaper

Using a paint roller

A roller will apply paint three times faster than a brush. Use a long-pile roller for heavy textures, and one with a medium pile for lightly textured or smooth walls. Rollers wear out very quickly on rough walls, so have a spare sleeve handy. When painting with a roller, vary the angle of the stroke to ensure even coverage; use a brush to cut into angles and obstructions.

A paint tray is difficult to use at the top of a ladder unless you fit a tool support. Better still, erect a platform from which to work.

Use a long-pile roller on a textured wall

Using a spray gun

Spray-painting columns
Columns – such as those forming part of a front-door portico – should be painted in a series of overlapping vertical bands. Apply the bands by moving the spray gun from side to side as you work down the column.

Spraying is the quickest and most efficient way to apply paint to a large expanse of wall, but you will have to mask all the parts you don't want to paint, using newspaper and masking tape, and erect plastic screening to prevent overspray.

Thin the paint by about 10 per cent; and set the spray gun according to the manufacturer's instructions, to suit the particular paint. It's advisable to wear a respirator.

Hold the gun about 225mm (9in) away from the wall and keep it moving with even, parallel passes. Slightly overlap each pass and try to keep the gun pointing directly at the surface (tricky while standing on a ladder). Trigger the gun just before each pass, and release it at the end of the stroke.

To cover a large blank wall evenly, spray it with vertical bands of paint, overlapping each band by 100mm (4in).

Spray external corners by aiming the gun directly at the apex, so that paint falls evenly on both surfaces. When two walls meet at an internal angle, treat each surface separately.

Spray internal corners as separate surfaces

Spray onto the apex of external corners

SEE ALSO > Preparing masonry 42–6, Work platforms 516

Painting interior walls and ceilings

Unless your house is newly built, most of the interior walls and ceilings will be plastered and probably papered or painted, too. Preparation varies, but the methods for painting them are identical and they can be considered smooth surfaces in terms of paint coverage. Emulsion paint, in its many forms, is the most practical finish for interior walls and ceilings – but use an acrylic or solvent-based paint on wall-fixed joinery such as skirtings, architraves and picture rails.

Emulsion is the obvious choice for walls and ceilings

Emulsion paints

Emulsion paint is most people's first choice for internal decorations: it is relatively cheap and practically odourless.

Vinyl emulsions are the most popular and practical paints for walls and ceilings. They are available in liquid or thixotropic consistencies, with matt or satin (semi-gloss) finishes.

A satin emulsion is less likely to show fingerprints or scuffs. Non-drip thixotropic paints have obvious advantages when painting ceilings.

One-coat emulsion

If you are to avoid a patchy, uneven appearance, you need to apply two coats of a standard emulsion paint, perhaps thinning the first coat slightly when decorating porous surfaces. A one-coat high-opacity emulsion is intended to save you time – but you won't get satisfactory results if you try to spread the paint too far, especially when overpainting strong colours.

New-plaster emulsions

These emulsions are formulated for painting newly plastered interior walls and ceilings, to allow moisture vapour to escape. Standard vinyl emulsions are not sufficiently permeable.

Anti-mould emulsion

This low-odour emulsion contains a fungicide to ward off mould growth.

Colour-fugitive emulsion paint

When repainting white walls and ceilings it can be difficult to see whether you have covered the surfaces evenly. A colour-fugitive emulsion goes on pink, but in less than an hour it dries to a brilliant white.

Solid emulsion

Non-drip solid emulsion is spread straight from the tray in which it is supplied. It can be brushed onto the wall or ceiling, but it is best applied with a short-pile roller.

Gloss and satin paint

Paints primarily intended for woodwork can also be applied to walls and ceilings that require an extra degree of protection. Similar paints are ideal for decorating the disparate elements of a period-style dado – wooden rail, skirting and embossed wallcovering. Gloss paints tend to accentuate uneven wall surfaces, so most people prefer a satin (eggshell) finish.

You can use any of the standard spirit-thinned paints on walls and ceilings; but if fast drying is a priority, choose a water-based acrylic paint.

Textured paints

Provided the masonry or plaster is basically sound, you can obliterate any unsightly cracks with just one coat of textured paint. A coarse high-build paint will cover cracks up to 2mm (1/16in) wide. There are also fine-texture paints for areas where people are likely to brush against a wall. Available in either a matt or satin finish, the paint is normally applied with a coarse-foam roller. You can use a synthetic-fibre roller if you want to create a finer texture.

Cement paint

This inexpensive exterior finish is also ideal for a utilitarian area indoors such as a cellar, garage or workshop. Sold in dry-powder form, it has to be made up with water and dries to a matt finish.

Finishes for bare masonry

Interior walls may be left unplastered for the sake of appearance, or because it is considered unnecessary to clad the walls of rooms such as a basement, workshop or garage. Sometimes they are deliberately stripped for effect. A brick or stone chimney breast, for example, can act as a focal point in a room, while an entire wall of bare masonry may make a dramatic impression.

If you want to finish brick, concrete or stone walls, follow the methods described for exterior walls. However, because in this case they do not have to withstand any weathering, you can use paints designed for interiors. Newly stripped masonry requires sealing with a stabilizing primer, in order to bind the surface.

It could be a mistake to apply modern masonry paint to exposed stone or brick in a period property. Limewash may be acceptable, but get advice from your local Building Control Office if you live in a listed building or your house is built in a conservation area.

SEE ALSO > Primers 40–41 Preparation 48–51, Cement paint 65, Anti-condensation paint 251

Applying paint

Even the most experienced decorator can't help dripping a little paint, so always paint the ceiling before the walls. Erect a work platform, placing it so that you can cover as much of the surface as possible without changing position – you will achieve a better finish and be able to work in safety.

● Black dot denotes compatibility.
All surfaces must be clean, sound, dry, and free from organic growth.

FINISHES FOR INTERIOR WALLS AND CEILINGS	Emulsion	One-coat emulsion	New-plaster emulsion	Solvent-based paint	Acrylic paint	Textured paint	Cement paint
Suitable to cover							
Plaster	●	●	●	●	●	●	●
Wallpaper	●	●	●	●	●		
Brick	●	●	●	●	●	●	●
Stone	●	●	●	●	●	●	●
Concrete	●	●	●	●	●	●	●
Previously painted surface	●	●	●	●	●	●	
Drying time in hours							
Touch dry	1–2	3–4	1–2	2–4	1–2	24	1–2
Recoatable	4		4	16–18	4		24
Thinners							
Water	●	●	●		●	●	●
White spirit				●			
Number of coats							
Normal conditions	2	1		1–2	1–2	1	2
Coverage							
Sq metres per litre	9–15	8	11	15–16	10–14	2–3	
Sq metres per kg							1–6
Method of application							
Brush	●	●	●	●	●	●	●
Roller	●	●	●	●	●	●	●
Spray gun	●	●	●	●	●		

Dip only the first third of the bristles in the paint

Place fingers on ferrule with thumb behind

Applying paint by brush

Choose a good-quality brush for painting walls and ceilings. Cheap brushes tend to shed bristles – which is annoying and also less economical in the long run. A brush about 200mm (8in) wide will allow you to cover a surface relatively quickly, but if you are not used to handling a large brush your wrist will soon tire. You may find a 150mm (6in) brush, plus a 50mm (2in) brush for the edges and corners, more comfortable to use. However, the job will take longer.

Loading the brush

Don't overload a brush with paint; it leads to messy work, and ruins the bristles if the paint is allowed to dry in the roots. Dip no more than the first third of the brush into the paint, wiping off excess on the inside of the container to prevent drips. When using thixotropic paint, load the brush and apply paint without removing excess.

Using a brush

You can hold the brush whichever way feels comfortable to you, but the 'pen' grip is the most versatile, enabling your wrist to move the brush freely in any direction. Hold the brush handle between your thumb and forefinger, with your fingers on the ferrule (metal band) and your thumb supporting it from the other side.

Apply the paint in vertical strokes, then spread it at right angles to even out the coverage. Finish oil paints with light upward vertical strokes, to avoid leaving brushmarks in the finished surface. This technique – known as 'laying off' – is not necessary when applying emulsion paint.

Applying paint by roller

A roller with interchangeable sleeves is an excellent tool for applying paint to large areas. Choose a roller about 225mm (9in) long for walls and ceilings. Larger ones are available, but they become tiring to use.

There are a number of different sleeves to suit the type of paint and texture of the surface. Long-haired synthetic-fibre or sheepskin sleeves are excellent on textured surfaces. Choose a shorter pile for smooth surfaces, and when using gloss or satin paints. Disposable plastic-foam rollers can be used to apply some specialist paints, but they soon lose their resilience.

Special rollers

Rollers with long detachable extension handles are ideal for painting ceilings without having to erect work platforms. Narrow rollers for painting behind radiators are invaluable if the radiators cannot be removed from the wall.

Loading a roller

You will need a special paint tray to load a standard roller. Dip the sleeve lightly into the paint reservoir and roll it gently onto the ribbed part of the tray to coat the roller.

Apply in zigzags, but finish in one direction

Using a roller

Use zigzag strokes with a roller, painting the surface in all directions to achieve even coverage. Keep the roller on the surface at all times – if you let it spin at the end of a stroke, it will spatter paint onto the floor or adjacent surfaces. When applying solvent-based paint, finish in one direction – preferably towards prevailing light.

SEE ALSO > Decorating tools 481–6, Work platforms 516

Applying paint by pad

Paint pads for large surfaces have flat rectangular faces covered with a short mohair pile. A plastic-foam backing gives the pad flexibility, so that the pile will always be in contact with the wall, even on a rough surface.

The exact size of the pad will be determined by the brand you choose, but one about 200mm (8in) long is best for applying paint evenly and smoothly on walls and ceilings. You will also need a small pad for cutting in at corners and ceilings.

Loading a pad

Load a pad from its own special tray, drawing the pad across the captive roller so that you pick up an even amount of paint. Be careful not to spin the roller.

Using a paint pad

To apply the paint consistently, keep the pad flat on the wall and sweep it gently and evenly in any direction. However, to prevent streaking, finish with vertical strokes when using solvent-based paints.

Load the pad by drawing it across the tray roller.

Sweep the pad gently in any direction

Painting the ceiling

Starting in a corner near the window, carefully paint along the edges of the ceiling with a small paintbrush (**1**). Working from the wet edges, paint in bands 600mm (2ft) wide, working away from the light (**2**). Whether you are using a brush, pad or roller, apply each fresh load of paint just clear of the previous application then blend in the junctions for even coverage.

1 Paint around the edges first

2 Blend in the wet edges

Painting the walls

Use a small brush to paint the edges, starting at a top corner of the room. If you are right-handed, work from right to left; and vice versa. Paint an area about 600mm (2ft) square at a time. When using emulsion, you can paint in horizontal bands; but apply gloss paints in vertical strips, because the junctions are more likely to show unless you blend in the wet edges quickly.

Always finish a complete wall before you take a break, otherwise a change of tone is likely to show between separate painted sections.

Electrical fittings

Remember to switch off at the mains before exposing electrical connections.

Painting around electrical fittings

Unscrew a ceiling-rose cover so that you can paint right up to the backplate with a small brush. Loosen the faceplate or mounting box of socket outlets and switches so you can paint behind them.

Loosen the face plates of socket outlets and switches

Unscrew a ceiling rose in order to keep it clean

Paint emulsion onto a wall in horizontal bands

Apply solvent-based paints to a wall in vertical strips

SEE ALSO > Primers 40–41, Repairing plaster 48–50, Stripping wallpaper 51, Consumer unit 296, Work platforms 516

Finishing woodwork

Paint is the most common finish for woodwork in and around the house, offering as it does a protective coating in a choice of colours and surface finishes. However, stains, varnishes, lacquers and polishes give an attractive, durable finish to joinery, enhancing the colour of the woodwork without obliterating the beauty of its grain. When choosing a finish, bear in mind the location of the woodwork and the amount of wear it is likely to get.

Painted woodwork
Paint, in its many guises, is one of the most versatile mediums available for home decorating.

Paint finishes

Solvent-based paints

Traditional solvent-based paints (oil paints) are available in high-gloss and satin finishes, with both liquid and thixotropic consistencies. Indoors they will last for years, with only the occasional wash-down to remove fingermarks. One or two undercoats are essential – especially outside, where durability is considerably reduced by the action of sun and rain. Outdoors, you should consider redecorating every 4 to 6 years.

A one-coat paint, with its creamy consistency and high-pigment content, can protect primed wood or obliterate existing colours without undercoating. Apply the paint liberally and allow it to flow freely, rather than brushing it out like a conventional oil paint.

Low-odour solvent-based finishes have largely eradicated the smell and fumes associated with drying paint.

Acrylic paints

These have a number of advantages over conventional oil paints. Being water-based, they are non-flammable and practically odourless and constitute less of a risk to health and the environment. They also dry very quickly, so that a job can often be completed in a single day. This means you have to work swiftly when decorating outside in direct sunlight – in order to avoid leaving brushmarks in the rapidly drying paintwork.

Provided they are applied to adequately prepared wood or keyed paintwork, acrylic paints form a tough flexible coating that resists cracking and peeling. However, in common with other water-based finishes, acrylic paints will not dry satisfactorily if applied on a damp or humid day. Even under perfect conditions, don't expect to achieve a high-gloss finish.

SEE ALSO > Colour and texture 32–3, 36, Primers 40–41

Painting woodwork

Each kind of wood has its own grain pattern and a different rate of absorption; and some species include knots that may ooze resin. These qualities all have a bearing on the type of paint you choose when decorating and the techniques and tools needed to apply it.

Basic application

Removing specks and bristles
Don't attempt to remove brush bristles or specks of fluff from fresh paintwork once a skin has started to form. Instead, let the paint harden, then rub down with wet-and-dry paper. The same applies if you discover runs.

It is essential to prepare and prime all new woodwork thoroughly before applying the finishing coats.

If you're going to use conventional solvent-based paint, apply one or two undercoats, depending on the covering power of the paint. As each coat hardens, rub down with fine wet-and-dry paper to remove blemishes, then wipe the surface with a cloth dampened with white spirit.

Apply the paint with vertical brush-strokes, and then spread it sideways to even out the coverage. Finish with light strokes ('laying off') in the direction of the grain. Blend in the edges of the next application while the paint is still wet. Don't go back over a painted surface that has started to dry, or you will leave brushmarks in the paintwork.

Use a different technique for spreading one-coat or acrylic paints. Simply lay on the paint liberally with almost parallel strokes, then lay off lightly. Blend wet edges quickly.

Best-quality paintbrushes are the most efficient tools for painting woodwork. You will need 25 and 50mm (1 and 2in) brushes for general work, and a 12mm (½in) brush for painting narrow glazing bars.

The order of work

Using fast-drying paints, you may be able to complete a job in a single day – but if you are using oil paints, plan your work to make sure the paint will be dry enough to close doors and windows by nightfall.

Inside

Paint windows early, followed by doors and skirting boards.

Outside

Don't paint in direct sunlight, as it dries water-based paints too quickly. Never paint on wet or windy days: rain specks will pit the finish and airborne dust may ruin it.

Painting a panel
When painting up to the edge of a panel or door, brush from the centre out – if you flex the bristles against the edge, the paint will run. Similarly, mouldings tend to flex bristles unevenly, so that too much paint flows: spread it well, taking extra care at corners of moulded panels.

Painting skirtings
Use a simple plastic shield to protect the floor when painting skirting boards. Alternatively, cover the edges of fitted carpet with wide low-tack masking tape.

Painting a straight edge
To finish an area with a straight edge, use one of the smaller brushes and place it a few millimetres from the edge. As you flex the bristles, they will spread to the required width, laying on an even coat of paint.

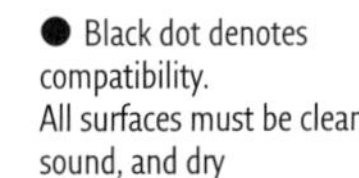

● Black dot denotes compatibility.
All surfaces must be clean, sound, and dry

FINISHES FOR WOODWORK

	Solvent-based paint	Acrylic paint	Wood dye	Protective wood stain	Coloured preserver	Varnish	Acrylic varnish	Cold-cure lacquer	Oil	Wax polish	French polish
Suitable to cover											
Softwoods	●	●	●	●	●	●	●	●	●	●	
Hardwoods	●	●	●	●	●	●	●	●	●	●	●
Oily hardwoods	●	●	●	●		●	●	●	●	●	●
Planed wood	●	●	●	●	●	●	●	●	●	●	●
Sawn wood					●						
Interior use	●	●	●	●		●	●	●	●	●	●
Exterior use	●	●		●	●	●	●		●		
Drying time in hours											
Touch dry	4	1–2	0.5	0.5–4	1–2	2–4	0.5	1	1		0.5
Recoatable	16	4–6	6	4–16	2–4	14	2	2	6	1	24
Thinners											
Water		●	●	●	●		●				
White spirit	●		●	●	●	●			●	●	
Methylated spirit											●
Special thinner								●			
Number of coats											
Interior use	1–2	1–2	2–3	1–2		2–3	3	2–3	3	2	10–15
Exterior use	2–3	1–2		1–2	2	3–4	3–4		3		
Coverage											
Sq metres per litre	15–16	10–14	16–30	10–25	4–12	15–16	15–17	16–17	10–15	variable	variable
Method of application											
Brush	●	●	●	●	●	●	●	●	●	●	●
Paint pad	●	●	●	●		●	●	●			
Cloth pad (rubber)			●			●	●		●	●	●
Spray gun	●	●		●	●	●	●	●			

SEE ALSO > Primers 40–41, Preparing wood 52–6

Painting doors

Doors have a variety of faces and conflicting grain patterns, all of which need to be painted separately – yet the end result needs to look even in colour, with no ugly brushmarks or heavily painted edges.

Glazed doors
To paint a glazed door, begin with the glazing bars, then follow the sequence recommended for panelled doors.

Remove the door handles and wedge the door open so that it cannot be closed accidentally, locking you inside the room. Keep the handle in the room with you.

It's a good idea to paint the door and its frame separately, so there's less chance of touching wet paintwork when passing through a freshly painted doorway.

Sequence for a flush door

To paint a flush door, start at the top and work down in sections, blending each one into the other. Lay on the paint, then finish each section with light vertical strokes. Finally, paint the edges, taking extra care to avoid paint runs.

Painting each side a different colour

Make sure all the surfaces that face you when the door is open are painted the same colour. Paint the architrave (**1**) and doorframe (**2**) up to and including the edge of the doorstop one colour. Paint the face of the door and its opening edge (**3**) the same colour.

On the opposite side of the door, paint the architrave and frame up to and over the doorstop (**4**) the second colour. Paint the opposite face of the door and its hinged edge (**5**) with the second colour.

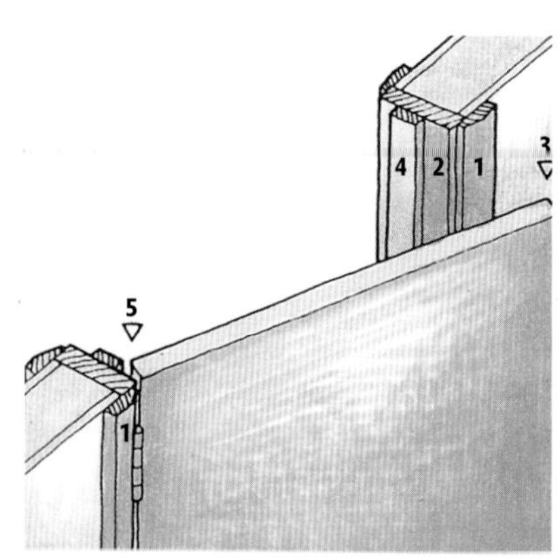

Using two different colours
Each side of the frame should match the corresponding face of the door.

Sequence for a panelled door

You need to paint the various parts of a panelled door in a logical sequence, and finish each part with strokes running parallel to the direction of the grain.

Whatever style of panelled door you are painting, start with the mouldings (**1**), followed by the panels (**2**). Paint the muntins (central verticals) next (**3**), and then the crossrails (**4**). Finish the face by painting the stiles – the outer verticals (**5**). Last of all, paint the edge of the door (**6**).

An alternative method, favoured by professional decorators, will enable you to achieve a superior finish. Paint the muntins, rails and stiles together, picking up the wet edges of the paint before they begin to dry.

When painting each side of a panelled door a different colour, use the method described above for flush doors.

Painting melamine doors
Refurbish old kitchen cupboards using a melamine paint and the specially formulated compatible primer. With a one-coat paint, no primer is needed.

Flush door
Apply paint in sections, working down from the top. Lay off with light vertical brushstrokes, picking up the wet edges for a good blend.

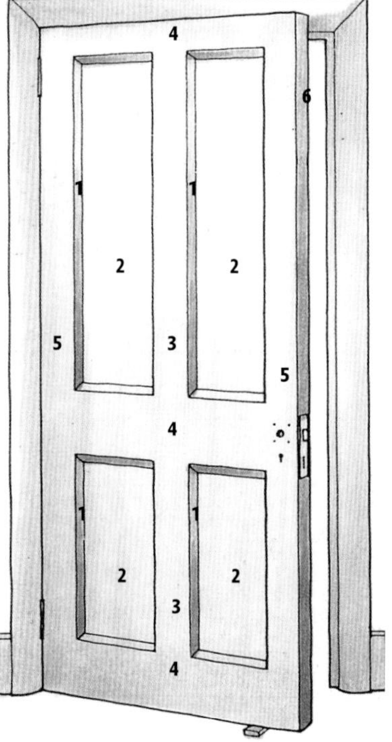

Panelled door: basic method
Follow the numbered sequence for painting the various parts of the door, finishing each part with strokes along the grain to prevent streaking.

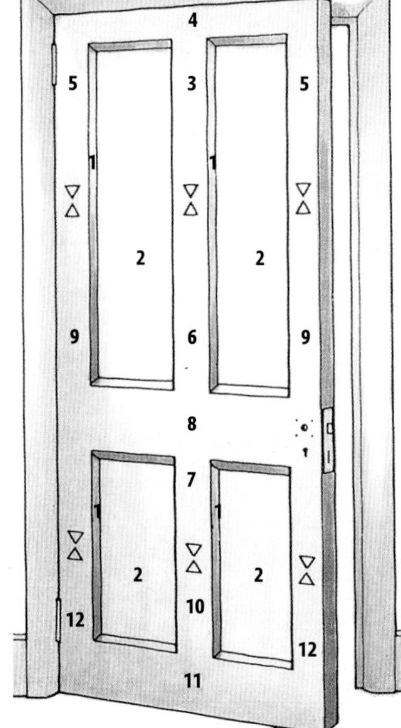

Panelled door: professional method
Working rapidly, follow the alternative sequence – which produces a finish free from joins between sections.

SEE ALSO > Primers 40–41, Preparing wood 52–6, Preparing paintwork 58–9, Staining a door 74, Doors 182–91

Painting window frames

Like doors, window frames need to be painted in sequence – so that the various components will be coated evenly and also so you can close the windows at night. Clean the glass thoroughly before painting a window.

Cutting-in brush
Paint glazing bars with a cutting-in brush. The bristles are cut at an angle to help you work right up to the glass.

Painting a sash window

The following sequence describes the painting of a sash window from the inside. To paint the outside face, use a similar procedure – but start with the lower sash. If you are using different colours for each side, the demarcation lines are fairly obvious: when the window is shut, all the visible surfaces from one side should be the same.

Painting sequence

Raise the bottom sash and pull down the top one. Paint the bottom meeting rail of the top sash (**1**) and the accessible parts of the vertical members (**2**). Reverse the position of the sashes, leaving a gap top and bottom, and complete the painting of the top sash (**3**). Paint the bottom sash (**4**), and then the frame (**5**) except for the runners in which the sashes slide.

Leave the paint to dry, then paint the inner runners (**6**) plus a short section of the outer runners (**7**), pulling the cords aside to avoid brushing paint on them, as this will make them brittle and shorten their working lives. Before the paint has time to dry, check that the sashes slide freely.

Raise bottom sash and lower top one **Reverse position of sashes** **Lower both sashes for access to runners**

Painting a casement window

A casement window hinges like a door – so if you are planning to paint each side a different colour, follow a procedure similar to that recommended for painting doors and frames.

It's best to remove the stay and catch before you paint the window – but so that you can still operate the window without touching wet paint, drive a nail into the underside of the bottom rail and use it as a makeshift handle.

Painting sequence

First paint the glazing bars (**1**), cutting into the glass on both sides. Carry on with the top and bottom horizontal rails (**2**), followed by the vertical stiles (**3**). Finish the casement by painting the edges (**4**), then paint the frame (**5**).

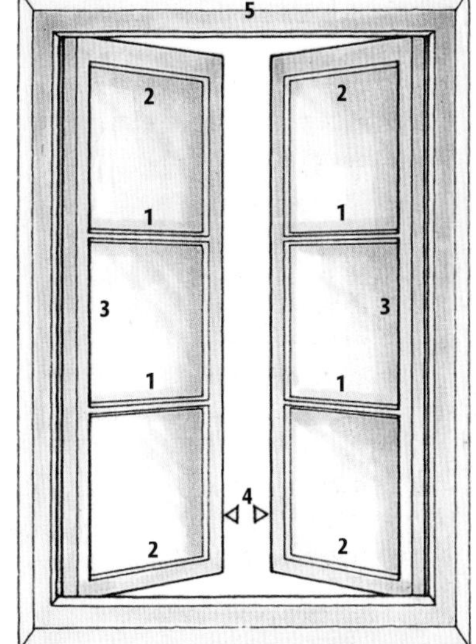

Painting sequence for casement windows

• **UPVC paint and restorer**
To clean ingrained dirt from UPVC windows and doors, use a proprietary surface-restorer on a damp cloth. If that doesn't revive the colour, you can redecorate badly weathered UPVC windows and doors with a special fast-drying gloss paint.

Window-painting tips

It is easy to smear the glass with paint unless you restrict the window's movement and use the correct tools.

Keeping the window open

With the catch and stay removed, there's nothing to stop a casement window closing. Tie a length of stiff wire to a screw driven into the underside of the bottom rail. Bend a hook in the other end, and slot it into one of the screw holes in the frame.

Protecting the glass

When painting the sides of glazing bars, overlap the glass by about 2mm (1/16in) to prevent rain or condensation seeping between the glass and woodwork.

If you find it difficult to achieve a satisfactory straight edge, use a proprietary plastic or metal paint shield, holding it against the edge of the frame, to protect the glass.

Alternatively, run masking tape around the edges of the windowpane, leaving a slight gap so that the paint will seal the join between glass and frame. When the paint is touch-dry, carefully peel off the tape – don't wait until the paint is completely dry, or the film may peel off with the tape.

Scrape the glass with a sharp blade to remove any dry paint spatters. Most DIY stores sell plastic handles to hold blades for this purpose.

Using a paint shield
A plastic shield enables you to paint a straight edge.

SEE ALSO > Primers 40–41, Preparing wood, 52–6, Preparing paintwork 58–9, Windows 192–204

Staining wood

Paint, which colours the wood by depositing a relatively dense layer of pigment on the surface, also provides a protective coating. A true penetrating wood stain or dye soaks into the wood, taking the colour deep into the fibres, but provides no protection at all.

Applicators
To apply penetrating stains, use paint pads, paintbrushes or a wad of soft cloth. Wear PVC gloves and old clothes or an apron when applying wood stains.

Wood stains and dyes

Modern stains often contain translucent pigments that lodge in the pores of the wood. Successive applications of these stains gradually darken the wood. Applying more than one coat of a non-pigmented stain has less effect on the colour.

Solvent or oil stains

The most widely available penetrating stains, made from oil-soluble dyes, are thinned with white spirit. Known as solvent stains or oil stains, these wood dyes are easy to apply evenly, won't raise the grain, and dry relatively quickly. Oil stains are made in a wide range of wood-like colours, which you can mix to achieve intermediate shades.

Spirit stains

Traditional spirit stains are made by dissolving aniline dyes in methylated spirit. The main disadvantage of spirit stains is their extremely rapid drying time, which makes it difficult not to leave darker patches of overlapping colour in an attempt to achieve even coverage. You can buy spirit stains in powder form, which you mix with meths and a little thinned shellac. Some manufacturers supply ready-mixed stains.

Water stains

Water stains are available from specialists as ready-made wood-colour dyes. You can also buy them as crystals or powders for dissolving in hot water so that you can mix any colour you want. Water stains dry slowly – which means there is plenty of time to achieve an even distribution of colour, but you must allow enough time for the water to evaporate before you apply a finish. They also raise the grain, leaving a rough surface, so it is essential to wet the wood and sand down before applying the stain.

Acrylic stains

The latest generation of water stains, based on acrylic resins, are emulsions that leave a film of colour on the surface of the wood. They raise the grain less than traditional water stains, and are more resistant to fading. Acrylic stains need diluting by about 10 per cent when used on dense hardwoods.

Making a test strip

Pigmented stain

Non-pigmented stain

Make a test strip to see how the wood will be affected by the stain you intend to use. It is important that the test strip is sanded smooth – coarsely sanded wood absorbs more dye and will therefore appear darker than the same piece of wood prepared with a finer abrasive.

Apply a coat of stain and allow it to dry – stains tend to look lighter once they have dried. Apply a second coat to see if it darkens the wood, leaving part of the first application exposed for comparison. If you apply more than two full coats of stain, the colour may become patchy.

A second coat of non-pigmented stain may not change the colour appreciably, but you can modify it by overlaying with a stain of a different colour.

Once the stain is dry, paint one half of the test strip with the intended finish to see how it affects the colour of the stain.

Preparing the wood for staining

Sand the wood well, making sure there are no scratches or defects that will absorb more stain than the surrounding wood. In addition, scrape off any patches of dried glue, as they could affect absorption.

Setting up for staining

Plan the work sequence to minimize the possibility of stain running onto adjacent surfaces, or one area of colour drying before you can 'pick up' the wet edges. If you have to colour both sides of a workpiece, stain the least important side first, immediately wiping off any dye that runs over the edges. If possible, set up the workpiece so that the surface to be stained is horizontal. It's best to lay a large panel or door on a pair of trestles, so you can approach it from all sides.

It is sometimes convenient to stain components before assembly, setting them aside to dry while you complete the batch. To colour a number of adjustable shelves, for example, drive two screws into each end. Support each shelf by resting the screws on a pair of battens placed on a workbench, to raise the shelf off the surface. Having stained each side in turn, stand the shelf on end against a wall until the stain is dry.

Staining a door
Place a door on a pair of trestles so you can approach it from all sides.

SEE ALSO > Using grain filler 52, Preparing wood 52–6

Preparing end grain

Because of the orientation of the cells, end grain readily absorbs penetrating stain. So that it won't look too dark, paint the end grain with a coat of white shellac or sanding sealer, which will reduce the amount of colour absorbed.

Alternatively, you can use thinned varnish – but wait 24 hours before you stain the wood.

Paint white shellac or thin varnish onto end grain

Applying wood stains

Pour enough stain to colour the entire workpiece into a shallow dish, so that you are able to load your applicator properly.

Staining a flat surface

Brush or swab the stain onto the wood in the direction of the grain, blending in the wet edges before the dye has time to dry. When you have covered the surface, take a clean cloth pad and mop up excess stain, distributing it evenly across the workpiece. If you splash stain onto the wood, blend it in quickly to prevent a patchy appearance.

If powdery deposits are left on the surface of the dry wood dye, wipe them off with a coarse, dry cloth, before applying a second coat.

Leave the dye to dry overnight, then proceed with the clear finish of your choice to seal the colourant.

Staining turned spindles

Apply stain to banisters and spindles with a rag or a non-woven polishing pad. Rub the dye well into beads and fluting, then cup your rag or pad around the leg or spindle and rub it lengthways. Since turned work often exposes end grain, it can be difficult to obtain even coverage.

Stain a flat surface with a paint pad

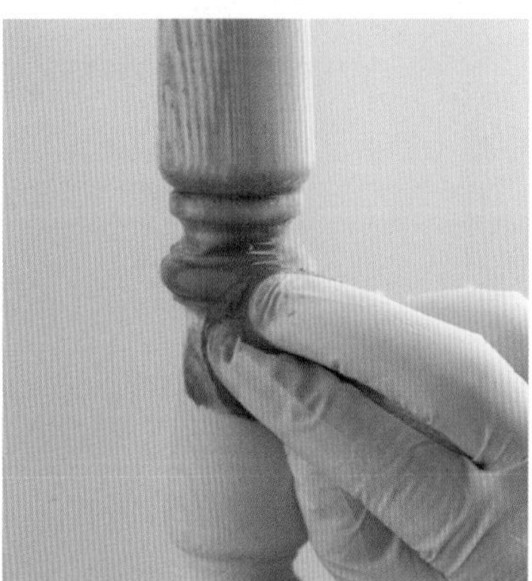

Use a rag to rub stain into a turned banister

Staining floors

Because a wooden floor is such a large area, it is more difficult to blend the wet edges of the dye.

Work along two or three boards at a time, using a paintbrush and finishing at the edge of a board each time.

Woodblock floors are even trickier; so work with an assistant, to cover the area quickly, blending and overlapping sections with a soft cloth.

Stain two or three floorboards at a time

Exterior wood stains

Certain products enable you to modify the colour of wood and provide a protective finish at the same time. Stained finishes do not have the same clarity as penetrating wood dyes and, because they lie on the surface of the wood, applying too many coats tends to obscure the grain. All these exterior finishes are brushed onto the wood.

Colour exterior woodwork with a protective stain

Protective wood stains

Protective wood stains are translucent finishes for exterior joinery. Being water-vapour permeable, they allow the wood to exude moisture while protecting it against adverse weather conditions. As a result, protective wood stains are long-lasting finishes that resist flaking and cracking.

The majority of protective wood stains are tinted, but there is also a clear variety for refurbishing previously stained wood without altering the colour. Protective wood stains are either water-based or solvent-based, and some are one-coat finishes. The water-based variety may not dry properly if applied during wet or humid weather.

Varnish stains

Varnish stains are basically tinted polyurethane or acrylic varnishes that contain colouring agents in the form of translucent pigments or oil-soluble dyes. They are ideal for putting colour back into dowdy woodwork that is already varnished. Although these varnishes provide a tough finish, it pays to overlay them with clear varnish, to prevent scratches and heavy wear that will reveal the paler wood beneath the layer of colour.

SEE ALSO > Preparing wood 52–6, Stripping wood 58–9, Wood preservers 246

Varnish and lacquer

Modern production methods have made available a large range of varnishes and lacquers, each with its own specific properties – durability, weather resistance, ease of application, drying speed, and so on. Such is their versatility that there's almost certainly a varnish or lacquer to meet your requirements.

Oil varnishes

Traditional oil varnish is composed of fossilized tree resins blended with linseed oil and thinned with turpentine. In the manufacture of modern oil varnishes, these natural resins have been superseded by synthetic ones, such as phenolic, alkyd and polyurethane resins, with white spirit as the solvent.

Oil varnishes – frequently referred to as solvent-based varnishes – dry as a result of oxidation. When the solvent has evaporated, the oil absorbs oxygen from the air, chemically changing the varnish in such a way that applying white spirit does not soften the dried film.

The ratio of oil to resin has an effect on the properties of the varnish. Varnishes with a high percentage of oil – known as long oil varnishes – are relatively tough, flexible and water-resistant, making them suitable for finishing exterior woodwork. Short oil varnishes – also called rubbing varnishes – are classed as interior woodwork finishes. Made with less oil and a higher proportion of resin than long oil varnishes, they dry more quickly, with a harder film, and can be polished to a gloss finish.

The choice of resin affects the characteristics of a varnish. Exterior-grade varnishes, for example, are often made from alkyd resin blended with tung oil to provide resilience and weather resistance. Manufacturers adopt terms such as marine varnish to describe superior-quality exterior finishes that will cope with polluted urban environments and coastal climates.

Polyurethane resin is favoured for interior oil varnishes, including floor sealers that need to be tough enough to withstand hard knocks and resist abrasion.

Oil varnishes are normally supplied ready for use, except for those containing pigments or matting agents, which need to be stirred first.

SEE ALSO > Colour and texture 32–3, 36, Preparing wood 52–6, Stripping wood 58–9, Applying varnishes 78–9

Acrylic varnishes

An acrylic varnish is composed of acrylic resins dispersed in water to form an emulsion. The varnish is milky white when applied, but becomes a clear transparent finish after going through a two-stage evaporative process.

Acrylic varnish contains a small percentage of solvents known as coalescing agents which, after the water has evaporated, fuse the particles of resin into a cured film. This process can only take place in a relatively warm dry atmosphere. In very humid or damp conditions, the coalescing agents may evaporate before the water does, leaving a film that cannot set properly.

Acrylic varnishes are non-toxic and practically odourless, and you can wash out your brushes in ordinary tap water.

Interior varnish
Oil varnishes are suitable for most interior wood surfaces.

Cold-cure lacquers

Cold-cure lacquers – which set hard by a process known as cross-polymerization – require the addition of an acid catalyst to start the reaction. When the resin cures, the molecules are bonded chemically, forming an extremely tough nonreversible film that is highly resistant to solvents, heat and abrasion. Because cold-cure lacquers do not rely on evaporation of the solvent or on oxidation for setting, they can be applied in relatively thick coats.

Some of these lacquers are supplied precatalysed, so that the curing process begins automatically as soon as the solvent evaporates. Others are supplied in two parts, requiring the user to add the acid hardener before applying the finish.

Cold-cure lacquers are usually manufactured with butylated urea-formaldehyde resins, plus melamine for heat resistance and alkyd resin as a plasticizer. The lacquer forms an exceptionally clear film that does not yellow with time. Opaque white and black finishes are also available.

Floor sealers
Hardwearing clear varnishes are made specifically for finishing floors.

Two-pack polyurethane varnishes

In order for this varnish to set hard, the user has to mix in a precise amount of isocyanate curing agent just before application. The result is a clear tough finish that is better than standard oil varnish in terms of durability and resistance to heat, alcohol and other chemicals. Its one disadvantage is that during the curing process the varnish exudes extremely unpleasant fumes, which can be injurious to health. Consequently, many countries have banned the use of two-pack polyurethane varnishes except in controlled industrial premises fitted with adequate exhaust ventilation.

Always read the safety advice and application instructions printed on the packaging before buying a two-part polyurethane varnish.

Fast-drying varnish
Acrylic varnish dries so rapidly you can complete most tasks in a day.

SEE ALSO > Colour and texture 32–3, 36, Preparing wood 52–6, Stripping wood 58–9, Applying varnishes 78–9, Applying lacquer 79

Applying varnishes

Applying oil varnish

Most people find it easiest to brush varnish onto the surface of the wood, but some manufacturers recommend using a soft absorbent pad, which they supply with their varnish.

Varnishing mouldings
When finishing a panelled door, varnish the mouldings first and then the panel, brushing out from each corner towards the centre. To prevent the varnish running, brush along the mouldings, not across them.

Varnishing a flat panel

Supporting a large panel horizontally on a pair of trestles makes varnishing slightly easier, but there are few problems with finishing a hinged door or fixed panel *in situ*, provided you guard against the varnish running.

When applying the first sealer coat to bare wood, thin oil varnish by about 10 per cent and either brush the varnish onto the wood or rub it into the grain with a soft cloth (**1**).

Leave the sealer coat to harden overnight, then inspect the varnished surface under a good source of light. Rub down the sealer coat lightly in the direction of the grain (**2**), using a folded piece of fine wet-and-dry paper dipped in water. Then wipe the surface clean, using a cloth moistened with white spirit, and dry it with a paper towel.

Follow up with a coat of full-strength varnish, brushing first with the grain and then across it to spread the finish evenly (**3**). Always brush towards the area you have just finished, to blend the wet edges. Work at a fairly brisk pace, as varnish begins to set after about 10 minutes and rebrushing tends to leave permanent brushmarks.

Finally 'lay off' along the grain with very light strokes – using just the tips of the bristles to leave a smoothly varnished surface (**4**). When varnishing vertical surfaces, lay off with upward strokes.

Two full-strength coats of oil varnish should be sufficient for most purposes. For a perfect finish, rub down lightly between each hardened coat.

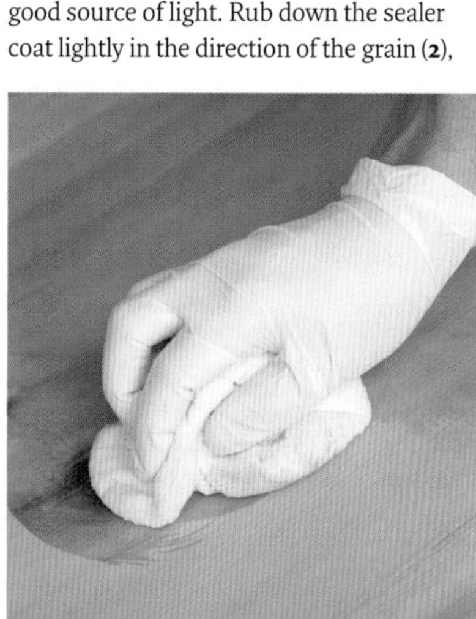
1 Apply a sealer coat of varnish

2 Rub down, using wet-and-dry paper

3 Spread full-strength varnish evenly

4 Lay off, using the tips of the bristles

Dealing with dust

Minor imperfections and particles of dust stuck to the varnished surface can be rubbed down with fine wet-and-dry paper between coats. If you are not satisfied with your final finish, wait until it is dry and then dip very fine wire wool in wax polish and rub the varnish with parallel strokes in the direction of the grain. Buff the surface with a soft duster. This treatment removes a high gloss, but it leaves a pleasant sheen on the surface with no obvious imperfections.

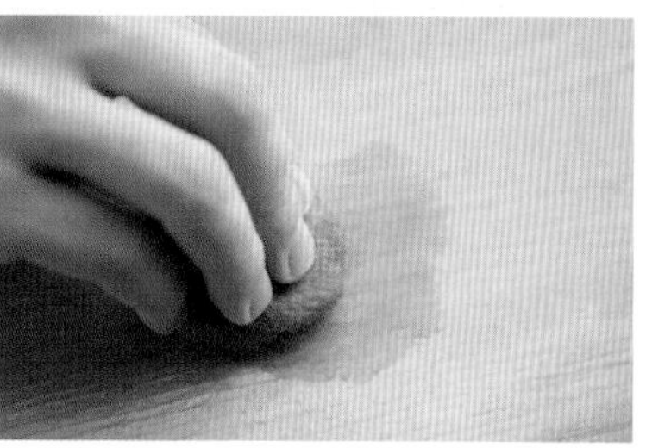
Remove dust particles with wire wool

Varnishing floors

Varnishing a floor is no different from varnishing any other woodwork; but due to the size of the area being treated in a confined space, oil varnishes can produce an unpleasant concentration of fumes. Open all the windows, to provide maximum ventilation, and wear a respirator while you are working.

Start in the corner furthest from the door and work back towards it. Brush the varnish out well, so that it does not collect in pools.

Alternatively, apply the varnish with a paint pad on an extended handle. Some manufacturers supply this type of pad with their floor varnishes.

Varnishing with a long handle is less tiring

SEE ALSO > Preparing wood 52–6, Stripping wood 58–9, Varnish and lacquer 76–7, Wax polishes 81

Applying acrylic varnish

Many of the techniques employed when applying oil varnish are equally relevant to acrylic varnish. As with oil varnish the aim is to achieve a flat, even coating without runs or brushmarks, but the chemical properties of acrylic varnish make it behave slightly differently.

Grain-raising characteristics

When a piece of wood absorbs water, its fibres swell and stand up proud of the surface. Water-based acrylic varnish has the same effect, making the final finish less than perfect. The solution is either to wet the wood first and sand it smooth before applying the varnish, or to sand the first coat of varnish with fine wet-and-dry paper dipped in water before recoating the work. Either way, wipe up the dust with a cloth dampened with water - a tack rag may leave oily deposits, which would spoil the next coat of varnish.

Applying the varnish

Acrylic varnish must be applied liberally. As with oil varnish (see opposite), brush across the grain first and lay off evenly.

Acrylic varnish dries in 20 to 30 minutes - so you need to work fast, especially on a hot day, to avoid leaving permanent brushmarks in the finish.

You can apply a second coat of varnish after 2 hours. A total of three coats is sufficient for maximum protection.

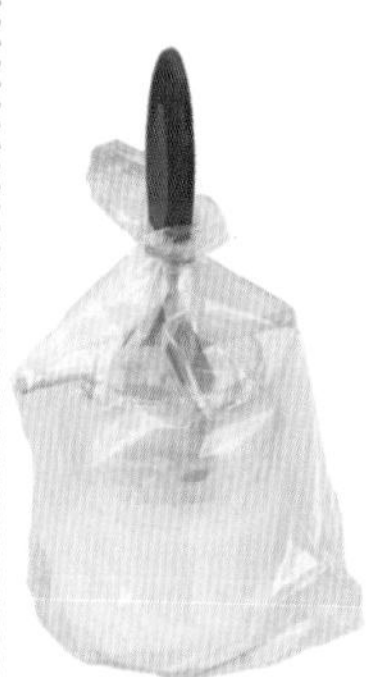

Brush care
Wash your brushes in special lacquer thinner as soon as the work is complete. You can leave a brush suspended in the mixed lacquer between coats if the whole container, including the brush, is wrapped in polythene.

Applying cold-cure lacquer

This is a very different finish from conventional varnish. Although cold-cure lacquer is no more difficult to apply, it is important to be aware of how the curing process can be affected by inadequate preparation.

Mixing cold-cure lacquer

Mix recommended amounts of hardener and lacquer in a glass jar or polythene container. Metal containers and other plastics may react with the hardener, preventing the lacquer from curing.

Once mixed, some cold-cure lacquers are usable for about 3 days. However, you can extend the pot life to about a week by covering the jar with polythene, held in place with an elastic band.

This type of lacquer will last even longer if you keep the sealed container - clearly marked in order to avoid accidents - in a refrigerator.

Mix the lacquer in a glass or polythene container

Applying the lacquer

The wood must be smooth and clean. Be sure to remove any trace of wax, which might prevent the lacquer curing. Any wood dye applied to the work must be compatible with the acid catalyst in the lacquer, so check the manufacturer's recommendations before colouring the workpiece.

Adequate ventilation is important - especially when you are lacquering a floor - but maintain a warm temperature.

Brush on the lacquer liberally, using a flowing action and blending in wet edges as you go. Apply it relatively thickly, taking care to avoid runs.

The lacquer will be touch-dry in about 15 minutes; apply a second coat after about an hour. If a third coat is required, apply it the following day.

Except to remove blemishes, there is never any need to rub down between coats. If you use stearated abrasives - those lubricated with powdered soap - wipe the sanded surface with special lacquer thinner.

Modifying the finish

To achieve a perfect gloss finish, let the last coat harden for a few days then sand it smooth, using wet-and-dry paper with water, until the surface appears matt all over (a shiny patch indicates a hollow). Finally, using a burnishing cream on a slightly damp cloth, buff the surface to a high gloss and then rub it with a duster.

To create a satin finish, rub the hardened lacquer with 000-grade steel wool lubricated with wax polish and finish by burnishing gently with a duster. For a matt finish, use coarser steel wool.

Apply a liberal coat of lacquer

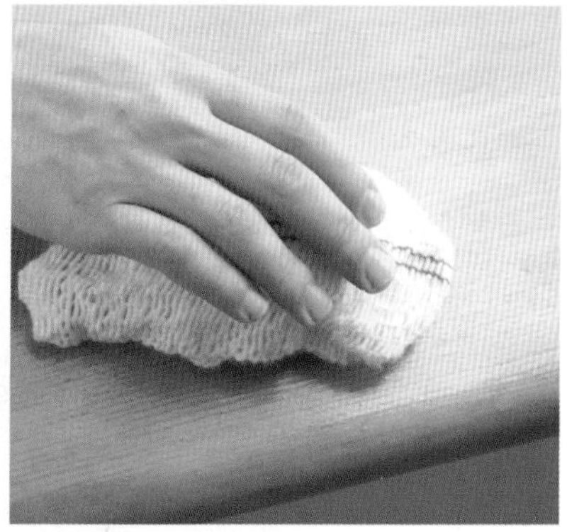

You can buff the surface to a high gloss

SEE ALSO > Preparing wood 52–6, Stripping wood 58–9, Varnish and lacquer 76–7, Wax polishes 81

Oiling wood

Unlike varnish and paint, which lie on the surface, wood-finishing oil penetrates deeply into the pores, forming a resilient finish that will not crack, peel or chip. Most oil finishes require no more than annual maintenance to preserve their appearance.

A natural appearance
A pine staircase in exceptional condition finished with hardwearing gelled oil. Apply a varnish first for extra durability.

Types of oil finish

Some woodworkers consider oil finishes suitable only for hardwoods such as teak or afrormosia – but oil makes a handsome finish for any timber, especially pine, which turns a rich golden colour when oiled.

Linseed oil

Traditional linseed oil is rarely used nowadays for finishing wood, mainly because it can take as long as 3 days to dry. However, modern manufacturers have been able to reduce drying time to about 24 hours, by heating the oil and adding dryers to produce 'boiled linseed oil'.

Tung oil

Also known as Chinese wood oil, tung oil is obtained from nuts grown in China and parts of South America. A tung-oil finish – which is resistant to water, alcohol and acidic fruit juice – takes about 24 hours to dry and is suitable for both interior and exterior woodwork.

Finishing oils

Commercial wood-finishing oils, which are based on tung oil, include synthetic resins to improve durability. Depending on temperature and humidity, finishing oils dry in about 6 hours. Often referred to as teak oil or Danish oil, finishing oils are suitable for any environment and can also be used as a sealer coat for oil varnish or paint.

Gelled oil

A blend of natural oils and synthetic resin is available as a thick gel that behaves more like a soft wax polish. It is packed in tubs so that the gel can be picked up on a cloth pad. Gelled oil can be applied to bare wood and, unlike other oil finishes, can also be applied over existing finishes such as varnish and lacquer.

Applying a finishing oil

Oil finishes other than gelled oil (see above right) cannot be applied to a prevarnished or lacquered workpiece. When finishing previously oiled timber, use white spirit to clean old wax from the surface.

Applying the oil

Apply the first coat of oil using a fairly wide brush to wet the surface thoroughly (**1**). Leave it for about 10 to 15 minutes to soak in, then ensure that coverage is even by wiping excess oil from the surface with a soft cloth pad.

After 6 hours, use an abrasive nylon-fibre pad to rub oil onto the wood in the general direction of the grain (**2**). Wipe excess oil from the surface with a paper towel or cloth pad, then leave to dry overnight. Apply a third coat in the same way.

1 Apply the first coat of oil with a brush

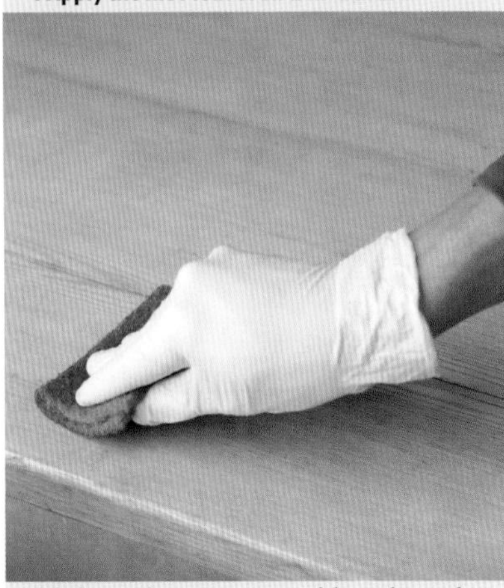

2 Rub on subsequent coats with a nylon pad

Disposing of oily rags

Oil-soaked rags are a fire hazard. Keep them in a sealed tin while the job is in progress, then unfold them and leave them outside to dry before throwing them away.

Using gelled oil

Use a soft cloth pad to rub gelled oil vigorously in the direction of the grain until the surface is touch-dry. Two coats are usually sufficient; but if the surface will be subjected to heavy wear or hot dishes, apply more oil. Allow 4 hours between coats. Gelled oil dries naturally to a soft sheen, so there's no need to burnish the workpiece again – but allow a full 48 hours before you put it to use.

Use a pad to apply gelled oil

SEE ALSO > Preparing wood 52–6, Stripping wood 58–9

Waxing wood

Waxing wood is a long-established tradition, especially for finishing period furniture. Thanks to the subtle qualities of wax polish, it can also be used to advantage as a finish for open-grain timbers or as a dressing over lacquer or varnish.

Commercial polishes

Most commercially prepared wax polishes are a blend of relatively soft beeswax and hard carnauba wax, reduced to a usable consistency with turpentine or white spirit.

Paste wax polish

The most familiar form of wax polish is sold as a thick paste, in flat tins or foil containers. Paste wax, applied with a cloth pad or fine steel wool, serves as an ideal dressing over another finish.

Liquid wax polish

When you want to wax a large area of wood – oak panelling, for example – it is often easiest to brush on liquid wax polish, which has the consistency of a cream.

Floor wax

A liquid polish formulated for hardwearing surfaces, floor wax is usually available as a clear polish only.

Coloured polishes

White to pale-yellow polishes do not alter the colour of the wood to a great extent, but there is also an extensive choice of darker polishes – sometimes referred to as staining waxes – that can be used to modify the colour of a workpiece or to hide scratches and minor blemishes. Dark-brown to black polish is a popular finish for oak; it enhances the patina of old wood and, by lodging in the open pores, accentuates the grain pattern. There are warm golden-brown polishes made to put the colour back into stripped pine, and orange-red polishes for enriching faded mahogany.

Applying one polish over another creates even more subtle shades and tints. It is not a good idea to wax chairs with dark-coloured polishes, in case your body heat should soften the wax and your clothes get stained. The same goes for finishing the insides of drawers: long-term contact could discolour fabrics.

Waxing bare timber

Before applying a wax polish, sand the wood smooth and then wipe the surface with white spirit to remove any traces of grease. Although there's no need to fill the grain, it is always best to seal the wood with a sanding sealer or a coat of clear varnish. Rub down the sealer coat with fine wet-and-dry paper.

Applying paste polish

Dip a cloth pad into the polish and apply the first coat using overlapping circular strokes to rub the wax into the grain (1). Cover the surface evenly, then finish by rubbing in the direction of the grain. If the polish proves difficult to spread, warm the tin slightly on a radiator.

After about 15 to 20 minutes, use 000-grade steel wool or an abrasive nylon pad to rub on more wax polish, this time working in the direction of the grain (2). Put the work aside for 24 hours, so the solvent can evaporate. On new work, apply four or five coats of wax in all, allowing each one to harden overnight.

Once the wax has hardened thoroughly, burnish vigorously with a soft cloth pad. Finally, rub over all polished surfaces with a clean duster.

1 Use overlapping circular strokes

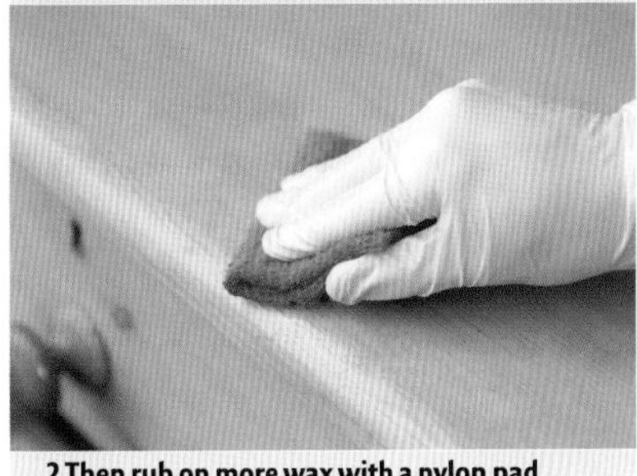

2 Then rub on more wax with a nylon pad

Brushing on liquid polish

Decant some of the liquid polish into a shallow dish and brush it liberally onto the wood, spreading the wax as evenly as possible. Then put the work aside to let the solvent evaporate for about an hour.

Apply a second coat of wax with a soft cloth pad, using circular strokes at first and finishing by rubbing in the direction of the grain. An hour later, apply a third coat if required.

Leave the polish to harden, preferably overnight; then burnish the workpiece, in the direction of the grain, with a clean soft duster.

Brush liquid polish onto the wood

Applying a wax dressing

If you want to achieve the mellow sheen typical of wax polish but need the finish to be more hard-wearing, you can apply a thin wax dressing over polyurethane varnish or cold-cure lacquer.

Dip 000-grade steel wool or an abrasive nylon pad into paste polish and rub the finished surface, using straight strokes in the direction of the grain. After 15 to 20 minutes, polish the hardened wax with a cloth.

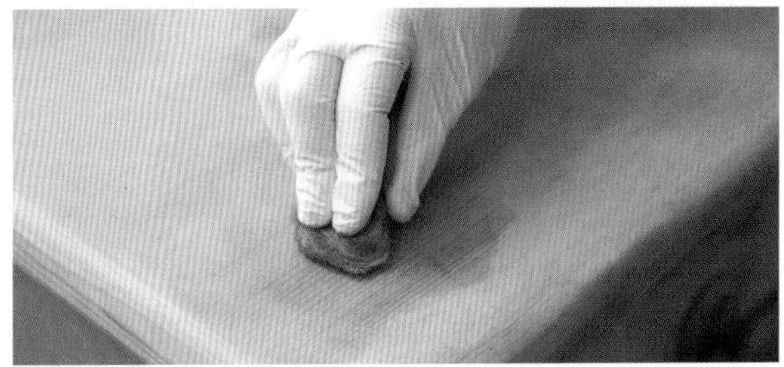

Modify the sheen of varnish with a wax dressing

SEE ALSO > Preparing wood 52–6, Stripping wood 58–9, Varnish and lacquer 76–7

Finishing metalwork

Ferrous metals that are rusty will shed practically any paint film rapidly – so the most important aspect of finishing metalwork is thorough preparation and priming, in order to prevent the corrosion returning. After that, applying the finish is virtually the same as when painting woodwork.

Protecting metalwork
There's no need to apply a primer when painting cast-iron railings with a one-coat hammered-finish paint.

FINISHES FOR METALWORK

● Black dot denotes compatibility.
All surfaces must be clean, sound and dry.

	Solvent-based paint	Hammered-finish paint	Metallic paint	Bitumen-based paint	Security paint	Radiator enamel	Black lead	Lacquer	Bath paint	Non-slip paint
Drying time in hours										
Touch-dry	4	0.5	4	1–2		0.5		0.25	6–10	4–6
Recoatable	14	1–3	8	6–24		4			16–24	12
Thinners										
Water				●		●				
White spirit	●		●	●	●		●		●	●
Special		●								
Cellulose thinners								●		
Number of coats										
Normal conditions	1–2	1	1–2	1–3	1	2	variable	1	2	2
Coverage										
Sq metres per litre	12–16	3–5	10–14	6–15	2.5	15	variable	18	13–14	3–5
Method of application										
Brush	●	●	●	●	●	●	●	●	●	●
Paint pad	●	●		●						
Spray gun	●	●		●				●		
Cloth pad (rubber)							●			

Finishes for metalwork

Solvent-based paints

Conventional solvent-based paints are suitable for use on metal. Once it has been primed, metalwork needs undercoating before a top coat is applied.

Hammered-finish paint

Consisting of a combination of heat-hardened glass flakes, aluminium particles and resins, hammered-finish paint is applied as one coat only. There's no need for a primer or undercoat, even when painting previously rusted metal. A smooth-finish paint with the same properties is also available.

Bitumen-based paints

Bitumen-based paints give economical protection for exterior storage tanks and piping. Standard bituminous paint is black, but there is also a limited range of colours, plus 'modified' bituminous paint, which contains aluminium.

Security paints

Non-setting security paint, used primarily for rainwater and waste downpipes, remains slippery to prevent intruders from climbing the pipe. Only use it for pipework more than 2m (6ft) or so above the ground.

Radiator enamels

Fast-drying water-based radiator enamel can be applied to previously painted radiators, provided the surfaces are thoroughly cleaned and lightly sanded. Bare metal or factory-primed radiators must be coated with a compatible primer.

Turn off the heating and allow the radiators to cool before painting them. Some radiator enamels are applied with a synthetic brush; others are supplied in aerosols for easier application.

Alternatively, paint your radiators with ordinary emulsion and then apply a special clear coating that keeps the painted surface clean and scratch-free.

Black lead

A cream used for cast ironwork, black lead is a mixture of graphite and waxes. It is reasonably moisture-resistant, but is not suitable for exterior use.

Lacquer

Virtually any clear lacquer can be used on polished metalwork without spoiling its appearance; however, many polyurethane lacquers have a tendency to yellow with age. For long-term protection of chrome, brass and copper, inside or outdoors, use a clear acrylic metal lacquer.

Non-slip paints

Designed to provide secure footholding on a wide range of surfaces, including metal, non-slip paints are ideal for metal staircase treads and exterior fire escapes.

SEE ALSO > Primers 40–41, Preparing metals 60–61

Methods of application

With the exception of black lead, you can use a paintbrush to apply metal finishes. In general, the techniques are similar to those used for painting woodwork.

Some paints can be sprayed, but there are few situations where this is advantageous, except perhaps in the case of intricately moulded ironwork such as garden furniture, which you can paint outside. Indoors, good ventilation is essential when spraying.

A roller is suitable for large flat surfaces. Pipework requires the use of a special V-section roller, designed to coat curved surfaces.

Door and window furniture
Remove metal door and window furniture before you paint it. Suspend the fittings on wire hooks to dry. Make sure sharp edges are coated properly, or you may find the finish wears thin relatively quickly.

• Fridge paint
Refurbish old washing machines, dishwashers and refrigerators by spraying them with white or satin-chrome enamel paint specially formulated for appliances. Surfaces must be clean, dry and rust-free.

Metal casement windows

Paint metal casement windows using the sequence described for wooden casements. Make sure you allow enough time for the paint to dry so you can close the window at night without spoiling a freshly painted surface.

Gutters and downpipes

It is best to coat the inside of gutters with a bitumen-based paint for thorough protection against moisture, but you can finish the outer surfaces with oil paint or security paint.

To protect the wall behind a downpipe, slip a scrap of card between pipe and wall before painting the back of the pipe.

Protect the wall behind a downpipe

Painting radiators and pipes

Leave radiators and hot-water pipes to cool before you paint them. The only problem with decorating a radiator is how to paint the back. The best solution is to remove the radiator completely or, if possible, to swing it away from the wall. After you have painted the back, reposition the radiator and paint the front.

If this is inconvenient, use a special radiator roller or brush. These are also ideal for painting in between the leaves of a double radiator. It is difficult to achieve a perfect finish – so aim at covering the areas you are likely to see when the radiator is fixed in position, rather than a complete application.

Don't paint over radiator valves or fittings – otherwise, you won't be able to operate them afterwards.

Paint pipework lengthwise rather than across, or runs are likely to form. The first coat on metal piping will be streaky, so be prepared to apply two or three coats. Allow the paint to harden thoroughly before turning on the heat.

Using a radiator brush or roller
A long slim-handled radiator brush or miniature roller enables you to paint between the leaves of a radiator. You can use the same tools to paint the back of the radiator without having to remove it from the wall.

Lacquering metalwork

Polish the metal to a high gloss, then use a nailbrush to scrub it with warm water containing some liquid detergent. Rinse the metal in clean water, then dry it thoroughly with an absorbent cloth.

Apply acrylic lacquer with a large, soft artist's paintbrush, working swiftly from the top. Let the lacquer flow naturally, and work all round the object to keep the wet edge moving.

If you do leave a brushmark in partially set lacquer, finish the job and then warm the metal (by standing it on a radiator, if possible). As soon as the blemish disappears, remove the object from the heat and allow it to cool gradually in a dust-free atmosphere.

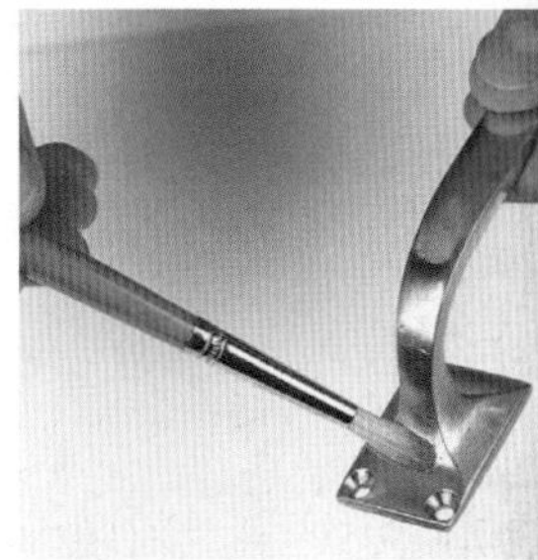

Applying lacquer
Use a large, soft artist's paintbrush.

Blacking cast iron

Black lead produces an attractive finish for cast iron. It is not a permanent or durable finish, and will have to be renewed periodically. It may transfer if rubbed hard.

Black lead comes in a tube similar to a toothpaste tube. Squeeze some of the cream onto a soft cloth and spread it onto the metal. Use an old toothbrush to scrub it into decorative ironwork, to achieve the best coverage.

When you have covered the surface, buff it to a satin sheen with a clean, dry cloth. Build up several applications of black lead to create a patina and provide a moisture-resistant finish.

Applying black lead
Use an old toothbrush to scrub the cream into intricate surfaces.

SEE ALSO > Primers 40–41, Preparing metals 60–61, Painting a casement window 73, Removing radiators 415

Wallcoverings

Although wallcoverings are often called 'wallpaper', by no means all of them are made solely from wood pulp. Indeed, there is a huge choice of paper-backed fabrics, ranging from exotic silks to coarse hessians and natural textures such as cork or woven grass. Plastics have widened the choice still further: there are paper-backed or cotton-backed vinyls, and plain or patterned foamed plastics. Before wallpaper became popular, fabric wall hangings were commonly used to decorate interiors – and this is still done today, using unbacked fabrics glued or stretched across walls.

Ensuring a suitable surface

Before hanging any wallcovering, make sure the surface of the wall or ceiling is clean, sound and smooth. If damp and organic growth are present, they must be eradicated.

Also, consider whether you should size the surface to reduce paste absorption.

Coverings that camouflage

Although a poor surface should be repaired, some coverings hide minor blemishes, as well as providing a foundation for other finishes.

Expanded-polystyrene sheet

Thin polystyrene sheet is used for lining a wall before papering. It reduces condensation and also bridges hairline cracks and small holes. Polystyrene dents easily, so don't use it where it will take a lot of punishment. There is a patterned version for ceilings.

Lining paper

This is a cheap buff-coloured wallpaper for lining uneven or impervious walls prior to hanging a heavy or expensive wallcovering. It provides an even surface for emulsion paint.

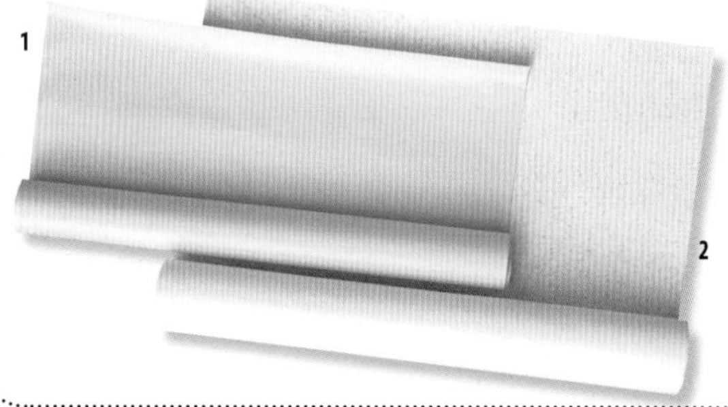

Top right
1 Lining paper
2 Expanded polystyrene

Above
3 Hand-printed
4 Machine-printed

Far right
5 Lincrusta
6 Embossed-paper wallcovering
7 Blown vinyl

Printed wallpapers

One advantage of ordinary wallpaper is the superb range of printed colours and patterns, which is much wider than for any other wallcovering. Most of the cheaper papers are machine-printed.

The more costly hand-printed papers are prone to tearing when wet, and the inks have a tendency to run if you smear paste on the surface. They are not really suitable for walls exposed to wear or condensation. Pattern matching can be awkward, because hand printing isn't as accurate as machine printing.

Relief papers

Some wallpapers, known as reliefs, have deeply embossed patterns. These papers are invariably painted, with satin-finish oil paints, emulsion or water-based acrylics.

Lincrusta – which was the first embossed wallcovering – consists of a solid film of linseed oil and fillers fused onto a backing paper before the pattern is applied with an engraved steel roller. It is still available, though many people prefer embossed-paper wallcoverings or the superior-quality versions made from cotton fibres.

Lightweight vinyl reliefs are also popular. During manufacture they are heated in an oven, which 'blows' or expands the vinyl, creating deeply embossed patterns.

SEE ALSO > Colour and pattern 32–3, 37, Sizing a wall 48, Repairing plaster 48–50, Mould growth 51, Stripping wallcoverings 51

Washable papers
These are printed papers with a thin impervious glaze of PVA to make a spongeable surface. Washables are suitable for bathrooms and kitchens. The surface must not be scrubbed, or the plastic coating will be worn away.

Vinyl wallcoverings
A base paper, or sometimes a cotton backing, is coated with a layer of vinyl on which the design is printed. Heat is used to fuse the colours and vinyl. The result is a durable, washable wallcovering ideally suited to bathrooms and kitchens.

Grass cloth
Natural grasses are woven into a mat and glued to a paper backing. While these wallcoverings are very attractive, they are fragile and difficult to hang.

Flock wallcoverings
Flock papers have the major pattern elements picked out with a fine pile produced by gluing synthetic or natural fibres such as silk or wool to the backing paper. The pattern stands out in relief, with a velvet-like texture.

Standard flock papers are difficult to hang, as contact with paste will ruin the pile. Vinyl flocks are less delicate and can be hung anywhere.

You can sponge flock paper to remove stains, but brush them to remove dust from the pile. Vinyl flocks can be washed without risk of damage.

Cork-faced paper
This is surfaced with thin sheets of coloured or natural cork. It is not spoiled as easily as other special papers.

Paper-backed fabrics
Finely woven cotton, linen or silk on a paper backing has to be applied to a flat surface. They are expensive and not easy to hang, so it is advisable to hire a specialist decorator. Most fabrics are delicate, but some are plastic-coated to make them scuff-resistant.

1 Washable papers
2 Flock paper
3 Paper-backed fabrics
4 Vinyl wallcoverings

SEE ALSO > Colour and pattern 32–3, 37, Sizing a wall 48, Repairing plaster 48–50, Mould growth 51, Stripping wallcoverings 51

Estimating quantities

Calculating the number of rolls of wallcovering you need will depend mainly on the size of the roll – both the length and width. However, you also need to take into consideration the pattern repeat and make allowance for cutting around obstacles such as windows and doors.

The width of a standard roll of wallcovering is 520mm (1ft 9in), the length 10.05 metres (33ft). Use the two charts on this page to estimate how many rolls you are likely to need for walls and ceilings.

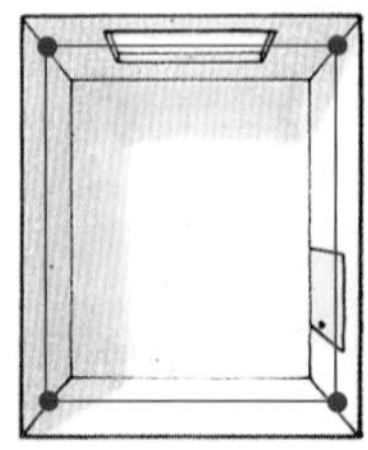

Measuring walls for standard rolls
A standard roll of wall-covering is 520mm (1ft 9in) wide and 10.05 metres (33ft) long. To be on the safe side, you may want to include windows and doors in your estimate.

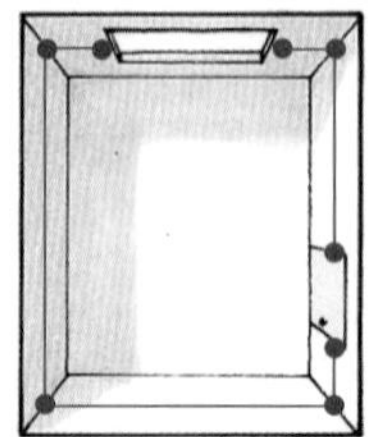

Measuring walls for non-standard rolls
Do not include doors and windows when estimating for expensive materials. Allow for short lengths after making your main calculation.

Non-standard rolls

If the wallcovering you prefer is not cut to a standard size, calculate the amount you need the following way:

Measuring the walls

Measure the height of the walls from skirting to ceiling. Divide the length of the roll by this figure to find the number of wall lengths you can cut from a roll.

Measure around the room, leaving out windows and doors, to determine how many widths fit into the total length of the walls. To estimate how many rolls you will need, divide this number by the number of wall lengths you can get from one roll.

Make an allowance for short lengths above doors and under windows.

Measuring ceilings

Measure the length of the room to determine the length of a single strip of paper. Work out how many roll-widths fit across the room. To estimate how many rolls you need, multiply the two figures and divide the answer by the length of a roll. Check for waste and allow for it.

Checking for shading

If rolls of wallcovering are printed in one batch, there should be no problem with colour-matching one roll with another. When you buy, look for the batch number printed on the wrapping.

Make a visual check before hanging the covering, especially when using hand-printed papers or fabrics. Unroll a short length of each roll and lay the rolls side by side. You may be able to obtain a better colour match by changing the rolls round. If the colour difference is too obvious, ask for replacement rolls.

Walls: Standard rolls
Measure your room, then look down the height column and across the wall column to estimate the number of standard rolls required.

MEASUREMENT IN METRES AROUND WALLS, INCLUDING DOORS AND WINDOWS	HEIGHT OF ROOM IN METRES FROM SKIRTING							
	2–2.25m	2.25–2.5m	2.5–2.75m	2.75–3m	3–3.25m	3.25–3.5m	3.5–3.75m	3.75–4m
Walls	Number of rolls required for walls							
10m	5	5	6	6	7	7	8	8
10.5m	5	6	6	7	7	8	8	9
11m	5	6	7	7	8	8	9	9
11.5m	6	6	7	7	8	8	9	9
12m	6	6	7	8	8	9	9	10
12.5m	6	7	7	8	9	9	10	10
13m	6	7	8	8	9	10	10	10
13.5m	7	7	8	9	9	10	10	11
14m	7	7	8	9	10	10	11	11
14.5m	7	8	8	9	10	10	11	12
15m	7	8	9	9	10	11	12	12
15.5m	7	8	9	9	10	11	12	13
16m	8	8	9	10	11	11	12	13
16.5m	8	9	9	10	11	12	13	13
17m	8	9	10	10	11	12	13	14
17.5m	8	9	10	11	12	13	14	14
18m	9	9	10	11	12	13	14	15
18.5m	9	10	11	12	12	13	14	15
19m	9	10	11	12	13	14	15	16
19.5m	9	10	11	12	13	14	15	16
20m	9	10	11	12	13	14	15	16
20.5m	10	11	12	13	14	15	16	17
21m	10	11	12	13	14	15	16	17
21.5m	10	11	12	13	14	15	17	18
22m	10	11	13	14	15	16	17	18
22.5m	11	12	13	14	15	16	17	18
23m	11	12	13	14	15	17	18	19
23.5m	11	12	13	15	16	17	18	19
24m	11	12	14	15	16	17	18	20
24.5m	11	13	14	15	16	18	19	20
25m	12	13	14	15	17	18	19	20
25.5m	12	13	14	16	17	18	20	21
26m	12	13	15	16	17	19	20	21
26.5m	12	14	15	16	18	19	20	22
27m	13	14	15	17	18	19	21	22
27.5m	13	14	16	17	18	20	21	23
28m	13	14	16	17	19	20	21	23
28.5m	13	15	16	18	19	20	22	23
29m	13	15	16	18	19	21	22	24
29.5m	14	15	17	18	20	21	23	24
30m	14	15	17	18	20	21	23	24

Ceilings: Standard rolls
Measure the perimeter of the ceiling. The number of standard rolls required is shown next to the overall dimensions.

Dimensions
All dimensions are shown in metres (1m = 39in).

CEILINGS: NUMBER OF ROLLS REQUIRED							
Measurement around room	Number of rolls	Measurement around room	Number of rolls	Measurement around room	Number of rolls	Measurement around room	Number of rolls
11m	2	16m	4	21	6	26m	9
12m	2	17m	4	22	7	27m	10
13m	3	18m	5	23	7	28m	10
14m	3	19m	5	24	8	29m	11
15m	4	20m	5	25	8	30m	11

SEE ALSO > Wallcoverings 84–5, Papering a wall 88–91, Papering a ceiling 94

Choosing paste

Most wallpaper pastes are supplied as powder or flakes for mixing with water. Some come ready-mixed.

All-purpose paste
Standard wallpaper paste is suitable for most lightweight to medium-weight papers.

Heavy-duty paste
This is specially prepared for hanging embossed papers, paper-backed fabrics and other heavyweight wallcoverings.

Fungicidal paste
Pastes often contain a fungicide to prevent the development of mould under impervious wallcoverings, such as vinyls, washable papers and foamed-plastic coverings.

Thixotropic paste
Tubs of ready-mixed thixotropic paste are specially made for heavyweight wallcoverings and fabrics.

Stain-free paste
Use with delicate papers that could be stained by conventional pastes.

Repair adhesive
For sticking down peeling edges and corners. Will glue vinyl to vinyl.

Trimming and cutting

Most wallcoverings are machine-trimmed to width so that you can join adjacent lengths accurately. Some hand-printed papers are left untrimmed. These are usually expensive coverings, so don't attempt to trim them yourself – ask the supplier to do this for you.

Cutting plain wallcoverings

Measure the height of the wall where you're going to hang the first 'drop'. Add an extra 100mm (4in) for trimming top and bottom.

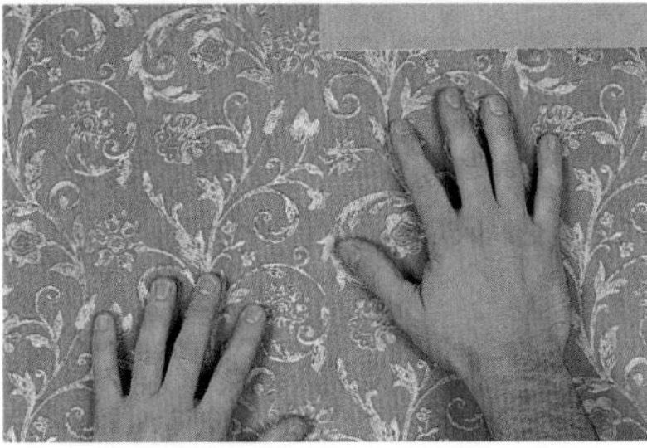

Allowing for patterned wallcoverings
You may have to allow extra on alternate lengths of patterned wallcoverings to match patterns.

Pasting wallcoverings

You can use any wipe-clean table for pasting, but a narrow fold-up pasting table is a good investment if you are doing a lot of decorating. Lay several cut lengths of paper face down on the table to keep it clean. To stop the paper rolling up while you are pasting, tuck the ends under a length of string tied loosely round the table legs.

Applying the paste

Use a large, soft wall brush or pasting brush to apply the paste. Mix the paste in a plastic bucket and tie string across the rim to support the brush, keeping its handle clean while you hang the paper.

Align the wallcovering with the far edge of the table (**1**), to avoid brushing paste on the top – where it could be transferred to the face of the wallcovering. Apply the paste by brushing away from the centre (**2**). Paste the edges and remove any lumps.

If you prefer, apply the paste with a short-pile paint roller. Pour the paste into a roller tray and roll it onto the wallcovering in one direction only, towards the end of the paper.

Pull the wallcovering to the front edge of the table and paste the other half. Fold the pasted end over – don't press it down – gently and slide the length along the table to expose an unpasted section (**3**).

Paste the other end, then fold it over to almost meet the first cut end. The second fold is invariably deeper than the first – a handy way to tell which is the bottom of patterned wallcoverings. Fold long drops concertina-fashion (**4**).

Hang vinyls and lightweight papers immediately; drape other wallcoverings over a broom handle spanning two chair backs, or other supports, and leave to soak. Some heavy or embossed wallcoverings need to soak for 15 minutes.

Pasting the wall

Instead of pasting the back of exotic wallcoverings, paste the wall, to reduce the risk of marking their delicate faces. Apply a band of paste just wider than the length of wallcovering, so you won't have to paste right up to its edge for the next length. Use a brush or roller.

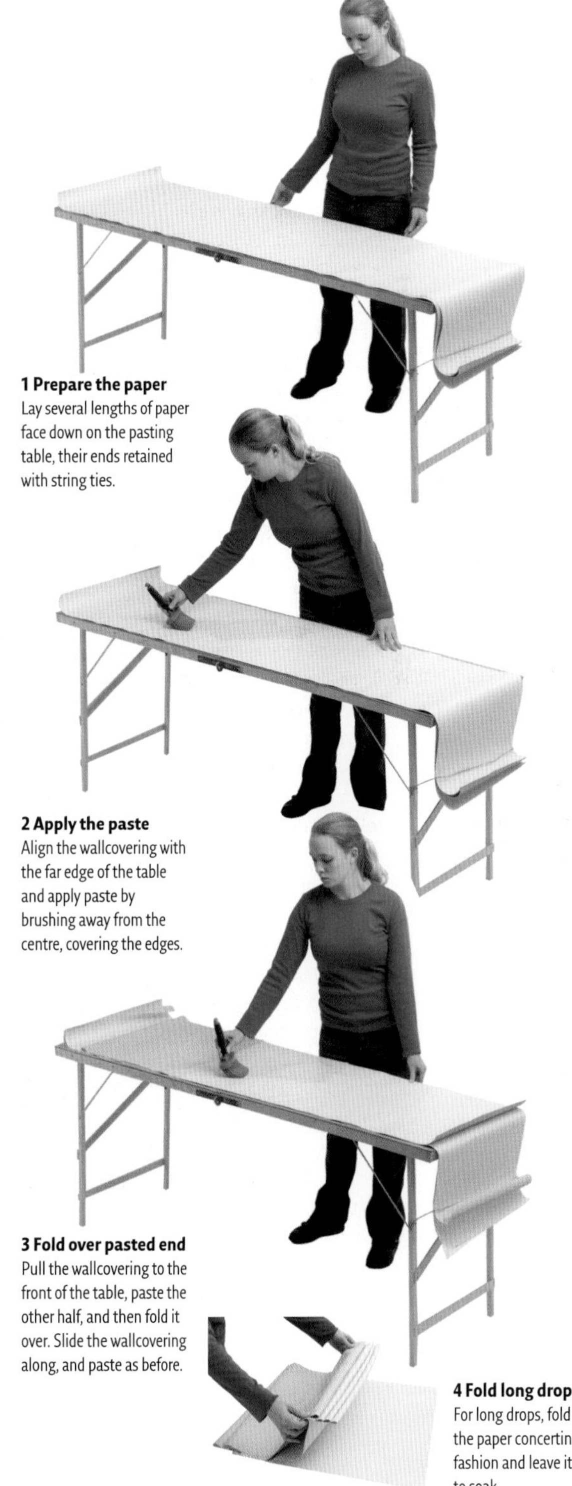

1 Prepare the paper
Lay several lengths of paper face down on the pasting table, their ends retained with string ties.

2 Apply the paste
Align the wallcovering with the far edge of the table and apply paste by brushing away from the centre, covering the edges.

3 Fold over pasted end
Pull the wallcovering to the front of the table, paste the other half, and then fold it over. Slide the wallcovering along, and paste as before.

4 Fold long drops
For long drops, fold the paper concertina-fashion and leave it to soak.

SEE ALSO > Wallcoverings 84–5, Papering a wall 88–91, Papering a ceiling 94

Papering a room

Don't apply a wallcovering of any kind until all the woodwork in the room has been painted or varnished, and the ceiling painted or papered. Since you can only hang one length of paper at a time, it is perfectly feasible to work from a single stepladder, but it is still an advantage to set up a platform from which to work.

Coordinated pattern
Most of the larger suppliers offer ranges of coordinated fabrics and wallcoverings, which make it particularly easy to unify a room.

Centre a large motif over a fireplace

Butt two lengths between windows

Where to start

The traditional method for papering a room is to hang the first length next to a window close to a corner, then work in both directions away from the light. But you may find it easier to paper the longest uninterrupted wall first, so you get used to the basic techniques before tackling corners or obstructions.

If your wallcovering has a large regular motif, centre the first length over the fireplace for symmetry. You could also centre this first length between two windows – unless that means you will be left with narrow strips each side, in which case it's better to butt two lengths on the centre line.

Hanging lining paper

Lining a wall prior to papering is a necessary first stage if you are hanging embossed or luxury wallcoverings, or if the wall has imperfections that might show through a thin wallpaper. Hang lining paper horizontally, so the joins cannot align with those in the top layer.

Mark a horizontal line on the wall one roll-width from the ceiling. Holding the concertina-folded length in one hand, start at the top right-hand corner of the wall if you're right-handed (if you're left-handed, start from the top left), aligning the bottom edge with the marked line. Smooth the paper onto the wall with a paperhanger's brush, working from the centre towards the edges of the paper.

Work along the wall gradually, unfolding the length as you do so. Take care not to stretch or tear the wet paper. Use the brush to gently tap the paper into the corner at each end.

Use the point of a pair of scissors to lightly mark the corner, peel back the paper, and trim to the line. Brush the paper back in place. You will have to perform a similar operation along the ceiling if the paper overlaps slightly. Work down the wall, butting each strip against the last or leaving a minute gap between the lengths.

Trim the bottom length to the skirting. Leave the lining paper to dry out for 24 hours before covering.

Lining prior to painting

If you are lining a wall for emulsion painting, hang the lining paper vertically, as you would with other wallcoverings.

Hanging lining paper horizontally
Hold the concertina-folded paper in one hand and smooth it onto the wall, starting top right if you are right-handed. Butt the strips of paper together, or leave a slight gap.

SEE ALSO > Repairing plaster 48–50, Painting wood 71–3, Wallcoverings 84–5, Papering a ceiling 94

Hanging paper on a wall

The walls of a room are rarely truly square, so mark a vertical guide against which to hang the first length of wallpaper. Start at one end of the wall and use a roll of paper to mark the vertical line one roll-width away from the corner less 12mm (½in), so the first length will overlap the adjacent wall. Use a plumb line to extend the line from ceiling to skirting (**1**).

Allowing enough wallcovering for trimming at the ceiling, unfold the top section of the pasted length and hold it against the plumbed line. Brush the paper gently onto the wall, working from the centre in all directions in order to squeeze out any trapped air (**2**).

When you're sure the paper is positioned accurately and smoothly brushed onto the wall, lightly draw the point of your scissors along the ceiling line, then peel back the top edge and cut along the crease (**3**) to remove the excess paper. Smooth the paper back and tap it down with the brush.

Unpeel the lower fold of the paper and smooth it onto the wall with the brush, then tap it into the corner (**4**). Crease the bottom edge against the skirting and peel away the paper, then trim and brush it back against the wall.

Hang the next length in the same manner. Slide it with your fingertips to align the pattern and produce a perfect butt joint. Wipe any paste from the surface with a damp cloth, then run a seam roller along the butt joint to ensure the edges of the paper adhere firmly to the wall (**5**).

Continue to the other side of the wall, allowing the last drop to overlap the adjoining wall by 12mm (½in).

Losing air bubbles

Slight blistering usually flattens out as wet paper dries and shrinks slightly. If a blister remains, you can inject a little paste through it and roll it flat. Alternatively, cut across it in two directions (**6**), then peel back the triangular flaps and paste them down.

1 Mark a line for the first length of paper

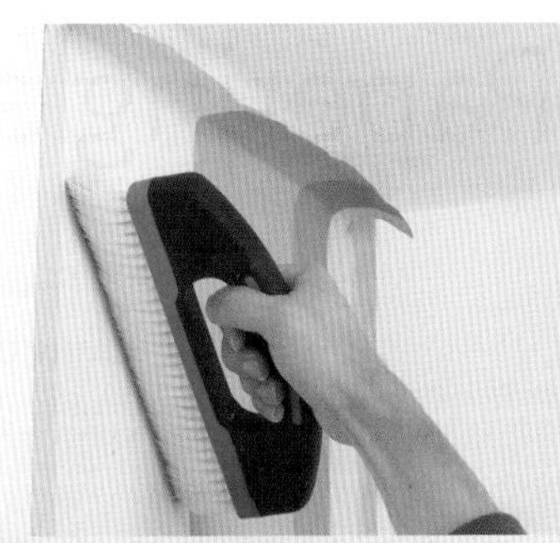

2 Brush from the centre in all directions

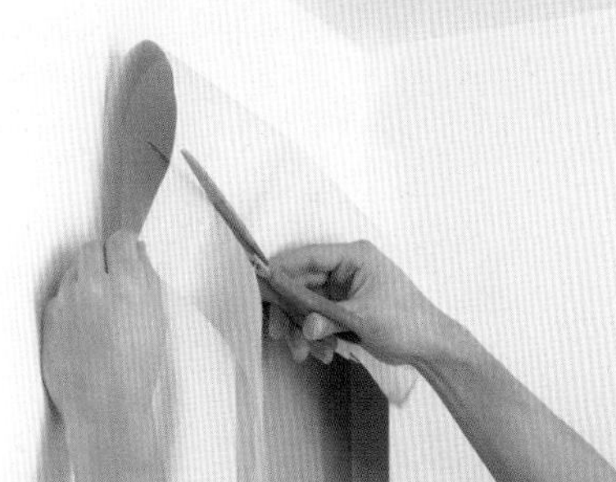

3 Cut along the crease to remove excess paper

4 Tap the paper against the top of the skirting

5 Run a seam roller along each butt joint

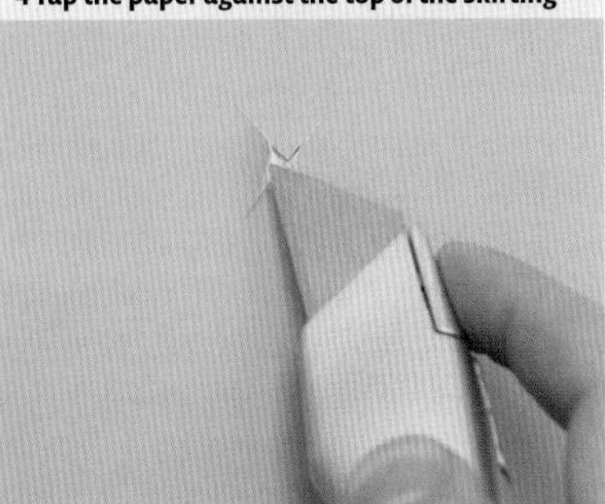

6 Cut the paper to release an air bubble

Papering around corners

Turn the corner by marking another plumbed line so that the next length of paper covers the overlap from the first wall. If the piece you trimmed off at the corner is wide enough, use it as your first length on the new wall.

If there's an alcove on both sides of the fireplace, you will need to wrap the paper around the external corners. Trim the last length so that it wraps around the corner, lapping the next wall by about 25mm (1in). Plumb and hang the remaining strip with its edge overlapping the first drop.

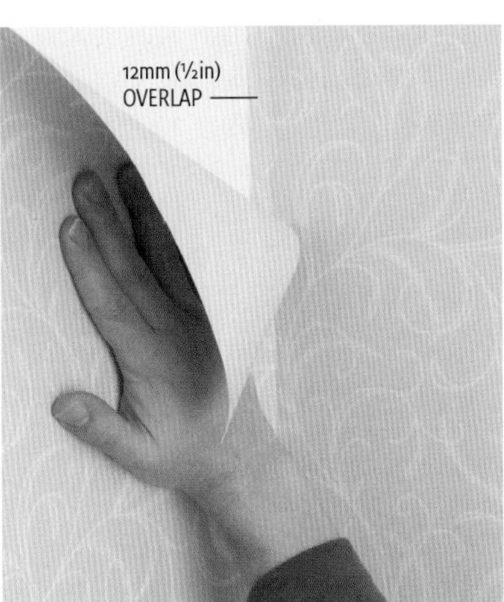

Papering round an internal corner

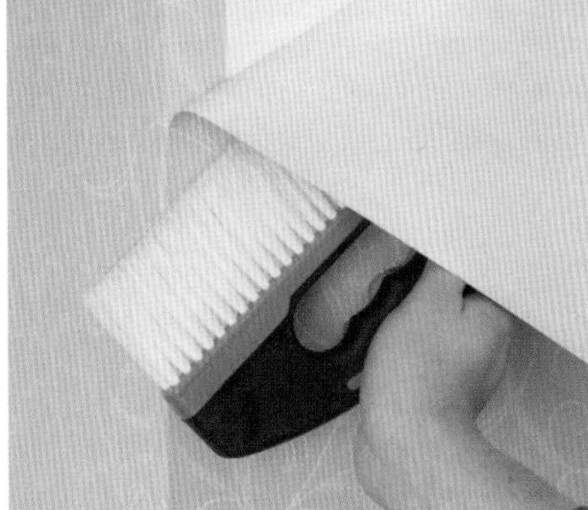

Papering round an external corner

Papering a chimney breast (right)
A chimney breast poses the problem of papering around both internal and external corners.

• **Hide a join in a corner**
When using a wallcovering with a large pattern, try to finish in a corner, where it will be less noticeable if the pattern doesn't quite match.

SEE ALSO > Repairing plaster 48–50, Wallcoverings 84–5

Papering around obstacles

Papering the walls is fairly straightforward, but every room has doors and windows that have to be accommodated, and you will also have to deal with papering around light switches and sockets.

Papering around switches

Turn off the electricity at the mains. Hang the wallpaper over the switch or socket, then make diagonal cuts from the centre of the fitting to each of its corners and tap the excess paper against the edges of the faceplate with the brush. Trim off the waste paper, leaving about 6mm (¼in) all round. Loosen the faceplate and tuck the margin behind, then retighten the plate. Don't switch the power back on until the paste is dry.

Trim off the waste and tuck the paper behind the faceplate

Papering around doors and windows

When you get to the door, hang the length of paper next to a doorframe, brushing down the butt joint to align the pattern and allowing the other edge to loosely overlap the door.

Make a diagonal cut in the excess towards the top corner of the frame. Crease the waste down the side of the frame with scissors, peel it back and trim off, and then brush back. Leave a 12mm (½in) strip for turning on the top of the frame.

Fill in with short strips above the door, then butt the next full length of paper over the door and cut the excess diagonally into the frame, pasting the rest of the strip down the other side of the door. Mark and cut off the waste.

Papering window reveals

Treat a flush window frame in a similar way to a doorframe. But if the window is set into a reveal, hang the length of wall-covering next to the window and allow it to overhang the opening. Make a horizontal cut just above the edge of the window reveal. Make a similar cut near the bottom, then fold the paper around to cover the side of the reveal. Crease and trim along the window frame and sill.

To fill in the window reveal, first cut a strip of wallcovering to match the width and pattern of the overhang above the reveal. Paste it, slip it under the overhang, and fold it around the top of the reveal (**1**). Cut through the overlap with a smooth wavy stroke, then remove the excess paper and roll down the joint (**2**).

To continue, hang short lengths on the wall below and above the window, wrapping top lengths into the reveal.

At a door, cut the overlap diagonally into the frame

1 Paper the top of the reveal

2 Cut excess, leaving wavy edge

SEE ALSO > Repairing plaster 48–50, Wallcoverings 84–5, Turning off the power 296

Papering around a fireplace

Papering around a fireplace is similar to fitting wallpaper around a doorframe.

Make a diagonal cut in the waste overlapping the fireplace, cutting towards the corner of the mantel shelf. Now tuck the paper in all round for creasing and trimming to the surround.

If the surround is fairly ornate, first brush the paper onto the wall above the surround, then trim the paper to fit under the mantel shelf at each side; brush the paper around the corners of the chimney breast to hold it in place.

Gently press the wallcovering into the shape of the fire surround, peel it away, and then cut round the impression with nail scissors. Smooth the paper back down with the brush.

Papering archways

Arrange strips to leave even gaps between the sides of the arch and the next full-length strips. Hang strips over the face of the arch, cut around the curve leaving an extra 25mm (1in) margin for folding onto the underside (snip into this margin to prevent creasing), then brush it in place. Fit a strip on the underside to reach from the floor to the top of the arch. Repeat on the opposite side.

Papering behind radiators

If you can't remove a radiator, turn off the heating and allow it to cool. Use a steel tape to measure the positions of the brackets fixing the radiator to the wall. Transfer these measurements to a length of wallcovering and slit it from the bottom to the top of the bracket. Feed the pasted paper behind the radiator and down both sides of the brackets. Use a radiator roller to press it to the wall. Crease and trim to the skirting board.

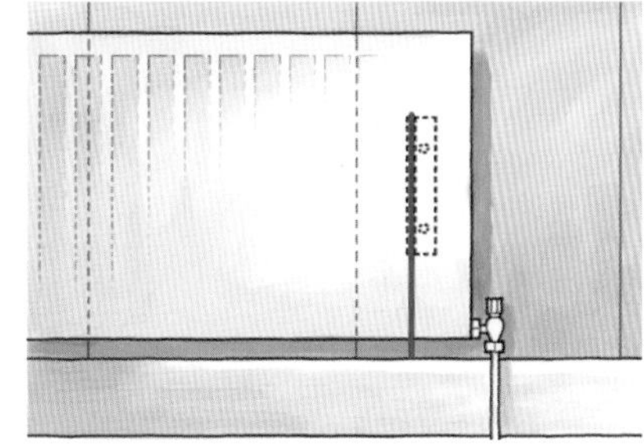

Cut a slit up to the top of the wall bracket

Papering stairwells

The problem when papering a stairwell is having to handle the extra-long drops on the side walls; and for this, you need to build a safe work platform over the stairs. Plumb and hang the longest drop first, lapping the head wall above the stairs by 12mm (½in).

Carrying the long drops of wallcovering - sometimes as much as 4.5m (15ft) long - is awkward. Paste the covering liberally, so it's not likely to dry out while you hang it, then fold it concertina-fashion; drape it over your arm while you climb the platform. You may need an assistant to support the weight of the pasted length while you apply it. Unfold the flaps as you work down the wall.

Crease and cut the bottom of the wallcovering against the angled skirting (don't forget to allow for this angle when cutting each piece to length). Work away from this first length in both directions, then paper the head wall.

To avoid making difficult cuts, it pays to arrange the strips so that the point at which the banister rail meets the wall falls between two butted joints. Hang the drops to the banister rail and cut horizontally into the edge of the last strip at the centre of the rail, then make radial cuts so the paper can be tapped in around the rail. Crease the flaps, then peel away the wallcovering and cut them off. Smooth the covering back in place.

Hang the next drop at the other side of the rail, butting it to the previous piece, and make similar radial cuts.

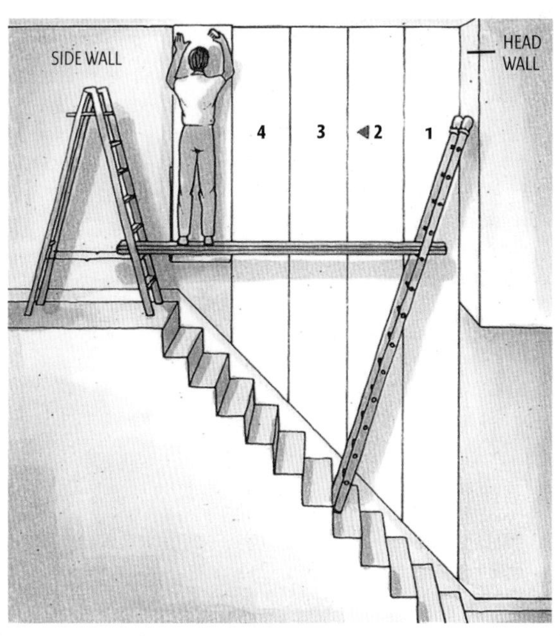

SEE ALSO > Repairing plaster 48–50, Wallcoverings 84–5, Removing radiators 415, Work platforms 516

Hanging special wallcoverings

No matter what kind of wallcovering you are using, most of the standard wallpapering techniques previously described hold good. However, there are some additional considerations and special techniques involved in applying some types of wallcovering.

Period dado
Modern embossed-paper wallcoverings can be used to recreate this type of period-style dado.

Hanging relief wallcoverings

Line the wall before hanging embossed-paper wallcoverings. Apply a heavy-duty paste liberally and evenly to the wallcovering, but try not to leave too much paste in the depressions. Allow each piece to soak for 10 minutes (15 minutes for cotton-fibre wallcoverings) before you hang it.

Tap down butt joints with a paperhanger's brush, to avoid flattening the pattern with a seam roller (**1**).

Don't turn a relief wallcovering around corners. Instead, measure the distance from the last drop to the corner and cut your next length to fit (**2**). Trim and hang the offcut to meet at the corner. Once the paper has dried thoroughly, fill external corners with cellulose filler.

Traditional Lincrusta is still available in a limited range of original Victorian patterns for re-creating period-style decorative schemes. In the long run it pays to leave hanging this expensive material to an expert, since it requires special techniques that are difficult to master.

Hanging vinyl wallcoverings

Paste paper-backed vinyls in the normal way. Cotton-backed vinyl hangs better if you paste the wall and then leave it to become tacky before you apply the wallcovering. Use a fungicidal paste.

Hang and butt-join lengths of vinyl, using a sponge instead of a brush to smooth them onto the wall. Crease each length top and bottom, then trim it to size with a sharp knife.

Vinyl will not normally stick to itself, so when you turn a corner use a knife to cut through both pieces of paper where they overlap. Peel away the surplus wallcovering and rub down the vinyl to produce a perfect butt joint. Alternatively, glue the overlap, using a repair adhesive.

Cut through the overlap and remove the surplus vinyl wallcovering

1 Tap down the joints with a paperhanger's brush

2 Cut the wallcovering to fit into the corner

SEE ALSO > Repairing plaster 48–50, Wallcoverings 84–5, Repair adhesive 87

Lining with expanded polystyrene

Paint or roll ready-mixed heavy-duty adhesive onto the wall. Hang the covering straight from the roll, smooth it gently with the flat of your hand, and then roll over it lightly with a dry paint roller.

Provided that the edges are square, butt adjacent drops. If they become crushed or have crumbled, overlap each join and cut through both thicknesses with a sharp trimming knife. Peel away the offcuts and rub the edges down.

Trim top and bottom with a knife and straightedge. Leave to dry for 72 hours, and then hang a subsequent wallcovering over the polystyrene, using a thick fungicidal paste.

Hang polystyrene straight from the roll

Use fabric wallcoverings for texture and pattern

Unbacked fabrics

To make a special feature of one wall or an alcove, for example, you might consider using unbacked fabric. You could paste a plain-coloured medium-weight fabric directly to the wall. For greater control, try stretching it onto panels of lightweight insulation board 12mm (½in) thick – which gives you the double advantage of insulation and a pinboard – and attach the boards directly to the wall.

Applying fabric with paste

Test an offcut of fabric to make sure the adhesive will not stain. Use a ready-mixed paste and roll it onto the wall.

Wrap a cut length of the fabric round a cardboard tube and gradually unroll it onto the pasted surface, smoothing it down with a dry paint roller. Take care not to distort the weave.

If you need to paste two lengths side by side, overlap the joins – but, in case the fabric shrinks, don't cut through them until the paste has dried. Then remove the excess, reapply the paste and close the seams. Similarly, press the fabric into the ceiling line and skirting, then trim away the excess when the paste has set.

Making wall panels

Stretch the fabric across each panel and wrap it round the edges, then use latex adhesive to stick it to the back of the panel. Hold the fabric temporarily with drawing pins while the adhesive dries.

Either use a general-purpose adhesive to glue the panels to the wall or pin them, tapping the nailheads through the weave of the fabric to conceal them. Another method is to use brass screws and screw cups, which are attractive enough to be visible on the face of the panels.

Hanging flock paper

Protect delicate flocking with a piece of lining paper as you smooth out air bubbles with a paperhanger's brush. If the paper is not machine-trimmed, overlap joining lengths slightly, then cut through both thicknesses of overlapping strips and remove the surplus. Press back the edges to make a neat butt joint.

Protect a delicate surface with lining paper when brushing

SEE ALSO > Repairing plaster 48–50, Wallcoverings 84–5

Papering a ceiling

Papering a ceiling isn't as difficult as you might think. The techniques are basically the same as for papering a wall, except that the drops are usually longer and so more unwieldy to hold while brushing the paper into place.

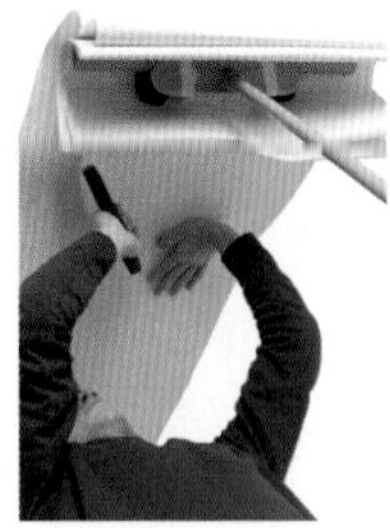

Working from a ladder
If you have to work from a stepladder, get an assistant to support the paper on a home-made support made by taping a cardboard tube to a broom.

Set up a safe work platform – it's virtually impossible to work from a single stepladder – and enlist a helper to support the folded paper while you position one end and then progress backwards across the room. Use a chalked line to mark out the ceiling accurately before you start hanging the paper.

Marking out the ceiling

Arrange your work platform before you begin to mark out the papering sequence for the ceiling. The best type of platform to use is a purpose-made decorator's trestle, but you can manage with a pair of scaffold boards spanning two stepladders.

Now mark the ceiling to give a visual guide to positioning the strips of paper. Aim to work parallel with the window wall and away from the light, so you can see what you are doing and so that the light will not highlight the joins between strips. If the distance is shorter the other way, then it's easier to hang the strips in that direction.

Mark a guideline along the ceiling one roll-width minus 12mm (½in) from the side wall, so that the first strip of paper will lap onto the wall.

Putting up the lining paper

Paste the paper as when papering a wall and fold it concertina-fashion. Drape the folded length over a spare roll and carry it to the work platform. You will find it easier if a helper supports the folded paper, leaving both your hands free for brushing the paper into place.

Hold the strip against the guideline, using a brush to stroke it onto the ceiling. Tap it into the wall angle, then gradually work backwards along the scaffold board, brushing the paper on as your helper unfolds it.

If the ceiling has a cornice, crease and trim the paper at the ends. Otherwise leave it to lap the walls by 12mm (½in), so that it will be covered by the wallcovering.

Work across the ceiling in the same way, butting the lengths of lining paper together. Cut the final strip roughly to width, and trim it to lap onto the wall as you did at the beginning.

Papering a ceiling
The job is much easier if two people work together from a sturdy platform.

Light fittings and centrepieces

Unlike walls, where you have doors, windows and radiators to contend with, there are few obstacles on a ceiling to make papering difficult. But problems may occur where there is a pendant light fitting or a decorative plaster centrepiece.

Cutting around a pendant light

Where the paper passes over a ceiling rose, cut several triangular flaps so that you can pass the light fitting through the hole. Tap the paper all round the rose with a paperhanger's brush, then continue on to the end of the length. Return to the rose and cut off the flaps with a knife. Be sure to switch off the power if you expose the wiring.

Papering around a centrepiece

If there is a decorative centrepiece, work out the position of the strips so a join will pass through the centre. Cut long flaps from the side of each piece, so you can tuck it in all round.

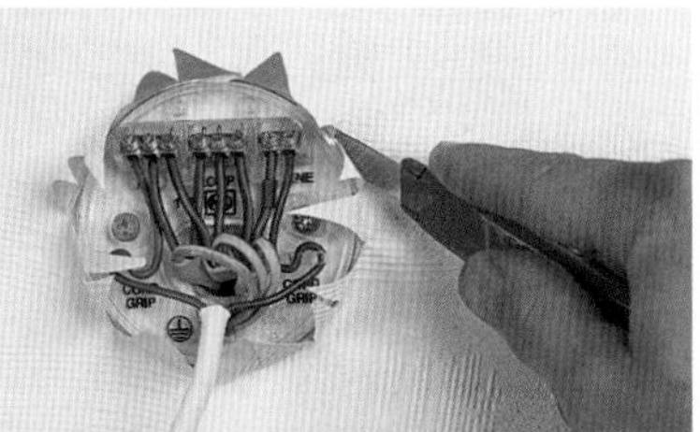

Cut off triangular flaps when the paste is dry

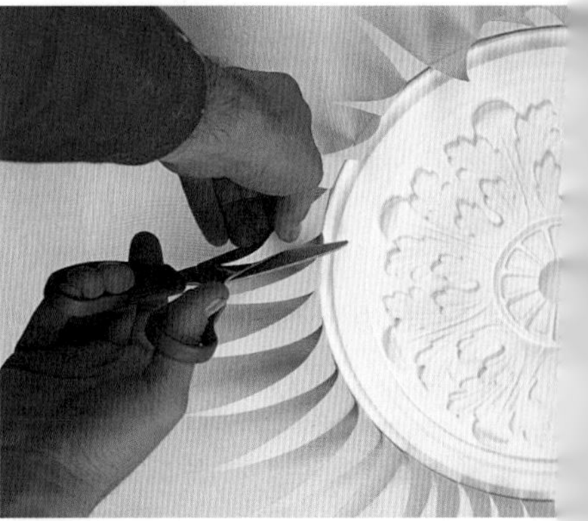

Cut long strips to fit round a decorative moulding

SEE ALSO > Repairing plaster 48–50, Wallcoverings 84–5, Pasting and folding paper 87, Turning off the power 296, Work platforms 516

Choosing tiles

With an almost inexhaustible range of colours, textures and patterns to choose from, tiling is one of the most popular methods for decorating walls and floors.

Ceramic wall tiles

Most ceramic wall tiles are coated with a layer of glaze that makes them durable, waterproof and relatively easy to cut. Unglazed tiles are generally more subtle in colour, and may need to be sealed to prevent them absorbing grease and dirt.

Machine-made tiles are regular in shape and colour, and are therefore simple to lay and match. With hand-made tiles, there is much more variation in shape and colour, which adds to their appeal.

The majority of wall tiles are 100 or 150mm (4 or 6in) square. As well as a wide range of plain colours, you can buy printed and high-relief moulded tiles in both modern and traditional styles.

Narrow border tiles create visual breaks that relieve the monotony of large areas of regular tiling. You can also buy purpose-made skirting and cornice tiles.

Ceramic floor tiles

Floor tiles are generally larger and thicker than wall tiles, so they can withstand the weight of furniture and foot traffic. As with wall tiling, square and rectangular tiles are the most economical ones to buy and lay, but hexagonal and octagonal floor tiles are also available and are often used in combination with small shaped inserts to create regular patterns. Tiles with interlocking curved edges require careful setting out in order to achieve a satisfactory result. Choose non-slip ceramic tiles for bathrooms and other areas where the floor is likely to become wet.

Small unglazed encaustic tiles are laid individually to create intricate patterns that re-create the styles of Victorian and Edwardian tiled floors. They are made in a range of plain colours and with patterns that are fired deep into the tiles.

Mosaic tiles

These are in effect small versions of the standard ceramic tiles. To lay them individually would be time-consuming and lead to inaccuracy, so they are usually joined, either by a paper covering or a mesh backing, into larger panels. Square tiles are the most common, but rectangular, hexagonal and round mosaics are available too. Because they are small, mosaics can be used on curved surfaces and fit irregular shapes better than large ceramic tiles do.

Quarry tiles

Thick unglazed quarry tiles are ceramic tiles with a mellow appearance. The colours are limited to browns, reds, black and white. Hand-made quarries are uneven in colour, producing a beautiful mottled effect.

Round-edge tiles are used as treads for steps; and there are shaped tiles for creating a skirting around a quarry-tile floor.

Field tiles
These are the standard square or rectangular tiles that are used to create main areas of tiling. Most glazed field tiles are so-called universal tiles, which have two glazed edges so that they can be used for edging half-tiled walls and splashbacks. Cross-shape plastic spacers are used to maintain regular gaps between field tiles.

Tile selection
The examples shown on the left are a typical cross-section of commercially available ceramic tiles.
1 Printed ceramic
2 Glazed ceramic wall tiles
3 Decorative strips
4 Quarry tiles
5 Ceramic floor tiles
6 Hand-printed tiles
7 Encaustic tiles

SEE ALSO > Colour and pattern 32–3, 37, Applying wall tiles 99–101, Applying floor tiles 106–7

Stone and slate flooring

A floor laid with natural stone or slate tiles will be exquisite but expensive. Sizes and thicknesses vary according to the manufacturer, and some will even cut to measure. These materials are so costly that you should consider hiring a professional to lay them.

Carpet tiles

These have advantages over wall-to-wall carpeting. An error is less crucial when cutting a single tile to fit; and being loose-laid, worn, burnt or stained tiles can be replaced instantly. However, you can't substitute a brand-new tile several years later, because the colour won't match. It's worth buying several spares initially and swap them around regularly to even out the wear and colour change. Most types of carpet are available as tiles, including cord, loop and twist piles, both in wool and a range of man-made fibres. Carpet tiles come mostly in plain colours or small patterns. Some have an integral rubber underlay.

A selection of carpet tiles
Tiles are used extensively for contract carpeting, but they are equally suitable as a floorcovering in the home.

Vinyl tiles

Vinyl can be cut easily; and provided the tiles are firmly glued with good butt joints between them, the floor will be waterproof. They are also among the cheapest and easiest floorcoverings to lay. A standard coated tile has a printed pattern sandwiched between a vinyl backing and a harder, clear-vinyl surface. Solid-vinyl tiles are made entirely of the hardwearing plastic.

Some vinyl tiles have a high proportion of mineral filler. As a result, they are stiff and must be laid on a perfectly flat base. Unlike standard vinyl tiles, they will resist some rising damp in a concrete subfloor. Most tiles are square or rectangular, but there are interlocking shapes and hexagons. There are many patterns and colours to choose from, including embossed textures that simulate wood, ceramic, brick or stone tiling.

Carpet tiles are hardwearing and easy to lay

SEE ALSO > Colour and pattern 32–3, 37, Applying floor tiles 104–5

Rubber tiles

These were originally made for use in shops and offices - but, being hardwearing yet soft and quiet to walk on, they also make ideal domestic floorcoverings. Rubber tiles are usually studded or textured to improve the grip.

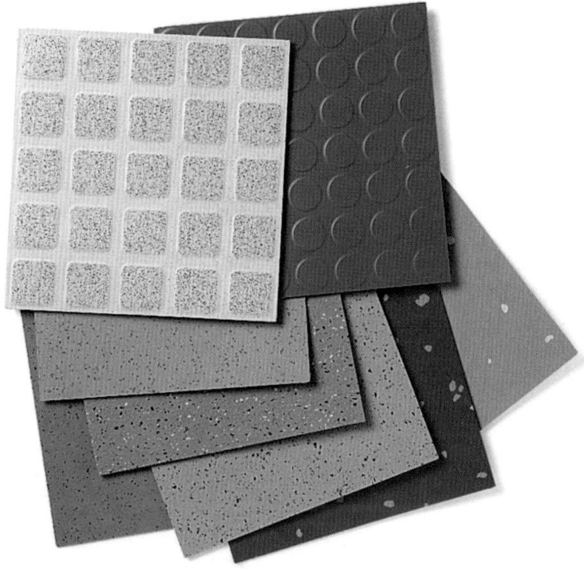

Cork tiles

Cork is a popular covering for walls and floors. It is easy to lay with contact adhesive, and can be cut to size and shape with a knife. A wide choice of textures and warm colours is available. Presanded but unfinished cork will darken in tone when you varnish it. Alternatively, you can buy ready-finished tiles with various plastic and wax coatings.

Mineral-fibre tiles

Ceiling tiles made from compressed mineral fibre are dense enough to be sound-insulating and heat-insulating. They are normally fitted into a suspended grid system that may be exposed or concealed, depending on whether the tile edges are rebated or grooved. Fibre tiles can also be glued directly to a flat ceiling.

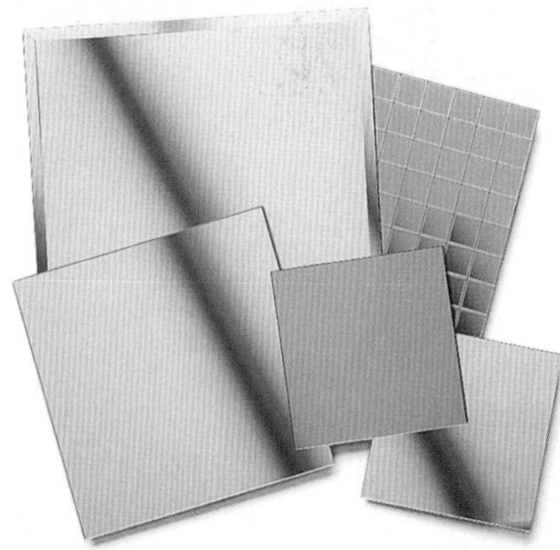

Mirror tiles

Square and rectangular mirror tiles are attached to walls by means of a self-adhesive pad in each corner. Both silver and bronze finishes are available. Mirror tiles will present a distorted reflection unless they are mounted on a perfectly flat surface.

SEE ALSO > Colour and pattern 32–3, 37, Applying wall tiles 99–101, Suspended ceiling 102, Applying floor tiles 105

Renovating wall tiles

A properly tiled surface should last for many years, but the appearance is often spoiled by discoloured grouting or cracked tiles. Or perhaps you just want a change of colour. However, there is usually no need to retile the wall, as these problems can be solved fairly easily.

Painting ceramic wall tiles

You can change the appearance of glazed ceramic tiles with a water-resistant one-coat tile paint. Clean the surfaces thoroughly, and scrub the grout lines with a nailbrush to remove traces of grease or mould growth. Dry the tiles, then apply the paint with a natural-bristle brush (1). If you want to pick out individual tiles, protect the surrounding tiles with masking tape. You may have to apply a second coat of paint to cover dark colours or heavily patterned tiles.

When the paint has dried, redraw the grout lines with a compatible grout pen (2). You can use a similar pen to brighten up discoloured grout without having to repaint the tiles.

1 Renovate old wall tiles with tile paint

2 Retouch the joints with a grout pen

Replacing a cracked ceramic tile

Scrape the grout from around the damaged tile, then use a small cold chisel to chip out the tile, working from the centre. Wear protective goggles, and take care not to dislodge neighbouring tiles.

Scrape out the old adhesive, and brush debris from the recess. Butter the back of the replacement tile with adhesive, then press it firmly in place. Wipe any excess from the surface, and allow the adhesive to set before renewing the grout.

Setting out wall tiles

Having prepared the wall for tiling, the next stage is to measure each wall accurately, to determine where to start tiling and how to avoid having to make awkward cuts. The best way is to mark a row of tiles on a straight batten, which you can use as a gauge stick for setting out the walls.

Making a gauge stick

Make a gauge stick from 50 x 18mm (2 x 3/4in) softwood to help you plot the position of the tiles on the wall. Lay several tiles along the stick, inserting plastic spacers between them, and mark the position of each tile on your gauge stick.

Mark tile increments along a gauge stick

Setting out the walls

The setting-out procedures described here are applicable to the following tiles: ceramic, cork, mosaic and mirror tiles. On a plain uninterrupted wall, use the gauge stick to plan horizontal rows of tiles, starting at skirting level. If you are left with a narrow strip at the top, move the rows up half a tile-width to create a wider margin. Then mark the bottom of the lowest row of whole tiles.

Temporarily nail a thin guide batten to the wall aligned with the mark (1). Make sure the batten is horizontal by placing a spirit level on top of it.

Mark the centre of the wall (2), then use the gauge stick to set out the vertical rows on each side of the line. If the margin tiles measure less than half a width, reposition the rows sideways by half a tile. Use a spirit level to position a guide batten against the last vertical line, and nail it to the wall (3).

Plotting a half-tiled wall

If you are tiling part of a wall only - up to a dado rail, for example, set out the tiles to leave a row of whole tiles at the top (4).

If you are incorporating skirting tiles or border tiles, plan their positions first and use them as starting points for setting out the wall.

Arranging tiles around a window

For nicely balanced tiling, you should always use a window as your starting point, so that the wall tiles surrounding it are equal in size but not too narrow. If possible, begin a row of whole tiles at sill level (5). When tiling a window reveal, position cut tiles at the back, next to the window frame (6).

If necessary, fix a guide batten over a window opening to support a row of tiles temporarily (7).

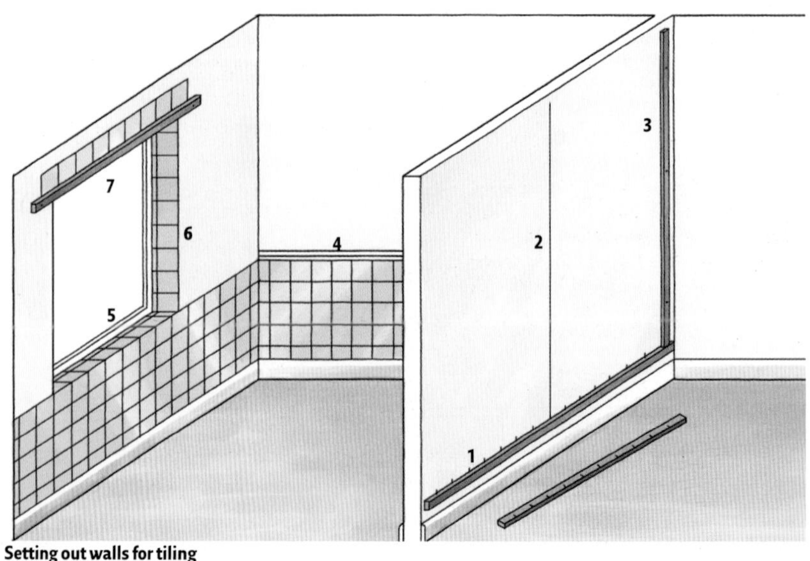

Setting out walls for tiling

SEE ALSO > Flaky paint 46, Repairing plaster 48–50, Stripping wallpaper 51, Wall tiles 95

Fixing ceramic wall tiles

Start by tiling the main areas with whole field tiles, leaving the narrow gaps around the edges to be filled with cut tiles later. This will allow you to work relatively quickly and to check the accuracy of your setting out before you have to make any tricky cuts.

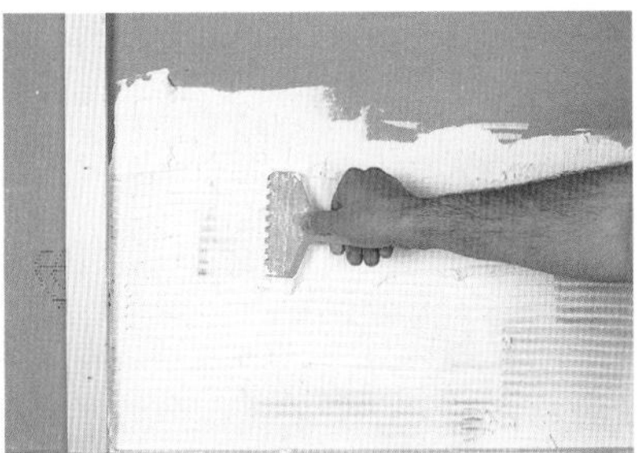
1 Form ridges with a notched spreader

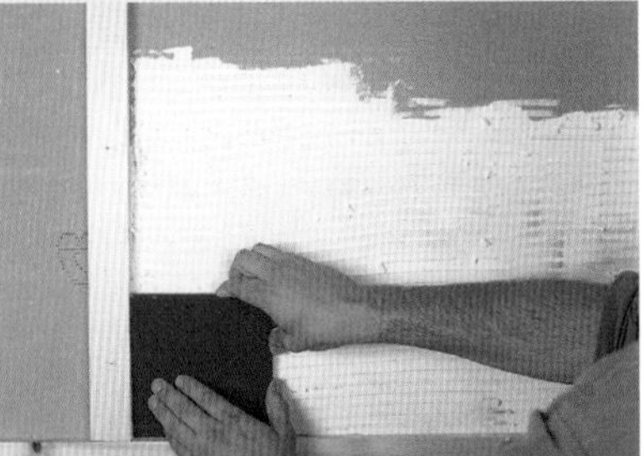
2 Stick the first tile against the setting-out battens

3 Mark the back of a margin tile

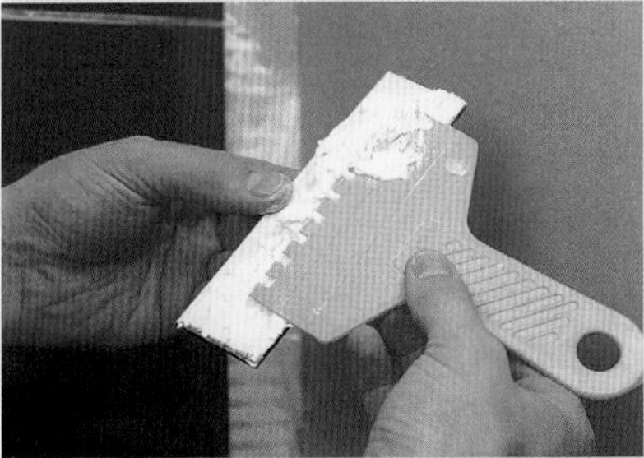
4 Butter adhesive onto the back of a cut tile

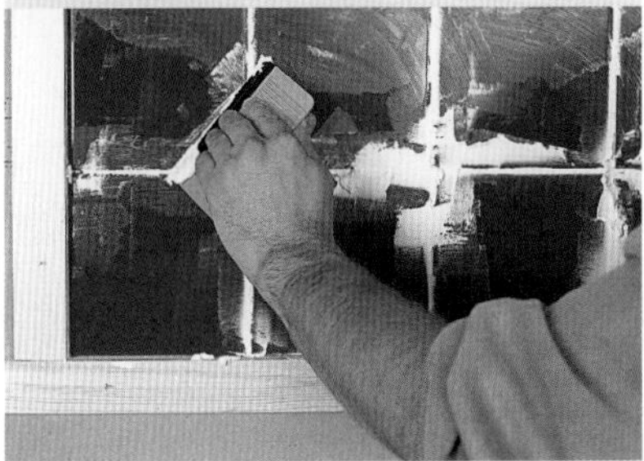
5 Press grout into the joints with a rubber spreader

Choosing tile adhesive and grout

Ceramic tiles are stuck to the wall with special adhesives that are generally sold ready-mixed, although a few need to be mixed with water to form a paste. The tubs or packets will state the coverage.

Grout is a similar material that is used to fill the gaps between the tiles. Unless you have specific requirements, it is convenient to use one of the many adhesives that can be used for both jobs.

Most tile adhesives and grouts are water-resistant - but check that any material you are planning to use for tiling shower surrounds is completely waterproof and can be subjected to the powerful spray generated by a modern shower. If tiles are to be laid on a wallboard, make sure you use a flexible adhesive. Heat-resistant adhesive and grout may be required in the vicinity of a cooker or around a fireplace. You should use an epoxy-based grout for worktops to keep them germ-free.

Tiling around pipes and fittings
Use the gauge stick to check how the tiles will fit round socket outlets, light switches, pipes and other obstructions. Make slight adjustments to the position of the main field in order to avoid difficult shaping around these features.

Applying ceramic tiles

A serrated plastic spreader is normally supplied with each tub of adhesive, but if you are tiling a relatively large area it pays to buy a notched metal plasterer's trowel for applying the adhesive to the wall.

Use a straight-edged spreader or the trowel to spread enough adhesive to cover about 1 metre (3ft) square; then swap to the notched tool and drag the edge through the adhesive so that it forms horizontal ridges (1).

Press the first tile into the angle formed by the setting-out battens (2). Press the next tile into place with a slight twist until it is firmly fixed, using plastic spacers to form the grout lines between the tiles. Lay additional tiles to build up three or four rows at a time, then wipe any adhesive from the surface of the tiles, using a clean damp sponge.

Spread more adhesive, and continue to tile along the batten until the first rows of whole tiles are complete. From time to time, check that your tiling is accurate by holding a batten and spirit level across the faces and along the top and side edges.

When you have completed the entire field, scrape adhesive from the margins and allow the rest to set firm before removing the setting-out battens.

Marking and fitting margin tiles

Because walls are never truly square, the margins are bound to be uneven. It's therefore necessary to cut tiles one at a time to fit the gaps between the field tiles and the adjacent walls.

Mark each margin tile by placing it face down over its neighbour with one edge against the adjacent wall (3); make an allowance for the normal spacing between the tiles. Transfer the marks to the edges of the tile, using a felt-tip pen.

Having cut it to size (see overleaf), spread adhesive onto the back of each tile (4) and press it into the margin.

Tiling around a window reveal
Tile up to the edges of a window, then stick universal tiles into the reveal so that they lap the edges of the surrounding tiles. Fill in the spaces behind the edging tiles with cut tiles.

Grouting the tiles

Standard grouts are white, grey or brown, but there is also a range of coloured grouts to match or contrast with the tiles. Alternatively, mix coloured pigment with dry powdered grout before adding water.

Leave the tile adhesive to harden for 24 hours, then use a rubber-bladed plastic spreader or a tiler's rubber float to press the grout into the open joints (5). Spread it in all directions to make sure every joint is well filled.

Using a barely damp sponge, wipe grout from the surface before it sets. Sponging alone is sufficient to finish the joints, but compressing each joint helps guarantee a waterproof seal: do this by running the end of a blunt stick along each joint. When the grout has dried, polish the tiles with a dry cloth.

To make sure the grout hardens thoroughly, don't use a newly tiled shower for about 7 days.

SEE ALSO > Repairing plaster 48–50, Wall tiles 95, Cutting tiles 100

Cutting ceramic tiles

For any but the simplest projects, you will have to cut tiles to fit around obstructions, such as window frames, electrical fittings and handbasins, and to fill the narrow margins around a main field of tiles.

Cutting glazed tiles is relatively easy, as they snap readily along a line scored in the glaze. But unglazed tiles can be tricky to cut, and you may have to buy or hire a special powered wet saw. Whatever method you adopt, protect your eyes with safety spectacles or goggles when cutting ceramic tiles.

Reducing tile width
To reduce the width of a tile, use tile nibblers to chop off the waste a little at a time. Smooth the cut edge of the tile with a tile sander or small slipstone.

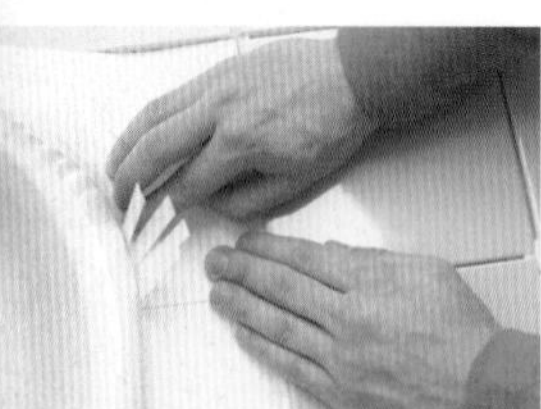

Cutting a curve
To fit a tile against a curved shape, make a template from thin card and use it to mark the curve on the face of the tile. Remove the waste with a tile saw – a thin rod coated with hard abrasive particles.

Making straight cuts

It is possible to scribe and snap thin ceramic tiles using an inexpensive plastic jig that you use to guide a hand-held scorer, then snap the tile with a special pincer-action tool. However, if you anticipate having to cut a lot of tiles or ones that are relatively thick, it is worth investing in a sturdy lever-action jig. A good-quality jig will be fitted with a tungsten-carbide cutting wheel and angled jaws that can snap most tiles effortlessly. Mark each end of the line on the face of a glazed tile with a felt-tip pen (use a pencil on unglazed tiles), then place the tile against the jig's fence, aligning the marks with the cutting wheel. With one smooth stroke, push the wheel across the surface to score the glaze (**1**).

Place the tile in the jig's snapping jaws, aligning the scored line with the arrow marked on the tool, then press down on the lever to snap the tile (**2**).

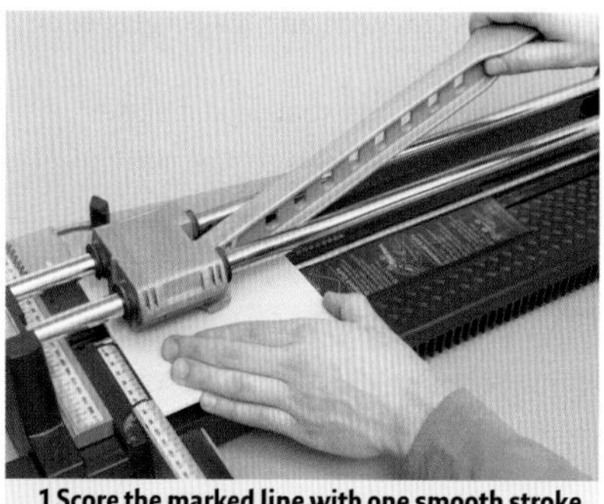

1 Score the marked line with one smooth stroke

2 Snap the tile by pressing down on the lever

Using a powered wet saw

Use a powered wet saw to cut thick unglazed tiles, and to cut the corner out of tiles that have to fit around an electrical socket or switch. The saw has a diamond-coated blade that runs in a bath of water to keep it cool and an adjustable fence that helps you make accurate cuts. You can adjust the angle of the blade in order to mitre thick tiles that meet in a corner. When using a wet saw, tuck in loose clothing and remove any jewellery that could get caught in the blade.

Adjust the fence to align the marked cut line with the blade, and tighten the fence clamp. Switch on the saw and feed the tile steadily into the blade, keeping your fingers clear of the cutting edge (**1**). When removing a narrow strip, use a notched stick to push the tile forwards.

To cut a corner out of a tile, make two cuts. Make the shortest cut first, and then slowly withdraw the tile from the blade. Switch off and readjust the fence, then make the second cut to remove the waste (**2**).

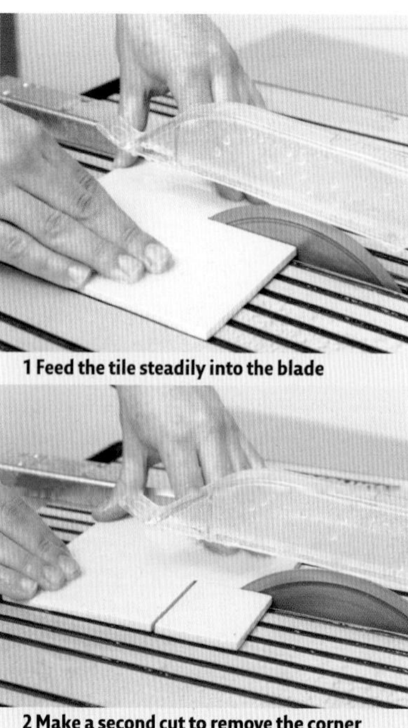

1 Feed the tile steadily into the blade

2 Make a second cut to remove the corner

Sealing gaps

Don't use grout to fill the gap between a tiled wall and a shower tray, bath or basin: a rigid seal can crack and allow water to seep in. Instead, use a flexible silicone sealant to fill gaps up to 3mm (⅛in) wide. Cartridges of clear sealant and a range of colours are available.

Using flexible sealant

Fit the cartridge into its applicator, then trim the tip off the plastic nozzle at an angle (the amount you remove dictates the thickness of the bead).

Clean the surfaces with a paper towel wetted with methylated spirit. Then to apply a bead of sealant, start at one end by pressing the tip into the joint and pull backwards while slowly squeezing the applicator's trigger (**1**). When the bed is complete, smooth any ripples by dipping your finger into a 50/50 mix of water and washing-up liquid and running it along the joint (**2**). If you have sensitive skin, use the handle of a wetted teaspoon.

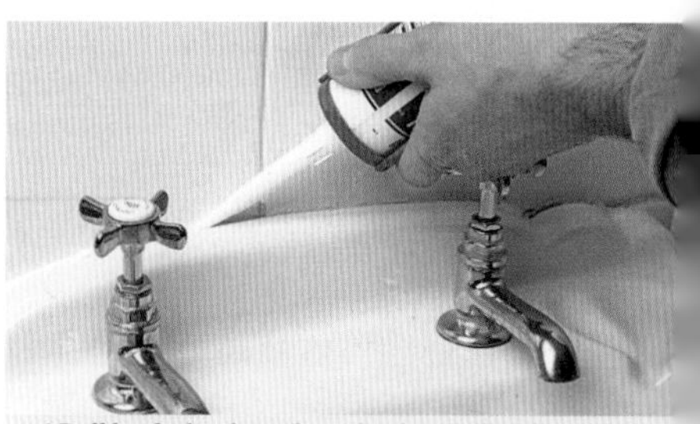

1 Pull back slowly to deposit a bead of sealant

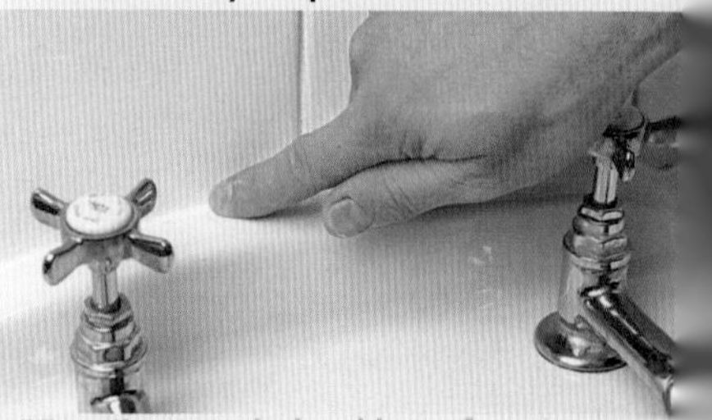

2 Smooth out any ripples with your fingertip

Removing old sealant

Brush a proprietary sealant remover onto a dirty or discoloured joint, and 15 minutes later scrape the sealant off the surface, using a plastic tool.

SEE ALSO > Wall tiles 95

Fixing other wall tiles

Ceramic tiles are ideal in bathrooms and kitchens, where at least some of the walls will inevitably get splashed with water – but in other areas of the home you may decide to use tiles for reasons other than practicality.

Mosaic tiles

When applying mosaic tiles to a wall, use adhesives and grouts similar to those recommended for standard ceramic tiles. Some mosaics have a mesh backing, which is pressed into the adhesive. Others have facing paper which is left on the surface until the adhesive sets.

Fill the main area of the wall, spacing the sheets to match the gaps between individual tiles. Place a carpet-covered board over the sheets and tap it with a mallet to bed the tiles into the adhesive.

Fill margins by cutting strips from the sheet. Use nibblers to cut individual tiles when fitting awkward shapes around obstructions.

If necessary, soak off the facing paper with a damp sponge; then grout the tiles.

Bedding mosaics
Tap mosaics to bed them into the adhesive.

Mirror tiles

It is difficult to cut glass except in straight lines – so avoid using mirror tiles in an area which would entail complicated fitting. If necessary, either mark up the tile to be cut or make cardboard templates of the shapes you need and have a glazier cut the tiles for you.

Mirror tiles are usually fixed close-butted, using self-adhesive pads supplied with the tiles. No grouting is necessary. Set out the wall with guide battens, as for ceramic tiles.

Peel the protective paper from the pads and lightly position each tile. Check its alignment with a spirit level, then press it firmly into place, using a soft cloth.

Finally, clean and polish the tiles, to remove any unsightly fingermarks.

Placing mirror tiles
Position each tile before pressing it onto the wall.

Tiling curved surfaces
The small size of mosaic tiles enables you to clad curved surfaces with a hardwearing waterproof material.

Cork tiles

Set up a horizontal guide batten to make sure you lay cork tiles accurately. However, it isn't necessary to fix a vertical batten, as the relatively large tiles are easy to align without one. Simply mark a vertical line centrally on the wall and hang the tiles in both directions from it.

You will need a rubber-based contact adhesive to fix cork tiles (use a glue that allows a degree of movement when positioning them). If any adhesive gets onto the face of a tile, clean it off immediately with the recommended solvent on a cloth.

Spread adhesive thinly and evenly onto the wall and the back of the tiles, and leave it to dry. As you lay each tile, place one edge only against either the batten or the neighbouring tile, holding the rest of it away from the glue-covered wall for the time being. Then gradually lower and press the tile against the wall, and smooth it down with your palms.

Cut cork tiles with a sharp trimming knife. Since the edges are butted tightly, you will need to be very accurate when marking out margin tiles; use the same method as for laying cork and vinyl floor tiles. Cut and fit curved shapes using a template.

Unless the tiles are precoated, apply two coats of varnish after 24 hours.

Bending a cork tile
In older houses some walls may be rounded at the external corners. Most flexible tiles will bend easily into a tight radius, but cork will snap if bent too far. Cut a series of shallow slits down the back of a cork tile with a tenon saw, then bend the tile gently to the curve required.

SEE ALSO > Repairing plaster 48–50, Wall tiles 95, Setting out wall tiles 98, Grouting 99, Trimming margin tiles 104

Suspended tiled ceiling

You can reduce your heating bills by lowering the ceiling in a kitchen, bathroom, workshop or utility room – and at the same time provide a distinctive feature . Manufactured suspended-ceiling systems are made from slim metal sections, which provide a lightweight structure to house acoustic tiles or translucent panels. They are quick and easy to fit, and do not require specialist tools. Systems vary, but the description below is a guide to what is involved.

The basic system

The framework is made from three basic elements: angled sections that are fixed to the walls; stiff main-bearers running at right angles to the ceiling joists above; and lighter T-section cross bearers that bridge the spaces between the main bearers.

The loose tiles rest on the flanges provided by the bearers. Normally tiles 600mm (2ft) square are used for suspended-ceiling systems, but larger ones may be available. The standard tiles can be lifted out easily, to provide access to ducting or to service light fittings concealed above them. You need a space of at least 200mm (8in) above the framework in order to fit the tiles.

1 Tiles aligned

2 Tiles staggered

3 Tiles aligned

4 Tiles staggered

Setting out the grid

Before fitting the framework, draw a plan of the ceiling on squared graph paper to ensure that the borders are symmetrical (see left). Draw a plan of the room, and include two lines taken from the halfway point on each wall to bisect at the centre. Lay out a row of tiles on your plan, starting from the shorter bisecting line (**1**); and then move the row sideways by one half-panel (**2**) to see which arrangement provides the widest margin tiles. Plot the position of the tiles across the room (**3**, **4**), using the same method. Try to get the margin tiles even on opposite sides.

Fitting the framework

Mark the height of the suspended ceiling on the walls with a continuous levelled line. Use a hacksaw to cut a strip of angled section to fit the length of each wall; file the cut ends smooth. Drill and plug the walls at 300mm (1ft) intervals, using the angled section as a guide, then screw into place (**1**).

Measure and cut the main bearers to span the room, paying careful attention to the slots in the uprights, which must be kept in line. One way to do this is to stretch a length of string across the room where the first row of prepunched slots needs to be. Place the ends of the main bearers on the angled sections (**2**). Support the main bearers with wire hangers at about 1200mm (4ft) centres and 300mm (1ft) from the walls. Fix each wire through a hole in the bearer, and hang it from a ceiling bracket provided or from a screw eye driven into a ceiling joist.

Install 1200mm (4ft) cross bearers, fitting them into the slots in the main bearers, then install 600mm (2ft) bearers between the cross bearers, all to form 600mm (2ft) squares (**3**).

Working from the centre, drop in full-size tiles (**4**) until the grid is square and rigid.

Cut and fit the perimeter cross bearers. Measure and cut the border tiles, then drop them into place.

Spanning wide rooms

Some ceiling systems can be extended. A joint-bridging piece is provided if the ends of the bearers are not made to lock together.

1 Screw angled sections to the walls

2 Position the main bearers

3 Fit the shorter bearers

4 Install the tiles

SEE ALSO > Mineral-fibre tiles 97, Turning off the power 296, Ceiling roses 324–5, Wall fixings 535–6

Setting out soft floor tiles

Soft tiles – such as vinyl, rubber, cork and carpet – are relatively large, so you can cover the floor fairly quickly. Also, they can be cut easily, with a sharp trimming knife or even with scissors, so fitting to irregular shapes isn't difficult.

Marking out the floor

It's possible to lay soft tiles onto either a solid-concrete or a suspended wooden floor, provided the surface is level, clean and dry. Most soft tiles are set out in a similar way: find the centre of two opposite walls, and snap a chalked string between them to mark a line across the floor (1). Lay loose tiles at right angles to the line up to one wall. If there's a gap of less than half a tile-width, move the line sideways by half a tile in order to create a wider margin.

To draw a line at right angles to the first, using string and a pencil as an improvised compass, scribe arcs on the marked line at equal distances each side of the centre (2).

From each point, scribe arcs on both sides of the line (3) that bisect each other. Join the points to form a line across the room. As before, lay tiles at right angles to the new line to make sure margin tiles are at least half-width. Nail a guide batten against one line, to help align the first row of tiles.

Plotting margin width

Lay loose tiles to make sure there is a reasonable gap at the margins. If not, move the line half a tile-width to the left.

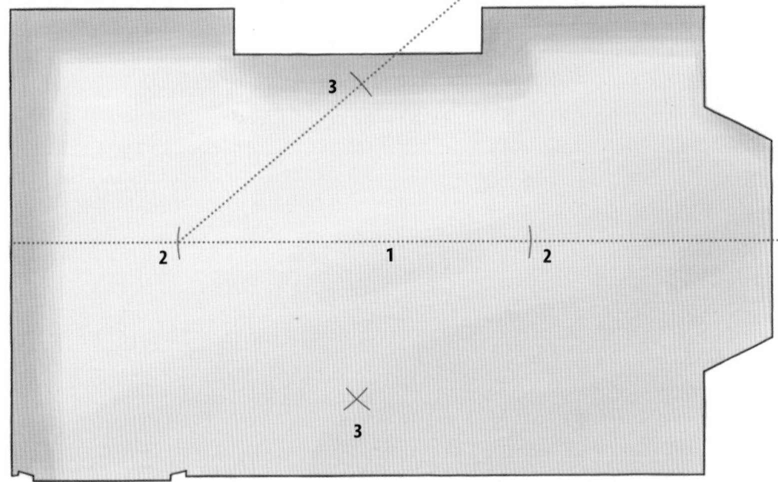

Dividing the room into quarters

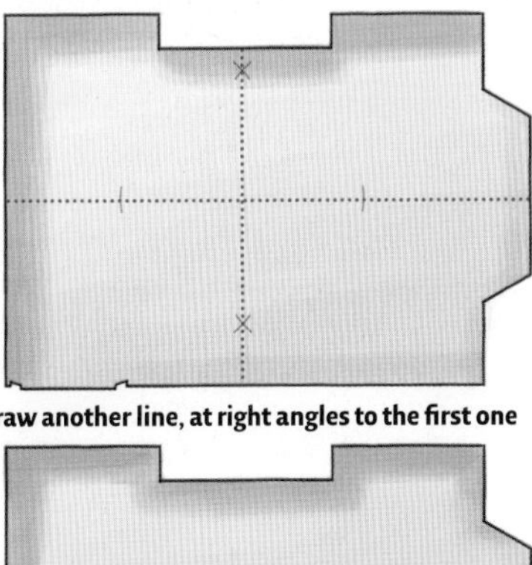

Draw another line, at right angles to the first one

Plotting the margin tiles

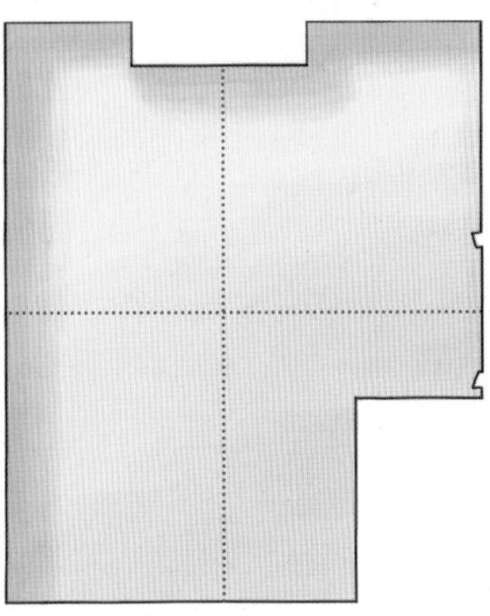

Setting out an irregular-shape room
If the room is noticeably irregular in shape, centre the first line on the fireplace or the door opening.

Setting out for diagonal tiling

Period-style hallway
Vinyl tiles laid diagonally across this spacious hallway are in keeping with the age and style of the house.

Arranging tiles diagonally can create an unusual decorative effect, especially if your choice of tiles enables you to mix colours. Setting out and laying the tiles off centre is not complicated – it's virtually the same as fixing them at right angles, except that you will be working towards a corner instead of a straight wall.

Mark a centre line, and bisect it at right angles, using an improvised compass (see left). Next, draw a line at 45 degrees through the centre point. Dry-lay a row of tiles to plot the margins, and mark another line at right angles to the first diagonal. Check the margins as before. Fix a batten along one diagonal as a guide to laying the first row of tiles.

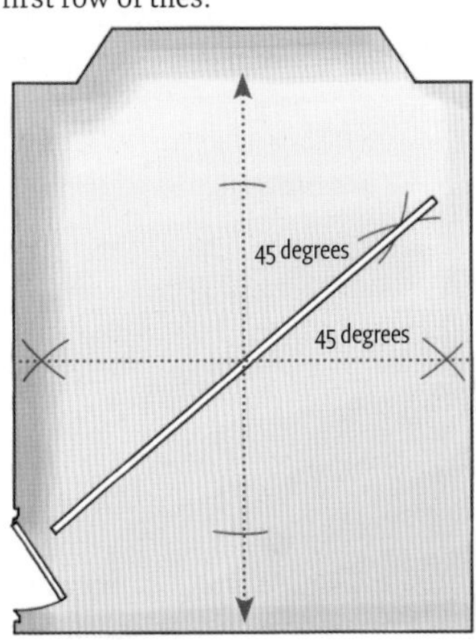

Setting out a floor diagonally
Bisect the quartered room at 45 degrees.

SEE ALSO > Levelling concrete 47, Levelling a wooden floor 57, Floor tiles 96–7

Laying vinyl floor tiles

Tiles precoated with adhesive can be laid quickly and simply. If you decide not to use self-adhesive tiles, follow the tile manufacturer's instructions concerning the type of adhesive to use.

Vinyl tiles in a kitchen
It is easy to fit vinyl tiles around kitchen appliances and floor-standing cupboards.

Gluing vinyl tiles
Spread adhesive thinly but evenly across the floor, using a notched spreader. Cover an area for about four tiles at a time. Lay the tiles carefully, and wipe adhesive from their faces.

Fixing self-adhesive tiles

Stack the tiles in the room for 24 hours before you lay them. If the tiles have a directional pattern, make sure you lay them the correct way; some tiles have arrows printed on the back to guide you.

Remove the protective paper backing from the first tile (1), then press its edge against the guide batten, aligning one corner with the centre line (2). Gradually lower the tile onto the floor and press it down.

Lay the next tile on the other side of the line, butting against the first tile (3). Form a square with two more tiles. Lay tiles around the square to form a pyramid (4). Continue in this way to fill one half of the room, then remove the batten and tile the other half.

1 Peel backing paper from self-adhesive tiles

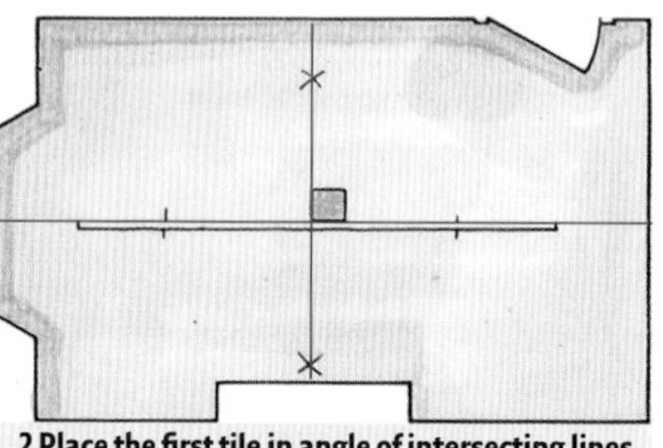

2 Place the first tile in angle of intersecting lines

3 Butt up the next tile on the other side of the line

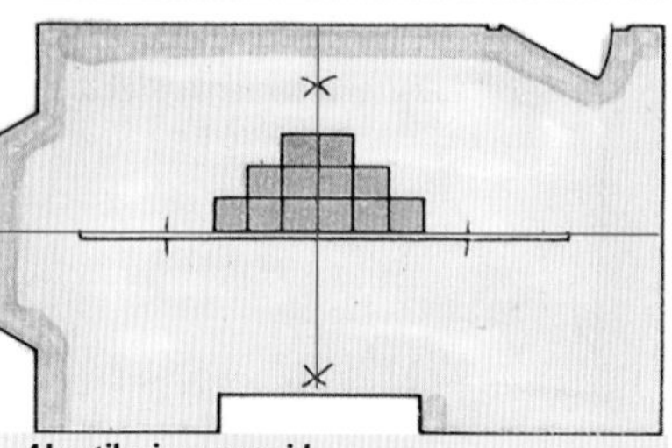

4 Lay tiles in a pyramid

Cutting tiles to fit

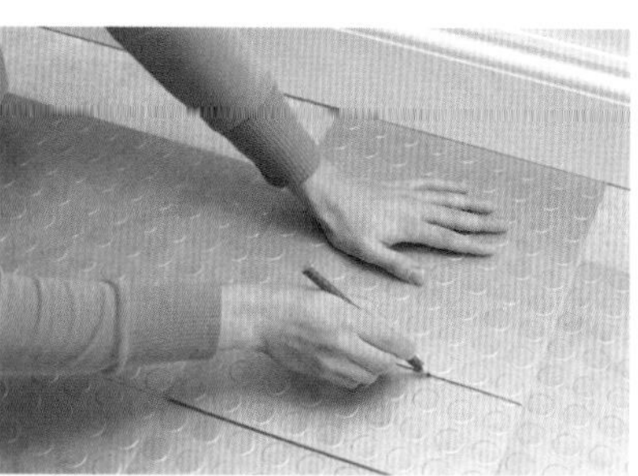

Trimming margin tiles
Floors are usually out of square, so you have to cut margin tiles to fit the gaps next to the skirting. To make one, lay a loose tile exactly on top of the last full tile. Place another tile on top, but with its edge touching the wall. Draw along the edge of this tile with a pencil to mark the tile below. Remove the marked tile and cut along the line.

Cutting irregular shapes
To fit curves, make a template out of thin card. Cut fingers that can be pressed against the object to reproduce its shape. Transfer the template to a tile and cut it to shape.

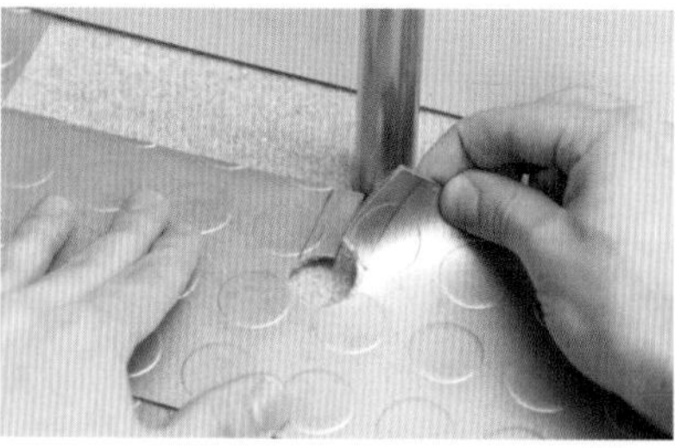

Fitting around pipes
Mark the position of the pipe on the tile. Starting from the perimeter of the circle, draw two parallel lines to the edge of the tile. Cut the hole for the pipe, using a home-made punch (see opposite), then cut a slit between the marked lines. Fold the tile back so you can slide it into place behind the pipe.

SEE ALSO > Levelling concrete 47, Levelling a wooden floor 57, Vinyl tiles 96

Laying other soft floor tiles

The procedures for laying floor tiles made from carpet, cork and rubber are similar in many respects to those described opposite for vinyl tiles. The differences are outlined below.

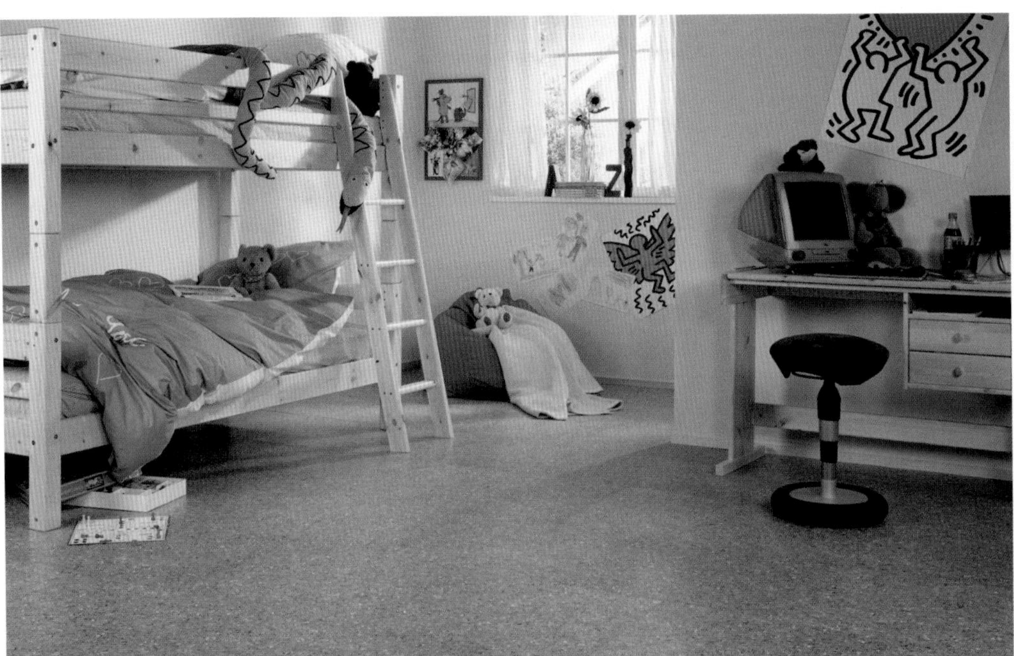

Cork is a relatively soft, sound-absorbing floorcovering for a child's bedroom

Covering a plinth

You can make kitchen base units or a bath panel appear to float above the ground by running floor tiles up the face of the plinth. Hold carpet tiles into a tight bend with gripper strip, but glue other types of soft floor tile in place to create a similar detail.

Glue a plastic moulding (normally used to seal around the edge of a bath) behind the floorcovering to produce a curve.

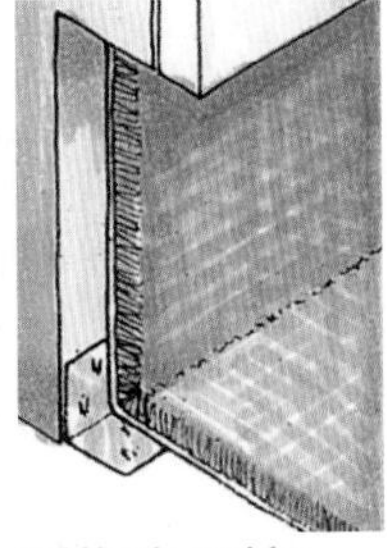

Hold in place with a gripper strip

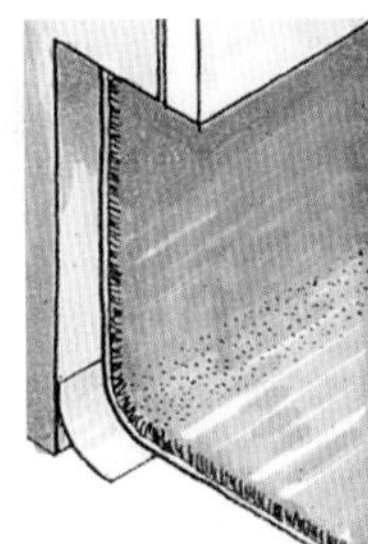

Curved detail for easy cleaning

Carpet tiles

Carpet tiles are laid the same way as vinyl tiles, except that they are not usually glued down. Set out centre lines on the floor, but don't fit a guide batten. Carpet tiles have a pile that has to be laid in the correct direction. This is sometimes indicated by arrows marked on the back of each tile.

Some tiles have ridges of rubber on the back, so they will slip easily in one direction but not in another. Lay these tiles in pairs, so one prevents the other from moving. In any case, stick down every third row of tiles, using double-sided carpet tape, and tape all squares in areas of heavy traffic.

Cut and fit carpet tiles as described for vinyl tiles.

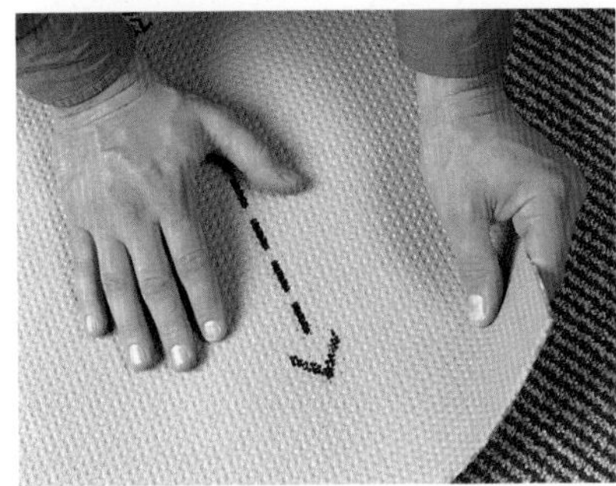

Arrows indicate direction of pile

Rubber tiles

Bed rubber floor tiles onto latex flooring adhesive. Place one edge and corner of each tile against its neighbouring tiles before lowering it onto the adhesive.

Cork tiles

Use a contact adhesive when laying cork tiles: thixotropic adhesives allow a degree of movement as you position the tiles. Make sure the tiles are level by tapping down the edges with a block of wood. Unfinished tiles can be sanded lightly to remove minor irregularities. Vacuum then seal unfinished tiles, applying two to three coats of clear varnish.

Bed down glued cork tiles, using a block of wood

Cutting holes for pipes

With most soft floor tiles you can use a home-made punch to cut neat holes for central-heating pipes. Cut a 150mm (6in) length of pipe with the relevant diameter, and sharpen the inside of the rim at one end with a metalworking file. Mark the position for the hole on the tile, then place the punching tool on top. Hit the other end of the punch with a hammer to cut through the tile cleanly, then cut a straight slit up to the edge. With some carpet tiles you may have to cut round the backing to release the cutout, then prevent fraying with carpet tape.

Punch holes for pipes with a sharpened offcut

SEE ALSO > Levelling concrete 47, Levelling a wooden floor 57, Carpet tiles 96, Cork tiles 97, Rubber tiles 97

Laying ceramic floor tiles

Ceramic floor tiles make a durable surface that can be extremely decorative. Laying the tiles on a floor is similar to hanging them on a wall – although, being somewhat thicker, floor tiles are generally more difficult to cut. Consequently, when setting out the tiles, it's worth making adjustments to avoid having to fit them around awkward obstructions.

Tiles with irregular edges, brindled colours and a well-used patina

Laying a mosaic floor

Set out the floor for tiling with mosaics as described for standard ceramic floor tiles. Spread adhesive on the floor, then lay the tiles, using spacers that match the gaps between the individual pieces. Paper-faced tiles should be laid paper uppermost. Press the sheets into the adhesive, using a block of wood to tamp them level. Leave for 24 hours, then remove the spacers and, where appropriate, soak off the paper facing with warm water. Grout as normal.

Cut out enough pieces of mosaic to fit a sheet around an obstruction, then replace individual pieces to fit the shapes.

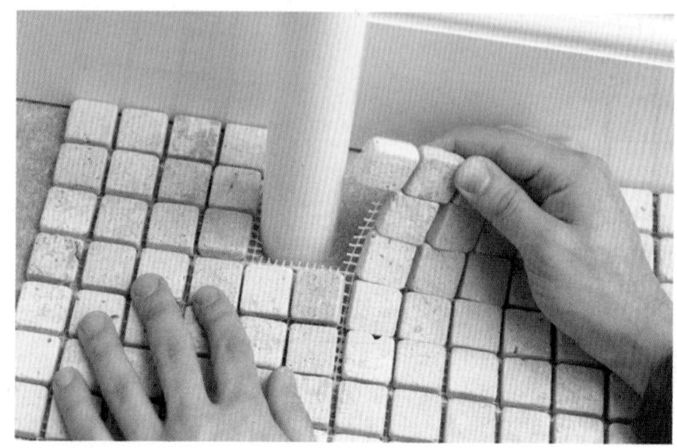

Remove mosaic pieces to fit around a pipe

Setting out

Mark out the floor as for soft floor tiling and work out the spacing to achieve fairly wide even margins. Use masonry nails to pin two softwood guide battens to the floor, set at 90 degrees and aligned with the last row of whole tiles on the two adjacent walls farthest from the door (1). Even a small error will become obvious by the time you reach the other end of the room, so check the angle by measuring three units – each say 300mm or 1ft in length – from the corner along one batten and four along the other. Measure the diagonal between the marks – it should measure five units if the battens form a right angle (2). Make a final check by dry-laying a square of tiles (3).

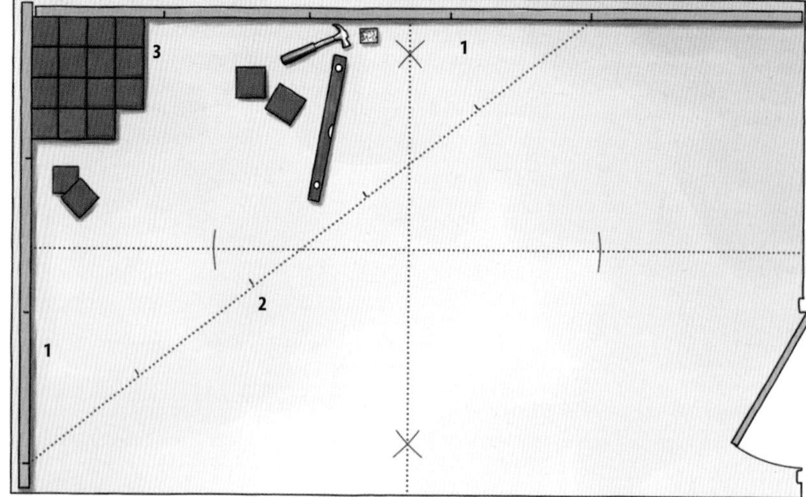

Setting out a floor for ceramic tiles

Laying the tiles

Use a waterproof and slightly flexible floor-tile adhesive. Spread it on, using a notched trowel. The normal procedure is to apply adhesive to the floor for the main area of tiles, and to butter the backs of cut tiles.

Spread enough adhesive on the floor to cover about a square metre (square yard). Press the tiles into the adhesive, starting in the corner. Work along both battens, then fill in between to form the square, using floor-tile spacers to create regular joints.

Wipe adhesive off the surface of the tiles with a damp sponge. Then check their alignment with a straightedge, and make sure they are lying flat by checking them with a spirit level. Work your way along one batten, laying one square of tiles at a time; and then tile the rest of the floor the same way, working back towards the door. Don't forget to scrape adhesive from the margins.

Allow the adhesive to dry for 24 hours before you remove the guide battens and fit the margin tiles. Even then, it's a good idea to spread your weight with a board or plank.

Cutting and grouting floor tiles

Measure the margin tiles as described for wall tiles, then score and snap them with a tile-cutting jig. With thick floor tiles, you may have to resort to using a powered wet saw – even for simple straight cuts. Seal around the edge of the floor with a dark-coloured flexible sealant.

Using a hard-rubber float, spread a grey grout over an area of about a square metre (square yard) at a time, pressing it firmly into the joints. Wipe grout off the surface with a barely damp sponge, then compress the joints with a blunt stick. Polish the tiles with a dry cloth when the grout is hard.

SEE ALSO > Levelling concrete 47, Levelling a wooden floor 57, Floor tiles 95, Cutting ceramic tiles 100, Marking and fitting margin tiles 104

Laying quarry tiles

Being tough and hardwearing, quarry tiles are an ideal choice for floors that receive heavy use. However, they are relatively thick and making even a straight cut requires a wet saw – so use quarry tiles only in areas that do not require a lot of complex shaping.

Don't lay quarry tiles on a suspended wooden floor: replace the floorboards with 18 or 22mm (¾ or ⅞in) exterior-grade plywood to provide a sufficiently flat and rigid base. A concrete floor presents no problems, so long as it is free from damp. You can lay quarries using a floor-tile adhesive, but the traditional method of laying the tiles on a bed of mortar takes care of slightly uneven floor surfaces.

Hard-wearing quarries
It is difficult to find tougher flooring for areas of heavy foot traffic than traditional quarry tiles.

Setting out the floor for tiling

Set out two guide battens at right angles to each other in a corner of the room, as described for ceramic floor tiles (opposite). The depth of the battens should measure about twice the thickness of the tiles, to allow for the mortar bed. Use long masonry nails to fix them temporarily to a concrete floor (**1**). The level of the battens is vital, so check with a spirit level and pack out under the battens with scraps of hardboard or card where necessary. As a guide to spacing, mark tile-widths along each batten, leaving 3mm (⅛in) gaps between for grouting.

Dry-lay a square of 16 tiles in the angle (**2**), then nail a third batten to the floor, butting against the tiles and parallel with one of the other battens (**3**). Level and mark it as before.

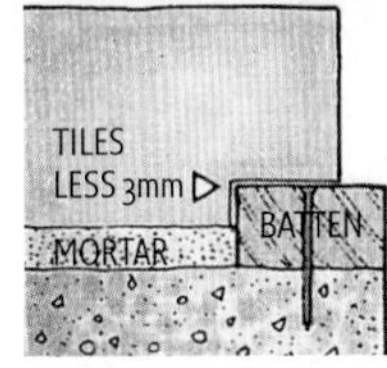

Notching the levelling board
Cut matching notches at each end of the board for levelling the mortar.

Setting out a quarry-tiled floor

Levelling the mortar
With a notch located over each guide batten, drag the levelling board towards you.

Laying the tiles

Lay quarry tiles on a bed of mortar made from 1 part cement : 3 parts builder's sand. When water is added, the mortar should hold an impression when squeezed. Soak the quarry tiles in water prior to laying.

Cut a board to span the parallel battens: this will be used to level the mortar bed and tiles. Cut a notch in each end to fit between the battens; its depth should match the thickness of a tile less 3mm (⅛in).

Spread the mortar to a depth of about 12mm (½in) to cover the area of 16 tiles. Level the mortar by dragging the notched side of the board across it. Dust dry cement on the mortar, then lay the tiles along three sides of the square against the battens. Fill in the square, spacing the tiles by adjusting them with a trowel. Tamp down the tiles with the unnotched side of the board until they are level with the battens. If the mortar is too stiff, brush water into the joints. Wipe mortar from the faces of the tiles.

Fill in between the battens, then move one batten back to form another section of the same size and level it to match the first. Tile section by section until the main area is complete. When the mortar is firm, lift the battens and fill the margin with cut tiles.

Levelling mortar for margin tiles
Mark up margin tiles as described for wall tiling, and cut them with a powered wet saw. Use a notched piece of plywood to level the mortar, then tamp down the tiles with a block.

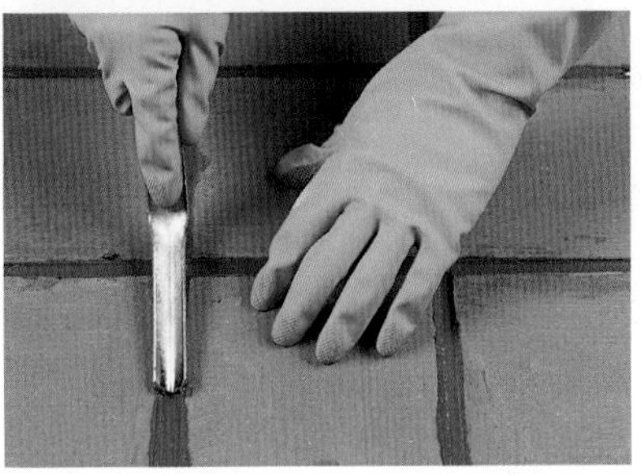

Grouting quarry tiles
Push grout into the joints with a pointing trowel, and compress the grout with a blunted stick or a bricklayer's jointer. Keep the tiles as clean as possible, wiping excess grout off the surface with a damp sponge. When the grout has set, brush the floor clean.

SEE ALSO > Damp floors 47, Levelling concrete 47, Levelling a wooden floor 57, Floor tiles 95, Cutting tiles 100, Mixing mortar 441

Wood flooring

Traditional parquet flooring made from short strips of solid wood is a highly prized floorcovering. It was expensive both to buy and have laid, but less costly alternatives made from real and simulated wood have reintroduced the fashion for wood-strip flooring. Modern wall-to-wall wood flooring is hardwearing and easy to keep clean, and provides sympathetic backgrounds for colourful or natural-fibre rugs and runners.

1 Laminate wood flooring
2 Laminate tiling
3 Engineered boarding
4 Solid-hardwood flooring
5 Bamboo flooring

Laminate flooring

A high-density fibreboard core is covered with a thin strip of material that perfectly simulates a wide range of softwoods and hardwoods. This decorative layer is sealed with a clear protective coating that is highly resistant to abrasion and spillages. Laminates are also available with a moisture-resistant core for use in bathrooms, kitchens and utility rooms.

As well as simulated wood effects, you can buy laminates that resemble ceramic tiles, slate, marble and other natural-stone flooring, complete with convincing joints and grouting.

Most laminates are made with patent locking edges that snap together to form a continuous 'floating' floor that requires neither glue nor nails to hold it in place.

Real-wood flooring

You can buy strips of genuine tongued and grooved wood that you either glue together to form a floating floor or nail down to a wooden subfloor. You can choose from a selection of European and American hardwoods, such as ash, beech, oak, walnut and cherry, as well as a few tropical hardwoods. Before buying hardwood flooring, it is important to check that the timber comes from sustainable sources. A responsible supplier will be able to give you this information.

Engineered boarding

This type of flooring provides the beauty and warmth of a real hardwood surface, but it is cheaper than the solid wood boards just described. A softwood core is sandwiched between a thick veneer of decorative hardwood and a balancing veneer of softwood on the underside. The hardwood surface comes ready-finished with a durable coating of lacquer. Engineered boarding is manufactured as snap-together strips that make real-wood flooring as easy to lay as laminates.

Bamboo flooring

If you prefer to avoid using timber from any source, you can opt for similarly attractive flooring made from bamboo. Being a grass, stocks of bamboo are easily replenished.

Underlays

Subfloors must be clean, dry and level before you lay wood flooring. Floorboards must be reasonably flat with all fixing nails driven below the surface. If necessary, level the floor with hardboard or plywood. Concrete and hard-tiled surfaces must be free from rising damp, and any very uneven areas filled with a self-levelling compound.

All laminates and wood flooring must be cushioned with an underlay to even out any slight irregularities in the subfloor. The standard underlay comprises strips of very thin plastic foam that are rolled out over the floor and cut to fit with scissors or a sharp knife, leaving a 10mm (3/8in) gap around pipes. Butt the strips together and join them with self-adhesive ducting tape.

A slightly thicker underlay incorporates a moisture barrier for laying over a concrete floor. It is fitted and joined like the standard underlay. You can lay a sheet of polythene over a concrete subfloor and then use the standard foam underlay on top, but the combined underlay and moisture barrier is a more convenient solution.

If you feel you need superior sound proofing and thermal insulation under your flooring, lay panels of 7mm (5/16in) felt or wood fibreboard as an underlay. You must lay a polythene moisture barrier over a concrete floor before you use this type of underlay. Stagger the joints, leaving a 5mm (1/8in) gap between the panels and a 10mm (3/8in) expansion gap around the edges of the room. Check whether the combined thickness of underlay and flooring will require you to cut the bottom off the room door and possibly raise the skirtings.

Expansion gaps

Before you start laying wood flooring, decide how you plan to cover the expansion gap left all round a floating floor. You can remove the skirtings and take the boarding up to within 10mm (3/8in) of the wall, then replace the skirtings at a higher level to cover the gap. Alternatively, leave the skirtings in place and, when the flooring has been laid, pin or glue a narrow wood moulding to the skirting (not the floor) to hide the gap. The moulding can match the colour of the flooring, or you can paint it the same colour as the skirting.

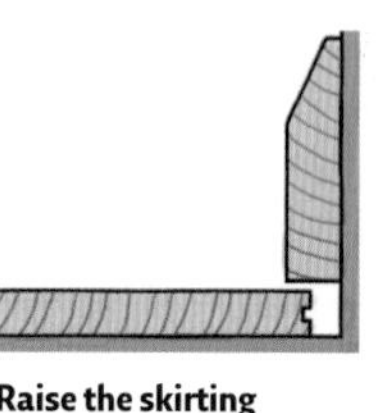

Raise the skirting

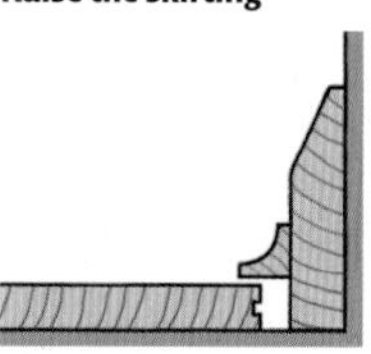

Pin on a cover moulding

SEE ALSO > Levelling concrete 47, Levelling a wooden floor 57, Preparing floorboards 54

Laying laminate flooring

It is necessary to allow laminates (and solid-wood flooring) to acclimatize to the ambient temperature and humidity of the room where they are to be laid. Bring the room up to normal living temperature and stack the laminates horizontally in the room for 48 hours prior to laying.

Laying the boards

With the subfloor prepared and the underlay in place, begin in one corner of the room, next to the longest straight wall. Lay the first board parallel with the long wall, and place spacers between it and the skirting or wall (**1**). The board's shorter tongue should face the wall. Holding the next board at about 30 degrees to the floor, hook one end under the end of the first board and press down to lock the two together (**2**). Continue in the same way up to the far wall, where you will probably have to cut a board to fit. Measure the space left between the end of the previous board and the wall, allowing for the expansion gap. Mark the cut line on the infill board, using a try square (**3**). Saw the board to length and lock it in place to complete the first row. If necessary, hook the tapping bar over the end of the cut board and strike the other end of the bar to close up all the end joints in the row (**4**).

Start at the far end again, laying the offcut you have just made against the first row – this will automatically stagger the end joints from row to row. Lay more boards end to end as before and, when the row is complete, offer it up to the first row at 30 degrees so you can lock the two longer edges together (**5**). You may find it easier to enlist help in locking long rows together.

Continue across the room and, at the far wall, cut boards lengthways to fit in the gap remaining, using the tapping bar to drive the locking edges together (**6**).

Nail or glue a moulding to the skirting to cover the expansion gap (see opposite).

Laminate flooring used to simulate rustic-pine boards

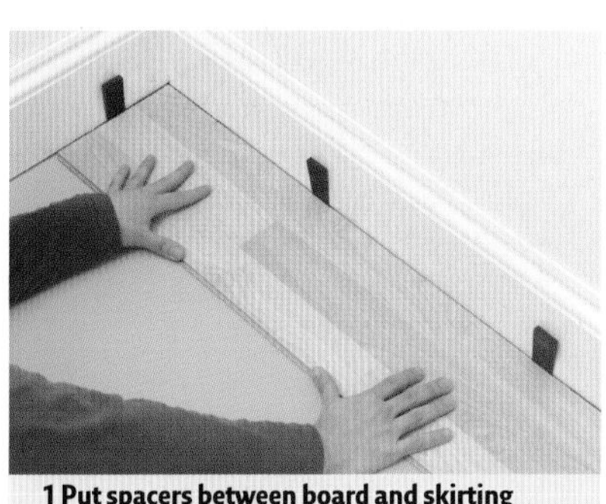

1 Put spacers between board and skirting

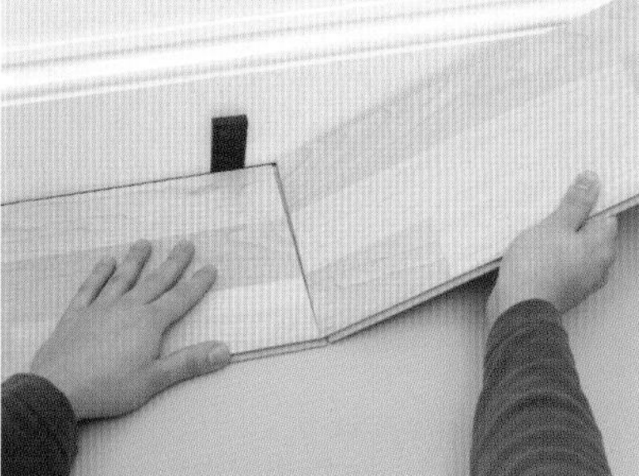

2 Lock the ends together

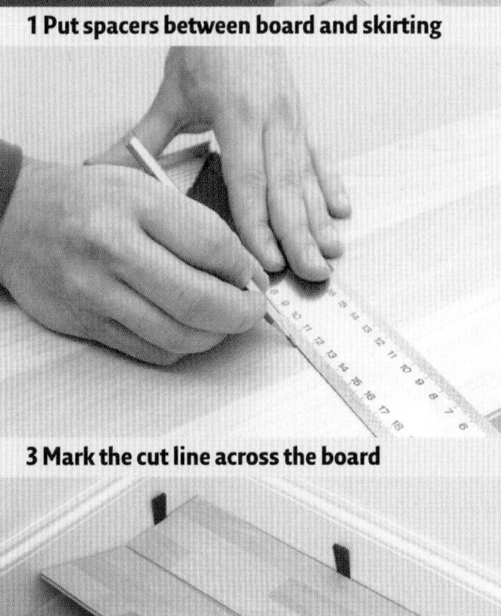

3 Mark the cut line across the board

4 Close up the end joints

5 Lock the edges together

6 Use a tapping bar to close up the gaps

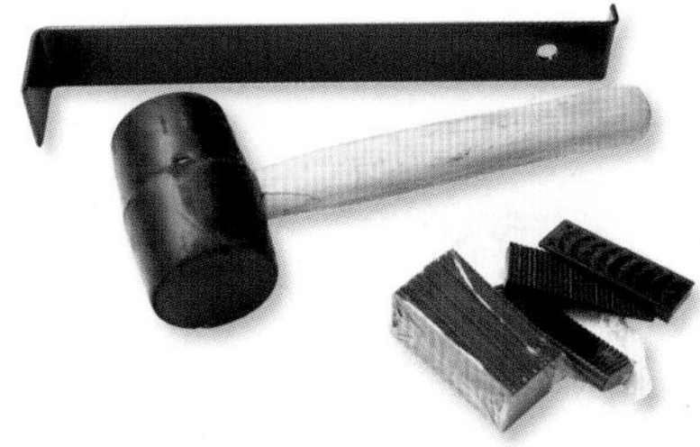

Special tools
When laying laminated flooring you will need a tapping bar (available from flooring suppliers) and hammer or mallet for closing up end joints. You can buy packs of spacers to help you maintain an even expansion gap all round the room.

Cutting around pipes

Measure and mark the position of a pipe that protrudes through the floor. Drill a hole slightly larger than the pipe, then cut out a tapered section of the laminate to accommodate the pipe. Lock the laminate in place and glue the wedge-shape offcut behind the pipe.

You can buy colour-matching covers that surround the pipe and conceal the hole drilled through the laminate.

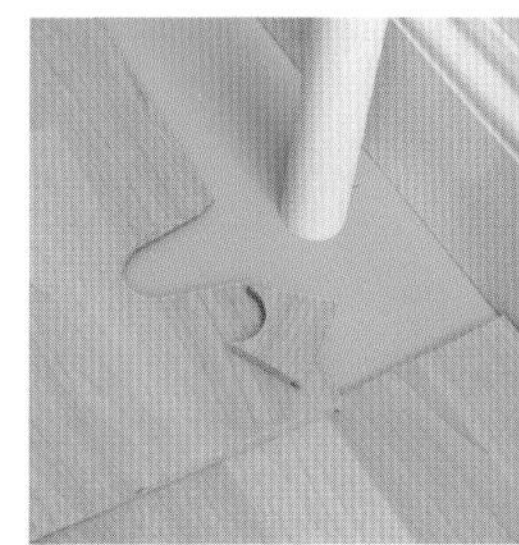

Cut a notch for a pipe

Fitting to a doorway

When you reach the doorway, use an offcut of laminate to support a panel saw in order to cut off the bottom of the doorframe. The flooring will fit neatly under the frame when you cut the boards to shape. Fit a suitable threshold bar across the door opening to cover the edge of the laminate.

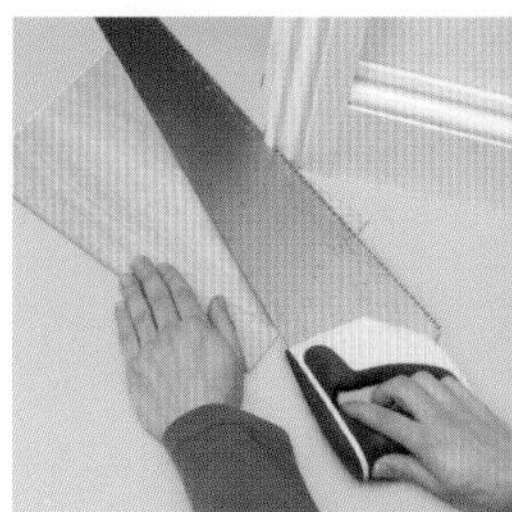

Cut away the doorframe

SEE ALSO > Levelling concrete 47, Levelling a wooden floor 57, Preparing floorboards 54

Laying a floating wood floor

It is possible to glue solid-wood flooring directly to a concrete subfloor, but it is an added complication that is probably best left to a professional floorer. It is much simpler to construct a floating floor that does not have to be fixed in any way to the subfloor. Fit an underlay that incorporates a moisture barrier over the concrete before you lay the flooring.

Laying tongued-and-grooved boards

Special tools
When laying a floating floor you will need a tapping bar and tapping block (both available from flooring suppliers) and a hammer or mallet to drive the glued joints together. You will also need spacers to maintain an even expansion gap around the room as the boards are laid.

The edges and ends of solid-wood boards are machined with tongues and grooves that slot together. These edges are glued as you lay a floating floor, but the boards are not glued down to the subfloor. Use standard PVA wood glue unless the flooring manufacturer recommends another type of adhesive. Because it can be difficult to dismantle the joints once the glue begins to set, dry-lay the flooring three rows at a time so you have plenty of time to cut and fit the boards before you apply adhesive.

Start in one corner of the room, against the longest straight wall, and lay the first board with its tongued edge facing the wall. You can remove this tongue with a plane, but it is only necessary if the edge moulding or skirting is not able to conceal it. Place spacers between the board and the skirting or wall (1) to create an expansion gap of between 10 and 15mm (depending on the flooring manufacturer's recommendation).

Add boards end to end up to the far wall, where you will need to measure and cut an infill board to complete the first row. Remember to allow for the expansion gap when measuring the board. Use a try square to mark the line accurately, and then cut the board to length with a tenon saw (2).

Use the offcut to start the next row so that the end joints between boards are staggered by between 150 and 300mm (6in and 1ft). Fit each length of flooring, one to another, using the tapping block to make sure the joints fit snugly (3). Once you have completed the first three rows, dismantle the joints and then re-lay the boards, this time squeezing a bead of glue along the groove (4) as you reassemble each joint. Tap the joints together as you lay the boards, and use a damp cloth to wipe surplus glue from the surface of the wood. Use the tapping bar to close up end joints (5).

Work across the room, dry-laying three rows at a time before you apply adhesive to the joints. For the last row, cut the boards lengthways to fit the space remaining, allowing for the expansion gap. Run a bead of glue along the joint and lower the cut board between the previous board and the skirting or wall. Using the tapping bar, close up the joint (6) and wipe excess glue from the surface. Leave the adhesive to harden overnight before you fit the cover moulding.

Engineered boards

The simplest way to construct a hardwood floating floor is to use snap-together engineered boards, which have a top layer or real wood. These boards are laid and cut to fit in the same way as laminates. Since there is no need to glue these boards edge to edge, they can be laid relatively quickly and can be lifted easily in order to rectify any errors.

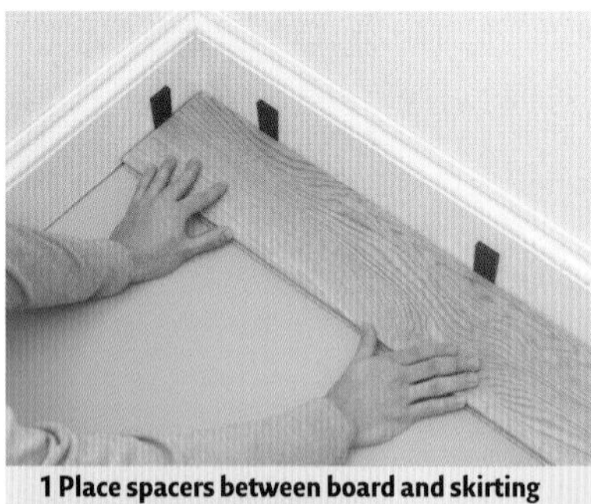

1 Place spacers between board and skirting

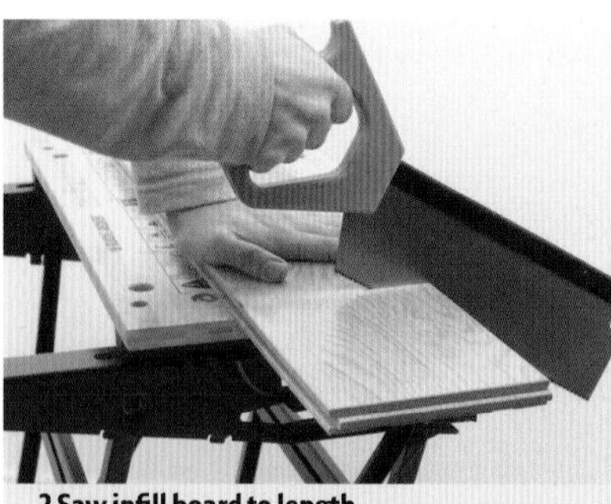

2 Saw infill board to length

3 Tap the joints together

4 Apply a bead of woodworking adhesive

5 Close up the end joints

6 Drive the joints home

SEE ALSO > Levelling concrete 47, Levelling a wooden floor 57, Expansion gaps 108, Laying laminate flooring 109

Nailing solid-wood flooring

If you plan to lay solid-wood flooring over an existing suspended wood floor, you can nail down the tongue-and-groove boards instead of gluing them edge to edge. If you want to use this method over a concrete floor, you need to install a damp-proof moisture barrier under a subfloor of 18mm (3/4in) exterior-grade plywood, leaving an expansion gap of 15mm (5/8in) all round.

Secret-nailing board flooring

Solid-wood flooring can be laid directly over existing floorboards, provided they are reasonably flat and even. Nail down any loose floorboards and drive all fixings below the surface, using a nail set. If the floorboards are not sufficiently flat to be used as a subfloor, cover them with 6mm (¼in) exterior-grade plywood, allowing for the expansion gap all round. Cover either subfloor with an underlay before you nail down the flooring.

The first row of boards must be straight and fixed securely to the subfloor. If the wall or skirting is not sufficiently straight to be used as a guide, snap a line across the floor the equivalent of one board's width plus 15mm (5/8in).

Prepare the first boards by drilling starter holes for the nails every 250 to 300mm (6in to 1ft), just inside the grooved edge (**1**). Starting in one corner, lay the first board against the line marked across the floor and with its grooved edge facing the wall. Drive nails through the predrilled holes into the subfloor below (**2**), and then sink the nailheads below the surface of the wood (**3**).

Nail down the tongued edge of the same board by driving nails at an angle of 45 degrees through the base of the tongue (**4**). Drive these nailheads just below the surface, using the nail set.

Tap the next board onto the end of the nailed board, making sure it follows the line marked on the subfloor, then fix it down with nails in the same way. Saw the final board in the row to fit the gap, allowing for the expansion gap. Drive the cut board into place with the tapping bar (**5**) and nail it down.

Continue across the floor, tapping the joints together before nailing each board through the tongue only.

Cut the final row of boards lengthways to fit the space remaining, allowing for the expansion gap. Drill starter holes (see left) through each cut board, then lower it into the space and drive the joint together, using the tapping bar (**6**). Fix the board in place by hammering nails through the predrilled holes into the subfloor.

Either replace the skirting to cover the expansion gap or nail a moulding around the edge of the room.

Quality flooring
Oak looks superb, even when newly laid, and it continues to improve with age.

1 Drill starter holes for the nails

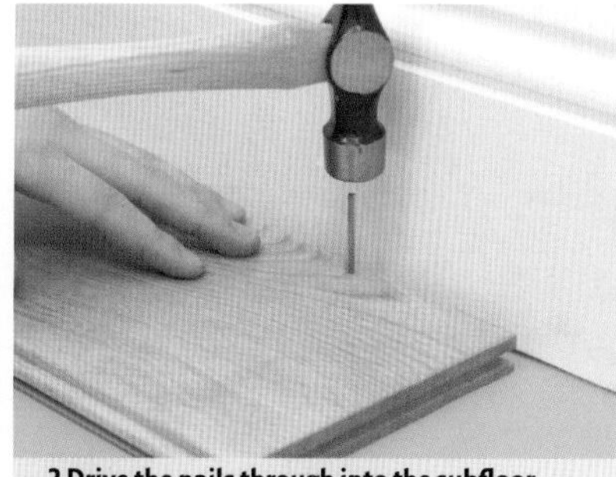

2 Drive the nails through into the subfloor

3 Sink the nailheads with a punch

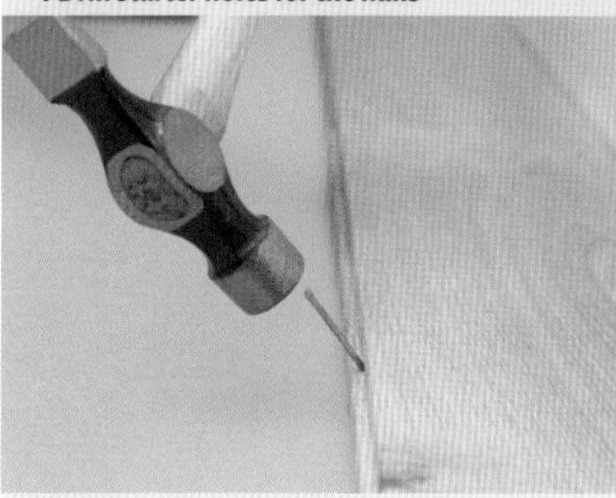

4 Drive nails at an angle through base of tongue

5 Drive the cut board into place

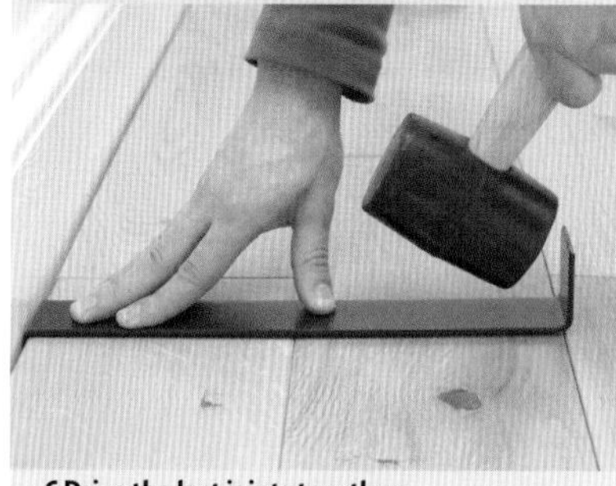

6 Drive the last joints together

SEE ALSO >Levelling a wooden floor 57, Preparing floorboards 54, Expansion gaps 108

Carpets

Originally piled carpets were made by knotting strands of wool or other natural fibres into a woven foundation, but gradually, with the introduction of machine-made carpets and synthetic fibres, a wide variety of different types has been developed. There is a good choice available for virtually all areas of the house, whether the need is for a luxurious floorcovering or one that's practical and hardwearing.

When selecting carpet, consider your options carefully. The floor area is an important element in the style of an interior, and the wrong choice could be an expensive mistake.

A well-laid good-quality carpet will last for many years - so unless you can afford to change your floorcovering every time you redecorate, take care to choose one that you will be able to live with after a change of colour scheme or furnishings. Neutral or earthy colours are easiest to accommodate. Plain colours and small repeat patterns are suitable for rooms of any size; large, bold designs are best reserved for spacious interiors.

If you are planning to carpet adjoining rooms, consider using the same carpet to link the floor areas. This provides a greater sense of space and harmony.

You can use patterned borders in combination with plain carpet to create a distinctive customized floorcovering in specific areas.

1 Cut pile
2 Velvet pile
3 Looped pile
4 Underlay
5 Sisal
6 Saxony pile
7 Twisted pile
8 Cord Pile

Natural-fibre rugs and runners

Though rarely laid as fitted carpets these days, natural fibres, such as jute, hemp, coir and sisal, are used to weave carpet squares, rugs and runners. Their warm textured surfaces are especially attractive when laid over real-wood flooring or laminates.

Rugs are also made from strips of bamboo sewn to a woven backing.

Natural-fibre floorcoverings cannot be cut to fit unless they have a latex backing that prevents fraying. They exude a fairly strong odour when new, but this usually fades with time.

Open-weave rugs and runners harbour grit and dust and should be lifted regularly for gentle beating outside. Sweep the floor beneath.

Natural-fibres tend to stain easily and may not be a wise choice for areas where liquids could be spilled.

An attractive combination

SEE ALSO > Colour, texture and pattern 32–3, 36, 37, Levelling floors 47, 57, Laying carpet 114

Choosing carpet

When shopping for carpets there are various factors to consider, including fibre content, type of pile and durability. Although wool carpet is luxurious, synthetic-fibre carpets also have a lot to offer in terms of finish, texture, comfort underfoot and value for money.

Fibre content of carpets

The best carpets are made from wool or a mixture of wool with a percentage of man-made fibre. Wool carpets are expensive, so manufacturers have experimented with a variety of fibres to produce cheaper but durable and attractive carpets. Materials such as nylon, polypropylene, acrylic, rayon and polyester are all used for carpet making, either singly or in combination.

Synthetic-fibre carpets were once inferior substitutes, often with an unattractive shiny pile and a reputation for building up a charge of static electricity that produced mild shocks when anyone touched a metal door knob. Nowadays, manufacturers have largely solved the problem of static, but you should still seek the advice of the supplier before you buy.

As for appearance, a modern carpet made from good-quality blended fibres is hard to distinguish from one made from wool. Certain combinations produce carpets that are so stain-resistant that they virtually shrug off spilled liquids. To their disadvantage, synthetic fibres tend to react badly to burns, shrivelling rapidly from the heat, whereas wool tends only to smoulder.

Rush, sisal, coir and jute are natural vegetable fibres used to make coarsely woven rugs or strips.

Which type of pile?

The nature of the pile is just as important to the feel and appearance of a carpet as the fibre content.

Piled carpets are either woven or tufted. Axminster and Wilton are names used to describe two traditional methods of weaving the pile simultaneously with the foundation, so that the strands are wrapped around and through the warp and weft threads. With tufted carpets, continuous strands are pushed between the threads of a prewoven foundation. Although secured with an adhesive backing, tufted pile isn't as permanent as a woven pile.

The column on the right explains the various ways tufted and woven piles are created. See below for durability.

The importance of underlay

A carpet undoubtedly benefits from a resilient cushion laid between it and the floor – it is more comfortable to walk on and the carpet lasts longer. Without an underlay, dust may emerge from the divisions between the floorboards and begin to show as dirty lines.

An underlay can be either a thick felt or a layer of foamed rubber or plastic. If you buy a foam-backed or rubber-backed carpet, there's no need for a separate underlay. However, additional protection (see margin note) will prevent the carpet sticking to the floor and, especially with cheaper carpets, will avoid the possibility of floorboards showing through.

Choosing a durable carpet

Whether it is woven, tufted or bonded, a hardwearing carpet must have a dense pile. When you fold the carpet and part the pile, you shouldn't be able to see the backing. The British Carpet Classification Scheme categorizes floorcoverings according to their ability to withstand wear. If the classification is not stated on the carpet, ask the supplier how it is classified.

DURABILITY RATING	
CLASSIFICATION	**APPLICATION**
Light domestic	Bedrooms
Medium domestic	Light traffic only (dining room, well-used bedrooms)
General domestic	Living rooms
Heavy domestic	Hallways/stairs

How carpets are made

Tufted and woven carpet pile is treated in a number of ways to give different qualities of finish. With some types, the strands are left long and uncut; with others, the looped pile is twisted together to give a coarser texture. Very hardwearing carpets have their looped pile pulled tight against the foundation. Cut, velvety and shaggy carpets have the tops of their loops cut off.

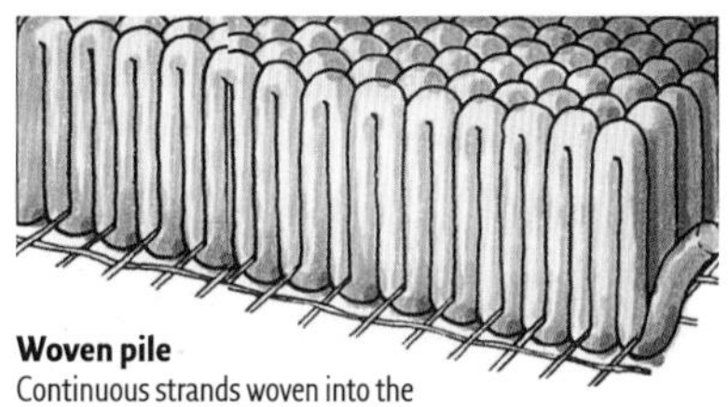

Woven pile
Continuous strands woven into the warp and weft threads of the foundation.

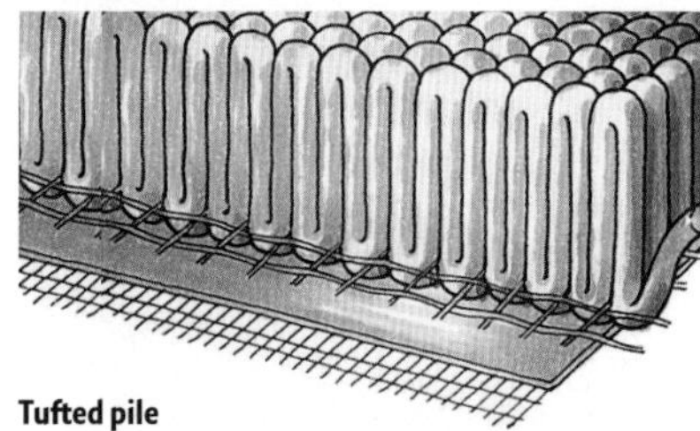

Tufted pile
Continuous strands pushed through a woven foundation and secured on an adhesive backing.

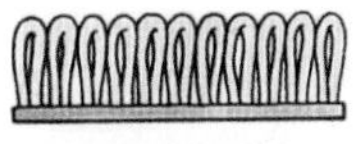

Looped pile
Ordinary looped pile gives a smooth feel.

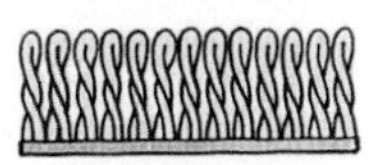

Twisted pile
Looped pile twisted for a coarser texture.

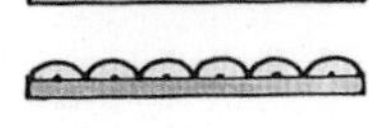

Cord pile
Loops are pulled tight against the foundation.

Cut pile
Loops are cut, giving a velvety texture pile.

Velvet pile
Loops are cut short for a close-stranded pile.

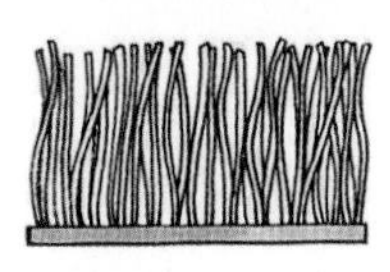

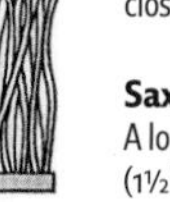

Saxony pile
A long cut pile, up to 38mm (1½in) long.

Fibre-bonded pile

A modern method of carpet production makes use of synthetic fibres packed tightly together and bonded to an impregnated backing. The texture is like coarse felt.

• Additional protection
As well as a conventional underlay, it is worth laying rolls of brown paper or synthetic-fibre sheet over the floor to stop dust and grit working their way into the underlay or to prevent a rubber-backed carpet sticking to the floor.

Fibre-bonded pile
A tough low-cost carpet, mostly used for commercial interiors.

SEE ALSO >Colour, texture and pattern 32–3, 36, 37, Levelling floors 47, 57, Carpet tiles 96, Laying carpet 114

Laying carpet

Some people loose-lay carpet, relying on the weight of the furniture to stop it moving around. However, a properly stretched and fixed carpet looks much neater.

Fixing carpet
Use one of three methods:

Fold tacked to floor

Double-sided tape

Gripper strip

Methods of fixing

There are different methods for holding a fitted carpet firmly in place, depending on the type of carpet you are laying.

Carpet tacks

A 50mm (2in) strip can be folded under along each edge of the carpet and nailed to a wooden floor with cut tacks about every 200mm (8in). You can usually cover the tack head by rubbing the pile with your fingertips. With this method, the underlay should be laid 50mm (2in) short of the skirting to allow the carpet to lie flat along the edge.

Double-sided tape

Use double-sided adhesive tape for rubber-backed carpets only. Stick 50mm (2in) tape around the perimeter of the room; then, when you are ready to fix the carpet, peel off the protective paper layer from the tape.

Gripper strips

These wooden or metal strips have fine metal teeth that grip the woven foundation. They are not really suitable for rubber-backed carpets, although they are used. Nail the strips to the floor, 6mm (¼in) from the skirting, with the teeth pointing towards the wall. Cut short strips to fit into doorways and alcoves.

Glue gripper strips to a concrete floor. Cut underlay up to the edge of each strip.

Joining at a doorway
Use one of these bars:

Double threshold bar

Single threshold bar

Using a knee kicker
The only special tool required for laying carpet is a knee kicker, for stretching it. This has a toothed head, which is pressed into the carpet while you nudge the end with your knee. You can hire a knee kicker from a carpet supplier or tool-hire company.

Laying standard-width carpet

If you are laying a separate underlay, join neighbouring sections of the underlay with short strips of carpet tape or secure them with a few tacks to stop them moving.

Roll out the carpet, butting one machine-cut edge against a wall: fix that edge to the floor. A pattern should run parallel to the main axis of the room. Stretch the carpet to the wall directly opposite and temporarily fix it with tacks, or slip it onto gripper strips. Don't cut the carpet yet. Work from the centre towards each corner, stretching and fixing the carpet; then do the same at the other sides of the room.

Cut a triangular notch at each corner, so the carpet lies flat. Adjust the carpet until it is stretched evenly, then fix it permanently.

When you are using tape or gripper strips, press the carpet into the angle between the skirting and the floor with a bolster chisel; then trim with a knife held at 45 degrees to the skirting. Tuck the cut edge behind a gripper strip with the bolster.

Cutting to fit

Cut and fit carpet into doorways and around obstacles, as described for sheet vinyl. Join carpets at a doorway with a threshold bar.

Joining carpet

Join seams with latex adhesive, as described for sheet vinyl; for rubber-backed carpets, use adhesive tape. Have expensive woven carpets sewn and laid by a professional.

Carpeting a staircase

Use standard-width narrow carpet on a staircase. Order an extra 450mm (1ft 6in), so that the carpet can be moved at a later date to even out the wear. This allowance is turned under onto the bottom step.

You can fit carpeting across the width of the treads, or stop short to reveal a border of polished or painted wood. With the latter method, you can use traditional stair rods to hold the carpet against the risers.

Alternatively, tack the carpet to the stairs every 75mm (3in) across the treads. Push the carpet into the angle between riser and tread with a bolster chisel while you tack the centre, then work outwards to each side.

Unless it's rubber-backed, you can use gripper strip to fix the carpet in place.

Fitting an underlay

Cut underlay into separate pads for each tread. Fix each pad next to the riser, using tacks or gripper strip; and tack the front edge under the nosing.

Laying a straight run

The pile of the carpet should face down the stairs. Gauge the pile by rubbing your palm along the carpet in both directions – it will feel smoother in the direction of the pile.

Starting at the bottom of the stairs, lay the carpet face down on the first tread. Fix the back edge with tacks, or nail a strip over it. Stretch the carpet over the nosing, and fix it to the bottom of the riser by nailing through a straight gripper strip. Run the carpet up the staircase, pushing it firmly into each gripper strip with a bolster. Nail the end of the carpet against the riser on the last tread, then bring the landing carpet over the top step to meet it.

Carpeting a straight run **Carpeting winding stairs**

Straight stairs
1 Underlay pads
2 Carpet tacked face down
3 Tacked to base of riser
4 Carpet runs upstairs and fixed to grippers

Winding stairs
Don't cut the carpet, but fold the excess under and fix to the risers with stair rods or long carpet tacks. To install fitted carpet, cut a pattern for each step and carpet it individually.

SEE ALSO > Levelling floors 47, 57, Sticking and joining sheet vinyl 116

Estimating sheet vinyl and carpet

Measure the floor area and draw a free-hand plan, including the position of doors, window bay, alcoves and so on, plus the full width of the doorframe. Make a note of the dimensions on the plan and take it to the flooring supplier, who will advise you on the most economical way to cover the floor.

The ideal solution is to achieve a seamless wall-to-wall covering; but this is often impossible, either because a particular width is unobtainable or the room is such an irregular shape that there would be too much wastage if it were cut from one piece. In these circumstances, carpet or sheet-vinyl widths have to be butted together – but try to avoid seams in the main walkways. You also have to consider matching the pattern and the direction of carpet pile: they must run in the same direction, or each piece of carpet will look different. Remember to order 75mm (3in) extra all round for fitting.

Standard widths

Most manufacturers produce carpet or vinyl to standard widths. Some can be cut to fit any shape of room, but the average wastage factor is reflected in the price. Not all carpets are available in the full range of widths and you may have difficulty in matching a colour exactly from one width to another, so ask the supplier to check. Carpet and vinyl are made to metric sizes, but the imperial equivalent is normally quoted.

AVAILABLE WIDTHS	
Carpet	**Vinyl**
0.69m (2ft 3in)*	2m (6ft 6in)
0.91m (3ft)	3m (9ft 10in)
2.74m (9ft)	4m (13ft)
3.66m (12ft)	
4m (13ft)*	
4.57m (15ft)*	

*rare

Carpet widths of 2.74m (9ft) and over are known as broadlooms; narrower widths are called body or strip carpets.

Carpet squares

Carpet squares – not to be confused with tiles – are large, rectangular loose-laid rugs. Simply order whichever size suits the proportions of your room. Carpet squares should be turned round from time to time to even out wear.

Sheet-vinyl floorcovering

Sheet vinyl makes an ideal wall-to-wall floorcovering for kitchens, utility rooms and bathrooms, where you are bound to spill water from time to time. It is straightforward to lay, provided you follow a systematic procedure.

Vinyl flooring
Being hardwearing and waterproof, sheet vinyl is one of the most popular floorcoverings for bathrooms and kitchens.

1 Vinyl
2 Vinyl carpet

Types of sheet-vinyl

There's a variety of sheet-vinyl floor-coverings to choose from.

Unbacked vinyl

Sheet vinyl is made by sandwiching the printed pattern between a base of PVC and a clear protective PVC covering. All vinyls are relatively hardwearing, but some have a thicker, reinforced protective layer to increase their durability.

Backed vinyl

Backed vinyl has similar properties to the unbacked type, with the addition of a resilient underlay to make it warmer and softer to walk on. The backing is usually a cushion of foamed PVC.

Vinyl carpet

Vinyl carpet – a cross between carpet and sheet vinyl – was originally developed for contract use but is now available for the wider market. It has a velvet-like pile of fine nylon fibres embedded in a waterproof expanded-PVC base, and is popular for kitchens as spillages are washed off easily with water and a mild detergent. It comes in 2m (6ft 7in) wide rolls.

Linoleum

Traditional linoleum, made from linseed oil, wood flour, chalk and pine resin, is being manufactured again. It is a durable superb-quality floorcovering, suitable for any room in the home.

Preparing the floor

Before laying a sheet-vinyl floorcovering or linoleum, make sure the floor is flat and dry. Vacuum the surface, and nail down any floorboards that are loose. Take out any unevenness by screeding a concrete floor or hardboarding a wooden one. A concrete floor must have a damp-proof membrane, while a ground-level wooden floor must be ventilated below. Don't lay vinyl over boards that have recently been treated with preserver.

SEE ALSO > Colour, texture and pattern 32–3, 36, 37, Levelling floors 47, 57, Laying sheet vinyl 116

Laying sheet vinyl

Leave the vinyl sheet in a room for 24 to 48 hours before laying, preferably opened flat – or at least stood on end, loosely rolled. Make a scribing gauge by driving a nail through a wooden lath about 50mm (2in) from one end. You will use this gauge for fitting the sheet against the skirtings.

Fitting and cutting sheet vinyl

Assuming there are no seams, start by fitting the sheet against the longest wall. Pull the vinyl away from the wall by approximately 35mm (1½in); make sure it is parallel with the wall or the main axis of the room. Use the scribing gauge to score a line that follows the skirting (**1**). Cut the vinyl with a knife, then slide the sheet up against the wall.

To get the rest of the sheet to lie as flat as possible, cut a triangular notch at each corner. At external corners, make a straight cut down to the floor. Remove as much waste as possible, leaving 50 to 75mm (2 to 3in) turned up all round.

Using a bolster, press the vinyl into the angle between the skirting and the floor. Align a metal straightedge with the crease and run a sharp knife along it, held at a slight angle to the skirting (**2**).

Trimming to fit a doorway

To fit the vinyl around the frame, crease it against the floor and trim off the waste. Make a straight cut across the opening, and fit a threshold bar to cover the edge.

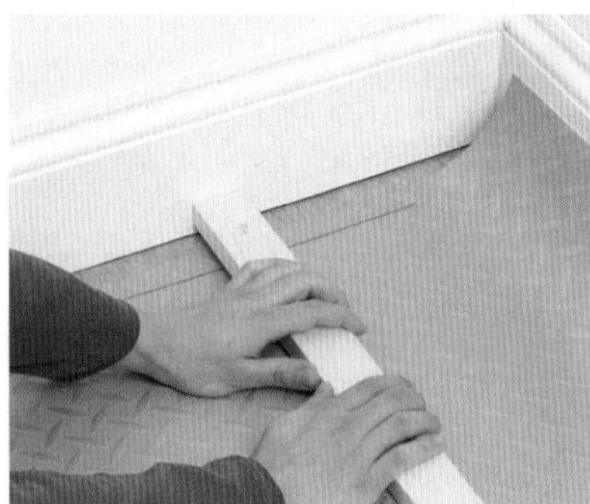
1 Fit to the wall by scribing with a nailed strip

2 Press the folded edge to the skirting and cut

Positioning sheet vinyl
Lay the vinyl on the floor so that it laps the skirting all round, then start by fitting the sheet to the longest, uninterrupted wall. Cut notches at each corner, so the sheet will lie flat, and make a straight cut across the door opening.

Sticking and joining sheet vinyl

Sheet-vinyl floorcoverings can be loose-laid, but you may prefer to at least glue the edges, especially across a door opening.

Peel back the edge and spread a band of the recommended flooring adhesive, using a toothed spreader; or apply double-sided adhesive tape, 50mm (2in) wide, to the floor.

Joining strips of vinyl

If you have to join widths of vinyl, overlap the free edge with the second sheet until the pattern matches exactly. Cut through both pieces with a knife, then remove the waste strips. Without moving the sheets, fold back both cut edges and apply tape or adhesive, then press the join together.

Secure butting edges on a bed of adhesive

Cutting to fit a curve

To fit around a WC pan or basin pedestal, fold back the sheet and pierce it with a knife just above floor level; draw the blade up towards the edge of the sheet. Make triangular cuts around the base, gradually working around the curve until the sheet can lie flat on the floor. Crease, and cut off the waste.

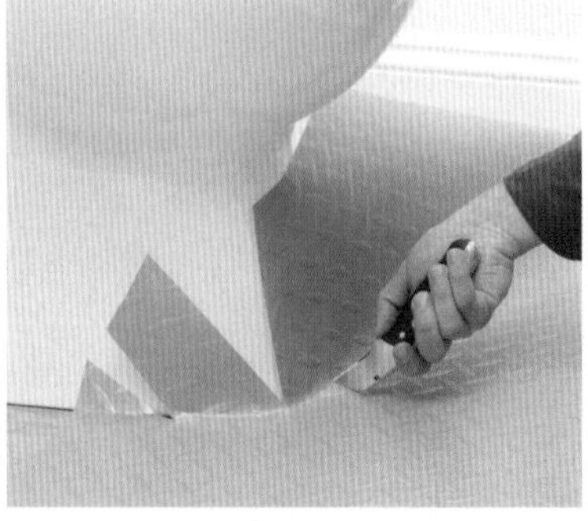
Make triangular cuts around a curve

SEE ALSO > Levelling floors 47, 57, Sheet vinyl 115

Repairs and Improvements

The construction of your house

If you want to repair or improve your home, you need to understand how it's put together. Most pre-1970s houses are built in brick or blockwork and have a roof made from timber rafters covered with tiles or slates.

Brick-built house

Pitched roof

Pitched roofs comprise angled timber rafters (**1**) meeting at a ridge board (**2**). They are braced by purlins (**3**), struts and ties, and their lower ends rest on timber wall plates (**4**). The roof is usually lined with roofing felt (**5**), and covered with tiles or slates (**6**) fixed to timber battens (**7**).

External walls

These walls are loadbearing; they support the roof and the floors. Older houses have solid walls. Houses built since about 1920 have cavity walls (**8**), which consist of two skins of masonry, braced with metal ties. A damp-proof course (DPC) above ground level (**9**) stops moisture rising up the walls. Door and window openings are spanned by supporting beams called lintels (**10**).

Chimneys

A chimney is a hollow brick structure with a flue for each fireplace (**11**). Where it passes through the roof, metal strips called flashings (**12**) weatherproof the opening. Each flue is topped by a pot (**13**).

Internal walls

These walls may be loadbearing or non-loadbearing. The former are built of brick (**14**) or blockwork and support the roof and floors. The latter are room dividers, and are built of lightweight blocks (**15**) or with timber (**16**) or metal frames.

Floors

Ground floors may be a slab of concrete or a suspended structure of timber joists (**17**) supported by low brick walls (**18**). The ground beneath a suspended floor is usually covered with a layer of concrete (**19**). Upper floors are formed of timber joists supported by the external walls and by loadbearing internal ones (**20**). They are covered with floorboards (**21**) or chipboard.

Foundations

The weight of the house is supported on its foundations. Older houses usually have a strip foundation (**22**). More recent houses may have a trench foundation (**23**), with concrete rather than masonry filling the trench, or a raft foundation (**24**).

SEE ALSO > Roof coverings 123–5, Walls 138–55, Lintels 139, Floors 172–81, DPCs 247, Building brickwork 442–49

Timber-framed house

Modern timber-framed houses differ from their brick-built counterparts in that the loadbearing walls are made from prefabricated panels clad externally with brickwork, boards or tiles.

Prefabricated roof

Timber-framed houses have roofs constructed from prefabricated trussed rafters (**1**). These are triangulated frames that combine the functions of rafters, struts and ceiling joists (**2**). They are fixed to the tops of the loadbearing timber wall frames, and are connected with a number of transverse braces and binders to keep the structure stiff. Special ladder frames are used at gable ends (**3**).The roof is felted, battened and tiled as for a traditional pitched roof (**4**).

Loadbearing walls

The external walls are similar to the cavity walls of a brick-built house. The inner skin of the wall is loadbearing, and is constructed from a series of prefabricated timber wall frames (**5**) that are fixed to timber sole plates (**6**) at ground level, and to each other as the structure rises. The frames are faced on the outside with plywood to stiffen them (**7**). Breather paper is fixed over this to act as a moisture barrier (**8**). A polythene vapour barrier is fitted on the inside (**9**), and the space in between is filled with insulation (**10**) and covered with plasterboard (**11**). Timber lintels span door and window openings (**12**). The outer skin of the wall may be a single thickness of brickwork, attached to the wall frames with metal ties (**13**), or may be covered with lightweight cladding such as tile hanging or weatherboarding.

Internal walls

These walls are all timber-framed room dividers. Downstairs walls carry the weight of the upper floors, so are loadbearing (**14**). Upstairs room dividers are built off the first floor platform; they are not loadbearing and can be positioned anywhere relative to the walls downstairs (**15**).

Floors

The ground floor is either a solid slab or a suspended concrete floor, as for a modern brick-built house(**16**). It incorporates rigid polystyrene insulation and a damp-proof membrane (DPM) (**17**). The first floor is built as a platform on top of the ground-floor wall frames (**18**), and supports the first-floor wall frames (**19**) and the upstairs room dividers.

Foundations

Because there is far less solid masonry in a timber-framed house, it does not need such massive foundations as a brick-built one. The foundations are usually in the form of a solid concrete raft with the edges and other areas thickened to support the various external and internal loadbearing walls (**20**).

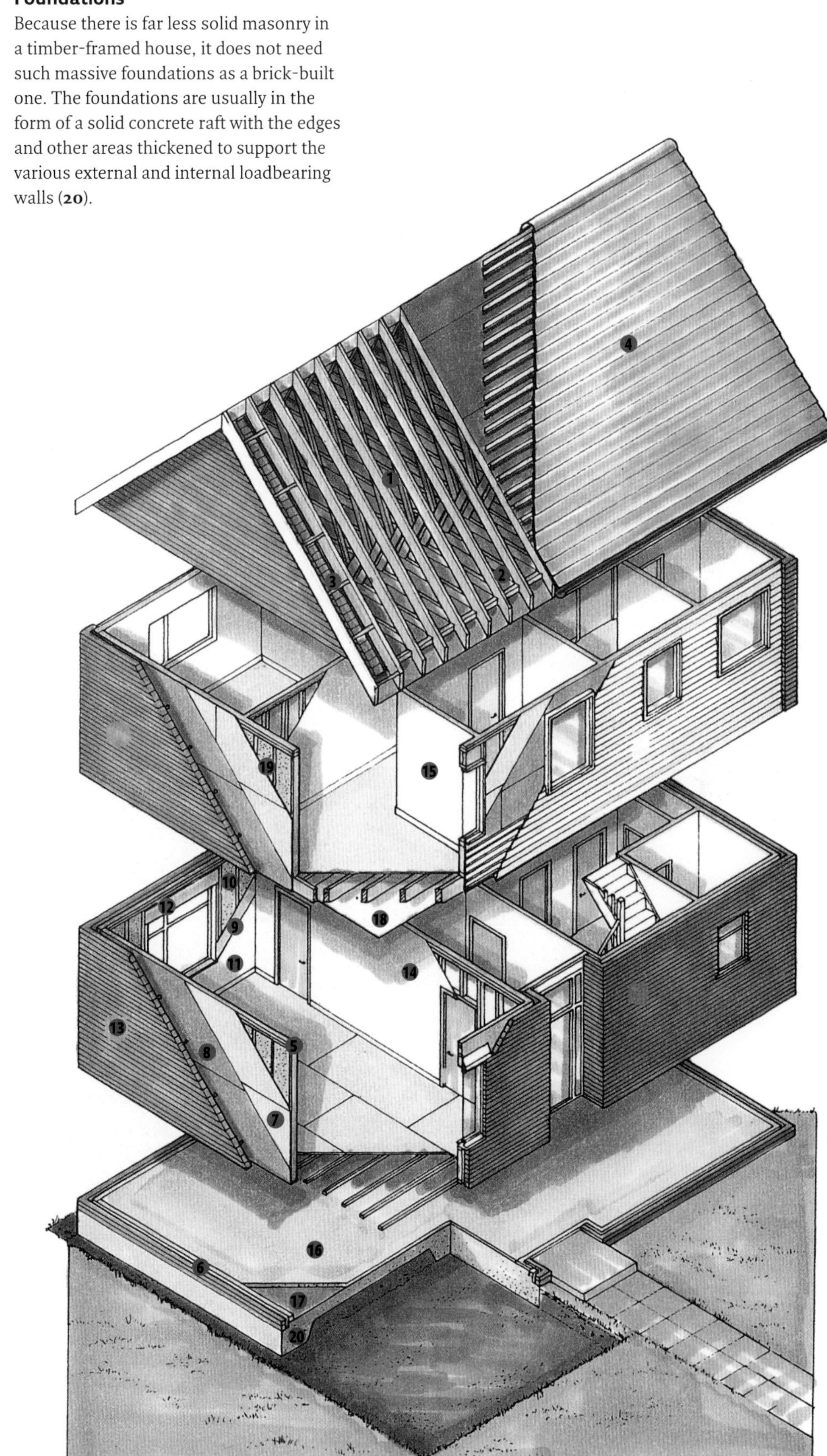

SEE ALSO > Roof coverings 123–5, Walls 138–55, Lintels 139, Floors 172–81, DPCs 247, Building brickwork 442–49

Pitched roofs

Pitched roofs were once built on site from individual lengths of timber, but to save time and materials most builders now use prefabricated frames called trussed rafters. These are specifically designed to meet the loading requirements of a given house and, unlike traditional roofs, are not usually suitable for conversion because to remove any components would weaken the structure.

Roof features

The simplest pitched roof is the gabled roof, with two slopes meeting at the ridge. The angle of the roof slope is commonly between 25 and 40 degrees. The triangular part of each end wall is the gable. The side edge of each roof slope is the verge. The roof slope may finish flush with the gable wall and the verges, or may project beyond them. The lower edge of each roof slope forms the eaves.

Roofs with four slopes are called hipped roofs. The two end slopes are triangular in shape, and each is bounded by two hips which meet at the ridge.

On an L- or T-shaped building, the roof slopes on each wing of the building meet at right angles to form sloping valleys, often containing a valley gutter. Where a roof meets a wall or chimney stack, the junction between them is called an abutment and is weatherproofed with a flashing, usually made of lead or mortar.

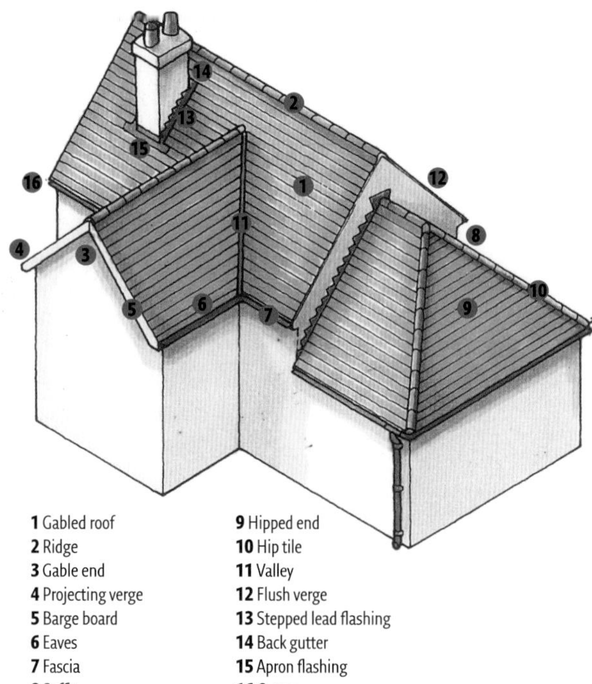

1 Gabled roof
2 Ridge
3 Gable end
4 Projecting verge
5 Barge board
6 Eaves
7 Fascia
8 Soffit
9 Hipped end
10 Hip tile
11 Valley
12 Flush verge
13 Stepped lead flashing
14 Back gutter
15 Apron flashing
16 Gutter

Single roof

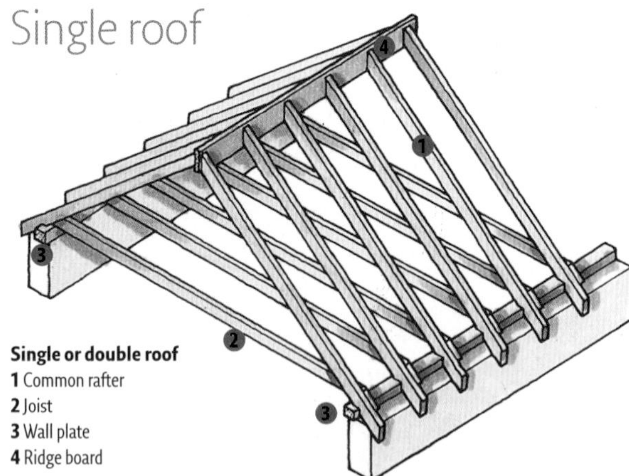

Single or double roof
1 Common rafter
2 Joist
3 Wall plate
4 Ridge board

The framework of an ordinary pitched roof is based on a triangle, the most rigid and economical form for a loadbearing structure. The weight of the roof covering is carried by the common rafters – the sloping members, which are set in opposing pairs, with their heads meeting at a central ridge board. The lower ends of the rafters are fixed to timber wall plates, which are bedded on the exterior walls and distribute the weight uniformly.

To stop the weight of the roof pushing the walls out, horizontal joists (ties) are fixed to the wall plates and to the ends of each pair of rafters, forming a simple structure known as a close-couple single roof. It is suitable only for relatively short spans.

Double roof

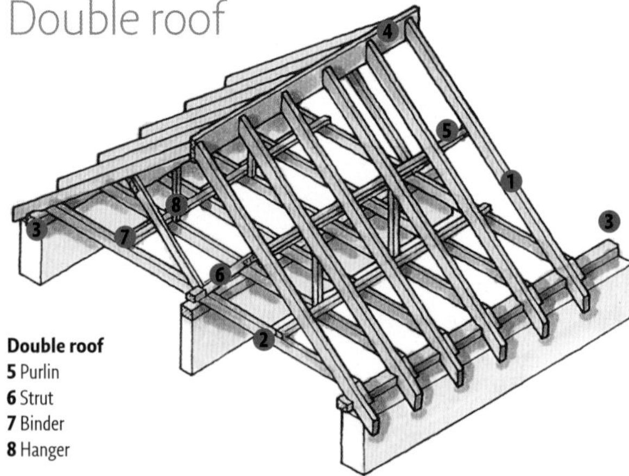

Double roof
5 Purlin
6 Strut
7 Binder
8 Hanger

In a double roof, horizontal beams called purlins link the rafters. They usually run midway between foot and ridge or at no more than 2.5m (8ft) intervals. The ends of the purlins are supported on the brickwork of a gable wall or, in a hipped roof, by hip rafters (see opposite). This effectively reduces the span of the rafters.

In order to keep the size of the purlins to a minimum, diagonal struts are set in opposing pairs to brace them at every fourth or fifth pair of rafters. The struts transfer some weight back to the centre of the ceiling joists, which are supported there by a load-bearing internal wall. Intermediate binders and hangers may also be used to give support to relatively lightweight ceiling joists.

SEE ALSO > Walls 138–55, Pitched roof coverings 123–4, Roof battens 124

Trussed-rafter roof

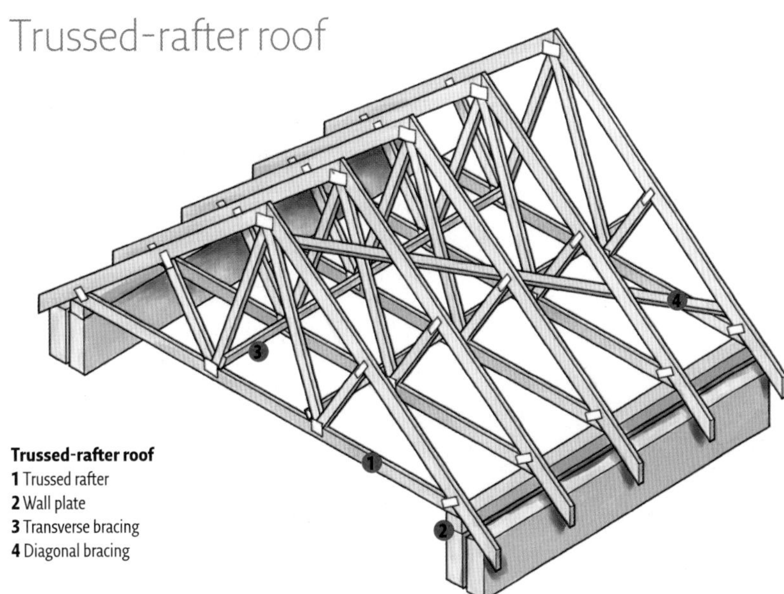

Trussed-rafter roof
1 Trussed rafter
2 Wall plate
3 Transverse bracing
4 Diagonal bracing

Trussed rafters allow for a relatively wide span and dispense with the need for a loadbearing interior wall. As main bearers for the roof, they transmit its weight to the exterior walls.

Trussed rafters are computer-designed for economy plus rigidity. Each truss combines two common rafters, a joist and angled strut bracing in a single frame; the members are butt-jointed and fixed with special nailed plate connectors. Individual trusses are spaced a maximum distance of 600mm (2ft) apart, and are linked with horizontal and diagonal bracing members. Such roofs are relatively lightweight, and are usually fixed to the walls with steel anchor straps to resist wind pressure.

Some older-style roofs embody rigid triangular trusses that carry purlins, which in turn support the rafters. Very few trussed roofs can be converted, and you should not try to cut into them.

Hipped roof

Gable and hipped roofs
Shown here is a hipped-end roof attached to a gable roof, using traditional construction.
1 Gable end
2 Hipped end
3 Hip rafter
4 Jack rafter
5 Crown rafter
6 Cripple rafter
7 Lay board

Hipped roofs are more complicated to build than gabled roofs, as their ends are pitched at an angle – so additional timbers have to be used in their construction. These are called hip rafters, jack rafters, crown rafters and cripple rafters. The illustration shows a gable roof and a shorter hipped-end roof, forming valleys at the points where they meet. Hips are sometimes used at the ends of main roofs.

Eaves and verges

The style of a roof is determined not only by its overall shape but also by the detailing of its eaves and verges.

Flush eaves

Eaves of this type result when the ends of the rafters are cut flush with the walls. A horizontal fascia board is nailed across the ends of the rafters, flush with the wall surface below, to protect them and to support the guttering.

Flush eaves

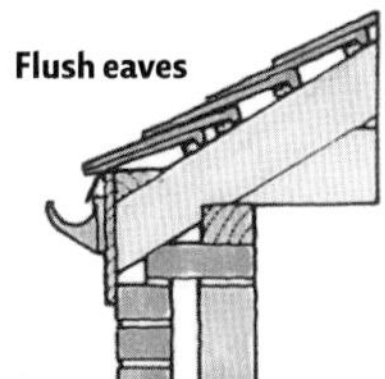

Open eaves

With open eaves, the exposed ends of the rafters project beyond the house walls. Gutter-fixing brackets are screwed to either their sides or top edges before the roof is tiled.

Open eaves

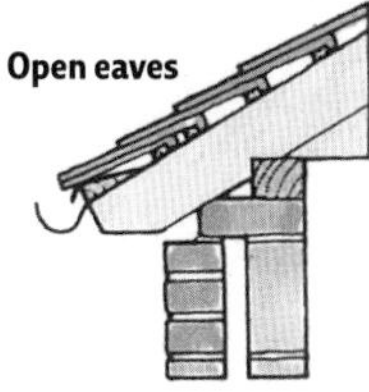

Closed eaves

Projecting rafters are sometimes clad with a fascia board grooved to take a soffit, enclosing the eaves. If the loft is insulated, a roof with closed eaves must be ventilated (see right).

Closed eaves

Eaves vents
Various types of vent are available for fitting above or below the fascia board to provide ventilation for an insulated roof.

The verge

The verge can end flush with the gable wall or project over it. With a flush verge, the end rafter fits inside the wall but the roof covering extends over it. A projecting verge is constructed with the roof timbers extending beyond the wall to carry an external rafter with a barge board fixed to it. To enclose a projecting verge, there is often a sloping soffit board behind the barge board.

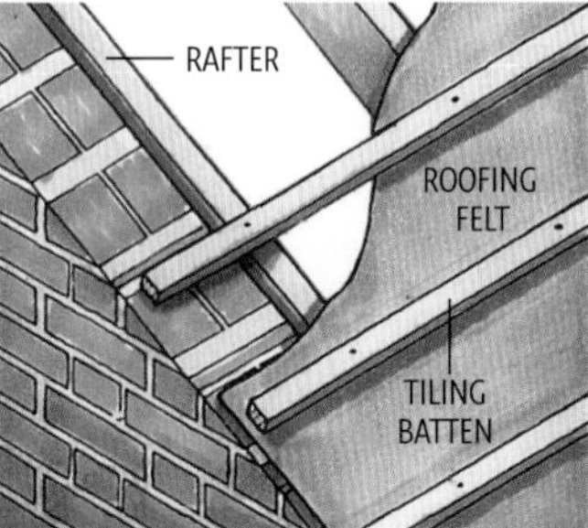

Flush verge

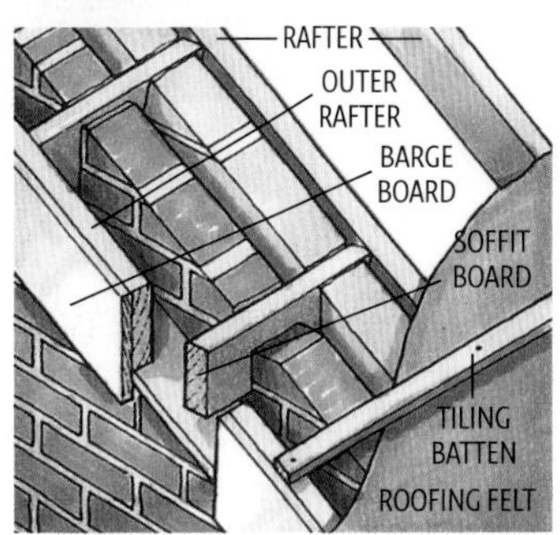

Projecting verge

SEE ALSO > Walls 138–55, Pitched roof coverings 123–4, Roof battens 124

Checking your roof structure

The timber structure of a roof can fail over time as a result of timber decay caused by poor weatherproofing, condensation or insect attack. It can also suffer from overloading if the original roof covering has been replaced using materials that are too heavy for the structure. This shows up as undulations across the surface of the roof slopes, and sometimes the ridge can sag along its length as well. Although a sagging roof is often visible from street level, it is better to inspect the structure closely from inside.

Inspecting your roof

Use an inspection lamp to check the roof

Inspect your roof annually to check that it's still weatherproof and that there is no woodworm infestation. Unless there's a window in the loft, buy a powerful torch or rig up a mains-powered extension lead with a caged lamp. In an unboarded attic, place planks across the joists to walk on.

It is a good idea to inspect your loft in different weather conditions. A check after a period of heavy rain will reveal any water penetration via defects in the structure, and a check in cold winter weather will show whether condensation within the roof space is a serious problem.

Strengthening a roof

A sagging roof will not necessarily require bracing if the structure is sound and weatherproof. Old houses with slightly sagging roof lines are often stable, but you should consult a surveyor if you suspect that your roof is weak.

The walls under the eaves should be inspected for bulging and checked with a plumb line. Bulging tends to occur where window openings are positioned close to the eaves. However, it is sometimes caused by an inadequately braced roof structure that is spreading and pushing the walls outwards. If this is the case, call in a roofing contractor to do the repair work.

A lightly constructed roof can be strengthened by adding extra timbers. The method depends on the type of roof, its span, loading and condition. It may be possible to add bracing from inside, provided the new timbers are not too large.

Damp, rot and infestation

Check the tile battens on an unfelted roof

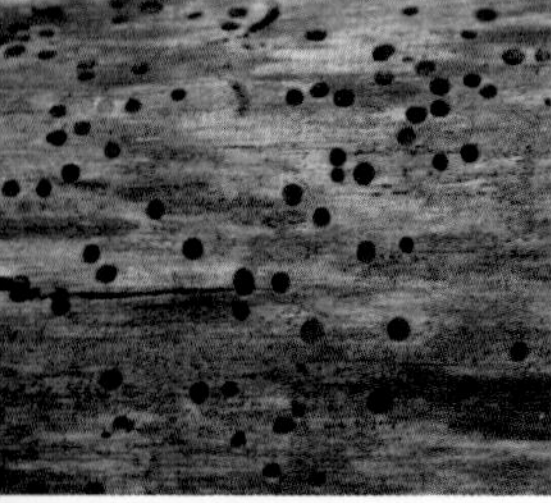

Check for woodworm damage to the timbers

If you find any damp patches on the roof timbers, small areas of sodden loft insulation or any evidence of rotten wood, inspect the underside of the roof slope closely in daylight. On a felted roof, look for tears or holes in the felt. If it is not felted, you will be able to see the roof battens and the undersides of the tiles or slates. Check whether any are visibly damaged or displaced, allowing light in.

Remember that on a pitched roof, water may penetrate at a higher level and run down the rafters, so the site of the leak may not be immediately obvious. If you find rot close to an abutment wall, the flashing may have failed.

Another frequently occurring cause of rot is long-term condensation in the roof space. If the loft floor is insulated, the most obvious evidence of this is damp or sodden insulation occurring over a wide area rather than in smaller, localized spots; it may even stain ceilings below. Better ventilation of the roof space is usually the remedy. Take expert advice from a roofing contractor about how best to provide this.

Rot in the roof structure is a serious problem which should be rectified by experts. When you employ contractors to treat the rot, get them to carry out any necessary structural repairs as well. Their rot treatment work will be covered by a guarantee, which could be invalidated if you attempt to deal with these yourself.

Serious woodworm infestation also needs to be treated by professionals. Severely infested wood may have to be replaced, and the whole structure will have to be sprayed with an eradicator. Again, the work will be guaranteed.

Water penetration can lead to serious rot damage

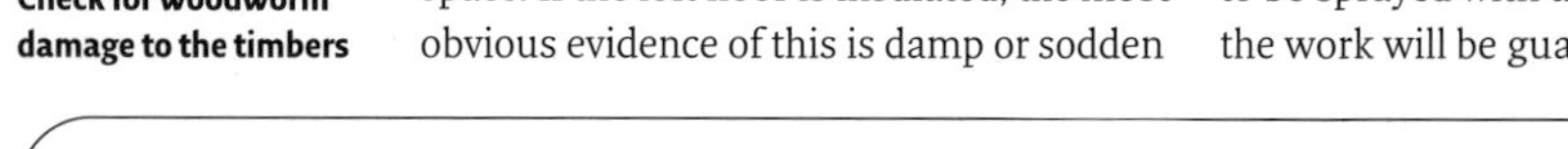

SEE ALSO > Pitched roofs 120–1, Flashings 132–3, Guttering 134–7, Treating woodworm 242, Wet and dry rot 245, Ventilation 273–80

Pitched roof coverings

Coverings for domestic pitched roofs follow a long tradition, but despite the development of new materials the older ones have not changed radically. Materials used for roofing were generally of local origin, leading to a great diversity of coverings. For centuries they were hand-made and had their own characteristics, visible in various regional styles.

During the late nineteenth century, mass production took over for the more durable roofing materials such as tiles and slates, and regional diversity began to be lost as the developing railway network carried them across the country.

Roof coverings are manufactured by moulding clay, mineral particles or concrete into various profiles or by splitting natural materials such as slate or stone into thin, flat sheets.

Today, concrete tiles are the most widely used roof covering, for several reasons. They are cheaper than clay tiles; they can be laid at a shallower pitch (slope angle); and the larger types can be laid more quickly. Clay and concrete tiles are hard to distinguish when they are first laid, but over time concrete tiles tend to weather and fade more quickly than clay ones.

Slate, the favourite roof covering on Victorian houses, is now as expensive as top-quality plain clay tiles. Cheaper imported slates are available, but they are of variable quality. There are also several man-made slate substitutes on the market. The cheapest are made from fibre cement; better types are made from reconstituted slate dust.

Most roofing materials are laid across the roof in courses (rows), so that the bottom of each course overlaps the top of the one below. Alternate rows are offset by half the width of the tile or slate, creating a waterproof covering. Each alternate row is started with a half-width tile or slate to maintain the offset. They are laid course by course, working from the eaves up the slope of the roof to the ridge.

Specially shaped tiles are available for capping the ridge and hips, to weather-proof the junctions of the slopes. Where the roof covering meets a wall or chimney, the junction between the two is protected with flashing, usually made of lead or mortar. The former is far more durable.

Types of roofing

Tiles and slates are rectangles made in a range of standard sizes. Most are plain, but pantiles are available in both clay and concrete and there is a wide range of profiles in interlocking concrete tiles.

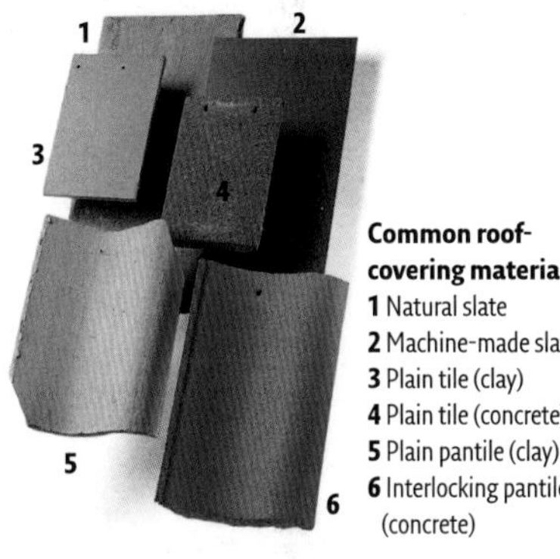

Common roof-covering materials
1 Natural slate
2 Machine-made slate
3 Plain tile (clay)
4 Plain tile (concrete)
5 Plain pantile (clay)
6 Interlocking pantile (concrete)

TYPICAL COVERINGS FOR PITCHED ROOFS

TYPE OF COVERING	Material	Common sizes	Finish	Colour	Fixing	Approx weight kg/m²	Minimum pitch in degrees
NATURAL SLATE	Split metamorphic sedimentary rock	Length: 400 to 600mm Width: 200 to 300mm	Natural	Natural Blue Grey Green	Two nails	27.5 to 70	17.5°
MACHINE-MADE SLATE	Fibre cement or slate dust	Length: 500, 600mm Width: 250, 300mm	Acrylic coating	Grey Blue/Black Brown Terracotta Mottled Heather	Two nails plus copper-disc rivet	20 to 21	20°
STONE SLAB	Split sandstone or limestone sedimentary rock	Random sizes and as natural slate	Natural	Natural	Two nails	90	20°
	Machine-made concrete	Length: 200 to 550mm Width: 100 to 500mm		Weathered buff		84 to 110	25° to 30°
PLAIN TILE	Hand-moulded or machine-moulded clay or machine-made concrete	Length: 265mm Width: 165mm	Sanded Smooth	Brown Red Grey Blue Green	Two nails or loose-laid on nibs	64 to 87	35°
INTERLOCKING TILE	Hand-moulded or machine-moulded clay or machine-made concrete	Length: 380, 410, 430mm Width: 220, 330, 380mm	Sanded Smooth Glazed	Red Brown	Loose-laid on nibs, nailed or clipped	40 to 57 depending on profile	22.5° (clay) 12.5° to 30° (concrete)

SEE ALSO >Roof-covering systems 124–5, Roof maintenance 126–7, Flashings 132–3, Ventilation 273–80, Fixings 532–6

Roof-covering systems

If you are going to make roof repairs yourself, you will need some knowledge of the roof-covering system used on a common pitched roof. This will also be of help if you have to commission contractors, either for repairs or extensive reroofing, as you will benefit from an understanding of the work to be carried out.

Tile clip

Nailed tile clip

Eaves clip (flat)

Eaves clip (contoured)

Verge clip (flat)

Copper rivet

Felt underlay

To comply with the Building Regulations, new or re-covered pitched roofs must be lined with a weather-resistant felt underlay, commonly called sarking.

The underlay was traditionally a reinforced bituminous felt, but this is now being superseded by various types of breathable membrane. The underlay presents a barrier to any moisture that penetrates the outer covering, and also improves the roof's insulation value. Breathable types allow water vapour in the roof space to pass through them, so help to combat condensation problems.

Like roofing tiles, the sarking is laid horizontally, working up the slope of the roof from the eaves, each strip being overlapped by the one above it.

Roof battens

The roof covering is supported on sawn softwood battens that are nailed across the rafters, over the sarking. The battens are pretreated with a preserver. When the roof is close-boarded, there should be vertical counterbattens fixed to the top edges of the rafters, under the horizontal battens, in order to provide ventilation under the tiles and to allow any moisture to drain freely down the roof.

The battens are nailed over the sarking

Close-boarded roofs should have vertical counterbattens

Fixings

Most roof coverings are fixed in place with nails or clips. Slates are all fixed individually, usually with a pair of nails placed halfway up each slate – although sometimes they are nailed near the top. Modern fibre-cement slates are fixed with two centrally placed nails and a copper rivet to hold down the tail (see left).

Roof tiles are made with nibs on the back that hook over the battens. With some types, this is all that holds them on the roof, apart from their weight. Others are fixed with nails or clips. The number of fixings used is determined by the type and size of tile, the pitch of the roof, and the prevailing weather conditions.

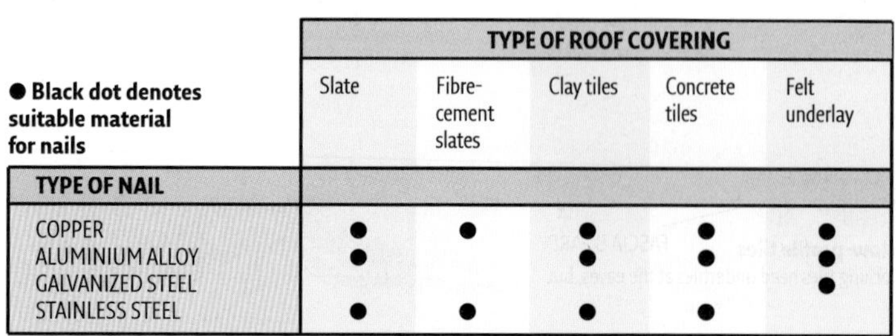

● **Black dot denotes suitable material for nails**

TYPE OF NAIL	Slate	Fibre-cement slates	Clay tiles	Concrete tiles	Felt underlay
COPPER	●	●	●	●	●
ALUMINIUM ALLOY	●		●	●	●
GALVANIZED STEEL					●
STAINLESS STEEL	●	●	●	●	

Lapping coverings

Double-lap coverings

Plain tiles and slates are 'double-lap' coverings. This means that at any point on the roof each vertical joint has a whole tile or slate both below and above it. The upper one covers the upper part of the joint, and any water penetrating the exposed lower part runs off the surface of the tile or slate beneath it.

Tiles and slates are essentially flat sheets laid with their side edges butting together, not overlapping. The joints are staggered on alternate courses.

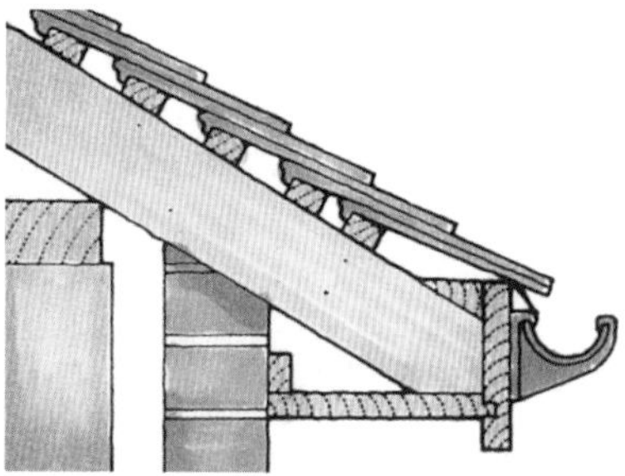

Double-lap covering

Single-lap coverings

Nearly all tiles made of moulded clay or concrete are single-lap coverings, which means that each tile overlaps its neighbour on one side and each course just overlaps the one below. This type of tile is made with ridges and grooves along the long edges that interlock when the tiles are laid, to prevent moisture penetrating the joint. Earlier single-lap roof coverings, such as clay pantiles, used the curved shape of the tile to form a weatherproof overlap at the edges.

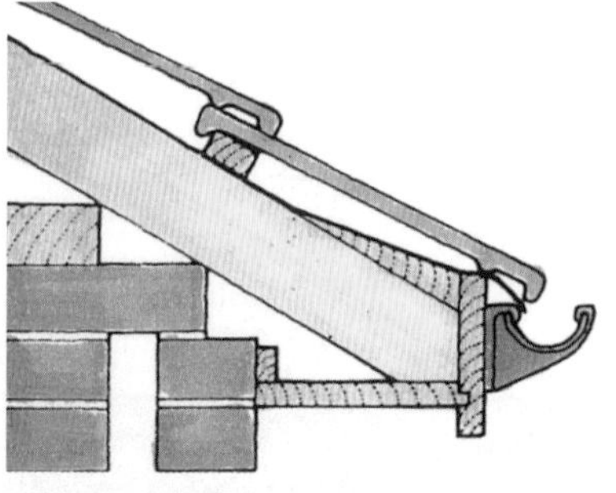

Single-lap covering

SEE ALSO > Types of roofing 123, Roof maintenance 126–7

Hips

The junction between adjacent roof slopes is weatherproofed in one of three ways: with hip tiles; with overlapping hip bonnet tiles; or in slates, with a close-mitred hip.

Hip tiles

The hip is covered with a row of butt-jointed tiles, similar to ridge tiles but often with a slightly different profile. They are bedded on mortar and supported at the eaves with a metal hip iron, which is nailed to the end of the hip rafter.

Bonnet hip tiles

These small shaped tiles are used to cover the hip on roofs laid with plain tiles, and match the courses in which the roof tiles are laid. Each bonnet hip tile is bedded on mortar and secured to the hip rafter with a single nail.

Close-mitred hip

The end slate in each course is cut so it meets its neighbour on the adjoining roof slope precisely over the centre line of the hip rafter. To waterproof the open joint, lead soakers are fixed to the rafter beneath and are concealed as the next course of slates is laid.

Edge details and junctions

If the verges, eaves and valley edges are constructed properly, your roof will be thoroughly weatherproof. Well-detailed edges and junctions also add to the overall appearance of a roof.

Verges

The verge is usually formed by laying an 'undercloak' of plain tiles or slates bedded onto the masonry or – in the case of an overhanging verge – nailed to the timber frame. The roof covering is then bedded in mortar on top of the undercloak and finished flush.

Special dry-fixed verge tiles are available for use with single-lap concrete tiles and fibre-cement slates.

Eaves

The detailing at the eaves depends on the type of roof covering. Plain tiling begins with a course of short undertiles, nailed to a batten and projecting 38 to 50mm (1½ to 2in) beyond the fascia board. The first course of whole tiles is laid with staggered joints over the undertiles, with their tail edges flush. Similarly, when the covering is natural slate a double course is laid at the eaves – in which case, a course of short slates is covered by a course of full ones.

With fibre-cement slates, a third nailed course is laid beneath the double course in order to support the tail rivets used with this type of covering.

Single-lap low-profile tiles are usually laid directly over and supported by the fascia board. However, some types, such as pantiles, are backed up with an undercloak of plain tiles.

Valleys

Double-lap roof coverings of plain tiles may use shaped valley tiles (see right) or, as with slate, they may be formed into so-called swept or laced valleys. The latter are difficult and expensive to make. Most valleys are formed as open gutters, using a sheet metal or glass fibre lining. Single-lap roofing may have sheet metal valleys or interlocking trough tiles (see below).

Verge detail at ridge
The ridge tile is set flush with the verge and its end is filled with bedding mortar. One or more small pieces of tile are sometimes set into this mortar.

• Dry fixings
Tile manufacturers have in recent years introduced various dry systems for securing verge, ridge and hip tiles. They use a variety of mechanical fixings – a low-maintenance alternative to mortar bedding. They are, however, more expensive.

Valley tiles
Valleys on plain-tiled roofs may be laid with shaped valley tiles that course with the roof tiles, instead of having a sheet metal gutter.

Verges
An undercloak course projects slightly and gives a neat finish to a verge.

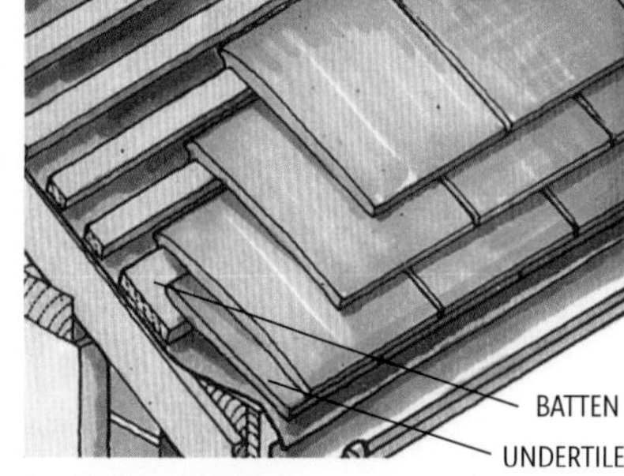

Double-lap plain tiles
The undertiles are nailed to a batten. The joints between them are covered with full tiles.

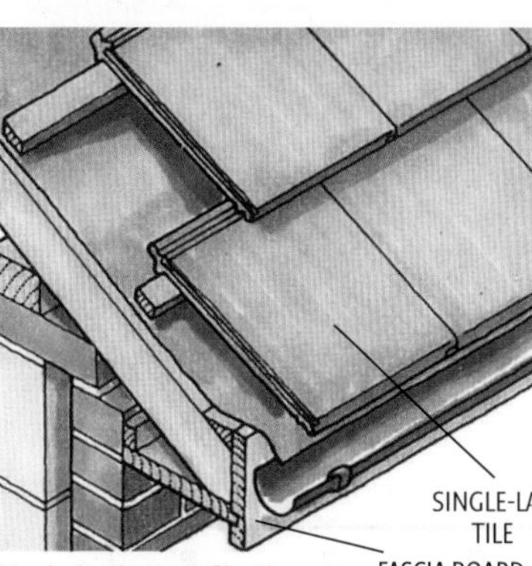

Single-lap low-profile tiles
Not all interlocking tiles need undertiles at the eaves, but the fascia board must support the eaves course at the correct angle.

Trough tiles
Roofs laid with single-lap tiles may have valleys formed with matching interlocking trough tiles.

SEE ALSO >Types of roofing 123, Flashings 132–3, Work platforms 514–6

Maintaining a pitched roof

Roof coverings have a limited life. How long they last depends on the quality of the materials and workmanship and exposure to severe weather. An average roof might be expected to give good service for 40 to 60 years – but certain types of material can last for 100 years or more, although some deterioration of the fixings and flashings is inevitable. To retain the character of your roof, if possible reuse the old materials.

Patch repairs may be of limited value; and once patching becomes a recurrent chore, it's time for the roof to be re-covered. This involves stripping off the original material and possibly reusing it, if it is in sound condition, or perhaps replacing it with a new covering similar to the old. Major roof work is not something you should tackle yourself. A specialist contractor can do it more quickly than you can, using safe and suitable access equipment, and will also guarantee that the work is carried out to a professional standard.

Reroofing sometimes qualifies for a repair grant, so check with your local authority to see if you are eligible before carrying out any work. Most grants are now available only to groups such as the elderly or disabled. Planning permission will not be required unless you live in a listed building or a conservation area.

Inspecting the roof

The roofs of older houses are likely to show their age and should be checked at least once a year. Start by taking a look at the roof from ground level. Slipped tiles or slates can usually be spotted easily. The colour of any newly exposed unweathered tile or slate will also pinpoint a fault.

Look at the ridge against the sky to check for misalignment and gaps in the mortar jointing. Follow this with a closer inspection through binoculars, checking the state of the flashings at abutments and around the chimney.

From inside an unlined roof, you will be able to spot chinks of daylight that indicate breaks in the covering. Use a torch to check the roof timbers for water stains; they may show as dark or white streaks. Trace the stain along the rafters to find the source of the leak.

Replacing a roof tile

Individual tiles can be difficult to remove because of the retaining nibs on the back of the top edges and their interlocking shape, which holds them together.

To remove a plain tile, lift the nibs clear of the batten then pull it out. This is easier if you raise the overlapping tiles first, using wooden wedges inserted at both sides of the broken tile. If the tile is also nailed, try rocking it loose. If this fails, you will have to break it out carefully. You may then have to use a slater's ripper to extract or cut any remaining nails.

Use a similar technique for a single-lap interlocking tile, but in this case you will also have to wedge up the tile to the left of the one being removed so you can lift the tile clear of the interlock.

If you are removing tiles in order to put a roof vent in, then you can afford to smash the one you are replacing. Use a hammer to do so, taking care not to damage any of the adjacent tiles. The remaining tiles should be easier to remove once the first is removed.

Obtain a suitable replacement tile and slide it into place, engaging its nibs over the roofing batten underneath the course of tiles above. Remove the wedges you used earlier.

Lift overlapping tiles with wedges

Lift the interlocking tile above and to the left

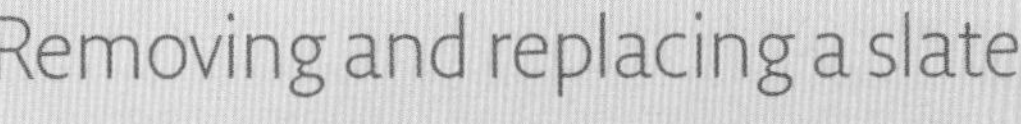

Removing and replacing a slate

A slate may slip out of place because the nails have corroded or because the slate itself has split. Whatever the cause, slipped or broken slates should be replaced as soon as possible, before a high wind lifts the neighbouring slates and strips them off the roof.

Use a slater's ripper to remove the trapped part of a broken slate. Slip the ripper under the slate and locate its hooked end over one of the fixing nails (**1**), then pull down hard on the tool to extract or cut through the nail. Remove the second nail in the same way. Even where an aged slate has already slipped out completely, you may have to remove the nails in the same way to allow the replacement slate to be inserted.

You will not be able to nail a new slate in place because the batten to which the original slate was nailed is covered by the slates in the course above. Instead, use a copper strip, a plastic clip, or cut a strip of lead, 25mm (1in) wide, to the length of the slate lap plus 25mm (1in). Attach the strip to the batten by driving a nail between the slates of the lower course (**2**), then slide the new slate into position and turn back the end of the lead strip to secure it (**3**).

1 Pull out nails

2 Nail strip to batten

3 Fold strip over edge

Temporary repair

If a slate has cracked or slipped out of position, you can fix it back in place temporarily with a strip of self-adhesive flashing tape. Apply the primer to the surface of the slate and bed a length of tape into it to secure the slate in place.

SEE ALSO > Flashings 132–3, Ventilating the roof space 275, Slater's ripper 513, Roofing nails 532

Rebedding ridge tiles

When the old mortar breaks down, a whole row of ridge or hip tiles can be left with practically nothing but their weight holding them in place.

Lift off the ridge tiles and clear all the crumbling mortar from the roof and from the undersides of the tiles. Soak the tiles in water before refixing them.

Mix 1 part cement : 3 parts sand, to make a stiff mortar. Load a bucket about half full and carry it onto the roof. Dampen the top courses of the roof tiles or slates and lay a thick bed of mortar on each side of the ridge, following the line left behind by the old mortar (**1**). Lay mortar for one or two tiles at a time.

Press each ridge tile firmly into the mortar and use a trowel to slice off mortar that has squeezed out. Try not to smear any on the tile itself.

Build up a bed of mortar to fill the hollow end of each ridge tile, inserting pieces of tile or slate to prevent the mortar slumping (**2**). Press the next tile in place, squeezing out enough mortar to fill the narrow end joint flush (**3**).

Build a similar mortar joint between an end ridge tile and a wall or chimney stack.

1 Apply bands of mortar on each side

2 Insert pieces of slate in the mortar

3 Press the next tile in place

Working safely

Working on a roof can be hazardous, and if you feel insecure working at that height you should hire a contractor.

Access

If you decide to do it yourself, don't use ladders alone to reach the roof. Hire a sectional scaffold tower and scaffold boards to provide a safe working platform complete with toe boards.

Roof coverings are fairly fragile and may not bear your weight - hire special roof ladders to gain access. A roof ladder must be able to reach from the scaffold tower to the ridge of the roof and hook over it. Wheel the ladder up the slope and then turn it over to engage the hook over the ridge.

Roof ladders are made with rails that keep the treads clear of the roof surface and spread the load - but if you think the roof covering is in poor condition, use additional padding in the form of sacks stuffed with paper or filled with sand to help spread the load further.

Tool safety

Carry your tools in a tool belt; and if you have to put them down, do so within the roof-ladder framework. When you finish work, make sure you bring every tool down from the roof.

Roll a roof ladder up to the ridge

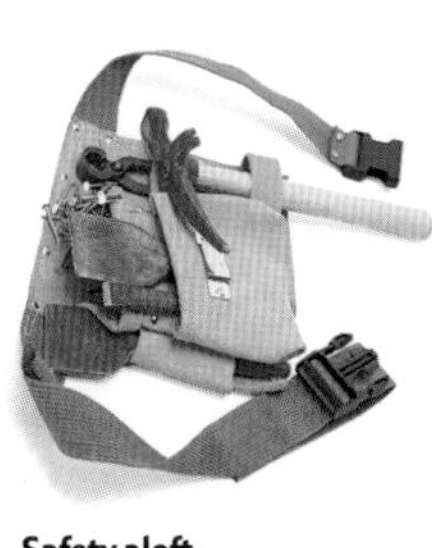

Safety aloft
A tool belt leaves your hands free so you can climb safely onto a roof.

Then turn the ladder over to engage the hook

Scaffold tower
Set up a hired scaffold tower next to the house wall so it reaches eaves level. This will provide safe access onto the roof slope and its deck can be used for stacking materials.

Repairing verges

Where tiles overhang a gable wall, the joint is filled with mortar. This can crack or fall out with age, allowing water in. You can seal small cracks with roof-and-gutter sealant, applied with a cartridge gun.

If the damage is more extensive, chip away the old mortar, using a chisel and club hammer, then brush away the dust. Mix up some prepacked bricklaying mortar, using water to which you have added PVA bonding agent (mixed 1:5 with the water).

Dampen the verge with water from a garden spray gun. Press the mortar firmly into the gap between the roof tiles and the undercloak, then smooth it off flush.

Fill the gap with mortar and finish it flush

Repairing metal valleys

The sheet metal used to line many valley gutters may split or develop holes as a result of corrosion, allowing rainwater to penetrate and run down the hip rafters inside the roof.

You can repair splits in metal valleys using self-adhesive flashing tape. First, clean the damaged area with a wire brush and medium-grade wet-and-dry abrasive paper. Then brush the flashing primer onto the cleaned metal and leave it to become tacky.

Cut a strip of flashing tape long enough to cover the damaged area, peel off the backing tape and press it onto the primer. Rub it down well with a cloth pad or a wallpaper seam roller.

If the valley has become porous due to corrosion, you can waterproof it temporarily by coating its entire length with a bitumen waterproofing compound. Clear the valley of debris and wire-brush the metal surface to remove dirt, then apply a generous coat of waterproofer.

Press the strip of tape down onto the primer

SEE ALSO > Roof coverings 124–5, Flashings 132–3, Ladders 514–15

Flat roofs

Timber-framed flat roofs are often used for rear extensions and outbuildings. Most have joists carrying stiff wooden decking, and these usually cross the shorter span of the roof. The joists may be fixed to a timber wall plate on loadbearing walls or supported by metal joist hangers. Metal restraint strips tie the ends of the joists down to the outer walls.

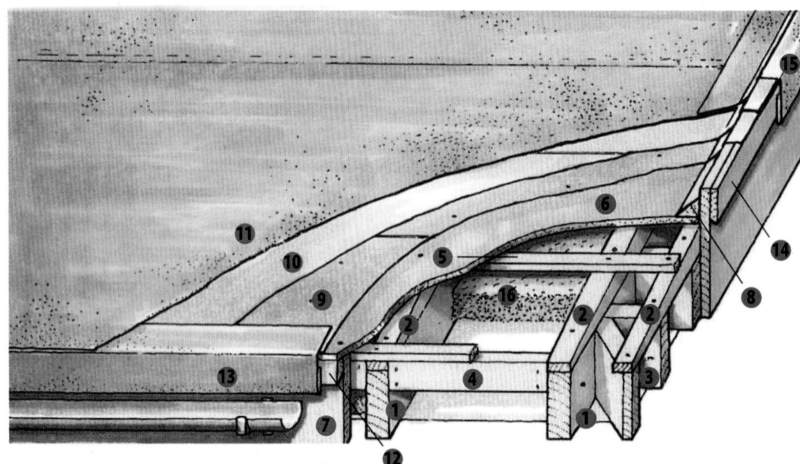

The components of a flat roof
1 Joists
2 Furring
3 Return joist
4 Nogging
5 Counterbattens
6 Decking
7 Fascia board
8 Angle fillet
9 First felt layer
10 Second felt layer
11 Cap sheet
12 Eaves drip batten
13 Felt eaves drip
14 Verge drip batten
15 Felt verge drip
16 Insulation

Furring methods

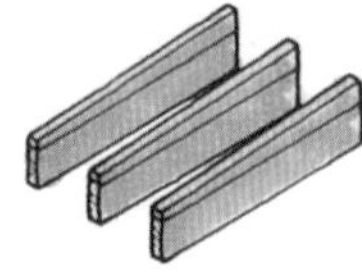

1 Tapered furrings fixed in line with joist.

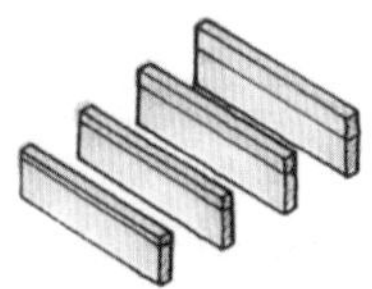

2 Furrings strips of decreasing size fitted across the fall.

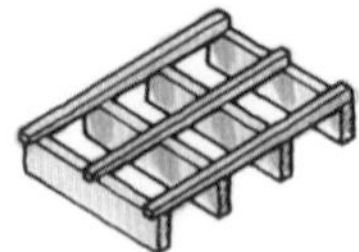

3 Tapered furrings fixed across joists.

Establishing the fall

The fall of a flat roof should be at least 1:80 for smooth surfaces like metal or plastic, and 1:60 for coarser materials such as roofing felt. The fall is designed to shed water – but if the slope is too shallow, puddles will form. Thermal movement of the decking can then cause the covering to break down and let standing water through.

To achieve the required fall, tapered strips of wood called furrings are nailed to the tops of the joists (**1**). Alternatively, the joists may be set across the line of the fall, with parallel furring strips of decreasing thickness nailed to them (**2**); or tapered strips may be fixed across them (**3**). The latter provide better cross-ventilation of the roof void. Counterbattens also provide ventilation for an internally insulated roof.

Roof decking

Either exterior WBP (weather-and-boil-proof) plywood or another type of exterior-grade man-made board is fixed to the joists to make a flat base for the roof covering. Older flat roofs were usually decked with tongue-and-groove softwood boards.

The panels – normally 18mm (¾in) thick – are laid with their longer edges running across the joists; their ends are centred over a joist for support. The butt joints should be staggered. Timber noggings may be fitted between the joists to give extra support to the longer edges of the panels, depending on their thickness and the joist spacing.

For a felted roof, you could start with prefelted decking. This surface-treated board is laid with 3mm (⅛in) gaps between the panels to allow for thermal expansion, and is fixed down with either nails or screws. If you are unable to apply a felt covering straightaway, this type of decking can be temporarily waterproofed by sealing the gaps between the boards with a cold-bonding mastic and then covering the joints with roof-sealing tape.

Covering the deck

Whatever type of decking is used, it must be fully waterproofed either with asphalt or with layers of roofing felt (see right).

To reflect some of the sun's heat, the roof can be coated with special paint or covered with a layer of pale-coloured chippings 12mm (½in) thick.

Flat-roof coverings

Bitumen-based coverings fall into two types: asphalt and bituminous felt. Felt coverings are now generally used for domestic buildings, instead of the more expensive lead, zinc or copper coverings seen on some older houses.

Mastic asphalt

This waterproof material, made from bitumen, weathers very well. It is melted in a cauldron and, while hot, spread over the roof. When set, it forms an impervious layer. Laying it is a skilled professional job.

Roofing felts

These bitumen-impregnated sheet materials are applied in layers to produce 'built-up' roofing. The layers may be bonded to each other with hot or cold bitumen, or may be self-adhesive. Several types are available (see chart opposite).

The choice will affect a roof's cost and longevity. British Standard (BS 747) felts are classified by their base material and finish, indicated by a number and letter. A colour strip identifies the base material at a glance. Traditional felts are not as tough as modern high-performance ones, which are made from bitumen reinforced with either glass-fibre or polyester fabric.

Making a roof of this kind with hot bitumen is best left to professionals. You could lay felt with a cold bitumen adhesive, but nowadays it's easier to use self-adhesive felt laid in two layers.

Dry-laid roof coverings

Butyl and EPDM roof coverings are single-ply flexible membranes that promise much longer life than roofing felts. They are simple to lay and provide a strong, maintenance-free covering.

One type is made to order in one piece, with fixing flaps welded to the underside of the sheet so that intermediate nail fixings won't penetrate the covering. Another is self-adhesive, and is bedded down into a coat of special primer. Its overlapping joints are heat-sealed, using a hot-air gun and a steel roofing roller.

SEE ALSO > Strutting 172–3, Renewing a felt roof 130, Flat-roof repairs 131, Roof insulation 261–4, Fixings 532–6

Abutments and parapets

Leaks can occur wherever a flat roof abuts a house or parapet wall. The roof covering is therefore usually turned up the wall to form a skirting, which may be covered by coping stones on top of the wall or tucked into the mortar bed of the brickwork or covered by flashing.

Parapet walls are particularly prone to damp, so the top edge is usually finished with a brick, stone or tile coping, which should overhang the faces of the wall to throw off rainwater. In addition, a damp-proof course is set in the mortar bedding beneath the coping (1).

A parapet wall that is no more than 350mm (1ft 2in) high may have an asphalt skirting taken up the face and continued under the full width of the coping (2) to form a damp-proof course. Alternatively, the roof covering is taken up two courses of bricks only and built into the wall to form the DPC (3).

Often, a flexible damp-proof course, such as lead or high-performance felt, is set in the bed joint before the roofing is laid and then dressed down to form a flashing over the skirting (4).

Relatively tall cavity walls will need a cavity-wall tray, in order to prevent water penetrating and running down the inside. The tray is formed by taking the damp-proof course up in a step from the inside leaf across the cavity to the outer leaf (5).

LEAD FLASHING
FELT SKIRTING

A dressed flashing normally laps the skirting

1 Solid and cavity walls need DPCs under copings

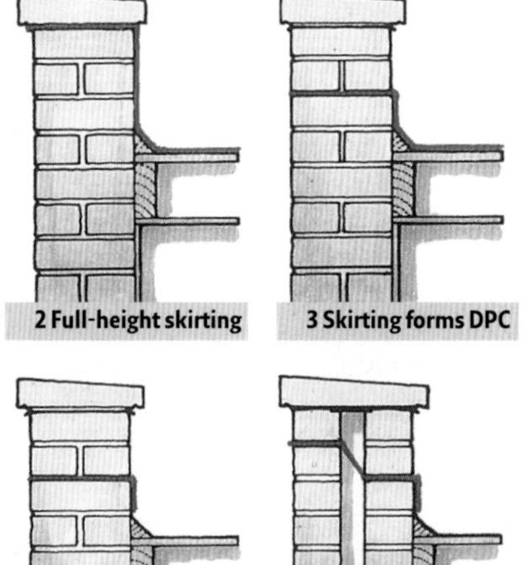

2 Full-height skirting

3 Skirting forms DPC

4 Flashing DPC

5 Cavity-tray DPC

Filling a cavity tray

A cavity wall abutted by an extension roof needs a cavity tray to protect it from damp. Normally this would be built-in, but for a new extension added onto an existing building, special cavity-tray units can be inserted from the outside by removing a course of bricks.

Moulded cavity trays
Straight and angled sections are available from most builders' merchants.

Inserting the units

Remove three bricks from the third course above the proposed roof level. Then lay a length of lead flashing wide enough to project 50mm (2in) into the wall and also to cover the roof skirting by 75mm (3in) when it is dressed down. Trap the flashing with the first tray unit, pushing it into one end of the opening (1). Lay two bricks in the tray (2), then fill the top joint with mortar. Leave a weep hole at the base of the joint between the bricks to drain moisture from the cavity.

Cut out two more bricks, leaving a three-brick opening (3). Roll out the flashing and insert a second unit. Join the two units with the clip provided (4). Lay two more bricks in the opening. Continue in this manner until the cavity tray is long enough to protect your new extension. Once the mortar is firm, point the new work to match the existing wall.

1 Trap the flashing

2 Replace two bricks

3 Cut out two bricks

4 Join the two trays

Felt type British Standard ref.	Base	Surface finish	Colour code	Weight	Properties and uses
BITUMINOUS FELTS FOR FLAT ROOFS					
BS 747 1B BS 747 1E	Fibre Fibre	Sand Mineral	White White	15kg (33lb) 15kg (33lb)	Least expensive type. Relatively weak. Good for roofing outbuildings. Not recommended for permanent buildings.
BS 747 3B BS 747 3E	Glass fibre Glass fibre	Sand Mineral	Red Red	18kg (40lb) 32kg (70lb)	Rot-proof, inexpensive, unsuitable for nailing. Good for 2-layer or 3-layer systems.
BS 747 3G	Glass fibre	Grit underside Sand topside	Red	26kg (57lb)	Perforated first layer for partial-bonding systems using hot bitumen.
HIGH-PERFORMANCE FELTS					
NO *BS NUMBERS*	Glass/polyester Glass/polyester	Sand Mineral		36kg (79lb) 28kg (62lb)	Rot-proof, tough, good weathering. Can be nailed. Use for 2-layer or 3-layer systems.
BS 747 5U BS 747 5B BS 747 5E	Polyester Polyester Polyester	Sand Sand Mineral	Blue Blue Blue	18.5kg (41lb) 20-42kg (44-92lb) 36-47kg (79-104lb)	More expensive than glass/polyester, but better performance. Use for 2-layer or 3-layer systems. Excellent for house extensions.
Elastomeric	Polyester Polyester Polyester	Sand Mineral Mineral		32kg (70lb) 40kg (88lb) 38kg (84lb)	Most expensive, but superior durability makes it long-lasting and cost-effective. Use for 2-layer or 3-layer systems. Excellent for house extensions.

SEE ALSO > Flashings 132–3, Ventilating the roof space 261–4

Renewing a felt roof

Applying a built-up felt system, which involves using hot bitumen, and 'torching' (using a gas-powered torch to soften bitumen-coated felt) is a technique best left to professionals. However, a competent amateur can confidently replace the old felt on a garage roof using a two-layer self-adhesive roofing system. The following example describes how to roof a detached garage with a solid-timber deck.

1 Overlap the underlay

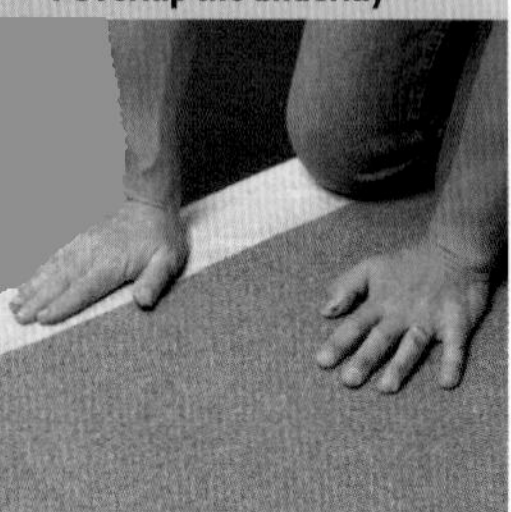
2 Lay the first top strip

3 Overlap the second strip

4 Bond the overlap

Replacing perished felt

Wait for dry weather, then strip off the old felt. Pull out any clout nails, and check the deck for damaged boards. Replace any you find, using galvanized wire nails to hold the new ones in place. Check the condition of the fascia boards, verge upstands and drip battens; and renew them if necessary.

To provide a smooth, flat surface for the self-adhesive felt underlay, nail an exterior-grade plywood decking, 6mm (¼in) thick, over the boards.

Preparing the surfaces

Cut hardboard formers for the eaves and verge drips (see far right). Apply special roofing-system primer to all surfaces to be covered, including the formers and any wall abutments.

Applying the underlay

Measure the length of the roof along the gutter edge, including the verge upstands at each end. The covering is laid at right angles to the slope of the roof. Measure and cut sufficient lengths of felt to cover the roof. If you need to join pieces end to end, allow a 75mm (3in) overlap where the ends meet.

Cut the first strip in half lengthways, so you will be able to stagger the joins when you lay the top layer of felt. Lay one of the half-width lengths flat on the roof, level with the gutter edge. Roll one end of this strip back to the centre of the roof and then, using a sharp craft knife, carefully cut across the release-paper backing that protects the felt's adhesive surface. Peel back the release paper, then roll out and press the underlay back onto the deck, pushing out any trapped air. Roll back the other half of the strip and repeat the procedure.

Lay the other strips working up the slope of the roof in a similar way, overlapping the first and subsequent strips by 50mm (2in) along their length (1). Cut and lap internal corners, and press them down with a steel roofing seam roller. If the covering meets a wall, take it up to form a skirt covering the first two courses of brickwork.

Applying the top layer of felt

Before laying the top layer, prepare and fit the eaves drip (see right). Measure the length for the roof between the verge upstands and cut the required number of strips to cover the area of the roof. Following the procedure used for the underlay, but starting with a full-width strip, lay the plain edge of the first length 50mm (2in) back from the gutter edge (2). There is a self-adhesive band along the top edge for bonding the next strip.

Lay the next length lapping the one below (3). Peel off the release paper from the adhesive band and bond the joint (4).

Use mastic to bond the top sheet where it laps the eaves, and also to join short lengths where they overlap. Cut the verge drips (see right) and bond them to the top sheet with mastic.

Making roof drips

Drips are used at the eaves and verge to shed rainwater clear of the walls.

Eaves drips

Cut felt strips 1m (3ft 3in) long. To calculate their width, measure the depth of the drip batten and add 25mm (1in), then double this and add at least 100mm (4in). Cut 50mm (2in) from one corner. Cut hardboard formers around which to fold the strips. Nail the felt to the drip batten, then nail on the formers. Fold each of the strips back over the former and bond it onto the underlay (1).

Cutting the corners

Where the drip meets the verge, cut the corners to cover the end of the upstand (2). Fold and bond the tabs.

Verge drips

Cut and fix the verge drips next. Cut the strips 1m (3ft 3in) long and calculate their width as with the eaves drip. Cut and fold the end of the first strip at the eaves (3); nail the strip then the former, and bond the remainder in place (4).

At the rear corners, cut and fold the strip covering the side verge (5). Cover the rear verge last, cutting and folding the corners to lap the side pieces (6).

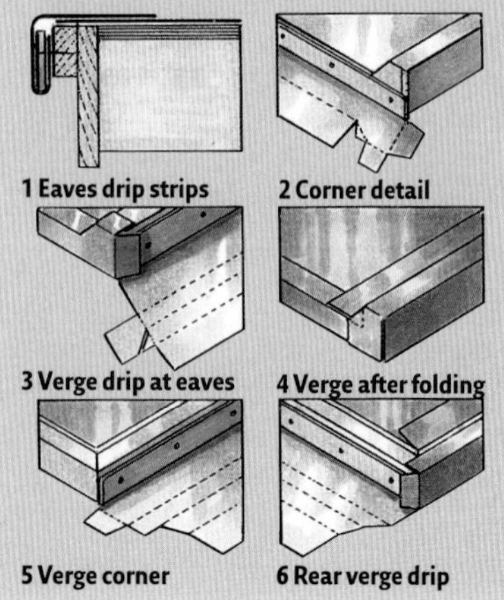
1 Eaves drip strips
2 Corner detail
3 Verge drip at eaves
4 Verge after folding
5 Verge corner
6 Rear verge drip

Fitting a dry-laid roof covering

Dry-laid roofing
Brush the old roof clean then:
1 Lay a felt underlay.
2 Nail covering to drip battens.
3 Nail down fixing flaps.
4 Attach cover trims.

Butyl and EPDM are tough rubber-based roofing materials that can be used for new roofs or to provide a watertight covering over an old felted roof.

One-piece types are fixed to the roof with special nails driven through welded-on fixing flaps, These flaps are concealed as the covering is laid (see left). Others are self-adhesive, and are laid in a similar way to roofing felt. The lengths are bonded to the roof deck with special primer.

To lay one-piece types over old felt, simply brush the surface of the felt clean and cover it with a loose-laid underlay felt. Nail drip battens all round the roof. Nail the sheeting to one of the battens, then unfold it and, if it is provided with fixing flaps, nail them to the roof. Fold the other edges over and nail them to the drip battens, taking care not to stretch the covering. Finally, finish the edges of the roof by attaching cover trims.

SEE ALSO > Fixings 532–6, Felt types 128, Flashings 132–3, Guttering 134–7, Roof insulation 261–4

Repairing a flat roof

The best approach for repairing a flat roof depends not only on its age and general condition but also on the extent of the damage. You can tackle minor repairs yourself – but if the covering has deteriorated across a wide area, then it may be best to call in a contractor and have the roof completely re-covered.

Fault-finding

If flat roofs are allowed to deteriorate, they inevitably leak. Damp patches on the ceiling are a clear sign that the roof needs attention, though the source of the problem is not always so obvious.

Locating the leak

If damp patches are close to a wall against which the roof abuts, the flashing has probably failed. However, a leak anywhere else in the roof may be hard to find, as the water can run downhill from its entry point before dripping onto the ceiling. Measure the distance between the damp patch and the edges of the ceiling, then locate the same point on the roof surface and work from there up the slope to find the source.

Splits and blisters

Splits and blisters on the smooth surface of an asphalt or bitumen-felt covering may be obvious, but chippings on the covering can obliterate the cause of a leak. Use a blowtorch or hot-air paint stripper to soften the bitumen, so that you can scrape the chippings away. The surface must be smooth if it is to be patch-repaired.

Splits in the covering caused by movement of the substrate can be recognized by the lines they follow. Press blisters formed by trapped moisture to locate pinholes or other blemishes, which will show up as the moisture is expelled. These must be sealed with patches. You can leave an undamaged blister for the time being, but deal with the cause as soon as possible.

Patch repairs

Localized damage such as small splits and blisters can be repaired with specialized materials. Their effectiveness relies on good adhesion, so take care to clean the roof surface thoroughly. If visible from above, a patched roof can be an eyesore, but you can improve its appearance with reflective paint or with bitumen and chippings.

Dealing with splits

You can use self-adhesive repair tapes to mend splits in all types of roof coverings. First remove any chippings, then clean the split and the surrounding surface. Fill a wide split with a mastic compound before taping. Apply the special primer supplied with the tape over the area to be covered, and leave it for an hour. Even where only a short split has occurred along a joint in the board substrate, prepare the whole line of the joint for covering with tape.

Peel back the protective backing and apply the tape to the primed surface (1). If you are repairing short splits, cut the tape to length first – otherwise, unroll the tape as you work along the repair. Press it down firmly and, holding it in place with your foot, roll it out and tread it into place as you go. Cut it off at the end of the run. Ensure that all the edges are sealed (2).

1 Apply the tape

2 Press tape firmly

Dealing with blisters

Any blisters in an asphalt or felted roof covering are best left alone unless they contain water or have been causing the covering to leak.

To repair a blister in an asphalt roof, heat the area with a blowtorch or hot-air stripper and, when the asphalt is soft, try to press the blister flat with a block of wood and a hammer. If the blister contains water, cut into the asphalt to open the blister up, and let the moisture dry out. Apply gentle heat before pressing the asphalt back into place. Work roof-repair mastic into the opening before closing it, then cover the repair with a patch of self-adhesive repair tape.

On a felted roof, make two intersecting cuts across a blister (1) and peel back the covering. Heating the felt will make this easier. Dry and clean out the opening, apply bitumen adhesive (2), and when it's tacky nail the covering back into place with galvanized clout nails (3).

Cover the repair with a patch of roofing felt, bonded on with bitumen adhesive; cut the patch to lap at least 75mm (3in) all round. Alternatively, you can use self-adhesive repair tape.

1 Open up felt blisters

2 Add mastic under tongues

3 Nail tongues down

Treating the whole surface

A roof that has already been patch-repaired and is in poor condition can be given an extra lease of life by means of a liquid waterproofing treatment.

One type of treatment uses a cold-applied bitumen-based emulsion that can be reinforced with an open-weave glass-fibre membrane.

First sweep the roof, then treat the surface with a fungicide to kill off any traces of lichen and moss. Following the manufacturer's instructions, apply a coat of primer and leave to cure.

Apply the first coat of waterproofer with a brush or broom then lay the glass-fibre fabric into the wet material and stipple it with a loaded brush. Overlap the edges of the fabric strips by at least 50mm (2in) and bed them down well with the waterproofer.

Allow the first coat to dry before brushing on the second. When the last coat becomes tacky, cover it with fine chippings. If you plan to apply a solar-reflective coating, let the waterproofer dry thoroughly.

• Condensation
Condensation can be a serious problem within flat roofs. If warm moist air permeates the ceiling, the vapour condenses under the cold roof and encourages rot in the roof timbers. It will also saturate any blanket insulation in the roof space, rendering it useless. In this case, upgrade the ceiling with a vapour barrier and fit some type of ventilation. Otherwise, have the roof re-covered and include new insulation at the same time.

SEE ALSO > Organic growth 42, Abutments and parapets 129, Flashings 132–3, Condensation 250–51, Ventilating the roof space 261–4, Hot-air stripper 481, Gas torch 521

Flashings

Flashings are used to weatherproof junctions between the roof and other parts of a building. Typically, these occur at abutments with walls and chimneys, and where one roof meets another.

Flashing materials

The most common flashing materials are lead, zinc, roofing felt and mortar fillets. Of all these materials, lead is by far the best, because it weathers well and is easily worked. It can be applied in any situation and to any type of roof covering.

Zinc is a cheaper substitute for lead, but it is not so long-lasting, nor so easy to work into shape. It's worth using lead whenever a zinc flashing needs replacing. In return for the extra outlay, the new flashing will last considerably longer.

Bitumen felt may be used for flashings on felted roofs, but it cannot be shaped easily and so is normally used for the more simple cover flashings that overlap the skirtings of felt roofs.

Mortar flashings, sometimes with inset cut tiles, are common on the pitched roofs of older houses. Although they tend to shrink and cause problems later, mortar flashings are still used, as they are cheap and easy to apply.

Where flashing is used
Places where flashing is commonly fitted on pitched and flat roofs.
1 Valley
2 Apron
3 Wall abutment
4 Parapet abutment
5 Chimney abutment

Apron flashing

The head of a lean-to roof is weatherproofed with a lead apron flashing, with its top edge pointed into a mortar joint two courses above the roof. The lead is dressed down onto the roof and should overlap the roof covering by 150mm (6in) or more.

Special moulded flashing units are available for use with corrugated-sheet roofing. These are shaped to fit the contour of the corrugated material. Plastic types have flat hinged upstands that can be adapted to fit any roof slope. The upstand is either lapped with a lead flashing or sealed with self-adhesive flashing tape.

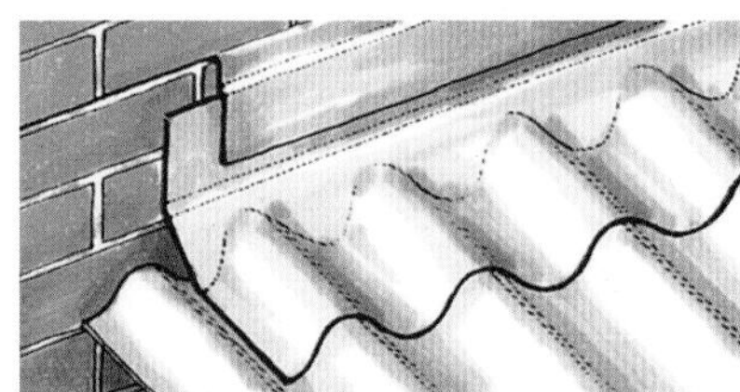

Moulded apron flashing for corrugated roofing

Flashing construction

Double-lap flashing

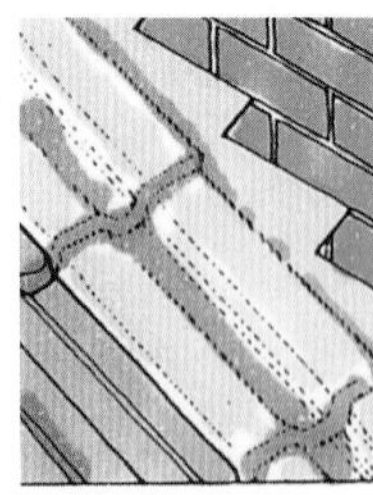

Single-lap flashing

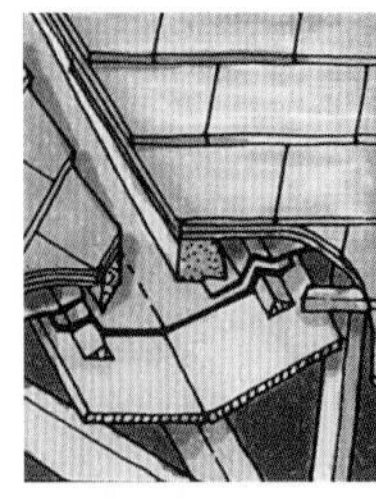

Valley flashing

The design of a flashing is determined by the particular details at the roof/wall junction and by the materials used. Three common situations are described here, using lead as the flashing material.

Double-lap flashing

Slate or plain-tiled roofs with a pitch of 30 degrees or more normally use soakers and a cover flashing. Soakers are lead or zinc pieces, equal in length to a tile's overlap, folded at right angles lengthways. The part that lies on the tiles should be at least 100mm (4in) wide and the upstand 75mm (3in); the back edge turns down over the tile's top edge. A soaker is laid over the end tile or slate as a course is laid. The upstand lies flat against the brickwork and is lapped by a stepped flashing dressed down over it. The top edges of the flashing are turned into the bed joints, held by lead wedges and pointed with mortar or mastic.

Single-lap flashing

Contoured single-lap tiles can be treated at abutments with a one-piece flashing. The lead is tucked into the brick wall, using the stepped method, and dressed down over the tile. The amount of overlap depends on tile contour and roof pitch; on a shallow pitch, it should be at least 150mm (6in). The lead is dressed to the tile's shape and the step at each course, and its free edge is carried over the nearest raised tile contour.

Valley flashing

Some tiled roofs have valley tiles that take the tiling into the angle, but most tiled and slated roofs have metal valley flashings made by laying a lead lining on boarding that runs from eaves to ridge, following the angle of the valley.

The lead is dressed over wooden fillets nailed to the boarding to form an upstand. Where two valleys meet at the ridge, a lead saddle is formed. The edges of the tiles or slates are cut to follow the angle of the valley and to leave a gap of no less than 100mm (4in) between them.

Slate coverings should overhang the supporting valley fillet by 50mm (2in). Contoured tiles should be bedded in mortar and finished flush with the edge of the tiles to form a watertight gutter.

Chimney flashing

The flashing where a roof meets a chimney is similar to that at an abutment, but there are junctions all round the stack.

An apron flashing is fitted at the front. The upstand is folded round the corner onto the sides of the stack, and its top edge set in a joint in the brickwork.

Stepped flashings are fitted to the sides of the stack. At the back, there's a timber-supported back gutter. Its front edge is turned up the back face of the stack, and its ends are folded over the side flashings. Its back edge is lapped by the tiles. A separate cover flashing is dressed over the upstand at the rear of the stack.

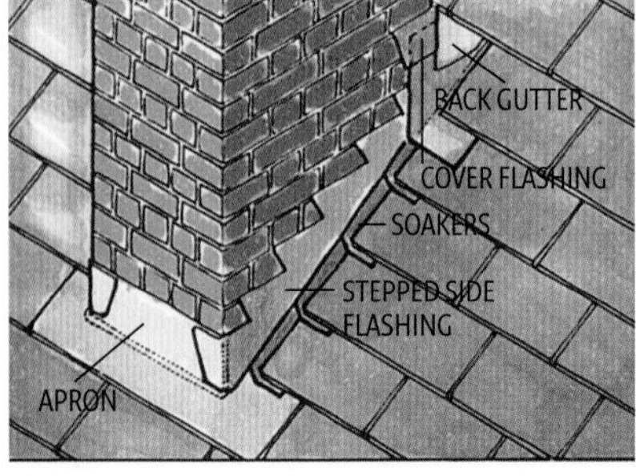

Chimney flashing for a slate roof

SEE ALSO > Repointing masonry 43, Roof coverings 123–4, Valley tiles 125

Flashing repairs

There are many problems associated with flashings, generally caused by the flashing corroding or a breakdown of the joints between the flashing and the structure of the house. A perished flashing should be stripped out and replaced. If this requires craft skills, the work should be done by a specialist contractor – but in many cases leaks are caused by shrinkage cracks, which you can repair with mastic or self-adhesive flashing tapes.

Sealing mortar fillets with mastic

Mortar fillets often shrink away from wall abutments. If the fillets are otherwise sound, you can simply fill the gap with a gun-applied flexible mastic. If possible, choose a colour that matches the fillet. Brush the surfaces to remove any loose material before injecting the mastic. Fill the crack generously to ensure a good seal.

Applying flashing tape

Prepare the surfaces by removing all loose and organic material. A broken or crumbling cement fillet should be made good with mortar.

Make sure that the surfaces are dry. If necessary, apply a primer (supplied with some tapes) to the roof and wall surfaces about an hour before you use the tape (1).

Cut the tape to length, and peel away the protective backing as you press the tape into place. Finally, rub over the surface of the tape with a cloth pad, applying firm pressure to exclude any air trapped beneath it (2). Make sure the edges are firmly stuck down.

1 Apply a primer with a 50mm (2in) paintbrush

2 Press tape with a pad to exclude air bubbles

Repointing a flashing joint

Rake out joint and repoint with fresh mortar

Metal flashings that are tucked into masonry often work loose when the old mortar becomes badly weathered.

If the flashing is otherwise sound, rake out the mortar joint, tuck the lead or zinc back into it, and wedge it there with rolled strips of lead spaced about 500mm (20in) apart. Then repoint the joint (alternatively, you can apply a mastic sealant).

While you have your access equipment in place, rake out and repoint any failed mortar joints in the adjacent brickwork.

Patching lead flashing

Lead doesn't readily corrode, but splits can occur where it has buckled through expansion and contraction. Flashing tape can be used to repair lead, and you can mend a split with solder. For a more substantial repair, it is possible to cut away a weak or damaged portion and join on a new piece of lead by 'burning' or welding. However, this is a job for a specialist, not one you can do yourself.

Repairing glazed roofs

Traditional porches and timber-framed conservatories and greenhouses all tend to suffer from leaks caused by a breakdown of the seal between the glass and glazing bars. Minor leaks should be dealt with promptly, because trapped moisture can lead to timber decay and expensive repairs.

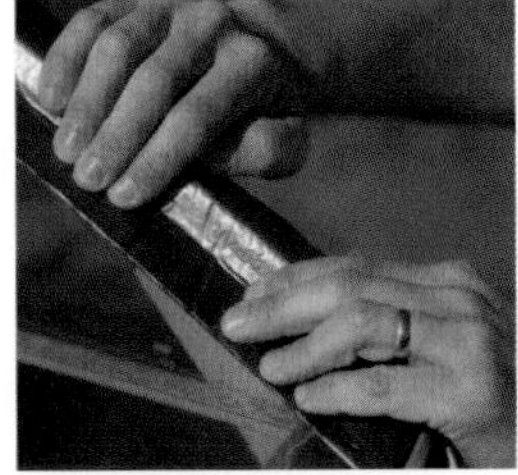

Mould the tape over the glazing bar

Using aluminium tape

You can waterproof glazing bars with self-adhesive aluminium tape.

Clean out the old putty from both sides of the glazing bars and let the wood dry out, then apply wood primer or linseed oil. When the primer is dry, fill the rebates with putty or mastic.

The tape must be wide enough to cover each glazing bar and lap the glass on each side by about 18mm (¾in). Start at the eaves and work up the roof, moulding the tape to the shape of each glazing bar and excluding air bubbles.

At a step in the glass, cut the tape and make an overlap. Mould the cut end over the stepped edge, then start a new length, lapping the stuck-down end by 50mm (2in).

At the ridge, either cut the tape to butt against the framework or lap onto it. Cover the ends with tape, applied horizontally. Where a lean-to roof has an apron flashing, tuck the tape under it.

The tape can be painted to match the woodwork or left its natural colour.

Taping cracked glass

To make a temporary repair to cracked glass, you can use clear self-adhesive waterproofing tape. Clean the glass and apply the tape on the outside, over the crack. If you apply the tape promptly, it will make an almost invisible repair.

Self-adhesive waterproofing tape can also be used to seal the overlap on translucent corrugated-plastic roofing.

SEE ALSO > Primers 40–41, Repointing masonry 43, Glass 195, Mastic guns 481

Guttering

Guttering and downpipes collect the rainwater that runs down your roof and discharge it into a drain. A well-installed and efficient system helps prevent damp finding its way into the house.

Moulded ogee guttering in a period setting

Roof drainage

The size and layout of a roof-drainage system should be designed to collect and discharge all the water from a given roof area efficiently. If you need to replace all or part of an old system, make sure you install components of the same size as the existing ones, or perhaps slightly larger.

If you are installing a new system on an extension, measure the roof area it is to serve and take the figures to your supplier, who will advise you on the correct gutter and downpipe sizes to install.

Types of rainwater guttering

The guttering on houses is adapted in various ways to suit the design of the roof.

Eaves gutters

Most houses have gutters fixed to the fascia boards along the eaves of the roof which discharge rainwater directly into a series of downpipes. They are made in many materials and designs (see below).

Parapet gutters

Older houses with raised parapet walls have wooden gutters lined with lead or asphalt that drain the roof behind the parapet. They often discharge through openings in the wall into decorative hopper heads and downpipes.

Valley gutters

Valley gutters are either tiled or lead-lined wooden gutters, used at the internal junctions between adjacent sloping roofs. They direct the rainwater either into eaves gutters or into parapet gutters.

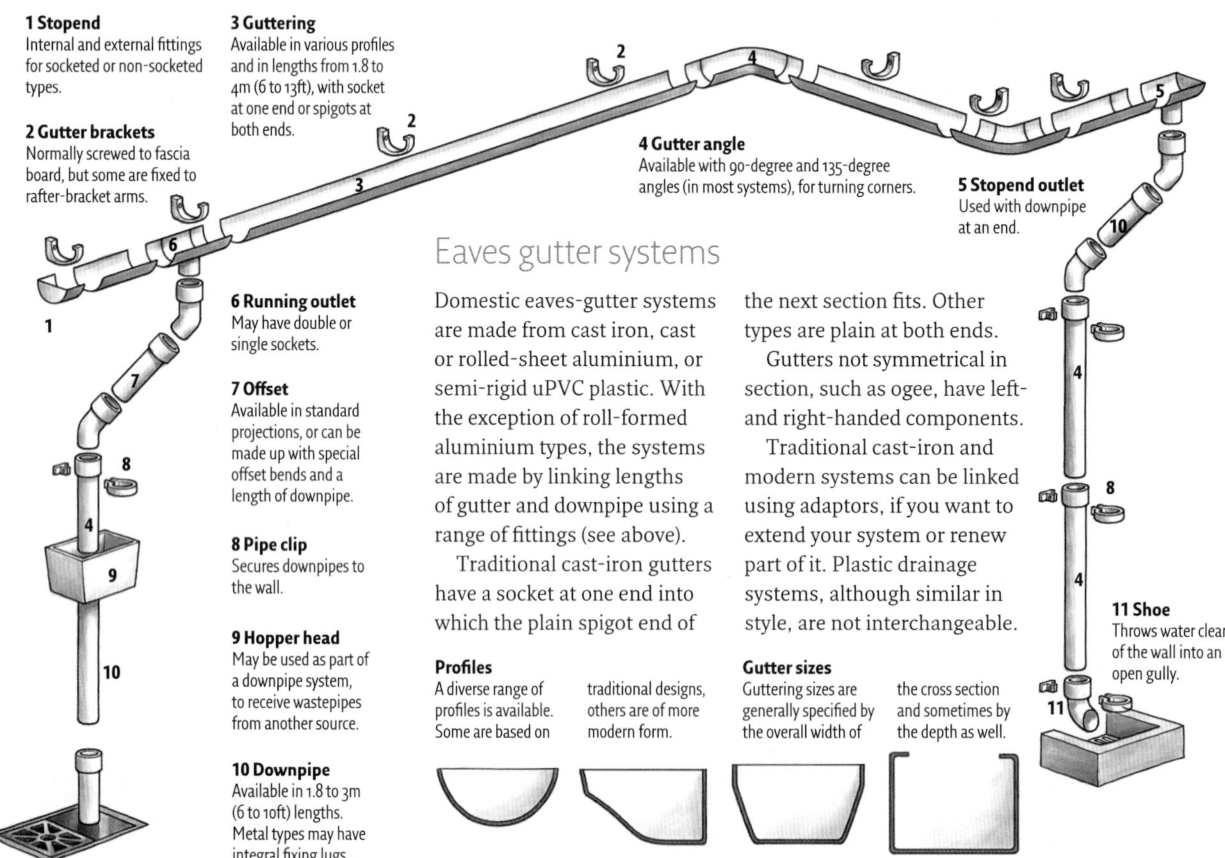

Eaves gutter systems

Domestic eaves-gutter systems are made from cast iron, cast or rolled-sheet aluminium, or semi-rigid uPVC plastic. With the exception of roll-formed aluminium types, the systems are made by linking lengths of gutter and downpipe using a range of fittings (see above).

Traditional cast-iron gutters have a socket at one end into which the plain spigot end of the next section fits. Other types are plain at both ends.

Gutters not symmetrical in section, such as ogee, have left- and right-handed components.

Traditional cast-iron and modern systems can be linked using adaptors, if you want to extend your system or renew part of it. Plastic drainage systems, although similar in style, are not interchangeable.

Profiles
A diverse range of profiles is available. Some are based on traditional designs, others are of more modern form.

Gutter sizes
Guttering sizes are generally specified by the overall width of the cross section and sometimes by the depth as well.

SEE ALSO > Valleys 125, Fitting guttering 136–7, Ladders 514–15

Guttering materials

Plastic guttering is widely available from the larger DIY outlets, but you will need to go to a builders' merchant for most other types – or even to an architectural salvage company to match cast-iron guttering.

Cast iron

The cast-iron rainwater systems that are often found on old houses are mostly of the ogee (OG) type. They are fixed to the fascia board with short mushroom-headed screws that pass through the back of the gutter above the water line.

Each 1.8m (6ft) standard length of the guttering has a socket end into which the plain 'spigot' end of the next piece fits (**1**). Short bolts secure the joint, and a bed of putty forms a seal when the bolts are tightened (**2**).

Cast iron is both heavy and brittle, so installing or dismantling such a system needs two people. The iron can be cut with a hacksaw and drilled with twist drills in a power tool.

The guttering needs regular painting, and a bituminous paint applied inside helps to preserve the metal. If it is left unprotected, it will rust – usually along the back edge, around the screws. Badly rusted guttering should be replaced, as it's likely to collapse.

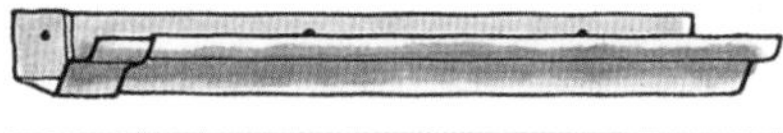

1 A standard gutter has a socket at one end

2 The joint is sealed with putty then bolted

Cast aluminium

Cast-aluminium guttering comes in a wide range of profiles. It is assembled in a similar way to cast-iron guttering, with bolted joints; but a flexible mastic is used, instead of putty, to make the seals. The guttering may be fitted to the fascia with screws through the back or with gutter brackets, and the fixings should either be sherardized or plated with zinc or cadmium. Cast aluminium is much lighter than cast iron – it is only about a third of the weight – and can be left unpainted, although in some situations it will corrode. If this type of guttering is used to replace part of a cast-iron system, all the aluminium surfaces must be protected with zinc phosphate or with a bituminous paint to prevent corrosion.

Rolled-sheet aluminium

Rolled-sheet aluminium guttering is a moulded lightweight system made from thin, prepainted flat-sheet aluminium, which is roll-formed to the gutter shape by a portable machine. This is done on site by the suppliers, and continuous lengths are made to measure. The stopends and angles are supplied as separate items and crimped to the ends of the gutter sections. Outlets are formed by forming holes in the bottom. Simple metal fixing brackets are clipped to the front and back edges of the guttering and attached to the fascia with drive screws.

The metal will not corrode, but you can paint it to improve its appearance.

Unplasticized PVC

Unplasticized PVC (uPVC) is now the most widely used type of guttering, both for new buildings and for replacing older systems. Available in a range of profiles and sizes, it is self-coloured and so does not need painting.

The various lightweight systems employ either clip-fastened joints or unions with in-built synthetic-rubber gaskets to form the watertight seals. Downpipe joints may be push-fit, solvent-welded or sealed with an O-ring. The guttering is supported by brackets; but with some systems, the joint unions, outlets and angle fittings are attached to the fascia board with screws, to provide additional support.

Maintaining guttering

Cast-iron and cast-aluminium guttering sections are rigid and may support a ladder; but it's much safer to use a ladder stay or, better still, a scaffold tower. Never be tempted to prop a ladder against either plastic or roll-formed aluminium gutters.

Inspect and clean out gutters regularly. Gutters concentrate dirt and sometimes collect sand washed down from the tiles by rain. This builds up quickly if the flow of water is restricted by leaves or twigs. Birds' nests can effectively block the guttering or downpipes, too.

The weight of water standing in plastic guttering can distort it; and if a blockage causes the gutter to overflow, damp may penetrate the wall below.

Avoiding damage
Use a ladder stay to hold a ladder away from the gutter so you do not damage it.

Removing debris

First block the gutter outlet with a rag. Using a shaped piece of plastic packaging, scrape the silt into a heap, scoop it out with a garden trowel, and deposit it in a bucket hung from the ladder. Sweep the gutter clean with a stiff handbrush. Remove the rag, and flush the gutter with a bucket of water. Fit a mesh guard along the guttering, or a wire or plastic balloon in the end of the downpipe, to prevent a blockage in the future.

Avoiding blockages
Fit a metal or plastic balloon into a gutter outlet to prevent the downpipe being blocked.

Repairing leaking joints

You can repair joints in metal gutters using roof and gutter mastic applied with a cartridge gun. Plastic gutters have flexible seals. Identify your brand of gutter from the markings on it, and obtain a matching replacement. Prise out the old seal and fit the new one.

Snow and ice
Plastic guttering can be badly distorted by the weight of snow and ice. If you can reach it safely, try dislodging the build-up with a broom from an upstairs window. If that's not a possibility, you will have to climb a ladder to remove it. If you find snow and ice are a regular seasonal problem, fit a snow board to the fascia so it projects above the gutter.

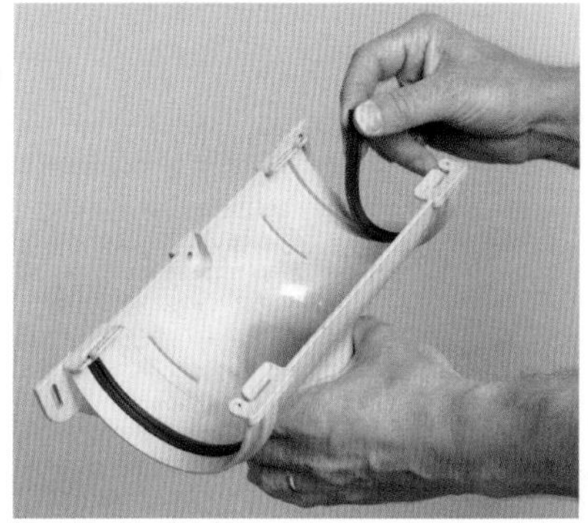

Prise out the old seal and fit a replacement

Seal metal joints with mastic

SEE ALSO > Primers 40–41, Finishing metalwork 82–3, Ladders 514–15

Fitting new guttering and downpipes

When your rainwater system reaches the end of its useful life, if possible replace it with one in the same style. Removing the old system and installing the new one is a two-person job. Make sure you have two ladders available that are long enough to reach the eaves and, ideally, fitted with ladder stays.

Estimating quantities

Measure round the base of the house walls to determine the total length of gutter required. Measure the downpipe lengths from a ladder. Choose the brand of rainwater system you want to install, and find out what gutter and downpipe lengths are available.

The commonest sizes are 3m (10ft) for gutters and 2.5m (8ft) for downpipes. From these, work out how many lengths of each you will need. Also note the number and type of brackets and fittings required to replace the existing system.

Positioning outlets and brackets

With the aid of a plumb line, mark the position of each gutter outlet (directly over the existing gullies) on the fascia board (**1**).

At the upper end of each gutter run, tap a nail into the fascia board just below the level of the eaves tiles. Tie string to it and pull it to the other end of the gutter run. Lower this end to give a fall of at least 25mm (1in) in 15m (50ft), then fix another nail at this level and tie the string to it. Screw the gutter outlet (or its support bracket) to the fascia (**2**), level with the lower end of the string and aligned with the mark you made on the fascia.

Fix a gutter bracket at the high end of the run, level with the string (**3**). Fix the rest of the brackets to follow the slope of the string, spacing them no more than 1m (3ft 3in) apart (**4**).

System components
Check that you have sufficient guttering and downpipe for the installation – plus all the necessary brackets and connectors.

Fitting the gutter

Start work at the top end of the run. Tuck the back edge of a length of gutter under the roofing felt and into the rear lips of the brackets, then attach the front of each bracket in turn (**5**). Add a stopend (**6**).

Fit a union bracket to the other end and connect the second length of guttering (**7**). Compress the rubber seal firmly, and leave a 6mm (¼in) expansion gap between the end of the gutter and the shoulder of the bracket. Clip the gutter into its brackets.

1 Use a plumb line to mark the outlet position

2 Fix the outlet to the fascia board

3 Fit a gutter bracket at the high end of the run

4 Fit the other brackets to a sloping string line

5 Fit the highest length of gutter into its clips

6 Add a stopend to it

7 Fit a union bracket and add the next length

8 Cut the final length to size with a panel saw

SEE ALSO > Fascia board 121, Guttering materials 135, Hacksaws 518

Cutting the gutter to fit

You will almost certainly have to cut the final length of gutter to fit between the last union bracket and the outlet. Measure the distance between them, mark the gutter and cut it squarely with a panel saw (**8**). File the cut end smooth and fit it into place (**9**).

Turning corners

Use the principles described here to set out and fit gutter runs that turn internal or external corners. Make sure that falls are maintained, and fit the appropriate type of corner angles as required.

Connecting to existing guttering

Renewing guttering on a terraced house may entail joining your system to your neighbour's. Left-hand and right-hand adaptors are available to link existing metal or plastic gutters to new systems.

Remove the old guttering to the nearest joint between the houses. Bolt the adaptor on, sealing the joint with mastic, then fix the new plastic gutter into it.

9 Fit the last length into the running outlet

10 Fit the top downpipe and measure the offset

Fitting the downpipes

Work downwards from the gutter outlet. If the eaves overhang, you will need to make up an angled connection, called an offset, between the outlet and the downpipe.

Fit a clip to the top of a length of downpipe. Hold it against the wall and measure the distance from its centre to a plumb line dropped through the centre of the outlet (**10**). You may be able to buy an offset to fit, but you will probably have to make one up with two offset bends and a short length of pipe. Assemble it dry and test its fit at the outlet. When you are happy that it will reach the downpipe, bond the parts together with solvent-weld cement. Assemble the offset on a table, to ensure that the bends lie in the same plane.

Fit the offset to the outlet, and the downpipe to the offset (**11**). Adjust the pipe so that the clip's backplate falls on a mortar joint. Mark the fixings, drill and plug the wall, then fix the pipe and clip with plated roundhead screws.

Mark and fix the lower lengths of pipe in the same way, with a 6mm (¼in) expansion gap between each pipe and the socket shoulder. Fit extra clips at the centre of pipes more than 2m (6ft 6in) long. Cut the lowest pipe section to length, and fit an angled shoe to its bottom end if it discharges over an open gully (**12**). If the pipe is jointed into a back-inlet gully (**13**) or a drain socket, you may have to work upwards from the bottom.

11 Make up the offset and fit it in place

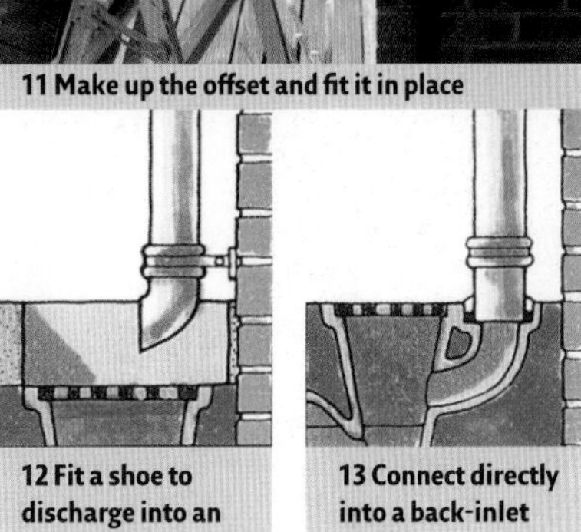

12 Fit a shoe to discharge into an open gully

13 Connect directly into a back-inlet gully

Saving rainwater

If you want to save rainwater for your garden, fit a plastic diverter into the downpipe and connect it, via a filler tube, to an adjacent water butt.

How the diverter works

There are various diverters available, but they all work on much the same principle. Water running down the inside of the downpipe is collected in a circular channel and diverted into a filler tube that runs to the water butt. When the butt is full, the channel overflows into the lower section of the downpipe and into the drain.

Fitting a diverter is a straightforward job. Decide where you want the filler pipe, mark and cut the downpipe (**1**) and slip the diverter into place (**2**). Then connect the filler tube to it (**3**).

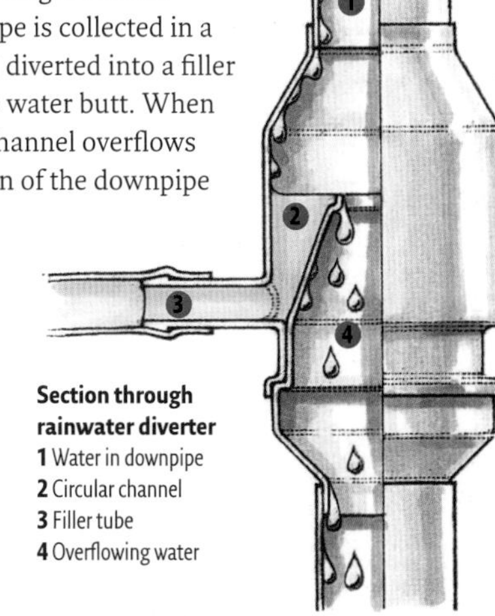

Section through rainwater diverter
1 Water in downpipe
2 Circular channel
3 Filler tube
4 Overflowing water

1 Remove a short section of the downpipe

2 Fit the diverter into the downpipe

3 Connect the filler pipe to the diverter

SEE ALSO > Fascia board 121, Guttering materials 135, Hacksaws 518

External walls

Typically, solid external walls are made of brick, blocks or natural stone. All provide good sound insulation, but traditional materials and methods of construction do not retain heat efficiently. Cavity walls, which have been widely used since the 1920s, are more effective in preventing moisture penetration and heat loss.

How solid walls are built

Solid walls are generally built from bonded brickwork or concrete blocks, although local natural stone is also found in many areas. The walls are usually at least 225mm (9in) thick – the length of a standard brick – but are sometimes a brick and a half thick if exposed to severe weather conditions.

Moisture resistance

Evaporation prevents moisture from penetrating to the inside surface of a solid wall; rainwater absorbed by the masonry is normally drawn out before it reaches the inner surface. Moisture is prevented from being absorbed from the ground by an impervious damp-proof course (DPC), usually consisting of bituminous felt, set in a mortar joint of the brickwork at least 150mm (6in) – two brick courses – from ground level.

Weatherproofing qualities

Many solid walls are cement-rendered, or otherwise clad, to weatherproof the brickwork. Thick exterior-grade concrete blocks can be left exposed, but their appearance and performance is improved by rendering. Natural stone walls are usually left bare – so weatherproofing relies solely on the thickness and density of the material.

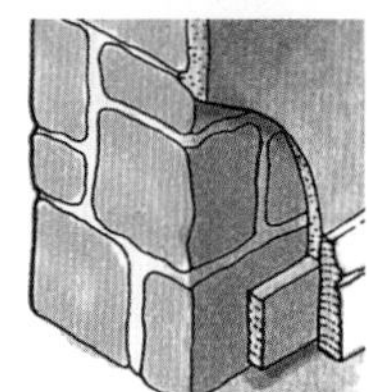

Solid walls
Traditional brick and stone walls will vary in thickness depending on the age and size of the building.

How cavity walls are built

Typical cavity walls consist of two walls or 'leaves', each 100mm (4in) thick, separated by a gap at least 50mm (2in) wide. They may be constructed from bricks, concrete blocks, or timber framing, or a combination of these. The two leaves of the wall must be tied together with metal wall ties (see left) to make them stable.

For the cavity to work as a moisture barrier, it's essential that the gap is not bridged. This can happen if mortar collects on the ties during construction.

Where openings occur, at doorways and windows, the cavity is closed at the sides – and on quality work, across the base – and DPCs are provided to stop moisture seeping in. Depending on the type of lintel used to bridge the opening, there may be a special DPC called a cavity tray installed above the lintel to stop any water that penetrates the outer leaf from soaking into the head of the opening (see below right). Weep holes – unmortared vertical joints between every third or fourth brick – are usually provided in the outer leaf above lintels and below the main DPC. Their function is to drain any moisture from the cavity that penetrates the outer leaf.

Since the 1970s thermal insulation has been incorporated within the cavity during construction. It may fill the whole cavity, or may be held flat against the inner leaf in a wider cavity by special clips fitted over the wall ties. Older houses may have the existing cavity filled with an insulating material which is injected or blown in through holes drilled in the outer leaf of the wall. In timber-framed houses, the insulation is fitted within the timber frame.

Cavity ties
Cavity-wall ties are laid in the mortar joints at 900mm (3ft) intervals horizontally and 450mm (1ft 6in) vertically. They are staggered on alternate brick courses.

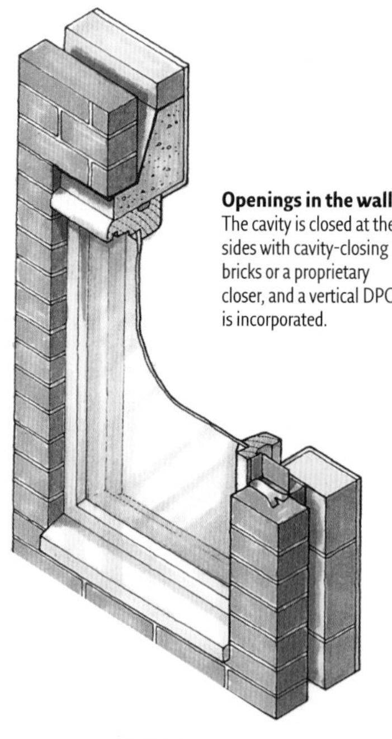

Openings in the wall
The cavity is closed at the sides with cavity-closing bricks or a proprietary closer, and a vertical DPC is incorporated.

Cavity walls
These have replaced solid walls in modern houses. A combination of brick, blocks and timber framing may be used to construct a cavity wall; brick is usually used for the outer leaf.

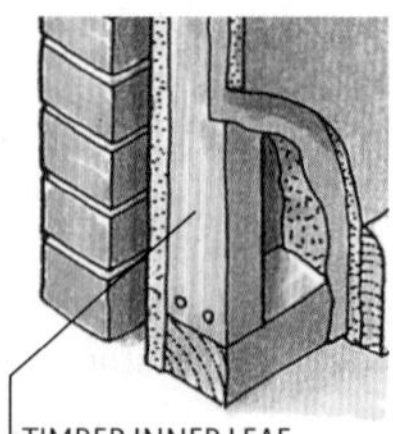

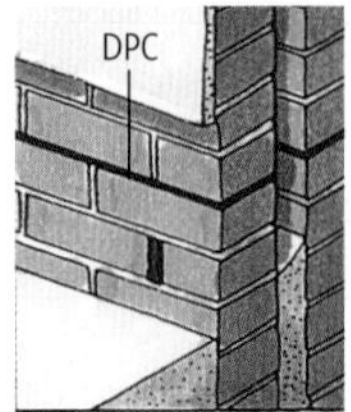

Weep holes are provided below the main DPC.

SEE ALSO > Party Wall Act 27, DPC 247, Cavity insulation 265, Brick types 438, Concrete blocks 439, Bonding brickwork 442

Loadbearing walls

The external walls of a house are loadbearing – they transmit the weight of the floors and the roof to the foundations. Roof braces, floor and ceiling joists and room partitions may also be supported on loadbearing internal walls.

A wall that supports floor joists will have the floorboards running parallel to it. Floor joists usually run in the direction of the shortest span.

Loadbearing walls are usually made of brick or of loadbearing concrete blocks. Occasionally, wooden stud walls in older homes may carry some weight. A wall may also be termed loadbearing or structural where it is not actually carrying a load but is adding to the stability of the structure.

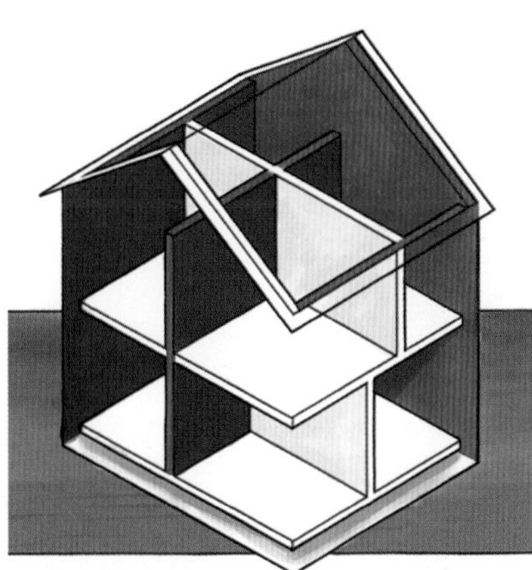

Loadbearing walls
These support parts of the house structure – such as the first-floor joists and room dividers or the roof structure.

Non-loadbearing walls

Walls that divide the floor space into rooms and are not intended to support the structure of the building are known as non-loadbearing walls. They may be made of brick, lightweight concrete blocks, timber or metal studding, or cellular-core wallboard, and are usually only a single storey high. If the floorboards run under the wall, it is likely that the wall is non-loadbearing.

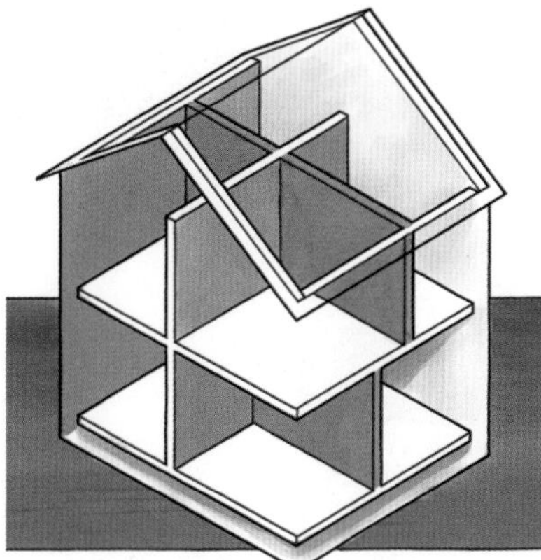

Non-loadbearing walls
These walls divide the internal space into smaller rooms, and are relatively lightweight.

Types of lintel

A lintel bridges the gap above an opening and carries the weight of the masonry above it. The type used depends on the age of the house, the type of wall involved and the size of the opening.

Wood

Wooden lintels were commonly used in the exterior brick walls of older houses – often behind a stone lintel or brick arch – and to bridge internal door openings. Those in external walls can suffer from rot due to penetrating damp. Wooden lintels are now used only in the inner leaf of timber-framed houses.

Stone

Stone is not strong in tension and cannot be used for wide spans. The stone lintels seen in older houses do not normally support the full thickness of the wall; timber lintels are inserted behind them.

Brick

Brick arches are used as an external design feature in many older houses, again with a timber lintel behind them. Flat brick arches in modern homes are supported by a steel lintel.

Concrete

Concrete lintels are used for exterior and interior openings. Concrete is good in compression but not in tension. To overcome this, metal rods are embedded in the lower portion of the beam to reinforce it. Concrete lintels are made in a range of sizes to match brick and block courses and to suit various wall thicknesses. Although they can span large openings, their weight can make handling awkward. Prestressed concrete lintels, reinforced with wire strands set in the concrete under tension, are lighter.

Steel

Galvanized pressed-steel lintels are widely used for external and internal openings. There are versions for cavity or solid walls built of bricks or blocks, and for timber-framed construction. Standard sections and lengths are available. They are fairly light in weight, and some are perforated to provide a key for a plaster finish. External steel lintels in all new homes are filled with thermal insulation.

Rolled-steel joists (RSJs) are used when an internal load-bearing wall is removed to convert two rooms into one.

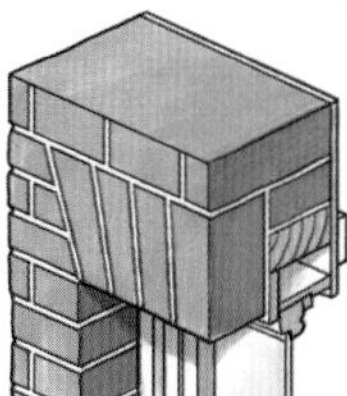

Old solid walls
A brick arch and timber beam span the opening.

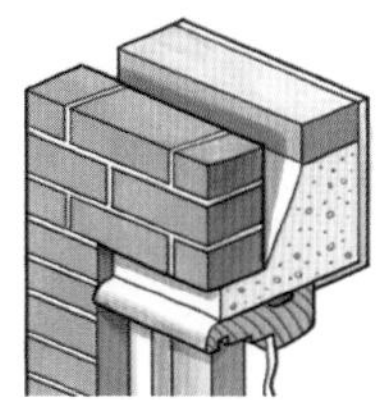

Cavity walls
A concrete boot lintel or hollow steel lintel is used.

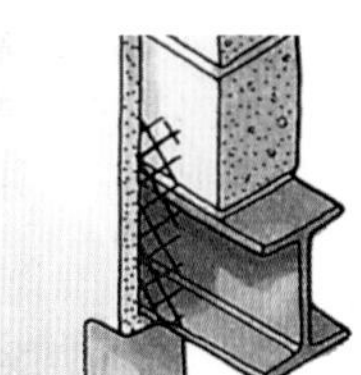

Internal walls
A rolled-steel joist (RSJ) carries the wall above.

Concrete and steel lintels

Modern lintels are made from either reinforced concrete or galvanized steel or a combination of both. These can support masonry over a considerable span, enabling large picture windows and patio doors to be installed without additional support. The hollow section of steel lintels contains thermal insulation.

The front face of some concrete lintels is visible. Where a brick facing is required, a steel lintel is installed and the bricks are laid on the lintel's thin metal front ledge.

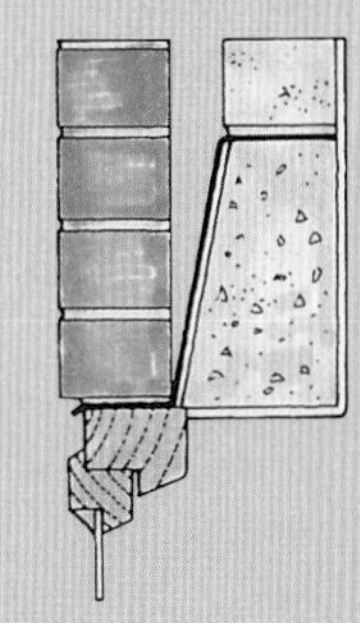

Steel and concrete
The concrete part supports the inner leaf only. No longer used in new houses.

Pressed steel
Hollow insulated lintel with mesh backing for internal plastering.

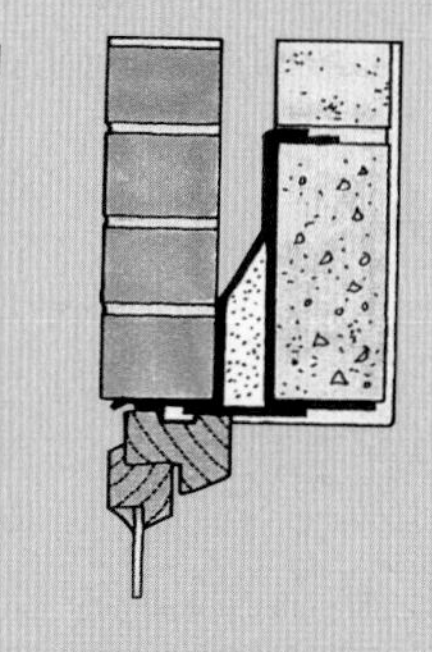

Steel and block
Lintel carries internal blocks above the opening. The hollow part is filled with insulation.

Cavity trays

In recently-built houses a special type of damp-proof course called a cavity tray is installed above the lintel spanning a door or window opening. Its purpose is to stop any moisture that penetrates the outer leaf of the wall and runs down within the cavity above the opening from soaking the inner leaf of masonry or the window frame. The trays incorporate end returns to stop water running off them into the cavity at either side of the opening. The water escapes to the outside through plastic weep holes that are built into the lowest course of brickwork above the opening.

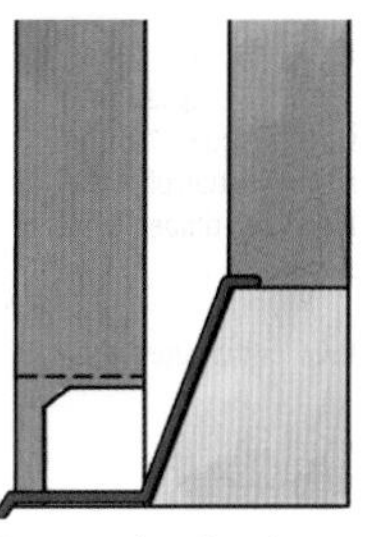

Tray over box lintel

Tray over top-hat lintel

SEE ALSO > DPC 247, Cavity insulation 265, Brick types 438, Concrete blocks 439, Bonding brickwork 442

Internal walls

There are two types of internal wall: structural party walls (which divide houses built side by side) and partition walls, which divide up the space within a house and may be loadbearing or non-loadbearing. Party walls are shared solid or cavity walls that divide semidetached or terraced houses. To curb the spread of fire and provide good sound insulation, they separate the properties throughout the entire height of the building. Any alteration work involving a party wall is subject to the Party Wall Act 1996, so always obtain professional advice.

Partition walls

Internal partition walls can be loadbearing or non-loadbearing, but are usually relatively lightweight and not more than 100 to 150mm (4 to 6in) thick.

Partition walls may be made from brick, concrete blocks, timber or metal framing, cellular-core wallboard or even glass blocks. Most ground-floor partition walls are built in solid masonry, and support the first-floor joists. Most upstairs partitions are timber-framed, unless they support part of the roof structure. In that case, there is likely to be a loadbearing masonry wall extending up to the roof from ground-floor level.

A plaster finish is usually applied to brick or block partition walls to provide a smooth surface. Walls with timber or metal framing are clad on both sides with plasterboard.

Stud partition walls

Timber-framed partitions (called stud partition walls) are common in both new and old houses. They are usually made from 100 x 50mm (4 x 2in) sawn softwood. The vertical timbers, known as studs, are placed 400 or 600mm (1ft 4in or 2ft) apart from centre to centre. Horizontal braces called noggings may be included for strength.

In older houses, laths (thin strips of wood nailed horizontally to the studs) are used as a key for a covering of plaster. However, plasterboard has long since replaced lath-and-plaster on this type of wall. Metal studding is another modern variant, with plasterboard sheets screwed to hollow metal channelling instead of to solid wood.

Stud walls of all types are usually non-loadbearing, but they may have a lateral stiffening effect on the house's structure and this must be taken into account if such a wall is being removed. Some upstairs stud walls may support a platform for water-storage tanks sited in the roof space.

Hollow stud walls offer a convenient duct for running services such as plumbing and wiring. Insulation can be incorporated within their structure to reduce sound transmission between adjacent rooms.

Glass blocks

Hollow glass blocks can be used to create an attractive light-sharing non-loadbearing feature wall. Both square and rectangular blocks are commonly supplied in thicknesses of 80 and 100mm (3¾ and 4in), and are available in a wide range of surface patterns, finishes and colours. The blocks can be laid in mortar, bonded with silicone sealant, or dry-fixed into a wooden frame. A kit frame system is made for dry fixing.

Lightweight concrete blocks

The blocks widely used for modern partition walls are nominally 150 to 225mm (6 to 9in) high and 450mm (1ft 6in) long. The most common size is 225 x 450mm (9in x 1ft 6in); a range of thicknesses, from 75 to 350mm (3 to 14in), is available. Blocks 100mm (4in) thick are often used for partition walls, as they correspond to standard brick bonding – being the equivalent of three brick courses high and two bricks long. Blocks are made from cement and lightweight aggregate. They are fireproof and provide good sound and thermal insulation.

Fixings can be made at any point on the wall, and pipework and wiring can be channelled into the surface. Blocks are cut with a bolster or a power masonry saw.

Cellular-core wallboards

These manufactured wall panels are made from two sheets of plasterboard with a gridded cardboard core bonded between them. They are available in similar sizes to standard plasterboard sheets and are 57 or 63mm (2¼ or 2½in) thick. The cell structure makes a light but rigid partition that's simple to install and which can be decorated directly or finished with plaster. Their use is not widespread in residential property – they are more commonly found in commercial buildings.

All fixings to this type of wall require a screwed cavity device unless wooden plugs are fitted when the wall is being installed.

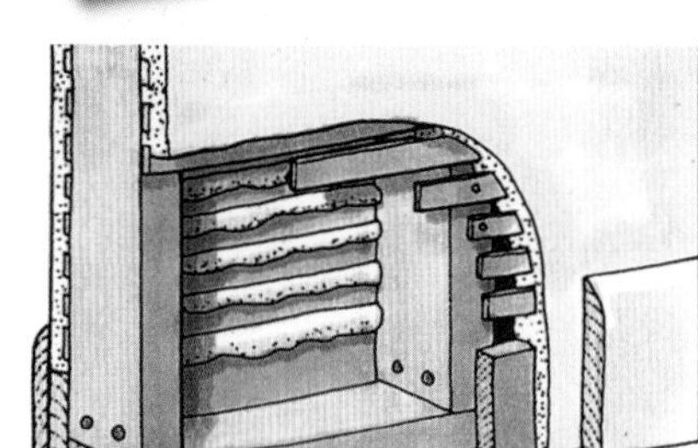

Lath-and-plaster stud partition

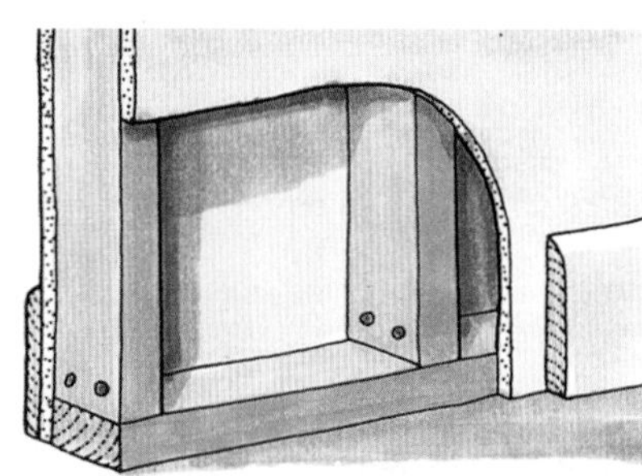

Plasterboarded stud partition

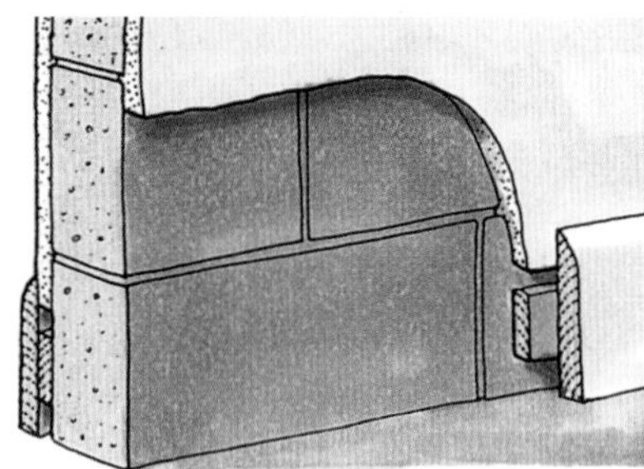

Plastered concrete block partition

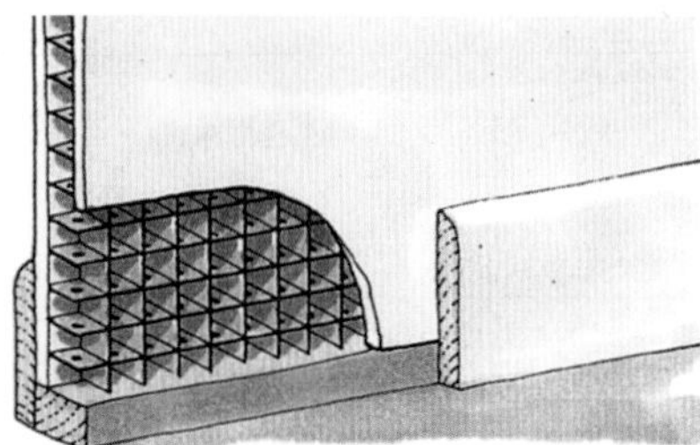

Cellular-core wallboard partition

SEE ALSO > Building a stud partition wall 151–3, Fixing to stud partition walls 154

Blocking up a doorway

If you are altering the internal layout of your home, you may have to block up a door opening. You will want the patch to be invisible, so take care when plastering or filling plasterboard joints and refitting skirtings.

Choosing the right materials

Nail ties

Frame cramp

Wall-connector system

It's generally better to fill in the opening with the type of materials used in the construction of the wall. This prevents cracks forming due to differential movements in the structure (for this purpose, you can consider bricks and blocks to be the same). It is possible to fill an opening in a brick wall with a wooden-stud frame covered on both sides with plasterboard, but it will not have the same acoustic properties as a solid infill, and cracks are difficult to prevent or disguise.

Removing the door lining

Remove the architraves, then saw through the side door-jamb linings close to the top and prise them away from the brickwork with a wrecking bar. If the linings were fitted before the flooring, the ends may be trapped; in which case, cut them flush with the floor. Next, prise the soffit board away from the top.

Bricking up the opening

Cut back the plaster about 150mm (6in) all round the opening. There's no need to cut straight or neat edges; an irregular outline helps disguise the shape of the doorway.

To bond the new brickwork into the old, cut out a half-brick on each side of the opening at every fourth course, using a power drill or a club hammer and bolster chisel. If the wall is made from concrete blocks, remove a quarter block from alternate courses.

However, if you don't want to cut blocks or bricks to fit, tie new and old masonry together using 100mm (4in) cut clasp nails driven dovetail fashion into the bed joints of the side brickwork. If you prefer, use metal frame cramps or a wall-connector system (see left). Fix them to the side walls, aligning on every fourth brick.

Lay the bricks or blocks in mortar, following the original courses. If a wooden suspended floor runs through the opening, lay the bricks on a timber sill nailed across the opening. When the mortar has set, spread on a basecoat of plaster, then follow it with a finishing top coat.

Fit two complete new lengths of skirting – or if you are able to match the original, replace the skirting using shorter pieces. To help disguise the opening, make sure the joints in the skirting do not align with the original door opening.

Cut out half-bricks

Lay bricks into the courses

Cut blocks to match bonding

Stud-wall openings

You can close off an opening in a stud partition by fitting new studding and covering it with plasterboard.

Filling the opening

Remove the door lining, as described left. Trim the lath-and-plaster or plasterboard back to the centre line of the door-jamb studs and head member, using a saw or trimming knife. Lever out the old nails with a claw hammer, then fix the cut edges of the plasterwork with nails.

Nail a matching sill to the floor between the studs. Nail a new stud centrally between head and sill. Cut and nail noggings between the studs across the opening. Cut plasterboard to fit on both sides of the opening, leaving a 3mm (1/8in) gap all round. Apply plaster or fill and tape the board joints, then finish as required.

Nail the sill, stud and noggings

SEE ALSO > Plastering a wall 158–61, Plasterboarding a wall 163–8

Spanning openings in walls

The top of a door or window opening in a loadbearing wall must be capable of carrying the structure above it. Even cutting a hole in a non-loadbearing brick partition necessitates supporting the masonry above.

Where supports are required

Doorframes and window frames are not designed to carry weight, so the load from the structure above is supported by a rigid beam called a lintel, which acts as a bridge and transmits the weight to the walls on each side of the opening. Wider or room-width openings call for stronger beams, such as rolled-steel joists (RSJs). There are numerous kinds of beam, but all of them function in a similar way.

The forces on a beam

When a load is placed at the centre of a beam that is supported at each end, the beam will bend because the lower part is being stretched and is in tension, while the top part is being squeezed and is in compression. In addition, the beam is subjected to shear forces at the points of support (the side walls), where the vertical load is trying to sever the beam. A beam must be able to resist all these forces. This is achieved by the correct choice of both material and beam depth in relation to the superimposed load and the overall span of the opening.

Choosing a lintel

The purpose of a lintel is to carry the load of the structure above the door or window opening. The load may be relatively light, being no more than a number of brick or block courses, but it is more likely that other loads from upper floors and the roof will also bear on the lintel.

The lintel must be of suitable size and shape for the job it has to do. The size should be derived from calculations based on the weight of the materials used in the construction of the building. Calculation for specifying a beam is, strictly speaking, a job for an architect or structural engineer. Tables relating to the weight of the materials are used to do this.

In practice, for typical situations, a builder can use his experience to advise on the required type and size of lintel. A Building Control Officer may be happy to accept this type of specification, but he can insist that proper calculations are submitted with your application for Building Regulations approval.

Do you need a temporary support?

Whenever you cut an opening in a masonry wall, you need to install a lintel. However, if the opening is no wider than 900mm (3ft) across and the wall is non-loadbearing, you can cut the hole without having to support the wall above while you fit the lintel. The only area of brickwork that is likely to collapse is roughly in the shape of a 45-degree triangle directly above the opening, leaving a self-supporting stepped arch of brickwork.

This effect is known as self-corbelling - see right. The darkest bricks are the only ones that are likely to fall before the lintel is installed, because of this effect. In theory the lintel supports the weight of materials within the 60-degree triangle, plus any superimposed floor or roof loading - but when the side walls (piers) are narrow, the load on the lintel is increased to encompass the area of the shaded rectangle.

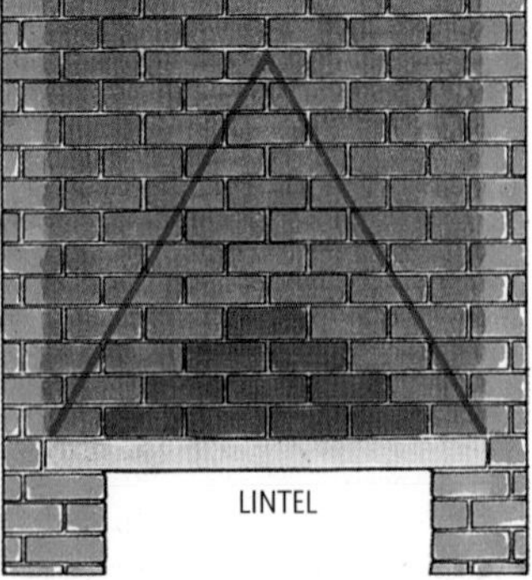

Self-corbelling

Before making any opening in a loadbearing wall, you will need to erect adjustable props as temporary supports while you fit a lintel or RSJ (see above right).

Propping the wall

To remove part of a loadbearing wall it is necessary to provide support for the wall above the opening. Hire adjustable steel props and scaffold boards to spread the load across the floor. Support the brickwork that remains below ceiling level with sawn timber bearers (known as 'needles'), at least 150 x 100mm (6 x 4in) in section and about 1.8m (6ft) long. For a door opening, one needle or metal support will suffice. Place the support centrally over the opening, about 150mm (6in) above the lintel. For wider openings use two supports no more than 900mm (3ft) apart.

Chop a hole in the wall for each needle, slot them through, and support the ends with props, placed on scaffold boards, no more than 600mm (2ft) from the wall.

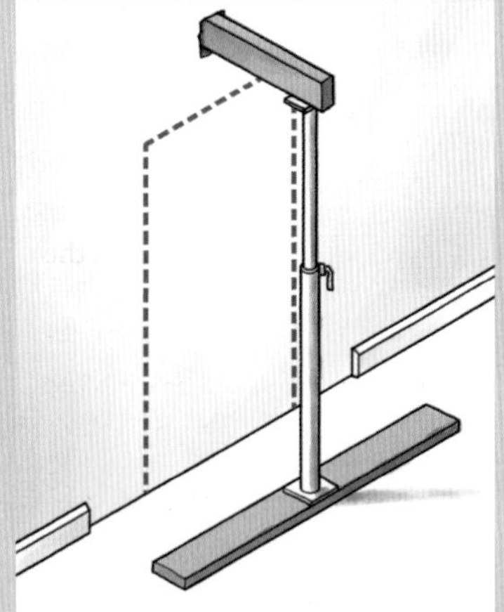

Support the needle with props

Alternatively, hire metal supports to carry the load. These devices are hammered into slots chopped in the wall and are supported on props.

Drive metal wall support into mortar joint

SEE ALSO > Building Regulations 22, Loadbearing walls 139, Types of lintel 139

Cutting internal openings

You may need to make a new doorway if you are changing the use of a room. This is often necessary as part of the process of converting a kitchen. When creating a new doorway, a lintel has to be installed to ensure the stability of both the wall itself and any load bearing on it.

Cutting through a brick or block wall

Fix galvanized ties

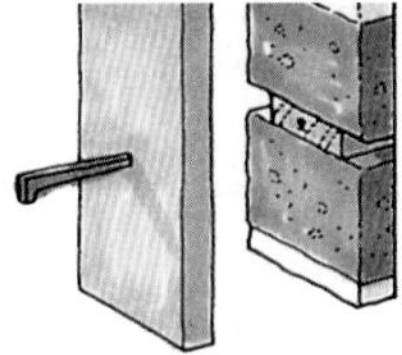

Nail to wedges

First check whether the wall is non-loadbearing or loadbearing. If it is the latter, seek approval from your local Building Control Officer (BCO). Begin by marking the opening on one side of the wall, then examine the coursing of the bricks or blocks by exposing a small area. If necessary, move the opening to align with the vertical mortar joints.

The height of the opening needs to allow for the height of the door plus a 9mm (3/8in) tolerance, the thickness of the soffit lining, and a new concrete or steel lintel. The width should be the width of the door plus a 6mm (1/4in) tolerance and twice the thickness of the door-jamb lining. Allow a further 12mm (1/2in) for fitting the lining.

Carefully prise off the skirtings from both sides of the wall. They can be cut and reused. Support the wall and fit the lintel (see right), then leave it overnight for the mortar to set hard.

The next day, starting from just below the lintel, chop out individual bricks, using a club hammer and bolster chisel. If the wall is built from lightweight blocks, use an all-purpose handsaw or a masonry saw to slice through the wall. At the bottom, chop out the masonry to just below floor level, so that you can continue the flooring through the doorway.

Stack sound whole bricks out of the way for reuse, then scoop up and bag the rubble in stout plastic sacks for disposal.

Fitting the door lining

The next step is to fit a timber frame, to which you can attach the stop bead, door and architrave. Make the frame from planed timber 25mm (1in) thick, with the width equal to the depth of the wall. Fix the lining to the sides of the opening, using metal frame cramps or ties mortared into slots cut in the brickwork. Alternatively, fit wooden wedges in the mortar joints and nail the frame to them.

Installing the lintel

Draw the position for the lintel and chop away the plaster with a club hammer and bolster chisel. Cut a hole above and either fit a supporting needle and adjustable props or use metal supports (see opposite); then cut the slot below for the lintel.

Bed a concrete lintel in a mortar mix of 1 part cement : 3 parts sand on the surface that is to bear it – which needs to be no less than 150mm (6in) wide – at each side of the slot. Level the lintel, if necessary packing pieces of slate under it. Replace loose bricks, and fill any gaps with the same mortar mix. After you have removed the needle, fill the hole above.

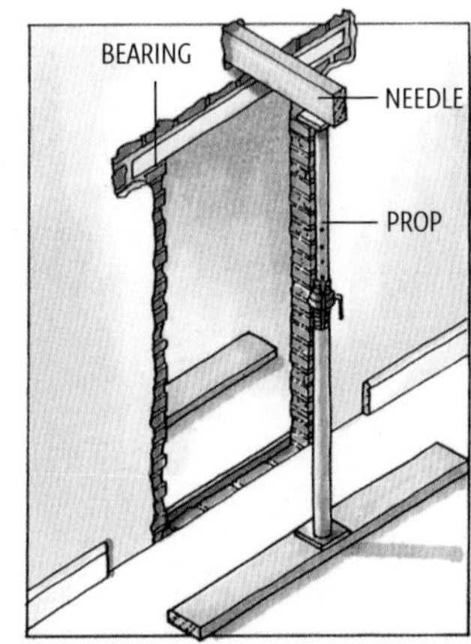

Fit a needle supported by props

Cutting an opening in a stud wall

First, locate the positions of the studs to determine the optimum position for the new doorway.

Prise off the skirting. Mark the position of the opening on the wall, then remove the cladding to expose the studs.

Door aligned with one stud

If one side of the door position you require coincides with one of the existing studs, you will have to cut away the next two studs at the level of the door head to create the new door opening.

Mark the height of the new opening on the studs, allowing for the thickness of the new door head and door lining, and cut them off squarely. Level up and skew-nail the new door head into place between the remaining full-height studs. Also skew-nail it to the bottom ends of the cut studs above it.

Mark the width of the door opening on the floor plate, cut through the plate and prise it up. Cut a new stud to fit between the door head and the floor plate, and then skew-nail it into place. Check that it is truly vertical. Fit a nogging between the new stud and the adjacent existing stud to brace it and keep it rigid.

Door centred between studs

If the door position falls between the positions of the existing studs, prepare the opening and fit the new door head as already described. Then cut and nail two new studs (which will form the door jambs) between the head and the sill. Fit noggings between the new and original studs. Cut away the floor plate to match the width of the new door opening.

With the door framing complete, cut and nail plasterboard panels in place to fill the gaps between the original wall cladding and the new studs. Tape and fill all the joints.

Cut and fit the door lining within the new opening, and add the door stops. Then fit the architraves to cover the edges of the doorframe and replace the skirting boards. Finally hang the new door.

Making the frame
Which method you adopt for the frame will depend on the positions of the studs. The diagrams illustrate typical solutions.

Door aligns with one stud   Door centred

SEE ALSO > Building Regulations 22, Loadbearing walls 139, Types of lintel 139

Converting two rooms into one

Making a through room is the best way to improve access between frequently used areas – the dining and living rooms, for example – and provides an opportunity to redesign your living space. In principle, the job is similar to making a new doorway, though on a larger scale. Removing a dividing wall – whether it is structural or a non-loadbearing partition – is a major undertaking, but it needn't be daunting. Provided you follow some basic safety rules, much of the job is straightforward. It will, however, be both messy and disruptive. Before you start, plan out your requirements and consult the at-a-glance flow chart below.

Removing a wall: planning ahead

Do you really want a through room?
Before you go ahead and demolish the wall between the two rooms, pause to consider how the new space is likely to function, its appearance, how long it will take you to carry out the work, and the cost you will incur. In particular, ask yourself the following questions.

• Will the shape and size of the new room suit your needs? If you have a young family, bear in mind that your needs are likely to change as they grow up.

• Will most of the family activities be carried out in the same room – eating, watching TV, playing music, reading, conversation, pursuing hobbies, playing with toys, doing homework?

• Will removing the wall deprive you of privacy within the family, or from passers-by in the street outside?

• Will the new room feel like one unit and not a conversion? For example, do the skirtings and mouldings match? Are the fireplaces acceptable when seen together, or should one be removed? If the doorways are close together, will one need to be blocked up?

• Will the loss of a wall make furniture arrangements difficult – particularly if radiators take up valuable wall space?

• Will the heating and lighting need to be modified?

• Will the proposed shape of the opening be in character? And will it be in proportion to the room?

• **Hiring professionals**
If in doubt about doing the whole job yourself, hire a professional builder. To save costs, you may be able to undertake some of the labour or preparation and clearing work.

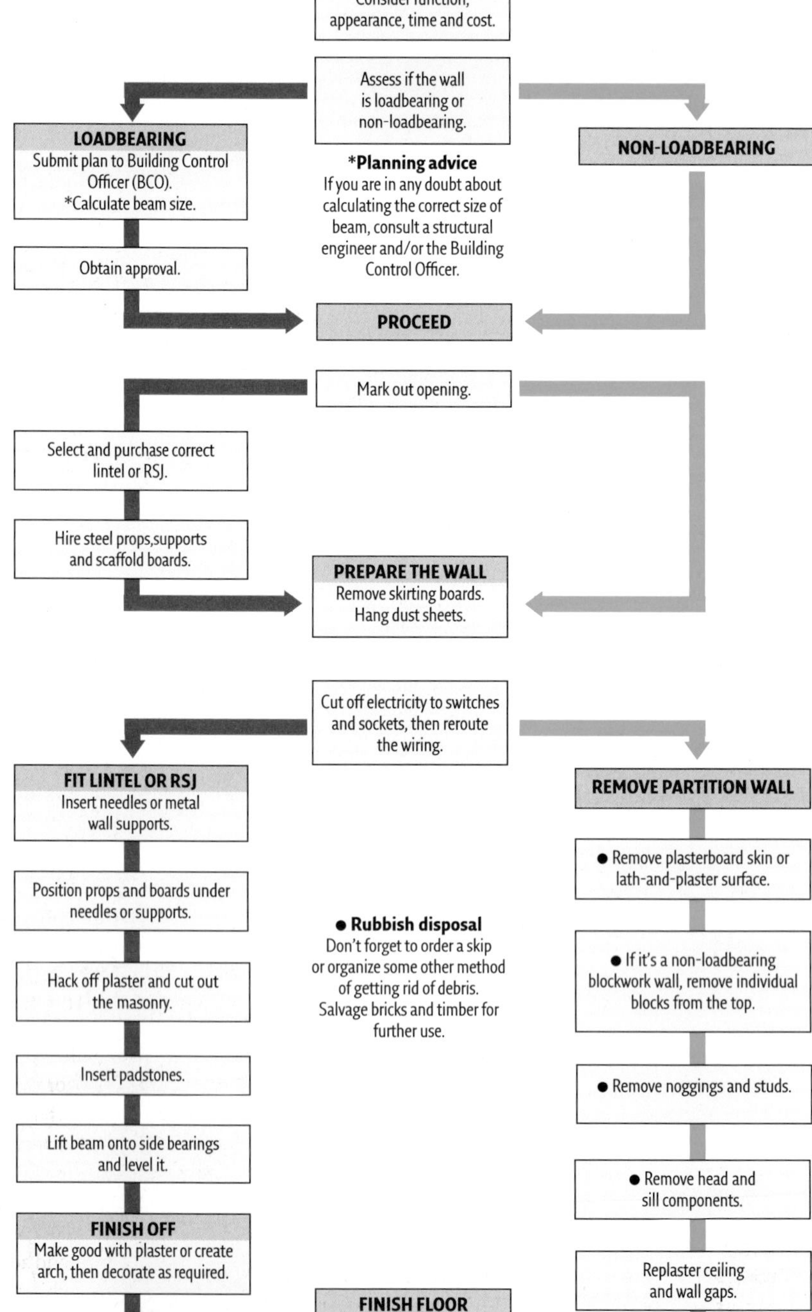

SEE ALSO > Building Regulations 22, Seeking approval 23–7, Removing walls 146–7

Supporting the wall

Once you are satisfied that the opening will be an improvement to the layout of your home, consider the practical problems. First, determine whether the wall is loadbearing or a non-loadbearing partition: bear in mind that a loadbearing wall will need a beam spanning the opening and resting on bearings at each end. Mark out the proposed opening on the wall with chalk to help you visualize its size and proportion.

Choosing a beam

The most suitable beam is usually a rolled-steel joist, although RSJs require preparation before they can be plastered over. Reinforced or prestressed concrete lintels can be used for openings up to about 3m (10ft) wide, but over a wider span their weight makes them difficult to handle. Prestressed types are lighter, but are more suitable for single door openings rather than wide spans. Pressed-steel box lintels – available in lengths up to 5.4m (about 18ft) – are also lighter than concrete and can be plastered directly.

What size beam?

Builders use a rule-of-thumb guide for sizing RSJs, making the beam 25mm (1in) deep for every 300mm (1ft) of the span. However, the size you use must always be approved by the Building Control Officer. For pressed-steel box lintels, refer to the manufacturer or supplier for sizes.

Applying for permission

Before any work is started on removing a loadbearing wall, you must seek approval from your local authority's Building Control Officer. The BCO will require you to submit a drawing showing the proposed opening and its overall height and width, and how the structure above the opening is to be supported.

This drawing does not have to be prepared by a professional – but it must be clear. Provided that the work complies with the Building Regulations, approval is unlikely to be withheld. The BCO must be satisfied that the removal of the wall will not weaken the structure of the house or any buildings attached to it in any way, and that it will not unduly encourage the spread of fire.

Where a party wall is involved, a formal notice must be presented to your neighbour to gain approval. A surveyor will advise you about this procedure.

Height of the opening

The height of the opening that is left when a dividing wall is removed is determined by the height of the existing ceiling and by the depth of the beam you are installing. The beam depth depends on the width of the opening it is to span and the load it has to carry; the wider the span, the deeper the beam has to be. Consult an architect or structural engineer who, for a fee, will calculate this for you.

In a room with a high ceiling, some brickwork can remain below ceiling level. If the ceiling is low, the beam can be positioned level with the undersides of the ceiling joists.

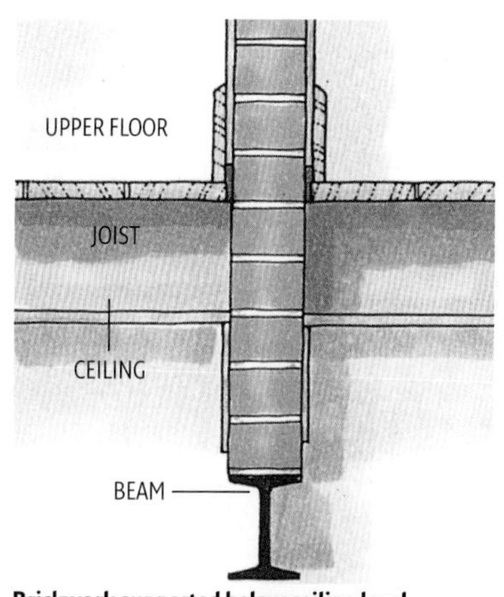

Brickwork supported below ceiling level

Brickwork supported directly under ceiling

How a beam is supported

The supports are usually brick piers, which are in effect columns attached to the side walls and formed from the remainder of the old wall. Concrete padstones are required on which to sit the beam. The BCO may want the piers increased in thickness to give sufficient support to the beam and the side walls.

Ideally, it is better if no piers are used, as they interrupt the line of the side walls running through. It may be possible to run the ends of the beam into the walls, eliminating the need for piers – but this is subject to Building Regulations approval. It requires a horizontal concrete beam called a spreader to be set in the wall, so that it will distribute the load across more of the wall.

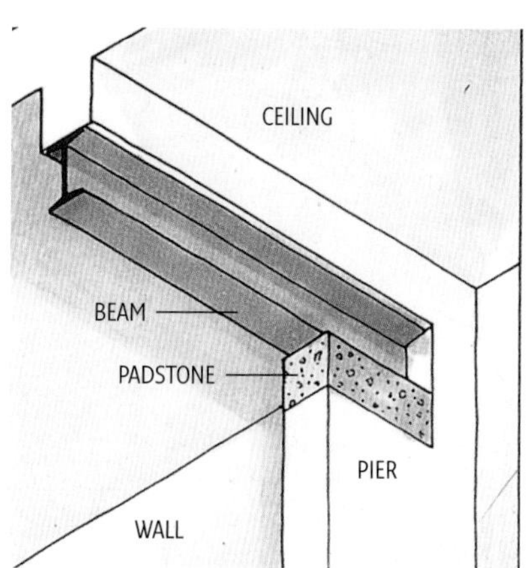

Pier capped by padstone supports the beam

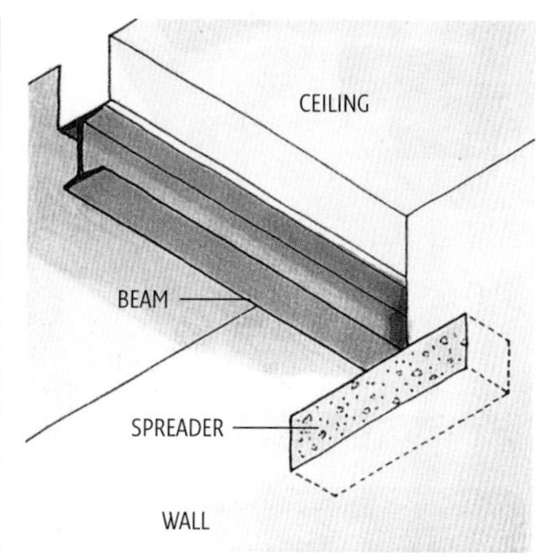

Concrete spreader distributes the load

SEE ALSO > Building Regulations 22, Party Wall Act 27, Loadbearing walls 139, Types of lintel 139, Partition walls 140

Removing the wall

To remove part of a loadbearing wall, you must temporarily support the walling above the opening. Hire adjustable steel props and scaffold boards on which to support them.

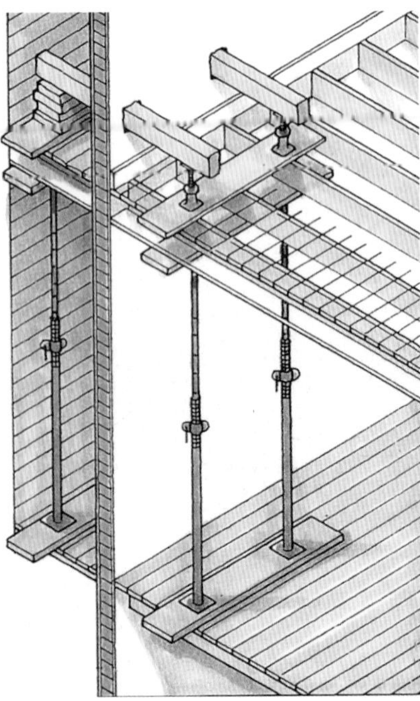

1 Layout for removing wall flush with ceiling

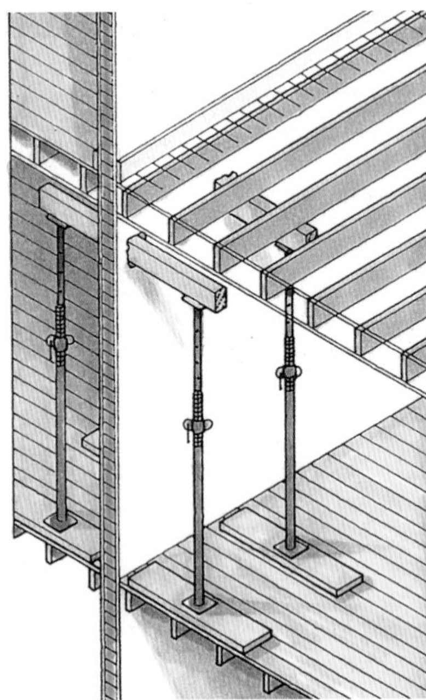

2 Layout for removing wall below ceiling

Erecting supports

When the beam is to be placed at ceiling level, hire extra boards to support the ceiling (**1**). Generally, you will have to pass needles through the wall below the ceiling in order to transfer the load to the props (**2**). The needles must be at least 150 x 100mm (6 x 4in) in section.

Hire sufficient adjustable props to space them not more than 900mm (3ft) apart across the width of the opening.

Marking out

First remove the skirting boards from both sides of the wall. On one side of the wall, mark the position of the beam in pencil. Use a steel tape measure, spirit level and straightedge for accuracy.

Inserting the needles

To help contain the inevitable airborne dust, hang dust sheets on the other side of the wall, around the area that is to be removed; attach the sheets with battens nailed over them at the top. Seal gaps around all doors with masking tape to prevent the dust travelling throughout the house. Open windows in the rooms you are working in.

Mark the positions for the needles on the wall, then cut away the plaster locally and chisel a hole through the brickwork at each point. Finish level with the bottom of a course of bricks. Make the holes slightly oversize, so you can pass the needles through easily.

Position a pair of adjustable props under each needle, not more than 600mm (2ft) from each side of the wall. Stand them on scaffold boards, in order to spread the load over the floor. Adjust the props to take the weight of the structure, and nail their base plates to the supporting boards to prevent them being dislodged.

Supporting the ceiling

If the ceiling needs supporting, stand the props on scaffold boards at each side of the wall and adjust them so they run virtually to ceiling height – they should be placed 600mm (2ft) from the wall. Place another plank on top of each pair of props and adjust simultaneously until the ceiling joists are supported.

Dismantling the wall

Hack off the plaster using a club hammer and bolster chisel, then start to cut out the brickwork, working from the top. Once you have removed four or five courses, cut the bricks at the side of the opening. Chop downwards to cut the bricks cleanly.

Remove all the brickwork down to one course below the floorboards. As you work, load the rubble into stout plastic sacks; it may be worth hiring a skip. The job is laborious, unless you hire a power brick-cutting saw; use this method only if you have had experience of using machine tools.

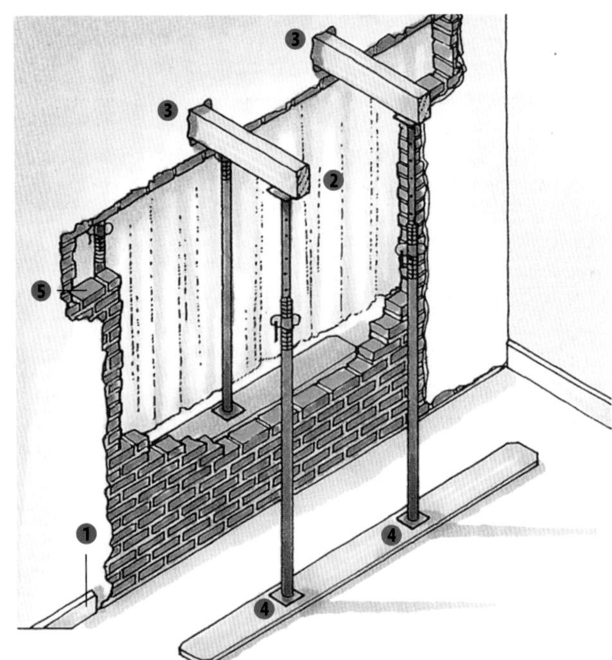

Cutting the opening
1 Remove or cut back the skirting and mark the beam's position.
2 Hang dust sheets around the work area.
3 Cut openings and insert needles.
4 Stand props on scaffold boards and adjust them to support the needles.
5 Cut away the plaster. Then chisel out the bricks, starting from the top of the opening.

Transferring the load to the sub-floor

If the floor appears to spring when you jump on it, check with a builder that the floor can carry the weight imposed. You may have to lift some floorboards and set the props on the foundations.

In older houses, where there is no concrete below the floor, scaffold boards must be placed under the props to spread the load over the ground.

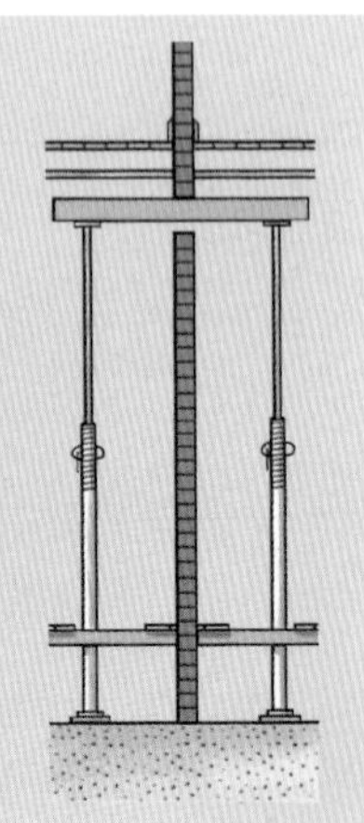

Props passing through a suspended floor

SEE ALSO > Adjustable props 142

Placing the beam

If the wall you are removing is deemed unsuitable as a basis for the supporting piers, you have two other choices. Where the adjacent wall is of double-brick thickness, you may be able to cut a hole to take the end of the beam, allowing the weight to be distributed to the existing foundations. If this is not possible, then you will have to build new piers with their own foundations.

Building piers

The piers must be built below the floor, resting on cast-concrete foundations. They must also include a DPC, and must be bonded in single-brick or double-brick thickness and toothed at every fourth course into the existing brickwork of the adjoining wall. The Building Control Officer will tell you the size for the piers.

Installing the beam

You need to cast a pair of concrete padstones on which to bed the RSJ – the BCO will recommend the optimum size. Make two wooden forms or boxes from thick plywood or softwood. Mix the concrete to the proportions 1 part cement : 2 parts sand : 4 parts aggregate, and fill the boxes. When the concrete has set, bed the padstones in mortar at the top of each pier.

Build a work platform by placing doubled-up scaffold boards between sturdy stepladders, or hire scaffold-tower sections. You will need help to lift the beam into position.

Apply mortar to the padstones, then lift and set the RSJ in place. Pack pieces of slate between the beam and the brickwork above to fill out the gap. Alternatively, 'dry-pack' the gap with a mortar mix of 1 part cement : 3 parts sand, which is just wet enough to bind it together. Where the gap can take a whole brick or more, apply a bed of mortar and rebuild the brickwork on top of the beam. Work the course between the needles, so that when the timbers are removed the holes can be filled in to continue the bonding. Allow 2 days for the mortar to set; then remove the props and needles, and fill in the holes.

When the beam is fitted against ceiling joists, you can use a different method. Support the ceiling with props and a board to spread the load on each side of the wall (see opposite). Cut away the wall, then lift the beam into position and fit a pair of adjustable props under it. Apply mortar to the top of the beam, and then screw up the props to push it against the joists and brickwork above. Bed the supporting padstones in mortar, as before.

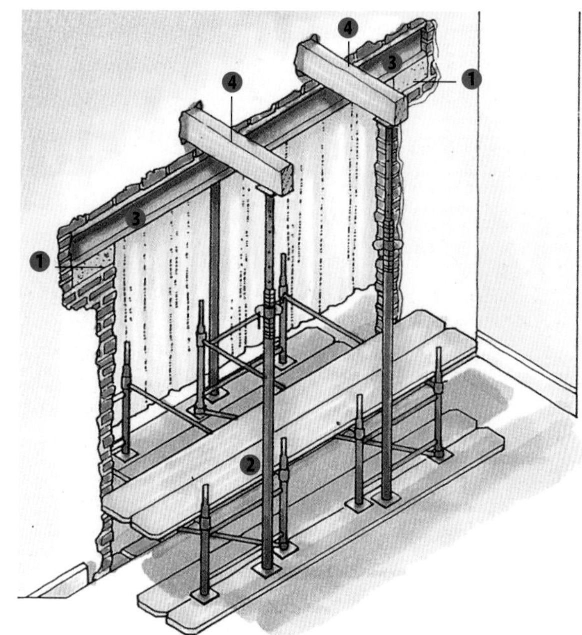

Installing the beam
1 Cast-concrete padstones set on brickwork piers.
2 Set up a secure platform to enable two people to work safely side by side.
3 Place the beam on the mortared padstones and check the level. Fill the gaps between the beam and the brickwork.
4 When set, remove the props and needles, then fill the holes.

Finishing the beam

A steel beam must be enclosed to provide protection from fire – which would cause it to distort – and to give a flat surface that can be decorated. Traditional wet plaster, plasterboard or other fireproof board can be used.

Cladding with plaster

To provide a key for plaster, clad an RSJ with galvanized expanded-metal mesh. Fold the mesh around the beam, then lap it up onto the brickwork above and secure it with galvanized nails (1). Alternatively, wedge 'soldiers' (shaped wooden blocks) into the recessed sides of the beam and nail the expanded metal to these (2).

Apply a stiff mix of bonding undercoat plaster in 9mm (3/8in) layers. Bond metal beading along the edges, to reinforce the corners. Then cover the beam with finish plaster, flush with the original surface.

1 Clad the beam with expanding mesh

2 Nail the mesh to wooden blocks

Making good with plasterboard

To box in the beam with plasterboard, you will need to fit shaped wooden blocks, wedged into the sides. Fix wooden battens to these (3), nailed together to make fixings for the plasterboard panels. Set the board about 3mm (1/8in) below plaster level, to allow for a skim coat to finish flush with the surrounding wall. Fill and seal the corner joints with tape. Plaster the piers. Then apply the finish plaster to the beam and piers.

3 Fix battens and nail on plasterboard

SEE ALSO > Plasterwork 158–61, Plasterboard 162–9, Door casings 183, Mixing concrete 455

Making arched openings

Removing a dividing wall – to create a through living and dining room, for example – leaves you with a rectangular opening formed by the RSJ and its piers. If you prefer a curved archway, you can buy ready-made metal-mesh formers, which are fitted in the corners of the opening and then plastered over.

Fibrous-plaster arches

Prefabricated decorative mouldings made from fibrous plaster are available to finish off rectangular openings. The mouldings are normally fixed with screws to wooden battens at the top and sides of the opening. To complete an authentic-looking period interior, there are ornate fibrous-plaster accessories such as corbels (supporting brackets), pillars and pilasters with which to clad the piers on either side of the opening.

Ornate corbels
These decorative supporting blocks can be fixed into the angle at each side of a rectangular opening.

Deciding on the arch profile

It's advisable to plan for the installation of an arch before you begin to make the opening. Choose the style of arch you want with care: the shape will effectively lower the height of the opening at the sides, which might be impracticable or result in a poorly proportioned room.

Corner and elliptical arches round off the angles and do not encroach on headroom. Semicircular types give a full rounded shape, but eat into headroom at the sides. Pointed arches make a distinctive shape without taking up valuable headroom at the middle of the opening.

Metal-mesh arch formers

Expanded-metal-mesh arch formers are available from builders' merchants. Various profiles are made – typically semicircles, corner quadrants and ellipses, although classical pointed arches are available, too.

One-piece mesh frames are sold, but they are suitable only for walls 112mm (4½in) thick. Segmented formers – half the face and half the soffit (underside) – are more versatile; some have a separate soffit strip and can fit any wall.

Fitting the former

You may first have to hack off a margin of plaster at the sides, so the mesh can be fixed flat against the bricks. Next, wedge a timber batten across the top of the opening, to which you can attach the mesh formers with nails. Hold the former in position and set it squarely, using a spirit level (1). Secure the mesh to the piers with galvanized masonry nails. Hold a spirit level diagonally against the fold of mesh at the curves and the hard plaster surface on the pier to check that it is set at the correct depth (2).

If you are fitting mesh segments, fit one half then the other; and then tie the soffit strips together with galvanized or copper wire (3) to prevent the mesh sagging under the weight of the plaster. On a thick wall, insert a soffit strip and tie it to the side pieces.

Mix some bonding plaster and spread a rough key coat onto the soffit with a plasterer's steel trowel, working from bottom to top from both sides (4). Don't press too hard, or too much plaster will be forced through the mesh. Apply plaster to the face of the arch, scraping it just below the hard plaster edge on the pier and the rigid mesh fold on the arch curve. When the plaster has stiffened, apply a thin coat of finish plaster. Apply a second coat, and trowel it smooth.

Arch-formers
Expanded-metal-mesh arch formers are made in standard shapes and are easy to install. The shapes can be modified by adding a soffit strip.

Semi-circular

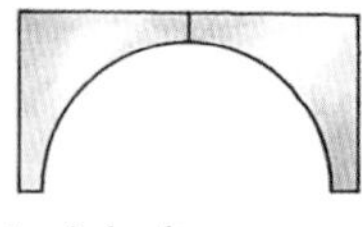

Pointed

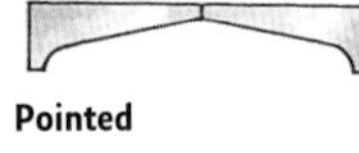

Elliptical

1 Set the former squarely within the opening

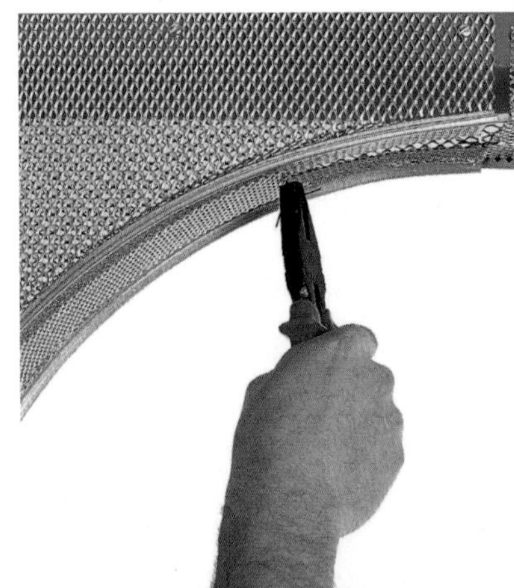

2 Tie the soffit strips together with wire

3 Plaster the sides and the soffit first

4 Use the same technique to plaster the walls

SEE ALSO > Mixing plaster 157, Plastering techniques 158–9, Plasterer's trowel 510, Spirit level 511

Removing a partition wall

Lightweight non-loadbearing partition walls can be removed without having to obtain local-authority approval, and without the need to add temporary supports. However, you must be absolutely certain that the wall is not structural, as some partitions offer partial support.

Dismantling a stud partition

Remove the skirting boards and any picture-rail mouldings from both sides of the wall. If there are any electrical switches or socket outlets attached to the wall, they must be disconnected and the wiring rerouted before work begins.

Removing the plasterwork

Use a claw hammer or wrecking bar to hack off the plasterboard or lath-and-plaster covering the wall frame. This is a dusty job, so protect yourself and seal the room. Bag up the debris and remove it.

Removing the framework

First knock away any nailed noggings from between the studs. If the studs are nailed to the head and sill, they can be knocked free. If they are housed or mortised in place, saw through them at an angle (this prevents the saw jamming). If you make the cuts close to the joints, you will be left with handy lengths of reusable timber.

Prise off the head and sill members from the ceiling joists and floor. The end studs are likely to be secured to the walls with masonry fixings. Undo these if you can; otherwise you will have to prise them away with a wrecking bar.

Finishing off

Replaster the gap left in the ceiling and walls; you may need to fit a narrow strip of plasterboard. If the floorboards are not continuous, fit new boards to fill the gap in the floor (see right).

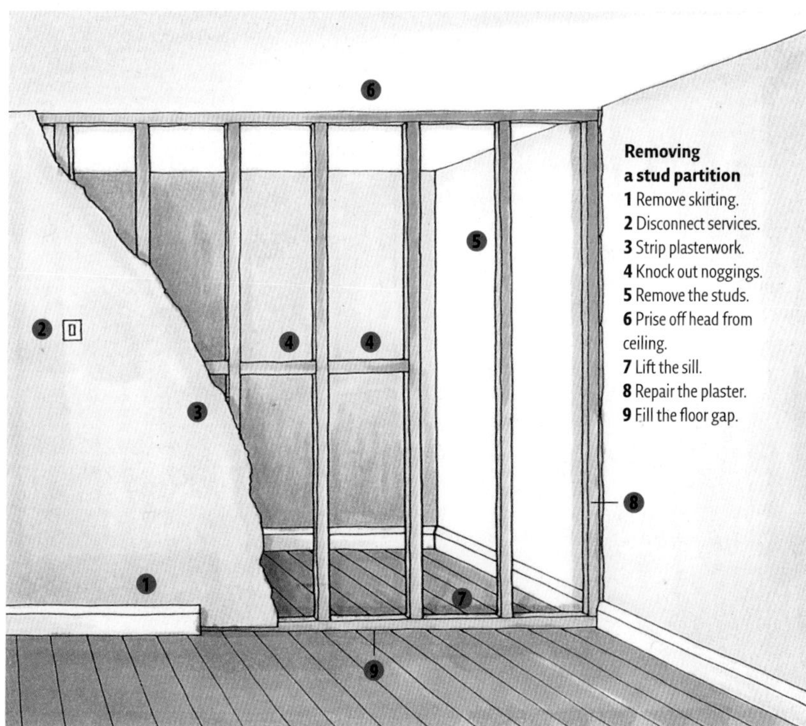

Removing a stud partition
1 Remove skirting.
2 Disconnect services.
3 Strip plasterwork.
4 Knock out noggings.
5 Remove the studs.
6 Prise off head from ceiling.
7 Lift the sill.
8 Repair the plaster.
9 Fill the floor gap.

Dismantling a blockwork wall

Partition walls are sometimes made using lightweight concrete blocks. To remove a blockwork wall, start by cutting away the individual units from the top, using a bolster chisel and club hammer. Work from the centre out towards the sides. Chop off an area of plaster first, so you can locate the joints between blocks, and then drive your chisel into the joints to lever out individual blocks.

Closing the gap

When you remove a dividing wall that penetrates the floor, you are left with a gap between the floors on each side. The floorboards may run parallel with the line of the wall or at right angles to it. Filling the gap with pieces of matching floorboard is usually straightforward.

Boards running parallel

When the boards are parallel with the wall, the supporting joists may rest on a wall plate on the lower wall. Cut a board matching the thickness of the existing boards to fill the gap. Nail the board to the joists.

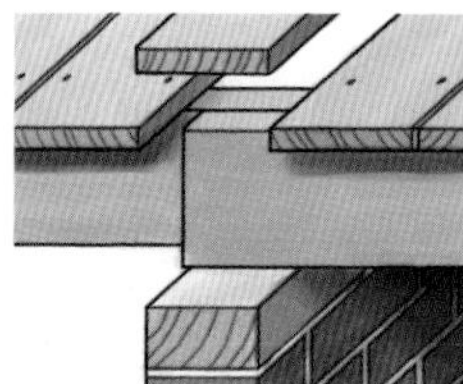

Cut boards to fit the gap and nail them to the joists

Boards at right angles

When the boards are at right angles to the gap, the ends will be supported on joists that run parallel with the wall. Cut the ends of the boards flush with the joists. Nail 50 x 25mm (2 x 1in) sawn softwood battens to the sides of the joists, level with the underside of the boards. Cut short lengths of matching floorboards to bridge the gap, and nail them in place.

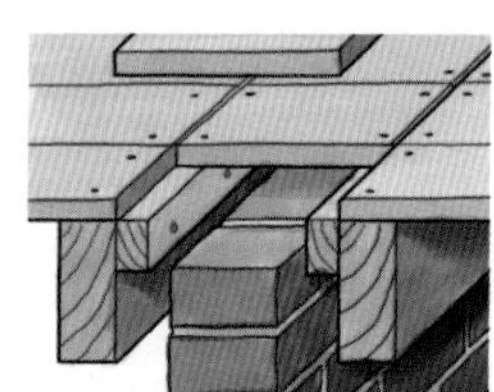

Cut short lengths of matching board to bridge the gap

Boards not at same level

A misalignment of up to 18mm (3/4in) can be accommodated by short lengths of board cut to span the gap: although acceptable, the slope will be apparent. Where the difference in level is large, you may have to create a step.

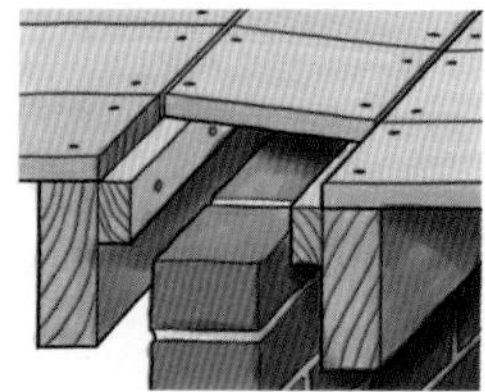

Fit short sloping boards across the gap

Creating a step

Trim the ends of the floorboards on the higher side flush with the joist, and nail a batten to it. Trim the boards on the lower side in the same way, but screw a planed softwood riser, 38mm (1½in) thick, to the side of the joist to finish level with the batten on the higher floor.

If the boards are to be covered, cut and nail short lengths to form the tread of the step. Where you want a bare-wood floor, a single board run across the width of the step will look better.

Make a step if the difference in level is large

SEE ALSO > Wall plate 126, Non-loadbearing walls 139, Replacing skirtings 218, Switching off the power 296, Running cable 303–5, Concrete blocks 439, Bolster chisel 513

Making one room into two

Building a partition to divide a large area into two smaller rooms is quite straightforward. You can build a frame of timber studs, as shown here, or use metal studding. Clad the wall and plaster it so that the new addition looks an integral part of the house. Before going ahead, however, you may need to seek Building Regulations approval from your local authority.

Complying with the Building Regulations

Before you begin to build a partition wall, check with your local authority to make sure the space you are creating complies with the Building Regulations. These state that if a new room is to be 'habitable' – a living room, dining room, bedroom or kitchen, for example – it must meet the ventilation requirements.

The regulations stipulate that there must be an open space outside the window to provide sufficient ventilation to the room. The openable area of the windows of each room must be not less than a twentieth of the room's floor area. (To check this, divide the area of the floor by the area of the window's sash or top vent.) Also, part, if not all, of the top vent must be at least 1.75m (5ft 9in) above the floor.

Alternative and additional means of ventilation can be provided by a mechanical ventilator direct to the open air. It may be permissible for a fanlight to connect to a vented lobby.

If you plan to partition a large bedroom to make an en suite shower or WC on an internal wall, natural light is not a requirement – but you must install ventilation. Consider the positioning of the new room in relation to existing plumbing.

Bear in mind the size and shape of the rooms in relation to the furniture – for example, if you're planning to make a large bedroom into two smaller units, allow sufficient space for making the beds. You may also need to create a corridor if you want the two rooms to be self-contained.

Constructing a stud partition wall

Parts of a stud partition
1 Head plate
2 Sill (sole plate)
3 Wall stud
4 Intermediate studs
5 Noggings

Timber-framed non-loadbearing walls are usually made from 100 x 50mm (4 x 2in) or 75 x 50mm (3 x 2in) sawn softwood. The partition comprises a head or ceiling plate (this forms the top of the wall and is fixed to the ceiling joists); a matching length, nailed to the floor, which forms the sill or sole plate; studs that fit between the plates, spaced equally at about 400mm (1ft 4in) centre to centre and fixed with nails; and short noggings, which are nailed between the studs to make the structure rigid. Noggings are required where horizontal joints occur in the cladding.

Positioning the partition

If the new partition is to run at right angles to the floor and ceiling joists, it can be fitted at any position. Each joist will share the load and will provide a solid fixing.

If the wall is to run parallel with the joists, it should stand directly over one of them. Locate the floor joist and check whether stiffening is required. If so, reinforce it by fixing an additional joist on each side. If the wall has to be sited between the joists, you must fit bearers between them.

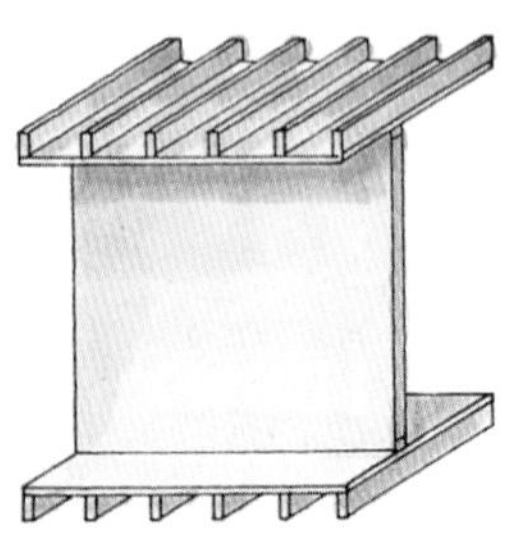

Right-angle alignment
A partition set at right angles to joists is well supported.

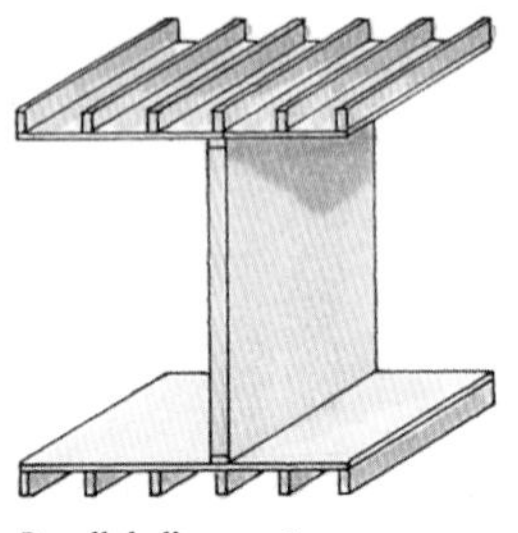

Parallel alignment
A partition parallel with the joists must be supported by one of them.

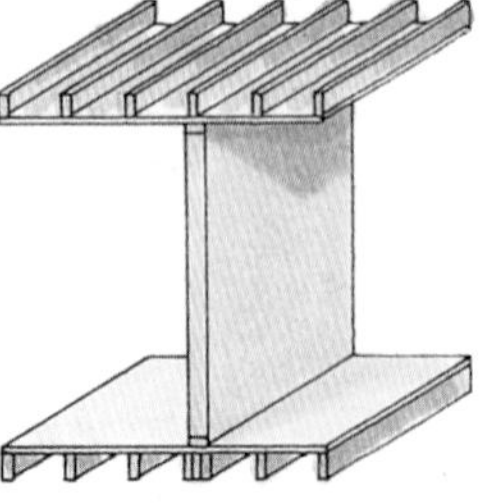

Reinforcement
The floor joist may need stiffening to bear the extra weight of the partition (see right).

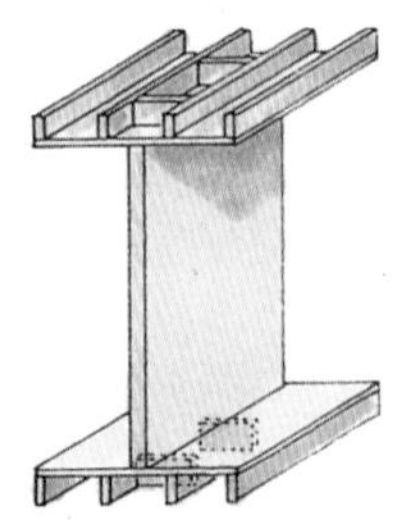

Between joists
You can fit timber bearers between the floor joists and ceiling joists to add support.

Reinforcing a joist

If a joist needs strengthening, you can reinforce it with new joists fixed at each side of it.

Using joist hangers

Remove the skirting and lift the floorboards. Screw metal joist hangers to the walls at each end – using screws 50mm (2in) long – to support the reinforcing joists flush with the original joist. Cut two joists to fit between the hangers.

Use coach bolts 12mm (½in) in diameter to clamp the joists together. Drill the holes for them slightly larger than their diameter and space them no more than 900mm (3ft) apart, working from the centre.

Using timber connectors

Instead of using joist hangers, you can fit double-sided timber connectors 75mm (3in) in diameter between the joists' meeting faces. If you have room, and a drill bit long enough, drill through all three joists while they are held together with cramps. If not, clamp one in place and drill through the two. Remove the reinforcing joist and clamp the other on the opposite side. Drill through it using the holes in the original joist as a guide. Bolt the reinforcing joists together.

Replace the boards on which the partition is to be erected.

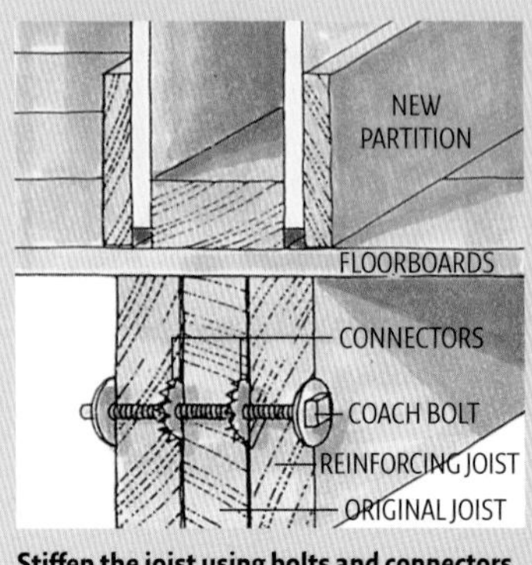

Stiffen the joist using bolts and connectors

SEE ALSO > Building Regulations 22, Metal stud partitions 155, Suspended floors 172, Joist hangers 174

Building a stud partition wall

When building a stud partition wall, you can include a doorway or a glazed area to borrow light from an existing window. Erect the partition directly on the floorboards, butted against the wall surface at each end.

Marking out and spacing the studs

With chalk, mark the position of the partition wall on the floor, using the sill member – a length of 100 x 50mm (4 x 2in) sawn softwood – as a guide to draw the lines. Continue the guide lines up the walls at each side of the room, using a spirit level and straightedge or a plumb line. Mark guide lines on the ceiling by snapping a distinct chalk line onto the surface with a taut string (**1**).

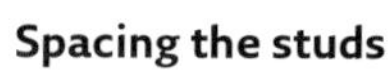

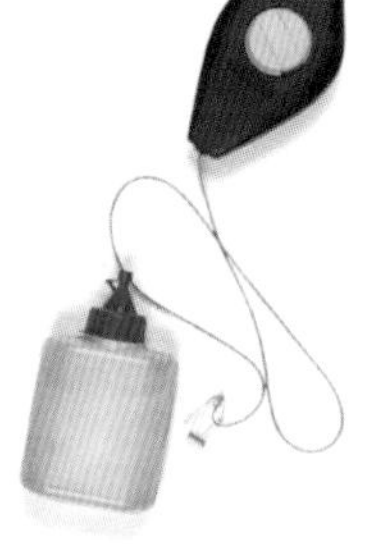

Using chalked string
A retractable self-coating chalk line makes marking out easier.

Spacing the studs

Lay the sill and head members side by side, with their face side uppermost. Mark the positions of the studs at 400 or 600mm (1ft 4in or 2ft) centres, working from the centre if the wall will not include a door. Opt for 400mm spacing to support thin wallboards or plasterboard 9.5mm (3/8in) thick, but choose 600mm spacing if you are using plasterboard 12.5mm (½in) thick or tongue-and-groove (T&G) boards. Square the lines across both members, using a try square (**2**).

Marking out a doorway

If there is to be a doorway in the wall, make an allowance for the opening. The studs that form the sides of the opening must be spaced apart by the width of the door plus a 6mm (¼in) tolerance gap and the thickness of both door linings.

Mark the width of the opening on the head plate, then mark the positions for all the studs, working away from the opening. Take the dimensions for the two sills from the head plate and cut both sills to length. The door studs will overlap the ends of the sills, which must be cut back to allow for them to fit.

1 Snap a chalk line on the ceiling

2 Mark the sill and head plate together

Fixing the framework

Secure a sill to the floor on each side of the door opening, using nails 100mm (4in) long or No10 countersunk woodscrews 75mm (3in) long. Use the head plate as a guide to keep the two sills in line. Holding the head plate on its line, prop it against the ceiling (**3**), then use a plumb line to check that the marks for the studs are directly above those marked on the sill. Nail or screw the head plate to the ceiling joists.

Measure the distance between the head and sill at each end and cut the outer wall studs to length: they should be a tight fit between the sill and head plate. Check that they are truly vertical. Fix them to a masonry wall with frame fixings, not less than 100mm (4in) long, or screw-fix them to a stud wall.

Fixing the door studs

Cut the door studs to fit between the head plate and the floor. Wedge them in place and check that they are vertical, but don't fix them in position yet.

Add together the door height and the thickness of the head lining, plus 9mm (3/8in) for tolerance, then mark the position of the door head on the edge of one stud. Hold a spirit level on this mark and transfer it accurately to the other door stud.

Fixing the door head

Remove the studs, then mark and cut a housing 12mm (½in) deep to receive the 50mm (2in) door head.

Reposition and skew-nail the door studs to the head plate, and dovetail-nail them into the ends of the sills.

Locate the door-head member in its housing and nail it through the studs (**4**). Fit a short stud between the head plate and door head.

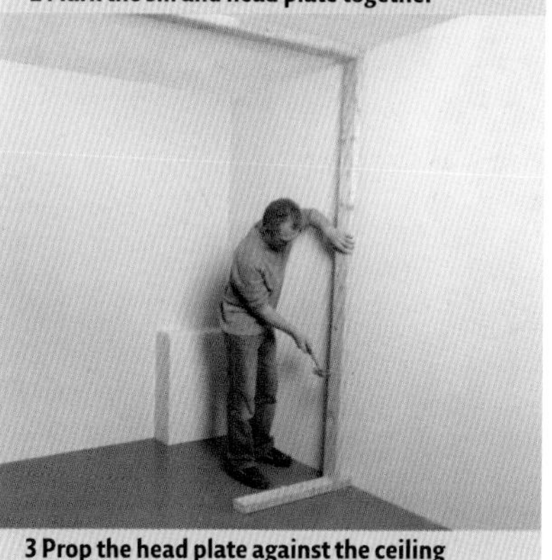

3 Prop the head plate against the ceiling

Alternative fixing for door studs

Another way to fix door studs in place is to cut them to the required door height and double up with studs that run the full height of the wall between the sill and the head plate. Nail each pair of studs together, then nail the door head to the top of both door-height studs. Cut and fit a short length of studding vertically between the centre of the head plate and the door head.

Double door studs
1 Door-height studs
2 Full-height studs
3 Door head

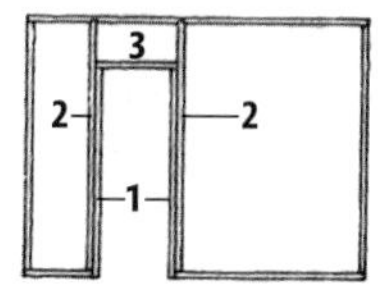

4 Nail the studs to the door head

SEE ALSO > Metal-stud partitions 155, Door casings 183, Dovetail nailing 505, Housing joints 507–8

Nailing techniques

Skew-nailing
Skew-nail a butt joint.

Supporting joint
Battens fixed to each side brace the joint.

Housing joints
Housing joints ensure a true and rigid frame.

There are a number of simple techniques for fixing wall studs top and bottom.

Use two round wire nails 100mm (4in) long to skew-nail each butt joint, driving one nail through each side. Temporarily nail a batten behind the stud to prevent it moving sideways when you are driving in the first nail.

Battens cut to fit between each stud can be permanently nailed in place to provide extra support.

Alternative stud-fixing method

For a particularly rigid fixing, set the studs into housings 12mm (½in) deep, notched into the head and sill plates before you fix these in position.

Cut the sides of the housings to one third of the depth of the head and sill plates, using a panel saw or circular saw, then chop out the waste wood with a wide chisel and a mallet. Insert the stud and fix it with nails.

Erecting studs and fixing noggings

Measure and cut each full-length stud and fix it in its marked position. Cut noggings to fit between the studs. Working from the wall, skew-nail the first end to the wall stud, then dovetail-nail through the next stud into the end of the nogging. One or two rows of noggings may be required; if you're going to fit plasterboard horizontally, space the centres of the noggings 1.2m (4ft) apart, working down from the ceiling. When the boards are to be fitted vertically, space the line of noggings mid-way between the head and sill plates. If you prefer, you can stagger them to make driving the nails easier.

Space studs equally and nail top and bottom

Nail noggings between studs to stiffen them

Attaching plasterboard vertically

Start at the doorway, with the edge of the first board flush with the stud face. Before nailing it in place, cut off a strip 25mm (1in) wide, running from the top edge of the board down to the bottom of the door-head member. Fix the board with 30mm (1¼in) or 40mm (1½in) plasterboard nails, not more than 150mm (6in) apart.

Fit a board on the other side of the doorway, cutting out a similar strip, as described above. Nail both boards, then cut and fit a section of plasterboard to fill the space above the opening (see below), allowing a 3mm (⅛in) gap at the cut joint. Then fit the remaining boards, scribing the last two boards where they butt against the walls.

Fixing to an existing stud wall

Stud walls are frequently used to divide up the first floor of a house into separate bedrooms. If your new partition butts against one of these timber-framed walls, try to fix it to one of the existing studs. Tap the old wall until you hear a dull thud that indicates the position of a stud, then drill a series of small holes through the cladding to find its centre.

If the position of the new partition falls between two studs, fix its first stud to the noggings, head and sill of the original wall. Construct the new partition as described above, but in this instance cut the first wall stud to fit between the floor and the ceiling, and fix it to the side wall before you nail or screw the sill and head plate into place.

Attaching plasterboard horizontally

Start by nailing the top row of boards to the frame. Cut a strip from the edge of the boards on each side of the doorway, to allow the short board over the door to be fixed to the studs.

To support a board while you nail it, fix a horizontal batten to the studs 3mm (⅛in) below the centre line of the noggings. Rest the bottom edge of a board on the batten and nail it to the studs. Nail out from the centre of every board.

Remove the temporary batten and proceed to fit the bottom row of boards. Hide cut edges behind the skirting, and stagger the vertical joints.

Fixing plasterboard vertically
Start at the doorway and work away from it.

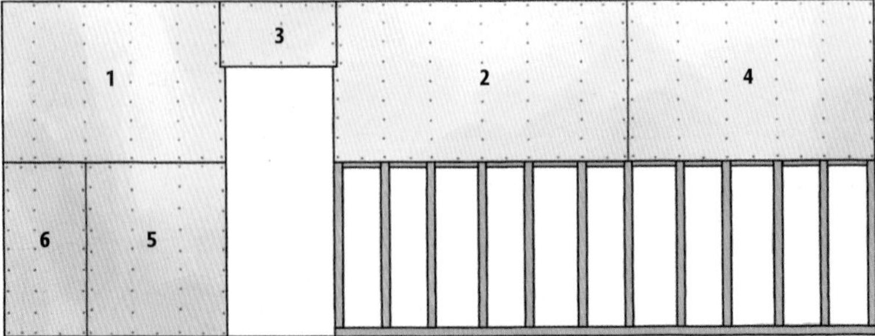

Fixing plasterboard horizontally
Fix the top row first. Stagger the joints in the second row.

SEE ALSO > Plasterboarding a wall 163, Scribing plasterboard 164, Finishing plasterboard 168

Staggered partitions

You can divide a large room in two and provide built-in storage at the same time. Constructing a staggered partition with a door at one end and a pair of spacious storage alcoves makes good use of available space. Build the partition just like a straight one, but with right-angle junctions for the alcoves.

Positioning the wall

First mark out the thickness of the main partition across the floor, then mark the position of the 'recessed' partition parallel with it. If you're going to create standard-depth wardrobes in the storage alcoves, set the two partitions 600mm (2ft) apart.

Next, calculate the length of the partitions by setting them out on the floor. Starting from the wall adjacent to the new doorway, measure off the thickness of a stud, the door lining, the width of the door, a second door lining and a second stud. Also add 6mm (¼in) for clearance around the door. This takes you to the face of the first short partition that runs at right angles to the wall. Measure from this point to the other wall and divide the dimension in two. This gives you the line for the other short partition. Mark all the sill plate positions on the floor.

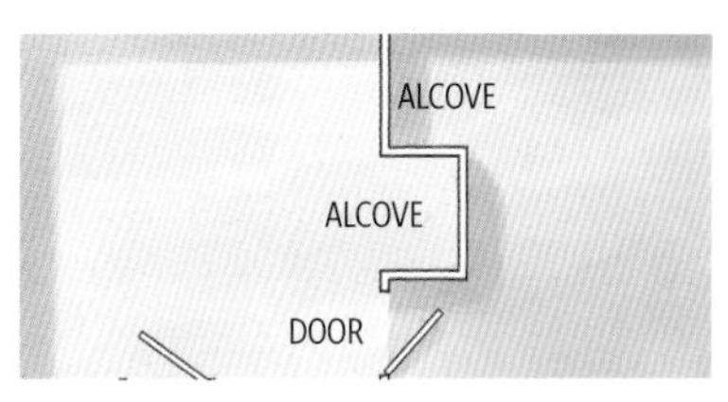

Staggered partition
The partition forms storage alcoves on each side, one for each room.

Fixing the sill and head plates

Mark the positions for the head plates on the ceiling. Use a straightedge and spirit level or a plumb line to ensure that the marks on the ceiling exactly correspond with the ones you marked on the floor for the sill plates.

Cut and fix the sill and head plates to the floor and ceiling respectively, as for building a straight partition. Cut and fit the studs at the required spacing to suit the thickness of the cladding. Form the right-angled junctions as shown (right).

Building the wall
1 Mark out partitions.
2 Transfer the marks to the ceiling.
3 Cut the sills and fix them to the floor.
4 Fix the head plates to the ceiling.
5 Make corners from three studs.
6 Fix the other studs at required spacing.
7 Fit noggings, then fix the boarding.
8 Fit doorframe and complete the boarding.
9 Fit door lining, door and mouldings (not shown here, but see right).

Completing the wall

The right-angled corners and the end of the short partition supporting the doorframe need extra studs to provide a fixing for the plasterboard.

Making up the posts

Form each corner from three studs arranged as shown and nailed in place. Fit offcuts of studding to pack out the gap; fix these offcuts level with the noggings.

For the end of the short partition next to the doorway, fit two studs 50mm (2in) apart with offcuts nailed between them.

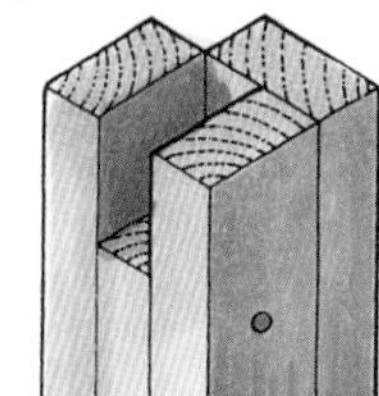

Corner post
Use three studs at the partition corners.

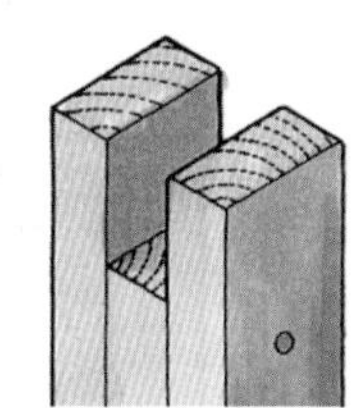

End post
Use two studs at the end of the partition.

Cladding the partition

Clad the staggered partition with sheets of plasterboard, overlapping the boards at each external and internal corner. At the door opening, leave the last stud exposed until the doorframe is fitted.

Cut the door studs, head plate and door head to length. Nail the head plate to the ceiling, and fix one stud to the new partition and the other to the room wall (below). Fit the door head and a short vertical stud above it.

Attach plasterboard above the doorway and to the side faces of the studs, including the end of the new partition. Finally fit a door lining, the doorstops and the architrave.

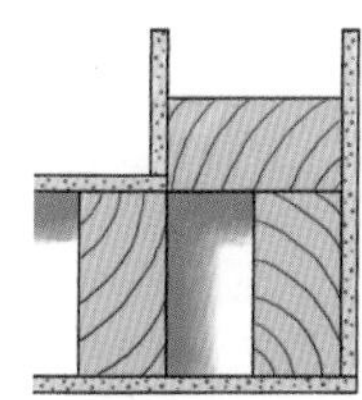

Wall cladding
Overlap the plasterboard at corners

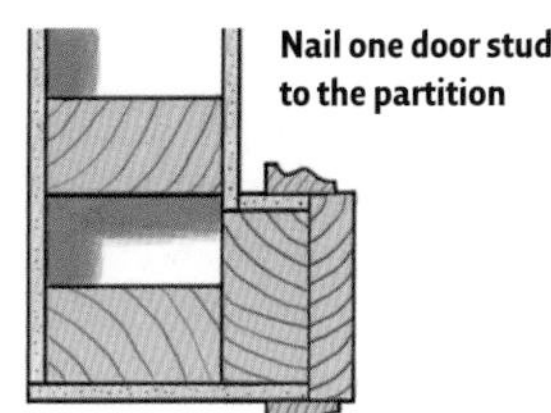

Nail one door stud to the partition

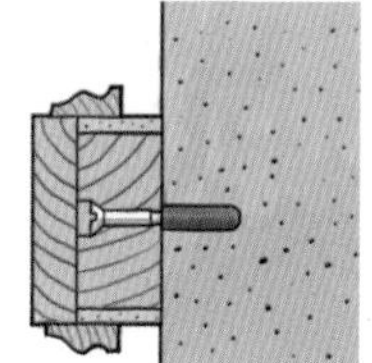

Screw-fix the other stud to the room wall

SEE ALSO > Building a stud partition wall 151–2, Plasterboarding a wall 163, Scribing plasterboard 164, Finishing plasterboard 168

Fixing to stud partition walls

Unlike masonry walls, stud walls are largely hollow – a problem that has to be overcome when wall fixtures are to be hung from them. On the other hand, when it comes to installing plumbing or electrical wiring, hollow walls are a real advantage.

Hanging fixtures

Wherever possible, these should be fixed directly to the structural stud members for maximum support. However, if the positions of fixtures are preplanned, extra studs, noggings or mounting boards can be included before the cladding is applied.

Mounting a hand basin

A wall-mounted basin needs a sound fixing to carry the weight of the basin and that of someone leaning on it.

The best way of providing this is to fix a panel of 18mm (¾in) thick plywood between the studs at the basin position. Cut away the plasterboard down to floor level and screw the panel to battens fixed to the sides of the studs. Set the panel back so plasterboard can be fixed over it once you have installed the basin's supply and waste pipes within the wall framework, but before the basin is fixed in place.

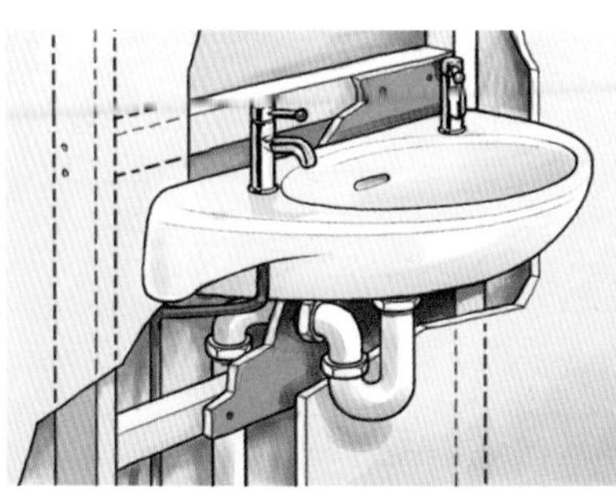

Fix a wall-mounted hand basin to a plywood panel fixed between adjacent studs

Fix shelf brackets directly to studs

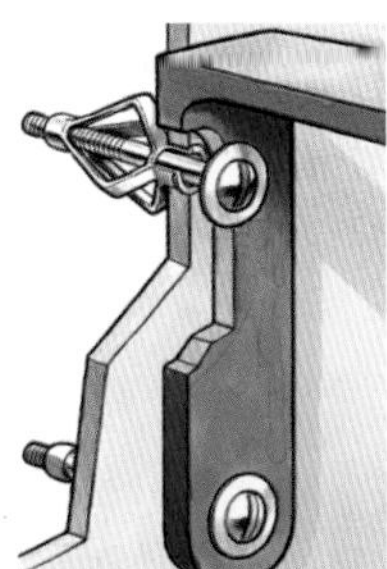

Otherwise, use metal collapsible anchors

Use strong metal cavity wall fixings such as collapsible anchors to mount a heavy cupboard

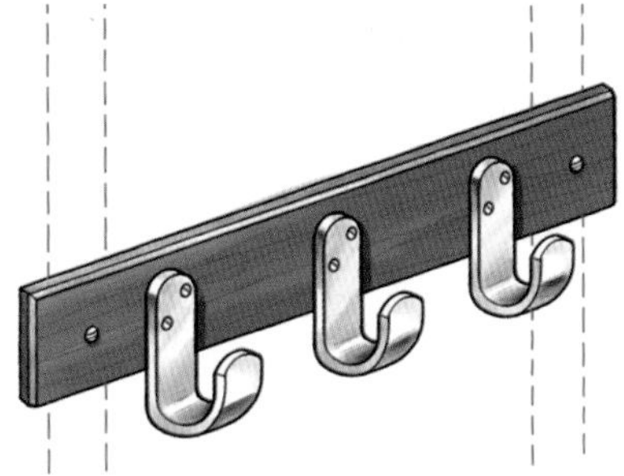

Mount fixtures such as coat hooks on a batten and screw it to adjacent studs

Fitting a wall cupboard

It's not always possible to fix to the studs, because walls tend to be put up long before furnishings are considered. If there are no studs just where you want them, you will have to use cavity fixings instead. Choose a type such as an expanding metal anchor that will adequately support the weight of the cupboard.

Hanging shelves

Wall-mounted bookshelves have to carry a considerable weight and must be fixed securely, especially to stud partitions. Use a shelving system that has strong metal uprights into which adjustable brackets are slotted, so the uprights spread the load across all the wall fixings. Screw into studs if you can, otherwise use suitable metal cavity fixings such as collapsible anchors or spring toggles.

If the studs are spaced at 400mm (1ft 4in) centres, fix the shelving uprights to alternate studs. If spaced at 600mm (2ft), fix to each in turn.

Another possibility is to fit individual shelves that clip into extruded-aluminium shelf-supports screwed horizontally across the studs.

Hanging small fixtures

Load-carrying fixtures with a small contact area can crush the plaster and strain the fixings. Mount coat hooks, for example, on a batten to spread the load, then screw the batten to two studs.

Small pictures should be hung on picture hooks secured with steel pins, preferably fixed to a stud (use larger pins with two-pin hooks). To hang a large mirror or picture on the wall, use mirror plates fixed to the frame. Heavy frames need to be suspended from stranded wire – not picture cord, which can stretch.

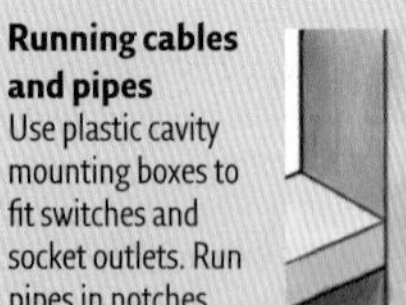

Running cables and pipes
Use plastic cavity mounting boxes to fit switches and socket outlets. Run pipes in notches cut into the studs, reinforcing cutouts over large pipes.

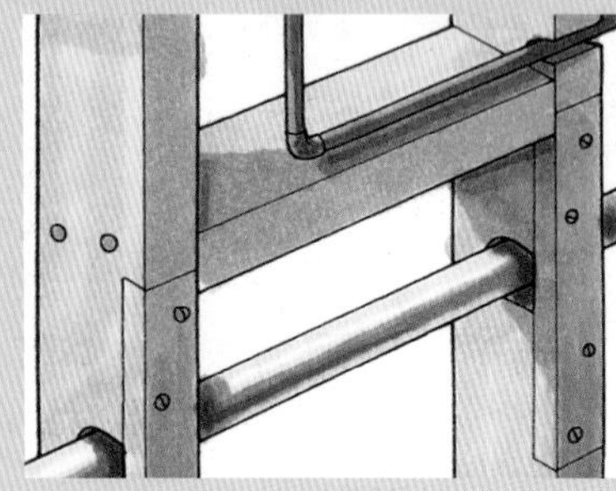

Installing services

It's easy to plan and fit pipes and wiring inside a new stud partition wall before lining it.

Drill holes for electrical cable at the centres of the studs for horizontal runs and in noggings for vertical runs, then run the cable to the point where you plan to mount a switch or socket outlet. With the plasterboard lining in place, mark and cut an opening for a plastic cavity mounting box and feed the cable into it. Push the box into its opening and rotate or release the box's side flanges to grip the cladding.

Drill holes for supply pipes close to the front edges of the studs, then saw in towards the holes to make notches. Larger notches for waste pipes must be reinforced to prevent them weakening the studs. Drill the holes, then cut housings for lengths of 50 x 25mm (2 x 1in) softwood to bridge the notches. Cut the notches and set the waste pipe in place, then screw on the bridging pieces.

SEE ALSO > Metal stud partitions 155, Shelving 222–7, Plumbing in a basin 373, Cavity wall fixings 536

Metal-stud partition walls

A partition-wall system employing a framework of metal studding is available from DIY suppliers. Metal studding is lightweight yet strong and stable; when clad in plasterboard and sealed, it offers good fire and sound resistance. The studs are preslotted to accommodate cables or water pipes.

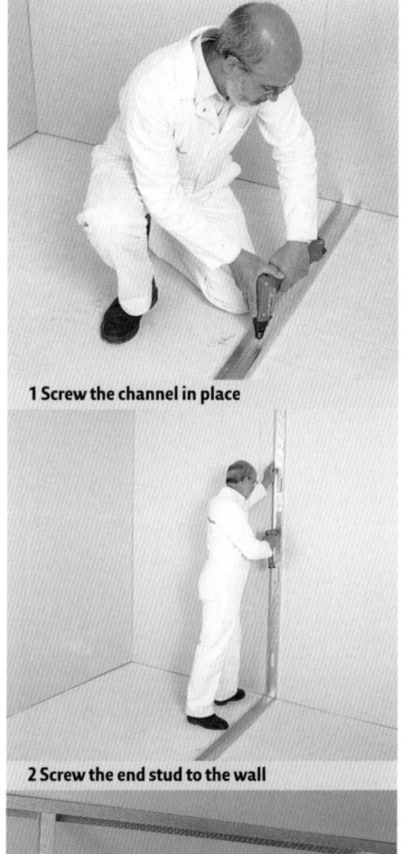

1 Screw the channel in place

2 Screw the end stud to the wall

3 Fit the prepared head member to the studs

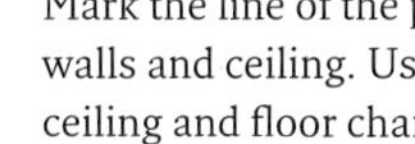

The basic system

Metal studs are made from plated-steel sheet folded into a C-shaped profile. They are produced in lengths of 2.4 to 4.2m (8 to 14ft) and are available in four widths: 48, 60, 70 and 146mm (1⅞, 2⅞, 2¾, and 5¾in). The ceiling and floor channels for them are made in corresponding sizes but the channels are 2mm (1⁄16in) wider, in order to allow the studs to fit inside them, and are 3.6m (12ft) long.

A fixing channel screwed across the studs provides support for wall-hung fixtures, if their positions can be planned in advance. Where required, a fixing strap is used to back up horizontal joints in the plasterboard lining.

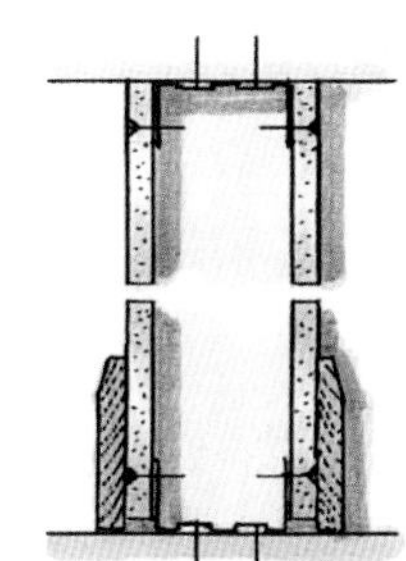

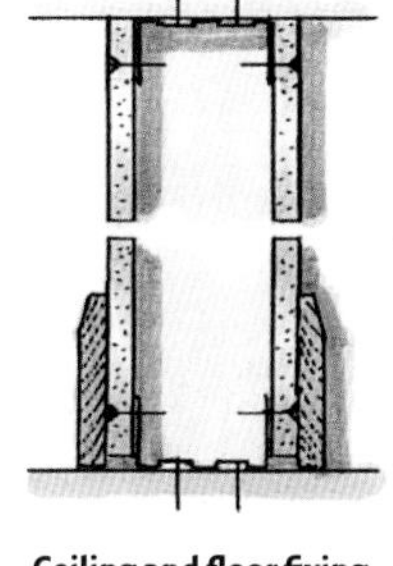

Ceiling and floor fixing

Erecting the metal framework

Mark the line of the partition on the floor, walls and ceiling. Using a hacksaw, cut the ceiling and floor channels to length, and screw them in place (1). Space the screws 600mm (2ft) apart, and stagger them when fixing channels of 72mm (2⅞in) and over. If the floor is uneven, fit a wooden sill of the same width first. Cut the studs to fit into the floor and ceiling channels; make sure the service cutouts will align. Screw the first channel to the side wall (2). Space the intermediate studs at 600mm (2ft) centres and fix them to the channel with special self-tapping wafer-head screws. Fix the wall stud similarly. Make sure all the studs face the same way. Fit extra studs, if required, for heavy wall-hung fixtures.

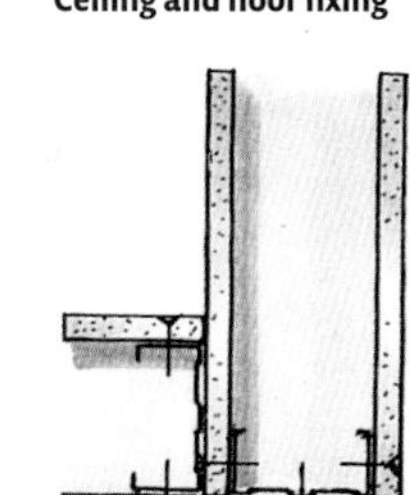

Corner assembly

Making a door opening

When calculating the width of the doorway, allow for the door, door linings, and wooden grounds fixed to the studs. Fit full-height studs at each side. Cut a section of channel to span the opening plus 150mm (6in) at each end. Saw through the side flanges of the channel and bend the ends at right angles to form the door-head member. Fit the head and screw the turned-down ends to the studs at the required height (3), allowing for the upper door lining and ground. Cut and fit a short stud above. Cut the wooden grounds and fix them into the opening.

Lining the wall

Line the framework with 12.5mm (½in) plasterboard, driving dry-wall screws directly into the studs (4); fit two layers of the board with their joints staggered. Fit the door linings and finish the surround with an architrave moulding.

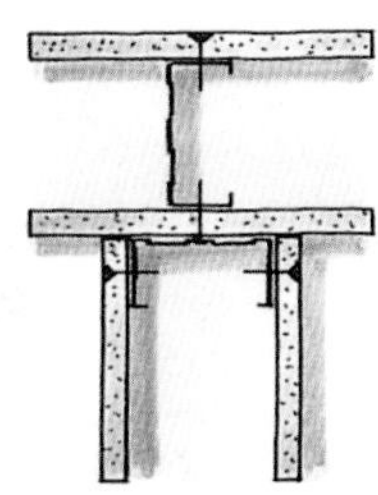

T-junction assembly

Running services
The metal studs are provided with cutouts that can be used for routing plumbing and electrical cables. Cables must be run in conduits to prevent abrasion.

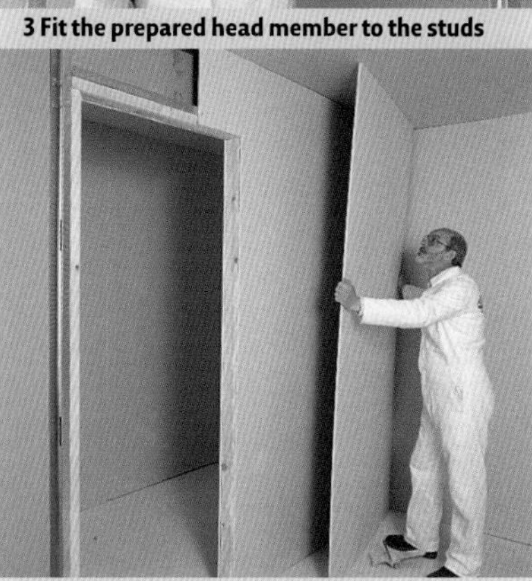

4 Fix the plasterboard to the studs

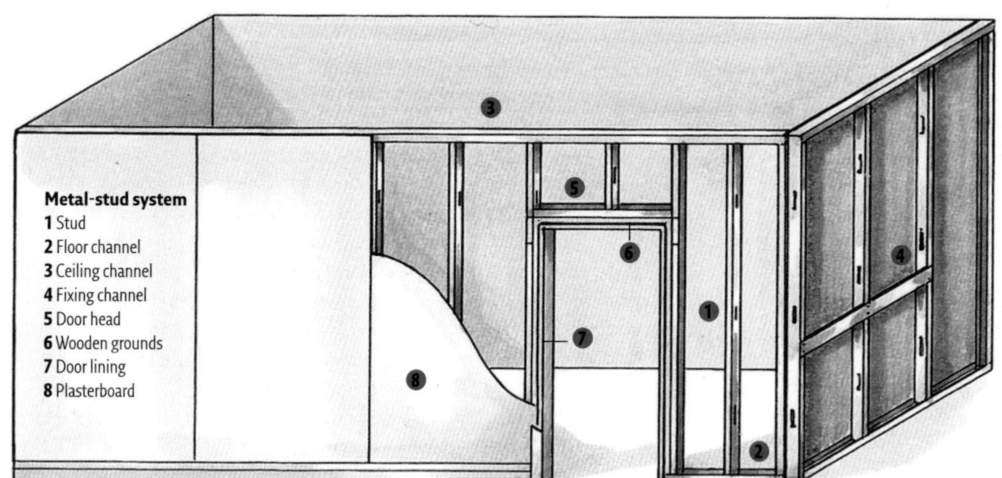

SEE ALSO > Marking out 151, Cutting plasterboard 162, Finishing plasterboard 168

Interior plasterwork

Plasterwork is used to provide internal walls and ceilings with a smooth, flat surface suitable for decorating. Plaster also provides sound and thermal insulation and protection from fire. There are two methods of providing a plaster finish: traditional wet plastering and the use of plasterboard (known as 'dry-lining').

Buying plaster
Plaster powder is sold in 25kg (55lb) paper sacks. Smaller sizes are available for repair work. Try to buy only as much plaster as you need for a job. Ready-mixed plaster is sold in plastic tubs. It is more expensive than dry plaster, but is easier for the amateur to use and keeps well.

Storing plaster
Store plaster powder in dry conditions. Keep an opened bag in a plastic sack sealed with tape. Discard plaster powder that contains lumps.

Traditional plastering

Traditional plastering uses a mix of plastering material and water, which is spread with a trowel over the rough background in one or two, or sometimes three, layers and then levelled. When set, the plaster forms an integral part of the wall or ceiling. It can be applied directly to a solid masonry wall. To plaster a timber-framed wall or ceiling, thin strips of wood called laths are nailed to the timber framework to support the plaster. As the plaster is applied, it is forced between the laths and forms projecting nibs that bond the plaster to the laths.

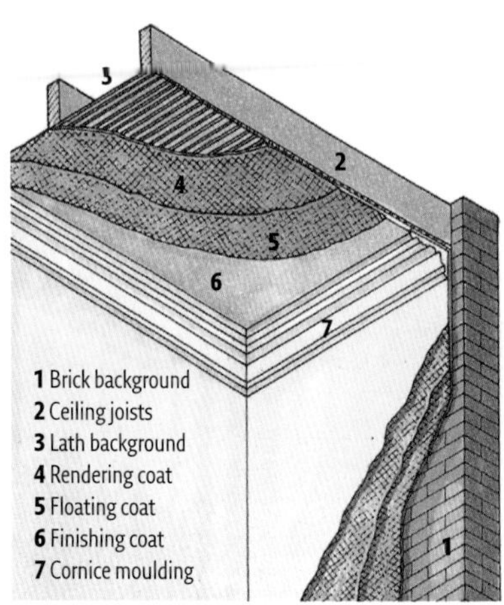

Dry-lining with plasterboard

Manufactured boards of paper-covered plaster are used both for dry-lining walls and ceilings in modern homes and for renovations. Plasterboard obviates the drying-out period required for wet plasters and requires less skill to apply. The large, flat boards are nailed, screwed or bonded to walls and ceilings to provide a separate finishing layer. On masonry walls, the boards are fixed to timber battens or bedded in dabs of plaster. The surface of plasterboard can be decorated directly once the boards are sealed, or it can be covered with a thin coat of finish plaster.

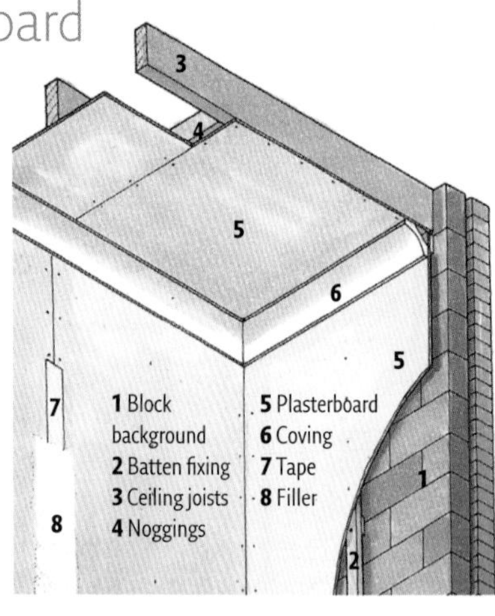

Preparing the background

A well-prepared background is the first step to successful plastering.

Background absorbency
Brush down the surface of a masonry background, in order to remove loose particles, dust and efflorescent salts. Test the absorption of the background by splashing on water; if it stays wet, you can consider the surface 'normal'. This means that it will only require light dampening with clean water prior to applying the plaster.

A dry background that absorbs the water immediately will take too much water from the plaster, so it is difficult to work. It also prevents the plaster from setting properly and may cause cracking. If the masonry is dry, soak it with clean water, applied with a brush or garden sprayer.

Prime very absorbent surfaces, such as aerated concrete blocks, with 1 part PVA bonding agent : 5 parts clean water. When this is dry, apply a bonding coat consisting of 3 parts bonding agent : 1 part water. Apply the plaster when the bonding coat is tacky.

Choosing plaster for interior work

The type of plaster you need depends on the nature of the work and on the surface you are plastering.

Ready-mixed plaster
For small-scale repair work on walls and ceilings, buy ready-mixed patching plaster. It can be applied to any background, and dries to a white finish.

One-coat plaster
You have to mix one-coat powder plaster yourself, but it will stay workable for longer than most powder plasters and it can be put on in a relatively thick single layer. It can be used on any wall background and dries to a white finish.

Undercoat plaster
If you are plastering old or new bare masonry, you need undercoat plaster to form the first layer (called the floating coat or basecoat) on the wall. This is usually about 10mm (3/8in) thick. So-called 'browning' plaster is used on masonry with average suction, such as brick and blockwork. 'Bonding' plaster is used on low-suction backgrounds, such as engineering bricks and surfaces that have been sealed with PVA bonding agents. Hardwall plaster is another undercoat plaster that can be used on most masonry backgrounds. The commonest types of undercoat plaster are Carlite and Thistle plasters.

Finish plaster
The undercoat layer is covered with a finish coat (topcoat) 2–3mm (about 1/8in) thick. Use Carlite Finish plaster over a Carlite undercoat, and Thistle Multi-finish over a Thistle undercoat.

Plastering plasterboard
Stud partition walls clad with square-edged plasterboard are given an overall smooth plaster finish coat 2–3mm (about 1/8in) thick, using a product such as Thistle Board Finish plaster. Where tapered-edge boards are used, the joints are taped and filled with joint filler, but the board surface is not plastered. It may be decorated directly, or given a skim coat of plaster.

SEE ALSO > Types of plasterboard 162, Fixing plasterboard 163, 166

Mixing plaster

Having prepared the background, the next step is to mix the plaster. This can be a messy job, so put down plastic or fabric dust sheets in the room where you are working and remember to wipe your feet when leaving the room.

1 Add plaster to water
2 Stir the plaster
3 Tip out the plaster

You should mix only as much plaster as you can apply in about 20 minutes - beyond that time it begins to set and starts to become unworkable. As you become more skilled at plastering, you can make up larger batches.

Old plaster stuck to your tools or other equipment can shorten the setting time and reduce the strength of newly mixed plaster. Discard any plaster that has begun to set in the bucket or on your spot board (see right) and wash them with clean water. Then make a fresh batch. Never rework old plaster by adding more water.

Mixing undercoat plaster

Mix undercoat plaster for patching work in a large plastic bucket. Use a trowel for small quantities, and a power stirrer with an electric drill for larger amounts. Pour the plaster slowly into the water and stir it to a smooth but fairly stiff consistency (it should resemble porridge). You will need about three quarters of a litre (1⅓ pints) of water to mix 1kg (2lb 4oz) of plaster.

For mixing larger quantities, buy a plasterer's trough from a builders' merchant and use a power mixer, to enable you to achieve a uniform mix.

Mixing finish plaster

Mix finish plaster in a plastic bucket. Pour no more than 2 litres (3½ pints) of water into the bucket, then sprinkle the plaster into the water (**1**) and stir it until it reaches the creamy consistency of melting ice cream (**2**). Tip it out onto a clean spot board (**3**), ready for use.

Mixing plaster fillers

Pour out a small heap of cellulose filler onto a flat board or tile. Scrape a hollow in the centre with your filling knife and pour in water. Gradually drag the powder into the centre until it absorbs all the water, then stir the mix to a creamy thickness; if it seems too runny, add a little more powder. To fill deep holes and cracks, begin with a stiff mix but finish off with creamy filler.

You can use 6mm (¼in) exterior-grade plywood to make a useful board for mixing and carrying filler. Cut out a 300mm (1ft) square with a projecting handle, or make a thumb hole as in an artist's palette. Seal the surface with varnish, or apply a plastic laminate for a smooth finish.

Plaster coverage
- A 25kg (55lb) bag of undercoat plaster will cover about 3.5sq m (4sq yd) at a thickness of 10mm (⅜ in).
- A similar quantity of finish plaster will cover an area of about 10sq m (12sq yd) at a thickness of 2–3mm (⅛ in).

Boards for mixing plaster

You need to place mixed plaster on a flat surface so you can load it onto your hawk.

Spot board

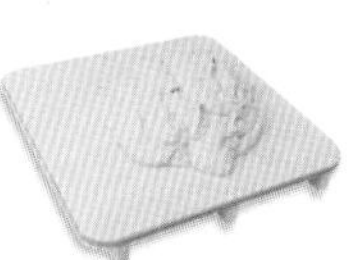

After mixing a quantity of plaster, tip it out onto a spot board. This is a piece of exterior-grade plywood, 18mm (¾in) thick and about 900mm (3ft) square. Round off the corners, and screw three lengths of 50 x 25mm (2 x 1in) softwood to the underside of the board.

Using a stand

To help you pick up the mixed plaster easily, use a stand that will support the spot board at table height - about 700mm (2ft 4in) from the ground.

To construct a folding stand, use 50 x 38mm (2 x 1½in) softwood for the legs and 75 x 25mm (3 x 1in) softwood for the rails and braces. Make one of the leg frames to fit inside the other, and bolt them securely together at the centre.

Alternatively, use a portable folding bench, with the board's central batten gripped in the vice jaws.

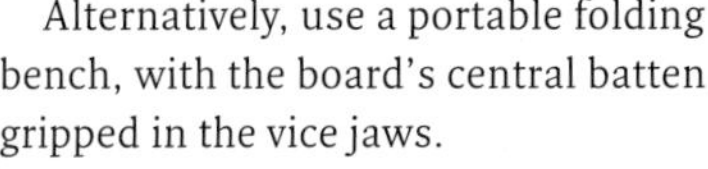

Using bonding agents

Bonding agents are based on polyvinyl acetate (PVA). They are used to modify the suction of the background or to improve the adhesion of the plaster. When using a bonding agent, don't apply a basecoat plaster any thicker than 10mm (⅜in) at a time. If you need to build up the thickness, scratch the surface of the first coat of plaster to provide an extra key, and allow at least 24 hours between coats.

Bonding agents can be mixed with plaster to fill cracks. Brush away any loose particles from the surface and then use a brush to apply a priming coat of 1 part agent : 3 to 5 parts water.

Mix the plaster to a stiff consistency, using 1 part bonding agent : 1 part water. Apply the filler with a trowel, pressing it well into the cracks.

SEE ALSO > Choosing plaster 156

Plastering techniques

Plastering can seem a daunting business to the beginner and yet it has only two basic requirements: that the plaster should stick well to its background and that it should be brought to a smooth, flat finish. Thorough preparation and careful choice of plaster and tools should ensure good adhesion, but the ability to achieve a smooth, flat surface will come only after some practice. It is a good idea to tackle a small-scale patch for your first attempt at plastering.

Problems to avoid

Sanding uneven surfaces

Many amateurs tackle plastering with the idea of levelling the plastered surface by rubbing it down when it has set. This approach creates a lot of dust, which can permeate other parts of the house, and invariably produces a poor result.

It is far better to try to achieve a good surface finish as you apply the plaster, using wide-bladed tools to spread the material evenly on the wall. Ridges left by the corners of a trowel or filling knife can be carefully shaved down before the plaster sets, using the knife.

When covering a large area with finish plaster, it's not always easy to see if the surface is flat as well as smooth. You can check this by looking obliquely across the wall surface, or by shining a light across it from one side to detect any irregularities.

Crazing

Fine cracks in finished plaster may be due to a sand-and-cement undercoat shrinking as it dries out. This type of undercoat must be fully dry before the finish plaster goes on. However, if the dried plaster surface is sound, the fine cracks can be concealed by a covering of lining paper.

Top-coat and undercoat plaster can also crack if it is made to dry out too fast. Never heat plaster to dry it.

Loss of strength

Gypsum plaster sets by chemical action when it is mixed with water. If it dries out before full setting has taken place, the surface will be weak and crumbly, having not yet developed its full strength. If this happens, you will have no option but to strip the wall and replaster it.

Picking up plaster

Hold the edge of your hawk below the spot board and use your trowel to scrape a manageable amount of plaster onto its surface (1). Take no more than a trowelful to start with.

Tip the hawk towards you and, in one movement, cut away about half of the plaster with the trowel, scraping and lifting it off the hawk and onto the face of the trowel (2). Keep this horizontal.

Applying the plaster

Hold the loaded trowel horizontally, then tilt it at an angle to the face of the wall (1). Apply the plaster with a vertical upward stroke, pressing firmly so that plaster is fed onto the wall surface. Flatten the angle of the trowel as you go (2) – but never let its whole face come into contact with the plaster, or it may induce suction and pull it off the wall.

1 Load the hawk

1 Tilt the trowel

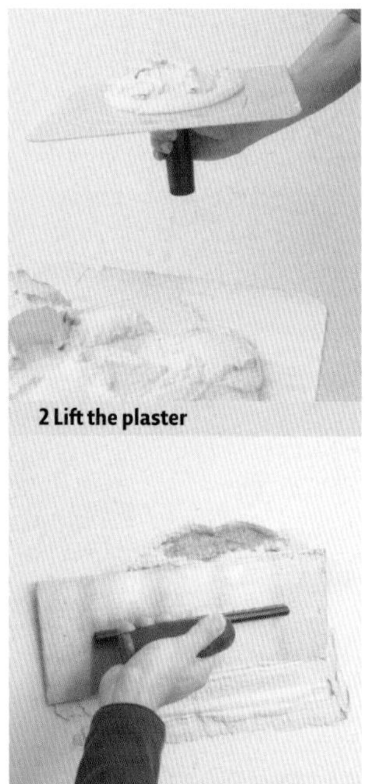

2 Lift the plaster

2 Apply the plaster

Levelling up

Build a slight extra thickness of plaster with the trowel, applying it as evenly as possible. Use a straightedged rule to level the surface. Hold the rule against the original plaster when filling a patch, or against wooden screeds (guides) when plastering a whole wall. Work the rule upwards while moving it from side to side, then lift it carefully away, taking the surplus with it. Fill in any hollows, with more plaster from the trowel, then level the surface again. Allow one-coat plaster to stiffen before you smooth it finally with a trowel. For two-coat work, scrape back the edges slightly, ready for the finish coat.

Work the rule up the wall to level the surface

Finishing the plaster

Apply the finish coat as soon as the undercoat has set. A cement-based sanded plaster must be allowed to dry out completely. The papered face of plasterboard can be finished immediately.

Use a plasterer's trowel to apply the finish plaster, spreading it evenly to a thickness of 2mm ($\frac{1}{16}$in) – and not more than 3mm ($\frac{1}{8}$in) – judging this by eye.

As the plaster stiffens, brush it or lightly spray it with water, then trowel the surface so as to consolidate it and produce a smooth matt finish. Avoid pressing too hard or overworking the surface. Sponge off surplus water.

Spray plaster occasionally as you smooth it

SEE ALSO > Types of plaster 156, Spot boards 157, Hawk 510, Plasterer's trowel 510

Reinforcing a corner

Plastered corners are vulnerable, particularly in corridors, and often need reinforcing.

Using corner beading

If damage to a corner extends along most of the edge, you can reinforce the repair with a metal or plastic corner beading. As well as strengthening the new corner, it will speed up the repair work considerably, because it dispenses with the need to use a board as a guide.

You can obtain beading from any good builders' merchant or DIY store. Cut it to length with snips and a hacksaw. Metal beading has a protective galvanized coating, and the cut ends must be sealed with a metal primer or bituminous paint.

Cut back the damaged plaster, wet the brickwork, and apply patches of undercoat plaster each side of the corner. Press the wings of the beading into the plaster patches (**1**), using your straightedge to align its outer nose with both of the original plaster surfaces. Alternatively, check for plumb with a builder's level. Allow the plaster to set.

Build up the undercoat plaster, but scrape it back with your trowel to 2mm (1/16in) below the old finished level (**2**).

Apply the finish coat, using the beading as a level to achieve flush surfaces. Take care not to damage the beading's galvanized coating with your trowel – or rust may come through later and stain wallcoverings. To be on the safe side, brush metal primer over the new corner before decorating.

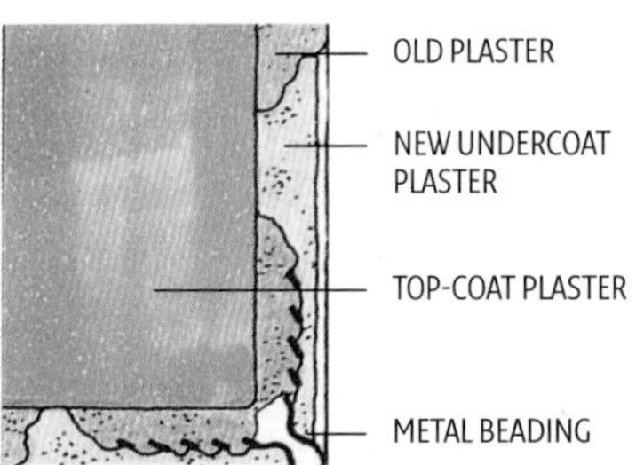

Section through a repaired corner

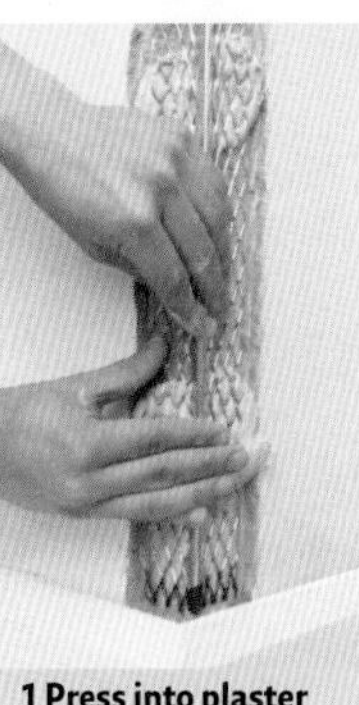

1 Press into plaster

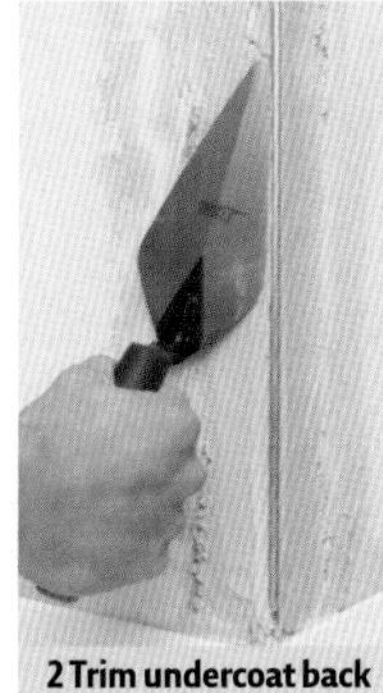

2 Trim undercoat back

Repairing damaged plaster

Once you start tackling jobs that are more ambitious than simple patch repairs – such as removing fireplaces and taking down walls – you will need to develop some of the professional plasterer's skills, in order to refurbish larger areas satisfactorily.

Plastering over a fireplace opening

A bricked-in fireplace provides an area that's large enough for the amateur to practise on without the work becoming unmanageable. Jobs of this kind can be undertaken with one-coat plaster, or you can apply an undercoat plaster followed by a top coat of finish plaster.

Using a one-coat plaster

Prepare the background by cutting away any loose plaster above and around the brickwork. Dampen the background with clean water and, before you start, place a strip of hardboard against the foot of the wall to catch dropped plaster.

Tip the plaster onto a spot board, then scoop some onto a hawk and, with a trowel (or the spreader provided), apply the plaster to the brickwork.

Work in the sequence shown on the right, starting at the bottom of each section and spreading the plaster vertically. Work each area in turn, blending the edges, then level the plaster with a rule. Fill any hollows, and level again.

Leave the plaster to stiffen for about 45 minutes – by which time firm finger pressure should leave no impression.

At this stage, lightly dampen the surface with a close-textured plastic sponge, and then use a wet trowel or spreader to smooth the plaster to a 'polished' finish. Use firm pressure, sweeping the trowel from side to side and then up and down until you have the perfect surface. Keep the trowel wet.

Let the plaster dry thoroughly before decorating.

Two-coat plastering

Apply undercoat and finish-coat plasters as described above – but scrape back the undercoat to allow for the thickness of the finishing coat.

Plastering sequence
Divide the area into manageable portions and apply the plaster in the sequence shown.

Repairing a chipped corner

When the plaster covering an external corner breaks away, it usually reveals unsightly patches of masonry. Repair the damage with one-coat or two-coat plaster, using a wide board nailed on one side as a guide to help you achieve a neat corner.

With a bolster chisel, cut away the plaster near the damaged edge to reveal about 75mm (3in) of masonry on each side of the corner.

If you are using two-coat plaster, nail the guide board on one side of the corner, so that the board's edge is set back about 3mm (1/8in) from the surface of the plaster on the other side of the corner (**1**). Mix up the undercoat plaster, wet the brickwork and the broken edge of the old plaster, then fill one side of the corner up to the edge of the board but not flush with the wall (**2**). Scratch-key the new plaster with your trowel.

When the plaster has become stiff, remove the board, pulling it straight from the wall to prevent the plaster breaking away. The edge thus exposed represents the finished surface – so, to allow for the top coat, scrape the plaster back about 3mm (1/8in), using the trowel and a straightedge as a guide (**3**).

For the next stage, a professional would simply hold the guide board over the new repair and fill the second side of the corner with plaster. An easier method for the amateur is to let the new plaster harden, then nail the board in place before applying and keying fresh plaster as before (**4**).

Let the undercoat set, then nail the board to the wall as before, but this time aligning its edge with the original plastered surface, and fill level with finish plaster. If necessary, dampen the undercoat to reduce the suction. When both sides are firm, polish the new plaster with a wet trowel, rounding over the edge slightly, and leave the plaster to dry out.

If you are using one-coat plaster for the repair work, set the guide board flush with the finished surface on each side of the corner.

1 Set board back

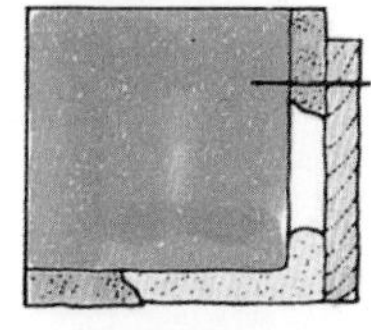

2 Fill flush with board

3 Scrape back edge

4 Fill second side

SEE ALSO > Repairing plaster 48–50, Preparing the background 156, Removing a fireplace 398

Patching a ceiling

A misplaced foot in the attic, a roof leak that has gone unnoticed, or a leaking water pipe can all damage a plasterboard ceiling. Fortunately, serious damage is usually localized and is easily repaired.

Check the direction in which the ceiling joists run and whether there is any electrical wiring close to the damaged area. Use a hammer to knock a hole through the centre of the damage: you will find that it's possible to look along the void with the help of a torch and a mirror.

Use a mirror and torch to inspect the void

Mark out a square or rectangle on the ceiling, enclosing the damaged area; then cut away an area of the plasterboard slightly larger than the damage, working up to the sides of the nearest joists. Use a padsaw – or if there is wiring nearby, a craft knife that will just penetrate the thickness of the plasterboard.

Cut and skew-nail 50mm (2in) noggings between the joists at the ends of the cutout, with half their thickness projecting beyond the cut edges of the plasterboard (1). Nail 50 x 25mm (2 x 1in) softwood battens to the sides of the joists, flush with their bottom edges (2).

Cut a plasterboard patch to fit the opening, leaving a 3mm (⅛in) gap all round. Nail the patch to the noggings and battens, then fill and tape over the joints to give a flush surface.

1 Nail in noggings

2 Nail in battens

Dealing with minor damage

It is not necessary to patch a ceiling that has minor damage. Eradicate the source of the problem and leave the ceiling to dry out, then use cellulose filler to make repairs to the plasterboard next time you decorate the room.

Repairing lath-and-plaster

When the plaster of a lath-and-plaster wall deteriorates, it often loses its grip on the laths. The plaster will probably bulge and may crack in places. It will sound hollow when tapped and tends to flex when you press against it. Loose plaster should be replaced.

Repairing holes in lath-and-plaster walls

Cut out loose plaster with a bolster and hammer. If the laths are sound, you can replaster over them.

After dampening the laths and plaster edges around the hole (1), apply a one-coat plaster, using a plasterer's trowel. Press the plaster firmly between the laths (2), building up the coating until it's flush with the original plaster. Level off with a rule. Let the plaster stiffen, then smooth it with a damp sponge and a trowel. Alternatively, apply the plaster in two coats. Scratch-key the first coat (3) and let it set, then apply the second coat and finish as before.

For larger repairs, use two coats of lightweight gypsum undercoat plaster, followed by a compatible finish plaster. For a small repair, press cellulose filler onto and between the laths.

If laths are damaged, cut them out and either replace them, using metal mesh, or cover the studs with plasterboard. Then finish with plaster.

1 Dampen edges of old sound plaster

2 Press plaster in between the laths

3 Scratch-key the undercoat

Repairing a ceiling

A leaking roof or pipe above a lath-and-plaster ceiling can cause localized damage to the plaster but should not damage the laths. Repair the ceiling with an undercoat plaster, finishing off with a top-coat of gypsum plaster.

Carefully cut back the damaged plaster to sound material. Dampen the background and apply the undercoat (1). Don't build up a full thickness. Key the surface and let it set. Give the ceiling a second coat, then scrape it back 2mm (1⁄16in) below the surface and lightly key it. When it has set, use a plasterer's trowel to apply a finish coat (2).

1 Apply a thin first coat with firm pressure

2 Level top coat over keyed undercoat

SEE ALSO > Repairing plaster 48–50, Types of plaster 156, Taping joints 168, Switching off the power 296

Plastering a wall

New work is more easily carried out with plasterboard, but there are times when repairs arising from problems with damp or structural alterations require fairly large areas to be plastered. It is possible to tackle plastering of this sort yourself, although some previous experience, such as patching up damaged plaster, would be an advantage. The key to success is to divide the wall into manageable areas.

Applying the plaster

Use the face of a plasterer's trowel to scrape a couple of trowel-loads of plaster onto the hawk, and start the undercoat plastering at the top of the wall. Holding the trowel at an angle to the face of the wall, apply the plaster with vertical strokes. Work from right to left if you are right-handed; if you're left-handed, work from left to right.

Using firm pressure to ensure good adhesion, apply a thin layer first; then follow it with more plaster, building up to the required thickness. If the final thickness of the plaster needs to be greater than 10mm (3/8in), key the surface with a scratcher and let it set, then apply a second or 'floating' coat.

Fill the area between two screed battens (see right), but there's no need to pack the plaster tightly up against them. Level the surface with a rule laid across the battens, sliding the rule from side to side as you work upwards from the bottom of the wall. Fill in any hollows, and then level the plaster again. Scratch the surface lightly, to provide a key for the finishing coat, and let the plaster set.

Work along the entire wall in this way, and then remove the battens. Fill the gaps, levelling the plaster with the rule or trowel.

With gypsum plasters, the finish coat can be applied as soon as the undercoat is set. Cement undercoats must be left to dry out for at least 24 hours, in order to allow for shrinkage. Wet the undercoat before the top coat is applied.

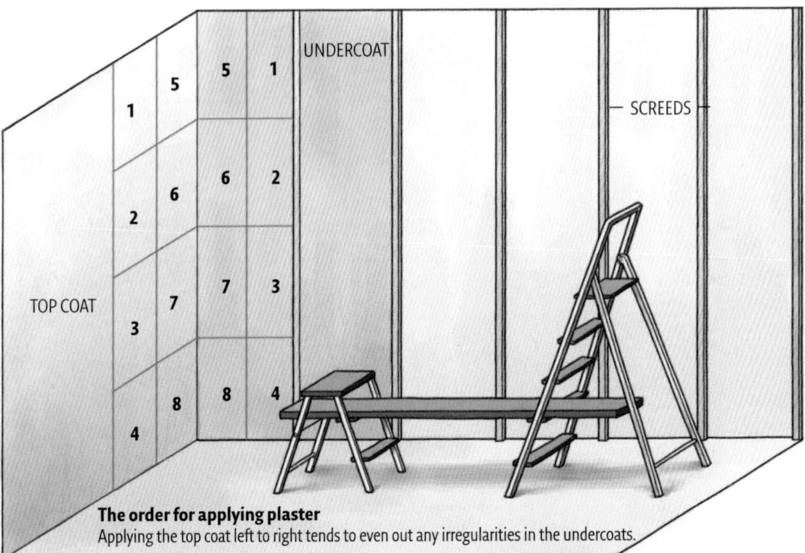

The order for applying plaster
Applying the top coat left to right tends to even out any irregularities in the undercoats.

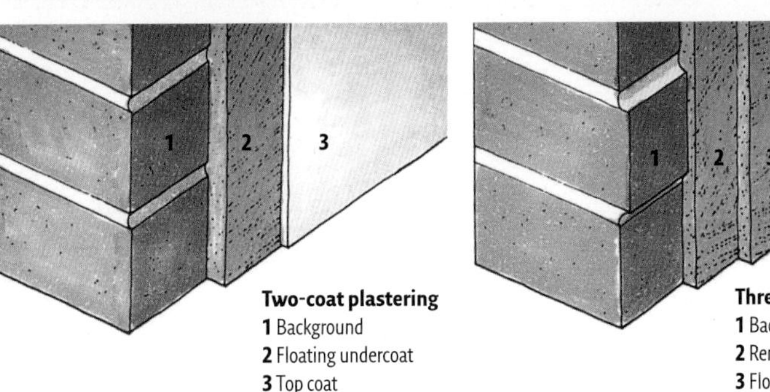

Two-coat plastering
1 Background
2 Floating undercoat
3 Top coat

Three-coat plastering
1 Background
2 Rendering undercoat
3 Floating undercoat
4 Top coat

Preparing to plaster

In addition to specialized plasterer's tools, you will need a spirit level and some lengths of planed softwood battening 10mm (3/8in) thick. The battens, known as screeds, are nailed to the wall to act as guides when it comes to levelling the plaster. Professional plasterers form 'plaster screeds' by applying bands of undercoat plaster to the required thickness. These can be laid vertically or horizontally.

After preparing the background, fix wooden screeds vertically to the wall with masonry nails. Drive most of the nails home fully to make it easier to work with the trowel, but leave one or two nails protruding slightly so you can remove the screeds afterwards. The screeds should be spaced no more than 600mm (2ft) apart. Use the spirit level to get them truly plumb, packing them out with strips of hardboard as need be.

Mix the undercoat plaster to a thick, creamy consistency and, to begin with, measure out two bucketfuls. You can increase this to larger amounts when you become more proficient.

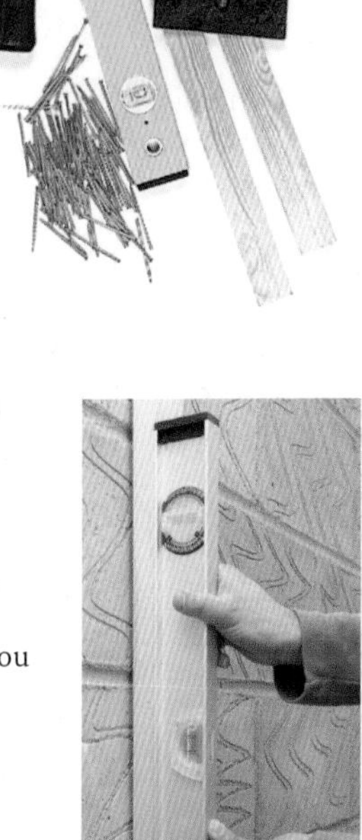

Plumb the screeds
Pack out the screed battens at the fixing points as required.

Finishing

Cover the undercoat with a thin layer of finish plaster, working from top to bottom, using even, vertical strokes. Work from left to right, if you are right-handed; if you are left-handed, work from right to left. Hold the trowel at a slight angle, so that only one edge is touching.

Make sweeping horizontal strokes to level the surface further. You can try using the rule to get the initial surface even – but you may risk dragging the finish coat off. Use the trowel to smooth out any ripples.

Wet your trowel and work over the surface with firm pressure, to consolidate the plaster. As it sets, trowel it to produce a smooth matt finish – but don't overwork it. Use a damp sponge to wipe away any plaster slurry that appears.

SEE ALSO > Preparing surfaces 156, Plastering techniques 158–9

Plasterboard

Plasterboard provides a quick and simple method of cladding walls or ceilings with a smooth surface for decorating. It is easy to cut and to fix, either by bonding or by nailing it into place. It is made in a range of thicknesses and sheet sizes, with either square or tapered edges.

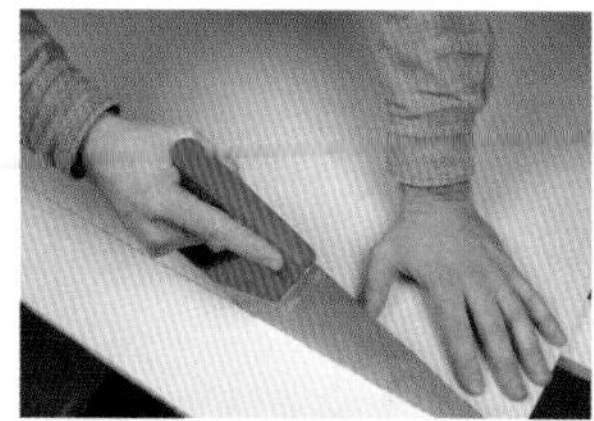

Cutting with a saw Support the sheet at either side of the cut, and saw it with the blade held at a shallow angle to the board.

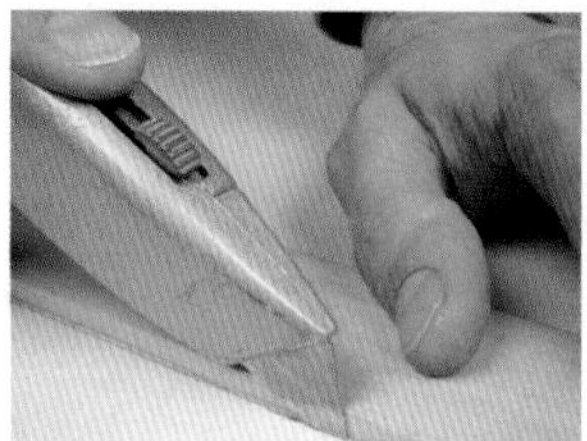

Cutting with a knife Use a slim timber batten as a straightedge to guide the knife blade.

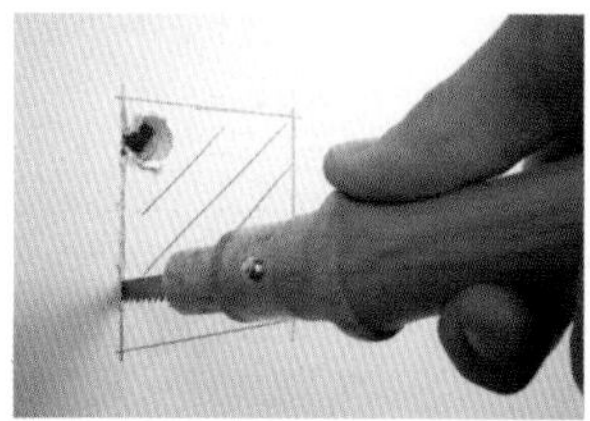

Cutting openings Drill a hole within the waste area to admit the blade of a padsaw or jigsaw, then make the cutout.

Plasterboard is available both from DIY stores and from builders' merchants. It is made with a core of aerated gypsum plaster and covered on both sides with strong paper. Standard boards have a grey-paper backing, but are covered on the outer face with ivory-coloured paper that provides an ideal surface for decorating. However, if you want to replicate a traditional plastered surface, you can apply a skim coat of wet plaster to the ivory-coloured face.

Storing and cutting plasterboard

Plasterboard is fragile and possesses very little structural strength until it is fixed to a supporting framework. But despite its fragility full-size sheets are quite heavy, and they are awkward to handle – so always get someone to help you carry them. Carry each sheet upright, supporting the long lower edge.

Plasterboard suppliers store sheets flat in stacks, but this is inconvenient at home. Store them on edge instead, leaning them at a slight angle against a wall, with their ivory-coloured faces together. Indoor storage is better than keeping them in a garage, where they may quickly become damp.

Handle and stack the sheets carefully, to avoid damaging their fragile corners and edges.

Cutting plasterboard

Cut plasterboard with a saw or craft knife. When sawing plasterboard, support either side of the cut with battens and hold the saw at a shallow angle to the surface of the sheet. Get a helper to support a large offcut as you approach the end of the cut, to prevent the sheet breaking.

When using a knife, cut deeply into the material, following a straightedge, then snap the sheet along the cutting line over a length of wood. Cut through the paper facing on the other side to separate the two pieces.

Use a keyhole saw, power jigsaw or stiff-blade craft knife to cut openings in plasterboard for electrical fittings. After cutting, remove any ragged edges with abrasive paper.

Plasterboard edges Tapered edges are filled and taped to provide smooth seamless joints that won't show under a wallcovering or coat of paint. Square edges need to be filled and taped, too, to ensure sound joints, although square-edged boards are primarily used for walls that are to be surfaced with a skim coat of wet plaster.

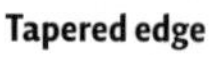

Tapered edge

Square edge

PLASTERBOARD SPECIFICATIONS

TYPE AND USAGE	WIDTHS	LENGTHS	THICKNESS	EDGE FINISH
Standard wallboard and plank				
This material is generally used for dry-lining walls and ceilings. It is produced in a range of lengths and, although most suppliers stock only a limited selection, other sizes can be ordered. One side is ivory-coloured for decorating or plastering.	900mm (3ft) 1.2m (4ft) Plank 600mm (2ft)	1.8m (6ft) to 3.6m (12ft) *Commonly stocked in 2.4m (8ft) lengths.* 2.35m (7ft 8½in) to 3m (9ft 10in)	9.5mm (⅜in) 12.5mm (½in) 15mm (⅝in) 19mm (¾in)	Tapered or square Square
Baseboard				
Baseboard is a square-edged plasterboard that is lined with grey paper. It is produced as a backing for a plaster finish and is used mainly for plastered ceilings. A vapour-check grade is also available (see below).	900mm (3ft)	1.2m (4ft)	9.5mm (⅜in)	Square
Thermal-insulation board				
Thermal-insulation boards are standard sheets of plasterboard with a backing of either expanded polystyrene, extruded polystyrene, phenolic resin or mineral-wool laminate. The surface may be ivory-coloured for direct decoration or plastering.	900mm (3ft) 1.2m (4ft)	2.4m (8ft) 2.7m (8ft 10¼in)	22mm (⅞in) to 55mm (2⅛in)	Tapered
Vapour-check plasterboard				
These boards have a tough metallized polyester-film backing, which is vapour-resistant and provides reflective thermal insulation. They are used as an internal lining to prevent warm moist air condensing on or inside structural wall or ceiling materials.	900mm (3ft) 1.2m (4ft)	1.8m (6ft) to 3m (9ft 10in)	*Stocked in same thicknesses as standard wallboard.*	Tapered or square

N.B. Metric sizes are actual, imperial sizes approximate.

SEE ALSO > Finishing plasterboard 168, Insulating walls 265–6

Plasterboarding a wall

Plasterboard can be nailed to the timber studs of a partition wall or screwed to metal ones; it can also be nailed to battens fixed to a masonry wall, or bonded directly onto solid walls with plaster or an adhesive. The boards can be fitted horizontally if it's more economical to do so, but generally they're placed vertically. All of the edges should be supported. When plasterboarding the ceiling and walls of a room, tackle the ceiling first.

Methods for fixing plasterboard

Fixing to a stud partition

Partition walls may be plain room dividers or may include a doorway (or doorways). If you are plasterboarding a plain wall, start fitting the boards from one corner of the room and work across to the other corner. If the wall includes a doorway, start there and work away from the doorway in both directions towards the adjacent corners.

Starting from a corner

Using a footlifter (see below right), hold the first board in position. If necessary, mark and scribe the edge that meets the adjacent wall. Then fix the board into position, securing it to all of the frame members (see FIXINGS, right).

Fix the rest of the plasterboard sheets in place, working across the partition. Butt the edges of tapered-edge boards, but leave a gap of 3mm (⅛in) between square-edge boards that are to be coated later with a board-finishing plaster.

If necessary, scribe the edge of the last board to fit the end corner before fitting it.

Cut a skirting board, mitring the joints at the corners or scribing the ends of the new board to the original, and fit it.

Starting from a doorway

Using the footlifter, hold the first board flush with the door stud and mark the position of the underside of the door head on the edge of the board. Between this mark and the board's top edge cut out a strip 25mm (1in) wide, so the board edge will lie over the centre of the stud above the door head. Reposition the board and fix it in place, securing it to all the frame members. Fix the rest of the boards in place between the doorway and the room corner, as described earlier.

Cover the rest of the wall – on the other side of the doorway – in a similar way, starting by cutting a strip 25mm (1in) wide from the edge of the first board, as you did on the other side of the doorway.

Cut a plasterboard panel to go above the doorway, fitting it into the cutouts you made in the boards on each side of the door. Sand away any ragged paper at the edges before fitting the panel.

Clad the other side of the partition wall with sheets of plasterboard in the same way.

When all of the plasterboard is in place, fill and finish the joints. Cut and fit solid-wood door linings, and cover the edges with an architrave moulding.

Cut and fit skirting boards, nailing or screwing through the plasterboard into alternate studs behind.

Fixings

Use special galvanized plasterboard nails – the table below lists recommended lengths. Space the nails 150mm (6in) apart and place them not less than 9mm (⅜in) from the paper-covered edge, and 12mm (½in) from cut ends. Drive the nails in straight, so that their heads sink just below the surface without tearing through the paper lining.

Board thickness	Nail length
9.5mm (⅜in)	32mm (1¼in)
12.5 or 15mm (½in or ⅝in)	40mm (1⅝in)
19 or 22mm (¾in or ⅞in)	50mm (2in)
30 to 40mm (1⅛in to 1⅝in)	65mm (2½in)
42 to 55mm (1¾ to 2⅛in)	75mm (3in)

Fixing to metal studs

To fix to metal studs, use special self-tapping dry-wall screws in similar sizes to the nails above. Space them similarly. You can also use these screws for fixing plasterboard to wooden studs.

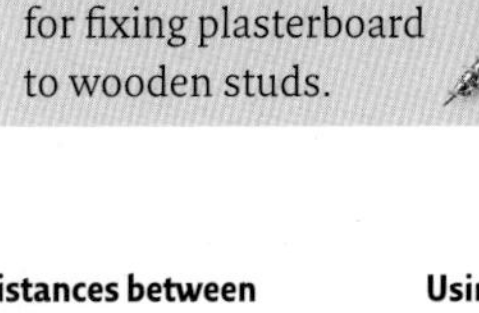

Distances between stud centres
Maximum distance between stud centres: for board 9.5mm (⅜in) thick, 450mm (1ft 6in); for board 12.5mm to 50mm (½ to 2in) thick, 600mm (2ft). When you're building a new partition, it is more economical to apply board 12.5mm (½in) thick to studs set 600mm (2ft) apart.

Procedure for plasterboarding
On a plain wall, work away from a corner. Otherwise, work away from a doorway.

Using a footlifter
A footlifter is a tool that holds the board against the ceiling, leaving both hands free for nailing. You can make one from a block of wood 75mm (3in) wide. Cut each board about 16mm (⅝in) shorter than room height, to provide clearance for the footlifter.

SEE ALSO > Scribing plasterboard 000, Finishing plasterboard 164, Door casings 183, Skirtings 218, Fitting architraves 217

Scribing plasterboard

If the inner edge of the first sheet of plasterboard butts against an uneven wall, or its other edge does not fall on the centre of the stud, the board must be scribed to fit. This involves tracing the wall or stud profile onto the sheet, then cutting it along the marked line.

Scribing the first board

Begin by trying the first board in position (1). The illustration shows an uneven wall pushing the right-hand edge of the sheet of plasterboard beyond the stud to which it is to be fixed.

Next, reposition the board so that its left-hand edge lies exactly on the centre of this stud. Hold it at the required height, using a footlifter, and tack it in place with plasterboard nails driven partway into the intermediate studs.

With a pencil and a batten, cut to the exact width of the board, trace a line that reproduces the profile of the wall onto the face of the plasterboard (2). Make sure you keep the batten level as you slide it down.

Take the board down carefully and use a craft knife or saw to trim the waste away. Cut just on the inside of the scribed line, to leave a 3mm (⅛in) gap next to the wall.

Place the board in the corner again, lift it up tightly against the ceiling and fix it to the studs with plasterboard nails (3). Use screws if you are fixing to metal studding.

Continue to fix whole boards one by one across the wall. If the stud spacing is standard, each board edge should fall on the centre of a stud.

Tools for scribing
Use straight timber battens and a pencil to mark wall profiles on the boards. Hold a spirit level on top of the batten if you wish, to help you keep it horizontal

Scribing the last board

Temporarily fix the board to be scribed directly over the previously fixed board (4), ensuring that their edges lie flush.

With a pencil and batten (as above), trace a pencil line down the face of the board to be scribed, using the batten as a guide. Remove the marked board and cut away the waste, then fix the board to the studs (5). Fill and tape the joints.

Lifting boards into place

Use a wedge-like tool called a footlifter to raise each board off the floor so its top edge is tight against the ceiling, ready for nailing. The gap at floor level will be covered by a skirting board.

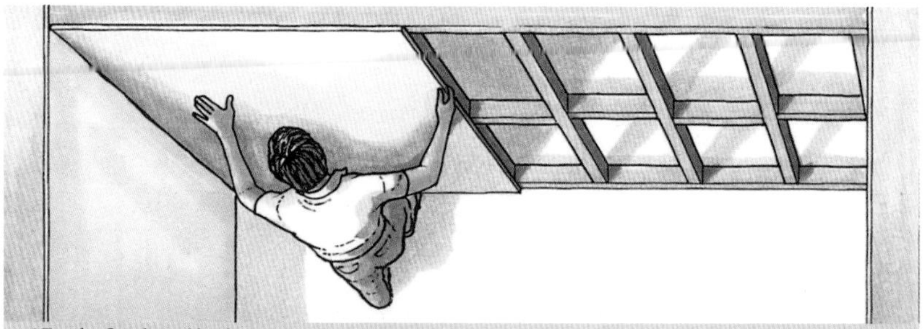

1 Try the first board in the corner

2 Reposition the board and mark the cutting line

3 Cut the board to size and nail it in place

4 Temporarily nail on the last whole board and scribe it to fit the wall

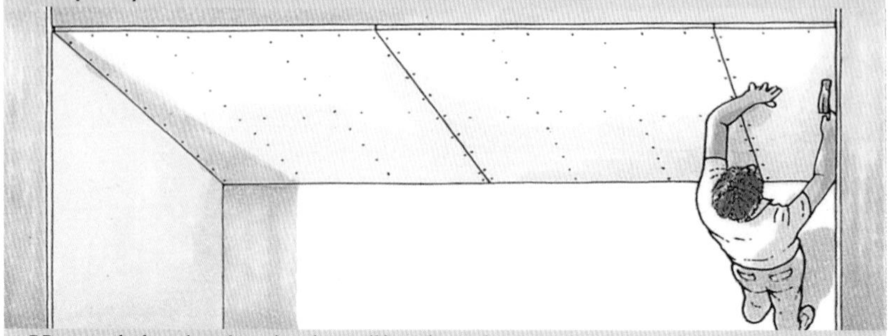

5 Remove the board, cut it to size, then nail it to the studs

SEE ALSO > Building a stud partition 151–3, Cutting plasterboard 162, Fixing plasterboard 163,166, Using a footlifter 163, Finishing plasterboard 168

Dry-lining a solid wall

Plasterboard can't be nailed directly to masonry walls, so battens of sawn timber – known as furring strips – are used to provide a fixing for the nails and to counter any unevenness of the wall surface. The battens should be treated with a wood preserver. You can cover old plaster if it is sound, otherwise it's best to strip back to the brickwork. If the wall is damp, treat the cause and let the wall dry out before lining it with plasterboard. Plan any pipe runs and electrical installations before fitting the battens to the wall.

Marking out

Using a straightedge as a guide, chalk the position of the vertical furring strips on the wall. Place the lines at 400mm (1ft 4in), 450mm (1ft 6in) or 600mm (2ft) centres, depending on the width and thickness of the plasterboard that is being used. Start marking out at any doorway or window opening, and bear in mind that sheets of plasterboard must meet on the centre lines of the strips. Don't forget to allow for the thickness of the plasterboard and furring strips at window reveals.

Fixing the furring strips

Cut the required number of furring strips from 50 x 32mm (2 x 1¼in) softwood. The vertical strips need to be cut 150mm (6in) shorter than the height of the wall. Make horizontal strips to run along the tops and bottoms of the vertical ones, including any short vertical infill battens above and below openings (see below).

Nail the vertical furring strips first, setting their bottom ends 100mm (4in) above the floor. Fix them with masonry nails or cut nails, with the face of each batten level with the guide line marked on the floor (see right). Also, check with a straightedge and spirit level that each strip is flat and plumb, and pack it out as necessary.

Now nail the horizontal strips along the tops and bottoms of the vertical members, inserting packing to bring them all to the same level.

Fixing the plasterboard

To fix plasterboard to furring strips, follow the procedure described for nailing to a stud partition. However, there's no need to notch the boards at the sides of windows and doorways, because you can place short furring strips just where you need them above the openings (see below). Follow the usual procedure for filling and finishing the joints between boards.

Cut the skirting board to length and nail it through the plasterboard to the bottom horizontal furring strip. If it is a high moulded skirting of the type used in period houses, it can be nailed to the strips.

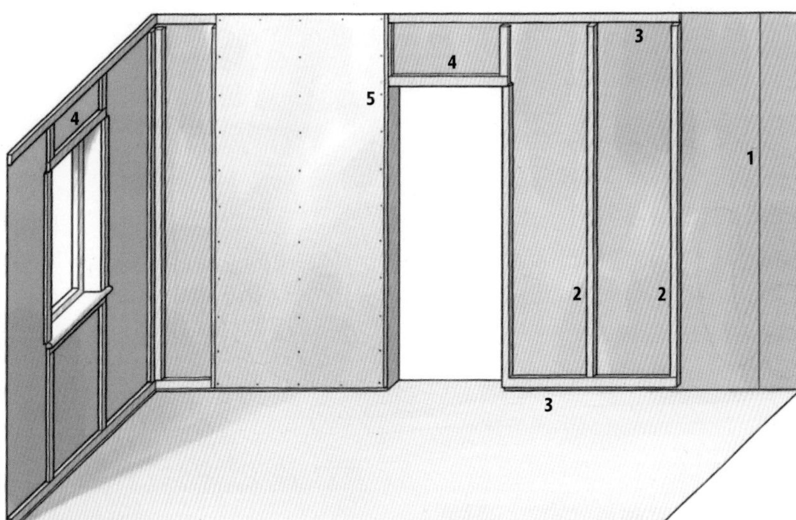

Attaching furring strips to a wall
1 Mark the positions of furring strips.
2 Fix vertical strips.
3 Attach horizontal strips.
4 Fix short pieces over doors and windows, offsetting the short vertical ones to avoid having to cut notches in the boards.
5 Nail boards in place, beginning next to a doorway or window.

Levelling the furring strips

Masonry walls are rarely flat – so if the plasterboard lining is to finish flat and straight, any unevenness has to be taken into account.

To check if the wall is flat, hold a long straightedge horizontally against it at different levels. If it is uneven, make a note of which vertical chalk line is the closest to the point where the wall bulges most (**1**).

Hold a straight furring strip against the marked chalk line, using a straightedge and spirit level to keep the strip plumb, then mark the floor (**2**) where the edge of the straightedge falls. Draw a straight guide line across the floor (**3**), passing through this mark to meet the walls at each end at right angles. Align all the furring strips with this line.

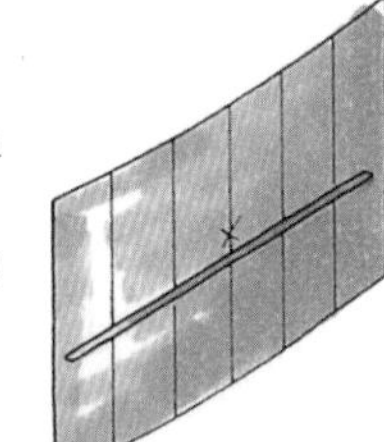

1 Check the wall

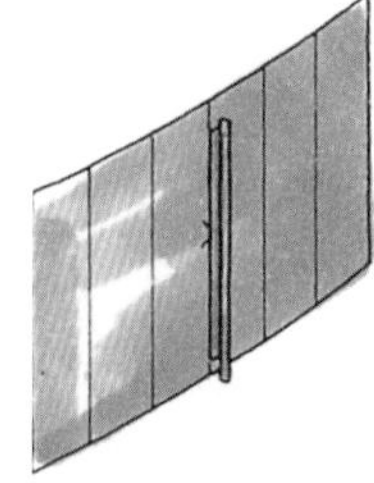

2 Mark the high point

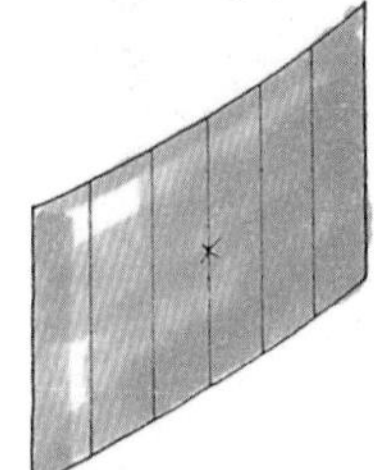

3 Draw line on floor

Marking the floor
Use a straightedge to plot a mark on the floor.

Metal furring strips

Folded-metal furring strips are used in a similar way to wooden strips. They are bonded in place at 600mm (2ft) centres, using a gypsum adhesive. Dabs of the adhesive are applied in horizontal and vertical lines; then the strips are pressed into place and levelled. Fix the plasterboard to the furring strips with screws.

SEE ALSO > Plasterboard 162, Fixing plasterboard 163, 166, Angles and openings 167, Finishing plasterboard 168

Bonding to a solid wall

As an alternative to using furring strips for dry-lining a solid wall, tapered-edge plasterboard can be bonded directly to the wall with thick dabs of gypsum adhesive. The boards are pressed into place and then, with the aid of a stiff straightedge, aligned along guide lines marked on the floor and ceiling. Boards 900mm (3ft) wide are normally used for this technique. The wall must be dry and sound, and the surface dust free.

Marking out

Set out vertical chalk lines on the wall, 450mm (1ft 6in) apart for 900mm (3ft) boards, working from either a corner or an opening.

Using a straightedge (as described for levelling furring strips), determine where the wall bulges most and mark the floor, using a straightedge and spirit level. From the mark, measure 10mm (3/8in), plus the thickness of the board, away from the wall and draw a short line on the floor. Extend this line across the floor, as described for levelling furring strips.

Transfer the line to the ceiling, using a plumb line to make sure that it is directly above the line marked on the floor. These lines will be used as guides when pressing the sheets of plasterboard into place.

Fixing the plasterboard

Starting from an opening or a corner, apply enough adhesive to fix one board at a time. Start by applying a continuous band of adhesive along the edges of the wall or opening, then apply thick dabs of the adhesive down the chalked centre line and about 25mm (1in) inside the marked joint lines, so as not to bridge the joints with adhesive (**1**). Space the dabs about 75mm (3in) apart vertically (**2**). Apply a horizontal row of closely spaced dabs just below ceiling level, and do the same at skirting-board level (**3**).

Place offcuts of plasterboard at the base of the wall to support the weight of the boards while the adhesive sets. Position the first board with its bottom edge resting on the packing, then press it into contact with the adhesive (**4**).

Use a straightedge to tap the board firmly into place until its face is level with the pencil guide lines drawn on the floor and ceiling.

Continue to apply adhesive and fix the rest of the boards in a similar way. If necessary, scribe and cut a board to width to fit at the end of a run. Work round angles and openings (see opposite) and, when all the surfaces have been covered, fill and finish the joints.

Bonding plasterboard to a wall
1 Mark dab lines.
2 Mark guide lines on floor and ceiling.
3 Apply adhesive bands to perimeter.
4 Apply dabs of adhesive to the wall.
5 Place plasterboard on packing and press into place.

1 Apply thick dabs of adhesive with a trowel

2 Continue to apply adhesive dabs. Add a continuous band at ceiling level

3 Apply another band at skirting level

4 Position board on packing and press into place

SEE ALSO > Preparing masonry 42–4, Scribing to fit 164, Levelling furring strips 165, Finishing plasterboard 168

Dealing with angles and openings

Whether the dry-lining plasterboard is being fixed to furring strips or held in place with dabs of adhesive, use the following suggestions for dealing with door and window openings and the corners of the room.

Window openings

Cut plasterboard linings to fit the soffit and the window reveals, and attach them before you dry-line the wall itself. Align the front edges of the window linings with the faces of the furring strips, or allow for dabs of adhesive.

Apply evenly spaced dabs of adhesive to the back of the soffit lining, then press it into place (1) and prop it there while the adhesive sets. Fit the reveal linings in the same way (2).

Beginning next to the window, fix the wall boards so that their papered edges lap the cut edges of the reveal lining. The panels for above and below the window are cut and fitted last. Sand off rough edges of paper, and leave a 3mm (⅛in) gap between boards for filling.

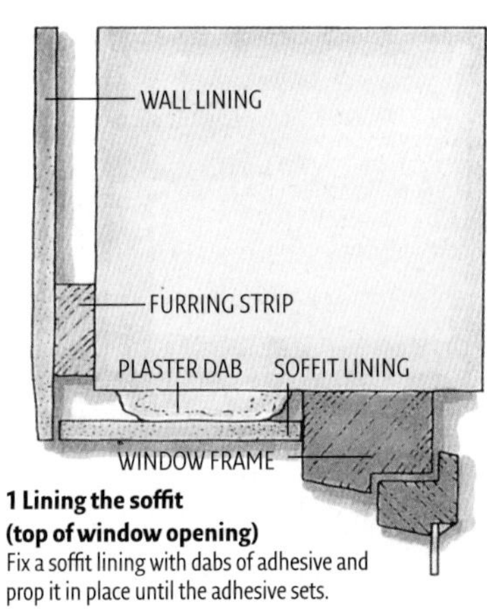

1 Lining the soffit (top of window opening)
Fix a soffit lining with dabs of adhesive and prop it in place until the adhesive sets.

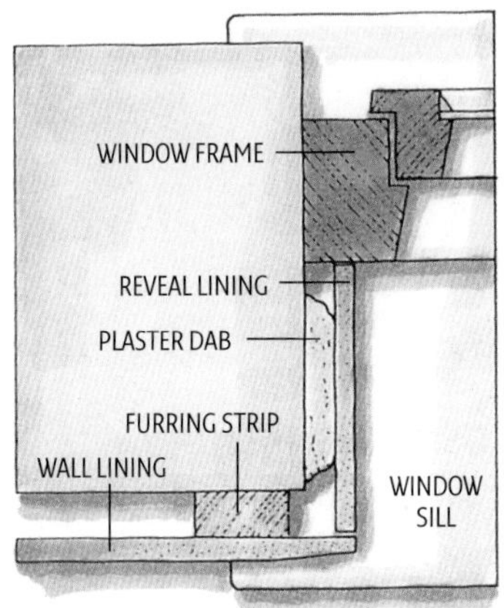

2 Lining the reveal (side of window opening)
As with the soffit lining, cut and fix the reveal so that the wall lining overlaps its cut edge.

Internal angles

Fix a pair of furring strips or place dabs of plasterboard adhesive close to the corner. Whenever possible, hide the cut edges of the plasterboard lining within the corner.

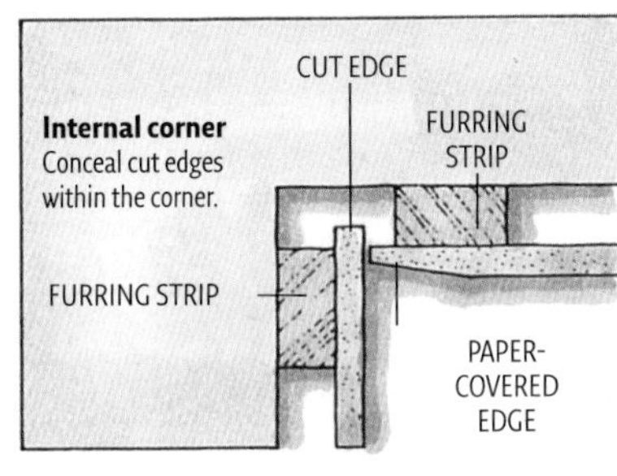

Internal corner
Conceal cut edges within the corner.

External angles

Attach furring strips or apply dabs as close to the corner as possible. Use screws and wallplugs when fixing wooden strips, to prevent the corner breaking away. At least one of the boards should have a paper-covered edge, which should lap the other.

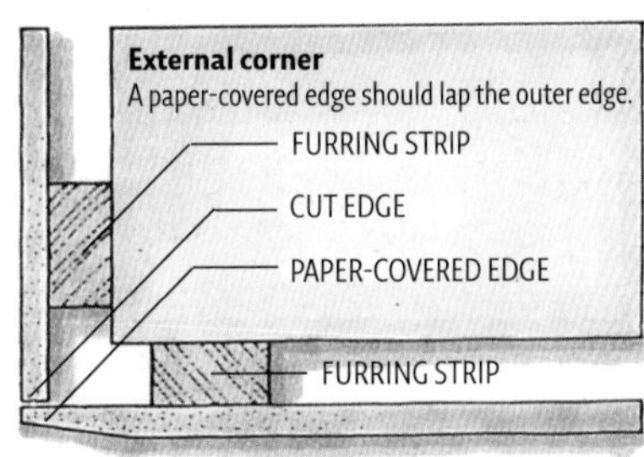

External corner
A paper-covered edge should lap the outer edge.

Door openings

Line the reveals and soffits of doorways in exterior walls as described for window openings (see far left). In the case of interior door openings, place the furring strips or adhesive dabs level with the edge of the wall; and then nail, screw or bond the plasterboard linings in place.

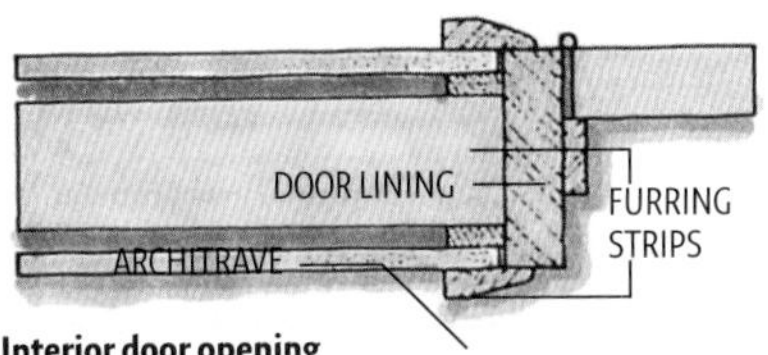

Interior door opening
Fit a new door lining, and cover the joint between the lining and the plasterboard with an architrave moulding.

Electrical fittings

Either chase the wall or pack out the mounting box so it finishes flush with the face of the plasterboard lining. Fix short lengths of furring strip on each side of the box.

Cut the opening for the box before fixing the board. Alternatively, remove the fitting from its mounting box and take an impression by placing the board in position and pressing it against the box.

Fix the plasterboard panel in place, then replace the electrical fitting.

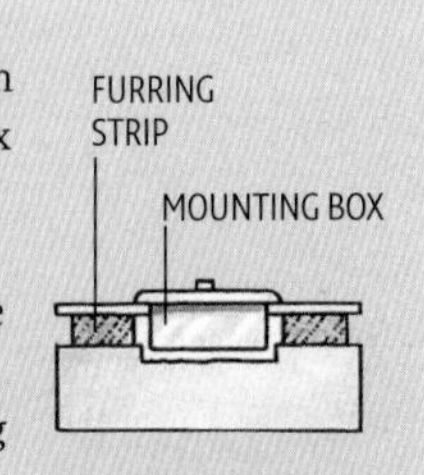

Electrical fittings
Turn off the power before you dismantle electrical fittings. Either chase the wall or pack out the mounting box to set it flush with the plasterboard.

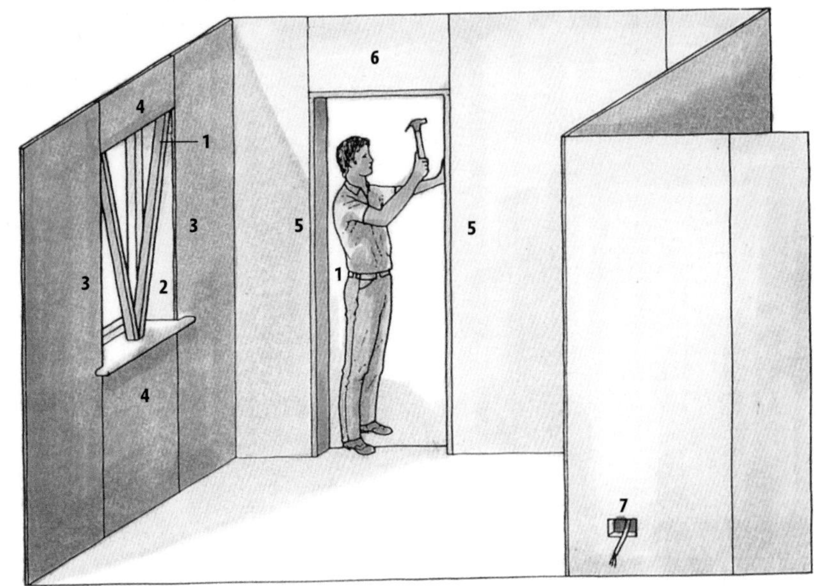

Lining door and window openings
1 Prop soffit lining.
2 Fit reveal lining.
3 Fit boards, working away from window.
4 Fit panels above and below window.
5 Fit boarding, working away from doorway.
6 Cut and fit panel above doorway.
7 Cut openings for electrical fittings before fixing boards in place.

SEE ALSO > Cutting plasterboard 162, Electrical fittings 306–7, 310, 329

Finishing plasterboard

All joints between boards and any indentations left by nailing must be filled and smoothed before the ivory-coloured surface of plasterboard is ready for decorating. You will need jointing tape, joint filler, and a special cement that leaves a smooth feathered joint.

Tools and materials

The filler and cement are either mixed with water or come ready mixed in tubs. Paper jointing tape is 53mm (2⅛in) wide with feathered edges, and is creased along its centre. It is used for reinforcing flat joints and internal corners. Special paper jointing tape is available for covering and reinforcing external corners. This tape has thin metal strips on each side of its central crease in order to strengthen the corner.

Professional plasterers use purpose-made tools, but the only tools you will need are filling knives, a plasterer's trowel and a close-textured plastic sponge.

Filling tapered-edge joints

1 Press tape into filler

2 Apply a wide band

3 Apply a thin layer

Apply a continuous band of filler, about 60mm (2½in) wide, down the length of each joint. Press paper tape into the filler, using a medium-size filling knife or plasterer's trowel to bed it in well and exclude any air bubbles (**1**). Apply another layer of filler in a wide band over the tape to level the surface (**2**).

When the filler has stiffened slightly, smooth its edges with a damp sponge, then allow it to set completely before filling any small hollows that remain.

When all the filler has set, coat it with a thin layer of joint cement applied in a broad band down the joint (**3**). Before the cement sets, feather its edges with a dampened sponge, using a circular motion.

Once the cement has set hard, lightly sand it and then apply another thin but wider band over the first application, again feathering the edges with the sponge.

Covering nails or screws

Fill the indentations left by nailing or screwing the boards in place. Use a filling knife to apply and then smooth the filler. When the filler has set, apply a thin coating of joint cement and feather it off at the edges with a damp sponge.

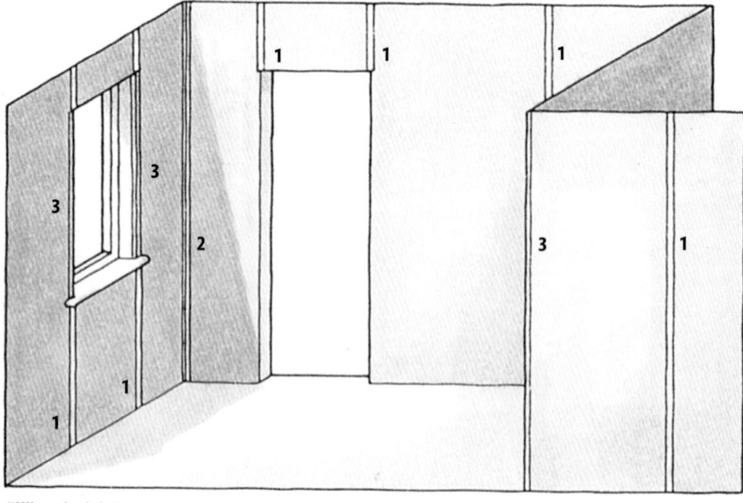

Filling the joints
1 Use the tape flat for flush jointing.
2 Fold the tape for internal corners.
3 Use metal-reinforced tape or beading on external corners.

Glass-fibre tape

A meshed glass-fibre tape can be used instead of traditional paper tape for jointing new plasterboard or making patch repairs. Being self-adhesive, the 50mm (2in) wide tape doesn't need filler to bond it in place. The tape is applied first, and then joint filler is pressed through the mesh.

Applying the tape

If the board edges have been cut, rub them with the handle of your filling knife to remove all traces of rough paper.

Starting at the top, centre the tape over the joint, then unroll it and press it in place as you work down the wall. Cut it off, to length, at the bottom. If you have to make a join in the tape, butt the ends (an overlap will show through the filler).

Mix the filler and press it through the tape into the joint, using a filling knife. Level off the surface so that the mesh of the tape is visible. Allow the filler to set.

Complete the joint with feathered joint cement, as with paper tape.

Cut or square edges

When a square-cut plasterboard edge butts against a tapered-edge board, fill the joint flush before you apply the jointing tape and joint cement (**1**).

Where two cut edges meet (**2**), press filler into the gap. When the filler has set, apply a thin band of joint cement to it and press the paper tape tight against the board. Cover this with a wide but thin coat of joint cement, then feather the edges. Finish off as before.

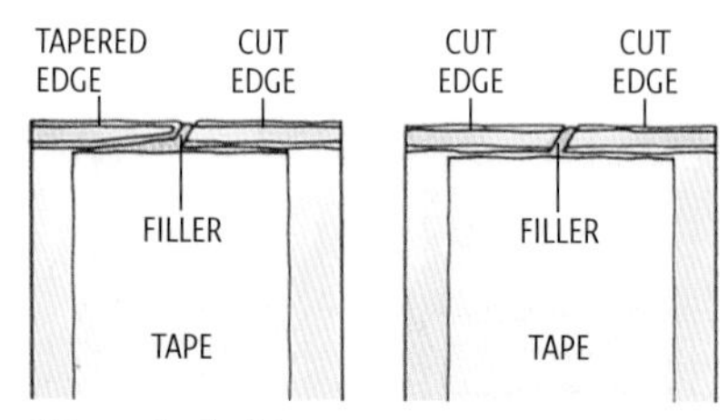

1 Tapered-edge joint **2 Square-edge joint**

SEE ALSO > Plasterboard 162, Dealing with angles and openings 167, Filling knife 481

Finishing internal corners

The internal corners of dry-lined walls are finished by a method similar to that used for flat joints. Any gaps are first filled flush with filler; and if necessary, a band of PVA bonding agent is applied to the original ceiling or wall plaster to reduce its suction.

Cut the paper tape to length and fold it down its centre. Brush a thin band of joint cement onto each side of the corner and press the tape into it. Use a square-section length of wood to press down both sides of the tape at the same time, in order to remove any air bubbles (1).

Apply a band of cement 75mm (3in) wide to both sides of the corner, and feather the edges with a damp sponge (2). When the cement has set, apply a second, wider coat and feather the edges again.

1 Press into the corner with a wooden block

2 Apply wide bands of cement and feather edges

Finishing external corners

Use metal-reinforced tape to finish an external corner. Cut it to length and fold it down its centre, then apply a band of filler, 50mm (2in) wide, down both sides of the corner. Press the tape onto the filler, using a wide filling knife. Press the tape down well, so that the metal strips are bedded firmly against the face of the plasterboard. If you have used a tapered-edge board on one side of the corner, however, square it up with filler before you apply the tape (1). Apply two coats of joint cement over the tape, feathering the edges as described for internal corners.

Protect a vulnerable corner with a length of metal or plastic angle bead. Apply a coating of filler to each side of the corner, then bed the angle bead in it, smoothing the filler flush with a knife before leaving it to set (2).

Apply a second coat of filler to both sides in a wide band and feather it off with a damp sponge. When set, apply two coats of joint cement, feathering off as before.

1 Fill out a tapered-edge board, then bed tape

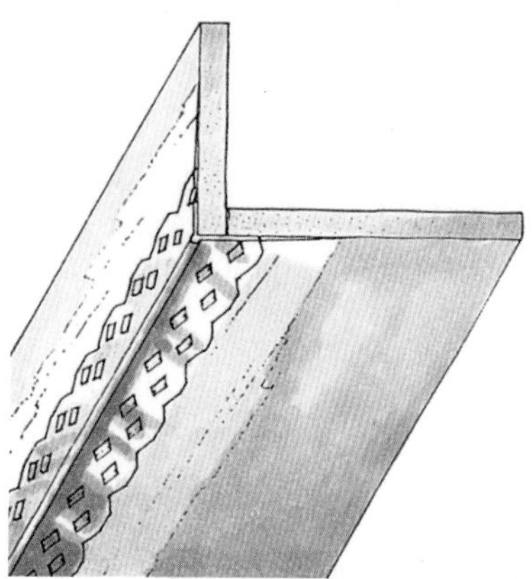

2 Embed metal bead in filler and feather edges

Plastering or decorating

Having fixed the plasterboard securely and finished the joints with tape and filler, you can now prepare the surfaces for decoration. This can be achieved either with a thin coat of plaster applied with a trowel or by brushing on a coat of sealer or primer.

Finishing with plaster

If you don't want to apply paint or a wall-covering directly to the papered surface of the plasterboard, you can apply a thin coat of board-finish plaster instead. This may be necessary if you want to match the characteristics of adjacent plastered surfaces.

Applying a thin finishing coat is not an easy technique to master. Unless you are prepared to put in some practice, it is probably best to hire a professional, especially for ceilings. If you decide to attempt the work yourself, study the section on plastering thoroughly before you begin.

All the gaps and joints between the boards must be filled with finish plaster and reinforced with tape, as described opposite, though in this case there's no need to feather the edges. The plaster should be left to set (but don't let it dry out completely), before the surface is covered with a thin coat of finish plaster.

Decorating directly

Before plasterboard can be decorated, it must be sealed by the application of a primer. One coat of general-purpose primer evens out the absorption of the board and joint fillers, and provides a sound surface for most decorative treatments. It also protects the board when steam-stripping wallpaper.

An alternative is to use a proprietary sealer coat, applied with a brush or roller. It is suitable for use with most decorative treatments. Two coats will serve as a vapour barrier, and will also provide a more durable finish.

Apply a primer to even out absorption

SEE ALSO > Types of plaster 156, Bonding agent 157, Reinforcing a corner 159, Plasterboarding a ceiling 170

Plasterboarding a ceiling

Plasterboard is widely used for making new ceilings, but it can also be employed to replace an old lath-and-plaster ceiling that has deteriorated beyond repair. Any competent amateur can fix the boards in place and finish them ready for decorating, but applying a coat of finish plaster is best left to a skilled plasterer.

Fixing plasterboard to the ceiling

1 Working on your own
Support the boards with simple T-shaped props known as deadmen.

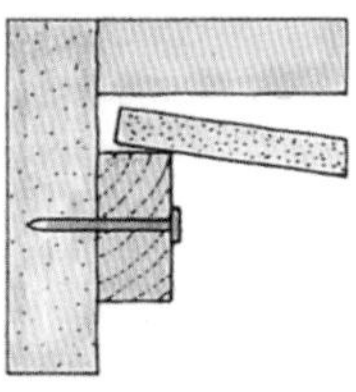

2 Temporary support
Nail a batten to the wall to give temporary support to the long edge of the board.

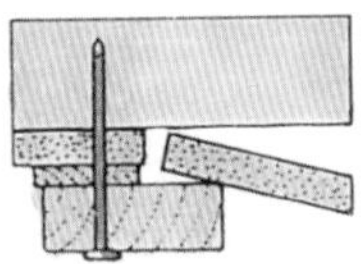

3 Supporting the next row of boards
Nail a temporary support batten to the ceiling joists when butting boards.

Measure the ceiling area and select the most economical size of boards to cover it. The boards should be fitted with their long edges running at right angles to the joists. The butt joints between the ends of the boards should be staggered on each row, and supported by a joist in every case.

Skew-nail perimeter noggings between the joists against the walls, and fit a series of intermediate ones in lines across the ceiling to support the long edges of the boards. These noggings should be at least 50mm (2in) thick, and should be fitted so the edges of the boards will coincide with the centres of the noggings.

Start fixing the boards, working from one corner of the room. Plasterboard is a relatively heavy material and it normally takes two people to support a large sheet while it is being fixed. However, if you have to work on your own, use support battens and T-shaped props, known as 'deadmen', to hold the boards in place while you are nailing them. Make a pair of props that are slightly longer than the overall height of the room, using 50 x 50mm (2 x 2in) softwood. Nail a crosspiece and a pair of diagonal struts to one end of each prop (**1**).

For the time being, nail a 50 x 25mm (2 x 1in) batten close to the top of the wall to support the long edges of the first row of boards (**2**). Support the next row with a batten that overlaps the edges of the first boards. Before you nail it to the joists, fit packing under the batten to provide clearance for the edges of the new boards (**3**).

Use galvanized plasterboard nails to fix each board in place, working from the middle outwards and driving in the nails at 150mm (6in) centres. This prevents the boards from sagging in the middle, which is likely to happen if their edges are nailed first.

If the boards are to be plastered, leave 3mm (1/8in) gaps all round. For direct decoration you can butt the paper-covered edges together, though you still need to leave 3mm (1/8in) gaps between the ends of the boards.

Finish the joints, using the method described for plasterboarding walls. This will ensure that cracks do not open up across the ceiling later.

Stripping old ceilings

Start by stripping away the damaged plaster and laths, and pulling out all the nails. Trim back the top of the wall plaster, so the edge of the new plasterboard can be tucked in.

This is a messy job, so wear a pair of goggles, a face mask and protective clothing while working. It is also a good idea to seal the gaps around the door, to prevent dust escaping into the rest of the house. You will need to dispose of a lot of waste material, so have some strong plastic sacks available and hire a skip.

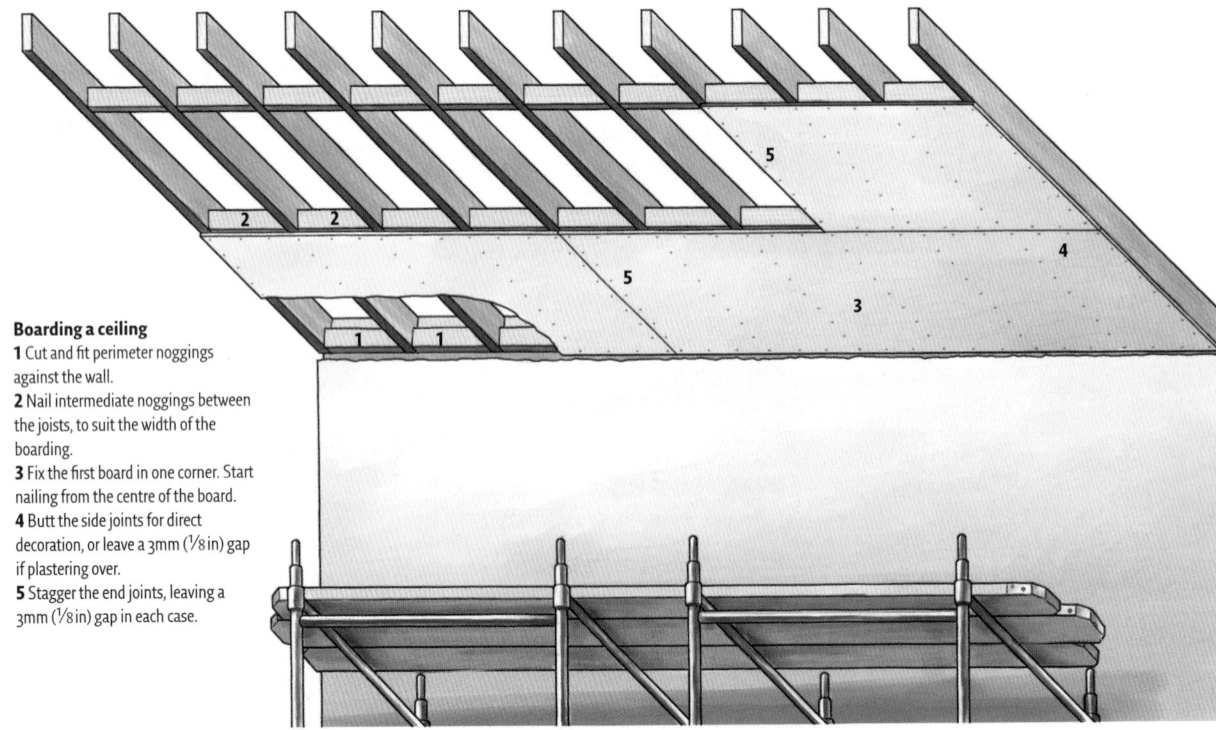

Boarding a ceiling
1 Cut and fit perimeter noggings against the wall.
2 Nail intermediate noggings between the joists, to suit the width of the boarding.
3 Fix the first board in one corner. Start nailing from the centre of the board.
4 Butt the side joints for direct decoration, or leave a 3mm (1/8in) gap if plastering over.
5 Stagger the end joints, leaving a 3mm (1/8in) gap in each case.

SEE ALSO > Noggings 152, Types of plasterboard 162, Plasterboarding a wall 163–4, Finishing joints 168, Woodworm 242–3, Rot 245

Fitting cornices and coving

Either a decorative plaster cornice or a plain concave coving is often used to finish the edges of a ceiling where it meets the walls. Paper-covered gypsum coving is widely available, though in a fairly limited range of profile sizes and lengths. However, you can buy a greater number of period-style cornices in fibrous plaster or moulded foamed plastic, many of which are exact copies of Georgian and Victorian originals. A template or a mitre box is essential for cutting the internal and external mitre joints accurately.

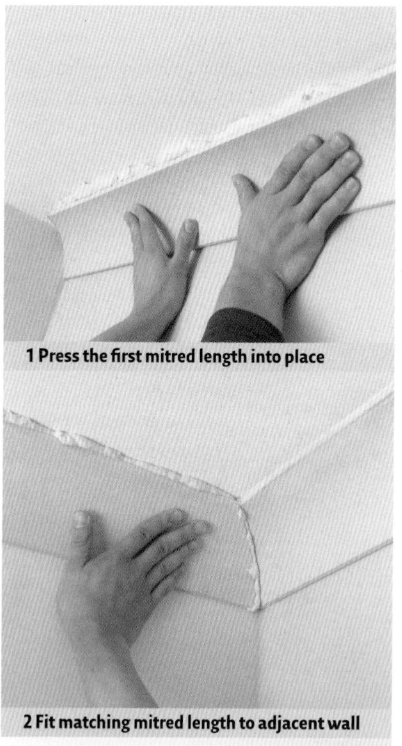

1 Press the first mitred length into place

2 Fit matching mitred length to adjacent wall

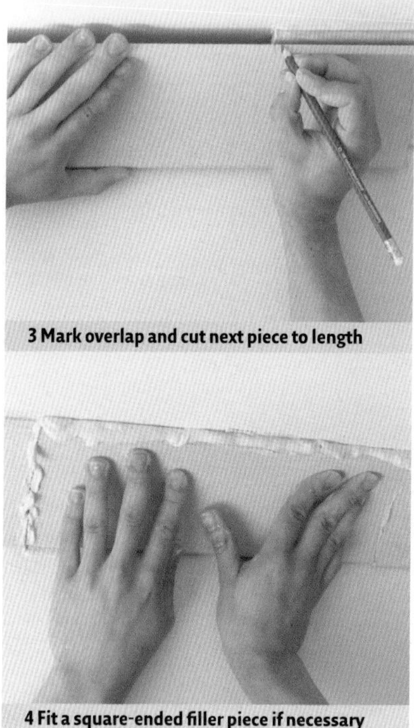

3 Mark overlap and cut next piece to length

4 Fit a square-ended filler piece if necessary

Fitting coving

Mark parallel guide lines for the coving along the wall and ceiling, using an offcut to set the dimensions. Scratch the plastered surfaces within the lines, to provide a good key for the adhesive. Remove wallpaper from the area.

The coving is stuck in place with adhesive, which is available ready-mixed or as a powder. If you are using a powder adhesive, mix it with water and stir it to a smooth paste. It should remain usable for about 40 minutes.

Start work at an internal corner. Mark a mitre (see right) on one end of the first length. Cut it with a fine-toothed saw, sawing from the face side.

Use a filling knife to apply adhesive liberally to the back faces of the coving that will be in contact with the wall and ceiling. Press it into the angle and align it with the guide lines (**1**). Scrape away any surplus adhesive before it sets. If the coving sags when in place, support it with nails driven into the wall beneath its bottom edge. Remove them when the adhesive has set.

Fix a second mitred length to the adjacent wall and fill the corner joint with adhesive (**2**). Repeat the process for the other internal corners. If any wall will take less than two lengths, cut the mitre on the end of the second length, hold it in place and mark the overlap on the first length. (**3**). Cut it squarely at the mark and stick it in position. If the wall requires more than two lengths, stick the second mitred length in place and fill the gap between with square-ended pieces as required (**4**). Use excess adhesive to fill all the joints as the work progresses.

Wipe along the edges of the coving with a damp sponge to remove any traces of adhesive. Once it has set, prime the coving ready for painting.

Remember that when you are cutting mitres for outside corners, the coving needs to be longer than the wall and must extend up to the line of the return angle drawn on the ceiling.

Cutting the mitres

Some makers of plaster coving supply a paper or card template or a plastic mitre guide with their products, which enables you to mark mitred corners more easily.

Mark the coving to length on one edge, bearing in mind whether you are mitring for an internal corner or an external one. Position the template or guide over the coving in line with the mark. Select the appropriate edge of the template for the mitre you require and draw along that edge with a pencil to mark the cutting line on the face and edges of the coving. Cut the mitre with a fine-toothed saw.

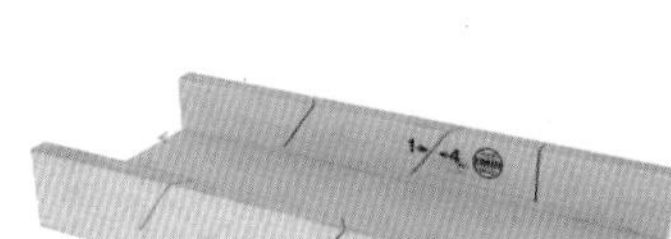

Special mitre boxes are ideal for cutting coving

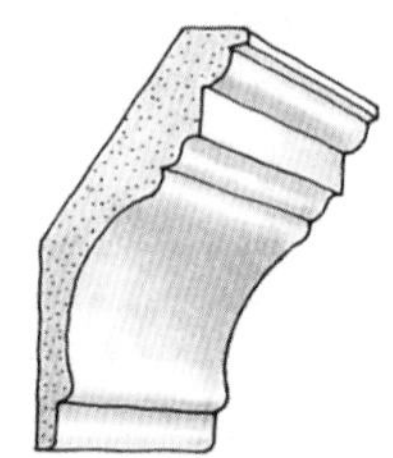

Cornice profile

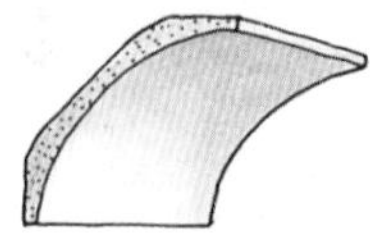

Coving profile

Using a mitre box

If you intend to fit a lot of coving, it's worth buying a proprietary coving mitre box to help you cut joints accurately.

Lay the coving on the mitre box, with its ceiling edge downwards and with the end to be cut facing in the right direction for either an external or an internal mitre (see right). Holding the coving firmly so it cannot move, place the blade of the saw in the appropriate slot in the mitre box, and cut the coving to size.

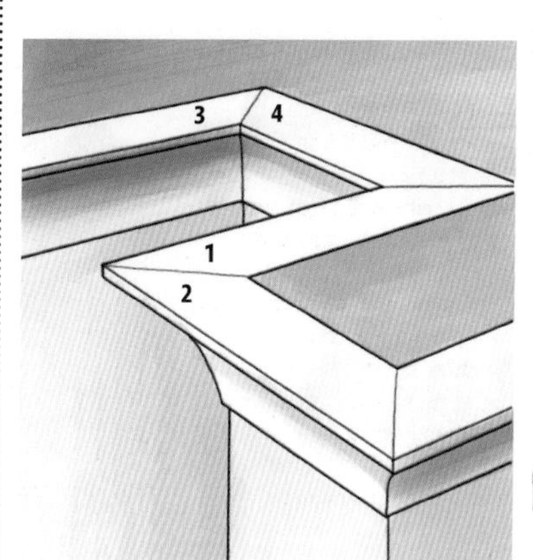

Identify each length and cut it correctly

External mitre

1 Left-hand piece

2 Right-hand piece

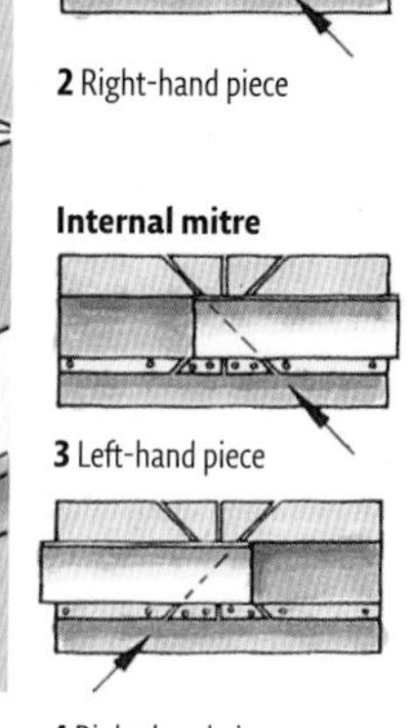

Internal mitre

3 Left-hand piece

4 Right-hand piece

SEE ALSO > Primers 40–41, Filling knife 481, Combination square 487, Erecting work platforms 516

Suspended floors

In a great many buildings floor construction is based on timber beams known as joists. These are rectangular in section, placed on edge for maximum strength – usually about 400mm (1ft 4in) apart – and supported at their ends by the walls. Such suspended floors contrast with solid floors made of concrete and supported over their whole area by the ground, which are commonly found in basements and also widely used at ground level in modern houses. Traditional suspended floors are usually boarded with tongue-and-groove or plain-edged wood planks, though in modern houses flooring-grade chipboard is often used for both types of floor.

Ground floors

The joists of a suspended ground floor are usually made from 100 x 50mm (4 x 2in) sawn softwood. Their ends and centre portions are nailed to lengths of 100 x 75mm (4 x 3in) softwood – called wall plates – that distribute the load from the joists to the walls, which support the weight of the floor.

In older houses various methods were employed for supporting the wall plates. At one time it was common for the ends of the joists to be slotted into the walls and set on wall plates built into the masonry. Alternatively, the wall plates were supported on masonry ledges called offsets.

The relatively lightweight joists tend to sag in the middle of long spans, and are therefore usually supported by additional wall plates set on three or four courses of honeycombed masonry, known as sleeper walls. The spaces left in the masonry allow air to circulate under the floor. Sleeper walls are usually spaced at intervals of about 2m (6ft), and are sometimes used to support the ends of the joists.

Beneath a fireplace in a room with a suspended ground floor will be found a solid masonry wall built to the same height as the sleeper walls. It retains and supports the concrete hearth. This fender wall carries a wall plate along its top edge to support the ends of the floor joists that run up to it.

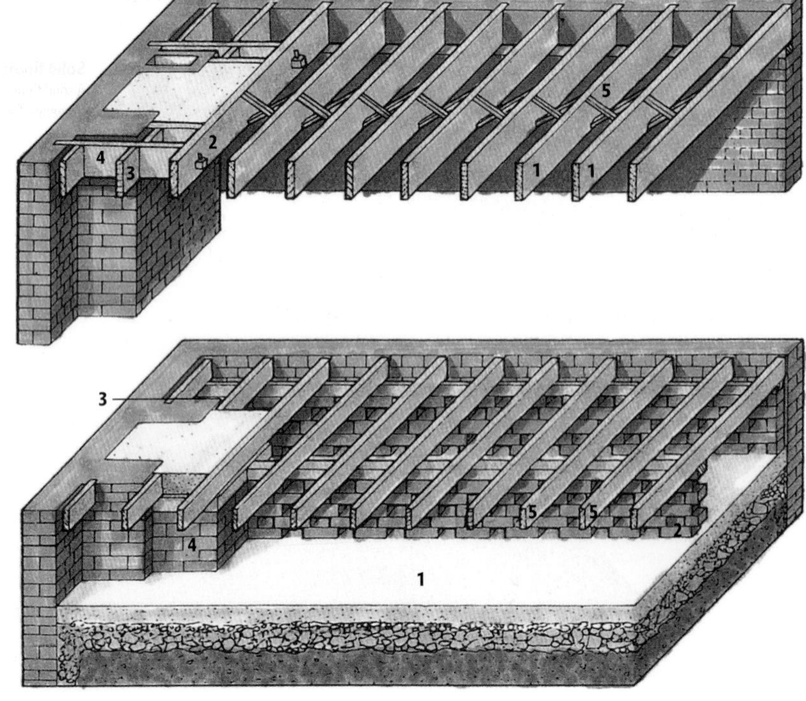

TRADITIONAL FLOOR CONSTRUCTION

First floor
1 Joists
2 Trimming joist
3 Trimmed joist
4 Trimmer
5 Herringbone strutting

Ground floor
1 Oversite concrete
2 Sleeper walls
3 Wall plate
4 Fender wall
5 Floor joists

Upper floors

The first-floor joists and those of other upper floors can be supported only at their ends, so they are usually laid in the direction of the shortest span. Also, as they can have no intermediate support, such joists are made deeper, to give them greater rigidity. These 'bridging joists' are usually 50mm (2in) thick, but their depth will be determined by the distance they have to span.

Where floor joists cannot run right through – as around a fireplace or at a stairway opening – a thicker joist is used to bear the extra load of the short joists (see below left). The thicker joist is known as a 'trimming joist'; the short ones parallel to it are called 'trimmed joists'; and the crosspieces joining them together are known as 'trimmers'.

In older properties the upstairs joists may be supported on wall plates that are built into solid walls, but damp is not a problem here.

With modern cavity-wall construction, the ends of the joists may also be built in, though they are more likely to be supported on metal joist hangers. Other metal fittings, such as straps and anchors, may also be used.

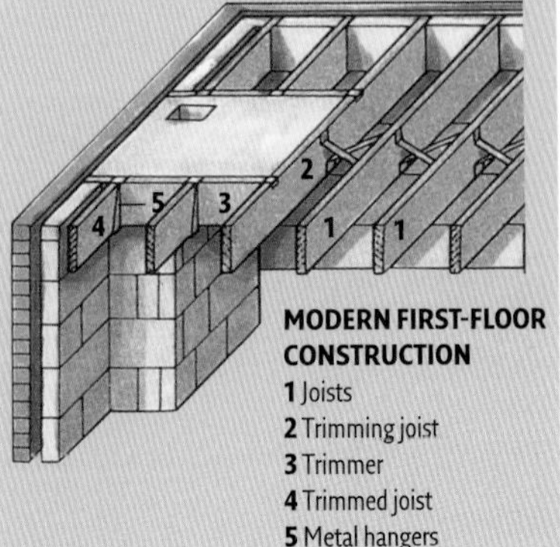

MODERN FIRST-FLOOR CONSTRUCTION
1 Joists
2 Trimming joist
3 Trimmer
4 Trimmed joist
5 Metal hangers

SEE ALSO > Lifting floorboards 179, Metal fittings for floors 174, Repairing joists 175, Laying pipes 177, Treating woodworm 242, Damp-proof course 247, Insulating floors 266

Bracing floor joists

For extra stiffness, the joists of an upper floor are braced with solid strutting – sections of timber nailed between them (1) – or with diagonal wooden braces known as herringbone strutting (2), which consists of 50 x 25mm (2 x 1in) softwood. With modern construction methods, joists are strutted with ready-made metal herringbone units (3). These are usually made with a drilled flange at each end for nailing to joists set at 400, 450 or 600mm (1ft 4in, 1ft 6in or 2ft) centres.

Herringbone strutting is preferable, as it is able to compensate for timber shrinkage. Wedges or packing blocks are placed in line with the strutting between the outer joists and the walls, in order to keep the joints tight.

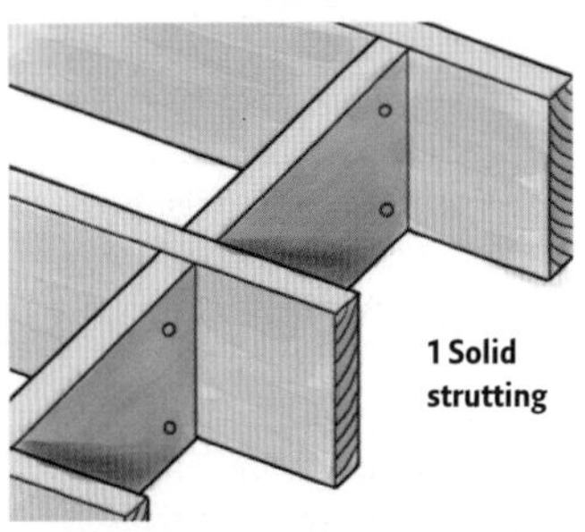

1 Solid strutting

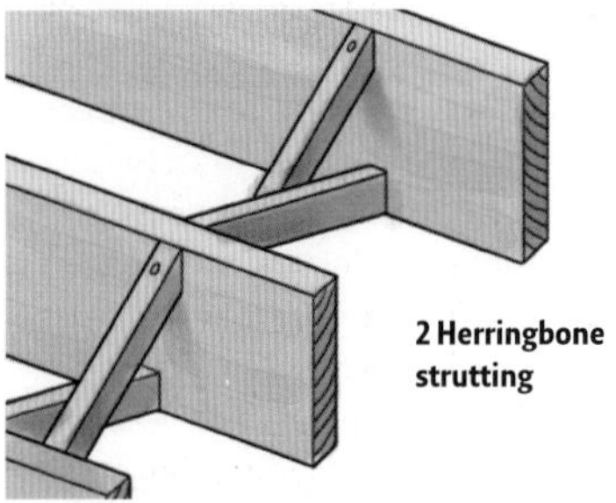

2 Herringbone strutting

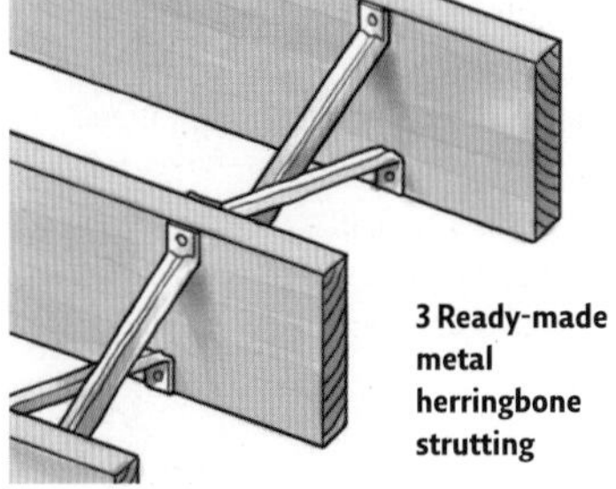

3 Ready-made metal herringbone strutting

Solid floors

A solid ground floor is essentially a concrete slab laid on a substratum of hardcore (coarse rubble). It is the usual floor construction used in all modern houses and is sometimes found in older properties.

To lay such a floor, the topsoil is first removed then a layer of hardcore is laid to consolidate the ground and level up the site. The rough surface of the hardcore is filled ('blinded') with a thin layer of sand, which is then rolled flat. This sand layer prevents the cement draining out of the concrete and into the hardcore, which would result in the concrete being weakened.

Concrete-slab floor

The concrete slab is usually about 100 to 150mm (4 to 6in) thick and is either laid on top of or covered by a continuous layer of moisture-resistant material – the damp-proof membrane (DPM). This membrane may be either a thick sheet of polythene or the more traditional liquid coating of asphalt or bituminous material. However it is laid, the damp-proof membrane must be joined to the damp-proof course (DPC) set in the walls.

Concrete raft

A concrete-raft foundation can be laid in two ways. It may form a solid base onto which the walls are built. Alternatively, where strip or trench foundations are used, the concrete slab may be laid over the ground contained within the walls.

The floor must first be covered with a smooth screed of sand and cement before it can be overlaid with a floorcovering. When the DPM is below the concrete slab, the screed can be 44mm (1¾in) thick – but when a membrane is laid over the slab, the screed should be at least 63mm (2½in) in thickness.

A suspended solid floor is composed of rows of precast concrete beams – set on sleeper walls at DPC level – infilled with lightweight concrete blocks.

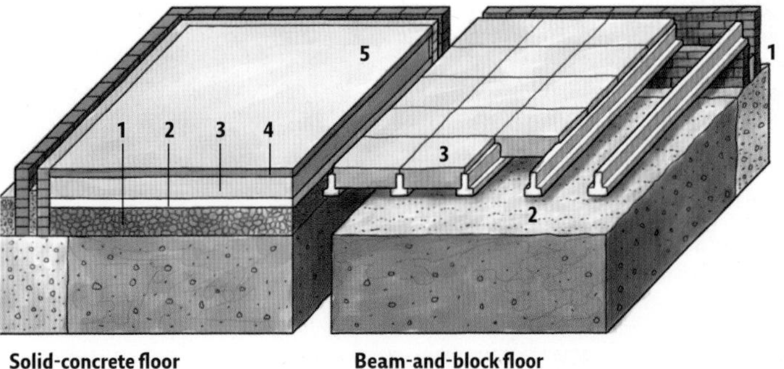

Solid floors
A solid floor is often used in preference to a suspended wooden floor, as it can be cheaper to construct. A concrete floor can be laid after the foundations and first courses of brickwork are built above ground level, or it can be built up using a beam-and-block system. It can also be an integral part of a reinforced-concrete foundation, forming a raft (see below left).

Solid-concrete floor
1 Hardcore
2 Insulation
3 Concrete slab
4 Damp-proof membrane
5 Concrete screed

Beam-and-block floor
1 Damp-proof course
2 Concrete beams
3 Concrete blocks

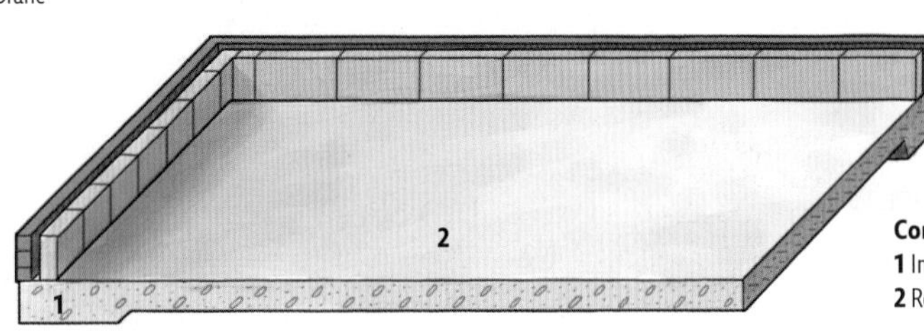

Concrete raft
1 Integral foundation
2 Reinforced-concrete slab

SEE ALSO > Metal fittings for floors 174, Laying a concrete floor 176–7, Damp-proof membrane 176, 247

Metal fittings for floors

Floor construction is one of the many areas in which builders have been able to substitute the use of factory-made fittings for traditional methods of construction. They are used to support and connect the joists and to tie the floor structure to the loadbearing walls of the building to provide strength and stability.

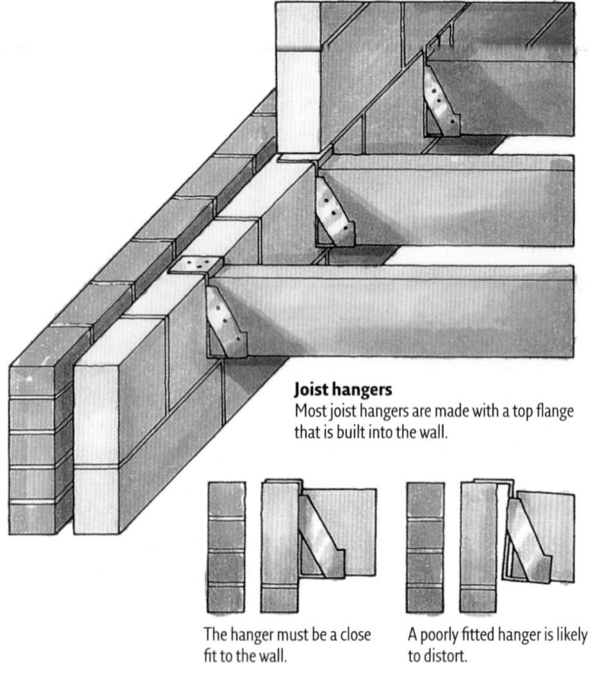

Joist hangers
Most joist hangers are made with a top flange that is built into the wall.

The hanger must be a close fit to the wall.

A poorly fitted hanger is likely to distort.

Joist hangers

Galvanized-steel joist hangers are brackets used in the construction of upper-storey timber floors. They are fixed to masonry walls in order to support the ends of the joists clear of the masonry. There are various versions for securing joists to solid or cavity walls; and there are special brackets that form a similar function when constructing timber-to-timber joints. The use of metal joist hangers allows brickwork or blockwork to be built before joists are fitted, and saves having to cut infill blocks between built-in joist ends.

Joist hangers need to be fitted properly - with the top flange sitting squarely on the bricks or blocks, and the rear face of the bracket fitting closely against the face of the masonry. The ends of the joists are fixed into hangers using 32mm (1¼in) sherardized twisted nails or plasterboard nails driven through the holes provided in the side gussets.

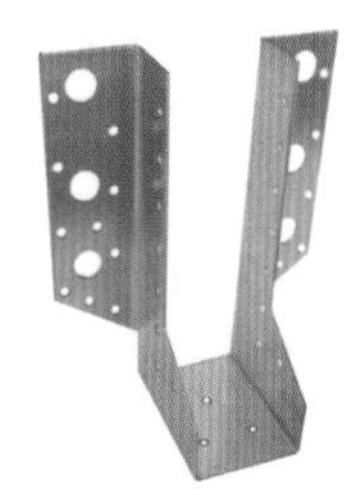

Face-fixing hanger

Straight-flange hanger

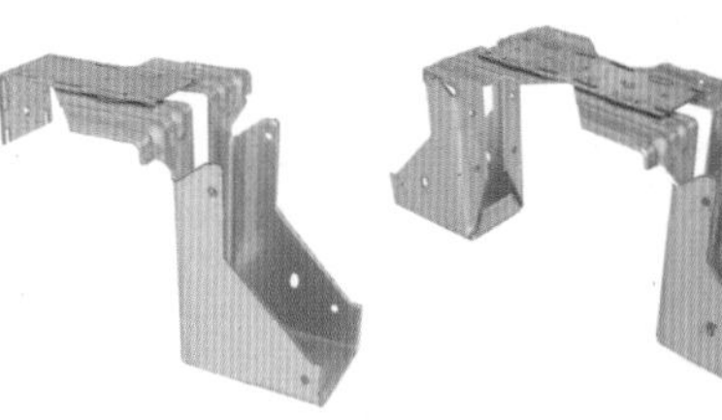

Hooked-flange hanger **Double hanger**

Framing anchors
These are fixed in place with relatively short nails driven in squarely. As a result, there is little risk of the wood splitting.

Framing anchors

Framing anchors are steel brackets used in the construction of butt joints between flooring timbers that meet at right angles. Builders use these brackets mainly for fixing trimmed joists, in order to avoid having to cut complicated joints.

Left-handed and right-handed framing anchors are available

Lateral-restraint straps

While the walls carry the weight of the floor, the floors contribute lateral stiffness to the walls. In areas where the force of the wind could threaten the stability of modern lightweight walls, lateral-restraint straps are used to provide ties between walls and floors. They are rigid strips of galvanized steel that are perforated for nail fixing and bent in various ways to suit the direction of the floor joists.

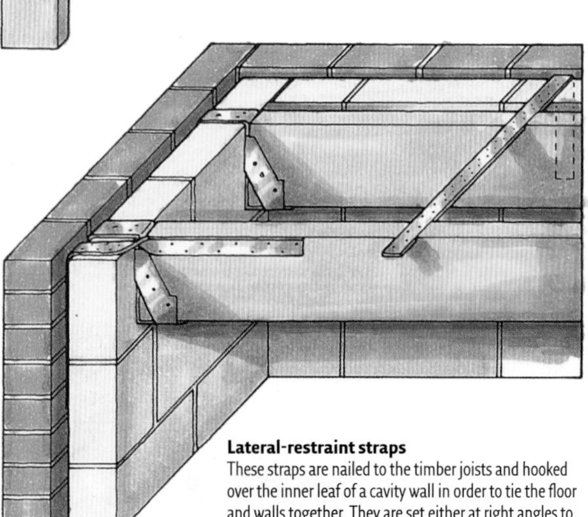

Lateral-restraint straps
These straps are nailed to the timber joists and hooked over the inner leaf of a cavity wall in order to tie the floor and walls together. They are set either at right angles to or parallel with the line of the joists.

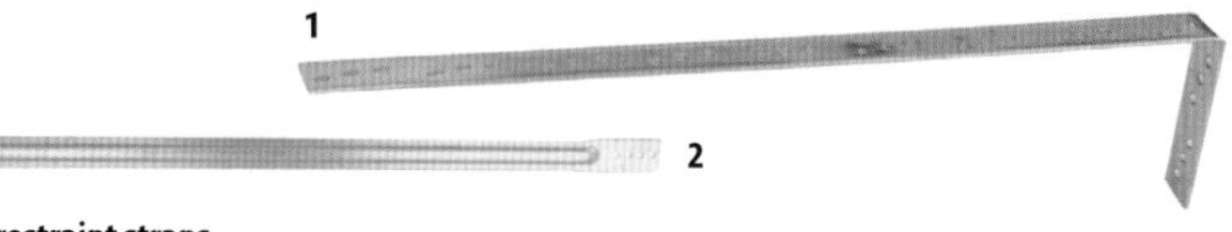

Lateral-restraint straps
1 For tying joists parallel to an external wall
2 For tying joists on either side of an internal wall

SEE ALSO > Reinforcing a joist 150, Trimmed joists 172, Repairing floor joists 175

Repairing floor joists

Since all floor joists are loadbearing, their size and spacing in new structures must satisfy a Building Control Officer. However, calculations are not necessary for most domestic repairs – matching new timber for old should suffice. Use only 'strength-graded' timber, which has been examined visually or machine-tested.

Fitting services

Service runs such as heating pipes and electric cables can run in the void below a suspended ground floor. But in upper floors those running at right angles to the joists have to pass through the joists, which are covered by flooring above and a ceiling below.

So as not to weaken the structure, bore holes for cables through the centre of a joist – or at least 50mm (2in) below the top edge, in order to clear floor nails. Try to place the holes within the middle two-thirds of the joist's length (**1**).

Notches for pipe runs in the top edge of the joist should be no deeper than one-eighth of the joist's depth. These notches should be confined to an area not more than a quarter of the joist's span at each end, and not closer to the end than 0.07 of the joist's span (**2**).

Fitting services
1 Make holes for cables within red area.
2 Place notches for pipes within red area.

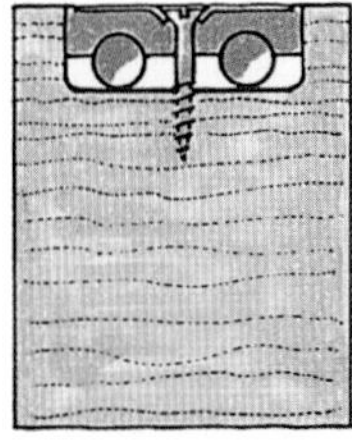

Accommodating pipes
Drill and saw notches for pipes, and cover them with a protector.

Replacing a joist
The stages for repairing a damaged joist are combined in the illustration.
1 Cut away old joist.
2 Drill and cut out damaged wall plate.
3 Fit new wall plate.
4 Cut and fit new joist, and brace the joint with bolted joist timbers.

Replacing floor joists

Floor joists that have been seriously attacked by wet or dry rot or by insect infestation have to be cut out and replaced. Such attacks usually occur at ground-floor level because of its proximity to the damp soil.

Remove the skirting boards and lift the floorboards covering the infected area until you reach a sleeper wall. Test the condition of the joists with a sharp knife. If the blade penetrates easily, the wood will have to be replaced. Sound wood can be treated with chemical preserver to kill rot spores and woodworm larvae.

Preparation

All infected timbers must be removed in an area extending at least 450mm (1ft 6in) beyond the last visible signs of attack, and all surrounding masonry must be treated with a fungicide. The following assumes that the end of a joist and also the wall plate are affected.

Saw through and remove the infected end of the joist, cutting it back to the centre of the nearest sleeper wall. If the wall plate that has been supporting the joist is also affected, cut it away too.

Replacement

Cut a new length of wall-plate timber to fill the gap. If the original mortar bed joint and damp-proof course are sound, apply a coating of liquid bituminous damp-proofing over it and then fit the new section of wall plate into place.

If necessary, re-lay the bed joint and insert a new length of DPC, making sure that its ends overlap the ends of the old one (if present) by at least 150mm (6in). Then reseat the wall plate.

Now cut a length of new joist, to sit on the repaired wall plate and meet the cut end of the old joist on the sleeper wall. To ensure that it is level with the other joists, trim its underside or pack it with slate or DPC felt. Brace the joint with two 900mm (3ft) lengths of joist timber on each side, and bolt through with four coach bolts and two timber connectors for each bolt. Finally replace the floorboards and skirtings.

Fitting joist hangers

Sections of infected wood can be replaced with metal joist hangers to support the ends of the repaired joists.

Having removed the damaged joist and section of wall plate (see above), lay bricks in the resulting slot. Before laying the mortar, check on the condition of the DPC and, if you think it necessary, reinforce it with an extra layer of DPC felt or a liquid damp-proofing material.

Set the brickwork to support the flange of the joist hanger at the required level, using slate packing under the flange if necessary. Allow the mortar to harden before fitting the new section of joist, as described above.

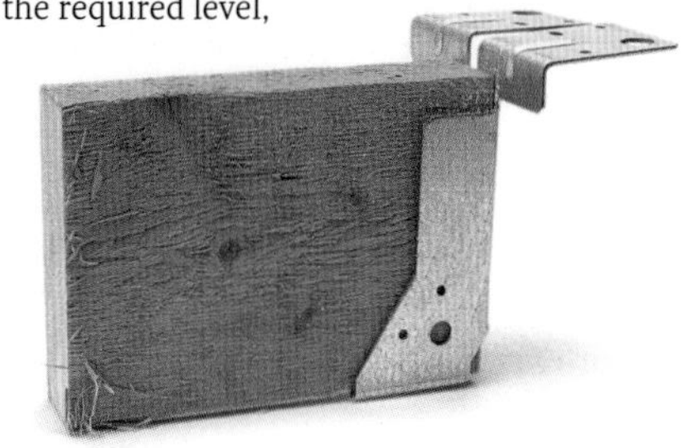

SEE ALSO > Joist hangers 174, Lifting floorboards 179, Replacing skirtings 218, Curing damp 247–54

Laying a concrete floor

A suspended timber floor that has been seriously damaged by rot or insect infestation can be replaced with a solid-concrete floor, provided the space below it needs no more than 600mm (2ft) of infill material. If it requires more, a new suspended floor will have to be fitted, as a concrete floor would be liable to damage through the settlement of so much infill.

Before taking any action, consult your local Building Control Officer. The converting of one floor can affect the ventilation of another, and it is also likely that insulation will be required.

If the work may interfere with the electrical main service cable or gas or water supply pipes, check with the relevant authorities. Wiring and heating pipes should be rerun before infill is laid.

Preparing the ground

Strip out all the infected timbers and burn them. Also remove the door of the room. Treat the ground and all the surrounding masonry thoroughly with a strong fungicide. Fill in any recesses left in the walls, as a result of removing the timbers, with bricks and mortar. Mark the walls with a levelled chalk line indicating the level of the finished floor, allowing for the floorcovering if you intend to use a thick material such as quarry tiles or wood blocks.

About 50mm (2in) below this line, mark another one, the space between them representing the thickness of the screed. Then mark a third chalk line 100mm (4in) further down, indicating the thickness of the concrete slab. Mark a fourth line below that, to indicate the required thickness of insulation board.

Insulating the floor
The degree of insulation required varies according to the area of the floor and its construction. Check with your local BCO, or ask an architect to calculate how much insulation is required.

The infill

Lay the infill material to the required depth in layers of no more than 225mm (9in), compacting each layer thoroughly and breaking up larger pieces with a sledgehammer (**1**). You can use brick and tile rubble for the infill – or, better still, gravel rejects (coarse stones from quarry waste). Discard any wood and fragments of plaster, which could react with cement. Bring the surface up to within 25mm (1in) of the chalk line for the insulation, then 'blind' the surface with a layer of sand, tamped or rolled flat.

Spread a polythene damp-proof membrane of 1000-gauge or 1200-gauge thickness over the surface of the sand, turning its edges up all round and lapping it up the walls to form a tray. Make neat folds at the corners and hold them temporarily in place with staples or paperclips. If the floor needs more than one sheet of polythene to cover it, the sheets must overlap by at least 200mm (8in) and the joints should be sealed with special waterproof tape, available from builders' merchants.

1 Preparing the ground
Mark the walls with chalk lines indicating the level of the finished floor, the thickness of the screed, and the thickness of the concrete slab and insulation. Fill the floor area with hardcore to within 25mm (1in) of the bottom line; compact each layer thoroughly with a sledgehammer. Cover the hardcore with sand up to the line, then lay a damp-proof membrane over it.

Including insulation

Lay closely butted polystyrene boards on the DPM and tape the joints. As the work progresses, place strips of insulant between the concrete and the walls to eliminate cold bridging.

Laying the concrete

Mix a medium-strength concrete, consisting of 1 part cement : 2½ parts sand : 4 parts aggregate. Don't add too much water – the mix should be fairly stiff.

Lay the concrete in bands about 600mm (2ft) wide, working towards the doorway. Tamp the concrete with a length of 100 x 50mm (4 x 2in) timber to compact it, and finish level with the chalked line (**2**). Slight unevenness will be taken up by the screed, but check the surface of the concrete from time to time, using a straightedge and spirit level, and fill in any hollows. Leave the concrete to cure for at least 3 days under a sheet of polythene, to prevent shrinkage caused by rapid drying.

Laying the screed

Mix a screed mortar from 3 parts sharp sand : 1 part Portland cement. Dampen the floor and prime with a cement grout mixed to a creamy consistency with water and bonding agent in equal parts. Working from one wall, apply a 600mm (2ft) band of grout with a stiff brush.

Apply a bedding of screed mortar at each end of the grouted area to take 38 x 38mm (1½ x 1½ in) screed battens. True them with a spirit level and straightedge, so that they are flush with the surface-level lines on the walls.

Lay mortar between the battens and tamp it down well (**3**). Level the mortar with a straightedge laid across the battens, then smooth it with a wooden float. Lift out the battens carefully, fill the hollows with mortar, and level again with the float.

Repeat the procedure, working your way across the floor in bands 600mm (2ft) wide. When the screed is firm, cover the finished floor with a sheet of polythene and leave it to cure for about a week. As soon as the floor is hard enough to walk on, trim the damp-proof membrane to within 25mm (1in) of the floor and fit the skirtings to cover its edges (**4**).

The floor will not be fully dry for about 6 months. Allow a month for every 25mm (1in) of thickness – and in the meantime don't lay an impermeable floorcovering.

SEE ALSO > Solid ground floors 173, Wet and dry rot 245, Curing damp 247–54, Running cable 303–5, Plumbing 346–94

2 Laying the concrete
Working towards the doorway, lay concrete in bands not more than 600mm (2ft) wide. Tamp down the concrete to consolidate it, and bring it level with the chalked line. Place strips of insulant between the concrete and the walls.

3 Laying the screed
Apply a band of cement grout, 600mm (2ft) wide, to the concrete base and set levelled screed battens in mortar at each end of it. Lay the screed in bands not more than 600mm (2ft) wide, and level the surface with a straight-edge and float. Lift out the battens and fill the hollows left by them. Then lay the next band.

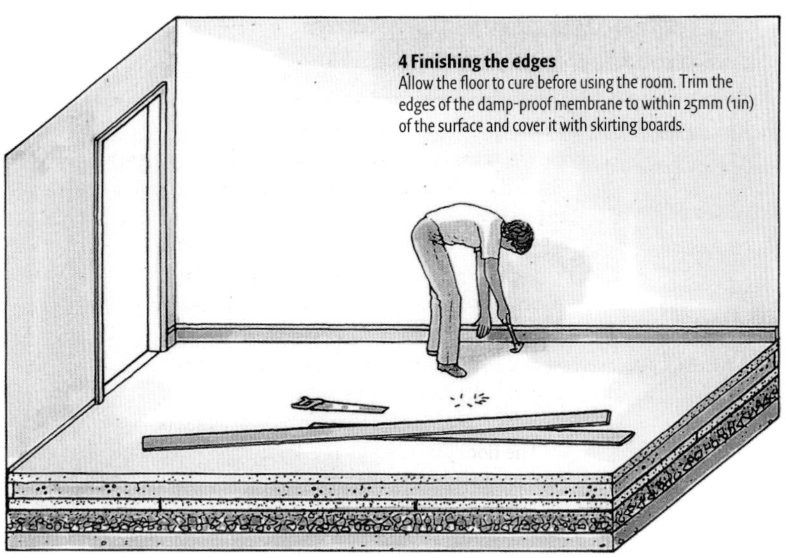

4 Finishing the edges
Allow the floor to cure before using the room. Trim the edges of the damp-proof membrane to within 25mm (1in) of the surface and cover it with skirting boards.

Chipboard floating floor

The most common way of finishing off a concrete floor is to lay a so-called floating floor, using flooring-grade chipboard. To meet current Building Regulations, a thick layer of rigid-polystyrene insulation must be placed over the final screed. This is overlaid with a continuous polythene vapour barrier; and the chipboard sheets, glued edge to edge, are placed on top. The floating floor is held in place by its own weight and by skirting boards nailed to the walls to cover the necessary expansion gap round the perimeter of the floor.

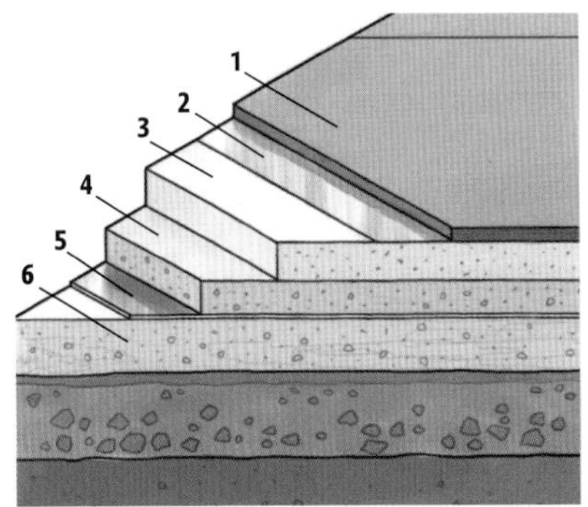

Chipboard floating floor
1 Chipboard flooring
2 Vapour barrier
3 Polystyrene insulation
4 Concrete screed
5 DPM
6 Concrete slab

Buried pipework

House conversions sometimes call for pipework to be run across a room. If the floor is solid, that will mean setting the pipework into the concrete floor.

Although the latter method was once common practice, water bylaws now stipulate that pipes must not be embedded directly in a solid-concrete floor. However, it is possible to conceal pipes inside moulded-plastic ducting laid in the floor.

After the pipework has been fitted and tested, a cover panel is screwed to the lipping of the duct to finish flush with the floor. Ideally, any decorative floorcovering laid over the ducting should be loose-fitted, or else detailed to provide easy access.

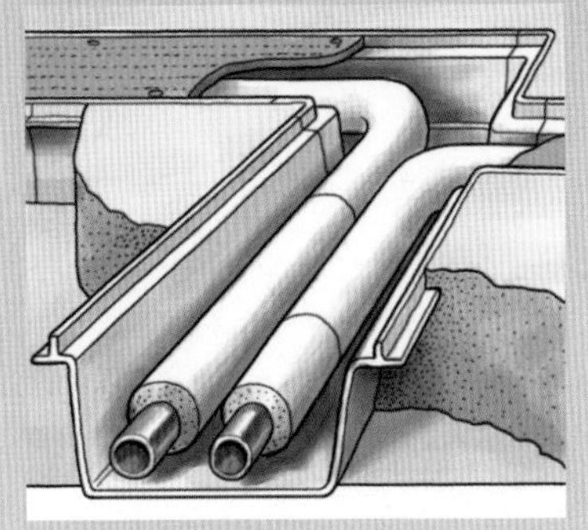

Plastic ducting for floor-run pipes

SEE ALSO > Using bonding agents 157, Replacing skirtings 218, Mixing concrete 455

Flooring

Flooring is the general term used to describe the boarding laid over the floor joists or over a concrete floor. It may consist of hardwood or softwood planks, or take the form of man-made boards.

Floorboards

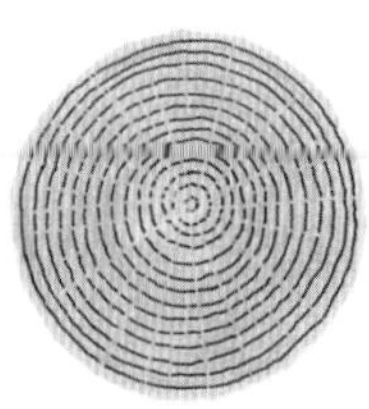

1 Quarter-sawn boards
Shrinkage does not distort these boards.

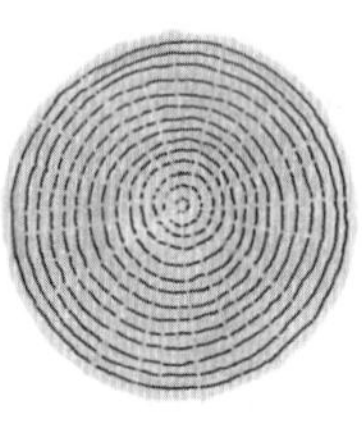

2 Tangentially sawn boards
Shrinkage can cause these boards to 'cup'.

Floorboards are usually made from softwoods and are sold planed all round (PAR), with square or tongue-and-groove edges. Standard sizes are specified as 125 x 25mm (5 x 1in) or 150 x 25mm (6 x 1in) nominal – although floorboards as narrow as 75mm (3in) and others as wide as 280mm (11in) may be found in some houses. Narrow boards produce superior floors, because any movement due to shrinkage is less noticeable. However, installation costs are high, so they tend to be used in the more expensive houses only. Hardwoods such as oak or maple are also used for high-grade flooring, but they add even more to the cost.

The best floorboards are quarter-sawn (**1**) from the log, a method that diminishes distortion due to shrinkage. But because this method is wasteful of timber, floorboards are more often cut tangentially (**2**), to reduce costs. However, boards cut in this way tend to 'cup' (bow) across their width and should be fixed with the concave side facing upwards, as there is a tendency for the grain on the other side to splinter. The cut of a board – tangential or quarter-cut – can be checked by looking at the annual-growth rings on the end grain (see left).

The joint on tongue-and-groove boards is not at the centre of the edges but closer to one face, and these boards should be laid with the offset joint nearer to the joist. Although tongue-and-groove boards are nominally the same sizes as square-edged boards, the edge joint reduces their floor coverage by about 12mm (½in) per board.

In some old buildings you may come across original floorboards bearing the marks left by an adze on the underside. Such old boards have usually only been trimmed to the required thickness where they sit over the joists, so that they lie level with each other.

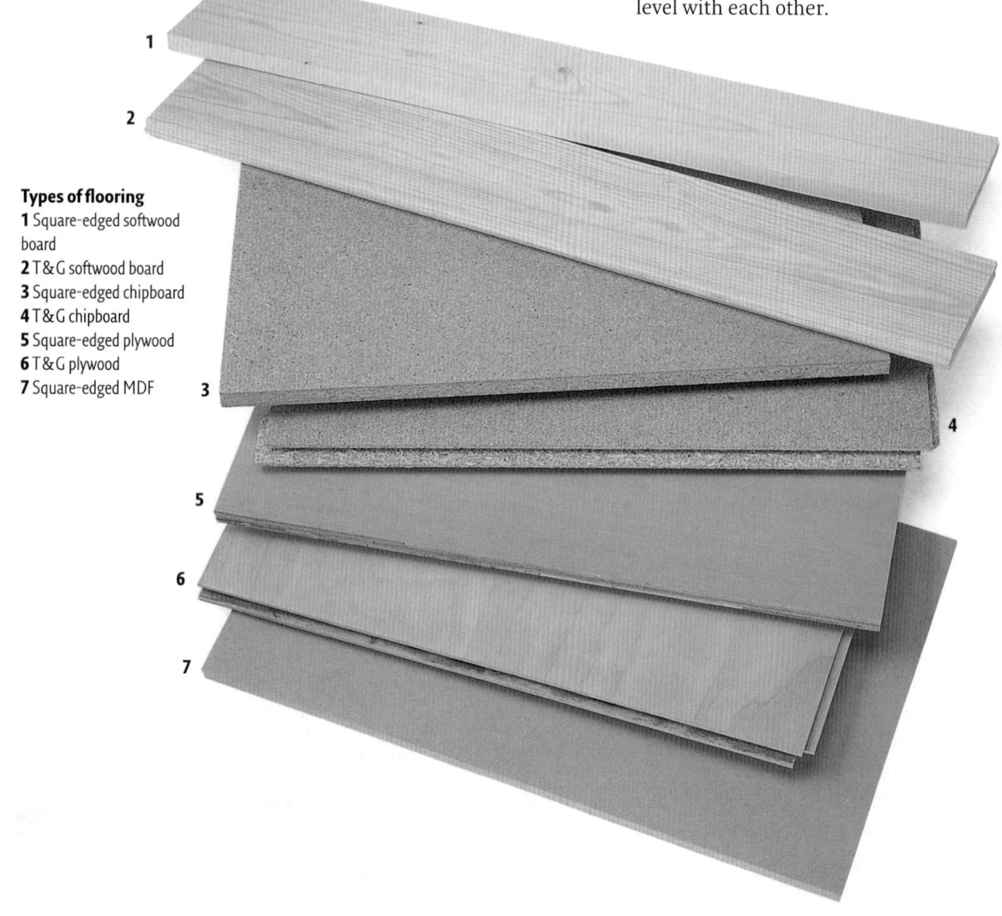

Types of flooring
1 Square-edged softwood board
2 T&G softwood board
3 Square-edged chipboard
4 T&G chipboard
5 Square-edged plywood
6 T&G plywood
7 Square-edged MDF

Sheet flooring

Softwood and hardwood boards provide a durable floor that takes on an attractive colour when sealed and polished. Sheet materials such as flooring-grade plywood or particle boards are merely functional, and are normally used as to provide a flat, stable sub-base for other floorcoverings.

Plywood

Any exterior-grade plywood boards (known as WPB bonded plywood) can be used for flooring. The ones sold as flooring-grade boards are either square-edged or may be tongued and grooved on all four edges.

If it is to be laid directly over the joists, plywood flooring should be 16 to 18mm (⅝ to ¾in) thick. When it is laid over an existing floor surface – to level it or to serve as an underlay for floor tiles – it can be 6 to 12mm (¼ to ½in) in thickness.

Chipboard

Chipboard is made from bonded chips of wood. Only proper flooring-grade chipboard – which is compressed to a higher density than the standard material – should be used for flooring. You can buy either square-edged or tongue-and-groove boards. The square-edged boards measure 2.44 x 1.22m (8 x 4ft) and are 18mm (¾in) thick. The tongue-and-groove boards are available in flooring-standard and moisture-resistant grades. Both grades come in sheets that are 2.4m x 600mm (8 x 2ft) and 22mm (⅞in) thick. The moisture-resistant type should always be used where damp conditions may occur.

The 18mm (¾in) thick boards are suitable for laying on joists that are spaced no more than 400mm (1ft 4in) apart. Where the joists are at 600mm (2ft) intervals, 22mm (⅞in) boarding should be used to avoid sagging.

Medium-density fibreboard

Medium-density fibreboard (MDF) is a dense material made from fine compressed wood fibres. It is produced in standard, moisture-resistant and exterior grades, and is suitable for flooring where a plain, smooth finish is required. MDF is available in 2.44 x 1.22m (8 x 4ft) square-edged sheets in a range of thicknesses. It costs more than chipboard, but is cheaper than plywood.

SEE ALSO > Wood flooring 108–11, Replacing floorboards 180, Laying chipboard flooring 181

Lifting floorboards

Floorboards are produced in lengths that are intended to run from wall to wall. In practice this rarely happens, because shorter lengths are often laid in order to save on materials. When lifting floorboards, start with these shorter pieces if possible. In older homes, a number of boards will probably have been lifted already in the past for access to services and may not have been refixed securely.

Lifting tongue-and-groove boarding

To lift a tongue-and-groove board, you first have to cut through the tongue on each side of the board. Use a circular saw if you have one (1), or a floorboard saw (2). Set the cutting depth to about 12mm (½in) and saw as close to the skirting boards as the saw will allow. Make the final cuts with a padsaw. Then saw across the board and lift it as you would a plain square-edged one.

1 Use a circular saw if you have one

2 Alternatively, use a floorboard saw

Square-edged boards

Tap the blade of a bolster into the gap between the boards, close to the cut end (1). Lever up the edge of the board, but try not to crush the one next to it. Fit the bolster into the gap at the other side of the board and repeat the procedure.

Ease the end of the board up in this way, then work the claw of a hammer under it until there is room to slip a cold chisel under the board (2). Lift the next pair of nails, and proceed in the same fashion along the board until it is free.

1 Lever up the board with a bolster chisel

2 Place a cold chisel under the floorboard

SAFETY WARNING

Be aware that pipes and cables are often run beneath floorboards. Use an electronic detector to check for them before cutting floorboards, especially if using a power saw.

Lifting a continuous board

Floorboards are fixed before the skirting is added, so the ends of a continuous board will be trapped under it. Consequently, you will have to cut across the board before you can lift it.

Locate a joist by the position of the nails fixing the board to it. Mark a line about 25mm (1in) to one side of the nail positions and drill a test hole 3mm (⅛in) in diameter through the board to check that you are clear of the joist side. Then make an access slot for a jigsaw blade by drilling three or four 3mm holes close together through the board, parallel with the joist (1). Break out the wood between the holes with a chisel and insert the jigsaw blade.

Saw across the board to one edge (2), then reverse the cutting direction and saw to the other edge. Prise up the cut end of the floorboard with a bolster, until you can slip a cold chisel under the board to lift it as described above. Then prise up the other section of board and lift it out.

With tongue-and-groove boards, the joints will have to be cut beforehand (see above left). When refixing the boards, you will need to support one end on a softwood block (see below left).

1 Find the joist's side

2 Saw across the board

Refitting a cut board

Board ends usually meet over a joist (1). However, a board that has been cut flush with the side of a joist must be supported below when it is replaced. Cut a piece of 50 x 50mm (2 x 2in) softwood and screw it to the side of the joist. Screw the end of the floorboard to the support (2).

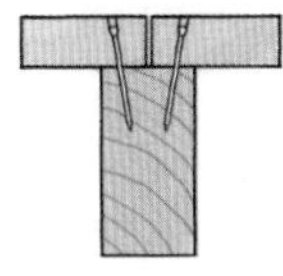

1 Meeting over a joist

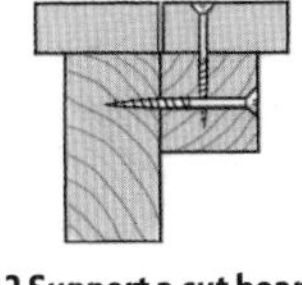

2 Support a cut board

Freeing the end of a board

To release the end of a floorboard that is trapped under the skirting, lift it until it is almost vertical and then pull it out of the gap between the skirting and the joist (1).

Before you can raise a floorboard that runs beneath a partition wall, you will have to cut it close to the skirting (2). Drill an access hole to enable you to insert the blade of a padsaw. Alternatively, buy a handsaw designed for cutting floorboards (3). It has a curved cutting edge that allows you to saw through floorboards without lifting them completely.

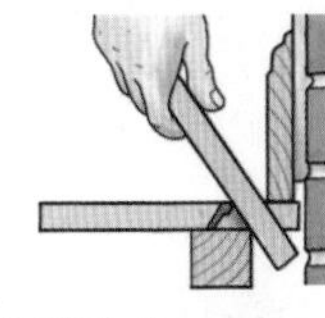

1 Lift the board clear

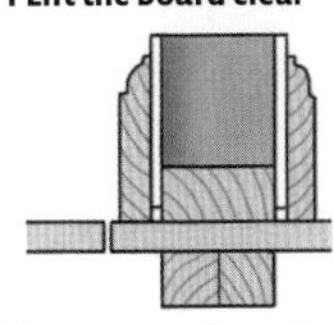

2 Cut close to the wall

3 If need be, use a floorboard saw

SEE ALSO > Saws 488–91, 512, Bolster 513, Cold chisel 513

Replacing floorboards

Although floors are subjected to a great deal of wear, it's usually water damage or timber decay (which could also affect the joists) that results in a floor having to be re-laid or even renewed entirely. Before laying a new floor, measure the room and buy your materials in advance. Leave the floorboards or sheet materials to acclimatize – ideally in the room where they are to be laid – for at least a week before laying.

Removing the flooring

To lift an entire boarded floor, you must first remove the skirting boards from the walls. If you intend to re-lay the existing boards, number them with chalk before lifting them. Remove the first few boards as described earlier, starting from one side of the room, then prise up the remainder by working a bolster chisel between the joists and the undersides of the boards. When lifting tongue-and-groove boards for re-laying, carefully ease them up two or three at a time to avoid breaking the joints and then pull them apart.

Pull all the nails out of the boards and joists, and scrape any accumulated dirt from the tops of the joists. Clean the edges of the boards too, if they are to be reused. Check all timbers for rot or insect infestation, and treat or repair them as required.

Laying floorboards
Work from a platform of loose boards, and proceed in the following order:
1 Fix the first board parallel to the wall.
2 Cut and lay up to six boards, clamp them together and nail them to the joists.
3 Lay the next group in the same way, and continue across the floor. Cut the last board down in width to fit.

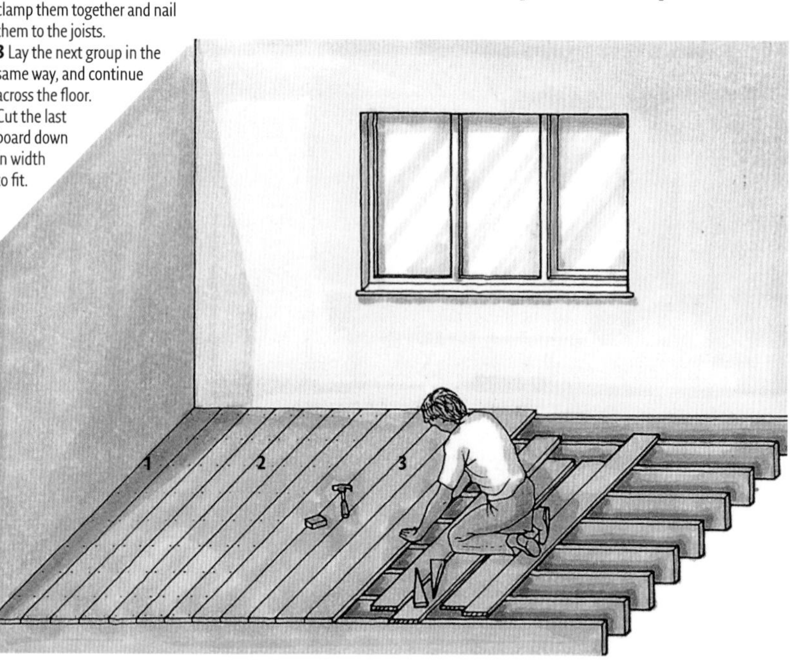

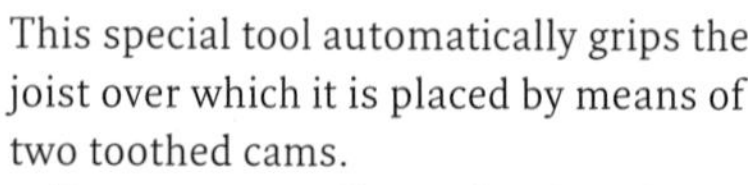

Floorboard cramp

Hire a special cramp to re-lay floorboards

This special tool automatically grips the joist over which it is placed by means of two toothed cams.

Drop a group of loose floorboards in place, then slide the cramp up close to the edge of the first board. Turning the tommy bar operates a screw ram, which applies pressure to the floorboards. Having nailed the boards, release the cramp and relay the next group.

Laying new floorboards

Although these instructions describe how to fix tongue-and-groove boards, the basic method applies equally to square-edged floorboards.

First lay a few loose floorboards together to act as a work platform. Measure the width or length of the room – whichever is at right angles to the floor joists – and cut your boards to stop 9mm (3/8in) short of the walls at each end. Lay four to six boards at a time.

Where two shorter floorboards are to be butted end to end, cut them so that the joint will be centred over a joist. It pays to arrange several boards at a time, so that you are not left with butt joints occurring side by side.

Laying the first board

Fix the first board with its grooved edge no more than 9mm (3/8in) from the wall, and nail it in place with cut floor brads or lost-head nails at least twice as long as the board's thickness.

Place the nails in pairs, one about 25mm (1in) from each edge of the board and centred on the joists. Use a nail punch to drive them about 2mm (1/16in) below the surface; or if you opt for secret nailing, drive nails diagonally through the tongued edge instead.

Fixing the other boards

Lay the other cut boards in place and clamp them to the one that has been fixed, to close up the edge joints. Special floorboard cramps can be hired for this (see below left), but wedges cut from 400mm (1ft 4in) offcuts of board will work just as well.

To clamp the boards with wedges, temporarily nail another floorboard just less than a board's width away from them. Insert pairs of wedges in the gap, resting on every fourth or fifth joist; then, using two hammers, tap the wedges toward each other (**1**). After nailing the clamped floorboards in place as before, remove the wedges and repeat the procedure with the next group of boards, continuing in this way across the room.

At the far wall, cut the last board to fit by removing its tongued edge – it should be cut to leave a gap equal to the width of the tongue or 9mm (3/8in), whichever is less. If you can't slide it onto the previous board's tongue, cut away the bottom section of its grooved edge, so it will drop into place (**2**).

Finally, replace the skirting boards all round the room.

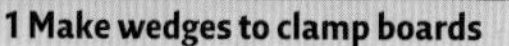

1 Make wedges to clamp boards

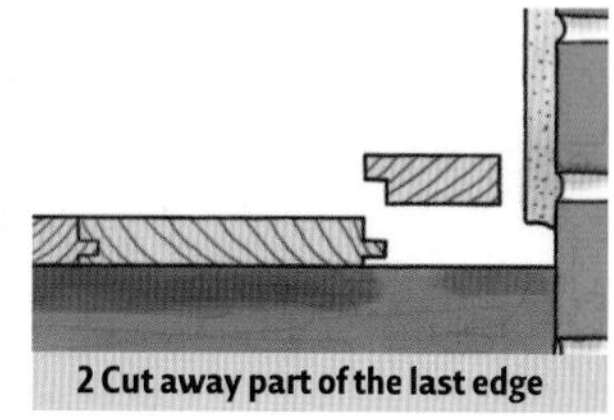

2 Cut away part of the last edge

SEE ALSO > Secret-nailing 111, Repairing floor joists 175, Lifting floorboards 179, Replacing skirtings 218, Woodworm 242, Nails 532–3

Laying chipboard flooring

Chipboard is an excellent material for a floor that is going to be invisible beneath some kind of covering, such as vinyl, cork, or fitted carpet. It can be laid relatively quickly and is a lot cheaper than the equivalent amount of timber flooring. It comes square-edged or tongued and grooved.

Laying square-edged boards

All the edges of square-edged sheet flooring need to be supported. Lay the boards with their long edges along the joists and nail 75 x 50mm (3 x 2in) softwood noggings between the joists to support the ends of the boards. The noggings against the wall are inserted in advance; those supporting joints between boards can be nailed into place as the boards are laid.

Start with a full-length board in one corner and lay a row of boards the length of the room, cutting the last one to fit, as required. Leave an expansion gap of about 9mm (3/8in) between the outer edges of the boards and the walls. The boards' inner edges should fall on the centre line of a joist. If necessary, cut the boards to width – but remove the waste from the edges that will be positioned next to the wall, preserving the machine-cut edges to make neat butt joints with the next row of boards in the centre of the room. Nail down the boards, using 50mm (2in) ring-shank nails, spaced about 300mm (1ft) apart along the joists and noggings. Place the nails about 9mm (3/8in) from the board edges. Cut and lay the remainder of the boards, with the end joints staggered on alternate rows.

Laying tongue-and-groove boards

Tongue-and-groove boards are laid with their longer edges running across the joists. Noggings are required only to support the outer edges close to the walls. The ends of the boards should be supported by joists.

Working from one corner, lay the first board with its grooved edges about 9mm (3/8in) from the walls and nail it in place. Apply PVA wood adhesive to the joint along the end of the first board, and then lay the next one in the row. Knock it up to the first board with a hammer for a good, close joint, protecting the edge with a piece of scrap wood. Nail the board down as before, then wipe any surplus adhesive from the surface before it sets, using a damp rag.

Continue in this way across the floor, gluing all of the joints as you go. Cut boards to fit at the ends of rows or to fall on the centre of a joist, and stagger end joints on alternate rows.

Finally, fit the skirting boards, which will cover the expansion gaps around the perimeter of the floor.

Cutting boards to fit

When laying wide square-edged boards, you may have to reduce them slightly in width (**1**) so that their long edges will butt together precisely on the centre lines of the floor joists.

When laying tongue-and-groove boards, only the last ones need cutting down in width in order to fit against the wall (**2**).

If possible, make all the saw cuts with a powered circular saw for accuracy. Alternatively, use a sharp universal handsaw.

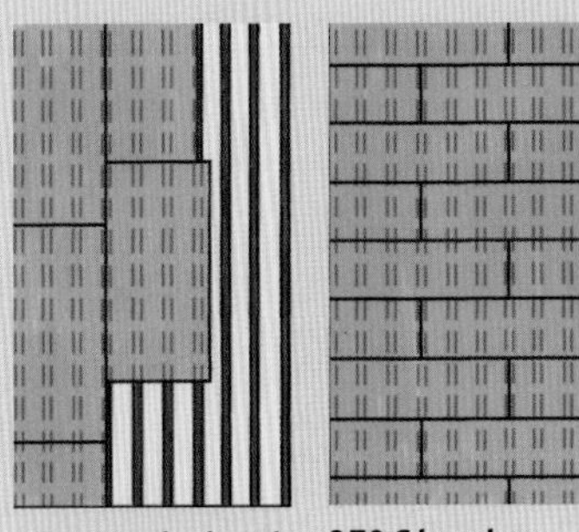

1 Square-edge boards **2 T&G boards**

Laying square-edged boards
The long edges rest on joists and the ends are supported by noggings.

Laying tongue-and-groove boards
Lay T&G boards across the joists, with cut ends centred on a joist.

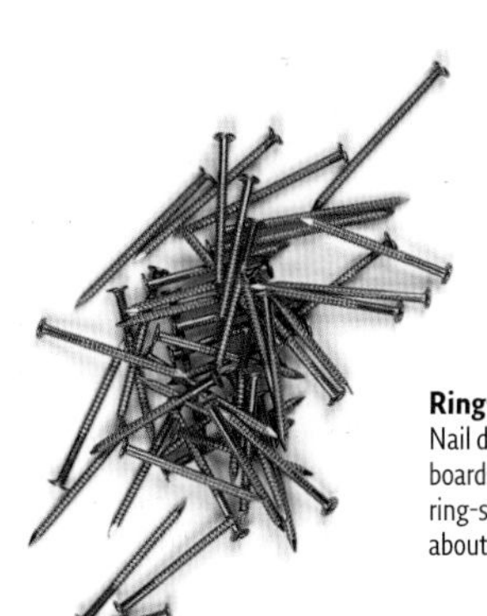

Ring-shank nails
Nail down square-edged boards, using 50mm (2in) ring-shank nails, spaced about 300mm (1ft) apart.

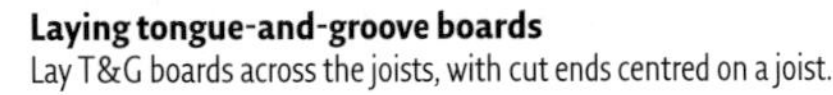

SEE ALSO > Floorcoverings 103–16, Chipboard flooring 178, Replacing skirtings 218, Nails 532–3

Doors: types and construction

At first glance there appears to be a great variety of doors to choose from – but most of the differences are purely stylistic and they are, in fact, all based on a relatively small number of construction methods. The vast range of styles sometimes tempts householders into buying doors that are inappropriate for the house they live in. If you need to replace your front door, it's especially important to choose one in keeping with the architectural style of your house.

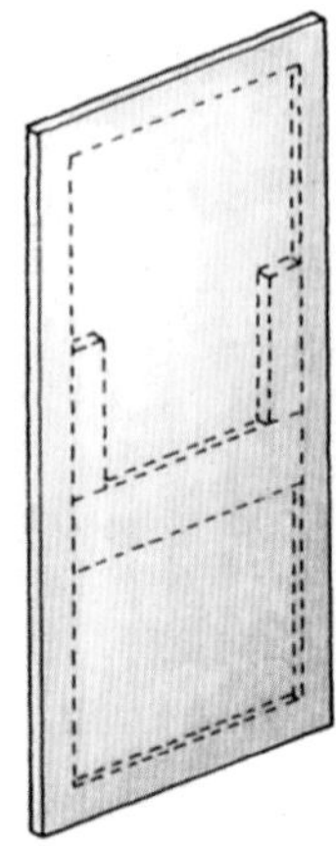

External flush door
A central rail is fitted to take a letter plate.

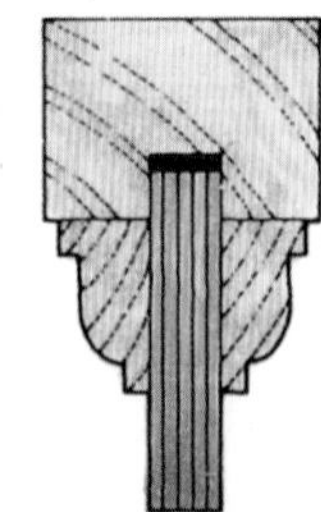

Planted moulding

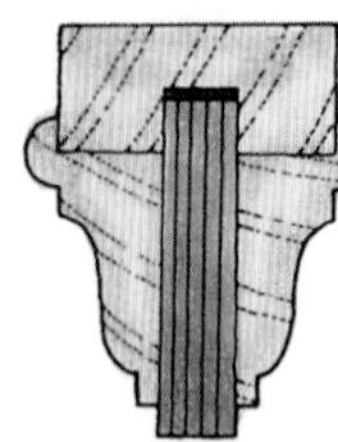

Bolection moulding

Buying a door

You can buy internal and external doors made from softwood or hardwood, the latter usually being reserved for special rooms or entrances where the natural features of the wood can be appreciated. Softwood doors are for more general, workaday use and are intended to be painted. However, some people prefer to apply a clear finish.

Glazed doors are often used for front and rear entrances. Traditionally these are of wooden-frame construction, though modern aluminium-framed and uPVC plastic doors can be bought in standard sizes, complete with double glazing and fitments.

Frame-and-panel doors are supplied in unfinished wood, and mostly require trimming, glazing and fitting with hinges, locks and letter plates.

Door sizes

Doors are made in several standard sizes, which meet most domestic needs. Standard heights are 2m (6ft 6in), 2.03m (6ft 8in) and occasionally 2.17m (7ft). Widths range from 600 to 900mm (2 to 3ft), in steps of about 75mm (3in). Thicknesses vary from 35 to 44mm (1³/₈ to 1³/₄in).

Older houses often have relatively large doors to the main rooms, but modern homes tend to have standard-size joinery throughout. The standard is usually 2m x 762mm (6ft 6in x 2ft 6in) – except for front doors, which are invariably larger in order to fit the proportions of the façade.

When replacing a door in an old house – where the openings may well be of non-standard sizes – have a door made to measure or buy one of the nearest available size and trim it to fit, removing an equal amount from each edge to preserve its symmetry.

Panel doors

Panel doors have a hardwood or softwood frame made with mortise-and-tenon or dowel joints. The frame is rebated or grooved to house the panels, which can be of solid wood, plywood or glass. Doors constructed from moulded-hardboard panels, pressed steel and ABS plastic fixed to a rigid frame are also available.

1 Muntins
These are the central vertical members of the door. They are jointed into the three cross rails.

2 Panels
These may be of solid wood or of plywood. They are held loosely in grooves in the frame to ensure they can shrink without splitting. They stiffen the door.

3 Cross rails
The top, centre and bottom rails are tenoned into the stiles. In cheaper doors, the mortise-and-tenon joints are replaced with dowel joints.

4 Stiles
These are the upright members at the sides of the door. They carry the hinges and lock.

Panel-door mouldings
Panel mouldings are either machined on the frame before assembly or machined separately and pinned on. A planted moulding (see far left) can shrink away from the frame, making cracks in the paintwork. A bolection moulding, which laps the frame, helps overcome this problem.

Panel door

Flush doors

Most flush doors have a softwood frame faced with sheets of plywood or hardboard on both sides and infilled with a hollow-core material. Mostly located internally, they're simple, lightweight and cheap, but lack character. External flush doors have a central rail to take a letter plate. Fire-resistant flush doors have a solid core.

1 Top and bottom rails
These are tenoned into the stiles.

2 Intermediate rails
These lighter rails, joined to the stiles, are notched to allow the passage of air, in order to prevent the panels sinking.

3 Lock blocks
A softwood block able to take a mortise lock is glued to each stile.

4 Panels
The panels are left plain for painting or finished with a wood veneer.

Core material
A cardboard honeycomb is often sandwiched between the panels in place of intermediate rails. A solid fire-retardant material forms the core of fire-check doors.

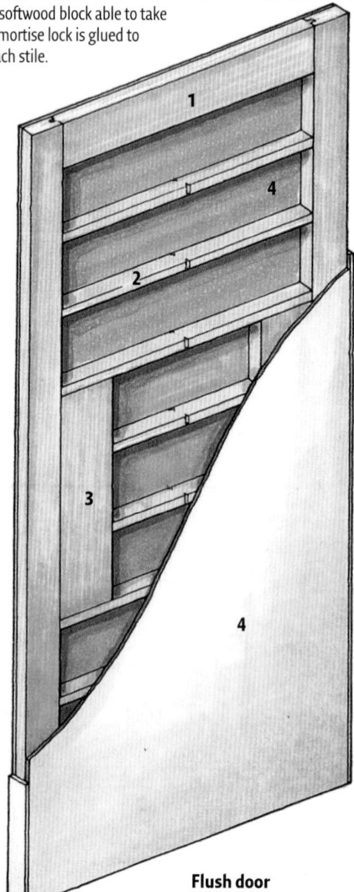

Flush door

SEE ALSO > Painting a door 72, Fitting a door 184–5, Weather bar 185, Door furniture 186, Fire-resistant doors 191, Fitting locks 235–6

Ledged-and-braced doors

These doors have a rustic look and are often found in outbuildings, garden walls and older houses. They are strong, secure and cheap, though sometimes a little crude. A superior framed version is tenon-jointed or dowelled, instead of being merely nailed or stapled. The door must be hung the right way round (see below) for the braces to be effective.

1 Battens
Tongue-and-groove boards are nailed to the ledges.

2 T-hinges
Butt hinges will not hold in the end grain of the ledges, so long T-hinges are used to take the weight.

3 Braces
These diagonals, preferably notched into the ledges, transmit the weight of the door to the hinges and stop it sagging.

4 Ledges
These are the cross rails to which the battens are nailed.

Framed ledged, braced and battened door

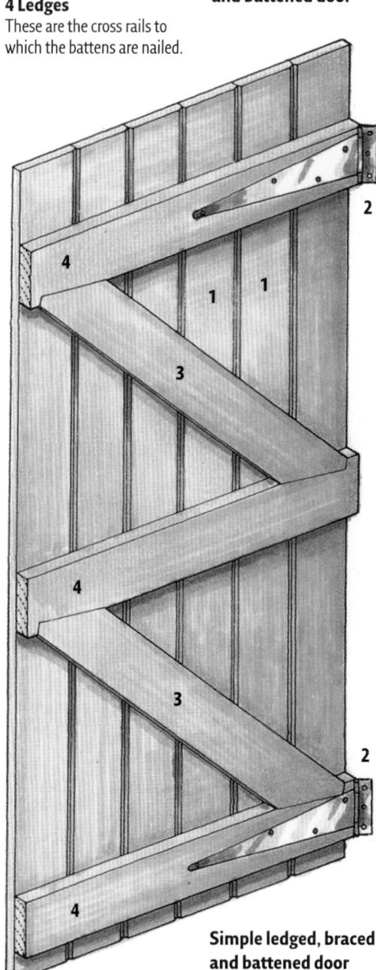

Simple ledged, braced and battened door

Frames and casings

External doorframes and internal door casings both serve the same purpose: to provide a secure mounting for the door within the structure of the wall. They are usually made of softwood or hardwood.

External frames

Typically an exterior door is fitted into a wooden frame, consisting of the head (1) at the top; the sill (2), with a water-repellent weather bar, at the bottom; and, mortised and tenoned between them, two rebated side posts (3). The head extends by 50mm (2in) on each side of the frame (4). These projections, known as 'horns', are built into the masonry to hold the frame in place. Pallets are wooden plugs, also built into the masonry, for nail-fixing the frame. Metal brackets (5) provide another way of fixing a doorframe.

Aluminium and uPVC door sets are supplied with an extruded frame and sill, and include all the door furniture, glazing and weatherstripping. Frame fixings hold the assembly in place.

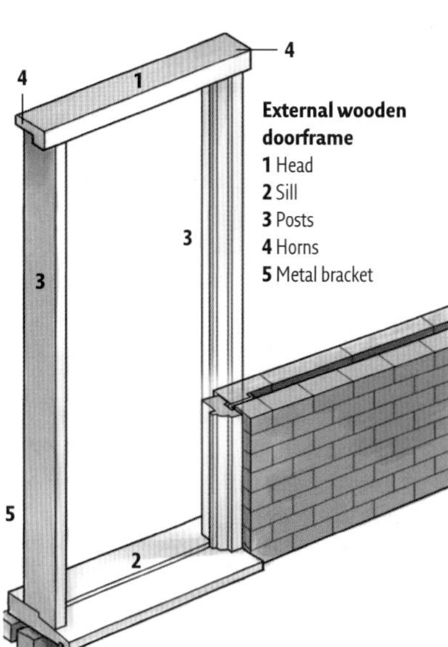

External wooden doorframe
1 Head
2 Sill
3 Posts
4 Horns
5 Metal bracket

Front door
External doors are often framed and panelled.

Internal casings

Internal doors are hung in a timber frame made up from three members: the soffit casing (1) at the top and jamb casings (2) on either side of the opening. These are jointed together at the corners with tongue-and-groove joints (3). The jambs were traditionally nailed to pallets (wooden plugs) set in the masonry (4). Frame fixings are now commonly used instead. An architrave (5) covers the joints between the casings and wall. The door closes against applied doorstops (6), which form a rebate.

In better-quality buildings, hardwood casings are often nailed to softwood grounds (see below). These are rough-sawn lengths of timber nailed in place to form a frame around the door opening. The soffit grounds (7) are nailed to the front of the lintel, and the jamb grounds (8) to wooden plugs in the masonry. The grounds provide a level for the plaster, and a secure fixing for the architrave moulding.

Internal door casing
1 Soffit casing
2 Jamb casing
3 Barefaced T&G joint
4 Pallet (wooden plug)
5 Architrave
6 Doorstop

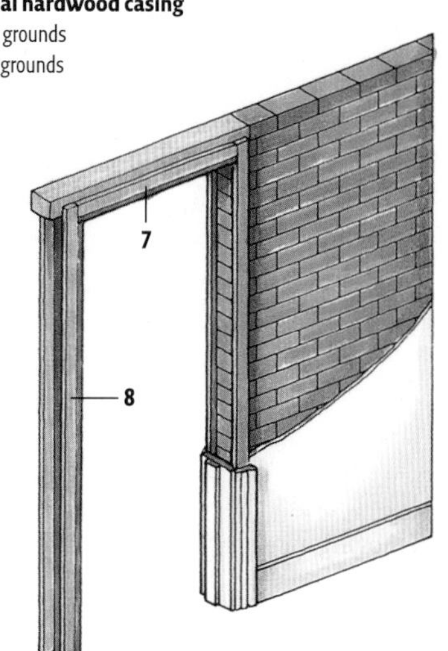

Internal hardwood casing
7 Soffit grounds
8 Jamb grounds

Room door
Modern internal doors are often moulded to simulate panelled doors.

SEE ALSO > Painting a frame 72, Fixing a casing 188, Repairing frames 188, Fire-resistant frame 191

Fitting and hanging doors

Whatever style of door you decide to fit, the procedure is similar, with only minor differences to contend with. Two good-quality 100mm (4in) butt hinges are enough to support a standard door; but a third (central) hinge should be added to a heavy hardwood door or a fire door. You will have to hang a door in its frame several times in order to obtain a perfect fit, so you will need to have someone working with you or else use wedges to hold the door temporarily in position.

Fitting a door

Before attaching the hinges to a new door, make sure that it fits well into its frame. It should have a clearance of 2mm (1/16in) at the top and sides, and should clear the floor by at least 6mm (1/4in), and by 12mm (1/2in) for a carpeted floor.

Measure the height and width of the door opening, and the depth of the rebate in the frame into which the door has to fit. Ideally, choose a door that is the right size – but if you can't get one that fits the opening exactly, select one large enough to be trimmed down.

Cutting to size

New doors are often supplied with 'horns' – extensions to their stiles that prevent the corners being damaged while the doors are in storage. Cut these off with a saw before trimming the door to size (1).

Transfer the measurements from the opening to the door, making allowance for the necessary clearances all round.

To reduce the width of the door, support it on edge, latch stile up, in a portable bench, and plane the stile down to the marked line. If a lot of wood has to be removed, take some off each stile – this is especially important in the case of panel doors, in order to preserve their symmetry.

If you need to reduce the height of the door by more than 6mm (1/4in), remove the waste with a saw and finish off with a plane. Otherwise, just trim it to size with the plane (2) – which must be extremely sharp to deal with the end grain of the stiles. To avoid 'chipping out' the corners, work from each corner towards the centre of the bottom rail.

Supporting the door on shallow wedges (3), try it in the frame. If it still does not fit, take it down and remove more wood where appropriate.

1 Trim door to size

2 Plane to size

3 Wedge the door

Fitting hinges

The upper hinge is set about 175mm (7in) down from the top edge of the door, and the lower one about 250mm (10in) up from the bottom. The recesses into which they fit are cut to equal depths into the stile and doorframe. Wedge the door in its opening, and – with the wedges tapped in to raise it to the right floor clearance – mark the positions of the hinges on both the door and frame.

Creating the hinge recesses

Stand the door on edge, hinge stile uppermost. Open a hinge and, with its knuckle projecting from the edge of the door, align it with the marks and draw round the flap with a pencil (1). Set a marking gauge to the thickness of the flap and mark the depth of the recess (2).

With a chisel, make a series of shallow cuts across the grain (3) and pare out the waste down to the scored depth line (4). Repeat the procedure with the second hinge; then, using the flaps as guides, drill pilot holes for the screws and fix both hinges into their recesses (5).

Wedge the door in its frame in the open position, aligning the free hinge flaps with the marks on the doorframe you made earlier. Make sure that the knuckles of the hinges are parallel with the frame, then trace the recesses on the frame and cut them out as you did the others (6).

Adjusting and aligning the door

Hang the door with one screw holding each hinge, and see if it closes smoothly.

If the latch stile rubs on the frame, you may have to make one or both recesses slightly deeper.

If the door appears to strain against the hinges, it is said to be hingebound. If this is the case, insert thin cardboard beneath the hinge flaps to pack them out.

When you're satisfied that the door opens and closes properly, drive in the rest of the screws (7).Make sure their heads fit neatly into the hinge countersinks.

1 Mark round the flap with a pencil

2 Mark the flap thickness on the door edge

3 Cut across the grain with a chisel

SEE ALSO > Fitting locks 235–6, Draught-proofing doors 258–9, Marking gauge 487, Folding bench 504

4 Pare away the wood down to the depth line

5 Drill pilot holes and attach the hinges

6 Mark and cut the hinge recesses on the frame

7 Wedge the door open and attach the hinges

Fitting rising butt hinges

Rising butt hinges – which lift a door as it is opened – prevent it dragging on a thick-pile carpet. These hinges are made in two parts: a flap with a fixed pin is screwed to the doorframe, and a flap with a single knuckle is fixed to the door. The knuckle pivots on the pin.

Rising butt hinges are designed to be fixed one way up only, and are therefore made specifically for left-hand or right-hand opening. The countersunk screw holes in the fixed-pin flap indicate which side it is intended for.

Fitting the hinges

Trim the door to size and mark the positions for the hinges (see opposite) – but before fitting them, plane a shallow bevel at the top outer corner of the hinge stile, so that it will clear the frame as it opens. Because the stile runs through to the top of the door, plane from the outer corner towards the centre, to avoid splitting the wood. The top strip of the doorstop will mask the bevel when the door is closed.

Fit the hinges to the door and frame; and then, taking care not to damage the architrave above the opening, locate the door leaf onto the leaf with the hinge pins and lower it into place.

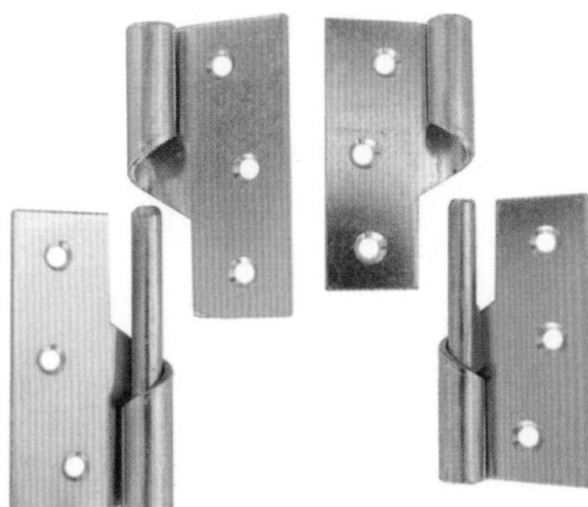

Left-hand opening **Right-hand opening**

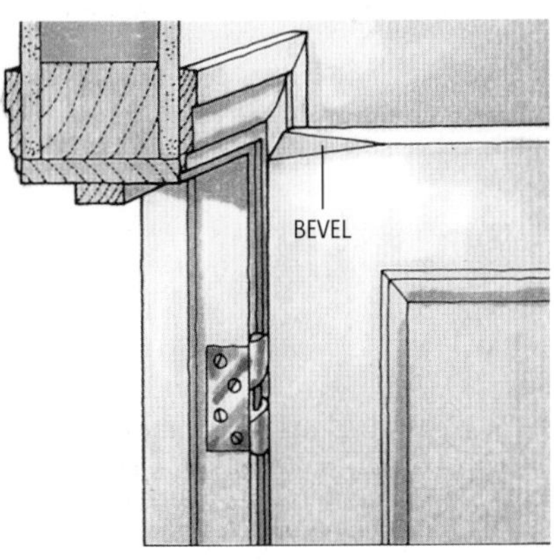

Plane a shallow bevel to clear the doorframe

Weatherproofing doors

Fitting a weatherboard

A weatherboard is a timber moulding, fitted to the bottom of an external door to shed rainwater away from the threshold. To fit one, measure the width of the opening between the doorstops and cut the moulding to fit, cutting one end at a slight angle where it meets the doorframe on the latch side. This will allow it to clear the frame as the door swings open.

Use screws and a waterproof glue to attach a weatherboard to an unpainted door. When fitting one to a door that is already finished, apply a thick coat of primer to the back surface of the weatherboard to make a weatherproof seal, then screw the moulding in place while the primer is wet. Fill or plug the screw holes before you paint the weatherboard.

Allowing for a weather bar

Although a rebate cut into the head and side posts of an external doorframe provides a seal round an inward-opening door, a rebate cut into the sill at the foot of the door would merely encourage rainwater to penetrate into the house.

A door in an exposed position needs to be fitted with a weather bar to prevent rainwater running underneath. This is a metal or plastic strip, set into the step or sill. If you are putting in a new door, cut a rebate across the bottom of the door in order to clear the bar.

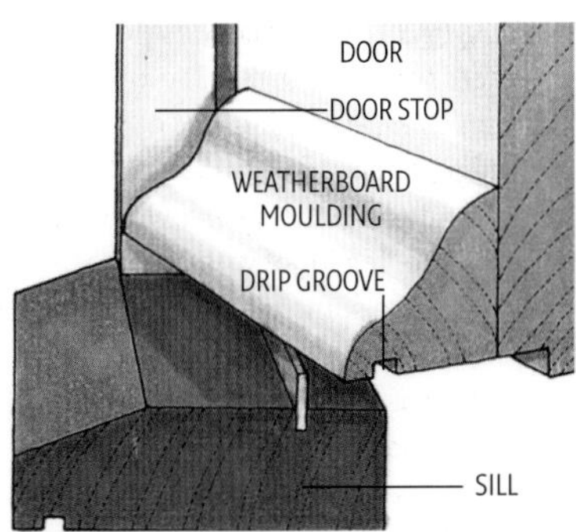

Door fitted with a weatherboard

Effects of weathering
A sadly neglected panel door that could have been preserved by applying a weatherboard before the deterioration had become so widespread.

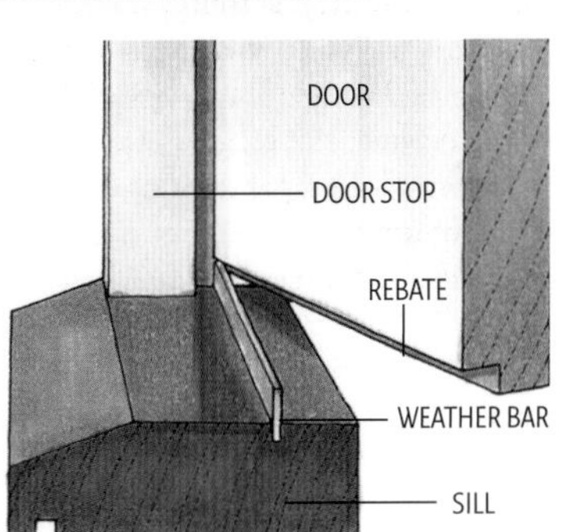

Sill fitted with weather bar

SEE ALSO > Door construction 182–3, Power saw 491, Router 495, Plug cutter 500

Door furniture

The term 'door furniture' describes the hardware that's fitted to an external or internal door to improve its function or appearance. It includes door knockers, letter plates, handles, knockers and door pulls.

Reproduction door furniture
1 Brass 'Georgian' letter plate
2 Brass 'Georgian' knocker
3 Brass 'Georgian' door knob
4 Black-iron door knob
5 Black-iron knocker
6 Black-iron letter plate

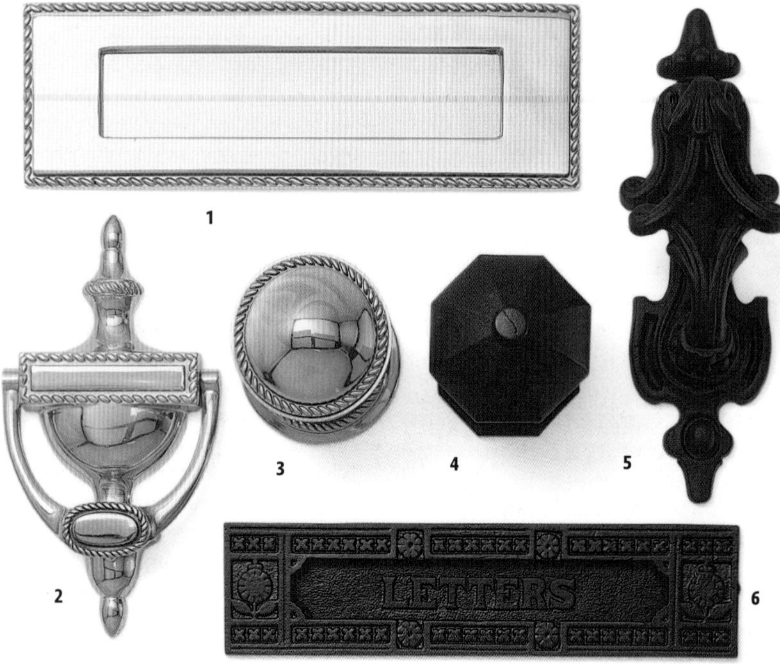

Fitting a door knocker

A complete set of reproduction exterior-door furniture in the traditional manner comprises a letter plate, a door knob and a knocker. Being the most ornate item in the set, a door knocker is more often regarded as an optional decorative feature rather than an essential item – especially since, from the functional point of view, electric door bells have made door knockers virtually obsolete.

On a panel door, fit a knocker to the muntin at about shoulder height. Mark a vertical centre line on the muntin at the required height and drill a counterbored clearance hole for the fixing screw, as described for fixing a door pull (see below left). Plug the counterbored hole on the inside after fixing the backplate.

Reproduction brass fittings are now usually finished at the factory with a clear lacquer to prevent tarnishing.

Fitting finger plates
Designed to protect the paintwork on interior doors, finger plates are screwed to each side of the lock stile, just above the centre rail.

Fitting a door pull

A period-style iron or brass door knob makes an attractive feature on a panelled door. Such knobs are reproduced in many traditional styles and patterns.

An external door pull in the form of a knob is usually fitted on the centre line of a panel door. If a letter plate occupies the middle rail, place the knob on the muntin above it.

Drill a counterbored hole from the inside of the door to take the head of the fixing screw.

The backplate of the knob has a locating peg on the reverse that stops the knob turning when the screw is tightened. Drill a shallow recess for the peg, then fit the knob and tighten the screw. For a neat finish, plug the counterbored hole.

Counterbore the hole for the fixing screw and conceal it with a wooden plug

Fitting a letter plate

Letter plates are available in a variety of styles and materials – solid brass, stainless steel, plated, cast iron and aluminium. They are designed either for horizontal or for vertical fitting. The fitting of a horizontal letter plate is described here, but the same method is applicable to the vertical type fitted into the door stile.

Mark out the rectangular opening on the centre of the cross rail. The slot must be only slightly larger than the hinged flap on the letter plate. Drill a 12mm (½in) access hole in each corner of the rectangle for the blade of a padsaw or power jigsaw. After cutting out the slot (**1**), trim the corners with a chisel and clean up the edges.

Mark and drill the fixing holes, then attach the letter plate (**2**). You may have to shorten the screws if the door is thin. Plug or fill the counterbored holes that house the screwheads.

Better still, fit an internal flap cover. Made from metal or plastic, these are held in place with small woodscrews. A flap cover reduces draughts, looks neat, and allows the letter plate to be removed more conveniently if it's to be machine-polished from time to time.

1 Use a jigsaw to cut out the letter-box opening

2 Fit the letter plate and tighten the fixing nuts

SEE ALSO > Preparing and cleaning metalwork 60–61, Finishing metalwork 82–3, Door construction 182–3, Door bells 313, Padsaw 489, Power jigsaw 491

Repairing doors

Doors suffer from several problems (many of which develop with age), including binding edges – which make the door difficult to open or close – and rattling against the doorstop when the door is closed.

Easing a binding door

The most common cause of doors binding in their frames is regular redecorating, which produces a thick build-up of paint on the door edges. The solution is to remove the excess paint, using a sharp bench plane or a Surform plane to avoid damaging the paint film on the door faces (1). Then test whether the door still binds in the frame. If it does, plane the edge a little more before priming and painting the stripped edge.

If the door binds on a floorcovering as it opens, you will need to remove a little wood from the bottom edge of the door. First use a wood offcut and a pencil to mark a cutting line on the face of the door that will clear the surface of the floorcovering. Unscrew the door from its hinges and lay it across two trestles or other supports. Use a handsaw or power saw to cut along the marked line (2), then sand the cut edge smooth. Re-hang the door and check that it now clears the floor.

1 Shave off excess paint from the door edge

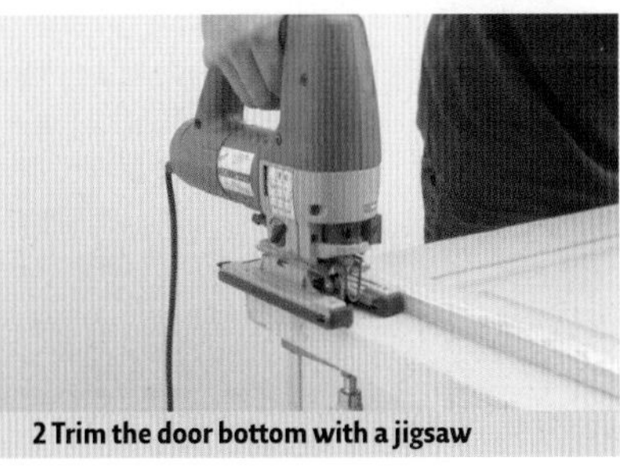

2 Trim the door bottom with a jigsaw

Curing a rattling door

The most common reason why doors rattle in their frames is that the striking plate into which the door latch engages is too far away from the door stop bead.

Repositioning the striking plate a little closer to the stop bead (1) will hold the closed door tightly against it.

Moving the striking plate can also be the solution if the latch will not engage when the door is closed, but in this case you may need to move the striking plate away from the stop bead, or up or down a little.

The new screw positions may be too close to the existing screw holes for you to drill pilot holes. Drill out the existing holes and glue hardwood dowels into them (2). Trim them off flush with the frame and drill the new pilot holes into them.

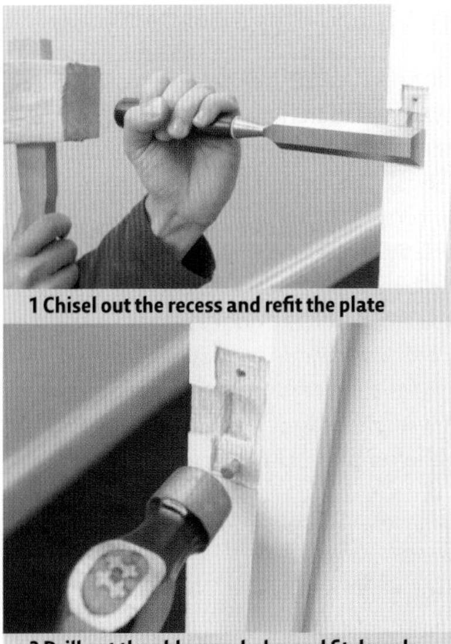

1 Chisel out the recess and refit the plate

2 Drill out the old screw holes and fit dowels

Easing a hard-to-close door

After years of use, hinges wear and the pins can become slack, allowing the door to drop so it becomes hard to close. In this case, either fit new hinges or save money by swapping the old hinges, top for bottom, which reverses the wear on the pins.

Doors may also bind if hinges are set too deep in their recesses. If this is the case, unscrew the affected hinge and insert thin pieces of cardboard packing into the recess.

Repairing a forced door

A solid-wood panelled door is commonly used for the main entrance to a house. This type of door should give trouble-free service over the years. However, even sound doors can be seriously damaged when a housebreaker uses brute force to gain entry.

Although relatively strong, practically any entrance door can be kicked in or smashed open with a sledgehammer, the weakest point often being down the hinged edge of the door rather than the well-fortified area where the locks have been installed.

When the stiles or panels are badly splintered, the easiest course is to replace the whole door. However, if the door is unique and therefore worth preserving, you can insert pieces of new wood to repair the damage.

Rebuilding the edge

If the hinge stile has been split, the wood may have failed in the vicinity of the hinge screws and may even have broken out from the front face of the door. If the splintered wood can be clamped back into place, glue the break with exterior wood adhesive. Cover the repair with a piece of polythene sheeting and place wooden blocks under the cramp heads to spread the forces over the damaged area. Glue dowel plugs into the old screw holes, so you can refix the door. Clean up the repair with a plane and fill any hollows in the surface with a wood filler prior to repainting.

However, it is likely that the split will be beyond repair. In which case, replace the damaged material with new wood. Use a chisel to cut back the damaged stile to sound wood, forming a regular recess. Undercut the ends to 45 degrees. Shape a block of similar wood to fit the length of the recess, but leave it oversize in width and thickness. Glue it in place and, when the glue has set, plane the repair block flush. Cut the housings for the hinges.

Rehang the door, and fit hinge bolts to the door stile and the frame to help prevent the door being forced again in the future.

SEE ALSO > Painting doors 72, Door construction 182–3, Hinge bolts 236, Wood preservers 246, Saws 488–91, Routers 495

Replacing a doorframe

Because external doorframes are built into the masonry, having to replace one inevitably damages the plaster or rendering. In older houses these frames are recessed into the masonry, with the inside face of the frame flush with the plasterwork and an architrave moulding covering the joint. Modern houses may have frames close to or flush with the outer face of the masonry. Measure the door and either buy a standard frame to fit or make one yourself from standard frame sections.

1 Cut back to expose the back of the frame

2 Cut through the frame fixings

3 Saw through the frame to remove it

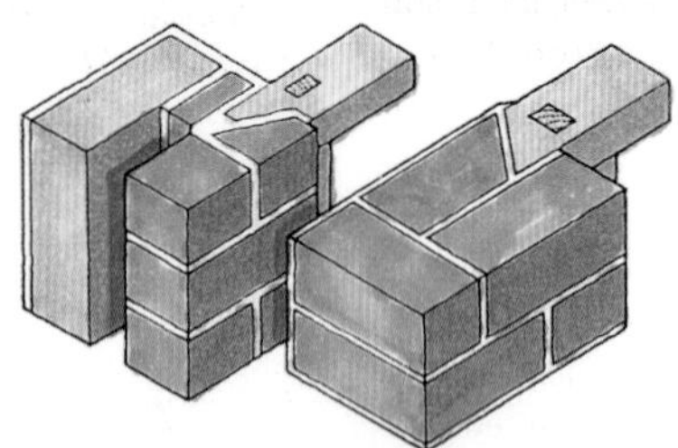

4 Shape the horns rather than cut them off

5 Screw the frame to the plugged wall

Removing the old doorframe

Chop back the plaster or rendering with a cold chisel to expose the back face of the doorframe (**1**). With an all-purpose saw (**2**), cut through the metal fixings holding the frame to the masonry on each side. You will find a fixing about 225mm (9in) from the top and bottom, and another situated between the two. Saw through the jambs halfway up (**3**); and if necessary, cut the head member and the sill. Lever the frame members out, using a crowbar. Clear any loose material from the opening; and repair a vertical DPC in a cavity wall with gun-applied mastic, in order to keep moisture out of the gap between the inner and outer layers of brickwork.

Fitting the new frame

Removing the horns makes fitting a frame easier, but it also weakens it. Where possible, retain the horns and shape them like the old ones (**4**).

Wedge the frame into position, checking that it is central, square and plumb. Drill three counterbored clearance holes in each jamb for the fixing screws, positioned about 300mm (1ft) from the top and bottom, with one halfway. Try to avoid drilling into mortar joints. Run a masonry drill through the clearance holes to mark their positions on the masonry.

Remove the frame, drill the holes in the masonry, and insert No12 wallplugs. Replace the frame and fix it with 100mm (4in) No12 steel screws, then plug the counterbored holes. Alternatively, use nailable-plug frame fixings – which avoids removing the frame to drill the wall.

Pack any gap under the sill with mortar. Make good the masonry, rendering or plasterwork, and apply mastic sealant round the outer edge of the frame to seal any small gaps.

Replacing a door casing

An internal door opening is finished off with a casing. If an existing casing is warped or damaged, replacing it is a relatively straightforward job. Simply remove the architraves and prise the old casing away from the wall.

Door casings are usually made from softwood – either 25mm (1in) thick if an applied doorstop is used, or 38mm (1½in) thick when the doorstop is rebated to take the door. The width of the casing should equal the thickness of the finished wall.

Joinery suppliers sell door casings as unassembled kits for standard door sizes. If your door is not standard, you can make a lining yourself, using a barefaced tongue-and-groove joint (**1**).

Fitting the new casing

Wedge the assembled and braced frame in the opening (**2**); and if necessary, place hardboard or plywood packing between the lintel and the soffit casing at each end. Check that the edges are flush with both faces of the wall, and then fix the soffit in place with two pairs of screws or nails.

Plumb one jamb casing, using a straightedge and spirit level (**3**), then pack it in place. Start fixing about 75mm (3in) from the bottom and work upward, checking for true as you go. Place the fixings for it about 450mm (1ft 6in) apart.

Make a 'pinch rod' from two laths to fit closely between the jamb casings at the top of the frame, then place it across the bottom (**4**) and pack out the unfixed jamb to fit. Check that this jamb is plumb. Fix the casing in place, and use the pinch rod to check the distance between the jamb members at all levels.

Fitting the architrave and doorstop

Repair any damage done to the wall surface around the opening, and cover the joint on both sides with a mitred architrave moulding. Fit the doorstop battens in their correct positions on the inside of the casing and hang the door.

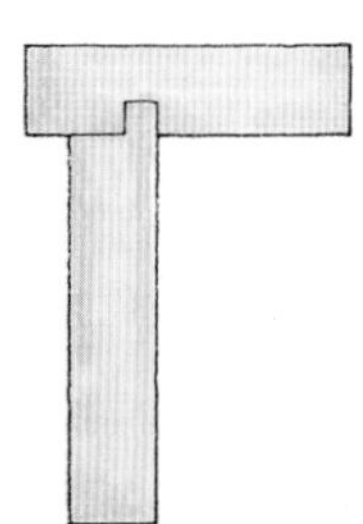

1 Barefaced T&G joint

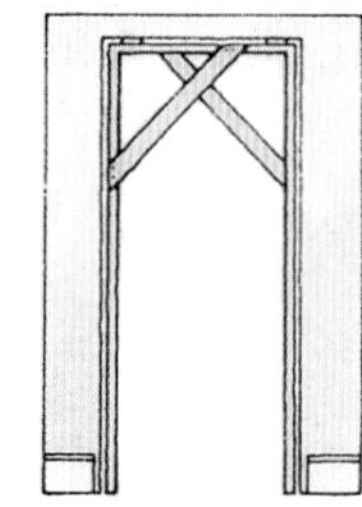

2 Wedge in position

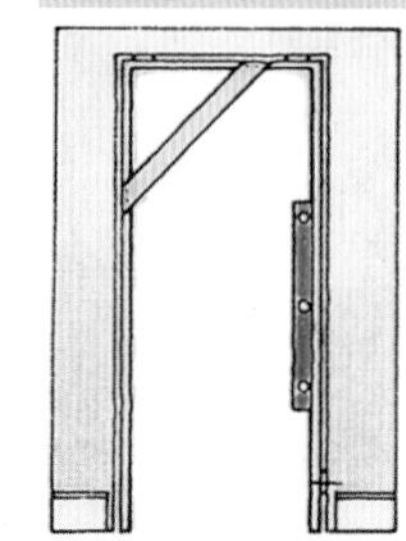

3 Plumb one jamb

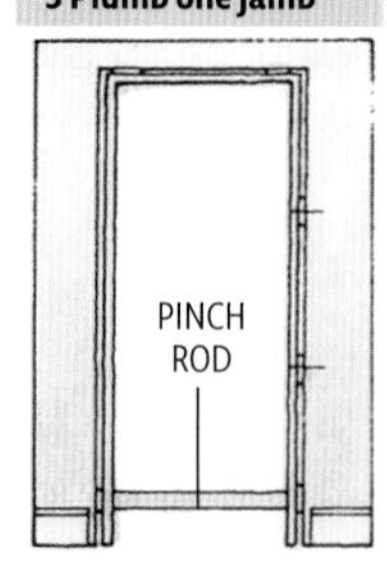

4 Pack out to fit

SEE ALSO > Patching plaster 159–60, Fitting a door 184–5, Sealing gaps 249

Repairing a rotten doorframe

Most external doorframes are made from softwood, and if regularly maintained they will give years of good service. However, if the ends of the doorsills and frame posts are subjected to continual wetting, they are vulnerable to wet rot. This can happen when the frame has moved because the timber has shrunk, or where old pointing has fallen out and left a gap where moisture can penetrate.

Prevention is always better than cure, so check round the doorframe for any gaps and apply a mastic sealant where needed. Keep all pointing in good order. A minor outbreak of wet rot can be treated with the aid of a proprietary repair kit and a chemical preserver. It is possible for the sill to rot without the doorposts being affected – in which case replace only the sill. But if the posts have been affected too, repair them at the same time (see right). In some cases, the ends of the doorposts are tenoned into the sill and fitted as a unit.

Replacing a sill

You can buy 150 x 50mm (6 x 2in) softwood or hardwood doorsill sections that can be cut to the required length. If your sill is not of a standard-shaped section, you can have a replacement made to order.

Taking out the old sill

Take the door off its hinges. The posts are usually tenoned into the sill, so split the sill lengthways with a wood chisel in order to dismantle the joints. A sawcut across the centre of the sill makes the job easier.

The ends of the sill are usually set into the masonry on each side of the opening. To release the sill, chop out the mortar joints carefully, using a plugging chisel, then pull out a brick from each side. Keep the bricks for replacing later.

The new sill has to be inserted from the front so that it can be tucked under the posts and into the brickwork. Cut off the tenon at the base of each post, level with the joint's shoulder line (1). Cut away the doorstop down to the depth of the rebate in each post (2). Then mark and cut shallow housings for the ends of the posts in the top of the new sill. The housings must be deep enough to accommodate the notched ends of the posts; this may mean that the new sill has to be fitted slightly higher than the original one, in which case you will have to trim a little off the bottom of the door.

Fitting a new sill

Try the new sill for fit and check that it is level. Before fixing it, apply two coats of all-purpose wood preserver to its underside and to both ends; and, as a precaution against rising or penetrating damp, apply two or three coats of bitumen-latex emulsion to the masonry that will be in contact with the sill.

When the wood is dry, glue the sill to the posts, using an exterior-grade woodworking adhesive. Wedge the underside of the sill with pieces of roofing slate to push it up against the ends of the doorposts. Skew-nail or screw the posts to the sill, then leave it for the adhesive to set.

Pack the gap between the underside of the sill and the masonry with a stiff mortar made with 3 parts sand : 1 part cement, then rebond and point the loose bricks. Finally, treat the wood with a preserver and seal any gaps around the doorframe with mastic.

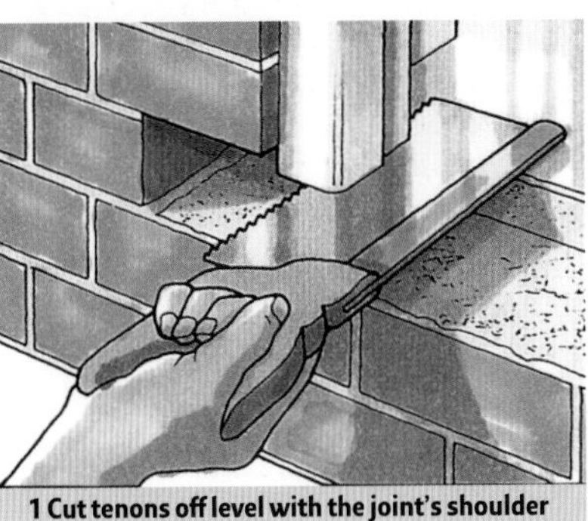

1 Cut tenons off level with the joint's shoulder

2 Notch the posts and cut housings in the sill

Repairing doorposts

Rot can attack the ends of doorposts where they meet stone steps or are set into concrete, especially in a doorway that is regularly exposed to driving rain.

If the damage is not too extensive, the rotten end can be cut away and replaced with a new piece, either scarf-jointed or halving-jointed into place. If your sill is made of wood, combine the following instructions with those given for replacing a sill (see left).

Splicing in new wood

First remove the door, then saw off the end of the affected doorpost, back to sound timber. For a scarf joint, make the cut at 45 degrees to the face of the post (1); for a halving joint, cut it square. If the post is located on a metal dowel set into the step, chop out the dowel with a cold chisel.

Measure and cut a matching section of post to length, allowing for the overlap of the joint. Then cut the end to 45 degrees for a scarf joint, or mark and cut both the post and the repair section to form a halving joint (2).

Drill a hole in the end of the new section for the metal dowel, if it is still usable. If not, make a new one from a piece of galvanized-steel rod and prime it to prevent corrosion. Treat the new wood with a preserver and insert the dowel. Set the dowel in mortar, and glue and screw the joint (3 and 4).

If a dowel is not used, fix the post to the wall with counterbored screws. Place hardboard or plywood packing behind it, if necessary, and plug the screw holes.

Apply a mastic sealant to the joints between the doorpost, wall and base.

1 Scarf joint

2 Halving joint

3 Set dowel in mortar as you close up joint

4 Do the same if you use a halving joint

SEE ALSO > Metal primers 41, Wood preservers 246, Damp-proof course 247, Bitumen emulsion 254, Housing joint 507–8

Garage doors

Traditional garage doors are constructed from softwood, hinged at either side, and may be solid or fitted with windows. Their modern counterparts may be made from wood, metal or glass-reinforced plastic (GRP), and as their name implies they open by moving up and over the garage interior.

Traditional hinged garage door (right)

Up-and-over door (far right)
Modern garage doors are made from wood, glass-reinforced plastic (GRP) or metal, in a range of styles.

Hinged doors
Traditional hinged doors require considerable floor space in which to open.

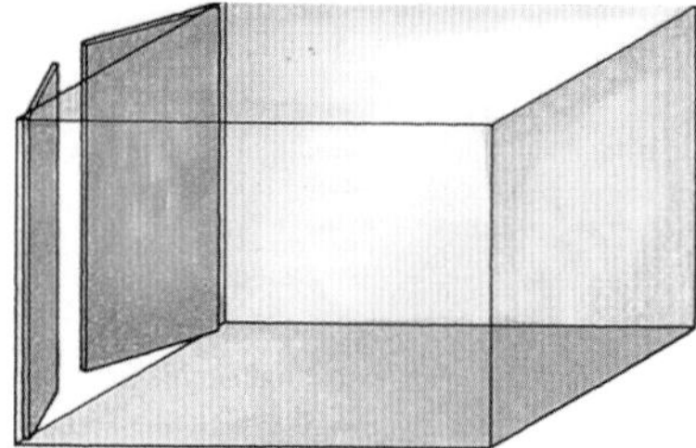

1 Hinged garage doors

Up-and-over door
These counterbalanced doors are tracked vertically or horizontally and are fully or partially retracting.

2 Up-and-over garage door

Sectional overhead garage door
A sectional overhead door retracts within its own space and can be used in a situation where a door must not swing out. Roller doors provide similar features, but do not retract so far into the garage.

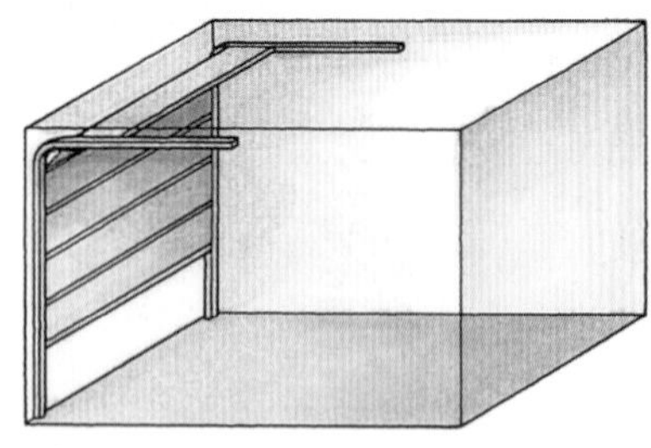

3 Sectional overhead garage door

Automatic-opening garage door
A remote-controlled automatic door-opening mechanism can be attached to most retracting garage doors.

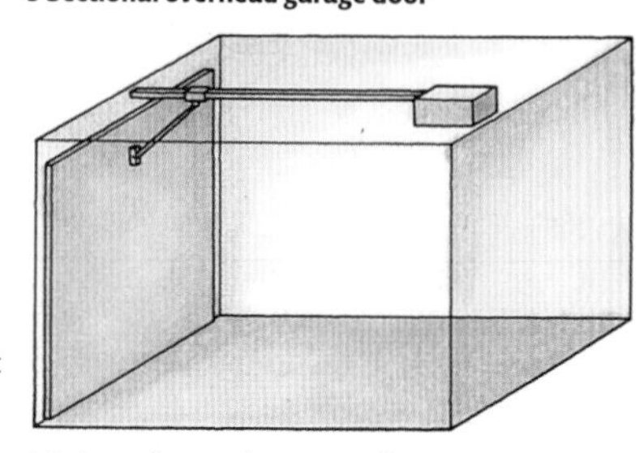

4 Automatic-opening garage door

Traditional hinged doors

Traditional garage doors (1) are made from softwood on the ledged, braced and battened principle, and may be solid or fitted with windows. To hang this type of door to the frame at either side of the opening, you need heavyweight hinges of the kind known as 'bands and hooks'.

These doors give long service if they are painted regularly, but they have a tendency to weaken after a time due to their weight. The frame drops and the doors begin to bind on the ground, absorbing moisture and quickly succumbing to wet rot.

Up-and-over doors

The modern alternative is an up-and-over door (2), which is manufactured as a single panel and is available in a wide range of styles. The door is counterbalanced, usually by springs, and is lifted upwards and backwards to clear the opening.

Depending on the design of the mechanism, when the door is opened it may retract fully into the garage or may remain partly projecting out from the doorframe. The latter type is known as a canopy up-and-over door. The vertically tracked canopy-type door is usually the simplest to install, as it involves no horizontal guide tracks. A non-protruding type should be used where the garage opening is level with your boundary line.

Sectional overhead door

Another type of garage door is the sectional overhead door (3). This consists of hinged horizontal sections that run on wheels on a continuous track, from the vertical position to horizontal. Similarly, a roller door has narrow slats that allow it to roll up inside the door opening.

Automatic opening doors

An automatic door-opening system is available for most types of door (4). The electrically operated mechanism is worked by remote control from inside the car, using a hand-held radio transmitter.

Each door mechanism has a coding system that enables it to be set to different combinations. Once set, it can only be activated by a transmitter set to the same frequency. Usually, a switch fixed to the garage wall will also operate the door mechanism. A manual override is a common safeguard, in case there should be a power failure or malfunction.

The system also incorporates an automatic safety device, which will stop or reverse the action immediately if the door should come into contact with an obstacle left in the doorway.

Automatic doors should not be regarded as merely a novel luxury. As well as saving time, they can provide easier, safer access to a garage facing a busy or narrow road.

SEE ALSO > Running power to outbuildings 342–3

Buying up-and-over doors

Up-and-over doors are manufactured in a range of standard sizes. These are specified in terms of the nominal size of the door opening - the distance between the frame posts and the height measurement between the floor and the head member, including a tolerance for fitting. There must also be room at the sides and top of the opening for the operating mechanism.

Most up-and-over doors require a wooden frame to provide a solid fixing. Some companies produce doors complete with a metal frame that simply needs screwing to the masonry. When a frame is included, the dimensions of the opening size and overall frame are specified.

If you are replacing old timber doors with an up-and-over door, your frame may not be a standard size. However, most firms supply made-to-measure doors.

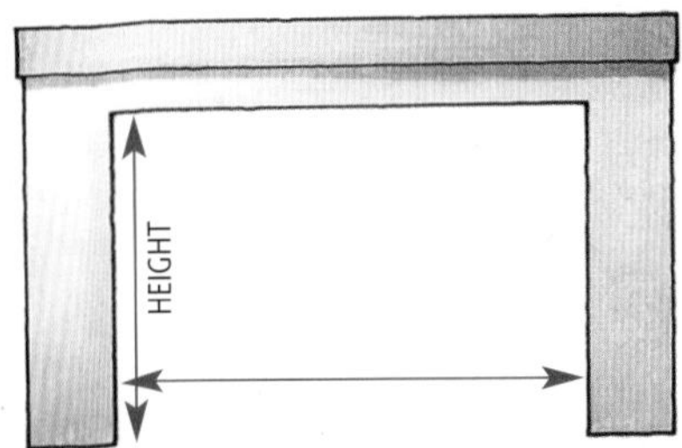

Key dimensions when ordering a door

Fixing arrangements

Most types of up-and-over doors can have their frame posts, or jambs, fitted between the walls or set behind them (**1**). Similarly, the head member of the frame can be fitted behind the lintel or underneath it (**2**).

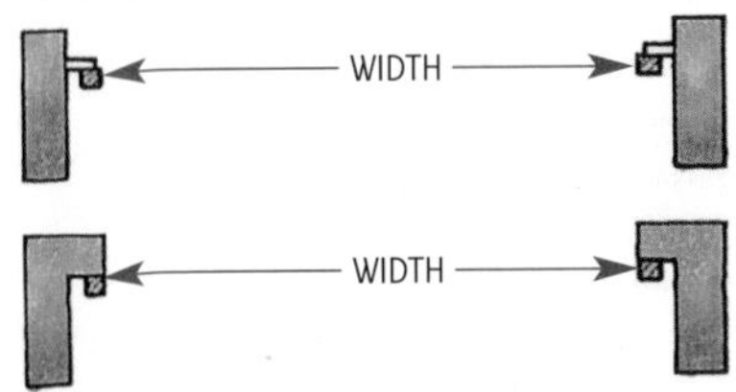

1 Fixing arrangements
A door can be set between or behind the walls.

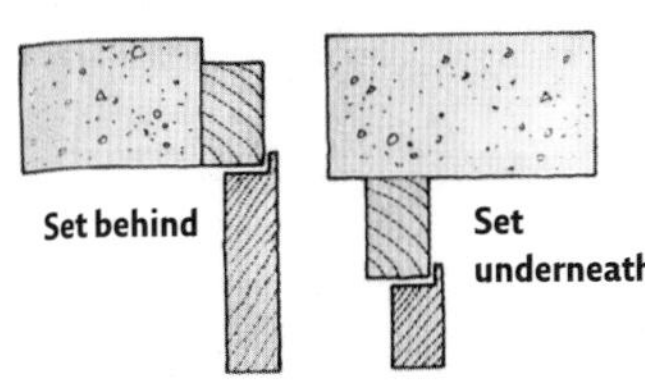

2 Head fixing
There is more headroom if the frame is set behind the opening than when set underneath it.

Fire-resistant doors

Fire-resistant doors help prevent the spread of fire. Although still known as half-hour or one-hour fire-check doors, their ratings are now designated with the prefix FD. An FD30 door, for example, has a 30-minute rating. An S suffix indicates an ability to resist smoke.

Fire-resistant doors: types and construction

Fire-resistant doors - usually flush doors made from wood - have a core of solid board material. They are available in standard sizes, in thicknesses of 44mm (1¾in) for the FD30 grade and 54mm (2⅛in) for the FD60. Simulated panel doors with moulded facings are also obtainable. Doors with window openings must be glazed with fire-rated plain or wired glass that is bedded in an intumescent material.

Fire-resistant doorframes have an integral stop in the form of a deep rebate. An intumescent strip (**1**) on the inside face of the rebate swells when heated and, in so doing, seals the gaps round the door. Some strips include a low-temperature smoke seal.

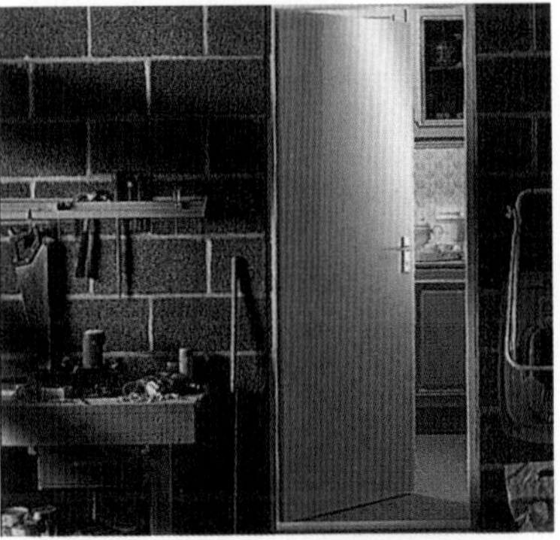

A fire door is required for an attached garage

Moulded-panel fire door

1 Doorframe
A fire-resistant doorframe member is machined from a single piece of wood and has an intumescent strip set within the rebate.

Fitting a door

A fire-resistant interior door can be fitted in place of a standard door to help prevent the spread of fire - but if it is to be effective, the frame must be upgraded. The simplest way to do this is to strip off the old solvent-based paint and finish the frame with a flame-retardant paint. The addition of a band of intumescent paste or an intumescent strip set in a groove routed round the edge of the door will also help.

Another option is to remove the old lining altogether and replace it with a fire-resistant frame that has an integral intumescent strip. This is not usually as wide as a standard door lining and so will need an extra section of lining glued to it (**2**). Fill the gap between the new woodwork and the walling with plaster or with fire-resistant mineral-wool packing under the architrave.

Trim the new door to fit the opening and hang it on three good-quality metal butt hinges; fix the hinges with steel screws that are at least No8 gauge and 32mm (1¼in) long. Fit the smallest mortise lock and latch available - since a large mortise cut in the stile would reduce the door's fire resistance. Also, fit a good-quality door closer.

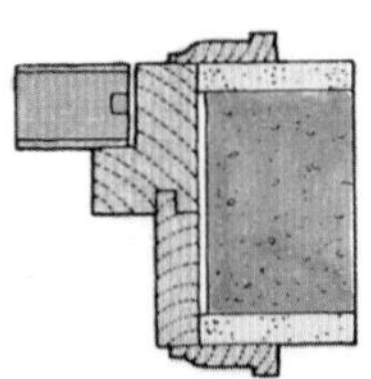

2 Extended frame lining

Hinges
Fire-door hinges must have a melting point of at least 800°C (1472°F). Light-alloy or plastic hinges are not suitable.

Building Regulations

The Building Regulations stipulate that certain doors must meet at least the FD20 level of fire-resistance and be self-closing.

This requirement primarily concerns dwellings of three or more storeys and is designed to prevent fire spreading to staircases and to other escape routes. It can also apply to the entrance door of a flat if it leads from a common area. The door between your home and an attached garage must meet this standard, too. Consult your Building Control Officer.

SEE ALSO >Door types 182-3, Fitting a door 184-5, Rising butt hinges 185, Door repairs 187-9, Fitting locks 235-6

Windows

Traditionally windows have been referred to as lights, and the term 'fixed light' is still used to describe a window or part of one that does not open. The part that opens – the sash – is a separate glazed frame that either slides vertically or is hinged on one edge. Hinged windows are often referred to as 'casements'. In some instances a single sash pivots horizontally; this type is commonly found in roof windows.

Wooden casement

Casement windows

Of all the various types of window, the simple hinged or casement window is the most widely used. Traditional casement window frames made of wood are constructed in much the same fashion as a doorframe. A vertical jamb at each side of the frame is joined by means of mortise-and-tenon joints to the head member at the top and a sill at the bottom (see below). Depending on the size of the window, the frame is sometimes divided vertically by a mullion or horizontally by a transom.

Modern window frames are sometimes fitted with trickle ventilators that provide a constant supply of fresh air.

A side-hung casement is usually attached with butt hinges, but sometimes 'easy-clean' extension hinges are used instead, in order to give better access to the outside of the glass for cleaning. A cockspur, or lever fastener, holds the casement closed. A casement stay fixed to the bottom rail holds the window open in various positions. With a top-hung casement, the stay also secures the window in the closed position.

Glazing bars – lightweight moulded strips of wood – are often fitted to divide the glazed areas into smaller panes.

Mild-steel casement windows have slim welded frames and sashes. They are strong and durable, but will rust unless protected by galvanizing or a primer. Modern versions are galvanized, using a hot-dip process, then finished with a coloured polyester coating.

• Window frames
Most frames and sashes are made up from moulded sections of solid wood. However, steel-reinforced plastic, mild steel and aluminium are also used. Metal frames are often fixed to the masonry by means of wooden subframes.

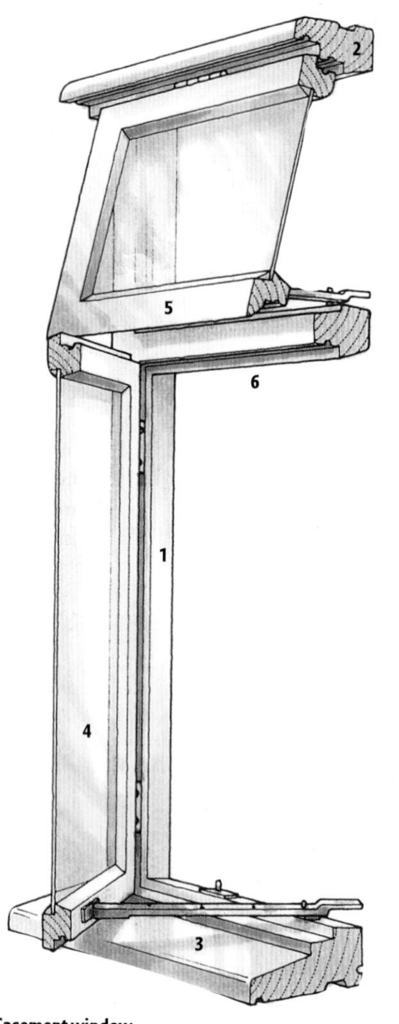

Casement window
1 Jamb
2 Head
3 Sill
4 Side-hung sash
5 Top-hung sash (vent)
6 Transom

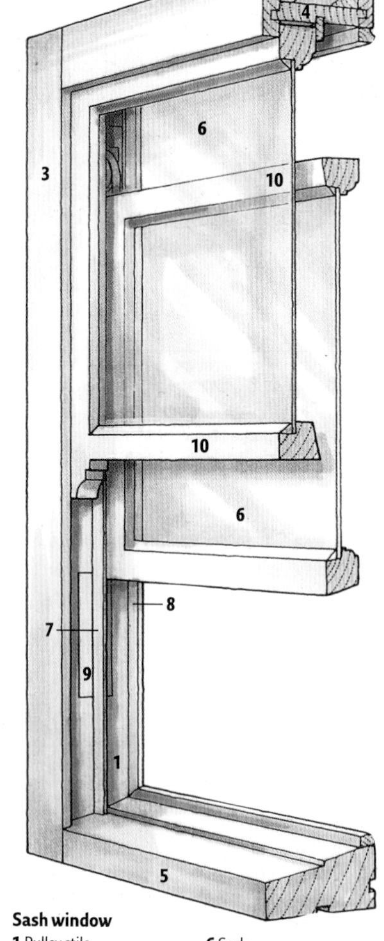

Sash window
1 Pulley stile
2 Inner lining
3 Outer lining
4 Head
5 Sill
6 Sash
7 Parting bead
8 Staff bead
9 Pocket
10 Meeting rail

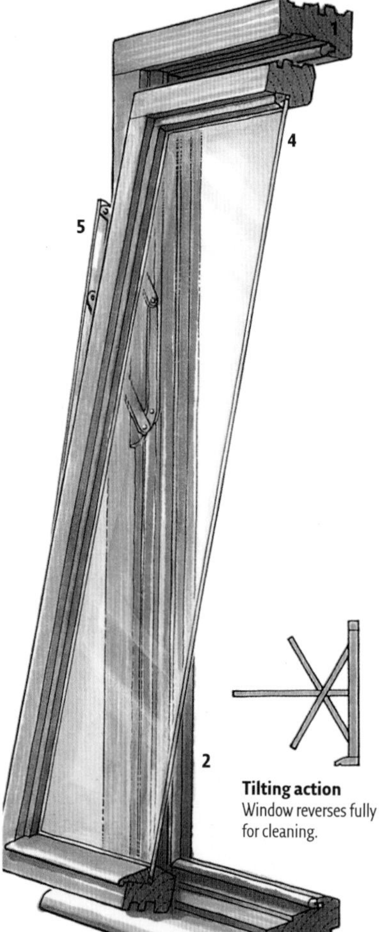

Tilting action
Window reverses fully for cleaning.

Pivot window
1 Head
2 Jamb
3 Sill
4 Sash
5 Pivot mechanism

SEE ALSO > Painting windows 73, Repairing windows 198–203, Securing windows 237–8, Draughtproofing 260, Double glazing 197, 267–9

Sash windows

Vertically sliding windows are usually known as sash windows. When both the top and bottom sash can be opened, they are known as double-hung sash windows. Traditional wooden sash windows (see opposite) are constructed with a box frame in which the jambs are made up from three boards – the pulley stile and the inner and outer linings. A back lining completes the box that houses the sash counterweights. The head is made up in a similar way but without the back lining, and the sill is cut from solid wood. The pulley stiles are jointed into the sill, and the linings are set in a rebate.

The sashes of a double-hung window are held in tracks formed by the outer lining, a parting bead and an inner staff bead. Both beads can be removed in order to service the sash mechanism. Each sash is counterbalanced by two cast-iron or lead weights – one at each side – which are attached by strong cords or chains that pass over pulleys in the stiles. Access to the weights is through pockets – removable pieces of wood set in the lower part of the stiles.

The top sash slides in the outer track and overlaps the bottom sash at their horizontal meeting rails. The closing faces of the meeting rails are bevelled, and their wedging action helps to prevent the sashes rattling. This also allows both rails to part easily as the window is opened, and improves security when it is locked. The sashes are secured by two-part fasteners of various types, which are screwed to the meeting rails.

Spiral balances

Modern wooden, aluminium or plastic sliding sashes have spring-assisted spiral balances. The balances are fixed to the faces of the frame stiles.

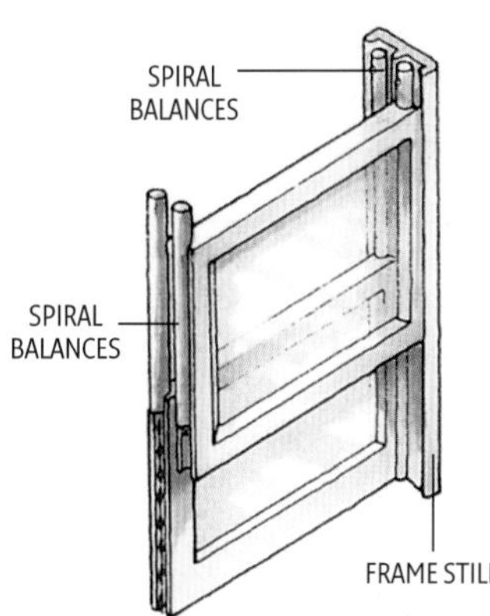

Spiral balances
The exposed balances are fixed to the frame stiles and set in grooves cut in the sash stiles.

Sash window

Pivot windows

Wooden-framed pivot windows (shown opposite) are constructed in a similar way to casement windows, but the special hinge mechanism allows the sash to be rotated so that both sides of the glass can be cleaned from inside. Using the built-in safety catch, the sash can be locked when ajar or when fully reversed.

Similar pivoting windows are made for installing in pitched roofs with slopes between 15 and 90 degrees. The windows are usually double-glazed with sealed units, and ventilators are incorporated in the frame or sash. The wood is protected on the outside by a metal covering, and a flashing kit provides a weatherproof seal between the window and roof.

Pivot windows
Centre-hung pivot windows offer a convenient source of ventilation while retaining a degree of privacy

Aluminium and plastic windows

Aluminium windows

Aluminium window frames first became popular in the 1960s as a taste developed for uncluttered 'picture windows'. They were fitted in new houses, and were also widely used to replace existing wooden windows in older homes. They suffered badly from condensation, both on the glass and on the frames, which were excellent conductors of heat and cold. They are now obsolete, but some remain in use.

To overcome these problems, the frames were engineered into complex sections to hold double-glazed sealed units and to incorporate integral draught strips. The hollow sections were filled with insulation material to act as a thermal break, so greatly reducing the condensation problems. This type was usually installed in a wooden subframe.

Aluminium-framed picture windows
The slim-framed windows offered excellent light, but suffered seriously from condensation on the frames

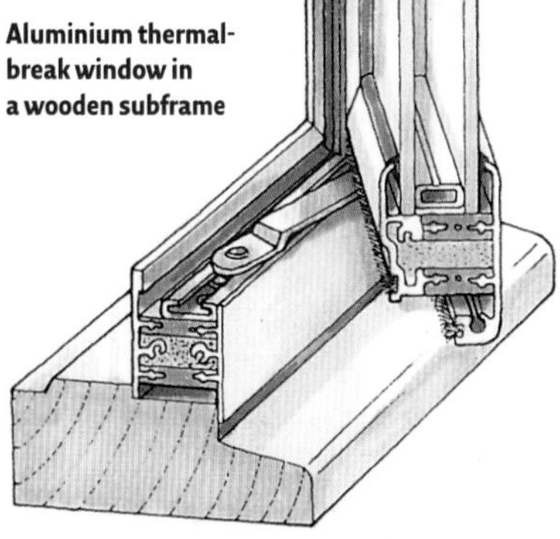

Aluminium thermal-break window in a wooden subframe

Plastic (uPVC) windows

Plastic windows are similar in style to aluminium ones, but have thicker sections and incorporate internal steel reinforcement. They are typically made in white or wood-coloured plastic and, once installed, require only minimal maintenance. They are widely used both in new buildings and as replacement windows in older homes.

Plastic windows
These are made from unplasticized polyvinyl chloride (uPVC). The casements have mitred corners.

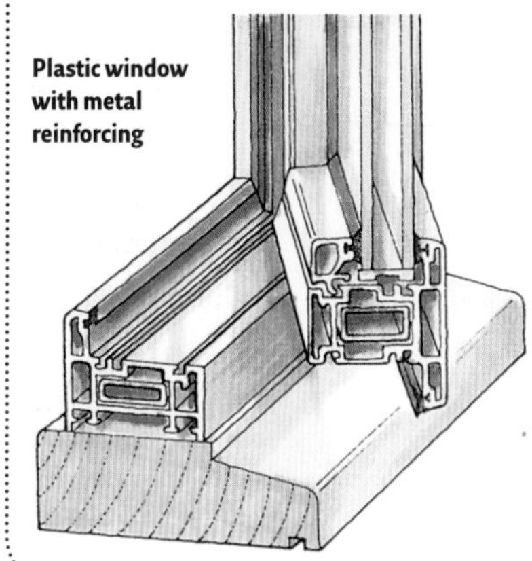

Plastic window with metal reinforcing

SEE ALSO > Spiral balances 201, Roof windows 204, Securing windows 237–8, Draughtproofing 260, Double glazing 197, 267–9

How windows are fitted

Casement windows are generally built with the face of the frame inset slightly from the face of the wall and the sill projecting beyond it. Sash windows in older houses are set back by the width of a brick, and the wooden sill sits on a projecting stone subsill.

Solid walls

In older houses it was a common practice to install the window-frame jambs (sides) in recesses built on the inside of the masonry. Once the windows had been fitted, their frames were nailed or screwed into wooden plugs set in the masonry. Vertical damp-proof courses were never fitted – it was thought that evaporation would keep the walls dry and so no extra protection would be needed to prevent rot.

Window frames in a solid wall 225mm (9in) thick were flush with the inside. In a 340mm (1ft 1½in) wall, they were set back from the inner surface. All windows had subsills, usually of stone, on the outside. Above a window opening, the masonry is usually supported by a stone lintel or, in some cases, by a brick arch. A true arch is curved, but window openings were often built with so-called 'flat' arches, made with tapered bricks. As a rule, flat arches are one brick thick, with wooden lintels placed behind them to help support the wall. Arches built with a shallow curve are constructed similarly.

Decorative motifs are often carved into stone lintels above windows. The relative weakness of the material ensured that such openings were fairly narrow unless they were subdivided by columns.

SASH WINDOW

Traditional method
The box frame of a sash window is set into the brickwork and is flush on the inside.
1 Sashes
2 Frame
3 Reveal
4 Brick arch
5 Wooden lintel
6 Stone subsill

Cavity walls

The window frames in modern houses are usually fixed into place as the brickwork is erected, using metal brackets known as frame cramps. The cramps are screwed to the sides of the frame and set in the mortar bed joints. There are usually three such cramps on each side of the frame.

Cavity walls must have a vertical damp-proof course. This is sandwiched between the external leaf of the wall and the cavity-closing bricks of the inner leaf. The window frame, which is set forward in the opening, covers the joint. Sometimes the damp-proof courses are fastened to the window frames. Moulded insulated cavity closers are now widely used to reduce the effects of cold bridging the cavity.

With a window frame in this situation, much of the wall's thickness is exposed on the inside of the house. The sides of the opening, known as reveals, are finished off with plaster, as is the top, or soffit. The ledge at the bottom is finished with a window board that is tongued into a groove along the back of the frame sill.

Depending on the type of lintel used, there may be a line of weep holes built into the outer leaf of the wall to allow any water that gets into the cavity above the window opening to drain away to the outside.

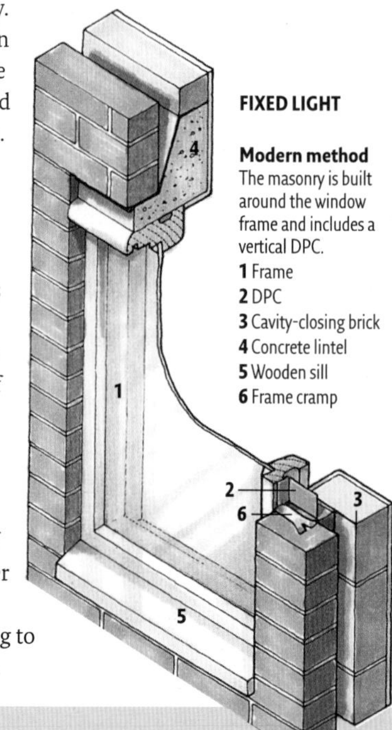

FIXED LIGHT

Modern method
The masonry is built around the window frame and includes a vertical DPC.
1 Frame
2 DPC
3 Cavity-closing brick
4 Concrete lintel
5 Wooden sill
6 Frame cramp

Buying glass

You can buy most types of glass from glass merchants, who will advise you on the thickness needed for the window concerned and will also cut the glass to your requirements. Most glass merchants will deliver large panes and multi-pane orders.

Glass thickness

Although there are no regulations concerning the thickness of glass to be used in repair work, Part N of the Building Regulations requires the use of either safety glass or small robust panes in certain critical areas – see opposite. The thickness of glass required depends on the area of the pane, its exposure to wind pressure, and the vulnerability of its situation. When buying, tell your supplier what the glass is for – a door, a window, a shower screen – and whether it is in a critical location.

Measuring up

Measure the height and width of the opening to the inside of the frame rebate. Check each dimension by measuring from at least two points. Also check that the diagonals are the same length. If they differ significantly, indicating that the frame is out of square, make a cardboard template of the opening and take it to your glass merchant. In any case, deduct 3mm (⅛in) from the height and width to give a tolerance for fitting.

When you order patterned glass, specify the height before the width, to ensure that the glass is cut with the pattern running in the right direction. When ordering an odd-shaped pane, make a template and tell your supplier which is to be the outside face. You can then fit the glass with the smooth side out, which will make it easier to clean.

SEE ALSO > Sash windows 192–3, Repairing sills 199, Replacing windows 202–3, Cold bridge 251

Types of glass

The type and quality of glass produced for windows is determined by the method used for processing at the molten stage. Ordinary window glass is known as 'annealed glass'. Special treatments during manufacture give glass particular properties, such as heat-resistance or extra strength.

Float glass

Float glass is made by floating the molten glass on a bath of liquid tin to produce a sheet with flat distortion-free surfaces. It has virtually replaced plate glass, which was rolled glass polished on both sides.

Clear float glass is manufactured in a range of thicknesses, from 3mm (1/8in) up to 25mm (1in). For windows, it is generally stocked in three thicknesses: 3mm (1/8in), 4mm (5/32in) and 6mm (1/4in).

Patterned glass

One side of patterned glass is embossed with a texture or a decorative design, and the transparency of the glass depends to a large extent on the density of the pattern. The glass is available as clear or tinted sheets, in thicknesses of 3mm (1/8in), 4mm (5/32in) and 6mm (1/4in).

Patterned or obscured glass is often used to provide a degree of privacy in bathroom windows, without reducing the level of natural light. Only toughened or laminated versions (see right) should be used for bath or shower screens.

Solar-control glass

Special glass that reduces heat transmission is often used for roof lights. This tinted glass, which can be of the float, laminated or textured type, also reduces glare, though at the expense of reducing the level of illumination. Solar-control glass is available in thicknesses ranging from 4 to 12mm (5/32 to 1/2in), depending on the type. Glass 6mm (1/4in) thick is the size most commonly used.

Low-emissivity glass

Low-E glass is a clear float glass with a special coating on one surface. It is used primarily for the inner pane of double glazing. The coating, which must be on the inside of the cavity, optimizes heat gain from sunlight, but helps prevent heat loss from the room. The glass provides a high level of natural illumination. The outer pane of the double-glazed unit can be of any other type of glass.

Non-reflective glass

This type of glass is used primarily for glazing picture frames. Its slightly textured surface eliminates the surface reflections associated with ordinary polished glass yet the glass appears completely transparent. Non-reflective glass is 2mm (3/32in) thick.

Safety glass

Glass that has been strengthened with reinforcement or by means of a toughening process is known as safety glass. It should be used whenever the glazed area is relatively large or where its position makes it especially vulnerable. For example, in domestic situations it must be used for glazed doors and low-level windows (see below right) and shower screens.

Fire-resistant glass

Wired glass is a roughcast or clear annealed glass 6mm (1/4in) thick, with a fine steel wire mesh incorporated during manufacture. Though the glass may crack, the mesh serves to hold the pane together, preventing the spread of smoke and flames. Formerly called Georgian wired glass, it is now known as Pyroshield. A laminated type of fire-resistant glass is also made.

Toughened glass

Toughened glass is ordinary glass that has been heat-treated to improve its strength. It is sometimes referred to as tempered glass. When it breaks, toughened glass shatters into relatively harmless granules. It is impossible to cut toughened glass – cutting holes and drilling for screw fixings must be done before the toughening process. Suppliers of doors and windows usually stock toughened glass to fit standard-size frames.

Laminated glass

Laminated glass is made by bonding together two or more layers of glass with clear tear-resistant plastic film sandwiched between them. The plastic interlayer not only helps to absorb the energy from an impact, it reduces the risk of injury from fragments of flying glass. One beneficial side effect of using laminated glass is that it helps prevent fading of textiles, wallcoverings and carpets by absorbing 99 per cent of harmful ultra-violet radiation.

Laminated glass is made in a range of thicknesses – from 4mm (5/32in) up to 13.5mm (17/32in), depending on the type. Clear, tinted and patterned versions are all available.

Patterned and tinted glass
Embossed and tinted glass is often used for restoring windows in older houses, but it also makes for attractive glazing in new installations.

Etched glass
As a result of the increased interest in restoring period houses, glass with a range of traditional acid-etched patterns is once again available. Etched glass is made in 4 and 6mm (5/32 and 1/4in) thicknesses; it can be toughened or laminated for safety.

Using safety glass

Building Regulations stipulate that safety glass is required for new and replacement glazing in certain areas.

1 For windows, or glazed openings in partition walls, within 800mm (2ft 7½in) of the floor.

2 For glazing in doors and adjacent glazed side panels that are within 300mm (1ft) of the door, up to a height of 1500mm (4ft 11in) from the floor.

If only part of the glazing falls within these dimensions, safety glass must be used for the entire panel or window.

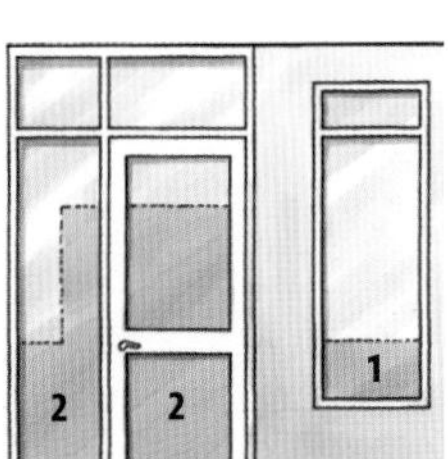

Glazing in small panes
Small panes held in glazing bars may be of float glass 6mm (1/4in) thick – so long as their smaller dimension does not exceed 250mm (10in) and the area does not exceed 0.5sq m (5.4sq ft).

SEE ALSO > Double-glazed units 197

Repairing a broken window

Even when no glass is missing, a cracked windowpane constitutes a safety hazard. Broken panes are a security risk and are no longer weatherproof, so replace them promptly.

Glazing putty

Traditional linseed-oil putty is made for glazing wooden frames. It dries slowly and is hard when set. All-purpose putty for wood and steel frames has similar properties. Both of these putties tend to crack if they are not protected with paint. Modern acrylic-based glazing putty is an all-purpose type that is easy to use and dries quickly, ready for painting.

Butyl rubber-based compound can be used with beaded wooden or metal window frames, but is not suitable for use in plastic frames or for fixing proprietary plastic glazing sheets.

Replacing glass in wooden frames

• Temporary repairs
For temporary protection from the weather, tape a sheet of polythene over the outside of the window frame, or hold it in place with nailed battens until you can replace the glass. If the window is merely cracked, it can be repaired temporarily using a special clear self-adhesive waterproof tape.

Glass fixed with putty

Wooden bead fixing
Some wooden frames feature screwed-on beading bedded into compound to hold and seal the panes in place. Unscrew the beading and scrape out the old compound. Bed the new glass in fresh compound and replace the beading.

In wooden window frames, the glass is set into a rebate cut in the frame's moulding and is then bedded in putty. Small wedge-shaped nails, known as sprigs, are also used to hold the glass in place. These are covered with a further bead of putty on the outside.

Removing the glass

If the glass in a window pane has shattered completely, leaving jagged pieces set in the putty, grip each piece separately and try to work it loose. Wear thick protective gloves and start working from the top of the frame. Wrap and discard the broken glass.

Although old putty that is dry will usually give way, if it's strong it will have to be cut out, using a glazier's hacking knife and a hammer (**1**). Alternatively, use a blunt wood chisel. Work along the rebate to remove the putty and glass. Pull out the old sprigs with pincers (**2**).

If the glass is merely cracked, run a glass cutter round the perimeter of the pane about 25mm (1in) from the frame, scoring the glass (**3**). Fasten strips of self-adhesive tape across the cracks and scored lines, then tap each piece of glass until it breaks free and is held only by the tape (**4**). Carefully remove individual pieces of glass, working from the centre of the pane.

Clean remnants of old putty out of the rebates, then seal the wood with wood primer. Measure the height and width of the opening to the inside of the rebates, and have your new glass cut 3mm (1/8in) smaller on each dimension to provide a tolerance for fitting.

1 Remove broken glass and cut away the old putty

2 Pull out the old sprigs

3 Score glass before removing a cracked pane

4 Tap the glass to break it free

Fitting new glass

Purchase new sprigs and enough putty for the frame. Your glass merchant should be able to advise you about this - but as a guide, 500g (1lb) of linseed-oil putty will fill an average-sized rebate about 4m (13ft) in length.

Working with putty

Knead a palm-sized ball of putty to an even consistency. Use your thumb to press a continuous bead of putty into the rebate all round. This is the bedding putty. Lower the edge of the new pane onto the bottom rebate, then press it into the putty. Press close to the edges only, squeezing the putty to leave a bed about 2mm (1/16in) on the inside, then secure the glass with sprigs about 200mm (8in) apart. Tap them into the frame so that they lie flat with the surface of the glass (**1**). Trim the surplus putty from the back of the glass with a putty knife.

Apply more putty to each rebate on the outside. Using a putty knife (**2**), work the putty to a smooth finish at an angle of 45 degrees. Wet the knife with water to prevent it dragging, and make neat mitres in the putty at the corners. Let the putty set and stiffen for about 3 weeks, then paint the frame as required.

1 Tap in new sprigs

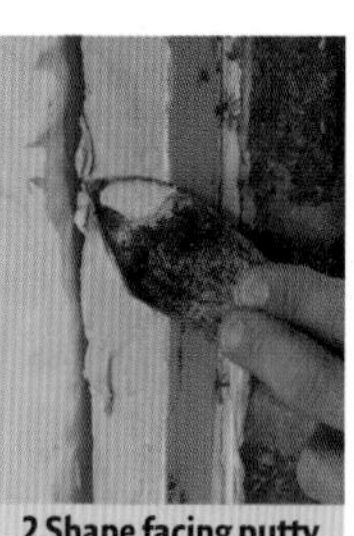

2 Shape facing putty

Using acrylic glazing putty

Acrylic glazing putty is supplied in a cartridge and is easily applied with a sealant gun. Run a bead of putty into the rebate. Bed the glass in place and secure it with sprigs. Then apply a continuous bead of putty all round the frame, and smooth it to a 45-degree angle with a wetted putty knife. Allow it to cure, then trim off any excess before painting it.

SEE ALSO > Painting windows 73, Hacking knife 512, Putty knife 512, Scaffold tower 514, 516

Glazing metal-framed windows

Mild-steel window frames are made with galvanized-metal sections that form a rebate for the glass. This type of window is glazed in the same way as a wooden-framed window, using all-purpose putty or acrylic glazing putty. The glass is secured in the frame with spring clips, which are set in the putty and located in holes in the frame. To replace the glass in a metal frame, follow the sequence described for wooden frames but use clips instead of sprigs. Before fitting the glass, treat any rust and apply a metal primer.

Modern aluminium and plastic double-glazed frames use a dry-glazing system that includes synthetic-rubber gaskets. These are factory-installed and should be maintenance-free. If you break a pane in a window of this type, consult the manufacturers, as they usually have their own patent repair system.

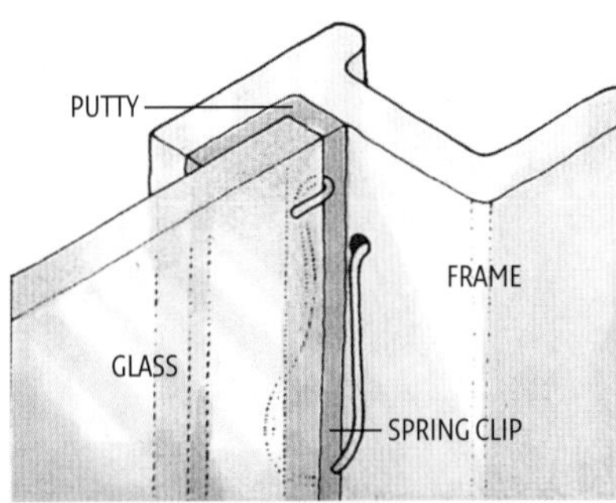

Use spring clips to hold the glass in place

Fitting double-glazed units

Stepped sealed units are designed to fit into existing window frames with shallow rebates that originally held a single thickness of glass. Square-edged units require a deeper rebate.

Fitting stepped sealed units

Set stepped sealed units in a bed of butyl compound, then place packing pieces of resilient material (supplied with the units) in the rebate to support the weight of the double glazing. Weatherproof the frame with putty, as when fitting new glass.

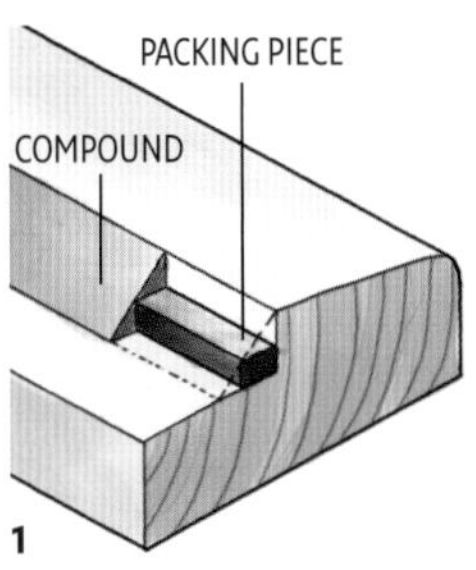

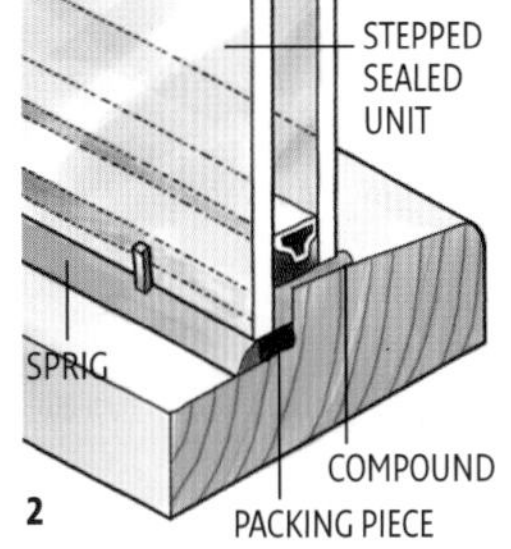

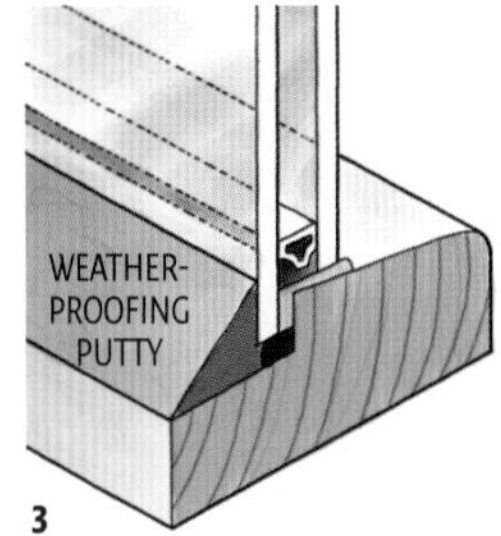

Fitting stepped units
Follow this sequence when fitting stepped double glazing.
1 Set the packing in butyl glazing compound.
2 Fit the glazing and secure with sprigs.
3 Weatherproof the glass with putty.

Fitting square-edged units

Square-edged units are sealed with either glazing tape or non-setting butyl glazing compound and held in place with beading. For the conventional method shown here, you will need glazing compound, glazing blocks as packing, and fixings for the beading (see below).

Lay a bed of the non-setting compound in the rebate. To prevent the glass moving, place the packing blocks on the bottom of the rebate and place the spacer blocks against the back of the rebate.

Set the sealed unit into the rebate and press it firmly in place. Apply an outer layer of the compound and place another set of spacers against the glass.

Press each bead against the spacers and screw it in place with countersunk brass or plated screws. Countersink the holes in the beading, or use screw cups.

Placing packing
For fixed windows, place the packing in the bottom rebate only. For side-hung sashes, place additional blocks near the bottom of the hinge-side rebate and diagonally opposite on the outer top corner.

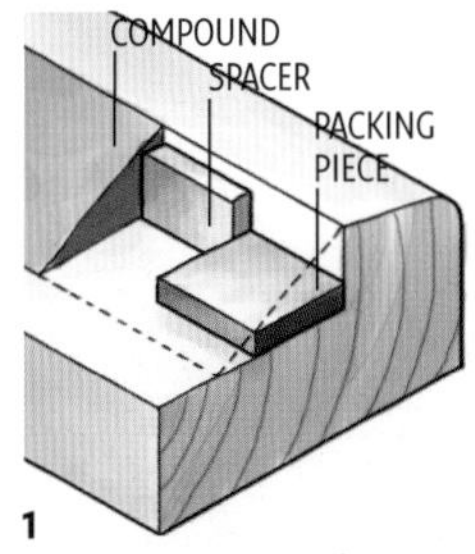

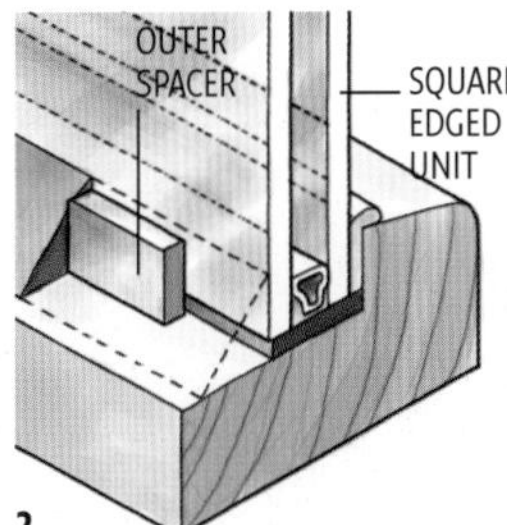

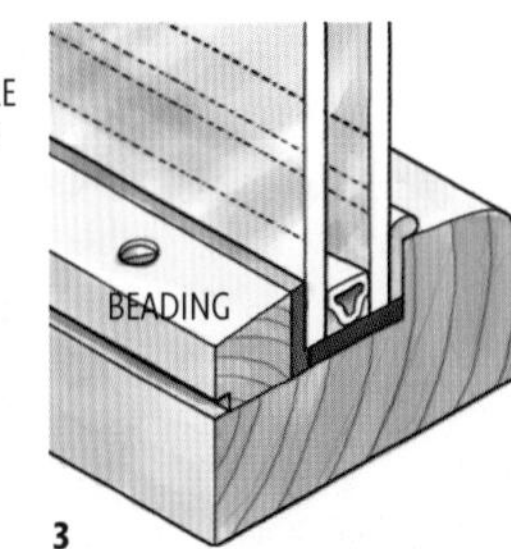

Using beading
Set square-edged units in a non-setting compound.
1 Set the packing and spacers in compound.
2 Fit the unit, apply more compound, and place spacers behind the screw-fixing points for the beading.
3 Press the beading against the spacers and fix in place with screws.

Curing sticking and rattling windows

If you have a casement window that sticks persistently in all weathers, it may be due to a thick build-up of paint. If this is the case, strip the old paint from the meeting edges of the sash and/or the frame rebate and apply fresh paint. You may also have to plane the edge a little.

The tolerances on vertically sliding wooden sashes are such that they do not stick unless they have been painted while shut or the staff or parting beads have been badly positioned.

Curing rattling windows

The rattling of a casement window is usually caused by an ill-fitting lever fastener. If the fastener is worn, you can either replace it with a new one or reset the plate on the frame into which the fastener locates.

Old wooden sash windows are notorious for rattling. Most often the cause is a sash - usually the bottom one - being a loose fit in its tracks. To cure it, remove and replace the inner staff bead with a new length, so it makes a close sliding fit against the sash.

If the top sash is rattling, pack it out and adjust the position of the catch to pull the sashes together.

SEE ALSO > Metal primers 41, Painting windows 73, Sash windows 192–3

Repairing windows

Old wooden casements and sash windows will, inevitably, have deteriorated to some extent, but regular maintenance and prompt repairs can preserve them almost indefinitely. New frames and ones that have been stripped should be treated with a clear wood preserver before you paint them.

Regular maintenance

The bottom rail of a sash is particularly vulnerable to rot – especially if it is left unprotected. Rainwater seeps in behind old shrunken putty, and moisture is gradually absorbed through cracked or flaking paintwork. Carry out an annual check and deal with any faults. Cut out old putty that has shrunk away from the glass and replace it. Remove flaking paint and make good any cracks in the wood with flexible filler.

Replacing a rotten sash rail

Removing glass
When removing the glass, be prepared for it to break. As a precaution, apply adhesive tape across the glass. Chisel away the putty to leave a clean rebate, then pull out the sprigs. Work the blade of a putty knife into the bedding joint on the inside of the frame to break the grip of the putty. Steady the glass and lift it out when it is free.

Where the rot is so severe that the rail is beyond repair, cut it out and replace it. This should be done before the rot spreads to the stiles, otherwise you will eventually have to replace the whole sash frame.

Remove the sash by unscrewing the hinges; or if it's a sliding-sash window, remove the beading.

It is possible to make the repair without removing the glass – though it is safer to remove it if the window is large. In any event, cut away the putty from the damaged rail.

The bottom rail is tenoned into the stiles (**1**), but it can be replaced using bridle joints. Saw down the shoulder lines of the tenon joints (**2**) from both faces of the frame and remove the rail.

Make a new rail, or buy a length of moulding if it is a standard section, then mark and cut it to length with a full-width tenon at each end. Position the tenons to line up with the mortises in the stiles. Cut the shoulders of the tenons to match the rebated sections of the stiles (**3**); or if there is a decorative moulding, pare the moulding from the stile to leave a flat shoulder (**4**). Cut slots in the ends of the stiles to receive the new tenons.

Glue the new rail securely into place with a waterproof resin adhesive, and reinforce the two joints with pairs of 6mm (¼in) stopped dowels. Drill the stopped holes for the dowels from the inside of the frame and stagger them.

When the adhesive is dry, plane the surface as required and treat the new wood with a clear wood preserver. Reputty the glass, and apply primer and paint as soon as the putty is firm.

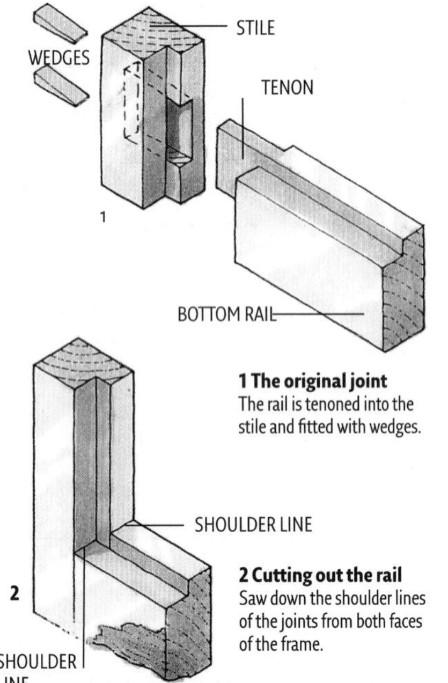

1 The original joint
The rail is tenoned into the stile and fitted with wedges.

2 Cutting out the rail
Saw down the shoulder lines of the joints from both faces of the frame.

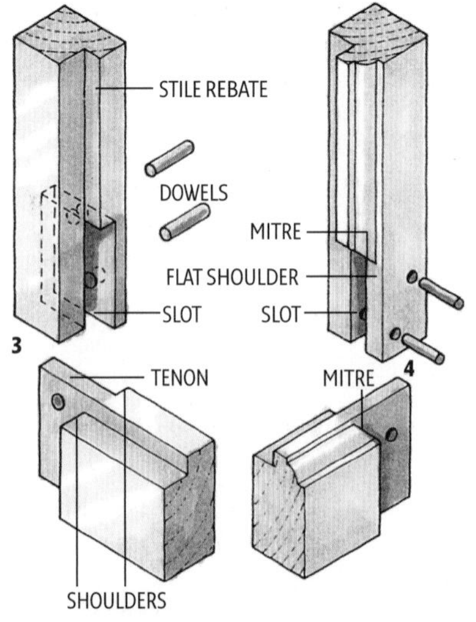

3 Cutting the joint
Cut tenons at each end of the rail, making sure that the shoulders of the joint accommodate the shape of the stile.

4 Moulded frames
Pare away the moulding on the stile to receive the square shoulder of the rail. Mitre the moulding.

Fixed-window rails

The frames of some fixed windows are made like sashes but are screwed permanently to the jamb and mullion. Unless you can unscrew and remove the frame, it must be repaired *in situ*.

First remove the putty and the glass, then saw through the rail at each end, close to the stile. Use a chisel to pare away what remains of the rail and to chop out the tenons from the stiles. Cut a new length of rail to fit between the stiles, and cut housings at both ends of its top edge to take loose tenons (**1**). Place the housings so that they line up with the mortises, and make each housing twice as long as the depth of the mortise.

Cut two loose tenons, to fit the housings, and two packing pieces. The latter should have one sloping edge (**2**).

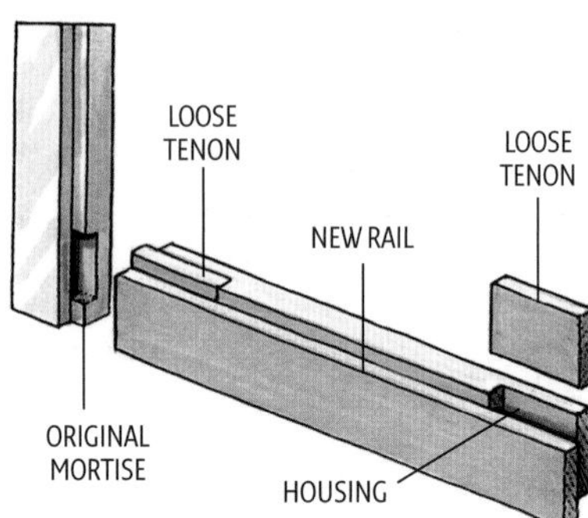

1 Cut housings for loose tenons at each end

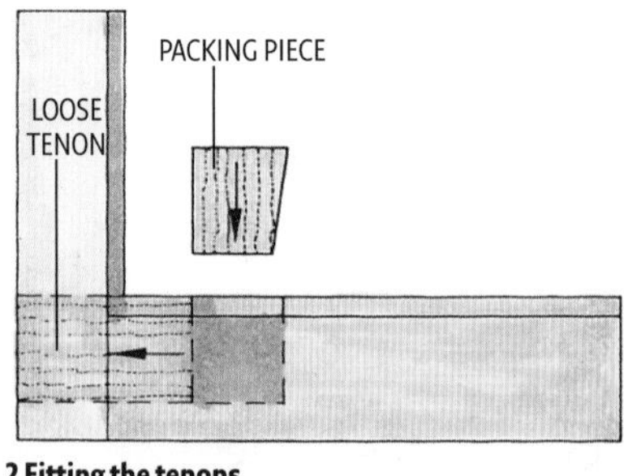

2 Fitting the tenons
Insert the loose tenons, push them sideways into the mortises, and wedge with packing pieces.

Reassembling the frame

Glue the rail between the stiles, insert the loose tenons into the mortises and drive in the packing pieces to lock them in place. When the adhesive has set, trim them flush with the rebate in the rail and replace the glass. Repaint once the putty is firm.

SEE ALSO > Sash windows 192–3, Fitting new glass 196, Removing glass 196, Bridle joints 507, Dowel joints 508

Repairing rotten sills

A rotten sill must be replaced. The frame of a casement window is made rather like a doorframe, and the sill can be repaired in a similar way once all the glass has been removed. See below for how to go about replacing the sill of a sash window. Make sure the damp-proof course between the underside of the sill and the wall is maintained. Gun-applied mastic makes this job relatively easy.

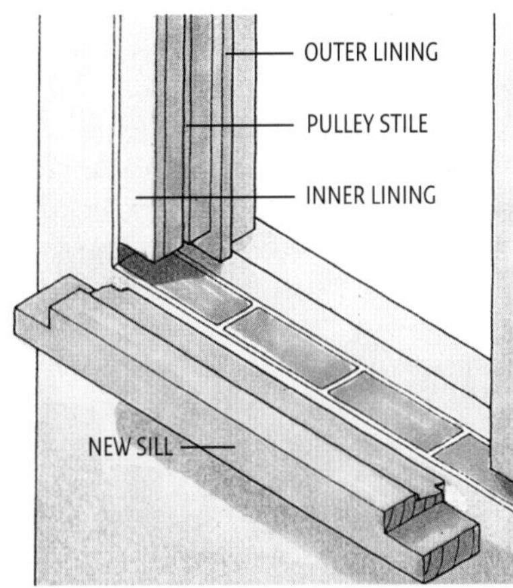

Cut the new sill to fit the frame

Replacing a wooden sill for a sash window

Don't simply replace a sill by cutting through it and fitting a new section between the jambs. Even if you seal the joints with mastic, any breakdown of the sealant will allow water to penetrate the masonry and the end grain of the wood - so you may find yourself having to do the job all over again.

If a sill is seriously rotted, you may have to take the whole frame out. Make and fit a new sill, using the old one as a pattern. Treat the new sill with a wood preserver, and take the opportunity to treat the old wood - which is normally hidden by the masonry. Apply a bead of mastic sealant to the sill, then replace the complete frame in the opening from inside. Make good the damaged plaster.

It is possible to replace the sill from the inside, leaving the frame in place (see left). Saw through the sill close to the jambs and remove the centre portion. Cut away the bottom ends of the inner lining level with the pulley stiles and remove the ends of the old sill. Cut the new sill to fit round the outer lining and under the stiles and inner lining. Fit the sill and nail or screw the stiles to it.

Decaying window sills
Renovate deteriorating sills and subsills before serious decay sets in.

Repairing a stone subsill

The traditional stone sills found in older houses may become eroded by weathering. They are also liable to crack if the wall subsides.

Repair cracks and eroded surfaces with a ready-mixed quick-setting waterproof mortar. Rake out the cracks to clean and enlarge them. Dampen the stone with clean water and work the mortar well into the cracks, finishing flush with the top surface.

To help the mortar adhere, undercut any depressions caused by erosion - a thin layer of mortar simply applied to a shallow depression in the surface will not last for long. To do this, use a cold chisel to cut away the surface of the sill to at least 25mm (1in) below the finished level; then remove all traces of debris and dust with a stiff brush.

Make a wooden former to the shape of the sill and temporarily nail it to the masonry. Dampen the stone, trowel in the mortar and tamp it level with the former, then smooth it out. Leave the mortar to set for a couple of days before removing the former. Allow it to dry thoroughly before applying paint.

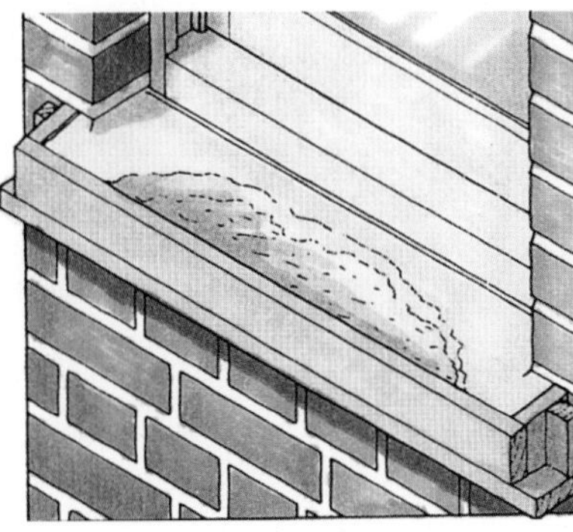

Make a wooden former to the shape of the sill

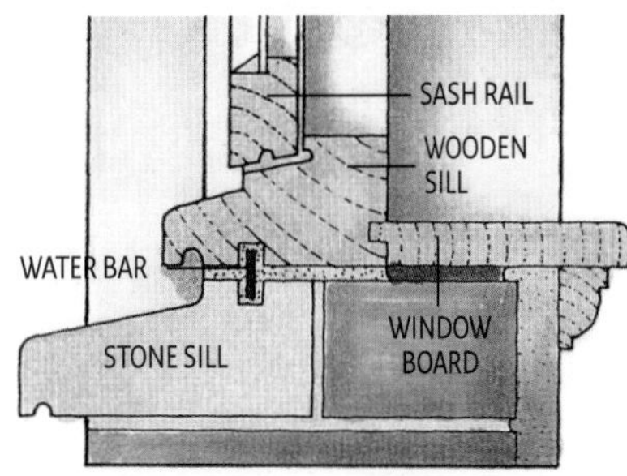

Traditional frame with stone subsill
If you are replacing the sill without removing the frame, you may have to discard the metal water bar and rely on a mastic bead to keep the water out.

Casting a new subsill

Cut out what remains of the old stone sill with a cold chisel and hammer. Make a wooden mould with its end pieces shaped to the same section as the old sill. The open top of the mould represents the underside of the sill.

Fill two-thirds of the mould with fine-aggregate concrete, tamped down well. Add two lengths of painted mild-steel reinforcing rod, judiciously spaced to share the volume of the sill, then fill the remainder of the mould. Set a narrow piece of wood, such as a dowel, into notches cut in the ends of the mould. This is to form a 'throat', or drip groove, in the underside of the sill.

Cover the concrete with polythene sheeting, or dampen it regularly for 2 to 3 days to prevent rapid drying. When the concrete has set (allow about 7 days), remove it from the mould and lay the new sill in the wall, on a bed of mortar. Pack the subsill up against the wooden sill, using pieces of slate.

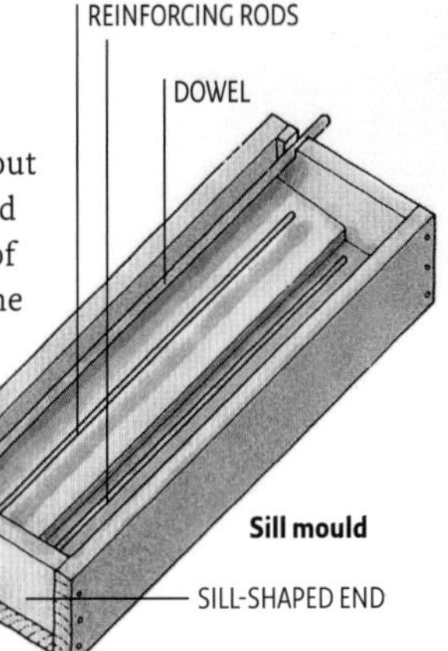

Sill mould

SEE ALSO > Painting masonry 66, Replacing a doorsill 189, Casement windows 192, Sash windows 192–3, Mixing concrete 455

Replacing broken sash cords

In time, the cords from which sliding sashes are suspended will wear or break. It is worth replacing both cords, even if only one has broken. Waxed sash cording is normally sold in standard hanks, although some suppliers sell it by the metre. Each sash requires two lengths of cord, measuring about three-quarters the height of the window.

Double-hung sash window

1 Pulleys
2 Bottom sash
3 Staff bead
4 Top sash
5 Parting bead
6 Bottom sash weight
7 Pocket pieces
8 Top sash weight

Prise off staff beads

Remove pocket pieces

Removing the sashes

Lower both sashes and cut through the cords with a knife to release the weights - holding onto the cords and lowering the weights as far as possible before allowing them to drop. Use a wide-bladed paint scraper to prise off the side staff beads from inside the frame, bending them in the middle until their mitred ends spring out.

Lean the inner sash towards you and mark the ends of the cord grooves on the face of the sash stiles (**1**). Reposition the sash and transfer the marks onto the pulley stiles. The sash can now be pulled clear of the frame. Carefully prise out the two parting beads from their grooves in the stiles. You can then remove the top sash, after marking the ends of the grooves as before. Place the sashes safely aside.

To gain access to the weights, take out the pocket pieces, which were trapped by the parting bead. Reach into the openings to lift out the weights. Pieces of thin wood, known as parting strips, are usually suspended inside the box stiles to separate each pair of weights. Push the strips aside to reach the outer weights.

Remove the old sash cords from the weights and sashes, set the weights aside after noting where each one was fitted, and clean up the wood ready for the new cords.

Refitting the sashes

The top sash is fitted first, but not before all the sash cords and weights are in place.

Tie a length of fine string to one end of the hank of sash cord. Weight the other end of the string with small nuts or a piece of chain. Thread the weight - known as a 'mouse' - over a pulley (**2**), then pull it and the string out through the pocket opening until the cord is also pulled through. Attach the end of the cord to the sash weight with a special knot (see below left).

Pull on the other end of the cord to hoist the weight up to the pulley, and then let it drop back about 100mm (4in). Hold it temporarily in this position with a nail driven through the cord into the stile just below the pulley. Cut the cord level with the mark on the pulley stile (**3**). Repeat this procedure for the cord on the other side, and similarly for the bottom sash.

Replace the top sash on the sill, lean it towards you, and locate its cords in the grooves in the stiles. Nail the cords in place, using three or four 25mm (1in) round wire nails. Nail only the bottom 150mm (6in), not all the way up (**4**). Lift the sash to check that the weights do not touch bottom.

Replace the pocket pieces and pin the parting beads in their grooves. Fit the bottom sash the same way. Finally replace the staff beads.

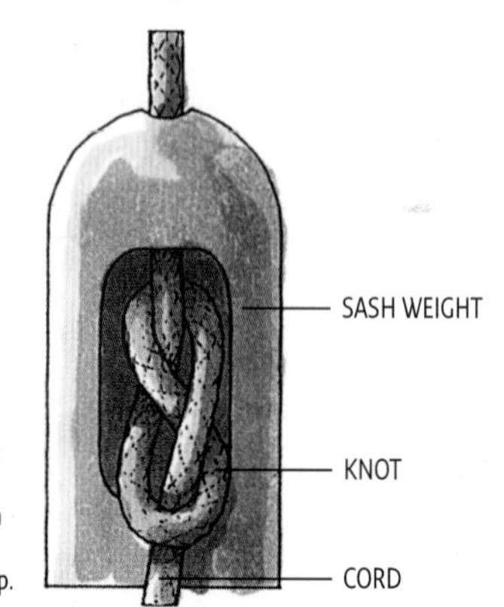

How to tie a sash-weight knot
Make a loop in the cord, about 75mm (3in) from the end. Take the end round the back of the cord to form a figure-of-eight, and then pass it through the first loop.

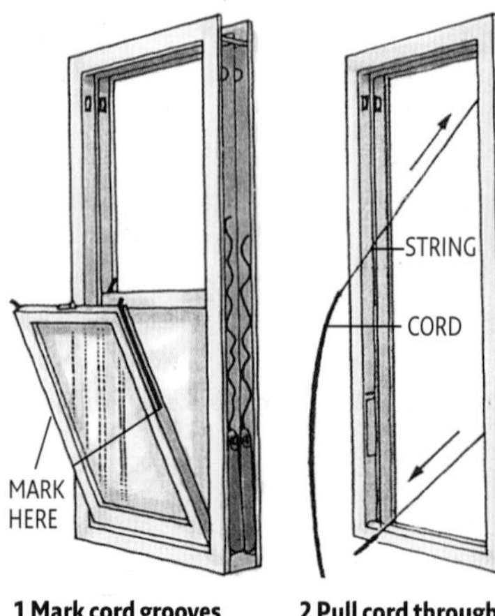

1 Mark cord grooves

2 Pull cord through

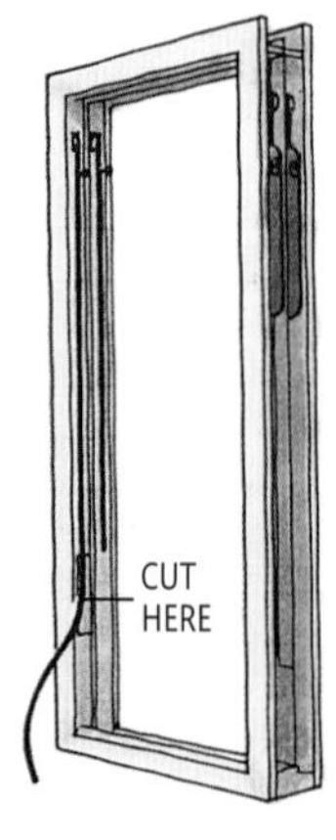

3 Cut cords at mark

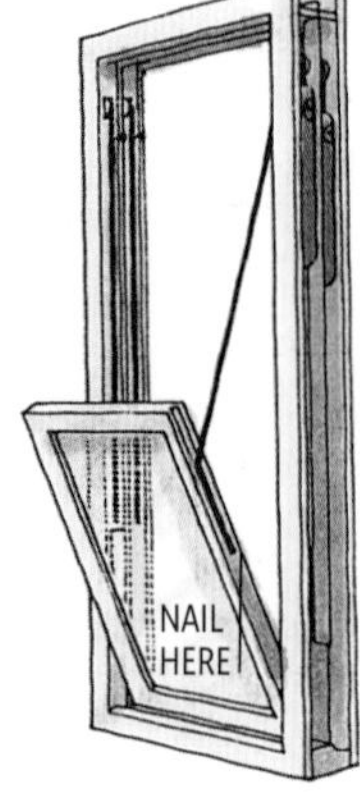

4 Nail cord to sash

SEE ALSO > Sash windows 192–3, Craft knife 485

Spiral balances

Instead of counterweights and cords, modern sash windows use spiral balances, which are mounted on the faces of the frame stiles, eliminating the need for traditional box frames. Pairs of balances are made to match the size and weight of individual glazed sashes and can be ordered through builders' merchants or direct from the manufacturers.

Spiral-balance components

Each balance consists of a torsion spring and a spiral rod housed in a tube. The top end is fixed to the frame stile, and the inner spiral to the bottom of the sash. The complete unit can be housed in a groove in the sash stile or in the window frame.

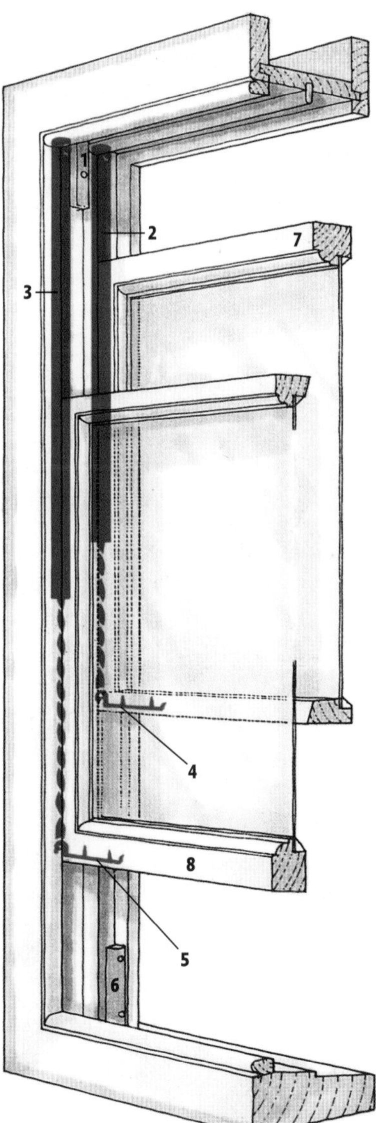

Sash window fitted with balances

1 Top limit stop
2 Top sash balance
3 Bottom sash balance
4 Fixing plate
5 Fixing plate
6 Bottom limit stop
7 Top sash
8 Bottom sash

Fitting the balances

You can fit spiral sash balances to replace the weights in a traditionally constructed sash window.

Remove the sashes and weigh them on your bathroom scales. Place your order, giving the weight of each sash together with its height and width, plus the height of the window frame. Refit the sashes temporarily until the balances arrive, then take them out and remove the pulleys.

Plug the holes and paint the box-frame stiles. Cut grooves, as specified by the manufacturers, in the stiles of each sash to take the balances (1). Also cut a housing at each end of their bottom edges to receive the spiral-rod fixing plates. Fit the fixing plates with screws (2).

Sit the top sash in place, resting it on the sill, and fit the parting bead. Take the top pair of balances, which are shorter than those for the bottom sash, and insert each into its groove (3). Fix the top ends of the balance tubes to the frame stiles with the screw-nails provided (4). Make sure the ends of both balances are tight against the window head.

Lift the sash to its full height and prop it with a length of wood. Hook the wire 'key' provided by the makers into the hole in the end of each spiral rod and pull it down about 150mm (6in). Keeping the tension on the spring, add three to five turns anticlockwise (5). Locate the end of each rod in its fixing plate and test the balance of the sash. If it drops, add another turn on the springs until the sash is perfectly balanced. Take care not to overwind the balances.

Fit the bottom sash the same way, refitting the staff bead to hold it in place. Fit the stops that limit the full travel of the sashes in their respective tracks, nailing them in place.

1 Cut a groove in the sash stiles

2 Fix each plate in its housing with screws

3 Fit the sash and insert the tube in its groove

4 Nail the top end of the tube to the stile

5 Tension the springs with the key provided

Spiral-balance unit

SEE ALSO > Parting bead 192

Replacing windows

The style of the windows is important to the appearance of any house. If you are replacing windows in an older building it's preferable – and needn't be more expensive – to have new wooden frames made to order, rather than change to modern plastic windows.

Ready-made windows

Joinery suppliers offer a range of ready-made window frames in both hardwood and softwood. Some typical examples are shown below.

Casement windows

Vertical sliding-sash windows

Construction details

Manufactured wooden frames are treated with preserver, and some are ready-primed for painting or prestained for final finishing. Most frames are rebated to take double-glazed sealed units, as well as single glazing.

In addition to stays and fasteners (normally supplied with the frames), some windows have either the top rail of the opening sash or the frame itself slotted to take a ventilator kit. This is in order to comply with current Building Regulations that require background ventilation in all habitable rooms.

High-performance windows also have integral draughtstripping fitted in the rebates into which the casements close.

Planning rules and Building Regulations

Window conversions don't normally require planning permission, since they come under the heading of house improvements. However, if you are planning to alter the appearance of your windows significantly (for example, by bricking one up or by making a new window opening), consult your local Building Control Officer – and if you live either in a listed building or in a conservation area, you will need to check with your local planning authority before making any changes to your windows.

All authorities require minimum levels of ventilation to be provided in the habitable rooms of a house. This normally means that the area of the openable part of the window(s) must be equal to at least one twentieth of the floor area of the room. Also, part, if not all, of a top vent must be 1.75m (5ft 9in) above the floor. Trickle ventilators with an opening area of 4000 or 8000sq mm (6½ to 13sq in) – depending on the size of the window – are also required for new window installations.

Buying replacement windows

Try to maintain the character of an older house by preserving the original joinery. If you have to replace a window, copy the style of the one that is to be replaced. If you are unable to find a standard ready-made window that's a suitable match, a specialist joinery firm will make up a new wooden frame to match the original, although this may be an expensive option if you need more than one or two new windows. If you choose this route, specify either an appropriate hardwood or, for a paint finish, softwood impregnated with wood preserver.

Alternatively, you can approach a replacement window company, though this may limit your choice to plastic (uPVC) frames. These are generally available in white or in a limited choice of natural timber colours. Ready-glazed units can often be fitted into your old timber subframes if these are sound, or into new hardwood ones supplied by the installer.

The majority of replacement window companies install the windows they supply, and their service should include disposing of the old windows and all debris, as well as weatherproofing the windows outside and making good indoors.

This method saves time and effort, but you should carefully consider the compatibility of such windows with the style of your house. Choose a frame that reproduces the proportions and method of opening of the original window as closely as possible.

Replacing casements

Measure the width and height of the window opening. If the replacement window needs a timber subframe and the existing one is in good condition, take your measurements from inside the frame. Otherwise, take them from the masonry. You may have to cut away some of the rendering or internal plaster in order to obtain accurate measurements. Order your replacement window accordingly.

Remove the old window by taking out the sashes first, and then remove the panes of glass in any fixed lights. Remove exposed fixings, such as screws or metal brackets, or chisel away the plaster or rendering and cut through the fixings with a hacksaw.

It should be possible to knock the frame out in one piece. If not, saw through it in several places and lever the pieces out with a crowbar (**1**). Clean up the edges of the opening with a bolster chisel.

1 Lever out the pieces of the old frame

If necessary, cut the horns off the new frame. Wedge the frame in the window opening and check that it is plumb (**2**). Drill screw holes through the stiles into the masonry (**3**); then remove the frame and plug the holes, or use frame fixings. Attach a strip of damp-proofing material to the jambs and sill. Refit the frame, checking that it is plumb before you screw it firmly into place.

Repair the wall with mortar and plaster. Gaps of 6mm (¼in) or less can be filled with mastic. Glaze the new frame as required.

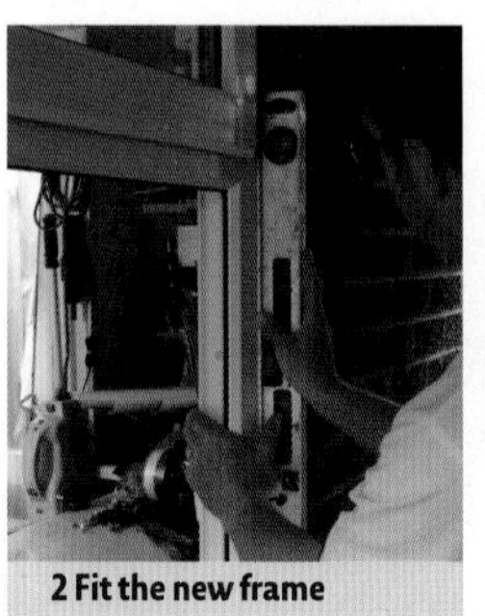

2 Fit the new frame

3 Drill fixing holes

SEE ALSO > Getting approval 24, Types of windows 192–3, DPC 138, Fitting new glass 196, Hacksaws 518

Bay windows

A bay window is a combination of window frames built out from the face of the building. The side frames may be set at 90-degree or 45-degree angles to the front of the house. Curved bays are made with equal-sized frames set at a very slight angle to each other to form a faceted curve.

The masonry structure that supports the window frames may continue up through all the storeys, finishing with a gable roof. Alternatively, the bay might have a masonry base only and a flat or pitched roof.

Bay windows can break away from the main wall as a result of subsidence caused by poor foundations or by differential ground movements. Once the movement has stabilized, minor damage can be repaired by repointing the masonry and applying mastic sealant to gaps round the woodwork. However, any damage from extensive or persistent movement should be dealt with by a builder. Consult your local Building Control Officer and inform your insurance company.

Fitting the frame

Where the height of the original window permits, a replacement can be made up from standard window frames. Various combinations of frames can be joined with shaped corner posts to set the side frames at an angle of 90 or 45 degrees, or with shaped mullions for curved bays. A sealant is used to weatherproof the joints between the posts and frames.

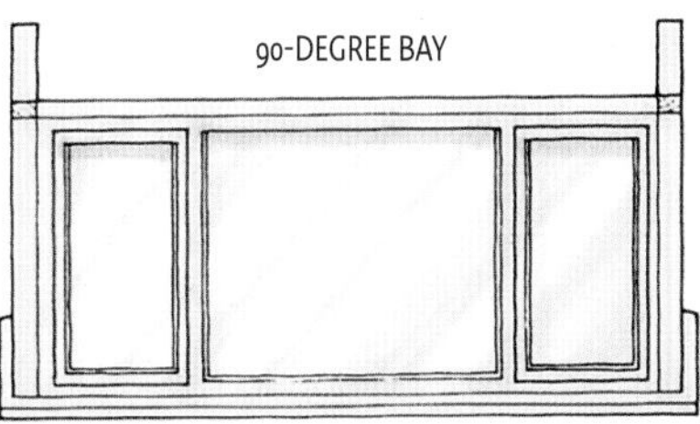

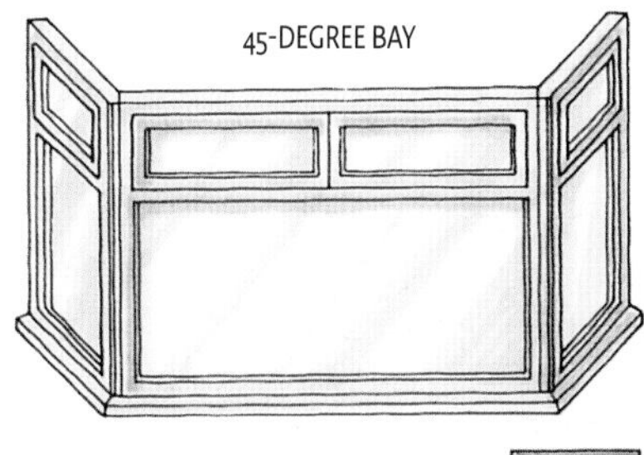

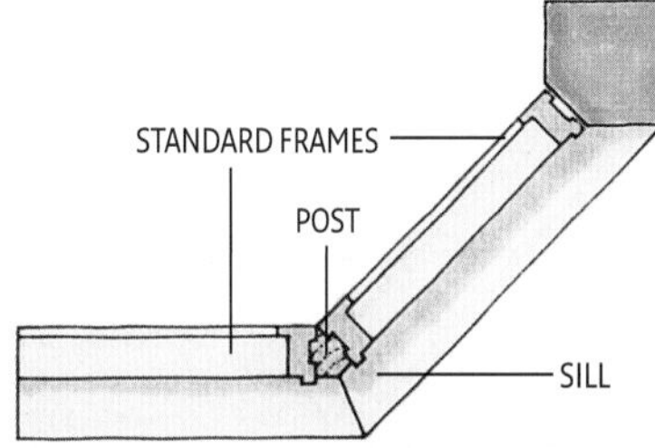

Standard frames joined with posts

Modern angled bay with decorative lead flashing

Bow windows

These windows are constructed on a shallow curve and normally project from a flat wall. Complete hardwood bow-window frames are available from joinery suppliers, ready for installation in a masonry opening. A flat-topped moulded-plastic canopy is available for weatherproofing the gap at the top of the window, in place of a traditional lead-sheet covering.

Modern bow window with fine glazing bars

Fitting the frame

Tack damp-proof-course material to the sides of the frame and the underside of the sill, then fit both the frame and the canopy into the wall opening, with the outer edges of the frame set flush with the wall. Screw the frame to the masonry. The vertical damp proofing should overlap any damp-proof course built into the wall.

Weatherproof the canopy with a lead flashing, cut into the wall and dressed over the upturned rear edge of the canopy. Use mastic to seal the joints between the frame and the masonry.

Fitting the window sill

Cut a shaped sill from exterior-grade plywood or moisture-resistant MDF to form the internal window sill.

Replacing a sash window

Traditional boxed-sash windows fitted with cords and counterweights are available from window specialists, who can also fit them for you. Alternatively, you may decide to replace an old vertical sliding-sash window with a new frame and spiral-balance sashes.

Removing the frame

Remove the sashes, then take out the old frame from inside the room. Do this by prising off the architrave, then the window boards, chopping away the plaster as necessary. Most frames are wedged in their openings, and you can loosen one by simply using a heavy hammer and a block of wood to hit the sill on the outside. Lift out the frame (**1**) and remove any debris from the opening.

Fitting a replacement

Fit a replacement for a traditional sash-window frame exactly as the original. Make sure the wood is treated with preserver.

Set a new spring-balance type (which has a slimmer frame) centrally in the window opening. Check the frame for plumb, and then wedge the corners at the head and sill. Make up the space left by the old box stiles by filling in with masonry (**2**).

Metal brackets screwed to the new frame's jambs can be set in the mortar joints to secure the frame.

When the mortar has set, replaster the interior wall and replace the architrave. Glaze the sashes and, to keep rainwater out, apply a mastic sealant to the joints between the outside walls and the frame.

1 Lift out old frame **2 Fill gaps with brick**

SEE ALSO > Repointing masonry 43, Sash windows 192–3, Removing sashes 200, Flashings 132–3, Sealing gaps 249

Roof windows

Double-glazed roof windows are popular for modernizing old attic skylights and are often included as part of a full loft conversion. They are supplied ready-glazed and fully equipped with catches and ventilators. Flashing kits designed to suit high-profile or low-profile roofing materials are also available.

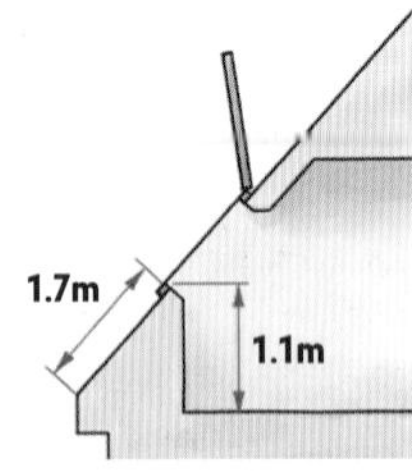

Fire-escape route
To satisfy the Building Regulations, one roof window in a loft conversion must serve as an 'egress window' in case of fire. Its height and width must be at least 450mm (18in), and its sill no more that 1.1m (3ft 7in) above floor level. To allow a ladder to be used for rescue purposes, the distance between the sill and the house eaves must not exceed 1.7m (5ft 7in).

Centre-pivoting sashes can be used for roofs with pitches of between 15 and 90 degrees. Top-hung roof windows are available for pitches between 15 and 75 degrees. A combined top-hung and centre-pivoting variety is also made, which provides a large opening that can be used as an emergency exit.

Roof windows can usually be installed from within the roof space, and the glass can be cleaned conveniently from inside.

Selecting the optimum size

Take into consideration the total area of glass that will be needed to provide a suitable level of daylight in the loft room. The manufacturers of roof windows offer a standard range of sizes.

The height of the window is quite important, too, though this is largely determined by the pitch of the roof. Manufacturers produce charts that show the recommended dimensions according to roof pitch. Ideally, if the window is to provide a reasonable outlook, the bottom rail should not obstruct the view from normal seat height, nor should it cut across the line of sight of someone who is standing. This means that the shallower the pitch of the roof, the taller the window needs to be. However, it is essential that the top of the window should be within easy reach.

In order to create a larger window, standard-size windows can be set side by side or placed one above the other. The widest single window available measures about 1.3m (4ft 4in). When deciding on the size of a window, bear in mind its proportions and position in relation to the building's appearance.

You will probably not need planning permission to install windows of this type - but check this, especially if you live in a listed building or a conservation area. However, the structural alterations will require Building Regulations approval, as would a complete loft conversion.

The manufacturers of roof windows supply fixing instructions to suit installation in all situations. The following information is a summary of one type of window fitted in a slate-covered roof. The frame for a tiled roof would have a different flashing kit.

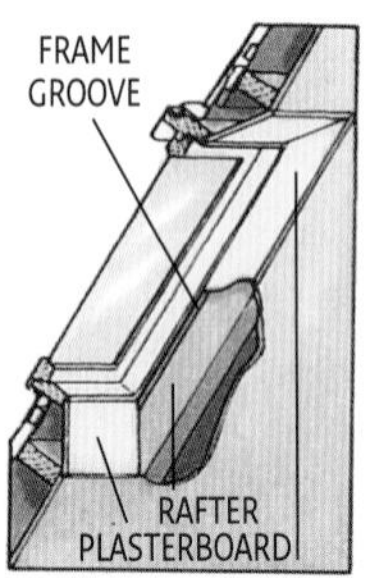

Lining the opening with plasterboard
Section through a window seen from the inside, showing the lining on the side, top and bottom of the opening. Prefabricated linings are available from some suppliers.

Fitting a window

Start by stripping off the slates over the window position. This will be determined by the position of the rafters and the roofing materials. Start by setting the bottom of the frame at the specified distance above the nearest full course of slates, and position it so as to have half or whole slates on each side.

Next, cut through the slating battens, roofing felt and rafters to make the opening, following the dimensions given by the window manufacturer. Cut and nail horizontal trimmers between the rafters to set the height of the opening, and a vertical trimmer or trimmers to set the width.

With the glazed sash removed, screw the window frame in place, using the brackets provided. A guide line is clearly marked round the frame, and you must set this level with the surface of the roofing battens. Check that the frame is square by measuring across its diagonals to ensure they are equal.

Complete the outside work by fitting the slates and flashing kit, working up from the bottom of the frame. Replace the glazed sash.

Cut and nail plasterboard to the sides of the rafters on the inside; and then fill in the top and bottom of the opening with plasterboard nailed to the timbers of the roof structure. Finish off the joints with filler and tape, ready for decoration.

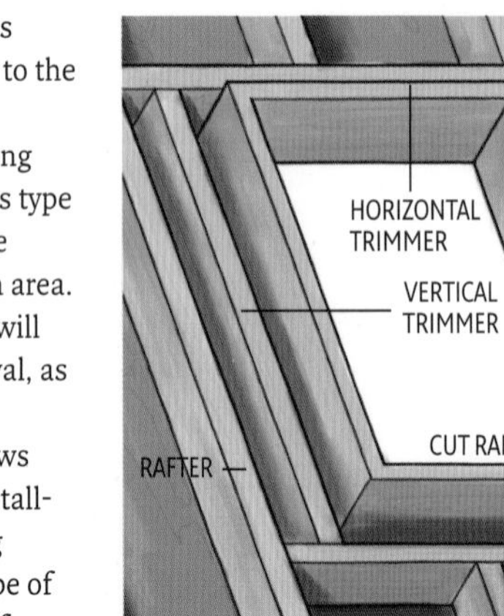

Cut the opening and fit trimmers

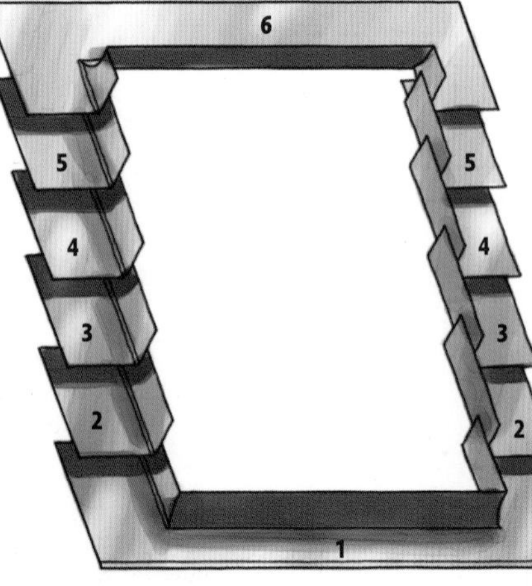

Flashing kit showing order of assembly

SEE ALSO > Roofs 120–37, Flashings 132–3, Plasterboard 162

Interior shutters

Louvred wooden shutters provide an attractive and practical alternative to fabric curtains or blinds, adding a touch of exotic style to an interior. Made from light-coloured fine-grained woods, they can be varnished to retain their natural appearance, or stained or painted to complement any colour scheme.

Adjustable-louvre shutters

Ready-made louvred shutters can be bought from specialist suppliers in both standard and made-to-measure sizes. The adjustable slats are connected by a slim vertical wooden bar that enables the entire bank of louvres to be set at the same angle. This action controls the level of natural light falling through the window. When shutters are fully closed and fastened together they provide privacy and also a certain degree of security.

Shutter combinations

The arrangement of shutters is largely determined by the size of the window opening. A single tier of panels or shutters is a common combination, comprising between one and four panels of uniform width. Two pairs of hinged panels, forming bifold shutters, is perhaps the most popular arrangement. Where the shutters would exceed 1120mm (3ft 8in) in height, each of the panels is made with an intermediate cross rail to stiffen the frame.

Alternatively, two or three shorter tiers can be stacked one above the other in order to cover tall windows. With this arrangement, you can have one or more tiers closed, while folding back the upper tier or tiers to illuminate the room. When planning for multi-tiered shutters, try to arrange the horizontal divisions between the panels to align with the main cross rails of the window frame.

Half-height or café-style shutters allow for a degree of privacy, but give less control over the level of illumination.

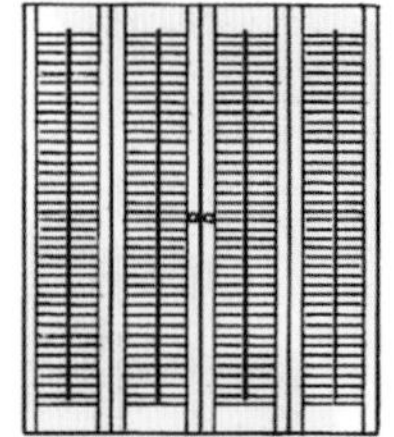

Single-tier bifold

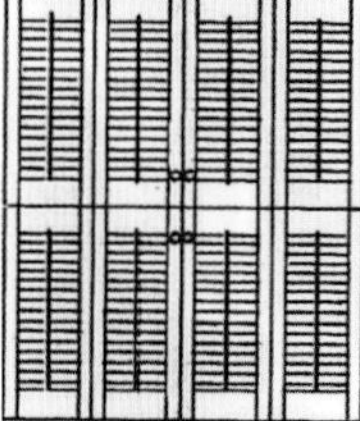

Multi-tiered shutters

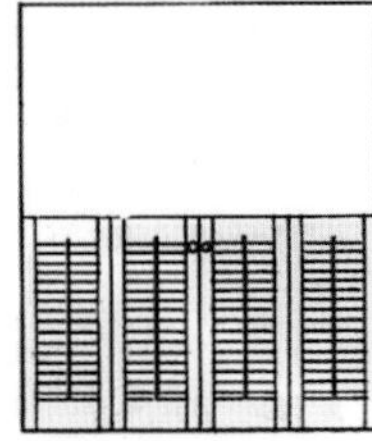

Café-style shutters

Mounting the shutters

The shutters are supplied hinged to a fixing batten for screwing to the wall or window frame. You can mount them to the face of the wall, so they span the window opening (1). Alternatively, if you have a deep-reveal window, you may prefer to fix the batten either to the inside of the recess (2) or to the sides of the window frame (3). Large shutters, as required for French windows, can be top-hung on a bifold door track.

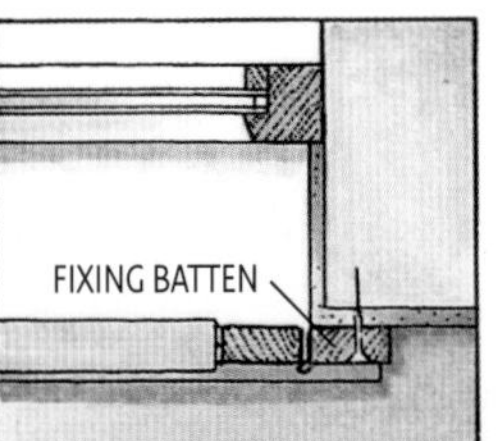

1 Face mounting

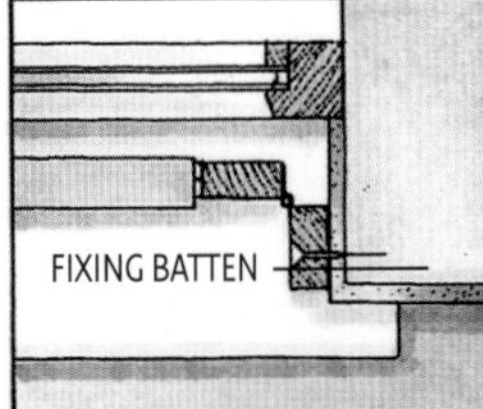

2 Recess mounting

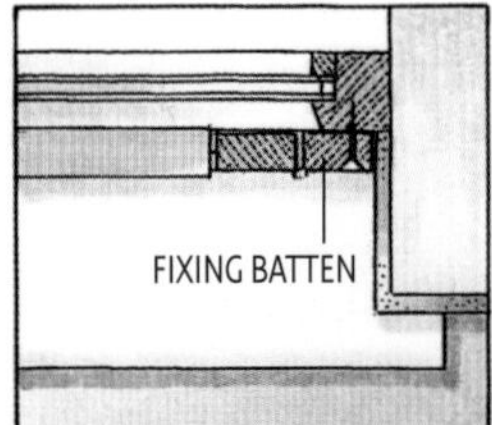

3 Window-frame mounting

Finishing shutters

Shutters are generally sold fine-sanded for finishing. You can use a brush to apply the finish, but covering the numerous faces and edges is time-consuming and it's difficult to avoid leaving runs. Consequently, it's preferable to spray a finish onto shutters. You can hire professional spray equipment, though for just one or two shutters you will probably be able to make do with pressurized spray cans.

Checking sizes

Face mounting

For shutters to be fixed to the face of a wall (see below left), measure the height from the sill and the width of the window opening. Remember to make an allowance for the shutters to overlap the wall at the top and sides of the opening; and check that the fixing screws won't be too close to the edges of the opening.

When fitting shutters over sliding-sash windows, measure to the inside of the existing architrave moulding.

Recess mounting

For shutters that are to be mounted in a window recess, measure the width of the opening between the reveals. Check the width top and bottom, and measure the height at both sides of the reveal. Take the smaller dimension in each case. You need to allow for the thickness of the fixing battens at each side (check this with your supplier).

To determine the size of individual shutters, divide the measured area by the number of shutters you want for each window.

Prefinished shutters
Shutters in a natural or plain-coloured finish provide a stylish window treatment for any room.

SEE ALSO > Sash windows 192–3, Paint-spraying equipment 484, Wallplugs 535

Fitting curtain rails and poles

Window treatments play an important part in interior design. Although the existing size and shape of the window itself cannot be altered easily, you can emphasize or modify its proportions by careful dressing, using curtains or blinds of an appropriate style.

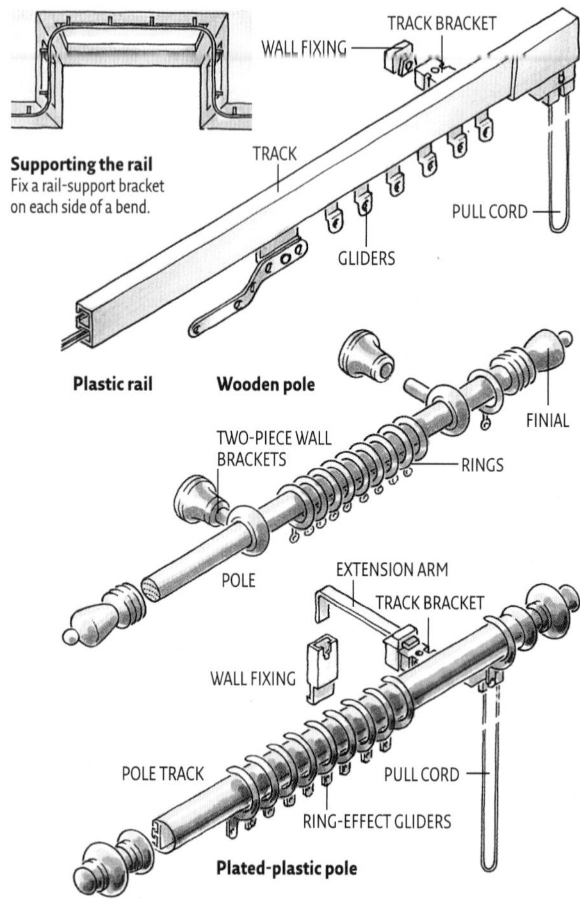

Supporting the rail
Fix a rail-support bracket on each side of a bend.

Curtain rails

As well as providing privacy, curtains help insulate the room from the sun, cold, draughts and noise. They are sold ready-made in a variety of fabrics and sizes, or you can make your own. Both the choice of material and the method used for hanging them contribute to the decorative style.

Modern curtain rails are made from plastic, aluminium or painted steel. They are available in various styles and lengths, and come complete with fixing brackets and glider rings or hooks. Some are supplied ready-corded - which makes drawing the curtains easier and minimizes soiling due to handling.

Although typically used in straight lengths, most rails can be shaped to fit a bay window. Depending on the tightness of the radius, you'll probably need more brackets to support a plastic rail in a bay than a metal one. Rails vary in rigidity, which dictates the minimum radius to which they can be bent. Plastic bends more easily when warm.

Curtain poles

Curtain poles, which were a feature of heavily draped Victorian interiors, are a popular alternative to modern track systems. Made from metal, plastic or wood, they come in a range of plated, painted or polished finishes. Traditional-type poles are supported on decoratively shaped brackets, and are fitted with end-stop finials and large curtain rings. Some modern derivations conceal corded tracks, providing the convenience of up-to-date mechanisms while retaining old-world charm.

A pair of wall-mounted decorative brackets are normally used to support curtain poles, but a central bracket may be required to support heavy fabrics or extra-wide poles. Modern plated-plastic tracked versions, with ring-effect gliders, are mounted on angle brackets. Slim lightweight poles are also made for sheer or net curtains. These are fitted with side-fixing or face-fixing sockets, and are commonly used to hang café curtains.

Fixing to the ceiling

Joists that run at right angles to the wall offer a fixing for placing curtain tracks at any convenient distance from the wall (1). Joists that run parallel to the wall need noggings nailed between them at the required fixing points (2). Skew-nail the noggings flush with the ceiling.

If the required position is close to the original joist, nail a 50 x 50mm (2 x 2in) batten to the face of the joist to provide fixing points (3).

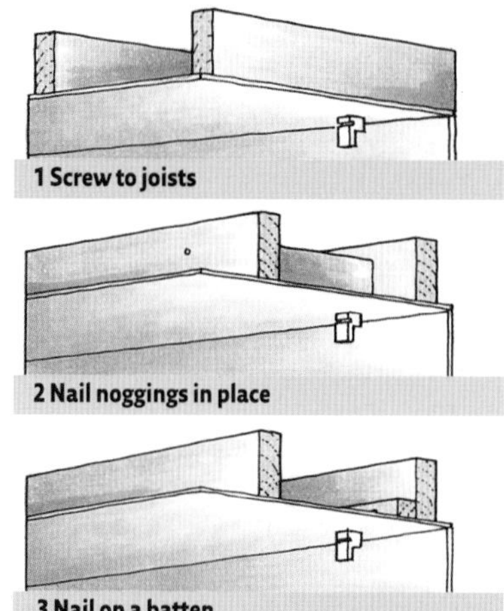

1 Screw to joists

2 Nail noggings in place

3 Nail on a batten

Fixing to the wall

Draw a guideline at a suitable height above the window opening. Plot the positions for the brackets along the line. Drill fixing holes and fit wallplugs if you are fixing into a masonry wall. Screw directly into wood framing, and use self-tapping screws or cavity fixings for metal lintels (4).

If it proves difficult to get a secure fixing at all the marked positions, screw a 25mm (1in) thick batten to the wall on which to mount the brackets.

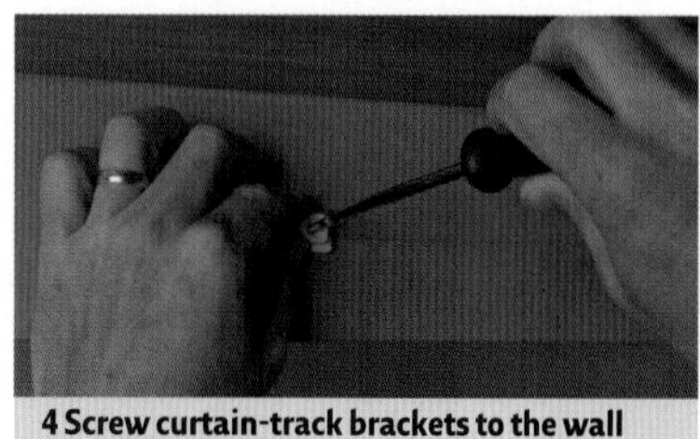

4 Screw curtain-track brackets to the wall

SEE ALSO > Noggings 152, Lintels 139, Wall fixings 535-6

Hanging blinds

Blinds provide a simple, attractive and sophisticated way of screening windows. Most standard types can be cut to size, and you can have blinds made to measure in a fabric of your choice. Some types incorporate refined opening and closing mechanisms.

Roller blinds

Low-cost roller blinds can be bought in a range of fabric designs and colours, ready-made or in kit form. A typical kit consists of a metal or plastic roller with two end caps (one of which includes the pull-cord mechanism), a narrow lath, a pull cord and two support brackets. You can buy the fabric separately and cut it to width and length. The rollers come in several lengths. Unless you can find a roller that fits your window exactly, get the next largest size and cut it to fit.

Components of a roller-blind kit

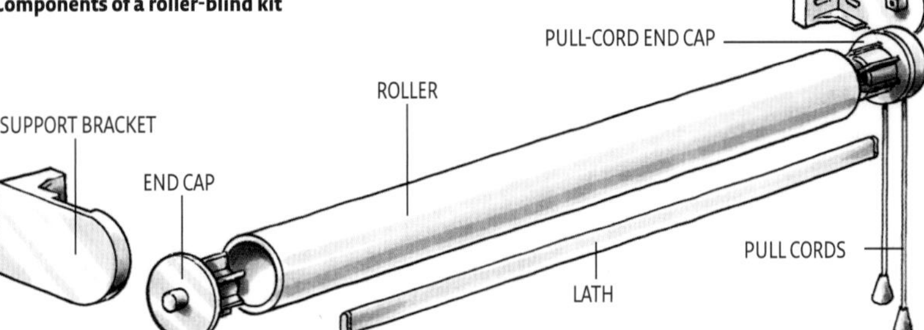

Cutting to size

A blind can be hung within the window recess or across the front of it. If fitting the roller inside, place the brackets in the top corners of the frame or opening. Ensure the pull-cord control bracket is at the end from which you intend to operate the blind. Measure and cut the roller to fit between the brackets.

If you are fitting the blind outside the window recess, you will need to cut the roller about 100mm (4in) longer than the width of the opening. Fit the brackets by drilling and plugging the wall, using the roller as a guide.

Fitting the fabric

Ideally the fabric should be non-fraying, to avoid having to sew side hems. Cut the width of the blind to finish 3mm (⅛in) less than the length of the roller; it should be long enough to cover the window, plus an extra 200mm (8in). Make a bottom hem 6mm (¼in) deep, then turn it up to form a sleeve for the lath. Stick the other end of the fabric to the self-adhesive strip on the roller, taking care to align the top edge of the fabric with the roller's axis.

Fitting the blind

With the fabric rolled on the roller, engage the square hole of the pull-cord end cap onto the control bracket, with the cords hanging down. Clip the other end into the opposite bracket. Identify the cord that lowers the blind, fit a knob on the end of it, then pull the cord down level with the sill.

Remove the blind and unwind the fabric till it reaches the sill or its lowest point. Refit the blind and raise it to the open position, using the other cord, then fit its knob. Check that the blind operates smoothly and, if necessary, adjust the length of the cords.

Vertical blinds

Vertical blinds suit simple modern interiors, and work well with patio doors. The blinds hang from a headtrack, which you can screw to the ceiling or to the wall above the window. The vertical vanes, which clip into hooks on the headtrack, are linked together by short chains at the bottom. The vanes are weighted so that they hang straight.

Mark a guide line on the wall, ceiling or soffit. Check that the rotating vanes will clear obstacles such as handles. Screw the mounting brackets in place and clip the track into them. Hang the preassembled vanes on the headtrack hooks, checking that the hooks are facing the same way, and that you are attaching the vanes with their seams all in the same direction.

Venetian blinds

Venetian blinds provide a stylish treatment for most windows. They come in a range of standard sizes, and can be made to measure. They are usually made of metal, and are available in a range of coloured finishes. Versions with wooden slats are also made.

Fitting a Venetian blind

If the blind is to be fitted into a window recess, measure the width at the top and bottom of the opening. Allow for a clearance of about 9mm (⅜in) at each end. Screw the brackets in place so that the blind will clear any handles or catches. Set the end brackets 75mm (3in) in from the ends of the headrail.

Mount the headrail in the brackets. Some are simply clamped, while others are locked in place by a swivel catch on each bracket (1). Raise and lower the blind to check that the mechanism is working freely. To lower the blind, pull the cord across the front of the blind to release the lock mechanism, then let it slide through your hand. Tilt the slats by rotating the control wand.

Fitting at an angle

Venetian blinds can be specified for use on a sloping window. They are supplied with cords that prevent the blind sagging. When threaded through the holes punched in the slats, both cords are fixed to the headrail and are held taut by fixing brackets at the bottom (2).

1 Locate headrail on brackets

2 Fix guide-line brackets to the wall

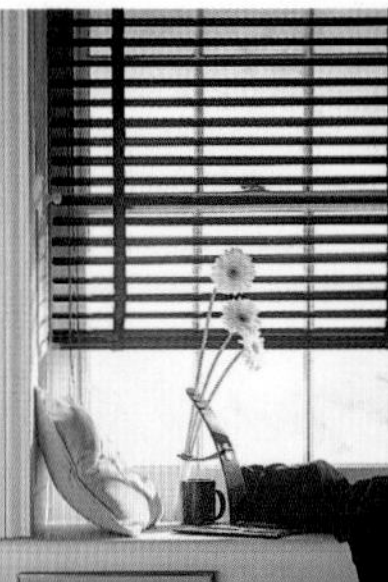

Roller and Venetian blinds
Blinds look at home in both traditional and modern settings.

SEE ALSO > Wall fixings 535–6

Staircases

The shape and decorative features of a staircase contribute greatly to the character of a house. Most stairs are made from softwood, although hardwoods are sometimes used for features such as newel posts and handrails. Stone and metal are also used – though they are rare in the average house, other than in the form of spiral staircases or basement steps.

Types of staircase

The simplest staircase is a straight flight of steps running from one floor to another – but where floor space is limited, the flight can change direction through 90 or 180 degrees, with a landing (or landings) provided between the two floors.

Flight configurations

There are a number of common flight configurations: the dog-leg, the open well, the quarter-turn and the half-turn are just some of the variants (see below). Most domestic stairs use newel posts in their construction at the end of each flight and at points where the flight changes direction, and they are known as newel stairs. Stairs of this type usually have parallel-sided treads. However, tapered treads, known as winders, are sometimes used at the top or bottom of a flight in order to turn a corner.

Straight flight with storage space below

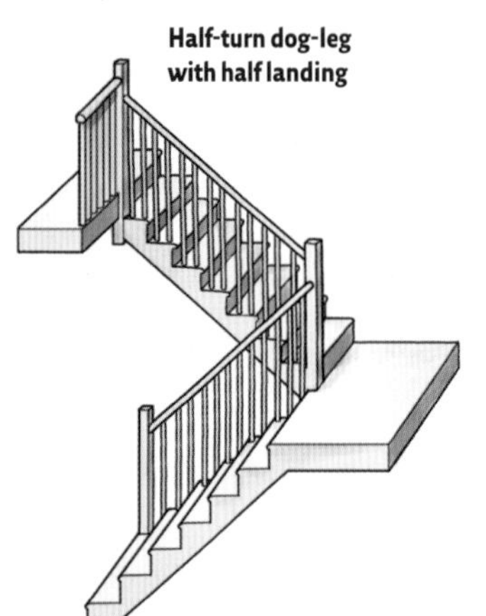
Half-turn dog-leg with half landing

Half-turn open-well with quarter landings

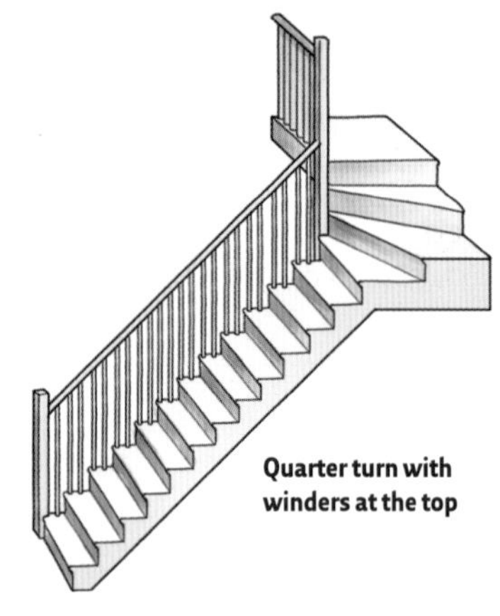
Quarter turn with winders at the top

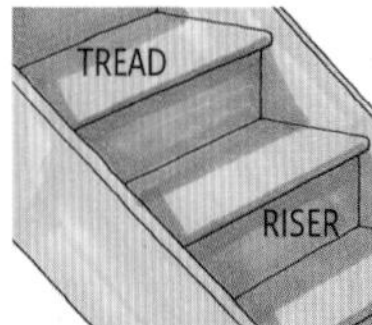

Most staircases have treads and risers

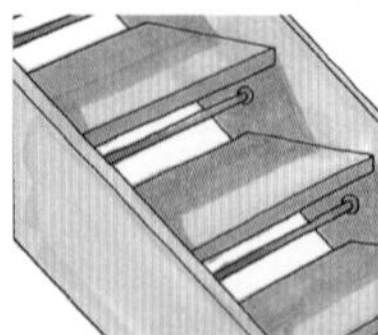
Open-tread stairs are fitted with tie rods

Treads and risers

Each step of an ordinary straight flight of wooden stairs is made from two boards: the vertical riser, which forms the front of the step, and the horizontal tread on which you walk. The riser is a stiffening member and is fixed between two treads, giving support to the front edge of one and the rear of the other.

Treads and risers may be butt-jointed together or joined with housings or with tongue-and-groove joints. Triangular blocks glued into the angles between the risers and treads reinforce the joint to provide greater stiffness.

Open-tread stairs have thick treads but no risers. In order to comply with the Building Regulations, metal tie rods or wooden rails must be fitted horizontally between open treads to restrict the vertical gap to less than 100mm (4in).

A closed string has long parallel edges

An open string is cut into step shapes

Strings

The steps are fixed at each end to wide parallel boards known as strings. These are the main structural members of the staircase and run from one floor level to another. The board attached to the wall is known as the wall string; the board on the open side of the staircase is called the outer string.

The appearance of a staircase is affected by the style of the strings, of which there are two types. A closed string has long parallel edges, while a cut or open string has its top edge cut away to conform to the shape of the steps. The closed version is always used for the wall string and picks up the line of the skirting boards in the hall and landing. The outer string can be either a simple closed type or a cut version, the latter being more often found in older dwellings.

SEE ALSO > Balustrades 215

Staircase construction

The principles of staircase construction have changed little over the past couple of centuries, although mass production and the requirements of the Building Regulations have led to a greater degree of standardization in recent years.

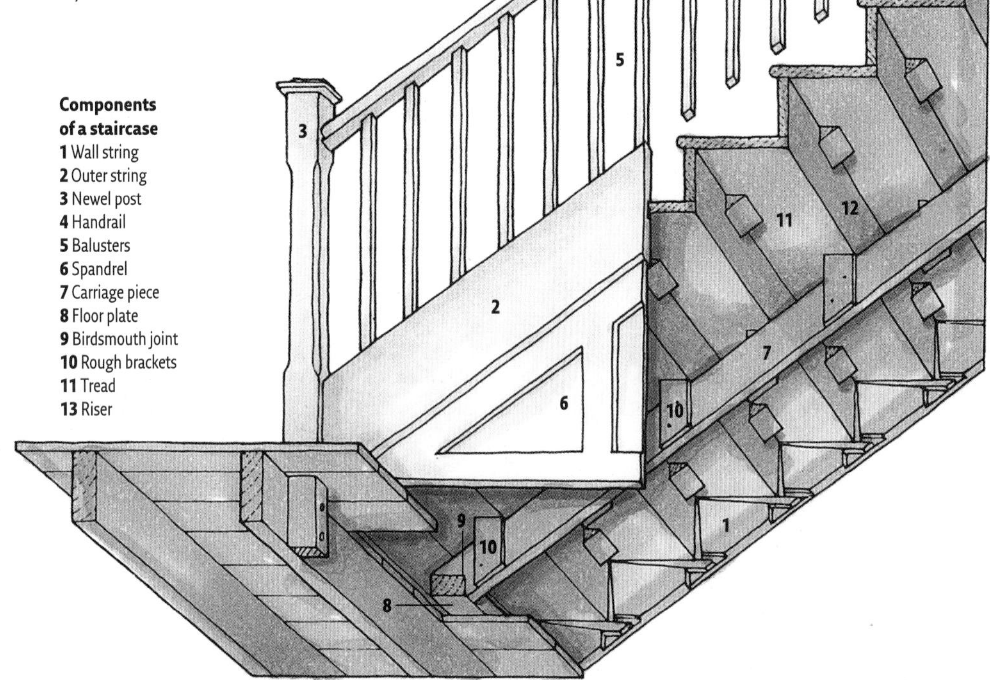

Components of a staircase
1 Wall string
2 Outer string
3 Newel post
4 Handrail
5 Balusters
6 Spandrel
7 Carriage piece
8 Floor plate
9 Birdsmouth joint
10 Rough brackets
11 Tread
13 Riser

Newel posts

The wall string is screwed to the wall at various points beneath the treads, and the outer string is tenoned into newel posts at each end. Newel posts – which are at least 100 x 100mm (4 x 4in) in section – give support to the staircase, securing it to the floor at the bottom and to the structural trimmer of the floor or landing above. The post at the top of the stairs and the central newel of a stair with a landing usually continue down to the floor. The handrail is nailed or tenoned into the newel posts.

Balustrade

The space between the handrail and the outer string may be filled with traditional balusters, framed panelling or modern balustrade rails. The entire assembly is known as the balustrade or banisters. The dimensions of a balustrade must meet certain safety requirements, which are specified by the Building Regulations (see REPAIRING BALUSTERS).

Storage space

The space underneath a staircase is often enclosed to make a cupboard. The infilling between the outer string and the floor is called the spandrel. Made with a plastered surface or wood panelling, the spandrel is not structural and can be removed if required. However, an under-stair cupboard is a sensible use of a space that is otherwise often of little value.

The central bearer

Traditional staircases over 900mm (3ft) wide should be supported by a central bearer or carriage piece fixed beneath the steps. This is a length of 100 x 50mm (4 x 2in) timber that is fixed by means of birdsmouth joints to a 100 x 50mm (4 x 2in) floor plate at the bottom and to the floor joist at the top. Short lengths of board 25mm (1in) thick, known as rough brackets, are nailed to alternate sides of the bearer to support each tread.

If the underside of the staircase is finished with lath-and-plaster, the central bearer also provides support for the laths. The ends of the laths are nailed either to the edges of the strings or to additional bearers mounted beside them. On stairs where no bearers are fitted, laths are sometimes nailed longitudinally to the underedges of the treads.

When a central bearer is fitted, wide strings are needed to match it. The string may be cut from a single wide board or made up from two narrower ones.

Step-and-string joints

The treads and risers of a staircase are set in housings cut into the face of a closed string and secured with glued wedges. The wedges are driven in from the underside to make a tight joint. Each vertical wedge is driven in first and is held in place by the horizontal wedge below it.

In the case of an open string, the outer ends of the risers are mitred into the vertical cut edges and the treads are nailed onto the horizontal edges. The nosing – the rounded edge of the tread – is returned by a matching moulding that covers the tread's end grain and usually has a scotia moulding beneath it.

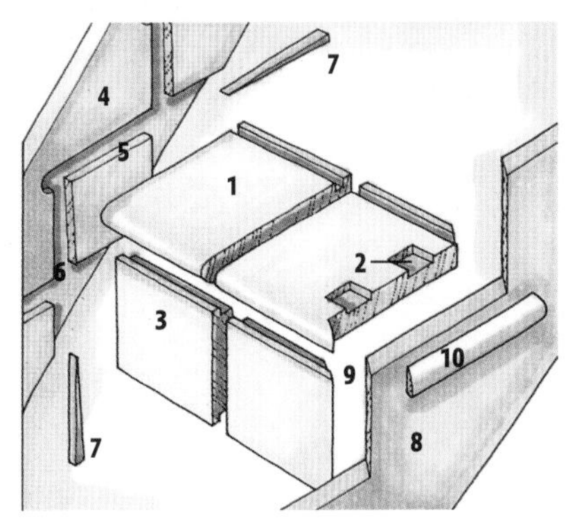

Step assembly with typical stair joints
1 Grooved tread
2 Baluster housing
3 Tongued riser
4 Wall string
5 Tread housing
6 Riser housing
7 Wedge
8 Open string
9 Mitred butt joint
10 Moulding

SEE ALSO > Upper floors 172, Repairing balusters 213, Fitting a handrail 214, Replacing a balustrade 215

Repairing worn steps

Old softwood stair treads are likely to show wear if they haven't been adequately protected by a floorcovering. Worn treads and nosings are dangerous and should be repaired promptly. If all the treads are badly worn, then it may be worth getting a builder to replace the staircase. Treads fitted between closed strings can be replaced only from below. If the soffit of the staircase is enclosed with lath-and-plaster or plasterboard, you will have to cut an opening to reach a worn-out tread. Where a central bearer is fitted, the work can be extensive and it is worth seeking advice from a builder.

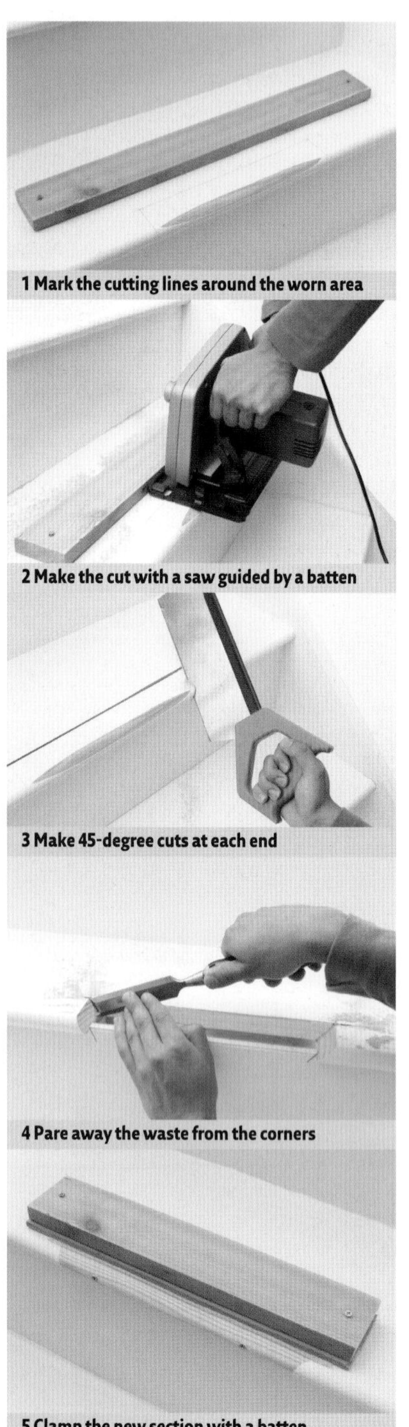

1 Mark the cutting lines around the worn area

2 Make the cut with a saw guided by a batten

3 Make 45-degree cuts at each end

4 Pare away the waste from the corners

5 Clamp the new section with a batten

Renewing a nosing

Wear on the nosing is usually concentrated around the centre of the step, and you may be able to repair it without having to renew the entire tread.

Mark three cutting lines just outside the worn area, one parallel with the edge of the nosing and the other two at right angles to it (1). Adjust the blade depth of a portable circular saw to the thickness of the tread. In order to guide the edge of the saw's base plate, pin a batten the required distance from and parallel to the long cutting line.

Cutting out the waste

Position the saw nose down, then switch on and make the cut by gradually lowering the blade into the wood (2). Try not to overrun the short end lines. Once you've made the cut, remove the guide batten.

Use a tenon saw to make the end cuts at 45 degrees to the face of the tread (3). Try not to saw beyond the circular-saw cut.

Cut away the waste with a chisel, working with the grain and taking care to avoid damaging the riser tongue if it has tongue-and-groove joints. Pare away the waste in the uncut corners (4).

Replacing the nosing

Plane a groove in the underside of a new section of nosing to receive the tongue of the riser, and cut the ends of the new section to 45 degrees. Check its fit in the opening, then apply wood adhesive to all meeting surfaces and fix it in place. Clamp it down with a batten screwed at each end to the tread (5). Place a packing strip of hardboard under the batten to concentrate the pressure, plus a piece of polythene to prevent the hardboard sticking.

Drill and insert glued dowels 6mm (¼in) in diameter into the edge of the nosing to reinforce the butt joint; then when the adhesive has set, plane and sand the repair flush. Refix any glued blocks that may have fallen off.

Replacing treads

Most stairs have tongue-and-groove joints between their risers and treads. However, in some cases the tops of the risers are housed into the undersides of the treads; and in others, simple butt joints are secured with nails or screws.

You can determine which type of joint you are faced with by trying to pass a thin knife blade between the shoulders of the joint. It will help if you first remove any nails or screws. Drive old nails into the wood with a nail punch. A butt joint will allow the blade to pass through, while a housed or tongue-and-groove joint will obstruct it.

Because the joints effectively lock the treads and risers together, those that are in contact with the damaged tread must be freed before the tread can be removed. A butt joint is relatively easy to dismantle, whereas a housed or tongue-and-groove joint has to be cut.

Dismantling a butt joint

To take a butt joint apart, first take out any screws or punch nails through with a nail punch. If adhesive has been used, give the edge of the tread a sharp tap with a hammer to break the old, hardened adhesive, or prise the tread up with a chisel. Remove the triangular glued blocks in a similar way.

Cutting a tongue

Work from the front of the step when cutting the tongue of a riser jointed into the underside of a tread. Where the riser's tongue is jointed into the top of the tread below, it must be cut from the rear. If there is a scotia moulding fitted under the nosing, try to prise it away first, using an old wood chisel.

Before cutting a tongue, remove any screws, nails and glued reinforcement blocks, then drill two or three 3mm (⅛in) holes just below the shoulder of the joint, so you can insert the blade of a padsaw. Begin the sawcut and then, when the kerf is long enough, continue with a panel saw, using the underside of the tread to guide the blade.

The method you use to remove the tread will depend on whether it is fitted between closed strings or has an open string at one end (see opposite).

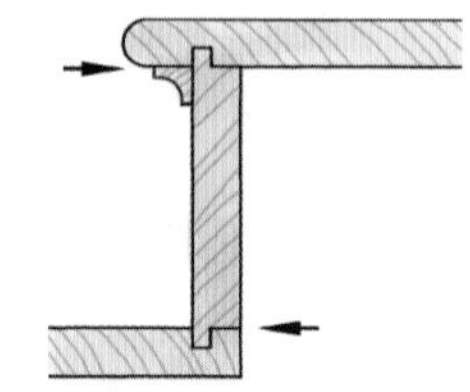

Cut tongue from the front or rear

Initiate the cut with a padsaw

SEE ALSO > Stair construction 209, Glued blocks 224, Saws 488, 491

Removing the tread from a closed string

To continue with the repair, work from the underside of the stair and chisel out the retaining wedges from the string housings at the ends of the tread (1). Free the joints by giving the tread a sharp tap from above with a hammer and block.

Drive the tread backwards and out of its two housings by alternately tapping one end and then the other (2).

Next, make a replacement tread to fit, shaping its front edge to match the nosing of the other steps, and cut a new pair of wedges. Slide the new tread and wedges into place from below. Measure the gaps left by the sawcuts at its front and back (3), and cut wooden packing strips or pieces of veneer to fill them.

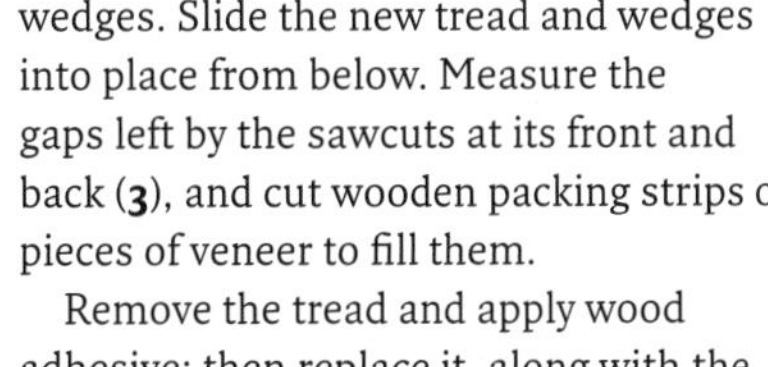

Remove the tread and apply wood adhesive; then replace it, along with the wedges and packing pieces. Secure the tread with 38mm (1½in) countersunk woodscrews, screwed into both risers.

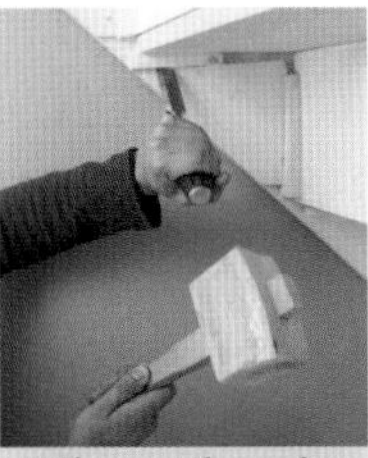
1 Chop out the wedges

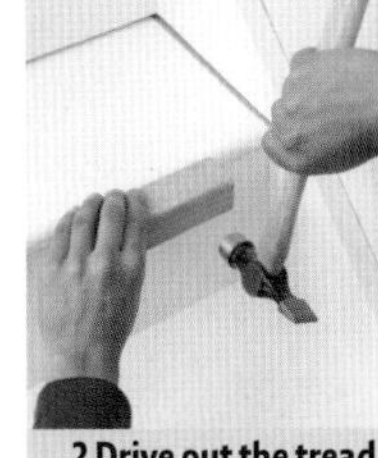
2 Drive out the tread

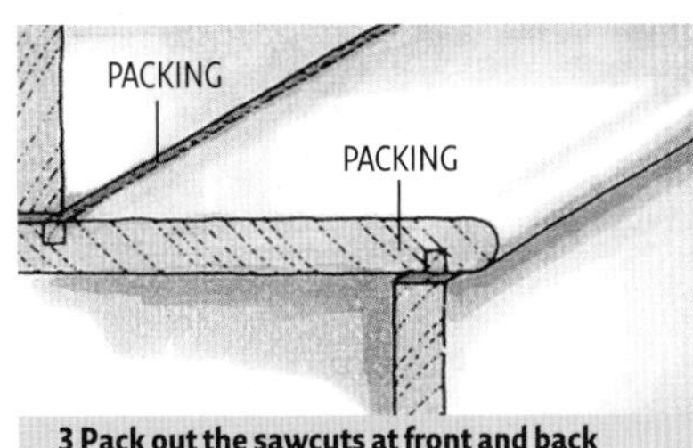

3 Pack out the sawcuts at front and back

Removing the tread from an open string

This type of staircase requires a different approach. Use a chisel to prise off the return moulding (which covers the end of the tread), taking care not to split it (1); and then remove the two balusters.

Chisel the wedge out of the wall-string housing, to free the inner end of the tread. Then drive the tread out from the rear of the stair (2), using a hammer and a wood block on its back edge. You will have to cut through or extract any nails that fix the tread to the outer string before it can be pulled completely clear.

Making use of the original tread as a template, mark its shape on a new board, then cut the board accurately to size. Take care to preserve the exact shape of the nosing, which must be the same as that of the original the return moulding prised from the end of the old tread.

Mark out and cut a pair of housings in one end of the tread for the balusters (3), and make a new hardwood wedge for the inner-tread housing. Treat all the new wood with a chemical preserver.

Fit the tread from the front, insert packing strips, then glue and screw it, following the method described for a closed-string tread (see above).

Apply adhesive to the balusters and replace them. Finally, pin and glue the return moulding to the end of the tread and replace any scotia moulding.

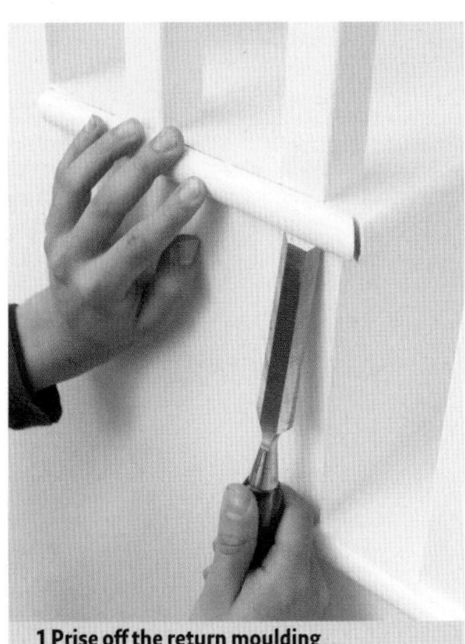
1 Prise off the return moulding

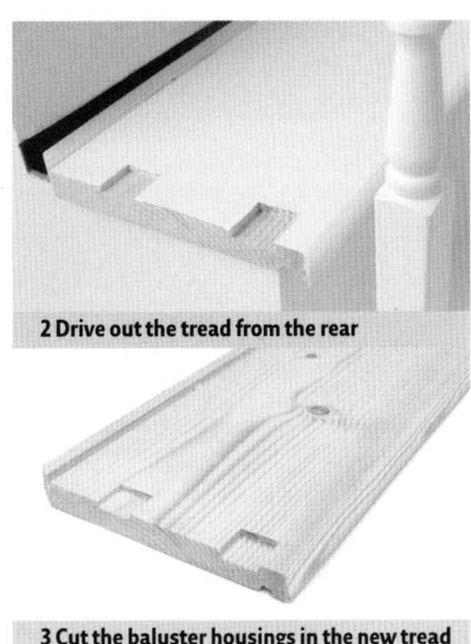
2 Drive out the tread from the rear

3 Cut the baluster housings in the new tread

Repairing a riser

Risers suffer much less wear and tear than treads and rarely have to be replaced. A riser that has been seriously affected by woodworm should always be replaced.

Closed-string staircase

In the case of a closed-string staircase, remove the tread below the damaged riser, using the method described left; and then saw through the tongue at the top of the riser. Knock the wedges out of the riser housings and prise out the riser itself (1).

Measure the distance between the strings; and also measure the distance from the underside of one tread to the top of another. Cut a new riser to fit. Although you could make tongue-and-groove joints, it is easier to join it to the treads with glued butt joints (2).

Glue and wedge the new riser into the string housings, then glue and screw the upper tread to its top edge.

If yours is a staircase where the steps are not carpeted, counterbore the screw holes and use wood plugs to conceal the screws. Another way to secure a glued butt joint is to screw and glue blocks into the right angle formed between the two components.

Refit the tread as described left, but note that you need pack out only the front sawcut, as the new riser has been made to fit exactly. Then glue and screw the tread to the lower edge of the new riser.

1 Prise out the riser

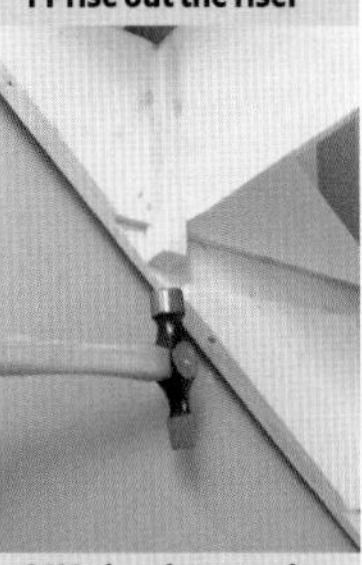
2 Wedge the new riser

Open-string staircase

If there is a scotia moulding fitted under the nosing, remove it. Then saw through the tongues at the top and bottom of the infected riser and remove the wedge from its wall-string housing.

Knock apart the mitred joint between the end of the riser and the outer string by hammering it from behind. Once the mitred joint is free, pull the inner end of the riser out of its housing.

Make a new riser to fit between the treads, mitring its outer end to match the joint in the string. Apply adhesive and fit the riser from the front. Then rewedge the inner housing joint, screw the treads to the riser, nail the mitred end, and replace the scotia moulding.

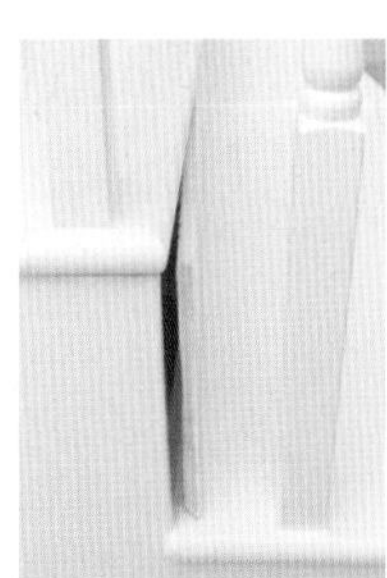
Free the mitred joint
On open-string stairs, knock the joint apart.

SEE ALSO > Stair joints 209, Repairing balusters 213, Treating woodworm 242, Plug cutter 500

Curing creaking stairs

Wood invariably shrinks when it dries out. When the wooden components of a staircase shrink, the joints become loose and creak when anyone mounts the stairs. Wear and tear may augment the problem. How you set about curing this irritating problem depends on whether you have access to the back of the treads. A better repair can be carried out from the back – that is, from below the stairs – but if that is going to mean cutting into a plastered soffit, then it's probably best to work from above.

Working from above

To identify the problem, remove the stair carpet and walk slowly up the stairs. When you reach a creaking tread, shift your weight to and fro to discover which part is moving and mark it with chalk.

Loose nosing joint

To cure a loose tongue-and-groove joint between the riser and tread nosing, drill clearance holes in the tread for 38mm (1½in) countersunk screws centred on the thickness of the riser. Inject some PVA woodworking adhesive into the holes and work the joint a little to encourage the adhesive to spread into it, then pull the joint up tight with the screws.

If the screws cannot be concealed by stair carpet, counterbore the holes so as to set the screw heads below the surface of the tread, and then plug the holes with matching wood (see left).

Cover the screws with a plug made from matching wood

Loose riser joint

A loose joint at the back of the tread cannot be repaired easily from above. You can try working PVA woodworking adhesive into the joint, but you cannot use woodscrews to pull the joint together.

Another approach is to reinforce the joint by gluing a section of 12 x 12mm (½in x ½in) triangular moulding into the angle between the tread and the riser (see below). This is viable so long as it does not reduce the remaining depth of the tread to less than the minimum Building Regulation requirement of 220mm (8¾in).

Unless the stair carpet covers the full width of the treads, it's best to cut the moulding slightly shorter than the width of the carpet for the sake of appearance.

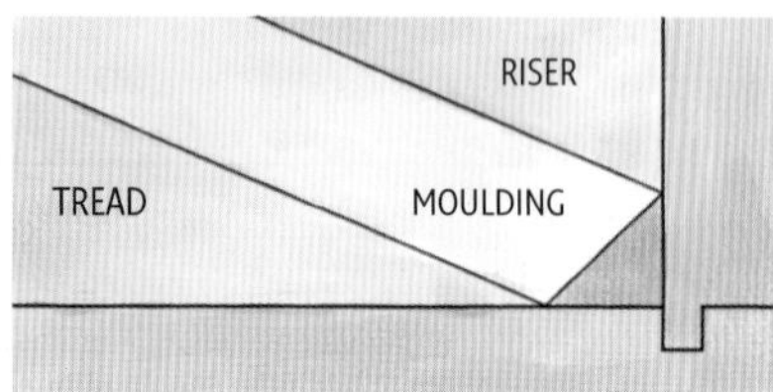

Glue a triangular moulding into the angle

Working from below

If it's possible to get to the underside of the stairs, have someone walk slowly up the steps, counting them out loud. From your position under the staircase, note any loose steps and mark them with chalk. Get your assistant to step on and off the loose treads while you inspect them to discover the source of the creaking.

Loose housing joints

If the tread or riser has become loose in its string housing, the glued wedge may have worked loose. Remove the wedge (**1**), clean it up, and apply PVA woodworking adhesive. Then rewedge the joint (**2**). If the old wedge is damaged, make a new one from hardwood.

Loose blocks

Check the triangular blocks that fit in the angle between the tread and riser. If the adhesive has failed on any of the faces, remove the blocks and clean off the old adhesive. Before replacing the blocks, prise the shoulder of the tread-to-riser joint slightly open, using a chisel, then apply adhesive to the joint (**3**) and rub-joint the glued blocks back into place in the angle (**4**).

If suction alone proves insufficient, use panel pins to hold the blocks in place while the adhesive sets (try to avoid treading on the repaired steps in the meantime).

If you find some of the blocks are missing, make new ones from a length of 50 x 50mm (2 x 2in) softwood.

1 Prise out the old wedge with a chisel

3 Prise open the joint and inject adhesive

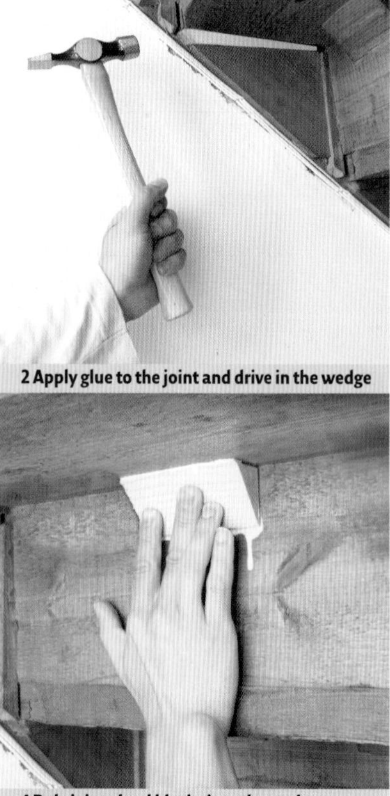

2 Apply glue to the joint and drive in the wedge

4 Rub-joint glued blocks into the angle

SEE ALSO > Carpeting stairs 114, Step-and-string joints 209, Plug cutter 500

Repairing balusters

A broken baluster is potentially dangerous and should be repaired or replaced promptly. If the baluster is a decorative one, it should be preserved if at all possible. Damage that is not too extensive can be repaired *in situ*. Otherwise, if the baluster is beyond repair, a new one can be made to replace it.

Buying and fitting balusters

Ready-turned balusters in a variety of traditional patterns are available from joinery suppliers. These can be used to create an authentic-looking balustrade, if made-to-measure replicas of the originals would be too costly.

They also make useful replacements for old square balusters – adding a touch of character to what would otherwise be a rather utilitarian staircase.

Balusters are usually either housed or tenoned into the underside of the handrail, and also into the edge of a closed string or the treads of an open string. Sometimes they are simply butt-jointed and secured with nails, or are housed at the bottom but nailed at the top. You can detect a nail fixing by examining or feeling the surface of the baluster, where you will find a slight bump or hollow. If the wood is stripped, the fixing will be obvious. A light shone across the joint can also reveal a nail fixing.

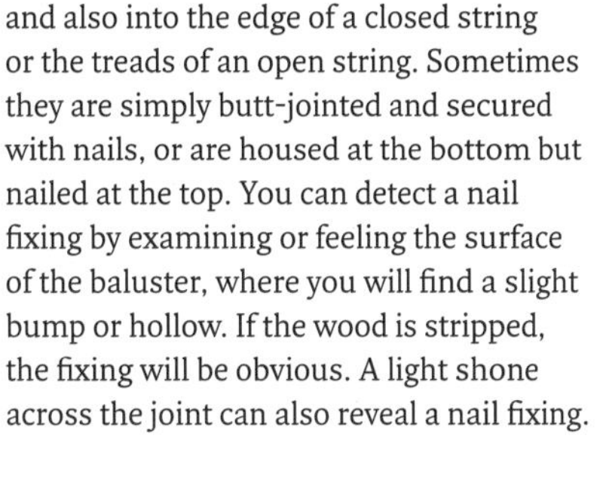

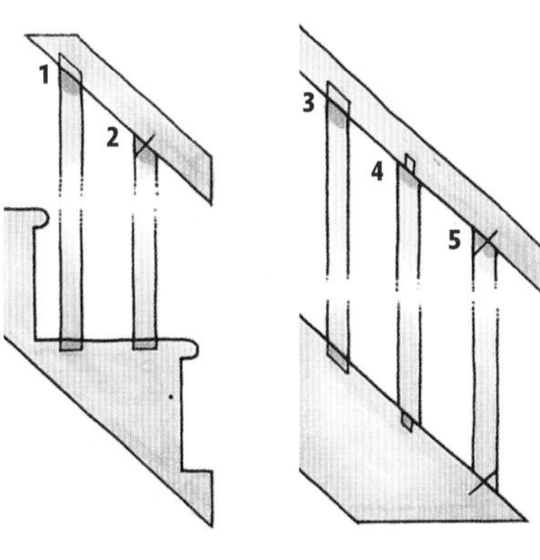

Baluster joints in open and closed strings
1 Housed at both ends. **2** Housed below and nailed above. **3** Housed at both ends. **4** Stub-tenoned. **5** Nailed.

Replacing a baluster

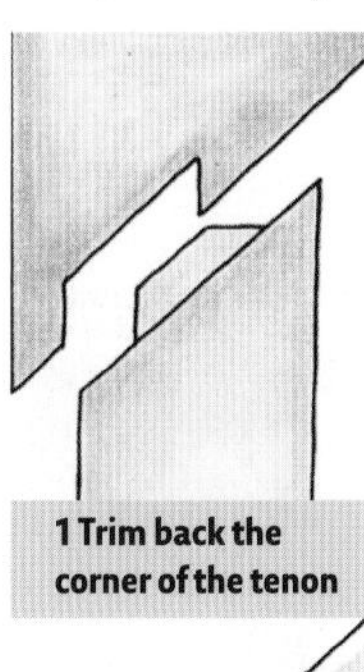

1 Trim back the corner of the tenon

2 Swing into place

A damaged baluster that is butt-jointed and nailed can be knocked out by driving its top end backwards and its bottom end forwards. If it is housed at the bottom, it can be pulled out of the housing once the top has been freed.

A baluster housed at both ends can be removed only by first cutting through the shoulder line of the joint on the underside of the handrail. It can then be pulled out of the lower housing.

When a baluster is fitted into an open string, carefully prise off the moulding covering the end of the tread. Knock the bottom end of the baluster sideways out of its housing, then pull it downwards to disengage it from the handrail housing.

Fitting a new baluster

Mark the required length on the new baluster, then mark out and cut the ends, using the old baluster as a guide. Fit and fix the new baluster in the reverse order to the way the old one was removed.

To replace a baluster that is housed at both ends in a closed-string stair, first trim off the back corner of the top tenon (**1**), then place the bottom tenon in its housing and swing the top end of the baluster into position (**2**) and nail it to the handrail.

Building Regulations

Sensible staircase design prevents unnecessary accidents. The position and dimensions of balustrades and handrails are therefore governed by the Building Regulations.

Essential dimensions

Building Regulations stipulate that the height of a stair balustrade must be no less than 900mm (3ft) and no more than 1m (3ft 3in), the measurement being taken vertically (**1**) from the pitch line (**2**) – the imaginary line formed by the stair nosings. Similarly, a balustrade protecting a landing or upper floor (**3**) must be no less than 900mm (3ft) high.The spaces between the balusters or balustrade rails should not allow a 100mm (4in) sphere to pass between them at any point (**4**), and children must not be able to climb the barrier.

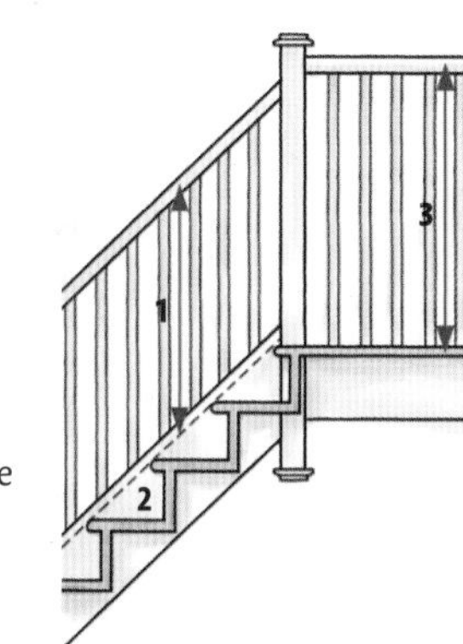

Balustrade with balusters
Can be used with closed or cut-string stairs. The pitch line is shown as a dotted line.

Staircase width

The Regulations require a staircase less than 1m (3ft 3in) wide to have at least one handrail; stairs wider than this must have two – one on each side. If the staircase is less than a 1m (3ft 3in) wide and has 'winders' (tapered treads), a handrail must be provided on the side where the treads are widest.

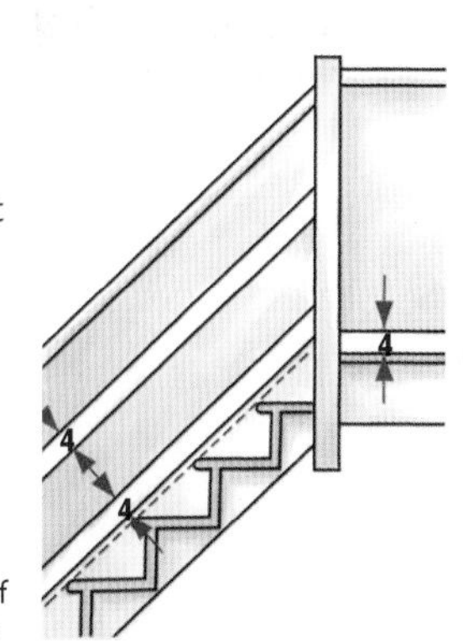

Balustrade with rails
To comply with the Regulations, this type of balustrade is used with a closed string only.

Mending a baluster

A baluster that has split along the grain can generally be repaired *in situ*. Open the split up carefully and work PVA glue into it, then squeeze the parts together and wipe any surplus glue from the surface with a damp rag. Bind the repair tightly with self-adhesive tape until the glue has set (right). Remove the binding and sand the repair smooth.

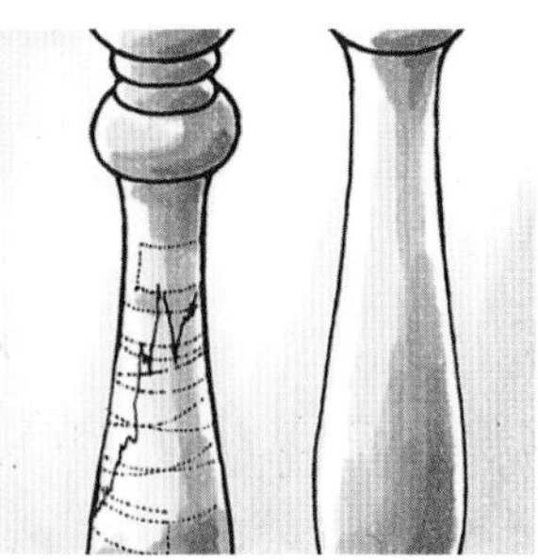

Apply glue to a split baluster and reinforce the repair with tape

SEE ALSO > Strings 209

Fitting a handrail

Handrails in hardwood and softwood, including curved sections used to change the direction of the handrail, are available from specialist joinery suppliers. The various parts are bolted together, using special steel handrail bolts; the assembled rails are then fixed to the wall with handrail brackets.

Handrail components
In addition to ordinary handrail mouldings, you can buy special matched components such as turns, ramps and caps. These are joined to straight sections with steel handrail bolts.

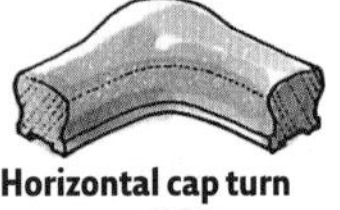
Horizontal cap turn

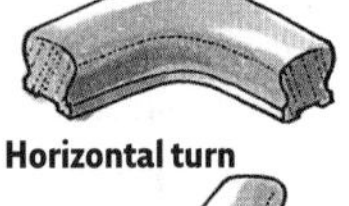
Horizontal turn

Opening cap

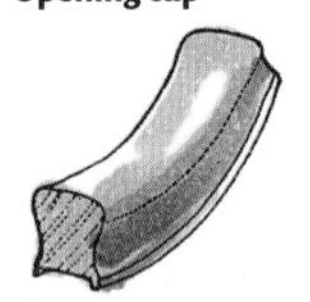
Concave ramp

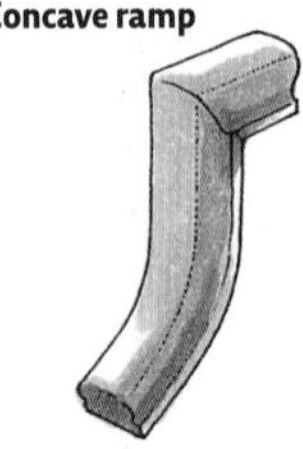
Goose neck

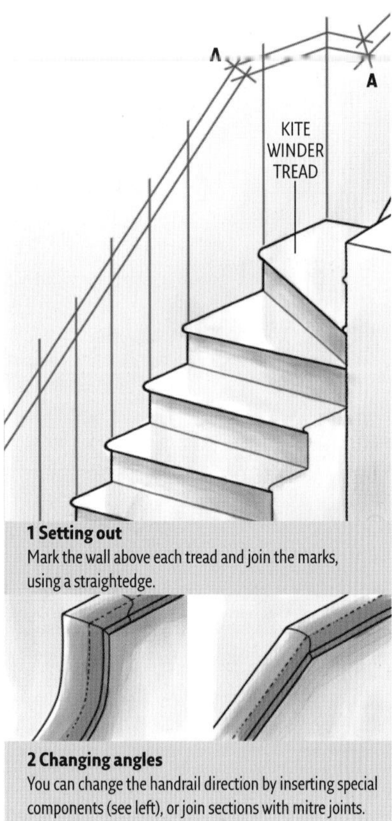

1 Setting out
Mark the wall above each tread and join the marks, using a straightedge.

2 Changing angles
You can change the handrail direction by inserting special components (see left), or join sections with mitre joints.

Measuring and marking

Mark a line on the wall to represent the top of the handrail, gauging the height in accordance with the Building Regulations. On a straight flight, set out the line by marking a series of points measured vertically from the nosing of each tread. Where tapered treads occur, take the same measurement from the central kite winder tread and the landing above (1).

Marking out

Using a straightedge, join up the marks to produce the line of the handrail; then draw a second line below and parallel to it at a distance equal to the thickness of the handrail. Where the rail changes direction, draw lines across the intersections (A) to find the angles at which the components must be cut (2).

Measure the run of the handrail and buy the required lengths, including special sections such as turns, ramps and the opening cap (see far left). Buy enough handrail brackets so you can space them at intervals of about 1m (3ft 3in).

Assembling and fitting

Cut the components to the correct lengths and angles, then dowel and glue short sections together, or use handrail bolts. These require clearance holes to be drilled in the ends of each component, and housings to be cut in the undersides for the nuts. If you are using handrail bolts, you will also need to fit locating dowels (3) to stop the sections rotating as they are pulled together. Assemble the handrail in manageable sections.

Screw the brackets to the rail and hold it against the wall while a helper marks the fixing holes. Drill and plug the wall. Then screw the handrail in place using No10 or No12 screws at least 63mm (2½in) long – long enough to make a secure fixing in the masonry and not just into the plaster (4).

Rub down the handrail and finish it with clear varnish or paint.

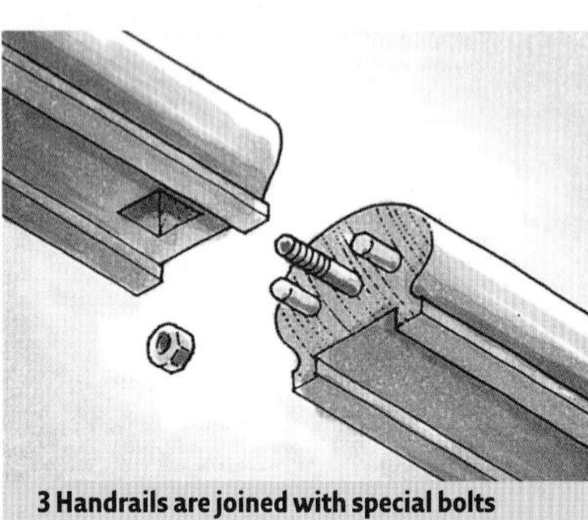
3 Handrails are joined with special bolts

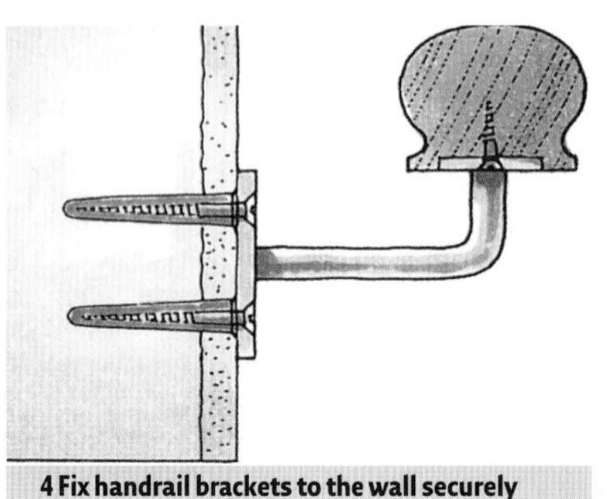
4 Fix handrail brackets to the wall securely

Fixing a loose balustrade

If the whole balustrade – including the handrail and newel post – feels loose, that usually indicates a breakdown of the joints between the steps and the outer string. You should attend to it as soon as possible, before someone leans heavily against the balustrade and the whole structure collapses.

To refix a loose string, first of all remove the wedges from the tread and riser housings. Then, having injected some glue into the joints, work along the face of the string with a hammer and wood block to knock it back into place and reseat the joints (1). If the string tends to spring away, hold it in place with lengths of timber braced between it and the opposite wall (2). Secure the joints by driving in glued hardwood wedges.

Reinforce the joint between the bottom step and the newel post with glued blocks rubbed into the angle on the underside of the staircase. Alternatively, screw metal angle plates into the corners (3).

1 Use a hammer and block to reseat joints

2 Brace the string against the opposite wall

3 Reinforce the bottom joint

SEE ALSO > Stair construction 209, Loose housing joints 212, Building Regulations 213

Replacing a balustrade

While the staircase contributes greatly to the character of a house, the character of the staircase itself is to a large extent determined by the design of the balustrade.

Older houses were often fitted with attractive decorative features such as turned newel posts and balusters, but over the years many of these old balustrades have been modernized.

Sometimes this has been done by simply panelling over the open balusters, sometimes by replacing turned balusters with straight ones, and sometimes even by cutting away all the balusters to achieve an open-plan appearance, perhaps with the addition of one or more intermediate rails or some open wrought ironwork.

Aesthetics apart, the latter arrangement does not comply with the current Building Regulations, and a new balustrade should be fitted for your own safety.

It is perfectly possible to carry out this work yourself (see right), but if you are unsure of your ability to do the job properly and safely, it is better to call in a professional carpenter to carry it out for you. This will ensure that the new balustrade is completely safe and that it conforms to the Building Regulations.

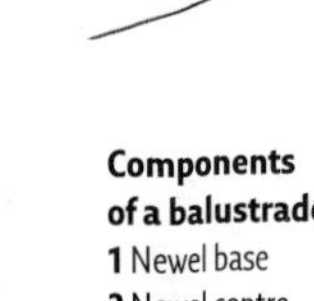

Components of a balustrade
1 Newel base
2 Newel centre
3 Decorative knob
4 Turned balusters
5 Handrail
6 Base rail
7 Spacer fillets
8 Metal brackets
9 Cover buttons

Using a kit to replace a balustrade

A typical kit consists of newel posts made up of three parts - a base section (**1**), a turned centre section (**2**) and a decorative knob (**3**) - plus turned balusters (**4**) and a handrail (**5**) and a machine-grooved base rail (**6**) in which to fit them. Spacer fillets (**7**) fill the gaps between the balusters. There are special metal brackets (**8**) for joining the ends of the handrails to the posts. Most types of balustrade can be constructed from a kit of parts; a straight flight is shown below as a typical example.

Preparation

Strip off any old hardboard or plywood panelling, and remove old balusters and handrails that aren't suitable.

Fitting newel posts

The simplest way to replace damaged or modified newels is to cut them off, leaving intact the joints between their bases and the outer string. Then mark diagonal lines across the cut ends to find their centres, and drill out central holes to receive the spigots on the ends of the new posts. Set the new posts in position, but don't yet glue them.

Fitting the rails

With a sliding bevel, take the angle of the stair string where it meets the base of the newel. Hold the balustrade base rail against the staircase, following the angle of the string exactly, and make a mark at each end where it meets the newels. Mark out mitres at these points, using the bevel and a try square, and cut the rail to length.

Mark and cut the handrail to length in the same way, or use the base rail as a guide if it's the same length. Screw the base rail to the string. Then fit the handrail, using the special handrail brackets bolted to the newel posts; take up the slack with a spanner.

Check that the newels are upright and that the rails fit properly, then glue the newels in place, using a PVA woodworking adhesive or, if the joints are slack, a gap-filling synthetic-resin glue. Tighten the handrail-bracket bolts; and when the adhesive has set, fit cover buttons (**9**) to conceal the nuts.

Balusters
A range of typical hardwood and softwood balusters.

Fitting the balusters

Calculate the number of balusters you need; allow for two per tread, except for the tread adjacent to the bottom newel post, where you will need only one. In any event, none of the components should be spaced more than 100mm (4in) apart. To find out how many infill fillets will be required, double the number of balusters and add four.

Next, measure the vertical distance between the groove in the handrail and the groove in the base rail, then transfer this dimension to a baluster. Mark it out, using the sliding bevel to achieve the exact angle. Cut the baluster to size and check it for fit, then cut the others to suit and sand them ready for finishing.

Pin and glue in place the balusters and precut spacer fillets. When the adhesive has set, finish the bare wood with paint or with coloured wood dye and clear varnish.

SEE ALSO > Stair construction 209, Building Regulations 213, Pitch line 213

Architectural mouldings

Interior wooden mouldings – generally referred to as architectural mouldings – are a legacy of the classically proportioned panelled walls found in grand houses. They include moulded skirting boards, dado rails, picture rails and decorative cornice mouldings. Mouldings are usually made from selected softwood, certain hardwoods, or from MDF which is often factory-primed ready for painting.

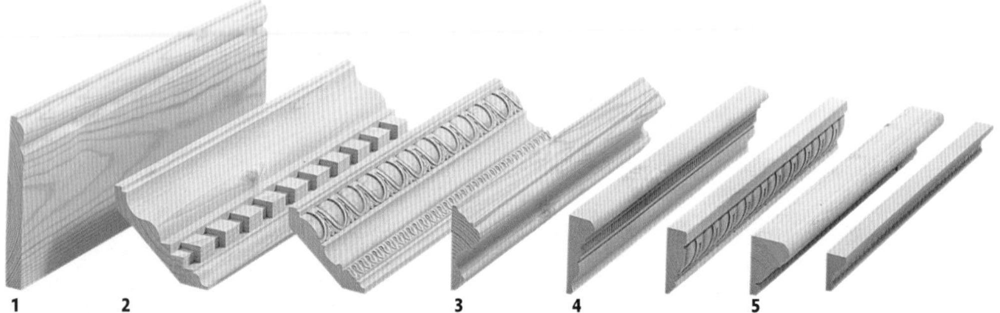

Types of moulding
1 Torus skirting
2 Cornice mouldings
3 Straight-run dado rail
4 Carved dado mouldings
5 Small dado mouldings

Types of moulding

Skirtings

Architectural mouldings are primarily functional, but they also contribute to the visual style and proportion of a room. A relatively tall skirting acts as a base to the composition, in a similar way to the base of a classical column.

Dado rails

The dado rail, also known as a chair rail, is a reference to the waist-high dado panelling of earlier times. It provides a rubbing strip to protect the wall finish from chair backs and forms a border for textured wallcoverings.

Picture rails

Like the dado moulding, the picture rail is an echo from the earlier panelled walls. It is usually set about 300 to 500mm (1ft to 1ft 8in) below the ceiling cornice to form a frieze. Picture-rail mouldings have a groove in the top edge to hold hooks for hanging pictures.

Cornice mouldings

Cornice mouldings form a bold decorative feature where the walls of a room meet the ceiling, and can be likened to the decorative capital of a column. These mouldings are usually made from plaster, but are sometimes made from wood. Ornate mouldings are made in standard lengths with premitred external and pre-scribed internal corner pieces.

Making corner joints

When moulded profiles meet at a corner, it is necessary to mitre the ends where they meet. Alternatively, for an internal corner only, you can scribe one end to fit over the moulded profile of the other. Some mouldings are pre-scribed. Cut mitres using a tenon saw and mitre box, or a mitre saw. To scribe the end of a moulding, first mitre it; and then, with a coping saw, cut away the waste, following the line formed by the face and the mitred end (**1**). For larger mouldings, mark the profile on the back face, using an offcut as a template (**2**). Saw off the waste with the teeth of the coping saw facing backward, to prevent breakout of the fibres on the face of the moulding.

1 Cut along the line between mitre and profile

2 Use an offcut as a template

Fixing architectural mouldings

On a masonry wall, you can use nails, nailable plugs or woodscrews driven into wallplugs. If it is a cavity wall, drive nails or screws into the wooden studs, but use cavity fixings elsewhere. Alternatively, use gun-applied panel adhesive in all cases.

Some mouldings have a groove machined along the back to fit onto plastic clips screwed to the wall. This offers an invisible fixing that does not require filling. Simply set the clips on a levelled marked line and attach the mouldings.

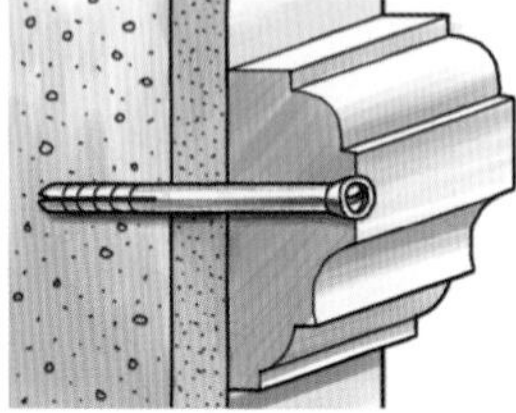
Nailable-plug fixing

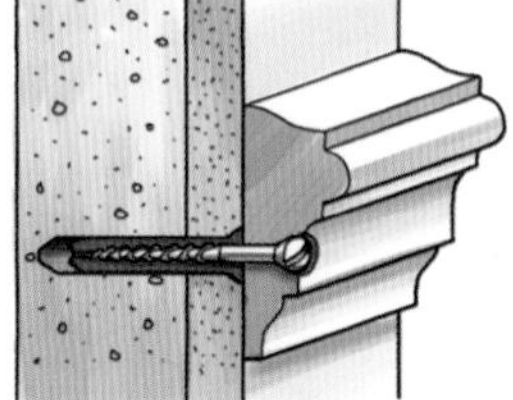
Plug-and-screw fixing

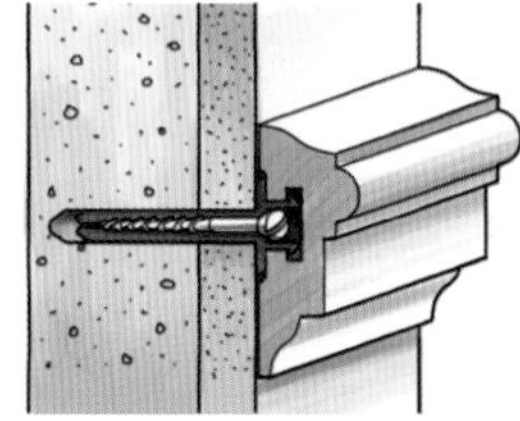
Plastic-clip fixing

SEE ALSO > Replacing skirtings 218, Wall fixings 535–6

Fitting architraves

An architrave moulding provides a decorative frame to a door, as well as concealing the joint between the door lining and the wall. Similar mouldings are used around sliding-sash windows. Standard architrave mouldings are stocked by DIY stores and timber merchants, but a variety of more elaborate and wider-than-average mouldings can be obtained from specialist joinery suppliers. If there's a particular profile you want to replicate, you can have mouldings machined to that pattern.

Fixing standard architraves

Hold a short length of the architrave moulding about 6mm (¼in) above the door opening; after checking that it is level, mark its width on the wall and on the front face of the door lining. Next, hold one slightly overlength upright in position, approximately 6mm (¼in) from the face of the door jamb. Transfer the marks previously made on the wall above to it (1).

Cut a 45-degree mitre on the marked end; then, using a spirit level to keep the upright vertical, nail it to the door jamb, inserting 500mm (2in) lost-head nails every 300mm (1ft) or so. Don't drive the nails in fully at this stage, in case you need to move the architrave. Cut and fix the second upright on the other side, using the same procedure.

Rest the top section of architrave upside down on the ends of the uprights and mark its length (2). Cut a mitre at each end and nail the moulding between the uprights (3). Drive a nail through the top edge into the mitred joint at each end (4). Drive all the nails below the surface with a nail set, then fill the holes and joints and sand them flush before priming and painting the woodwork.

If the architrave is hardwood and you are planning to finish it with a clear varnish, fill the nail holes with a coloured wood filler.

1 Mark the length of the upright

2 Mark the length of the top moulding

3 Nail the moulding to the door lining

4 Drive a nail into the mitred joint

Classical architraves

A classical-style architrave comprises a fluted moulding with decorative top and bottom blocks that avoid the need to cut mitre joints in the moulding. Some are made as kits for fixing with hidden plastic clips, but you can make your own from separate components and nail them in place to the door frame. It's not always necessary to fit skirting blocks.

However, if you are using skirting blocks, they should be fitted first (1). The upright architrave mouldings are then centred on them and fixed with nails. You will first have to calculate their length and cut the ends square, making an allowance for the top blocks. Fix the top blocks in place, centred over the architrave moulding (2). When both sides of the doorway are complete, measure the distance between the top blocks and cut the horizontal architrave moulding to fit, then nail it in place.

1 Nail skirting blocks

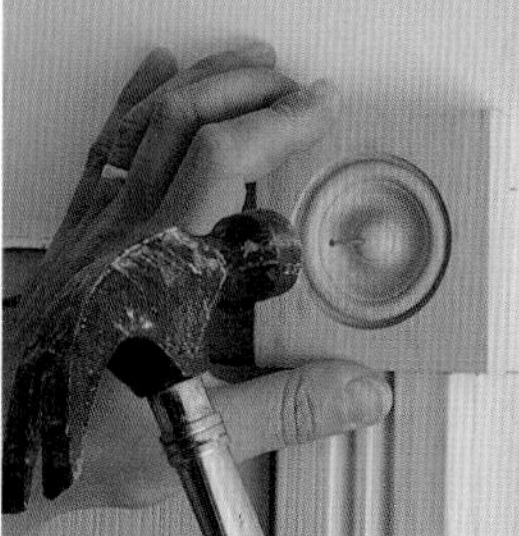

2 Pin the corner block

Out-of-square frames

If you are restoring an older house, you may find the doorways are out of square, and so 45-degree mitres will not butt together accurately.

In this situation, hold each architrave component in position parallel with the frame and mark along the edges (1). Mark a diagonal line where the lines cross (2), to give the required angle for the corner joint. Set an adjustable bevel to this angle, transfer it to the architrave components, and cut them accordingly.

1 Mark parallel lines

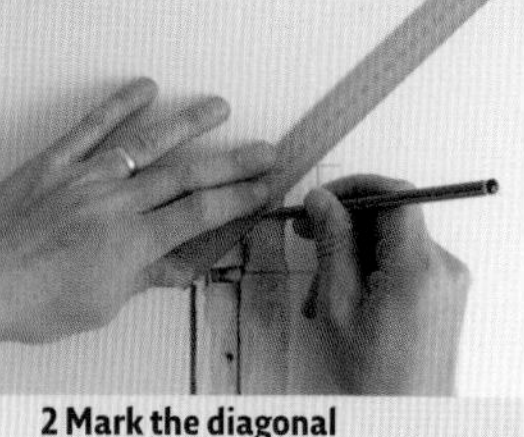

2 Mark the diagonal

SEE ALSO > Mitre joint 509, Tenon saw 488, Spirit level 511

Replacing skirtings

Skirtings are protective 'kick boards', usually moulded to form a decorative border between the floor and walls. Modern skirtings are relatively small and simply formed, with a rounded or bevelled top edge. Skirting repairs or replacement are an inevitable consequence of major repairs to a floor.

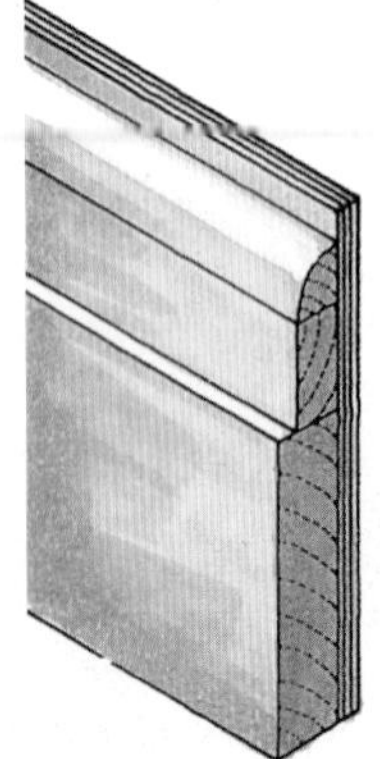

Making a skirting
If you are unable to find a length of skirting to match your original, have one machined or make one from various sections of wood.

In older houses, skirtings can be as tall as 300mm (1ft) and quite elaborately moulded. In most homes they are about 175mm (7in) tall and of either ovolo, torus, bevelled or rounded design. You can buy traditional skirtings from timber merchants, and some will supply more elaborate designs to special order. Traditionally skirting boards are nailed either directly to plastered masonry or to battens, known as 'grounds', fixed in place during the plastering stage. On partition walls they are nailed to the studs.

Removing the skirting

Lever the skirting board away from the wall. A continuous length of skirting, with ends that are mitred into internal corners, may have to be cut before it can be removed.

Tap the blade of a bolster between the skirting and the wall, and lever the top edge away sufficiently to insert the tip of a crowbar. Place a thin strip of wood behind the crowbar to protect the wall, then tap the bolster in again, a little to one side. Work along the skirting until the board is free.

Cutting a long skirting

A long stretch of skirting board may bend sufficiently for you to cut it *in situ*. Lever it away at its centre and insert blocks of wood, one on each side of the proposed cut, to hold the board about 25mm (1in) from the wall (**1**).

Make a vertical cut with a panel saw held at about 45 degrees to the face of the board (**2**). Saw with short strokes, using the tip of the blade only.

1 Prise skirting away from the wall and pack out

2 Cut through skirting with the tip of the saw

Standard skirting mouldings

Most standard skirting boards are made of softwood or MDF, ready for painting. Hardwoods are not so commonly used; they are usually reserved for special decorative mouldings and coated with a clear finish. Moulded-reverse skirtings are machined with a different profile on each side of the board.

Selection of skirting mouldings
1 Bevelled hardwood skirting
2 Bevelled/rounded reverse skirting
3 Torus/ovolo moulded-reverse skirting
4 Ovolo skirting
5 Torus skirting
6 Bolection skirting

Fitting a new skirting

Whenever possible, restore a damaged skirting, particularly if it is an unusual moulding for which there is no modern replacement. If that's not possible, you could try to make a replacement from standard moulded sections, all of which are readily available.

Cutting mitred joints

Measure the length of each wall, bearing in mind that most skirtings are mitred at the corners. Mark the length of the wall on the bottom edge of the new skirting, mark a 45-degree angle for the mitre, and extend the marked line across the face of the board, using a try square. Clamp the board on edge in a vice and carefully saw down the line at that angle, using a sharp panel saw.

Cutting scribed joints

Sometimes moulded skirting boards are scribed and butt-jointed at internal corners. To achieve the required profile, cut the end off one board at 45 degrees, as for a mitre joint (**1**); then, using a coping saw, cut along the contour line on the moulded face, so it will mate with its neighbour (**2**).

Fixing the boards

Use lost-head nails when attaching skirting boards to wooden grounds; but when nailing to brick or stone, fix the skirtings in place with cut clasp nails or masonry nails. Punch in the nailheads and fill the holes. It is also possible to fix skirtings with instant-grip adhesive, applied with a cartridge gun.

Saw a 45-degree mitre at the end

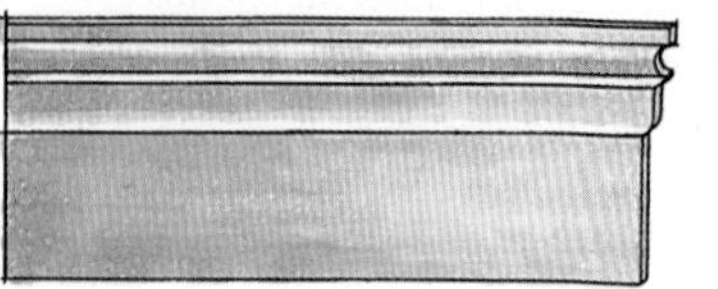

Cut the shape following the contour line

SEE ALSO > Finishing woodwork 70–81, Architectural mouldings 216, Try square 487, Panel saw 488, Coping saw 488–9, Nails 532

Interior panelling

Walls that are in poor condition – except those that are damp – can be covered with panelling to conceal them and to provide a decorative surface. Panelling can be practical in other ways, too, when used in conjunction with insulation.

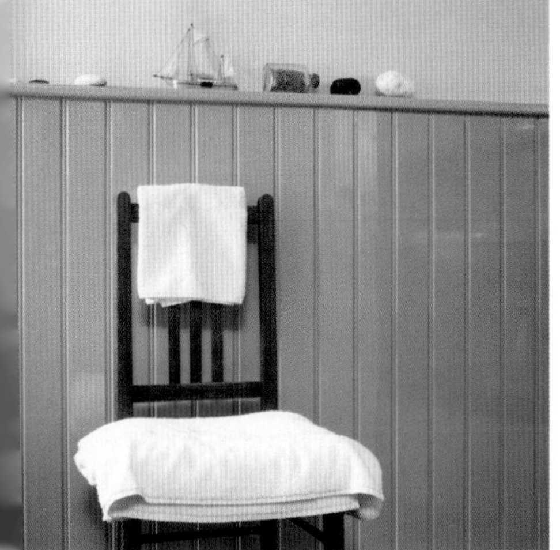

Tongue-and-groove boards

Solid-wood panelling is made from planks with a tongue along one edge and a matching groove on the other. The main function of this joint is to provide room for movement resulting from atmospheric changes, but it also allows for 'secret nailing' when fixing the planks to the wall.

The meeting edges of tongued, grooved and V-jointed (TGV) boards are machined to produce a decorative V-shaped profile, accentuating the junction between boards. Other types of tongue-and-groove boards have more-decorative profiles.

Shiplap has a rebate on the back face, which holds down the coved front edge of the next board.

Today a few hardwoods are available as panelling, but most boards are made from softwood (typically knotty pine).

Buy your boards in one batch

Make sure you buy enough TGV boards to complete the work. Boards from another batch may not be compatible, because the machine used to shape their edge joints was set to slightly different tolerances.

Tongue-and-groove planks are sold by most timber merchants in various lengths up to 3m (10ft); nominal dimensions are 100 x 12mm (4 x ½in). Prepacked bundles are available from some stockists.

Constructing a framework for panelling

Because most solid walls are fairly uneven, it is necessary to construct a frame from furring strips (softwood battens).

Before you start, carefully prise off the skirting boards, picture rails and coving, so that you can refix these on the panelling, if required. Erect the framework using 50 x 25mm (2 x 1in) planed or sawn softwood battens that have been treated with a proprietary wood preserver.

You can reduce heat loss through an external wall by fitting insulation between the furring strips. If you do this, staple polythene sheeting over the furring strips to act as a vapour barrier.

The battens should be fixed 400mm (1ft 4in) apart, using 50mm (2in) masonry nails or screws and wallplugs. Use a builder's spirit level to align each batten with its neighbour in order to produce a vertical flat plane. Pack out any hollows behind the furring strips, using card or thin strips of hardboard.

You can erect TGV boards horizontally or diagonally, but if you prefer traditional vertical panelling you should run the furring strips horizontally. Fit the lowest strip level with the top of the skirting, with short vertical strips below it for attaching a length of skirting board.

Vertical TGV panelling
Furring strips run horizontally across the wall.

Tongue-and-groove boards
Various profiles are machined from solid wood:
1 Moulded tongued, grooved and V-jointed (TGV)
2 Tongued, grooved and V-jointed
3 Rebated shiplap

Fixing the panelling

Mark out and saw the boards to length, then sand the outer surfaces smooth. With the grooved edge butted against the left-hand wall, plumb the first board with a spirit level. Nail it to the strips through the centre of its face, using 25mm (1in) panel pins.

Slide the next board onto the tongue and, protecting the edge with a strip of wood, tap it in place with a hammer. Fix to the battens by driving a pin at an angle through the inner corner of the tongue (**1**). Punch the head below the surface. Slide on the next board to hide the fixings (**2**), and nail it as before.

Use up short lengths of boarding by butting them end to end over a furring strip, but stagger such joints across the wall to avoid a continuous line.

When you reach the other end of the wall, you may have to cut the last board down its length to fit the gap. Nail it through its face. If it's a tight fit, spring the last two boards in at the same time: slot the penultimate board's groove onto the exposed tongue, and then push both into position. Pin a small quadrant cover strip down the vertical edges, nail the skirting in place, and fit a ceiling coving to conceal the edges of the boards.

1 Drive nails in at an angle through the tongue

2 Slide the next board onto the nailed tongue

SEE ALSO > Stud partitions 140, Woodworm 242, Insulant 261, 266, Vapour barriers 261, 266

Panelling details

Panelling a single plain wall is relatively simple, but if you want to clad adjacent walls with wood panelling, you will have to cope with corners. There may also be doors and windows or electrical fittings to deal with.

• **Panelling a ceiling**
It is relatively straightforward to panel a ceiling with TGV boards, following the methods described for cladding a wall. First locate the joists, then nail or screw the furring strips across them, ready to receive the boards. Finish the edges of the ceiling with timber coving.

To panel adjacent walls, shape the solid-wood strips to make neat internal or external corners.

Internal corners

Where two boards meet in an internal corner, cut the first board and nail it through its face onto the furring strips. Plane a chamfer along the meeting edge of the adjacent board, then pin that board to the furring strips.

External corners

To join the boards at an external corner, lap one board over the other and pin them together. Plane a chamfer on the outer corner for a neat finish.

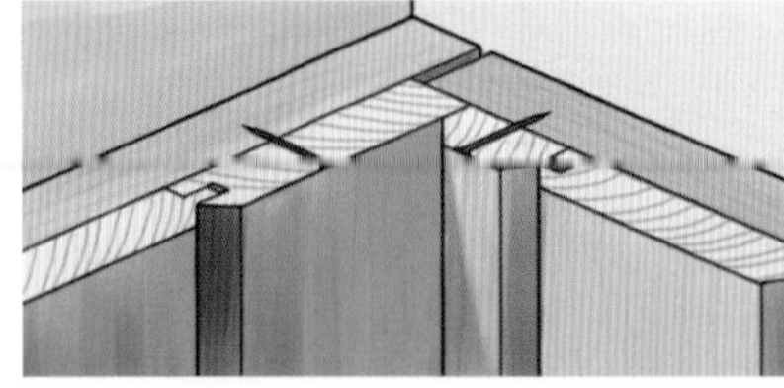

Fit chamfered board to make an internal corner

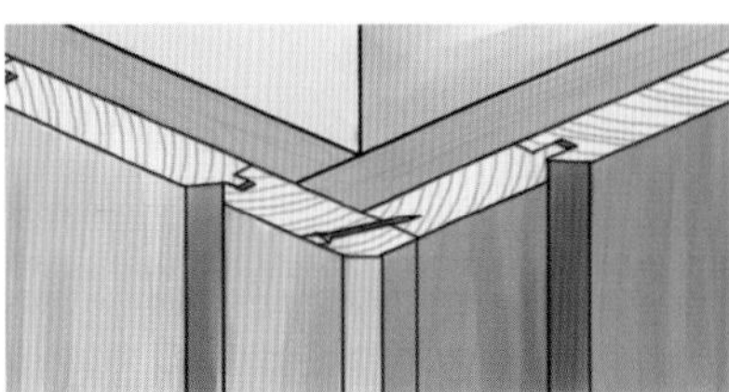

Lap one board over the other at an internal corner

Panelling around doors

It's possible to panel around doors and windows using similar techniques, but window reveals and sill mouldings add complications that make it a less practicable proposition.

When you panel up to a door, start by removing the architrave. Then nail vertical furring strips on both sides of the door so they just lap the frame (1). Continue by nailing the usual horizontal furring strips to the wall, with their ends butted up against the vertical strips on either side of the door (2). Nail one furring strip across the top of the doorframe.

Fix the panelling in place and cover the board edges and the furring strips with thin strips of wood (3).

Refit the original architraves (4) on top of the panelling. Paint the architraves, the cover strips and the doorframe to match.

1 Remove architraves and nail on vertical strips

2 Add horizontal strips at either side

3 Fix the panelling and cover the vertical strips

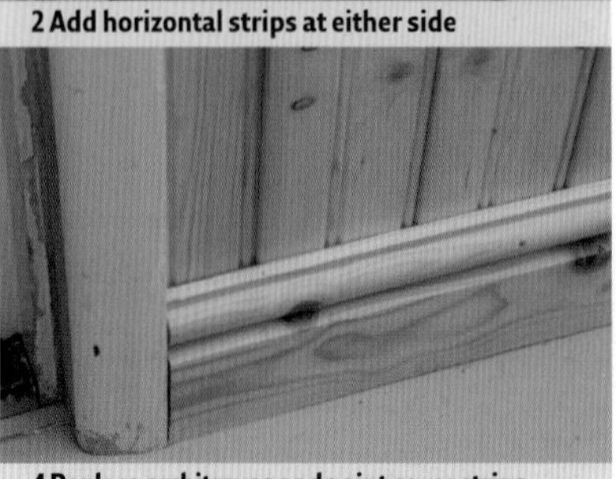

4 Replace architraves and paint cover strips

Dealing with electrics

Existing socket outlets and light switches must be adapted to fit the newly panelled wall. You can either refix surface-mounted fittings on the face of the new panelling or leave the fittings where they are and simply panel around them so their faceplates project through the panelling. Flush-mounted fittings need to be brought forward so that they are flush with the new surface.

Flush fittings

Turn off the power at the mains, then unscrew and disconnect the faceplate. There should be enough slack in the cable for you to be able to extract the metal mounting box from its recess in the wall and then move it slightly to one side. Screw the box to the face of the wall so that it will lie flush with the finished panelling. Nail short battens all round it.

Alternatively, fix the mounting box to the panelling itself, using a plastic box of the type used on hollow partition walls. These have flanges that project from two sides of the box and grip the rear face of the panelling when the box is inserted in a matching cutout.

Surface-mounted fittings

Nail short battens on each side of the cable to take the screws that hold the mounting box to the wall. Drill a hole in the panelling, pass the cable through, and then screw the mounting box to the battens. After wiring, fit the faceplate.

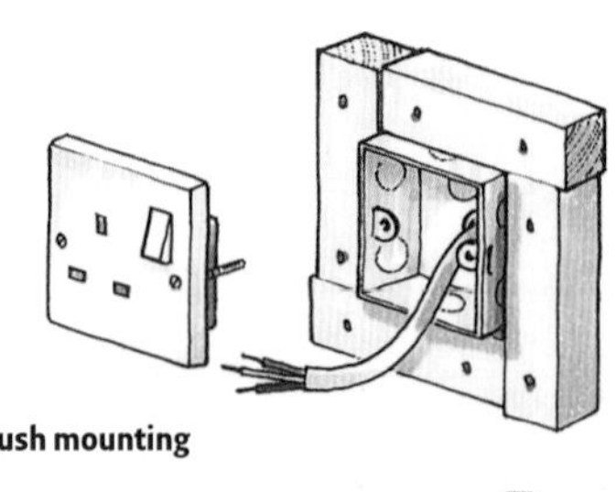

Flush mounting

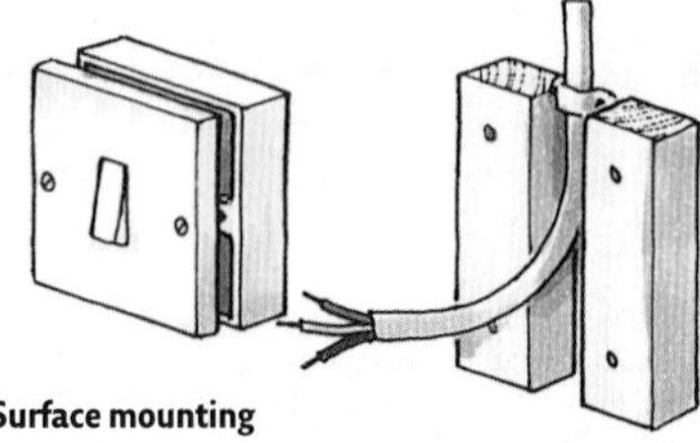

Surface mounting

SEE ALSO > Scribing 164, Turning off power 296

Storage

Shelving

Shelving can be anything from a set of chipboard or MDF planks on functional brackets to elegant spans of solid wood or plate glass on decorative supports. It is generally the cheapest and simplest form of storage you can find; and if you opt for an adjustable system, you can adapt your shelving to suit future requirements.

Wall-hung shelves

Shelves can be fixed in an alcove on support battens, or cantilevered off a wall with any one of a wide range of shelving brackets. The brackets may be made from pressed, cast or wrought steel or from moulded or extruded alloy.

Adjustable shelving systems have brackets that slot or clip into upright metal supports screwed to the wall. Most uprights have holes or slots at close intervals that take fixing lugs on the rear of each bracket. In one system, the upright is made with a continuous groove over its entire length, so that the brackets can be placed at any level.

One advantage of such systems is that the weight and stress of even heavily loaded shelves are distributed down the supporting uprights. Another factor in their favour is that once the uprights are in place shelving arrangements can be changed easily, and you can add extra shelves as the need arises without having to add extra fixings.

Use cheap, functional pressed-metal shelving for utilitarian purposes - in your garage or workshop, for example - and choose the more expensive and attractive bracket designs for your storage needs around the house.

Alcove shelves

The simplest way to make built-in open shelves is to fit them in alcoves, such as those flanking a chimney breast. However, you'll probably find the surface of the walls is not perfectly regular, and so you may have to trim each shelf to fit perfectly.

Fitting fixed shelves
Use slim battens fixed to the side walls of the alcove to support the shelves. You can add an extra batten to the back wall if they will carry a heavy load, such as books.

Fitting adjustable shelves
If you need your shelving to be adjustable to accommodate changing storage needs, the best solution is to use a track-and-bracket system that allows you to position the shelves at whatever level you require. The tracks are fixed to the wall at spacings to suit the shelf material and the load, and the brackets are slotted into them.

SEE ALSO > Putting up wall-mounted shelving 224–6

Choosing shelf materials

Ready-cut shelves made from solid timber or man-made board are available from DIY stores in a range of standard sizes. The latter are usually prepainted or covered with plastic or wood veneer. Shelves manufactured from glass or painted pressed steel are also widely available. If the standard range of shelving doesn't meet your requirements, make your own, using the following materials.

Materials for shelving

Solid wood

Softwood usually contains knots unless it is specially selected. Parana pine, however, is generally knot-free, has attractive colouring and is available in wide boards, but is relatively expensive.

Hardwoods, such as oak, beech, ash and possibly mahogany and teak, are available from some timber merchants, but their high cost limits their use to special features and furniture.

Blockboard

Blockboard is a relatively expensive stable man-made board constructed from strips of softwood glued and sandwiched between two layers of plywood-grade veneer. Blockboard is as strong as solid wood, provided the shelving is cut with the core running lengthways. You will need to lip the raw edges with veneer or solid wood to cover the core.

Plywood

Plywood is built up from veneers, with the grain alternating at right angles in order to provide strength and stability. The edges can either be left exposed or covered with a solid-wood lipping or veneer.

Chipboard

Being the cheapest man-made board, chipboard is frequently used for the core of manufactured veneered shelving planks. Chipboard shelves are liable to bend under sustained loads unless they're supported properly at the required bracket spacings.

Medium-density fibreboard

Medium-density fibreboard (MDF) is a dense, stable man-made board that is easy to cut and machine. It finishes smoothly on all edges and doesn't need to be lipped. MDF is ideal for painting or veneering.

Glass

Plate glass is an elegant material for display shelving. Use toughened glass, which is available to special order. Have it cut to size and the edges ground and polished by the supplier. Textured or wired glass can also make attractive shelving.

Choosing the correct span

Solid timber or blockboard, with its core running lengthways, is best for sturdy shelving – but a shelf made from either material will sag if its supports are too far apart. Veneered chipboard, though popular because of its low cost, availability and appearance, will eventually sag under relatively light loads, so it needs supporting at closer intervals than solid wood. Moving the supports in from each end of a shelf helps to distribute the load and reduces the risk of sagging.

The chart shows recommended maximum spans for shelves made from different materials. If you want to increase the length of the shelf, then either move the supports closer together, add another bracket, use thicker material, or stiffen its front edge.

RECOMMENDED SHELF SPANS

Material	Thickness	Light load	Medium load	Heavy load
Solid wood	18mm (¾in)	800mm (2ft 8in)	750mm (2ft 6in)	700mm (2ft 4in)
Blockboard/Plywood	18mm (¾in)	800mm (2ft 8in)	750mm (2ft 6in)	700mm (2ft 4in)
Chipboard	16mm (⅝in)	750mm (2ft 6in)	600mm (2ft)	450mm (1ft 6in)
MDF	18mm (¾in)	800mm (2ft 8in)	750mm (2ft 6in)	700mm (2ft 4in)
Glass	6mm (¼in)	700mm (2ft 4in)	Not applicable	Not applicable

Stiffening your shelves

A wooden batten, lipping or metal extrusion fixed to the underside or front edge of a shelf will increase its stiffness. Where appropriate, a wall-fixed batten may be fitted in order to support the back edge. A deep wooden front rail can be used to conceal a strip-light fitting; metal strip reinforcements are slimmer and much less noticeable.

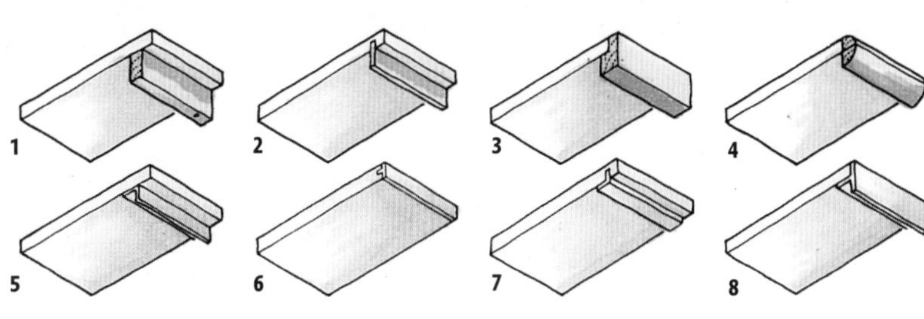

Wooden stiffeners
1 Wooden batten
2 Plywood strip
3 Rebated batten
4 Half-round lipping

Metal stiffeners
5 Screwed angle
6 Grooved T-section
7 Grooved angle
8 Screwed T-section

SEE ALSO > Wood and boards 528–9, Sawing wood 489, Cutting metal 518

Fitting shelves in alcoves

Alcoves – usually found at each side of a central chimney breast – are an ideal place to build shelves, as the alcove walls provide somewhere on which to fix the individual shelf supports. The only problem you may encounter is that alcove walls may not be at true right angles to each other.

- **The right screw**
Use screws 38mm (1½in) longer than the batten thickness for lightly loaded shelves, and ones 50mm (2in) longer for heavily laden shelves.

- **Check for cables**
If there is a wall light or socket outlet in the alcove, use a cable detector to track the cable route so you can avoid drilling through it. Expect cables to run vertically up or down the wall to the light or socket outlet.

- **Hide any gaps**
If your alcoves are not perfectly square, hide any gaps by sticking lengths of slim quadrant beading into the wall-shelf angle.

Fixing the battens

Shelves that will carry only light loads need a support batten at each end. Add a batten along the rear wall, too, for bookshelves. Use 50 x 19mm (2 x ¾in) or 50 x 25mm (2 x 1in) planed softwood.

Start by measuring the width of the alcove and cut the rear batten 10mm (⅜in) shorter than this measurement. Cut the side battens 50mm (2in) shorter than the depth of the shelves you intend to fit, and trim their ends at 45° so they will be less noticeable when installed (**1**).

Drill screw clearance holes through the face of each batten at about 300mm (12in) centres. Then drill two holes right through the depth of the side battens so you can screw the shelves to the battens later (**2**). Countersink all the holes.

Decide on the position of the first shelf and hold the rear batten up to the mark with a spirit level on top. When it's level, mark the wall through one end hole with a twist drill bit (**3**). Switch to a masonry bit, remove the batten and drill the hole. Plug it and drive the first screw in far enough to support the batten.

Raise the rear batten so it is level with the pencil line and mark the positions of the other fixing holes. Let the batten drop out of the way so you can drill and plug the holes (**4**), then raise it level and drive in all the fixing screws.

Hold the first side batten in line with the rear batten, level it and mark the wall below it as a guide (**5**). Mark the screw holes on the wall, drill and plug them and fix the batten in place. Repeat this for the second batten.

Fixing the shelves

Measure the alcove width at the front and back, and mark the shelf width to the smaller measurement. Cut the shelf to size, rest it on the battens, hold it down and drive two screws up into each end of the shelf through the clearance holes you drilled earlier in the battens to lock it securely in place (**6**).

Repeat this sequence of operations to fix the other shelves in the alcove.

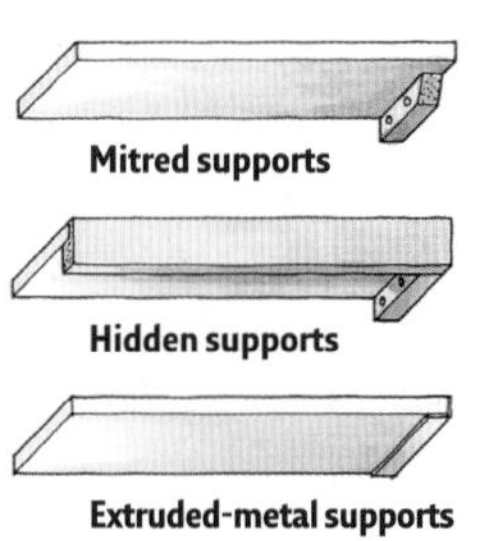

Mitred supports

Hidden supports

Extruded-metal supports

1 Cut side battens to length and angle the ends

2 Drill holes through the face and depth

3 Level the batten and mark the fixing holes

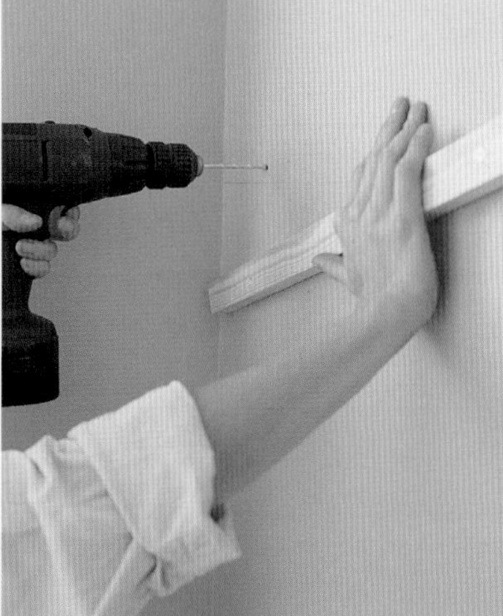

4 Drill the fixing holes for the rear batten

5 Level both side battens and mark the wall

6 Drive in screws to secure the shelf

SEE ALSO > Power drills 500, Drilling masonry 512, Masonry bits 512, Wall fixings 535–6

Fitting shelves with brackets

If you need just a single shelf in a particular location, the best way of supporting it is to use individual shelf brackets. These are available in a wide range of styles from ornate to utilitarian, and are screwed to the wall and the underside of the shelf. Strip supports that grip the rear edge of the shelf are another option.

Attaching the brackets

Start by choosing the material and size for your shelf, and select the bracket spacing to match the shelf width and likely load, using the chart earlier in this section. Select brackets with a horizontal arm equal to at least three-quarters of the shelf width.

Position the brackets on the underside of the shelf at the required spacing, with the end brackets about one quarter of the shelf width in from the ends. See below for the bracket positions if you are fixing the shelf to a timber-framed wall. Make sure their rear faces are aligned with the back edge of the shelf, and make pilot holes at the screw positions. Screw each bracket to the shelf, using relatively short screws that will penetrate no more than three-quarters of the shelf thickness (**1**).

Making wall fixings

You can fix the shelf anywhere on a masonry wall. Hold the shelf in position and make a mark on the wall through one fixing hole (**2**). Drill the hole with a masonry drill bit (**3**) and fit a wallplug.

Push a screw through the same fixing hole you used to mark the wall, locate it in the wallplug and drive it partway in to take the weight of the shelf while you do the levelling (**4**).

Hold the shelf up with one hand and place a spirit level on top. Adjust the shelf until it is truly level, then mark the other fixing screw positions on the wall (**5**). Undo the supporting screw and set the shelf aside. Drill and plug the remaining screw holes, lift the shelf into position and drive in all the screws (**6**).

Timber-framed walls

If you are fixing your shelf to a timber-framed wall, you can attach it anywhere using expanding metal wall anchors (but not plastic fixing devices) if it will be lightly laden. For heavy loads, you need to screw the brackets directly to the vertical frame members (the studs). These are usually at 400mm (1ft 4in) centres. You can locate them using a cable and stud detector (see below). Position the shelf brackets to match the stud spacings, and secure them with 50mm (2in) long screws. With brackets at these spacings, take care to select a shelf material that will not bow under the imposed load.

Using a cable detector

Before drilling any holes in a solid masonry wall, always check them for buried cables or pipework, using a battery-powered cable detector. This will also indicate the positions of the studs in timber-framed walls, by detecting the lines of nails fixing the plasterboard to the wall framework.

1 Screw the brackets to the underside of the shelf

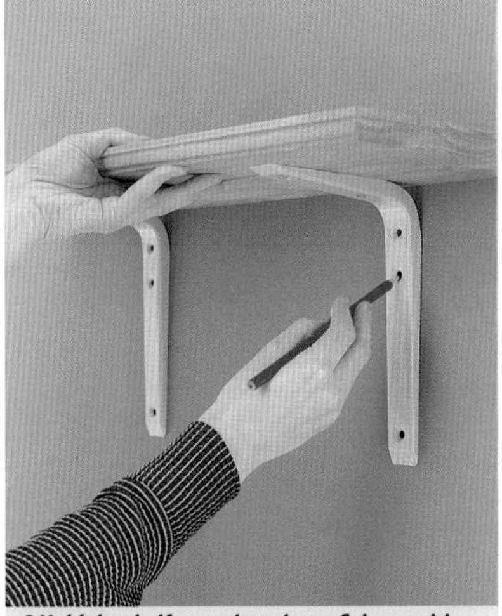

2 Hold the shelf up and mark one fixing position

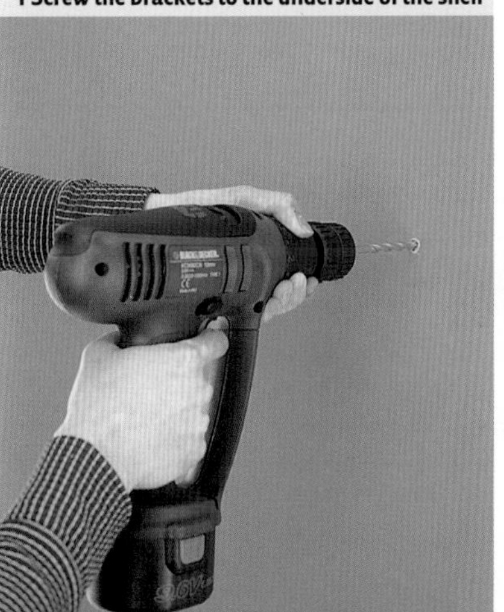

3 Drill and plug the hole for the first fixing screw

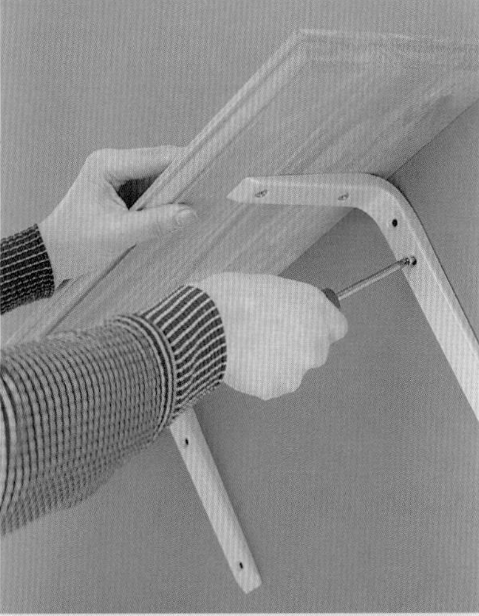

4 Drive in one screw to take the weight of the shelf

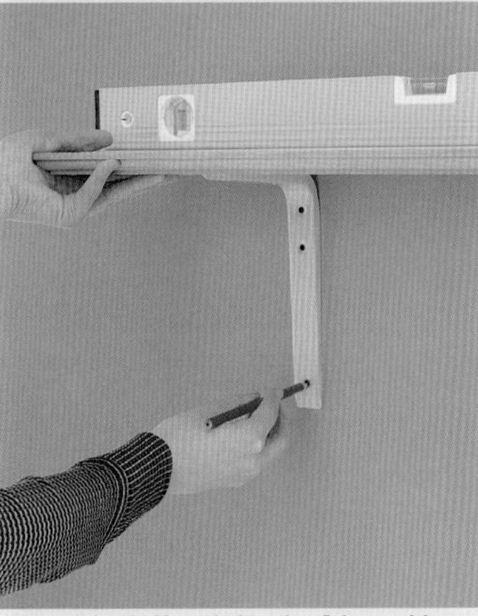

5 Level the shelf; mark the other fixing positions

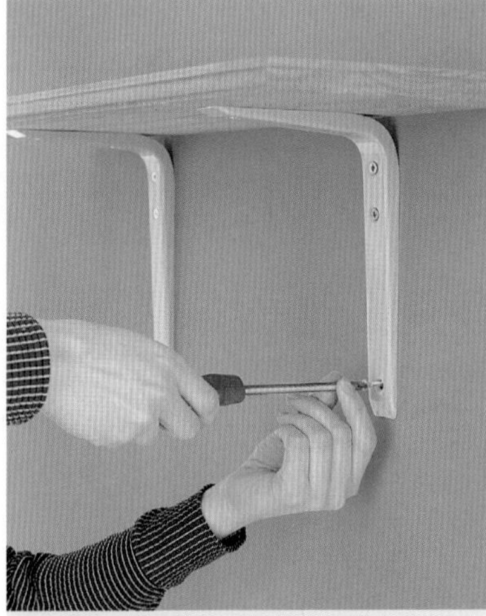

6 Drill the other holes and drive in all the screws

SEE ALSO > Wood and boards 528–9, Sawing wood 489, Electrical safety 285–9

Fitting track shelving

Shelving track is a system of vertical wall tracks and clip-in brackets that allows you to create an array of fully adjustable shelving. The tracks and brackets are available in a range of sizes and finishes, with brackets that fit into slots or into a continuous channel in the upright. They can be fixed to any type of wall.

Fitting the tracks

Decide on the number of shelves you want, the required spacings between the shelves and the overall width of the system. For wide systems, you can fix three or four parallel tracks, enabling you to fit shelves at different levels on each pair of tracks. Use the chart given earlier to match the bracket spacing to the likely load for a given shelf material.

Mark the position and level of the tracks on the wall. Hold up the first track to its mark and use a bradawl to mark the wall through the top hole in the track. Drill and plug the hole and drive the fixing screw in partway so the track hangs loosely (**1**).

The track should hang vertically. Check this with a spirit level, then mark the positions of the other fixing holes on the wall (**2**). Swing the track aside so you can drill holes at the marks (**3**). Insert a wallplug in each hole, swing the track back into position and drive in the rest of the screws, including the top one.

Hold your spirit level against the wall with one end resting on top of the first track. Make sure it is level, then hold the second track at its mark butting up against the spirit level and mark the position of its top fixing hole on the wall (**4**). You may need to enlist a helper for this stage. Then fix this and subsequent tracks to the wall as described for the first track.

Fitting the shelves

Fit the first pair of brackets into the track (**5**), counting slots up from the bottom or down from the top to set them level. If the tracks have a continuous channel, bridge the brackets with a spirit level to position them. Check that the brackets are securely engaged. Set the first shelf on its brackets (**6**). Then decide how far apart you want the others, and add more brackets and shelves to complete the system.

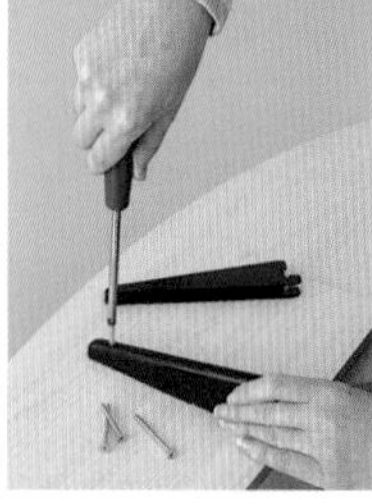

Secure brackets
Some shelf brackets can be screwed to the shelf to make them more secure. Place the shelf on its brackets and mark the fixing positions with a bradawl. Lift off the shelf and brackets and screw the brackets to the shelf. Make sure the screws will not penetrate the top surface of the shelf.

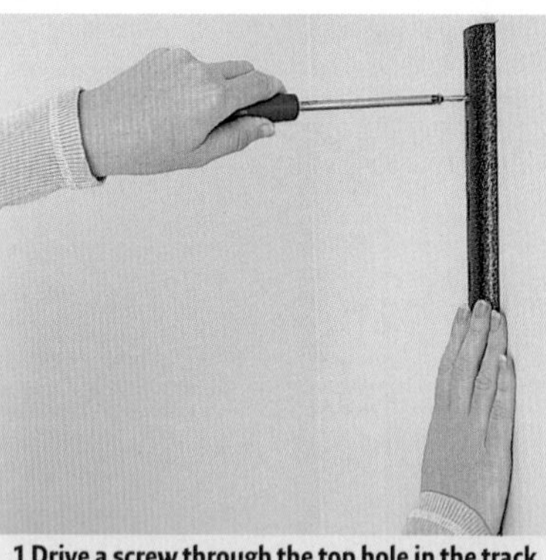

1 Drive a screw through the top hole in the track

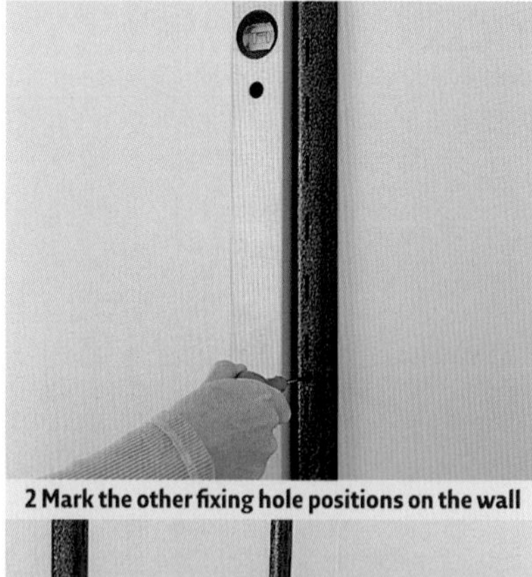

2 Mark the other fixing hole positions on the wall

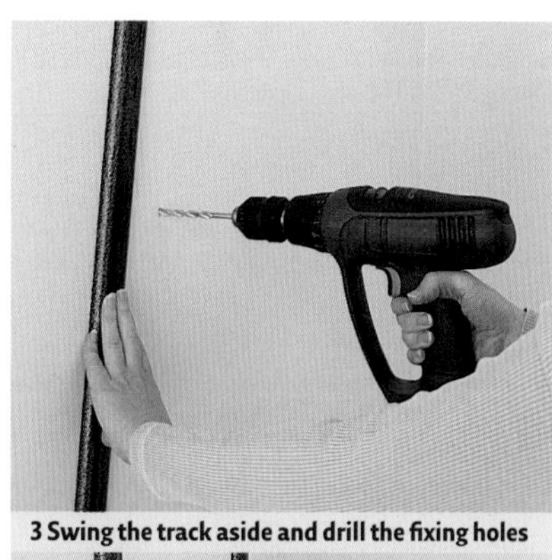

3 Swing the track aside and drill the fixing holes

4 Use a spirit level to position the second track

5 Fit the brackets into the track

6 Place the shelf on the brackets

SEE ALSO >Power drills 500, Drilling masonry 512, Masonry bits 512, Wall fixings 535–6

Assembling flat-pack furniture

A wide range of furniture is available in flat-pack form, from bookshelves and chests of drawers to full-size wardrobes. All rely on a small range of clever concealed fixing devices for their assembly.

The secret of success with assembling flat-pack furniture is to unpack everything, identify every component and check that nothing is missing. Separate screws and dowels from the other fixing devices and check their sizes; different ones are often used in different places. Then read the instructions carefully, and decide whether you will need an extra pair of hands – if not for the actual assembly, then for lifting the complete piece into place.

Dowels are widely used as locators rather than as fixing devices. Don't glue them into place if you think you will need to dismantle the piece in the future – when moving house, for example.

You will usually need screwdrivers, hex (Allen) keys and perhaps a small spanner or two. Hex keys and a small spanner may be included in the kit; if not, check that you have all the tools you need to carry out the assembly before you start work.

It is generally best to carry out the assembly with the piece on its front or back, to avoid putting any unnecessary strain on the corner joints. Add the back when the carcase is complete, to help keep the assembly square while you add features such as plinths or shelves. Check that all the fixing devices are fully tightened before lifting the piece into its final position.

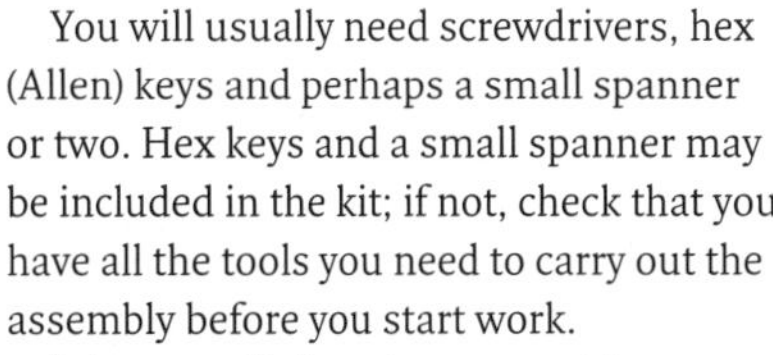

1 Unpack the kit and check all the parts

2 Hammer all the dowels into their holes

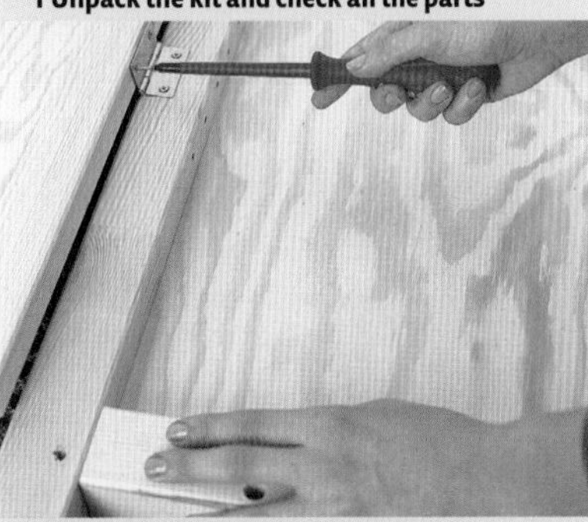

3 Fit any doors to their side panels

4 Fit dowelled panels to their matching parts

5 Do up the various fixing devices tightly

6 Add the back panel to keep the piece square

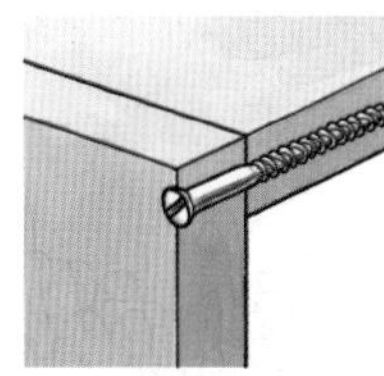

Screw connectors
These coarse-threaded countersunk screws are driven into a pilot hole drilled in the edge of the board.

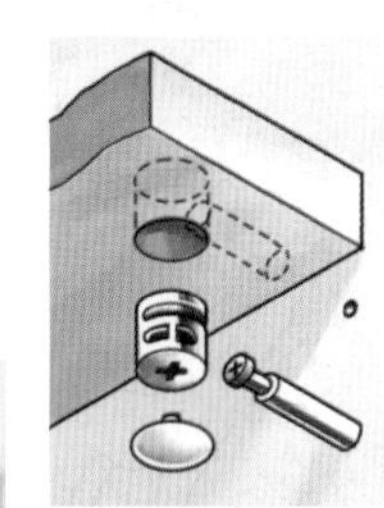

Cam fittings
The rounded end of a metal dowel projecting from one component locates in a slot in a cam-action boss dropped into a hole in the other component. Turning the boss with a screwdriver locks the two components together.

Another version has a cranked nylon peg that plugs into the edge of one component and fits into a circular boss recessed in the other. Turning the screw in the boss locks the peg.

Cabinet connectors
These two-part connectors link cupboards or wardrobes that are installed side by side.

Adjustable shelf supports

If you want adjustable shelving in a bookcase or cabinet, there are several ways of providing it. All are simple to fit, and are even more flexible than wall-mounted track shelving.

Bookcase strip

This metal strip has slots at regular intervals into which small metal shelf supports are clipped. Two strips are fitted at each side of the cabinet, and care must be taken to position them level with each other to ensure that the shelves will be truly horizontal.

Fit clips into slots

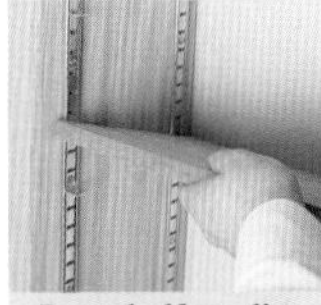

Rest shelf on clips

Magic wires

This system uses metal wires 3mm (⅛in) in diameter, shaped so their ends fit into holes drilled at regular intervals in the sides of the cabinet. Two wires support each shelf. In a flat-pack unit, mark and drill the holes before you assemble it.

Cut the shelf 3mm (⅛in) narrower than the cabinet. Cut a 10mm (⅜in) deep slot in each end with a circular saw, stopping it 25mm (1in) from the shelf's front edge. Engage the slots over the wires and push in the shelves.

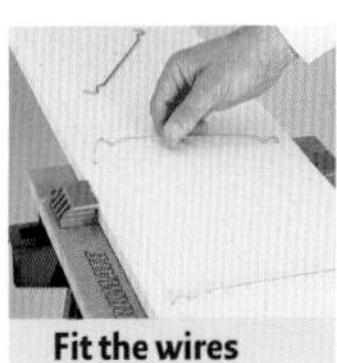

Fit the wires

Slide shelves in

Shelf studs

Small metal or plastic studs are fitted into holes drilled in the cabinet sides. Some have matching plugs. As with magic wires, it is best to mark and drill the holes before you assemble the cabinet, so you can ensure they are accurately aligned.

Types of shelf stud

Rest shelf on studs

SEE ALSO > Knock-down fittings 536

Assembling flat-pack kitchen units

Kitchen units are one of the most popular forms of flat-pack furniture. They come in a wide array of sizes and configurations, allowing you to plan and assemble a fully fitted kitchen for a fraction of the price of a professionally installed one. These instructions cover the assembly of a typical base unit; wall units are generally similar but simpler to put together.

Identify the parts
Lay out all the parts of the cabinet on a flat surface so you can see which part is which, and work out how they will be assembled.

Assembling base units

Start by unpacking and identifying all the components. Then carry out a dry run, fitting the components together so you can check how they are assembled and work out where the various fixing devices go (**1**).

Most kitchen units use a combination of glued dowels to locate components, and cam fixings to lock them together. Start by positioning all the dowels in their predrilled holes, gluing them in place and hammering them in fully (**2**).

Next, insert the cam studs in their holes in the panels with the dowels; screw them in until their shoulders meet the panel surface (**3**). Fit the locking cams into the larger holes drilled in the mating cabinet panels (**4**). Ensure that the embossed arrow on each cam points towards the end of the panel, so that the stud can pass into it as you assemble the carcase.

To begin the assembly, apply glue to all the exposed dowels (**5**) and bring the mating panels together. Tap their edges with a mallet to seat the dowels and cam studs fully in their holes, then tighten the cams by turning them through 90° with a screwdriver (**6**). Add the top front rail to make the carcase rigid, then check that the assembly is square.

The back panel usually slides into grooves pre-machined in the sides and base panel. Slide it into position (**7**) to complete the cabinet, ready for its doors to be hung and worktop to be positioned on top of it. Finally, attach the leg brackets (**8**) and push the legs into them (**9**).

1 Assemble the parts as a dry run

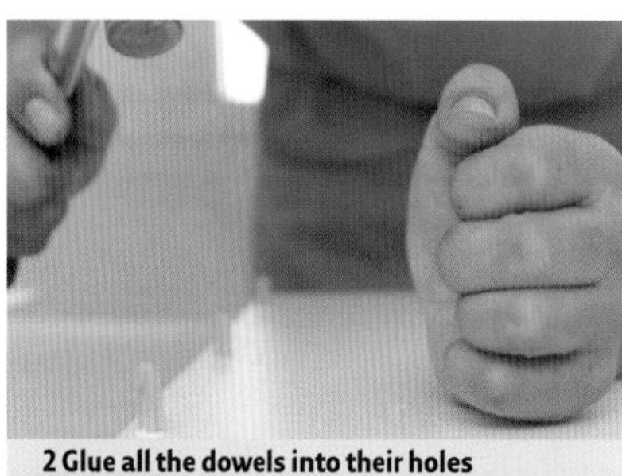

2 Glue all the dowels into their holes

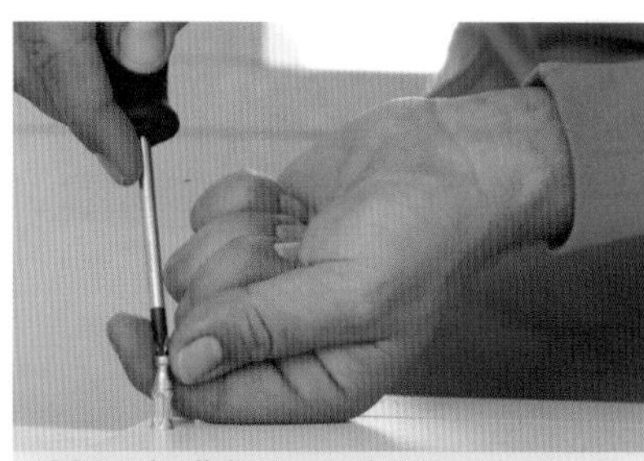

3 Screw in all the cam studs

Double cabinets
Add a vertical post to the centre of the front of a double cabinet to strengthen the unit and hide any gap between the two doors.

4 Position all the locking cams

5 Glue all the protruding dowels

6 Assemble the panels and tighten the cams

7 Slide the back panel into its grooves

8 Screw the leg brackets to the cabinets

9 Push the legs into their brackets

SEE ALSO > Knock-down fittings 536

Fitting flat-pack kitchen units

Installing a fitted kitchen is relatively straightforward once all the base and wall units are assembled and the old kitchen has been stripped out. These instructions cover the basics of installing the units themselves, ready to receive their worktops and appliances, for which installation instructions are always provided.

Installing base units

Start work in a corner of the kitchen, setting the corner unit in position. Adjust the legs to align the unit's top edge with the pencil guideline (see Setting out the levels, right), and to get it level both side-to-side and front-to-back (1). Repeat this process unit by unit until they are all in position, and check that each one is level with its neighbour by laying a spirit level across them both.

Either fix the base units together using connector screws, or screw them together with countersunk screws. Clamp the units together while you do this (2), then drill a clearance hole through one cabinet side. Make a pilot hole into the adjacent cabinet and drive in the screw. With all the base units in position and level, fix them to the wall by driving screws through metal angle fixing brackets (3).

Setting out the levels

Use a batten the same height as the base units to mark the wall at regular intervals where the units will stand. Then draw a horizontal datum line on the wall through the highest mark. Align the top of each base unit to this line as you install it to ensure that all the units are precisely level with each other.

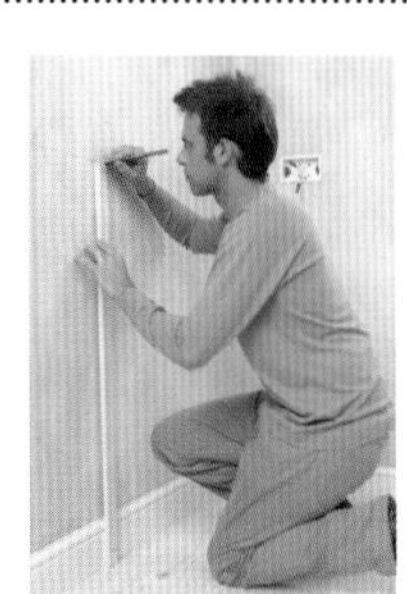

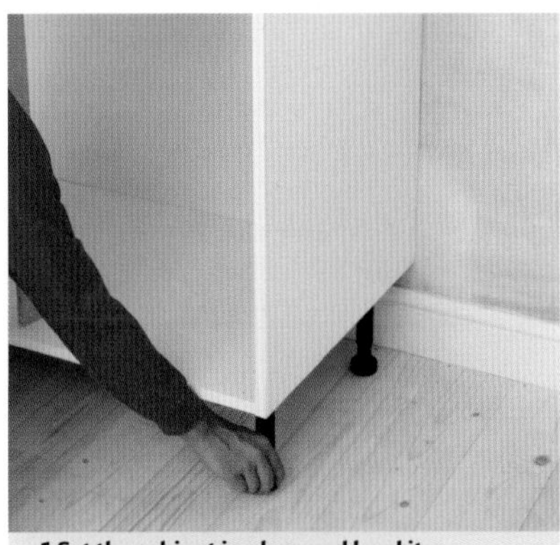

1 Set the cabinet in place and level it

2 Clamp adjacent cabinets together

3 Fix cabinets to the wall with brackets

Aligning doors
Line up each door with its neighbours using the two screws on the hinge arm. Loosen the rear screw to move the door in or out. Turn the front screw to move the door to the left or right.

Installing wall units

Mark a horizontal line on the wall to indicate the level of the bottoms of the wall units above the datum line, using a spirit level. If you are fitting the units single-handed, it helps to fix a temporary support batten to the wall with plugs and screws, level with this line. Then you can rest the units on the batten while you make the wall fixings. Remove the batten and fill the holes when the units are in place.

Most wall units are mounted using a fitting that fits inside the top corners of the cabinets and hooks onto a special bracket on the wall. The fitting incorporates an adjustment block, allowing you to adjust the level of the units precisely. Full fixing instructions are provided with the units for installing these fittings. Follow these to fix the brackets to the wall (1), and hook the cabinets onto them (2). Then adjust the screws in the adjustment block to level and align the unit (3). Finally, clamp the cabinets together and join them using connecting bolts or screws (4).

1 Fix the hanging brackets to the wall

2 Hook the unit onto its wall brackets

3 Adjust the position and level of the unit

4 Clamp and screw adjacent cabinets together

SEE ALSO > Wall fixings 535–6, Spirit level 511

Making a loft hatch

Many houses have a hatch in the ceiling that provides access to the roof space for servicing water tanks and maintaining the roof structure. If your house has a large roof space without access, installing a hatch will provide you with valuable extra room for storage.

In older houses cutting away part of the roof structure is usually not a problem, as the timbers are relatively substantial. In modern houses, however, lightweight timber is used to make strong triangulated trussed-roof structures. Since these are designed to carry the entire weight of the roof, with each part of the truss playing an important role, any alteration may weaken the structure.

Before you start work, check with your Building Control Officer that it is safe to proceed with the alterations.

If you have a choice, site the hatch over a landing (although not too close to the stairs) – rather than in one of the bedrooms, which is generally less convenient. Also, take into consideration the pitch of the roof, as you will need to have adequate headroom above the hatch.

Alternative ways to install hatch covers

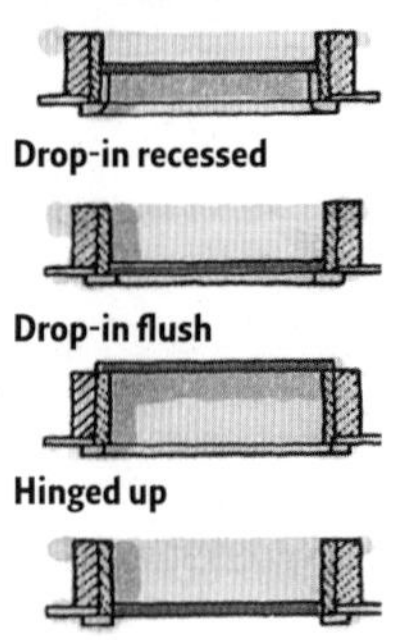

Drop-in recessed

Drop-in flush

Hinged up

Hinged down

Making the opening

If you are planning to fit a special folding loft ladder, the size of the new opening will be specified by the ladder's manufacturer. In general, aim to sever no more than one ceiling joist: these are usually spaced 350mm (1ft 2in) apart.

Locate three joists by drilling pilot holes in the ceiling. Mark out a square for the opening between the two outer joists. Cut an inspection hole inside the marked area to check that there are no obstacles in the way of the cutting line. Saw through the ceiling plasterwork and strip it away.

Pass a light up into the roof space, and climb up into it between the joists. Lay a board across the joists to support yourself. Saw through the middle joist, cutting it back 50mm (2in) from each edge of the opening. Cut two new lengths of joist timber, called trimmers, to fit between the joists; allow for a square housing joint 12mm (½in) deep to be cut at each end (see left). Nail the housed joints, and the butt joints between the trimmers and the ceiling joists. Use two 100mm (4in) round wire nails to secure each joint.

Nail the ceiling laths or plasterboard to the underside of the trimmers. Cut timber linings to cover the joists and the edges of the plaster. Make good the damaged edges of the plaster with filler. When it is set, nail mitred architrave moulding around the opening. Make a drop-in or hinged panel of plywood or blockboard.

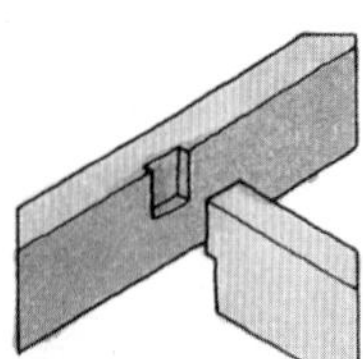

Housing joints
A housing joint will give better support to the trimmer joists than using nails alone.

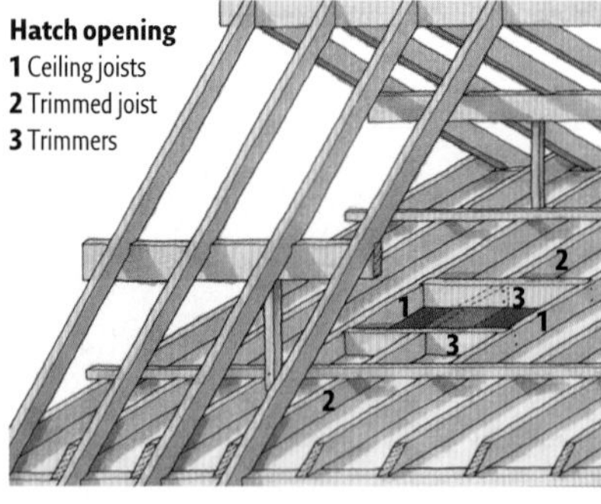

Hatch opening
1 Ceiling joists
2 Trimmed joist
3 Trimmers

Loft-access traps

Any openings made in the ceiling will encourage the flow of water vapour into the loft space. This can increase the risk of condensation, particularly if the loft is not well ventilated. Ready-made loft-access traps are available with seals to overcome this problem.

Each trap has a moulded frame that, when fixed in the trimmed ceiling opening (as described above), forms a seal with the ceiling all round. It also neatly covers the cut edges of the hole. The insulated trap door incorporates a flexible vapour seal between it and the hatch frame.

There are hinged trap doors and lift-out ones. Some of them are fire-resistant. Hinged types can be used in conjunction with an aluminium loft ladder that is available as an accessory.

Frame forms a seal when fixed to joist

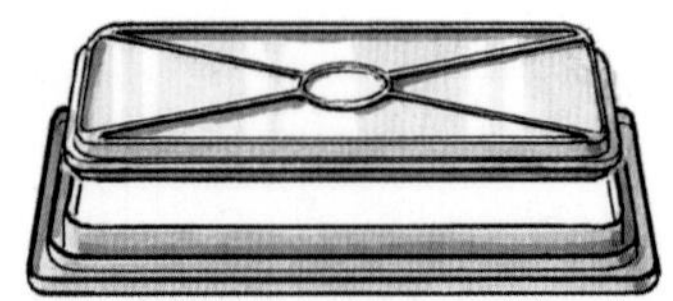

Frame and insulated trap form an airtight seal

Folding loft ladders

Access to the roof space is safer and more convenient if you install a folding loft ladder. Some come complete with built-in hatch cover, frame and fittings, ready to install in a new opening.

Normally, the length of the ladders suits ceiling heights of 2.3 and 2.5m (7ft 6in and 8ft 3in), although some can extend to 2.9 to 3m (9ft 6in to 10ft).

Concertina ladder

To fix a concertina ladder, screw the fixing brackets of the ladder to the framework of the opening. Fit the retaining hook to the framework to hold the ladder in the stowed position. To operate the ladder, you use a pole that hooks over the bottom rail. Fit the hatch door to the frame with a continuous hinge, and fix a push-to-release latch to the edge of the hatch door.

Ready-to-install folding ladder

Cut the opening and trim the joists to the size specified by the manufacturer. Insert the casing with built-in frame in the opening, then screw it to the joists.

A concertina ladder is simple to install

Folding ladders are easy to deploy

SEE ALSO > Repairing plaster 48–50, Pitched roofs, 120Patching a ceiling 160, Chipboard flooring 178

Home Security

Home security

It is, without doubt, well worth taking reasonable precautions to protect yourself and your family and property against the risks of fire and burglary. The cost and effort involved is small compared with the possible expense of replacement or even rebuilding – not to mention the grief caused by personal injury or the loss of items of sentimental value.

How a burglar gains entry

Many people innocently believe that they are unlikely to be burgled because they are not conspicuously wealthy. But statistics prove that most intruders are opportunists in search of one or two costly items, such as electrical hardware (typically CD players, television sets and computers), jewellery, or cash.

The average burglar takes only a few minutes to break into a house – often in broad daylight. Nevertheless, although it's virtually impossible to prevent a determined burglar from breaking in, you can do a great deal to make it difficult for inexperienced criminals.

The illustration below indicates the vulnerable areas of an average house, and the points listed opposite suggest methods for safeguarding them. Check out each point and compare them with your own home, to make sure your security is up to standard.

Vulnerable areas of a house

1 The front door
Inadequate locks invite forced entry.

2 Darkened porch
Makes identification of callers difficult.

3 Back and side doors
Often fitted with inadequate locks.

4 French windows
Can be sprung with one well-placed blow.

5 Downstairs windows
A common means of entry if unlocked. Weak putty allows a thief to remove glass silently.

6 Upstairs windows
Vulnerable if they can be reached and opened easily.

7 Trap door to attic
The only way to enter a house from the loft.

8 Skylight
A possible means of entry for a burglar if accessible from an adjacent building.

9 Unlocked gate
Provides a convenient exit for a burglar removing bulky items.

10 Garage or shed
A potential source of housebreaking tools.

11 Downpipe
As good as a ladder to an agile burglar.

12 Burglar alarm and CCTV
Valuable deterrents.

Seeking expert advice

If you require more detailed information about home security, you can obtain free advice tailored to your needs.

Crime Prevention Officer

Local police authorities appoint a full-time Crime Prevention Officer (CPO) who is responsible for advising both companies and private individuals on ways to improve the security of their premises. Telephone your nearest police station to arrange for a confidential visit from the CPO, who will discuss any aspect of home security.

Fire Prevention Officer

Contact the Fire Prevention Officer (FPO) at your local fire-brigade headquarters for advice on how to balance effective security measures against the need to provide adequate escape routes in case of fire. He will also explain the differences between the various types of simple firefighting equipment available to home owners. Some local authorities will fit smoke alarms free of charge in certain circumstances.

Insurance companies

Check with your insurance company that your home and its contents are adequately covered against fire and theft. Most household policies are now index-linked, the premium and sum insured being automatically adjusted each year to allow for inflation.

You can also opt for a 'new for old' policy that will guarantee the full replacement cost of lost or destroyed property. In some circumstances an insurance company may insist on certain precautions, such as a monitored alarm system, but they may also be willing to reduce your premium if you provide adequate security.

SEE ALSO > Securing doors 234–6, Securing windows 237–8, Protecting against fire 240

Guarding against intruders

You can reduce the likelihood of burglary by adopting security-conscious habits. Discourage opportunist burglars by closing and locking all windows and doors, even when you're only going to be out for a short time. Break-ins have been known to occur while the whole family is watching television – so lock up before sitting down for the evening. When you leave the house at night, close the curtains and leave a light on.

Don't open your front door to callers unless you know them or they've made a prior appointment. Even then, don't be afraid to ask for identification. Bona fide gas or electricity officials will expect to be challenged, so keep your security chain in place until you're satisfied that their identification is genuine.

When you go on holiday, cancel regular deliveries. Fit time switches to turn lights on and off, to give the impression that the house is occupied. Remove an internal letter-box basket, so mail won't pile up and prevent deliveries. Deposit your valuables with a bank. Don't put your home address on your luggage when travelling to your holiday destination.

Mark your possessions with your full post code plus your house number. You can buy an electric engraving tool, or use an ultraviolet marker pen – your coding will only be visible under a UV lamp. There are special marker pens for glass and china. Your local authority may be able to supply you with stickers to display in your windows to show that you have marked your belongings.

Photograph jewellery and paintings and other valuables that are difficult to mark; and, in case of fire, keep copies of the photos at the bank or with a trusted friend. You can buy a strong yet compact floor or wall safe for storing valuables and important documents.

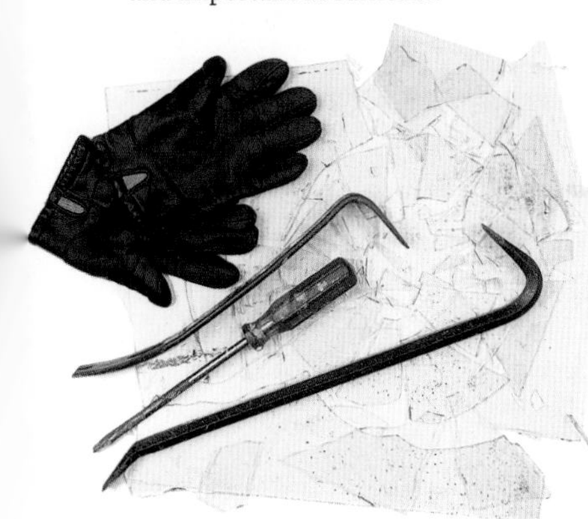

A checklist for guarding your home

1 Front door
Install a strong mortise lock that conforms to BS 3621, and fit a bolt top and bottom on the inside of your front door. Attach a security chain or similar fitting to prevent an intruder bursting in as you open the door a fraction. It's also worth fitting a peephole door viewer or CCTV, so you can identify callers.

If you live in a flat and the entrance door is the only vulnerable point of entry, consider having a multipoint lock fitted: it throws bolts into all four sides simultaneously. Make sure your door security will not prevent you escaping in the event of a fire.

2 Darkened porch
Fit a porch light, so that you can identify callers after dark. Security lighting may also make an intruder think twice before attempting to break in.

3 Back and side doors
A burglar can often work unobserved at the rear or side of a house. Consider security lighting, and fit mortise locks and bolts similar to those described for the front door. If the door opens outwards, fit hinge bolts – which will hold the door firmly in its frame.

4 French or patio windows
Insecure French windows can be sprung by a heavy blow or a kick. It is therefore essential to fit rack bolts, both top and bottom. Make sure sliding patio doors cannot be lifted off their runners.

5 Downstairs windows
These are always vulnerable – especially at the back and side of the house. Fit locks and catches to suit the material and style of the windows.

6 Upstairs windows
Even if these can only be reached with a ladder, to be on the safe side fit key-operated locks. Windows accessible by scaling a drainpipe, flat roof or wall should be secured the same way.

7 Trap door to attic
Fit a bolt on the trap door leading to your loft. Terraced and semi-detached houses sometimes have common lofts, and burglars have been known to break through dividing walls between houses.

8 Skylight
Windows at roof level are at risk only if they can be reached easily by means of drainpipes or from an adjacent building, but fit a lock or a bolt to deter thieves.

9 Side gate
If your house has a side gate, lock it to prevent burglars carrying away bulky items. Fitting a trellis above the gate may stop them vaulting over it.

10 Garages and sheds
Keep outbuildings locked to protect the contents, and to prevent burglars using your own tools to break into your house. Fit either a standard door lock or a padlock with a hasp that's close-fitting or concealed, so it cannot easily be cut. Either choose a design that covers the fixing screws or, if possible, substitute bolts for screws, to prevent the lock being prised off. Lock up your ladders, even if you have to chain them outside.

11 Downpipes
Paint downpipes with security paint to dissuade burglars from climbing them. The substance remains slippery, making it difficult to get a good grip.

12 Burglar alarm
Although an alarm is a useful deterrent, it should not be regarded as a sufficient safeguard on its own.

Outbuildings
Use a strong padlock and steel hasp to secure a garage or shed door.

Louvred windows
Use an epoxy adhesive to glue each pane into its fitting so it cannot be removed from outside.

• Security glass
Most people accept the risk that glass can be broken or cut. However, for greater security you can fit laminated glass or polycarbonate double glazing. Other alternatives are to cover ordinary glass with a metal grille or fit external security shutters operated from inside.

SEE ALSO > Security paint 82, Mortise locks 234–5, Time switches 235, Hinge bolts 236, Rack bolts 236, Window locks 237–8, Burglar alarms 239, Escape routes 240, Security lighting 337–8, CCTV 339–40

Securing doors

Doors are vulnerable to forcing and are often used by burglars for a quick exit. For both reasons, it's worth fitting strong locks and bolts. Don't just rely on an old-fashioned night latch, which offers no security at all – it is only as strong as the screws holding it to the door, and a thief can easily break a pane of glass to operate it or simply slide back the bolt with a credit card.

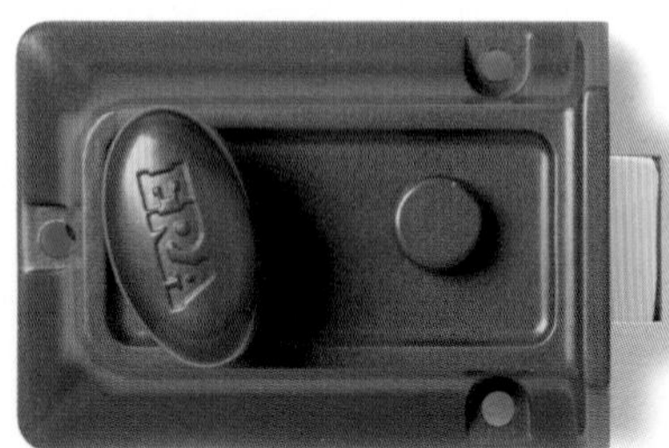

Night latch
This type of lock does not provide adequate security on its own.

Some locks and bolts are designed specifically for use on the door by which you leave the house - normally the front door. This needs a particularly strong lock because it can't be bolted from inside except when you are at home. Back and side doors need bolts top and bottom as extra security against them being forced open from outside. You should also fit a lock to these doors, to prevent thieves making an easy getaway with their spoils. The basic choice of locks is between mortise and rim types.

Deadlocking cylinder rim locks

A deadlocking cylinder rim lock can be fitted to a final-exit door as an alternative to a mortise lock – it locks automatically as the door is closed, so that the bolt cannot be forced back without a key except by turning the knob on the inside. One complete turn of the key prevents the lock being operated even from inside, so an intruder can't walk out of the front door with your property. The staple should be fixed into the edge of the doorframe with screws or a metal stud: if it's screwed to the face, a well-placed kick may rip out the screws.

• **Changing locks**
There's no need to buy a new lock just because a door key has been lost or stolen. Simply take the old one to a locksmith, who will swap the internal mechanism for one that comes complete with a different set of keys.

Mortise locks

A mortise lock is fitted into a slot cut in the edge of the door, so it cannot be tampered with easily. There are various patterns to suit the width of the door stile and the location of the door.

A mortise sashlock is suitable for back and side doors. It has a handle on each side to operate a springbolt, and a key-operated deadbolt that can't be pushed back once the door is closed.

Purely key-operated mortise locks are best for final-exit doors where no handle is necessary. Any exterior-door lock should conform to BS 3621. This ensures the lock has a minimum of 1000 key variations, is proof against 'picking', and is strong enough to resist drilling, cutting or forcing. Some locks are specifically intended for doors that open to the right or to the left.

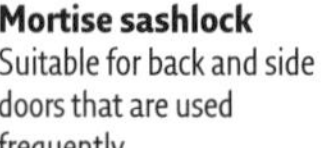

Mortise sashlock
Suitable for back and side doors that are used frequently.

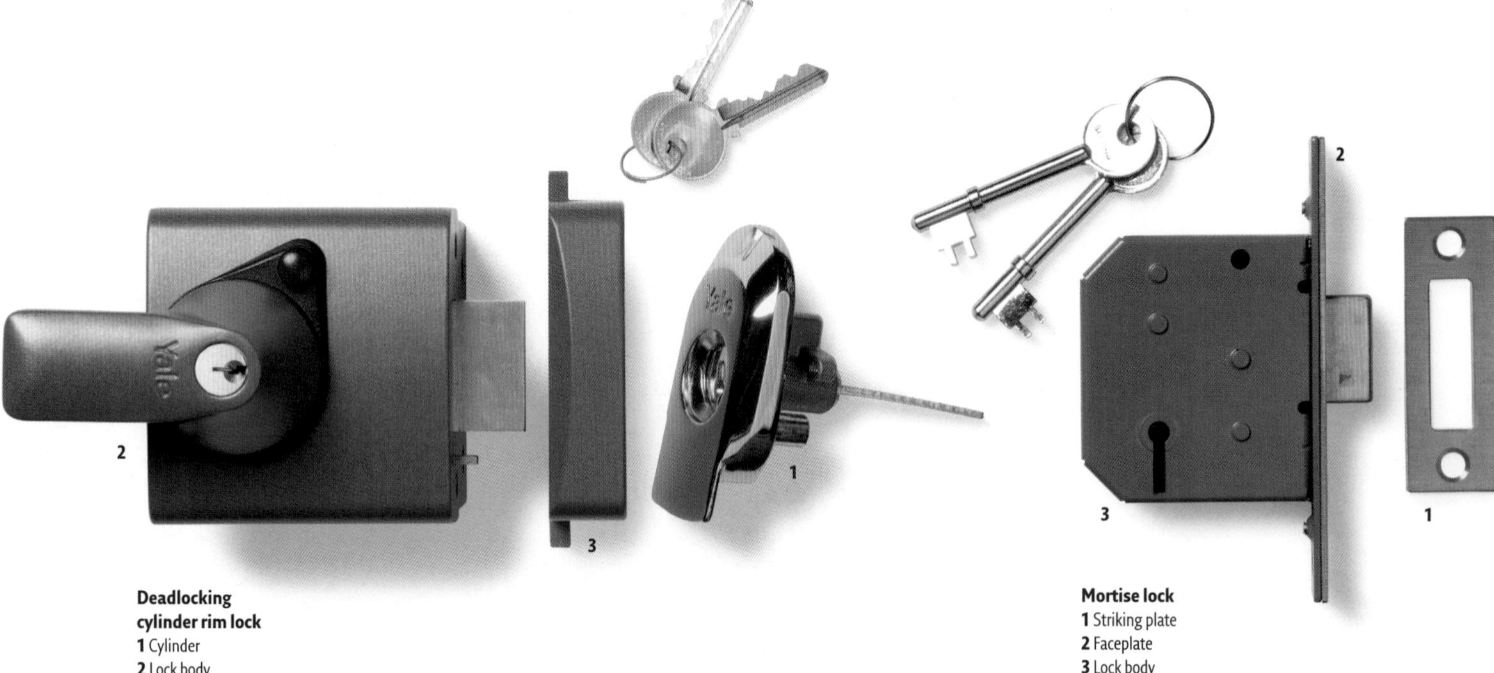

Deadlocking cylinder rim lock
1 Cylinder
2 Lock body
3 Staple

Mortise lock
1 Striking plate
2 Faceplate
3 Lock body

SEE ALSO > Fitting a porch light 336

Automatic timers

You can give the impression that someone is at home by using an automatic time switch, plugged into an ordinary electrical wall socket, to control a table lamp or radio.

Mechanical timers

The simplest type of timer is programmed manually to turn the lamp or radio on and off several times over a period of 24 hours. The minimum switching period for mechanical timers is usually 15 minutes, but there is also a manual override. Though extremely reliable, most mechanical timers simply repeat the same sequence each day.

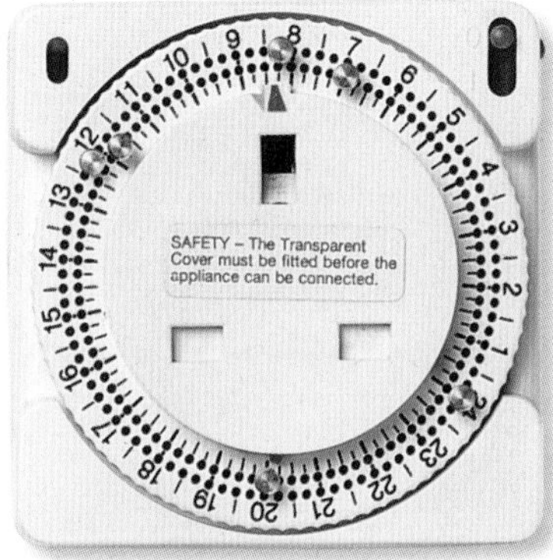

24-hour mechanical time switch

Electronic timers

If you want something more sophisticated, buy an electronic timer that switches lighting on and off at different times every day of the week. Some programmers also provide for random switching, which gives a more realistic impression that the house or flat is occupied.

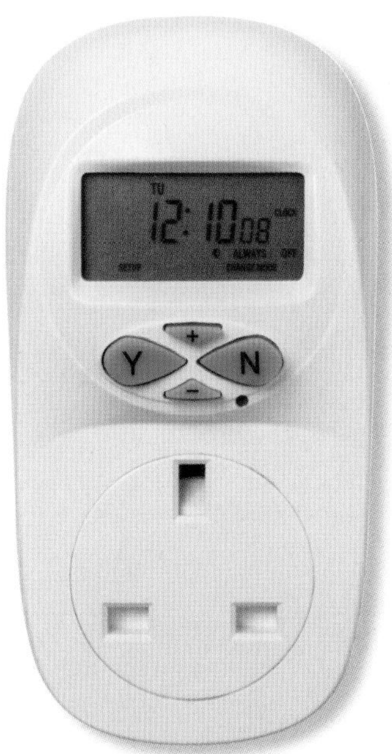

7-day electronic timer

Fitting door locks

Any competent woodworker will be able to fit mortise locks or cylinder rim locks satisfactorily. Fitting additional security devices, such as hinge bolts and rack bolts, is easier still.

Fitting a mortise lock

Scribe a line centrally on the edge of the door with a marking gauge, and use the lock body as a template to mark the top and bottom of the mortise (1). Choose a drill bit that matches the thickness of the lock body, and drill out the majority of the waste wood for the mortise between the marked lines.

Square up the edges of the mortise with a chisel (2), until the lock fits snugly in the slot. Mark around the edge of the faceplate with a knife (3), then chop a series of shallow cuts across the waste with a chisel. Pare out the recess until the faceplate is flush with the edge of the door.

Hold the lock against the face of the door and mark the centre of the keyhole with a bradawl (4). Clamp a block of scrap timber to the other side of the door, over the keyhole position, and then drill right through on the centre mark – the block prevents the drill bit splintering the face of the door as it bursts through on the other side. Cut out the keyhole slot on both sides.

Screw the lock into its recess and check its operation; screw on the coverplate, and then the escutcheons over the holes on each side of the door. With the door closed, operate the bolt to mark the position of the striking plate on the doorframe. If the bolt has no built-in marking device, shoot the bolt fully out, then push the door to, so you can draw round the bolt on the face of the frame (5).

Mark out and cut the mortise and shallow recess for the striking plate (6).

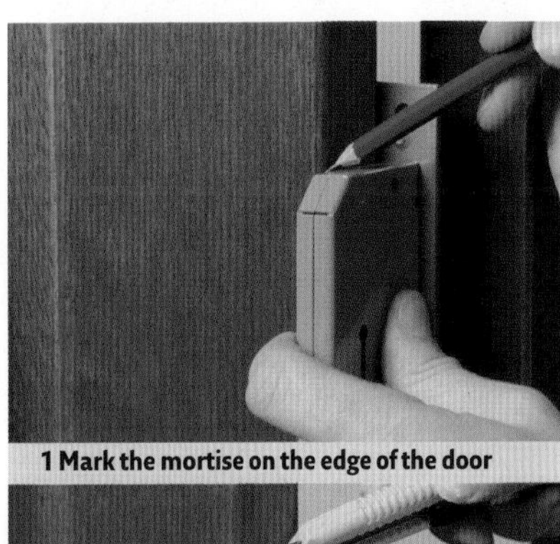

1 Mark the mortise on the edge of the door

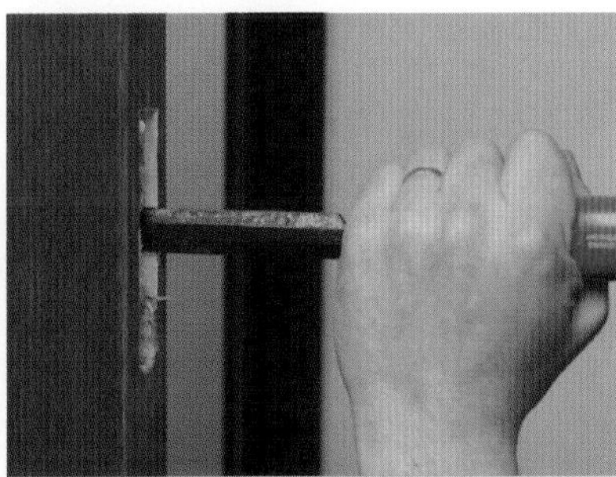

2 Chop out the waste with a sharp chisel

3 Mark around the edge of the faceplate

4 Mark the keyhole with a bradawl

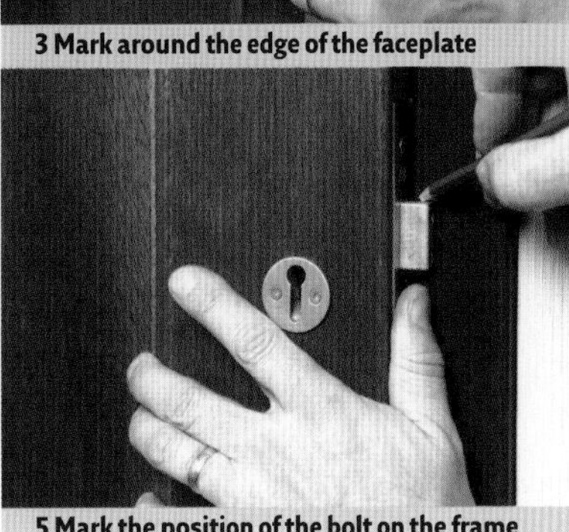

5 Mark the position of the bolt on the frame

6 Fit the striking plate

SEE ALSO > Woodworking tools 487–504, Junior hacksaw 518

Fitting hinge bolts
Fit at least two bolts per door and position them near the hinges. Drill a hole in the edge of the door for the bolt, and another one in the doorframe. Recess the locking plate in the frame.

Fitting a cylinder rim lock

Although fitting instructions vary from model to model, the following method shows how easy it is to fit a cylinder rim lock. Using the templates provided with the lock (1), mark then drill the holes for the cylinder. Hold the lock body against the door, so you can mark and cut a recess for its flange (2).

Pass the cylinder into the hole from the outside and check the required length of the flat connecting bar. If need be, cut it to size with a hacksaw (3). Bolt the cylinder to the door.

Screw the mounting plate for the lock on the inside of the door (4) and attach the lock body to it. Screw the lock's flange into the recess in the edge of the door, making sure it lies flush.

Use the fitted lock as a guide for positioning the striking plate on the door-frame. Chisel out a shallow recess for the staple, then screw it to the frame.

1 Use the template to mark the holes

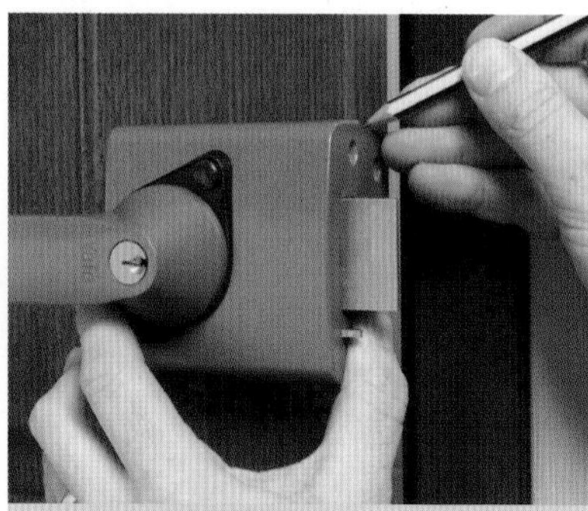

2 Draw round the flange

3 Cut the connecting bar to length

4 Fit the lock's mounting plate

Installing a door viewer

A peephole door viewer enables you to identify callers before admitting them. Select a viewer with as wide an angle of vision as possible – you should be able to see someone standing to the side of the door or even crouching below the viewer. Choose one that is adjustable to fit any thickness of door.

Drill a hole of the recommended size – usually 12mm (½in) – right through the centre of the door at a comfortable eye level. Insert the barrel of the viewer into the hole from the outside. Then screw on the eyepiece from inside.

A telescopic viewer fits doors of any thickness

Fitting rack bolts

The components of a standard rack bolt
1 Key
2 Barrel
3 Keyhole plate
4 Locking plate

There are many types of bolt for securing a door from the inside. Rack bolts can be fitted in the edge of the door and have the advantage of being unobtrusive as well as secure.

First, drill a hole – usually 16mm (⅝in) in diameter – in the edge of the door for the barrel of the bolt. Use a try square to transfer the centre of the hole to the inside face of the door. Allowing for the thickness of the faceplate, mark the keyhole then drill it with a 10mm (⅜in) bit and insert the bolt (1).

With the key holding the bolt in place, mark the recess for the faceplate (2); then pare out the recess with a chisel. Screw the bolt and keyhole plate to the door. Operate the bolt to mark the frame, then drill a hole 16mm (⅝in) in diameter to a depth that matches the length of the bolt. Fit the locking plate over the hole.

1 Drill holes for barrel and key, then fit the bolt

2 With the key in place, draw round the faceplate

Attaching a security chain

No special skills are needed to fit a security chain. Simply screw the fixing plates to the door and frame; the security chain should be positioned just below the lock.

Alternatively, fit a rigid door limiter. The sliding bar can be released only when the door is closed.

Identify a caller before releasing the chain

A door limiter is more substantial than a chain

SEE ALSO > Woodworking tools 487–504

Securing windows

Windows are particularly vulnerable, so it's worth making sure they're adequately secured. There are all sorts of locks for wooden and metal windows, including some that lock automatically when you close the window. Locks for metal frames are rather more difficult to fit, as you may have to cut threads for the screw fixings.

Fitting window locks

The type of lock suitable for a window depends on how the window opens. Sliding sashes are normally secured by locking the sashes together, whereas casement windows – which open like doors – should be fastened to the outer frame or locked by rendering the catches and stays immovable.

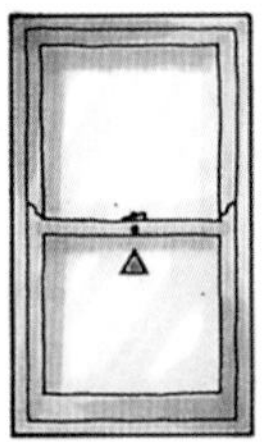

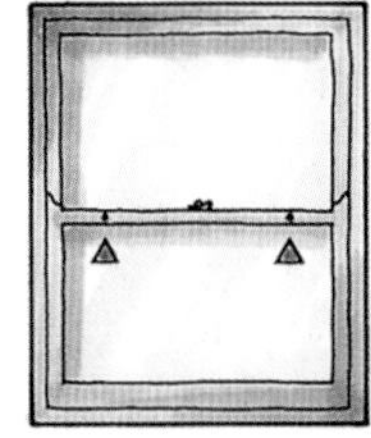

Where to place window locks
The black dots indicate the best positions for bolts or locks.

Window locks must be strong enough to resist forcing and have to be situated correctly for optimum security. On a small window, for example, fit a single lock as close as possible to the centre of the meeting rail or vertical stile; on larger windows, you will need two locks spaced apart.

Locks that can only be operated by a removable key are the most secure. Some keys will open any lock of the same design – an advantage in that you need fewer keys for your windows, though some burglars carry a range of standard keys. With other locks, there are several key variations.

Wooden windows need to be fairly substantial to accommodate mortise locks, so surface-mounted locks are frequently used instead. These are perfectly adequate and, being visible, act as a deterrent. If the fixing screws are not concealed when the lock is in place, you could drill out the centre of the screws, so they cannot be withdrawn.

Installing sash stops

When the bolt is withdrawn with a key, a sash stop fitted to each side of a window allows it to be opened slightly for ventilation. As well as deterring burglars, sash stops prevent children from opening the window any further. Fitting stops on both sides of a sash window prevents it being levered open by a determined burglar.

To fit a stop, drill a hole in the upper sash for the bolt, then screw the faceplate over the hole (1). On close-fitting sashes, you may have to recess the faceplate. If possible, tighten up the window's catch to prevent the upper sash moving while you pare out the recess with a chisel.

Screw the protective plate to the top edge of the lower sash, then withdraw the bolt, using the special key provided (2).

When redecorating, don't paint over sash stops or you may find it impossible to operate them.

1 Screw the faceplate to the upper sash

2 Withdraw the bolt to secure the window

Dual screws for sashes

Cheap but effective, a dual screw consists of a bolt that passes through both meeting rails so that the two sashes are immobilized. The screw is operated by a special key, and there is little to see when the window is closed.

With the window shut and the catch engaged, fit a dual screw by drilling through the inner meeting rail into the outer one; wrap tape around the drill bit to gauge the depth (1). Slide the sashes apart and tap the two bolt-receiving devices into their respective holes (2). Close the window again and insert the threaded bolt (3), then use the key to drive it flush with the window frame. If need be, saw the bolt to length.

1 Drill a hole in both meeting rails

2 Tap each part of the fitting into the hole

3 Insert the threaded bolt

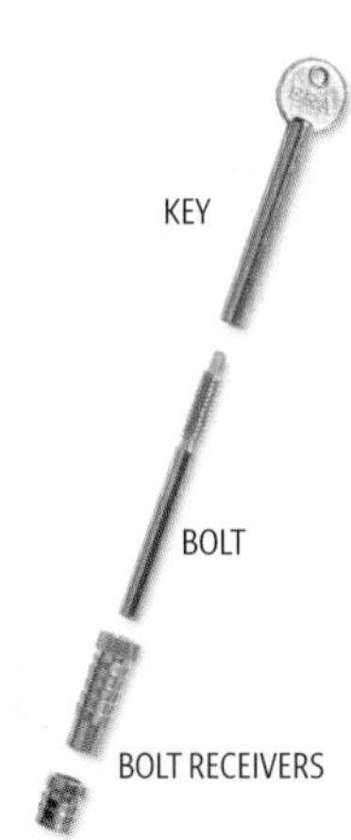

Dual screw
Inexpensive device that locks sliding sashes together until the bolt is withdrawn, using the key.

• **Fitting key-operated sash locks**
These are simple locks that screw to the top surface of the two meeting rails, effectively clamping the rails together. To secure an aluminium sash window, fit the type of lock recommended for securing fanlight windows.

SEE ALSO > Casement and sash windows 192–3, Rack bolts 236, Woodworking tools 487–504

Fitting locks to casement windows

Casement windows, which swing on hinges like doors, should be fitted with surface-mounted key-operated locks or bolts. Pivoting windows and fanlights are simply variations of the casement window.

Fitting a casement lock

A lock can easily be fitted to a wooden window frame: either the bolt is engaged by turning a simple catch or the lock may engage automatically when you close the window. It doesn't matter which type you choose, provided the lock can only be released with a removable key that can be kept out of reach of the window.

A similar device for metal windows is a clamp that shoots a bolt which hooks over the fixed frame.

A good casement lock has a removable key

Locking a cockspur handle

A cockspur handle, which secures the opening edge of the casement to the fixed frame, can be locked by means of an extending bolt that you screw to the wood just below the handle. However, make sure that the handle is not worn or loose – otherwise the lock may be ineffective.

Lockable handles that allow you to secure a window that's left ajar for ventilation can be substituted in place of a standard cockspur handle.

An extending bolt stops the handle turning

French windows and patio doors

Traditional French windows are large casements

French windows and other glazed doors are vulnerable to forcing (a burglar only has to break a pane to reach the handle or bolts inside), so key-operated locks are essential.

Each door of a French window needs a rack bolt both at the top and at the bottom. You have to take each door off its hinges in order to fit the lower bolt; if that's difficult, fit a lockable surface-mounted bolt instead.

Locking sliding patio doors

If you have sliding patio doors, fit locks at the top and bottom to prevent the sliding frame from being lifted off its track. These locks offer at least 1000 key variations.

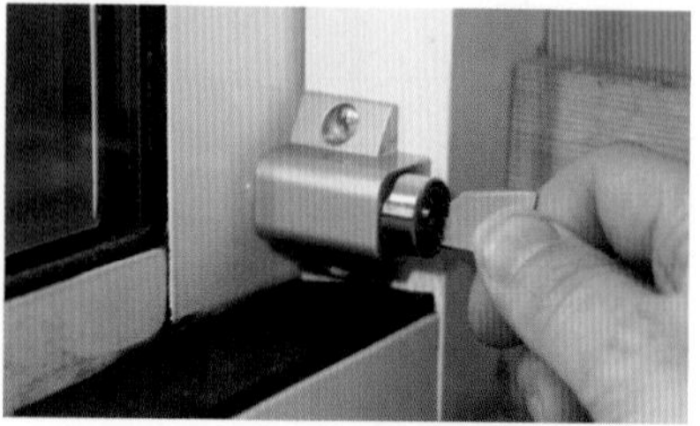

Fit a lock to the top and bottom of a sliding door

Pivot windows

If a pivot window is not supplied with an integral lock, use rack bolts or locks recommended for casement windows. Alternatively, fit the swing-bar lock suggested for fanlight windows.

Fanlight windows

You can buy a variety of casement locks, as well as devices that secure the stay to the window frame. The simplest kind is screwed below the stay arm to receive a key-operated bolt passed through one of the holes in the stay arm. Purpose-made lockable stays are also available.

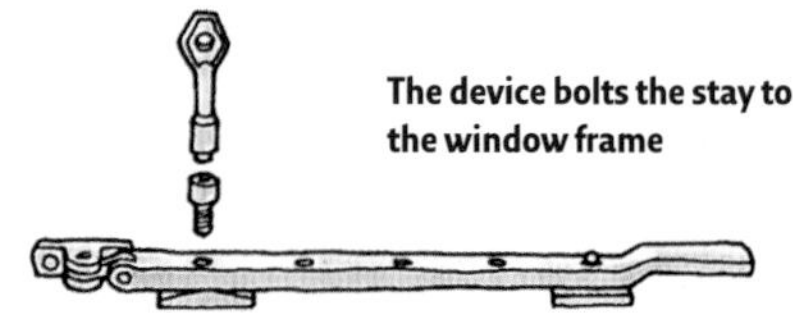

The device bolts the stay to the window frame

A better alternative is a swing-bar lock that clamps the window to the surrounding frame. Attach the lock first, then use it to position the staple.

Attach the lock first in order to locate the staple

SEE ALSO >Casement windows 192

Burglar alarms

Although it's no substitute for good locks and catches, an alarm system provides extra security and may help to deter intruders. The system itself must be reliable, and you and your family need to be disciplined in its use. If your neighbours are constantly subjected to false alarms, they are less likely to call the police in a genuine emergency. In many areas, the police will not respond unless they are alerted by a member of the public or the system is professionally monitored.

Typical alarm systems

Alarm systems differ greatly, but there are two basic kinds: hard-wired systems, where the various detectors and sensors are connected to a central control unit by fine cable, and wireless systems that utilize radio signals to perform a similar function. Both types include passive sensors that detect the presence of an intruder inside the house, and perimeter protection to guard likely means of entry. The best systems incorporate a combination of features in case perimeter detectors are bypassed.

Control unit

The heart of the system is the control unit, which triggers a siren when it receives an alarm signal from a detector. The control unit has to be programmed to allow sufficient time for legitimate entry and exit. If it has a zone-monitoring option, you can activate door contacts or sensors in selected parts of the house – to permit freedom of movement upstairs at night, for example, while entry doors and downstairs areas remain fully guarded.

The control unit must be tamper-proof, so that it will trigger the alarm if disarming is attempted by any means other than a key or the correct digital code. It is usually connected to mains power – but it should also have a rechargeable battery, in case of power failure.

Scanning devices

Infra-red sensors can be strategically positioned to scan a wide area and will detect the presence of an intruder by measuring body heat. If necessary, you can opt for sensors able to distinguish between household pets and human beings. Passive infra-red detectors are usually connected to the central control unit, but you can buy independent battery-operated sensors for protecting a single room.

Infrasonic alarm systems can detect the ultra-low noise levels created by the displacement of air caused by opening or closing doors and windows. Even when the alarm is set, neither you nor your pets will trigger it unless you open a door or window. Infrasonic alarms are particularly easy to install.

Detectors

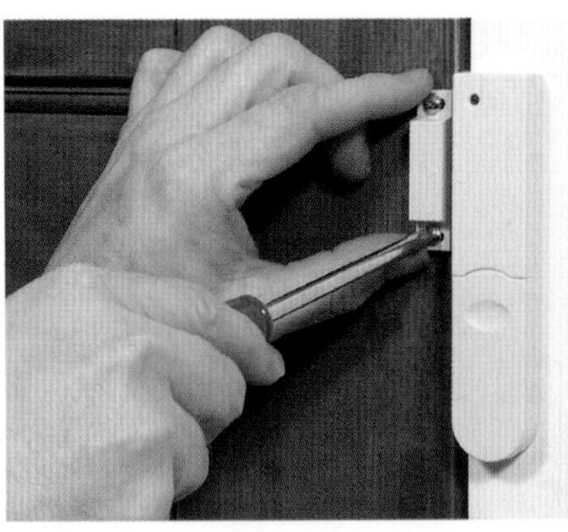

Entrances can be fitted with small devices that trigger the alarm when a magnetic contact is broken by someone opening a door or window. Other types of detector sense vibrations caused by breaking glass. A good detector is capable of distinguishing between a forced entry and vibration from other sources.

Exterior siren

Most alarms have a siren mounted on an outside wall. These switch off automatically after a set period, but some alarms are designed to continue signalling with a flashing light and some will automatically rearm themselves. It is important that the alarm is triggered by any attempt to tamper with it, either by dismantling or by cutting wires. Most sirens take their power from the control unit, but some are solar-powered. Many systems transmit a warning directly to a monitoring centre for a swift and reliable response to a break-in.

Personal-attack devices

With most systems you can have a 'panic button' installed beside entry doors to press in the event of an attack. There are also portable wireless devices that can be carried on the person to summon help in the case of emergency around your home and in the garden. These devices trip the alarm even when the system is disarmed.

DIY systems

If you want to avoid the expense of professional installation, there are several DIY alarm systems that are quick and easy to install. However, you may need advice from the supplier of the equipment on the choice and siting of sensors and detectors. Consult your insurance company to check whether your choice of alarm affects your policy in any way.

Make sure the system will enable you to select the type and number of detectors you require, and that it incorporates a reliable tamper-proof control unit.

Wireless systems – which use secure coded radio signals to trigger the alarm – avoid the need for extensive wiring and can be extended to monitor sheds and garages. During installation you can programme each piece of equipment, including the control unit, with your own personal numeric code.

SEE ALSO > Crime Prevention Officer 232, Security lighting 337–8, CCTV 339–40

Protecting against fire

No one needs to be reminded about the potential risk of fire – and yet nearly all domestic fires are caused by carelessness. Many fires could be prevented by taking sensible precautions.

Avoiding the risks

Smoke detectors
A detector provides an early warning of fire. Choose only those that comply with BS 5446 Part 1. Press your detector's test button once a week and vacuum dust from inside twice a year.

Make sure your electrical installations and equipment are safe and in good order. Don't overload power sockets with adaptors: fit more sockets instead. Don't trail long extension leads and flexes under carpets or rugs: if the wiring becomes damaged, it could overheat and start a serious fire.

Never leave fires or heaters unguarded, especially when there are children in the house. And don't dry clothes in front of a fire – they could easily fall onto the elements or flames.

Take particular care with smoking materials. Empty ashtrays at night, but dampen the contents before discarding them. Don't rest ashtrays on chair arms: a burning cigarette's centre of gravity shifts as it burns, which may cause it to topple off and ignite the upholstery. Never smoke in bed: fires are frequently caused by smokers falling asleep and setting light to the bedclothes.

Keep your workshop or garage clear of shavings and flammable rubbish – especially oily rags, which can ignite spontaneously. If possible, store flammable chemicals and paints in an outbuilding away from the house.

As a means of fighting a fire, install an all-purpose fire extinguisher in a prominent position, preferably on an escape route. Mount a fire blanket close to – but not directly above – the cooker. Your local Fire Prevention Officer will be able to recommend equipment for domestic use. Don't buy inferior items: they may not work in an emergency.

Carbon monoxide

Carbon monoxide is a toxic gas produced by poorly maintained or badly fitted heating appliances, such as gas fires and boilers. Because the gas is colourless and odourless, it's worth installing simple carbon-monoxide detectors, similar in size and appearance to a smoke detector.

One alarm should be installed near your bedrooms and it is worth having a second alarm where the boiler or heater is located, but at least 2 metres (6ft 6in) away from the appliance itself.

Screw each detector to a wall at eye level. When carbon monoxide is detected, a red LED comes on, accompanied by a loud siren.

Providing escape routes

Fire blankets and extinguishers
Portable extinguishers should comply with BSEN3, and fire blankets with BSEN 1869. Extinguishers must be serviced regularly.

Your first responsibility is to ensure that your family can escape safely if your house should catch fire. Before you go to bed, close internal doors – which will help to contain a fire – but don't lock them. Locked internal doors rarely deter burglars, anyway.

Although you shouldn't leave a key in an external lock, keep it close by but out of reach of the door or windows. Make sure everyone in the house knows where the key is kept, and always return it to the same place after use. Ensure some accessible part of double-glazed windows can be opened to afford an emergency escape route. Consider keeping a chain escape ladder in a bedroom or in a cupboard on your upstairs landing.

Keep stairs and hallways free from obstructions: they may be difficult to see in dense smoke. Avoid using oil heaters to warm these areas, in case they get knocked over during an escape and spread the fire further. Communal stairs to flats are especially important, so try to persuade neighbours to keep them clear.

In the event of a fire, get everyone out of the building quickly, alert neighbours and call the fire brigade. Never open a door that feels warm – it could be protecting you from a dangerous smouldering fire.

Tackling a fire

Don't attempt to tackle a fire yourself unless you discover it early – and then only with the right equipment. Make sure that everyone in your family knows what to do in the event of a fire.

Fat fire

Cooking oil ignites when it reaches a certain temperature – unattended chip pans cause a lot of domestic fires. Don't attempt to move a burning pan. Instead:

- Turn off the source of heat if it is safe to do so.
- Smother the fire with a close-fitting lid or a fire blanket. Alternatively, quickly soak a tea towel in water, wring it out, and drape it over the burning pan.
- Leave the pan to cool for at least half an hour.
- If you aren't able to extinguish the fire immediately, call the fire brigade.

Chimney fire

If there is a blaze in a chimney, phone the fire brigade, then stand a fireguard on the hearth and evacuate the house.

Smoke detectors

A smoke detector will identify the presence of smoke and fumes and sound a shrill warning. Although detectors can be incorporated into an alarm system, self-contained battery-operated units are easier to fit yourself. Change the battery at least once a year, and check that the detector is working by pressing its test button.

There are two basic types of detector. Photoelectric devices detect smoke from slow-burning fires, which give off large quantities of smoke. Ionization detectors are less sensitive to smouldering fires but are attuned to particles of smoke produced by hot, blazing fires, such as a burning chip pan. Some detectors combine both systems.

Siting a smoke detector

The best place for a smoke alarm is on the ceiling, at least 300mm (1ft) away from any wall or light fitting. If it's wall mounted, it should be 150 to 300mm (6in to 1ft) below the ceiling. Don't install a smoke detector in a kitchen or bathroom.

In a bungalow, mount a detector between the bedrooms and living area(s). In a two-storey home, fit one detector in the hallway, directly above the bottom of the stairs, and if possible fit a second one on the landing. Some smoke alarms can be linked – if one detects smoke, they are all triggered at once.

SEE ALSO > Fire-resistant doors 191, Fire-prevention officer 232, Checking electrics 290–91

Infestation, Rot and Damp

Eradicating pests

Our homes are sometimes invaded by voracious insect pests. Some of these are quite harmless, although they cause a great deal of annoyance and even alarm; but certain insects can severely weaken the structure of a building, and they often go unnoticed until the damage is done. At the first signs of infestation, try to identify and eradicate the pests as quickly as possible – before they seriously damage your home.

Woodboring insects
(Not drawn to scale)
These can destroy the timbers and furniture in your home. Urgent treatment is required.

Furniture beetle

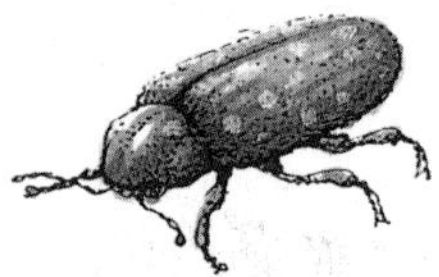

Deathwatch beetle

House longhorn beetle

Woodboring weevil

Attack by woodworm

Woodworm is the term used to describe all kinds of woodboring insects. The most common of these pests is the furniture beetle. The adult insect is a brown beetle about 3mm (⅛in) long – but the damage is caused by its larvae, which feed on the sapwood of household timbers. The beetle, which is most active in early summer, lays its eggs in the crevices of bare timber.

When the grubs hatch, they burrow into the wood for up to 3 years, then pupate just below the surface. The new adult emerges by chewing its way out, leaving the familiar round flight hole. These tiny holes, about 1 to 2mm (1/16in) in diameter, are generally the first signs of infestation – but there may be several generations of woodworm active inside the timber.

Other types of woodworm

The furniture beetle is said to inhabit about three-quarters of British homes – and most outbreaks of woodworm are certainly caused by this pest. However, there are other woodboring insects that can create even greater damage.

Both the deathwatch beetle and the house longhorn beetle bore much larger holes – from 3 to 6mm (⅛ to ¼in) in diameter. The environmental authorities are anxious to control the spread of these rarer insects, so contact your local Environmental Health Department if you suspect their presence in your home.

Another common pest is the weevil, which attacks wood at two stages in its life cycle. Both the adults and the grubs burrow into all types of timber – but only when it is already decaying and in a moist condition.

Locating woodworm

Check the unfinished parts of your furniture, particularly plywood drawer bottoms and backs of cabinets – as wood-boring insects have a taste for the glues used in their manufacture. Wickerwork and the wooden frames of upholstered furniture are other favourite habitats.

The structural timbers of your house are the place where woodworm can do most harm. Inspect roof timbers, stairs, floorboards and joists. The unpainted underedges of doors and skirtings are also common breeding grounds, as is the upper edge of picture rails.

Where the insects' flight holes are dark in colour, it may be that the timber has received treatment already – but clean holes, especially when surrounded by the fine pale-coloured dust known as 'frass', are evidence of recent activity. If the signs are extensive, push a knife blade into the infected timbers; if the wood crumbles, the infestation is serious and you need to seek the advice of a specialist contractor. The damaged woodwork will have to be cut away and replaced, then the new and old wood treated with a chemical preserver.

Treating minor outbreaks

Dealing with a minor woodworm outbreak in furniture and other small wooden items is a fairly simple task.

Use either a special aerosol applicator or a can with a pointed nozzle (**1**) to inject woodworm fluid into the insects' flight holes every 75 to 100mm (3 to 4in). Since the tunnels are connected, the fluid will penetrate deeply into the wood.

Continue the treatment by painting all unfinished timber with two coats of fluid (**2**). There's no need to paint fluid onto polished surfaces, although it will not harm them.

Use a pump-action spray can or an aerosol to coat the inside of confined spaces (**3**) and wickerwork.

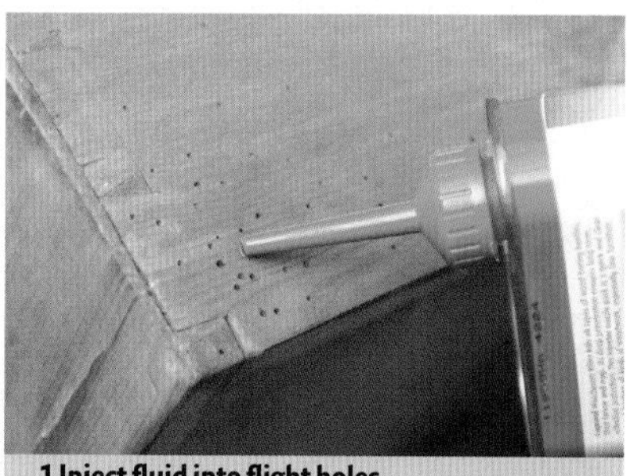

1 Inject fluid into flight holes

2 Paint bare timber with preservative

3 Spray fluid into confined spaces

Professional treatment for woodworm

Treating house timbers
Hire a specialist contractor to treat woodworm in structural timbers.

If woodworm is spotted by your surveyor when inspecting a house that you are thinking of buying, your mortgage company will insist that you hire a specialist firm to eradicate the pest who guarantee the work for 20 or 30 years.

Similarly, if you detect woodworm in your present home, have it inspected by a specialist firm who will advise you on the extent of the damage (which may not be obvious to the untrained eye) and quote a price for treating, and if need be replacing, the infested timber.

You can treat less serious infestations yourself, using a chemical insecticide. Most of these fluids are flammable; so don't smoke when applying them, and extinguish any naked flames. Wear protective gloves, goggles and a respirator. The initial smell of solvent-based eradicators can be unpleasant, but will gradually fade.

Water-based low-odour woodworm eradicators are solvent-free and non-flammable. This type of eradicator is suitable for use in bat roosts.

SEE ALSO > Surveyors 16–17

Disguising flight holes

After treatment, fill flight holes in painted woodwork with cellulose filler. Use sticks of wax to match the colour of polished or varnished wood. It is possible to use children's wax crayons, but sticks of harder wax are available from specialist wood-finish suppliers.

Cut off a piece of wax and put it on top of a radiator to soften. Using a pocket knife, press the wax into the woodworm holes (1) and leave it to harden. Scrape the repair flush with an old plastic phone card or credit card, then fold a piece of sandpaper and use the paper backing to burnish the wax filling (2).

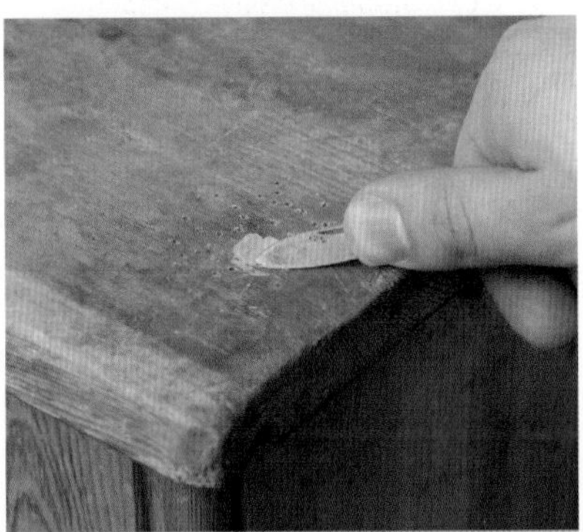

1 Press wax into the woodworm holes

2 Burnish the hardened wax

Preventive treatment

To protect new timber from attack, treat it with a chemical preserver. Once the wood is dry, it can be decorated in the usual way.

Furniture can be protected with an insecticidal polish. If you buy an old piece of furniture that shows any signs of infestation, treat it with a chemical preserver to be on the safe side.

Other insect pests

Insecticides can be dangerous if they are allowed to contaminate foodstuffs (they are also harmful to honey bees), so follow the manufacturer's instructions carefully when using them to eradicate insect pests of any kind.

Common household insect pests
(Not drawn to scale)
The insects shown below constitute a nuisance or health hazard, rather than a threat to the structure of your house.

Common black ant

Wasp

Housefly

Cockroach

Silverfish

Ants

Common black ants often enter buildings to forage for food. Once established, the worker ants follow well-defined trails. In summer, great numbers of winged ants emerge from the nest to mate, but the swarming is over in a matter of hours and the ants themselves are harmless. If the flying ants stray into your house, they can be overcome with an insecticidal spray.

To locate the nest, follow the trail of ants. The nest may be situated under a path, at the base of a wall, in the lawn or under a flat stone, perhaps as far as 6m (20ft) from the house. Destroy the nest by pouring boiling water into the entrances. Alternatively, seal the nest with a foam insecticide.

Wasps

Wasps are beneficial in spring and the early summer, as they feed on garden pests; but later in the year they destroy soft fruit. They have also been known to kill honey bees.

Trap foraging wasps in open jam jars containing a mixture of jam, water and detergent. You can kill flying wasps with an aerosol fly spray. Wasps can be destroyed in their nest by depositing insecticidal powder near and around the entrances – tie a spoon to a cane to extend your reach. Where there's no risk of fire, another alternative is to light a smoke-generating pellet, place it in the entrance and seal the opening.

Wasps sting when they are aroused or frightened.Treat a wasp sting with a cold compress soaked in witch hazel, or use an antihistamine cream or spray.

Flies

Houseflies breed in rotting vegetables, manure, and decaying meat and offal. They can carry the eggs of parasitic worms, and spread disease by leaving small black spots of vomit and excreta on foodstuffs.

Cover food, and keep refuse in a bin liner inside a garbage bin with a tight lid. Gauze screens fitted over windows and bead curtains in open doorways will help to keep flies out of the house. An aerosol fly spray will deal with small numbers; but for swarming flies – in a roof space, for example – use an insecticidal smoke generator (available from a hardware store or chemist). Large numbers in a living room can be sucked into a vacuum cleaner; then suck up some insecticidal powder and wait for a few hours before emptying.

Cockroaches

It is rare to find cockroaches in domestic premises, but they are sometimes attracted by warmth and a ready supply of food and water. Cockroaches are unhygienic, and smell unpleasant. Being nocturnal feeders, they tend to hide during the day in crevices in walls, behind cupboards, and above all in warm places – under cookers or fridges, for example, or near heating pipes.

A serious outbreak should be dealt with by professionals, but you can lay insecticidal powder between accessible food supplies and suspected daytime haunts – taking care not to sprinkle it near the food itself. Use a paintbrush to stipple powder into crevices and under skirting boards.

Once you have eradicated the pests, fill cracks and gaps to prevent a return.

Silverfish

Silverfish are tapered wingless insects about 12mm (½in) long. They like the moist conditions found in bathrooms, kitchens and cellars. You may discover them behind wallpaper, where they feed on the paste; or in bookshelves, as they also eat paper. Use an insecticidal spray or powder in these locations.

SEE ALSO > Preservers 246

Birds and animal pests

Insects are not the only pests that invade buildings. Mice and rats can be a menace, particularly in older houses where there are plenty of underfloor runs. These enable them to live and prosper uninterrupted, and to benefit from a plentiful supply of food by invading your living quarters. Mice are just a nuisance, but rats present a positive health hazard; eradication is therefore essential. Bats sometimes shelter inside houses, too, usually occupying the roof space. Although you may not relish sharing your home with them, they are harmless and are protected by law.

Electronic repellers
When plugged into a socket, electromagnetic and ultrasonic repellers discourage mice, rats and other pests from nesting. These small devices do not disturb cats, dogs or birds, but they are not suitable for homes with rodent pets, such as mice, rabbits and hamsters.

Mice

Mice are attracted by fallen scraps of food, so the easiest remedy is to keep floors spotlessly clean. However, mice can move from house to house, through roof spaces or wall cavities and under floors, and so may be difficult to eradicate. Consult your local Environmental Health Department if they persist.

You can obtain ready-poisoned bait - which should be sprinkled onto a piece of paper or a disposable dish, so you are able to remove uneaten bait safely. Keep pets and children away from the bait. If signs of mice are still evident after 3 weeks, resort to traps. Humane traps capture mice alive in a cage or box, enabling you to deposit them elsewhere. Although less humane, you can also use spring-loaded traps.

The best place to put traps is against the skirting board in a dark corner, or put them behind the plinth under your kitchen cupboards.

Bait mouse traps with porridge oats or chocolate moulded onto the bait hook. If necessary, dispose of the bodies by burying or burning them.

Domestic mouse
Not a serious threat to health, though mice are unhygienic rodents.

Rats

Serious rat infestation occurs rarely in the average domestic situation, but rats can be a problem in rural and inner-city areas or near rivers, canals and docks.

They can be killed with anti-coagulant poisons - but as rats are a health hazard, always contact your local Environmental Health Department for expert advice.

Common rat
A serious health risk. Seek expert advice.

Bats

Bats prefer to roost in uninhabited structures such as barns, caves, mines and tunnels, but occasionally they take up residence in houses. They do not present a health hazard (their droppings are dry insect skeletons), nor do they gnaw at wood or paintwork. In fact, they are an advantage in a roof space, as they feed on woodworm beetles.

Bats are becoming rare and are now a protected species. It is illegal to kill or injure bats, or disturb their roosting place or block their means of access. If you are alarmed by their presence, contact your local Environmental Health Department for advice. You must inform the same authority if you plan to have wood preservers or insect eradicators sprayed in a roof space inhabited by bats, since certain chemicals will harm them.

If a bat should fly into a room, try to keep calm. It will avoid you if it can. Open all the doors and windows immediately, so it is able to escape. A crawling bat can be picked up carefully in gloved hands and gently put outside.

Repelling birds
As well as being noisy, pigeons, gulls and starlings foul wherever they perch in significant numbers. You can buy self-adhesive strips of plastic spikes that dissuade the birds from alighting on ledges. Alternatively, spray the ledges with a foam that dries to form a sticky transparent surface, which deters the birds without harming them.

Handling poisons

Poisons designed to kill rodents are deadly to humans too - so it is vital to follow the manufacturer's handling and storage instructions to the letter. Store poisons where pets and other animals cannot get at them, and make sure they are kept out of reach of children. Never store poisons under the kitchen sink - where they could easily be mistaken for household products - or anywhere where they might contaminate food.

If poison is accidentally consumed by humans or animals, keep the container so that the poison can be identified by a doctor or vet. Wear protective gloves when you are handling poisons.

Handling poisons safely
Wear gloves when preparing poisoned bait.

Rodent damage
As well as posing a health risk, rodents can cause material damage, too.

Rats will chew through plumbing to get water

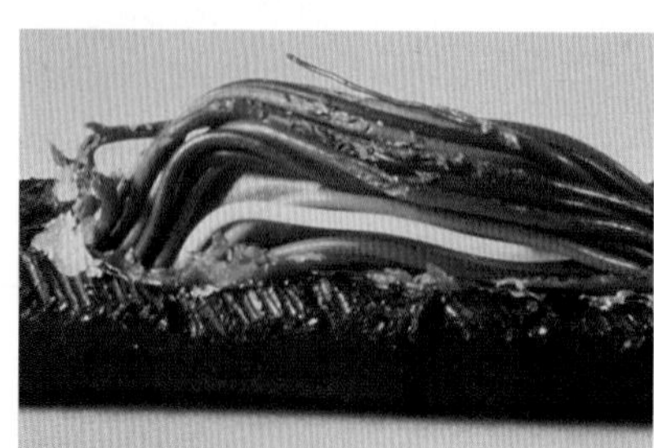

Electrical cable chewed by mice

Rat damage to old pipework

SEE ALSO > Insect pests 242–3

Wet rot and dry rot

Rot occurs in unprotected household timbers, outbuildings and fences that are subject to damp. Fungal spores – which are always present – multiply and develop in damp conditions, until eventually the timber is destroyed. Fungal attack can cause serious structural damage and requires immediate attention if costly repairs are to be avoided. The two most common scourges are wet rot and dry rot.

Recognizing rot

Signs of fungal attack are easy enough to detect – but certain strains are much more damaging than others, and so it is important to be able to identify them.

Mould growth

White furry deposits or black spots on timber, plaster or wallpaper are mould growths. Usually, these are the result of condensation. When they are wiped or scraped off, the structure shows no sign of physical deterioration apart from staining. Cure the source of the damp conditions, and treat the affected area with a fungicide or a solution of 16 parts warm water : 1 part household bleach.

Wet rot

Wet rot only occurs in timber that has a high moisture content. Once the cause of the moisture is eliminated, further deterioration is arrested. This type of rot often attacks the framework of doors and windows that have been neglected, allowing rainwater to penetrate joints or between brickwork and adjacent timbers.

The first sign of wet rot is often peeling paintwork. Stripping the paint reveals timber that is soft and spongy when wet, but dark brown and crumbly when dry. In advanced stages the grain splits and thin grey-brown or black fungal strands are evident on the timber. As the fungus grows, flat fruiting bodies may develop. Always treat wet rot as soon as practicable.

Wet rot – treat it at the earliest opportunity

Dry rot

Once it has taken hold, dry rot can be an extremely serious form of decay. Urgent treatment is therefore essential. It attacks timber with a much lower moisture content than wet rot, but only in dark, poorly ventilated spaces indoors – unlike wet rot, which thrives outdoors as well as indoors.

Dry rot exhibits different characteristics depending on the extent of its development. It spreads over timber and other materials as a network of fine tubular strands. These can spread very widely, even passing through cracks in building materials such as plaster, stone, brick and concrete. The rot can progress at an alarming rate – as much as 150mm (6in) in a month. Once established, dry rot develops wrinkled pancake-shaped fruiting bodies that are brown in colour with smooth white outer margins. When the spores are released, they cover surrounding timber and masonry with a layer of fine rust-red dust. You may detect a pungent, musty, mushroom-like smell, produced by the fungus.

Infested timber becomes dark brown and brittle, with deep cracks across and along the grain, causing it to break up into cube-like pieces. Painted wood may exhibit signs of buckling, and the surface may collapse due to decomposition of the wood.

Dry rot – urgent treatment is essential

Treating rot

Wear protective gloves, goggles and a respirator when handling preservatives.

Dealing with wet rot

Once you have eliminated the cause of the damp, cut away and replace wood that is badly damaged, then paint the new and surrounding woodwork with three liberal applications of chemical wet-rot eradicator. Brush it into the joints and end grain well.

Before decorating, you can apply a wood hardener to reinforce slightly damaged timber, then 6 hours later rebuild the surface with a special two-part wood filler.

Paint slightly damaged timber with hardener

Dealing with dry rot

Call in an independent expert who can identify the source of the damp and tell you what needs to be done. This often involves having to remove not only affected timbers but also much of the surrounding material.

Once the source of the moisture has been eliminated, the usual treatment involves replacing infected wood and stripping plastered surfaces up to 1m (3ft) beyond the last sign of fungal attack, and applying a fungicidal solution to sterilize all woodwork, masonry and associated materials in the area of the outbreak. You may have little choice but to accept such drastic measures if a treatment guarantee is required by your mortgage company. However, once the damp is eradicated and possibly extra ventilation provided, dry-rot growth will cease and chemical treatment may not be required. Before making a decision, you should get independent expert advice.

SEE ALSO > Eradicating mould growth 51, Repairing door and window frames 188–9, 198–9, Preventing damp 247–54

Preventive treatment

Because fungal attack can be so damaging, it is well worth taking precautions to prevent it occurring. Regularly decorate and maintain doorframes and window frames – where water is able to penetrate easily – and seal around them with mastic. Provide adequate ventilation between floors and ceilings, and also in the loft. Check and eradicate sources of damp, such as plumbing leaks. During routine maintenance, apply a chemical preserver to unprotected wood.

Protecting joints
Place preservative tablets close to the joints of a frame.

Preserving timberwork

Brush or spray two or three applications of a chemical preserver onto both new and existing timbers, paying particular attention to joints and end grain.

Protecting door and window frames

You can buy preserver in solid-tablet form. To protect timber frames, insert the tablets into holes drilled at regular 50mm (2in) intervals in a staggered pattern. If the timber becomes wet, the tablets will dissolve, placing preserver exactly where it is needed. Fill the holes with wood filler and paint as normal.

Immersing timbers

Timber that is to be in contact with the ground will benefit from prolonged immersion in preserver – you should, at least, stand fence posts on end in a bucket of preserver fluid overnight. For better protection, make a shallow bath from loose bricks and line it with thick polythene sheet. Fill the trough with the preserver and immerse the timbers, weighing them down with bricks to prevent them from floating (1). Leave the bath covered overnight. Next day, bury a bucket at one end of the trough and remove the bricks at that end, so the fluid will empty into the bucket (2).

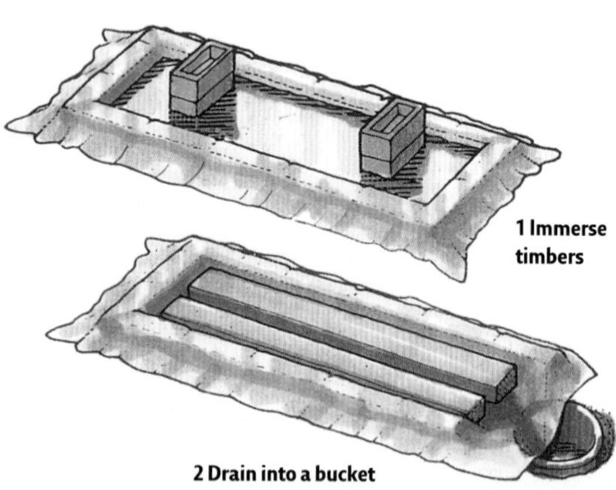

Safety with preservers

Solvent-based preservers are flammable – so don't smoke while you are handling or applying them, and extinguish any naked lights first. Wear protective gloves and goggles and a respirator when applying preservers. Provide good ventilation while working indoors, and don't sleep in a freshly treated room for 48 hours or so – in order to allow time for the fumes to dissipate completely. Wash spilt preserver from your skin and eyes with water immediately. Don't delay seeking medical advice if irritation persists.

Wood preservers

Most modern solvent-based products are harmless to plants when dry – but it makes sense to check before you buy. Water-based preservers are odourless and can safely be used on horticultural timbers.

You can use clear liquid preservers that protect timber from dry or wet rot only. Alternatively, use an all-purpose fluid that will also provide protection against woodboring insects. Clear preservers are useful when you want to retain the appearance of natural timber – oak beams or hardwood doors, for example. Usually, you can either varnish or paint the surface once the wood has dried.

Green preserver

There is a green solvent-based preserver that's traditionally used on horticultural timbers. Its colour helps identify treated timbers for the future. The green tint is due to the presence of copper, which is not a permanent colouring agent when used outdoors. The protective properties of this type of preserver nevertheless remain unaffected, even when the colour is washed out by heavy rain.

Coloured preservers

You can buy preservers formulated to protect sound exterior timbers against fungal and insect attack while staining the wood at the same time. There is a choice of brown shades intended to simulate common hardwoods, and one that is designed specifically to preserve the richness of cedarwood. The solvent-based types are made with light-fast pigments that inhibit fading. They don't penetrate as well as clear preservers, but generally provide slightly better protection than tinted preservers that are water-based.

There are ranges of colourful wood finishes for sheds and fences that render the wood water-resistant but offer no protection against insect or serious fungal attack. However, you can treat the wood beforehand, using a clear preserver.

SEE ALSO > Preparing wood 52–6, Finishing wood 70–81, Woodworm 242–3, Wet and dry rot 245

Types of damp

Damp can be detrimental to your health and to the condition of your home. So try to locate and eliminate the source of the problem as quickly as possible – before it promotes its even more damaging side effects, wet and dry rot. Unfortunately, this is sometimes easier said than done, as one form of damp may be obscured by another or may appear in an unfamiliar guise. The three main categories are penetrating damp, rising damp and condensation.

Principal causes of rising damp
- Missing DPC or DPM
- Damaged DPC or DPM
- DPC too low
- Bridged DPC
- Earth piled above DPC

Principal causes of penetrating damp
1 Broken gutter
2 Leaking downpipe
3 Missing roof tiles
4 Damaged flashing
5 Faulty pointing
6 Porous bricks
7 Cracked masonry
8 Cracked render
9 Blocked drip groove
10 Defective seals around frames
11 Missing weatherboard
12 Bridged cavity

Penetrating damp

Penetrating damp is the result of water permeating the structure of the house from outside. The symptoms only occur during wet weather or very soon after it has rained. A few days later, the damp patches dry out, often leaving stains.

As isolated patches are caused by a heavy deposit of water in one area, you should be able to pinpoint their source fairly accurately. General dampness usually indicates that the wall itself has become porous, but it could equally well be caused by some other problem.

Penetrating damp most frequently occurs in older homes that have solid walls. Relatively modern houses built with a cavity between two thinner brick skins are less likely to suffer from penetrating damp, unless the cavity is bridged in one of several ways.

DPC in a solid wall
A layer of impervious material is built into a joint between brick courses, 150mm (6in) above the ground.

Rising damp

Rising damp is caused by water soaking up from the ground into the floors and walls of the house. Most houses are protected by an impervious barrier built into the walls and under concrete floors, so that water cannot permeate above a certain level.

If either the damp-proof course (DPC) in the walls or the membrane (DPM) in a floor breaks down, water is able to seep into the upper structure. Alternatively, there may be something forming a bridge across the barrier, so that water is able to flow around it. Some older houses were built without a DPC.

This type of damp is confined to the lower sections of walls and to solid floors. It is a constant problem – even during dry spells – and gets worse with prolonged wet weather.

DPC and DPM in a cavity-wall structure
The DPM in a concrete floor is linked to the DPC protecting the inner leaf of the cavity wall. The outer leaf of the wall has its own damp-proof course.

SEE ALSO > Wet and dry rot 245

Seal leaky guttering

Flood prevention
If you live in an area that floods regularly, you may want to take preventive measures, such as fitting temporary but effective plastic barriers across external doors. Similarly, it may be worth fitting clip-on covers to prevent flood water entering your home via airbricks. For detailed advice, contact the Environment Agency Floodline (0845 988 1188) or consult their website, **www.environment-agency.gov.uk.**

Cover airbricks

Fit plastic door barriers

PENETRATING DAMP: PRINCIPAL CAUSES

CAUSE	SYMPTOMS	REMEDY
Broken or blocked gutter Rainwater overflows, typically at the joints of old cast-iron gutters, and saturates the wall directly below, preventing it from drying out normally.	Damp patches appearing near the ceiling in upstairs rooms, and mould forming immediately behind the leak.	Clear leaves and silt from the gutters. Repair the damaged gutters, or replace a faulty system with maintenance-free plastic guttering.
Broken or blocked downpipes A downpipe that has cracked or rusted douses the wall immediately behind the leak. Leaves lodged behind the pipe at the fixing brackets will eventually produce a similar effect.	An isolated patch of damp, often appearing halfway up the wall. Mould growth behind the downpipe.	Repair the cracked or corroded downpipe; or replace it, substituting a maintenance-free plastic version. Clear the blockage.
Loose or broken roof tiles Defective tiles allow rainwater to penetrate the roof.	Damp patches appearing on upstairs ceilings, usually after heavy rain.	Replace the faulty tiles, renewing any damaged roofing felt.
Damaged flashing The junction between the roof of a lean-to extension and the side wall of the house or around a chimney stack emerging from the roof is sealed with flashing strips. These are usually made of lead or zinc, but sometimes a mortar fillet is used instead. If the flashing or fillet cracks or parts from the masonry, water trickles down inside the building.	Damp patch on the ceiling extending from the wall or chimney breast; also on the chimney breast itself. Damp patch on the side wall near the junction with the lean-to extension; damp patch on the lean-to ceiling itself.	If the existing flashing appears to be intact, refit it securely. If it is damaged, replace it, using similar material or a self-adhesive flashing strip.
Faulty pointing Ageing mortar between bricks in an exterior wall is likely to crack or fall out; water is then able to penetrate to the inside of the wall.	Isolated damp patches or sometimes widespread dampness, depending on the extent of the deterioration.	Repoint the joints between bricks, then treat the entire wall with water-repellent fluid.
Porous bricks Bricks in good condition are weather-proof; but old soft bricks become porous and often lose their faces. As a result, the whole wall is eventually saturated, particularly on an elevation that faces prevailing winds or where a fault with the guttering develops.	Widespread damp on the inner face of exterior walls. A noticeable increase in damp during a downpour. Mould growth or stains appearing on internal plaster and decorations.	Repair bricks that have spalled, and waterproof the exterior with a clear water-repellent fluid.
Cracked brickwork Cracks in a brick wall allow rainwater (or water from a leak) to seep through to the inside face.	An isolated damp patch – on a chimney breast, for example, due to a cracked chimney stack.	Fill cracked mortar and replace damaged bricks.
Defective render Cracked or blown render encourages rainwater to seep between the render and the brickwork behind it. The water is prevented from evaporating and so becomes absorbed by the wall.	An isolated damp patch, which may become widespread. The trouble can persist for some time after rain ceases.	Fill and reinforce the crack. Hack off extensively damaged or blown render and patch it with new sand-cement render; then weatherproof the wall by applying exterior paint.
Damaged coping If the coping stones on top of a roof parapet are missing or the joints are open, water can penetrate the wall.	Damp patches on ceiling, near to the wall immediately below the parapet.	Bed new stones on fresh mortar and make good the joints.

SEE ALSO > Repointing 43, Waterproofing masonry 44, Repairing render 45, Painting exterior masonry 64–6, Abutments and parapets 129, Flashings 132–3, Guttering 134–7

PENETRATING DAMP: PRINCIPAL CAUSES

CAUSE	SYMPTOMS	REMEDY
Blocked drip groove Exterior windowsills should have a groove running longitudinally on the underside. When rain runs under the sill, the water falls off at the groove before reaching the wall. If the groove is bridged by layers of paint or moss, the water soaks the wall behind.	Damp patches along the underside of a window frame. Rotting wooden sill on the inside and outside. Mould growth appearing on the inside face of the wall below the window.	Rake out the drip groove. Nail a batten to the underside of a wooden sill to deflect drips.
Failed seals around windows and doorframes Timber frames often shrink, pulling the pointing from around the edges so that rainwater is able to penetrate the gap.	Rotting woodwork and patches of damp around the frames. Sometimes the gap is obvious where mortar has fallen out.	Repair the frame, and seal around the edges with a clear sealant. Seal gaps around UPVC frames, too.
No weatherboard An angled weatherboard across the bottom of a door should shed water clear of the threshold and prevent water running under the door.	Damp floorboards just inside the door. Rotting at the base of the doorframe.	Fit a weatherboard, even if there are no obvious signs of damage. Repair rotted wood at the base of the doorframe.
Bridged wall cavity Mortar inadvertently dropped onto a wall tie connecting the inner and outer leaves of a cavity wall allows water to bridge the gap.	An isolated patch of damp appearing anywhere on the wall, particularly after a heavy downpour.	Open up the wall and remove the mortar bridge.

Seal around windows and doorframes

RISING DAMP: PRINCIPAL CAUSES

CAUSE	SYMPTOMS	REMEDY
No DPC or DPM If a house is built without either a damp-proof course or damp-proof membrane, the walls are able to soak up water from the ground.	Widespread damp up to about 1m (3ft) above skirting level. Damp concrete floor surface.	Depending on the age of the property, you can fit a new DPC or DPM. If your house is pre-Victorian, obtain expert advice before fitting either.
Damaged DPC or DPM If the DPC or DPM has deteriorated, water will penetrate at that point.	Damp at skirting level (possibly isolated but spreading).	Repair or replace the DPC or DPM.
DPC too low If the DPC is lower than the necessary 150mm (6in) above ground level, heavy rain is able to splash above the DPC and soak the wall surface.	Damp at skirting level, but only where the ground is too high.	Lower the level of the ground outside. If it's a path or patio, cut a 150mm (6in) wide trench and fill with gravel, which drains rapidly.
Bridged DPC If exterior render has been taken below the DPC or if mortar has fallen within a cavity wall, moisture is able to cross over to the inside.	Widespread damp at and just above skirting level.	Hack off render to expose the DPC. Remove several bricks and rake out debris from the cavity.
Debris piled against wall A flower bed, rockery or area of paving built against a wall will bridge the DPC. Building material and garden refuse left there will also act as a bridge.	Damp at skirting level in area of bridge only, or spreading from that point.	Remove the earth, paving or debris and allow the wall to dry out naturally.

DPC too low

Render bridges DPC

Earth piled over DPC

SEE ALSO > Waterproofing masonry 44, New DPM 176–7, Repairing door and window frames 188–9, 198–9, Bridged cavity 250, Drip moulding 250, New DPC 252–3

Treating damp

Remedies for different forms of damp are suggested in the charts on the previous pages. The information below supplements these suggestions by providing more detailed advice on eradicating damp.

Waterproofing walls

Applying a repellent to the outside of a wall not only prevents rainwater soaking into the masonry but also reduces the possibility of interstitial condensation. This occurs when water vapour from inside the house penetrates the wall until it reaches the damp, colder interior of the masonry, where the vapour condenses. The moisture migrates back to the inner surface of the wall, causing stains and mould.

There are also damp-proofing liquids for painting onto the inside of walls, but these should be considered a temporary measure only, as they do not treat the source of the problem. Remove wallcoverings and make sure the wall surfaces are sound and clean. Treat any mould growth with a fungicide. Brush on two full coats of waterproofer over an area appreciably larger than the present extent of the damp. Once the wall is dry, you can decorate it with paint or a wallcovering.

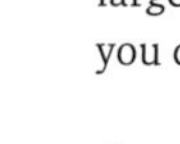

1 Water drips to the ground

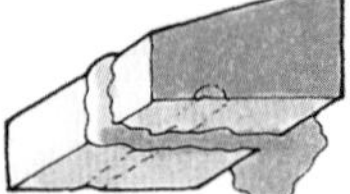

2 A bridged groove

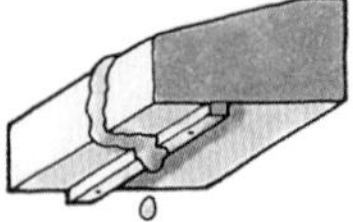

3 Drip moulding

Providing a drip moulding

Because water cannot flow uphill, a drip groove on the underside of an external windowsill forces rainwater to drip to the ground before it reaches the wall behind (**1**). When redecorating, scrape out old paint or moss from drip grooves before it forms a bridge (**2**).

If an external wooden windowsill does not have a precut drip groove, it is worth adding a drip moulding by pinning and gluing a hardwood strip 6mm (¼in) square 35mm (1½in) from the front edge of the sill (**3**). Finish the drip moulding to match the sill itself.

Sealing around window frames

Scrape out old or loose mortar from around the frame, and fill deep gaps with expanding-foam filler; then seal all around the frame with a flexible mastic. Mastic is available in cartridges, some designed for use with an applicator gun. Cut the end off the cartridge nozzle and run it along the side of the frame to form an even, continuous bead.

Most sealants form a skin and can be overpainted after a few hours, although they are waterproof without painting.

Bridged cavity

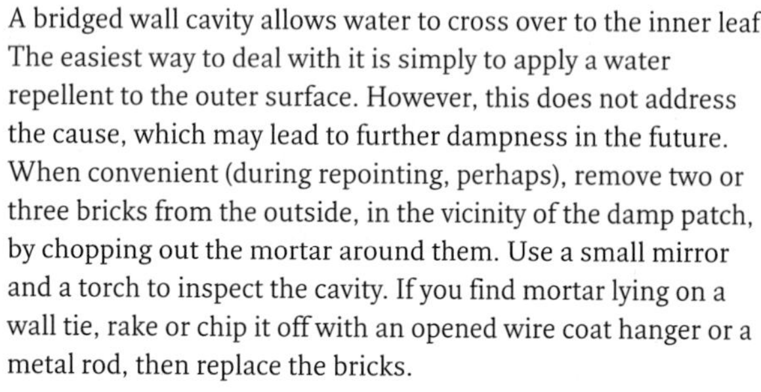

A bridged wall cavity allows water to cross over to the inner leaf. The easiest way to deal with it is simply to apply a water repellent to the outer surface. However, this does not address the cause, which may lead to further dampness in the future. When convenient (during repointing, perhaps), remove two or three bricks from the outside, in the vicinity of the damp patch, by chopping out the mortar around them. Use a small mirror and a torch to inspect the cavity. If you find mortar lying on a wall tie, rake or chip it off with an opened wire coat hanger or a metal rod, then replace the bricks.

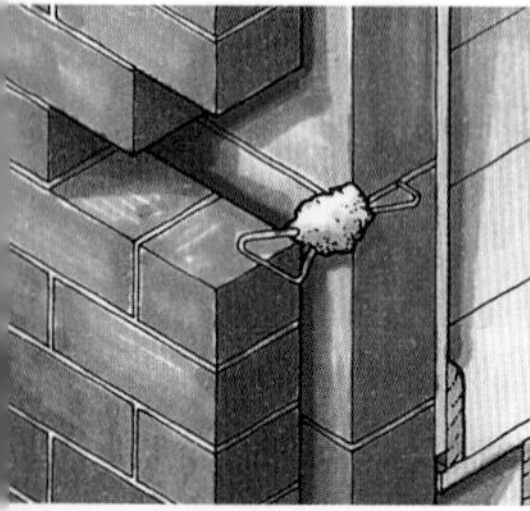

Exposing a bridged wall tie
Remove a few bricks in order to rake or chip off the mortar from the wall tie.

Condensation

Air carries moisture in the form of water vapour. The air's capacity depends on its temperature.

As air becomes warmer, it absorbs more water, rather like a sponge. When water-laden air comes into contact with a surface that is colder than itself, the air cools until it can no longer hold the water it has absorbed and – just like a sponge being squeezed – it condenses, depositing water in liquid form on the cold surface.

A great deal of moisture vapour is produced by cooking and by using baths and showers, and even by breathing. The air in a house is normally warm enough to hold the moisture without reaching saturation point – but in cold weather the low temperature outside cools the external walls and windows below the temperature of the heated air inside. When this happens, the moisture in the air condenses and runs down windowpanes and soaks into the wallpaper and plaster. Matters are made worse in the winter when windows and doors are kept closed, so that fresh air is unable to replace humid air before it condenses.

Damp in a fairly new house that is in good condition is almost invariably due to condensation.

The root cause of condensation is rarely simple – because it is the result of a combination of air temperature, thermal insulation, humidity and poor ventilation. Tackling just one of these problems in isolation may transfer the condensation elsewhere – or even exaggerate the symptoms. However, the chart opposite lists major factors that contribute to the total problem.

Condensation usually appears first on cold glass

SEE ALSO > Repointing 43, Waterproofing masonry 44

CONDENSATION: PRINCIPAL CAUSES

CAUSE	SYMPTOMS	REMEDY
Insufficient heat In cold weather the air in an unheated room may become saturated with moisture.	General condensation.	Heat the room to increase the ability of the air to absorb moisture without condensing – but don't use a paraffin heater (see below).
Paraffin heaters This type of heater produces as much water vapour as the paraffin it burns, causing condensation to form on cold windows, exterior walls and ceilings.	General condensation in rooms where paraffin heaters are used.	Substitute another form of heating.
Uninsulated walls and ceilings Moist air readily condenses on cold ceilings and exterior walls.	Widespread damp and mould. The line of ceiling joists is picked out because mould grows less well along the joists, which are relatively warm.	Install efficient loft insulation and/or line the ceiling with insulating tiles or polystyrene lining. Alternatively, apply anti-condensation paint.
Cold bridge Even when a wall has cavity insulation, there can be a cold bridge across the lintel over windows and the solid brick down the sides.	Damp patches or mould surrounding the window frames.	Line the walls and window reveals with expanded-polystyrene sheeting or foamed polyethylene.
Unlagged pipes Cold-water pipes attract condensation. The problem is often wrongly attributed to a leak when water collects and drips from the lowest point of a pipe run.	A line of damp on a ceiling or wall, following the pipework. An isolated patch on a ceiling, where water drops from plumbing. Beads of moisture on the underside of a pipe.	Insulate your cold-water pipes, either with plastic-foam lagging tubes or with mineral-fibre wrapping.
Cold windows When exterior temperatures are low, windows usually show condensation before other features do, because the glass is thin and is constantly exposed to the elements.	Misted windowpanes, or water collecting in pools at the bottom of the glass.	Double-glaze your windows. If condensation occurs inside a secondary system, place some silica-gel crystals (which absorb moisture) in the cavity between the panes.
Sealed fireplace If a fireplace opening is blocked up, the air trapped inside the flue cannot circulate and therefore condenses on the inside, eventually soaking through the brickwork.	Damp patches appearing anywhere on the chimney breast.	Ventilate the chimney by inserting a grille or airbrick at a low level in the part of the fireplace that has been blocked up. Treat the chimney breast with damp-proofing liquid.
Loft insulation blocking airways If loft insulation blocks the spaces around the eaves, air cannot circulate in the roof space and so condensation is able to form.	Widespread mould affecting the timbers in the roof space.	Unblock the airways and, if possible, fit a ventilator grille in the soffit or install tile/slate vents.
Condensation after building or repairs If you have carried out work involving new bricks, mortar and especially plaster, condensation may be the result of these materials exuding moisture as they dry out.	General condensation affecting walls, ceiling, windows and solid floors.	Wait for the new work to dry out, then review the situation before decorating or other treatment.

SEE ALSO > Lining with polystyrene 84, Lagging pipes 257, Insulating lofts 261–4, Insulating walls 265–6, Double glazing 267–9, Ventilating a fireplace 273, Soffit vents 275, Tile and slate vents 275, Extractor fans 277–8

Installing damp-proof courses

When an old damp-proof course (DPC) has failed, the only reliable remedy is to insert a new one. Of the options available, chemical injection is the only method you should attempt yourself. Even so, professional installation may be more cost-effective in the long run. Unless eradicated completely, rising damp can lead to other expensive repairs – so hiring a reputable company may be a wise investment (they normally provide a 30-year guarantee). Ask for a detailed specification to ensure that the work is carried out to approved standards.

Checking for rising damp

There's no substitute for a professional survey to determine the cause of rising damp, but you can use an inexpensive electronic moisture meter to check the condition of your walls.

Working on the inside, take readings at regular intervals along the entire length of a wall, not just in one spot. Systematically check an area extending from floor level to about 1m (3ft) above the floor. If rising damp is present, the meter should indicate a high moisture reading, which is likely to drop sharply above that level. Penetrating damp and condensation tend to show up either as isolated patches or as dampness that extends right up the wall. If you suspect rising damp, check that there is nothing bridging a perfectly sound damp-proof course before committing yourself to the cost of installing a new one.

It is sometimes possible to detect symptoms of rising damp even after the installation of a new DPC. This is almost always due to old salt-contaminated plaster – which should be removed and replaced with special renovating plaster.

Use a moisture meter to test for rising damp

A physical DPC

A traditional DPC consists of a layer of impervious material built into the wall at about 150mm (6in) – or two to three brick courses – above ground level. It is possible to install a DPC in an existing wall by cutting out a mortar joint with a chain saw or grinding disc. Copper sheet, polythene or bituminous felt is then inserted and the joint wedged and filled with fresh mortar. Experience is needed in order to avoid weakening the wall, and there's always a risk of cutting into a pipe or electric cable. Although a physical DPC is expensive to install, it is considered the most reliable method.

A physical DPC
A joint is removed to insert an impervious layer.

Porous tubes

Porous clay tubes are inserted into a row of closely spaced holes to increase the rate of evaporation. This has the effect of preventing moisture rising to too high a level. This is a simple and relatively inexpensive method.

Electro-osmosis

This method makes use of the principle that a minute electrical charge will prevent water rising by capillary action. A titanium wire is inserted in a continuous chase cut all round the building; anode points bent in the wire are inserted into holes drilled in the masonry at regular intervals. The wire is connected to an earthing rod buried in the ground, and the system's power unit plugs into a standard 13amp socket. This type of system can be placed internally or externally, but only by a professional fitter.

Electro-osmosis
A copper electrode is planted in the wall.

SEE ALSO > Rising damp 247

Injecting a chemical DPC

The most widely practised method of creating a DPC is to inject a waterproofing chemical to form a continuous barrier throughout the thickness of the wall. It is suitable for brick or stone walls up to 600mm (2ft) thick and is straightforward to install yourself, using hired equipment. Use the following as a guide, but modify the instructions and dimensions to follow the advice provided by the hire company or equipment manufacturer.

Preparing the wall for injection

If you decide to carry out the work yourself, hire a pressure-injection machine. You will need between 68 and 90 litres (15 to 20 gallons) of DPC fluid for every 30m (100ft) of a wall 225mm (9in) thick. Remove skirting boards, and hack off plaster and render to a height of 450mm (1ft 6in) above the line of visible damp. Repair and repoint the brickwork.

Drilling the injection holes

Drill a row of holes about 150mm (6in) above external ground level – but below a suspended wooden floor or just above one made of solid concrete. If the wall has an old DPC, set the new course just above it and take care not to puncture it when drilling. Use the size of masonry drill recommended to fit the equipment you are using. If possible, drill a row of identical holes from both sides of a wall 225mm (9in) or more thick, to provide a continuous DPC.

When you are drilling a 225mm (9in) solid-brick wall, the holes should be at 100mm (4in) centres, about 25mm (1in) below the upper edge of a brick course. Angle them downwards slightly. Drill 75mm (3in) deep – unless the treatment is to be limited to one side of the wall only, in which case you should drill to a depth of 190mm (7½in). Treat each leaf of a cavity wall separately, drilling to a depth of 75mm (3in) in each leaf. If the wall is made of impervious-stone blocks, you will need to drill into the mortar course around each block at the proposed DPC level, spacing the holes 75mm (3in) apart.

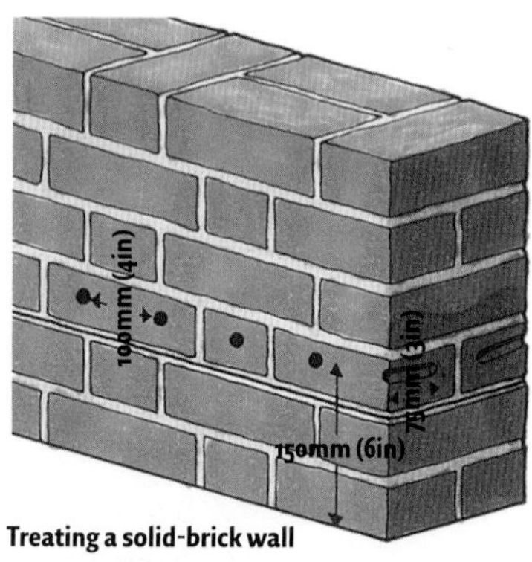

Treating a solid-brick wall

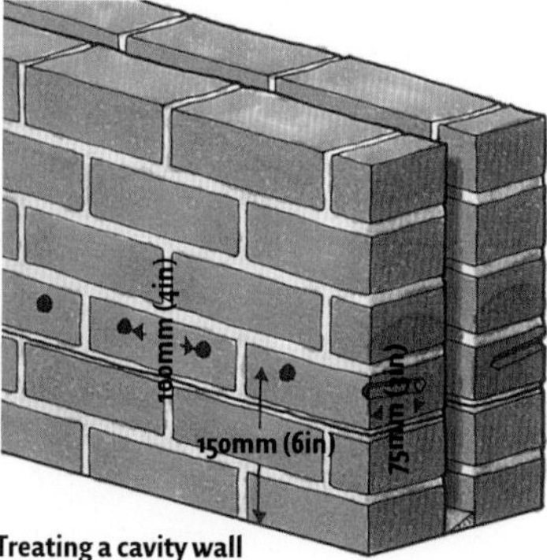

Treating a cavity wall

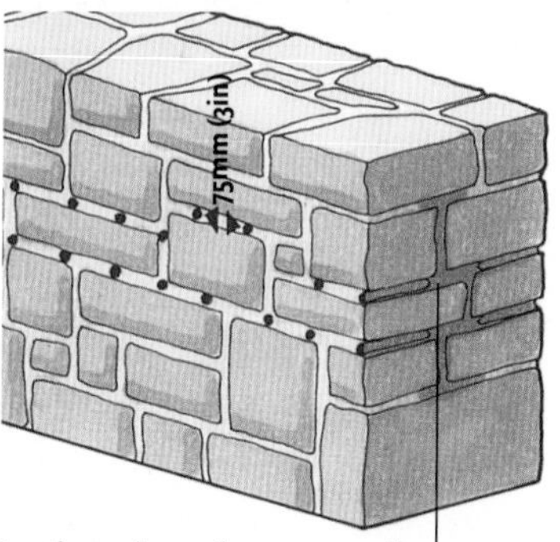

Treating an impervious-stone wall

At least one-third thickness. Seek local professional advice.

Injecting the fluid

Although there are various kinds of injection pump available, most of them work in basically the same way. With most types, the pump's filtered suction hose is inserted into a drum containing the chemical. Make sure that the valves controlling the injection nozzles are closed, then connect the pump to the mains electrical supply.

Pressure-injection machines usually have three to six nozzles. Connect the nozzles to the ends of the hoses and push them into the holes in the wall – if you are treating a thick wall, drill holes 75mm (3in) deep to begin with and start with the shorter nozzles. Tighten the wing nuts sufficiently to secure the nozzles and form a seal – but don't overtighten them, or you may damage the expansion nipples at their tips. Open the control valves on all the nozzles except for the one at the far end; then switch on the pump, so the fluid will circulate.

Bleed off some fluid into a container by opening the valve of the last nozzle, to expel air from the system. Switch off the pump and insert the nozzle into the wall. Reopen the valve and allow the fluid to be injected till it wets the surface of the bricks.

Maintain the pressure at 50–80psi (pounds per square inch) by adjusting the valve on the pump body. You may be advised in the hirer's literature to maintain a lower pressure, depending on the condition and age of the masonry.

Close off all the valves, then move the nozzles to the next series of holes and repeat the procedure. When you reach the other end of the wall, switch off the pump, return to the starting point and redrill the holes to a depth of 190mm (7½in). Swap the short injection nozzles for the longer 190mm (7½in) ones (if need be, wrapping PTFE sealing tape round the threads), then slot them into the wall, tighten their nuts, and inject the fluid. After use, flush the machine through with white spirit to clean out all traces of fluid.

Safety precautions

The hire company will provide you with detailed health and safety advice for handling the chemicals and equipment provided. Hire whatever protective clothing is recommended, but at the very least you should wear suitable gloves, goggles and an organic-vapour face mask or respirator.

Hiring equipment
A tool-hire firm will supply you with all the materials and equipment necessary for injecting a chemical DPC yourself. It is an economical method that requires careful work rather than experience. Flush the machine out thoroughly with white spirit before you return it.

SEE ALSO > Repointing 43, PTFE tape 362

Damp basements and cellars

Being at least partly below ground level, the walls and floors of a cellar or basement invariably suffer from damp to some extent. Because the problem can't be tackled from outside in the normal way, you have no option but to seal out the damp by treating the internal surfaces.

Rising damp in concrete floors, whatever the situation, can be treated as described below – but penetrating or rising damp in walls other than those of a cellar should be cured at source, since merely sealing the internal surfaces may encourage the damp eventually to penetrate elsewhere. In addition, ensure that a treated cellar is properly ventilated – and if need be, heat it to avoid condensation in the future.

Treating the walls

Damp-proof membrane (DPM)
If you are laying a new concrete floor, incorporate a damp-proof membrane (DPM) during construction. If an existing floor doesn't have a DPM, or the DPM has failed, seal the floor with a heavy-duty moisture-curing polyurethane.

Moisture-cured polyurethane can be used to seal the walls of a cellar or basement, as well as the floor (see bottom right). If you plan to use emulsion paint, decorate within 24 hours after treatment, to achieve maximum adhesion. Gloss paints can be applied at any time.

Use a heavy-duty paste to hang wallpaper. Before you hang vinyl or a heavily embossed wallcovering, apply lining paper.

Blind bitumen emulsion with dry sand

Bitumen emulsion

Where you plan to plaster or dry-line the basement walls, you can seal out the damp by using a relatively cheap bitumen emulsion. This is often used as an integral DPM under the top screed of a concrete floor or as a waterproof adhesive for some tiles and for parquet flooring – but is unsuitable as an unprotected covering, either for walls or floors.

Hack off old plaster to expose the brickwork, then apply a skim coat of mortar to smooth the surface. Paint the wall with two coats of the bitumen emulsion, joining with the DPM in the floor. Before the second coat dries, embed some clean, dry sand (blinding) into it to provide a key for subsequent coats of plaster.

Cement-based waterproof coating

In a cellar or basement where there is severe damp, apply a cement-based waterproof coating. Hack off old plaster or rendering to expose the wall.

In order to seal the join between a concrete floor and the wall, cut a chase with a width and depth of about 20mm (¾in). Brush out the debris and fill the channel with hydraulic cement (see right), finishing it off neatly as an angled fillet. Fill other cracks and holes with the same product, then wash the wall with clean water to remove dust and any loose particles.

Following the maker's instructions, mix the cement-based powder with water or the manufacturer's special acrylic solution.

Having dampened the wall, apply the first coat with a stiff-bristle brush – don't spread the material too thinly. If the brush begins to drag, don't thin the coating further, but dampen the surface a little more.

Leave the coating to cure overnight. Remove any condensation with a sponge before brushing on the second coat. For a decorative finish, lay off with vertical strokes. If you intend to plaster the surface, finish applying the coating with horizontal strokes to form a key. Never apply gypsum-based plaster over waterproof coating – use cement-based renovating plaster only.

Brush on cement-based waterproof coating

Patching active leaks

Before you damp-proof a cellar, patch any cracks that are active water leaks, using a quick-drying hydraulic cement. Supplied in powder form, ready for mixing with water, the cement expands as it hardens, sealing out the moisture.

Undercut a crack or hole, using a chisel and club hammer. Mix some cement and hold it in a gloved hand until it is warm, then push it into the crack. Hold it in place for 3 to 5 minutes, until it is hard.

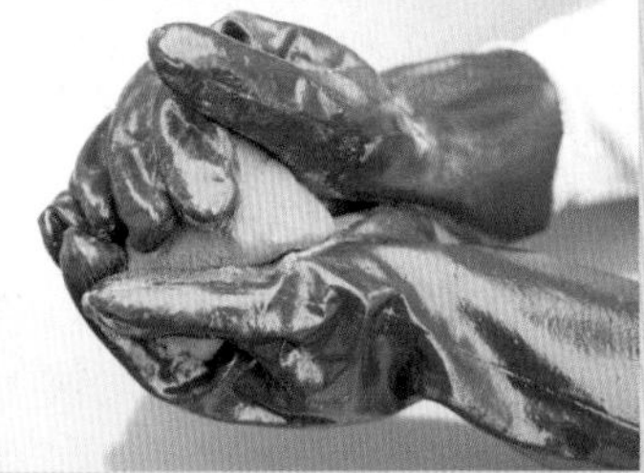

Hold cement in gloved hands until it is warm

Treating the floor

Make sure the floor is clean and grease-free. Before filling any cracks, prime them with a coat of moisture-cured polyurethane. When the surface is tacky, trowel in a filler made by mixing 6 parts of dry medium-sharp sand with 1 part urethane. Allow it to harden overnight. The floor must be as dry as possible, so force-dry a damp cellar with a fan heater before treatment.

Apply the first coat of the special urethane with a brush, using 1 litre to cover about 5sq m (50sq ft). If you're damp-proofing a room with a DPC in the walls, take the urethane coating up behind the skirting to meet the DPC.

When the first coat is touch dry, apply a second coat of polyurethane – don't allow more than 4 hours to elapse between coats. Apply three coats in all.

After 3 days, you can use the cellar and can lay a floorcovering. If you use an adhesive to stick down the floorcovering, make sure it is suitable for a non-porous surface. If you use a solvent-based adhesive, allow the urethane to harden for 7 days.

SEE ALSO > Efflorescence 42, Repairing concrete 47, Lining a wall 88, PVA bonding agent 157, New DPM 176–7, Rising damp 247, Condensation 250, Ventilation 273–80

Insulation and Ventilation

Insulating your home

No matter what fuel you use, the cost of heating a home continues to rise. Saving money is a major consideration – but of equal importance is the need to conserve energy in order to protect the environment. Even if such considerations could be ignored, the improved comfort and health of your family would more than justify the effort and expense of installing or upgrading insulation in your home.

Insulation grants

Because home insulation is of benefit to the economy, the government has made discretionary grants available through its Warm Front scheme to encourage people to insulate and draughtproof their houses and flats. However, the work has to be carried out by professional contractors, and these grants are not available at present for DIY insulation.

To find out whether you are eligible for a grant and how to process your application, phone the following numbers. If your home is in England, call 0800 316 6011. In Scotland, call 0800 316 1653. In Wales, call 0800 316 2815. In Northern Ireland, call 0800 181 667.

Kelvin
Kelvin is used as a measurement of the difference between one temperature and another, whereas Celsius is used to define the difference between zero and a given temperature.

Specifications

When comparing thermal insulating materials, you are likely to encounter certain technical specifications.

U-values

Elements of a building's structure and the insulation itself are often assigned a U-value. This indicates the rate at which heat is transmitted from one side of a wall or ceiling, for example, to the other. It is measured in watts per square metre per degree kelvin (W/m^2k).

For example, if a solid brick wall is specified as having a U-value of 2.0, it means that 2 watts of heat are conducted from every square metre of the wall for every degree difference in the temperature on each side of the wall. If the temperature outside is 10 degrees lower than inside, each square metre of the wall will conduct 20 watts of heat. The lower the U-value, the better the insulation.

R-values

A material may be given an R-value, which indicates the resistance to heat flow of a specified thickness. Materials with superior insulating qualities have the highest R-values.

Deciding on your priorities

Opinion differs on the exact figures, but it is estimated that from the average uninsulated house 35 per cent of the lost heat escapes through the walls, 25 per cent through the roof, 25 per cent through draughty doors and windows, and 15 per cent through the floor. At best, this is no more than a rough guide, as it is difficult to define an 'average' home in order to estimate the rate of heat loss. A terraced house, for example, will lose less than a detached house of identical size, even though their roofs have the same area and are in similar condition. And other factors are relevant, too – for instance, large ill-fitting sash windows permit far greater heat loss than tightly fitting casements.

Although these statistics identify the major routes for heat loss, they do not necessarily indicate where you should begin your insulation programme in order to achieve the quickest return on your investment – or, for that matter, the most immediate improvement in terms of comfort. In fact, it is best to start with relatively inexpensive measures.

1 Hot-water cylinder and pipes

Modern cylinders are manufactured with an outer layer of foam insulation, but if you have one of the older uninsulated cylinders you should begin by lagging it with a segmented mineral-fibre jacket. At the same time, lag the hot-water pipes that run through unheated areas of your house. These simple measures will constitute a considerable saving in a matter of only a few months.

2 Radiators

Fit a foil-faced lining behind radiators against external walls. This will reflect heat back into the room, instead of it being absorbed by the wall.

3 Draughtproofing

Eliminate heat loss around all windows and doors, including draughts between sliding sashes. In return for a modest outlay, draughtproofing helps reduce heating costs and provides increased comfort. It is also easy to accomplish.

4 Roof

Tackle the insulation of your roof next. Most householders will have installed loft insulation at some time, but in most cases the level of insulation will not be adequate to meet current recommended standards and if possible should be topped up.

5 Walls

Depending on the construction of your house, insulating the walls may be a sound investment. However, it's likely to be a relatively expensive operation and, unless you qualify for a substantial grant towards the cost of installation, it may take several years for you to recoup your initial outlay.

6 Floors

Floorcoverings such as carpets, tiles or parquet offer some degree of insulation. Whether you install extra insulation is likely to depend on the level of comfort you require, and also on whether you need to carry out other improvements to a floor. Floor insulation is a mandatory requirement for all new dwellings.

7 Double glazing

Contrary to the typical advertisements, double glazing will produce only a slow return on your investment, especially if you choose one of the more expensive glazing systems. However, it may help to increase the value of your property, and a double-glazed room is definitely cosier. In addition, you will be troubled by less noise from outside, especially if you choose to install triple glazing.

SEE ALSO > Draughtproofing 258–60, Insulating roofs 261–4, Insulating walls 265–6, Insulating floors 266, Double-glazing 267–9

Lagging pipes, cylinders and radiators

Some very effective measures, such as lagging the hot-water pipes and cylinder, are so simple they can be undertaken by householders who have had little practical do-it-yourself experience.

Insulating the cylinder

People used to think that an unlagged cylinder had the advantage of providing a useful source of heat in an airing cupboard – but in fact it squanders a surprising amount of energy. Even a lagged cylinder should provide ample heat in an enclosed airing cupboard; if not, an uninsulated pipe will do so.

Buying a water-cylinder jacket

Proprietary water-cylinder jackets are made from segments of mineral-fibre insulation, 75 to 100mm (3 to 4in) thick, wrapped in plastic. Measure the approximate height and circumference of the cylinder to choose the right size.

If need be, buy a jacket that is too large, rather than one that is too small. Make sure the quality is adequate by checking that it is marked with the British Standard Kite mark.

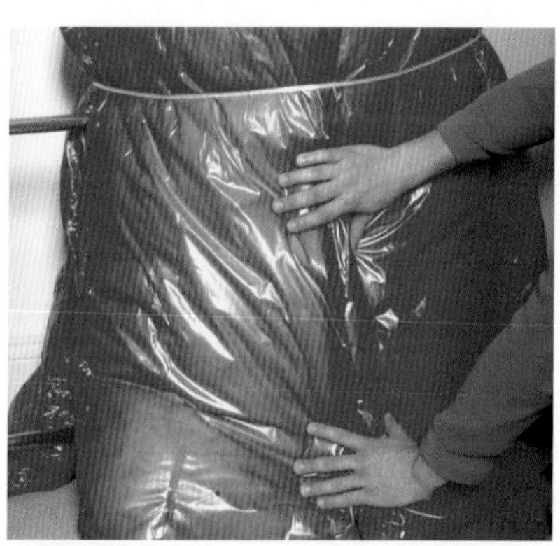

Fitting a jacket

Thread the tapered ends of the jacket segments onto a length of string and tie it round the pipe at the top of the cylinder. Distribute the segments evenly around the cylinder, then wrap the straps round it to hold the jacket in place. Don't pull the straps too tight. Spread out the segments to make sure the edges are butted together, and tuck the insulation around the pipes and the thermostat. Check that the cable running to the immersion heater is not trapped between the insulation and the cylinder.

Wrap foamed-plastic tubes (see above right) around the pipework, especially the vent pipe directly above the cylinder.

If you should ever have to replace the cylinder itself, consider substituting a preinsulated version.

Lagging pipe runs

You should insulate hot-water pipes in those parts of the house where their radiant heat is not contributing to the warmth of the rooms, and cold-water pipes in unheated areas of the building (where they could freeze). You can wrap pipework in lagging bandages (there are several types, some of which are covered in reflective foil), but it is generally more convenient to use foamed-plastic tubes designed for the purpose. This is especially true for pipes close to a wall, which may be awkward to wrap.

Foamed-plastic tubes are produced to fit pipes of different diameters: the foamed plastic varies in thickness from 12 to 20mm (½ to ¾in). The more expensive ones incorporate a metallic-foil backing that reflects some of the heat back into hot-water pipes.

Most tubes are preslit along their length, so that they can be sprung over the pipe (**1**). Butt successive lengths of tube end-to-end, and seal the joints with PVC adhesive tape.

At a bend, cut small segments out of the split edge, so that it bends without crimping. Fit it around the pipe (**2**) and seal the closed joints with tape. If two pipes are joined with an elbow fitting, mitre the ends of the two lengths of tube, then butt them together (**3**) and seal with tape. Cut lengths of tube to fit snugly around a T-joint, linking them with a wedge-shaped butt joint, and seal with tape.

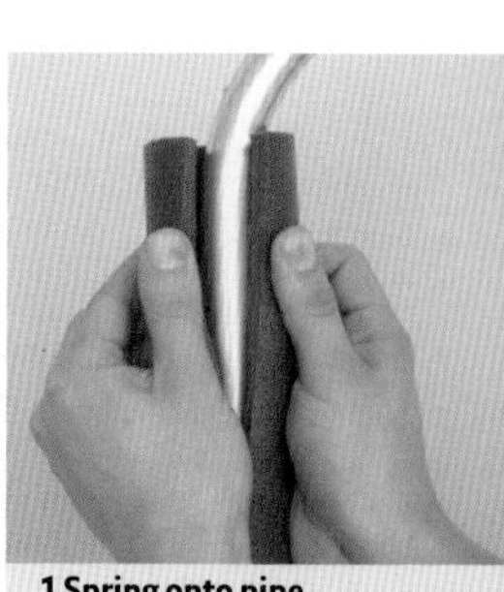

1 Spring onto pipe

2 Cut to fit a bend

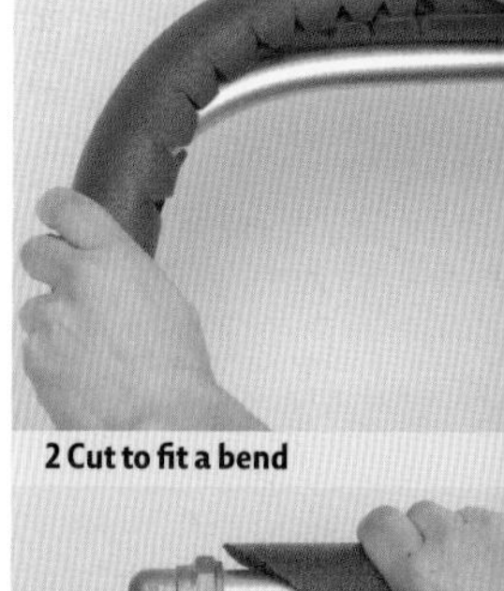

3 Cut mitres for elbows

Reflecting heat from a radiator

As much as 25 per cent of the radiant heat from a radiator placed against an outside wall is lost to the wall behind it. You can reclaim maybe half this wasted heat by applying a foil-faced expanded-polystyrene lining to the wall behind the radiator, to reflect the heat back into the room. The material is available as rolls, sheets or tiles. It is easiest to apply the lining to the wall when the radiator is removed for decorating, but you can do it with the radiator in place.

Turn off the radiator and measure it, making a note of the position of the brackets. Use a sharp trimming knife or scissors to cut the lining to size, so it is slightly smaller than the radiator all round. Cut narrow slots, as need be, to fit over the fixing brackets (**1**).

Apply heavy-duty fungicidal wallpaper paste to the back of the material, and then slide it behind the radiator (**2**). Smooth it onto the wall with a wooden batten or a small roller used for painting radiators. Allow the paste to dry before turning the radiator on again. Alternatively, you can fix the lining in place with double-sided adhesive pads.

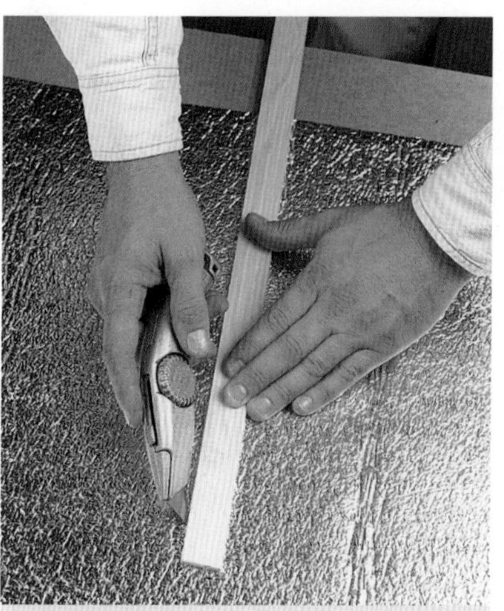

1 Cut slots to align with the wall brackets

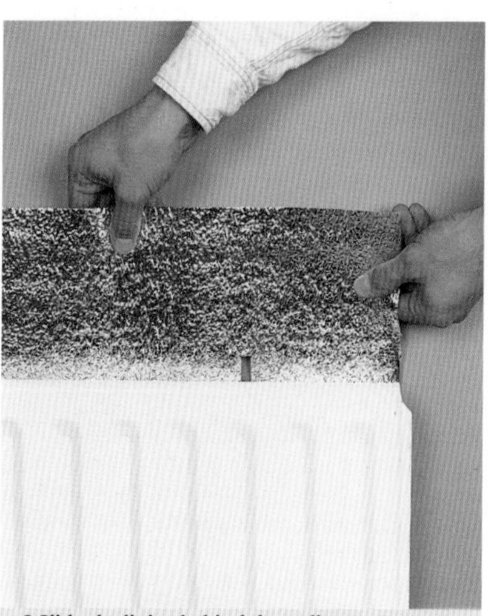

2 Slide the lining behind the radiator

SEE ALSO > Wallpaper paste 87, Hot-water cylinders 392–3, Radiator roller 483

Draughtproofing

A certain amount of ventilation is desirable to maintain a healthy environment and keep condensation at bay; it's also essential to enable some heating appliances to operate properly and safely. However, uncontrolled draughts are hardly an efficient way to ventilate a house – and besides accounting for quite a large proportion of the heat lost, they cause a good deal of discomfort. It is therefore worth spending a little money and effort on draughtproofing your home.

Locating draughts
A lighted joss stick will detect the slightest draught.

Locating draughts

Tackle the exterior doors and windows first. Seal only those interior doors that are the worst offenders, as there should be some 'trickle' ventilation from room to room.

Next, check other possible sources of draughts – such as spaces between floorboards, gaps in skirtings, loft hatches, fireplace openings, and the overflow pipes from sanitaryware. Locate draughts by holding a lighted joss stick near likely gaps. You may be surprised by how much air is whistling through, especially on a windy day.

Draught excluders are made by a variety of manufacturers and there are many variations. Nevertheless, the following examples illustrate the principles that are commonly employed.

Threshold draught excluders

If the gap between the bottom of a door and the floor is very large, it's bound to admit fierce draughts, so it pays to use a threshold excluder to seal the gap.

If you fit an excluder to an exterior door, make sure it is suitably weatherproof. If you can't buy a threshold excluder that fits the opening exactly, cut a longer one down to size.

Flexible-strip excluders

The simplest form of threshold draught excluder is a flexible strip of plastic or rubber that sweeps against the floor-covering to form a seal. Most excluders have a rigid-plastic or aluminium extrusion that is screwed to the face of the door to hold the excluder in contact with the floor. Flexible-strip excluders work best over smooth flooring.

Brush seals

A long nylon-bristle brush, set into a metal or plastic extrusion, can be used to exclude draughts under doors. This kind of threshold excluder is suitable for slightly uneven floors and textured floorcoverings. It is the only type that can be fitted to sliding doors as well as hinged ones. Brush-depth varies a great deal, but provided the pile is in contact with the floor surface it should still work efficiently.

Flexible arch

This type of excluder consists of an arched vinyl insert, fitted to a shallow aluminium extrusion, that presses against the bottom edge of the door. Because it has to be nailed or screwed to the floor, a flexible-arch excluder is difficult to use on a solid-concrete floor. For an external door, choose a version that has additional underseals to prevent rain seeping beneath it. To fit it, you may have to plane the bottom edge of the door.

Door kits

The best solution for an exterior door is to buy a kit combining an aluminium weather trim, which is designed to shed rainwater, and a weather bar fitted with a tubular draught excluder that's made of rubber or plastic. The trim is screwed to the face of the door, and the weather bar is fixed to the threshold. There are a great many variations to choose from, but all work on a similar principle.

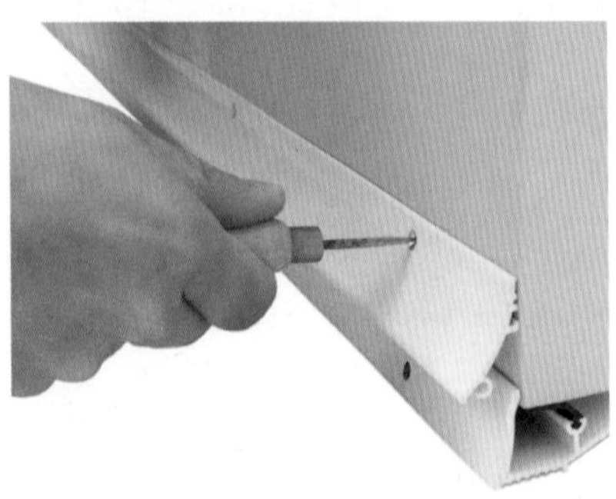

Screwing a weather trim to the door
Use a bradawl to mark the screw holes, especially on a hardwood door.

Flexible strip

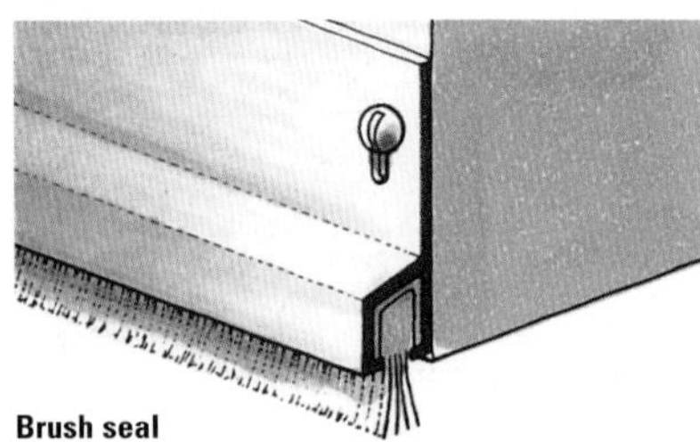

Brush seal

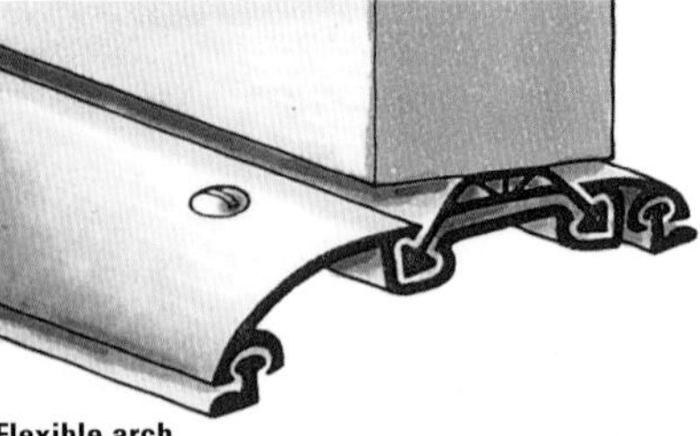

Flexible arch

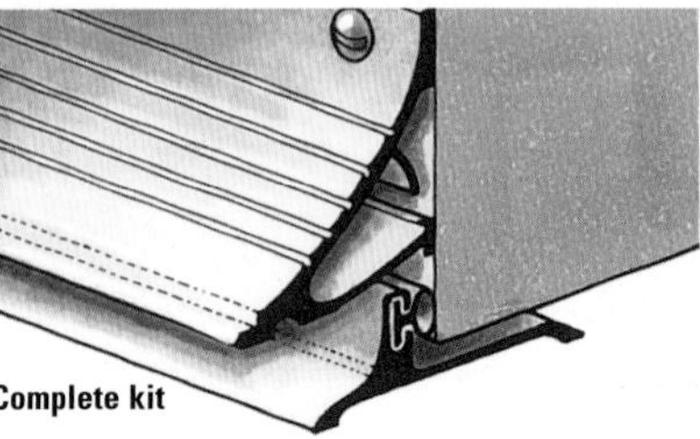

Complete kit

SEE ALSO > Condensation 250, Ventilating appliances 273, 407

Sealing gaps around doors and casement windows

A well-fitting door needs a 2mm (1/16in) gap at the top and sides so that it can be operated smoothly. However, a gap this large can lose a great deal of heat. There are several ways to seal it, some of which are described here.

Hinged casement windows and pivot windows can be sealed with similar draught excluders, but check the excluders are weatherproof.

The cheaper excluders may have to be renewed regularly.

Compressible strips

The most straightforward excluder is a self-adhesive foam-plastic strip, which you stick around the rebate; the strip is compressed by the door or window, forming a seal. The cheapest polyurethane foam will be good for one or two seasons (although it's useless if painted) and is suitable for interior doors only. The better-quality vinyl-coated polyurethane, rubber or PVC foams are more durable and, unlike their cheaper counterparts, don't perish on exposure to sunlight. When applying compressible excluders, avoid stretching them, as that reduces their efficiency. The door or window may be difficult to close at first, but the excluder will adjust after a short while.

V-strips

If it is too difficult to force a door or casement closed against a compressible excluder, fit a strip that is bent back to form a V-shape. The self-adhesive strip can be mounted to fill the gap around the door or window, or attached to the stop so that the door or window closes against it. V-strips are cheap and unobtrusive, but a good fit is essential to exclude draughts completely.

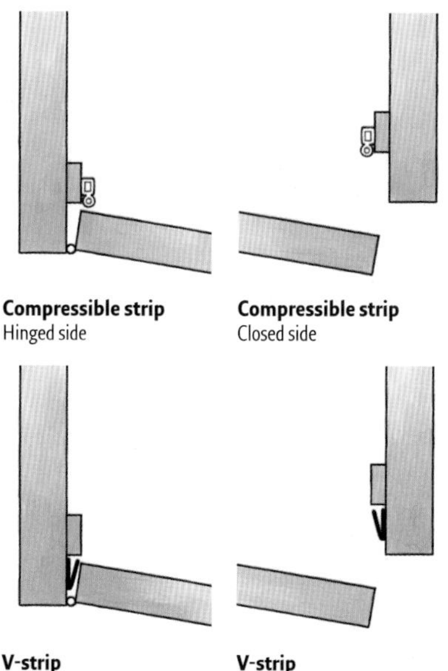

Compressible strip Hinged side

Compressible strip Closed side

V-strip Hinged side

V-strip Closed side

External-door sealer kits

1 Press strip against the door and insert screws

2 At each corner, cut a notch for a perfect fit

Foam strips are not suitable for external doors, although you can fit some of the rubber and plastic versions. Alternatively, buy an external-door sealer kit comprising three lengths of aluminium extrusion holding a plastic or rubber strip that presses against the outer face of the door across the top and down both sides. A flat strip is provided for fitting across the top and down the closing side. A curved strip is supplied for fitting to the doorframe down the hinged side. If you fit the strips to the wrong side of the door, the seal will be less effective.

Use a small hacksaw to cut each extrusion to size, taking an equal amount from each end. If the flexible strip gets wrinkled in the process, pinch one end of the extrusion onto the strip, using a pair of pliers. Pull on the other end of the strip to straighten it, and then pinch the extrusion at that end to keep the strip in tension.

With the door closed, hold the short extrusion against the top of the doorframe, with the flexible strip pressing against the door. Make sure the strip is pressed evenly across the door, then use a bradawl to mark the positions of the slotted fixing holes in the aluminium. Screw the extrusion in place (**1**). Make sure the strip seals properly across the door. If necessary, loosen the screws and adjust the position of the extrusion.

Repeat the process down both sides of the door, taking care to ensure the curved flexible strip on the hinged side does not get pinched by the edge of the door.

For a perfect seal, cut a notch out of both top corners to join the extrusions closely (**2**).

Keyholes and letter boxes

Keyhole coverplate
The coverplate is part of the escutcheon.

An external keyhole should be fitted with a coverplate to keep out draughts during the winter.

You can buy a hinged flap that screws onto the inside of the door to cover a letter box; some types have a brush seal behind the flap for extra draughtproofing.

Brush-seal excluder
An integral brush seal prevents draughts even when the letter box is open.

SEE ALSO > Doors 182–91, Letter plates 186

Draughtproofing sashes

Draughtproofing the sliding components of a sash window is more complicated than sealing hinged casements. It's necessary to fit different types of excluder to the various parts of the window.

Sealing a sash window

The top and bottom closing rails of a sash window can be sealed with a weatherproof compressible excluder, but choose one that allows you to operate the latch when the sashes are closed.

The sliding edges admit fewer draughts, but they can be sealed with a brush seal fixed to the frame – inside for the lower sash, outside for the top one. With the brush pressed against the sash, drive panel pins through the predrilled holes into the framework.

To seal the gap between the sloping faces of the central meeting rails of a traditional sash window, use a self-adhesive springy V-strip.

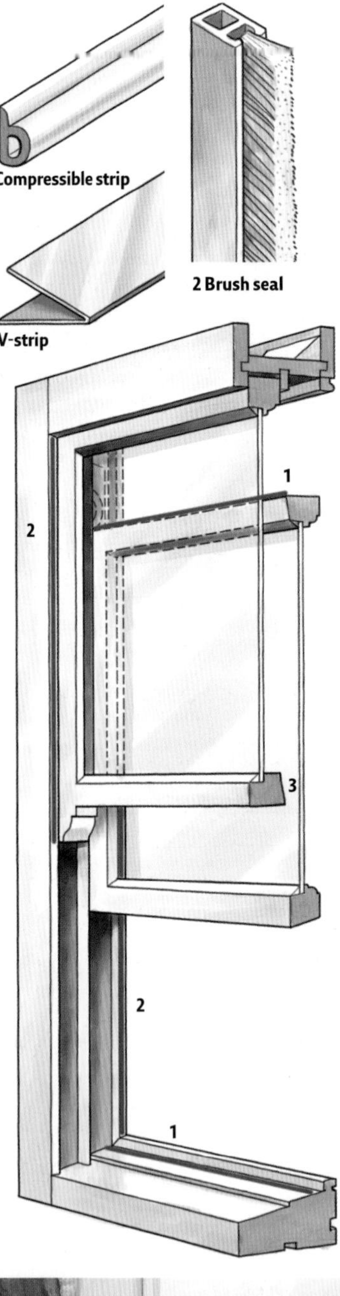

Pin a brush seal to the staff bead

Draughtproofed beads
Have a refurbishment company install beads made with integral brush seals.

Replacing the beads

Professional companies that specialize in refurbishing sliding-sash windows can replace the parting beads and the inner staff beads with new ones that have integral brush seals. This will cost you a lot more than a DIY solution – but, in addition to superior draughtproofing, the refurbished windows will slide more smoothly and rattles will be eliminated.

Filling large gaps

Large gaps left around newly fitted window frames (or doorframes) will be a source of draughts. The same is true of a hole made for pipework or an air vent. Use an expanding-foam filler to seal these gaps. When the filler has set, trim off the excess and then seal around the frame with flexible mastic.

Additional draughtproofing

The ventilated void below a suspended wooden floor is a common source of draughts that penetrate through large gaps between floorboards and under the skirting. Fill between floorboards or cover them with hardboard panels.

Seal gaps at the skirting boards with mastic applied with an applicator gun. Pin a quadrant or scotia moulding to the skirting to cover the sealed gap.

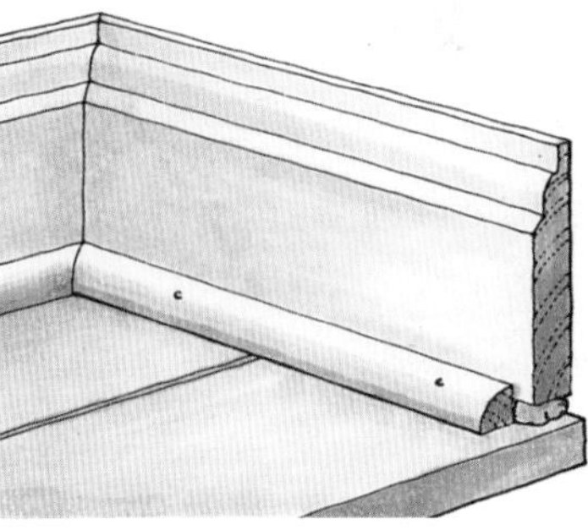
Seal the gap with mastic and wooden quadrant

Draughts from overflows

Overflow pipes leading directly from a lavatory cistern or cold-water storage tank frequently provide a passage for draughts when there's a strong wind blowing. This can cause pipes to freeze in harsh conditions.

The simplest solution is to cut the neck off a balloon and stretch it over the end of the pipe – the fabric will hang down to cover the opening but allow water to pass through unhindered.

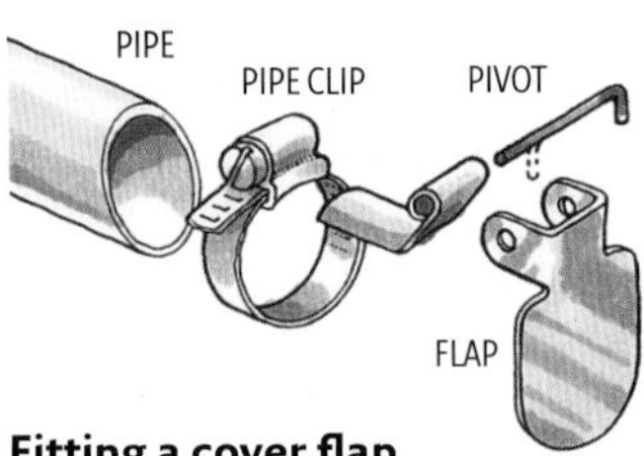

Fitting a cover flap

Another remedy is to cut a cover flap from a lightweight rustproof metal, such as zinc or aluminium. Make a simple pivot from the same metal and attach the flap to the end of the tube with a pipe clip.

Draughty fireplaces

To retain a disused open fireplace, cut a sheet of flame-retardant polystyrene to seal the throat of the chimney – leave a hole 50mm (2in) across for ventilation. If you use the fireplace again, don't forget to remove the polystyrene.

SEE ALSO > Levelling a wooden floor 57, Windows 192–207, Ventilating a fireplace 273, Ventilating below floors 274

Insulating roofs

Approximately a quarter of the heat lost from an average house goes through the roof, so minimizing this should be one of your priorities. Provided you are able to gain access to your loft space, reducing heat loss through the roof is just a matter of laying insulating material between the joists – which is cheap, quick and effective. If you want to make use of your attic, insulating the sloping surface of the roof is a straightforward alternative.

Types of roof insulation

There's a range of insulating materials available, so investigate which type will suit your circumstances best.

Blanket insulation

Blanket insulation – which is made from glass fibre, mineral wool or rock fibre – is widely available in the form of rolls that fit snugly between the joists. All types are non-flammable and are proofed against damp and vermin. Similar material, cut to shorter lengths, is also sold as 'batts'.

Some blanket insulation is wrapped in plastic that serves as a vapour barrier (see below right) and reduces direct contact with fibres that could irritate the skin. However, unbacked blanket is the cheapest and it is perfectly suitable for laying on the loft floor.

Blankets are usually either 100, 150, 170 or 200mm (4, 6, 6¾ or 8in) thick. Some kinds can be split into two to accommodate shallow joists or for topping up existing insulation. The rolls are normally 370 to 400mm (15 to 16in) wide, to fit snugly between the joists, and 6 to 8m (20 to 25ft) long. Wider rolls are available for non-standard joist spacing.

If you want to fit blanket insulation to the sloping part of a roof, buy semi-rigid batts or slabs of mineral fibre, between 50 and 75mm (2 and 3in) thick. Similar materials can be inserted between the wall studs when insulating an attic.

Rigid sheet insulation

Sheet insulation, of foamed polystyrene or polyurethane, can be fixed between the rafters of a sloping roof. It pays to install the thickest insulation possible, allowing sufficient ventilation between the insulating material and the roof tiles or slates to avoid condensation.

Some polystyrene panels are grooved longitudinally, which makes them easy to cut to width, using a small craft saw. The grooves also allow the panels to be compressed slightly, which makes for a snug fit between the sloping rafters.

Foiled quilts

If the rafters are too narrow to accommodate slab or rigid sheet insulation, you could staple a thin foiled quilt to the underside of the roof timbers.

One type of quilt is made of layers of foamed plastic interleaved with reflective foil. This is relatively expensive, but the U-value of a layer 25mm (1in) thick is equivalent to that of standard blanket insulation eight times thicker.

Other quilts have a layer of superior-quality 'bubble wrap' sandwiched between foil. The same quilt is suitable for laying between the joists when insulating suspended wooden floors.

Rigid-foam decking

If you plan to use your loft for storage, consider laying foamed polystyrene panels with flooring-grade moisture-resistant chipboard bonded to the top surface. The edges of the chipboard are tongued and grooved for positive location. The panels, which are narrow enough to pass through most loft hatches, are laid at right angles to the joists. For a better standard of insulation, the panel manufacturers recommend laying blanket insulation between the joists before you lay the panels on top and screw them to the joists. You should provide sufficient gaps to allow heat to escape from ceiling-mounted uplighters and electrical cable.

Blown-fibre insulation

Inter-joist fibrous insulation is blown through a large hose by professional contractors. It may not be suitable for a house in a windy location, but seek the contractor's advice. An even depth of 270mm (10½in) is required to meet current recommendations. Discuss with the contractor how best to avoid burying electrical cables and light fittings under the insulation.

Preparing the loft

Before installing any form of insulation, check roof timbers for woodworm and signs of rot, so they can be treated first. Make sure all the electrical wiring is sound, and carefully lift it clear so that you can lay insulation beneath it. In some cases it may be necessary to install longer cables with sufficient slack to accommodate thicker insulation.

The plaster or plasterboard ceiling below will not support your weight. You therefore need to lay a plank or two, or a chipboard panel, across the joists so you can move about safely. If there is no permanent lighting in the loft, rig up an inspection lamp on an extension lead and move it wherever it is needed – or hang the lamp high up to provide an overall light.

Most attics are very dusty, so wear old clothes and a gauze face mask. It is also advisable to wear protective gloves, especially if you're handling glass-fibre batts or blanket insulation, which may irritate sensitive skin.

Working safely
Place strong planks or chipboard panels over the joists to make safe walkways in the loft.

Vapour barriers

Installing roof insulation has the effect of making uninsulated parts of the house colder than before, so increasing the risk of condensation either on or within the structure itself. This could reduce the effectiveness of the insulation – and also promote dry rot in the roof timbers.

One way to prevent this happening is to ventilate those parts of the house that are outside the insulated area. Alternatively, install a vapour barrier on the warm (inner) side of the insulation, to prevent moisture-laden air passing through. The vapour barrier, which is usually a plastic or metal-foil sheet, is sometimes supplied along with the insulation. It's vital that the barrier is continuous and undamaged.

Some blankets are sleeved in plastic or foil and therefore do not require a separate vapour barrier. Other types of insulation have a closed-cell structure that resists the passage of water vapour – making it unnecessary to install a vapour barrier.

Installing a vapour barrier
Cut the sheet into strips about 75mm (3in) wider than the joist spacing, then staple each strip to the joist on each side. Overlap any joints and secure with self-adhesive tape. Cut holes in the sheet to accommodate light fittings that protrude into the loft.

SEE ALSO > Woodworm 242–3, Dry rot and wet rot 245, Condensation 250, Roof ventilation 275

Insulating a loft

One of the easiest ways to insulate a loft that isn't in use as a living space is to lay blanket insulation between the joists. No special skills are required and the job should take no longer than a day to complete.

Laying blanket insulation

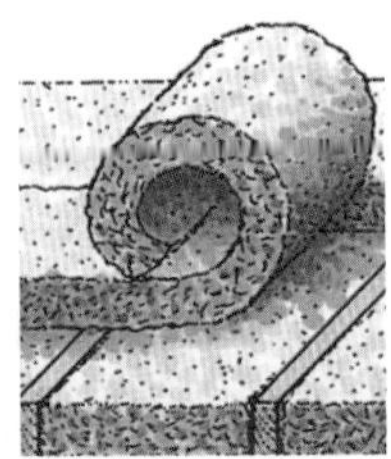

Cross-laying
Most modern ceiling joists are only 100mm (4in) deep. One way to install insulation of the recommended thickness is to lay two layers of blanket at right angles to each other.

Before starting to lay blanket insulation, seal gaps around pipes, vents or wiring entering the loft, using flexible mastic.

Remove the blanket's wrapping in the loft itself – the insulation is compressed for transportation and storage, but swells to its true thickness on being released – and begin by placing one end of a roll into the eaves. Make sure you don't cover the ventilation gap (trim the end of the blanket to a wedge shape, so that it doesn't obstruct the airflow), or fit eaves vents.

Unroll the blanket between the joists, pressing it down to form a snug fit – but don't compress it. Continue at the opposite side of the loft with another roll. Cut it to butt up against the end of the first roll, using either a large kitchen knife or a pair of long-bladed scissors. Continue across the loft until all spaces have been filled (to fit odd spaces, trim the insulation).

Don't cover the casings of any light fittings that protrude into the loft space, and don't be tempted to cover electrical cables – there's a risk that they could overheat. Instead, lay the cables on top of the blanket, taking care not to stretch them. If necessary, cut the blanket to leave a gap around and above a cable.

Don't insulate the area immediately below a cold-water tank – the heat rising from the room below will help to prevent freezing during the winter.

Cut a piece of blanket to fit the cover of the entrance hatch, and attach it with PVA adhesive or with cloth tapes and drawing pins. Fit foam draught excluder around the edges of the hatch.

• Ventilating the loft
Laying insulation between the joists increases the risk of condensation in an unheated roof space – but provided there are adequate vents or gaps at the eaves, there will be enough air circulating to keep the loft dry.

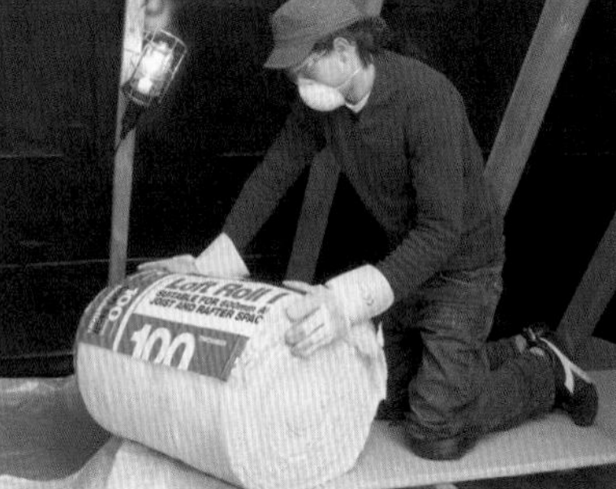

Unwrap blanket insulation in the loft

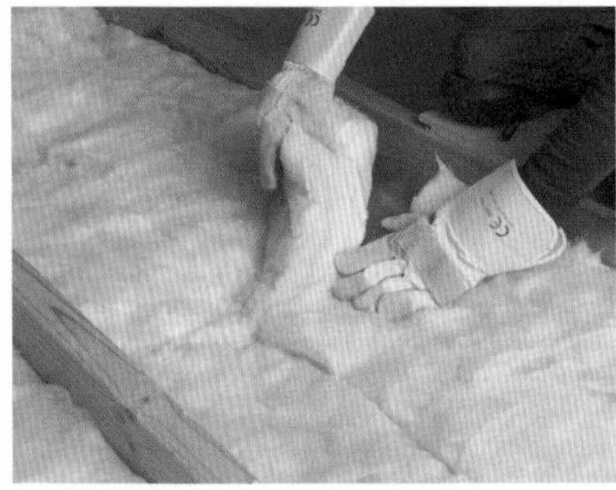

Cut lengths to fit and butt them together

Laying blanket insulation

Laying blanket insulation
1 Gaps around pipes, vents and wiring are sealed.
2 Allowance for ventilation at the eaves.
3 Proprietary eaves vents keep the airway open permanently.
4 Blanket insulation laid between joists.
5 Tank and cold-water pipes insulated separately.

Cross-laying insulation

The Building Regulations recommend a minimum thickness of 270mm (10½in) for loft insulation. Most ceiling joists are too shallow to accommodate blanket insulation of this thickness, and the only practical method of complying with the Regulations is to lay a second layer of insulation at right angles to the joists.

However, once the joists are covered it is impossible to walk in the loft without the danger of putting a foot through the plaster ceiling below. Even if you don't intend to use the loft for storage, you or a tradesman may have to enter the loft at some stage to service the plumbing or inspect the roof structure. Before laying a second layer of blanket insulation it makes sense to nail wooden spacers to the top of the joists in those areas where one may have to gain access, so you can place a chipboard flooring panel over the blanket and screw it down to the spacers. As you lay the blanket, cut it to fit around the spacers.

Tanks and pipes

Current bylaws require your cold-water-storage tank to be insulated. It's simplest to buy a Bylaw 30 kit, which includes a jacket and other equipment that is required. Insulate your central-heating expansion tank, too.

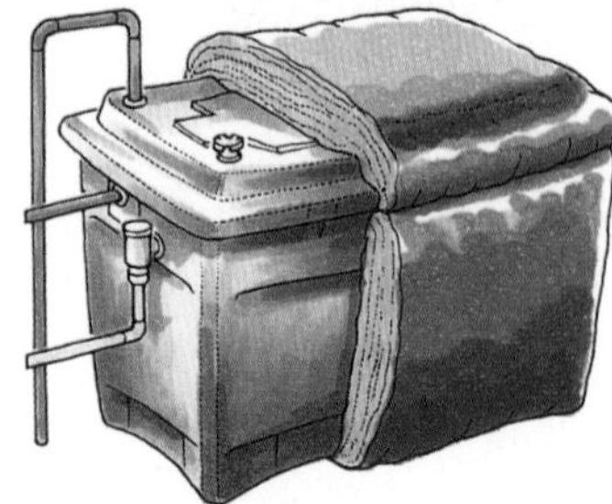

Buy a ready-made jacket to insulate a tank

Insulating pipes

If there are cold-water pipes running between the joists, prevent them from freezing by laying blanket insulation over them. If that's not practical, then insulate each pipe run separately, using foamed-plastic pipe lagging.

SEE ALSO > Lagging pipe runs 257, Draught excluders 259, Types of insulation 261, Ventilating the roof space 275

Insulating a sloping roof

If the attic is to be used as a room or rooms, you will need to insulate the sloping part of the roof in order to heat the living space. There's more than one solution to consider.

Insulating between the rafters

Repair the roof first, so the insulation won't become soaked in the event of leaks (it will also be more difficult to spot leaks after insulating).

Condensation often causes serious problems after installing insulation between the rafters, as the undersides of the roof tiles become very cold. It is vital to provide a 50mm (2in) gap between the insulant and the tiles, to promote sufficient ventilation to keep the space dry (this also determines the maximum thickness of insulation you can install). The ridge and eaves must be ventilated, and you should include a vapour barrier on the warm side of the insulation.

Attaching sheet insulation

Cut rigid sheet insulation as accurately as possible, to ensure a wedge-fit between the rafters. To maintain a 50mm (2in) gap behind the insulant, screw battens to the sides of the rafters (**1**); treat the new battens with a chemical preserver first.

Press the insulant in place, then staple a sheet of polythene vapour barrier over the rafters (**2**), making sure you double-fold the joints before stapling the polythene in place.

Lining with plasterboard.

Reduce heat loss still further by screwing insulated (thermal) plasterboard to the underside of the rafters. This is like ordinary plasterboard, but is backed up with a layer of insulating polystyrene. Insulated boards that have an integral vapour barrier do not require a separate plastic-sheet barrier. Screw the panels to the rafters, staggering the joints between.

1 Screw battens to the sides of each rafter

2 Staple a vapour barrier over the rafters

Insulating an attic from the inside
Fit sheet insulation between the rafters.
1 Minimum gap of 50mm (2in) between insulation and slates to provide ventilation.
2 Sheet insulant wedged between rafters.
3 Vapour barrier with double-folded joints stapled to rafters.
4 Thermal plasterboard screwed over vapour barrier.
5 Tile battens.
6 Tiles or slates.
7 Roof felt.

Installing a foiled quilt

Where it is difficult to install adequate insulation between narrow rafters, you can staple a foiled quilt to the underside of the rafters.

Unroll the quilt as you work, cutting it to length with sharp scissors. Having stapled the quilt in place, seal the joints with a special foil tape that is made with an acrylic adhesive for a strong watertight bond.

If you want to plasterboard or panel over the quilt, screw spacer battens 25mm (1in) thick to the covered joists; then screw the boards to these battens. Use thermal plasterboard if the quilt alone does not provide sufficient insulation.

Using foiled quilt
Staple a foiled quilt to the underside of the rafters.

Insulating the attic

If there's an attic room that was built as part of the original structure of your house, you probably won't be able to insulate the pitch of the roof unless you are prepared to hack off the old plaster before insulating between the rafters (see left). It may therefore be simpler to insulate from the inside (as for a flat roof), although you won't have a great deal of headroom.

Insulate the short vertical wall of the attic from inside the crawlspace, installing a vapour barrier on the warm inner side of the partition. At the same time, insulate between the joists of the crawlspace.

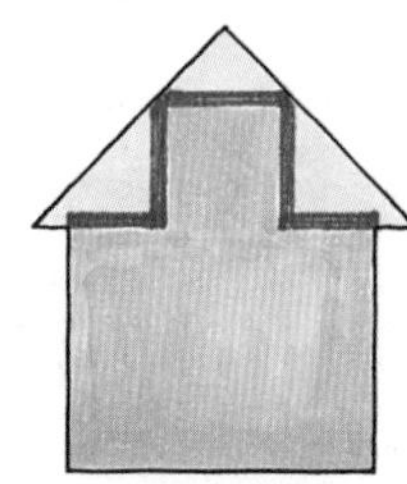

Insulating a room in the attic
Surround the room itself with insulation – but leave the floor uninsulated, so the attic will benefit from heat rising from the rooms directly below.

Fit batts between the wall studs

SEE ALSO > Plasterboarding 162–70, Wood preservers 246, Vapour barriers 261, Insulating flat roofs 264

Topping up

Most householders will have insulated the loft at some time in the past, but it is unlikely that existing insulation is thick enough to comply with the current recommendation of 270mm (10½in). You may wish to top up your present insulation to bring it up to standard.

Cross-laying

Heat diffuser

Laying a second layer of blanket insulation at right angles to the joists, which is described under insulating a loft, is a simple and effective way to reduce heat loss to a minimum.

Rigid-foam decking

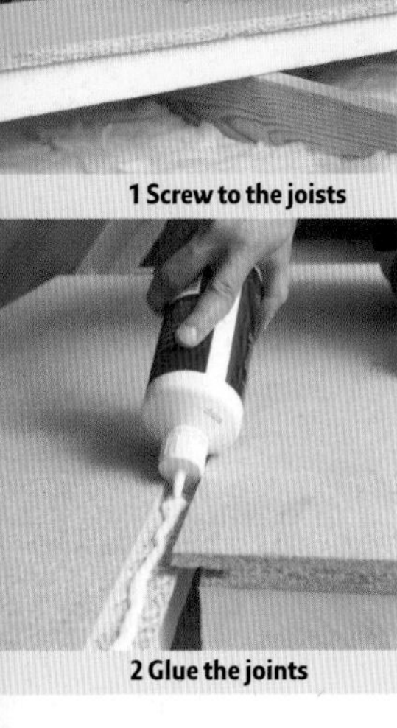

1 Screw to the joists

2 Glue the joints

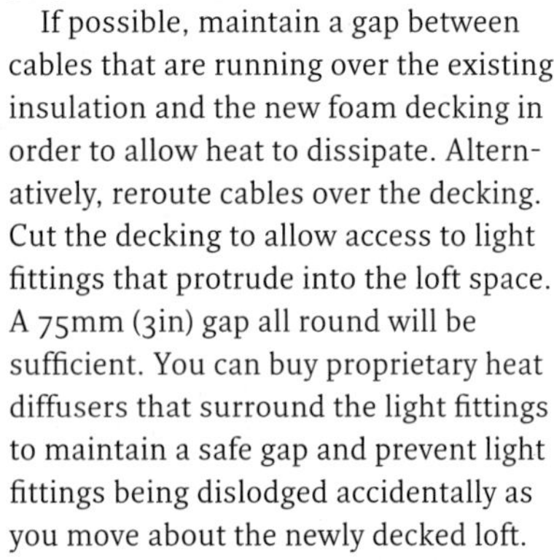

If you want to increase your insulation and, at the same time, convert your loft into a practical area for storage, you could install rigid-foam decking over your existing insulation. Make sure your ceiling joists are strong enough to take the additional load of insulation and any proposed storage.

If possible, maintain a gap between cables that are running over the existing insulation and the new foam decking in order to allow heat to dissipate. Alternatively, reroute cables over the decking. Cut the decking to allow access to light fittings that protrude into the loft space. A 75mm (3in) gap all round will be sufficient. You can buy proprietary heat diffusers that surround the light fittings to maintain a safe gap and prevent light fittings being dislodged accidentally as you move about the newly decked loft.

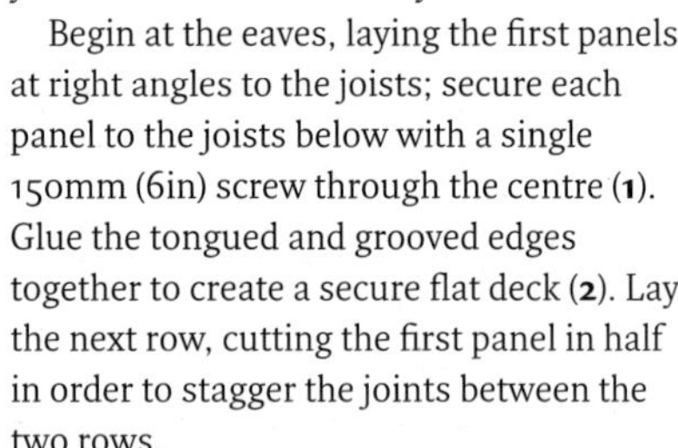

Begin at the eaves, laying the first panels at right angles to the joists; secure each panel to the joists below with a single 150mm (6in) screw through the centre (1). Glue the tongued and grooved edges together to create a secure flat deck (2). Lay the next row, cutting the first panel in half in order to stagger the joints between the two rows.

As you lay subsequent panels, mark the position of pipe runs and cables on the surface of the decking for future reference. Cut the insulated panels to fit around cold-water storage tanks.

Rafter insulation

If electrical wiring or plumbing make installing extra insulation at joist level impracticable, leave the existing insulation in place and supplement it with foiled quilt or rigid sheet insulation fixed to the sloping roof above.

Insulating flat roofs

Expert contractors can insulate a flat roof from above, but the only practical DIY solution is to apply a layer of insulation to the ceiling.

Treatment from above

One way of insulating a flat roof is to lay rigid insulating board on the original deck. The bonded 'warm-roof system' incorporates a vapour barrier – possibly just the old covering – that is laid under the insulation, which is then protected with a new waterproof covering. With a protected-membrane system, the insulation is laid over the covering and is held in place with paving slabs or a layer of pebbles. Both systems are best installed by contractors. Get them to check that the roof is weatherproof and can support the additional weight.

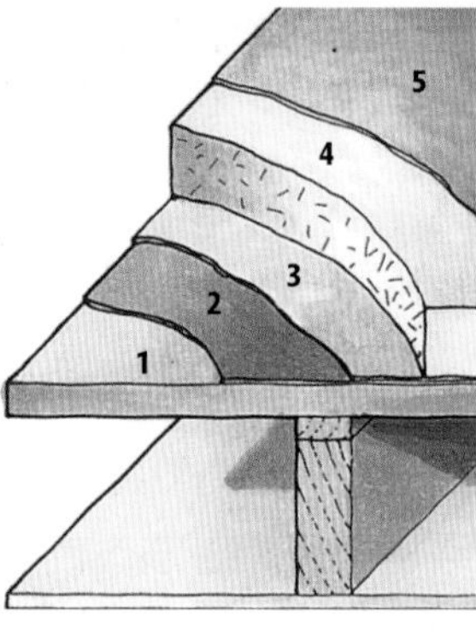

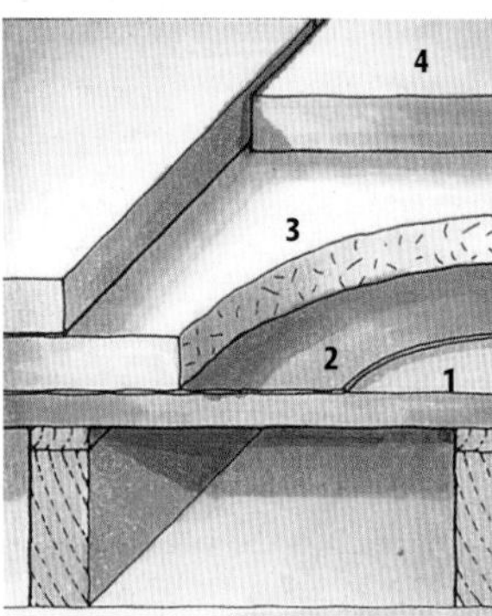

Warm-roof system (right)
1 Roof deck
2 Waterproof covering
3 New vapour barrier
4 Insulation
5 New waterproof covering

Protected-membrane system (far right)
1 Roof deck
2 Waterproof covering
3 Insulation
4 Paving slabs

Treatment from below

Another option is to insulate the ceiling below a flat roof. This is not a difficult task, provided the area is not too large, but you will have to relocate lighting and accommodate windows or fitted cupboards that extend to the ceiling.

Very often the space within the roof structure has little or no ventilation. It is therefore essential to include a vapour barrier on the warm side of the ceiling, below the insulation.

First of all, either nail thermal plasterboard to the joists or install fire-retardant expanded polystyrene, 50mm (2in) thick, between softwood battens screwed to the joists every 400mm (1ft 4in) across the ceiling. Fit the first of the battens against the wall at right angles to the joists, then fit one at each end of the room. Butt the polystyrene against the first batten, then coat the back of it with polystyrene adhesive and fix it to the ceiling. Continue with alternate battens and panels until you reach the other side of the room, finishing with a batten against the wall.

Install a polythene vapour barrier, double-folding the joints and stapling them to convenient battens. Fix plasterboard panels to the battens with galvanized plasterboard nails. Stagger the joins between the panels, then fill the joins and finish ready for decorating as required.

Insulating the ceiling
Insulate a flat roof by fixing insulant to the ceiling.
1 Existing plasterboard or lath-and-plaster ceiling.
2 Softwood battens screwed to the joists.
3 Insulation glued to existing ceiling.
4 Polythene vapour barrier stapled to the battens.
5 Plasterboard nailed to the battens.
6 If possible, provide cross-ventilation by installing vents equal to 0.4 per cent of the roof area.

SEE ALSO > Plasterboarding 162–70

Insulating walls

Once you have recouped the initial outlay, insulating the external walls of your home will reduce your heating costs considerably.

Consider the options

How you insulate the walls of your home is likely to be determined by several factors. Firstly, the type of construction.

Cavity or solid walls

Houses built after 1920, and certainly after 1950, usually have cavity walls – two skins of masonry, with a gap between them to reduce the likelihood of water penetration. Although heat loss is slightly slower through a cavity wall than one of solid brick, that does not substantially reduce the cost of home heating. However, filling the cavity with insulation prevents circulation, trapping the air in millions of tiny air pockets within the material. This can reduce heat loss through the wall by as much as 65 per cent.

Solid walls require different treatment. You can either employ a contractor to insulate the external face of the walls or line the inner surfaces yourself.

Cavity insulation

Cavity filling is most cost-effective for homes that have properly controlled central heating. Heating without controls simply increases the temperature, instead of saving on fuel bills. This type of insulation is not practical for flats unless the whole building is insulated at the same time.

Dry-lining

Another method – suitable for solid and cavity walls – is to line the inner surfaces of the walls with insulation. This may involve a great deal of effort, depending on the amount of alteration to joinery, electrical fittings and plumbing required – but it does provide an opportunity for selective insulation, concentrating on those rooms that are likely to benefit most. It is also the only form of wall insulation that can be carried out by the householder.

Exterior-wall insulation

Cladding the exterior of a house with insulation is expensive and also spoils the appearance of most buildings. External-wall insulation can be installed only by a contractor and should only be considered if the house is built with solid masonry walls.

Insulating cavity walls

When constructing a new house, builders either include a layer of insulation between the two masonry leaves of exterior walls or blow insulant into the cavity before the walls are plastered on the inside. These measures significantly increase the insulation of the building. However, in the past, millions of homes were built with cavity walls that were left empty, and bringing these homes up to current standards of insulation requires a skilled professional to introduce an insulant through holes cut in the outer brick leaf.

Professional installers

It is imperative to hire contractors who specialize in blown cavity-wall insulation. Before starting work, the contractor will assess the house to ensure that the walls are suitable for filling, with no evidence of frost damage, failed pointing or cracked render. Leaking gutters will have to be repaired, too.

Having carried out the inspection, the contractor will complete and submit on your behalf a Building Notice to the local Building Control Office. When the work is complete, the contractor will ask the Cavity Insulation Guarantee Agency (CIGA) to issue a guarantee that covers the installation for 25 years against defects in workmanship or materials. The guarantee is transferable to future owners of the house. CIGA will honour the guarantee, even if the contractor goes out of business.

All systems of cavity-wall insulation have been tested and approved by independent bodies such as the British Board of Agrément (BBA). Amongst other requirements, the insulation must be water-resistant and must fill adequately in order to satisfy the BBA. The Board also undertake continuous assessment and surveillance of their approved installers.

Materials for blown cavity insulation

The most common type of cavity-wall insulation is mineral wool, being either rock wool or glass wool. One alternative to mineral wool is expanded polystyrene, (EPS), which comes in the form of white or grey beads. Along with the EPS, an adhesive is sprayed at the point of injection to bond the beads together and prevent the insulation settling in the cavity. EPS does not affect the fire resistance of the wall.

Urea-formaldehyde foam (UF) is rarely used except in the less exposed parts of the UK. Mineral wool and expanded polystyrene are approved for use all over the country.

Polyurethane-foam systems are generally used as cavity-reinforcement foam (CRF) where wall ties have corroded. CRF is considerably more expensive than other systems, and a CIGA guarantee is not available for it.

Installing the insulant

Any installation should be completed within 2 to 3 hours and is undertaken from outside the house, although the contractor will need to make various checks and tests inside. He or she will begin by drilling holes in a defined pattern through the mortar joints in the external walls (**1**). Extra holes are drilled close to obstructions such as doors and windows.

A hose is then inserted into each hole (**2**) and the insulant is blown into the cavity, filling it from the base. After injection, the holes are filled with mortar to match the existing pointing.

1 Drilling holes in the outer leaf

2 Introducing the insulant

SEE ALSO > Interior panelling 219–20

Internal dry-lining

If you are planning to dry-line an external wall with some form of panelling, it is worth taking the opportunity to include blanket or sheet insulation between the wall-mounted furring strips.

Fix a polythene-sheet vapour barrier over the insulation by stapling it to the furring strips before you nail the panelling in place. Alternatively, use an insulated (thermal) plasterboard that has an integral vapour barrier.

Any form of panelling can be applied over blanket insulation, but you should use plasterboard to cover expanded-polystyrene insulant.

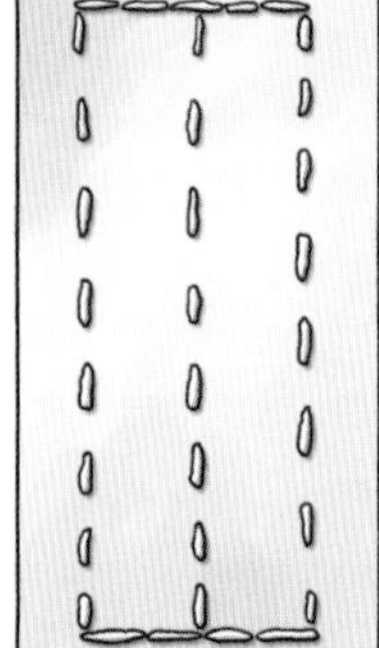

Insulated plasterboard
1 Insulant
2 Integral vapour barrier
3 Plasterboard lining

Gluing the plasterboard
Apply dabs of adhesive sealant to the wall in three rows.

Gluing directly to the wall

A simpler method is to use the board manufacturer's adhesive to glue insulated plasterboard directly onto the wall. This type of wall insulation has a layer of plasterboard backed by a layer of either expanded-polystyrene or phenolic foam. Make sure an integral vapour barrier is incorporated into the board.

Using a trowel, apply 250 x 75mm (10 x 3in) dabs of adhesive to the wall, in three vertical rows, with a continuous strip of adhesive at the top and bottom. Place packing pieces of wood about 12 to 18mm (½ to ¾in) thick at the foot of the wall to support the insulated board.

Resting the bottom edge of the board on the packing pieces, press it against the adhesive and tamp it down with a 100 x 50mm (4 x 2in) straightedge. Apply each board in a similar way, making sure they are flat and level. Use a fine-toothed saw to cut a panel to fit into a corner.

For additional security, wait until the adhesive sets, then drill through each board into the wall to insert three nailable plugs, two near the top of the board and one in the centre. Remove the packing pieces, then tape and fill all joints.

Detailed instructions regarding door and window mouldings can be found in the section on wall panelling. Glue the skirting board to the plasterboard and seal the gap at the bottom with a bead of mastic sealant.

Nailable plugs
Used to fix insulated plasterboard to the wall. Push each plug into a hole drilled through the board, then drive in the fixing to expand the plug and grip the masonry.

Insulating floors

It is possible to upgrade an existing concrete floor by installing an insulated floating floor on top of it. You can reduce draughts through a suspended wooden floor, using carpet and underlay – but really effective insulation entails additional measures.

Working from above

By lifting the floorboards you can lay a substantial amount of insulation between the joists. Staple some plastic netting to the sides of the joists as support for blanket insulation. Alternatively, nail battens to the joists to support panels cut from rigid sheet insulant.

Installing foiled quilt

Another method is to roll foiled quilt across the floor joists and push it down between each pair of joists to a depth of 50mm (2in). Then staple the quilt to both sides of each joist. Overlap joints in the quilt by 100mm (4in) and take the insulation 75mm (3in) up behind the skirting boards.

Staple foiled quilt to the sides of the joists

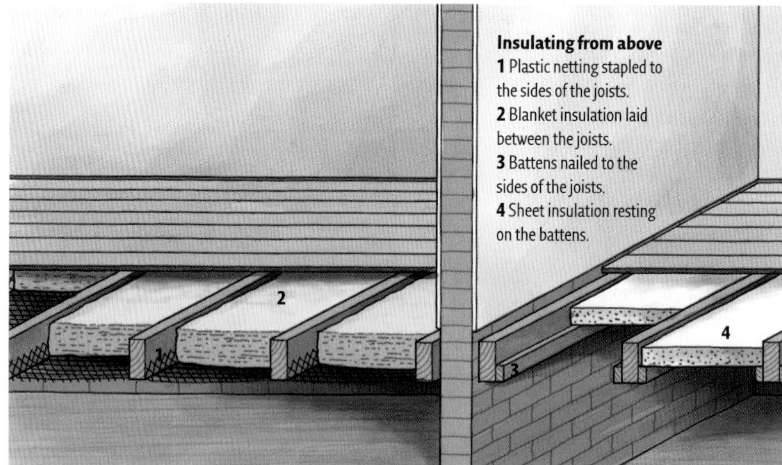

Insulating from above
1 Plastic netting stapled to the sides of the joists.
2 Blanket insulation laid between the joists.
3 Battens nailed to the sides of the joists.
4 Sheet insulation resting on the battens.

Working from below

If you can gain access from below, insulating a suspended wooden floor is easier still. Simply push insulating material between the joists and then staple plastic netting or wire mesh to the undersides to hold it in place.

Alternatively, run foiled quilt at right angles to the floor joists, stapling it to the undersides of the joists. Overlap the joints between strips of insulation by 100mm (4in).

Staple foiled quilt to the undersides of the joists

SEE ALSO > Levelling a wooden floor 57, Floating floors 177, Furring strips 219, Interior panelling 219–20, Taping joints 168, Damp 247–54, U-values 256, Types of insulation 261, Ventilating below floors 274

Double glazing

A double-glazed window consists of two sheets of glass separated by an air gap. The air gap provides an insulating layer that reduces heat loss and sound transmission. Condensation is also reduced, because the inner layer of glass remains warmer than the glass on the outside.

Both factory-sealed units and secondary glazing are used for domestic double glazing. Sealed units are unobtrusive; secondary glazing is a cheaper option that helps to reduce the intrusion of noise from outside. Both provide good thermal insulation.

What size air gap?

For heat insulation, a 20mm (¾in) gap will give the optimum level of efficiency. If the gap is less than 12mm (½in), the air can conduct a proportion of the heat across it. If it's greater than 20mm (¾in), there is no appreciable gain in thermal insulation, and air currents can transmit heat to the outside layer of glass.

For noise insulation, an air gap of 100 to 200mm (4 to 8in) is more effective. Triple glazing – a combination of sealed units with secondary glazing – may therefore prove to be the ideal solution.

Although the amount of heat lost through windows is relatively small, the installation of double glazing can halve the wastage. As a result, you will find there is a saving on your fuel bills.

But the benefit you will be aware of more immediately is the elimination of draughts. In addition, the cold spots associated with large windows (most noticeable when you're sitting still) are likely to be reduced.

Installing double glazing with good window locks will improve security against forced entry, particularly when sealed units or toughened glass are used. However, make sure that some accessible part of appropriate windows can be opened in order to provide an escape route in case of fire.

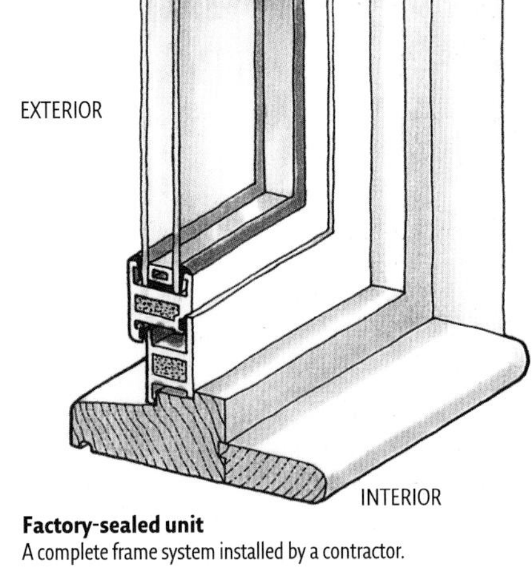

Factory-sealed unit
A complete frame system installed by a contractor.

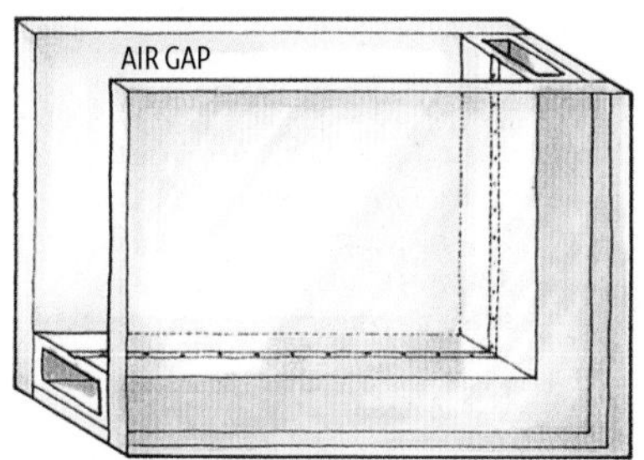

Double-glazed sealed unit

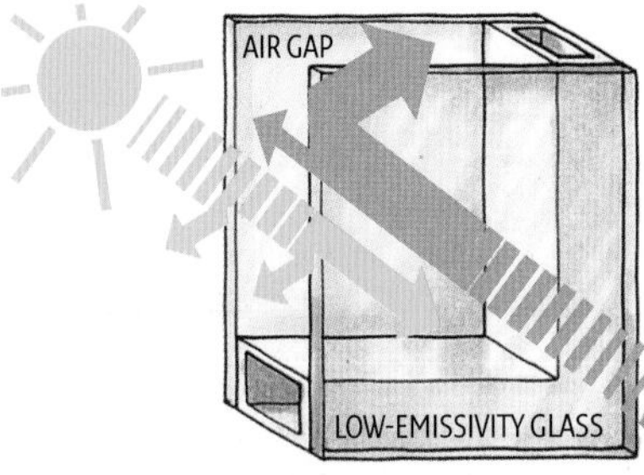

Heat-retentive sealed unit

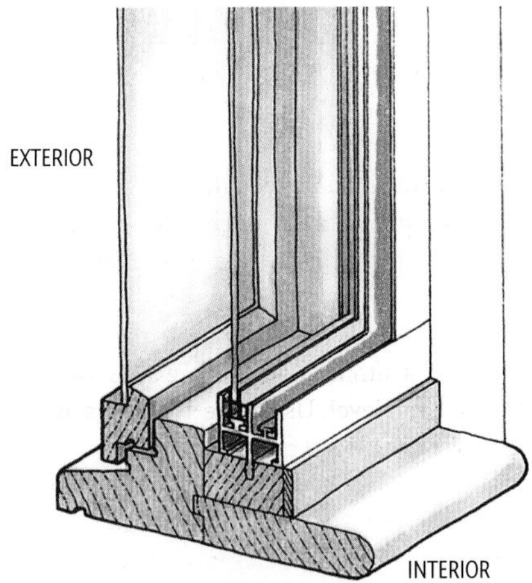

Secondary double glazing
Fitted in addition to an ordinary glazed window.

Double-glazed sealed units

Double-glazed sealed units consist of two panes of glass that are separated by a spacer and hermetically sealed all round. The gap may contain dehydrated air – which eliminates condensation between the two panes of glass – or inert gases, which also improve thermal and acoustic insulation.

The thickness and type of glass used are determined by the size of the unit. Clear float glass or toughened glass is commonly employed. When obscured glazing is required to provide privacy, patterned glass is used. Heat-retentive sealed units, incorporating special low-emissivity glass, are supplied by some double-glazing companies.

Generally, factory-sealed units are produced and installed by suppliers of ready-made double-glazed replacement windows. Square-edged units are available for frames with a deep rebate, and stepped units for window frames that were originally intended for single glazing.

Double-glazed sealed units with metal-reinforced uPVC frames are rarely suitable for older houses. A secondary system that leaves the original window intact is generally more appropriate – especially if you have attractive leaded windows, which should be preserved (sealed units with a modern interpretation of leaded lights are not an adequate substitute for the real thing).

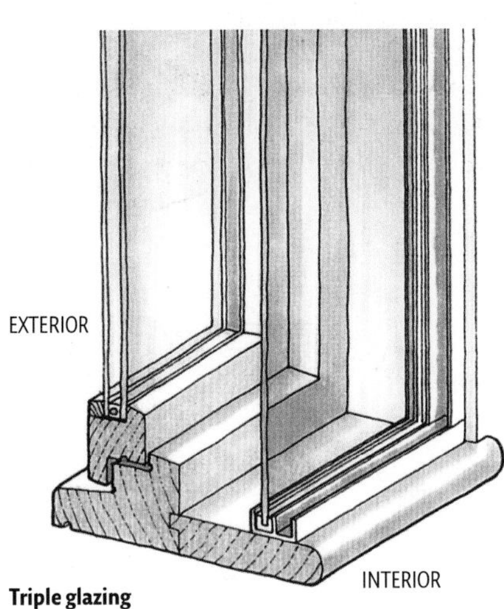

Triple glazing
A combination of secondary and sealed units.

SEE ALSO > Double-glazed units 197

Secondary double glazing

Secondary double glazing consists of a separate pane of glass or plastic fitted over an ordinary single-glazed window. It is normally fitted on the inside of the existing windows, and is one of the most popular methods of double glazing as it's relatively inexpensive compared with sealed units. You can install DIY secondary-glazing kits yourself or stretch plastic film over your existing windows.

Sash-fixed
Glazing fixed to opening part of window.

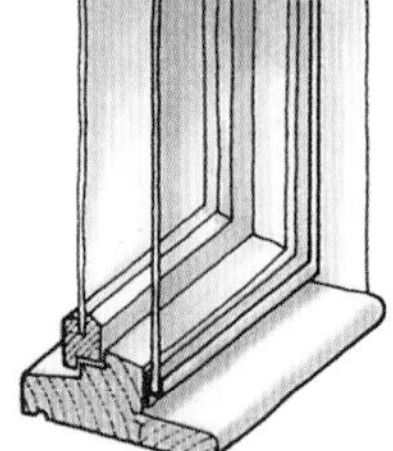

Frame-fixed
Glazing fixed to the structural frame.

Reveal-fixed
Glazing fixed to the reveal and interior windowsill.

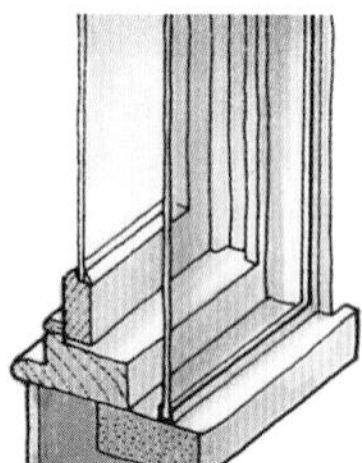

Exterior-fitted
Glazing fixed to the reveal and exterior windowsill..

Providing a fire escape
If you fit secondary glazing, make sure there is at least one window in every occupied room that can be opened easily.

How double glazing is fixed

Secondary glazing can be fastened to the sash frames or window frame or across the window reveal. The method depends on ease of fixing, the type of glazing chosen, and the amount of ventilation that is required.

Glazing fixed to the sash will reduce heat loss through the glass and provide accessible ventilation – but it won't stop draughts, whereas glazing fixed to the window frame has the advantage of cutting down heat loss and eliminating draughts at the same time. Glazing fixed across the reveal offers improved noise insulation too, since the air gap can be wider. Any system should be readily demountable, or preferably openable, to provide a change of air if the room does not have any other form of ventilation.

A rigid-plastic or glass pane can be fitted to the exterior of the window if secondary glazing fitted on the inside would look unsightly. Windows set in a deep reveal, such as the sliding-sash type, are generally the most suitable ones for external secondary glazing.

Glazing with renewable film

Cheap and effective double glazing can be achieved using double-sided adhesive tape to stretch a thin flexible sheet of plastic across a window frame. The taped sheet can be removed and thrown away at the end of the winter.

Clean the window frame and cut the plastic roughly to size, allowing an overlap all round. Apply double-sided tape to the edges of the frame (1), then peel off the backing paper.

Attach the plastic film to the top rail (2), then tension it onto the tape on the sides and bottom of the window frame. Apply light pressure until you have positioned the film, and then rub it down onto the tape.

Remove all wrinkles in the film, using a hairdryer set to a high temperature (3). Starting at an upper corner, move the dryer slowly across the film, holding it about 6mm (¼in) from the surface. When the film is taut, cut off excess plastic with a knife (4).

1 Apply double-sided tape to the fixed frame

2 Stretch the film across the top of the frame

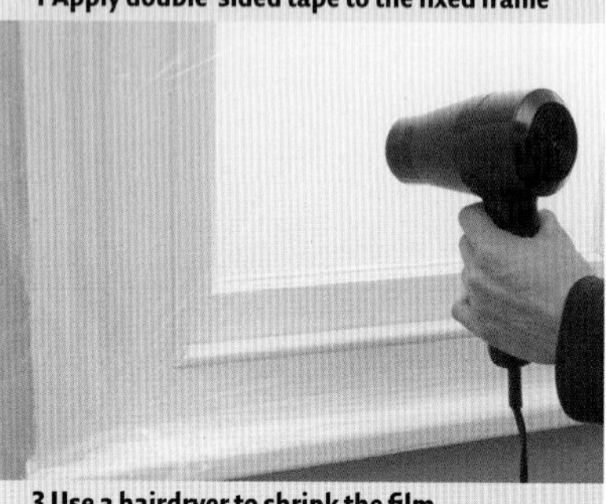

3 Use a hairdryer to shrink the film

4 Trim the waste with a sharp knife

Demountable systems

Other simple methods of interior secondary glazing use clear-plastic film or sheet. These lightweight materials are held in place by self-adhesive strips or rigid moulded sections, which form a seal. Most strip fastenings use magnetism or some form of retentive tape, thus allowing the secondary glazing to be removed for cleaning or ventilation. The strips and tapes usually have a flexible-foam backing, which takes up slight irregularities in the woodwork. You need to clean the windows and the surfaces of the window frame before installation. This type of secondary glazing can be left in place throughout the winter and removed for storage during the summer months.

Fitting demountable systems

To install the simplest systems, cut the plastic sheet to size, then hold it against the window frame and draw round it. Lay the sheet on a flat table. Peel back the protective paper from one end of the self-adhesive strip and stick it to the plastic sheet, flush with one edge. Cut the strip to length and repeat on the other edges. Cut the mating parts of the strips and stick them onto the window frame, following the guide lines marked earlier. Press the glazing into place.

When using rigid moulded sections, cut the sections to length with mitred corners. To fit an extruded clip-type moulding, stick the base section to the frame, then insert the outer section to hold the glazing in place.

Rigid plastic mouldings support the glazing

SEE ALSO > Draughtproofing windows 260

Hinged and sliding systems

The suppliers of hinged or sliding secondary-glazing kits provide detailed fitting instructions for every situation. The description below will give you some idea of the work involved and, if you prefer, you can ask the same companies to install similar systems for you. Sliding and hinged systems are intended to be permanent fixtures.

Glass or plastic

Self-assembly kits can incorporate glass of various thicknesses to suit the location, but if your window is close to the floor, or is vulnerable to impact damage for some other reason, you may prefer to use clear acrylic sheet instead.

Hinged systems

Hinged systems incorporate coated aluminium extrusions that form a frame for the glass or rigid-plastic sheet. The glazing sits in a flexible gasket lining the extrusions. Screw-fixed corner joints hold the sides of the frame together, and pivot hinges are inserted into one of the extrusions in order to make side-hung or top-hung units.

Hinged units are usually fitted to the face of a wooden window frame and secured by turn buttons. A flexible draughtproofing strip is fixed to the back of the frame. A self-locking stay can be fitted to keep the window open to provide ventilation.

Hinged system
1 Glazing
2 Glazing gasket
3 Corner joints
4 Hinges
5 Aluminium extrusion
6 Turn button
7 Draughtproofing strip

Sliding systems

A horizontally sliding system is used for casement windows, whereas a vertically sliding system is more suitable for tall double-hung sashes. Each of the panes is framed by an aluminium extrusion, which is jointed at the corners, and the glass is sealed into its frame with a gasket.

A horizontal system has two or more sliding panes, the number depending on the width of the window. They are held in a tracked frame, which is screwed to the window frame or to the reveal. Fibre or brush seals are fitted to the sliding-frame members to prevent draughts. The glazing is opened with an integral handle, and each pane can be lifted out for cleaning.

A vertically sliding system is similar in construction, but catches are incorporated to hold the panes open at any height.

Fitting a horizontally sliding system

As an example of what is involved, the following instructions describe the installation of a sliding system often used for casement windows. Suppliers provide more detailed instructions with their kits.

Measure your window opening and buy a kit of parts slightly larger than the opening. After cutting the vertical track members to size, using a hacksaw (1), screw them to either the reveal or the inside face of the window frame. Cut the top and bottom track members and screw them in place (2) after cutting notches in the extrusions to fit the shape of the side members (see right). This frame must be square and parallel if the glazed frames are to slide smoothly.

Measure the opening for the glazing and have it cut to size, following manufacturer's instructions regarding tolerances. Cut and fit the components of the glazing frames, including gaskets and seals. Join the four sides together with corner joints (3) – and lift the glazing into the sliding tracks (4).

Sliding system
1 Glazing extrusion
2 Glazing
3 Corner joints
4 Glazing gasket
5 Top track
6 Bottom track
7 Side track
8 Draught seal
9 Slides

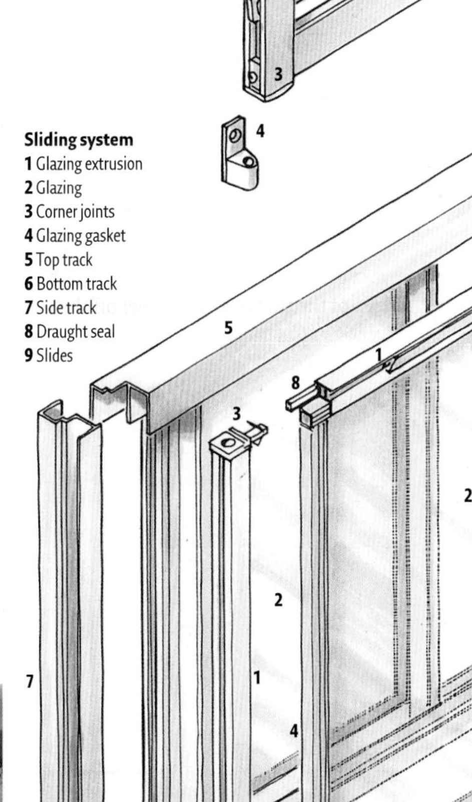

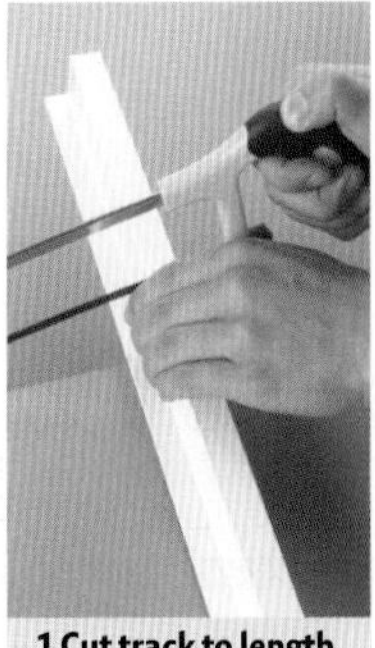
1 Cut track to length

2 Screw it in place

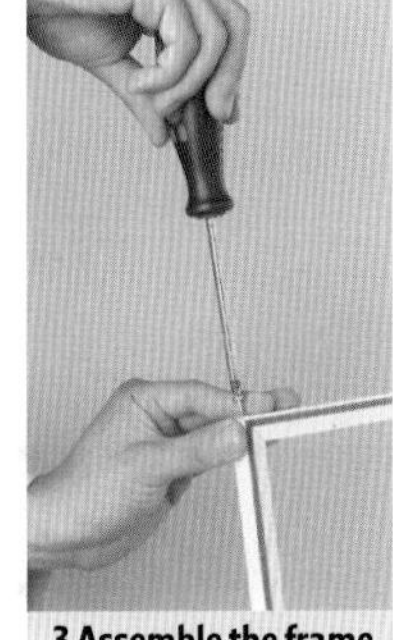
3 Assemble the frame

4 Fit it into the tracks

SEE ALSO > Woodworking tools 487–504

Soundproofing

Noise generated by road and air traffic or by industrial processes or thoughtless neighbours can make life distinctly unpleasant, if not intolerable. Although it's difficult to block out unwelcome sounds completely, it is possible to reduce intrusive noise levels in almost any house or flat.

Sound is produced as a vibration that sets up pressure waves. These are transmitted to different elements in a house, which in turn resonate, making the noise 'echo' through the building.

The materials that make up the house react differently to sound waves. Carpets and curtains, for example, act as insulators – whereas hard surfaces such as ceramic tiles and plastered walls reflect sound, and thin materials offer little resistance. In addition, loose-fitting doors and windows, holes in the roof and gaps between the floorboards or under skirtings all contribute to the problem of penetrating noise.

What's needed is an airtight barrier that has sufficient mass to be resistant to vibration – but lightweight modern housing materials, although thermally efficient, are not as soundproof as the denser materials used in the construction of older, traditionally built houses.

Soundproofing materials

It is possible to soundproof your home to some extent, using materials such as ordinary plasterboard and thermal-insulating blankets or batts, but to block sound transmission effectively you should use special acoustic boards, mineral wool and sealant, all of which can be ordered from specialist internet web sites and delivered to your door.

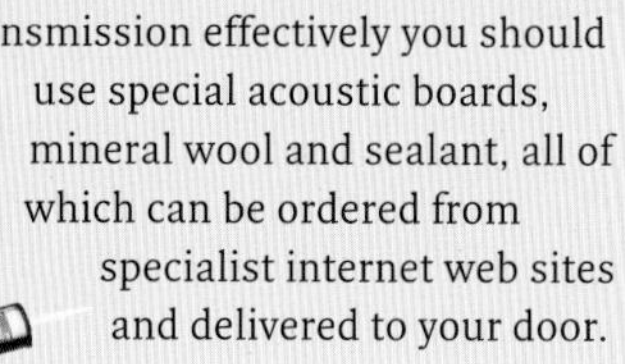

Partition walls

To reduce the noise that passes from room to room in your own home, line both sides of existing stud partitions with an additional layer of acoustic plasterboard 19mm (¾in) thick. Fill any gaps around the plasterboarded walls with a special acoustic sealant, then fill and tape the joints between the boards.

If you are building a new stud partition, install acoustic mineral-wool blanket between the studs and clad it with two layers of acoustic plasterboard.

Soundproofing a party wall

Noise can easily penetrate a shared wall between houses. Although neighbourly courtesy ought to rule out noise problems, in practice neighbours aren't always so considerate.

The soundproofing of a party wall can be greatly improved by various methods, although their effectiveness depends on factors such as the construction of the party wall, whether or not there is a fireplace, and the location of electrical fittings.

External walls can be soundproofed, too, but coping with windows makes it a more difficult proposition.

Minor improvements

Sealing gaps in the party wall is an important way to reduce airborne noise. If necessary, remove the skirting boards and floorboards close to the party wall so you can repoint poor mortar joints. At the same time, fill any gaps around the ends of the joists built into the masonry.

After replacing the skirting and floorboards, seal any gaps between them with a flexible acoustic sealant.

It may also be worth repointing the party wall in the loft and plastering it to add mass.

Lining with acoustic panels

Acoustic panels are made from plasterboard with a layer of acoustic mineral wool 42mm (1⅝) thick bonded to the back. They are simply cut to size with an ordinary handsaw, then glued to the party wall with an adhesive that can be supplied with the panels.

Preparing the party wall

Remove any loose or flaky material, including peeling wallpaper. Soundly fixed wallpaper can be left in place.

Switch off the electricity supply at the consumer unit, and replace any electrical fittings attached to the party wall with junction boxes in readiness for relocating the fittings on the new lining. Remove the skirting carefully and retain it for reuse.

Carry out the minor improvements described above before you install the panels.

Lining the wall

Lay each board face down and apply blobs of the adhesive in three vertical rows 400mm (16in) apart. Space the blobs vertically at 400mm (16in) centres. At each point, prime the mineral wool with an initial blob of adhesive that is smeared into the wool and then apply a second blob directly on top (**1**).

Press the glued panel against the wall, resting it temporarily on spacers to keep it between 3 and 5mm (⅛in to ¼in) off the floor (**2**). Leave a similar gap around the perimeter of the wall, but butt each panel tightly together.

Finally, fill the perimeter gap with acoustic sealant before gluing the skirting board in place and refitting any electrical fittings. Fill and tape the plasterboard joints in the usual way prior to decorating.

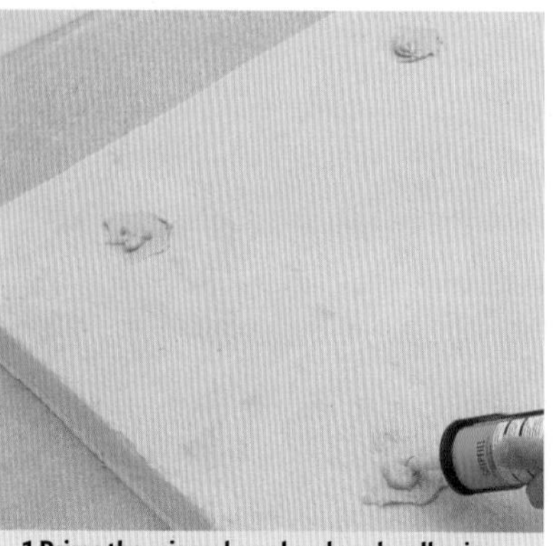

1 Prime the mineral wool and apply adhesive

2 Use spacers to keep the panel off the floor

SEE ALSO > Party-wall Act 27, Soundproofing doors and windows 272, Soundproofing floors and ceilings 272

1 Screw furring strips to the wall

2 Press acoustic blanket between the strips

3 Screw resilient bars across the furring strips

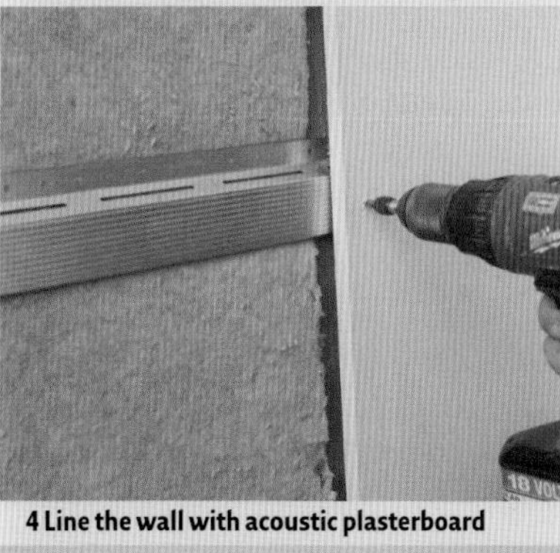

4 Line the wall with acoustic plasterboard

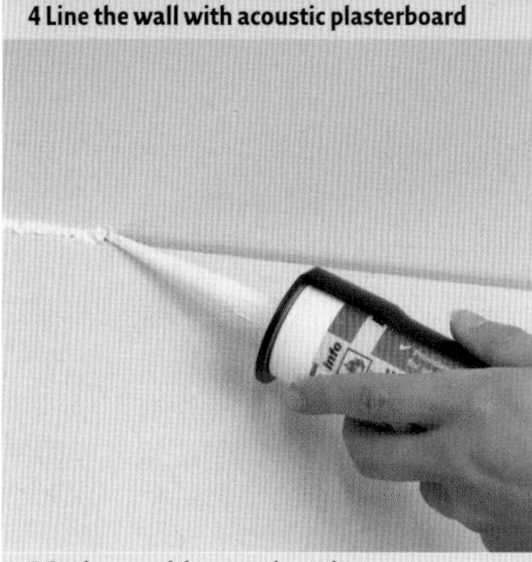

5 Seal gaps with acoustic sealant

Mineral wool and floating plasterboard

An alternative method for soundproofing a party wall is to line it with acoustic mineral wool, then mount the covering layers of plasterboard on lightweight resilient metal bars that eliminate any direct contact with the wall behind, dissipating sound that would normally be transferred through solid materials.

Attaching furring strips

Screw 50 x 50mm (2 x 2in) furring strips (wood battens) vertically to the wall (**1**). Leave a space of slightly less than 600mm (2ft) between the battens – in order to allow a snug fit for acoustic mineral-wool blanket 50mm (2in) thick, which you press in place against the wall (**2**).

Starting at approximately 100mm (4in) from the floor, screw resilient bars horizontally across the battens. Space the bars 400 to 600mm (16 to 24in) apart (**3**). You can cut the bars to length with tinsnips or a hacksaw, and overlap the ends by about 100mm (4in) if you have to join them. The final bar should be 50mm (2in) from the ceiling.

Lining the wall

Line the wall with sheets of acoustic plasterboard 19mm (¾in) thick, screwing them to the resilient bars with 32mm (1¼in) dry-wall screws (**4**). The screws should pass through the flange of each bar, but must not touch the wall or battens behind. Take care to leave a 3 to 5mm (⅛in to ¼in) gap around the perimeter of the wall.

Using 42mm (1⅝in) screws, install a second layer of acoustic plasterboard over the first. This time, use plasterboard 12.5mm (½in) thick and stagger the joints between the sheets in each layer.

Seal gaps all round with acoustic sealant (**5**), then refit the skirting board and prepare the plasterboard for decorating.

Building an independent stud wall

If the noise coming through a party wall is excessive, the best solution is to build an independent stud partition, leaving a 50mm (2in) gap between the partition and the party wall.

Construct the partition from 50 x 75mm (2 x 3in) timber. It must not be in contact with the party wall at any point, all fixings being made to the adjacent walls, floor and ceiling. Before you fix the partition in place, use acoustic mineral wool 100mm (4in) thick to line the party wall in the floor and ceiling voids immediately above and below the partition.

Sandwich acoustic mineral wool 100mm (4in) thick between the partition studs, then attach resilient bars and two layers of acoustic plasterboard as described above.

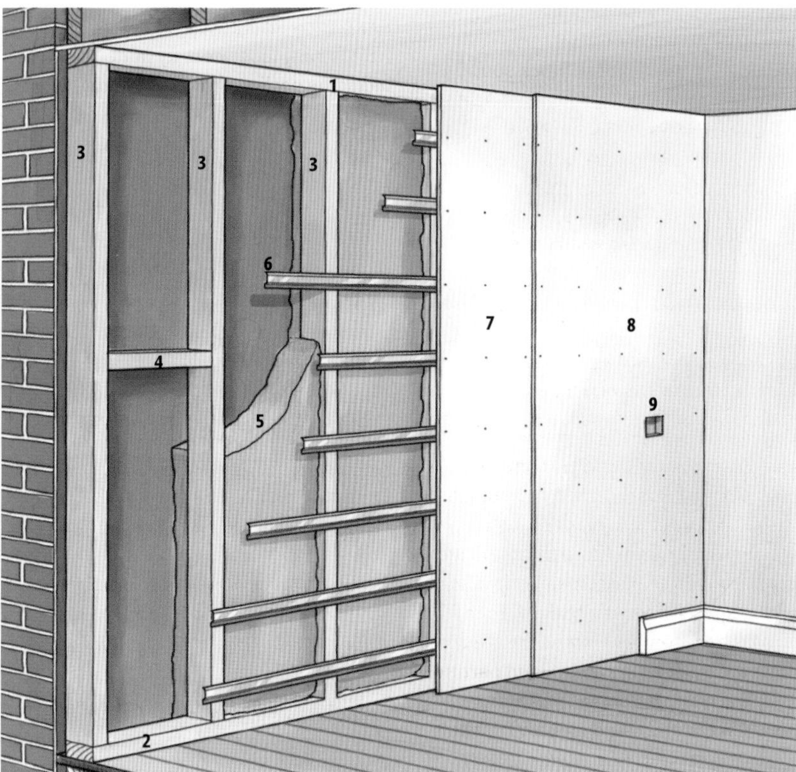

Independent stud wall
1 Head plate
2 Sole plate
3 Studs
4 Nogging
5 Acoustic blanket
6 Resilient bar
7 First layer of plasterboard
8 Second layer of plasterboard
9 Electrical fitting

SEE ALSO > Repointing masonry 43, Stud partitions 151–5, Plasterboarding 162–70, Soundproofing doors and windows 272, Soundproofing floors and ceilings 272, Electricity 282–344,

Soundproofing floors and ceilings

Preventing sound travelling between floors is a priority for most flat dwellers. How you achieve this depends on the level of nuisance you are subjected to and whether you have access above or below the floor.

Working from above

1 Lay acoustic blanket

2 Fill the gaps

Carpeting to muffle the sound

The easiest and most basic solution is to lay a good-quality carpet and underlay. Ideally, use a special-purpose acoustic carpet underlay consisting of 5mm (¼in) high-grade felt bonded to a 5mm (¼in) rubber base.

These measures will reduce impact-noise transmission to the floor below, but there are more effective methods to cut down airborne noise.

Filling the ceiling void

If you are able to lift the floorboards, place 100mm (4in) acoustic mineral wool on the ceiling below (**1**). The insulating blanket must be a snug fit between the joists.

Screw the floorboards back in place and fill gaps between them with acoustic sealant (**2**).

Including a layer of plasterboard

To provide additional acoustic insulation, you can install above the mineral wool a layer of acoustic plasterboard 19mm (¾in) thick supported on wood battens screwed to the sides of the joists. Squeeze a strip of acoustic sealant along the top edge of each support batten before laying the plasterboard between the joists.

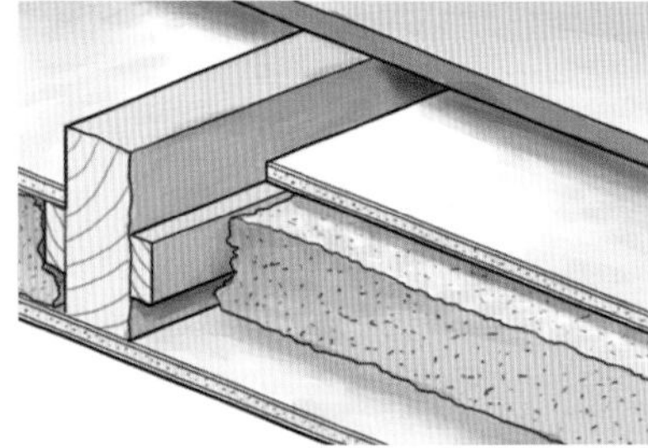

Install acoustic plasterboard above mineral wool

Suspended ceilings

If you are unable to gain access to the floor above, you may want to consider introducing soundproofing in the form of a suspended ceiling. The object of the exercise is to install acoustic mineral wool that will absorb airborne sound and detach the plaster ceiling from the joists to absorb impact noise.

Using resilient bars

If you have a plasterboard ceiling with very little headroom, consider using resilient bars screwed at 400mm (16in) centres across the ceiling at right angles to the joists. The one big disadvantage is having to remove the plasterboard so you can install mineral wool 100mm (4in) thick between the joists. Screw two layers of acoustic plasterboard to the bars, as described for soundproofing a wall. This method reduces the height of a room by less than 50mm (2in).

Acoustic hangers

A lath-and-plaster ceiling is a relatively good soundproofer, so don't take it down unless you have to. Instead, support 50mm (2in) square battens on special acoustic hangers screwed along each joist at 600mm (2ft) centres. Install 50mm (2in) acoustic mineral wool between the battens and affix a double layer of acoustic plasterboard to the battens. This method reduces the height of a room by about 75mm (3in).

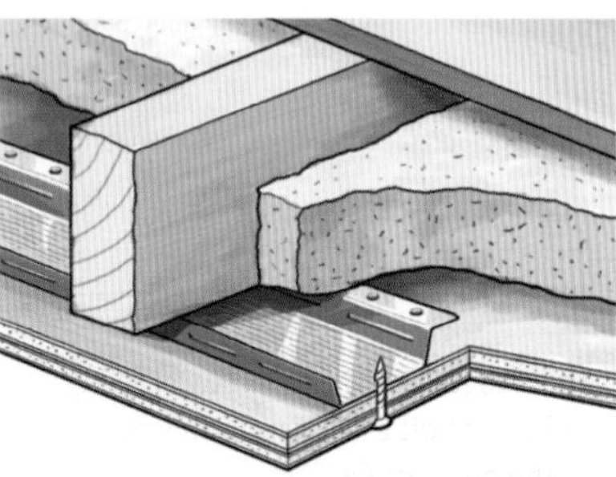

Using resilient bars to install insulation

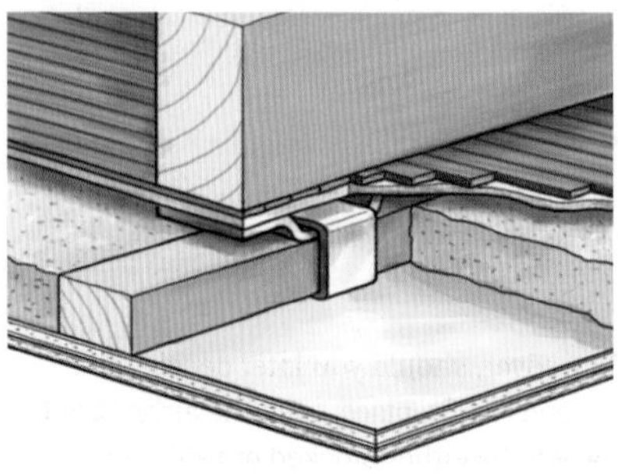

Suspend an insulated ceiling from acoustic hangers

Doors and windows

Because they are relatively large openings cut through the fabric of the building, doors and windows can admit a great deal of noise.

Soundproofing doors

To muffle noise from outside, draughtproof exterior doors and fit secondary double glazing to porch or entrance-hall windows, perhaps incorporating toughened glass to improve security. The joints between the surrounding doorframe and the masonry should be filled with acoustic sealant.

Draughtproofing your interior doors will have a similarly beneficial effect; and replacing lightweight hollow-core doors with heavy solid doors may help to reduce sound transmission between neighbouring flats.

Dealing with the windows

It is very likely that outside noise will penetrate through traditional single-glazed windows. Not only does sound find its way through gaps around the sashes (good draughtproofing is needed in order to make them airtight), but it also passes directly through the thin panes of glass. Double glazing will improve matters, but there must be a gap of at least 100mm (4in) between the panes for satisfactory sound insulation. This can be achieved by installing an airtight secondary-glazing system, but triple glazing (which includes a sealed unit) provides the optimum solution.

When fitting a secondary system, make sure that at least one window can be opened to provide an escape route in case of fire.

If your windows are the only source of ventilation, install a ventilator elsewhere in the room – preferably not connected directly to the outside. If that is not feasible, make sure the ventilator has a baffle that interrupts incoming sound.

SEE ALSO > Triple glazing 267, Double glazing 267–9, Acoustic materials 270, Soundproofing walls 270–71

Ventilation

Ventilation is essential for a comfortable atmosphere, but it has an even more important function – it affects the structure of our homes. This wasn't a problem when houses were heated with open fires, drawing fresh air through all the natural openings in the structure; but with central heating and thorough insulation and draughtproofing, well-designed ventilation is vital.

Initial considerations

Whenever you plan an improvement to your home that involves insulation in one form or another, take into account how it's likely to affect your existing ventilation. It may change conditions sufficiently to create a problem in areas outside the habitable rooms - so that damp and its side effects are able to develop unnoticed under floorboards or in the loft. If there is any likelihood that damp conditions might occur, provide additional ventilation.

Without a constant change of air, centrally heated rooms become stuffy, and the moisture content of the air soon becomes so high that water is deposited as condensation - often with serious consequences. There are various ways to provide ventilation: some are extremely simple, others much more sophisticated, giving total control.

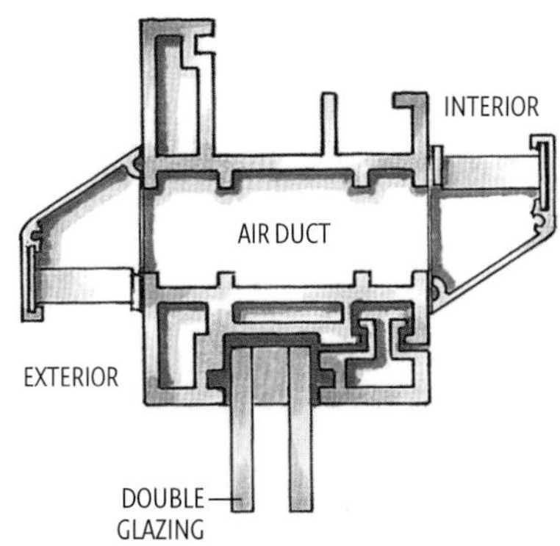

Combustion air vent
This type of trickle ventilator provides a permanent air supply for rooms containing a fuel-burning appliance.

Ventilating a fireplace

An open fire has to have oxygen if it is to stand any chance of burning well. If the air supply is reduced, perhaps by thorough draughtproofing or double glazing, then the fire smoulders and the slightest downdraught will blow smoke into the room. There may be other reasons why a fire burns poorly - such as a blocked chimney flue - but if you find that the fire picks up within a few minutes of partially opening the door to the room, you can be certain that inadequate ventilation is the cause of the problem.

One simple solution is to fit a slim trickle ventilator over the door or window. Ventilators with sliding grilles are suitable for a room with an open fireplace; but if you are heating a room with a fuel-burning appliance that is connected to a flue, the ventilator must be permanently open.

Some trickle ventilators are fitted with acoustic baffles to reduce noise penetration from outside.

Ventilating an unused fireplace

If you close off an unwanted fireplace with masonry or plasterboard, you should fit a vent, so air can flow up the chimney to dry out condensation or penetrating damp. Provided the chimney is uncapped, the moist warm air from inside the room will not condense on the cold surface of the flue - the updraught will simply draw the moisture-laden air to the outside.

To ventilate the fireplace, either cut a hole in the plasterboard or leave a single-brick aperture in the masonry, as appropriate. Screw a face-mounted ventilator over the hole; or use one that's designed to be plastered in.

Fitting an airbrick

An airbrick cut into the flue from outside is an even better solution. But it's much more difficult to accomplish, and impossible if you live in a terraced house. Moreover, should you later decide to reopen the fireplace, then the airbrick will have to be either blocked or replaced.

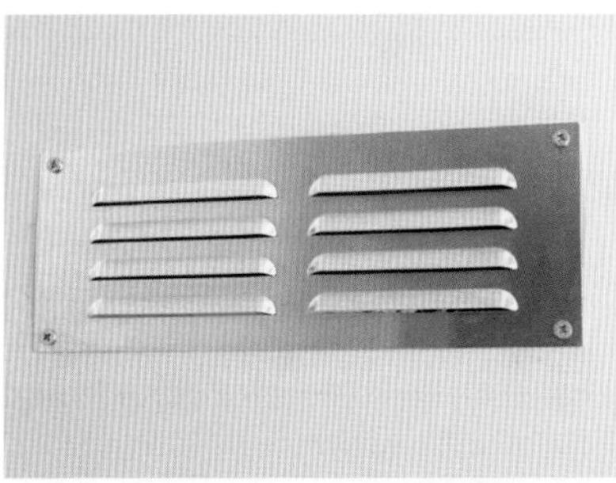

Face-mounted grille for an unused fireplace

Hide the fixings of a grille with plaster

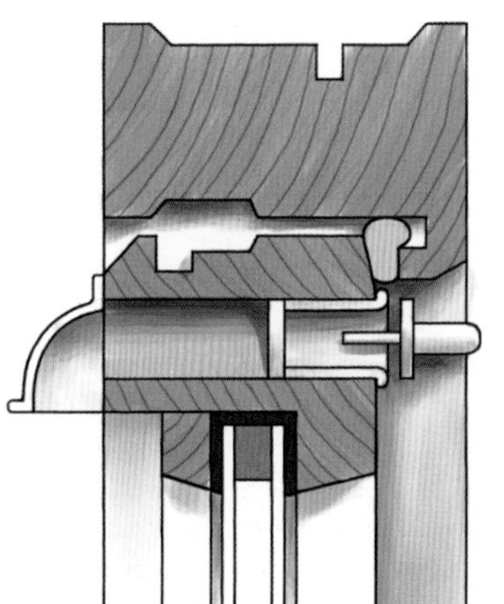

Trickle ventilation
Replacement windows can be supplied with a slot (either at the top of the fixed frame or in the movable sash) for a controllable trickle ventilator. This type of ventilator can also be fitted to an existing window in order to provide background ventilation when the window is closed.

Fixed window vents

You can provide continuous ventilation by installing an inexpensive fixed vent in a window. Well-designed ventilators of this kind usually have a windshield on the outside - which allows a free flow of air without causing draughts - and are totally reliable.

Some window ventilators are fitted with wind-driven fans - which can emit irritating squeaks as they begin to wear.

Have the recommended size of hole cut in the glass by a glazier. Then fit one of the vent's louvred grilles on each side of the window, clamping them together with the central fixing bolt, and bolt the plastic windshield to the outer grille.

SEE ALSO > Plastering 156–61, Condensation 250, Airbricks 274, Enclosing a fireplace 399, Ventilating appliances 407

Ventilating below a floor

Perforated openings known as airbricks are built into the external walls of a house to ventilate the space below suspended wooden floors. If they become clogged with earth or leaves, there's a strong possibility of dry rot developing in the timbers – so check their condition regularly.

Plastic and ceramic airbricks

Checking the airbricks

Ideally there ought to be an airbrick every 2m (6ft) along an external wall, but in a great many buildings there is less provision for ventilation without ill effect – in fact, sufficient airflow is more important than the actual number of openings in the wall.

Floor joists that span a wide room are supported at intervals by low sleeper walls made of brick. Sometimes these are perforated to facilitate an even airflow throughout the space – but in other cases there are merely gaps left by the builder between sections of solid wall. This method of constructing sleeper walls can lead to pockets of still air in corners where draughts never reach. Even when all the airbricks are clear, dry rot can break out in areas that don't receive an adequate change of air. If you suspect there are 'dead' areas under your floor – particularly if there are signs of damp or mould growth – fit an additional airbrick in a wall nearby.

Old ceramic airbricks sometimes get broken, and are often ignored because there is no detrimental effect on the ventilation. However, even a small hole can provide access for vermin. Don't be tempted to block the opening, even temporarily – instead, replace the broken airbrick with a similar one of the same size. You can choose from single or double-size airbricks, made in ceramic or plastic.

Bridging a cavity wall

To build an airbrick into a cavity wall, bridge the gap with a plastic telescopic unit, which is mortared into the hole from both sides. If need be, a ventilator grille can be screwed to the inner end of the telescopic unit.

Where an airbrick is inserted above the DPC, it is imperative to fit a cavity tray above the telescopic unit. This is to prevent water percolating to the inner leaf of the cavity wall.

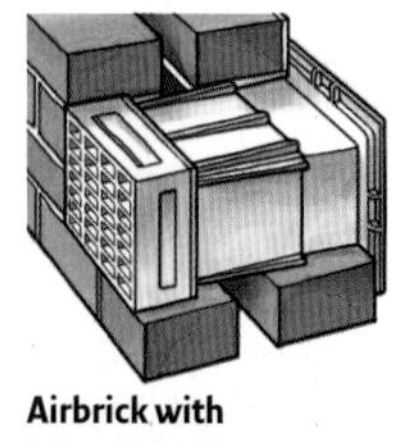

Airbrick with telescopic sleeve
Bridge a cavity wall with this type of unit.

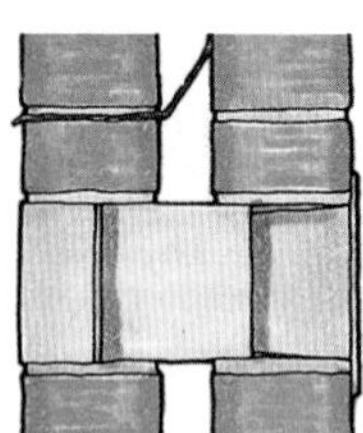

Cavity tray
A cavity tray sheds any moisture that penetrates the cavity above the unit. It is necessary only when the airbrick is fitted above the DPC.

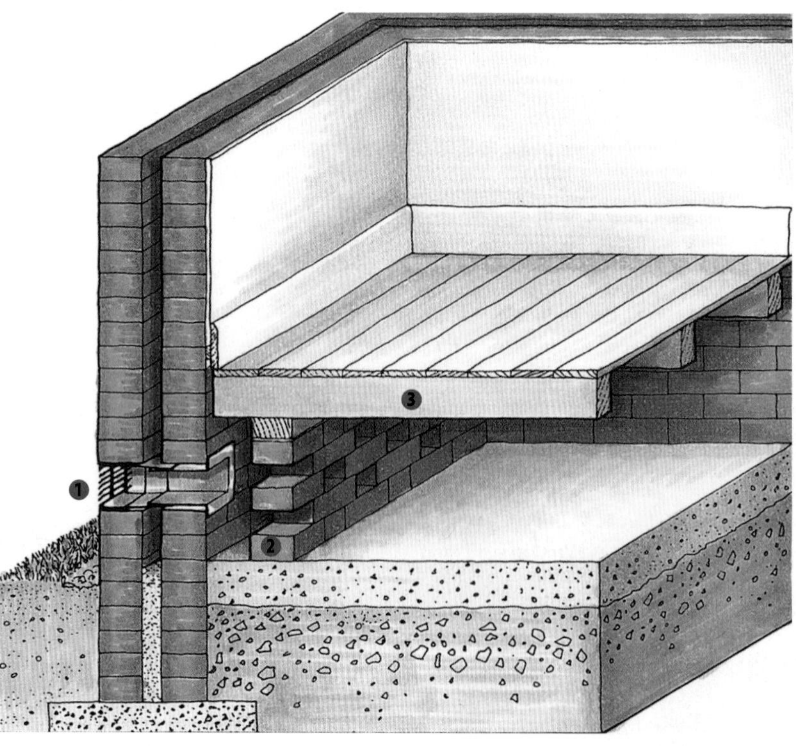

Replacing an airbrick

Use a masonry drill to remove the mortar surrounding the brick you are removing (1), and a cold chisel to chop out the brick itself. Spread mortar on the base of the hole, and along the top and both sides of the new airbrick (2). Push it into the opening, keeping it flush with the face of the brickwork, then repoint the mortar to match the profile used on the surrounding wall (3).

1 Remove the mortar from around the brick

2 Spread mortar onto the new brick

3 Repoint the mortar

Ventilating the space below a suspended wooden floor
The illustration (left) shows a cross section through a typical cavity-wall structure, with a wooden floor suspended over a concrete base. A house with solid-brick walls is ventilated in a similar way.
1 Airbrick fitted with telescopic sleeve.
2 Sleeper wall built with staggered bricks in order to allow air to circulate.
3 Floorboards and joists are susceptible to dry rot caused by poor ventilation.

SEE ALSO > Repointing masonry 43, Cavity tray 129, Dry rot 245, DPC 247, Cutting bricks 444, Laying bricks 444–9

Ventilating the roof space

When loft insulation first became popular as an energy-saving measure, householders were recommended to tuck insulant right into the eaves to keep out draughts. What people failed to recognize was that a free flow of air is necessary in the roof space to prevent moisture-laden air from below condensing on the structure.

Inadequate ventilation can lead to serious deterioration. Wet rot develops in the roof timbers and water drips onto the insulant, eventually rendering it ineffective as insulation. If water builds up into pools, the ceiling below becomes stained and there is a risk of short-circuiting the electrical wiring in the loft. For these reasons, efficient ventilation of the roof space is essential in every home.

Ventilating the eaves

The regulations governing new housing insist on ventilation equivalent to continuous openings of 10mm (3/8in) along two opposite sides of a roof that has a pitch (slope) of 15 degrees or more. If the pitch is less than 15 degrees or the roof space is habitable, ventilation must be equivalent to continuous openings of 25mm (1in). It makes sense to adopt similar standards when refurbishing a house of any age. The simplest method of ventilating a standard pitched roof is to fit soffit vents made with integral insect screens. To calculate how many vents you need, divide the specified airflow capacity of the vent you are planning to use into the recommended continuous gap. Space the vents evenly along the roof. Push the vents into openings cut with a hole saw or jigsaw.

If the opening at the eaves is likely to be restricted by insulation, insert a plastic or cardboard eaves vent between each pair of joists. Push the vent into the angle between the rafters and the joists, with the ribbed section uppermost. Vents can be cut to length with scissors for an exact fit. When you install the insulation, push it up against the vent.

Slate and tile vents

Certain types of roof construction do not lend themselves to ventilation from the eaves only, but the structure can be ventilated successfully by strategically replacing tiles or slates with specially designed roof vents. A range of colours and shapes is available to blend with various roof coverings.

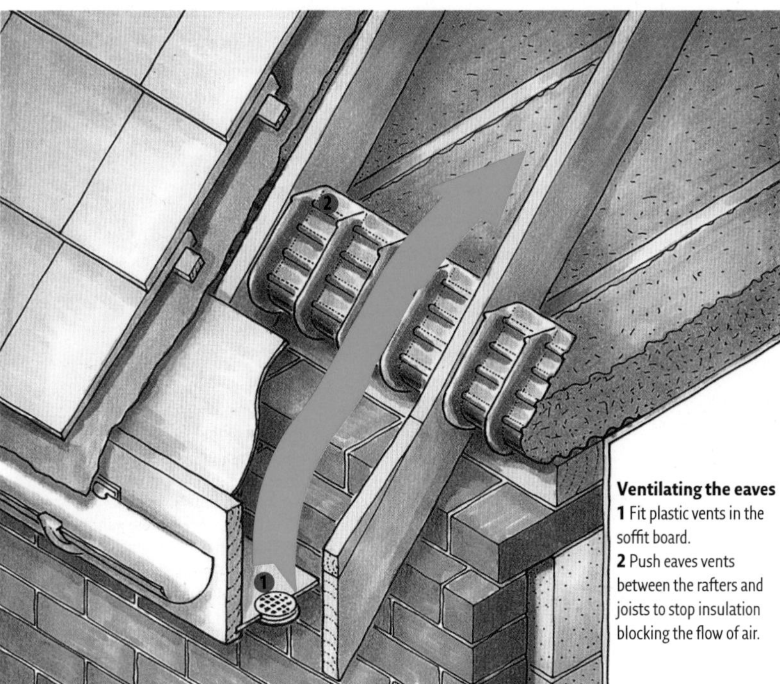

Ventilating the eaves
1 Fit plastic vents in the soffit board.
2 Push eaves vents between the rafters and joists to stop insulation blocking the flow of air.

Venting the roof

Eaves-to-eaves ventilation normally keeps the roof space dry, but tile or slate vents sometimes have to be fitted to draw air through the roof space.

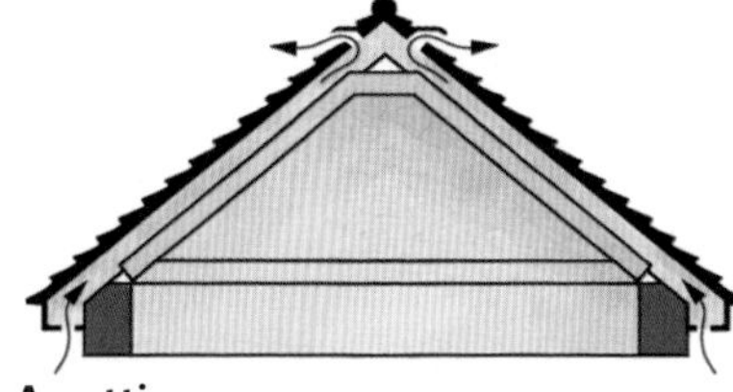

An attic space
If you insulate a sloping roof, you must provide a minimum 50mm (2in) airway between the insulant and roof covering. Fit soffit vents at the eaves, and replace some tiles or slates near the ridge with vents.

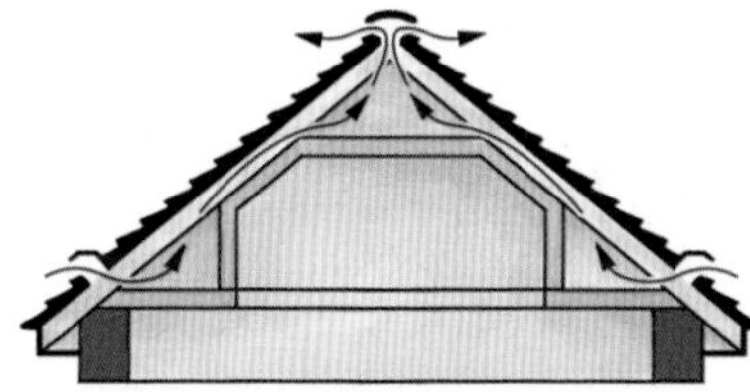

A room in the roof
Where a room is built into the attic, fit ridge vents and tile or slate vents near the eaves to draw air through the narrow spaces over the sloping ceiling.

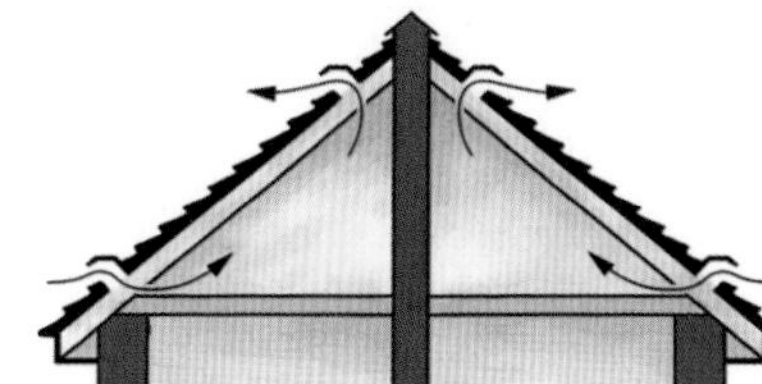

A fire wall or party wall
Fit slate or tile vents to ventilate your side of the wall (ideally, your neighbour should do the same). Use a similar arrangement to ventilate a mono-pitch roof over an extension or lean-to.

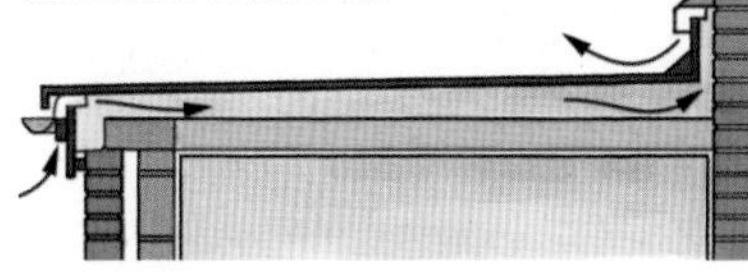

A flat roof
An insulated flat roof can be ventilated by fitting over-fascia ventilators at the eaves and at the wall abutment. On an existing roof, you need to modify the wall flashing.

Soffit vent

Slate/tile vents
Roof vents are made to resemble a variety of roof coverings.

Ridge vent

Slate vent

Double pantile vent

SEE ALSO > Wet rot 245, Insulating a loft 261–4, Insulating a sloping roof 263

Whole-house ventilation

If you are prepared to make the necessary investment, you can have a simple system installed to extract moisture-laden air and stale odours from the entire house. It works on the principle that natural convection draws the relatively warm air inside the house via ducts to the roof, where it escapes through ridge or tile vents. This type of system is self-regulating and, since there are no electrical connections, it costs absolutely nothing to run.

Passive stack ventilation

Extractors are fitted in rooms where there is likely to be the greatest concentration of moist or odour-laden air – usually the kitchen, bathroom and utility room. A single duct runs from each extractor by the most direct route to the roof, where the wind creates a suction effect that helps to draw the warm air through the duct, just like smoke being carried up a chimney. The stale air in neighbouring 'dry' rooms, such as living rooms and bedrooms, moves naturally towards the vented rooms where extraction takes place. Trickle vents, fitted in the windows or exterior walls of the dry rooms, provide a flow of fresh air.

Noise pollution
Because there are no fans running, passive stack ventilation is perfectly quiet. If there is a possibility of noise penetrating from outside, make sure the air-inlet vents are fitted with acoustic baffles.

Ventilation by demand

The inlet vents and extractors in each room are operated by humidity-sensitive controls, so that their flaps or louvres open and close progressively to admit or extract air as necessary, to maintain a perfect balance.

Unobtrusive installation

Provided that they are fitted with care, the system's slim external vents should be unobtrusive. Internally, ducting is normally either sited within fitted cupboards or run through stud partitions up to the roof space, where it must be insulated to prevent condensation forming inside the duct.

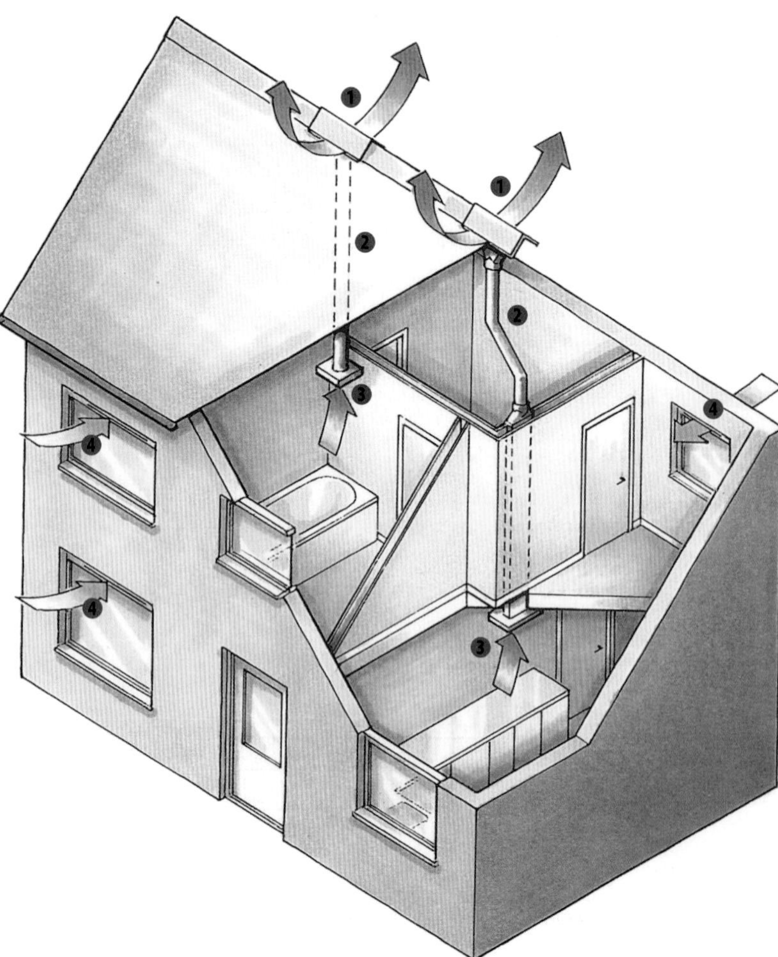

Combustion air
Rooms containing open-flued heating appliances must be ventilated permanently. Suitable vents can be installed as part of passive-vent systems.

Passive-vent system
This type of system is designed to ventilate the entire house without using electrically driven fans.
1 Stale moist air escapes through ridge vents (as shown) or through tile vents, which must be located no more then 50cm (20in) from the ridge.
2 Ducting takes the shortest route to the roof. Air is drawn through the vents by convection.
3 Extractors in the kitchen and bathroom draw air from surrounding rooms.
4 Trickle vents mounted in windows or exterior walls admit fresh air but without causing draughts.

Extracting radon

Radon is a radioactive gas that can seep into buildings from below ground. Mostly, radon levels are so low they are harmless, but where the gas is sufficiently concentrated it can be a health risk. When building new homes, contractors must prevent radon gas from entering the building. This is done by incorporating a gas-impermeable membrane in a solid concrete base. Below a suspended floor, ventilation is usually sufficient to disperse the gas. Where there are high concentrations, install a radon-collection sump below ground, vented to the roof.

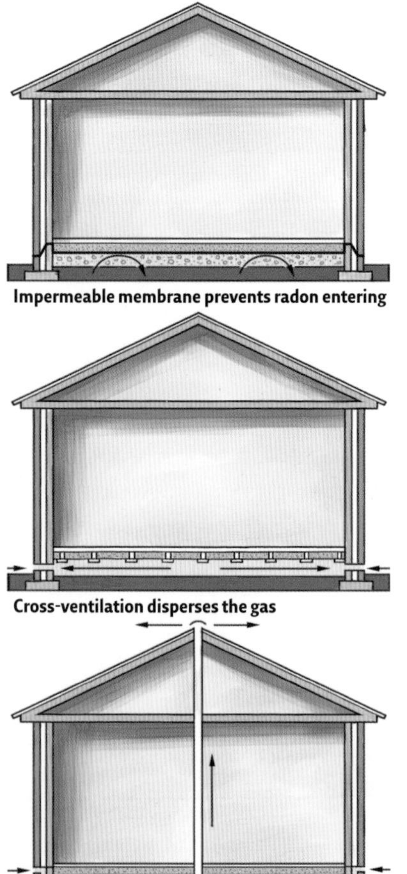

Impermeable membrane prevents radon entering

Cross-ventilation disperses the gas

A vented sump removes radon by convection

SEE ALSO > Trickle ventilators 273, Central-heating boilers 406–7

Extractor fans

Since kitchens and bathrooms are particularly prone to condensation, it's important to have some means of expelling moisture-laden air, together with unpleasant odours. An electrically driven extractor fan freshens a room quickly, and without creating draughts.

Positioning the fan

The best place to site a fan is either in a window or on an outside wall, but its exact position is more critical than that. Stale air extracted from the room must be replaced by fresh air - normally through a door leading to other areas of the house. But if the fan is sited close to the source of replacement air, it will promote local circulation while having little effect on the rest of the room. The ideal position for it is directly opposite the source of replacement air, as high as possible, to extract the hot air. In a kitchen, try to locate the fan adjacent to the cooker, so that cooking smells and steam will not be drawn across the room before being expelled.

If the room contains a fuel-burning appliance with a flue, you must ensure that there is enough replacement air to prevent fumes from the appliance being drawn down the flue when the extractor fan is switched on.The only exception is an appliance with a balanced flue, which takes its air directly from outside.

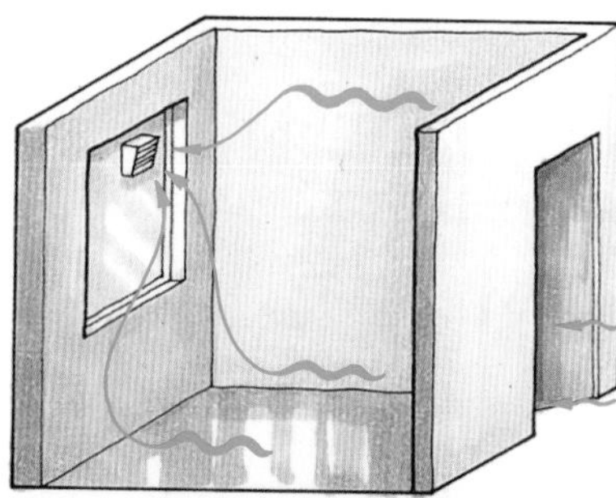

Fit extractor opposite replacement-air source

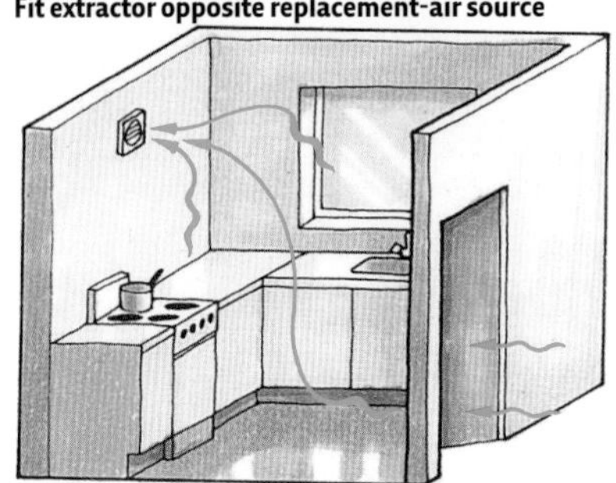

In a kitchen, place extractor near cooker

Types of extractor fan

Many fans have an integral switch. If not, a switched fused connection unit can be wired into the circuit when you install the fan. Some fans incorporate a built-in controller to regulate the speed of extraction, and a timer that switches off the fan after a certain interval. Some fans will switch on automatically when the humidity in the room reaches a predetermined level. Axial fans can be installed in a window; and with the addition of a duct, some models will extract air through a wall (to overcome the pressure resistance in a long run of ducting, you need a centrifugal fan). To prevent backdraughts, choose a fan with external shutters that close when the fan is not in use.

• **Building Regulations**
You must inform the Building Control Officer before undertaking any electrical wiring in a bathroom or kitchen – see BUILDING REGULATIONS ON ELECTRICAL WIRING.

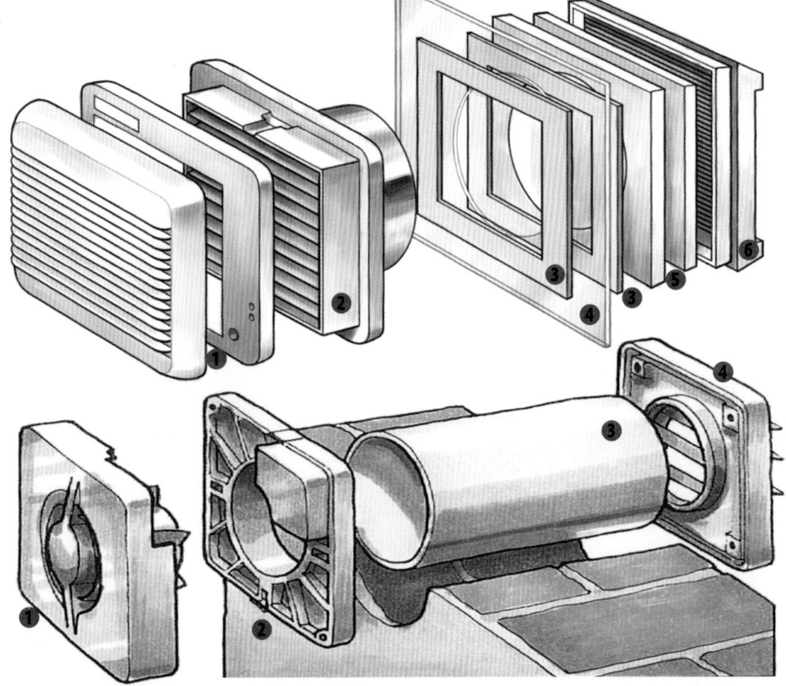

Window-mounted axial fan
1 Inner grille
2 Fan housing
3 Gasket
4 Glass
5 Spacers
6 Outer grille

Wall-mounted axial fan
1 Motor assembly
2 Interior backplate
3 Duct
4 Exterior grille

Choosing the size of a fan

The capacity of a fan should be determined by the type of room in which it is installed. A fan installed in a kitchen must be capable of changing the air completely 10 to 15 times per hour. A bathroom requires 6 to 8 air changes per hour, or 15 to 20 changes if a shower is installed, and a WC needs 6 to 10 changes. A living room normally requires about 4 to 6 changes per hour.

In order to determine the minimum capacity required, calculate the volume of the room and then multiply the volume by the recommended number of air changes per hour (see example below).

CALCULATING THE CAPACITY OF A FAN FOR A KITCHEN				
Size of kitchen				
Length		**Width**	**Height**	**Volume**
3.35m (11ft)		3.05 (10ft)	2.44m (8ft)	24.93cu m (880cu ft)
Air changes		**Volume**	**Fan capacity**	
15 per hour	x	24.93cu m (880cu ft)	= 374cu m per hour (13,200cu ft per hour)	

Low-profile fans
Because the motor and fan assembly are built into the duct immediately behind the grille, the face plate can be made ultra-slim.

• **Low-voltage fans**
A special low-voltage fan, which comes with its own transformer and sometimes a light fitting, is designed to be mounted directly above a shower.

SEE ALSO > Planning kitchens 15, External walls 138, Condensation 250, Installing a cooker hood 279, Building Regulations 284, Wiring small fixed appliances 311

Fitting extractor fans

There are so many different extractor fans on the market that it is impossible to describe them all, but the following instructions serve as a guide for installing typical fans in an exterior wall or window.

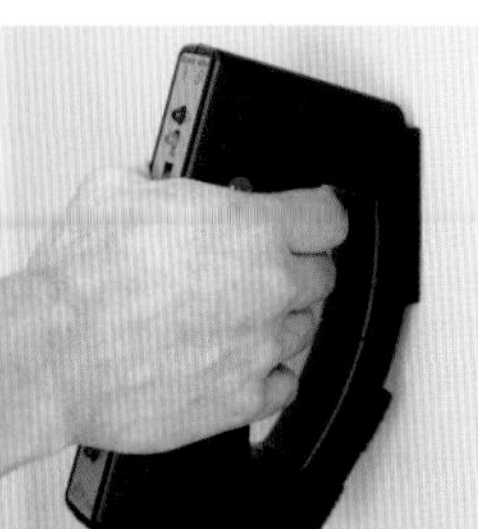

1 Use a metal detector

2 Drill out the hole

3 Seal the plate spigot

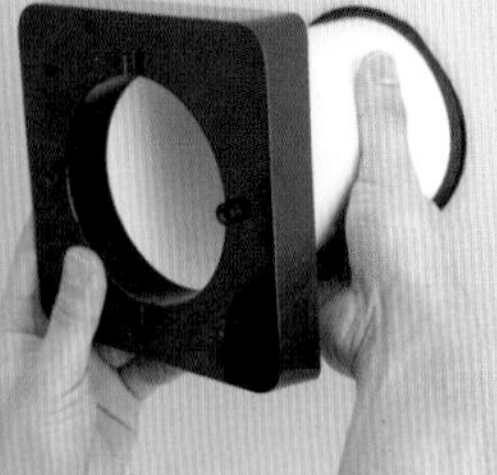

4 Insert the duct

5 Screw-fix the grille

Wall-mounted fans

Satisfy yourself there is no plumbing or electrical wiring buried in the wall, using an electronic sensor (1). Make sure there are no drainpipes or other obstructions.

Cutting the hole

Wall-mounted fans are supplied with plastic ducting for inserting in a hole cut through the wall. Plot the centre of the hole and draw its diameter on the inside of the wall. Use a long-reach masonry drill to bore a central hole right through. To prevent the drill breaking through the masonry on the outside, hold a stout plywood panel against the wall and wedge it with a strong plank supported by stakes driven into the ground.

Before cutting the masonry, drill holes close together around the inner edge of the hole (2). With a cold chisel, cut away the plaster, using the holes as a guide, and then continue to cut away the masonry (try to avoid debris falling inside a cavity wall). When you reach the centre of the wall, remove the panel; then use the same technique to finish the hole from outside.

Fitting the fan

Most wall fans are fitted in a similar manner, but check the instructions beforehand. Separate the components of the fan, then attach a self-adhesive foam sealing strip to the spigot on the backplate to receive the duct (3). Insert the duct in the hole so that the backplate fits against the wall (4). Mark the length of the duct on the outside, remembering to allow for fitting the spigot on the outer grille. Cut the duct to length with a hacksaw. Reposition the backplate and duct in order to mark the fixing holes on the wall. Drill and plug the holes, then feed the electrical supply cable into the backplate before screwing it to the wall. Stick a foam sealing strip inside the spigot on the grille. Position it on the duct, then mark, drill and plug the wall-fixing holes. Use a screwdriver to stuff scraps of loft insulation between the duct and the cut edge of the hole (or use a sprayed expanding foam), then screw on the exterior grille (5). If the grille doesn't fit flush with the wall, seal the gap with mastic. Wire the fan according to the manufacturer's instructions, then attach the motor assembly to the backplate.

Installing a fan in a window

An extractor fan can only be installed in a fixed window. If you want to fit one in a sliding-sash window, you will need to secure the top sash, in which the fan is installed, then fit a sash stop on each side of the window in order to prevent the lower sash damaging the casing of the fan.

If you plan to install an extractor fan in a hermetically sealed double-glazing system, ask the manufacturer to supply a special unit with a precut hole, which is sealed around the edges, to receive the fan. Some manufacturers supply a kit for adapting a fan so that you can install it in a window with secondary double glazing.
It allows the inner window to be opened without dismantling the fan.

Cutting the glass

Every window-mounted fan requires a round hole to be cut in the glass. The size is specified by the manufacturer. It is possible to cut a hole in an existing window, but stresses in the glass will sometimes cause it to crack. Also, there is always a security risk while the glass is removed for cutting, especially if you decide to take it to a glazier. All things considered, it is generally better to fit a new pane, which will be easier to cut and can be installed as soon as the old one has been removed.Cutting a hole in glass is not easy, and you may find that it's more economical to have it cut by a glazier – in which case, you will need to provide exact dimensions, including the size and position of the hole. Order 4mm (5/32in) glass that matches the existing glazing.

Installing the fan

The exact assembly may vary, but the following sequence is a typical example of how a fan is installed in a window.

Take out the existing windowpane and clean up the frame, removing retaining sprigs and traces of old putty; then fit the new pane with the precut hole as you would any other window glass.

From inside, fit the fan housing into the hole in the glass (1). On the outside, slide the plastic body or spacer over the fan housing (2). Then insert the threaded collar (3) to draw the entire assembly together, clamping the glass between the inner and outer components. Soft gaskets are usually supplied to cushion the glass on both sides.

Wire up the fan in accordance with the manufacturer's instructions, then fit both the outer and inner grilles (4) to the unit. Finally, switch on the fan to check that it runs smoothly, and that the backdraught shutter opens and closes automatically when the unit is switched on and off.

1 Fit the fan housing into the window

2 Slide the plastic body onto the fan housing

3 Screw the threaded collar in place

4 Fit grilles on both sides of the fan

SEE ALSO > Glass 195–6, Sash stops 236, Building Regulations 284, Consumer units 296, Wiring an extractor fan 311

Installing cooker hoods

Window-mounted and wall-mounted fans are primarily intended for overall room extraction – but the most effective way to rid your kitchen of steam and greasy cooking smells is to mount an extracting hood, which is designed specifically for this purpose, directly over your cooker.

Where to mount the cooker hood

Unless the manufacturer recommends otherwise, an extracting hood should be positioned between 600mm (2ft) and 900mm (3ft) above a gas or electric hob, or about 400mm (1ft 4in) to 600mm (2ft) above an eye-level grill.

Depending on the model, a cooker hood may either be cantilevered from the wall or screwed between or beneath fitted kitchen cupboards. With some kitchen ranges you can buy a cooker-hood unit that matches the style of the cupboards (opening the unit operates the fan automatically).

Most hoods have either two or three speed settings, and a built-in light fitting to illuminate the hob or cooker below.

Installing trunking

When a cooker hood is mounted on an external wall, air is extracted through the back of the unit into a straight duct passing through the masonry.

But if the cooker is situated against an interior wall, you'll need to connect the extracting hood to the outside by means of fire-resistant plastic trunking. The straight and curved components of the trunking – which simply plug into one another – form a continuous shaft running along the top of the wall cupboards.

To fit the trunking, begin by plugging the female end of the first component over the outlet spigot attached to the top of the cooker hood. Cut each of the components to length with a hacksaw or tenon saw and piece the rest of the trunking together, making the same female-to-male connections along the shaft. Some manufacturers print airflow arrows on the trunking to ensure that each component is oriented correctly; if you should accidentally reverse a component somewhere along the shaft, air turbulence may be created around the joint, reducing the effectiveness of the extractor. At the outside wall, cut a hole through the masonry for a straight piece of ducting and fit an external grille (see opposite).

Fitting a cooker hood

Cooker hoods are hung from brackets that come with them; these have screw-fixing points for attaching the brackets beneath or between wall cupboards or directly to the wall. Cut a ducting hole through the wall, as for a wall-mounted fan (see opposite), and wire the cooker hood following the maker's instructions.

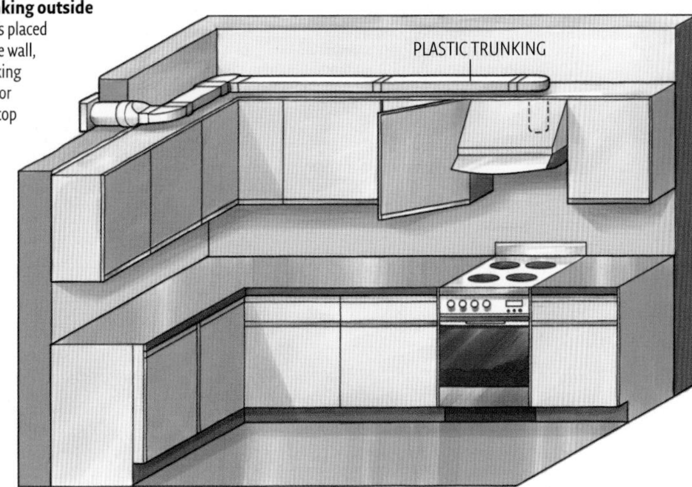

Running trunking outside
When a cooker is placed against an inside wall, run plastic trunking from the extractor hood along the top of wall-hung cupboards.

Recirculation or extraction?

Some cooker hoods filter out the odours and grease and then return the air to the room. Others dump stale air outside through a duct in the wall, in much the same way as a wall-mounted extractor fan. Because the air is actually changed, extraction is the more efficient of the two methods.

In order to install an extracting hood, it is necessary to cut a hole through the wall then fit ducting and an external grille. Although hoods that recycle the air are much simpler to install, they do not expel moisture from the room, nor do they filter out all of the grease and cooking odours.

To keep any cooker hood working at peak efficiency, it is essential to change the filters regularly.

Building Regulations
You must inform the Building Control Officer before undertaking any electrical wiring in a bathroom or kitchen – see BUILDING REGULATIONS ON ELECTRICAL WIRING.

Recirculation hoods return the air to the room

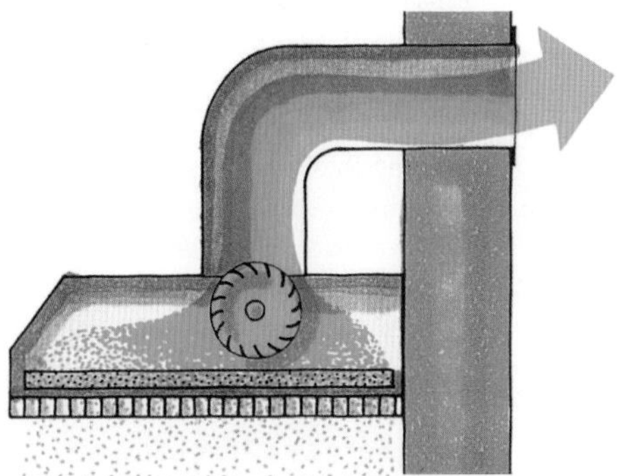

Extraction hoods suck air outside via trunking

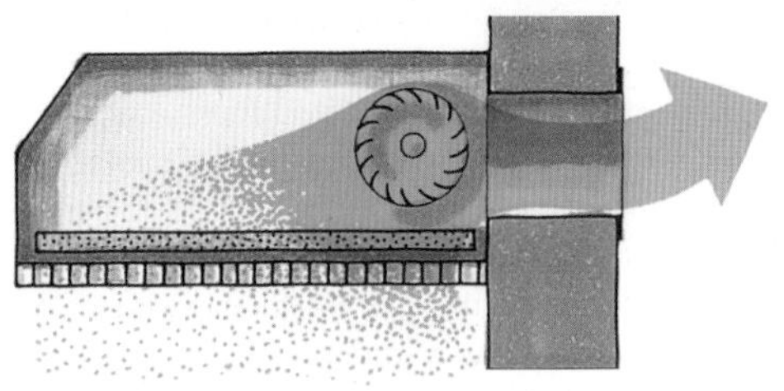

Alternatively, air is extracted through ducting

SEE ALSO > Planning kitchens 15, Condensation 250, Building Regulations 284, Wiring a cooker hood 311

Heat-recovery ventilation

It has been estimated that more than half the energy produced by burning fossil fuels is used simply to keep our homes warm. Although the installation of efficient insulation reduces heat loss to a minimum, a great deal of heat is still wasted as a result of necessary ventilation.

Heat-recovery ventilators

Heat-recovery ventilators are designed to balance the requirements of conserving energy and the need for a constant supply of clean fresh air. But in practice the cost of running the system may outweigh the benefits of heat recovery.

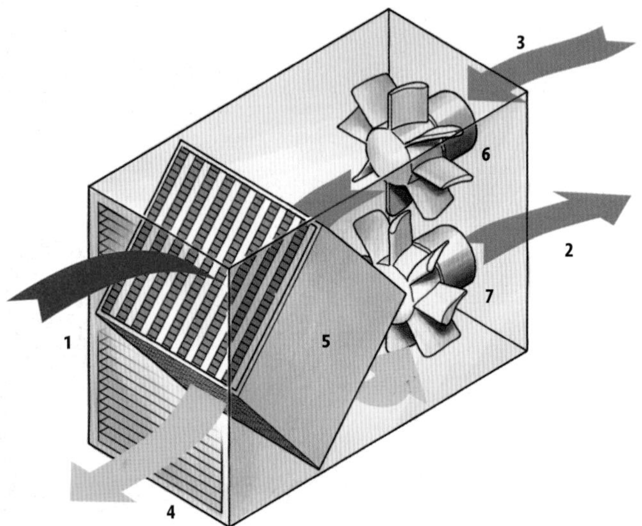

Heat-recovery ventilation unit
The diagram shows the layout of a typical wall-mounted heat-recovery ventilator.
1 Stale air from room
2 Stale-air exhaust
3 Fresh-air supply
4 Warmed fresh air
5 Heat exchanger
6 Induction fan
7 Extractor fan

How it works

Heat-recovery ventilation can range in scale from compact airbrick-size units, for continuous low-volume ventilation of individual rooms, to whole-house ducted systems. The simple ventilator shown below left contains two low-noise electric fans. Stale air from the interior is extracted by one fan through a highly efficient heat exchanger. This absorbs up to 70 per cent of the heat that would otherwise be wasted, and transfers it to a flow of fresh air drawn into the room by the second fan. Because the two airflows are not allowed to mingle, odours and water vapour are not transferred along with the heat.

Fitting a heat-recovery ventilator

Site a heat-recovery ventilator on an external wall, close to the ceiling and in a position where it will extract air most efficiently. Although they are typically set into a standard solid or cavity wall, you can install one in a thicker wall with the aid of a telescopic metal sleeve.

After marking out the aperture, cut away the masonry, as described in the section on fitting a standard extractor fan. Fit the unit into the hole and repair the masonry and plasterwork, sealing any gaps around the unit with a gun-applied sealant. Finally, wire up the controls of the ventilator, following the manufacturer's instructions.

Air-conditioning units

With increasing summer temperatures to contend with, people are looking for a simple means of installing air conditioning, even if only for one or two rooms. One solution is to fit a compact wall-mounted unit that can cool, warm or dehumidify the air at the press of a button on its remote controller.

The refrigerant system in this type of unit is factory-sealed, so installation does not involve having to connect pipes or hoses. All that is required are two 155mm (6in) holes bored at a slight downward angle through an external wall. Outside, there's no unsightly condensing unit but simply a pair of discreet grilles.

The unit is powered by electricity from a fused connection unit mounted inside the room.

Dehumidifiers control condensation

To combat condensation, you can either remove the moisture-laden air by ventilation or warm it so that it is able to carry more water vapour before it becomes saturated. A third possibility is to extract the water itself from the air, using a dehumidifier.

A dehumidifier works by drawing air from the room into the unit and passing it over a set of cold coils, so that the water vapour condenses on them and drips into a reservoir. The cold but now dry air is then drawn by a fan over heated coils before being returned to the room as additional convected heat.

The process is based on the simple refrigeration principle that gas under pressure heats up – and when the pressure drops, the temperature of the gas drops too. In a dehumidifier, a compressor delivers pressurized gas to the 'hot' coils, in turn leading to the larger 'cold' coils, which allow the gas to expand. The cooled gas then returns to the compressor for recycling.

A dehumidifier for domestic use is usually built into a floor-standing cabinet. It contains a humidistat that automatically switches on the unit when the moisture content of the air reaches a predetermined level. When the reservoir is full, the unit shuts down in order to prevent overflowing, and an indicator lights up to remind you to empty the water in the container.

When a dehumidifier is installed in a damp room, it should extract the excess moisture from the furnishings and fabric within a week or two. After that, it will monitor the moisture content of the air to maintain a stabilized atmosphere.

Working components of a dehumidifier
1 Incoming damp air
2 Cold coils
3 Water reservoir
4 Compressor
5 Hot coils
6 Fan
7 Dry warm air
8 Capillary tube where gas expands

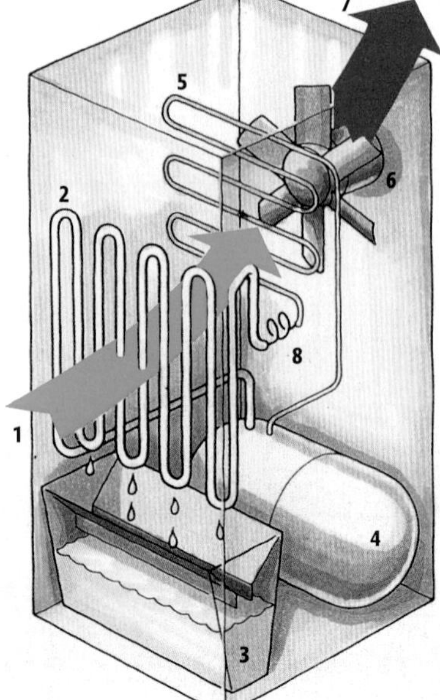

SEE ALSO >Condensation 259, Whole-house ventilation 276, Cutting a hole in masonry 278

Electricity

Reducing electricity bills

Pressures from all sides urge us to conserve energy. But even without such encouragement, our electricity bills would provide stimulus enough to make us find ways of using less power. Nobody wants to live in a poorly heated or dismally lit house without the comforts of hot water, refrigeration and other conveniences – but it is possible to identify where energy is wasted and find ways to reduce waste without compromising comfort or pleasure.

Insulation
Measures taken to save energy will have little effect unless you insulate your house as well as the hot-water cylinder and pipework. You can do most of the work yourself for a relatively modest outlay and a little effort.

Fitting controls to save money

As the chart opposite clearly shows, heating is by far the biggest consumer of domestic power. One way to reduce your electricity bills is to fit devices that regulate the heating in your home to suit your lifestyle, maintaining comfortable but economic temperatures.

Thermostats

Most modern heating has some form of thermostatic control - a device that will switch power off when surroundings reach a certain temperature. Many thermostats are marked out simply to increase or decrease the temperature, in which case you have to experiment with various settings to find the one that suits you best. If the thermostat settings are more precise, try 18°C (65°F) for everyday use - although elderly people are more comfortable at about 21°C (70°F).

As well as saving you money, an immersion-heater thermostat prevents your water from becoming dangerously hot. Set it at 60°C (140°F). See right for Economy 7 settings.

Time switches

Even when it's thermostatically controlled, heating is expensive if run continuously - but you can install an automatic time switch to turn it on and off at preset times, so you get up in the morning and arrive home in the evening to a warm house. Set it to turn off the heating about half an hour before you leave home or go to bed, as the house will take time to cool down.

A similar device will ensure that your water is at its hottest when needed.

Off-peak rates

Electricity is normally sold at a general-purpose rate, every unit used costing the same; but if you warm your home with storage heaters and heat your water electrically, then you can take advantage of the economical off-peak tariff. This system, called Economy 7, allows you to charge storage heaters and heat water at less than half the general-purpose rate for seven hours, starting between midnight and 1 a.m. Other appliances used during that time get cheap power too, so more savings can be made by running the dishwasher or washing machine after you've gone to bed. Each appliance must, of course, be fitted with a timer. The Economy 7 daytime rate is higher than the general-purpose one, but the cost of running 24-hour appliances such as freezers and refrigerators is balanced since they also use cheap power for seven hours.

For full benefit from off-peak water heating, use a cylinder that holds 182 to 227 litres (40 to 50 gallons), to store as much cheap hot water as possible. You will need a twin-element heater or two separate units. One heater, near the base of the cylinder, heats the whole tank on cheap power; another, about half way up, tops up the hot water during the day. Set the night-time heater at 75°C (167°F), the daytime one at 60°C (140°F).

The electricity companies provide Economy 7 customers with a special meter to record daytime and night-time consumption separately, plus a timer that automatically switches the supply from one rate to the other.

Monitoring consumption

Keep an accurate record of your energy saving by taking weekly readings. Note the dates of any measures taken to cut power consumption, and compare the corresponding drop in meter readings.

Digital meters

Modern meters display a row of digits that represent the total number of units consumed since the meter was installed. To calculate the number of units used since your last electricity bill, simply subtract the 'present reading' shown on your bill from the number of units now shown on the meter. Make sure that the bill gives an actual reading and not an estimate (indicated by the letter 'E' before the reading).

Reading dial meters

Older installations may incorporate a meter with a set of dials that indicate the consumption of electricity. With a bit of practice you will be able to read these meters yourself. Ignore the dial marked 1/10, which is only for testing. Start with the dial indicating single units (kWh) and, working from right to left, record the readings from the 10, 100, 1000 and finally 10,000 unit dials. Note the digits the pointers have passed. If a pointer is, say, between 5 and 6, record 5. If it's right on a number, say 8, check the next dial on the right: if that pointer is between 9 and 0, record 7; if it's past 0, record 8. Also, remember that adjacent dials revolve in opposite directions, alternating along the row.

Digital meter display

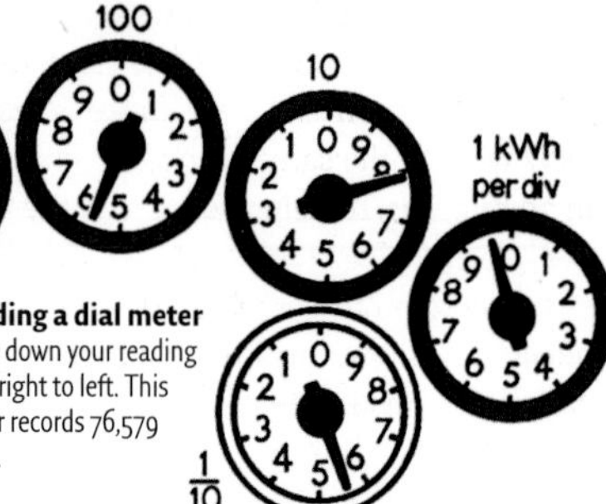

Reading a dial meter
Write down your reading from right to left. This meter records 76,579 units.

SEE ALSO > Time switches 235, Insulation 256–69, Immersion heaters 316–17, Heating controls 409

Lower running costs

In Britain there are now more than twenty companies who supply electricity and gas – which means that shopping around may help you find a better deal. Supply companies play no part in the actual generation and distribution of electricity and gas, even if their parent company is involved with these activities. Whichever supplier you go with, the responsibility for meters and incoming cables and pipes remains unchanged.

Buying your energy at the lowest price

The tariffs offered by all the energy-supply companies are a combination of a standing charge and unit costs for the energy supplied. Unit costs vary, depending on whether the energy is supplied during the day or at night, and block charges for consumption above a certain level may reduce unit costs still further. In addition, discounts are usually available if you adopt methods of payment such as direct debit that are more convenient for the supply companies. There is also some incentive to choose a company who can supply both electricity and gas. Every company seeks to make its tariffs seem more attractive than those of its competitors – but the only figure that is important to you, the customer, is the total you pay each year for your energy.

Comparing prices

The government website **www.energywatch.org.uk** provides a code to be followed by price-comparison websites. Examples of websites that adhere to this code are **www.energylinx.co.uk**, **www.which.co.uk** and **www.uSwitch.com** These sites will supply you with estimates of costs from each supplier and compare those against your present outgoings. Make sure you don't log on to a website created on behalf of one particular supplier. Once you have made the choice to switch to another supplier, it is often possible to make the transfer on-line.

You can use the same 'comparison' sites to check on how easy it is to make a transfer to a potential supplier and find out what policies they have in relation to environmentally sensitive issues.

To carry out a meaningful comparison you will need to supply:

- Your postcode
- Your present suppliers of gas and electricity
- The type of meter (normal or Economy 7)
- Your annual consumption of each fuel or your present annual bills.
- The units used at night (for Economy 7 customers) expressed as either a number of units or a percentage of the total units

Though most companies offer discounts for customers who take both gas and electricity from the same supplier, you may find that it is more economical to purchase each fuel separately. Try entering the same details for gas and electricity only and compare the results with a quote for a combined tariff.

Within the constraints imposed by the government watchdog, energy suppliers are continually adjusting their prices, and it may be worth comparing costs at about the same time each year.

Energy-efficiency labelling

When you're shopping for new appliances, look for the European Community Energy Label that must by law be available at the point of sale, including web sites on the internet. This labelling gives guidance on energy efficiency for electrical equipment from light bulbs to dishwashers, and the choice of an 'A' rating can make considerable savings in running costs.

European flower
Any appliance bearing this symbol will be the best in its class in terms of all environmental criteria.

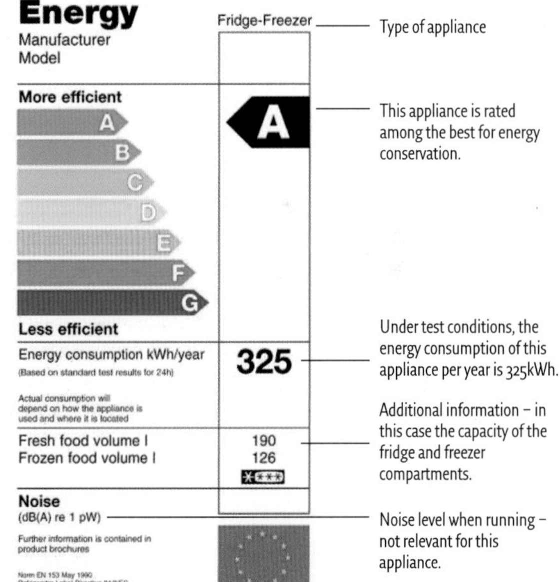

Type of appliance

This appliance is rated among the best for energy conservation.

Under test conditions, the energy consumption of this appliance per year is 325kWh.

Additional information – in this case the capacity of the fridge and freezer compartments.

Noise level when running – not relevant for this appliance.

Typical running costs

Apart from the standing charge, your electricity bill is based on the number of units of electricity you have consumed during a given period. Each unit represents the amount used in one hour by a 1kW appliance. An appliance rated at 3kW will use the same amount of energy in 20 minutes. To help you identify the heavy users of energy, the chart on the right groups typical appliances under headings for low, medium and high electricity consumption.

LOW ENERGY CONSUMERS Less than 100 units per year	MEDIUM ENERGY CONSUMERS 100 to 1000 units per year	HIGH ENERGY CONSUMERS More than 1000 units per year
Toasters	Refrigerators	Instant water heaters
Coffee percolators	Freezers	Dishwashers
Slow cookers	Cookers	Immersion water heaters
Cooker hoods	Electric kettles	Fan heaters
Microwave ovens	Extractor fans	Electric fires
VCRs and DVD players	Washing machines	Whole-house lighting using GLS lamps (ordinary bulbs)
Stereo systems	Tumble dryers	Whole-house electric heating
Electric blankets	Irons	
Shavers	Vacuum cleaners	
Hairdryers	Colour TVs	
Power tools	Compact fluorescent house lighting	
Hedge trimmers	Instant showers	
Lawn mowers	Heated towel rails	

SEE ALSO > Heating water 316–17, Comparing bulbs and tubes 327

First things first

Before you undertake any electrical work, familiarize yourself with the basic facts on how a domestic system works and make sure you understand how to proceed safely. You also need to be aware of the current regulations that cover electrical wiring in the home.

Understanding the basics

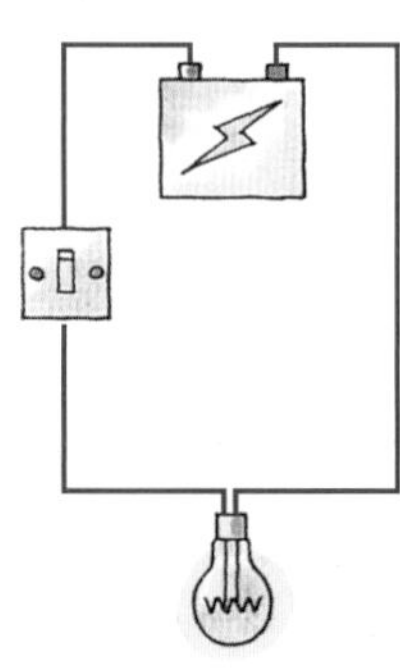

A basic circuit
Electricity runs from the source (battery) to the appliance (bulb) and then returns to the source. A switch breaks the circuit to interrupt the flow of electricity.

Electrical circuits are based on simple principles. For any electrical appliance to work, the power must be able to flow along a wire from its source to the appliance (say, a light bulb) and then back to the source along another wire. If the circuit is broken at any point, the appliance will stop working – the bulb will go out. Breaking the circuit – and restoring it as required – is what a switch is for. When the switch is in the 'on' position, the circuit is complete and the bulb operates. Turning the switch off makes a gap in the circuit, so the electricity stops flowing.

Mains electricity in your home flows through live or 'phase' wires linked to every light, socket outlet and fixed electrical appliance in your home. The current flows back out of the building through the neutral wires.

Earthing

Any material through which electricity can flow is known as a conductor. Most metals conduct electricity well, which is why copper is used for electrical wiring. The earth itself – the ground on which we stand – is also an extremely good conductor, which is why electricity always flows into the earth whenever it can, taking the shortest available route. This means that if you were to touch a live conductor, the current would divert and take the short route to the earth – through your body.

A similar thing can happen if a live wire accidentally comes into contact with any exposed metal component of an appliance, including its casing. To prevent this, a third wire is included in the system and connected to the earth, usually via the outer casing of the electricity company's main service cable. This third wire – called the earth wire – is attached to the metal casing of some appliances and to earth terminals in others, providing a direct route to the ground should a fault occur. This sudden change of route by the electricity – known as an earth fault – causes a fuse to blow or circuit breaker to operate, cutting off the current.

Measuring electricity

Watts measure the amount of power used by an appliance when working. The wattage of an electrical appliance is normally marked on its casing. One thousand watts (1000W) equal one kilowatt (1kW).

Amps measure the flow of current that is necessary to produce the required wattage for an appliance.

Volts measure the 'pressure' provided by the electricity company. This drives the current along the conductors to the various outlets. In this country 230 volts (formerly 240) is standard.

If you know two of these measurements, you can determine the other one.

$\frac{\text{Watts}}{\text{Volts}}$ = Amps	Amps x Volts = Watts
Use this method to determine what kind of fuse or flex is safe.	Indicates how much power is needed to operate an appliance.

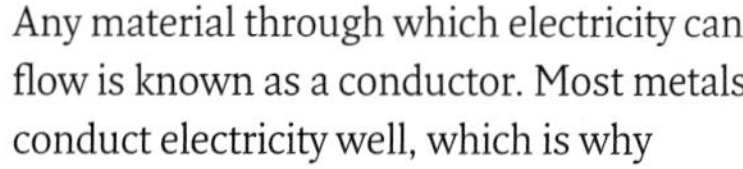

Double insulation
Appliances that are double-insulated – which usually means they have a plastic casing that insulates the user from metal parts that could become live – must not be earthed with a third wire. A square within a square, either printed or moulded on an appliance, means it is double-insulated and its flex does not need an earth wire.

Notifiable work
To help you decide which electrical work you can do yourself, all notifiable work shown in this book is marked with this symbol.

Building Regulations on electrical wiring

Regulations – known as Part P of the Building Regulations – have been introduced to promote better standards. Similar legislation for Scotland is covered by the Building Standards (Scotland) Regulations. These regulations do not prevent the DIY worker from undertaking electrical wiring, but they put strict limits on what can be done without supervision and inspection.

All local authorities have Building Control Officers (BCOs) who are responsible for monitoring the regulations. You should therefore contact your BCO to ascertain how exactly your particular authority applies the regulations.

Certain tasks can be undertaken without having to notify the authority, and most BCOs do not require any communication or paperwork for 'non-notifiable' electrical work. However, where similar work is carried out in locations such as kitchens and bathrooms or the wiring will be complicated or extensive, then the work becomes 'notifiable' and must be discussed with the BCO before it is carried out.

Non-notifiable work

A DIY worker can do the following, anywhere in the home without having to inform the BCO in advance:

- Replace sockets, fused connection units, switches and ceiling roses.
- Replace damaged cable for a single circuit.
- Refix or replace enclosures (mounting boxes for sockets and switches) on existing circuits.
- Provide mechanical protection in the form of conduit and plastic channel.

Also without having to inform the BCO in advance, a DIY worker can do the following anywhere in the home except in kitchens, bathrooms and utility rooms and in special locations – such as rooms with a bathtub or shower, swimming pools and paddling pools, hot-air saunas and outdoors – or when installing extra-low-voltage lighting:

- Add new light fittings and switches to existing circuits.
- Add new socket outlets to existing ring circuits and radial circuits.
- Add fused spurs to existing ring circuits and radial circuits.

Notifiable work

The BCO must be notified before a DIY worker undertakes any electrical work not listed above or if the work is categorized as one of the exceptions described above.

Although DIY electricians are permitted to carry out notifiable work, the cost and complexity of obtaining approval, testing, and certification from the BCO (see opposite) may make it more economical to have such work done by a professional electrician.

SEE ALSO > Testing circuits 288–9, Flex 292, Switching off 296, Earthing and bonding 297, Fuses and circuit breakers 299, Cable 302

Complying with the regulations

It is not necessary to involve the BCO when any work is undertaken by a professional electrician – that is a competent person registered with an electrical self-certification scheme. He or she will deal with all the paperwork required by the authority and, on completion of the work, should give you a signed Building Regulations Self-certification Certificate and a completed Electrical Installation Certificate.

If you feel competent to do any notifiable work yourself, you must tell your local BCO in advance exactly what you propose to do. Having obtained permission to proceed, once you have completed the work you must ask the BCO to send an inspector to test the installation and issue a certificate. A fee will be charged for inspection and testing. Most BCOs will offer some concession – such as including the electrical inspection in the general inspection costs for building a new extension. Some BCOs may ask you to arrange for a competent electrician to inspect and test the work.

Procedures are laid down for appeals, determinations, relaxations and dispensations, but the common-sense approach is to accept any advice or instruction given by your local Building Control Officer.

Provided you are competent to undertake non-notifiable work, you may proceed without supervision so long as the methods used comply with the the IEE Wiring Regulations (BS7671). Good workmanship and the use of proper materials are fundamental to these regulations. You should also keep a record of your work in the form of a Minor Electrical Works Certificate, which you can pass on to interested parties should you decide to sell your home in the future. Selling a house without appropriate paperwork may introduce delays and difficulties.

The methods and materials suggested in this book comply with the Wiring Regulations, but you should be aware that the rigorous final testing of installations, which has to be carried out by qualified persons using specialized equipment, falls outside the scope of this book. If you have any doubts about your ability to satisfy the requirements of the Wiring Regulations, then use this book to study the work involved so you can brief a professional electrician and agree an appropriate price for the job. Ensure that any electrician you hire is a member of an authorized competent-person self-certification scheme.

With safety in mind

Throughout this chapter you will find frequent references to the need for safety while working on your electrical system – but it cannot be stressed too strongly that you must also take steps to safeguard yourself and anyone else using the system. Faulty wiring and appliances are dangerous, and can be lethal.

- Never inspect or work on any part of an electrical installation without first switching off the power at the consumer unit and removing the relevant circuit fuse or locking off the miniature circuit breaker (MCB).
- Always unplug a portable appliance or light before doing any work on it.
- Always use the correct tools and use good-quality equipment and materials.
- Always double-check all your work (especially connections) before you turn the electricity on again.
- Fuses are vital safety devices. Never fit one that's rated too highly for the circuit it is to protect – and never be tempted to use any other type of wire or metal strip in place of proper fuses or fuse wire.
- Wear rubber-soled shoes when you're working on an electrical installation.

Colour coding

For purpose of identification, the coverings of live, neutral and earth wires in flex and mains cables are colour-coded. The live wires are brown and the neutral wires blue.

When an earth wire is included in a piece of flex, it is coded with a green-and-yellow covering. In a mains cable, the earth is a bare copper wire. Whenever the earth wire is exposed for linking to socket outlets or light fittings, it should be covered with a green-and-yellow sleeve.

Until recently the live and neutral wires in mains cables were coded with other colours. Live wires had a red covering, and neutral wires a black covering. There is no reason to replace old colour-coded cables, but whenever you need to join new cable to old, remember to connect the brown wire to the old red one, and the blue wire to the old black one.

Identifying conductors
The insulation used to cover the conductors in electrical cable and flex is colour-coded to indicate live, neutral and earth.

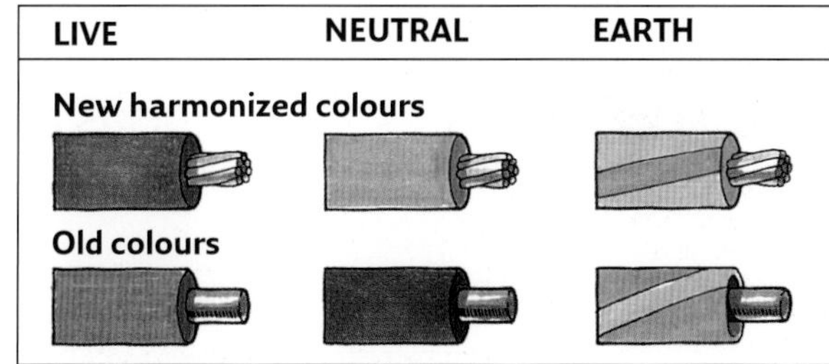

Fuses and circuit breakers

A conductor will heat up if an unusually powerful current flows through it. This can damage electrical equipment and create a serious fire risk if it is allowed to continue. As a safeguard weak links are included in the wiring, to break the circuit before the current reaches a dangerously high level.

Fuses

A very common form of protection is a fuse, a thin wire that's designed to break the circuit by melting at a specific current. This varies according to the part of the system that the fuse is protecting – an individual appliance, a single power or lighting circuit, or the entire domestic wiring system.

Miniature circuit breakers

Alternatively, a special switch called a circuit breaker is used that trips and cuts off the current as soon as an overload on the wiring is detected.

A fuse will 'blow' (or an MCB will trip) in the following circumstances:

- If too many appliances are operated on a circuit simultaneously, then the excessive demand for electricity will blow the fuse in that circuit.
- If the current reroutes to earth due to a faulty appliance, the flow of power increases in the circuit and blows the fuse (this is known as an earth fault).

SEE ALSO > Flex 292, Cable 302, Switching off the power 296, Fuses and circuit breakers 299

Bathroom safety

Because water is such a highly efficient conductor of electric current, water and electricity form a very dangerous combination. For this reason, in terms of electricity, bathrooms are potentially the most dangerous areas in your home. Where there are so many exposed metal pipes and fittings, combined with wet conditions, regulations must be stringently observed if fatal accidents are to be avoided.

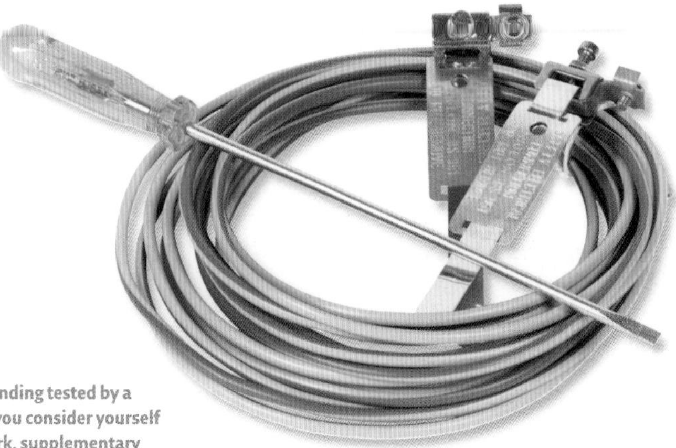

(N) If you undertake work marked with this symbol, you must inform the BCO before starting – see FIRST THINGS FIRST.

WARNING

Have your supplementary bonding tested by a qualified electrician. Unless you consider yourself fully competent to do the work, supplementary bonding must be installed by a professional.

GENERAL SAFETY

- Sockets must not be fitted in a bathroom – except for special shaver sockets that conform to BS EN 60742 Chapter 2, Section 1.
- The IEE Wiring Regulations stipulate that light switches in bathrooms must be outside zones 0 to 3 (see opposite). The best way to comply with this requirement is to fit ceiling-mounted pull-cord switches.
- When installing an electrical appliance in a bathroom, the relevant circuit should be protected by a 30 milliamp RCD.
- If you have a shower in a bedroom, it must be not less than 3m (9ft 11in) from any socket outlet, which must be protected by a 30 milliamp RCD.
- Light fittings in a bathroom must be well out of reach and shielded – so fit a close-mounted ceiling light, properly enclosed, rather than a pendant fitting.
- Never use a portable appliance, such as a hairdryer, in a bathroom – even if it is plugged into a socket outside the room.

Supplementary bonding (N)

In any bathroom there are many nonelectrical metallic components, such as metal baths and basins, supply pipes to bath and basin taps, metal waste pipes, radiators, central-heating pipework and so on – all of which could cause an accident during the time it would take for an electrical fault to blow a fuse or trip a miniature circuit breaker. To ensure that no dangerous voltages are created between metal parts, all these metal components must be connected one to another by a conductor which is itself connected to a terminal on the earthing block in the consumer unit. This is known as supplementary bonding and is required for all bathrooms – even when there is no electrical equipment installed in the room, and even though the water and gas pipes are bonded to the consumer's earth terminal near the consumer unit.

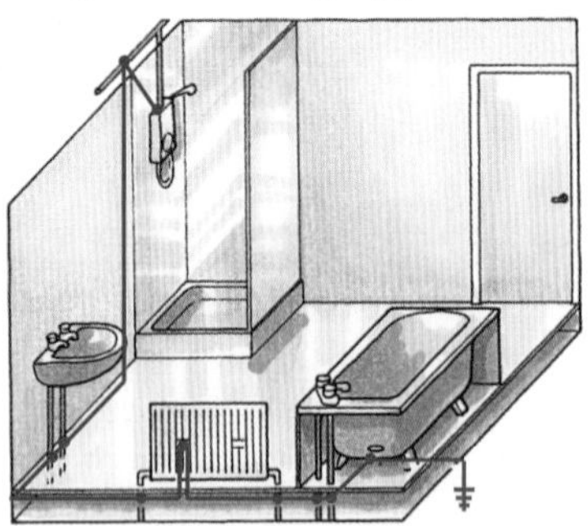

Supplementary bonding in a bathroom

When electrical equipment, such as a heater or shower, is fitted in a bathroom, that too must be bonded by connecting its metalwork – such as the casing – to the nonelectrical metal pipework.

Making the connections

The Wiring Regulations specify the minimum size of earthing conductor that can be used for supplementary bonding in different situations, so that large-scale electrical installations can be costed economically. However, 6mm² single-core cable, insulated with green-and-yellow PVC, is large enough to be safe for supplementary bonding in any domestic situation. For a neat appearance, the route of the bonding cable should be planned to run behind the bath panel, under floorboards, and through basin pedestals. If necessary, the cable can be run through a hollow wall or under plaster.

Connecting to pipework

An earth clamp is used for making connections to pipework. The pipe should be cleaned locally with wire wool to make a good connection between the pipe and clamp. Scrape or strip an area of paintwork if the pipe has been painted.

Attach an earth clamp to the pipework

Connecting to a bath or basin

Metal baths or basins are made with an earth tag. To connect the earth cable, the bared end of the conductor should be trapped under a nut and bolt with metal washers. Make sure the tag has not been painted or enamelled.

If an old metal bath or basin has not been provided with an earth tag, drill a hole through the foot of the bath or through the rim at the back of the basin; so that the cable can be connected with a similar nut and bolt, with metal washers.

Connecting to an appliance

The bonding cable must be connected to the earth terminal provided in the electrical appliance and then run to a clamp on a metal supply pipe nearby.

SEE ALSO > Building Regulations 284, Bonding to earth 296–7, Cable 302, Running cable 303–5, Wiring a shower 316

Zones for bathrooms

Within a room containing a bath or shower, the Wiring Regulations define areas, or zones, where specific safety precautions apply. The regulations also describe what type of appliances can be installed in each zone, and the routes cables must take. There are special considerations for extra-low-voltage equipment with separated earth.

The four zones

Any room containing a bathtub or shower is divided into four zones. Zone 0 is the interior of the bathtub or shower tray – not including the space beneath the tub, which is covered by other regulations (see right). Zones 1 to 3 are specific areas above and around the bath or shower, where only specified electrical appliances and their cables may be installed. Wiring outside these areas must conform to the IEE Wiring Regulations, but no specific 'zone' regulations apply.

ZONE	LOCATION	PERMITTED
Zone 0	Interior of the bathtub or shower tray.	No electrical installation.
Zone 1	Directly above the bathtub or shower tray, up to a height of 2.25m (7ft 5in) from the floor. (See also UNDER THE BATH, right.)	Instantaneous water heater. Instantaneous shower. All-in-one power shower, with a suitably waterproofed integral pump. The wiring that serves appliances within the zone.
Zone 2	Area within 0.6m (2ft) horizontally from the bathtub or shower tray in any direction, up to a height of 2.25m (7ft 5in) from the floor. The area above zone 1, up to a height of 3m (9ft 11in) from the floor.	Appliances permitted in zone 1. Light fittings. Extractor fan. Space heater. Whirlpool unit for the bathtub. Shaver socket to BS EN 60742 Chapter 2, Section 1. The wiring that serves appliances within the zone and any appliances in zone 1.
Zone 3	Up to 2.4m (7ft 11in) outside zone 2, up to a height of 2.25m (7ft 5in) from the floor. The area above zone 2 next to the bathtub or shower, up to a height of 3m (9ft 11in) from the floor.	Appliances permitted in zones 1 and 2. Any fixed electrical appliance (a heated towel rail, for example) that is protected by a 30 milliamp RCD. The wiring that serves appliances within the zone and any appliances in zones 1 and 2.

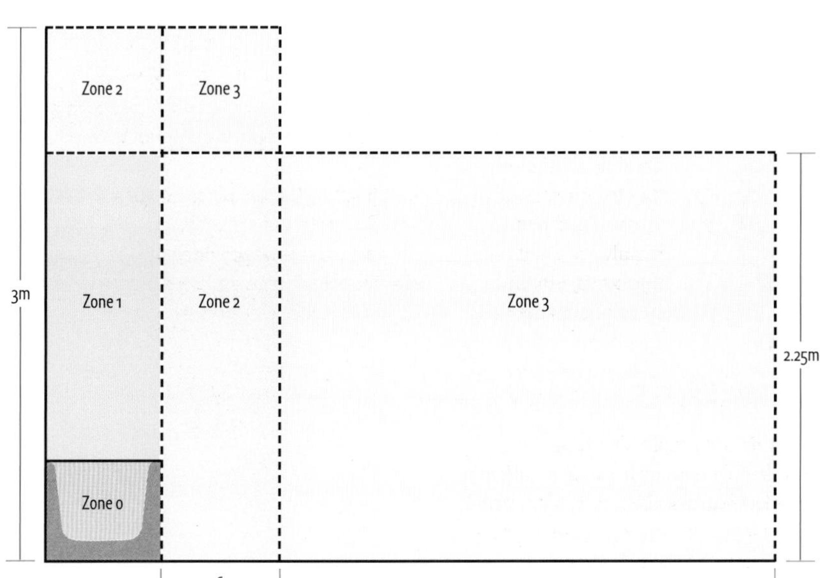

Zones within a room containing a bath or shower

Under the bath

The space under a bathtub is designated as zone 1 if it is accessible without having to use a tool – that is, if there is no bath panel or if the panel is attached with magnetic catches or similar devices that allow the panel to be detached without using a tool of some kind. If, however, the panel is screw-fixed, then the enclosed space beneath the bath is considered to be outside all zones.

Supplementary bonding

In bathrooms, nonelectrical metallic components must be bonded to earth (see opposite). In zones 1, 2 and 3, this bonding is required to all pipes, any electrical appliances and any exposed metallic structural components of the building. This does not include window frames, unless they are themselves connected to metallic structural components.

Supplementary bonding is not required outside the zones. In the case of a shower cubicle in a bedroom, supplementary bonding can also be omitted from zone 3.

Cable runs
You are not permitted to run electrical cables that are feeding a zone through another zone designated with a lower number. This includes cables buried in the plaster or concealed behind other wallcoverings.

Switches

Electrical switches, including ceiling-mounted switches operated by a pull cord, must be situated outside the zones. The only exceptions are those switches and controls incorporated in appliances suitable for use in the zones.

If the bathroom ceiling is higher than 3m (9ft 11in), pull-cord switches can be mounted anywhere. However, if the ceiling height is between 2.25 and 3m (7ft 5in and 9ft 11in), pull-cord switches must be mounted at least 0.6m (2ft) – measured horizontally – from the bathtub or shower cubicle. If the ceiling is lower than 2.25m (7ft 5in), switches must be outside the room.

13amp sockets
In the special case of a bedroom containing a shower cubicle, socket outlets are permitted in the room, but only outside the zones, and the circuit that feeds the sockets must be protected by a 30 milliamp RCD.

IP coding

Electrical appliances installed in zones 1 and 2 must be made with suitable protection against splashed water. This is designated by the code IPX4 (the letter X is sometimes replaced with a single digit). Any number larger than four is also acceptable as this indicates a higher degree of waterproofing. If in doubt, check with your supplier.

IP coding
Suitable equipment may be marked with this symbol.

SEE ALSO > Wiring a shower 316, Light switches 329

Testing circuits

For your own safety and for the safety of others using or working on your electrical installation in the future, carry out the tests recommended here each time you work on the fixed wiring of your home. Although these tests should not be regarded as substitutes for those required by Building Control Officers, if your work passes them it is likely to meet the requirements of the regulations.

Test instruments

Ohms and MegOhms
On some multimeters, Ohms are indicated by the symbol Ω and MegOhms (millions of Ohms) by MΩ.

There are many different testers to choose from, and those at the top end of the market may cost hundreds of pounds. However, reliable testers can be purchased for much less.

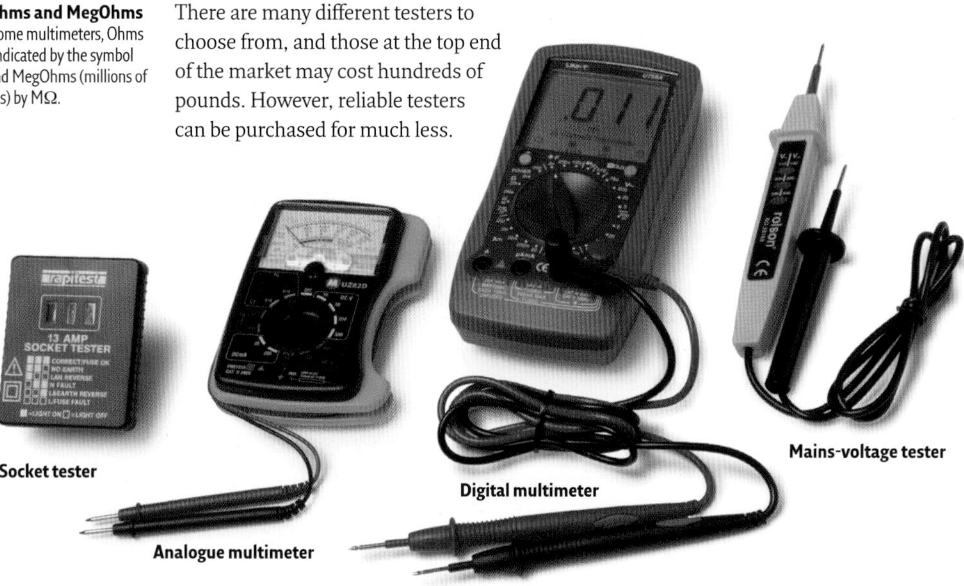

Socket tester

Analogue multimeter

Digital multimeter

Mains-voltage tester

1 Insulation resistance
Set the selector to the highest resistance scale.

2 Continuity
Set the selector to the lowest resistance scale.

Mains-voltage tester

Mains testers are designed to tell you whether a circuit is completely 'dead' after you have turned off the power at the consumer unit. Be sure to buy a tester that's intended for use with mains voltage - similar devices are sold in auto shops for 12V car wiring only.

Multimeters

There are digital multimeters that give readings on an LCD screen, and there are analogue instruments with a needle that moves across a scale on a dial.

Both types have a rotary selector for setting the meter to measure voltage, current, resistance and other values. When testing insulation resistance and continuity (see opposite), you want the meter to measure resistance. For insulation resistance, set the selector to the highest resistance range (**1**); for continuity, set it to the lowest resistance range (**2**). With some multimeters, you can select an audible signal to tell you when there is continuity.

With an analogue multimeter, a reading at the lower end of the scale indicates a continuous, unbroken circuit. A reading at the top end of the scale means there is an 'open' circuit - there's a break somewhere on the circuit.

With an analogue meter, satisfactory insulation resistance is indicated when the needle is at the top end of the scale, showing a reading of millions of Ohms (MegOhms).

When using a digital multimeter, for continuity you are looking for a low value - less than 10 Ohms. For satisfactory insulation resistance, you want a value of more than 10 million Ohms (10 MegOhms).

To test that a multimeter is working, touch the two probes together and the meter should read zero. Move the probes apart and it should read infinity. The manufacturers of digital multimeters use the figure 1 (with no other figures after the decimal point) to mean infinity - which simply indicates a very high resistance.

Socket tester

A simple plug-in device can be used to test the connections inside a 13amp socket outlet without having to turn off the power or expose internal wiring.

Required testing

Carry out the tests described opposite to check the effectiveness of the fixed wiring of your house. However, the Building Regulations require final testing with specialist equipment, which is used by Building Control inspectors and other professionals to provide readings that can be entered on the necessary certificates.

Is the power off?

Having turned off the power at the consumer unit, make sure an accessory is safe to work on by using an electronic mains-voltage tester to check whether terminals or wires are live, before you tamper with them. Always make sure the tester is functioning properly both before and after you use it, by testing it on a circuit you know to be live.

Following the manufacturer's instructions, place one probe on the neutral terminal and the other on the live terminal; if the indicator lights up, the circuit is live. If it doesn't illuminate, test again - this time between the earth terminal and each of the live and neutral terminals. If the indicator still doesn't light up, you can assume the circuit is not live - provided you have checked the tester.

Using a mains-voltage tester
Touch the neutral terminal with one probe and the live terminal with the other. The circuit is live if the indicator illuminates.

SEE ALSO > Building Regulations 284, Consumer units 298

Protective devices

As part of the testing required by Building Control Officers, an inspector uses equipment that checks whether protective devices (miniature circuit breakers and residual current devices) are operating within the times specified in the regulations. This is a procedure that falls outside the scope of this book.

However, you can at least ensure an RCD trips satisfactorily when you press its test button, and you can test that an MCB is working by operating its switch. Test these devices every time you carry out electrical work on your home, and also at regular intervals - say every three months or so.

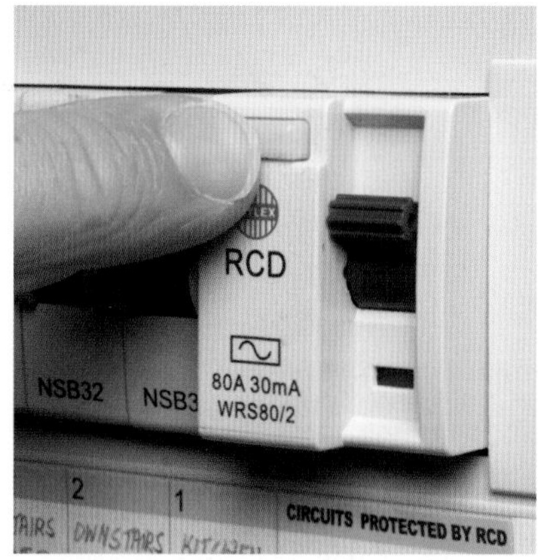

Press the test button on a residual current device

Checking polarity

Having worked on an electrical circuit, before replacing sockets, switches or faceplates, always double-check that the live, neutral and earth conductors are connected to their respective terminals.

Having switched the power back on, you can use a plug-in tester to check the wiring to your socket outlets. Switch on the socket; and if all three indicator lights come on, the socket is wired correctly.

If all three lights come on, polarity is correct

Testing for continuity

In simple terms, a continuity test is designed to check that there is an electrical connection between two points, say between the two ends of a length of wire. This is done with a multimeter set to its lowest resistance range. Place one of the instrument's probes on each end of the wire. A low reading on the dial or screen means the wire is continuous - there is continuity. A high reading means the wire is broken somewhere along its length - so there's no continuity.

You can use this test to check whether a cartridge fuse has blown, or whether a ring circuit is continuous or a heating element is working.

Testing a ring circuit

This is an important test because a ring circuit could still be functioning even when there's a break somewhere on the circuit. At the consumer unit, having first turned off the main switch, identify the two ends of the cable feeding the ring circuit; then remove the live, neutral and earth conductors from their terminals and separate all the wires.

Testing for continuity
Touch one end of the wire with one probe and the other end of the same wire with the other probe. A low reading (shown above) indicates that the wire is continuous.

Carry out the continuity test between the two ends of the live (red or brown) conductor. Repeat the test on the neutral (black or blue) conductor, and then on the earth (yellow-and-green) conductor. A low reading (low resistance) for each test means there is continuity on all three conductors - each is continuous, which is how it should be.

If you get a high reading, check every socket outlet, junction box and fused connection unit to make sure there are no loose connections and then perform the continuity test again.

Testing insulation resistance

This test is designed to make sure there is no current leaking through the insulation between two conductors, say live and neutral. If this is allowed to happen there is a danger of overheating - which could cause a fire. Alternatively, there could be a short circuit and the fuse protecting the circuit would blow or the MCB would trip.

You should test any circuit you have worked on. Make sure the power is turned off, then unplug every appliance on the circuit and check that all switches are turned off. This includes switches for all fixed appliances.

At the consumer unit, identify the cable feeding the relevant circuit and disconnect the conductors from their terminals. If you are installing a new circuit, do the test before making the final connections at the consumer unit.

With a multimeter set to its highest resistance range, place one probe on the live (red or brown) conductor and the other probe on the neutral (black or blue) conductor. If the reading shown on the meter is low, the insulation resistance is suspect and should be investigated. If the reading is high - in the order of MegOhms - the insulation resistance is satisfactory. Repeat the test between the live conductor and earth (green-and-yellow) conductor

Insulation resistance
Touch the neutral conductor with one probe and the live conductor with the other. A high reading (shown above) indicates satisfactory insulation resistance.

and then between the neutral and earth, looking for a high reading in each case.

Investigating a suspect circuit

With the power turned off, inspect the suspect wiring, including every accessory (socket, switch, junction box and so on), starting with the ones you have been working on. Typical causes of low insulation resistance are:

- A damp wall or water running into an accessory.
- A nail or screw driven through a cable.
- Rodent damage to cables.
- Old rubber-insulated cables connected to the circuit.
- Conductors crushed together by careless replacement of a socket outlet or switch.

SEE ALSO > Building Regulations 284, RCDs 297, 298, Consumer units 298, MCBs 299, Resetting an MCB 300, Checking fuses 300, Domestic circuits 301, Adding a spur to a ring 309, Wiring a cooker 314–15, Replacing an element 317

Assessing your installation

Inspect the electrical installation in your home to ensure that it is safe and adequate for your present and future needs. But remember, you should never examine any part of it without first switching off the power at the consumer unit. If you are in doubt about any aspect of the installation, don't hesitate to ask a qualified electrician for an opinion. If you get in touch with your electricity company, they will arrange for someone to test the whole system for you. It is recommended that you should have your house wiring tested at least every ten years.

Round-pin sockets
Replace old round-pin sockets with 13amp square-pin sockets.

Damaged sockets
Replace cracked or broken faceplates.

Questions	Answers
Do you have a modern consumer unit, or a mixture of old fuse boxes?	Old fuse boxes can be unsafe and should be replaced with a modern unit. Seek professional advice about this.
Is the consumer unit in good condition?	Replace a broken casing or cracked covers. Trip MCBs deliberately every three months or so to make sure they are in good working order. Check that fuse carriers are intact and that they fit snugly in their fuseways.
Are all your MCBs or circuit fuses of the correct ratings?	Seek the advice of an electrician about replacing suspect MCBs. Replace any fuses of the wrong rating. If an unusually large fuse is protecting one of the circuits, don't change it without getting professional advice – it may have a special purpose. If you find any wire other than proper fuse wire in a fuse carrier, replace it at once. If you have rewirable fuses, ask an electrician to quote for having them converted to cartridge fuses or MCBs.
Are all the cables leading from the consumer unit in good condition?	The cables should be fixed securely, with no bare wires showing. If the cables appear to be insulated with rubber, have the whole installation checked as soon as possible. Rubber insulation has a limited life, so yours could already be dangerous.
Is the earth connection from the consumer unit intact and in good condition?	If the connection seems loose or corroded, have the electricity company check whether the earthing is sound. You can check an RCD by pushing the test button to make sure it is working mechanically.
What is the condition of the fixed wiring between floors and in the loft or roof space?	If just a few cables appear to be rubber-insulated, have the entire system checked by a professional – it can be confusing, as old cable may have been disconnected but left in place during a previous upgrade. If cable is run in conduit, it can be difficult to check on its condition – but if it looks doubtful where it enters the accessories, have the circuit checked professionally. Wiring should be fixed securely and sheathing should run into all accessories, with no bare wire in sight. Junction boxes on lighting or power circuits should be screwed firmly to the structure and should have their covers in place.
Is the wiring unobtrusive and orderly?	Tidy all surface-run wiring into properly clipped straight runs. Better still, bury the cable in the wall plaster or run it under floors and inside hollow walls.

SEE ALSO > Switching off 296, Old fuse boards 297, Consumer units 298, Fuse ratings 299, Running cable 303–5

Scorch marks
Scorch marks on a socket or round the base of plug pins indicate poor connections.

Warm plug
This is another indication of loose connections.

Overloaded socket
If you have to use adaptors to power your appliances, you should fit extra sockets.

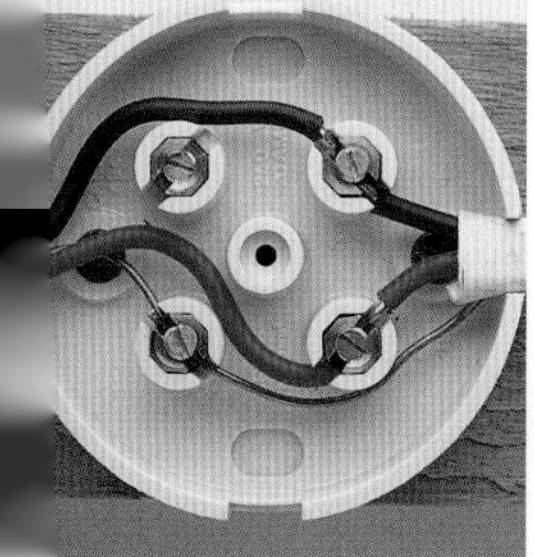

Red and black insulation
This is perfectly safe, and merely suggests the wiring was installed before 2005.

Questions	Answers
Are there any old round-pin socket outlets?	Replace old radial circuits with modern wiring and 13amp square-pin sockets as soon as possible.
Are the outer casings of all accessories in good condition and fixed securely to the structure?	Replace any cracked or broken components and secure any loose fittings.
Do switches on all accessories work smoothly and effectively?	If the switches are not working properly, replace the accessories.
Are all the conductors inside accessories connected securely to their terminals?	Tighten all loose terminals and ensure no bare wires are visible. Fit green-and-yellow sleeves to earth wires if not fitted already.
Is the insulation around wires inside any accessories dry and crumbly?	If so, it is rubber insulation in advanced decomposition. Replace the covers carefully and have a professional check the system as soon as possible.
Are the wires in some accessories covered with red and black insulation?	This is perfectly safe. Only homes rewired after 2005 are likely to have cables with brown and blue insulation.
Do any sockets, switches or plugs feel warm? Is there a smell of burning? Or are there scorch marks visible on sockets or around the base of plug pins? Does a socket spark when you pull out a plug? Or a switch when you operate it?	All these symptoms mean loose connections in the accessory or plug, or a poor connection between plug and socket. Tighten loose connections and clean all fuse clips, fuse caps and plug pins with silicon-carbide paper, then wipe them with a soft cloth. If the fault persists, try fitting a new plug. If that fails to cure the problem, replace the socket or switch.
Is it difficult to insert a plug in a socket?	The socket is worn and should be replaced.
Are your sockets in the right places?	Sockets should be placed conveniently round a room so that you need never have long flexes trailing across the floor or under carpets. Add sockets to the ring circuit by running spurs.
Do you have enough sockets?	If you have to use plug adaptors, you need more sockets. Replace singles with doubles or add spurs.
Is there old twisted twin flex hanging from the ceiling roses?	Replace it with PVC-insulated-and-sheathed flex.
Are there earth wires inside your ceiling roses?	If not, get professional advice on whether to replace the lighting circuits.
Is you lighting efficient?	Consider extra sockets or different light fittings to make your lighting more effective. Make sure you have two-way switches on stairs.
Is there power in the garage or workshop?	Detached buildings should have their own power supply.

SEE ALSO > Colour coding 285, Flex 292, Plugs 295, Switching off 296, Old fuse boards 297, Consumer units 298, Fuse ratings 299, Running cable 303–5, Sockets 306, Ceiling roses 324, Running power to an outbuilding 342–3

Simple replacements

You can carry out many repairs and replacements without having to concern yourself with the wiring system installed in your home. Many light fittings and appliances are supplied with electricity by means of flexible cords that plug into the system – so provided that they have been disconnected, there can be no risk of getting an electric shock while working on them.

WARNING

Never attempt to carry out electrical repairs without first unplugging the appliance or switching off the power supply at the consumer unit.

Flexible cord (flex)

All portable appliances and some of the smaller fixed ones, as well as pendant and portable light fittings, are connected to your home's permanent wiring system by means of conductors in the form of flexible cord, normally called 'flex'.

Each of the conductors in any type of flex is made up of numerous fine wires twisted together, and each conductor is insulated from the others by a covering of plastic insulation. So that the conductors can be identified easily, the insulation is usually colour-coded (brown = live; blue = neutral; and green-and-yellow = earth). Further protection is provided on most flexible cords in the form of an outer sheathing of insulating material enclosing the inner conductors.

Heat-resistant flex is available for enclosed light fittings and appliances with surfaces that become hot.

Twisted twin flex
This is similar to parallel twin flex (above right), but the insulated conductors are twisted together for extra strength. It was once used to support hanging light fittings, but nowadays must be replaced with a two-core sheathed flex when wiring pendant lights.

Types of electrical flex

Parallel twin
Parallel twin flex has two conductors, insulated with PVC (polyvinyl chloride), running side by side. The insulation material is joined between the two conductors along the length of the flex. This kind of flex should only be used for wiring audio-equipment speakers. One of the conductors will be colour-coded for identification.

Flat twin sheathed
Flat twin sheathed flex has colour-coded live and neutral conductors inside a PVC sheathing. This flex is used for double-insulated light fittings and small appliances.

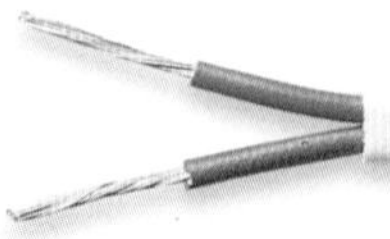

Two-core circular sheathed
This has colour-coded live and neutral conductors inside a PVC sheathing that is circular in its cross section. It is used for wiring certain pendant lights and some double-insulated appliances.

Three-core circular sheathed
This is like two-core circular sheathed flex, but it also contains an insulated and colour-coded earth wire. This flex is perhaps the most commonly used for all kinds of appliances. A special high-temperature flex is available for connecting immersion heaters, storage heaters and similar appliances.

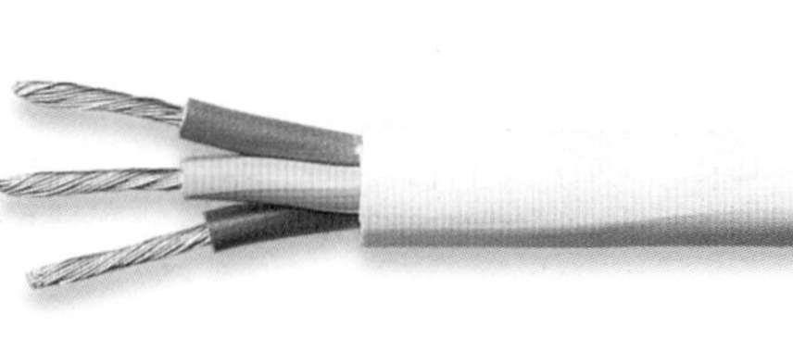

Unkinkable braided
This flex is used for appliances such as kettles and irons, which are of a high wattage and whose flex must stand up to movement and wear. The three rubber-insulated conductors, plus the textile cords that run parallel with them, are all contained in a rubber sheathing that is bound outside with braided material. This type of flex can be wound round the handle of a cool electric iron.

Coiled flex
A coiled flex that stretches and retracts can be a convenient way of connecting a portable lamp or appliance.

SEE ALSO > Colour coding 285, Extending flex 294

Connecting flexible cord

Although the spacing of terminals in plugs and appliances varies, the method of stripping and connecting the flex is the same.

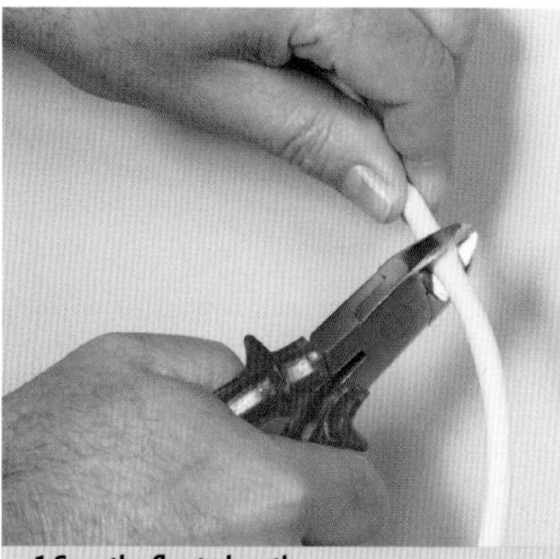
1 Crop the flex to length

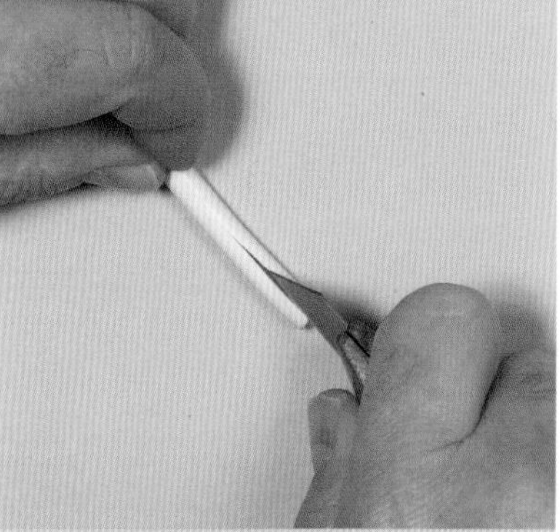
2 Slit sheathing lengthwise

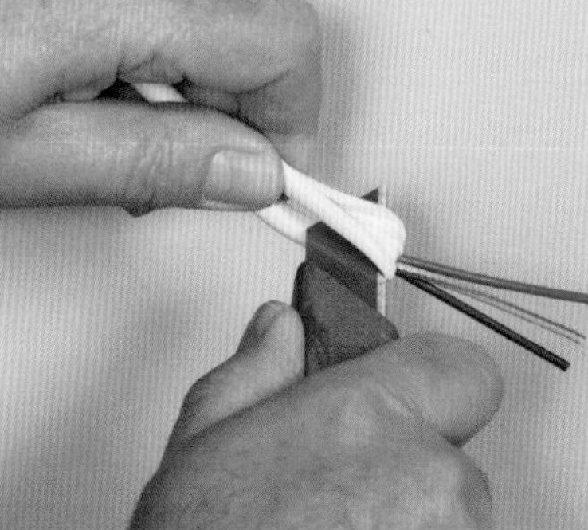
3 Fold sheathing over the blade and cut it off

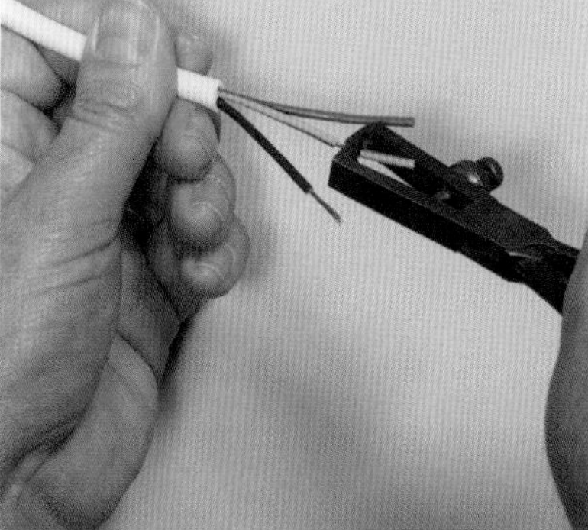
4 Strip insulation from conductors

Stripping the flex

Crop the flex to length (**1**). Slit the sheath lengthwise with a sharp knife (**2**), being careful not to cut into the insulation covering the individual conductors. Peel the sheathing away from the conductors, then fold it back over the knife blade and cut it off (**3**).

Separate the conductors, crop them to length and, using wire strippers, remove about 12mm (½in) of insulation from the end of each one (**4**).

Divide the conductors of parallel twin flex by pulling them apart before exposing their ends with wire strippers.

Connecting conductors

Twist together the individual filaments of each conductor to make them neat.

If the plug or appliance has post-type terminals, fold the bared wire (**1**) before pushing it into the hole. Make sure the insulation butts against the post and that all the wire filaments are enclosed within the terminal. Then tighten the clamping screw, and pull gently on the wire to make sure it is held quite firmly.

When you're connecting to clamp-type terminals, wrap the bared wire round the threaded post clockwise (**2**), then screw the clamping nut down tight onto the conductor. After tightening the nut, check that the conductor is held securely.

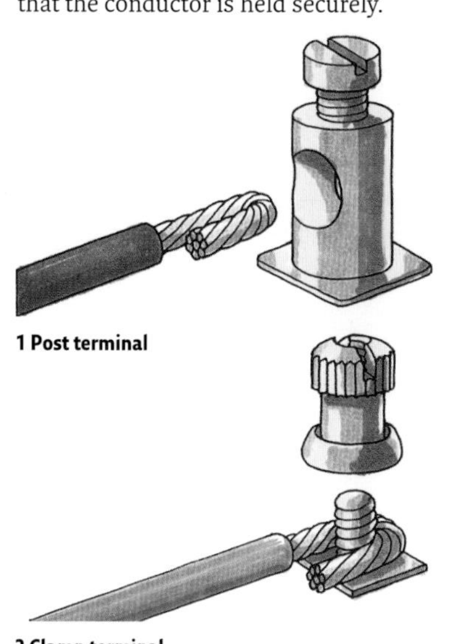
1 Post terminal

2 Clamp terminal

Choosing a flex

Not only is the right type of flex for the job important; the size of its conductors must suit the amount of current that will be used by the appliance.

Flex is rated according to the area of the cross section of its conductors, 0.5mm² being the smallest for normal domestic wiring. The flex size required is determined by the flow of current that it can handle safely. Excessive current will make a conductor overheat - so the size of the flex must be matched to the power (wattage) of the appliance that it is feeding.

Manufacturers often fit 1.25mm² flex to appliances of less than 3000W (3kW), since it is safer to use a larger conductor than necessary if a smaller flex might be easily damaged. It is advisable to adopt the same procedure when replacing flex.

Conductor	Current rating	Appliance
0.5mm²	3amp	Light fittings up to 690W
0.75mm²	6amp	Light fittings and appliances up to 1380W
1.0mm²	10amp	Appliances up to 2300W
1.25mm²	13amp	Appliances up to 2990W
1.5mm²	15amp	Appliances up to 3450W
2.5mm²	20amp	Appliances up to 4600W

Because they generate relatively high background temperatures, 3kW immersion heaters are wired with 2.5mm² heat-resistant flex (see WIRING AN IMMERSION HEATER).

Wire strippers

Special tools are available for removing the plastic insulation covering flex and cable conductors. Traditional wire strippers have shaped jaws that cut through the covering without damaging the conductors.

Modern wire strippers have jaws calibrated in millimetres and inches to measure the amount of insulation to be removed. The single action of squeezing the handles cuts through the covering and then removes it.

SEE ALSO > Immersion heaters 316–17, Extending flex 294

Extending flexible cord

When you plan the positions of socket outlets, try to ensure there will be enough – all conveniently situated, so it's never necessary to extend the flexible cord of a table lamp or other appliance. But if you do find that a flex will not reach a socket, extend it so it is not stretched taut, which could cause an accident. Never be tempted to join two lengths of flex by twisting the bared ends of wires together, even if you bind them with insulating tape. People often do this as a temporary measure then neglect to make a proper connection later.

Flex connectors

- **Two-part flex connectors**
Connectors with two pins, as shown right, must only be used with two-core flex and double-insulated appliances.

If possible, fit a longer flex, wiring it into the appliance itself. But if you can't do this or don't want to dismantle the appliance, use a flex connector. There are two-terminal and three-terminal connectors, which you must match to the type of flex you are using. Never join two-core flex to three-core flex.

Strip off just enough sheathing for the conductors to reach the terminals, and make sure the sheathed part of each cord can be secured under the cord clamp at each end of the connector.

Crop the conductors to length, then strip and connect the conductors – connecting the live conductor to one of the outer terminals, the neutral to the other, and the earth wire (if present) to the central terminal. Make sure that matching conductors from both cords are connected to the same terminals, then tighten the cord clamps and screw the cover in place.

In-line switches

- **Larger appliances**
Never extend the flex of large appliances, such as dishwashers or washing machines. And don't plug them into an extension lead or trailing socket.

If you plan to fit a longer continuous length of flex you can install an in-line switch that will allow you to control the appliance or light fitting from some distance away – a great advantage for the elderly and people confined to bed. Some in-line switches are luminous.

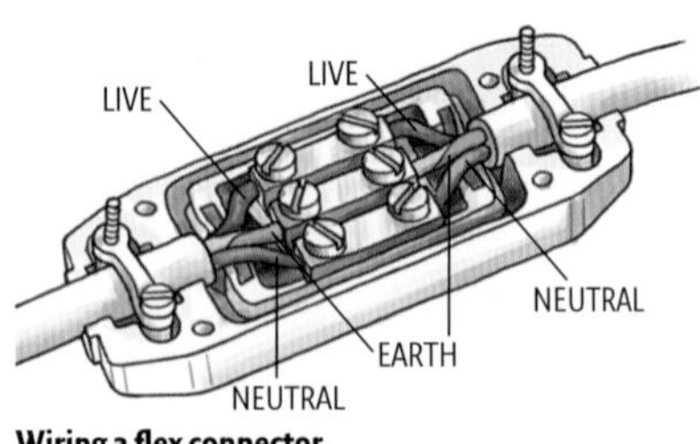

Wiring a flex connector

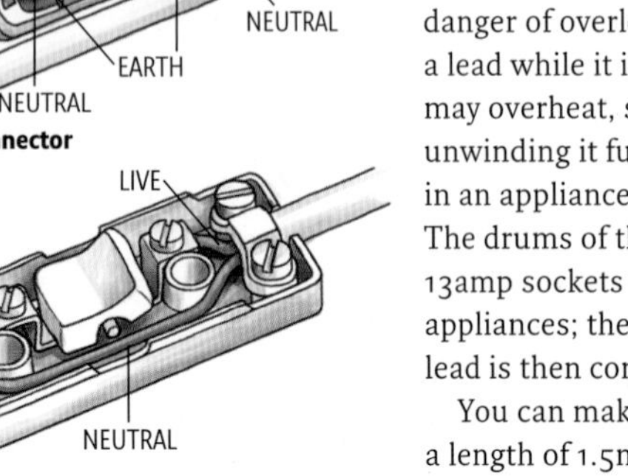

Wiring an in-line switch

Extension leads

If you fit a long flex to a power tool, it will inevitably become tangled and one of the conductors will eventually break, perhaps causing a short circuit. The solution is to buy an extension lead or make one yourself.

The best type of extension lead to be had commercially is wound on a drum. There are 5amp ones – but it's safer to buy one with a 13amp rating, so you can run a wider range of equipment without danger of overloading. If you use such a lead while it is wound on the drum it may overheat, so develop the habit of unwinding it fully each time you plug in an appliance rated at 1kW or more. The drums of these leads have built-in 13amp sockets to take the plugs of appliances; the plug at the end of the lead is then connected to a wall socket.

You can make an extension lead from a length of 1.5mm² three-core flex with a standard 13amp plug on one end and a trailing socket on the other. Use those with unbreakable rubber casings. A trailing socket is wired in a similar way to a 13amp plug (see opposite). Its terminals are marked to indicate which conductors to connect to them.

'Multi-way' trailing sockets will take several plugs and are ideal for hi-fi systems or computers with a number of individual components that need to be connected to the mains supply. Using a multi-way socket, the whole system is supplied with power from a single plug in the wall socket.

You can also extend a lead by using a two-part detachable flex connector. One half has pins that fit into the other half of the connector. When wiring a two-part flex connector, never attach the part with the pins to the extension lead. The exposed pins will become live – and dangerous – when the lead is plugged into the socket.

SEE ALSO > Types of flex 292, Connecting flex 293

Replacing a pendant lampholder

Because pendant lampholders hang on a flexible cord from the ceiling, they are in a stream of hot air rising from the bulb. In time this tends to make plastic holders brittle and more easily cracked or broken. Check their condition from time to time, and replace any that look suspect before they become dangerous.

Plastic lampholders

Plastic lampholders are the most common type. They have a threaded skirt that screws onto the actual holder (the part that takes the bulb). Some have an extended skirt. If you are going to use a close-fitting or badly ventilated shade, fit a heat-resistant version. Plastic holders are designed to take two-core flex only. Never fit one on a three-core flex, as there is no place to attach the earth wire.

Where possible, replace an old metal lampholder with a plastic version, substituting its three-core flex with a two-core circular sheathed type.

Fitting a lampholder

Before commencing work, remove the circuit fuse or remove (or lock off) the circuit breaker from the consumer unit so that no-one can turn the power on.

Unscrew the old holder's cap and slide it up the flex to expose the terminals. Loosen their screws and pull the wires out. If some wires are broken or brittle, cut back slightly to expose sound wires before fitting the new holder.

Slide the cap of the new fitting up the flex and attach it temporarily with adhesive tape. Fit the live wire into one of the terminals, and the neutral wire into the other one. Then loop the conductors round the supporting lugs of the holder, to take the weight off the terminals, and screw the cap down.

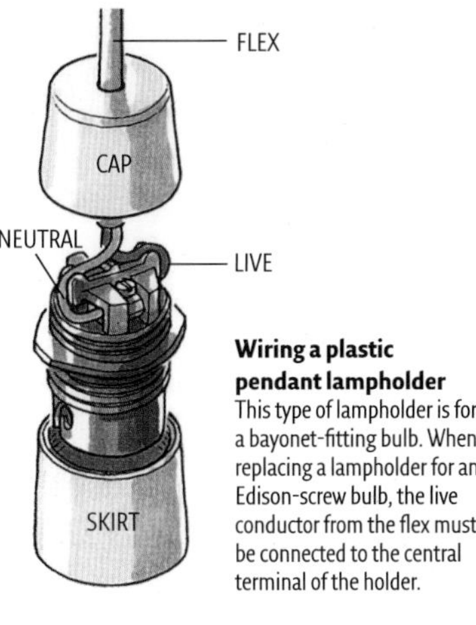

Wiring a plastic pendant lampholder
This type of lampholder is for a bayonet-fitting bulb. When replacing a lampholder for an Edison-screw bulb, the live conductor from the flex must be connected to the central terminal of the holder.

Three-pin plugs

Square-pin 13amp plugs are used to connect most portable light fittings and appliances to the mains supply. Their construction may vary slightly, but all 13amp plugs work on the same principle. They are available with plastic or rubber casings, and some have insulated pins to prevent the user getting a shock from a plug pulled partly from the socket. Use only plugs marked BS 1363.

Factory-fitted plugs

All new appliances are sold with a plug moulded onto the end of the flexible cord. This type of plug contains a small replaceable cartridge fuse within a retractable holder positioned between the pins. Factory-fitted plugs cannot be dismantled, so if you ever need to replace one that is damaged, cut through the flex and fit a rewirable plug.

Factory-fitted plug

Rewirable plug

Rewirable plugs

The plugs available in shops and DIY stores can be fitted onto any electrical flex. They too contain a replaceable cartridge fuse, which is accessible when the plug's cover is removed. All rewirable plugs have a cord clamp or grip that prevents the conductors being accidentally pulled out of their terminals.

• **Disposing of plugs** Before you discard a damaged plug, bend one of the pins to prevent it being plugged into a socket by a child.

Fuses for plugs

Use a 3amp (red) fuse for appliances of up to 720W, and a 13amp (brown) fuse for those of 720 to 3000W (3kW). There are also 2, 5 and 10amp fuses, but these are less often used in the home.

EARTH
FUSE
LIVE
NEUTRAL
CORD CLAMP

Rewirable post-terminal plug

Wiring a 13amp plug

Loosen the large screw between the pins and remove the cover. Position the flex on the open plug to gauge how much sheathing to remove (the cord clamp must grip sheathed flex, not the conductors). Strip the sheathing and position the flex on the plug again, so that you can cut the conductors to the right length. These should take the most direct routes to their terminals and lie neatly within the channels of the plug.

Strip and prepare the ends of the wires, then secure each to its terminal. If you are using two-core flex, simply leave the earth terminal empty.

Tighten the cord clamp to grip the end of the sheathing and secure the flex (a sprung cord grip tightens if the flex is pulled hard). Fit a fuse of the correct rating , then replace the plug's cover and tighten up the screw.

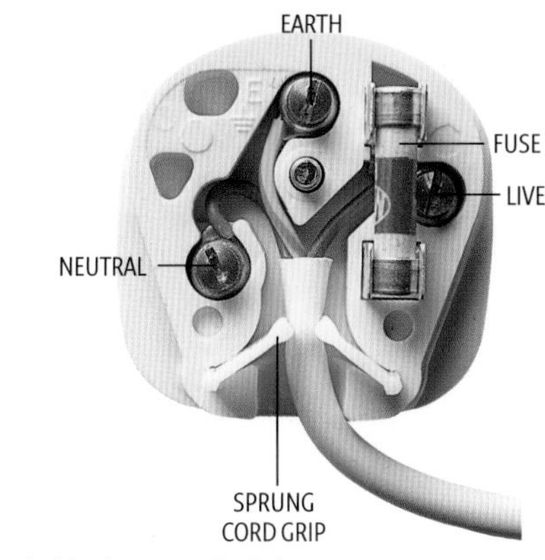

Rewirable clamp-terminal plug

SEE ALSO > Connecting flex 293, Switching off 296, Light bulbs 326–7

Main switch equipment

Electricity flows because of a difference in 'pressure' between the live wire and the neutral one, and this difference in pressure is measured in volts. Domestic electricity in this country is supplied as alternating current, at 230 volts, by way of the electricity company's main service cable. This normally enters your house underground, although in some areas electricity is distributed by overhead cables.

• Cross-bonding cable sizes
Single-core cables are used to cross-bond gas and water pipes to earth. An electrician can calculate the minimum size for these cables, but for any single house or flat it is safe to use 10mm² cable. (See also PME opposite).

The service head

The main cable terminates at the service head, or 'cutout', which contains the service fuse. This fuse prevents the neighbourhood's supply being affected if there should be a serious fault in the circuitry of your house. Cables connect the cutout to the meter, which registers how much electricity you consume. Both the meter and cutout belong to the electricity company and must not be tampered with. The meter is sealed in order to disclose interference.

If you are using cheap night-time power for electric storage heaters and hot water, a time switch will be supplied by the electricity company.

Consumer unit

Electricity is fed to and from the consumer unit by 'meter leads', thick single-core insulated-and-sheathed cables made up of several wires twisted together. The consumer unit is a box containing the fuseways that protect the individual circuits in the house. It also incorporates the main isolating switch, which you operate when you need to cut off the supply of power to the whole house. Not all main isolating switches operate the same way. Before you need to use it, check to see whether the main switch on your consumer unit has to be in the up or down position for 'off'.

In a house where several new circuits have been installed over the years, the number of circuits may exceed the number of fuseways in the consumer unit. If so, an individual switchfuse unit – or more than one – may have been mounted alongside the main unit. Switchfuse units comprise a single fuseway and an isolating switch; they, too, are connected to the meter by means of meter leads.

If your home is heated by off-peak storage heaters, then you will have an Economy 7 meter and a separate consumer unit for the heater circuits.

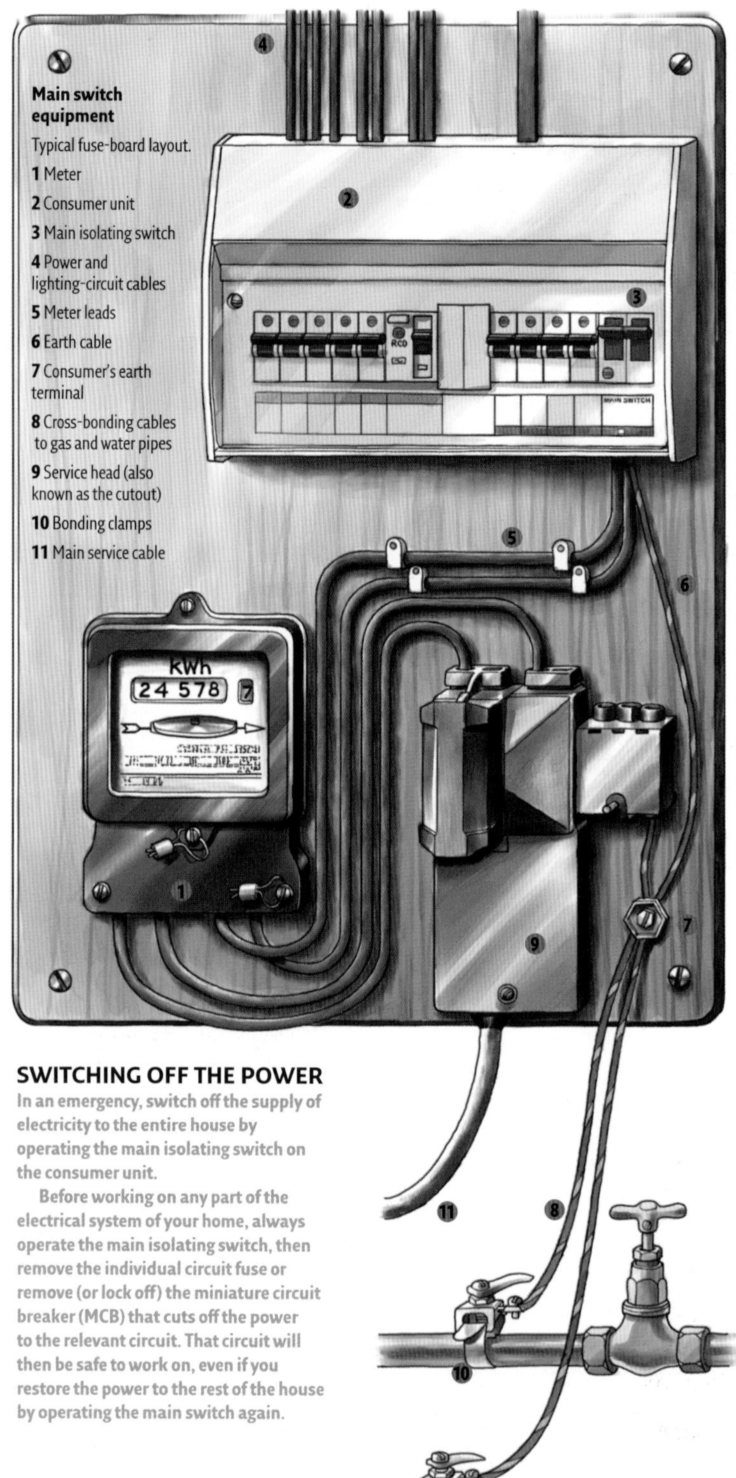

Main switch equipment
Typical fuse-board layout.
1 Meter
2 Consumer unit
3 Main isolating switch
4 Power and lighting-circuit cables
5 Meter leads
6 Earth cable
7 Consumer's earth terminal
8 Cross-bonding cables to gas and water pipes
9 Service head (also known as the cutout)
10 Bonding clamps
11 Main service cable

SWITCHING OFF THE POWER

In an emergency, switch off the supply of electricity to the entire house by operating the main isolating switch on the consumer unit.

Before working on any part of the electrical system of your home, always operate the main isolating switch, then remove the individual circuit fuse or remove (or lock off) the miniature circuit breaker (MCB) that cuts off the power to the relevant circuit. That circuit will then be safe to work on, even if you restore the power to the rest of the house by operating the main switch again.

SEE ALSO > Consumer units 298, Domestic circuits 301

Earthing and bonding

All of the individual earth conductors of the various circuits in the house are connected to a metal earthing block in the consumer unit. A single cable with a green-and-yellow covering runs from this earthing block to the consumer's earth terminal, which is mounted next to the cutout. In most urban houses a connection is provided from inside the cutout to an external earth-connection block, which is also wired to the consumer's earth terminal. This provides an effective path to earth, as it allows the current to pass along the sheath of the main service cable to the electricity company's substation, where it is solidly connected to earth. If the company does not provide an earth connection to its cable, the installation must be protected by an RCD.

In the past most domestic electrical systems were earthed to the cold-water supply, so earth-leakage current passed out along the metal water pipes into the ground in which they were buried. But nowadays more and more water systems use nonconductive, nonmetallic pipes and fittings. As a result, such a means of earthing is no longer reliable.

Despite this, you will find that your gas and water pipework is connected to the consumer's earth terminal. This ensures that the water and gas piping systems are cross-bonded, so earth-leakage current passing through either system will run without hindrance to the main earth without producing dangerously high voltages. The cross-bonding clamps must be as close as possible to the point where the pipes enter the house, but on the consumer's side (within 600mm) of the stopcock or gas meter.

Bonding clamp
This type of clamp (BS 951) is used to make connections to gas and water pipes. It must not be removed under any circumstances.

PME

The electricity company sometimes provides a different method of earthing the system, called 'protective multiple earth' (PME), by which earth-leakage current is fed back to the substation along the neutral return wire, and so to earth. Regulations regarding the earthing of this system are particularly stringent. With PME, cross-bonding cables to gas and water services are sometimes required to be larger. Check this with the electricity company.

RCDs

Although the local electricity company normally provides effective earthing for the electrical system of your home, safe earthing is the consumer's own responsibility. With this in mind, it is worth installing a residual current device (RCD) into the house circuitry.

When conditions are normal, the current flowing out through the neutral conductor is exactly the same as that flowing in through the live one. Should there be an imbalance between the two caused by an earth leakage, the residual current device will detect it immediately and isolate the circuitry.

An RCD can be either installed as a separate unit or incorporated into the consumer unit, sometimes together with the main isolating switch.

A residual current device is sometimes referred to as a residual current circuit breaker (RCCB). It was formerly known as an ELCB, or earth-leakage circuit breaker.

A separate unit containing an RCD

Old fuse boards

Domestic wiring systems were once very different from the ones used today. Besides lighting, water-heating and cooker circuits, each socket outlet had its own circuit and fuse, while further circuits would be installed from time to time as the needs of the household changed. Consequently, an old house may have a mixture of 'fuse boxes' attached to the fuse board, along with the meter.

You may find that the wiring itself is haphazard and badly labelled, with the serious danger that you may not safely isolate a circuit you're going to work on. Furthermore, you will not be able to tell whether a particular fuse is correctly and safely rated unless you know what type of circuit it is protecting.

Arrange for an inspection

If your home still has such an old-style fuse board, have it inspected and tested by a qualified electrician before you attempt to work on any part of the system. He or she can advise you as to whether your installation needs to be replaced with a modern consumer unit. At the same time, check that the cables are PVC-insulated. If everything does prove to be in good working condition, he or she can label the various circuits clearly to help you in the future.

An old-fashioned fuse board
This type of installation is out of date. A professional electrician may advise you to replace at least some of the components.

SEE ALSO > Bathroom safety 286

Consumer units

The consumer unit is the heart of your electrical installation: every circuit in your home has to pass through it. Although there are several different types and styles, all consumer units are based on similar principles.

• **Important notes**
Make a note of the last time you had your electrical installation checked professionally, and attach it as close as possible to the consumer unit. Similarly, jot down the next proposed date of inspection.

If your home is wired with both the old-style colour-coded cables and the newer ones, attach a note near the consumer unit to alert anyone working on the fixed wiring of your house in the future.

Every consumer unit has a large main isolating switch, which can turn off the entire electrical system of the house. On some units, the switch is in the form of an RCD that can be operated manually but which will also 'trip' automatically should any serious fault occur, isolating the whole system. There is greater emphasis these days on protecting only the most vulnerable circuits with an RCD. With these 'split' consumer units, the main isolating switch still turns off every circuit simultaneously.

Some consumer units are designed in such a way that it's impossible to remove the outer cover without first turning off the main isolating switch. Even if yours is not this type, always switch off the power before exposing any of the elements within the consumer unit.

Having turned off the main switch, remove the cover so that you can see how the unit is arranged. Remember that even when the unit is switched off the cable connecting the meter to the main switch is still live – so take care.

Take note of the cables that feed the various circuits in the house. The blue-insulated neutral wires run to a common neutral block, where they are attached to their individual terminals. Similarly, the green-and-yellow earth wires run to a common earth block. The brown-covered live conductors are connected to terminals on individual fuseways or circuit breakers.

Some wires will be joined together in a single terminal. These are the two ends of a ring circuit, and that is how they should be wired.

Split consumer unit with miniature circuit breakers
Only the circuits on the left are protected by the RCD.

SEE ALSO > Colour coding 285, Main switch equipment 296, Power failure 300, Domestic circuits 301, Cable 302

Fuses and circuit breakers

In some consumer units there is a fuseway for each circuit. Into each fuseway is plugged a fuse carrier, which is essentially a bridge between the main switch and that particular circuit. When the fuse carrier is removed from the consumer unit, the current cannot pass across the gap. In many consumer units you will find miniature circuit breakers (MCBs) instead of fuse carriers.

Identifying fuses

Pull any fuse carrier out of the consumer unit and turn it round to see what kind of fuse it contains.

At each end of the carrier you will see a single-bladed or double-bladed contact. An old rewirable carrier will have a thin wire running from one contact to the other, held by a screw terminal at each end. Fuse wire is made in various thicknesses, calculated to melt at given currents when a circuit is substantially overloaded, thus breaking the 'bridge' and isolating the circuit.

Alternatively, the carrier may contain a cartridge fuse, varying in size according to its rating. The cartridge is a ceramic tube containing a fuse wire packed in fine sand. The wire is connected to metal caps at the ends of the cartridge that snap into spring clips on the contacts of the fuse carrier.

Cartridge fuses provide better protection, since they blow faster than ordinary fuse wire; modern consumer units no longer contain rewirable fuses.

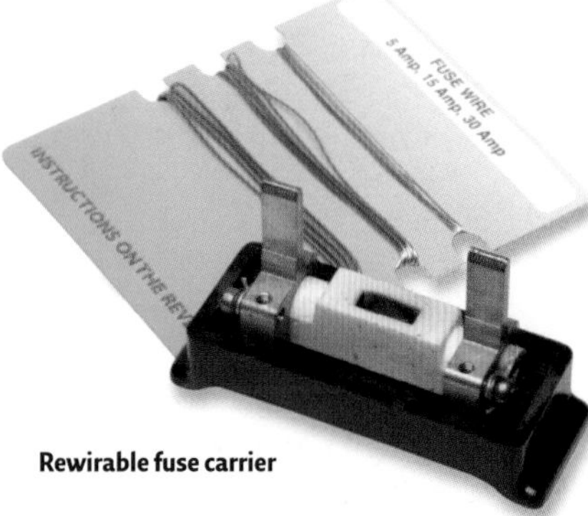

Rewirable fuse carrier

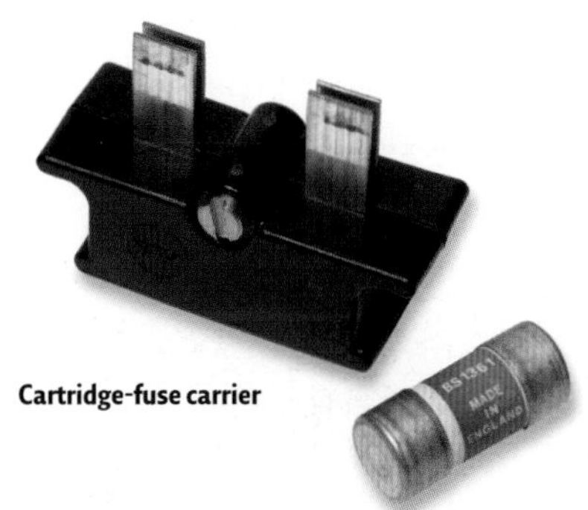
Cartridge-fuse carrier

Fuse ratings

Whatever the type of fuses used in the consumer unit, they are rated in the same way. Cartridge fuses are colour-coded and marked with the appropriate amp rating for a certain type of circuit. Fuse wire is bought wrapped round a clearly labelled card.

Never insert fuse wire that is heavier than the gauge intended for the circuit. To do so could result in a dangerous fault going unnoticed because the fuse wire fails to melt. And it is even more dangerous to substitute any other type of wire or metal strip; these provide no protection at all.

When you need to change a fuse, do not automatically replace it with one of the same rating. Check first that it is the correct type of fuse for the circuit. The fuse carrier should be marked and/or colour-coded. You can also look at the list of circuits printed on the inside of the consumer-unit cover to identify the carriers and their required ratings.

Keep spare fuse wire or cartridge fuses in or close to the consumer unit.

FUSE RATINGS

Circuit	Fuse	Colour coding
Door bell	5amp	White
Lighting	5amp	White
Immersion heater	15amp	Blue
Storage heater	15amp	Blue
Radial circuits – 20sq m maximum floor area 50sq m maximum floor area	20amp 30amp	Yellow Red
Ring circuits – 100sq m maximum floor area	30amp	Red
Shower unit	45amp	Green
Cooker	30amp	Red

Miniature circuit breakers

With MCBs a faulty circuit is obvious as soon as you inspect the consumer unit, as they switch to the 'off' position automatically. There are many types of miniature circuit breaker on the market, but only buy ones made to the required standards of construction and safety.

Make sure any MCB that you use is marked BS EN 60898, which is the relevant British Standard. There are also different classes of MCB (you need to look for Type B). And lastly, MCBs are classified according to the largest potential fault current they are able to clear; ask for M6 or M9, as these will clear any potential current likely to be met in a domestic situation.

MCB ratings

To conform to European standards, MCB ratings tend to vary slightly from circuit-fuse ratings (see CIRCUITS: MAXIMUM LENGTHS). However, if you have MCBs that match the slightly smaller ratings shown for circuit fuses, that is perfectly acceptable.

Button-operated miniature circuit breaker

Switch-operated miniature circuit breaker

A selection of circuit fuses
From left to right: 45amp fuse, 30amp fuse, 20amp fuse, 15amp fuse, 5amp fuse.

SEE ALSO > Power failure 300, Domestic circuits 301, Circuit lengths 344

In the event of a power failure

If there's a fault on a circuit or it is overloaded by having too many appliances plugged into it, the MCB protecting the circuit will 'trip' (switch to the 'off' position); or if the circuit is protected by a fuse, the fuse will 'blow' (melt). When everything on a circuit stops working, go to your consumer unit and look for a tripped MCB or a blown fuse. However, if all or any of the circuits are protected by an RCD, check first to see whether the RCD has switched off

Identifying the faulty circuit

If your RCD has tripped, turn off all the MCBs it is protecting and then reset the RCD. Now turn on each MCB in turn until the RCD trips again. Having identified the faulty circuit, turn off the consumer unit's main switch and tape it in the 'off' position while you are working. Inspect the sockets or light fittings and switches on the suspect circuit to see if a conductor has worked loose and is touching one of the other wires or terminals or the outer casing, causing a short circuit. If that doesn't solve the problem, keep the faulty circuit isolated (MCB locked off) and call in an electrician.

Resetting an MCB

Assuming your RCD is still switched on when you inspect your consumer unit, look next for a miniature circuit breaker that has switched automatically to the 'off' position; or if your MCBs are the press-button type, see whether a button has popped out. If so, turn off the consumer unit's main switch, and reset the MCB by moving the toggle switch to the 'on' position (1) or pressing the button back in. Then turn the main switch on again (2).

If the same MCB trips immediately, unplug or switch off everything on the circuit to make sure the cause is not simply overloading or a faulty appliance, then reset the MCB as before. If the MCB trips again, look for loose connections as described above and then, if necessary, get an electrician to trace and rectify the fault.

Regular testing
It is a good idea to check that all your MCBs and RCDs are in good working order by tripping them deliberately every three months or so. If an MCB has tripped frequently, have it replaced.

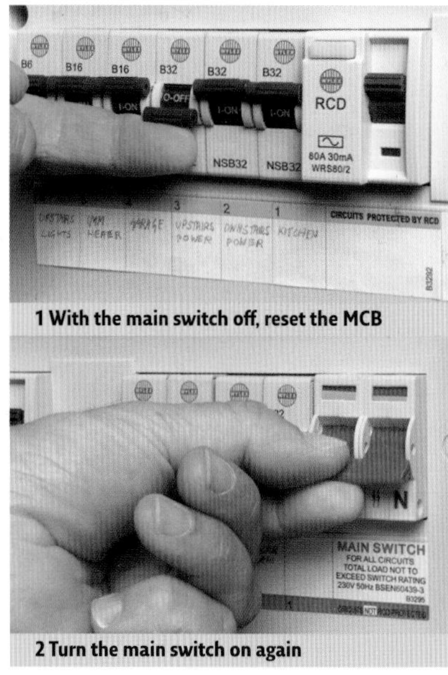

1 With the main switch off, reset the MCB

2 Turn the main switch on again

Replacing a cartridge fuse

Turn off the main switch on the consumer unit, take off the cover, and look for the failed fuse. To identify the relevant fuse, look at the list of circuits inside the cover. If there is no list, inspect the most likely circuits. If, for example, the lights blew when you switched them on, you need check only the lighting circuits, which are usually colour-coded white.

1 Remove the suspect cartridge fuse

2 Use a multimeter to check the fuse

Checking a cartridge fuse

With the power turned off, pull out the suspect fuse carrier and then, depending on the style of the fuse carrier, either dismantle the carrier to gain access to the cartridge fuse (1) or prise the fuse out of its spring clips.

Check the fuse with a multimeter set to its lowest resistance range. Place one of the meter's probes on each of the fuse's metal caps (2). If the meter reading is high (thousands of Ohms or more), the fuse has blown. Insert a new fuse of the appropriate rating and replace the carrier, then turn on the main switch.

Checking a rewirable fuse

Broken fuse wire is usually obvious, but if you can't be sure, pull gently on each end of the wire with the tip of a small screwdriver to see if the wire is intact (1).

Replacing fuse wire

To replace blown fuse wire, loosen the two terminals holding the old wire and extract the broken pieces. Wrap one end of a new length of the correct fuse wire clockwise round one of the terminals (2) and tighten the screw. Attach the other end to the second terminal, making sure you don't stretch the wire taut. Tighten the screw, cut off excess wire from the ends, then replace the fuse carrier. Turn on the main switch.

1 Pull the wire gently with a small screwdriver

2 Wind the wire clockwise round the terminal

Checking out a fault

If a fuse (of either type) blows again as soon as the power is restored, then there is either a fault or an overload on that circuit. Unplug or switch off everything on the circuit to make sure it isn't overloaded, then replace the fuse again. If the same fuse blows immediately, turn off the main switch and check for loose connections on the circuit as described above left. If you can't find the fault, call in an electrician.

SEE ALSO > Consumer units 298, Fuses and circuit breakers 299

Domestic circuits

Running from the consumer unit are the cables that supply the various fixed wiring circuits in your home. Not only are the sizes of the cables different, the circuits themselves also differ, depending on what they are used for and also, in some cases, how old they happen to be.

Ring circuits

The most common form of 'power' circuit for feeding socket outlets is the ring circuit, or 'ring main'. With this method of wiring, a cable starts from terminals in the consumer unit and goes round the house, connecting socket to socket and arriving back at the same terminals. This means that power can reach any of the socket outlets or fused connection units from both directions, which reduces the load on the cable.

Ring mains are always run in 2.5mm² cable and are protected by 30amp fuses or 32amp MCBs. Theoretically there is no limit to the number of socket outlets or fused connection units that can be fitted to a ring circuit provided that it does not serve a floor area of more than 100sq m (120sq yd) – a limit based on the number of heaters that would be adequate to warm that space. However, in practice two-storey houses usually have one ring main for the upper floor and another one for downstairs.

Spurs

The number of sockets on a ring main can be increased by adding extensions or 'spurs'. A spur can be either a single 2.5mm² cable connected to the terminals of an existing socket or fused connection unit (FCU), or it can run from a junction box inserted in the ring.

Each (unfused) spur can feed only one fused connection unit for a fixed appliance or one single or double socket outlet. You can have as many unfused spurs on a ring circuit as there were sockets or FCUs on it originally (note that for this calculation a double socket is counted as two).

The 30amp fuse (or 32amp MCB) that protects the ring main remains unchanged, no matter how many spurs are connected to the circuit.

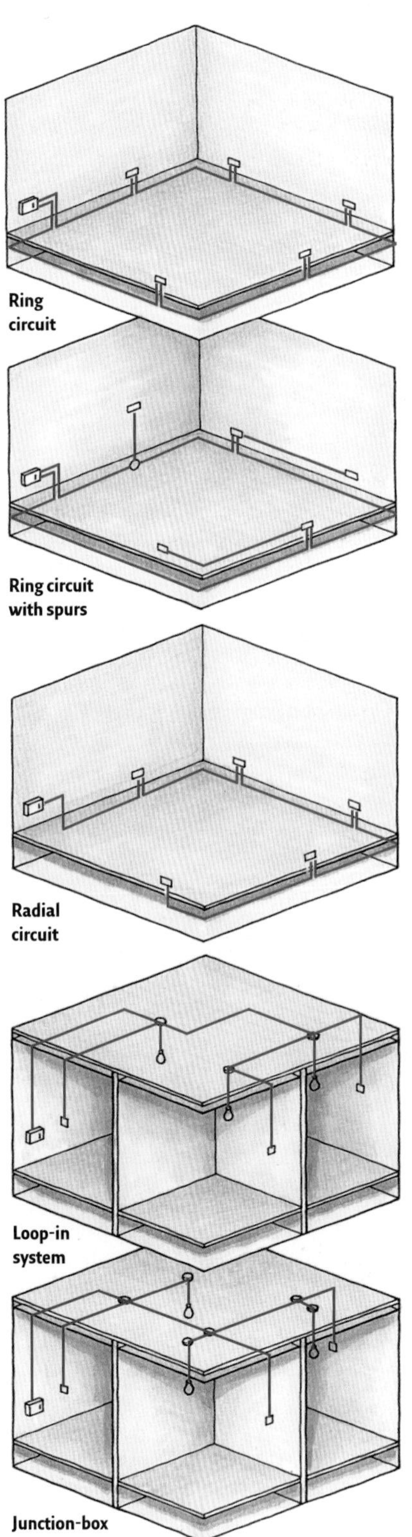

Ring circuit

Ring circuit with spurs

Radial circuit

Loop-in system

Junction-box system

Radial circuits

A radial power circuit feeds a number of sockets or fused connection units – but, unlike a ring circuit, its cable terminates at the last outlet. The size of cable and the fuse rating depend on the size of the floor area to be supplied by the circuit. In an area of up to 20sq m (24sq yd), the cable needs to be 2.5mm², protected by a 20amp MCB or a 20amp fuse of any type. For a larger area, up to 50sq m (60sq yd), you should use 4mm² cable with a 30amp cartridge fuse or 32amp MCB (a rewirable fuse is not permitted).

Any number of socket outlets can be supplied by one of these circuits, and spurs can be added if required. These circuits are known as multi-outlet radial circuits. A powerful appliance such as a cooker or shower unit must have its own radial circuit.

Lighting circuits

Domestic lighting circuits are of the radial kind, but there are two systems currently in use.

The loop-in system simply has a single cable that runs from ceiling rose to ceiling rose, terminating at the last one on the circuit. Single cables also run from the ceiling roses to the various light switches.

The junction-box system (which is the older of the two systems) incorporates a junction box for each light. The boxes are situated conveniently on the single supply cable. A cable runs from each junction box to the ceiling rose, and another from the box to the light switch. In practice, most lighting circuits are a combination of the two methods.

A single circuit of 1.5mm² cable is able to serve the equivalent of eleven 100W light fittings. Check the load by adding together the wattage of all the light bulbs on the circuit. If the total comes to more than 1200W, the circuit should be split. In any case, it makes sense to have two or more separate lighting circuits running from the consumer unit.

Lighting circuits must be protected by 5amp fuses or 6amp MCBs.

SEE ALSO > Fuse ratings 299, Cables 302, Sockets 306, Fused connection units 310, Cooker circuits 314, Shower circuit 316, Circuit lengths 344

Electrical cable

Cable supplies power to every socket, switch and fixed appliance in your home. The conductors or wires in modern cable are invariably made from copper, and are insulated and sheathed in PVC. The insulation is colour-coded to identify live, neutral and earth conductors.

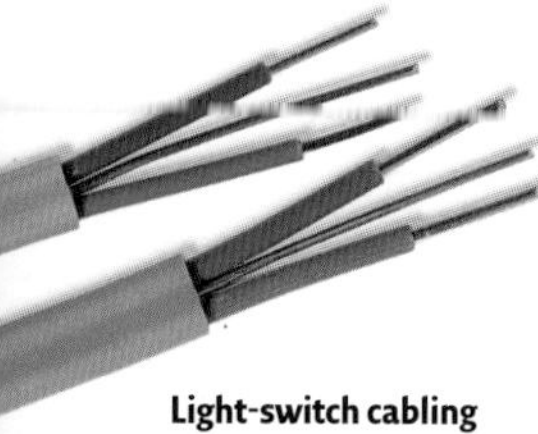

Light-switch cabling

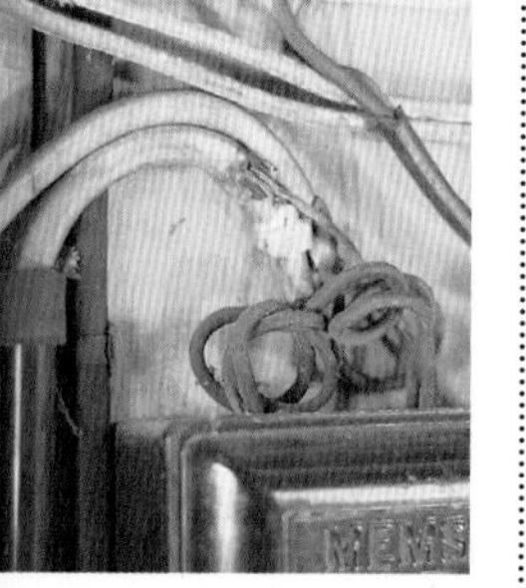

Prewar cable
Houses wired before World War II may still have old cable that is sheathed and insulated in rubber. Rubber sheathing is usually a matt black. It is more flexible than modern PVC insulation – unless it has deteriorated, in which case it will be crumbly. Old cable may be dangerous and needs to be replaced.

Types of domestic cable

A number of different types of electrical cable are found in domestic wiring.

Two-core-and-earth cable

Cable for the fixed wiring in your home usually has three conductors: the insulated live and neutral ones and the earth conductor lying between them, which is uninsulated except for the sheathing that encloses all three conductors. Cable up to 2.5mm² has solid single-core conductors; but larger sizes (up to 10mm²) wouldn't be flexible enough if they had solid conductors, so each one is made up of seven strands. The live conductor is insulated with brown PVC, and the neutral one with blue. If the earth wire is exposed, as in a socket outlet, it should be covered with a green-and-yellow sleeve. The PVC sheathing on the outside of the cable is usually white or grey.

Three-core-and-earth cable

This cable is used for a two-way lighting system, which can be turned on and off at different switches – at the top and bottom of a staircase, for example. It contains three insulated conductors – with brown, black and grey coverings – and a bare earth wire.

Single-core cable

Insulated single-core cable is used in buildings where the electrical wiring is run in metal or plastic conduit – a type of installation rarely found in domestic buildings. The cable is colour-coded in the normal way: brown for live, blue for neutral, and green-and-yellow for earth.

Single-core 16mm² cable insulated in a green-and-yellow PVC covering is used for connecting the consumer unit to the earth. Single-core cable of the same size is used for connecting the consumer unit to the meter. The meter leads are insulated in brown for the live conductor and blue for the neutral one.

Light-switch cabling

Wall-mounted light switches are usually wired with ordinary 1.5mm² two-core-and-earth cable. The live wire is colour-coded brown, and the switch-return wire blue. Because the blue wire carries live current back to the light fitting, it is normal to either attach a brown flag or slip brown sheathing over the wire to identify it. However, you can now buy special cable with two brown wires for wiring light switches.

Cable sizes

The chart below gives the basic sizes of cables used for wiring domestic circuits. For details of the maximum permitted lengths for circuits, see CIRCUITS: MAXIMUM LENGTHS. If the company fuse is larger than 60amps, 25mm² meter leads are required – but it is best to consult your electricity company for advice.

CIRCUIT-CABLE SIZES		
Circuit	**Size**	**Type**
Fixed lighting	1.5mm²	Two-core-and-earth
Bell or chime transformer	1.5mm²	Two-core-and-earth
Immersion heater	2.5mm²	Two-core-and-earth
Storage heater	2.5mm² & 4.0mm²	Two-core-and-earth
Ring circuit	2.5mm²	Two-core-and-earth
Spurs	2.5mm²	Two-core-and-earth
Radial – 20amp	2.5mm²	Two-core-and-earth
Radial – 30amp	4.0mm²	Two-core-and-earth
Shower unit	10.0mm²	Two-core-and-earth
Cooker	4.0mm² & 6.0mm²	Two-core-and-earth
Consumer earth cable	16.0mm²	Single core
Meter leads	16.0mm²	Single core

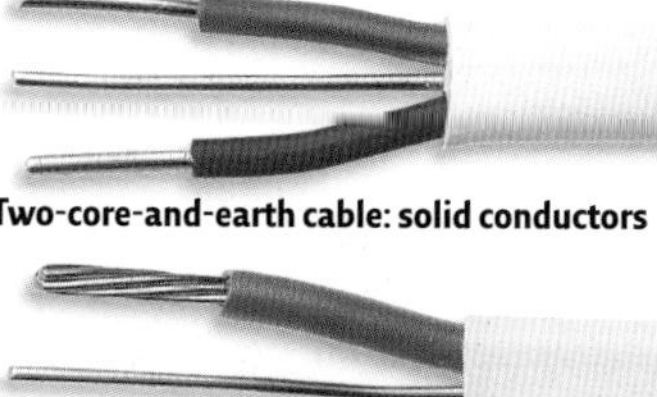

Two-core-and-earth cable: solid conductors

Two-core-and-earth cable: stranded conductors

Three-core-and-earth cable

Insulated single-core cable

Insulated-and-sheathed single-core cable

Stripping cable

When cable is wired to an accessory, some of the sheathing and insulation must be removed. Slit the sheathing lengthwise with a sharp knife, peel it off the conductors, then fold it over the blade and cut it off. Take about 12mm (½in) of insulation off the ends of the conductors, using wire strippers.

Cover the uninsulated earth wire with a green-and-yellow plastic sleeve, leaving 12mm (½in) of the wire exposed.

If two stranded conductors are to be inserted in the same terminal, twist the exposed ends together with pliers. Don't twist solid conductors; simply insert them together into the terminal. Tighten the fixing screws, and pull on each conductor to make sure it is held securely.

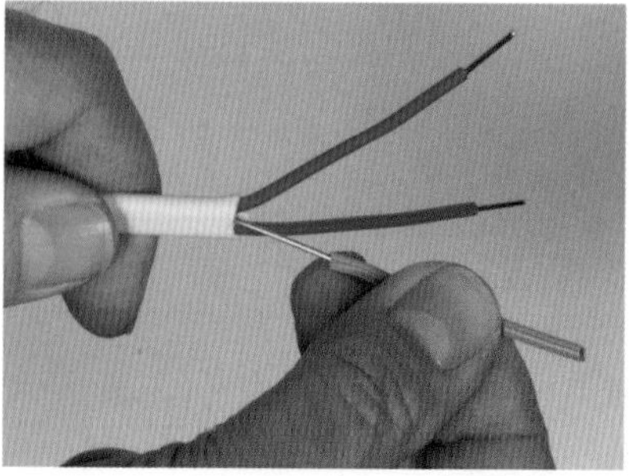

Slip colour-coded sleeving over the earth wire

SEE ALSO > Colour coding 285, Wire strippers 293, Earth lead 296, Meter leads 296, Two-way lighting 332, Circuit lengths 344

Running cable

Long runs of cable are necessary to carry electricity from the consumer unit to all the sockets, light fittings and fixed appliances in the home. Along its route the cable must be fixed securely to the structure of the house, except in confined spaces to which there is normally no access, such as inside hollow walls.

Surface fixing

Though it may be unsightly, PVC-sheathed cable can be fixed to the surface of a wall or ceiling without any further protection. Fix it with plastic cable clips or metal buckle clips every 400mm (1ft 4in) on vertical runs, and every 250mm (10in) on horizontal runs. Try to keep the runs straight, and avoid kinks in the cable by keeping it on the drum as long as possible. If you do have to remove kinks, pull the cable round a thick dowel held in a vice.

If a cable seems vulnerable, or you simply want to hide it, run it inside plastic mini-trunking. Screw or stick the trunking to the wall (see far right), then insert the cable and clip on the flexible cover strip.

Plastic cable clip

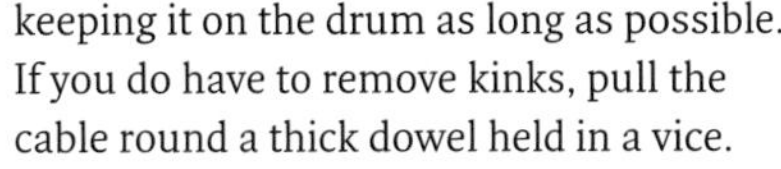

Metal buckle clip

Concealed fixing

While surface-fixed cable is acceptable in a cellar or in a garage or workshop, you wouldn't want to see it running across your living room walls or ceiling. From a decorative point of view, it's better to bury it in the plaster or hide it in a wall void. PVC-sheathed cable can be buried without further protection.

Where possible, run cable vertically to accessories such as switches or socket outlets, to avoid dangerous clashes with wall fixtures installed later. If that is not possible, you are permitted to run the cable horizontally directly from the switch or socket. However, if a cable isn't connected to a switch or socket on a wall in which it is concealed, then the cable must be within 150mm (6in) of the vertical or horizontal edges of the wall. Never, in any circumstances, run a buried cable diagonally across a wall.

Some people cover all buried cable with a plastic channel or run it inside conduit, but this is not required by the IEE Wiring Regulations. However, any cable that is buried in plastic conduit can, if necessary, be withdrawn later without having to damage the paintwork or wallcovering.

Mark out your cable runs on the plaster, making allowance for a 'chase', or channel, about 25mm (1in) wide for single cable. Cut both sides with a bolster and club hammer (**1**), and then use a cold chisel to hack out the plaster between the cuts. Normally, plaster is thick enough to conceal cable, but you may have to chop out some brickwork to get the depth. Clip the cable in the channel and, once you have checked that the installation is working properly, plaster over it (**2**). To avoid electric shock, ensure that the power is turned off before you use wet plaster round a switch or socket outlet.

1 Cut a chase in the plaster for the cable

2 Repair the plaster up to the switch or socket

Inside a hollow wall

To install a short cable run in a lath-and-plaster wall, hack the plaster away, fix the cable to the studs, and then plaster over again in the normal way.

Although you can run cable through the space between the two claddings of a partition wall, there is no way of doing this without at least some damage to the wall. Cut a hole in the plaster near the ceiling and directly above the spot where you are planning to position the switch, for example, and then drill a 12mm (½in) hole through the top head plate (**1**). Tap the wall directly below the hole to locate the nogging. Cut another hole in the plaster to reveal the top of the nogging, then drill a similar hole through it.

Pass a weight on a plumb line through both holes, down to where the switch will be. Tie the line to the cable, tape it and pull it through (**2**).

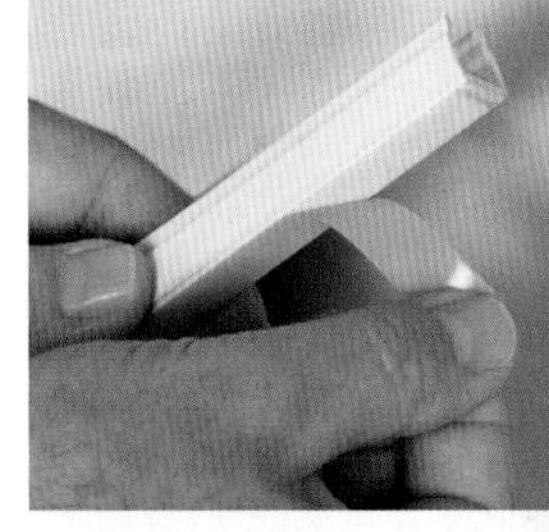

Plastic mini-trunking
Peel off the backing strip and stick the trunking to the wall plaster or paintwork.

1 Drill a hole through the head plate

2 Pull the cable through to the switch position

SEE ALSO > Repairing plaster 48–50, Head plate and noggings 151–2, Switching off 296

Running cable under floors

Power and lighting circuits are often concealed beneath floors. It isn't necessary to lift every floorboard to run a cable from one side of a room to the other: by lifting a board every 2m (6ft) or so, you should be able to pass the cable from one gap to the next with the help of a length of stiff wire bent into a hook at one end.

Lifting floorboards

Lifting tongued boards
Use a special floorboard saw to cut through the tongue on both sides of the board.

Drive a wide bolster chisel between two boards about 50mm (2in) from the cut end of one of them (**1**). Lever that board up with the bolster, then do the same on the other edge, working along the board until you have raised it far enough to wedge a cold chisel under it (**2**). Proceed along the board, raising it with the chisel, till the board is loose.

Full-length boards

If you have to lift a board that runs the whole length of the floor from one skirting to the other, start somewhere near the middle of the board, close to one of the floor joists – the nail heads indicate the positions of joists. Lever the board up and make a sawcut across it, centred on the joist, then lift the board in the normal way.

Lifting tongue-and-groove boards

You cannot lift a tongue-and-groove floorboard until you have cut through the tongues along both sides of the board with a floorboard saw, which has a blade with a rounded tip.

1 Prise up the floorboard with a bolster

2 Wedge the raised end with a cold chisel

Cutting a board next to a skirting

A joist that is fitted close to a wall may make it impossible to lift a floorboard in the normal way without damaging the bottom edge of the skirting.

In such a case, drill a starting hole through the floorboard alongside the joist, then insert the blade of a padsaw into the hole and cut across the board, flush with the side of the joist (**1**).

To support the cut end afterwards, nail a length of 50 x 50mm (2 x 2in) softwood to the joist. Hold the batten tightly against the undersides of the adjacent floorboards while you are fixing it, to ensure that the cut board will lie flush with the others (**2**).

1 Cut through a trapped board with a padsaw

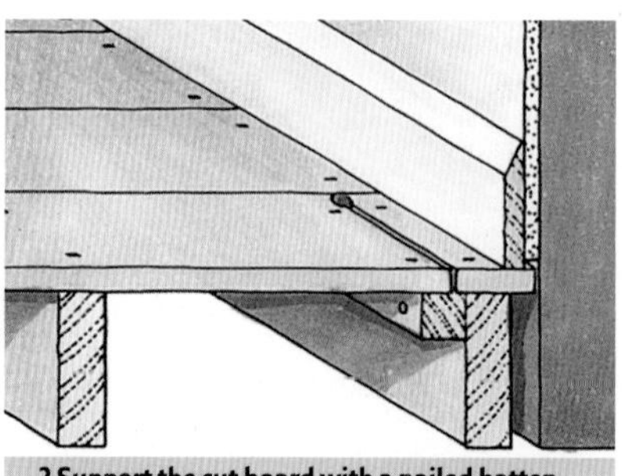

2 Support the cut board with a nailed batten

Solid floors

In a new concrete floor, you can lay conduit and then run cable through it before the concrete is poured.

In an existing solid floor, you can cut a channel for conduit, although it's hard work without an electric hammer and chisel bit; and if the floor is tiled, you will not want to spoil it for one or two socket outlets. An alternative is to drop spur cables, buried in the wall plaster, from the ring circuit in the upper floor.

Another way is to run cable through the wall from an adjacent area and channel it horizontally in the plaster just above the skirting. Yet another is to install plastic mini-trunking along the top of the skirting.

In the roof space

All wiring can be surface-run in the roof space; but as people may enter the space from time to time, you must make sure the cable is clipped securely to the joists or rafters. Run it through holes in the normal way, especially where joists are to be boarded over or in areas of access – around water tanks and near the entrance hatch, for example. If short lengths have to run on top of a joist, add mechanical protection.

Wiring overlaid by roof-insulation material has a slightly higher chance of heating up. Lighting circuits do not present a problem; but circuits on which there are heaters, cookers or shower units, for example, are more critical. Wherever possible, run cable over thermal insulation. If you cannot avoid running it under the material, use a heavier cable – but consult a qualified electrician to be on the safe side.

When expanded-polystyrene insulation is in contact with cable for a long time, it affects the plasticizer in the PVC sheathing on the cable. The plasticizer reacts with the polystyrene, forming a sticky substance on the cable. This becomes a dry crust, which can crack if the cable is moved. Although it gives the impression that the sheathing is cracking, scientific testing has shown that the cracking is in fact merely in the surface crust. On balance, however, it is best to keep cable away from polystyrene.

SEE ALSO > Removing skirting boards 218, Mini-trunking 303, Spur cables 301, 309, Padsaw 489

Running cable through the house
Use the most convenient method to run cable to sockets and switches.

1 Clip cable to battens nailed to roof timbers in the loft.

2 Junction boxes must be fixed securely.

3 In the joists near the hatch, run cable through holes.

4 Run cable over loft insulation.

5 To avoid damaging a finished floor, you can run a short spur through the wall from the next room.

6 When cable needs to run across the line of joists, drill holes 50mm (2in) below the joists' top edges.

7 When cable needs to run parallel to the joists, it can lie on the ceiling below.

8 Let cable drape onto the base below a suspended floor.

9 If it's impractical to run cable through a concrete floor, you can drop a spur from the floor above, but label the consumer unit accordingly.

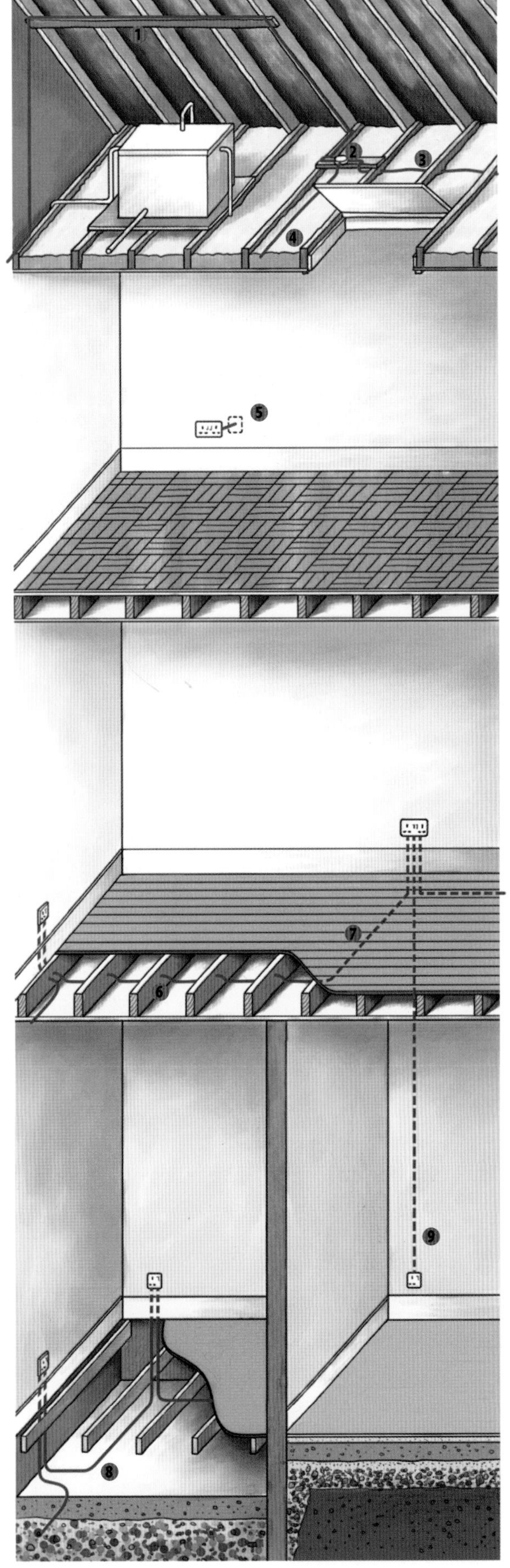

• **Labelling circuits**
If you have added sockets to a ring or radial circuit, make sure that the label in the consumer unit identifies the circuit to which the new sockets are connected.

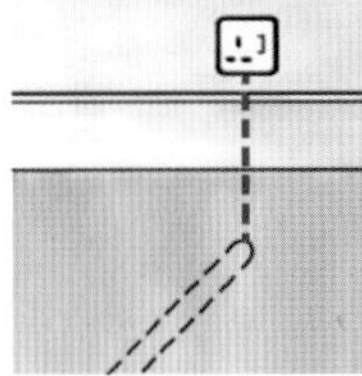

Burying cable in concrete
When you are laying a new concrete floor, take the opportunity to bury conduit for cable.

Running the cable

On the ground floor the cable can rest on the earth or on the concrete platform below the joists, provided that there won't normally be access to the space. Allow enough slack, so the cable isn't suspended above the platform, which might put a strain on fixings to junction boxes or socket outlets. For the same reason, beside junction boxes or other accessories, secure cable with clips to the side of the joist. Never attach circuit cable to gas or water pipes; and don't run it next to heating pipes, as the heat could melt the PVC sheathing and insulation.

When laying cable between a floor and the ceiling below, it can rest on the ceiling without any other fixing, so long as the cable runs parallel with the joists. If it runs at right angles to the joists, drill a series of 12mm (½in) holes, one through each joist along the intended cable run. The holes must be at least 50mm (2in) below the tops of the joists, so floorboard nails won't at some time be hammered through the cable. Similarly holes must be at least 50mm (2in) from the bottom edge of ceiling joists, in order to be certain that nails driven from below cannot pierce the cable. The space between joists is limited, but you can cut down a spade bit for use in a power drill.

Having marked out the position of a socket or fused connection unit, cut a channel from it down to the skirting board and, with a long masonry bit fitted in a power drill, remove the plaster from behind the skirting board. Use the drill at a shallow angle to loosen the debris, then finish the job with a slim cold chisel. Raking the debris out from below, with the same chisel, also helps to dislodge it.

Pass a length of stiff wire with one end formed into a hook down behind the skirting. Hook the cable and pull it through, at the same time feeding it from below with your other hand.

Drilling the joists
Shorten a spade bit so that your drill fits between the joists. Take care not to weaken joists.

Drilling behind skirting
Use an extra-long masonry bit to remove plaster behind a skirting board.

Preventing the spread of fire

Every time you cut an opening in the structure of the house for a cable, you are creating a potential route for fire and smoke to spread. After you have installed the cable, fill any holes between floors or rooms, using plaster or some other non-flammable material (not asbestos). Even where you pass a cable into a mounting box, you must fit a 'blind' grommet and cut a hole through it that is only just large enough for the cable.

SEE ALSO > Cable clips 303, Concealing cable 303, Fitting a grommet 307, Running a spur 309, Spade bit 500

Socket outlets

Whatever type of circuits exist in your home, only use 13amp square-pin sockets. All round-pin sockets are now out of date – and even if they are not actually dangerous at the moment, you should have them checked and consider changing your wiring to accommodate 13amp sockets. Before you start work on any socket, switch the power off at the consumer unit and remove the fuse or remove (or lock off) the MCB for the relevant circuit – then test the socket with a mains-voltage tester to make sure the power has been switched off.

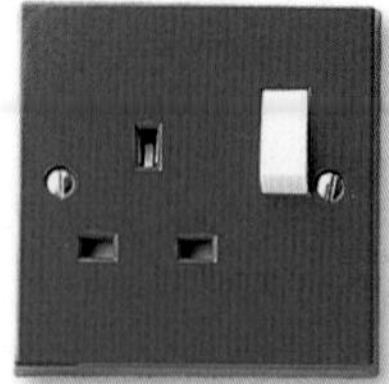

Switched single

Unswitched single

Single switched with indicator

Types of 13amp socket

Although all sockets are functionally similar, there are several variations to choose from. For most situations, you are likely to use either a single or double socket. Both are available switched or unswitched, and with or without neon indicators so you can see at a glance whether the socket is switched on. All of these are wired in the same way.

Another basic difference is in how the sockets are mounted. They can either be surface-mounted (screwed to the wall in a plastic box) or flush-mounted in a metal box buried in the wall, with only the faceplate visible.

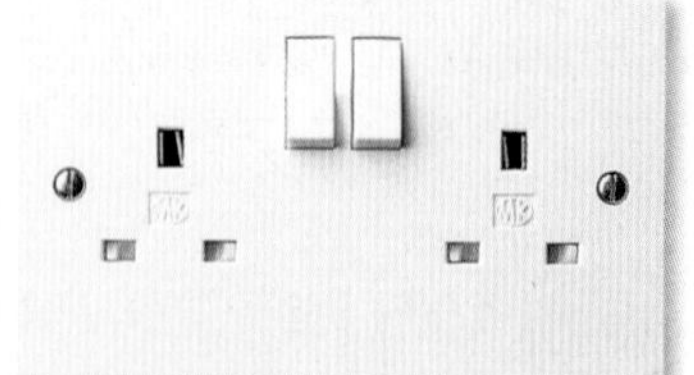

Switched double

Positioning socket outlets

Choose the most convenient positions for hi-fi and computer equipment, table lamps, television, and so on, and position your sockets accordingly. To avoid using adaptors or long leads, distribute the sockets evenly round living rooms and bedrooms, and wherever possible fit doubles rather than singles. Don't forget sockets for running a vacuum cleaner in hallways and on landings.

Most sockets are mounted just above the skirting, between 225 and 300mm (9in to 1ft) from the floor. There is a recommendation that sockets should be between 450mm and 1.2m (1ft 6in to 4ft) above the floor, to make them accessible to a person using a wheelchair. If you want to install additional sockets at this higher level, simply run short vertical spurs from existing sockets.

In the kitchen, fit at least four double sockets 150mm (6in) above the worktops. You will also need sockets for floor-standing appliances, such as refrigerators and dishwashers. You must inform your BCO before installing new sockets in a kitchen.

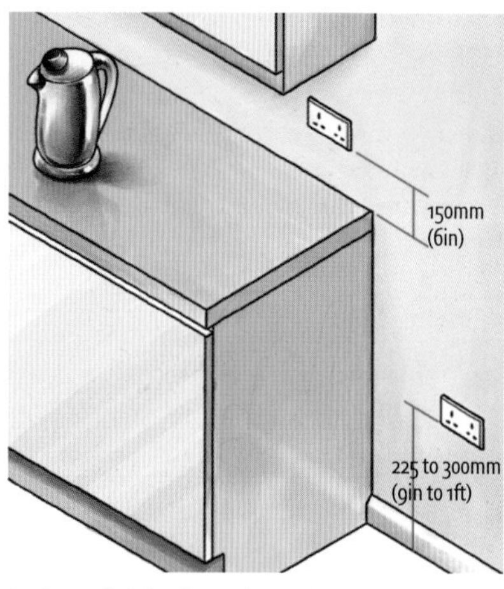

Optimum heights for socket outlets

Surface-mounted socket outlets

Triple sockets
Though relatively expensive, triple sockets are useful where several electrical appliances are grouped together.

Using a small screwdriver, break out the thin plastic webs that cover the fixing holes in the back of a plastic mounting box. Two fixings should be sufficient. The fixing holes are slotted to enable easy adjustment.

Hold the mounting box firmly against a masonry wall. Use a small spirit level to check that the box is upright, then mark the position of the fixing holes on the wall with a bradawl through the holes in the back of the box. Drill and plug the holes with No 8 wallplugs.

With a larger screwdriver and pliers, break out the plastic web covering the most convenient cable-entry hole in the box. For surface-run cable this will be in the side; for buried cable it will be the one in the base.

Feed the cable into the mounting box to form a loop about 75mm (3in) long, then fix the box to the wall with 32mm (1¼in) countersunk woodscrews. Finally, wire and fit the socket.

Leave a 75mm (3in) loop of cable at the box

Fixing to a hollow wall

On a dry-partition or lath-and-plaster wall, a surface-mounted box is fixed with any of the standard fixings used for hollow walls. Alternatively, use ordinary woodscrews if you are able to position the box over a stud, making sure you can feed the cable into the mounting box past the stud.

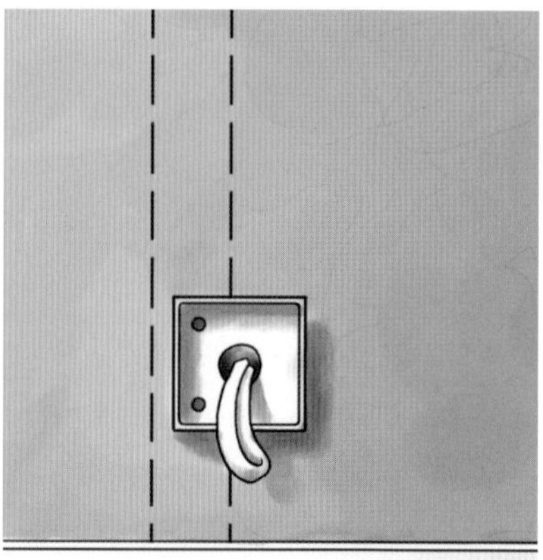

Feed the cable past the stud into the box

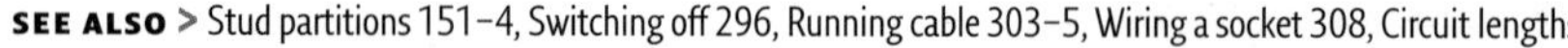

SEE ALSO > Stud partitions 151–4, Switching off 296, Running cable 303–5, Wiring a socket 308, Circuit lengths 344

Flush-mounted sockets

Sockets that are fitted flush with the wall are not only better in appearance but are also less likely to get broken by being struck with vacuum cleaners and children's toys.

Fixing to masonry

Hold the metal box against the wall and draw round it with a pencil (**1**), then mark a 'chase' (channel) running up from the skirting to the box's outline.

Using a bolster or cold chisel, cut away the plaster down to the masonry (**2**), within the marked area. With a masonry bit, bore several rows of holes down to the required depth across the recess for the box (**3**); then, using a cold chisel, cut away the masonry to the depth of the holes, so that the box will lie flush with the plaster.

Try the box in the recess. If it fits in snugly, mark the wall through the fixing holes in its back, then drill the wall for screw plugs. If you have made the recess too deep or the box rocks from side to side, apply some filler in the recess and press the box into it, flush with the wall and properly positioned. After about 10 minutes, ease the box out carefully and leave the filler to harden, so that you can mark, drill and plug the fixing holes through it.

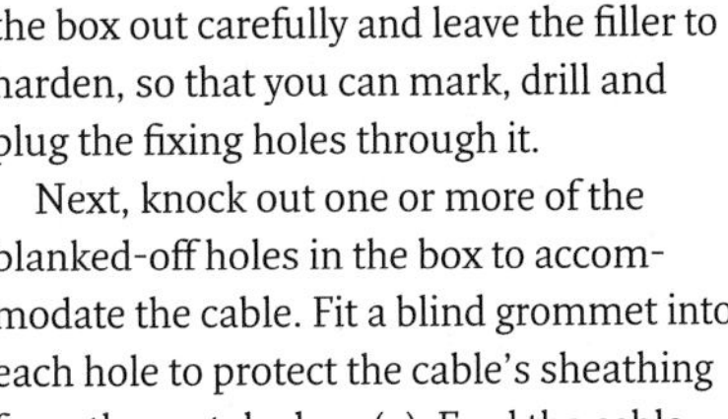

Next, knock out one or more of the blanked-off holes in the box to accommodate the cable. Fit a blind grommet into each hole to protect the cable's sheathing from the metal edges (**4**). Feed the cable into the box, and screw the box to the wall.

Plaster up to the box and over the cable chased into the wall; then, when the plaster has hardened, wire and fit the socket itself.

1 Draw round the mounting box

2 Chop away the plaster with a cold chisel

3 Drill out the blockwork with a masonry bit

4 Fit a soft grommet in the cable-entry hole

Fixing to plasterboard

In order to fit a flush socket to a wall made of plasterboard laid over wooden studs, trace the outline of the metal box on the wall and drill a hole in each corner. Then use a padsaw to cut out the recess for the box.

Punch out the blanked-off entry holes in the box and then line them with rubber grommets. Feed the cable into the box.

Clip dry-wall fixing flanges to the sides of the box – these will hold it in place by gripping the wall from inside (see also far right). Ease one side of the box, with flange, into the recess; and then, holding the screw-fixing lugs, manoeuvre the box until both flanges are behind the plasterboard and the box sits snugly in the hole. Wire and fit the socket and, as you tighten the fixing screws, the plasterboard will be gripped between the flanges and the faceplate.

Dry-wall fixing flanges clipped to a box

Lath-and-plaster

Older homes have partition walls covered with thin strips of wood, known as laths, that form a key for the wall plaster. If you want to fit a flush socket outlet in a lath-and-plaster wall, try to locate it over a stud or nogging.

Mark the position of the metal box, cut out the plaster, and saw away the laths with a padsaw. Try the box for fit, and if necessary chop a notch in the woodwork until the box lies flush with the wall surface. Feed in the cable; and screw the box to the stud before wiring and fitting the socket.

If you can't position the socket on a stud, cut away enough of the plaster and laths to make a slot in the wall running from one stud to the next. Between the studs, screw or skew-nail a stout softwood nogging to which you can fix the box. If necessary, set the batten back from the front edges of the studs, to make the mounting box lie flush with the wall surface. Feed the cable into the box and make good the surrounding plaster before you wire and fit the socket.

Notch a wall stud for the mounting box

Alternatively, nail a nogging between the studs

Cavity-wall box
Instead of fitting dry-wall fixing flanges to a standard mounting box, you can use a special cavity-wall box with integral hinged flanges that you push through the sides of the box after it is fitted.

SEE ALSO > Stud partitions 151–4, Repairing plaster 48–50, Switching off 296, Running cable 303–5, Wiring a socket 308

Replacing socket outlets

If you need to replace a broken or faulty socket, there are several options worth considering before you embark on the job. There is no need to notify your BCO before changing a damaged socket.

Simple replacement

Replacing a damaged socket with a similar one is a fairly straightforward job. A socket outlet of any style will fit into a metal mounting box, but check carefully when you substitute a socket that screws onto a surface-mounted plastic box. Although it will fit and function perfectly well, square corners and edges on either will not suit rounded ones on the other – in which case, you may also have to buy a new, matching box.

An unswitched socket outlet can be replaced with a switched one without any change to the wiring or fixing.

Switch off the power at the consumer unit and take out the circuit fuse or remove (or lock off) the MCB, then undo the fixing screws from the faceplate and pull the socket out of the box.

Loosen the terminals to free the conductors. Check that all is well inside the box, then connect the conductors to the terminals of the new socket. Fit the faceplate, using the original screws if those supplied with the new socket don't match the thread in the box.

Surface to flush

If you have to renew a surface-mounted socket for any reason, you may want to take the opportunity to replace it with a neater flush one.

Flying-earth leads
Short lengths of cable are sometimes found running from the earth terminal on the socket outlet to a terminal inside a metal mounting box. This does no harm and the leads can be left in place – but it is not necessary to provide them on your new wiring, provided the metal box has at least one fixed lug for attaching the faceplate. However, flying earths are necessary if the earth connection is provided by a metal conduit or sheath system.

Replacing a single socket with a double

One way to increase the number of socket outlets in a room is to substitute doubles for singles. Any single socket on a ring circuit can be replaced with a double without making any changes to the wiring.

A single socket on a spur can be replaced with a double one so long as it's the only socket on that spur – it needs to be connected to a single cable. To ensure that a socket fed by two cables is not one of two sockets on the same spur (which is no longer permitted), carry out the ring-circuit continuity test – see opposite.

Remember to switch off the power before making any alterations.

Surface to surface

Replacing a surface-mounted single socket with a surface-mounted double is easy.

Fixing a surface-mounted pattress over a flush box

Having removed the old socket outlet, simply fix the new, double box to the wall in the same place.

Flush to flush

Remove the old single socket and its metal box, then try the new double box over the hole. You can either centre the box over the hole or align it with one end, whichever is more convenient. Trace the outline of the box on the wall and cut out the brickwork.

Use a similar procedure to substitute a double socket for a single in a hollow wall, installing the socket by whichever method is most convenient.

Flush to surface

To avoid the disturbance to decor that is involved in installing a flush double socket, fit a special surface-mounted, pattress, which is made with two fixing holes that will line up with the fixing lugs on the buried metal box. You can use the blanked-off holes in the back of a standard plastic pattress for a similar purpose, but the special converter is much slimmer.

Surface to flush

To replace a single surface-mounted socket with a flush double, cut a recess for the metal box in the normal way.

Wiring a socket outlet

When a single cable is involved, strip off the sheathing in the normal way and connect the wires to the terminals: the blue wire to neutral – N; the brown one to live – L; and the earth wire, which you should insulate yourself with a sleeve, to earth – E (1). If necessary, fold the stripped ends over, so that no bare wire protrudes from a terminal.

Connecting to a ring-circuit cable

When connecting to a ring circuit, cut through the loop of cable and strip the sheathing from each half. Insert the bared ends of matching wires – live with live and so on – into the terminals (2). Slip sleeves onto the earth wires. After tightening the terminal screws, pull on each wire to ensure it is fixed securely.

Stiff cable can make it difficult to close the faceplate, so bend each conductor until it folds into the box. Locate the fixing screws and tighten them gradually in turn until the plate fits properly.

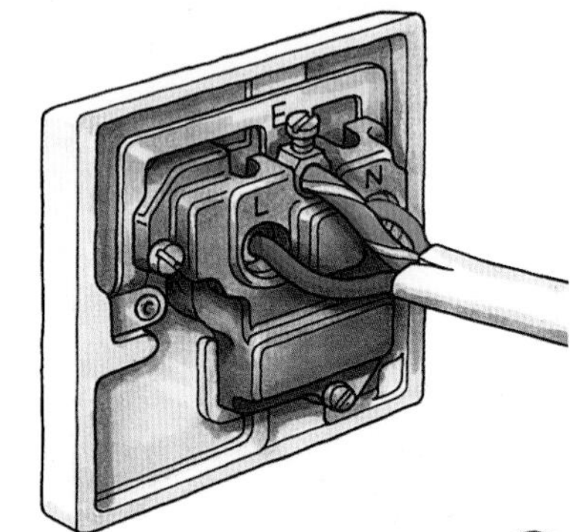

1 Wiring a socket outlet

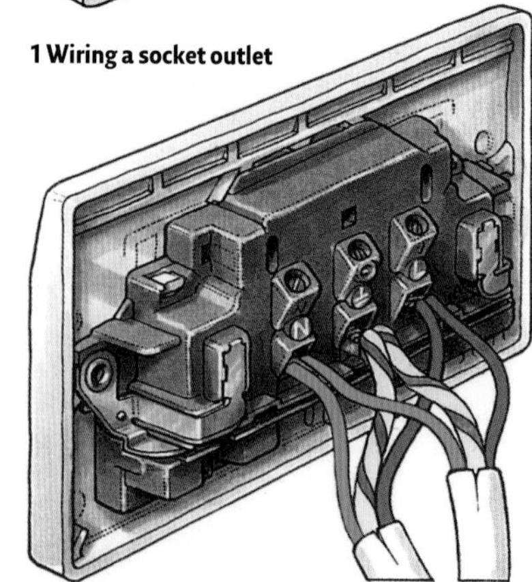

2 Connecting a socket to a ring circuit

SEE ALSO > Switching off 296, Stripping cable 302, Sockets 306, Mounting to a hollow wall 306–7, Recessing a mounting box 307

Adding a spur to a ring

If you need more socket outlets in a room, you can run 2.5mm² spur cables from a ring circuit and have as many unfused spurs as there are sockets or FCUs already on the ring. A spur can feed one single or one double socket.

A spur cable can be connected to any socket or fused connection unit on the ring circuit, or to a new junction box inserted in the circuit. If running a spur cable from an existing socket would mean disturbing the plaster, it will be more convenient to use a junction box; and if there is no socket outlet within easy reach of the proposed new one, using a junction box may save cable. If the cable is surface-run and you want to extend a row of sockets – behind a workbench, for example – then it will be simpler to connect the spur to a socket.

Examine the socket. If it is fed by a single cable, it is probably already on a spur; and if there are three cables in the socket, then it's already feeding a spur itself. What you need to look for is a socket that has two cables – but before you connect the spur to it, carry out a continuity test to make sure the socket is actually on a ring.

Testing for continuity

Isolate the ring circuit by switching off, then lock off the MCB or remove the fuse from the consumer unit. Unplug all appliances from the ring and switch off any fixed appliances connected to it.

Remove the socket, loosen the live terminal and separate the two red conductors. Leave the other wires in place. Using a multimeter set to its lowest resistance range, place one of the meter's probes on the socket's neutral terminal, and the other probe on the bared end of each red wire in turn. The meter reading should be high in each case.

Now touch one probe against the end of one of the red conductors, and the other probe against the end of the other red conductor. If the meter reading is low, you can be sure it is a ring circuit and you can safely add your spur.

Connecting to an existing socket

Fix the new socket, then wire it up in the normal way (see opposite) and run its spur cable to the existing socket outlet. Switch off the electricity and remove the existing socket. You may have to knock out another entry hole in order to feed the spur cable into the box. Prepare the conductors, and insert their bared ends together with those of the conductors of the ring circuit. Insert the wires in their terminals (brown/red – L; blue/black – N; and green-and-yellow – E). Replace the socket and switch the power on.

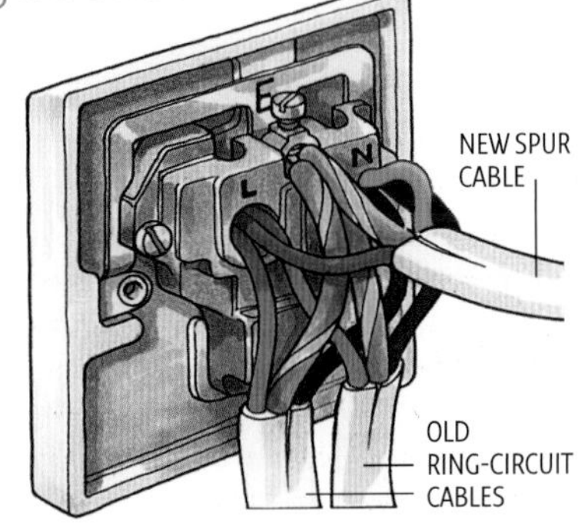

Taking a spur from an existing socket outlet

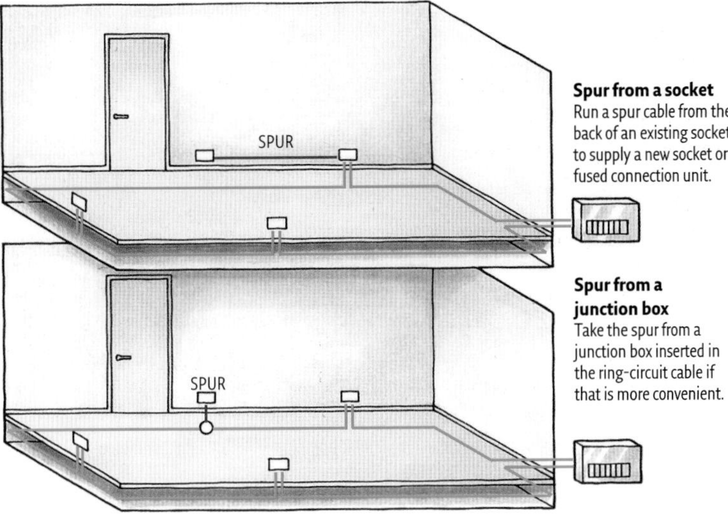

Spur from a socket
Run a spur cable from the back of an existing socket to supply a new socket or fused connection unit.

Spur from a junction box
Take the spur from a junction box inserted in the ring-circuit cable if that is more convenient.

Using a junction box

You will need a 30amp junction box with three terminals to connect to a ring circuit. It will have either knock-out cable-entry holes or a special cover that rotates to blank off unneeded holes. Lift a floorboard close to the new socket, so you can connect to the ring-circuit cable without stretching it.

Making a platform

Make a platform for the box by screwing a 100 x 25mm (4 x 1in) strip of wood to battens fixed to the joists (see right). Loop the ring-circuit cable over the platform before fixing it, so that the cable need not be cut for connecting up. Remove the cover, screw the junction box to the platform, and break out three cable-entry holes. If you do forget to loop the cable over the platform, simply cut the cable when you come to connect it up.

Connecting the ring-circuit cable

Turn off the power at the consumer unit, then rest the ring-circuit cable across the box and mark the amount of sheathing to remove. Slit it lengthwise and peel it off the conductors. Don't cut the live and neutral conductors, but slice away just enough insulation on each to expose a section of bare wire that will fit into a terminal (see right). Cut the earth wire and fit insulating sleeves on the two ends.

Remove the screws from all three of the terminals and lay the wires across them – with the earth wire in the middle terminal. Push the wires home with a screwdriver.

Connecting the spur

Having fitted and wired the new spur socket, run its cable to the junction box. Prepare the ends of the spur wires and attach them to the terminals of the box (see right). Attach the new brown wire to the terminal holding the old red ones, and the new blue wire to the terminal holding the old black ones. Connect all earth wires to the central terminal. Replace the terminal screws. Check that all the wires are secured, with the sheathing running into the junction box, then fit the cover.

Fix each cable to a nearby joist with cable clips, to take the strain off the terminals, then replace the floorboards. Switch the power back on and test the new socket.

Old colour coding
In a house built before 2005 you are likely to find that the existing cables are colour-coded black for neutral and red for live. The diagrams on this page show new-style spur cables being connected to old-style circuit cables.

Make a wooden platform for a junction box

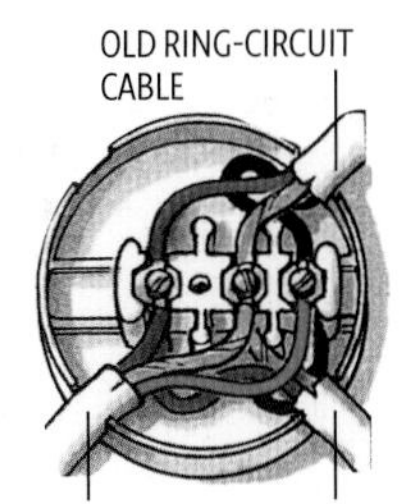

Taking a spur from a junction box

SEE ALSO > Testing circuits 288–9, Switching off 296, Important notes at consumer unit 298, Cables 302, Stripping cable 302, Running cable 303–5

Fixed appliances

Socket outlets are designed to enable portable appliances to be moved from room to room, but many electrical appliances are fixed to the structure of the house or stand in one position all the time. Such appliances may therefore just as well be wired into your electrical installation permanently. Indeed in some cases there is no alternative, and some require radial circuits of their own direct from the consumer unit.

Changing a fuse
With the electricity turned off, remove the retaining screw in the face of the fuse holder. Take the holder from the connection unit; prise out the old fuse and fit a new one; then replace the holder and the retaining screw.

Fused connection units

A fused connection unit (FCU) is basically a device for joining the flex (or sometimes cable) of an appliance to circuit wiring. The connection unit incorporates the added protection of a cartridge fuse similar to that found in a 13amp plug. If the appliance is connected by a flex, choose a unit that has a cord outlet in the faceplate.

Some fused connection units are fitted with a switch, and some of these have a neon indicator that shows at a glance whether they are switched on. A switched connection unit allows you to isolate the appliance from the mains.

All fused connection units are single (there are no double versions available) and have square faceplates that fit metal boxes for flush mounting or standard surface-mounted plastic boxes.

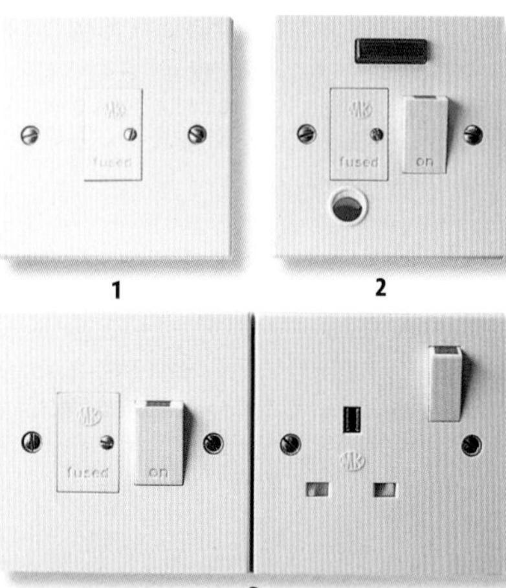

Fused connection units
1 Unswitched connection unit.
2 Switched unit with cord outlet and indicator.
3 Connection unit and socket outlet in a dual mounting box.

Mounting a fused connection unit

A fused connection unit is mounted in the same type of box as an ordinary socket outlet, and the box is fixed to the wall in exactly the same way. The unit can also be mounted in a dual box that is designed to hold two single units – for example, a standard socket outlet beside a connection unit. The socket is wired to the ring circuit, and the two units are linked together inside the box by a short 2.5mm² spur.

Dual mounting box

Wiring a fused connection unit

Before you wire a fused connection unit to the house circuitry, the power must be switched off at the consumer unit.

Fused connection units can be supplied by a ring circuit, a radial circuit or a spur. Some appliances are connected to the unit with flex, others with cable. Either way, the wiring arrangement inside the unit is the same. Units with cord outlets have clamps to secure the connecting flex.

An unswitched connection unit has two live (L) terminals – one marked 'Load' for the brown wire of the flex, and the other marked 'Mains' for the brown or red wire from the circuit cable. The blue wire from the flex and the blue or black wire from the circuit cable go to similar neutral (N) terminals; and both earth wires are connected to the unit's earth (E) terminal or terminals (**1**).

Switched connection units

A fused connection unit with a switch has two sets of terminals, too. Those marked 'Mains' are for the spur or ring cable that supplies the power; the terminals marked 'Load' are for the flex or cable from the appliance.

Wire up the flex side first, connecting the brown wire to the L terminal, and the blue one to the N terminal, both on the 'Load' side. Connect the green-and-yellow wire to the E terminal (**2**) and tighten the cord clamp.

Attach the circuit conductors to the 'Mains' terminals – brown or red to L, and blue or black to N; then sleeve the earth wire and take it to the E terminal (**2**).

If the fused connection unit is on a ring circuit, you need to fit two circuit conductors into each 'Mains' terminal and into the earth terminal.

Before screwing the unit to its box, make sure the wires are held firmly in the terminals and can fold away neatly.

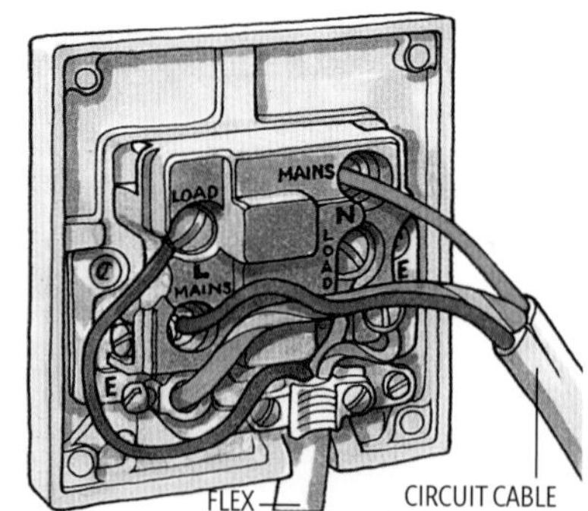

1 Wiring a fused connection unit

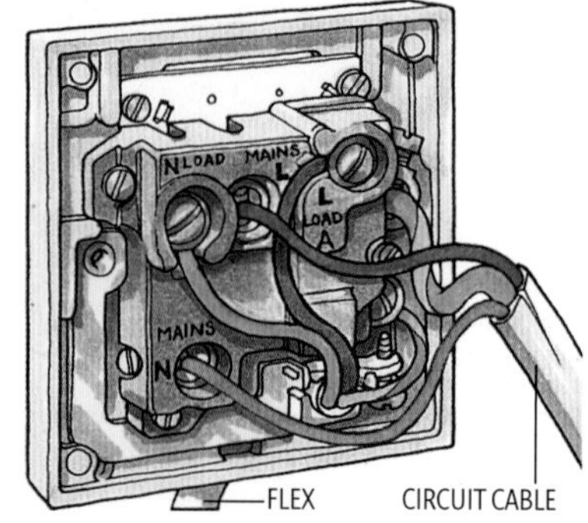

2 Wiring a switched fused connection unit

SEE ALSO > Stripping flex 293, Switching off 296, Power circuits 301, Stripping cable 302, Mounting boxes 306–7

Wiring small fixed appliances

Small permanent electrical appliances with ratings of up to 3000W (3kW) – wall heaters, extractor fans, cooker hoods and so on – can be wired into a ring or radial circuit by means of fused connection units. Although such appliances could be connected by means of 13amp plugs to socket outlets, the electrical contact would not be so good – and there is also some risk of fire with that type of permanent installation.

Flex outlets

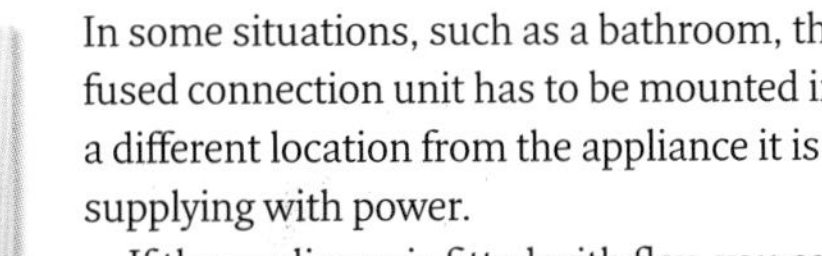

Flexible-cord outlet

In some situations, such as a bathroom, the fused connection unit has to be mounted in a different location from the appliance it is supplying with power.

If the appliance is fitted with flex, you can mount a flexible-cord outlet – 'flex outlet' next to the appliance – and then run a cable from the outlet to the FCU and connect it to the 'Load' terminals in the unit.

The flex outlet is mounted either on a standard surface-mounted box or flush on a metal box. At the back of the faceplate are three pairs of terminals to take the conductors from the flex and the cable.

(N) If you undertake work marked with this symbol, you must inform the BCO before starting – see FIRST THINGS FIRST.

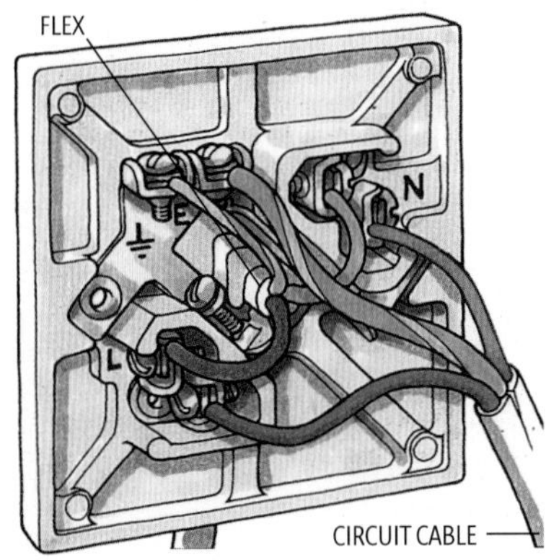

Wiring a flexible-cord outlet

Extractor fans (N)

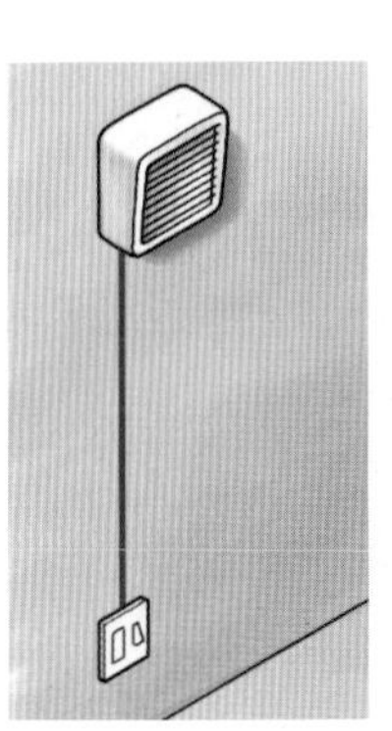

Wall-mounted fan
Run a 1.5mm² cable from a fused connection unit to a wall-mounted extractor fan.

To install a fan in a kitchen, mount a fused connection unit 150mm (6in) above the worktop. Run a cable to the fan or to a flexible-cord outlet next to it. If the fan has no integral switch, use a switched connection unit to control it. Fit a 3 or 5amp fuse, as recommended by the manufacturer.

If the fan's speed and direction are controllable, it may have a separate control unit – in which case you need to wire the connection unit to the control unit, following the manufacturer's instructions.

To install a fan in a bathroom, mount the fused connection unit outside the room and run the cable to the fan or flex outlet via a double-pole ceiling switch. The fan must be outside zones 0 and 1, and the circuit protected by a 30 milliamp RCD.

Fridges, dishwashers and washing machines (N)

There is no reason why you cannot plug an appliance like a fridge, dishwasher or washing machine into a standard socket outlet – except that in a modern kitchen such appliances are installed under worktops, and sockets mounted behind them are difficult to reach. It's therefore generally more convenient to mount a switched fused connection unit 150mm (6in) above the worktop, then connect it to the ring circuit and run a spur – using 2.5mm² cable – from the connection unit to a socket outlet mounted behind the appliance.

Cooker hoods (N)

Either mount a fused connection unit, fitted with a 3amp fuse, close to the cooker hood or mount the connection unit 150mm (6in) above the worktop and then run a 1.5mm² cable from the unit to a flexible-cord outlet beside the hood.

Instantaneous water heaters (N)

To provide an on-the-spot supply of hot water, you can install an instantaneous water heater above a washbasin or sink. Join a 3kW model by heat-resistant flex to a switched fused connection unit mounted out of reach of water splashes from the basin or sink.

If the heater is for use in a bathroom, wire it via a flex outlet to a ceiling pull-switch and then to a fused connection unit outside the bathroom. Fit a 13amp fuse in the unit.

Wire a 7kW water heater in the same way as a shower. If it is situated in the kitchen, you can use a double-pole wall switch to control it.

Waste-disposal units (N)

A waste-disposal unit is housed in the cupboard unit below the sink. Mount a switched fused connection unit 150mm (6in) above a worktop near the sink, but well out of reach of small children and splashes from the sink. From the unit, run a 1.5mm² cable to a flex outlet next to the waste-disposal unit. Clearly label the connection unit 'waste disposal', to avoid accidents. Fit a 13amp fuse.

Circuits for kitchen equipment
1 Connection units
2 Flex outlets
3 Socket outlets

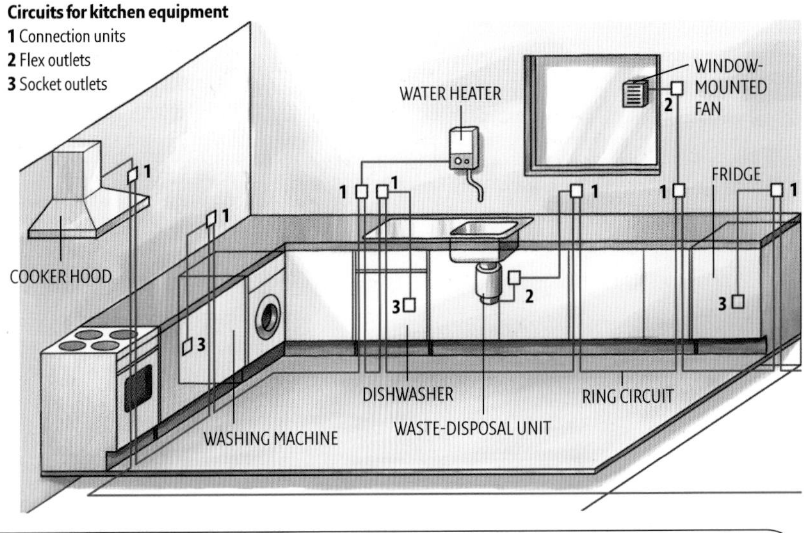

SEE ALSO > Building Regulations 284, Fans 277–8, Cooker hoods 279, Bathroom safety 286, Zones for bathrooms 287, Switching off 296, Fuses 299, Running cable 303–5, Running a spur 309, Double-pole switches 316, Circuit lengths 344, Waste-disposal units 388

Ⓝ If you undertake work marked with this symbol, you must inform the BCO before starting – see FIRST THINGS FIRST.

Shaver sockets Ⓝ

Special shaver socket outlets are the only kind of electrical socket allowed in bathrooms. This type of socket contains a transformer that isolates the user side of the unit from the mains, reducing the risk of an electric shock.

This type of socket has to conform to the exacting British Standard BS EN 60742 Chapter 2, Section 1. However, there are shaver sockets that do not have an isolating transformer and therefore don't conform to this standard. These are safe to install and use in a bedroom – but must not be fitted in a bathroom.

• **RCD protection**
When installing any electrical appliance in a bathroom, the circuit must be protected by a 30 milliamp RCD.

Shaver unit for use in a bathroom

You can wire a shaver socket from a junction box on an earthed lighting circuit or from a fused connection unit, fitted with a 3amp fuse, on a ring-circuit spur. If you're installing the shaver socket in a bathroom, then the fused connection unit must be positioned outside the room. Run a 1.5mm² two-core-and-earth cable from the connection unit to the shaver socket; then connect the conductors: brown to L and blue to N. Sheathe the earth wire with a green-and-yellow sleeve and connect it to the earth (E) terminal.

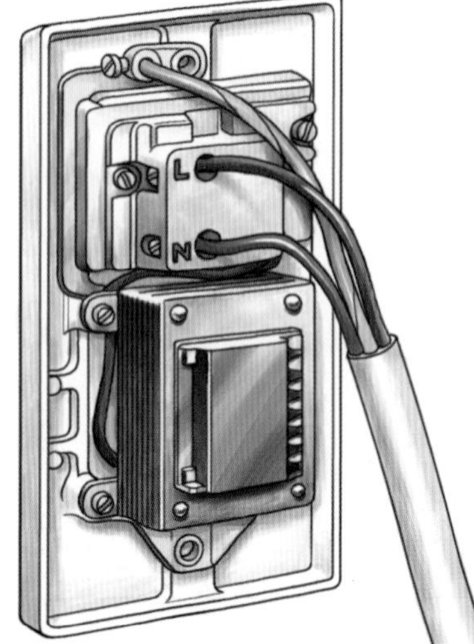

Wiring a shaver unit

Heated towel rails Ⓝ

When you're installing a heated towel rail in a bedroom, the appliance can be wired to a switched fused connection unit mounted next to the appliance, at a height of about 225 to 300mm (9in to 1ft) from the floor. For a towel rail of 1kW or less, fit a 5amp fuse in the connection unit; otherwise fit a 13amp fuse.

Heated towel rail in a bathroom

The Wiring Regulations covering other electrical equipment situated in bathrooms also apply to heated towel rails. The fused connection unit must be mounted outside the bathroom and wired to a convenient mains power circuit. Because the towel rail is mounted inside the bathroom, the circuit supplying power must be protected by a 30 milliamp RCD.

Run a spur cable from the fused connection unit to a flexible-cord outlet mounted beside the towel rail. Connect the cable's brown conductor to the flex outlet's live (L) terminal, and the blue conductor to the neutral (N) terminal.

Cover the bare copper earth wire with green-and-yellow sleeving and then attach it to the outlet's earth terminal.

Connect the flex from the towel rail similarly – brown conductor to live and blue to neutral. Connect the green-and-yellow-insulated earth conductor to the earth terminal.

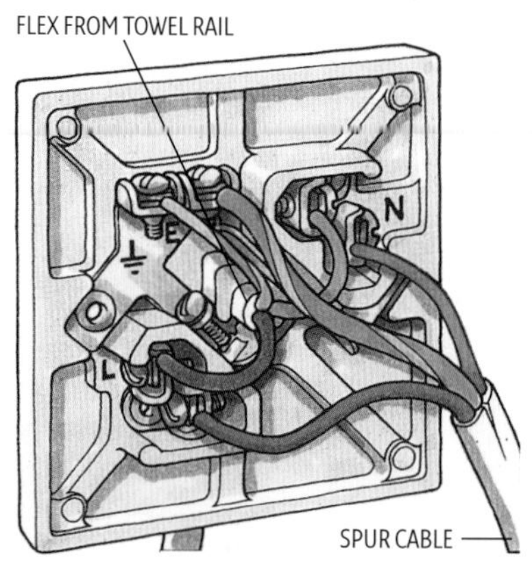

Wiring the flex outlet in a bathroom

Electric towel rail installed in a stylish modern bathroom

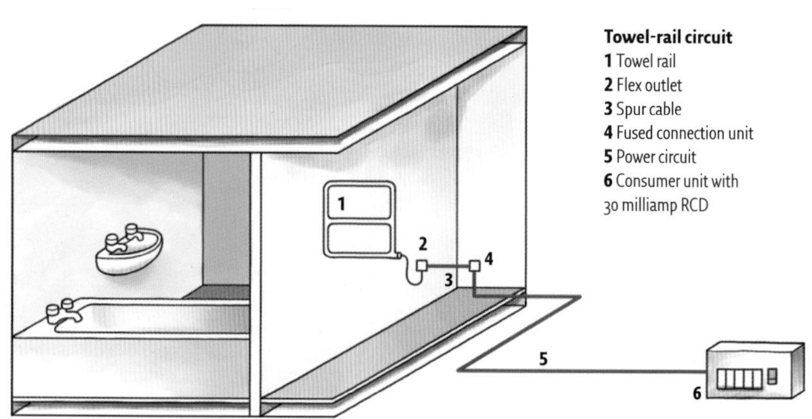

Towel-rail circuit
1 Towel rail
2 Flex outlet
3 Spur cable
4 Fused connection unit
5 Power circuit
6 Consumer unit with 30 milliamp RCD

SEE ALSO > Building Regulations 284, Bathroom safety 286, Zones for bathrooms 287, Switching off 296, Fuses 299, Running cable 303–5, Running a spur 309, Fused connection units 310, Flex outlets 311, Circuit lengths 344

Door bells and chimes

Whether you choose a door bell, a buzzer or a set of chimes, there are no practical differences that affect the way they are installed.

Wiring a bell push

Door bells

Most door bells are of the 'trembler' type. When electricity is supplied to the bell – that is when someone presses the button at the door – it activates an electromagnet, which causes a striker to hit the bell. But as the striker moves to the bell it breaks a contact, cutting off power to the magnet – so the striker swings back, makes contact again and repeats the process, going on for as long as the button is depressed. This type of bell can be operated by battery or (if it is an AC bell) by a mains transformer, which may be situated inside the unit or mounted separately.

Buzzers

A buzzer operates on exactly the same principle as a trembler bell, but in a buzzer the striker hits the magnet itself instead of a bell.

Wireless door chimes
You can continue using the socket even when a wireless door chime is plugged into it.

Chimes

A set of ordinary door chimes has two tubes or bars tuned to different notes. Between them is a solenoid, containing a spring-loaded plunger which acts like the trembler striker described above. Most chimes can be run from a battery or transformer.

Bell pushes

Pressing a bell push completes the circuit that supplies power to the bell. The bell push is in effect a switch that is operated by holding it in the 'on' position. Inside it are two contacts, to which the circuit wires are connected. One contact is spring-loaded, touching the other when the button is depressed, to complete the circuit, and then springing back again when the button is released.

Illuminated bell pushes incorporate a tiny bulb, which enables you to see the bell push in the dark. These have to be operated from a mains transformer – as the power to the bulb, although only a trickle, is on continuously and would soon drain a battery. Luminous types glow at night without a power supply.

Wireless bell pushes

To remove the need for wiring, use a bell push that sends a radio signal to its bell. The bell can be moved around the house; and you can add a second bell, if required.

Batteries or transformer?

Some bells and chimes house batteries inside the casing, while other types incorporate a built-in transformer that reduces the 230V mains electricity to the very low voltages needed for this kind of equipment. For many door bells or chimes you can use either method. Most of them take either two, three or four 1½V batteries, but some need a 4½V battery that is housed separately.

The transformers sold for use with door-bell systems have three low-voltage tappings (3V, 5V and 8V), to cater for various needs. Generally 3V and 5V connections are adequate for bells or buzzers; the 8V tapping is suitable for many sets of chimes.

However, some door chimes require a higher voltage, and for these you will need a transformer that has 4V, 8V and 12V tappings. A bell transformer must be designed in such a way that the full mains voltage cannot cross over to the low-voltage wiring.

Circuit wiring

The battery, bell push and bell are linked by two-core insulated 'bell wire'. This fine wire is usually surface-run, but can be run under floors. Bell wire is also used for connecting a bell and bell push to a transformer.

Connect a BS 3535 Part 2 double-insulated transformer to a junction box or ceiling rose on a lighting circuit with 1.5mm² two-core-and-earth cable. As no earth is required for a double-insulated transformer, cut and tape back the earth wire at the transformer end. Or you can run a spur from a ring circuit in 2.5mm² two-core-and-earth cable to an unswitched fused connection unit, fitted with a 3amp fuse; then run a 1.5mm² two-core-and-earth cable from the connection unit to the transformer's 'Mains' terminals.

Installing a system

The bell itself can be installed in any convenient position. Keep the bell-wire runs as short as possible, especially for a battery-operated bell. With a mains-powered bell you will want to avoid long runs of cable – so position the transformer where it can be wired simply. A cupboard under the stairs is usually a good place.

Drill a small hole in the doorframe and pass the bell wire through to the outside. Fix the conductors to the terminals of the bell push, then screw it over the hole.

If the battery is housed in the bell casing, there will be two terminals for attaching the other ends of the wires. Either wire can go to either terminal. If the battery is separate from the bell, run the bell wire from the push to the bell. Separate the conductors, cut one of them and join each cut end to a bell terminal. Run the wire on to the battery and attach it to the terminals.

Wiring to a transformer

If you are wiring to a transformer, proceed as above but connect the bell wire to whichever two of the three terminals combine to provide you with the necessary voltage. Some bells and chimes require separate lengths of bell wire, one from the bell push and another from the transformer. Fix the wires to terminals in the bell housing, following the maker's instructions.

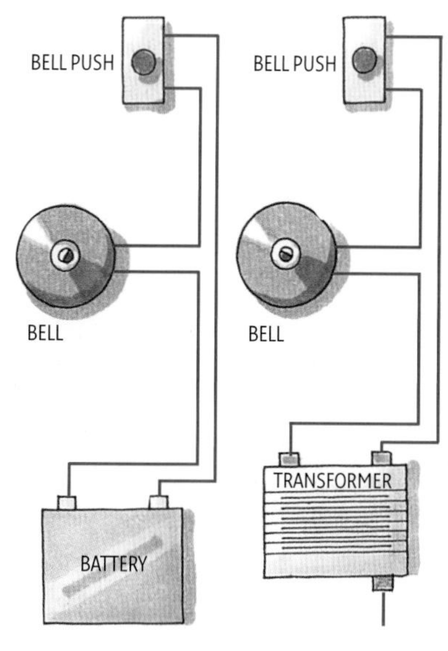

1 Battery circuit **2 Transformer circuit**

SEE ALSO > Switching off 296, Consumer units 298, Running cable 303–5, Running a spur 309, Fused connection units 310, Connection to a light circuit 331

Wiring a cooker

Appliances, such as cookers, that have a power load greater than 3000W (3kW) must have their own radial circuits connected directly to the consumer unit, with separate fuses protecting them.

Cooker circuits

Small table cookers and separate ovens that rate no more than 3kW can be connected to a ring circuit by a fused connection unit or even by means of a 13amp plug and socket. However, most cookers are much more powerful and must be installed on their own circuits.

Cooker control unit with socket

Basic control unit

Terminal outlet box

The radial circuit

A cooker must be connected to a radial circuit – a single cable that runs back to the consumer unit. Between the cooker and the consumer unit, you must install a cooker control unit (which is basically a double-pole isolating switch). Some cooker control units incorporate a single 13amp socket outlet that can be used for appliances such as an electric kettle.

When cookers up to 13.5kW are connected to a control unit that has a socket, the radial circuit must be run using $4mm^2$ two-core-and-earth cable and it must be protected by a 30amp fuse or a 32amp MCB. Larger cookers, up to 18kW, can be connected to a similar circuit, but you must use $6mm^2$ two-core-and-earth cable and a 40amp MCB – you cannot use a fuse. (See CIRCUITS: MAXIMUM LENGTHS).

With either of the circuits described above, it's safe to use a unit that does not have a socket outlet. In fact, if you use a socketless unit, the Wiring Regulations allow you to run longer circuit lengths and to use a fuse with the larger cookers (instead of an MCB). If either of these is desirable, consult an electrician.

Connecting to the consumer unit

You can either use an existing fuseway that is already protecting a cooker circuit or, if there's an empty fuseway in your consumer unit, you can use this for the new cooker circuit. If your consumer unit has fuses instead of MCBs, before installing the cooker circuit make sure they are cartridge fuses and not the rewirable type.

Positioning the cooker control unit

The control unit must be situated within 2m (6ft 6in) of the cooker. The unit must never be installed directly above a cooker, hob or oven, and it has to be easily accessible – so don't install the unit inside a cupboard or under a worktop.

A single control unit can serve both sections of a split-level cooker, with separate cables running to the hob and the oven, provided that the control unit is within 2m (6ft 6in) of both parts. (If this isn't possible with your cooker, you will need to install a separate control unit for each part.) The connecting cables must be of the same size as the cable used in the radial circuit. If the combined total of oven and hob exceeds 15kW, the circuits must be increased to $6mm^2$ two-core-and-earth cable

A freestanding cooker will have to be moved from time to time for cleaning, so wire it with sufficient cable to allow it to be moved well out from the wall. The cable is connected to a terminal outlet box, which is screwed to the wall about 600mm (2ft) above floor level. A fixed cable runs from the outlet box to the cooker control unit.

Circuit for freestanding cooker
1 Cooker
2 Terminal outlet box
3 Control unit
4 Radial circuit
5 Consumer unit

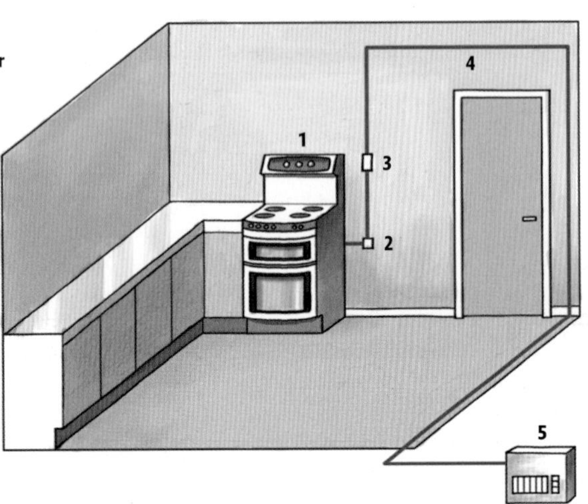

Circuit for separate hob and oven
1 Oven
2 Hob
3 Control unit
4 Radial circuit
5 Consumer unit

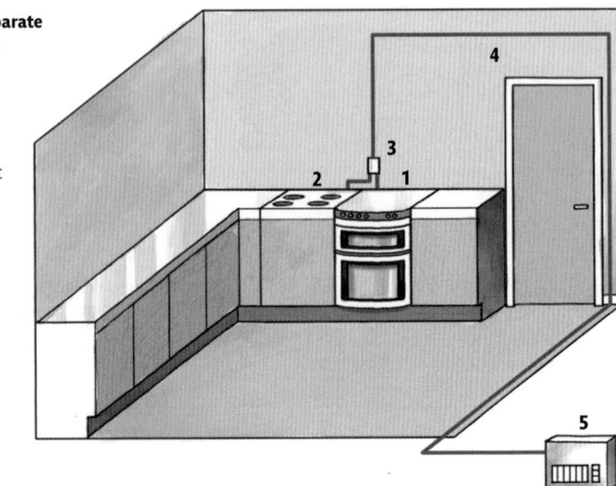

SEE ALSO > Consumer units 298, Circuits fuses 299, Circuit lengths 344

Wiring a freestanding cooker Ⓝ

Prepare a surface-mounted box for the cooker control unit by knocking out the cable-entry holes, and then screw it to the wall. If it's to be flush-mounted, cut a hole in the plaster and brickwork for a metal box. Cable-entry holes in metal boxes must be lined with blind grommets.

Running cable

Run the supply cable from the consumer unit, taking the most economical route to the cooker. If the cable is to be buried in the plaster, cut a vertical chase in the wall up to the cooker control unit, then cut a similar chase for the cable running to the terminal outlet box.

Connecting up the control unit

Feed the circuit cable and cooker cable into the control unit, then strip and prepare the conductors for connection.

There are two sets of terminals in the control unit: one marked 'Mains' for the circuit conductors, and the other marked 'Load' for the cooker cable. Run the brown wires to the L terminals, and the blue ones to the terminals marked N. Put green-and-yellow sleeves on both earth conductors and connect them to the E terminal (**1**). When all conductors are fixed securely, screw the faceplate to the mounting box.

1 Wiring the cooker control unit
The faceplate has to be removed in order to wire some cooker control units.

Wiring the terminal outlet box

Run the cable down the wall from the cooker control unit to the terminal outlet box. This box has a set of terminals for connecting both cables – the one from the control unit and the other from the cooker itself.

Prepare the wires from both cables and insert them in the same terminals (**2**), matching colour for colour. Secure the sheathed part of both cables with the clamp, and then screw the plastic faceplate onto the outlet box.

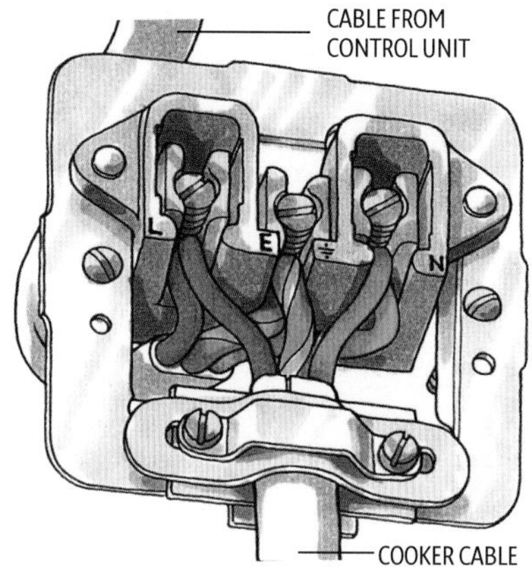

2 Wiring the terminal outlet box

Wiring the cooker

A panel on the back of the cooker has to be removed to gain access to the terminals. Prepare the end of the cable ready for connection, and release the cable clamp so that the cable can be slipped under it.

Undo the terminal nuts, so you can trap the bared end of each conductor under the terminal clamp; the brown cable conductor is connected to the live (L) terminal, and the blue conductor to the neutral (N) terminal (**3**); then tighten both terminal nuts. Sleeve the copper earth conductor and connect it to the earth (E) terminal.

Tighten the cable clamp and replace the back panel.

3 Connecting the cable to the cooker terminals

Wiring a hob and oven Ⓝ

The procedure for wiring a separate hob and oven is similar to that described for a freestanding cooker, but because the appliances are fixed permanently in place there is no need to provide terminal outlet boxes. Instead, the cables running from the cooker control unit are wired directly to the hob and oven.

Connecting the cables

At the cooker control unit, connect the incoming radial-circuit cable to the 'Mains' terminal, as described far left.

Feed the cables from the appliances into the cooker control unit, then strip the conductors and prepare them for connection. Connect the bared ends of both brown conductors to the same live (L) terminal on the 'Load' side of the control unit. Similarly, insert both of the blue conductors together into the same neutral (N) terminal.

Cover the two earth conductors with green-and-yellow sleeving and then connect them to the common earth (E) terminal. Check that all conductors are fixed securely, before you screw the faceplate in place.

Connecting to hob and oven

Connect the hob and oven to their respective cables as described left.

Ⓝ If you undertake work marked with this symbol, you must inform the BCO before starting – see FIRST THINGS FIRST.

At the consumer unit

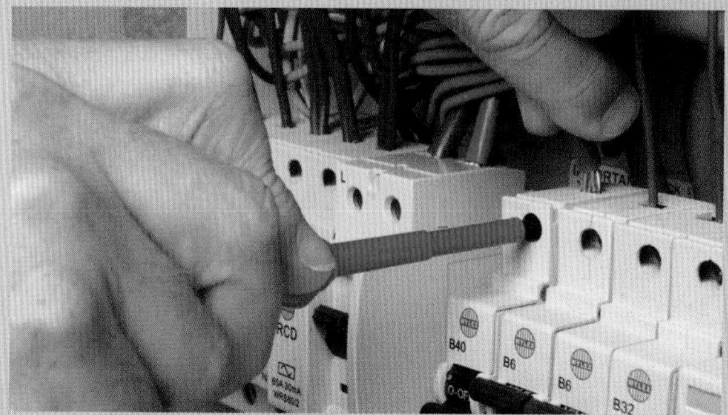

Once you have tested the new radial circuit yourself, you can connect the prepared cable to the consumer unit.

With the main switch turned off, remove the fuse carrier or switch off the MCB. You must turn off the control unit and cooker controls, too.

Sheathe the incoming earth conductor in green-and-yellow sleeving and then connect it to a spare terminal in the earth block. Connect the blue conductor to a spare terminal in the neutral block. Finally, connect the brown conductor to the 'Load' terminal on the MCB or fuseway.

Having ruled out any obvious faults yourself, ask the BCO to carry out the necessary tests before you switch on and use the new circuit.

SEE ALSO > Building Regulations 284, Testing circuits 288–9, Consumer units 298, Stripping cable 302, Running cable 303 – 5, Flush mounting 307,

Wiring a shower

An electrically heated shower unit is plumbed into the mains water supply. The flow of water operates a switch to energize an element that heats the water on its way to the shower sprayhead. Because there's so little time to heat the flowing water, instantaneous showers use a heavy load – from 6 to 10.8kW. Consequently, an electrically heated shower unit has to have a separate radial circuit, which must be protected by a 30 milliamp RCD. In addition, for showers up to 10.3kW the radial circuit must be protected by a 45amp MCB or fuse, either in a spare fuseway at the consumer unit or in a separate single-way consumer unit; a 10.8kW shower needs a 50amp MCB. The circuit cable needs to be $10mm^2$ two-core-and-earth.

The shower unit itself has its own on/off switch, but there must also be a separate isolating switch in the circuit. This must not be accessible to anyone using the shower, so you need to install a ceiling-mounted 45amp double-pole pull-switch (a 50amp switch is required for a 10.8kW shower). The switch has to be fitted with an indicator that tells you when the switch is 'on'.

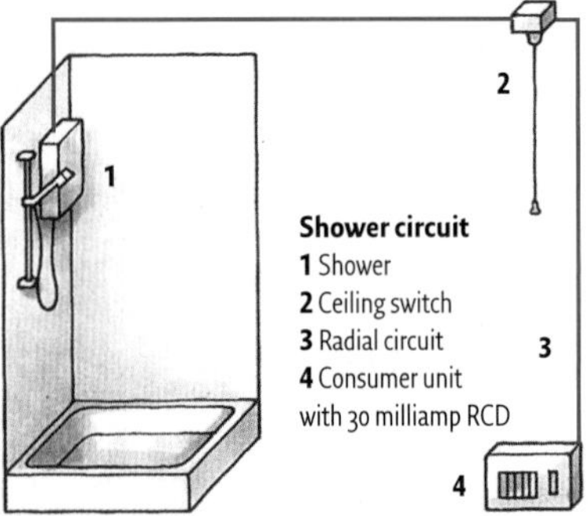

Shower circuit
1 Shower
2 Ceiling switch
3 Radial circuit
4 Consumer unit with 30 milliamp RCD

Connect the live and neutral conductors from the consumer unit to the switch's 'Mains' terminals, and those of the shower cable to the 'Load' terminals. Connect both earth wires, which have to be covered with green-and-yellow sleeving, to the single earth terminal on the switch.

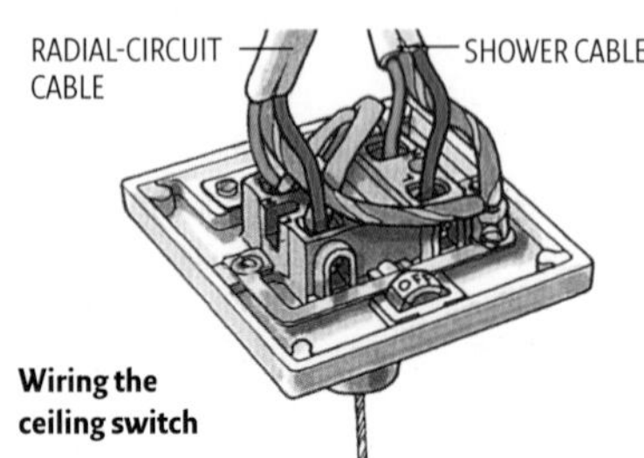

Wiring the ceiling switch

The shower unit itself must be wired according to the manufacturer's instructions. The unit and all metal pipes and fittings must be bonded to earth.

Immersion heaters

The water in a storage cylinder can be heated by an electric immersion heater, providing a central supply of hot water for the whole house. In many centrally heated homes the water is heated indirectly by the boiler, and an immersion heater is used as a backup for when the central heating has been switched off.

Types of immersion heater

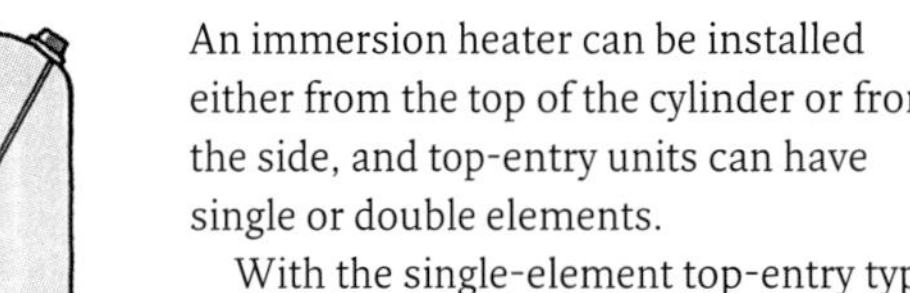

1 Single element

2 Double element

3 Side-entry elements

An immersion heater can be installed either from the top of the cylinder or from the side, and top-entry units can have single or double elements.

With the single-element top-entry type, the element extends down almost to the bottom of the cylinder, so that all of the water is heated whenever the heater is switched on (**1**).

For economy, one of the elements in the double-element type is a short one for top-up heating, while the other is a full-length element that heats the entire contents of the cylinder (**2**). A double-element heater that has a single thermostat is called a twin-element heater; one with a thermostat for each element is known as a dual-element heater.

Side-entry elements are of identical length. One is positioned near to the bottom of the cylinder, and the other a little above halfway up (**3**).

Adjusting the water temperature

The thermostat that controls the maximum temperature of the water is set by adjusting a screw inside the cap covering the terminal box.

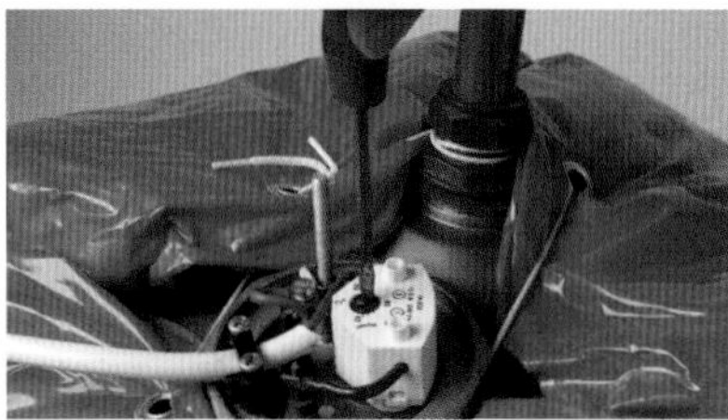
Adjusting the thermostat

Heating water on the night rate

If you have storage heaters, your electricity company supplies you with cheap-rate power for seven hours sometime between midnight and 8.00 a.m., the exact period being at the discretion of the company. This scheme is called Economy 7.

If you have a cylinder that is large enough to store hot water for a day's requirements, you can benefit by heating all your water during the Economy 7 hours. For the water to retain its heat all day, the cylinder must be insulated.

If your cylinder is already fitted with an immersion heater, you can use the existing wiring by fitting an Economy 7 programmer, a device that will switch your immersion heater on at night and heat up the whole cylinder. Then if you run out of hot water during the day, you can always adjust the programmer's controls to boost the temperature briefly. You can make even greater savings if you have two side-entry immersion heaters or a dual-element one. The programmer will switch on the longer element, or the bottom one, at night; if the water needs heating during the day, then the upper or shorter element is used.

Economy 7 without a programmer

You can have a similar setup without a programmer if you wire two separate circuits for the elements. The upper element is wired to the daytime supply, while the lower one is wired to its own switchfuse unit and operated by the Economy 7 time switch during the hours of the night-time tariff only. A setting of 75°C (167°F) is recommended for the lower element, and 60°C (140°F) for the upper one. If your water is soft or your heater elements are sheathed in titanium or incoloy, you can raise the temperatures to 80°C (175°F) and 65°C (150°F) respectively without unduly reducing the life of the elements.

Leave the upper unit switched on permanently. It will only heat up if the thermostat detects a temperature of 60°C (140°F) or less, which should happen rarely if the cylinder is properly insulated.

SEE ALSO > Reducing electricity bills 282–3, Building Regulations 284, Bonding to earth 286, Zones for bathrooms 287, Consumer units 298, Circuit fuses 299, Running cable 303–5, Circuit lengths 344, Plumbing a shower 383

The circuit

The majority of immersion heaters are rated at 3kW; but although you can wire most 3kW appliances to a ring circuit, an immersion heater is regarded as using 3kW continuously, even though rarely switched on all the time. A continuous 3kW load would seriously reduce a ring circuit's capacity, so immersion heaters must have their own radial circuits.

The circuit needs to be run in 2.5mm² two-core-and-earth cable protected by a 15amp fuse or 16amp MCB. Each element must have a special double-pole isolating switch mounted near the cylinder; the switch should be marked 'water heater' and have a neon indicator. A 2.5mm² heat-resistant flexible cord runs from the switch to the immersion heater.

If the cylinder is situated in a bathroom, the switch must be outside zones 0 to 2. If this precludes a standard water-heater switch, fit a 20amp ceiling-mounted pull-switch with a mechanical on/off indicator. When installing any electrical appliance in a bathroom, the circuit must be protected by a 30 milliamp RCD.

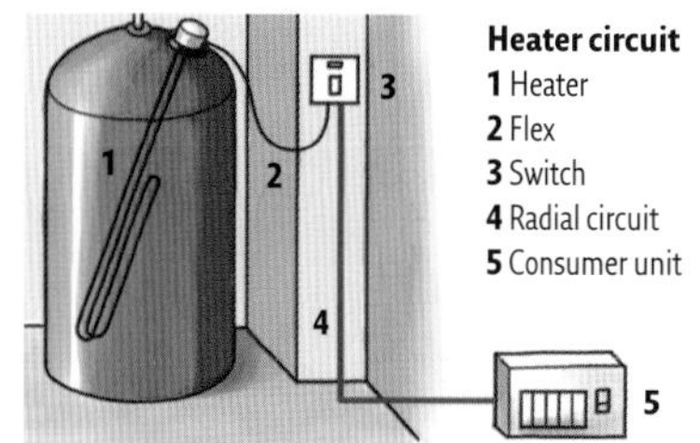

Heater circuit
1 Heater
2 Flex
3 Switch
4 Radial circuit
5 Consumer unit

20amp switch for an immersion heater

(N) If you undertake work marked with this symbol, you must inform the BCO before starting – see FIRST THINGS FIRST.

Wiring the switch and heater (N)

Feed the circuit cable into the switch mounting box fixed to the wall, and connect it to the 'Mains' terminals – brown to L, blue to N. Sheathe the earth wire in a green-and-yellow sleeve, then connect it to the common earth terminal (1). Prepare a heat-resistant flex for the switch. Connect the green-and-yellow earth wire to the common earth terminal and the other wires to the 'Load' terminals – brown to L, and blue to N. Tighten the flex clamp before screwing the switch faceplate in place.

The flex from the switch goes to the heater. Feed it through the hole in the cap, and then prepare the wires for connection.

Connect the brown flex wire to one of the terminals on the thermostat (the other one is already connected to the wire running to the live terminal on the heating element). Connect the blue wire to the neutral terminal, and the green-and-yellow wire to the earth terminal (2). Replace the cap, which covers all the heater terminals and the thermostat.

Connecting to the consumer unit

Run the circuit cable from the cylinder cupboard to the fuse board. With the power switched off, connect the cable to an empty fuseway in the consumer unit (see WIRING A COOKER). Although the consumer unit is switched off, the cable between the main switch and the meter will remain live – so take special care.

Having ruled out any obvious faults yourself, ask the BCO to carry out the necessary tests before you switch on and use the new circuit.

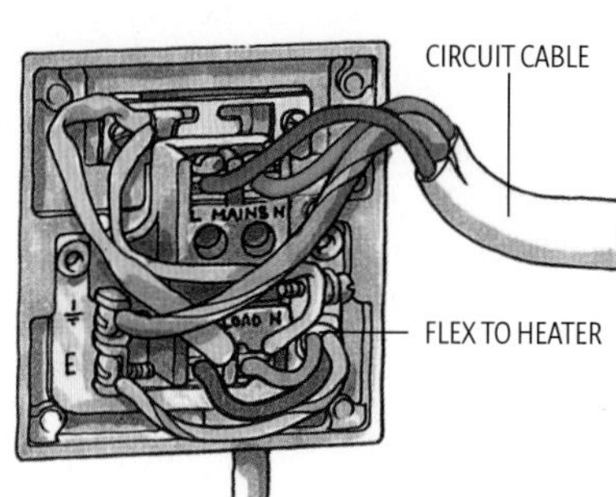

1 Wiring the switch

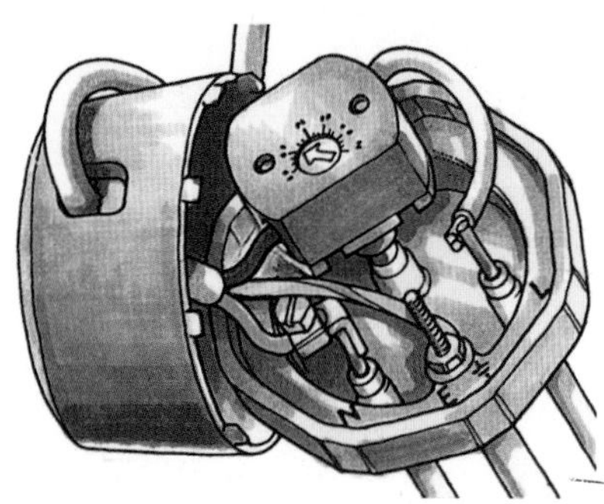

2 Wiring the heater

Replacing an element

With time, immersion heaters simply burn out and you are left without hot water. You can replace a heater yourself without notifying your BCO. First, check the circuit fuse or MCB; and if that isn't the source of the problem, isolate the heater circuit at the consumer unit and turn off the switch beside the cylinder. If your water is also heated by a boiler, switch that off, too.

Testing the immersion heater

Take the cap off the heater and, to test that the power has been switched off, touch the neutral terminal with one probe of a mains-voltage tester and the incoming live terminal on the thermostat with the other probe (1). Now do the same between incoming live terminal and the earth. If the power is off, make a note of the way the wires are connected to the heater, then disconnect the flex.

To check for a faulty thermostat, set it for maximum temperature and, using a multimeter set to its lowest resistance range, place one of the meter's probes on each of the thermostat terminals (2). If the meter shows no continuity, you only need to replace the thermostat – which saves having to drain the cylinder. If the thermostat seems to be functioning, place the probes on the heater terminals (3); and if there is no continuity, replace the heater.

Replacing the heater

To buy a replacement, estimate the diameter of the cylinder or the length of a top-entry heater. Heaters are usually supplied with the thermostat ready-fitted. You will also need to buy either an immersion-heater ring spanner or a special box spanner for turning an element surrounded by foam insulation.

Before you drain the cylinder, turn the heater very slightly with the spanner to free the threads (4). Now drain the cylinder, unscrew the heater and lift it out.

Fit the large washer supplied with the new heater, then screw the heater in place by hand until you feel the threads turning smoothly. The washer should prevent any leaks, but you can wrap PTFE tape around the heater threads as an extra precaution. Never smear it with sealant. Give a final turn with the spanner to tighten the heater, but don't apply too much force or you could distort the thin metal of the cylinder.

With the help of your notes, replace the wires on their terminals as they were on the old element (5); and then set the thermostat to the required temperature (see opposite). Replace the cap, refill the cylinder and check for leaks; then restore the power.

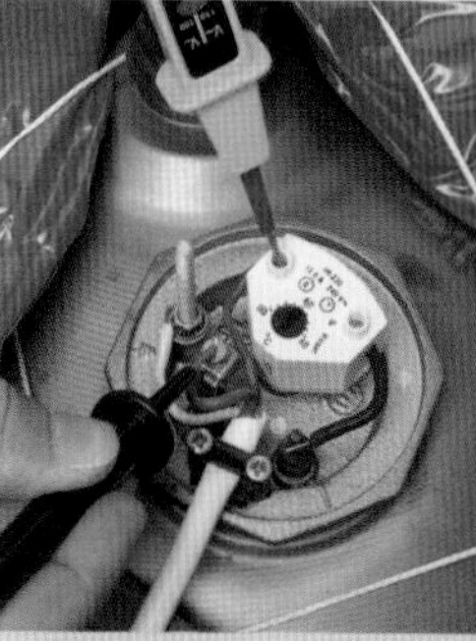

1 Check that the power is off

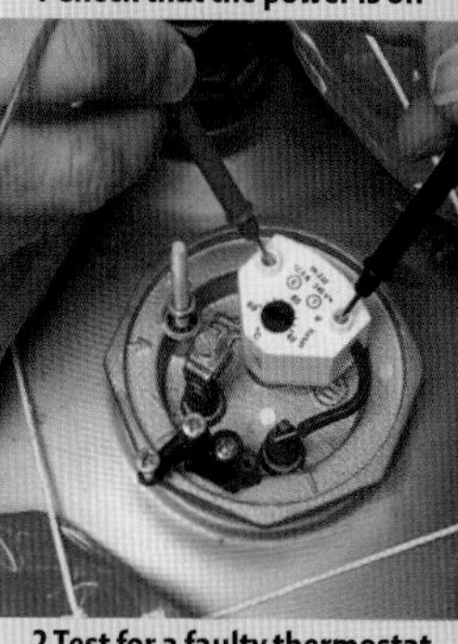

2 Test for a faulty thermostat

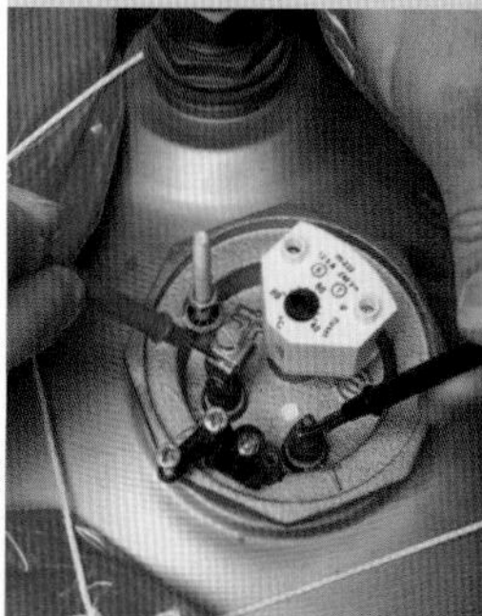

3 Test the heater

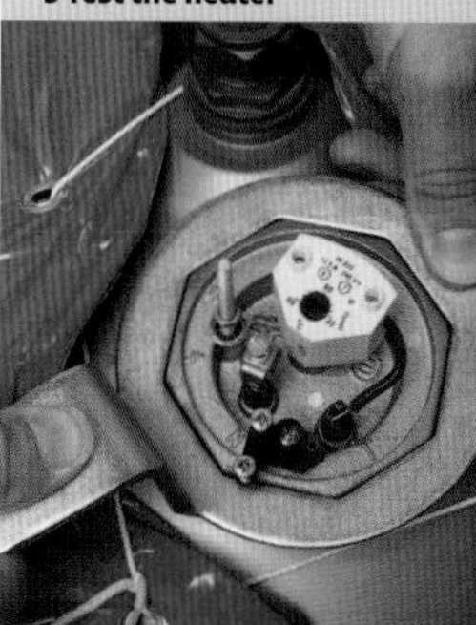

4 Free the heater threads

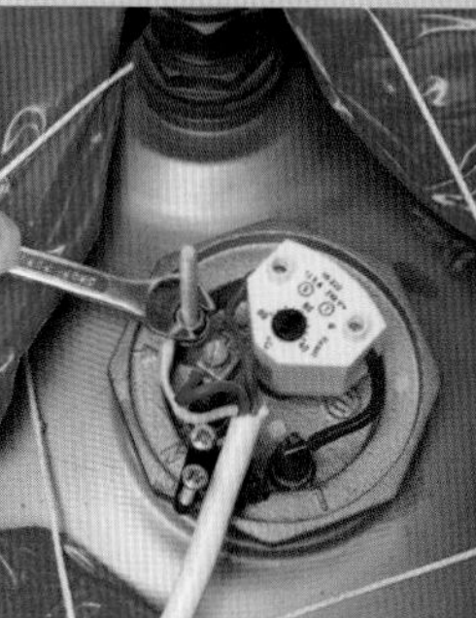

5 Replace the wires

SEE ALSO > Building Regulations 284, Zones for bathrooms 287, Testing circuits 288–9, Connecting flex 293, Stripping cable 302, Running cable 303–5, Switching off 296, Consumer units 298, Circuit lengths 344, Draining the system 348

Communication equipment

The modern British home is equipped with all manner of communication equipment, including telephones, computers, television sets and digital radios. No one but an expert would be advised to try to make major repairs to these appliances, but there's a lot you can do to boost their performance and to make using them more convenient.

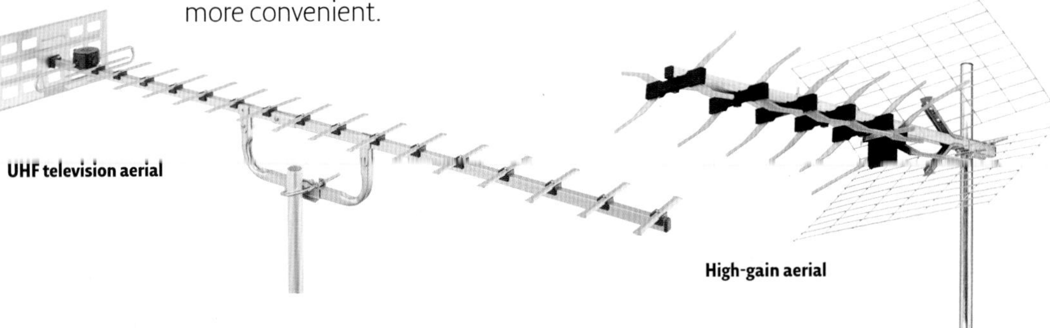

UHF television aerial

High-gain aerial

Outdoor aerials

Aerials mounted on the roof or clamped to a tall mast afford the best possible reception. An outdoor aerial can be installed in the loft, but - depending on the strength of the broadcast signal - picture quality may be reduced.

This type of aerial has a number of elements (crosspieces) and, as a rule, the more elements there are the better the reception. If you happen to live in an area where the incoming signal is weak, you may benefit from using a high-gain aerial, with an even greater number of elements designed to gather more of the available signal.

When directed towards a mains transmitter, an aerial should be mounted with its elements parallel to the ground. If it is receiving a signal from a relay transmitter, then the elements should be vertical.

Indoor aerials

If it's not possible to connect your TV set to an outdoor aerial, a good-quality set-top aerial may be the best solution. There are directional indoor aerials - which work best when aimed at the transmitter. Omnidirectional aerials are designed to receive signals from any angle, but in practice you may still have to try the aerial in different positions to get the best reception.

Television sets and aerials

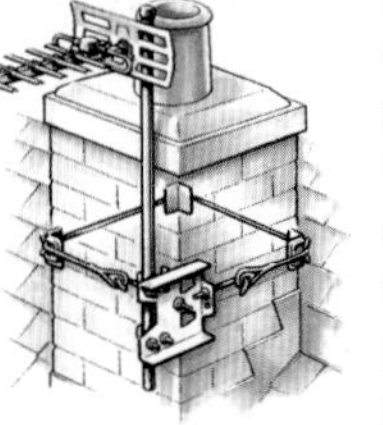

Outdoor aerial
TV aerials erected outside usually provide better reception than a similar aerial mounted in the loft.

The television set is probably the most widely used electronic appliance in the home, with most households boasting two or more large-screen or portable sets. This dependence on TV is becoming costly in terms of energy, with the larger plasma-screen sets consuming up to four times more power than the average television. The situation is greatly magnified by all the peripheral equipment, such as DVD players and recorders, especially when appliances are left on standby.

In Britain, the transmission of analogue TV signals is in the process of being phased out in favour of digital signals. However, at the moment our TV pictures and sound are broadcast in analogue format from about 1000 transmitters. Only a small percentage are high-power main transmitters, the majority being smaller low-power transmitters designed to relay the signals to homes outside the scope of the main transmitters. In order to receive these signals, a TV set must be connected to a suitable aerial.

Indoor aerial

Digital terrestrial broadcasting

By converting TV pictures and sound into binary code, digital broadcasters can transmit much more information than is possible with the analogue format. As a result, there are several advantages to be gained from a digital system:

- Sharp, clear pictures with CD-quality sound.
- Greater choice of programmes.
- Greatly enhanced Teletext service.
- Interactive TV.

Because the majority of terrestrial broadcasting operates on the same frequencies as analogue television, many households can continue using their existing outdoor aerials. However, the aerial may have to be realigned and, in some areas, a new wideband UHF aerial may be required.

Regardless of the aerial you use, in order to receive digital broadcasts you will either have to install a set-top box to decode the signals or buy a digital TV set with an integral decoder.

Digital radio

Digital Audio Broadcasting (DAB) converts sound into binary code. The benefits over FM and AM transmissions include almost CD-quality sound and interference-free reception.

To receive digital radio broadcasts, you require a digital receiver. If you need a separate aerial, a VHF aerial that covers Band 3 between 211.5 and 230MHz is usually recommended. Before you spend a lot of money on equipment, ask around to see what the reception is like in your area - with digital radio you invariably get an error-free signal or nothing at all.

Satellite broadcasting

Satellite broadcasters transmit low-power signals to a satellite in a geostationary orbit above the earth. The satellite amplifies the signals, converts them to a different frequency and transmits them back to earth. Signal strength is also affected by weather conditions, with cloud cover, rain and snow all tending to degrade quality of reception.

To receive a satellite signal, you need a dish of a suitable size and shape. As a rule, the weaker the signal the larger the dish required in order to receive acceptable pictures and sound. Large dishes, which have relatively narrow angles of reception, concentrate the signal and reduce interference but require more accurate alignment.

The low-noise block suspended in front of the dish reduces the signals to a lower frequency and sends them via a coaxial

SEE ALSO > Installing aerial sockets 320

cable to the satellite receiver – this is the unit that converts the signals into a format that can be displayed on the television screen.

Digital satellite broadcasting

A digital satellite broadcaster can transmit literally hundreds of channels, with a mixture of subscription and pay-as-you-view services. To receive digital satellite broadcasts, you need the appropriate set-top decoder or a TV set with an integral decoder, and you will probably have to get a smaller digital dish aerial. If you want to receive both analogue and digital transmissions, you will need two satellite dishes.

Installing a dish

Installing your own dish aerial is a simple DIY project, but it involves altering the direction of the aerial to obtain the strongest signal. In practice, this is probably best left to the TV supplier or satellite station, who usually offer free installation as part of the package.

Have a satellite dish installed by a professional

Cable TV

TV signals delivered by underground cables are not as susceptible to the sorts of interference that affect ordinary satellite reception. To receive them, you need the appropriate set-top or integral decoders – similar to but different from those required for satellite broadcasting.

Other services

Cable-TV suppliers can also provide broadband connection for your computer and an independent dedicated phone line. Installation is not a DIY job and the cable provider will make all the necessary connections and adjustments. It's worth asking your installer whether it is possible to avoid unsightly surface wiring, but be prepared to do some of the preparatory work yourself.

Signal boosters

In locations where the TV or FM radio signals are weak, a signal booster (amplifier) will improve reception appreciably. With the appropriate booster, you can distribute the signals to a number of TV sets and audio systems without loss of quality.

Masthead amplifiers

Masthead signal amplifier
1 High-gain outdoor aerial
2 Signal amplifier
3 Wall socket
4 Power-supply unit
5 Coaxial cable
6 Television set

In areas where reception is particularly poor, it would be worth having a high-gain outdoor aerial connected to a masthead signal amplifier. Mounted outside, the amplifier is powered by a special power-supply unit, which is plugged into an indoor wall socket.

If you ask the installer to fit a 'diplexer' alongside the amplifier, you can gather and distribute signals from both a TV aerial and an FM radio aerial.

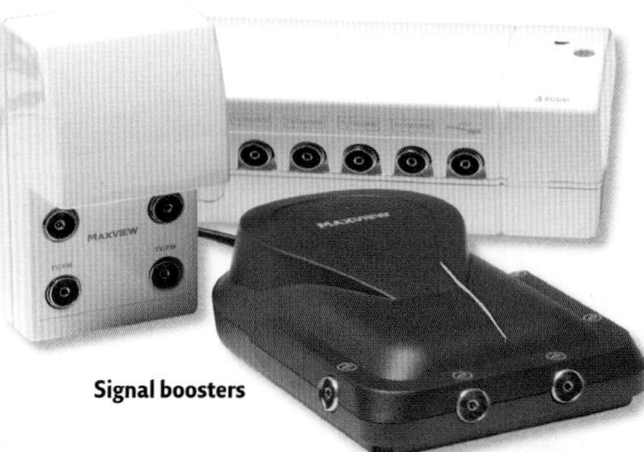

Signal boosters

Plug-in signal boosters

For best-quality reception a signal booster should be placed as close to the aerial as possible – but for sheer convenience it's hard to beat a booster that you simply plug into a socket next to the television set. Having plugged the incoming aerial cable into the booster, you can then connect up as many appliances as the booster is designed to accommodate.

Other signal boosters are fitted with a 13amp plug on the end of a short length of flex. This type can be left freestanding on a shelf close to your TV set and hi-fi system, or you can mount it on the wall. Some of these are 'fixed-gain' boosters, and some are made with a dial or switch that allows you to increase and decrease the signal gain as required.

Some indoor TV aerials are made with integral signal boosters.

Installing a booster

It's advisable to get a professional to put up a masthead amplifier, but you can install a booster yourself indoors. To fit a typical fixed-gain signal booster, screw the mounting box supplied with the booster to the wall or skirting board (**1**). Check that it's level before tightening the screws.

Connect the coaxial cables from your television sets and audio system, and also the aerial cable (**2**).

Screw the booster to the mounting box (**3**), then plug it into a 13amp wall socket and switch on.

1 Screw the mounting box to the wall

2 Plug in the aerial and the cables to your TV sets

3 Attach the booster to its mounting box

SEE ALSO > Wiring coaxial plugs 320

Installing aerial sockets

If you can't get satisfactory reception on every television set in your home, consider hooking all of them up to the main outdoor aerial. There are several ways to do this – including using a plug-in signal booster (already described). Another solution is to use surface-mounted aerial sockets to connect two TV sets to the same aerial.

Extending a TV aerial
1 Outdoor aerial
2 Splitter socket
3 Main TV set
4 Single aerial socket
5 Coaxial cable
6 Portable TV set

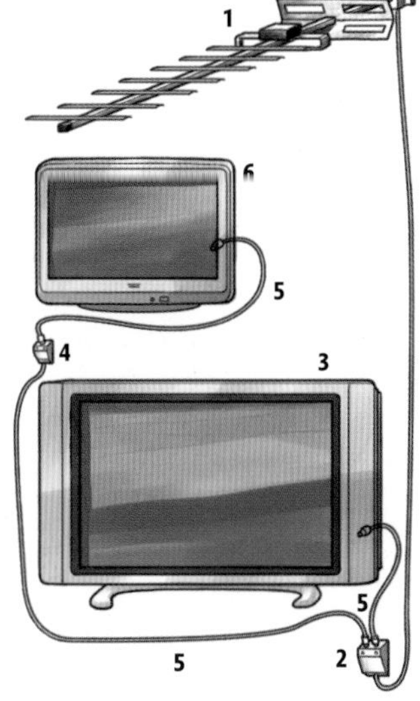

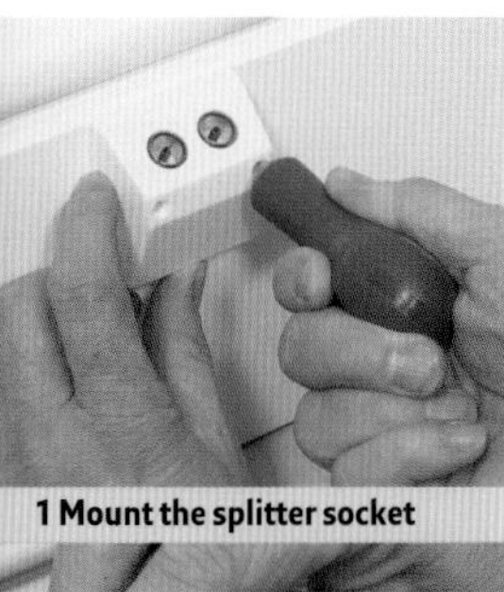

1 Mount the splitter socket

2 Remove the inner insulation

3 Clamp the braided copper

4 Connect to the splitter socket

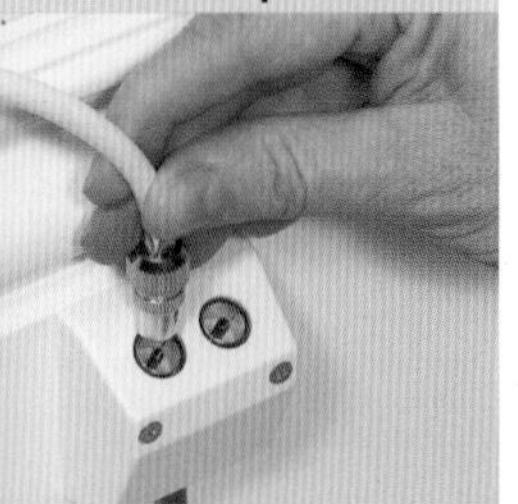

5 Plug in the cables

Extending a TV aerial

Using a bradawl, make holes for screwing a splitter socket to the skirting close to your main TV set (**1**). Do the same for a single aerial socket in a similar position in the room where you use your second set.

Cut a length of coaxial cable to run from one socket to the other. Attach this cable to skirting boards and architraves, using cable clips. Alternatively, run the coaxial cable under the floor or inside hollow walls - but not next to mains electricity cables.

At the single socket, strip about 18mm (¾in) of sheathing from the cable, fold back the copper strands and then remove about 16mm (⅝in) of insulation to reveal the inner conductor (**2**). Using the socket as a guide, trim the solid conductor to length.

Connect the conductor to the terminal in the socket and trap the braided copper and sheathing under the cable clamp (**3**). Tighten both screws, then screw the socket to the skirting. Fit a coaxial plug (see right) to the other end of the cable, ready for plugging into the splitter.

Remove the coaxial plug from the end of the existing incoming aerial cable and then connect the cable to the splitter socket (**4**), as described above. Screw the socket in place.

Plug in the new cable running from the single socket (**5**). Make or buy two coaxial (RF) leads for your TV sets and connect them, one from each box, to the 'antenna in' (ANT) socket on the back of each set.

Wiring coaxial plugs

A special insulated and shielded (coaxial) cable is required to pass the incoming signals to your TV sets. There are several types, but most electrical outlets stock the common 6mm (¼in) low-loss cable. Coaxial cable is either wired directly into the back of aerial sockets or fitted with single-pin coaxial plugs for insertion into the sockets. The ones shown here are solderless fittings made with simple screw fixings.

Cut the cable to length and slide the plug's locking ring onto one end. Strip off about 30mm (1¼in) of the outer sheathing, taking care not to sever the fine copper strands in the process (**1**).

Unravel the copper strands and fold them back over the sheathing. Wind the strands in a clockwise direction until they cover the first 6mm (¼in) of the sheathing (**2**).

Slide the cable gripper onto the end of the sheathing so that it covers the copper strands (**3**). Pinch the gripper onto the sheathing to contain the fine copper strands.

Strip all but about 3mm (⅛in) of the polythene insulation to reveal the solid copper conductor inside. Trim off excess conductor, leaving about 6mm (¼in) protruding from the insulation (**4**).

Loosen the fixing screw and insert the conductor into the plug's pin. Tighten the screw to secure the conductor (**5**).

Assemble the plug (**6**), making sure that none of the copper strands touch the inner conductor, then secure the fitting with the locking ring. Fit a similar plug to the other end of the cable.

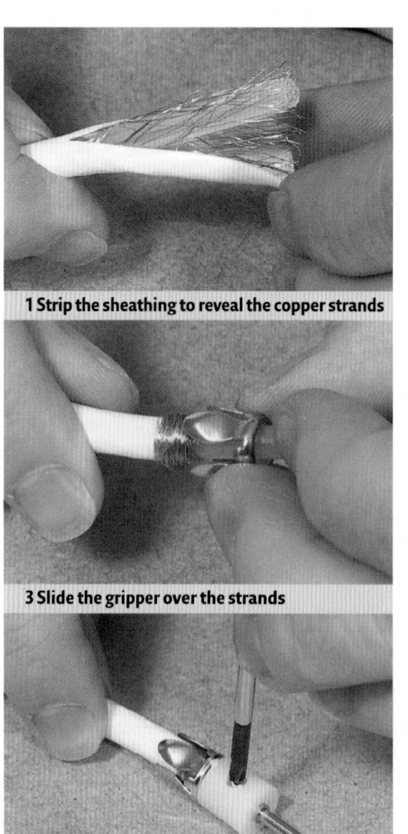

1 Strip the sheathing to reveal the copper strands

3 Slide the gripper over the strands

5 Clamp the conductor by tightening the screw

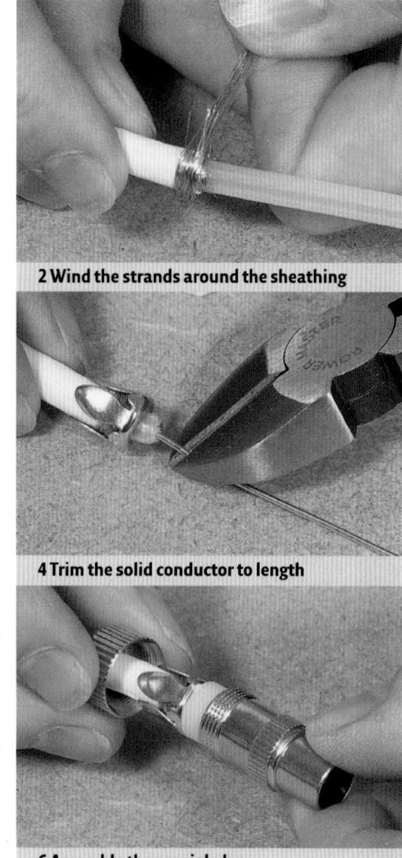

2 Wind the strands around the sheathing

4 Trim the solid conductor to length

6 Assemble the coaxial plug

SEE ALSO > TV sets and aerials 318, Signal boosters 319

Telephone extensions

Although a telephone company must be employed to install the master socket that's connected to the incoming network cable, you are permitted to install extension cables and sockets yourself. All the necessary equipment is available from DIY outlets and from electronics stores and telephone shops.

You can install as many telephone extension sockets as you want, so long as the total 'Ringer Equivalence Number' (REN) in your home does not exceed four. A telephone is normally allocated an REN of one – but it is advisable to check this before you decide which equipment to purchase. Telephones are made with either 'tone' or 'pulse' dialling, and modern phones can be switched from one to the other. The type of dialling does not affect the wiring of sockets.

Sockets and accessories
1 Single-socket faceplate
2 Surface-mounted socket
3 Socket doubler
4 Converter plug
5 British Telecom Linebox
6 Insertion tool

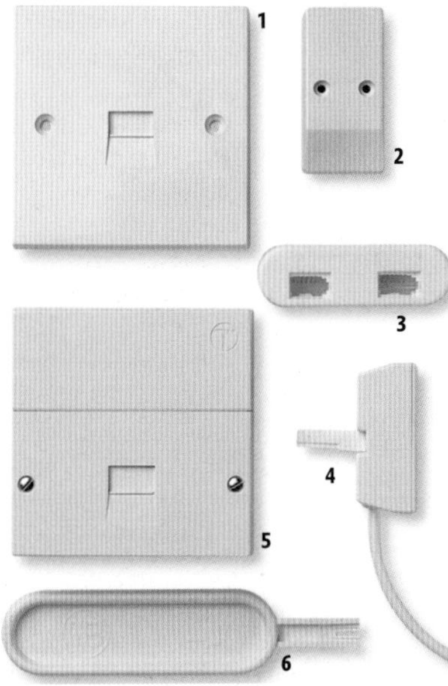

Telephone sockets

The single and double sockets that accept the small rectangular telephone plugs are made in the form of square faceplates (1) that fit standard electrical metal and plastic mounting boxes. Compact surface-mounted sockets are also available (2).

To operate two telephones or a telephone and an answering machine from a single socket without additional wiring, simply plug in a socket doubler (3).

You can run an extension from any master socket by means of a converter plug (4), which usually comes complete with several metres of cable. Another option is to wire your extension cable directly into a British Telecom Linebox (5), which has a removable cover for customer access.

Running the circuit

Run a length of cable from the existing master socket to each extension socket. The cable can be pinned to the top of skirtings or along picture rails and doorframes, using small plastic cable clips. Alternatively, you can conceal the cable under the floorboards or within walls, provided it does not follow exactly the same route used for mains wiring – maintain a minimum of 75mm (3in) between the telephone cable and mains cables. At each socket, feed a loop of cable into the mounting box, ready for connection.

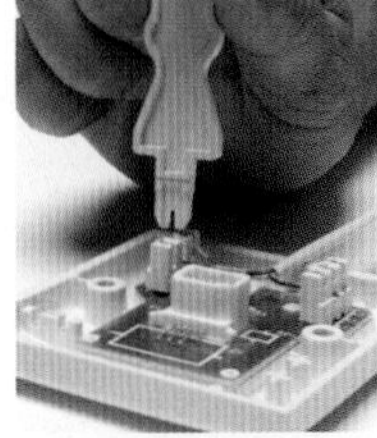

Connecting cable to blade terminals

Inserting wires into screw terminals

Connecting to the sockets

At each socket, cut the loop of cable and strip the sheathing to expose the colour-coded conductors, then separate the conductors and connect them to the appropriate numbered terminals.

Telephone-socket terminals usually comprise two opposing brass blades that cut into the cable's insulation and make contact with the wire core as the conductor is forced between them with an insertion tool. Lay the insulated conductor across its terminal and press it firmly to the base of the terminal. Trim the end of the wire.

Other sockets are made with screw terminals. Strip about 6mm (1/4in) of insulation from the end of each of the conductors, then insert the wire into the terminal and tighten the screw.

Sometimes, plastic cable ties are provided to secure the cable inside the socket, in order to prevent strain on the connections.

Telephone cable

Telephones, including extensions, are wired with extra-low-voltage cable.

Telephone cable usually comprises six colour-coded conductors sheathed in PVC. However, four-core cable is often sold for running domestic telephone extensions, and is perfectly adequate provided you match the colour-coded conductors to any existing wiring (see chart below).

Socket terminals are numbered 1 to 6. Always match the same colour coding to the same number terminal in each socket. If you are using four-core cable, ignore terminals 1 and 6.

Number	Colour coding
Terminal 1	Green with white rings
Terminal 2	Blue with white rings
Terminal 3	Orange with white rings
Terminal 4	White with orange rings
Terminal 5	White with blue rings
Terminal 6	White with green rings

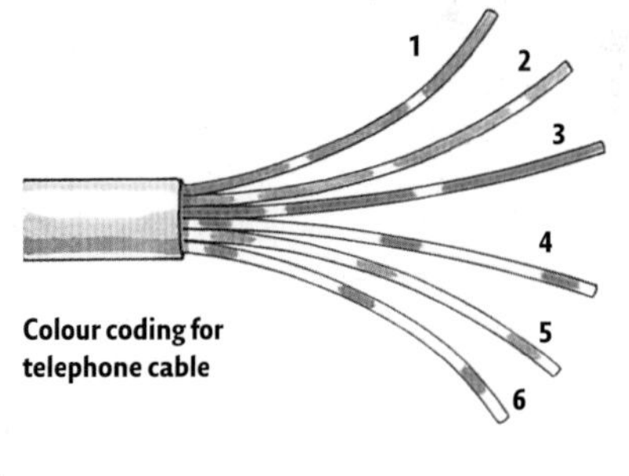

Colour coding for telephone cable

Wiring the master socket

Plugging a converter plug into the master socket will connect all your extensions to the telephone company network. To connect cable to a British Telecom Linebox, remove the front cover and use the insertion tool to introduce the conductors into the bladed terminals, as described left.

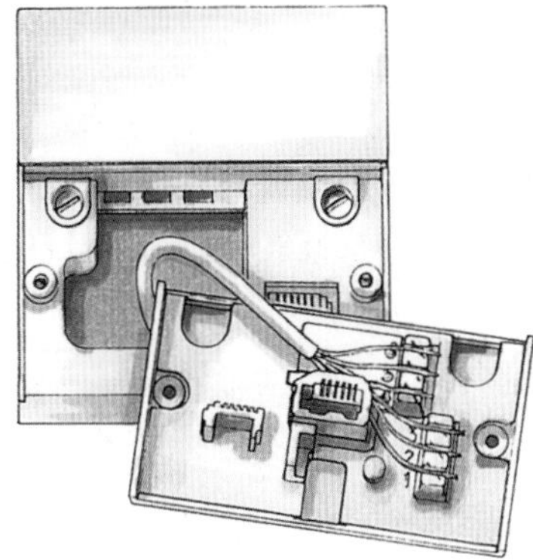

Connecting to a British Telecom Linebox

SEE ALSO > Running cable 303–5, Mounting boxes 306–7

An office at home

Working from home has become a practical option for a great many people. And even those who commute to the workplace usually need somewhere at home where they can catch up with extra work and sort out domestic accounts. Homework and hobbies place younger members of the family in a similar position. Increasingly, these activities are centred on a computer and a network of electronic equipment.

Whether you make do with a corner of the dining table or have the luxury of a dedicated workspace, some planning – and perhaps new wiring – will avoid a tangle of trailing flexes and overloaded socket outlets. To assess the number and positions of socket outlets, first plan your office layout to make the best use of the space available. Think about where your desk or worktable should be placed. You will probably want to take advantage of natural light – but before you make any permanent alterations, try out the position of your computer monitor to avoid distracting reflections from windows and fixed lighting.

Comfortable worktop
A desk with an adjustable worktop gives you the opportunity to have your keyboard at exactly the right height for comfort.

A worktop for your computer

Most people can work comfortably on a worktop that is 700mm (2ft 4in) from the floor. Ideally a computer keyboard should be slightly lower – which is why ready-made computer work stations are usually made with a slide-out work surface that can be stowed beneath the monitor. If your children are likely to use the same workspace, get a chair that is adjustable in height.

A fixed worktop needs to be at least 600mm (2ft) deep to provide enough room for the average computer and keyboard. But you may need a worktop 750mm (2ft 6in) deep to accommodate larger equipment, unless you can build an L-shape unit that allows the monitor, to be tucked into the corner.

Improved memory and screen quality has made the laptop computer a viable space saver for the home office.

Whatever computer you use, remember to provide extra worktop space for papers and reference books, plus shelves or drawers to store items such as stationery and computer disks.

Ancillary equipment

Even the most sophisticated computer is of limited use without a printer for accounts and correspondence, and to print out e-mails and downloads from the Internet. And you may want a scanner for putting your own photos and graphics onto the computer, which allows you to manipulate and recompose the images.

And as time goes by, you may require extra memory for data storage, which might mean a second hard drive for the computer. Handy USB memory sticks are a viable alternative, but they should not be relied upon for long-term storage.

Most offices are equipped with a paper shredder. Reduce the amount of paper you need to store by scanning documents onto your computer, then shred the paper.

The cable jungle

Each new piece of equipment needs a power supply and a connection to the computer – which is why so many home offices end up with a tangle of wires and overloaded sockets. You can tidy the cable runs with various cable ties and hoses, but having enough sockets positioned where needed is a better long-term solution.

Having to disconnect one appliance in order to use another is very inconvenient. Try connecting all your equipment to a USB hub plugged into the back of the computer.

A computer with wireless connection for e-mail and Internet downloads could help eliminate some cables.

Networking

If you have more than one computer, networking allows you to transfer data from one to the other. Similarly, printers and scanners can be shared. A network can be hard-wired, using Ethernet cables laid like ordinary mains cabling, but most people find a wireless network more convenient. For this, you will need a wireless router connected to the incoming Internet cable and to one of the computers. Any other computer can be connected by wireless receiver units, which plug into a USB socket or memory-card slot.

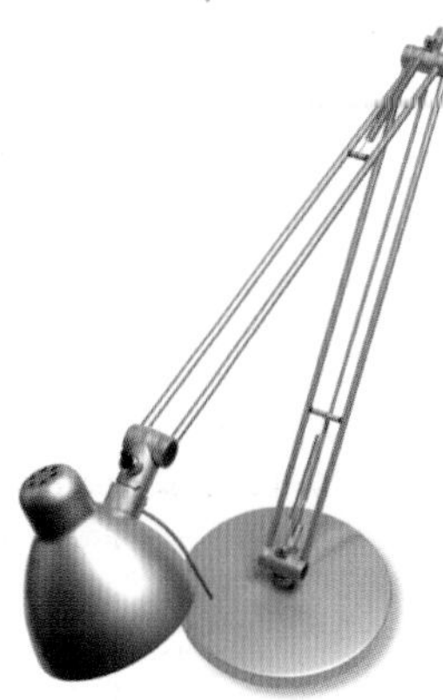

Lighting your office
Use dedicated task lighting to illuminate the work area without creating distracting reflections. A portable desk lamp is one option, or you could install a small spotlight or downlighter above the work station. A dimmer switch that controls the room lighting will allow you to set the optimum level of background illumination.

USB hub
A small USB hub allows you to connect several pieces of equipment to a single port on the back of your computer.

SEE ALSO > Light fittings 326–7

Providing extra sockets

Most householders just don't have the space to dedicate a room exclusively to working at home - but even if your study has to double as a spare bedroom from time to time, adding socket outlets will provide flexibility in the way you use your office or study and allow the room to be used for hobbies and games without compromising other activities.

Incorporate new socket outlets by adding spurs or extending the ring circuit. You will then be able to plug in as many appliances as you wish, including electric heaters, without fear of overloading the circuit. In addition, it will reduce the risk of a plug being pulled out accidentally, which could result in the loss of irreplaceable data.

Extending a ring circuit

With the power turned off, you can break into the ring circuit and connect a new length of cable, either to the existing sockets or by means of junction boxes. Sockets are relatively cheap - so be generous with the number you install and make sure you provide enough for all the equipment you are likely to need.

You'll probably need one or two extra socket outlets at skirting level, and two or three more at desktop height. This arrangement will provide you with the most direct route for connecting floor-standing and desktop equipment, without having to extend flexible cords. Where possible, rewire plugs - making the flex as short as practicable.

Label all the plugs that are connected to vulnerable equipment - including your computer. This simple precaution will reduce the risk of the equipment being unplugged inadvertently by another member of your family who wants to use the socket for another appliance.

Adding sockets
You could extend the ring circuit to add extra sockets at skirting level and to provide a source of power at desktop height.

EXTENDED CIRCUIT
OLD RING CIRCUIT
OLD RING CIRCUIT

Multi-way sockets

If extending your ring circuit is not a viable option, there are various ways of connecting more than one appliance to existing sockets outlets.

Trailing sockets

Trailing sockets are made with up to ten 13amp socket outlets, connected via a relatively short flexible lead to a single plug. With this type of device you can connect your computer and ancillary equipment to a single wall-mounted socket.

Look for trailing sockets fitted with surge suppressors (see right).

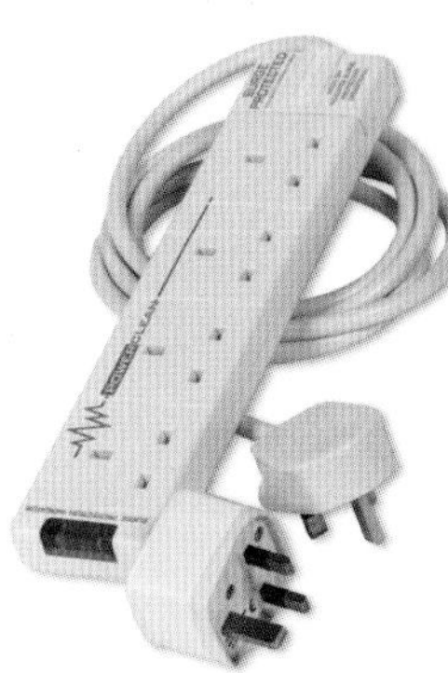

Surge protection
Sensitive electronic components in a computer can be damaged by voltage 'spikes' - short-duration peaks of high voltage. You can buy special plugs and trailing sockets fitted with surge suppressors designed to protect vulnerable equipment.

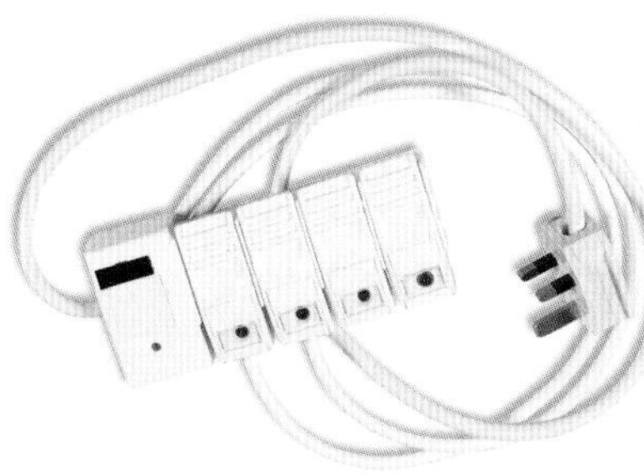

Miniature trailing sockets

There are special trailing sockets made with miniature plugs. They can be screwed to a skirting, or to the wall behind your desktop. There is one disadvantage with this equipment. Because the miniature plugs are not fused individually, a fault in any of the appliances connected to the trailing socket will cause the fuse in the 13amp plug to blow, and all of the appliances - including your computer - will be disconnected instantly. To protect vital data, have your computer plugged into its own wall socket and use the trailing socket for ancillary equipment only.

Wiring a miniature plug

Multi-adaptor

You can wire up to four appliances directly to a multi-adaptor, which has a short flex and 13amp plug for connecting to a single wall socket. The flex from each appliance is wired to its own set of terminals inside the adaptor, where it is protected by an individual fuse. Consequently, a fault on a single appliance is less likely to affect other equipment connected to the adaptor.

Each appliance is wired to a set of terminals

Telephones and modems

Unless your equipment utilizes wireless technology, you will need a telephone socket near your computer in order to access the Internet. To make better use of a single telephone socket, you can plug your phone and modem leads into a socket doubler.

British Telecom or similar telephone companies can advise you on broadband connection via the phone line or a network cable in order to receive faster downloads. This has the advantage of being able to use a single phone line for simultaneous phone and Internet use. If you use the phone a great deal, a 'voice over Internet' connection might save you money.

Most people use an answerphone to pick up messages when they're not at home or are unavailable. These need to be connected to a telephone socket, and to a power supply via a 13amp plug. It is worth labelling this plug, in order to avoid accidental disconnection and the subsequent inconvenience of having to reprogram the unit.

If you don't have a dedicated photocopier, you can equip your home office with a multipurpose printer/copier/fax machine or printer/copier/scanner, which are now relatively inexpensive.

SEE ALSO > Switching off 296, Cables 302, Running cable 303–5, Sockets 306–8, Adding a spur 309

Lighting circuits

Every lighting system needs a feed cable to supply power to the various lighting points, and a switch that can interrupt the supply to each point. There are two ways of meeting these requirements in your home: the junction-box system and the loop-in system. Your house may be wired with either one, though it's quite likely that there will be a combination of the two systems.

No earth wires
If you uncover an old lighting system that lacks earth wires, reconnect the other wires temporarily and get expert advice on rewiring the circuit.

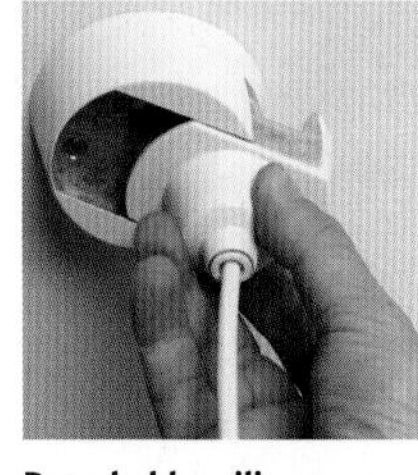

Detachable ceiling rose
If you use a modern detachable ceiling rose, you can slide out the centre section to change the light fitting without disturbing the fixed wiring. This type of rose can support a light fitting weighing up to 5kg (11lb).

Domestic systems

The junction-box system

With a junction box system, the feed cable runs from the consumer unit to a series of junction boxes, one for each lighting point. From each box a separate cable runs to the light itself, and another runs to its switch.

The loop-in system

With the loop-in system, the ceiling rose takes the place of the junction box. The cable from the consumer unit runs into each rose and out again, then on to the next. The switch cable and the flex to the bulb are connected at the rose.

Combined system

The loop-in system is now more widely used since it entails fewer connections. However, lights located at some distance from a loop-in circuit are often run from a junction box on the circuit; and lights added after the circuit has been installed are also often wired from junction boxes.

The circuits

Both the junction-box system and the loop-in system are, in effect, multi-outlet radial circuits. The cable runs from the consumer unit, looping in and out of the ceiling roses or junction boxes, and terminates at the last one. Unlike the cable of a ring circuit, it doesn't return to the consumer unit.

Lighting circuits require 1.5mm^2 two-core-and-earth cable, and each circuit needs to be protected by a 5amp circuit fuse or 6amp MCB in the consumer unit. A maximum of eleven 100W bulbs or their equivalent can therefore use the circuit.

In the average two-storey house the usual practice is to have two separate lighting circuits - one for the ground floor and the other for upstairs.

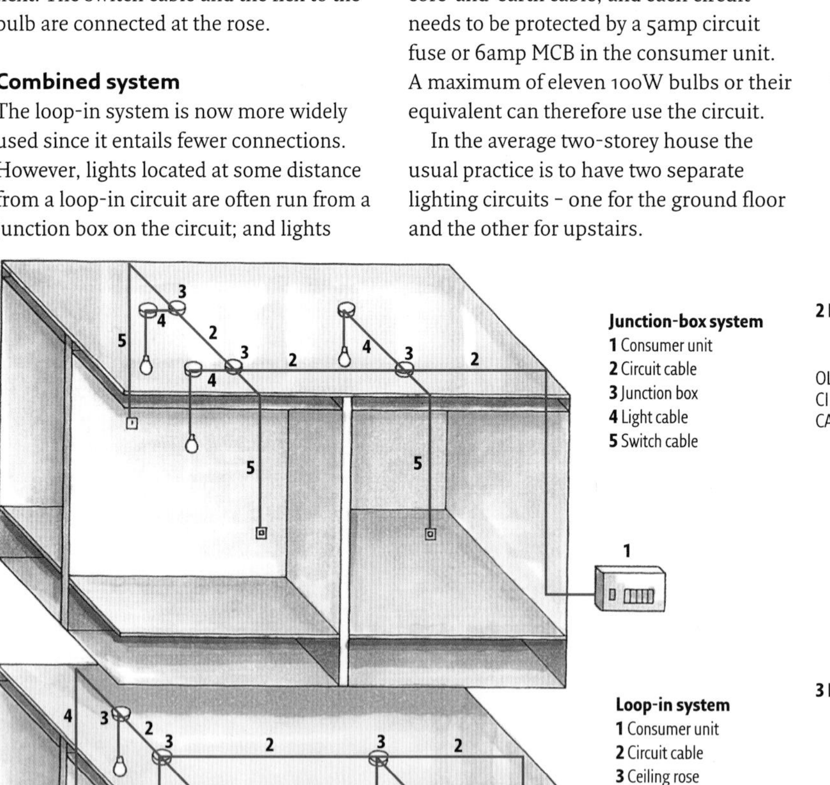

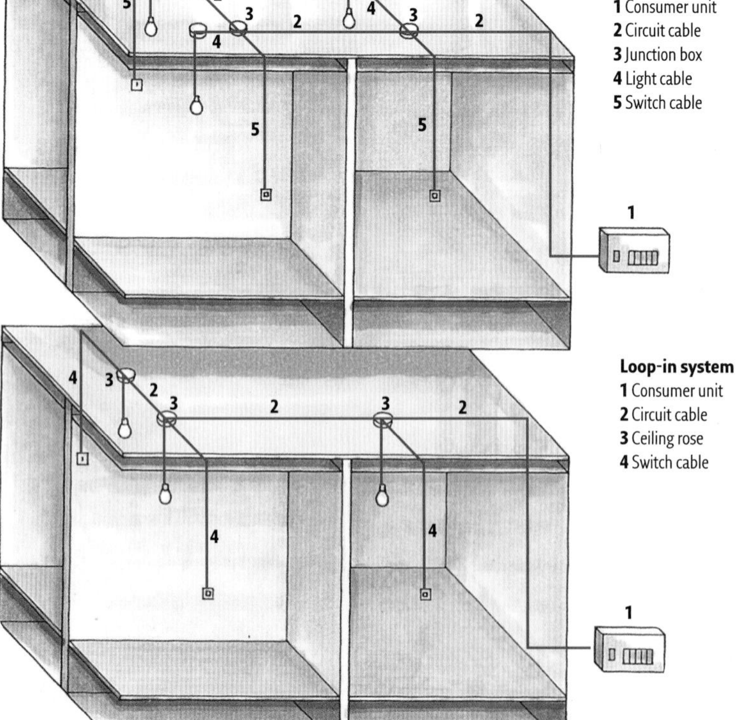

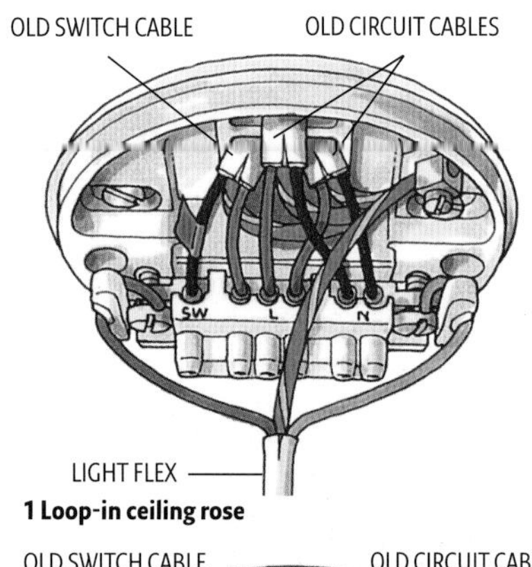

1 Loop-in ceiling rose

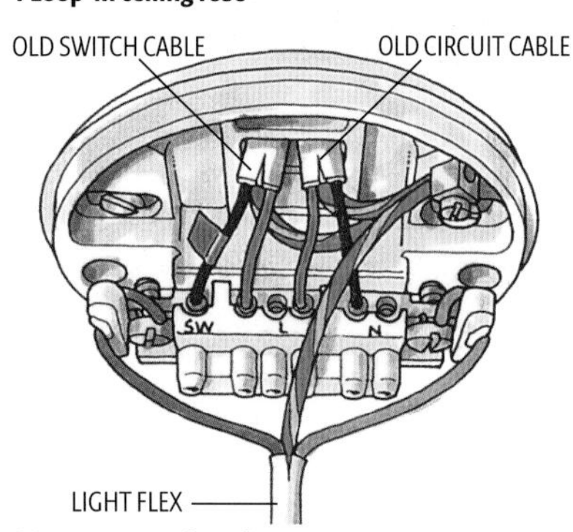

2 Last rose on a loop-in system

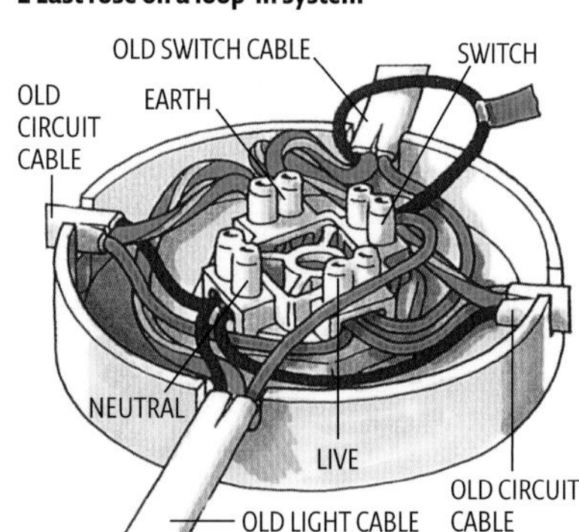

3 Lighting junction box

OLD LIGHT CABLE

SW L N

LIGHT FLEX

4 Ceiling rose on a junction-box system

SEE ALSO > Domestic circuits 301, Light fittings 326–7

Identifying connections

When you unscrew a ceiling rose, you can identify what sort of system has been used to wire it by examining the connections closely.

Loop-in system

A loop-in ceiling rose (1) has three terminal blocks, arranged in a row. The live (red or brown) wires from the two cut ends of the circuit-feed cable run to the central live block, and the neutral (black or blue) wires run to the neutral block on one side. The earth wires (green-and-yellow) run to a common earth terminal.

The live (red or brown) wire from the switch cable is connected to the remaining terminal in the central live block. The electricity runs through this wire to the switch, then back to the rose via the black 'switch-return' wire, which is connected to the third terminal block (the 'switch-wire block') in the ceiling rose. When the light is 'on', the switch-return wire is live – it is therefore identified by wrapping a piece of red or brown tape round it to distinguish it from the other black or blue wires, which are neutral. The earth wire in the switch cable goes to the common earth terminal.

The brown wire from the pendant flex connects to a terminal in the switch block, while the blue wire runs to the neutral block. If three-core flex is used, the green-and-yellow wire runs to the earth terminal.

When the circuit-feed cable terminates at the last ceiling rose on the circuit, only one set of cable conductors is connected (2).

Old colour coding
In a house built before 2005 you are likely to find that the existing cables are colour-coded black for neutral and red for live. The diagrams opposite show old-style lighting-circuit cables. For new-style circuits, substitute brown for red and substitute blue for black.

Junction-box system

The junction boxes on a lighting circuit have four terminals – for live, neutral, earth and switch connections. The live, neutral and earth wires from the circuit cable go to their respective terminals (3).

The live (red or brown) wire from the cable that runs to the rose is connected to the switch terminal; the black or blue wire to the neutral terminal; and the green-and-yellow wire to the earth terminal (3).

The red or brown wire from the switch cable is connected to the live terminal; the earth wire to the earth terminal; and the black or blue 'return' wire from the switch goes to the switch terminal (3). This last conductor must be identified with a piece of red or brown tape wrapped round it.

At the ceiling rose, the live cable wire is connected to one of the outer terminal blocks, and the neutral wire to the other one. The central block is left empty. The earth wire goes to the earth terminal (4).

The brown flex wire is connected to the same terminal block as the live cable wire; and the blue flex wire goes to the block holding the neutral cable wire. If the flex has an earth wire, it should be connected to the common earth terminal (4).

1 Screw a platform between the joists

2 Screw the new backplate to the ceiling

3 Loop the flex wires over the support hooks

Replacing a ceiling rose

Turn off the power and remove the circuit fuse or lock off the MCB. Switching off at the wall is not enough. Unscrew the rose cover and examine the connections. If it's a loop-in rose, identify the switch-return wire with red or brown tape. If there's only one live and one neutral wire, it's a junction-box system and there will be no switch cable.

If there are wires running into three terminal blocks, first look for the one with all red or brown wires and no flex wires. This is the live block, containing live circuit-feed wires and a live switch wire. The neutral terminal block takes the black or blue circuit-feed wires and the blue flex wire. The third block takes the brown flex wire plus a black or blue switch-return wire. All earth wires will run to one terminal.

Fixing the new rose

Draw a diagram of the connections before you disconnect the wires. Take down the old backplate. Knock out the entry hole in the new backplate and thread the cables through it; then fix the backplate to the ceiling. If the old fixings aren't secure, screw a piece of wood between the joists above the ceiling (1) and drill a hole through it from below for cable access. Screw the new rose backplate to the wood through the ceiling (2), and then reconnect the wires.

Slip the new cover over the pendant flex and connect the flex wires to the terminals in the rose – loop these wires over the rose's support hooks to take the weight off the terminals (3). Screw on the cover, then switch on the power and test the new light.

SEE ALSO > Colour coding 285, Replacing a pendant lampholder 295, Switching off 296, Lifting floorboards 304

Light fittings

There is a vast range of light fittings for the home – but, although they may differ greatly in their appearance, they can be grouped roughly into eight categories according to their functions.

Close-mounted light

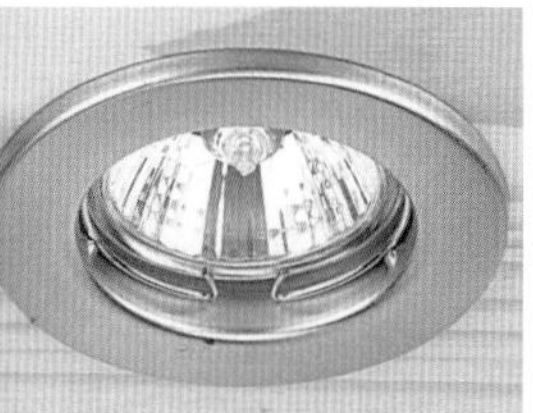
Recessed fitting

Directional recessed light

Wall light

Batten holder

Pendant lights

The pendant light is probably the most common fitting. At its most basic it consists of a lampholder, with a bulb and usually with some kind of shade, and is suspended from a ceiling rose by a length of flexible cord.

Many decorative pendant lights are designed to take more than one bulb and are much heavier than the simpler ones. Heavy pendant lights should never be attached to a standard plastic ceiling rose. However, they can be connected to a detachable ceiling rose.

Close-mounted ceiling lights

A close-mounted fitting is screwed directly to the ceiling, without a ceiling rose, most often by means of a backplate that houses the lampholder or holders. The fitting is usually enclosed by some kind of rigid light-diffuser, which is also attached to the backplate.

Recessed ceiling lights

The lamp housing itself is recessed into the ceiling void, and the diffuser either lies flush with the ceiling or projects only slightly below it. These discreet light fittings, which are ideal for modern interiors with low ceilings, are often referred to as downlighters.

Wall lights

Light fittings designed for screwing to a wall can be supplied either from the lighting circuit in the ceiling void or from a fused spur off a ring circuit. Among the most popular wall lights are uplighters, adjustable spotlights and various kinds of close-mounted fittings.

Batten holders

These basic fittings are fixed directly to the wall or ceiling. They are generally used in areas such as lofts or cellars where appearance is not important.

Track lights

Several individual light fittings can be attached to a metal track screwed to the ceiling or to a wall. Because a contact runs the length of the track, lights can be fitted anywhere along it.

Striplights

These slim lights are often mounted above mirrors and inside cupboards and display cabinets. They can be controlled by separate microswitches so the light comes on each time the cupboard door is opened. Striplights usually take 30W or 60W tubular tungsten-filament lamps with a metal cap at each end.

Some undercupboard striplights are designed to be linked with short lengths of cable so that they can all be powered from a single 13amp plug.

Display alcoves illuminated with striplights

Fluorescent light fittings

A fluorescent light features a glass tube containing mercury vapour. The voltage makes electrons flow between the electrodes at the ends of the tube and bombard an internal coating – which fluoresces, producing bright light.

Different types of coating make the light appear 'warmer' or 'cooler'. For domestic purposes, choose either 'warm white' or 'daylight' tubes.

Fluorescent lighting is unattractive in most domestic interiors, but it is very functional for workshops and garages, where good even illumination is an advantage. However, you should be aware that fluorescent lighting can create the illusion that moving parts of machinery (saw blades and lathe chucks) are stationary when they are still turning.

Light bulbs and tubes

There are numerous light bulbs and tubes designed for use in the various fittings described left.

General lighting service lamps (GLS)

This is the trade name for what we call a light bulb. It is technically known as a tungsten-filament lamp, as the thin metal filament inside the glass envelope glows brightly when heated by electricity.

GLS bulbs come with either an Edison screw or a bayonet fitting for securing the bulb to a lampholder.

The glass envelope can be clear, for fitting inside or behind a glass or plastic cover; or 'pearl', which provides a diffused light for pendant fittings and table lamps. There are also coloured GLS lamps, used mainly for outdoor decoration.

As well as the familiar domed and compact mushroom-shaped bulbs, there are decorative GLS lamps, including bulbs shaped to resemble candle flames.

Reflectors

Some tungsten-filament lamps are silvered to reflect the light forwards or backwards.

Halogen lamps

The filament inside a bulb containing halogen gas glows with an intense white light. As well as mains-voltage lamps, there are low-voltage fittings that have to be wired to a transformer – (see LOW-VOLTAGE LIGHTING).

Fluorescent tubes

Fluorescent tubes are more economical than GLS or halogen bulbs. Compact fluorescent lamps are designed as low-energy replacements for GLS bulbs. Though they are relatively expensive to buy, you are likely to recoup the additional cost within 6 to 12 months.

Light-emitting diodes (LEDs)

Formerly used only for indicator lights, LEDs are now often used in groups to create extremely durable light sources.

The chart opposite compares the features and efficiency of various bulbs and tubes.

SEE ALSO > Lighting circuits 301, Close-mounted lights 328, Fitting a downlighter 328, Fitting track lighting 328, Fluorescent lights 329, Adding wall lights 333, Low-voltage lighting 334–5, Mains-voltage halogen lamps 335

Comparing bulbs and tubes

• Lumens per watt – the higher the figure, the greater the efficiency (more light per unit of electricity). • Colour temperature (in degrees Kelvin) – the higher the figure, the colder (bluer) the light.		Common names	Normal range	Life expectancy in hours	Features	Typical lumens per watt	Colour temperature
General service lamp		Light bulb	40–150 watts	1000–2000	General-purpose bulbs in a range of shapes and colours.	12–18	2800
Decorative GLS		Candle, globe	25–60 watts	1000–2000	Bulbs designed to be visible.	7–12	2800
Crown-silvered lamp		Mirrored bulb	40–100 watts	1000–2000	Front of the bulb is coated to bounce light back against a reflective surface inside the light fitting.	8	2700
Internal-silvered lamp		Spotlamp	25–100 watts	1000–2000	The bulb is coated internally to reflect the light forward in a concentrated beam.	8–12.5	2800
Parabolic aluminized reflector		PAR	60–120 watts	1000–2000	Conical-shape reflector, often used for floodlighting.	8–13	3050
Architectural tube		Striplight	25–60 watts	1000–2000	Used to illuminate interior of cabinets and mounted above kitchen worktops.	7–12	2700
Fluorescent tube			13–125 watts	6000–7000	Gives bright, even illumination. A variety of warm and cool tones. Economical to run.	35–100	2700 to 6300
Compact fluorescent tube		Low-energy bulb	48–69 watts	6000–7000	Miniature tubes with Edison screw or bayonet fittings. Cheap to run, lasting 10 to 12 times longer than equivalent GLS bulbs.	6–30	2700 to 6300
Mains-voltage halogen lamp			20–50 watts	2000–4000	Less 'sparkle' than low-voltage halogen, but simpler to install. Popular for wall lights and recessed lighting.	12–16	3050
Linear mains-voltage halogen lamp		Double-ended halogen	100–500 watts	2000–4000	Mainly used for uplighters and floodlights. Tends to get very hot.	18–22	3050
Low-voltage halogen lamp			10–50 watts	2000–4000	Widely used for wall lights and recessed ceiling lights. Can be suspended from special plastic-insulated cable.	14–19	2900 to 3000
Light-emitting diode		LED	Up to 10 watts per light fitting	100,000	Often used for decorative fittings. Can be built into CCTV cameras. Does not get hot.	30–35	5500

SEE ALSO > Fluorescents under cupboards 329, Low-voltage lighting 334–5, Security lighting 337–8, CCTV 339–40

Close-mounted lights

N If you undertake work marked with this symbol, you must inform the BCO before starting – see FIRST THINGS FIRST.

Close-mounted light fittings often have a backplate that screws directly to the ceiling, in place of a ceiling rose. To fit one, switch off the power at the consumer unit and take out the circuit fuse or lock off the MCB, then remove the ceiling rose and fix the new backplate to the ceiling.

If only one cable feeds the light, attach its conductors to the terminals of the lampholder and connect the earth wire to the terminal on the backplate.

Since more heat is generated inside an enclosed fitting, slip heat-resistant sleeving over the conductors before you attach them to their terminals.

If the original ceiling rose was wired into a loop-in system, then you will find that a close-mounted light fitting won't accommodate all the cables. In which case, withdraw the cables into the ceiling void and wire them into a junction box screwed to a length of 100 x 25mm (4 x 1in) timber nailed between the joists; then run a short length of heat-resistant cable from the junction box to the new light fitting.

1 BESA boxes
Use a BESA box (also known as a conduit box) to house the connections when a light fitting is supplied without a backplate. A metal box must be earthed.

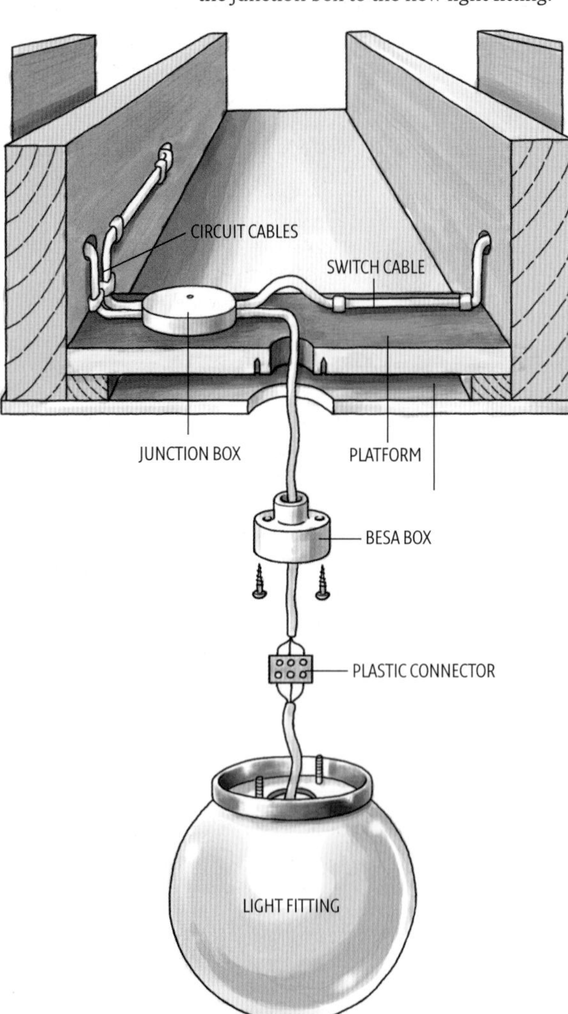

2 Accommodating a BESA box

Fittings without backplates

Sometimes close-mounted lights are supplied without backplates.

Wiring Regulations stipulate that all unsheathed wires and terminals have to be enclosed in a noncombustible housing – so if you plan to use a fitting without a backplate, you must find a means of complying. The best way is to fit a BESA box (**1**), a plastic or metal box that is fixed into the ceiling void so as to lie flush with the ceiling.

The screw-fixing lugs on the BESA box should line up with the fixing holes in the light fitting's coverplate, so check that they do so before buying the box. You will also need two machine screws of the appropriate thread for attaching the light to the box.

Accommodating a BESA box

Check that there isn't a joist directly above where you wish to fit the light (if there is one, move the light to one side until it fits between two joists). Then hold the box against the ceiling, trace round it, and carefully cut the traced shape out of the ceiling with a padsaw.

Cut a platform from timber 25mm (1in) thick to fit between the joists (**2**), and place it directly over the hole in the ceiling while an assistant marks out the position of the hole on the board from below. Then drill a cable-feed hole centrally through the shape of the ceiling aperture marked on the board. If there's a boss on the back of the BESA box, the hole must be able to accommodate it. Position the box and screw it securely to the platform.

Have your assistant press some kind of flat panel against the ceiling and over the aperture. Fit the BESA box into the aperture from above, so that it rests on the panel; drop the platform over the BESA box, and mark both ends on both joists. Screw a batten to each joist to support the platform at that level. Fix the platform to the battens and feed the cable through the hole in the centre of the BESA box.

For attaching the cable conductors, the light fitting will probably have a plastic connector, which may have three terminals. Alternatively, there may be a separate terminal for the earth conductor attached to the coverplate. After securing the conductors, fix the coverplate to the BESA box with the machine screws.

If the original ceiling rose was fed by more than one cable, connect them to a junction box in the ceiling void, as described previously.

Fitting a downlighter

Decide where you want the light, check from above that it falls between joists, and then use the cardboard template supplied with all downlighters to mark the outline of the circular aperture on the ceiling. Drill a series of 12mm (½in) holes just inside the perimeter of the marked circle to remove most of the waste, then cut it out with a padsaw.

Bring a single lighting-circuit cable from a junction box through the sawn opening and attach the cable to the downlighter, following the maker's instructions. You may have to fit another junction box into the void in order to connect the circuit cable to the heat-resistant flex attached to the light fitting.

Insert the downlighter into the opening and secure it there by adjusting the clamps that bear on the hidden upper surface of the ceiling.

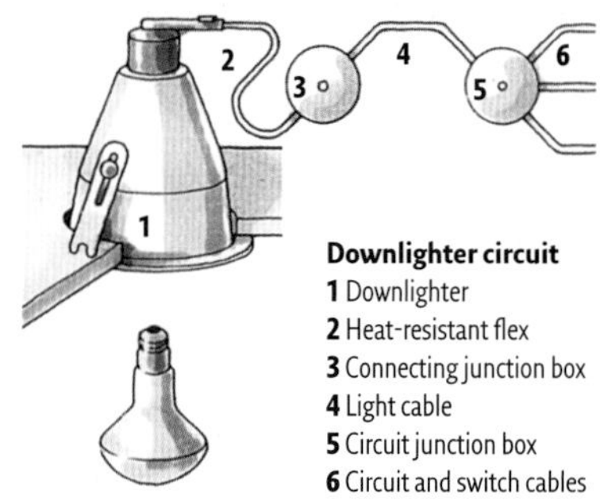

Downlighter circuit
1 Downlighter
2 Heat-resistant flex
3 Connecting junction box
4 Light cable
5 Circuit junction box
6 Circuit and switch cables

Fitting track lighting

Ceiling fixings are supplied with all track-lighting systems. Mount the track so that the terminal-block housing at one end is situated close to where the old ceiling rose was fitted. Pass the circuit cable into the fitting and wire it to the cable connector provided. If the circuit is a loop-in system, mount a junction box in the ceiling void to connect the cables.

Make sure that the number of lights you intend to use on the track will not overload the lighting circuit – which can supply a maximum of eleven 100W lamps (bulbs) or their equivalent.

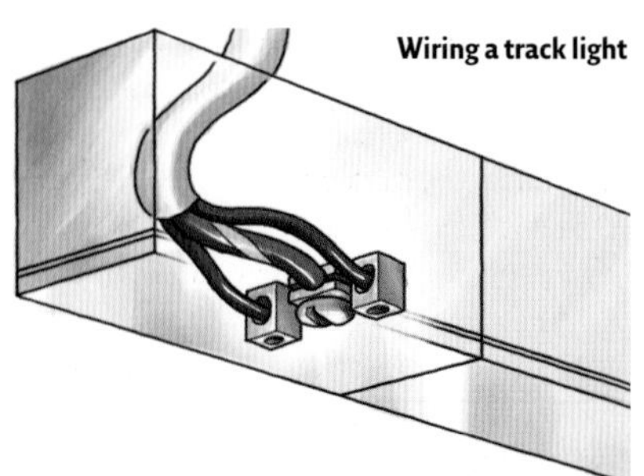

Wiring a track light

SEE ALSO > Building Regulations 284, Switching off 296, Loop-in system 324, Fixing to ceiling 325, Junction box 325, Close-mounted lights 326, Recessed lights 326, Track lights 326

Fluorescent lights

Remove the ceiling rose and then screw the new fluorescent light fitting to the ceiling, positioned so that the circuit cable can be fed into it conveniently.

Fluorescent light fittings are supplied with terminal blocks for connection to the mains supply. Each terminal block will take only three conductors - so either the fitting must be connected to a junction-box system or a junction box must be installed in the ceiling void to accommodate loop-in wiring, as for a close-mounted light (see opposite). Fluorescent lights normally need earth connections, so they can't be used with old systems that lack earth conductors.

You can mount a fluorescent unit by screwing directly into the ceiling joists or into boards nailed between the joists to provide secure fixings.

Replacing a starter

A fluorescent tube needs high voltage in order to start up, and then the voltage is reduced by a ballast unit. Some modern light fittings incorporate an electronic ballast to provide instant or rapid start-up. However, many models still have replaceable electromechanical starters. If the tube merely glows at each end when you switch on, try pressing in and unscrewing the small cylindrical starter, which is usually easily accessible. If that causes the tube to illuminate, buy a new compatible starter for the fitting.

Similarly, a flickering tube may indicate a faulty starter, but it may also mean the tube itself needs replacing. Perform the same test described above.

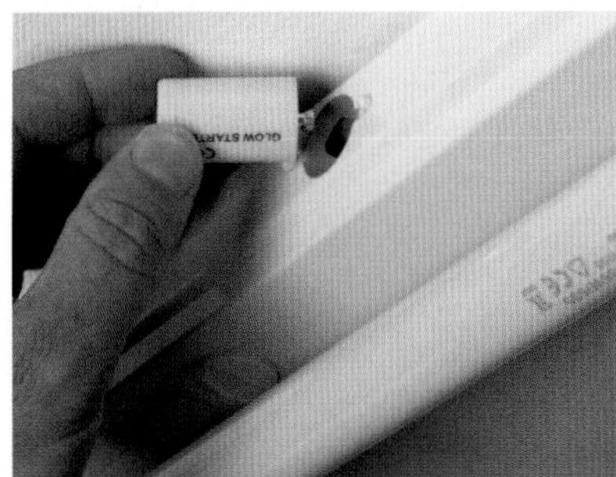

Replace a faulty starter

Fluorescents under cupboards (N)

You can fit fluorescent lighting underneath wall-mounted kitchen cupboards to illuminate the work surface below. The power is supplied from a switched fused connection unit with a 3amp cartridge fuse.

When installing a second fluorescent light fitting, you can supply it with power by wiring it into the terminal block of the first fitting.

Light switches

The type of switch that's most commonly used for lighting is the plate switch. This has a switch mechanism mounted behind a square faceplate with either one, two or three rockers. Although that's usually enough for domestic purposes, double faceplates with as many as four or six rockers are also available.

A one-way switch simply turns a light on and off. Two-way switches are wired in pairs so that the light can be controlled from two places - typically at the head and foot of a staircase. It's also possible to have an intermediate switch, to allow a light to be controlled from three places.

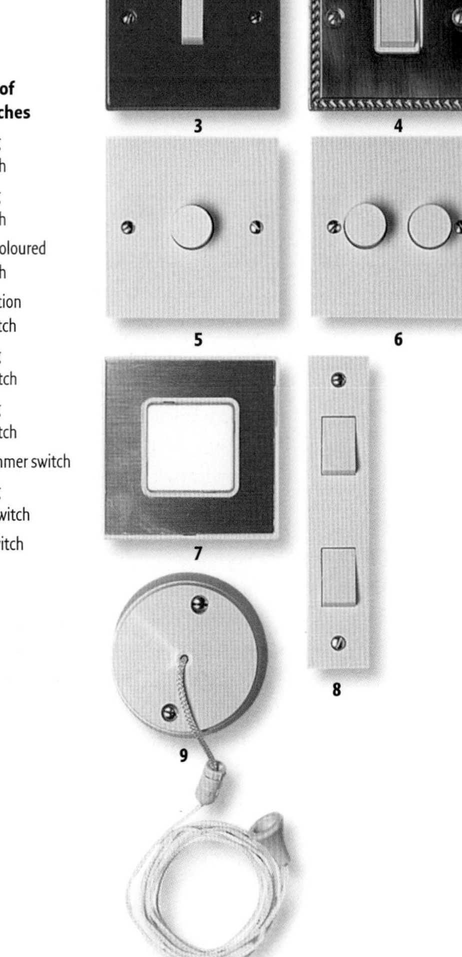

Selection of light switches
1 One-gang rocker switch
2 Two-gang rocker switch
3 Primary-coloured rocker switch
4 Reproduction antique switch
5 One-gang dimmer switch
6 Two-gang dimmer switch
7 Touch dimmer switch
8 Two-gang architrave switch
9 Ceiling switch

Any type of switch can be flush-mounted in a metal box buried in the wall plaster or surface-mounted in a plastic box. Boxes 16 and 25mm (5/8 and 1in) deep are available, to accommodate switches of different depths.

Where there is not enough room for a standard switch, a narrow architrave switch can be used. There are double versions with two rockers, one above the other.

As well as turning the light on and off, a dimmer switch controls the intensity of illumination. Some types have a single knob that serves as both switch and dimmer. Others incorporate a separate knob for switching, so the light level does not have to be adjusted every time the light is switched on. Some can be operated by remote control.

The Wiring Regulations forbid the positioning of a conventional switch within reach of a washbasin, bath or shower unit - so only ceiling-mounted double-pole switches with pull-cords must be used in bathrooms. With this type of switch, both live and neutral contacts are broken when it is off.

Installing light switches and cable

Light switches need to be installed in relatively accessible positions, which normally means just inside the door of a room, at about adult shoulder height.

In order to reach the switch, lighting cable is either run within hollow cavity walls or buried in the wall plaster.

Methods for fixing mounting boxes in place are similar to those described for fitting socket outlets.

Choosing switches

Most light switches are made from white plastic, but you can buy other finishes to compliment your decorative scheme. Coloured switches can look striking in a modern house, while reproductions of antique brass switches are both appropriate and attractive in a traditional interior.

SEE ALSO > Building Regulations 284, Fluorescent tubes 326, Replacing switches 330, Adding new switches 331, Two-and-three-way lighting 332

Replacing switches

Replacing a damaged switch is simply a matter of connecting the existing wiring to the terminals of the new switch – making sure that you connect the wires in exactly the same way as in the old one.

• **Switching off**
Always turn off the power and remove the relevant fuse or remove (or lock off) the MCB before you take off a switch faceplate to inspect the wiring.

Check that a new faceplate for a surface-mounted switch will fit the existing mounting box; otherwise, you will have to replace both parts of the switch. If you are able to use the box, attach the new faceplate with the old machine screws. You can then be certain of having screws that will match the threads.

If you want to replace a surface-mounted switch with a flush-mounted one, remove the old switch then hold the metal box over the position of the original switch and trace round it. Cut away the plaster to the depth of the box, then screw it to the brickwork. Take great care not to damage the existing wiring while you are working.

Replacing a one-way switch

• **Old colour coding**
In a house built before 2005 you are likely to find the existing cables are colour-coded black for neutral and red for live. The diagrams on this page show old-style switch cables. For new-style circuits, substitute brown for red and substitute blue for black.

(N) If you undertake work marked with this symbol, you must inform the BCO before starting – see FIRST THINGS FIRST.

Examine a one-way switch and you will see that it is serviced by a two-core-and-earth cable. The earth conductor, if there is one, will be connected to an earth terminal on the mounting box. The red (brown) and black (blue) conductors will be connected to the switch itself.

A true one-way switch has only two terminals, one situated above the other, and the red (brown) or black (blue) conductors can be connected to either terminal (**1**). The back of the faceplate is marked 'top' to ensure that you mount the switch the right way up, so the rocker is depressed when the light is on. The switch would work just as well upside down – but the 'up for off' convention is a useful one, as it tells you whether the switch is on or off even when the bulb has failed.

You may come across a light switch that is fed by a two-core-and-earth cable and operates as a one-way switch yet has three terminals (**2**). This is a two-way switch that has been wired for one-way function – something that's fairly common and perfectly safe. If the switch is mounted the right way up, then the red (brown) and black (blue) wires should be connected to the 'Common' and 'L2' terminals (**2**) – either wire to either terminal.

Replacing a two-way switch

A two-way switch will have at least one conductor in each of its three terminals. Without going into the complexities of two-way wiring at this stage, you will find that the most straightforward method of replacing a damaged two-way switch is simply to make a written note of which conductors run to which terminals before you start to disconnect the various wires.

Another simple method is to detach the wires from their terminals one at a time, and connect each one to the corresponding terminal on the new two-way switch before you deal with the next conductor.

Two-gang switches

A two-gang switch is the name for two individual switches mounted on a single faceplate. Each of the switches may be wired differently. One may be working as a one-way switch, and the other as a two-way (**3**). To transfer the wires from an old switch to the terminals of a new one, work on one switch at a time and use one of the methods for replacing a two-way switch described above.

Replacing a rocker switch with a dimmer switch

Examine the present switch in order to determine the type of wiring that feeds it, then purchase a dimmer switch that will accommodate the existing wiring. The manufacturers of dimmer switches provide instructions with them, but the connections are basically the same as for ordinary rocker switches (**4**).

Don't use a dimmer switch to control a fluorescent light.

How switches are wired

It is very easy to replace a damaged switch or to swap one for a different type of switch. The illustrations below show four common methods of wiring switches. If a switch appears to be wired differently, it is probably part of a two-way or three-way lighting system. Replace switches as described left.

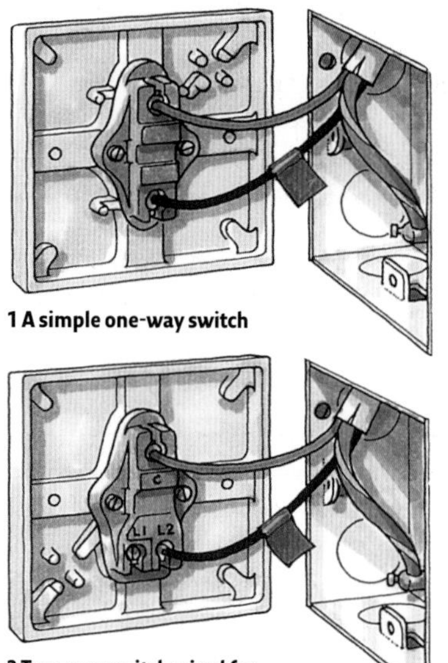

1 A simple one-way switch

2 Two-way switch wired for one-way function

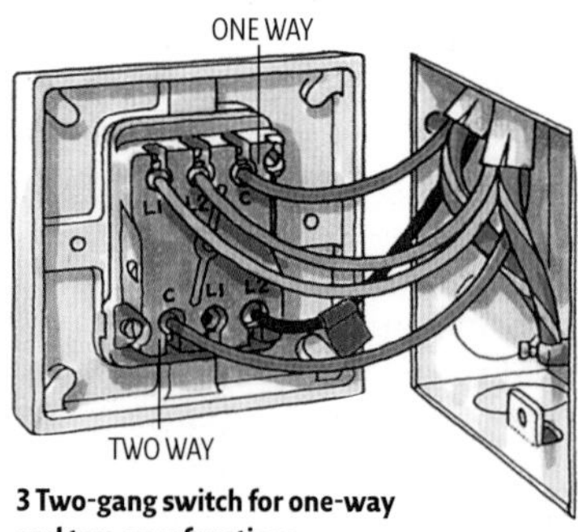

3 Two-gang switch for one-way and two-way functions

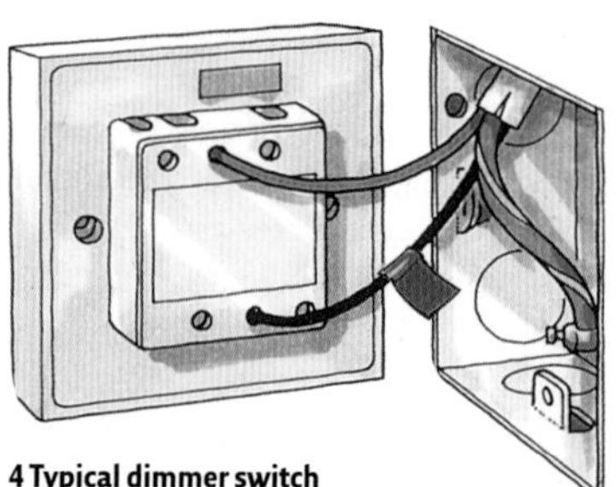

4 Typical dimmer switch

SEE ALSO > Building Regulations 284, Colour coding 285, Switching off 296, Flush mounting 307, Light switches 329, Two-and-three-way lighting 332

Adding new switches and circuits

When you want to move a switch or install a new one, you will have to modify the circuit cables or run a new spur cable from the existing lighting circuit to take the power to where it is needed.

Replacing a wall switch with a ceiling switch N

In a bathroom, light switches must be outside zones 0 to 3. If your bathroom has a wall switch that breaks this rule, replace it with a double-pole ceiling switch positioned at least 0.6m (2ft) horizontally from the bath or shower.

Turn off the power at the consumer unit, then remove the old switch. If the cable running up the wall is surface-mounted or in a plastic conduit, pull it up into the ceiling void. It needs to be long enough to reach the point where the new switch will be located.

If the switch cable is buried in the wall, trace it in the ceiling void and cut it. Then wire the remaining part that runs to the light into a three-terminal junction box fixed to a joist or to a piece of wood nailed between two joists. Connect the conductors to separate terminals (**1**), and from those terminals run a new 1.5mm² two-core-and-earth cable to the site of the ceiling switch.

Bore a hole in the ceiling to pass the cable through to the switch. Screw the switch to a joist if the hole is close enough; otherwise, fix a support board between the joists.

Knock out the entry hole in the back-plate of the switch and pass the cable through, then screw the plate to the ceiling. Strip and prepare the ends of the conductors, connecting the earth wire to the terminal on the backplate. Connect the brown and blue conductors to the terminals on the switch – either wire to either terminal (**2**). Finally, attach the switch to the backplate and make good any damage done to the plasterwork.

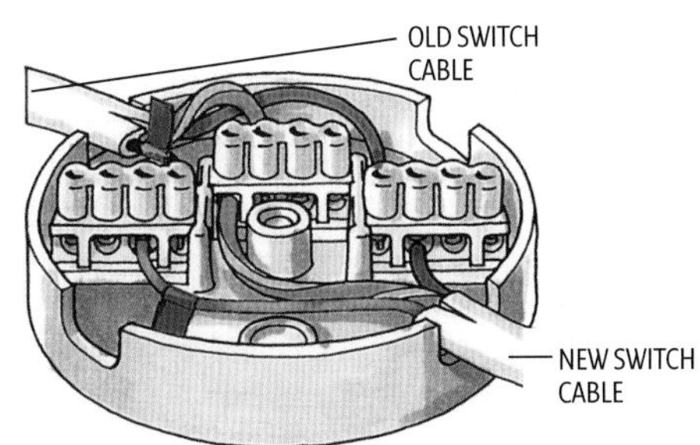

1 Link the switch cable with a junction box

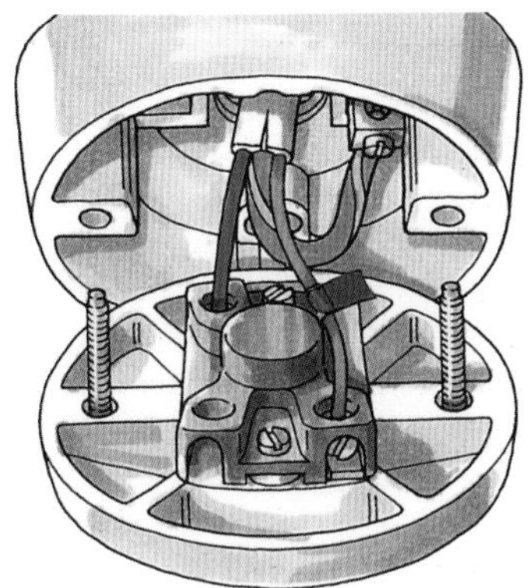
2 Wiring a ceiling switch

Old colour coding
In a house built before 2005 you are likely to find the existing cables are colour-coded black for neutral and red for live. The diagrams on this page show new-style cables being connected to existing old-style circuit cables.

Adding a new switch and light

Switch the power off at the consumer unit and inspect your lighting circuit to check whether it is earthed. If there's no earth wire, get professional advice.

Decide where you want to mount the light, and bore a hole through the ceiling for the cable. If the ceiling rose can't be screwed to a joist, nail a board between two joists to provide a strong fixing for the rose.

Bore another hole right above the site of the new switch and close to the wall. Push twists of paper through both holes, so you can find them easily from above. Screw the switch mounting box to the wall and cut a chase in the plaster for the cable, up to the hole already bored in the ceiling.

Your new light fitting can be supplied with power from a nearby junction box or ceiling rose that's already on the lighting circuit – or, if it's more convenient, from a new junction box wired into the lighting-circuit cable. From whichever of these sources you choose, run a 1.5mm² two-core-and-earth cable to the position of the new light fitting – but don't connect to the lighting circuit till the new installation has been completed. Push the end of the cable through the hole in the ceiling and identify it with tape marked 'Mains'.

The next step is to run a similar cable from the switch to the same lighting point and identify it with tape marked 'Switch'.

Strip and prepare the cable at the switch, connecting the earth wire to the terminal on the mounting box – and connect the brown and blue conductors, either wire to either terminal if it is a one-way switch. If you are using a two-way switch, connect the brown wire to the 'Common' terminal and the blue wire to 'L2'. Screw the switch to the box.

Knock out the cable-entry hole in the ceiling rose and feed both cables through it, then screw the rose to the ceiling.

Take the cable marked 'Mains' and connect its brown conductor to the live central block and its blue one to the neutral block. Slip a green-and-yellow sleeve over the earth wire and connect it to the earth terminal.

Connect the brown wire of the switch cable to the live block, and the blue wire to the switch-wire block: mark the blue wire with brown tape. Connect the switch earth wire to the earth terminal. Connect the pendant flex and screw on the rose cover.

With the power turned off, connect the new light circuit to the old one at the rose or junction box. The new conductors will have to share terminals with the old wires already connected: brown to live, blue to neutral, and earth to earth (see right) Finally, test and switch on the new circuit.

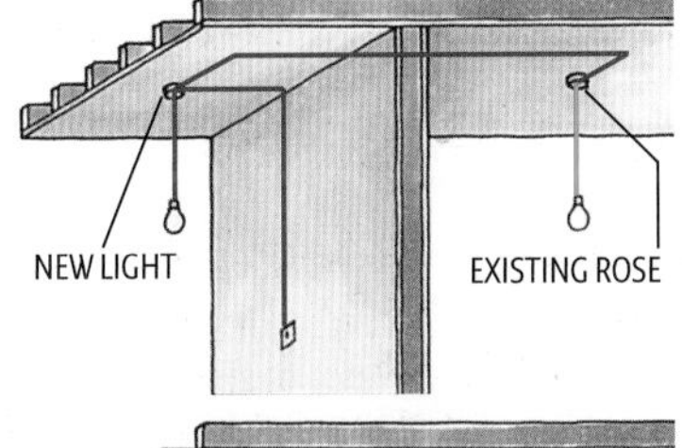

Circuit for a new light
You can take the power for a new light from an existing ceiling rose or junction box, or insert a new junction box into the existing lighting circuit.

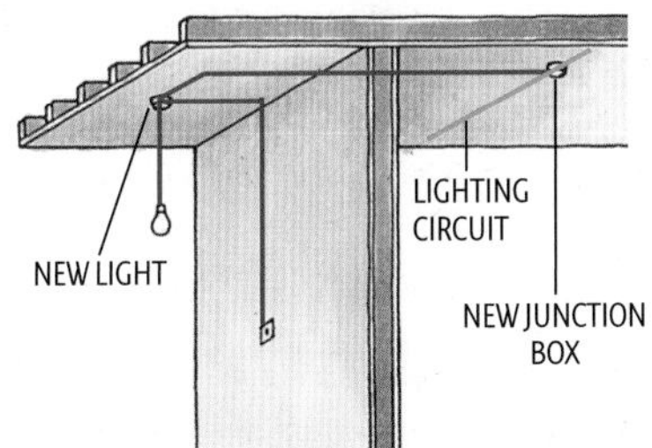

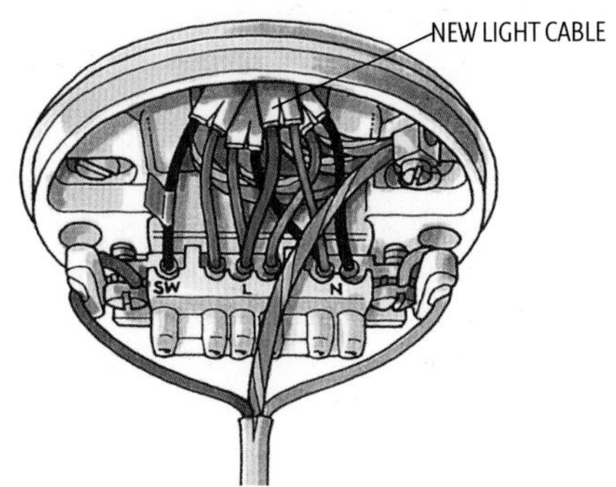

Lighting cable connected to a loop-in rose

SEE ALSO > Building Regulations 284, Bathroom zones 287, Testing circuits 288–9, Switching off 296, Important notes at consumer unit 298, Stripping cable 302, Running cable 303–5, Junction box 309, Lighting circuits 324, Wiring a rose 324–5, Fixing to ceiling 325, Circuit lengths 344

Two-and-three way lighting

There are situations in which a light should be controllable from two points. For example, a landing light needs to be controlled from both the top and bottom of the stairs.

Adding a two-way light

Installing a new two-way light is very similar to installing a one-way light, the only real difference being in the wiring of the switches.

First, mount the ceiling rose and both of the two-way switches, then run a 1.5mm² two-core-and-earth cable from the power source to the light and from the light to the nearest switch. Don't connect the new installation to the lighting circuit until all the wiring has been completed.

Run a 1.5mm² three-core-and-earth cable from the first to the second switch. Then strip the conductors and prepare them for connecting to the switches, slipping insulating sleeves over the bare earth wires.

At the first switch you will have two cables to connect: the switch cable from the light and the one linking the two switches. The switch cable has three conductors (brown, blue and green-and-yellow); the linking cable has four (brown, black, grey and green-and-yellow). Connect the green-and-yellow wires from both cables to the earth terminal on the mounting box (**1**). Next, connect the brown wire from the linking cable to the 'Common' terminal on the switch. Connect the black wire and either the brown or blue switch-cable wire to the 'L1' terminal. Connect the grey wire and the remaining switch-cable wire to 'L2' (**1**). Screw the switch's faceplate to the mounting box.

At the second switch, connect the linking cable's green-and-yellow wire to the earth terminal; its brown wire to the 'Common' terminal; its black wire to 'L1'; and its grey wire to 'L2' (**1**). Screw the switch's faceplate to the box.

Make sure the power is switched off, and then connect the installation to the lighting circuit at either a ceiling rose or a junction box. Finally, test the new installation.

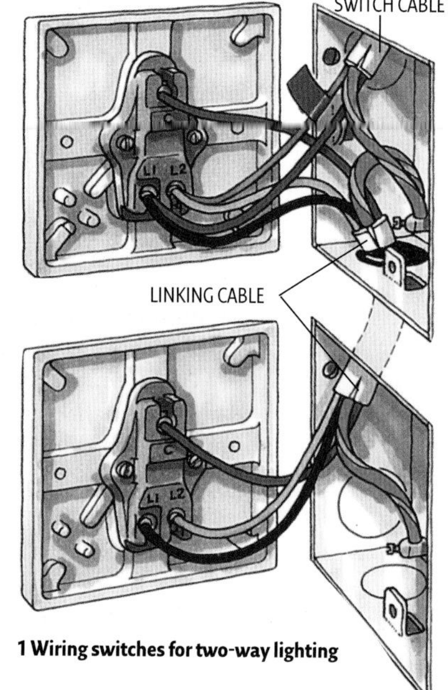

1 Wiring switches for two-way lighting

Three-way lighting

You can control a light from three places by adding an intermediate switch to the circuit described above. The intermediate switch interrupts the three-core-and-earth cable linking the other two. It has two 'L1' and two 'L2' terminals.

At its mounting box you will have two identical sets of wires – brown, black, grey and green-and-yellow. Connect the green-and-yellow wires to the earth terminal on the box (**2**) and join the two brown wires – which play no part in the intermediate switching – with a plastic connector (**2**).

Connect the grey and black wires of either cable to the 'L1' terminals on the new switch and those of the other cable to the 'L2' terminals (**2**). Then screw the faceplate to the mounting box.

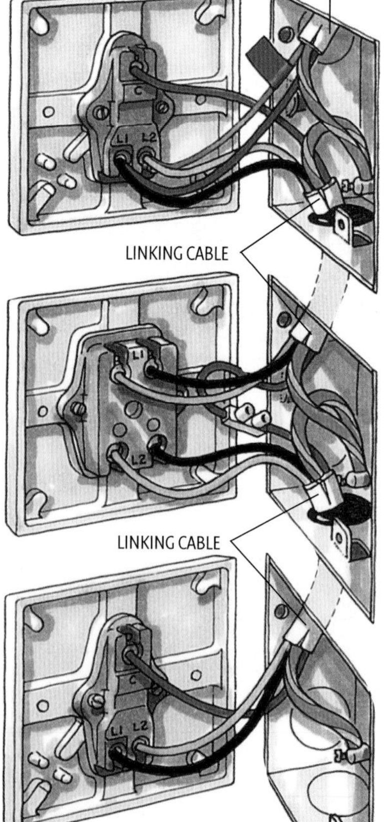

2 Wiring switches for three-way lighting

Two-way lighting
(right)
1 Consumer unit
2 Light fitting
3 Lighting-circuit cable
4 Switch cable
5 Switch
6 Linking cable
7 Junction box

Three-way lighting
(far right)
1 Consumer unit
2 Light fitting
3 Lighting-circuit cable
4 Switch cable
5 Switch
6 Intermediate switch
7 Linking cable
8 Junction box

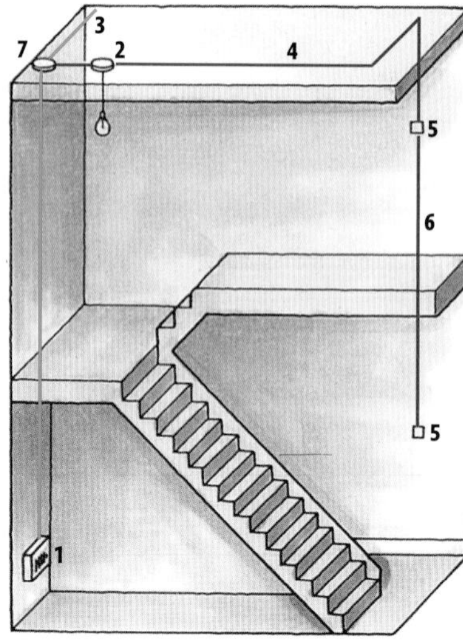

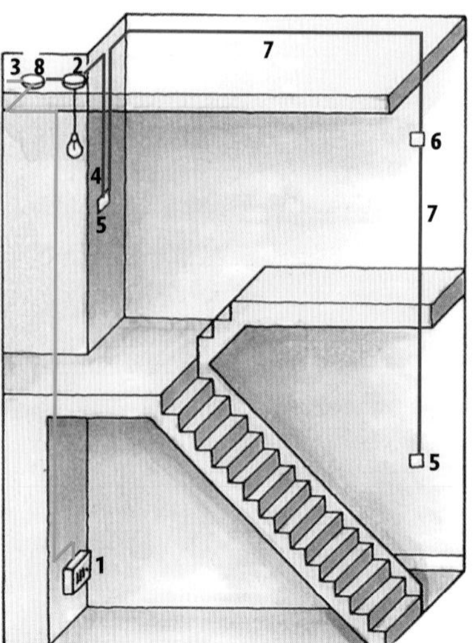

SEE ALSO > Testing circuits 288–9, Switching off 296, Cable 302, Running cable 303–5, Connecting to junction boxes 309, Lighting circuits 324, Adding new switch and light 331, Connecting to loop-in rose 331, Circuit lengths 344

Adding wall lights

Many wall lights are supplied without integral backplates to enclose the wires and connections. To comply with the Wiring Regulations, such a fitting must be attached to a noncombustible mounting such as a BESA box – a round plastic or metal box that's screwed to the wall in a recess chopped out of the plaster and brickwork.

Alternatively, you can use an architrave-switch mounting box. This is a slim box that will leave plenty of room on each side for the wallplug fixings needed for the light fitting. Both types of mounting box are fixed to the wall in the same way as the boxes used for flush-mounted socket outlets.

The basic circuit and connections

The simplest way to connect wall lights to the lighting circuit is via a junction box. The procedure is to complete the wall-light installation first, then switch off the electricity and connect the new installation to the junction box.

Wire up a one-way switch. All the wall lights in the room will be controlled by this switch – although lights with integral switches can be controlled individually, too.

Next, run a 1.5mm² two-core-and-earth cable from the junction box, looping in and out of each wall-light mounting to the last one, where the cable ends.

Prepare the cut ends of the conductors for connection. At each of the lights, slip green-and-yellow sleeving over the earth wires and connect them to the earth terminal on the mounting box.

Connect up the brown and blue wires to the block connector inside each light fitting – connecting the blue conductors to the terminal already holding the blue wire, and the brown conductors to the terminal already holding the brown wire.

The last wall-light mounting will have one end of the cable entering it; connect the wires as described above.

Using an architrave-switch mounting box

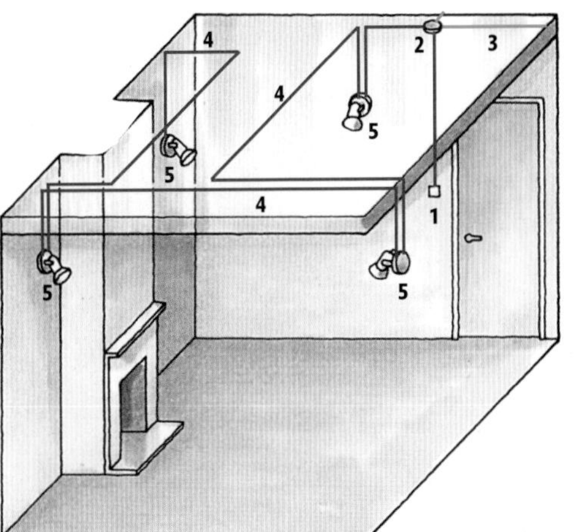

Basic wall-light circuit
The basic circuit and connections are as described above.
1 Switch
2 Junction box
3 Existing lighting circuit
4 1.5mm² wall-light cable
5 Wall light

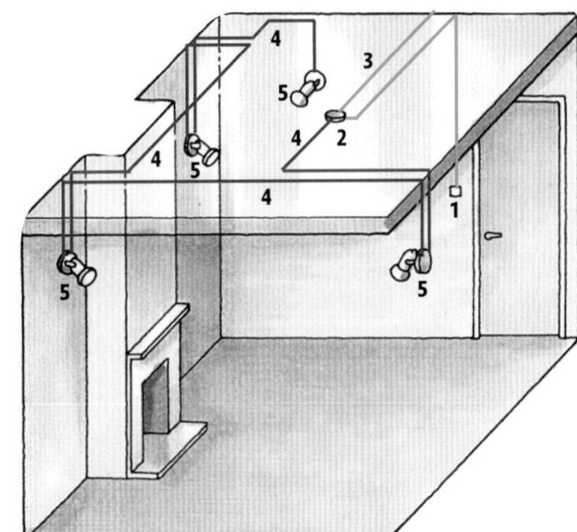

Replacing a ceiling light
You can dispense with a ceiling light in favour of wall lights, using the existing wiring and switch. Switch off the power, then remove the rose and connect up the wiring to a fixed junction box.
1 Existing switch and cable
2 Junction box replaces rose
3 Existing lighting circuit
4 1.5mm² wall-light cable
5 Wall light

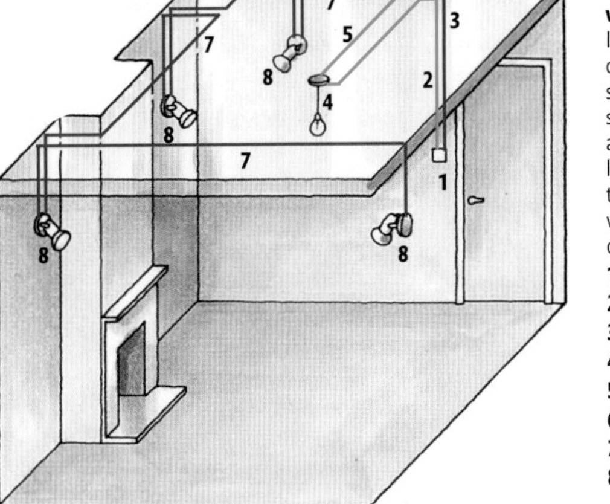

Ceiling light plus wall lights
If you want to retain your ceiling light, you can substitute a two-gang switch for the single one – and wire the present ceiling-light cable to one half of the switch, and the new wall-lighting cable to the other half.
1 Two-gang switch
2 Old switch cable
3 New switch cable
4 Ceiling light
5 Existing lighting circuit
6 Junction box
7 1.5mm² wall-light cable
8 Wall light

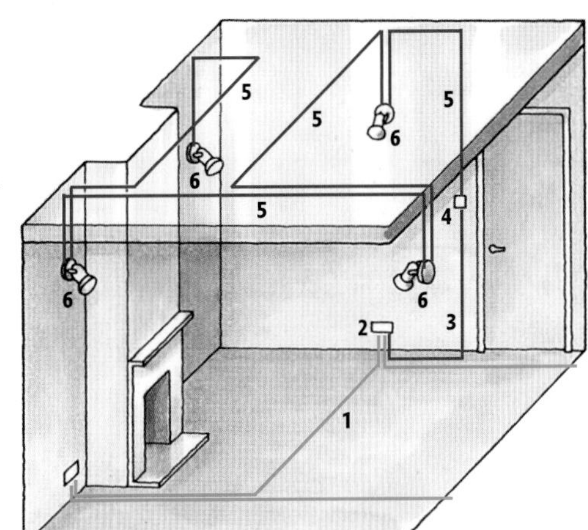

Using a spur
Wall lights can be wired to a ring circuit by means of a spur cable. Run a 2.5mm² two-core-and-earth spur from a nearby socket to a switched fused connection unit that has a 3amp fuse.
1 Ring circuit
2 Socket outlet
3 Spur cable
4 Fused connection unit
5 1.5mm² wall-light cable
6 Wall light

SEE ALSO > Testing circuits 288–9, Switching off 296, Cable 302, Running cable 303–5, Running a spur 309, Fused connection units 310, Lighting circuits 324, Light fittings 326, Light switches 329, Circuit lengths 344

Low-voltage lighting

Originally, low-voltage halogen light fittings were developed for illuminating commercial premises. Being small and unobtrusive, they blend into any scheme and the bright intense beams of light they produce are ideal for display lighting. The potential for dramatic effects and narrowly focused task lighting was not lost on home owners, and manufacturers were quick to respond with a range of low-voltage fittings.

N If you undertake work marked with this symbol, you must inform the BCO before starting – see FIRST THINGS FIRST.

The specially designed miniature bulb is the key to what makes low-voltage lighting so attractive. The light source is concentrated into a small filament, which enables accurate focusing of spotlight beams. The integral 'dichroic' reflector allows the heat generated by the filament to escape backward into the fitting, creating a cool but intense white light. Coloured bulbs are also available for special effects and mood lighting.

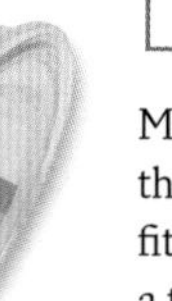

Low-voltage halogen bulb

Low-voltage light fittings

Miniature fixed or adjustable 'eyeball' downlighters recessed into the ceiling are among the most widely used low-voltage light fittings. They can be mounted individually or wired in groups to a transformer, which is also concealed in the space above the ceiling. Some fittings are made with integral transformers; these include table lamps and small spotlights. Others, such as track lights, combine several individual fittings connected to a single transformer. Unique to low-voltage lighting are fittings connected to exposed plastic-sheathed cables suspended across the room.

Optimum voltage

Even a small increase from the designed voltage can halve the life of a bulb. If the voltage is too low, light output drops and eventually the bulb blackens. Voltage can be affected in a number of ways, and you need to select your equipment accordingly.

Choose a transformer with an output that closely matches the combined wattage of the bulbs on the circuit. It's important to ensure that the total wattage of these bulbs is greater than 70 per cent of the transformer rating, or the bulbs will burn out relatively quickly. For example, a 50W transformer can supply two 20W bulbs or one 50W. A 200W transformer is perfect for four 50W bulbs, but not for six 20W bulbs (for these, you would want a 150W transformer). If you buy a low-voltage kit, you can be sure the transformer is suitable. Even with a perfectly matched transformer, replace a blown bulb as soon as possible to avoid overloading the other bulbs on the circuit.

Dimmer switches

Using ordinary dimmer switches is not advisable, because they too reduce voltage to an unacceptable level. For this type of control, check that the low-voltage fittings are suitable for dimming and only use dimmer switches specifically designed for low-voltage lighting.

Using separate components N

If you install a low-voltage lighting kit that comes ready-wired (see opposite), there is no need to notify your Building Control Officer except when it is fitted in a special location such as a kitchen or bathroom. However, if for some reason it is not convenient to use this type of kit, it is possible to install low-voltage lighting, using individual components, such as light fittings, transformer and cable. However this type of work is notifiable.

Having decided on the ideal location of each light fitting, choose a central position for the transformer.

The connections of the mains-voltage supply and switching would be the same as the kit system shown opposite. However, on the low-voltage side, use a separate 1.5mm² two-core cable for each light fitting, keeping this as short as possible – a maximum of 4 metres from each fitting to the output terminals of the transformer. Normally, each light fitting is supplied with a terminal block for connecting its heat-resistant flex to the cable.

If necessary, you can install longer cables to each light fitting, but this would involve calculating the larger cable sizes required.

Low-voltage fittings
These light fittings take their power from special plastic-coated low-voltage cable that stretches from wall to wall. This system is unique to low-voltage lighting.

SEE ALSO > Building Regulations 284, Cables 302, Dimmer switches 329

Installing a ready-wired lighting kit

There is no need to notify your Building Control Officer if you install a ready-wired low-voltage kit, provided it is CE marked and it is not in a special location, such as a bathroom or kitchen. The circuit described here includes a kit with a transformer, supplying three individual halogen lamps of equal wattage.

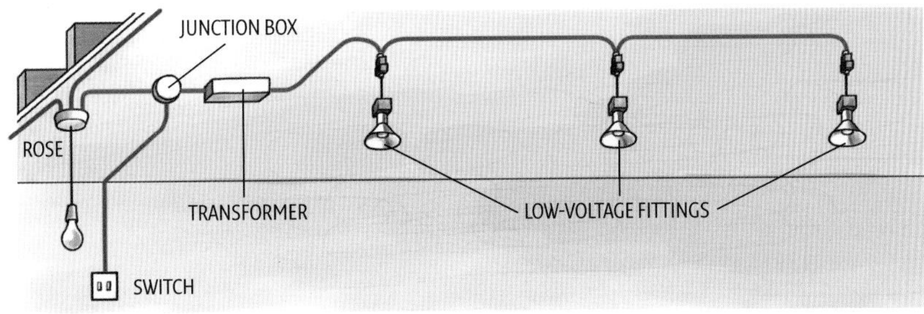

Take power from the nearest ceiling rose

Making the connections

Place the transformer at a convenient point for the light fittings – the maximum spacing of these fittings is limited by the length of the flex supplied. Screw the transformer to a joist, between the ceiling and the floorboards above. Clear any insulation from around the transformer.

Screw a four-terminal junction box to the joist close to the transformer. Prepare the flex already connected to the input side of the transformer and connect this to the switch-wire and neutral terminals in the junction box. From the same box, run a 1.5mm² two-core-and-earth cable to the switch position, and a circuit-feed cable of similar size to the nearest ceiling rose, where you will pick up the 230V mains supply (but don't make this connection yet). Make all the connections at the junction box as shown (**1**).

Each light fitting has a special plug attached to the back of the lamp by a short length of heat-resistant flex. Insert this plug into the matching socket on the flex supplied with the kit (**2**) – then clip this flex to a joist to make sure it cannot touch the back of any of the light fittings, which can become hot. Keep this low-voltage flex separate from any cable carrying mains-voltage electricity. At the transformer, connect the flex to the output terminals (**3**) as described in the manufacturer's instructions.

Fit an ordinary wall switch to control the lighting (**4**).

Connecting to the mains

Having turned off the power, connect the live, neutral and earth wires of the circuit-feed cable to the ceiling rose (**5**).

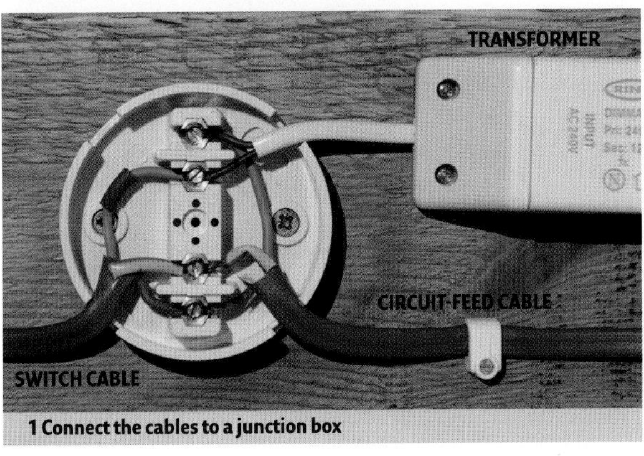

1 Connect the cables to a junction box

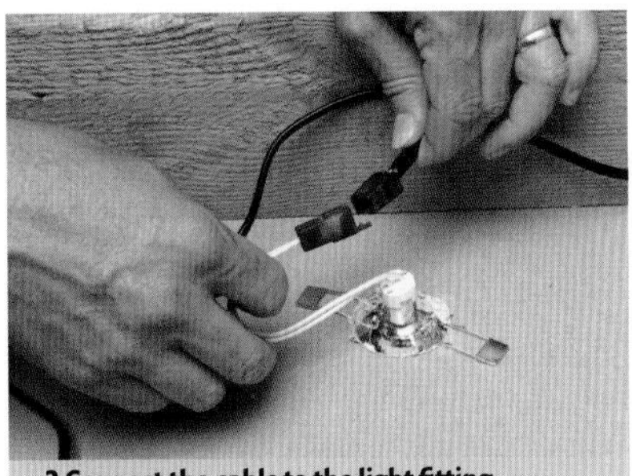

2 Connect the cable to the light fitting

3 Connect live and neutral wires to output terminals

4 Wire the wall switch

5 Switch off and connect cable to the ceiling rose

Mains-voltage halogen

You can buy mains-voltage halogen fittings that are very similar in appearance to the low-voltage versions. Their main advantage is that they don't require a remote transformer to reduce the power to 12V and can therefore be connected to existing wiring, like other mains-voltage fittings. However, the bulbs and fittings are generally more expensive than the low-voltage equivalents.

• 230V halogen
All extra-low-voltage wiring is notifiable, but wiring 230V fittings is only notifiable in special locations.

With some mains-voltage ranges, an electronic transformer is built into the base of each bulb. As a result, the filament within the bulb operates on 12V, just like any other low-voltage fitting. This type of bulb is usually made with an Edison-screw end cap.

Most ranges of mains-voltage fittings accommodate a bulb with two pins that engage a spring-loaded lampholder, similar in principle to the familiar bayonet-cap bulbs. These bulbs contain quartz burners that operate on 230V.

Mains-voltage fittings emit the same sort of bright, sparkling illumination that is normally associated with low-voltage lighting – but if you want a lamp with a relatively cool output, make sure you choose mains-voltage bulbs made with dichroic reflectors, rather than the aluminium-coated versions.

SEE ALSO > Building Regulations 284, Switching off 296, Cable 302, Running cable 303–5

Using electricity outdoors

Electrical work in the garden is subject to the same regulations that govern wiring inside the house. Indeed, you are required to notify the BCO before you install any exterior electrical fittings, except for ready-wired plug-in kits and solar powered lights and pumps.

Ⓝ If you undertake work marked with this symbol, you must inform the BCO before starting – see FIRST THINGS FIRST.

Despite these restrictions, there are good reasons for extending your electrical installation outside the house. First, and most important, it is safer to run electric garden tools from a convenient, properly protected socket than to trail long leads from unsuitable sockets inside the house – a practice that can lead to serious accidents. A garage or workshop is also safer and more efficient if it is equipped with good lighting and its own circuit from which to run power tools.

Finally, well-arranged lighting and waterfalls or fountains powered by electric pumps add to the charm of a garden or patio and can extend its use in summer by providing a pleasing background for barbecues and outdoor parties.

SAFETY OUTDOORS

The need for absolute safety outdoors cannot be overemphasized.

- The BCO must be notified in advance and permission granted before you install equipment other than plug-in kits or solar-powered fittings.
- Install only light fittings specifically made for outside use.
- Protect all outside installations with residual current devices (RCDs), as they provide an almost instantaneous response to earth-leakage faults.
- Always disconnect the power before servicing electrical equipment and tools. Don't handle pool lighting or pumps unless the power is off.
- Wear thick rubber-soled footwear when using electric garden tools.
- Choose double-insulated power tools for extra protection.

Installing a socket for garden tools Ⓝ

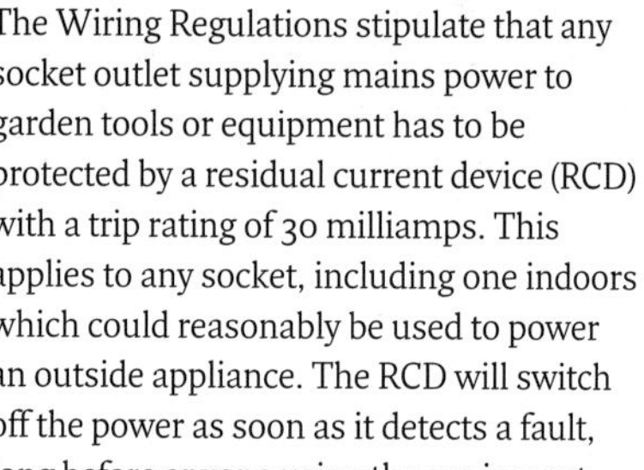

Socket with integral RCD

Adaptor RCDs plug into any socket outlet

The Wiring Regulations stipulate that any socket outlet supplying mains power to garden tools or equipment has to be protected by a residual current device (RCD) with a trip rating of 30 milliamps. This applies to any socket, including one indoors which could reasonably be used to power an outside appliance. The RCD will switch off the power as soon as it detects a fault, long before anyone using the equipment can receive a fatal electric shock.

Outdoors or indoors?

There are special external waterproof socket outlets. These are best installed by a qualified electrician able to satisfy the requirements of the BCO.

You can use an ordinary socket, provided it is protected by an RCD and is housed in a weatherproof workshop, garage, lobby or conservatory that's part of the house. Mount this type of socket high enough to prevent it being struck by a wheelbarrow or hidden by garden tools.

Providing RCD protection

You can provide RCD protection in several ways. Perhaps the best method is to have a consumer unit with its own built-in RCD, or to fit a separate RCD near the consumer unit so that it protects the whole ring circuit, including any spurs for garden equipment. Alternatively, install a socket that incorporates an RCD.

RCDs fitted in plug-in adaptors will provide some protection, but they do not satisfy the requirement for the socket itself to be protected.

Fitting a porch light Ⓝ

A light illuminating the entrance welcomes visitors to your home and helps them to identify the house. It also enables you to view unexpected callers before you open the door. Choose a light that is specifically designed for outdoor use – the fitting must be weatherproof, and the bulb has to be held in a moisture-proof rubber gasket or cup that surrounds the electrical connections.

If possible, position the porch light in such a way that the cable to it can be run straight through the wall or ceiling of the porch, directly into the back of the fitting. But if an ordinary cable has to be run along an outside wall, it must be protected by being passed through a length of plastic conduit.

A porch light can be installed by a procedure very similar to that for adding a new light indoors. Take the power from the nearest ceiling rose – probably in the entrance hall – and run it to a 5amp four-terminal junction box screwed to a board between ceiling joists. From the junction box, run a 1.5mm² two-core-and-earth cable to a switch mounted near the door and run a similar cable to the light fitting itself.

Bore a hole through the wall where you plan to position the light. Cement a short length of plastic conduit into the hole, using a soft rubber grommet to seal each end of the tube.

Run the cable through the conduit and wire it to the fitting, following the manufacturer's instructions. With the power switched off, connect the porch-light cable at the ceiling rose.

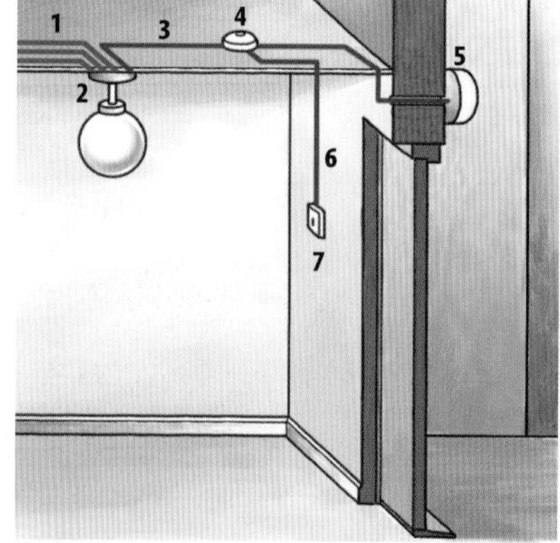

Porch-light circuit
1 Loop-in circuit and switch cables
2 Ceiling rose
3 1.5mm² lighting cable
4 Junction box
5 Porch light
6 Switch cable
7 Porch-light switch

SEE ALSO > Building Regulations 284, Testing circuits 288–9, Switching off 296, RCDs 297, 298, Running cable 303–5, Running a spur 309, Lighting circuits 324, Junction box 324, One-way switch 330, Adding a new light 331, Connecting to a loop-in rose 331, Circuit lengths 344

Security lighting

Any form of exterior lighting that illuminates the approaches to your house and garage allows you to move about your home with greater convenience and safety – and if it's controlled automatically, it saves you having to fumble with your door keys in the dark. However, probably higher on most people's list of priorities is the added security afforded by installing a system that will detect the presence of intruders and draw attention to their activities.

Dusk-to-dawn lighting

You cannot feel completely secure if you have to remember to switch on exterior lighting every evening. The simplest solution is to install exterior light fittings that are controlled automatically by the ambient light level. Known as dusk-to-dawn lights, these fittings create permanently illuminated areas during the hours of darkness. A photocell detects a change in the level of daylight, switching the lamp on at the approach of darkness and off again early in the morning. For larger properties, install a single photocell that controls a number of ordinary exterior light fittings.

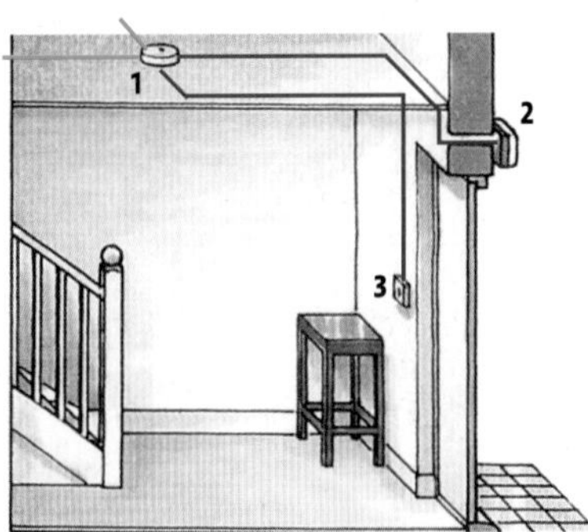

Wiring dusk-to-dawn security lighting
1 Junction box inserted in existing lighting circuit.
2 Light fitting with built-in photocell.
3 Wall switch.

The circuit

From a junction box installed in your domestic lighting circuit, run a 1.5mm² two-core-and-earth cable to the light fitting and another cable of the same size from the junction box to an ordinary wall switch. If you want to install more than one light fitting, run the cable from the junction box to each light in turn, using the single switch to control all of them.

Adjusting security lighting

A screw is usually provided for adjusting the sensitivity of the photocell. Wait till it is getting dark; then turn on the wall switch and gradually adjust the screw until the light comes on. The photocell will operate the lighting, provided the wall switch is left on.

Installing a light fitting (N)

Plan the installation carefully, making sure the light fitting is mounted high enough to prevent unauthorized interference. Drill a cable-access hole through the wall, and line it with a short length of plastic conduit (see FITTING A PORCH LIGHT, opposite). Pass a length of cable through the hole in the wall and into the back of the fitting. Screw the light fitting to the wall.

Inside the fitting, cut the separate conductors to length, leaving enough slack to reach their separate terminals. Connect the blue conductor to the neutral terminal and the brown one to the live terminal - these may have internal wiring already connected to them (1). Fit green-and-yellow sleeving over the bare earth conductor and connect it to the earth terminal. It may be necessary to connect internal wires to the photocell before the bulb is fitted and the cover replaced.

Now run the cable from the light fitting to where you are going to connect up to the lighting circuit.

Mounting the light switch

Cut the cable chase in the plaster and mount a plastic or metal box on the wall for the switch. Then run the cable into the mounting box, and connect the blue and brown conductors to the terminals of a simple one-way switch (2). Sleeve the earth conductor and connect it to the earth terminal in the mounting box. Screw the faceplate to the mounting box, then take the cable to the point in the lighting circuit where you plan to install the junction box.

1 Wiring the light fitting

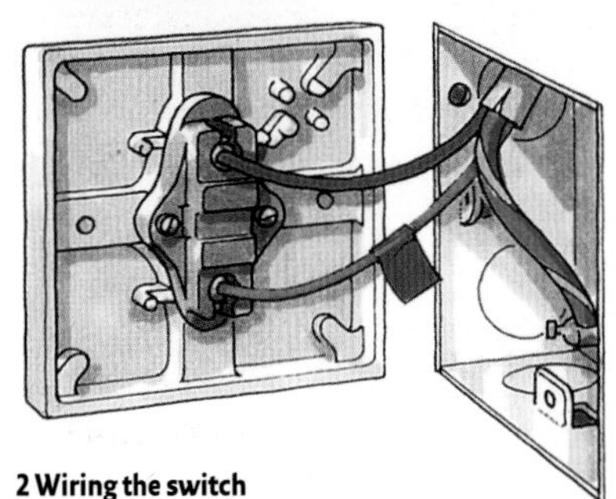

2 Wiring the switch

Connecting to the lighting circuit

The power must be switched off at the consumer unit, and the lighting-circuit fuse removed or the MCB removed or locked off. Cut the lighting cable in order to install a four-terminal junction box. Screw the box securely to a joist. The terminals in the box, which are normally unmarked, should be designated as live, neutral, earth and switch.

Prepare the cut ends of the lighting-circuit cable and connect the live, neutral and earth conductors to their respective terminals (3).

Prepare the end of the cable running from the light fitting and connect its brown conductor to the switch terminal (3). Connect its blue conductor to the neutral terminal, and its sheathed earth conductor to the earth terminal.

Prepare the end of the cable running from the switch and then connect its brown conductor to the live terminal, the sleeved earth conductor to the earth terminal, and the blue conductor to the switch terminal (3). Identify this last conductor by wrapping a piece of brown tape round it. Make sure all the connections are secure, and then refit the cover of the junction box.

If the new circuit tests satisfactorily, the power supply can be switched back on at the consumer unit.

• **Old colour coding**
In a house built before 2005 you are likely to find the existing cables are colour-coded black for neutral and red for live. The diagram below shows new-style cable being connected to existing old-style circuit cable.

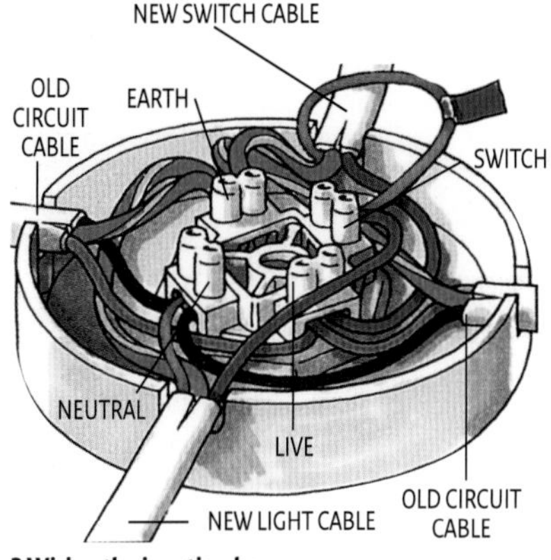

3 Wiring the junction box

SEE ALSO > Building Regulations 284, Testing circuits 288–9, Switching off 296, Important notes at consumer unit 298. Running cable 303–5, Lighting circuits 324, Infra-red lighting 338, Circuit lengths 344

Passive infra-red lighting

Exterior lights connected to a passive infra-red detector illuminate only when the sensor picks up the body heat of someone within range. The detector is also fitted with a photocell, so the lights operate only at night.

(N) If you undertake work marked with this symbol, you must inform the BCO before starting – see FIRST THINGS FIRST.

A passive infra-red system has two advantages over simple dusk-to-dawn lighting. A porch light, for example, switches on only as you or visitors approach the entrance, then switches off again after a set period. This means you're not wasting electricity by burning a lamp continuously all night. Secondly, remote passive infra-red detectors can be positioned to detect an intruder almost anywhere around your home and will switch on all your security lights or only those you think necessary. The effect is likely to startle intruders and deter them from approaching any further.

Light fittings and sensors

Because infra-red detectors are designed to be mounted about 2.5m (8ft) above ground level, light fittings made with integral detectors tend to be for porch lighting and most of them are styled accordingly. However, since the lighting needs to be operated for periods of no more than a few minutes at a time, remote infra-red detectors are often used to control powerful halogen floodlights. Floodlights are also available with built-in detectors, which simplifies the wiring.

Security lighting
1 Remote passive infra-red detector
2 Halogen floodlight
3 Porch light with integral detector

Positioning detectors

Unless you position detectors carefully, your security lighting will be activated unnecessarily. This can be a nuisance to neighbours and, as with any security device that's constantly giving false alarms, you will soon begin to mistrust it and ignore its warnings.

Infra-red detectors have sensitivity controls so that they won't be activated by moving foliage or the presence of small animals. However, if your house is close to a footpath, you will need to adjust the angle of the detectors so that the lights don't switch on every time a pedestrian passes by.

When fitting a remote detector, make sure it isn't aimed directly at a floodlight that it is controlling – or its photocell will try to switch it off as soon as it comes on and the likely result will be a light that simply flickers and never fully illuminates the scene.

It is also important not to position an infra-red detector above a balanced flue from a boiler, or any other source of heat that could activate the sensor.

The circuit

It is usually possible to wire infra-red security lighting in exactly the same way as dusk-to-dawn lighting. However, as some detectors are capable of controlling several powerful floodlights, you may not be able to run them from the domestic lighting circuit. In which case, you will need to run a 2.5mm² two-core-and-earth spur from a power circuit and control the lighting with a switched fused connection unit.

Use a 3amp fuse in the connection unit for a combined rating of up to 690W; a 13amp fuse for anything greater.

Wiring a remote sensor (N)

Unless the manufacturer's instructions suggest an alternative method, wire an individual light fitting with an integral infra-red detector in the same manner as a dusk to dawn fitting.

To wire a remote sensor controlling light fittings mounted elsewhere, take the incoming cable from the junction box or fused connection unit into the back of the fitting and connect its brown and blue conductors to the 'Mains' terminals. Run a second cable of the same size from the 'Load' terminals back through the wall and on to the first light fitting. Sleeve both bare copper earth conductors and connect them to the earth terminal.

Wire the first light fitting using the method described for a dusk-to-dawn fitting, then connect another cable to the same terminals and run it on to the second light fitting, and so on.

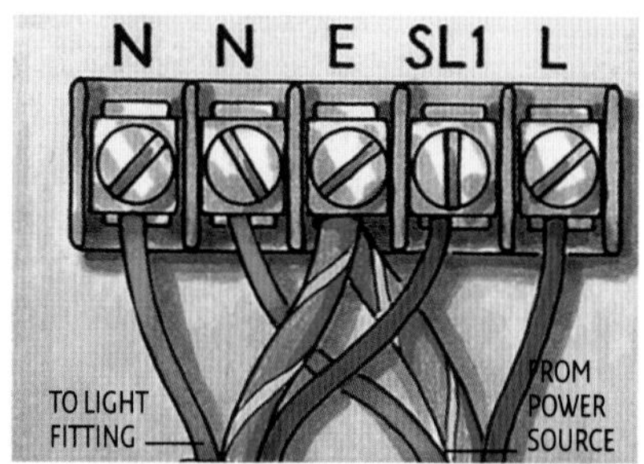

Wiring a remote sensor

Adjusting detectors

Once all the connections are made, you need to set the infra-red detector's adjustment knobs or screws. One of them is for setting the photocell so that the system operates only during the hours of darkness. A second control dictates the period of time that the lights will remain on – three or four minutes should be sufficient.

The final operation is to set the sensor's controls

SEE ALSO > Building Regulations 284, Switching off 296, Running cable 303–5, Running a spur 309, Fused connection units 310, Lighting circuits 324, Dusk-to-dawn lighting 337, Circuit lengths 344

Closed-circuit television

Surveillance by closed-circuit television acts as a deterrent to would-be intruders – and if you choose to record the output from your cameras, in the event of a burglary it may help the police to apprehend the perpetrator and recover your stolen property.

There are numerous CCTV systems at your disposal, including highly sophisticated equipment primarily designed for protecting commercial premises. You are required to notify the BCO before installing most types of CCTV system, but if you choose one of the relatively inexpensive but effective plug-in DIY kits you can install it yourself without notification. However, if a kit is installed as described overleaf then it is categorized as fixed wiring and is therefore notifiable.

Do-it-yourself kits

Not every CCTV kit contains the same equipment, but illustrated below is a selection of accessories sold for DIY installation. Light fittings are rarely, if ever, included in these kits, but since a great many attempted burglaries occur after dark, it's hardly worth the expense of installing CCTV unless you are prepared to buy and install compatible security lighting. A monitor is not required, as DIY kits are designed to be connected to ordinary television sets and video-cassette recorders.

Camera and cable

Power-supply unit

Scart connector

Switcher unit

Distribution box

Light and buzzer

Switcher unit remote control

VCR controller

Extension cable

Cameras
Up to four cameras can be connected to the average CCTV system. Black-and-white cameras are the least expensive and tend to give a sharper image in low light levels. Most cameras incorporate a microphone, and some have built-in PIR (passive infra-red) movement detectors.

Power-supply unit
CCTV power-supply units have built-in 13amp plugs. There are heater elements in the cameras to prevent condensation, so they have to be connected to the electrical supply permanently. Power consumption, however, is negligible.

Distribution box
This compact unit sends the signals from the camera to your television set. You can make the connection using phono plugs, but a Scart connector is preferable.

Switcher unit
You will only need a switcher unit if you have more than one camera. Connected to the distribution box, it has a socket for each camera input.

VCR controller
This device switches on your VCR when a camera detects movement in the vicinity of your house.

Audible warning
A buzzer will alert you when a camera picks up a possible intruder, even when your TV set is switched off. The unit, which also includes a small flashing light, plugs into the distribution box.

Cable
Special colour-coded multi-core cable transmits the signals from the camera to your TV set. It is supplied in standard lengths, and extension cables are available.

SEE ALSO > Building Regulations 284, Security lighting 337–9, Installing CCTV 340

Installing CCTV (N)

Although the type of plug-in kit described below is designed for DIY installation, the installation of such a system becomes notifiable if fixed wiring and external security lighting are used.

Installing a plug-in system

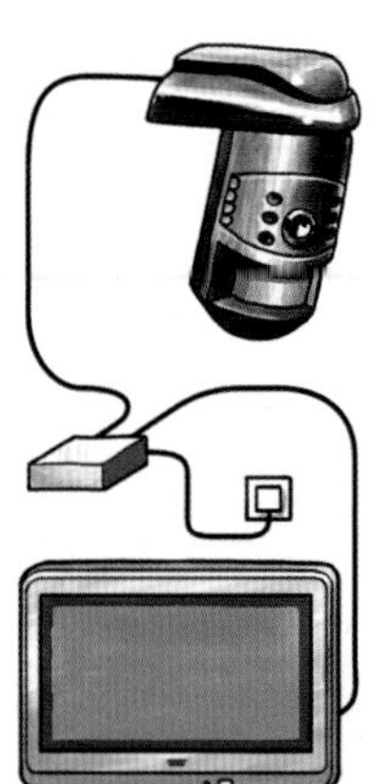

Single camera
The simplest CCTV installation consists of a single camera, a distribution box and a television set.

(N) If you undertake work marked with this symbol, you must inform the BCO before starting – see FIRST THINGS FIRST.

Try to cover the most likely approaches to your home. Adjust each camera so it is aimed at a slight angle to the route an intruder might take. It will then record film from several different angles as he passes by. This may help the police identify a known burglar.

Place your CCTV cameras out of reach – somewhere between 2.5 and 3m (8 to 10ft) from the ground. Point each camera down at an angle, never directly into the sun or towards a light fitting. If you have PIR detectors fitted to the cameras, make sure they are adjusted to avoid false alarms being triggered by passing animals and moving branches.

If you're in doubt about the suitability of a particular location, it may make sense to rig up a temporary connection and test the camera before you install it.

Running and connecting cable

Run the cable supplied with the kit from the camera to the television set, keeping as much of the wiring indoors as possible. Clip the cable to a sound surface at 1m (3ft) intervals, making sure it does not run alongside mains power cables.

To make it more difficult for anyone to tamper with the connections, feed the cable through a hole drilled directly behind the camera's housing.

It is inadvisable to coil up excess cable. Instead, cut it to length and feed the cut end though the grommet or seal in the camera mounting; then prepare and connect the colour-coded wires to the camera terminal box, following the manufacturer's instructions.

Installing the distribution box

Install the distribution box behind your television set. Plug the Scart connector into the back of the set, and the DIN connector on the camera cable into the distribution box. Connect the power-supply unit to the distribution box and plug it into a convenient 13amp socket.

Security lighting 

To use cameras effectively after dark, install porch lighting or, better still, floodlights fitted with PIR detectors. Since some cameras are particularly sensitive to infra-red, it pays to choose fittings that take halogen or tungsten bulbs rather than fluorescents. Try to achieve even illumination – it is difficult for a camera to cope with strong contrasts between, say, a dark carport and a well-lit pathway.

Alternatively, buy the type of camera that can detect an image in the very low level of illumination produced by light-emitting diodes mounted round the lens. No other form of security lighting is required with this type of camera.

Recording intruders

Recording the signals
With a more complex installation, you can have several cameras connected to a VCR or DVR so you can make a recording of would-be intruders.

If you want to tape the pictures transmitted from your cameras, plug the Scart connector into a video recorder instead of the TV set. Switch the TV to the video channel, and the VCR to the AUX (auxiliary) channel.This gives you the option to make recordings, even when you're not at home.

Switching channels

Provided that you leave your TV set switched to the video channel, your TV viewing will be interrupted to show you the scene outside as soon as a camera detects an intruder. You will still be able to switch from one TV channel to another, using the standard VCR remote controller.

Recording the scene

If you want the VCR to start recording whenever the camera's PIR detects movement, fit a special VCR controller to the distribution box and point its infra-red output at the port used by your standard VCR remote controller.

If you prefer, you can fit a small unobtrusive LED (light-emitting diode) extension to the controller, so that you can hide the main unit out of sight.

You can preset how long you want the VCR to continue recording before it automatically switches off.

Using a second VCR

With your VCR switched to the AUX channel, you won't be able to view a pre-recorded tape – so you may want to buy a cheap second-hand VCR that you can use solely for surveillance. You could install this VCR somewhere out of sight, so that a burglar is less likely to spot it and destroy the evidence.

Linking to several TV sets

You can use all the television sets in your home as surveillance monitors, but to do this the signals have to be transmitted via the TV aerial. For multi-set monitoring, you need to connect the distribution box to a device known as a modulator. Connect the TV aerial to the modulator, and the modulator to your existing aerial splitter socket.

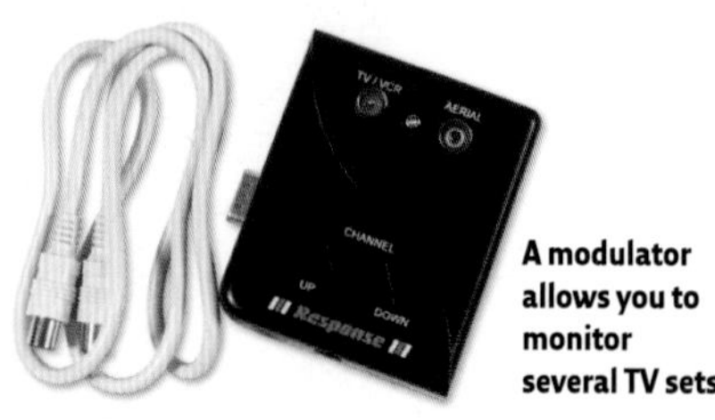

A modulator allows you to monitor several TV sets

SEE ALSO > Building Regulations 284, Installing aerial sockets 320, Security lighting 337–8

Garden lighting and pumps

Just a few outdoor lights can transform a garden. Spotlights or floodlighting can be used to emphasize particularly attractive features, at the same time providing functional lighting for pathways and steps.

Extra-low-voltage lighting

Some types of garden light fitting are connected directly to the mains supply. However, there are also very efficient systems that draw power via an extra-low-voltage transformer. Position the transformer close to a 13amp socket outlet in a garage or workshop, and connect it to the socket by an ordinary square-pin plug. The flex – which is normally supplied with the light fitting – is connected to the two 12V outlet terminals on the transformer.

Carry out the connections to the lights in accordance with the manufacturer's instructions.

Unless the maker states otherwise, extra-low-voltage flex supplying garden lights can be run along the ground without further protection – but inspect it regularly and don't let it trail over stone steps or other sharp edges likely to damage the PVC insulation if someone steps on it. If you have to extend flex, use a purpose-made waterproof connector.

Pool lighting

Pool lights are normally submerged so as to have at least 18mm (¾in) of water above the lens. Some are designed to float unless they're held down below the surface by smooth stones, carefully placed on the flex.

Submerged lights get covered by the particles of debris that float in all ponds. To clean the lenses without removing the lights from the water, simply direct a gentle hose over them.

You will find that occasionally you have to remove a light and wash the lens thoroughly in warm soapy water. Always disconnect the power supply before you handle the lights or take them out of the pond.

Run the flex for pool lighting under the edging stones via a drain made from corrugated plastic sheeting. The entire length of the flex can be protected from adverse weather by being run through a length of ordinary garden hose. Take the safest route to the power supply, anchoring the flex gently in convenient spots – but don't cover it with grass or soil in a place where someone might inadvertently cut through the flex with a spade or fork. Join lengths of low-voltage cable with waterproof connectors.

Floating pond lights illuminate this fountain

Pumps

Electric pumps can be used in garden pools to create fountains and waterfalls. A combination unit will send an adjustable jet of water up into the air and at the same time pump water through a plastic tube to the top of a rockery to trickle back into the pool.

Some pumps run directly from the mains supply, but there are also extra-low-voltage pumps that connect to a transformer (see left) shielded from the weather. So you can disconnect the pump without disturbing the extra-low-voltage wiring to the transformer, join two lengths of cable with a waterproof connector. Conceal the connector under a stone or gravel beside the pool.

Most manufacturers recommend you take a pump from the water at the end of each season and clean it thoroughly, then return it to the water immediately. To avoid corrosion, don't leave it out of the water for very long without cleaning and drying it. Never service a pump without first disconnecting it from the power supply. During the winter, run the pump for at least an hour every week, to keep it in good working order.

Beautifully constructed miniature waterfall

- **Connected kits**
You do not have to notify your Building Control Officer if you are installing a complete ready-connected lighting kit or pump that is CE approved and that is not part of the fixed wiring of the house.

- **'Extra-low-voltage'**
Strictly speaking, this is the correct term to describe equipment that runs on 50V or less. However, suppliers and manufacturers often use the term 'low-voltage' to describe equipment of this kind.

Waterproof cable connector
You can obtain suitable cable connectors from pump and lighting suppliers.

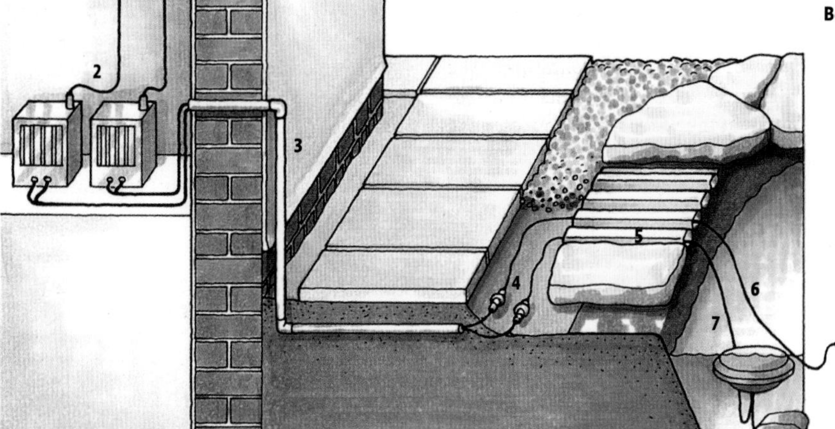

Low-voltage pump and lighting circuits
1 Socket outlet
2 Isolating transformers BS 3535 Type 3 (also numbered BS EN 60742).
3 Plastic conduit
4 Waterproof connectors
5 Home-made drain
6 Pump cable
7 Lighting cable

SEE ALSO > Building Regulations 284, Pond drain 475

Running power to outbuildings (N)

The power supply to a separate workshop, garage or tool shed can't be tapped from other domestic circuits. The cable has to run either from from its own fuseway in the consumer unit or a separate switchfuse unit, and pass safely underground or overhead to the outside location – where it can be wired into a switchfuse unit from which the various circuits in the outbuilding can be distributed as required.

(N) If you undertake work marked with this symbol, you must inform the BCO before starting – see FIRST THINGS FIRST.

Types of cable permitted outdoors

Three types of cable can be used outside. The type you choose will depend on how you wish to run the cable.

Armoured

Although insulated in the ordinary way, this two-core or three-core cable has additional protection in the form of steel-wire armour. There is also an outer sheath of PVC. With two-core cable, the metal armour provides the path to earth, but as some authorities insist on two-core-and-earth cable, check what is required before you buy your cable.

Armoured cable is expensive and has to be terminated at a special junction box at each end of its run, where it can be joined to ordinary PVC-insulated cable. It is fitted with threaded glands for attaching it to the junction boxes. When buried in the ground, this type of cable must be covered with cable covers or warning tape.

Mineral-insulated copper-sheathed

The bare copper conductors of mineral-insulated copper-sheathed (MICS) cable are tightly packed in magnesium-oxide powder within a copper sheathing. The copper sheathing can act as the earth conductor. Because the mineral powder absorbs moisture, special seals must be fitted at the ends of the cable.

Like armoured cable, MICS cable is costly and has to be terminated at special junction boxes so that cheaper cable can be used in the outbuilding itself. It must also be protected with cable covers or warning tape when it is buried below ground.

PVC-insulated-and-sheathed

Ordinary PVC-insulated two-core-and-earth cable can be run underground to an outbuilding – but only if it is protected with impact-resistant heavy-gauge conduit and paving slabs that will, together, provide at least the same degree of mechanical protection as armoured cable.

If the conduit has to go round corners, elbow joints can be cemented onto the ends of straight sections. The cable itself should be continuous.

PVC-insulated cable can also be run overhead quite safely – but only under certain specified conditions (see below).

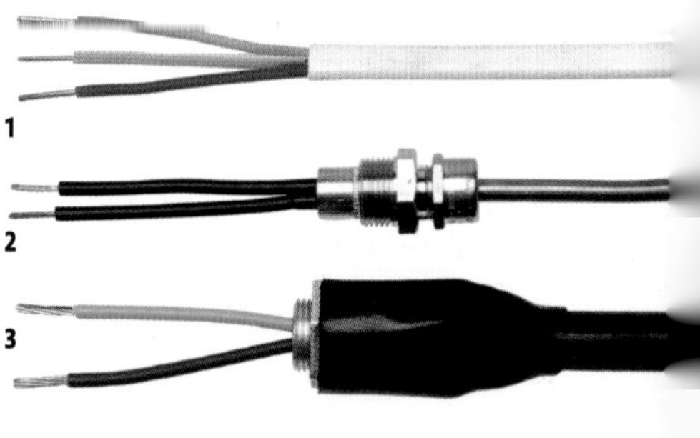

1
2
3

Outdoor cables
1 PVC-insulated-and-sheathed cable
2 Mineral-insulated copper-sheathed cable
3 Armoured cable

Ways of running outdoor cable

Underground

Running cable underground is usually the best way of supplying electricity to an outbuilding. You should bury the cable in a trench at least 500mm (1ft 8in) deep, or deeper still if the cable has to pass underneath a vegetable plot or flowerbed, or other areas where digging is likely to go on. It's best to plan the cable run so as to avoid such areas where possible. But extra protection can be provided for the cable by laying housebricks along both sides of it, supporting a covering of paving slabs. Line the bottom of the trench with finely sifted soil or sand.

Special black-and-yellow-striped tape should be buried above the cable to serve as a warning to anyone who happens to uncover the slabs at a later date.

Overhead

Ordinary PVC-insulated cable can be run from house to outbuilding provided it is at least 3.5m (12ft) above the ground or 5.2m (17ft) above a driveway that's accessible to vehicles. The cable may not be used unsupported over a distance of more than 3m (10ft), though the same distance can be spanned by running the cable through a continuous length of rigid steel conduit suspended at a height of at least 3m (10ft) above the ground or 5.2m (17ft) above a driveway. The conduit must be earthed.

Over greater distances, the cable must be supported by a taut metal catenary wire, which must be earthed. The cable needs to be clipped to it or hung from slings.

PVC-insulated cable can also be run through conduit mounted on a wall.

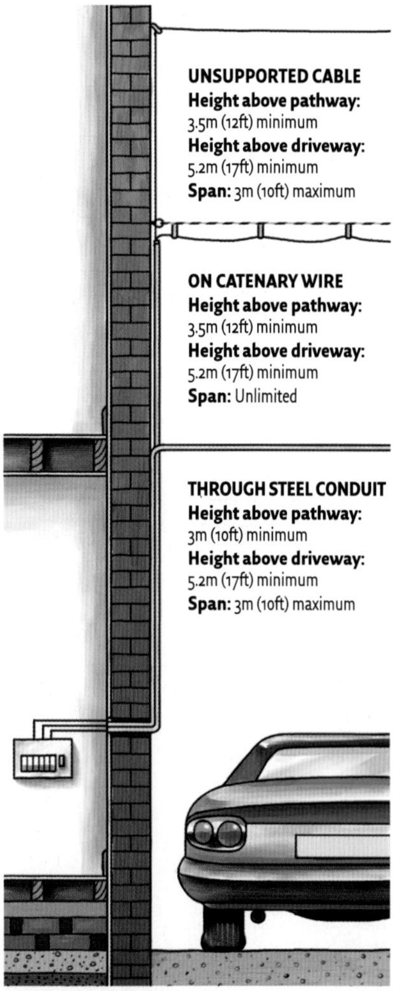

UNSUPPORTED CABLE
Height above pathway: 3.5m (12ft) minimum
Height above driveway: 5.2m (17ft) minimum
Span: 3m (10ft) maximum

ON CATENARY WIRE
Height above pathway: 3.5m (12ft) minimum
Height above driveway: 5.2m (17ft) minimum
Span: Unlimited

THROUGH STEEL CONDUIT
Height above pathway: 3m (10ft) minimum
Height above driveway: 5.2m (17ft) minimum
Span: 3m (10ft) maximum

Running cable overhead

SEE ALSO > Building Regulations 284, Cables 302

Running the circuit

There are various ways to run a circuit to a workshop or other outbuilding. The method described here suggests using PVC-insulated cable run from a fuseway in the consumer unit to a switchfuse unit in the outbuilding. If there's no spare fuseway in your consumer unit, the outgoing cable can run from a separate switchfuse unit – but the wiring is complicated by having to connect the unit to the meter, so is probably best left to a professional.

The cable is shown running underground in heavy-gauge plastic conduit protected by paving slabs. It must enter both buildings above the DPC. It's assumed here that both sockets and lighting are required in the outbuilding, so the lighting circuit is taken from the power cable via a junction box and an unswitched fused connection unit.

House end of the circuit

Ideally, the outgoing $4mm^2$ two-core-and-earth cable should run from a 32amp MCB or 30amp circuit fuse in the consumer unit. In addition, the circuit must be protected by an RCD.

Alternative arrangement

If there's no room for the new circuit in your consumer unit, mount a 30amp switchfuse unit containing a 30amp circuit fuse near the meter (see right). A separate residual current device must be installed between the unit and the meter. Use a $10mm^2$ two-core-and-earth cable to connect the RCD to the 'Mains' terminals of the switchfuse unit. Connect the outgoing $4mm^2$ to the 'Load' terminals of the switchfuse unit.

Connect a pair of $16mm^2$ meter leads – one brown and one blue – to the 'Mains' terminals of the residual current device. Wire a $16mm^2$ earth lead to the RCD in readiness for connection to the consumer's earth terminal.

After the BCO has made the necessary tests, the electricity company will make the connections to the meter and the company's earth.

Outbuilding end of circuit

Run $4mm^2$ two-core-and-earth cable through conduit from the house to the outbuilding, terminating at a 30amp switchfuse unit mounted on the wall.

Connect the incoming cable to the supply or 'Mains' terminals of the switchfuse unit, and run an outgoing $4mm^2$ cable from its 'Load' terminals to the outbuilding's sockets (**1**).

Insert a 30amp junction box at some point along the power cable (**2**), and run a $4mm^2$ spur from it to an unswitched fused connection unit fitted with a 3amp fuse. Run a $1.5mm^2$ two-core-and-earth cable from the connection unit to the light fitting and switch.

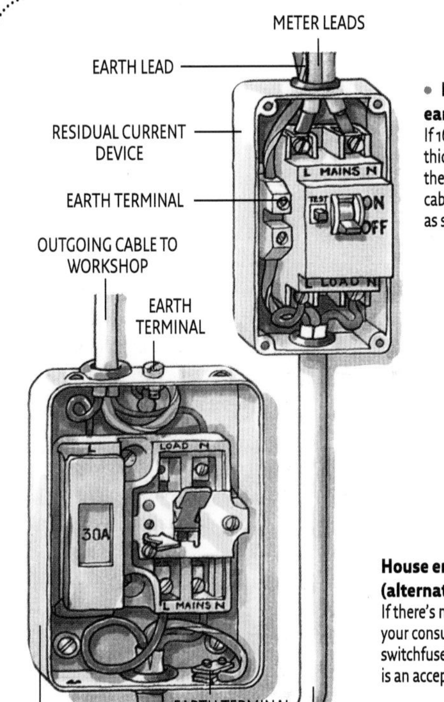

• Meter leads and earth lead
If $16mm^2$ cable is too thick for the terminals in the RCD, use $10mm^2$ cable – but keep the leads as short as possible.

House end of circuit (alternative arrangement)
If there's no spare fuseway in your consumer unit, a separate switchfuse unit wired to an RCD is an acceptable alternative.

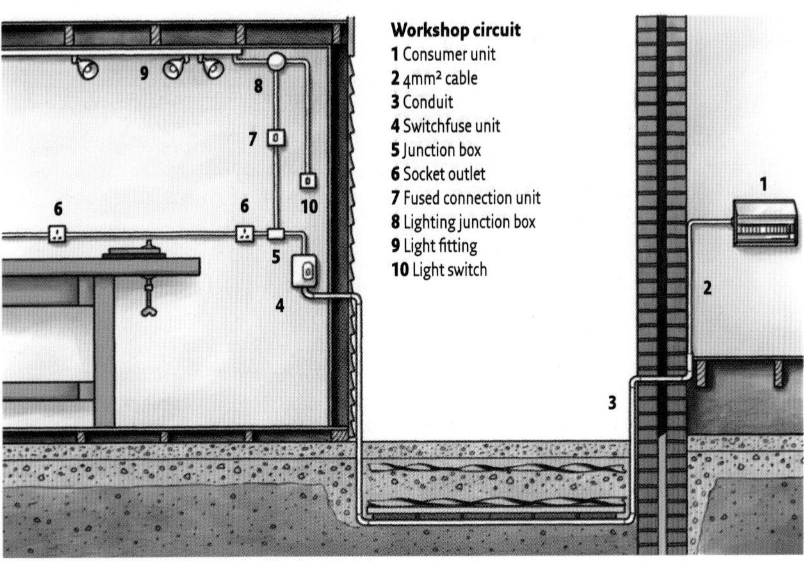

Workshop circuit
1 Consumer unit
2 $4mm^2$ cable
3 Conduit
4 Switchfuse unit
5 Junction box
6 Socket outlet
7 Fused connection unit
8 Lighting junction box
9 Light fitting
10 Light switch

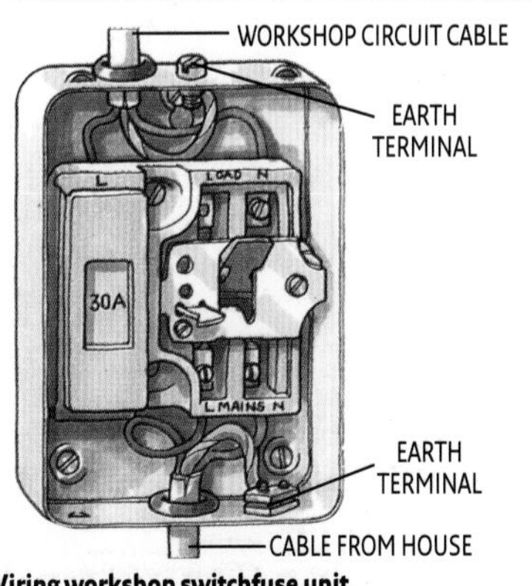

1 Wiring workshop switchfuse unit

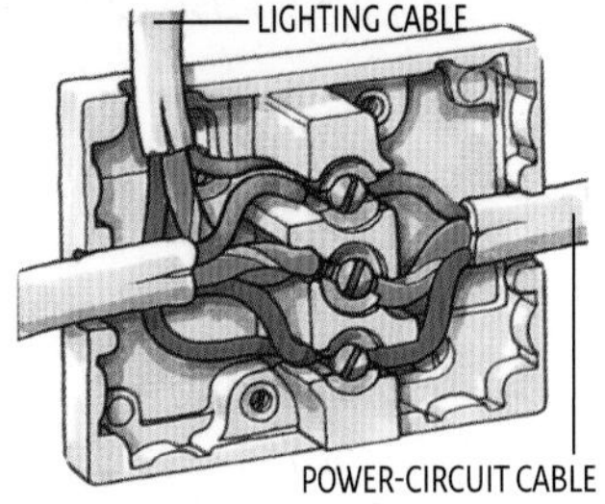

2 Wiring junction box on power circuit

SEE ALSO > Building Regulations 284, Testing circuits 288–9, Switching off 296, Running cables 303–5, Connecting sockets 308, Fused connection units 310, Lighting circuits 324, Fitting track lighting 328, One way-switch 320, New switch and light 331

Complete wiring (N)

When you are working on a single circuit the rest of the household can function normally, but to renew all the circuits means that every part of your home will eventually be affected. Few of us would contemplate taking on such a time-consuming task. And even if you do feel competent to undertake extensive rewiring, the additional burden of obtaining and paying for formal testing and certification might make you think again.

(N) If you undertake work marked with this symbol, you must inform the BCO before starting – see FIRST THINGS FIRST.

A full-time professional will be able to cope with every aspect of the job in such a way that inconvenience is kept to a minimum. So unless you are able to make the wiring a full-time commitment for at least a week or two, you would be well advised to employ an electrician who can undertake the work and deal with the paperwork on your behalf.

Perhaps he or she may allow you to work alongside – which could mean a saving on the cost if you are able to carry out some of the more mundane tasks, such as running cable under floorboards and channelling out plaster and brickwork.

Circuits: maximum lengths

The maximum length of a circuit is limited by the permitted voltage drop and the time it takes to operate the fuse or MCB in the event of an earth fault.

The method for calculation given in the Wiring Regulations is extremely complicated – but the table below will provide you with a simple method for determining the maximum cable lengths for common domestic circuits.

If necessary, plan to split up your circuits so that none of the indicated cable lengths are exceeded. If your requirements fall outside the limits of this chart, ask a professional electrician to make the calculations for you.

Rewirable fuses are not included, as they are subject to special restrictions – which makes them an unwise choice.

Most two-core-and-earth cables have a standard-size protective circuit conductor (earth wire). In each case, the chart below shows the size of earth wire used in the calculations.

The maximum circuit lengths given in the chart are based on the assumption that you won't install any electrical cables where the ambient temperature exceeds 30°C (86°F), that no cables will be bunched together, and that you will not cover any of the cables with thermal insulation.

The shower-circuit lengths assume that a 30 milliamp residual current device is used in the circuit.

The cooker-circuit lengths allow for using a cooker control unit with a built-in socket outlet. However, you can safely use the same figures for wiring a control unit without a built-in socket.

MAXIMUM LENGTHS FOR DOMESTIC CIRCUITS

TYPE OF CIRCUIT	Max. floor area in m^2	Cable size in mm^2	Size of earth wire in mm^2	Current rating of circuit fuse	Max cable length using cartridge fuse	Current rating of MCB	Max cable length using MCB
				USING FUSES		USING MCBs	
RING CIRCUIT	100	2.5	1.5	30amp	65	32amp	65
RADIAL CIRCUIT	20	2.5	1.5	15amp	60	20amp	60
COOKER up to 13.5kW with socket outlet		6	2.5	30amp	42	32amp	42
COOKER from 13.5 to 18kW		6	2.5	45amp	32	40amp	32
IMMERSION HEATER		2.5	1.5	15amp	39	16amp	39
SHOWER up to 9.2kW		10	4	45amp	31	40amp	52
SHOWER from 9.2 to 11.4kW		10	4		N/A	50amp	25
STORAGE HEATER up to 3.375kW		2.5	1.5	15amp	35	16amp	35
FIXED LIGHTING including switch drops		1.5	1	5amp	100	6amp	100

Note: Longer lengths may be permissible with detailed calculations, which will require system information from your supplier.

Designing your system

Before you set up a meeting with a professional, you need to form clear ideas about the kind of installation you want. A proper specification should enable you to avoid expensive modifications.

Choosing the best consumer unit

It is worth installing the best consumer unit you can afford. Choose one that has MCBs or cartridge fuses. and make sure it has enough spare fuseways for possible additional circuits.

Ask the electrician about the advantages of installing a split consumer unit, with a residual current device (RCD) protecting only the most vulnerable circuits

Power circuits

Ring circuits are better than radial circuits for supplying socket outlets. Provided that the floor area in question does not exceed 100sq m (120sq yds), you can have as many sockets as you want. Economizing on the cost of a few sockets now could cause you considerable inconvenience in the future – for example, there's little point in opting for a single socket outlet when you can fit a double for about the same price.

Lighting circuits

Modern domestic lighting is normally designed around a loop-in system; but you can supply individual lights from junction boxes if that is the most practical solution.

You should insist on a lighting circuit for each floor – so that you will never be left totally without electric lights if a fuse should blow. In the interests of safety, make sure you have two-way or three-way switches installed for lights in passageways and on landings and staircases.

Additional circuits

Decide what additional circuits you are going to need – such as a radial circuit for an immersion heater or for a hob-and-oven combination. Are you going to want lighting outdoors, or other exterior wiring? Now's the time to incorporate the work, rather than call in another electrician later.

SEE ALSO > Building Regulations 284, Consumer units 298, Fuses and MCBs 299, Domestic circuits 301

Plumbing

Plumbing systems

Plumbing is no longer the preserve of the professionals, thanks to a wide range of tools and fittings that are available to the DIY enthusiast. With the addition of easy-to-use plastic and metal fittings and pipework, successful repairs and modifications are easier – and faster – than ever.

The advantages of DIY plumbing

Being able to tackle your own plumbing installations and repairs can save you the cost of hiring professionals – and that can amount to a substantial sum of money. It also avoids the distress and inconvenience of ruined decorations, and the expense of replacing rotted household timbers where a slow leak has gone undetected. Then there's the saving in water. A dripping tap wastes litres of water a day – and if it's hot water, there's the additional expense of heating it. A little of your time and a few pence spent on a washer can save you pounds.

• **Wiring Regulations**
When making repairs or improvements to your plumbing, make sure you don't contravene the electrical Wiring Regulations. All metal plumbing has to be bonded to earth. If you replace a section of metal plumbing with plastic, it is important to reinstate the earth link. (See below.)

Water systems

Generally, domestic plumbing incorporates two systems. One is the supply of fresh water from the 'mains', and the other is the waste or drainage system that disposes of dirty water. Both of the systems can be installed in different ways (see opposite).

Stored-water system (Indirect)

The majority of homes are plumbed with a stored-water supply system. The storage tank in the loft and the cold-water tap in the kitchen are fed directly from the mains; so possibly are your washing machine, electric shower(s) and outside tap. But water for baths, washbasins, flushing WCs and some types of shower is drawn from the storage tank, which should be covered with a purpose-made lid to protect the water from contamination. Drinking water should only be taken from the cold-water tap in the kitchen.

Cold water from the storage tank is fed to a hot-water cylinder, where it is indirectly heated by a boiler or immersion heater to supply the hot taps. The water pressure at the taps depends on the distance ('head') from the tank to the tap.

A stored-water system provides several advantages. There is adequate water to flush sanitaryware during a temporary mains failure; the major part of the supply is under relatively low pressure, so the system is reasonably quiet; and because there are fewer mains outlets, there is less likelihood of impure water being siphoned back into the mains supply.

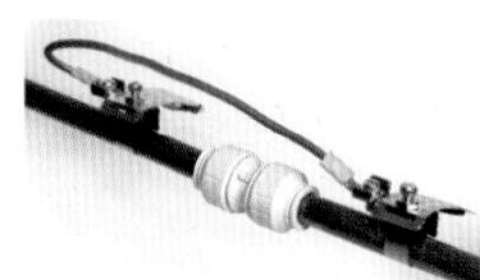

Reinstate the link
If you replace a section of metal plumbing with plastic, you may break the path to earth – so make sure you reinstate the link. Bridge a plastic joint in a metal pipe with an earth wire and two clamps. If you are in any doubt, consult a qualified electrician.

Mains-fed system (Direct)

Many properties now take all their water directly from the mains – all the taps are under high pressure, and they all provide water that's suitable for drinking. This development has come about as a result of limited loft space that precludes a storage tank and the introduction of non-return check valves, which prevent drinking water being contaminated. Hot water is supplied by a combination boiler or a multipoint heater; these instantaneous heaters are unable to maintain a constant flow of hot water if too many taps are running at once. Some systems use an unvented, pressurised cylinder, which stores hot water but is fed from the mains.

A mains-fed system is cheaper to install than an indirect one. Other advantages include mains pressure and drinking water at all taps. With a mains-fed system there's no plumbing in the loft to freeze.

Drainage

Waste water is drained in one of two ways. In houses built before the late 1950s, water is drained from baths, sinks and basins into a waste pipe that feeds into a trapped gully at ground level. Toilet waste feeds separately into a large-diameter vertical soil pipe that runs directly to the underground main drainage network.

With a single-stack waste system, which is installed in later buildings, all waste water drains into a single soil pipe – the one possible exception being the kitchen sink, which may drain into a gully.

Rainwater usually feeds into a separate drain, so that the house's drainage system will not be flooded in the event of a storm.

Water Regulations

The Water Supply (Water Fittings) Regulations 1999 (or Byelaws in Scotland) govern the design, installation and maintenance of plumbing systems, fittings and appliances that use water. These laws are intended to prevent the misuse, waste and contamination of water and apply from the point at which water enters your home's service pipe.

Owners, occupiers and anyone who installs plumbing or water fittings have a legal duty to ensure that systems meet the regulations and that water supplies aren't contaminated. They must also give advance notification to their local water supplier of various alterations to the system, including installation of a rim supply bidet; a bath with a capacity of more than 230 litres (50 gallons); shower pumps drawing more than 12 litres (2½ gallons) a minute; and garden watering systems.

Your local water supplier will provide you with the relevant information about other notifiable works, inspection requirements and possible certification for new work and for major alterations.

Drainage

The Building Regulations on drainage are designed to protect health and safety. Before undertaking work on your soil and waste pipes or drains (except for emergency unblocking) you need to contact the Building Control Office of your local authority.

SEE ALSO > Saving rainwater 137, Supplementary bonding 286, Earthing 297, Garden tap 390, Water bylaws 391

Direct and indirect systems

Stored-water system

Central heating omitted for clarity.

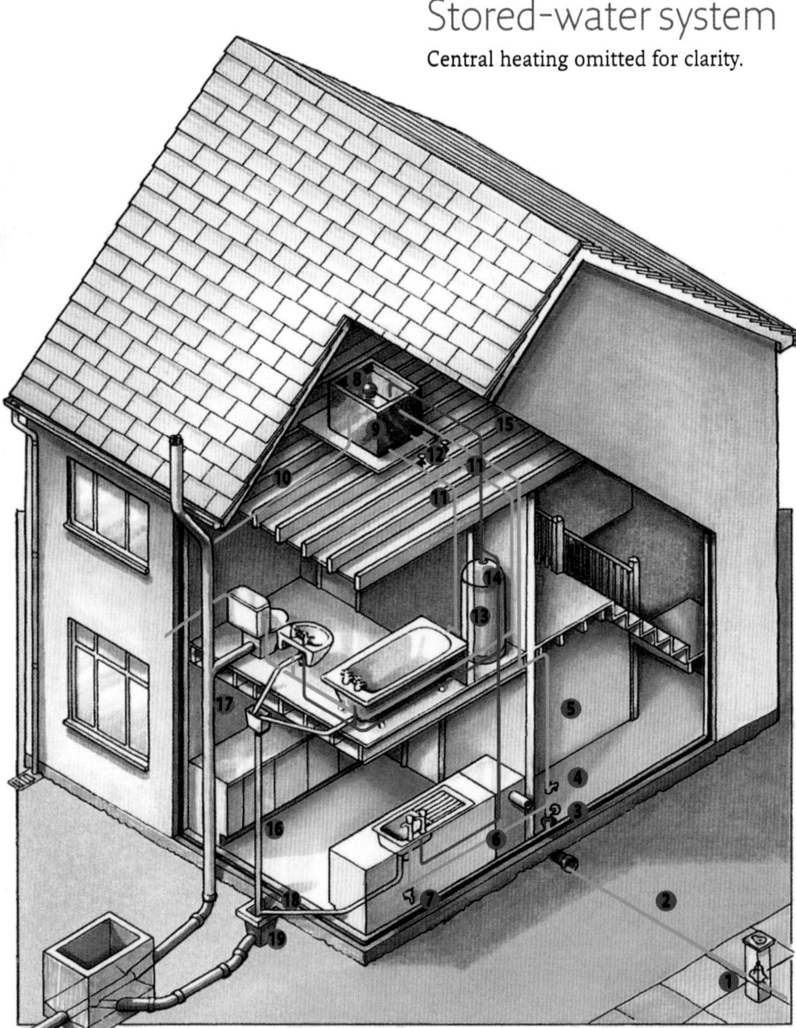

1 Water company stopcock
The water company uses this stopcock to turn off the supply to the house. Make sure it can be located quickly in an emergency.

2 Service pipe
From the water company stopcock onwards, the plumbing becomes the responsibility of the householder.

3 Household stopcock
The water supply to the house itself is shut off at this point.

4 Draincock
A draincock here allows you to drain water from the rising main.

5 Rising main
Mains-pressure water passes to the cold-water storage tank via the rising main.

6 Drinking water
Drinking water is drawn off the rising main to the kitchen sink.

7 Garden tap
The water company allows a garden tap to be supplied with mains pressure, provided it is fitted with a check valve.

8 Float valve
This valve shuts off the supply from the rising main when the cistern is full.

9 Cold-water storage tank
Stores from 230 to 360 litres (50 to 80 gallons) of water. Positioned in the roof, the tank provides sufficient 'head', or pressure, to feed the whole house.

10 Overflow pipe
Also known as a warning pipe, it prevents an overflow by draining water to the outside.

11 Cold-feed pipes
Water is drawn off to the bathroom and to the hot-water cylinder from the storage tank.

12 Cold-feed valves
Valves at these points allow you to drain the cold water in the feed pipe without having to drain the whole tank as well.

13 Hot-water cylinder
Water is heated and stored in this cylinder.

14 Hot-feed pipe
All hot water is fed from this point.

15 Vent pipe
Allows for expansion of heated water and enables air to be vented from the system.

16 Waste pipe
Surmounted by a hopper head, it collects water from basin and bath.

17 Soil pipe
Separate pipe takes toilet waste to main drains.

18 Kitchen waste pipe
Kitchen sink drains into same gully as waste pipe from upstairs.

19 Trapped gully

Mains-fed-water system

Central heating omitted for clarity.

1 Water-supplier's stopcock
May include water meter.

2 Service pipe

3 Main stopcock

4 Rising main
Supplies water directly to cold-water taps and WCs, etc.

5 Water heater or combination boiler

6 Unvented storage cylinder
(Not required for instantaneous heaters.)

7 Single-stack soil pipe
WC, handbasin, bath and shower drain into the stack. The stack may be fitted with an air-admittance valve terminating inside the house.

8 Sink waste
Water from the sink drains into a trapped gully.

9 Trapped gully

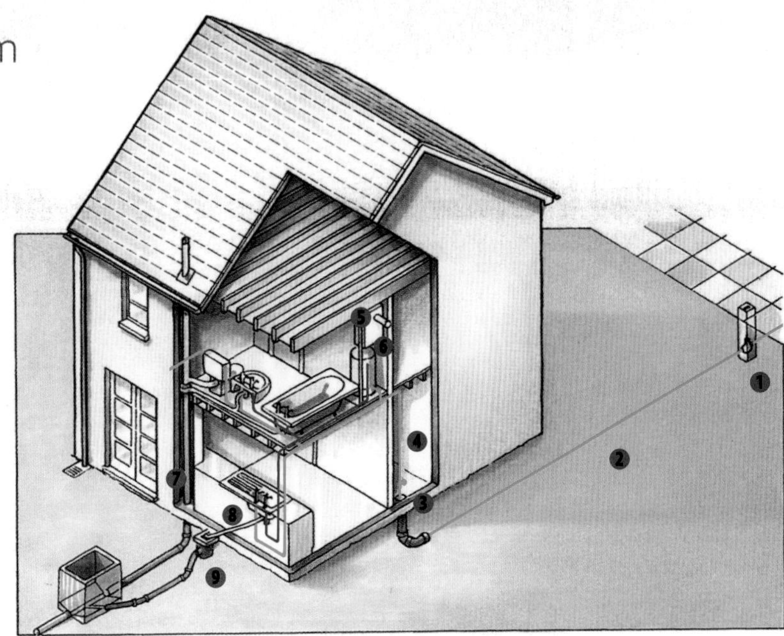

Water meters
Instead of paying a flat-rate water charge based upon the size of your home, you can opt to have your water consumption metered so you pay for what you use. For two people living in a large house, the savings can be considerable. Water meters are fitted to the incoming mains, usually outside at the supplier's stopcock, where they can be read more easily.

SEE ALSO > Wet central heating 405

Draining the system

You will have to drain at least part of any plumbing system before you can work on it; and if you detect a leak, you will have to drain the relevant section quickly. So find out where the valves, stopcock and draincocks are situated, before you're faced with an emergency.

Saving hot water
If your gate valve won't close off and you don't want to drain all the hot water, you can siphon the water out of the cold tank with a garden hosepipe. While the tank is empty, replace the old gate valve.

Draining cold-water taps and pipes

- Turn off the main stopcock on the rising main to cut off the supply to the kitchen tap (and to all the other cold taps on a direct system).
- Open the tap until the flow ceases.
- To isolate the bathroom taps, close the valve on the appropriate cold-feed pipe from the storage tank and open all taps on that section. If you can't find a valve, rest a wooden batten across the tank and tie the arm of the float valve to it. This will shut off the supply to the tank, so you can empty it by running all the cold taps in the bathroom. If you can't get into the loft, turn off the main stopcock, then run the cold taps.

Draining hot-water taps and pipes

- Turn off immersion heater or boiler.
- Close the valve on the cold-feed pipe to the cylinder and run the hot taps. Even when the water stops flowing, the cylinder will still be full.
- If there's no valve on the cold-feed pipe, tie up the float-valve arm, then turn on the cold taps in the bathroom to empty the storage tank. (If you run the hot taps first, the water in the tank will flush all the hot water from the cylinder.) When the cold taps run dry, open the hot taps. In an emergency, open hot and cold taps to clear the pipes as quickly as possible.

Draining a WC cistern

- To empty the WC cistern itself, tie up its float-valve arm and flush the WC.
- To empty the pipe that supplies the cistern, either turn off the main stopcock on a direct system or, on an indirect system, close the valve on the cold feed from the storage tank. Alternatively, shut off the supply to the storage tank and empty it through the cold taps. Flush the WC until no more water enters its cistern.

Draining the cold-water storage tank

- To drain the storage tank in the roof space, close the main stopcock on the rising main, then open all the cold taps in the bathroom. Bail out the residue of water at the bottom of the tank.

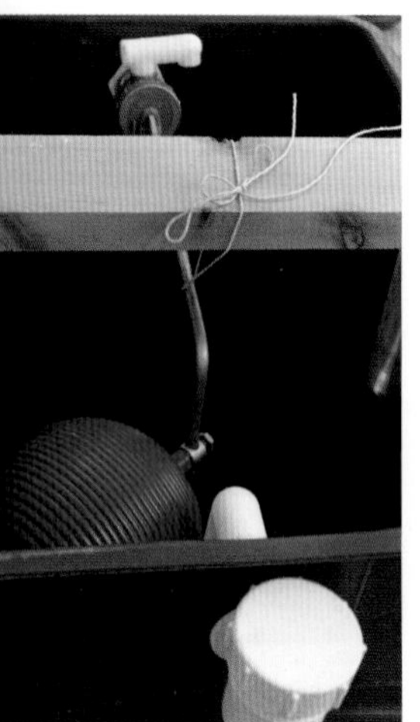

Closing a float valve
Cut off the supply of water to a storage tank by tying the float arm to a batten.

Draining the hot-water cylinder

- If the hot-water cylinder springs a leak (or you wish to replace it), first turn off the immersion heater and boiler, then shut off the cold feed to the cylinder from the storage tank (or drain the cold-water storage tank - see above). Run hot water from the taps.
- Locate a draincock from which you can drain the water remaining in the cylinder. It is probably located near the base of the cylinder, where the cold feed from the storage tank enters. Attach a hose and run it to a drain or sink that is lower than the cylinder. Turn the square-headed spindle on the draincock till you hear water flowing.
- Water can't be drained if the washer is baked onto the draincock seating, so disconnect the vent pipe and insert a hosepipe to siphon the cylinder.
- Should you want to replace the hot-water cylinder, don't disconnect all its pipework until you have drained the cylinder completely. If the water is heated indirectly by a heat-exchanger, there will be a coil of pipework inside the hot-water cylinder that is still full of water. This coil can be drained via the stopcock on the boiler after you have shut off the mains supply to the small feed-and-expansion tank in the roof space. Switch off the electricity to the central-heating system.

Adding extra valves

Unless you divide up the system into relatively short pipe runs with valves, you will have to drain off a substantial part of a typical plumbing installation even for a simple washer replacement.

- Install a gate valve on both the cold-feed pipes running from the cold-water storage tank. This will eliminate the necessity for draining off litres of water in order to isolate pipes and appliances on the low-pressure cold-and hot-water supply.
- When you are fitting new taps and appliances, take the opportunity to fit miniature valves on the supply pipes. In future, when you have to repair an individual tap or appliance, you will be able to isolate it in moments.

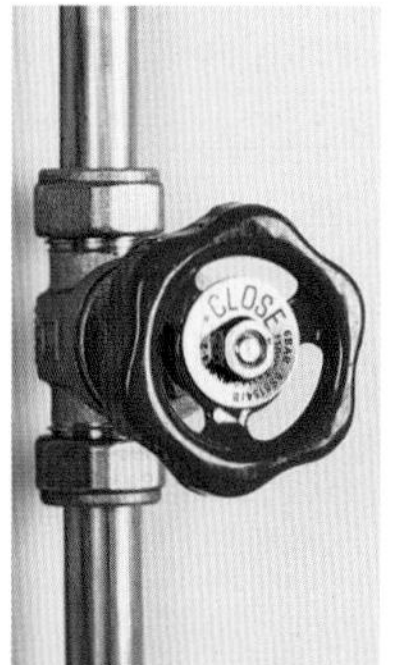

Gate valve
Fit a gate valve to the cold-feed pipes from the storage tank.

Miniature valve
Fit a miniature valve to the supply pipes below a sink or basin.

Sealed central-heating systems

A sealed system (see SEALED CENTRAL-HEATING SYSTEMS) does not have a feed-and-expansion tank - the radiators are filled from the mains via a flexible hose known as a filling loop. The indirect coil in the hot-water cylinder is drained as described left, though you might have to open a vent pipe that is fitted to the cylinder before the water will flow.

SEE ALSO > Consumer unit 296–8, Cylinders 392, Cylinder vent pipe 392, Sealed central heating 405, Radiators 407

Repairs and maintenance

It pays to master the simple techniques for coping with emergency repairs – in order to avoid the inevitable damage to your home and property, as well as the high cost of calling out a plumber at short notice. All you need is a simple tool kit and a few spare parts.

Draining and refilling the system

Partially drain the plumbing system if you are leaving the house unoccupied for a few days during winter and leave the central heating on a low setting. For longer periods away at any time of the year, it's wise to drain the system completely.

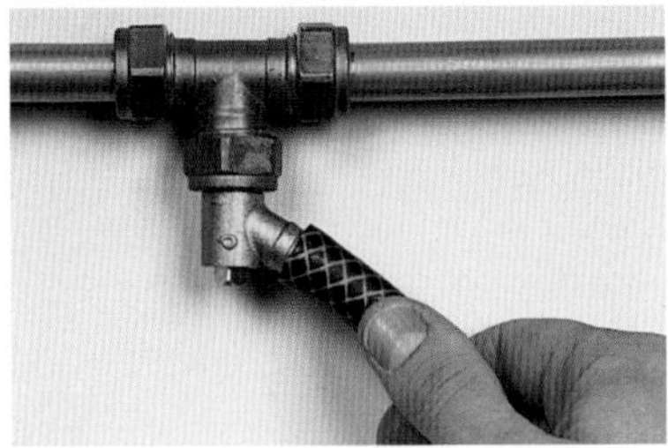

Attach hosepipe to draincock

Partial drain-down

- Add special antifreeze to the central-heating feed tank and set the heating to come on briefly twice a day.
- Turn off the main stopcock.
- Open all taps to drain the system.

Full drain-down

- Switch off and extinguish the water heater and/or boiler.
- Turn off the main stopcock and, if possible, the main stopcock outside.
- Open all taps to drain the pipework.
- Open the draincock at the base of the hot-water cylinder. If there are draincocks in the rising main or other pipework, open them too.
- Flush the WCs.
- Drain the boiler and radiator circuits at the lowest points on the pipe runs.
- Add salt to the WC pan to prevent the trap water freezing.

Refilling the system

- Close all taps and draincocks.
- Turn on the main stopcock.
- Turn on taps and allow water and air to escape. Bleed radiators and check that float valves are working properly.

Thawing frozen pipes

If water won't flow from a tap during cold weather, or a tank refuses to fill, a plug of ice may have formed in one of the supply pipes. The plug cannot be in a pipe supplying taps or float valves that are working normally, so you should be able to trace the blockage quickly. In fact, freezing usually occurs first in the roof space.

As copper pipework transmits heat quickly, use a hairdryer to gently warm the suspect pipe, starting as close as possible to the affected tap or valve and working along it. Leave the tap open, so water can flow normally as soon as the ice thaws. If you can't heat the pipe with a hairdryer, wrap it in a hot towel or hang a hot-water bottle over it.

Preventive measures

Insulate pipework and fittings to stop them freezing, particularly those in the loft or under the floor. If you're going to leave the house unheated for a long time during the winter, drain the system (see left). Cure any dripping taps, so leaking water doesn't freeze in your drainage system overnight.

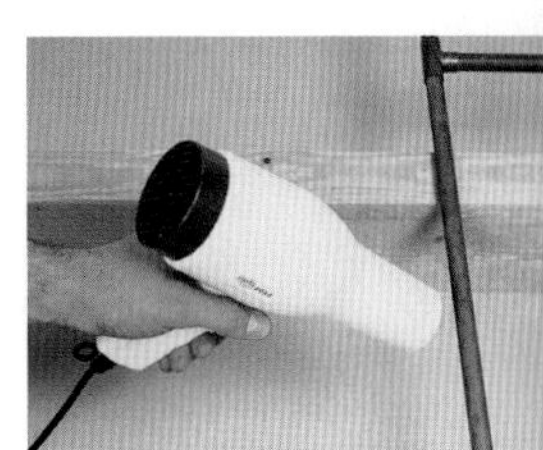

Thawing a frozen pipe
Play a hairdryer gently along a frozen pipe, working away from the blocked tap or valve.

Dealing with a punctured pipe

Unless you are absolutely sure where your pipes run, it is all too easy to nail through one of them when fixing a loose floorboard. You may be able to detect a hissing sound as water escapes under pressure, but more than likely you won't notice your mistake until a wet patch appears on the ceiling below, or some problem associated with damp occurs at a later date. While the nail is in place, water will leak relatively slowly, so don't pull it out until you have drained the pipework and can repair the leak. If you pull out the nail by lifting a floorboard, replace the nail immediately.

If you plan to lay fitted carpet, you can paint pipe runs on the floorboards to avoid such accidents in future.

Patching a leak

During freezing conditions, water within a pipe turns to ice, which expands until it eventually splits the walls of the pipe or forces a joint apart. The only other reason for leaking plumbing is mechanical failure - either through deterioration of the materials or because a joint has failed and is no longer completely watertight. Make a permanent repair if you can by inserting a new section of pipe or replacing a leaking joint (if it is a compression joint that has failed, try tightening it first). If you have to make an emergency repair, drain the pipe first. If it is frozen, make the repair before it thaws.

Sealing a split or pinhole

For a temporary repair, use a repair clamp, below, or special amalgamating tape which will work in wet conditions.

A push-fit repair pipe (see right), makes a fast, permanent repair if you have to remove a section of pipe.

Alternatively, a slip-on compression fitting (below left) will also make a permanent repair.

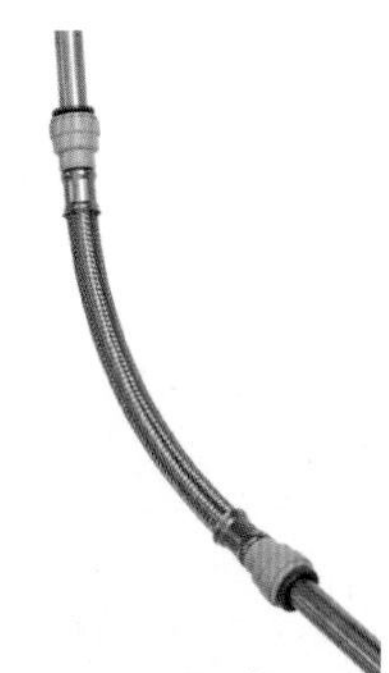

A push-fit repair pipe

A slip-on compression fitting makes a secure repair

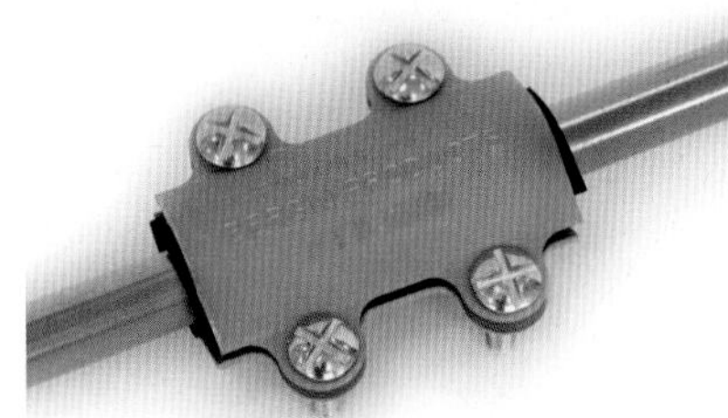

Fit an emergency repair clamp over the split

SEE ALSO >Insulating pipes 257, Joining pipes 361–7, Compression joints 362

Repairing leaking taps

Leaking taps aren't too difficult to deal with. When water drips from a spout, it usually points to a faulty washer. If the tap is old, its seat may be worn, too. If water leaks from beneath the head of the tap when it's in use, the O-ring needs replacing. When you are working on a tap, insert the plug and lay a towel in the bottom of the washbasin, bath or sink to catch small objects and protect the surface.

Replacing a washer

Traditional pillar tap
The components of a pillar tap
1 Capstan head
2 Metal shroud
3 Gland nut
4 Spindle
5 Headgear nut
6 Jumper
7 Washer
8 Tap body
9 Seat
10 Tail

To replace the washer in a traditional pillar tap, first drain the supply pipe, then open the valve as far as possible.

If the tap is shrouded with a metal cover, unscrew it by hand or use a wrench, taping the jaws to protect the chrome finish.

Lift the cover to reveal the headgear nut just above the body of the tap. Slip a spanner onto the nut and unscrew it (1).

The jumper to which the washer is fixed fits into the bottom of the headgear. In some taps the jumper is removed along with the headgear (2), but in other types it will be lying inside the tap body.

The washer itself may be pressed over a small button in the centre of the jumper (3) and can be prised off with a screwdriver. A securing nut can be hard to remove. Allow penetrating oil to soften any corrosion; then, hold the jumper stem with pliers and unscrew the nut with a spanner (4). If the nut sticks, replace the jumper and washer; otherwise, fit a new washer and retaining nut, then reassemble the tap.

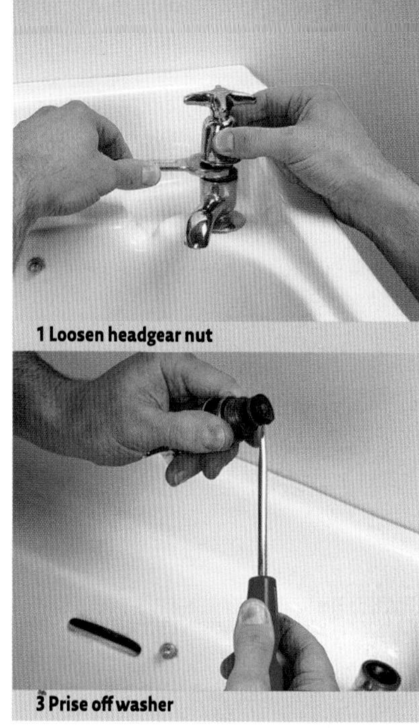

1 Loosen headgear nut

3 Prise off washer

2 Lift out headgear

4 Or undo securing nut

Curing a dripping ceramic-disc tap

1 Prise out the disc

2 Pull the head off

Getting inside a tap
On most modern taps the head and cover is in one piece. You will have to remove it to expose the headgear nut. Often a retaining screw is hidden beneath the coloured hot/cold disc in the centre of the head. Prise out the disc with the point of a knife or a small screwdriver (1). If there's no retaining screw, simply pull the head off (2).

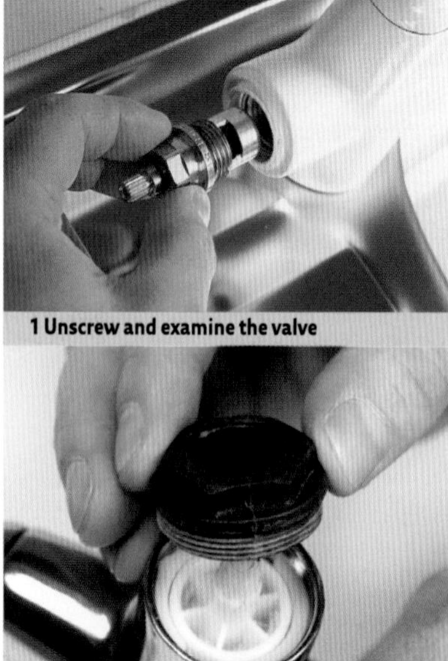

1 Unscrew and examine the valve

3 Unscrew retaining nut

2 Replace a worn rubber seal

4 Replace inlet seals

Ceramic-disc taps should be maintenance free, but faults can still occur. Since there's no washer to replace, you have to replace the whole valve when the tap leaks.

Turn off the water. Remove the headgear by turning it anticlockwise with a spanner. Remove the valve and examine it for wear or damage (1). Removing debris from the disc may do, but if disc is scratched, you will need a new valve. These are handed – left (hot), right (cold). Also examine the rubber seal on the bottom of the valve. If worn or damaged, it will cause the tap to drip. If need be, replace the seal with a new one (2).

Single-lever mixer taps have a cartridge that controls both flow and temperature. To replace it, remove handle cap. Use a socket spanner to undo the handle nut. Lift handle off, remove shroud and undo the cartridge-retaining nut (3), then lift out the cartridge. Fit new inlet seals on underside of cartridge if discs appear undamaged (4); replace the entire cartridge if they are visibly damaged.

SEE ALSO > Bib tap 360, Tap mechanisms 370, Spanners and wrenches 522

Repairing seats and glands

If replacing a washer doesn't solve the problem then the tap itself is probably worn. If you want to keep the taps, it is possible to renovate them.

Regrinding or renewing the seat

If a tap continues to drip after you have replaced the washer, the seat is probably worn, allowing water to leak past the washer. A simple way to cure this is to cover the old seat with a nylon liner that is sold with a matching jumper and washer (1). Drop the liner over the old seat, replace the jumper and assemble the tap. Close the tap to force the liner into position.

Alternatively, use a tap grinding tool (2) to put a new smooth surface on the seat. The tool uses serrated cutters to grind out any imperfections that might be allowing water past the washer.

With the headgear removed, insert the grinder (3) and screw the threaded bush to the tap to locate the tool securely.

Push down and twist the grinder clockwise. Resurfacing is complete when the whole seat is shiny and new looking.

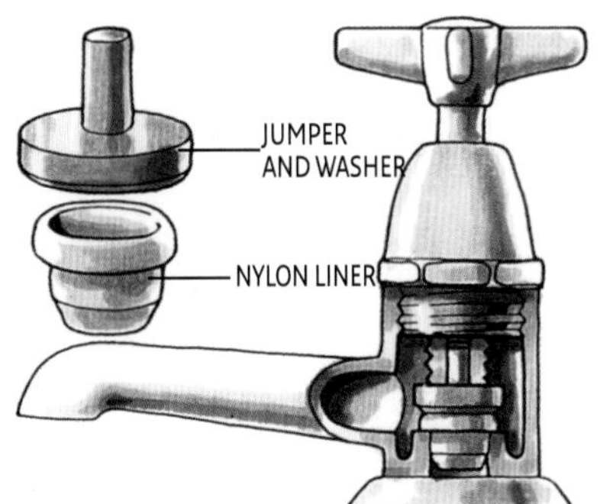

1 Repair a worn seat with a nylon liner

2 A tap grinding tool

3 Cut new seat

Stopcocks and valves

Stopcocks and gate valves are used rarely but often fail just when needed.

Make sure that they are operating smoothly by closing and opening them from time to time. Lubricate stiff spindles with penetrating oil. A stopcock is fitted with a standard washer, but as it is hardly ever under pressure it is unlikely to wear.

Penetrating oil or lubricant prevents seizure

Replacing O-rings

On a mixer tap each valve is usually fitted with a washer, as on conventional taps, but in most mixers the gland packing (see far right) has been replaced by a rubber O-ring. The base of a mixer's swivel spout is also sealed with a washer or O-ring. If water seeps from that, it needs replacing.

First remove the mixer spout - the retaining screw may be accessible from the front; if it's at the back, you may have to use a cranked screwdriver to remove it (1). Lift out the swivelling spout (2), then use a small screwdriver to prise out the O-ring from its groove (3). Take care not to scratch the metal. Lubricate a new ring with silicone grease (4), then carefully slide it into place before re-fitting the spout (5) and replacing the retaining screw.

1 Use a cranked screwdriver for rear screws

3 Remove the O-ring from the swivel spout

5 Replace spout

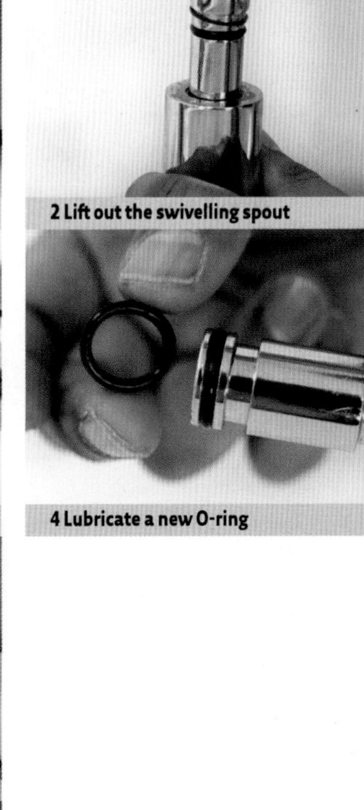

2 Lift out the swivelling spout

4 Lubricate a new O-ring

GLAND PACKING

Gland packing
Older-style taps are sealed with water-tight packing around the spindle.

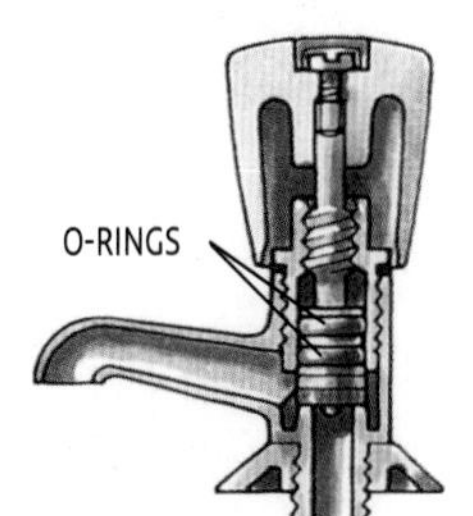

O-ring seal
Modern taps are sealed with rubber rings, in place of gland packing.

SEE ALSO > Tap mechanisms 370, Gate valve 360, PTFE tape 362, Stopcock 364

Maintaining cisterns and storage tanks

The mechanisms used in WC cisterns and storage tanks are probably the most overworked of all plumbing components, so servicing is required from time to time to keep them operating properly. You can get the spare parts you need from plumbers' merchants and DIY stores.

Direct-action WC cisterns

Most modern WCs are washed down by means of direct-action cisterns. Water enters the cistern through a valve, which is opened and closed by the action of a hollow float attached to one end of a rigid arm. As the water rises in the cistern, it lifts the float until the other end of the arm closes the valve and shuts off the supply.

Flushing is carried out by depressing a lever, which is linked by wire to a rod attached to a perforated plastic or metal plate at the bottom of an inverted U-bend tube (siphon). As the plate rises, the perforations are sealed by a flexible plastic diaphragm (flap valve), so the plate can displace a body of water over the U-bend to promote a siphoning action. The water pressure behind the diaphragm lifts it, so that the contents of the cistern flow up through the perforations in the plate, over the U-bend and down the flush pipe. As the water level in the cistern drops, so does the float - thus opening the float valve to refill the cistern.

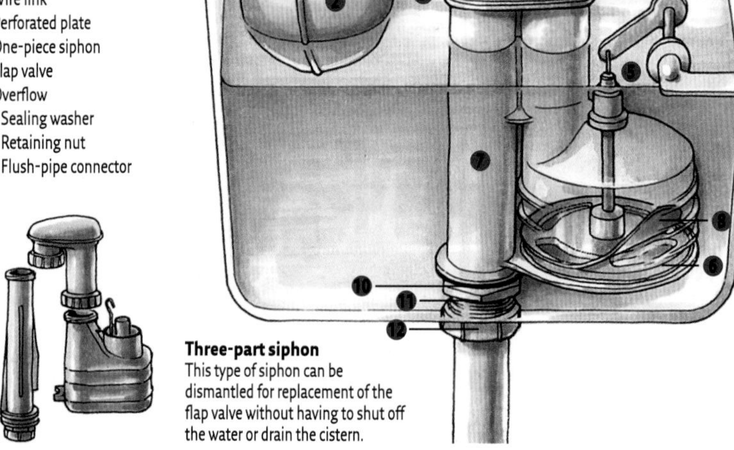

Direct-action cistern
The components of a typical direct-action WC cistern.
1 Float valve
2 Float
3 Float arm
4 Flushing lever
5 Wire link
6 Perforated plate
7 One-piece siphon
8 Flap valve
9 Overflow
10 Sealing washer
11 Retaining nut
12 Flush-pipe connector

Three-part siphon
This type of siphon can be dismantled for replacement of the flap valve without having to shut off the water or drain the cistern.

Servicing cisterns

The few problems associated with this type of cistern are easy to solve. A faulty float valve or poorly adjusted float arm will allow water to leak into the cistern until it drips from the overflow pipe that runs to the outside of the house. Slow or noisy filling can often be rectified by replacing the float valve. If the cistern will not flush until the lever is operated several times, the flap valve probably needs replacing (see below). If the flushing lever feels slack, check that the wire link at the end of the flushing arm is intact. When water runs continuously into the pan, check the condition of the washer at the base of the siphon.

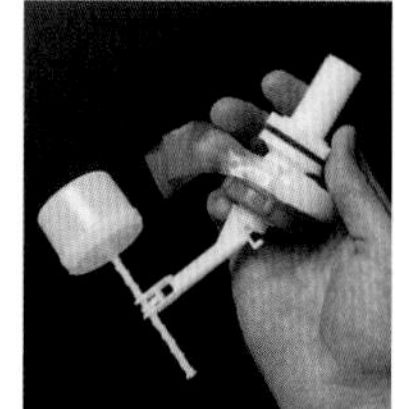

Miniature float valve
This type of float valve is designed for installing in WC cisterns only.

1 Wedge the float arm
2 Release flush pipe
3 Loosen retaining nut
4 Lift off flap valve

Replacing a flap valve

If a WC cistern will not flush first time, take off the lid and check that the lever is actually operating the flushing mechanism. If that appears to be working normally, then try replacing the flap valve in the siphon. Before you service a one-piece siphon, shut off the water by wedging the float arm with a bent wire across the cistern (**1**). Flush the cistern.

Use a wrench to unscrew the nut that holds the flush pipe to the underside of the cistern (**2**). Move the pipe to one side.

Release the retaining nut that clamps the siphon to the base of the cistern (**3**). A little water will run out as you loosen the nut - so have a bucket handy. You may find that the siphon is bolted to the base of the cistern, instead of being clamped by a single retaining nut.

Disconnect the flushing arm, then ease the siphon out of the cistern. Lift the diaphragm off the plastic plate (**4**) and replace it with one of the same size. Reassemble the entire flushing mechanism and reconnect the flush pipe to the cistern.

Making a new wire link

You won't be able to flush a WC cistern if the flushing lever has come adrift.

Make a replacement for a rusted link from thick wire; if the lever connecting the handle to the link has broken, the WC can be flushed by pulling the wire link upwards until you can get a new one.

Curing continuous running water

If you notice that water is running into the pan continuously, turn off the supply and let the cistern drain. If the siphon hasn't split, try changing the sealing washer.

If the water is flowing from the float valve so quickly that the siphoning action is not interrupted, fit a float-valve seat with a smaller water inlet.

SEE ALSO > Adjusting the float arm 354, Spanners and wrenches 522

Diaphragm valves

The pivoting end of the float arm on a diaphragm valve (known in the trade as a Part 2 valve) presses against the end of a small plastic piston, which moves the large rubber diaphragm to seal the water inlet.

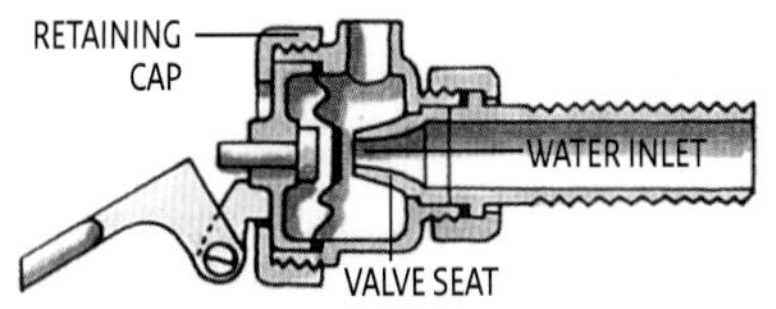

Diaphragm valve: retaining cap to the front

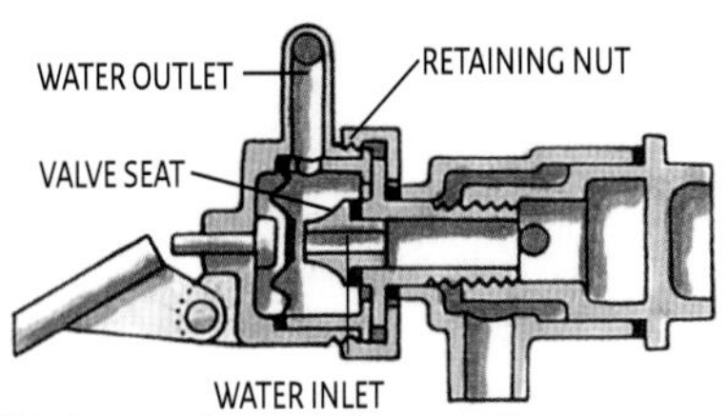

Diaphragm valve: retaining nut to the rear

Replacing the diaphragm

Turn off the water supply, then unscrew the large retaining cap. Depending on the model, the nut may be screwed onto the end of the valve or behind it (see above).

With the latter type of valve, slide out the cartridge inside the body (**1**) to find the diaphragm behind it. With the former, you will find a similar piston and diaphragm immediately behind the retaining cap (**2**).

Wash the valve, before assembling it along with the new diaphragm.

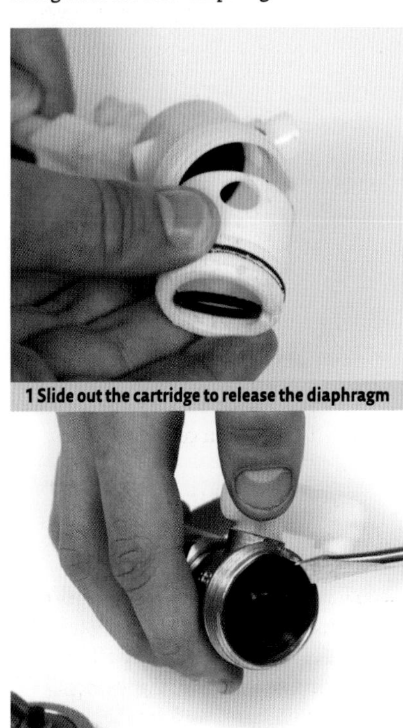
1 Slide out the cartridge to release the diaphragm

2 Undo the cap and pull float arm to find the valve

Close-coupled WCs and push-button cisterns

This modern style of WC does away with the pipe that connects the cistern to the pan. Water flows from the cistern through a moulded-in channel in the pan to the rim. The cistern is bolted directly to the pan and a rubber seal prevents leaks at the joint. This style often features compact cisterns with push-button action and lower water usage.

The cistern may incorporate a diaphragm valve, but it's becoming more common to find close-coupled WCs with push-button, 'continental'-style cisterns. Here, the traditional handle is replaced by a button on the top of the cistern. Usually the button is split, to give a dual flush facility of 4 or 6 litres (7 or 10½ pints), helping to save water.

Push-button cisterns use a different type of valve, which is activated via a cable release. A small float controls the level of water in the cistern. The valve usually incorporates an overflow, which allows water to flow into the toilet bowl – rather than outside via an overflow pipe – if there is a problem.

The mechanism inside the cistern is all plastic, so won't rust. As a result, there's less to go wrong, but if problems occur spare parts may be harder to find as there are many different types available.

These cisterns produce a faster flush, which doesn't give the same cleansing action as a slower, syphon-operated flush. However, they are quiet in operation and allow for a very slimline cistern, helping to reduce the 'footprint' of the WC.

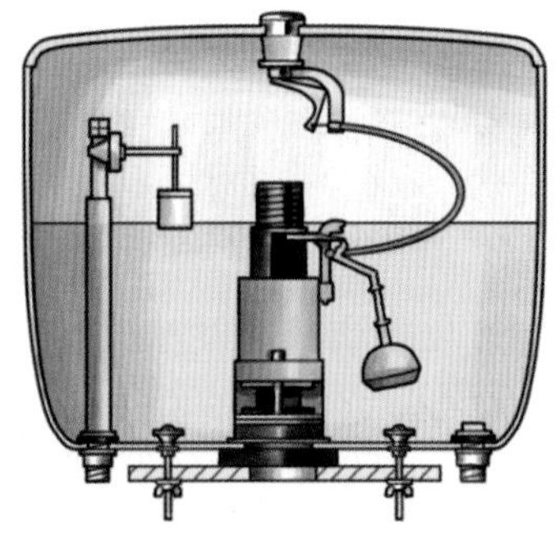
Push-button cistern mechanism

A close-coupled cistern with push-button operation

Flapper valve
This is a modern replacement for the siphon and can be operated by handle or push-button. It helps to save water because it only allows water to flush while the handle or button is depressed, unlike a siphon, which empties a full cistern every time. It has a built-in overflow, but as it lies in the bottom of the cistern it can be prone to limescale or debris interfering with the seal. It can be used in conjunction with all types of float valve.

Other types of cistern valve

A Fluidmaster valve converts a lever-operated siphon into a push-button cistern. A flap valve controls the flow of water into the WC. Quiet in use and water-efficient, it works well with low-capacity cisterns, but is not suitable for double-trap toilets. Two kits are available: one which replaces the lever and siphon; the other which also replaces the float valve.

The Torbeck valve can be used to replace the diaphragm or piston valve in most cisterns. Its all-plastic construction means there's nothing to corrode. After flushing, water enters the cistern through a tube which is mostly below water level, so there's no noise from splashing. The float is easily adjustable via a screw thread. Side and bottom entry versions are available, the latter with a built-in debris filter and flow control device.

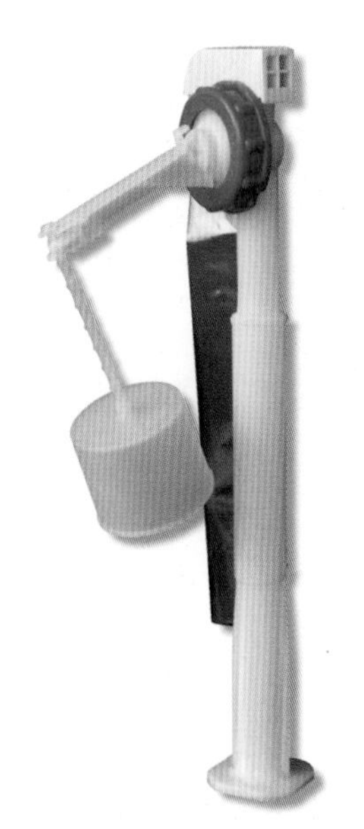
Torbeck valve

Fluidmaster valve

SEE ALSO > Turning off the water 348, Adjusting a float arm 354, Slip-joint pliers 525

Renovating valves and floats

A cistern or tank that doesn't work properly can prevent WCs flushing properly or cause noise throughout the plumbing system. Sorting the problem can be as simple as bending the float arm or adjusting a screw.

Adjusting the float arm

Adjust the float so as to maintain the optimum level of water, which is about 25mm (1in) below the outlet of the overflow pipe.

Bend the metal arm on a Portsmouth valve downward to reduce the water level, or straighten it to let in more water (1).

The arm on a diaphragm valve has an adjusting screw, which raises or lowers the arm to alter the water level (2).

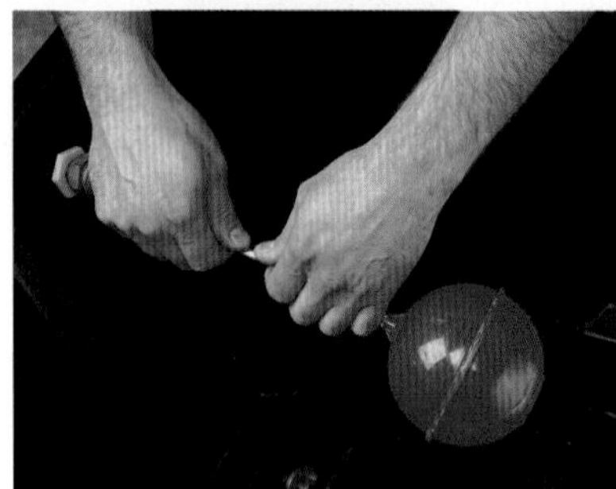

1 Straighten or bend a metal float arm

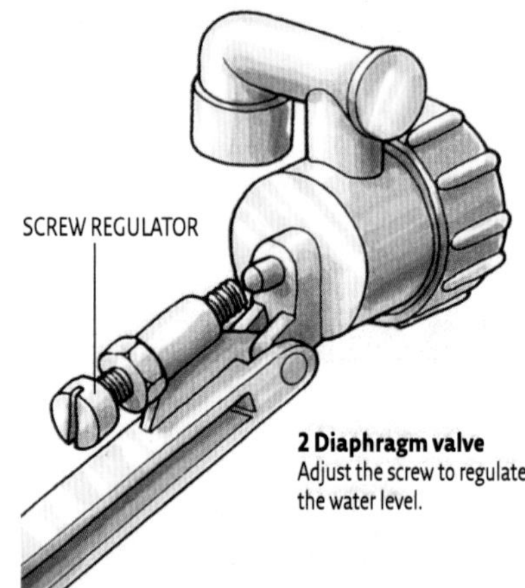

2 Diaphragm valve
Adjust the screw to regulate the water level.

Thumb-screw adjustment
Some float arms are cranked, and the float is attached with a thumb-screw clamp. To adjust the water level in the cistern, slide the float up or down the rod.

Float valve with flexible silencer tube

Replacing the float

Modern plastic floats rarely leak, but old-style metal floats eventually corrode and allow water to seep into the ball. The float gradually sinks, until it won't ride high enough to close the valve. Unscrew the float to see if there is water inside.

If you can't obtain a new float for several days, lay the ball on a bench, enlarge the leaking hole with a screwdriver and pour out the water. Cover the ball with a plastic bag, tying the neck tightly around the float arm, and then replace the float.

Curing noisy cisterns

Cisterns that fill noisily can be very annoying. It was once permitted to screw a pipe into the outlet of a valve so that it hung vertically below the level of the water. This solved the splashing problem, but concern about the possibility of water 'back-siphoning' through the silencer tube into the mains supply led to rigid tubes being banned in favour of flexible plastic silencer tubes (see far left), which seal by collapsing should back-siphoning occur.

A silencer tube can also prevent water hammer - a rhythmic thudding that reverberates along the pipework. This is often the result of ripples on the surface of the water in a cistern, caused by a heavy flow from the float valve. As the water rises, the float arm bouncing on the ripples 'hammers' the valve, and the sound is amplified and transmitted along the pipes. A flexible plastic tube will stop ripples by introducing water below the surface.

If the pressure through the valve is too high, the arm oscillates as it tries to close the valve - causing water hammer. This can be cured by fitting an equilibrium valve. As water flows through the valve, some of it is introduced behind the piston or diaphragm to equalize the pressure on each side, so that the valve closes smoothly and silently.

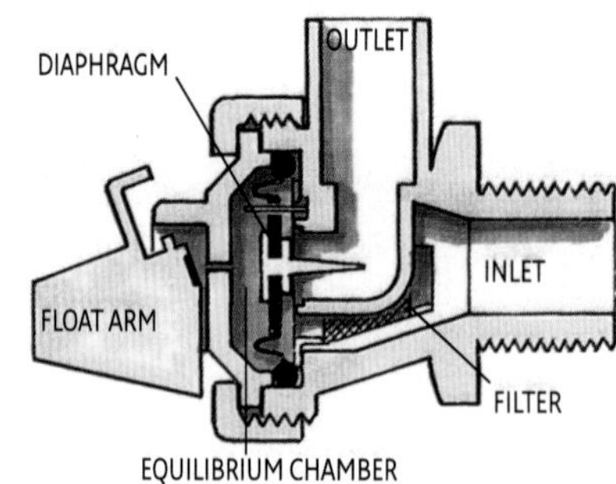

Diaphragm-type equilibrium valve

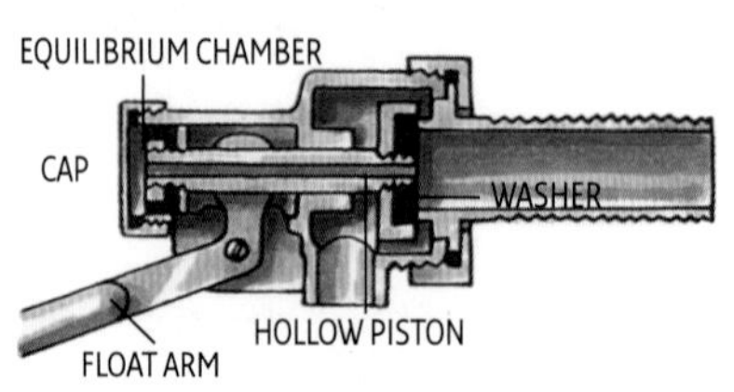

Piston-type equilibrium valve

Renewing a float valve

Turn off the supply of water to the cistern or tank, then use a spanner to loosen the tap connector joining the supply pipe to the float-valve stem. Remove the float arm, then unscrew the fixing nut outside of the cistern and pull out the valve.

Fit the replacement valve and, if possible, use the same tap connector to join it to the supply pipe.

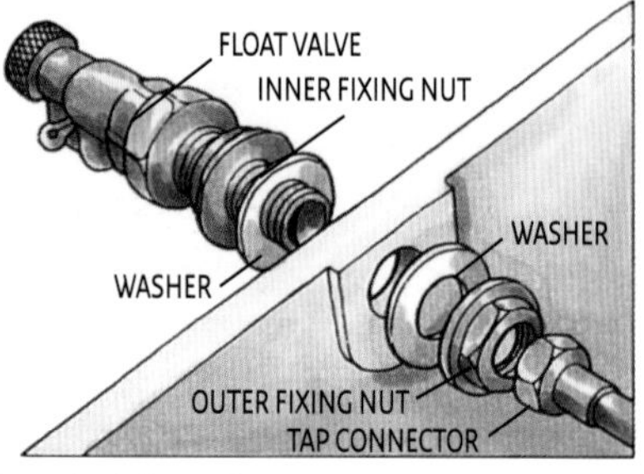

Renewing a float valve
Clamp the valve to the cistern with fixing nuts.

Choosing the correct pressure

Float valves are made to suit different water pressures: low, medium and high (LP, MP and HP). If the pressure is too low for the valve, the cistern may take a long time to fill; if too high, it may leak continuously. Most domestic WC cisterns require an LP valve; those fed direct from the mains need an HP valve. If the head (the height of the tank above the float valve) is greater than 13.5m (45ft), fit an MP valve; if over 30m (100ft), fit an HP valve. In an apartment with a packaged plumbing system (a storage tank built on top of the hot-water cylinder), the pressure may be so low that you will have to fit a full-way valve to the WC cistern in order to get it to fill reasonably quickly. If you live in an area where water pressure fluctuates a great deal, fit an equilibrium valve (see left).

To alter the pressure of a modern valve, simply replace the seat inside.

SEE ALSO > Float valves 353, Supporting pipes 368

Drainage systems

A drainage system is designed to carry dirty water and WC waste from the appliances in your home to underground drains leading to the main sewer. The various branches of the waste system are protected by U-bend traps full of water, to stop drain smells fouling the house. Depending on the age of your house, it will have a two-pipe system or a single stack. Because the two-pipe system has been in use for very much longer, it is still the more common of the two. Use similar methods to maintain either system.

Responsibility for the drains

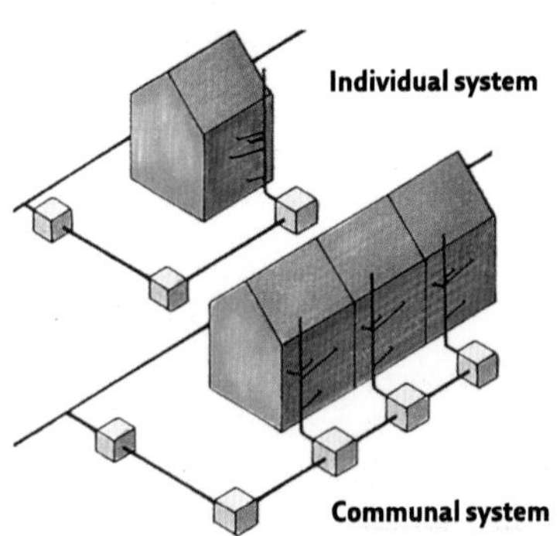

If a house is drained individually, the whole system up to the point where it joins the sewer is the responsibility of the householder. However, where a house is connected to a communal drainage system linking several houses, the arrangement for maintenance, including the clearance of blockages, is not so straightforward.

If the drains were constructed prior to 1937, the local council is responsible for cleansing but can reclaim the cost of repairing any part of the communal system from the householders. After that date, all responsibility falls upon the householders collectively, so that they are required to share the cost of the repair and cleansing of the drains up to the sewer, no matter where the problem occurs. Contact the Technical Services Department of your local council to find out who is responsible for your drains.

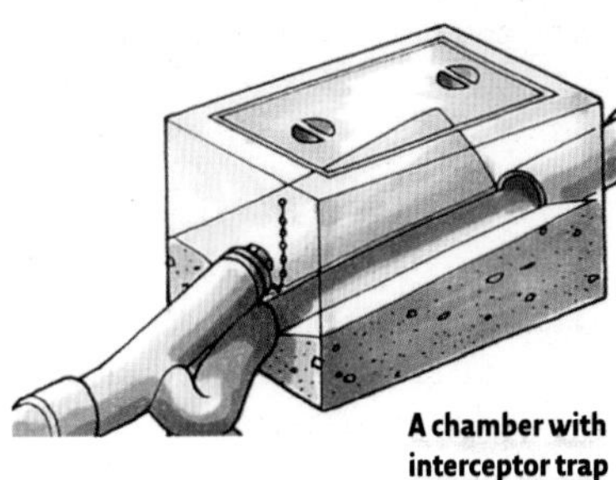

A chamber with interceptor trap

Two-pipe system

The waste pipes of older houses are divided into two separate systems. WC waste is fed into a vertical soil pipe that leads directly to the underground drains. To discharge drain gases at a safe height and make sure that back-siphoning cannot empty the WC traps, the soil pipe is vented to the open air above the guttering.

Individual branch pipes leading from upstairs washbasins and baths drain into an open hopper that funnels the water into another vertical waste pipe. Instead of feeding directly into the underground drains, this pipe terminates over a yard gully - another trap covered by a grid. A separate waste pipe from the kitchen sink normally drains into the same gully.

The yard gully and soil pipe both discharge into an underground inspection chamber, or manhole. These chambers provide access to the main drains for clearing blockages, and are located wherever the main drain changes direction on its way to the sewer.

At the last inspection chamber, just before the drain enters the sewer, there is an interceptor trap, the final barrier to drain gases and sewer rats.

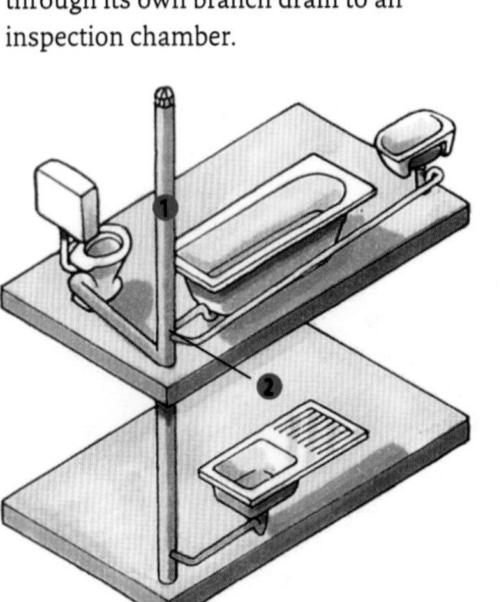

Two-pipe system
1 Soil pipe
2 Hopper
3 Waste pipe
4 Yard gully
5 Inspection chamber

Single-stack system

Since the late 1950s, most houses have been drained using a single-stack system. Waste from basins, baths and WCs is fed into the same vertical soil pipe or stack - which, unlike the two-pipe system, is often built inside the house. A single-stack system must be designed carefully to prevent a heavy discharge of waste from one appliance siphoning the trap of another, and to avoid the possibility of WC waste blocking other branch pipes. The vent pipe of the stack terminates above the roof and is capped with an open cage; or inside the house and is fitted with an air-admittance valve (see right).

The kitchen sink can be drained through the same stack, but it is still common practice to drain sink waste into a yard gully. Nowadays waste pipes must pass through the grid, stopping short of the water in the gully trap - so that if blocked with leaves, the waste can discharge unobstructed into the gully. Alternatively, it may be a back-inlet gully, with the waste pipe entering below ground level.

A downstairs WC is sometimes drained through its own branch drain to an inspection chamber.

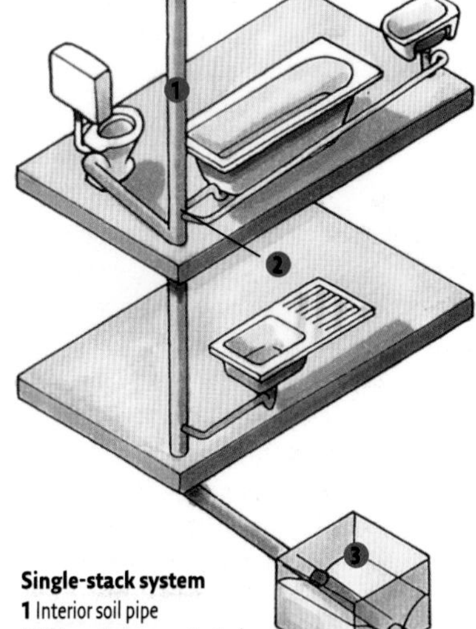

Single-stack system
1 Interior soil pipe
2 All branch pipes run to stack
3 Inspection chamber

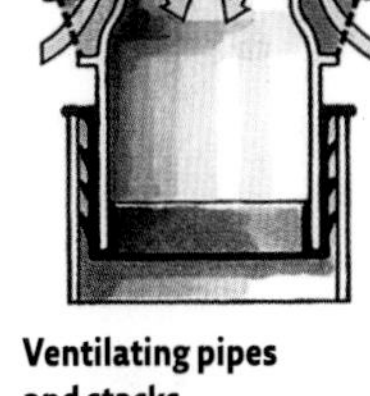

Ventilating pipes and stacks
An air-admittance valve seals off the vent pipe, but allows air into the system to prevent water being siphoned from the trap seals. This type of valve can only be used if the drainage scheme has been approved by the local authority.

Prefabricated chamber
On a modern drainage system, the inspection chambers may take the form of cylindrical prefabricated units. There may not be an interceptor trap in the last chamber before the sewer.

SEE ALSO > Plumbing systems 346–7, Blocked soil pipe 357, Yard gully 357, Blocked drains 358

Clearing blockages

Don't ignore the early signs of an imminent blockage in the waste pipe from a sink, bath or basin. If the water drains away slowly, use a chemical cleaner to remove a partial blockage before it becomes more serious. If a waste pipe blocks without warning, there are various ways to locate and clear the obstruction.

Cleansing the waste pipe

Grease, hair and particles of kitchen debris build up gradually within the traps and waste pipes. Regular cleaning with a proprietary chemical drain cleaner will keep the waste system clear and sweet-smelling.

If water drains away sluggishly, use a cleaner immediately. Follow the manufacturer's instructions carefully, with particular regard to safety. Always wear protective gloves and goggles when handling chemical cleaners, and keep them out of the reach of children.

If unpleasant odours linger after you've cleaned the waste, pour a little disinfectant into the basin overflow.

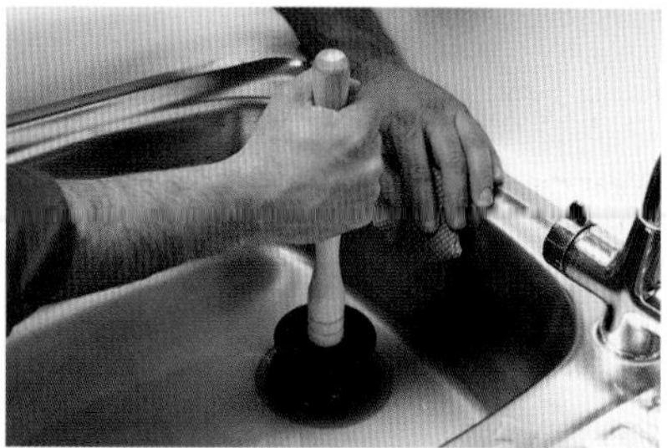

Use a plunger to force out a blockage

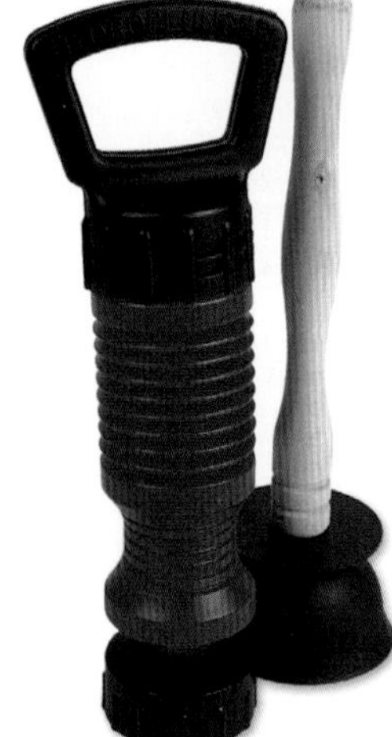

Using a plunger or pump

If one basin fails to empty while others are functioning normally, the blockage must be somewhere along its individual branch pipe. Before you attempt to locate the blockage, try forcing it out of the pipe with a sink plunger. Smear the rim of the rubber cup with petroleum jelly, then lower it into the blocked basin to cover the waste outlet. Make sure that there's enough water in the basin to cover the cup. Hold a wet cloth in the overflow with one hand and pump the handle of the plunger up and down a few times. The waste may not clear immediately if the blockage is merely forced further along the pipe, so repeat until the water drains away.

If it will not clear after several attempts, try hiring a hand-operated hydraulic pump to clear the pipe. Block the sink overflow with a wet cloth and fill the pump with water from the tap. Hold the pump's nozzle over the outlet, pressing down firmly, then pump up and down until the obstruction is cleared.

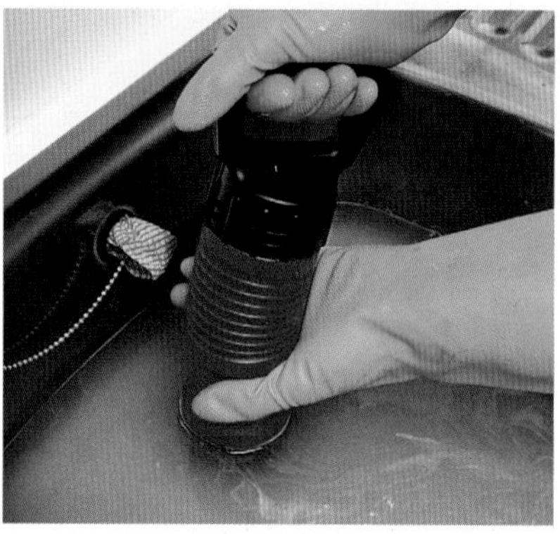

A pump forces a jet of water along the pipe

Clearing the trap

If you can't shift the blockage using a plunger or pump, dismantle the trap situated immediately below the waste outlet of a sink or basin. The trap is basically a bent tube designed to hold water to seal out drain odours. Traps become blocked when debris collects at the lowest point of the bend.

Place a bucket under the basin to catch the water, then use a wrench to release the cleaning eye at the base of a P-trap; on a bottle trap, remove the large access cap by hand. If there is no provision for gaining access to the trap, unscrew the connecting nuts and remove it.

Let the contents of the trap drain into the bucket, then bend a hook on the end of a length of wire and use it to probe the section of waste pipe beyond the trap. (It is also worth checking outside, to see if the other end of the pipe is blocked with leaves.) If you have had to remove the trap, take the opportunity to scrub it out with detergent before replacing it.

Cleaning the branch pipe

Quite often, a vertical pipe from the trap joins a virtually horizontal section of the waste pipe. Unscrew the access plug built into the joint and use a length of hooked wire to probe the branch pipe. If you locate a blockage that seems very firmly lodged, rent a drain auger from a tool-hire company to clear the pipework.

If there's no access plug, remove the trap and probe the waste pipe with an auger. If it's made with push-fit joints, it can be dismantled easily.

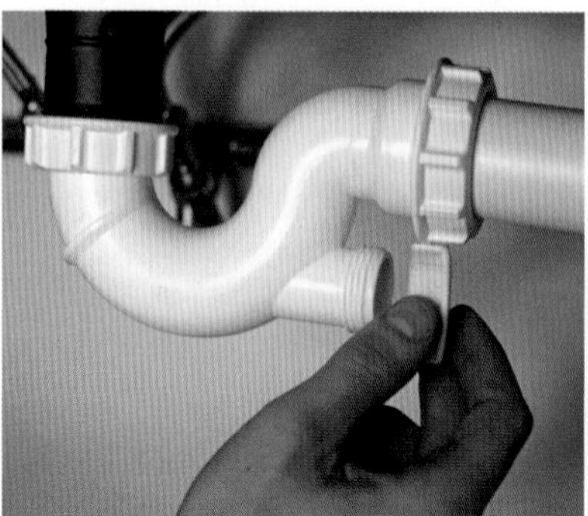

Undo the cleaning eye on a P-trap

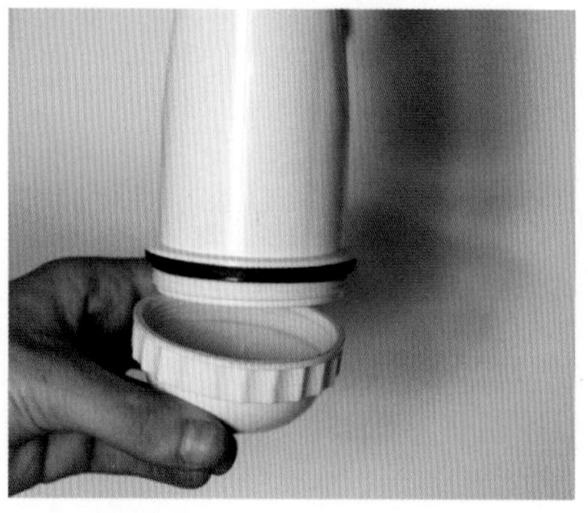

Unscrew the access cap on a bottle trap

Use an auger to clear a branch pipe

SEE ALSO > Frozen pipes 349, Drain auger 517, Hydraulic pump 517, Sink plunger 517

Blocked stacks or gullies

If several fittings are draining poorly, the vertical stack is probably obstructed. In autumn, the hopper, downpipe and yard gully may be blocked with leaves. The blockage may not be obvious when you empty a basin, but the contents of a bath will almost certainly cause an overflow. Clear the blockage immediately to avoid penetrating damp affecting your house.

Cleaning out the hopper and drainpipe

Wearing protective gloves, scoop out the debris from the hopper, then gently probe the drainpipe with a cane to check that it is free. Clear the bottom end of the pipe with a piece of bent wire. If an old cast-iron waste pipe has been replaced with a modern plastic pipe, you may find there are cleaning eyes or access plugs at strategic points for clearing a blockage.

While you're on the ladder, scrub the inside of the hopper and disinfect it to prevent odours entering the bathroom.

Unblocking a yard gully

Unless you decide to hire an auger, you have little option but to clear a blocked gully by hand. However, by the time it overflows the water in the gully will be quite deep, so try bailing some of it out with a small disposable container. Wearing rubber gloves, scoop out the debris from the trap until the remaining water disperses.

Rinse the gully with a hose and cleanse it with disinfectant. Scrub the grid as clean as possible, or burn off accumulated grime from a metal grid with a gas torch.

If a flooded gully appears to be clear and yet the water will not drain away, try to locate the blockage at the nearest inspection chamber.

Bail out the water, then clear a gully by hand

Unblocking a soil pipe

Unblocking a soil pipe is an unpleasant job, which can be doubly difficult because of access problems. A cast-iron external stack will almost certainly have to be cleared via the vent above the roof, while a stack running inside the house may be hard to reach and any mess could ruin carpets or wallpaper. In either case it may be best to call in a professional cleaning company.

You can clean an external plastic stack yourself, since there should be a large access plug or cleaning eye wherever branch pipes join the stack. Unscrew and open the cleaning eye to insert a hired drain auger. Pass the auger into the stack until you locate the obstruction, then crank the handle to engage it. Push or pull the auger until you can dislodge the obstruction to clear the trapped water, then hose out the stack. Wash and disinfect the surrounding area.

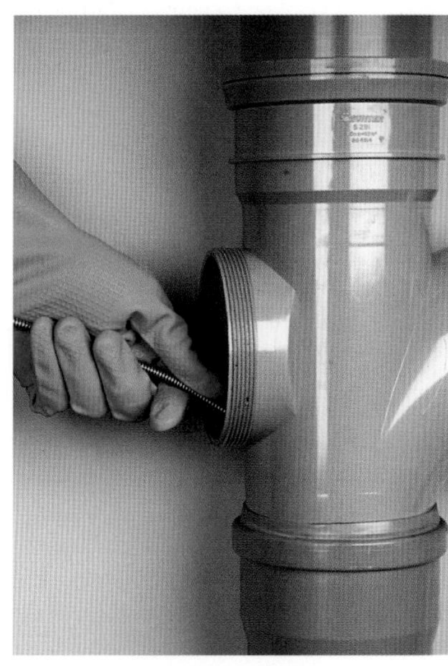

Use a hired auger to clear a soil stack

Unblocking a WC

If the water in a WC pan rises when you flush it, there's a blockage in the vicinity of the trap. A partial blockage allows the water level to fall slowly.

Hire a larger version of the sink plunger to force the obstruction into the soil pipe. Position the rubber cup of the plunger well down into the U-bend, and pump the handle. When the blockage clears, the water level will drop suddenly, accompanied by an audible gurgling.

If the trap is blocked solidly, hire a special WC auger. Pass the flexible clearing rod as far as possible into the trap, then crank the handle to dislodge the blockage. Wash the auger in hot water and disinfect it, before returning it to the hire company. A more serious blockage may require professional assistance.

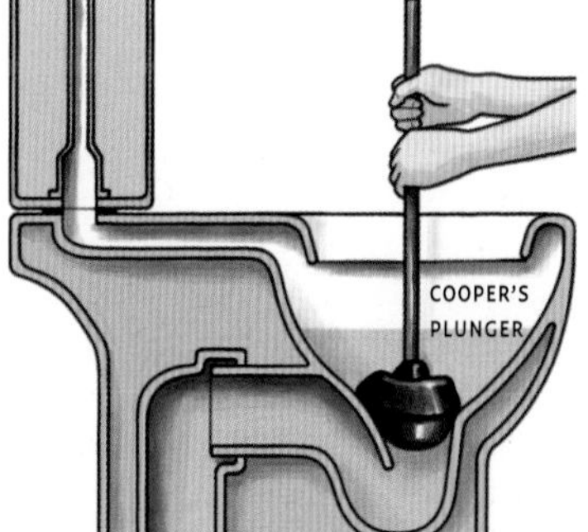

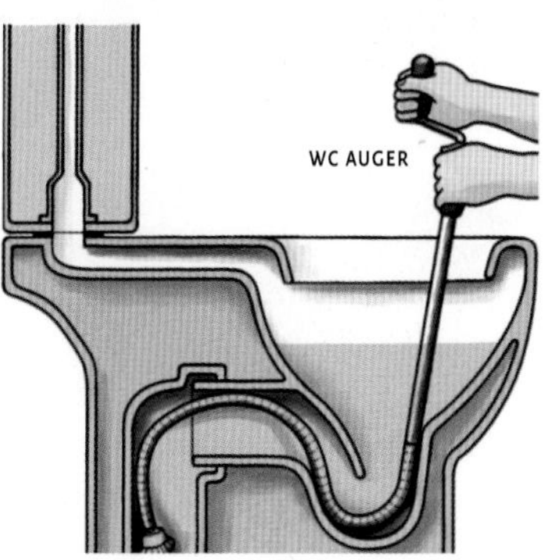

Clearing a blockage
Use a Cooper's plunger (top) to pump a blocked WC. Alternatively, clear it with a special WC auger (above).

• **Clearing a blockage with a hydraulic pump**
Shift a really stubborn blockage with a hired pump, similar to the one used for clearing a blocked sink (see opposite).

SEE ALSO > Guttering 134–7, Penetrating damp 247, Inspection chambers 358, Drain auger 517, WC auger 517, Gas torch 521

Rodding the drains

The first sign of a blocked drain may be an unpleasant smell from an inspection chamber, but a severe blockage may cause waste to overflow from a gully or inspection chamber. Before calling in the professionals, hire a set of drain rods – flexible rods made of plastic or wire, screwed end to end – to clear the blockage.

Rodding a drain
Use flexible drain rods to get at the blockage.

Locating the blockage

Lift the cover from the inspection chamber nearest to the house. If it's stuck or the handles have rusted away, scrape the dirt from around its edges and prise it up with a garden spade.

• If the chamber contains water, check the one nearer the road or boundary. If that chamber is dry, the blockage is between the two chambers.

If the chamber nearest the road is full, the blockage will be in the interceptor trap or in the pipe beyond, leading to the sewer.

• If both chambers are dry and a yard gully or downstairs WC will not empty, check for blockages in the branch drains that run to the first inspection chamber.

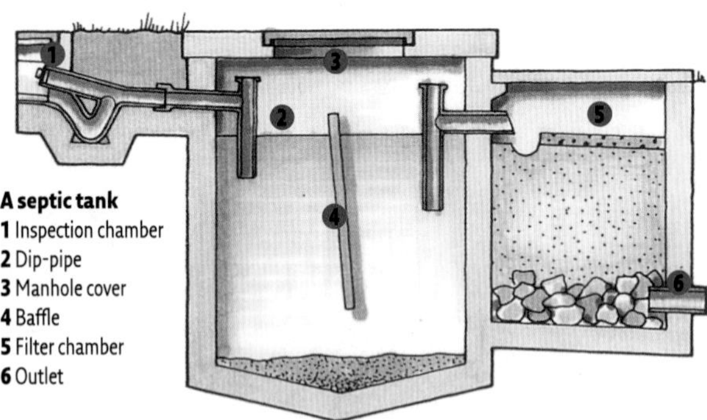

A typical cesspool
1 Inspection chamber
2 Dip-pipe
3 Manhole cover
4 Ventilator
5 Sludge

A septic tank
1 Inspection chamber
2 Dip-pipe
3 Manhole cover
4 Baffle
5 Filter chamber
6 Outlet

Rodding points

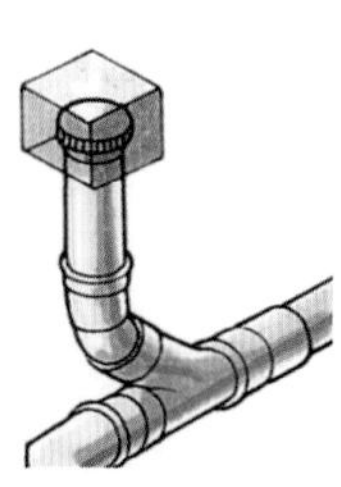

A modern drainage system is often fitted with rodding points to provide access to the drain. They are sealed with small oval or circular covers that may be a push or screw fit.

Rodding the drainpipe

Screw two or three rods together and attach a corkscrew fitting to the end. Insert the rods into the drain at the bottom of the inspection chamber, in the direction of the suspected blockage. If the chamber is full of water, use the end of a rod to locate the open channel running across the floor, leading to the drain opening.

As you pass the rods along the pipe, attach further lengths till you reach the obstruction, then twist the rods clockwise to engage the screw (don't twist the rods anticlockwise, or they will become detached). Agitate the obstruction until it breaks up, allowing the water to flow away.

Extract the rods, flush the chamber with clean water from a hose, and then replace the cover and clean the rods.

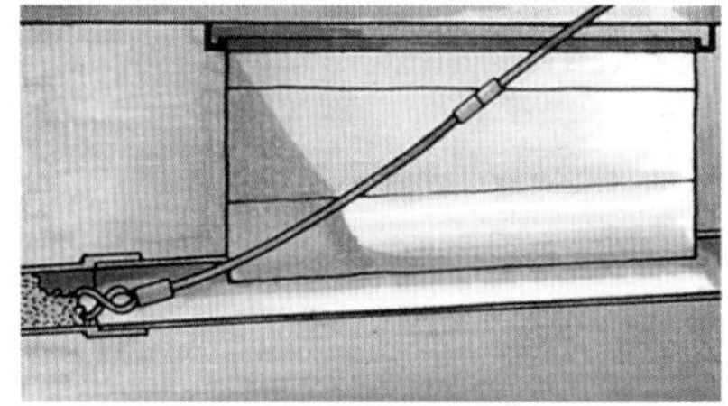

Use a corkscrew fitting to clear a drain

Clearing traps

Screw a rubber plunger to the end of a short length of rods and locate the channel that leads to the base of the trap. Push the plunger into the opening of the trap, then pump the rods a few times to expel the blockage. (This is also a useful technique for clearing blocked yard gullies.)

If the water level does not drop after several attempts, try clearing the drain leading to the sewer. Access to this drain is through a cleaning eye above the trap. It will be sealed with a stopper, which you will have to dislodge with a drain rod, unless it is attached to a chain stapled to the chamber wall. Don't let the stopper fall into the channel and block the trap. Rod the drain, then hose out the chamber before replacing the stopper and cover.

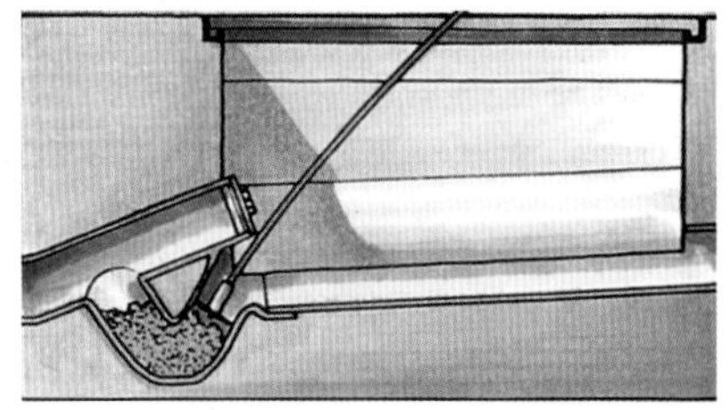

To rod an interceptor trap, fit a rubber plunger

Cesspools and septic tanks

Houses built in the country or on the outskirts of a town may not be connected to a public sewer. Instead, waste is drained into a cesspool or septic tank.

A cesspool simply acts as a collection point for sewage until it can be pumped out by the local council. A septic tank is a complete waste-disposal system, in which sewage is broken down by bacterial action before the water is finally discharged into a local waterway or distributed underground.

Cesspools

The Building Regulations stipulate that cesspools must have a minimum capacity of 18,000 litres (4,000 gallons), but many existing cesspools hold far less and require emptying perhaps once every two weeks. Water boards estimate usage at around 115 litres (25 gallons) per person per day.

Septic tanks

The sewage in a septic tank separates slowly: heavy sludge falls to the bottom to leave relatively clear water, with a layer of scum floating on the surface. Waste discharges below the surface, so that incoming water does not stir up the sewage. Bacterial action takes a minimum of 24 hours, so the tank has baffles to slow down the movement of sewage through it.

The partly treated waste passes out of the tank into some form of filtration system for further bacterial action. This may consist of another chamber, containing a deep filter bed; or the waste may flow underground through a network of drains, which disperses the water over a wide area to filter through the soil.

Modern packaged waste water treatment plants are electrically operated and produce very clean effluent.

SEE ALSO > Inspection chambers 355, Drain rods 517

Metal pipes

The ability to install a run of pipework, make watertight joints and connect up to fittings constitutes the basis of most plumbing. Without these skills, a householder is restricted to simple maintenance. Modern materials and technology have made it possible for anybody who is prepared to master a few techniques to upgrade and extend plumbing without having to hire a professional.

Metric and imperial pipes

Copper and stainless-steel pipes are now made in metric sizes, whereas pipework already installed in older houses will have been made to imperial measurements. If you compare the equivalent dimensions (15mm - ½in, 22mm - ¾in, 28mm - 1in), the difference seems obvious, but metric pipe is measured externally while imperial pipe is measured internally. In fact, the difference is very small - but enough to cause some problems when joining one type of pipe to the other.

When making soldered joints, an exact fit is essential. Imperial to metric adaptors are necessary when joining 22mm pipe to its imperial equivalent; and, although not essential, adaptors are convenient when you are working with 28mm pipes or with thick-walled ½in pipes. Adaptors are not required when using compression fittings, but when you are connecting 22mm to ¾in plumbing slip an imperial olive onto the ¾in pipe.

Typically, 15mm (½in) pipe is used for the supply to basins, kitchen sinks, washing machines, some showers, and radiator flow and returns. However, 22mm (¾in) pipes are used to supply baths, high-output showers, hot-water cylinders and main central-heating circuits; and 28mm (1in) pipe for larger heating installations.

Electrochemical action

Joining pipes made from different metals can accelerate corrosion as a result of electrolytic action. If you live in a soft-water area, where this problem tends to be pronounced, use plastic pipe and connectors when you're joining to old pipework - but make sure that the metal pipes are still bonded to earth, as required by the Wiring Regulations.

Metal supply pipes

Over the years, most household plumbing systems will have undergone some form of improvement or alteration. As a result, you may find any of a number of metals used, perhaps in combination, depending on the availability of materials at the time of installation or the preference of an individual plumber.

Copper

Half-hard-tempered copper tubing is the most widely used material for pipework. This is because it's lightweight, solders well, and can be bent easily (even by hand, with the aid of a bending spring). It is used for both hot-water and cold-water pipes, as well as for central-heating systems. There are three sizes of pipe generally used for domestic plumbing: 15mm (½in), 22mm (¾in), and 28mm (1in).

Stainless steel

Stainless-steel tubing is not as common as copper, but is available in the same sizes. You may have to order it from a plumbers' merchant. It's harder than copper, so cannot be bent as easily, and is difficult to solder. It pays to use compression joints to connect stainless-steel pipes, but tighten them slightly more than you would when joining copper.

Stainless steel does not react with galvanized steel (iron) - see Electrochemical action (bottom left).

Lead

Lead is never used nowadays for any form of new plumbing - but there are thousands of houses that still have a lead rising main connected to a modernized system.

Lead plumbing that's still in use will be nearing the end of its life, so replace it as soon as an opportunity arises. When drinking water lies in a lead pipe for some time, it absorbs toxins from the metal. If you have a lead pipe supplying your drinking water, always run off a little water before you use any.

Galvanized steel (iron)

Galvanized steel was once commonly used for supply pipes, both below and above ground, having taken over from lead. It was then superseded by copper.

There are two problems with this type of pipe. It rusts from the inside and resists water flow as it deteriorates. Also, when it is joined to copper, the galvanizing breaks down rapidly because of an electrolytic action between the copper and zinc coating.

Cast-iron waste pipes
All old soil pipes are made from cast iron, which is prone to rusting. If it weren't for their relatively thick walls, pipes of this kind would have rusted away long ago. Should you need to replace a cast-iron pipe, ask for one of the plastic alternatives.

Copper pipes
The economic choice for modern plumbing systems.

Stainless steel
Owing to its superior appearance and strength, stainless steel is used where pipe runs are exposed. It does not cause electrolytic action with galvanized-steel pipes.

Lead
This is still found in older houses. It can introduce toxins into the drinking-water supply, so should be replaced.

Iron
Iron pipes are used for mains water supply in some older systems. Iron is susceptible to furring-up and decay, which can result in low water pressure and leaks. Cast iron is used for waste pipes in older buildings.

SEE ALSO > Supplementary bonding 286, Main switch equipment 296, Soldered joints 361, Push-fit joints 362, Plastic waste pipes 364, Soft water 390

Metal joints and fittings

Joints are made to connect pipes at different angles and in various combinations. There are adaptors for joining metric and imperial pipes, and for connecting one kind of material to another. You need to consult manufacturers' catalogues to see every variation, but the examples on this page illustrate a typical range of joints. Plumbing fittings such as valves are made with demountable compression joints, so that they can be removed easily for servicing or replacement.

Straight connectors
To join two pipes end to end in a straight line.
1 For pipes of equal diameter – compression joint.
2 Reducer to connect a 22mm (¾in) pipe to a 15mm (½in) pipe – capillary joint.

Bends or elbows
To join two pipes at an angle.
3 90° – compression joint.

Tees (T-joints)
To join three pipes.
4 Equal tee, for joining three pipes of the same diameter – capillary joint.
5 Unequal tee, for reducing size of pipe run when connecting a branch pipe – compression joint.

Adaptors
To join dissimilar pipes.
6 Straight coupling for joining 22mm and ¾in pipes – compression joint.
7 Connector for joining copper to galvanized steel – compression joint for copper, threaded female coupling for steel.

Fittings
Identical jointing systems are used to connect fittings.
8 End cap, to seal pipes – compression joint.
9 Tap connector for connecting supply pipe to tap – capillary joint.
10 Tank connector, joins pipes to cisterns – compression joint.
11 Bib-tap wall plate, for fixing tap on outside wall.
12 Bib tap has threaded tail to fit wall plate.
13 Gate valve to fit in straight pipe run – compression joint.
14 Draincock for emptying a pipe run – compression joint.
15 Straight service valve for isolating a tap or float valve – compression joint.
16 Double-check non-return valve, used for outside taps and other outlets where contamination of water supply is possible – compression joint.

1 Equal-size connector

2 Reducer

3 Elbow 90°

4 Equal tee

5 Unequal tee

6 Straight coupling

7 Copper-to-steel connector

8 End cap

9 Tap connector

10 Tank connector

11 Bib-tap wall plate

12 Bib tap

13 Gate valve

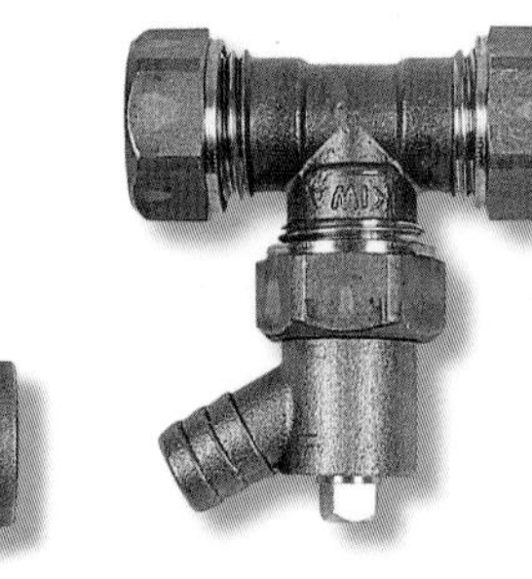
14 Draincock

15 Straight service valve

16 Double-check non-return valve

Pipe joints

It's not possible to make a strong, watertight joint by simply soldering pipes together, so capillary or compression joints are used to connect pipes or attach fittings such as tap connectors, valves and the like.

Capillary joints

Capillary joints are made to fit snugly over the ends of a pipe. The very small gap between the pipe and joint sleeve is filled with molten solder - when this cools, it holds the joint together and makes it watertight. Capillary joints are neat and inexpensive - but because you need to heat the metal with a gas torch, there is a risk of fire when working in confined spaces under floors.

Soldering capillary joints

Solder is introduced to each mouth of the assembled end-feed joint and flows by capillary action into the fitting.

The rings pressed into the sleeves of an integral-ring fitting contain the exact amount of solder to make perfect joints.

Compression joints

Compression joints are simple to use, but more expensive than capillary joints. They are also more obtrusive, and you may find it hard to manoeuvre a wrench where space is restricted. When the cap-nut is tightened with a wrench it compresses a ring of soft metal, known as an olive, to fill the joint between fitting and pipe.

Corrosion resistance
Corrosion can take place between brass fittings and copper pipes. Look for the symbol that denotes corrosion-resistant brass fittings.

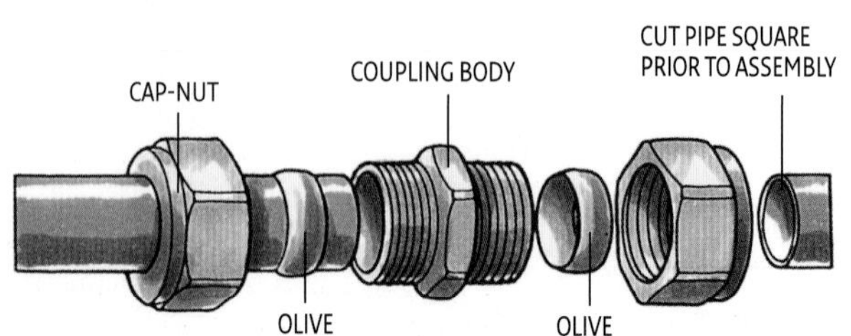

SEE ALSO > Metal plumbing 359

Cutting metal pipe

Calculate the length of pipe you need, allowing enough to fit into the sleeve of the joint at each end. Whatever type of joint you use, it's essential to cut the end of every length of pipe square.

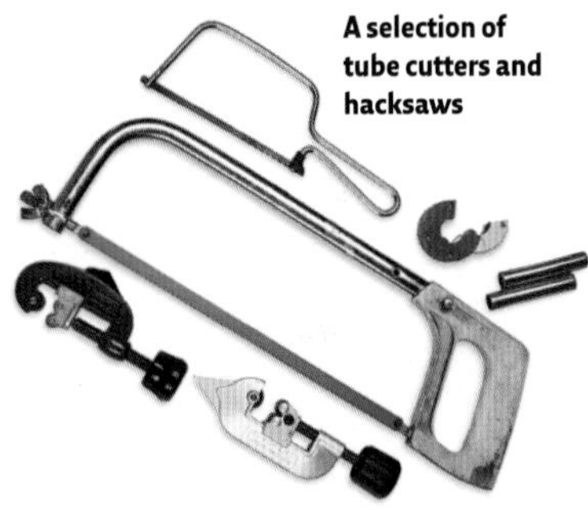
A selection of tube cutters and hacksaws

To ensure a perfectly square cut each time, use a tube cutter. Align the cutting wheel with your mark, and adjust the handle of the tool to clamp the rollers against the pipe (1). Rotate the tool around the pipe, adjusting the handle after each revolution to make the cutter bite deeper into the metal.

A tube cutter makes a clean cut on the outside of the pipe, but use the pointed reamer on the tool to clean the burr from inside the cut end (2).

If you use a hacksaw, make sure the cut is square by wrapping a piece of paper with a straight edge around the pipe. Align the wrapped edge and use it to guide the saw blade (3). Remove the burr, inside and out, with a file.

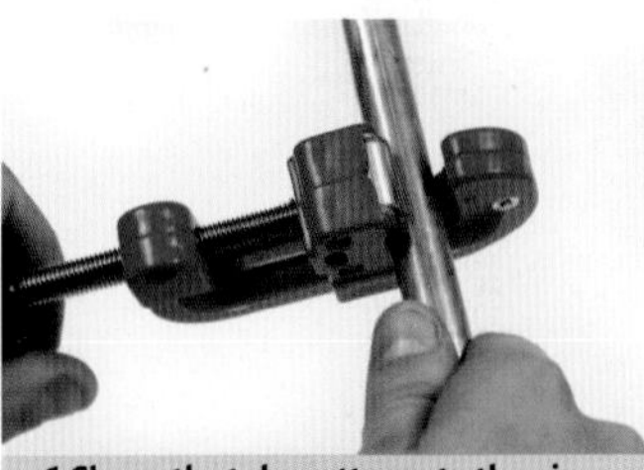
1 Clamp the tube cutter onto the pipe

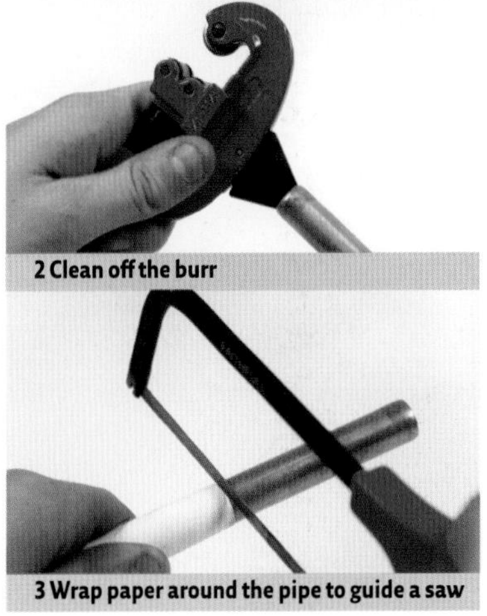
2 Clean off the burr

3 Wrap paper around the pipe to guide a saw

Making soldered joints

Soldering pipe joints is easy once you have had a little practice. The fittings are cheap, so you can afford to try out the techniques before you begin to install pipework. You need a gas torch to apply heat, some flux to clean the metal, and solder to make the joint. Make sure the pipe is perfectly dry before you attempt to solder a joint.

Solder and flux

Solder is a soft alloy manufactured with a melting point lower than that of the metal it is joining. Plumbers' solder is sold as wound wire.

Copper must be spotlessly clean and grease-free if it is to produce a properly soldered joint. Even when cleaned mechanically with wire wool, copper begins to oxidize immediately; a chemical cleaner known as flux is therefore painted onto the metal to provide a barrier against oxidation until the solder is applied. A non-corrosive flux in the form of a paste is the best one to use. On stainless steel use a highly efficient active flux - but wash it off with warm water after the joint is made, or the metal will corrode.

Gas torches

To heat the metal sufficiently for a soldered joint, most plumbers use a gas torch. Gas, liquefied under pressure, is contained in a disposable metal canister. When the control valve of the torch is opened, gas is vaporized to combine with air, making a highly combustible mixture. Once ignited, the flame is adjusted until it burns steadily with a clear blue colour.

Using end-feed joints

Clean the pipe with wire wool (1) then apply flux (2). Assemble the components (3), then heat the joint evenly. When the flux begins to bubble, remove the flame and touch the solder to two or three points around the fitting (4) - the joint is full of solder when a bright ring appears around each sleeve. Allow it to cool.

1 Clean the pipe with wire wool

3 Push components together

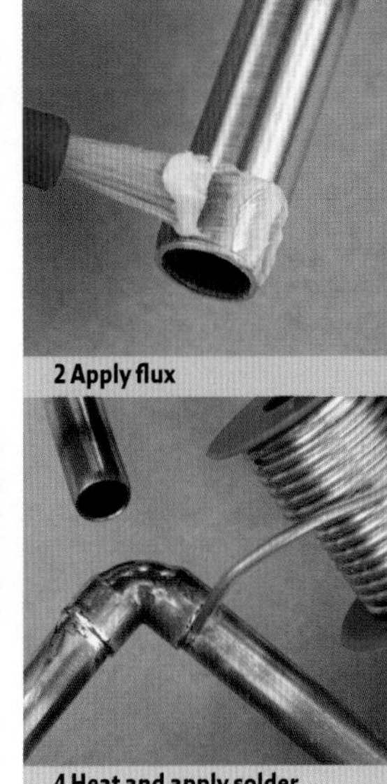
2 Apply flux

4 Heat and apply solder

Using integral-ring joints

Clean the ends of each pipe and the inside of the joint sleeves with wire wool or abrasive paper until the metal is shiny. Brush flux onto the cleaned metal and push the pipes into the joint, twisting them to spread the flux evenly. Push each pipe up against the stop in the joint.

If using elbows or tees, mark the pipe and joint with a pencil, to make sure they do not get misaligned during soldering.

Slip a ceramic tile or a plumber's fibre-glass mat behind the joint to protect flammable materials, then apply the flame of a gas torch to the area of the joint to heat it evenly. When a bright ring of solder appears at each end of the joint, remove the flame and allow the metal to cool for a couple of minutes before disturbing it.

Repairing a weeping joint

When you fill a new installation with water for the first time, check every joint to make sure they're watertight. If you notice water 'weeping' from a soldered joint, drain the pipe and allow it to dry. Heat the joint and apply some fresh solder to the edge of each mouth. If it leaks a second time, heat the joint until you can pull it apart with gloved hands. Either use a new joint or clean and flux all surfaces and reuse the same joint, adding solder as if you were working with a new end-feed fitting.

SEE ALSO > Pipe fittings 360, Plumbing tools 517-25

Compression joints

Using compression fittings is so straightforward that you will be able to make watertight joints without any previous experience. All that's required for success is to ensure that the pipes to be joined are clean and that the fitting is not overtightened.

Straight connector
Compression joint to join two pipes of equal diameter, end to end, in a straight line.

Elbow joint
A 90° elbow compression joint connects two pipes at an angle.

Assembling a joint

Cut the ends of each pipe square and clean them, along with the olives, using wire wool. Dismantle a new joint and slip a cap-nut over the end of one pipe, followed by an olive (1). Look carefully to see if the sloping sides of the olive are equal in length. If one is longer than the other, that side should face away from the nut.

Push the pipe firmly into the joint body (2), twisting it slightly to ensure it is firmly against the integral stop. Slide the olive up against the joint body, then tighten the nut by hand.

The olive must be compressed by just the right amount to ensure a watertight joint. As a guide, make a pencil mark on one face of the nut and on the opposing face on the joint body (3); then, holding the joint body steady with a spanner, use another spanner to turn the nut one complete revolution (4). Assemble the other half of the joint in exactly the same manner.

Some plumbers like to wrap a single turn of PTFE tape over the olive before tightening the nut, to make absolutely sure the joint is watertight. However, a properly tightened compression joint should be watertight without it.

1 Slip an olive onto the pipe after the cap-nut

2 Clamp the joint to the pipe with the nut

3 Mark the nut and joint with a pencil

4 Tighten the joint with two spanners

Fixing weeping joints

Crushing an olive by overtightening a compression joint will cause it to leak. Drain the pipe and dismantle the joint. Cut through the damaged olive with a junior hacksaw, taking care not to damage the pipe. Remake the joint with a new olive, restore the supply of water, and check for leaks once more.

Saw through a damaged olive

Metal push-fit joints

Metal push-fit joints are available as an alternative to the plastic variety. Made from brass alloy, they have a one-piece body that incorporates a stainless-steel grab ring to prevent the fitting coming loose under pressure. A release mechanism is incorporated to make them easy to remove. They are quick to use, less bulky than their plastic counterparts and better able to withstand higher water pressures, but they are more expensive, especially if you are carrying out a major project.

SEE ALSO > Metal joints and fittings 360, Plumbing adaptors 364, Wrenches 522

Bending pipes

You can change the direction of a pipe run by using an elbow joint, but there are occasions when bending the pipe itself will produce a neater or more accurate result. A simple bending spring is all that is required to make bends in small copper pipework; you can hire or buy special tools for more substantial stock.

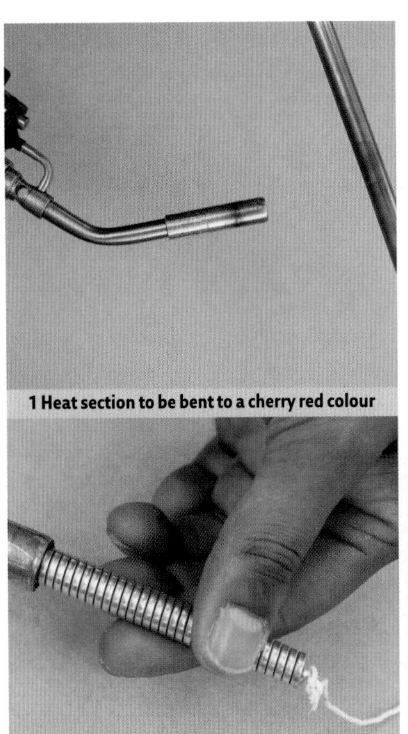
1 Heat section to be bent to a cherry red colour

2 Lubricate spring and tie string to end

If you want to carry a pipe over a small obstruction (another pipe, for example), a slight kink in the pipe will be less of an obstruction to the flow of water and create less noise than two elbows within a few centimetres of each other. If you need to to run pipes into a window alcove where the walls meet at an unusual angle, bending the pipes accurately will allow you to fit the pipes neatly against the alcove walls.

Using a bending spring

A bending spring is the cheapest and easiest tool for making bends in small pipe runs. It is a hardened-steel coil spring that supports the walls of copper tube to stop it kinking. Most bending springs are made to fit inside the pipe, but some slide over it.

Soften the section to be bent by heating first (**1**) and cooling, then slide the spring (see below) into the tube (**2**), so it supports the area to be bent. Hold the tube against your padded knee and bend to required angle (**3**). The tube will grip the spring, but slipping a screwdriver into the ring at one end and turning it anticlockwise will compress the spring so it can be pulled out.

If you make a bend some distance from the end of a tube, you won't be able to withdraw the bending spring with a screwdriver. Either use an external spring or tie string to the ring and lightly grease the spring with petroleum jelly before you insert it. Slightly overbend the tube, open it out to the correct angle to release the spring, then pull it out with the string.

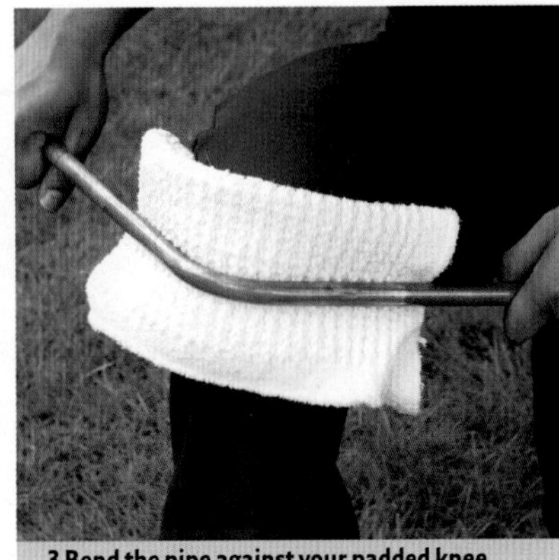
3 Bend the pipe against your padded knee

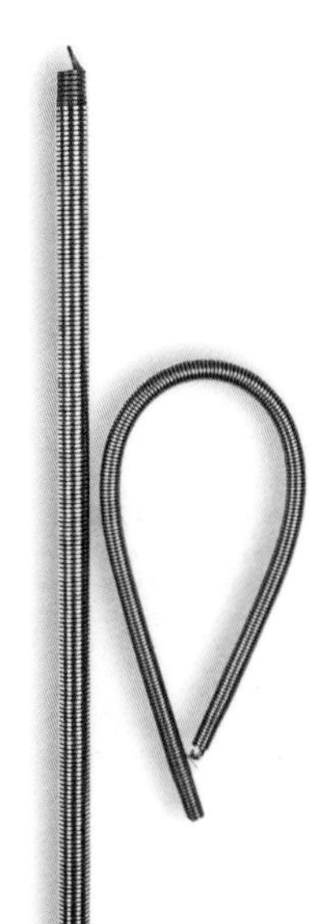
Plumbers' bending springs

Using a pipe bender

Although you can hire bending springs to fit the larger pipes, it isn't easy to bend 22 or 28mm (3/4 or 1in) tube over your knee – so it is well worth hiring a pipe bender to do the job. Ensure that you fit the correct former to suit the pipe diameter.

Hold the pipe against the radiused former and insert the straight former to support it. Pull the levers towards each other to make the bend, and then open up the bender to remove the pipe.

1 A pipe bender makes accurate bends

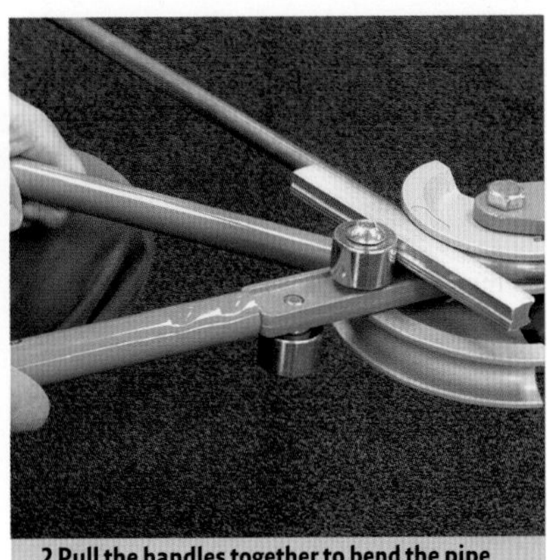
2 Pull the handles together to bend the pipe

Getting the bends in the right place

It is difficult to position two or more bends accurately along a single length of pipe. In an alcove, it's easier to bend lengths of pipe to fit each corner, then cut the tubes where they overlap and insert joints.

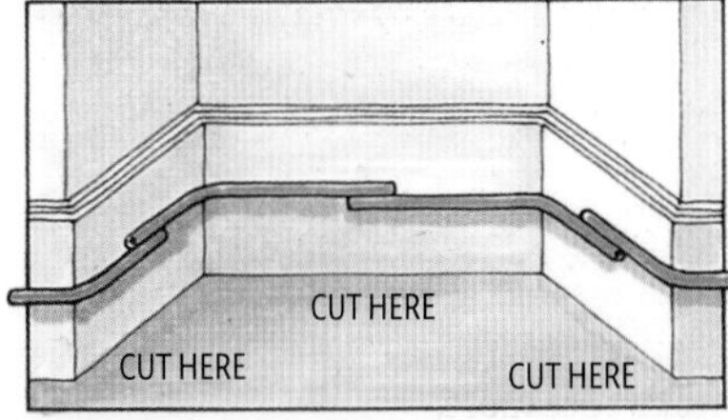

Formers are marked to aid bends to common angles

SEE ALSO > Connecting plastic to metal plumbing 365

Plastic plumbing

Plastic plumbing is lightweight and extremely simple to assemble. It doesn't burst when frozen, corrode, or adversely affect other materials; and, depending on the type of plastic, it can be used both for cold water and hot, including central-heating pipework. Most plastic systems can be connected to existing metal pipes.

Plastic joints and fittings are similar to the ones used for metal plumbing, but are typically larger in size. Joints and pipes are for the most part manufactured from the same material, but there are several specialized connectors available for joining plastic plumbing to taps, tanks and existing metal plumbing. To see the huge variety of plastic joints, you need to browse through manufacturers' catalogues, but the selection below shows some of the most common types.

Straight connectors
For joining two pipes end to end.
1 For pipes of equal diameter – push-fit.

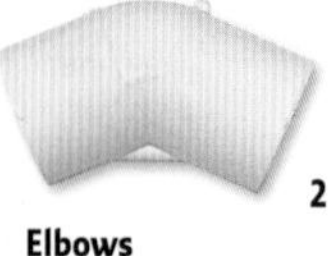

Elbows
For joining two pipes at an angle.
2 Elbow 45° – solvent weld.
3 Elbow 90° – push-fit.

Tees
For joining three pipes.
5 Equal tee for joining 15mm (½in) branch pipes – push-fit.

Adaptors
To join dissimilar pipes.
4 Plastic-to-copper connector – push-fit and compression joint.

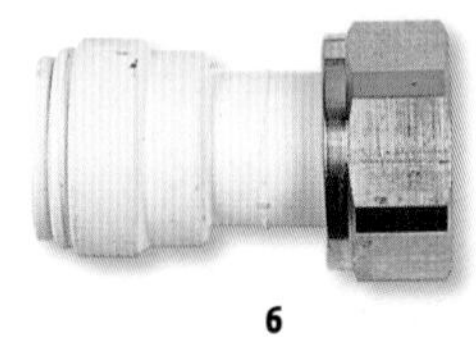

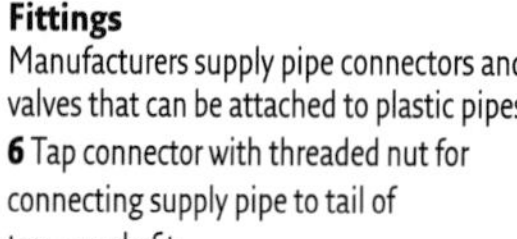

Fittings
Manufacturers supply pipe connectors and valves that can be attached to plastic pipes.
6 Tap connector with threaded nut for connecting supply pipe to tail of tap – push-fit.
7 Tank connector joins pipes to storage tanks and cisterns – push-fit.
8 Stopcock – push-fit.

• **Oxygen-diffusion barriers**
There's some concern that a small amount of oxygen drawn through the walls of plastic central-heating pipes contributes to the corrosion of the system. To prevent this happening, an oxygen-diffusion barrier is built into the walls of the pipe.

Bending plastic pipes

Flexible pipes can be bent cold to a minimum radius of eight times the pipe diameter. Use a pipe clip at each side of the bend to hold the curve, or use a plastic or metal cold forming bend. It is easy to thread flexible pipe around obstacles or under floorboards.

Rigid plastic pipe can be bent by heating it gently with a gas torch. Keep the flame moving and revolve the pipe. When the pipe is soft enough, bend it by hand on a flat surface. Hold it still till the plastic hardens again. Wear thick gloves when handling hot plastic.

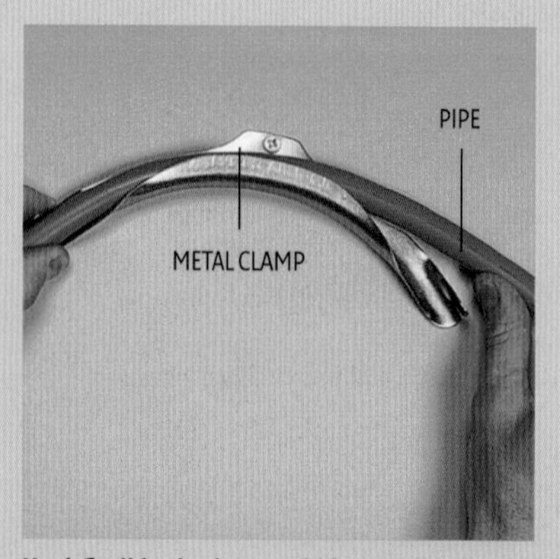

Hook flexible pipe into a cold forming bend

Plastic supply pipes

Plastic supply pipes are made to the same standard sizes as metal pipework, but there may be a slight variation in wall thickness from one manufacturer's stock to another.

Chlorinated polyvinyl chloride (cPVC)

A versatile plastic suitable for hot and cold supply. It can even withstand the temperatures that are required for central-heating systems.

Polybutylene (PB)

A tough, flexible plastic pipe used for hot and cold supply, and central heating. Available in standard lengths or continuous coils, PB resists bursting when frozen. It will sag if unsupported.

Cross-linked polyethylene (PEX)

Although it expands considerably when it is heated, PEX is used to make pipes that supply hot and cold water and for under-floor heating systems. However, it tends to sag, so is unsuitable for surface running. A PEX pipe resists bursting when subjected to frost. Twin-wall PEX, with an oxygen-diffusion barrier (see far left) in the form of an aluminium layer sandwiched between the walls, is semi-rigid.

Medium-density polyethylene (MDPE)

Widely used for underground domestic supply pipes, the pipes, normally coloured blue, can be laid in continuous lengths and are resistant to pressure and corrosion.

SEE ALSO > Solvent-weld joints 367

Joining plastic supply pipes

Some plastic supply pipes can be connected using solvent-weld joints (as described for waste systems), but it is easier and more convenient to use the push-fit connectors shown below.

Push-fit joints

When the pipe is inserted, an O-ring seals in the water in the normal way and (depending on the model) a special plastic grab ring, or a collet with stainless-steel teeth, grips the tube securely to prevent water under mains pressure forcing the joint apart. Joints fitted with collets can be disconnected easily, but to dismantle the other type of push-fit joint, it's necessary to remove the retaining cap and prise open the grab ring, using a special tool.

Push-fit joints are more obtrusive than their solvent-welded equivalents - but are much faster to assemble.

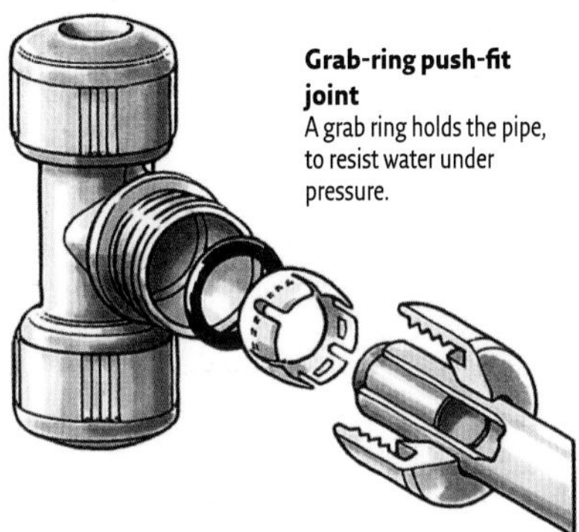

Grab-ring push-fit joint
A grab ring holds the pipe, to resist water under pressure.

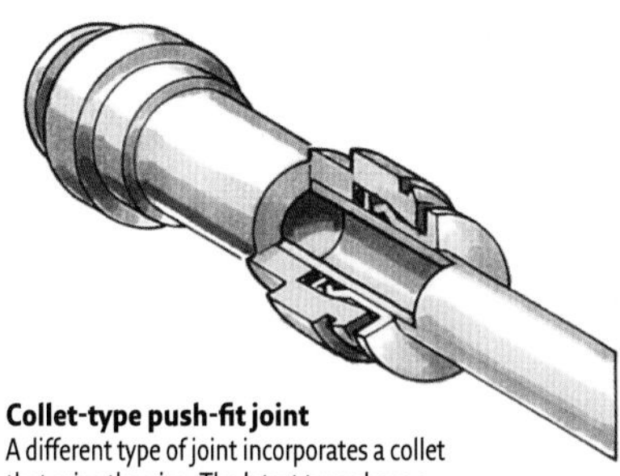

Collet-type push-fit joint
A different type of joint incorporates a collet that grips the pipe. The latest types have a screw cap that locks the pipe in position and applies more compression to the rubber seal.

Using grab-ring joints

Cut polybutylene pipe to length with the special shears that are supplied by the manufacturer (**1**); alternatively, use a sharp craft knife. Provided that you make the cut reasonably square, the joint will be watertight.

Push a metal support sleeve into the pipe (**2**), and, if necessary, smear a little silicone lubricant around the end of the pipe and inside the socket (**3**).

Push the prepared pipe firmly a full 25mm (1in) into the socket (**4**). As the joint can revolve freely around the pipe after connection without breaking the seal, there is no problem when aligning tees and elbows with other pipe runs.

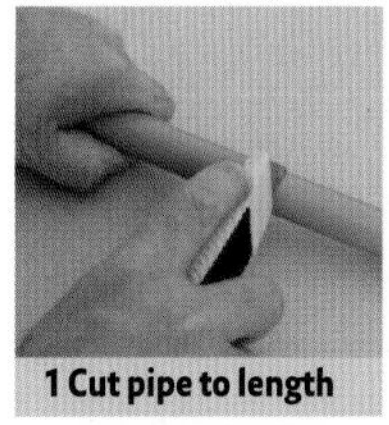

1 Cut pipe to length

2 Insert metal sleeve

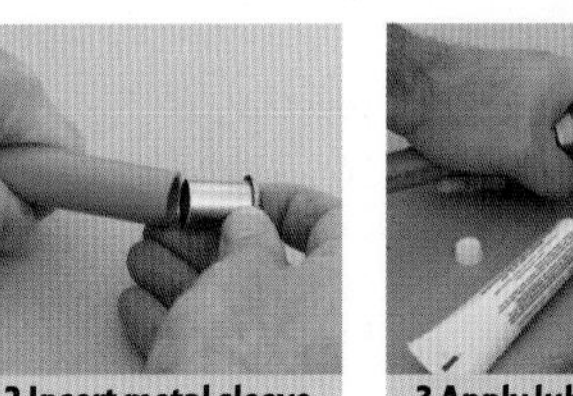

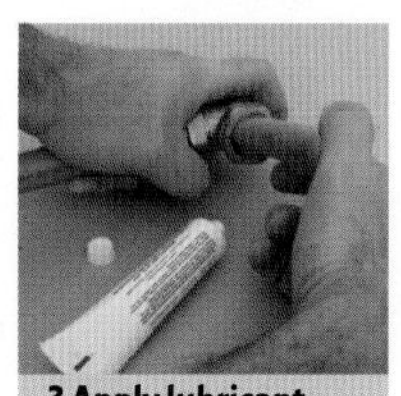

3 Apply lubricant

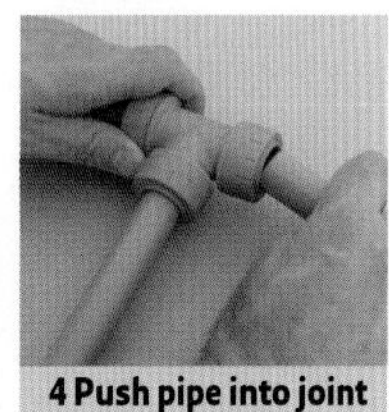

4 Push pipe into joint

Dismantling a joint

To dismantle a joint, unscrew the cap and pull out the pipe. Slide off the rubber O-ring, then prise off the grab ring, using a special demounting tool (see below left). Grab rings are not reusable and you must use new ones when re-assembling the joint using the technique described above. Never try to assemble the fitting like a compression joint, or it will blow out under pressure.

If the type of fitting is no longer available, use another brand that closely matches the original. Given that there are small differences between brands of pipe, there is a risk that the new fitting won't seal properly, so you may have to replace the length of pipe and several fittings.

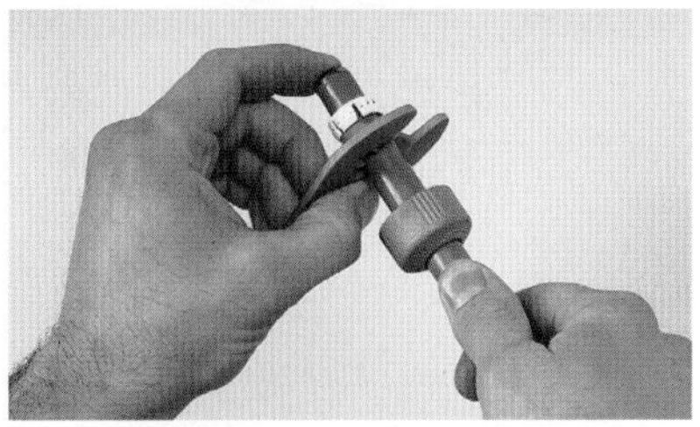

Prise open the grab ring, using a special tool

Connecting metal to plastic plumbing

Special adaptor couplings are needed in order to connect most types of plastic pipe to copper or galvanized-steel plumbing. To join polybutylene pipe to copper, insert a metal support sleeve, then use a standard brass compression joint; or use a push-fit connector to join copper pipes to a polybutylene run. Cut and deburr the copper pipe carefully before pushing it into the joint.

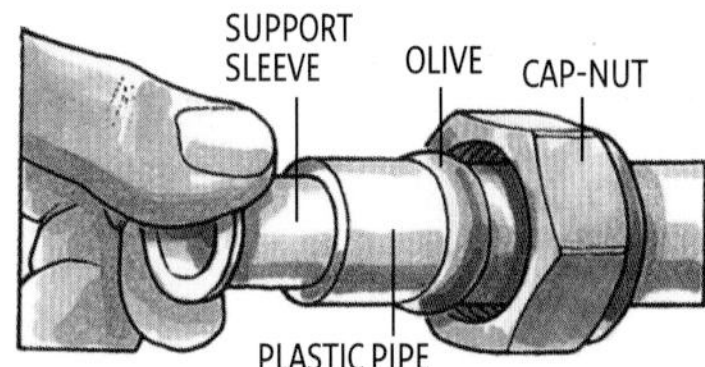

Joining plastic pipe with a compression fitting
Insert support sleeve before tightening the joint.

• Repairing a weeping joint
A push-fit joint on a supply pipe may leak if the pipe is not pushed home fully, or if the O-ring is damaged. A plastic pipe that has not been cut square or has scratches in the joint area may leak, too. Take the joint apart and check all the components, replacing any that are damaged, then reassemble carefully, pushing the pipe fully home.

Collet-type joints

Push-fit joints that incorporate collets are particularly easy to assemble. Cut the end of the pipe square, push it into the socket until it comes up against the internal stop, then pull back to check that it is secure.

If you need to dismantle a joint, hold the collet in with your fingertips (**1**) and pull the pipe out of the socket.

Join metal pipes the same way, but remove burrs and sharp edges to prevent tearing the O-ring. Provide extra grip by twisting the outer collar to lock it (**2**).

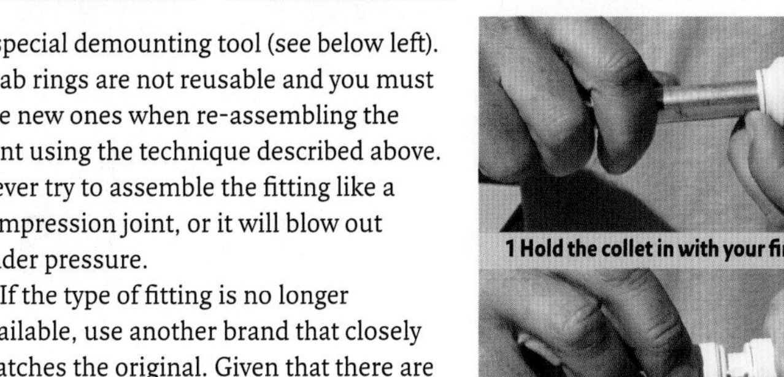

1 Hold the collet in with your fingertips

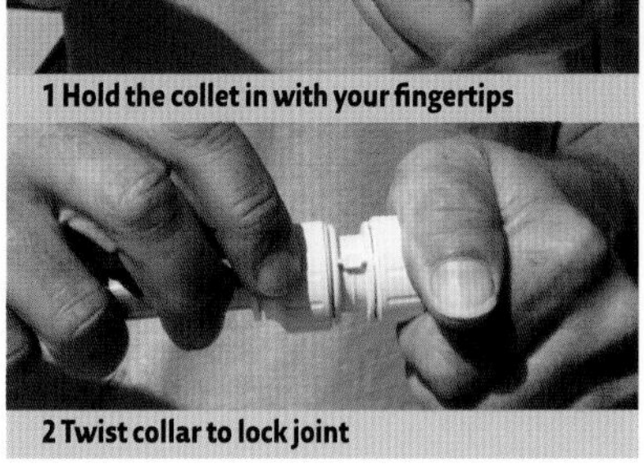

2 Twist collar to lock joint

Cutting plastic pipe
Polybutylene pipe is easy to cut, using special shears.

SEE ALSO >Supporting pipes 368, Adaptor couplings 364, Solvent-weld joints 367, Hacksaws 518, Files 524

Plastic waste pipes

Plastics are complex materials, each having its own properties. Consequently, a technique or material that is suitable for joining one plastic may not be suitable for another. To make watertight joints, it's vital to follow the manufacturer's instructions carefully, and to use the recommended solvents and lubricants.

Types of plastic

Plumbing manufacturers have a wide variety of plastics to draw upon, each with its own special characteristics.

Modified unplasticized polyvinyl chloride (MuPVC)

A hard plastic, used for solvent-weld waste pipe and fittings. It is resistant to most domestic chemicals, and is not affected by ultra-violet light when used outdoors. It is slightly more flexible than uPVC, which is used for soil pipes with push-fit and solvent-weld joints.

Polypropylene (PP)

A slightly flexible plastic with a slightly waxy feel, used for waste systems. It's impossible to glue PP, so it is assembled with push-fit joints.

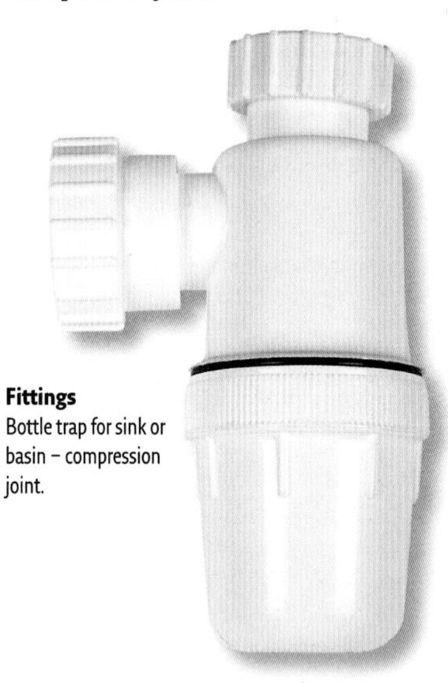

Fittings
Bottle trap for sink or basin – compression joint.

PLASTIC WASTE-PIPE SIZES

Overflow pipes	22mm (¾in)
Washbasin waste pipes	32mm (1¼in)
Bath/shower and sink waste pipes	40mm (1½in)
Soil pipe	100mm (4in)

Acrylonitrile butadiene styrene (ABS)

A very tough plastic that is equally suited to hot and cold waste. It can be either solvent-welded or compression-jointed.

Joints and fittings

As well as the usual types of joint, waste systems also include easy-flow swept bends and tees for efficient drainage. The swept part of the fitting should face downhill to aid water flow.

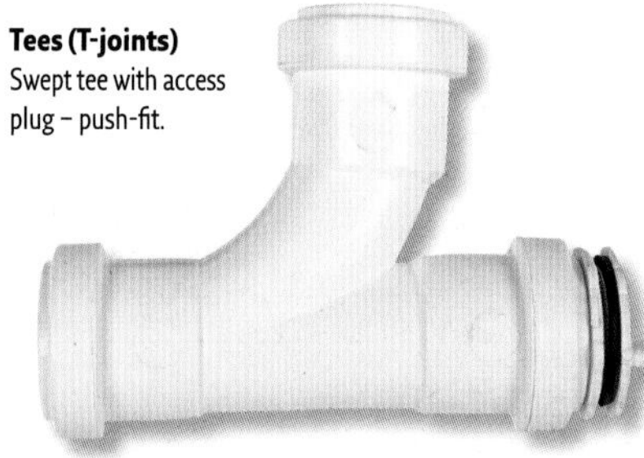

Tees (T-joints)
Swept tee with access plug – push-fit.

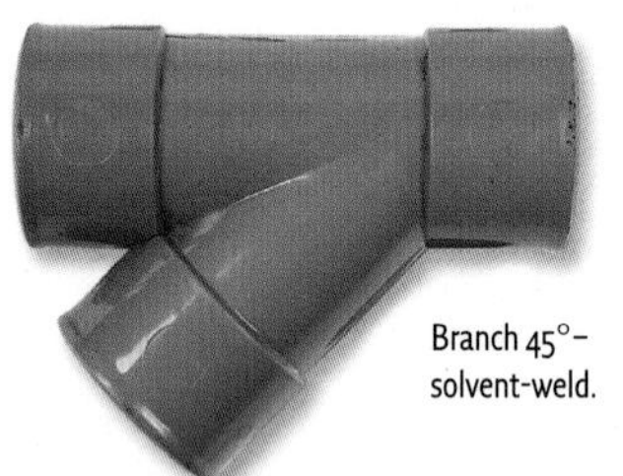

Branch 45° – solvent-weld.

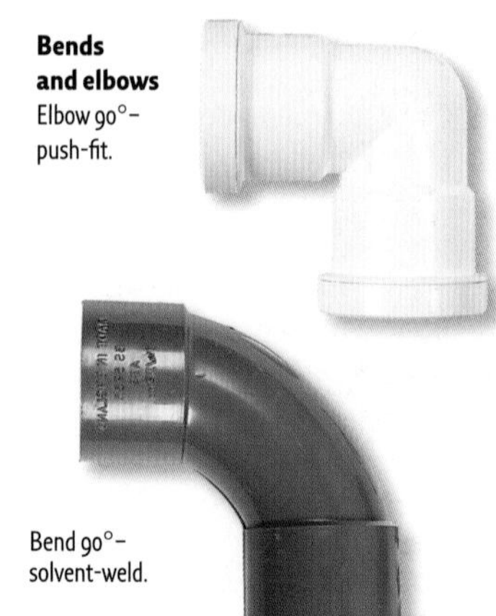

Bends and elbows
Elbow 90° – push-fit.

Bend 90° – solvent-weld.

Waste-pipe joints

Solvent-weld joints

Lengths of pipe are linked by simple socketed connectors coated with solvent which dissolves the surfaces of the mating components. As the solvent evaporates, the joints and pipes are literally fused together into one piece of plastic.

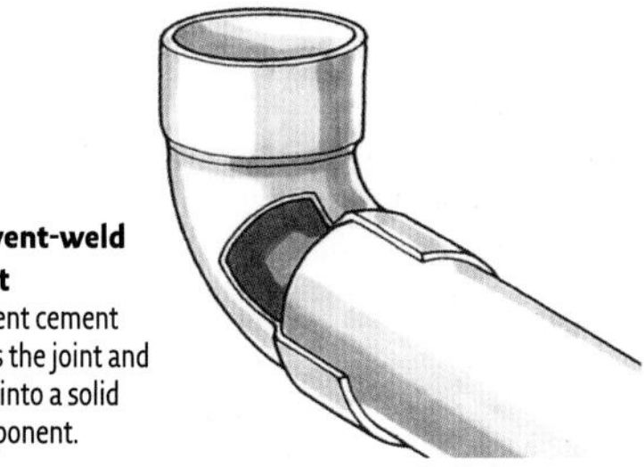

Solvent-weld joint
Solvent cement fuses the joint and pipe into a solid component.

Compression joints

So that they can be dismantled easily, sink, bath and washbasin traps are often connected to the pipework by means of compression joints that use a rubber ring or washer to make the joint watertight.

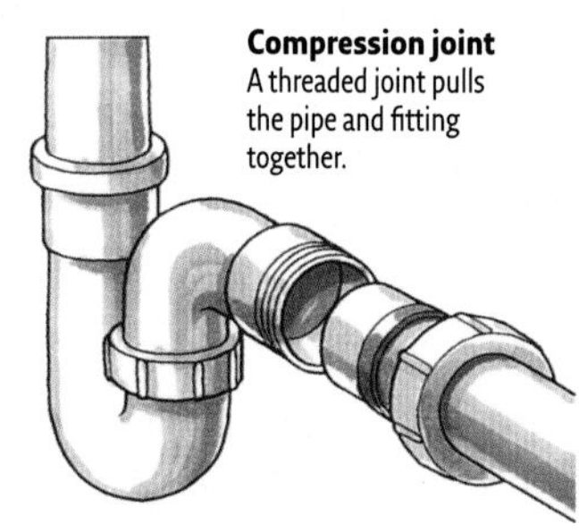

Compression joint
A threaded joint pulls the pipe and fitting together.

Push-fit joints

Because a waste system is never under pressure, a pipe run can be constructed by simply pushing plain pipes into the sockets of the joints. A captive rubber seal in each socket holds the pipe in place.

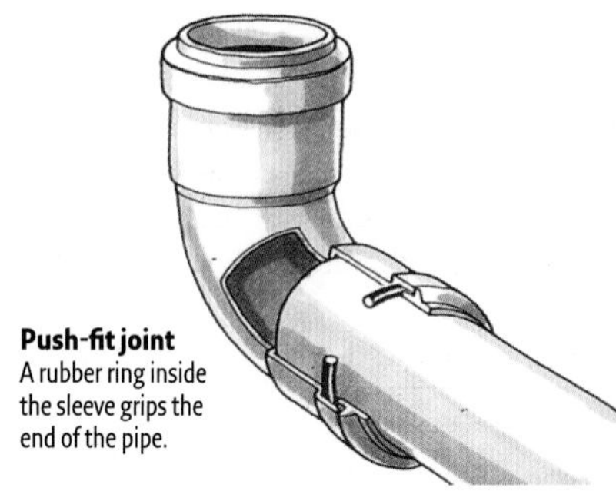

Push-fit joint
A rubber ring inside the sleeve grips the end of the pipe.

SEE ALSO > Plastic supply pipes 564

Joining plastic pipes

It's important to follow the instructions supplied with any particular brand of pipe or fitting, but the methods given below and on the facing page describe the basic techniques for connecting plastic pipes.

Work carefully and avoid spilling solvent cement – it will etch the surface of the pipework and damage some other plastics, as well.

Making solvent-weld joints

While the sequence of illustrations on the right shows large-diameter waste pipe, the methods described are equally valid for joining plastic supply pipe.

Cut the pipe to length with a fine-tooth saw, allowing for the depth of the joint socket. To make sure your cut is square, wind a piece of notepaper round the tube, aligning the wrapped edge as a guide (1). Revolve the pipe away from you as you cut it. Smooth the end with a file (2).

Welding the joint

Push the pipe into the socket to test the fit, then mark the end of the joint on the pipe with a pencil (3). This will act as a guide for applying the solvent. You need to key both the outside of the pipe and the inside of the socket with fine abrasive paper before using some solvents (check the manufacturer's instructions).

Before dismantling elbows and tees, mark the pipe and joint with a pencil (4), to help you align them correctly when you reassemble the components.

Use a clean rag to wipe the surface of the pipe and fitting with the recommended spirit cleaner. Brush solvent evenly onto both components (5), then immediately push home the socket. (Some manufacturers recommend that you twist the joint to spread the solvent.) Align the joint properly and leave it for 15 seconds.

The pipe is ready for use with cold water after an hour. But don't pass hot water through the system until at least four hours have elapsed (depending on the manufacturer's recommendations) or, preferably, longer.

Repairing a weeping joint

If a joint leaks, leave it to dry out naturally. Then apply a little more of the solvent cement to the mouth of the socket, allowing it to flow into the joint by capillary action.

You will have to drain a supply pipe before you can make this repair.

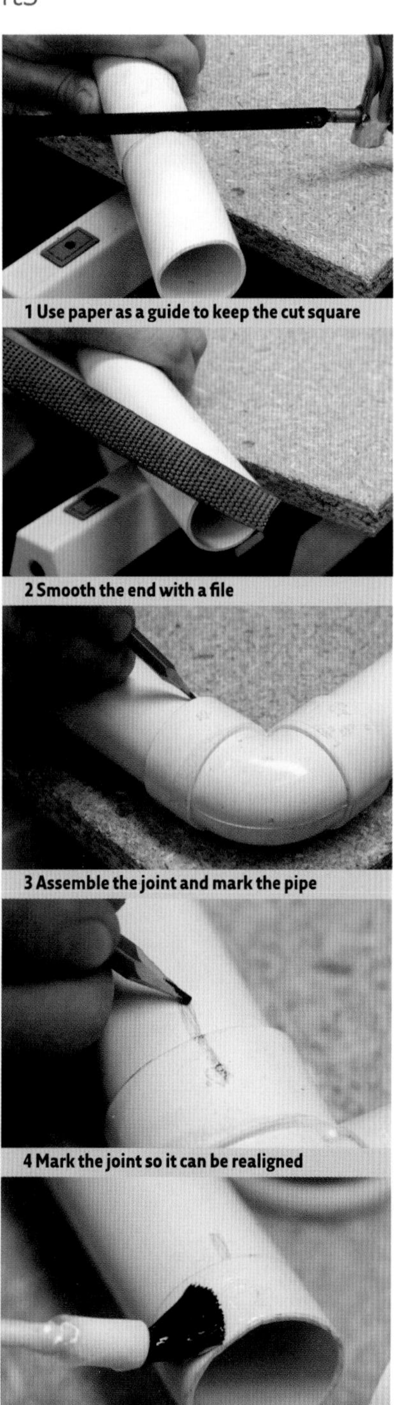

1 Use paper as a guide to keep the cut square

2 Smooth the end with a file

3 Assemble the joint and mark the pipe

4 Mark the joint so it can be realigned

5 Paint solvent up to the pencil mark

Making push-fit joints

Cut the pipe to length and chamfer the end, as for solvent-weld joints. Wipe the inside of the socket with the recommended cleaner, and lubricate the pipe with some silicone lubricant.

Push the pipe into the joint right up to the stop, and mark the edge of the socket on the pipe with a pencil (1).

Withdraw the pipe about 9mm (3/8in) (2), to allow the pipe to expand when subjected to hot water.

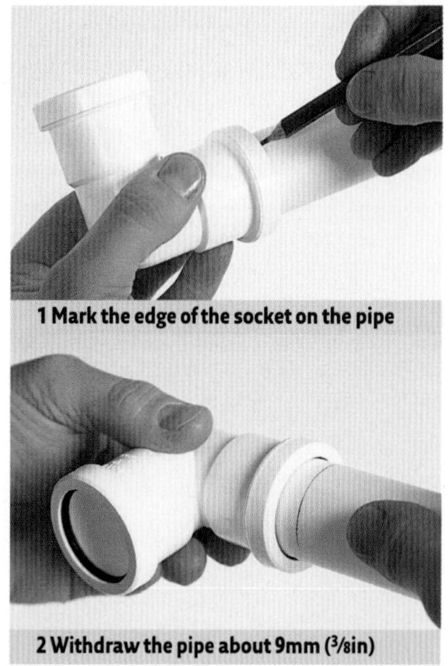

1 Mark the edge of the socket on the pipe

2 Withdraw the pipe about 9mm (3/8in)

Repairing a weeping push-fit joint

A push-fit joint will leak if the rubber seal has been pushed out of position. Dismantle the joint and check the condition of the seal.

Making compression joints to traps

Traps with compression joints are made for connecting directly to a plain waste pipe (see opposite). Just slip the threaded nut onto the waste pipe, followed by the washer and then the rubber ring. Push the pipe into the socket of the trap and tighten the compression nut.

SEE ALSO > Hacksaws 518, Files 524

Running and concealing pipework

The most difficult part of many plumbing jobs is not the actual plumbing itself but the work required to run and conceal the associated pipework. This may involve lifting floorboards and drilling through walls and joists, so spend time working out which is the least disruptive route. You may also have to consider how to hide pipework from view where it has to be run across a wall.

• Supporting pipe runs
The spacing of pipe clips will vary depending on the direction the pipe is running, the material it's made from and its diameter. Horizontal runs will need more clips than vertical ones.

On a horizontal run, plastic pipes up to 15mm (½in) diameter need to be supported every 300mm (1ft); 22mm (¾in) pipes every 500mm (1ft 8in). Vertical runs require spacings of 500mm (1ft 8in) and 800mm (2ft 8in) respectively.

Horizontal runs of 15mm (½in) copper pipe should be supported every 1.5m (5ft); for 22mm (¾in) the spacing is 2m (6½ft). Vertical runs require spacings of 2m (6½ft) and 2.5m (8ft 3in) respectively.

Supporting pipework

It's important that all pipework used in waste, supply or central heating applications is supported or secured at regular intervals.

Unsecured pipework will place undue strain on joints, increasing the risk of joint failure. It may also be noisy, due to excess movement caused by expansion and contraction, and, if visible, will sag and look unsightly.

There's a wide variety of clips for securing surface run pipework. Copper pipes are usually secured with push-in plastic clips, which are screwed in place. The most common clip has an open top (see below) but some have a hinged latch which clips over the pipe for added security. Nail-in clips that resemble cable clips are available for small-bore pipes, while copper clips - known as saddles - with two screw fixings are often used on exterior runs, where their lower profile and extra strength are desirable.

Saddle-style clips are generally used for plastic waste pipe, though standard pipe clips can be used for 15mm or 22mm (½in or ¾in) plastic supply pipes.

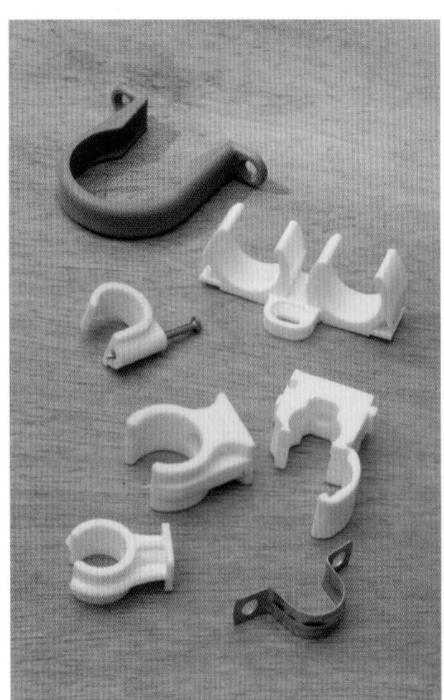
A selection of pipe clips

Pipes in floors

Pipes running across the direction of the joists can be set into notches cut into the top of the timbers.

The notches should only be made in the top of the joist and should be no deeper than 0.125 times the depth of the joist to avoid weakening it. Notches should also be no closer to the joist supports than 0.07 times the span of the joist, or further than a quarter of the length of the joist away. This is to avoid the areas of maximum stress or bending in the timber.

The notches should be just wider and deeper than the diameter of the pipe to avoid contact between pipe, joist and floorboards. Lining the notch and covering the top of the pipe with foam mat will prevent noise as the pipe expands or the board above is trodden on.

If you can arrange for the pipe to be under the centre line of the board covering it, you can nail the board back either side of the notch.

Drilling joists

If you have to drill holes through the joist for pipes - a convenient way to run flexible plastic pipes - then the holes should be drilled on the centre line of the joist and have a diameter no bigger than a quarter of the joist's depth. Multiple holes should be spaced at least three times the largest diameter permitted apart.

Drilling large holes between joists can be tricky as there isn't enough room for the power drill and bit. You can hire or buy a special right-angled drill specially designed for this job, which will make drilling straight, level holes simple.

Pipes running parallel to joists can be clipped to the joists or supported with a 'bridge' made from battens and plywood to bridge the gap between two joists.

Once you've run a pipe under floorboards, mark its route with a felt pen or paint on the surface of the boards so you know where it is in future.

Chisel out the notch

Pipes should lie beneath the board level

Drill holes between joists with an angled drill

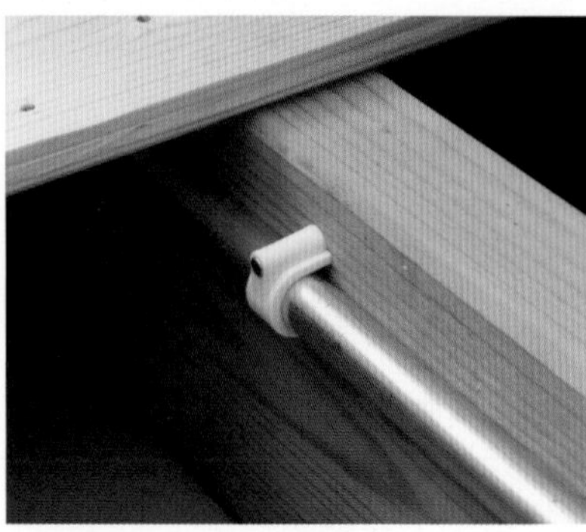
Pipes running parallel to joists can be clipped

SEE ALSO > Lifting floorboards 179

Concealing pipework

With carefully designed pipe runs, it should be possible to plumb your house without a single pipe being visible. In practice, however, there are always situations where you have no option but to surface-run some pipes.

You can minimize the effect by taking care to group pipes together neatly and keeping runs both straight and parallel. When painted to match the skirtings or walls, such pipes are barely visible.

Alternatively, using softwood battens and plywood, you can make your own accessible ducting to bridge the corner of a room; or construct a false skirting that is deep enough to contain the pipes.

For total accessibility, you can use proprietary ducting made from PVC. This is manufactured in a range of sizes, to contain grouped or individual pipes (see below).

Make sure that gate valves or service valves remain accessible - you may have to construct removable panels in order to ensure access. These could be hinged or attach with magnetic cupboard clips.

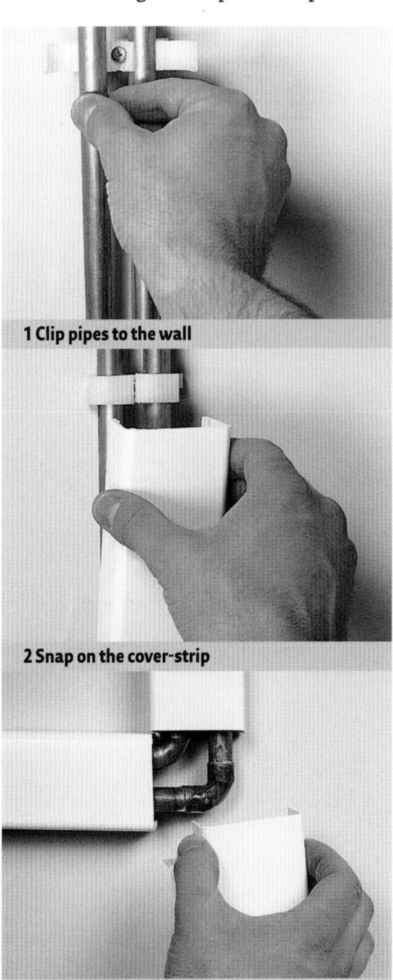

1 Clip pipes to the wall

2 Snap on the cover-strip

3 Snap on corner covers

Drilling through walls

Use a core bit for large diameter holes

Drill several small holes, then chop out waste

Where pipes have to pass through walls - perhaps for a waste from a washing machine or a supply pipe for a garden tap - you'll need a suitable hole.

For smaller pipes up to 15mm (½in) or so, you can use a large-diameter masonry bit in an ordinary power drill - the bit will have a reduced diameter shank to fit the drill's chuck.

However, larger diameter holes are best made with a core bit. These are available in a range of diameters and can even be used to cut holes for 100mm (4in) diameter waste pipe. Diamond or carbide tipped, core bits are expensive and best hired; for bigger holes you'll need to hire a suitably powerful drill as your own probably won't be up to the job. Holes should slope slightly downward from the inside to the outside to prevent any risk of rainwater running along the pipe.

Copper pipes should be sleeved with a piece of plastic pipe for protection where they pass through the wall. Any space around the pipe can be filled with mortar, silicone sealant or expanding foam filler.

If you don't want to hire a core drill, you can form a larger hole by drilling a series of small holes with a standard masonry bit, then using a hammer and cold chisel to chop out the masonry between the holes. Cut from the outside in to avoid any risk of breaking the surface brickwork around the hole.

Allow space for insulation

Exterior supply pipes must be insulated and standard pipe clips don't leave enough room between the wall and the pipe for foam insulation. You can buy spacers to suit most pipe clips which distance the clip from the wall and leave space for the insulation to fit comfortably.

Waste pipe to soil pipe

A proprietary pipe boss is used to connect a basin waste pipe to a single-stack plastic soil pipe. There are various ways of connecting the boss, one of the simplest being to clamp it with a strap.

Mark where the basin waste meets the soil pipe, and use a hole saw to cut a hole of the recommended diameter (1). Smooth the edge of the hole with abrasive paper.

Wipe both contacting surfaces with the manufacturer's cleaner, then apply gap-filling solvent cement around the hole. Strap the boss over the hole and tighten the bolt (2).

Insert the rubber lining in the boss, in preparation for the waste pipe (3).

Lubricate the end of the pipe and push it firmly into the boss (4). Clip the pipe to the wall.

1 Cut a hole in the pipe with a hole saw

3 Insert the rubber lining

2 Strap the boss over the hole

4 Push the waste pipe into the boss

SEE ALSO > Cold chisel 513, Core drill 523

Selecting taps

Taps can be fashionable as well as functional and come in a huge variety of different styles and finishes. Not all taps are built to last, so check the quality if you are buying for the long term. Chromium-plated brass taps are the most durable. Check that the taps you are considering will fit the holes in your chosen appliance.

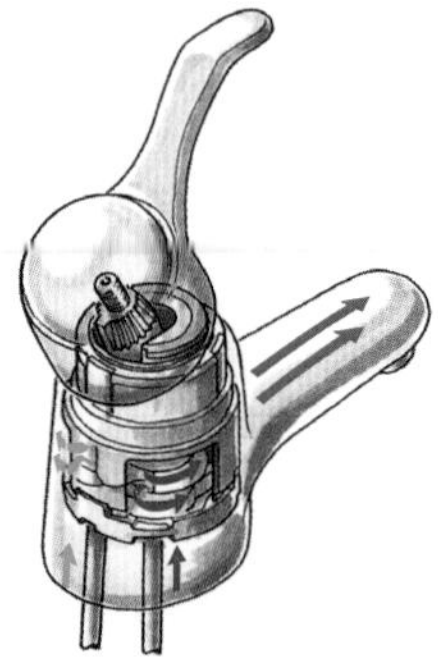

Single-lever mixer tap
Moving the lever up and down turns the water on and off. Swinging it from one side to the other alters the temperature, by mixing the hot water with the cold. These taps have smaller, 10mm (3/8in)feed pipes, which will need adaptors to connect to 15mm (1/2in) supply pipes.

• The right pressure
Some taps imported from the Continent have relatively small inlets and are intended for use with mains-pressure supply only. These taps will not work efficiently if they are connected to a low-pressure tank-fed supply.

Types of tap

The majority of washbasins are fitted with individual taps for hot and cold water. While capstan-head taps are still manufactured for use in period-style bathrooms, most modern taps have a shrouded head made of metal or plastic.

A lever-head tap turns the water from off to full on with one quarter turn only, useful for those who may have difficulty in manipulating other taps.

In a mixer tap, hot and cold water are directed to a common spout. Water is supplied at the desired temperature by adjustment of the two valves. With a single-lever mixer tap, flow rate and temperature are controlled by adjusting one lever, which moves up to control the flow and sideways to alter temperature.

Washbasin mixer taps sometimes incorporate a pop-up waste plug. A series of interlinked rods, operated by a button or small knob on the centre of the mixer, open and close the waste plug in the basin.

Normally, the body of the tap (which connects the valves and spout) rests on the upper surface of the washbasin. But it is also possible to mount it in its entirety on the wall above the basin. Another alternative is for the valves to be mounted on the basin and divert hot and cold water to a spout mounted on the wall above.

Tap mechanisms

Over recent years there have been some revolutionary changes in the design of taps, which have made them easier to operate and simpler to maintain.

Rising-spindle taps

This traditional tap design has a washer on the end of a spindle that rises as the tap is turned on. It is a simple, rugged mechanism that lasts for years.

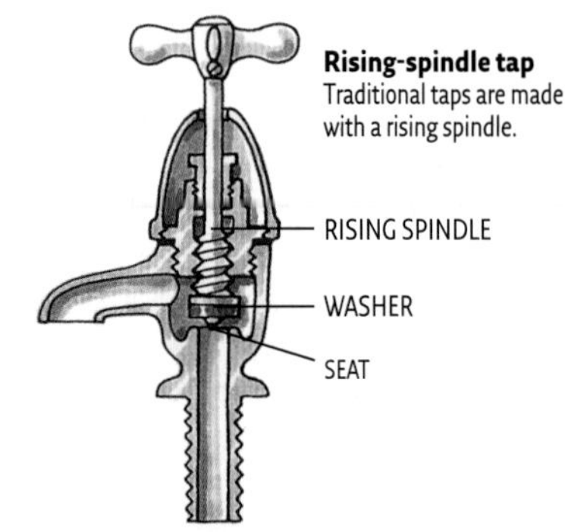

Rising-spindle tap
Traditional taps are made with a rising spindle.

Non-rising-spindle taps

Theoretically, these taps should exhibit fewer problems than rising-spindle taps, because the mechanism imposes less wear on the washer. In practice, however, the spindle's fine thread is prone to wear, and misalignment may be caused by the circlip that holds the mechanism in place.

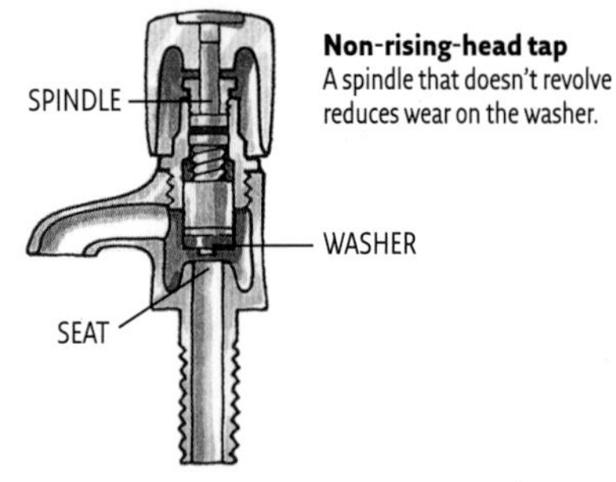

Non-rising-head tap
A spindle that doesn't revolve reduces wear on the washer.

Ceramic-disc taps

With these taps, precision-ground ceramic discs are used in place of the traditional rubber washer. One disc is fixed and the other rotates until the waterways through them align and water flows. There is minimal wear, as hard-water scale or other debris is unlikely to interfere with the close fit of the discs. However, if a problem does develop, the entire inner cartridge and the lower seal can be replaced.

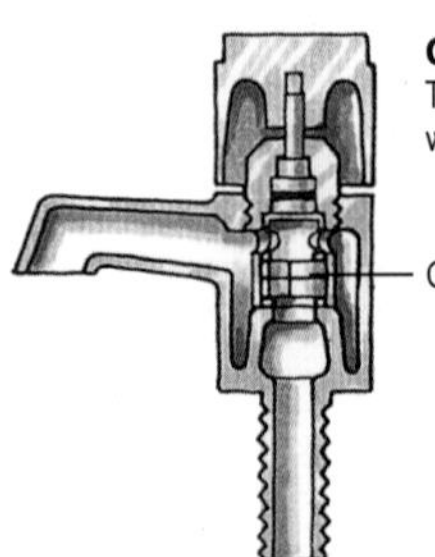

Ceramic-disc tap
The rubber washer is replaced with rotating ceramic discs.

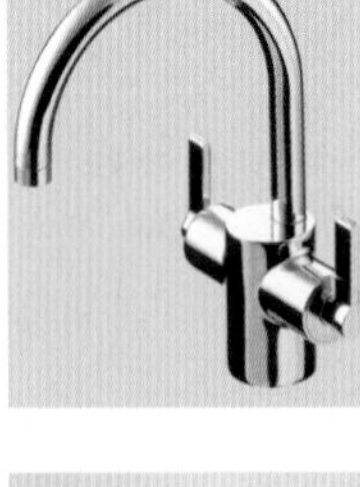

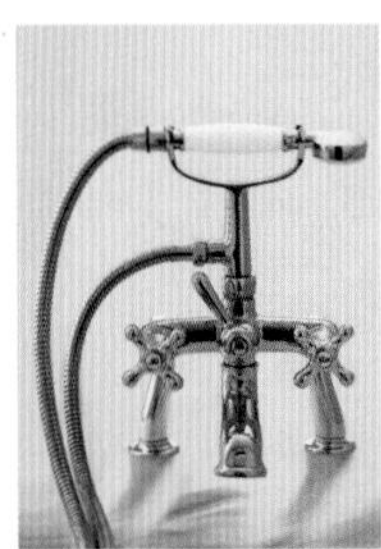

Basin and bath taps
(top row – left to right)
One-hole basin mixer
Single shrouded head pillar taps
Single-lever mixer with pop-up waste

(bottom row – left to right)
Shower-mixer deck
Monobloc bath mixer
Remote spout bath mixer

SEE ALSO > Repairing taps 350–51

Removing old taps

When replacing taps, you will want to use the existing plumbing if possible, but disconnecting old, corroded fittings can be difficult.

Apply some penetrating oil to the tap connectors and to the back-nuts that clamp the tap to the basin. While the oil takes effect, shut off the cold and hot water supply to the taps.

If necessary, apply heat with a gas torch to break down the corrosion - but wrap a wet cloth around nearby soldered joints, or you may melt the solder. Take care that you do not damage plastic fittings and pipes, and protect flammable surfaces with a ceramic tile. Try not to play the flame onto a ceramic basin.

Cranked spanners

It is not always possible to engage the nuts with a standard wrench. Instead, use a special cranked spanner designed to reach into the confined spaces below a basin or bath. You can apply extra leverage to the spanner by slipping a stout metal bar or wrench handle into the other end.

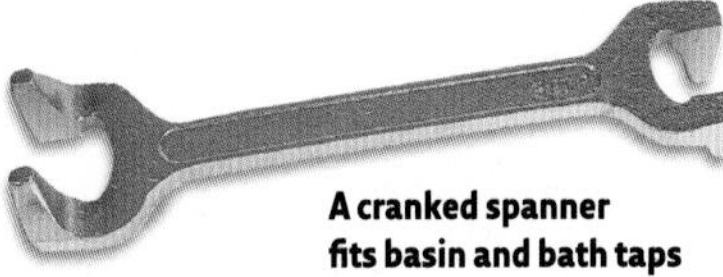

A cranked spanner fits basin and bath taps

Removing a stuck tap

Even when you have disconnected the pipework and back-nut, you may find that the taps are stuck in place with putty. Break the seal by striking the tap tails lightly with a wooden mallet. Clean the remnants of putty from around the holes in the basin, then fit new taps. If the tap tails are shorter than the originals, buy special adaptors designed to take up the gaps.

Releasing a tap connector
Use a special cranked spanner to release the fixing nut of a tap connector.

Fitting new taps

If you're installing a new bath or basin, it's much easier to fit the taps before the sanitaryware is in position since access to hard-to-reach nuts will be much better.

Most taps are made to standard sizes, so you shouldn't have any difficulty with new baths or basins, but if you're replacing the taps on an older fitting, check that they will cover the holes adequately or, if you're using a two-hole tap, fit in the holes. Check that the spout is long enough to deliver water properly - there must be enough overhang to wash your hands underneath a basin tap, for instance.

Basin taps

Taps are supplied with flexible anti-rotation washers to stop the tap moving as it is turned on or off. Slip the washer onto the tap tail (1) and insert the tap through the hole (put the hot tap on the left). Add the back-nut (2) then hold the tap steady as you tighten it with a cranked spanner.

While you have the water turned off, fit service valves so that the taps can be serviced in future without having to turn off the water. These can be fitted in the supply pipe or you can get versions that double as tap connectors (3).

Single-hole mixers often come with small-bore flexible hose (4) tails, which make connecting the supply pipes much easier.

Some mixers feature a control that operates a pop-up waste. Adjust the rods carefully to ensure (5) that the plug seats and lifts correctly.

Bath taps

Two-hole mixers are fitted in much the same way as basin taps. If you're fitting *in situ*, remove the overflow fitting to give you more access. Mixers are supplied with flexible washers to seal the holes - if the washer colour doesn't suit your decor, use silicone sealant instead (6).

1 Slip the anti-rotation washer over the tap tail

3 Service valves make future maintenance easy

5 Adjust the linkage for smooth operation

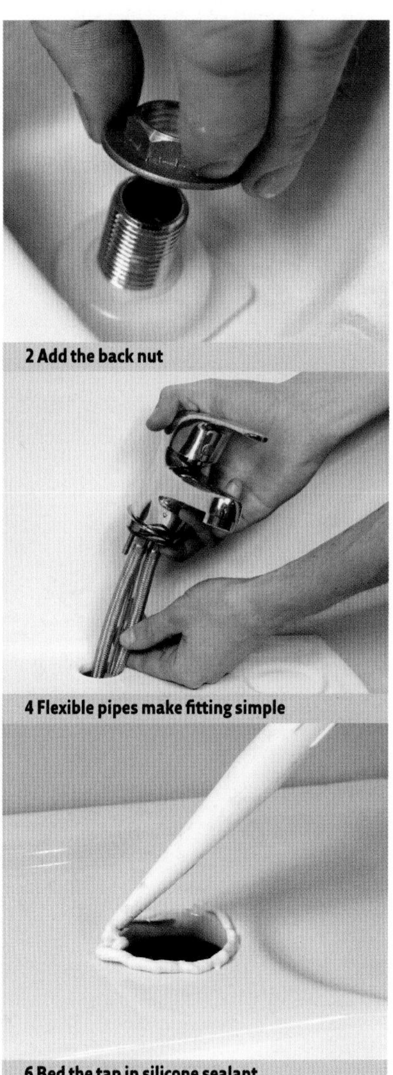

2 Add the back nut

4 Flexible pipes make fitting simple

6 Bed the tap in silicone sealant

SEE ALSO > Turning off the water 348, Connecting pipes 361–2, 365, Hacksaws 318, Gas torch 521, Spanners and wrenches 522

Choosing a washbasin

Whether you're modifying existing plumbing or running pipework to a new location, fitting a washbasin in a bathroom or guest room is likely to present few difficulties provided you give some thought to how you will run the waste to the vertical stack. The pipe must have a minimum fall or slope of 6mm (1/4in) for every 300mm (1ft) of pipe run and should not be more than 3m (10ft) long.

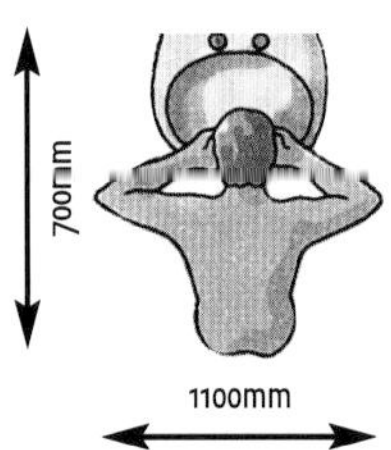

Space for a basin
Recommend dimensions for comfortable use

Selecting a washbasin

Wall-hung and pedestal washbasins are invariably made from vitreous china, but basins that are supported all round by a counter top are also available in pressed steel and plastic.

Select the taps at the same time, to ensure that the basin of your choice has holes at the required spacing to receive the taps – or no holes at all if the taps are to be wall-mounted.

Pedestal basins

The hollow pedestal provides some support for the basin and it conceals the unsightly supply and waste pipes. The basin is secured to the wall with screws, but the pedestal supports much of the weight.

Wall-hung basins

Older wall-hung basins are supported on large, screw-fixed brackets, but a modern concealed mounting is just as strong provided the wall fixings are secure. Check that you can screw into the studs of a timber-frame wall or hack off the lath-and-plaster and install a mounting board. If you want to hide pipes, consider some form of panelling.

Pedestal basin

Wall-hung basin

Corner basins

Handbasins that fit into the corner of a room are space-saving, and the pipework can be run conveniently through adjacent walls or concealed by boxing them in across the corner.

Recessed basins

In a cloakroom or WC where space is very limited, a small handbasin can be recessed into one of the walls. Also, you can recess a standard basin to conceal the plumbing.

Counter-top basins

In a large bathroom or bedroom, you can fit a washbasin or pair of basins into a counter top as part of a built-in vanity unit. Cupboards below provide storage.

Recessed basin

Counter-top basin

Corner basin

Removing a washbasin

If you want to use existing plumbing, loosen the compression nuts on the tap tails (**1**) and then remove the trap and waste pipes (**2**). Otherwise, cut through the waste and supply pipes at the point where you can most easily connect new plumbing.

Next, remove the pedestal (**3**), which may be screwed to the floor, and then undo any screws or brackets holding the basin to the wall. These may be corroded and hard to remove – there may be no option but to lever the basin off the wall.

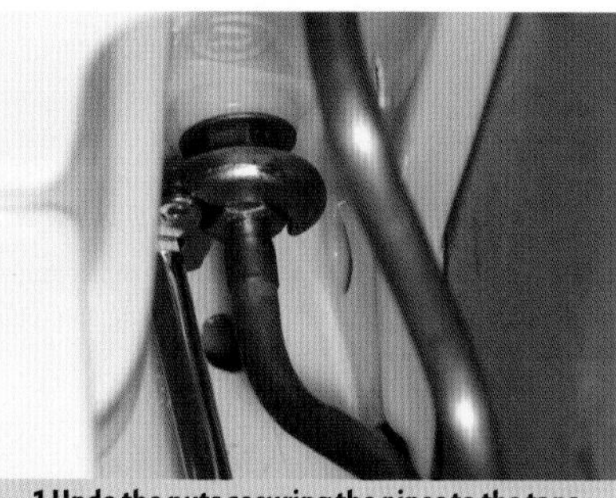

1 Undo the nuts securing the pipes to the taps

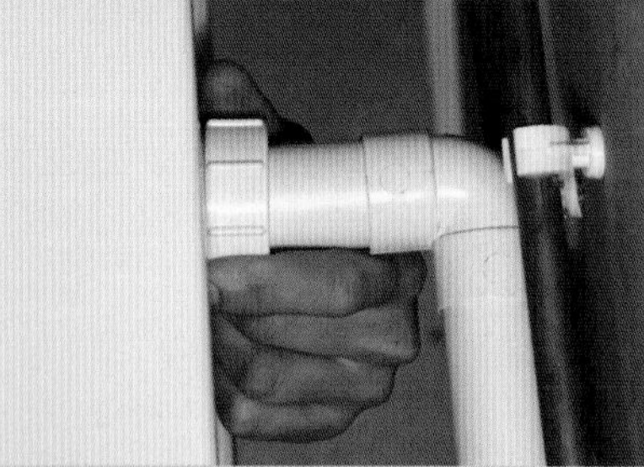

2 Remove the trap and waste pipes

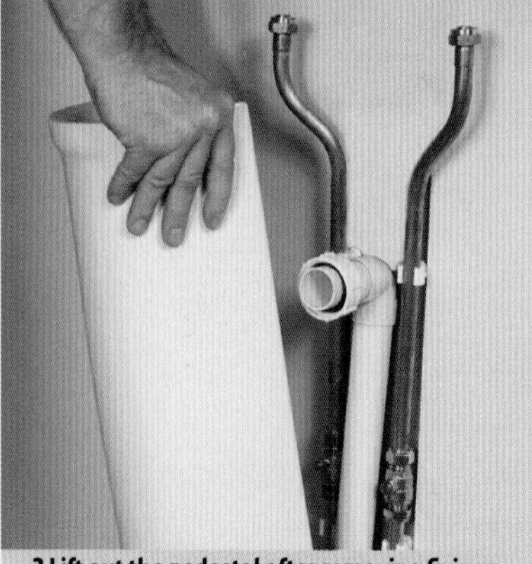

3 Lift out the pedestal after removing fixings

SEE ALSO > Bathroom planning 14

Connecting a washbasin

Plan the location for your basin carefully, ensuring that there is sufficient space around it for comfortable use – ideally in an area at least 800mm (2ft 8in) wide and 700mm (2ft 4in) deep. If wall-mounted, it should be no higher than 1100mm (3ft 10in) to be suitable for all members of the family. Wall-mounted basins need to have subtantial fixings – ensure the wall is in good condition, with something solid to take the weight.

Fixing basin to the wall

Get an assistant to hold a wall-hung basin against the wall at the required height while you use a spirit level to check that it is horizontal.

Mark the fixing holes for the basin (**1**), then drill and plug the holes (**2**). Insert the special screw-in bolts and place the sink over the bolts. Add the washers and tighten the nuts (**3**).

For a pedestal basin, place the pedestal in position, then sit the basin on it and mark the fixing holes.

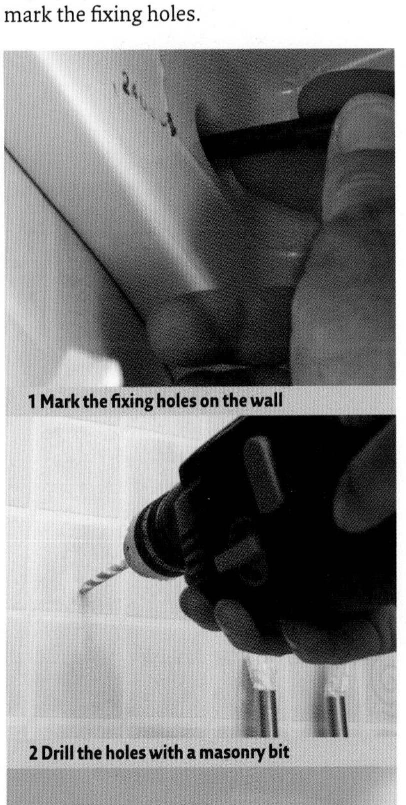

1 Mark the fixing holes on the wall

2 Drill the holes with a masonry bit

3 Fix the basin to the wall

Fitting trap and waste

Fit the waste outlet into the bottom of the basin as described for taps, using washers or a silicone sealant to form a watertight seal. The basin will probably have an integral overflow running to the waste - if this is the case, ensure that the slot in the waste outlet aligns with the overflow. Tighten the back-nut under the basin, while holding the outlet still by gripping its grille with long nose pliers.

If you can use the existing waste pipe, connect the trap to the waste outlet and to the end of the pipe. A two-part trap provides some adjustment for aligning with the old waste pipe.

To run a new 32mm (1¼in) waste pipe, cut a hole through the wall with a masonry core drill. Run the pipe, with sufficient fall - 6mm (¼in) per 300mm (1ft) run - to terminate over the hopper on top of the outside downpipe, or feed into a soil pipe. Fix the waste pipe to the wall with saddle clips.

Connecting the taps

You can run standard 15mm (½in) copper or plastic pipes to the taps and join them with tap connectors, but it is easier to use short lengths of flexible corrugated copper pipe designed specially for tap connection. They can be bent by hand to allow for any slight misalignment between the supply pipes and tap tails, and they are easy to fit behind a pedestal. Each pipe has a tap connector at one end and a capillary or compression joint at the other for connection to the plumbing system.

Connect the corrugated pipes to the tap tails, leaving them hand-tight only. Then run new branch pipework to meet the corrugated pipes, or connect them to the existing plumbing. Make soldered or compression joints to connect the pipes. Use a cranked spanner to tighten the tap connectors. Turn on the water supply and check the pipes for leaks; if you need to repair a weeping soldered joint, drain the system, clean the joint with wire wool and coat with flux prior to heating and adding more solder.

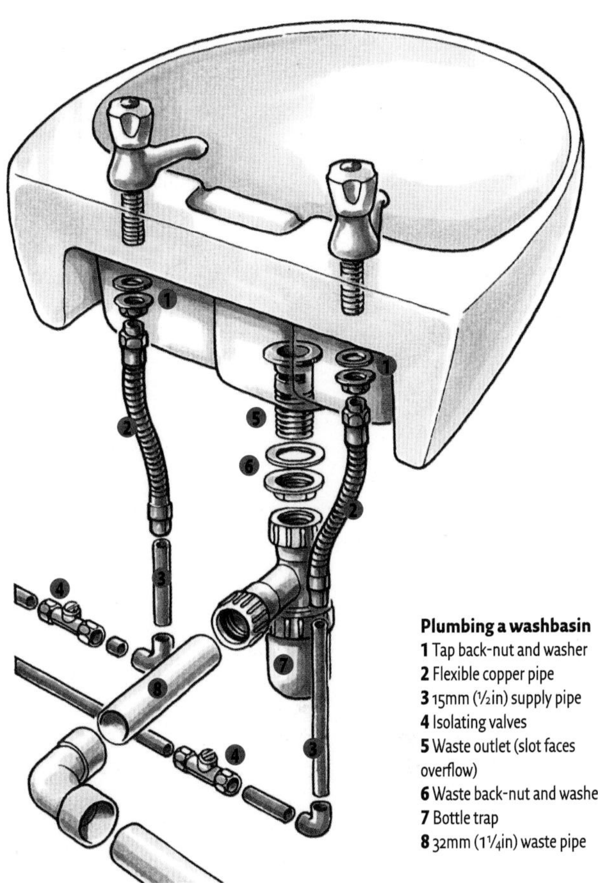

Plumbing a washbasin
1 Tap back-nut and washer
2 Flexible copper pipe
3 15mm (½in) supply pipe
4 Isolating valves
5 Waste outlet (slot faces overflow)
6 Waste back-nut and washer
7 Bottle trap
8 32mm (1¼in) waste pipe

Basin details

Pedestal basins

Run pipework up to and behind a pedestal. Fix the basin to the wall with screws. Some basins are attached to the pedestal with clips, or bonded with silicone sealant. Screw the pedestal to the floor.

Pressed-metal basin

When you fit taps to a pressed-metal basin, slip built-up 'top-hat' washers onto the tails to cover the shanks. The basin itself may be supplied with a rubber strip to seal the joint with the counter top.

Top-hat washer
These large washers cover the shank of a tap fitted to a pressed-metal basin.

Counter-top basin

A template is supplied for cutting the hole in the counter top to receive the basin. Run mastic around the edge to seal the basin, and clamp it with the fixings supplied.

SEE ALSO > Draining the system 348, Connecting pipes 361–2, 365, Fitting taps 371, Cranked spanner 522

Choosing a new bath

Whether your bathroom is cupboard-like or palatial, there's a huge range of baths available to suit every conceivable location - and pocket. Built-in or freestanding, materials include acrylic, glass-fibre, pressed steel, cast iron, or even stone, with a wide variety of shapes and sizes to make bath time a real experience.

Selecting a bath

Access to a bath
Allow a 1100 x 700mm (3ft 8in x 2ft 4in) space beside a bath so that it's possible to climb in and out safely, and for bathing younger members of the family.

Nowadays, the majority of baths are made from acrylic or glass-reinforced plastic - light and relatively cheap materials offering a wide variety of shapes. The surfaces are warm to the touch, and some freestanding models are 'double glazed' with an insulated twin-skin construction to help retain heat. The surfaces are vulnerable to abrasive cleaners and bleach, however, and care needs to be taken when using a blowtorch nearby for plumbing.

With their enamelled surfaces, pressed-steel and cast-iron baths are much tougher. They are heavy and it will take two people to carry a steel bath, and perhaps more for a cast-iron bath. Resin/stone composite baths are becoming more popular and are warm and practical.

Baths can be built in, panelled, sunken or freestanding. Corner baths can allow a bigger bath in a smaller space, while for very small bathrooms there are compact units just 1200mm (3ft 11in) long. There are also side-opening baths for those who have mobility problems.

Many baths can now be supplied fitted with a spa facility, where a powerful pump circulates water through a series of nozzles fitted in the sides of the bath - DIY kits are available to convert existing baths.

• Selecting taps for a bath
In design and style, bath taps are identical to basin taps; but they are proportionally larger, with 22mm (3/4 in) tails. Some bath mixers are designed to supply water to a sprayhead, either mounted telephone-style on the mixer itself or hung from a bracket mounted on a wall above the bath.

Rectangular bath

A standard rectangular bath is still the most popular and economical design. Baths vary in size from 1.5 to 1.8m (5 to 6ft) in length, with a choice of widths from 700 to 800mm (2ft 4in to 2ft 8in).

Corner bath

A corner bath occupies more floor area than a rectangular bath of the same capacity, but because it is fitted across the corner it may take up less wall space. A corner bath usually provides some shelf space for essential toiletries.

Round bath

A round bath is likely to be impractical in most bathrooms - but if you are converting a spare bedroom, you may decide to make the bath a feature of the interior design as well as a practical appliance.

Freestanding bath

The Victorian roll-top bath is the best example of this style, though there are many modern variations on the theme.

An acrylic bath

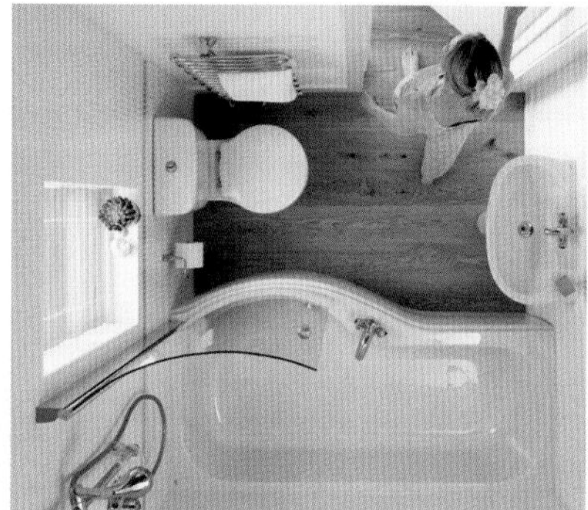

Plastic can be moulded into attractive shapes

Corner baths make good use of space

Roll top baths are still popular

If space is tight you can fit a compact bath

Illuminated bath panels give a modernist look

Supporting a frame-mounted plastic bath

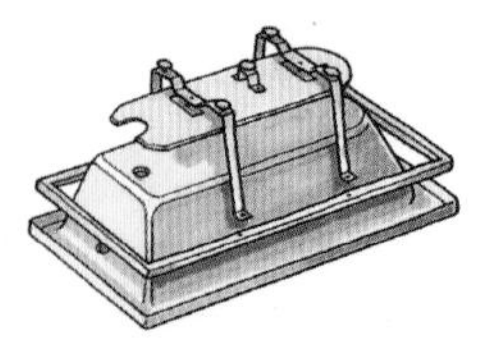

Assembling the cradle
Turn a bath onto its rim to fit the cradle.

A frame with adjustable feet is supplied to cradle a flexible plastic bath. The parts need to be assembled before the bath is fitted into place. To avoid any movement, it's important to ensure the feet are level and resting on a firm surface.

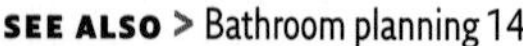

SEE ALSO > Bathroom planning 14

Plumbing a bath

Once a bath is fitted close to the wall, it can be difficult to make the joints and connections – so fit the taps, overflow and trap before you push the new bath into position. Set the adjustable feet to raise the rim of the bath to the required height, and check it for level along its length and width. If the bath has small feet, cut two boards to go under them to spread the point load over a wider area.

Removing and installing

Turn off the water supply before you drain the system.

Removing an old bath

Have a shallow bowl ready to catch any trapped water, then use a hacksaw to cut through the old pipes. The overflow pipe from an old bath will almost certainly exit through the wall, so saw through the overflow at the same time.

If the bath has adjustable feet, lower them and then push down on the bath to break the mastic seal between the bathroom walls and the rim. Pull the bath away from the walls.

If a cast-iron bath is beyond restoration, it is easier to break it up *in situ* and carry it out in pieces. Drape a dust sheet over the bath; then, wearing gloves, goggles and ear protectors, smash it with a heavy club hammer.

Installing a new bath

Either run new 22mm (¾in) supply pipes or attach spurs to the existing ones, ready for connection to the flexible pipes already fitted on the bath taps.

Slide your new bath into position and adjust the height of the feet with a spanner. Use a spirit level to check that the rim is horizontal. Adjust the flexible tap pipes and join them to the supply pipes. Connect a 40mm (1½in) waste pipe to the trap and run it to the external hopper or soil stack, as for a washbasin.

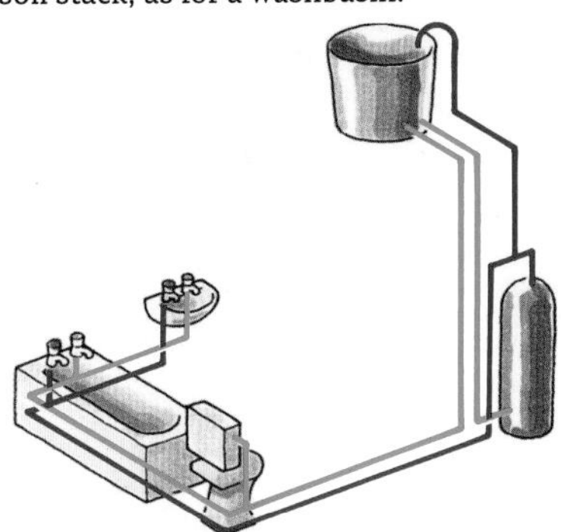

Typical tank-fed bathroom pipe runs
Red: Hot water. **Blue:** Cold water.

Fitting the taps

Fit individual hot and cold taps as for a washbasin. Fitting a mixer tap is a similar procedure, but some mixers are supplied with a long sealing gasket that slips over both tails. Lower the tails through the holes in the rim, then slip top-hat washers onto them and tighten both back-nuts to clamp the mixer securely to the bath.

Fit a flexible 22mm (¾in) copper pipe onto each tail. These flexible pipes allow for the easy adjustment that will be necessary if the joints are slightly misaligned. Alternatively, attach short lengths of standard 22mm (¾in) copper or plastic pipe with tap connectors, in preparation for jointing to the pipe run.

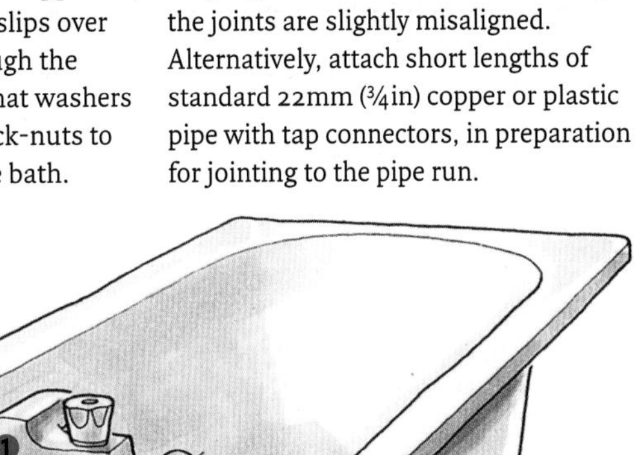

Plumbing a bath
1 Mixer tap
2 Mixer-tap gasket
3 Mixer back-nut and washer
4 Flexible copper pipe
5 Overflow unit
6 Waste outlet
7 Waste back-nut and washer
8 Deep-seal trap to 40mm (1½in) waste pipe
9 Supply pipes – 22mm (¾in)

Fitting waste and overflow

With a combined waste and overflow, a flexible plastic hose takes water from the overflow outlet at the foot of the bath to the waste outlet or trap. If you use a 'banjo' unit, you must fit the overflow before the trap; but the flexible pipe of a compression-fitting unit connects to the trap itself (see above).

Put silicone sealant under the rim of the waste outlet, or fit a circular rubber seal. Before inserting its tail into the hole in the bottom of the bath, seal the thread with PTFE tape. On the underside, add a plastic washer; then tighten the large back-nut, bedding the outlet down onto the sealant or the rubber seal. Wipe off excess sealant.

Connect the bath trap (see above) to the tail of the waste outlet and fit the banjo overflow unit at the same time.

Pass the threaded boss of the overflow hose through the hole at the foot of the bath. Slip a washer seal over the boss, then use a pair of pliers to screw the overflow outlet grille on.

Waste/overflow units
A flexible tube takes any overflow water to the trap.

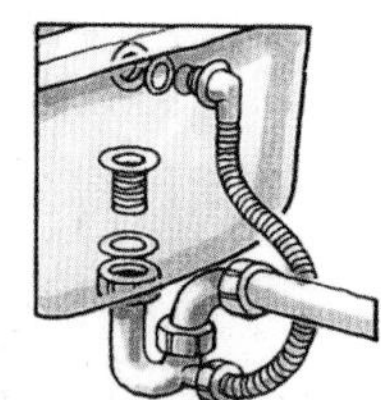

Compression unit
Runs to the cleaning eye on the trap.

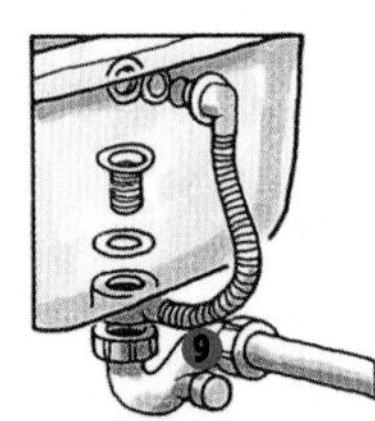

Banjo unit
Slips over the tail of the waste outlet.

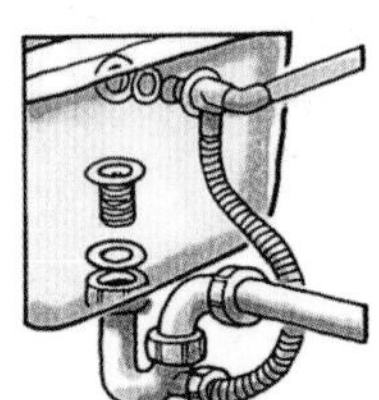

WC and bath overflow
Overflow from a WC joins the bath unit.

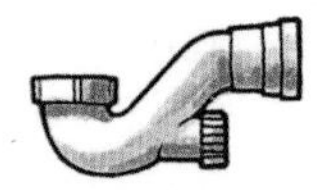

Shallow-seal trap
Use this type of trap when space is limited. It must discharge to a yard gully or hopper, and not to a soil stack.

SEE ALSO > Draining the system 348, Connecting pipes 361–2, 365, Fitting taps 371, Cranked spanner 522

Replacing a WC suite

Replacing an old WC with a modern suite is a relatively straightforward procedure, provided you can connect it to the existing branch of the soil pipe. However, if you are going to move a WC, or perhaps install a second one in another part of your home, you will have to connect to the main soil pipe itself or run the waste into the underground drainage system. In either case, hire a professional plumber to make these connections.

Cisterns

From antique-style high-level cisterns to discreet close-coupled or concealed models, the choice is so wide that you're bound to find one to suit your requirements. Before buying, make sure the equipment carries the British Standard 'Kite mark' or complies with equivalent EC standards.

High-level cistern

If you simply want to replace an old-fashioned high-level cistern without having to modify the pipework, comparable cisterns are still available from plumbers' merchants.

Standard low-level cistern

Many people prefer a cistern mounted on the wall just above the WC pan. A short flush pipe from the base of the cistern connects to the flushing horn on the rear of the pan, while inlet and overflow pipes can be fitted to either side of the cistern. Most low-level cisterns are manufactured from the same vitreous china as the WC pan.

Compact low-level cistern

Where space is limited, use a plastic cistern, which is only 114mm (4½in) from front to back.

Concealed cistern

A low-level cistern can be completely concealed behind panelling. The supply and overflow connections are identical to those of other types of cistern, but the flushing lever is mounted on the face of the panel. These plastic cisterns are utilitarian in character, with no concession to fashion or style, and are therefore relatively inexpensive. Don't forget that you will need to provide access for servicing.

Close-coupled cisterns

A close-coupled cistern is bolted directly to the pan, forming an integral unit. Both the inlet and overflow connections are made at the base of the cistern. An internal standpipe rises vertically from the overflow connection with the pan to protrude above the level of the water.

WC pans

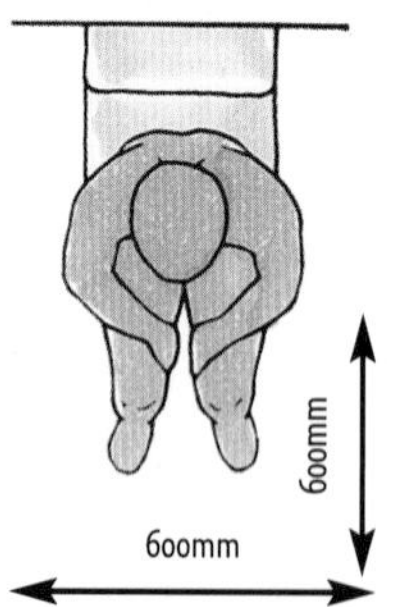

Space for a WC
You will need to allow a space at least 600mm (2ft) square in front of the pan.

When visiting a showroom, you are confronted with many apparently different WC pans to choose from, but in fact there are usually only two variations on the washdown pan – those where the cistern is connected by a pipe, and close-coupled units where the cistern bolts on directly.

Your bathroom may have an older, siphonic type of WC, but these are now obsolete due to their higher water usage.

WC pans are now made to reduce the amount of water needed to flush them. This is a legal requirement for new installations, but it is still possible and legal to buy an older-style pan with a higher water content.

New pans use the same trap seal depth and the waste pipe bore; they reduce the water content by having a shallow section rather like the shallow end of a swimming pool.

Washdown pans

Washdown pans work by displacement of waste by fresh water falling from the cistern. They are inherently more reliable than siphonic pans, but make considerably more noise when flushed.

Floor or wall exit?

When replacing a WC pan, check to see whether the new one needs to have a floor-exit or wall-exit trap.

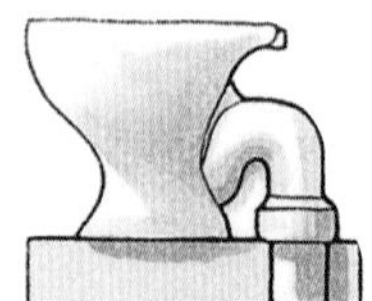

Floor-exit trap
S-traps are connected to a soil pipe that is then passed through the floor.

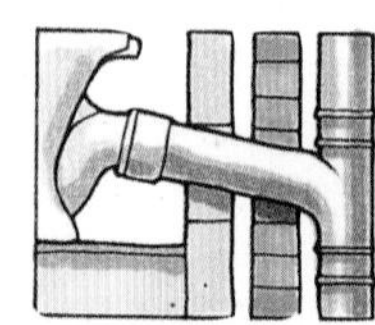

Wall-exit trap
The outlet from a P-trap connects to a soil-pipe branch located behind the pan.

Choosing a WC cistern

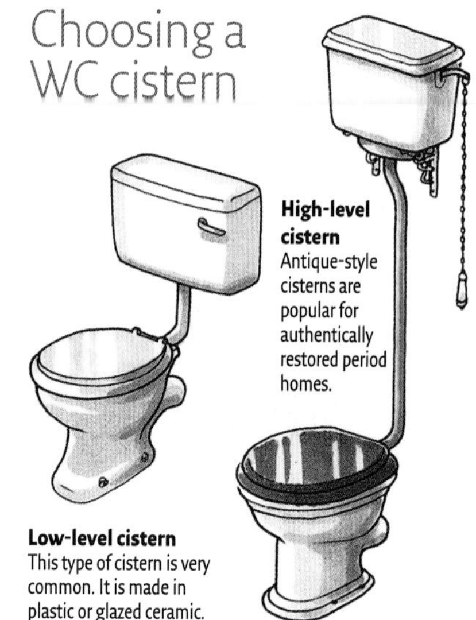

High-level cistern
Antique-style cisterns are popular for authentically restored period homes.

Low-level cistern
This type of cistern is very common. It is made in plastic or glazed ceramic.

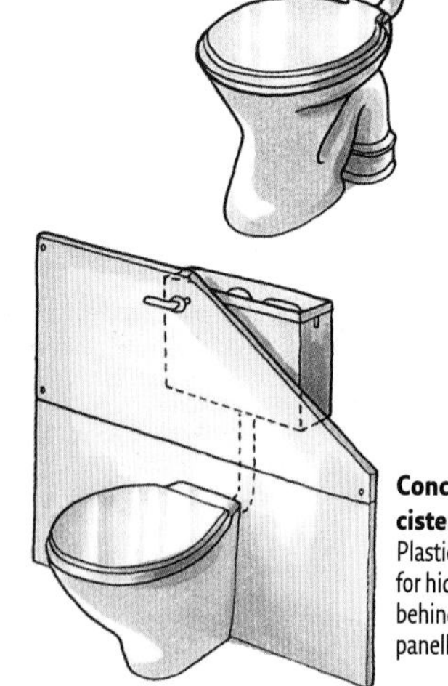

Compact cistern
Very slim plastic cistern, for use where space is limited.

Concealed cistern
Plastic cistern for hiding behind panelling.

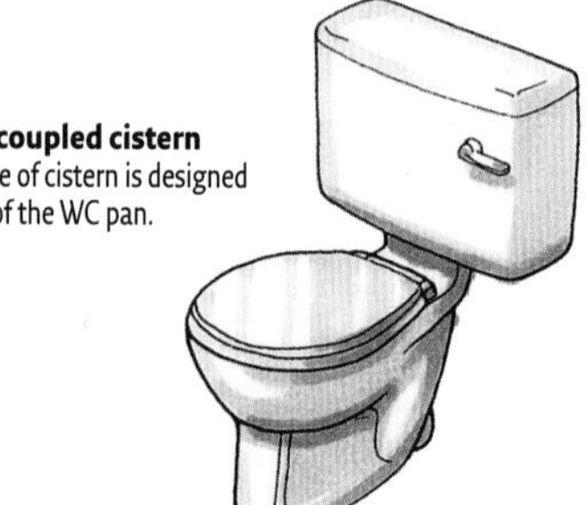

Close-coupled cistern
This type of cistern is designed as part of the WC pan.

SEE ALSO > Bathroom planning 14, Cisterns 364–5

Removing an old WC

Cut off the water supply, then flush the cistern to empty it. If you are merely renewing a cistern, you will have to disconnect the supply and overflow pipes with a wrench and loosen the large nut connecting the flush pipe to the base of the cistern. These connections are often corroded and painted – so if you intend to replace the entire suite it is easier to hacksaw through the pipes close to the connections.

Choosing a WC pan

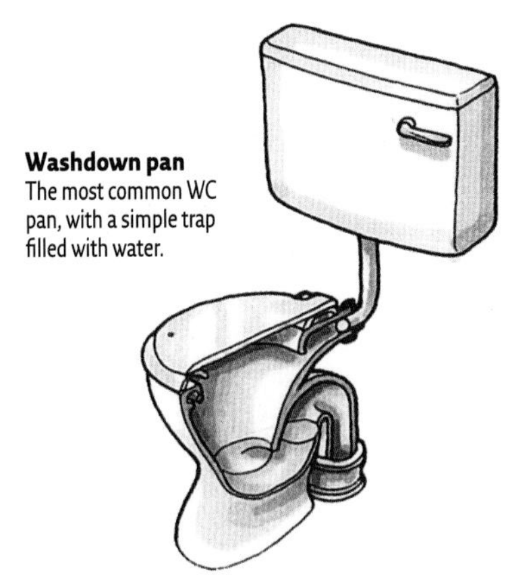

Washdown pan
The most common WC pan, with a simple trap filled with water.

Close-coupled pan
This washdown pan is neater than a pan with a separate cistern. The cistern bolts onto the back of the pan. P- or S-trap versions are available, though many are only made with a horizontal P-trap that can be connected to the soil pipe in the floor with a right-angled pan connector.

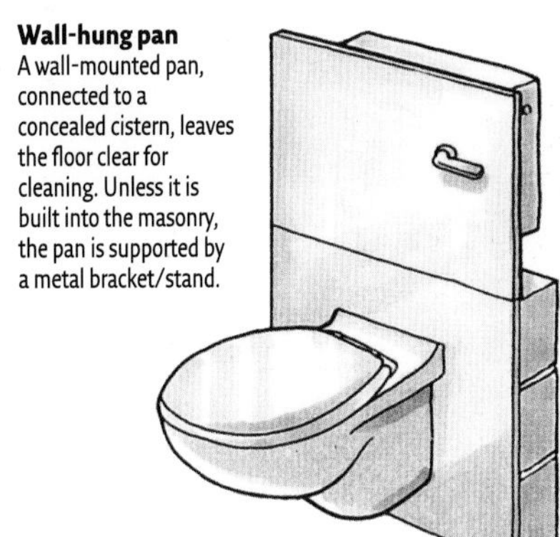

Wall-hung pan
A wall-mounted pan, connected to a concealed cistern, leaves the floor clear for cleaning. Unless it is built into the masonry, the pan is supported by a metal bracket/stand.

Removing the old pan and cistern

Remove the fixing screws through the back of the cistern, or lift it off its support brackets and remove them. Lever the brackets off the wall with a crowbar if necessary.

Cut the overflow pipe from the wall with a cold chisel. Repair the plaster when you decorate the bathroom.

If the pan is screwed to a wooden floor, it will probably have a P-trap connected to a nearly horizontal branch soil pipe. Remove the pan's floor-fixing screws and scrape out the old putty around the pipe joint. Attempt to free the pan by pulling it towards you while rocking it slightly from side to side.

If the joint is fixed firmly, smash the pan outlet just in front of the soil pipe with a club hammer (**1**). Protect your eyes with goggles. Stuff rags into the soil pipe to prevent debris falling into it, then chip out the remains of the pan outlet with a cold chisel (**2**). Work carefully, to preserve the soil pipe.

Smash an S-trap in the same way – and if the pan is cemented to a solid floor, drive a cold chisel under its base to break the seal. Chop out the broken fragments as before, and clean up the floor with a cold chisel.

If you crack the end of the soil pipe, cut it off square with a hired chain-link pipe cutter (**3**) or an angle grinder fitted with a masonry cutting disk. The cut-down pipe will still be able to accept a push-fit flexible connector, which should be lubricated before inserting into the pipe (**4**).

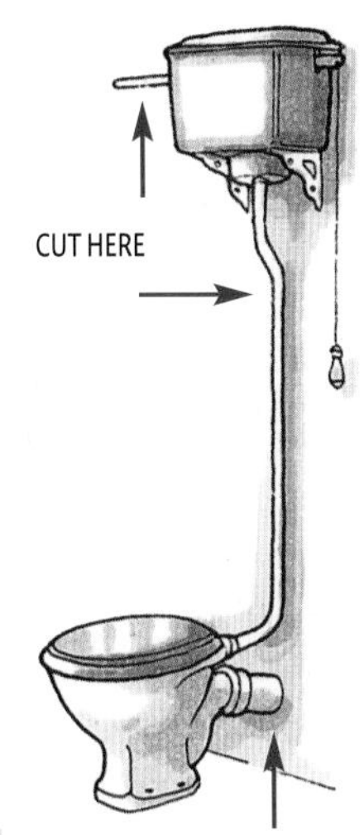

Removing an appliance
If fittings are corroded, remove the appliance by cutting through the flush pipe, overflow and pan outlet.

1 Break the outlet of the pan with a hammer

2 Use a cold chisel to cut out the remnants

3 Cut a damaged soil pipe with a hired cutter

4 The cut pipe will accept a flexible connector

• **Lubricating connectors**
When installing plastic soil-pipe connectors, smear the surfaces lightly with a silicone lubricant.

Pan to soil-pipe connection

Before you install the new suite, choose a push-fit flexible connector to join the pan to the soil pipe. There are connectors to suit most situations, even when the two elements are slightly misaligned. You may need an angled connector to join a modern horizontal-outlet pan to an old P-trap branch pipe (see opposite).

When selecting a connector, make a note of the following dimensions: the external diameter of the pan outlet, the internal diameter of the soil pipe, and the distance between the outlet and the pipe when the pan is installed.

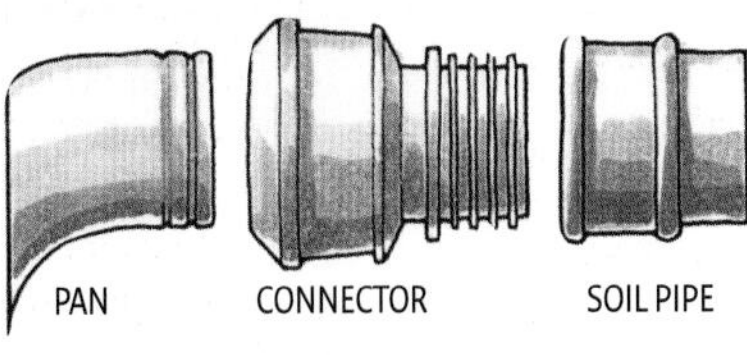

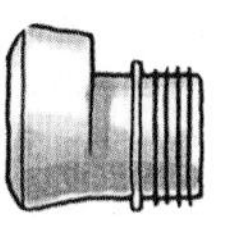

SEE ALSO > Turning off the water 348, Cisterns 364–5, Cold chisel 513, Spanners and wrenches 522

Installing a new WC suite

Clean the floor and make good any damage before you begin to install a new WC suite. It's important to make sure that no debris enters the soil pipe while the WC is disconnected, so stuff it with an old cloth, or tape a carrier bag over it.

• Fixing a new WC pan to the floor
All manufacturers advise against the old-fashioned method of cementing a WC pan to a concrete floor. In fact, guarantees are usually invalidated if cement or a strong adhesive is used. If you can't screw the pan in place, just rely on the bed of silicone sealant to bond the pan to the floor.

Fitting and plumbing the suite

Make up the new cistern with the siphon or valve and the inlet fill valve.

Not all cisterns come with instructions, but most have an illustration showing the position of the seals. Do not overtighten the nuts. Use enough pressure to press the rubber washers onto the ceramic, but not so much that the washers are squeezed out. If the washers get wet, it is best to dry them before tightening because the water lubricates them and helps them squeeze out from under the nut.

The pan is held onto the cistern with nuts and bolts. There will be a series of washers to seal the bolts and protect the ceramic surfaces. The golden rule is to avoid metal touching ceramic otherwise there's a risk of cracking.

The pan should be fixed to the floor with brass screws. Take care to align them correctly and avoid overtightening. The cistern should be fixed against the wall with screws that are cushioned with tap washers or a cistern fixing kit.

Alternatively, fix the cistern with a couple of dobs of silicone sealant - this reduces the possibility of the cistern cracking if there is any movement between the wall and floor.

On most cisterns the overflow now runs into the pan through an internal route. It is important to adjust the dump valve height so the cistern fills to the water line marked on the inside of the cistern.

In many cases this is set in the factory so you won't need to adjust it. If you are fitting a new dump valve, then you will often need to make an adjustment.

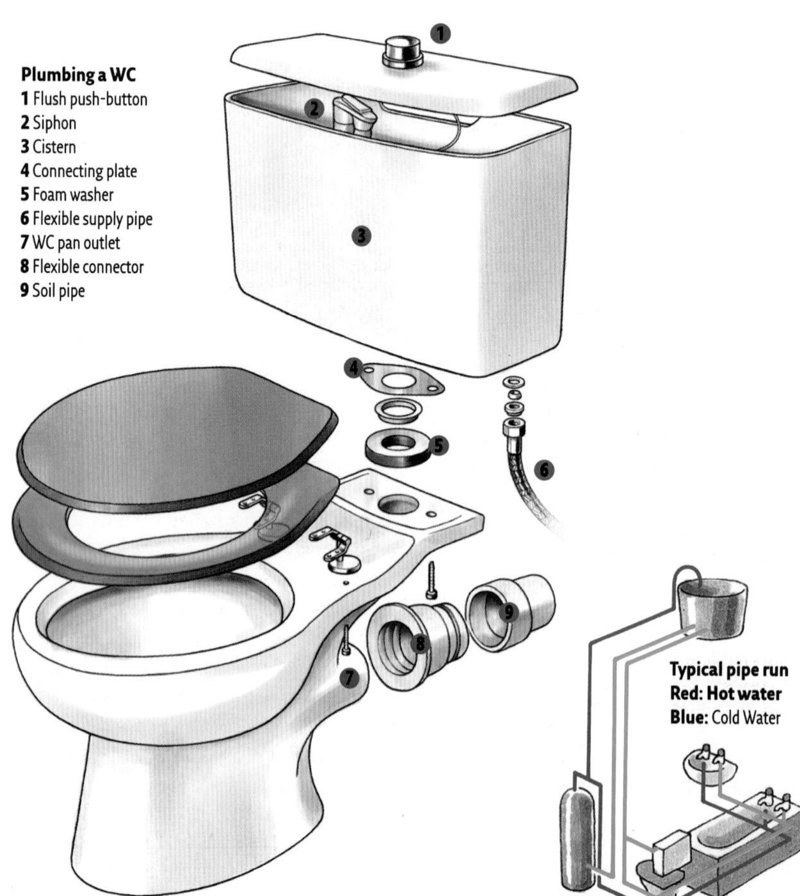

Plumbing a WC
1 Flush push-button
2 Siphon
3 Cistern
4 Connecting plate
5 Foam washer
6 Flexible supply pipe
7 WC pan outlet
8 Flexible connector
9 Soil pipe

Small-bore waste systems

The siting of a WC is normally limited by the need to use a conventional 100mm (4in) soil pipe and to provide sufficient fall to discharge the waste into the soil stack. By using an electrically driven pump and shredder unit, you can discharge WC waste through a 22mm (¾in) pipe up to 50m (55yd) away from the stack. The shredder will even pump vertically, to a maximum height of about 4m (12ft).

You can run the small-bore pipework through the narrow space between a floor and ceiling. Consequently, a WC can be installed as part of an en-suite bathroom, in a basement, even under the stairs, so long as the space is adequately ventilated.

The unit is designed to accept any conventional P-trap WC pan. It is activated by flushing the cistern, and switches off about 18 seconds later. It must be wired to a fused connection unit - via a suitable flex outlet if it is installed in a bathroom.

The waste pipe can be connected to the soil stack using a 32mm (1¼in) pipe boss, provided the manufacturer supplies a 22 to 32mm (¾ to 1¼in) adaptor. A WC waste pipe must be connected to the soil stack at least 200mm (8in) above or below any other waste connections.

It's wise to check that these systems are approved by your local water supplier.

Small-bore waste system for a WC
The shredding unit fits neatly behind a P-trap WC pan. When fitted in a bathroom, the unit must be wired to a flex outlet. Otherwise, it can be connected to a fused connection unit.

SEE ALSO > Building Regulations on electrical wiring 284 Fused connection units 310, Flex outlet 311

Choosing a shower

All showers, except for the most powerful, use less water than required for filling a bath. And because showering is generally quicker than taking a bath, it helps to alleviate the morning queue for the bathroom. For even greater convenience, install a second shower somewhere else in the house – this is one of those improvements that really does add value to your home. Improvements in technology have made available a variety of powerful, controllable showers. However, many appliances are superficially similar in appearance, so it's important to read the manufacturers' literature carefully before you opt for a particular model.

Pressure and flow

When choosing a shower, bear in mind that pressure and flow are not the same thing. For example, an instantaneous electric shower delivers water at high mains pressure, but a relatively low flow rate is necessary to allow the water to heat up as it passes through the shower unit.

A conventional gravity-fed system delivers hot water from a storage cylinder under low pressure, but often has a high flow rate when measured in litres per minute. Adding a pump to this type of system can increase both pressure and flow rate. Alter the flow and pressure ratio by fitting an adjustable showerhead with a choice of spray patterns, from needle jets to a gentle 'champagne' cascade .

This showerhead provides a choice of spray patterns

Gravity-fed showers

In most homes cold water is stored in a tank in the loft and fed to a hot-water cylinder at a lower level. Both the hot-water and cold-water pressures are determined by the height (or 'head') of the cold-water storage tank above the shower. A minimum of at least 1 metre (3ft) head should give reasonable flow rate and pressure. If flow and pressure are insufficient for a good shower, you could improve the situation by raising the tank or fitting a pump in the system.

Mains-pressure showers

Some types of shower are fed directly from the mains: one of the simplest to install from a plumbing point of view is an instantaneous electric shower, which needs a dedicated electricity supply.

Another alternative is to install a thermal-store cylinder. Mains-pressure water passes through a rapid heat exchanger inside the cylinder (see right). Yet another option is to store hot water in an unvented cylinder – which will supply high-pressure water to a shower without the need for a booster pump.

Nowadays showers are often supplied from combination boilers, though these often need to run at full flow to keep the boiler firing properly. Before buying a shower, check with the manufacturer of your boiler to ascertain whether there's likely to be a problem.

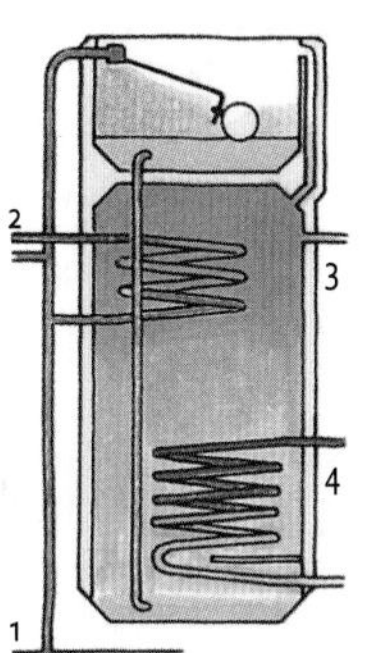

Thermal-store cylinder
Mains-fed water passes through a rapid heat exchanger on its way to the shower.
1 Mains feed
2 To shower
3 Other outlets
4 Boiler connections

Shower enclosures
If space permits, choose an enclosed shower cubicle (centre left). However, there are a number of screens and plumbing options, which make an over-the-bath shower almost as efficient.

Drainage

Draining the used water away from a shower can be more of a problem than running the supply.

If it is not possible to run the waste pipe between the floor joists or along a wall, then you may have to consider relocating the shower. In some situations it may be necessary to raise the shower tray on a plinth in order to gain enough height for the waste pipe to fall (slope) towards the drain. Another way to overcome the problem is to install a special pump to take the waste water away from the shower.

Shower traps

When running the waste pipe to an outside hopper, you can fit a conventional trap – but these are relatively large, creating problems when installing the shower tray.

You could cut a hole in the floor, or substitute either a smaller, shallow-seal or compact trap that includes a removable grid and dip tube for easy cleaning. Another possibility is to fit a running trap in the waste pipe at a convenient location, or install a self-sealing valve in the pipe.

A shower trap that is connected to a soil stack must have a water seal not less than 50mm (2in) deep. The best solution is to fit a compact trap, which is shallow enough to fit under most modern shower trays, but is designed to provide the necessary water seal. Alternatively, fit either a running trap or a self-sealing valve.

Wet rooms
Wet rooms do away with shower trays and have drainage through the floor. They create a clean, uncluttered look, but need careful waterproofing to avoid problems with leaks

SEE ALSO > Planning a bathroom 14, Shower mixers and sprayheads 380, Booster pumps 384, Thermal-store cylinders 393, Unvented cylinders 393

Shower mixers and sprayheads

Installing an independent shower cubicle with its own supply and waste systems requires some prior experience of plumbing – but if you use an existing bath as a shower tray, then fitting a shower unit can involve little more than replacing the taps.

Bath/shower mixers

This type of shower is the simplest to install. It is connected to the existing 22mm (¾in) hot and cold pipes in the same way as a standard bath mixer, and the bath's waste system takes care of the drainage. Once you have obtained the right temperature at the spout by adjusting the hot and cold valves, you lift a button on the mixer to divert the water to the sprayhead via a flexible hose. The sprayhead can be hung from a wall-mounted bracket to provide a conventional shower, or hand-held for washing hair.

Bath/shower mixer
Fit this type of shower unit like an ordinary bath mixer.

Because the supply pipes for this type of shower are part of the overall house system, it's impossible to guard against fluctuating pressure – and potentially scalding temperatures – unless the mixer is fitted with a thermostatic valve. An unregulated shower could be a real hazard if there are very young or elderly residents. Installing a pressure-equalizing valve in the pipework will add convenience and safety – if the pressure is insufficient, fit a booster pump.

Don't fit a bath/shower mixer unless both the hot and cold water is under the same pressure, either high or low. This type of shower has controls that are uncomfortably low to reach.

Dual-lever mixer
With this type of mixer, one lever controls flow and the other temperature.

Manual shower mixers

A manual shower mixer can be located over a bath or in a separate shower cubicle. Manual mixers require their own independent hot and cold supply.

Simple versions are available with individual hot and cold valves, but most manual shower mixers have a single control that regulates the flow and temperature of the water. Single-lever ceramic-disc mixers operate exceptionally smoothly and, having few moving parts, are less prone to hard-water scaling.

You can choose a surface-mounted unit, or a nearly flush mixer with the pipework, connections and shower mechanism all concealed in the wall.

Thermostatic mixers

A thermostatic shower mixer is similar in design to a manual mixer, but it has an extra control incorporated to preset the water temperature. If the flow rate drops on either the hot or cold supply, a thermostatic valve rapidly compensates by reducing the flow on the other side. This is primarily a safety measure, to prevent the shower user being scalded should someone run a cold tap elsewhere in the house. A thermostatic shower should be supplied by means of branch pipes from the bathroom plumbing – but try to join them as near as possible to the cold tank and hot cylinder. The mixer can't raise the pressure of the supply, so you still need a booster pump if the pressure is low.

Thermostatic mixer mechanisms are usually based on wax-filled cartridges or bimetallic strips. Brand-new thermostatic valves respond extremely quickly to changes of temperature, but the rate slows down as scale gradually builds up inside the mixer. Even when new, reaction time will be slower if the mixer is expected to cope with exceptionally hot water (above 65°C/149°F). At such high temperatures the hot-water ports are almost fully closed and the cold ones almost wide open, so there is little margin for more adjustment.

The majority of thermostatic mixers can be used with the existing gravity-fed hot and cold supply, but it may be necessary to fit a booster pump. Check the manufacturer's literature – some showers don't perform well at low pressures.

Thermostatic mixer
This unit prevents excessive fluctuations in water temperature.

Sprayheads

There's a wide range of sprayheads available and many are adjustable to offer a variety of spray patterns. If you're thinking of upgrading an existing shower by installing an electric pump, it's worth finding out whether you can also replace the sprayhead.

In addition to the standard shower spray, a simple adjustment is all that is needed to produce an invigorating, pulsing jet to wake you up in the morning or a soft bubbly stream that is ideal for small children. Some sprayheads can also be adjusted to deliver a very light spray while you soap yourself or apply shampoo.

Rubber nozzles
Rub the the rubber nozzles on a modern sprayhead occasionally with your hand to help to shift lime scale accumulation.

Cleaning a sprayhead

Gradually, accumulation of lime scale blocks the holes in the sprayhead, and eventually this affects the performance of your shower. The harder the water, the more often it will need cleaning.

Remove the entire sprayhead from its hose or unscrew the perforated plate from the showerhead. Leave the sprayhead or plate to soak in a proprietary descalant until the scale has dissolved, then rinse thoroughly under running cold water.

Before you reattach the sprayhead or plate, turn on the shower to flush any loose scale deposits from the pipework.

SEE ALSO > Choosing a shower 379, Fitting a bath mixer 375

Instantaneous showers

An instantaneous electric shower is designed specifically for connection to the mains water supply, using a single 15mm (½in) branch pipe from the rising main. A non-return valve must be fitted close to the unit.

Incoming water is heated within the unit, so there is no separate hot-water supply to balance. The shower is thermostatically controlled to prevent fluctuations in pressure affecting the water temperature and will switch off completely if there is a serious pressure failure. Some units have a shut-down facility: when you switch off, the water continues to flow for a little while to flush any hot water out of the pipework. This ensures that someone stepping into the cubicle immediately after another user isn't subjected to an unexpectedly hot start to their shower.

The electrical circuit

An instantaneous shower requires a separate circuit from the consumer unit. A ceiling-mounted double-pole switch is connected to the circuit to turn the appliance on and off.

Surface-mounted or concealed

With most instantaneous showers, all plumbing and electrical connections are contained in a single mixer cabinet that is mounted in the shower cubicle or over the bath. However, you can buy showers with a slim, flush-fitting control panel that is connected via a low voltage cable to a power pack installed out of sight – for example, under the bath behind a screw-fixed panel.

Fit a stopcock or miniature isolating valve in the supply pipe to allow the shower to be serviced.

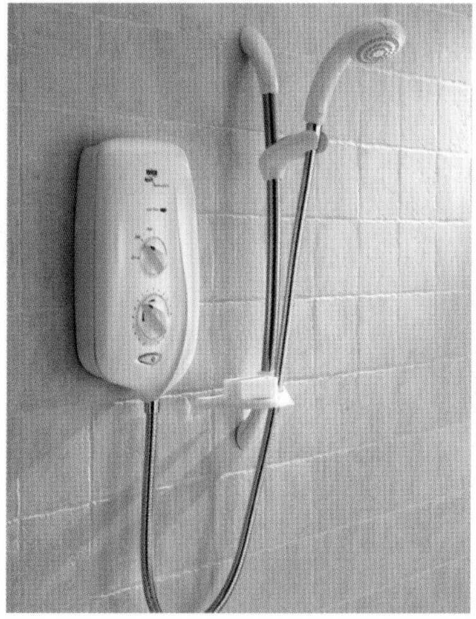

Pump-assisted showers

The pump-assisted 'power' shower is perhaps most people's concept of the ideal shower. The pump delivers water at a constant pressure and flow rate, eliminating the need for the minimum pressure normally required for a gravity-fed shower.

Most power showers need a head of about 75 to 225mm (3 to 9in) to activate the pump when the mixer control is turned on. A pump can be used to boost the pressure and flow rate of stored hot and cold water, but not mains-fed water.

Ideally, the cold supply should be taken directly from the storage tank – not from branch pipes that feed other taps and appliances. The hot-water supply can be connected to the cylinder by means of a Surrey or Essex flange, which helps to eliminate the tendency for the pump to suck in air from the vent pipe.

If the water is heated by an electric immersion heater, make sure the cylinder is fed by a dedicated cold feed and that the cold-feed gate valve is fully open. This is to prevent the top of the cylinder running dry and perhaps burning out the heater. If the cylinder is heated from a boiler, make sure the water temperature is controlled by a thermostat. If the water is too hot, the shower could splutter.

Many power showers resemble instantaneous units, with the mixer controls and pump enclosed in a waterproof casing mounted on the shower cubicle wall.

Other pumps are designed for remote installation in the pipes feeding the shower mixer. These freestanding pumps can also be used to improve the performance of an existing installation. They're usually located next to the hot-water cylinder in an airing cupboard – as low as possible, so that the pump remains full of water. There are also pumps that are designed to perform satisfactorily when mounted at a high level – even in a loft. In such situations, a single-impeller pump is best.

Water Regulations

If the shower is mounted in such a way that the sprayhead could dangle below the rim of the bath or shower tray, you have to fit double-seal non-return valves in the supply pipes to prevent dirty water being siphoned back into the system. Most shower sets come with a bracket to prevent the hose reaching that far.

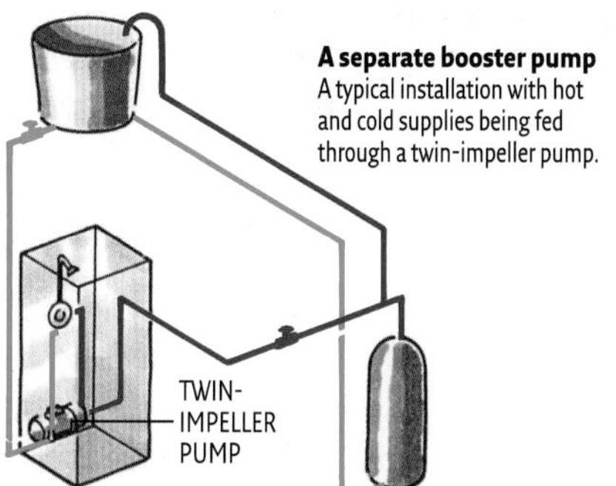

All-in-one power shower
The cold supply comes from the storage cistern, and the hot supply from the hot-water cylinder.

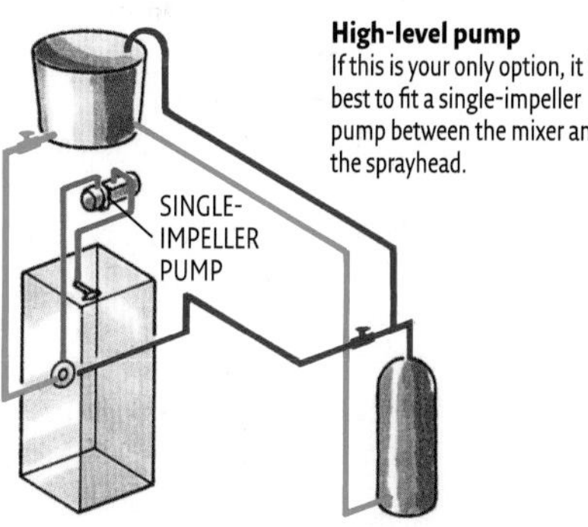

A separate booster pump
A typical installation with hot and cold supplies being fed through a twin-impeller pump.

High-level pump
If this is your only option, it is best to fit a single-impeller pump between the mixer and the sprayhead.

Computer-controlled showers

Computerized showers allow for the precise selection of temperature and flow rates, using a touch-sensitive control panel. Most panels also include a memory program, so that each member of a family can select their own preprogrammed ideal shower.

These showers have real advantages for the disabled and for elderly people since they are exceptionally easy to operate – and the control panel can even be mounted outside the cubicle, so that it's possible to warm up the shower before you get in, or operate it for someone else.

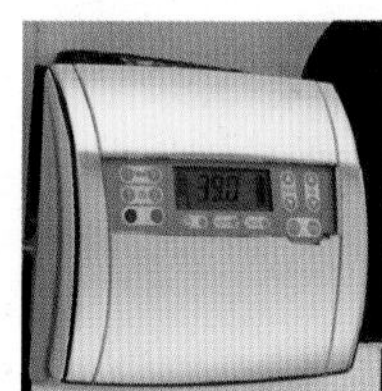

Touch-sensitive computerized panel

SEE ALSO > Building Regulations on electrical wiring 284, Wiring electric showers 316

Building a shower enclosure

The simplest way to acquire a shower cubicle is to install a factory-assembled cabinet, complete with tray and mixer, together with waterproof doors or a curtain to contain the spray from the sprayhead. Once you have run supply pipes and drainage, the installation is complete. However, factory-built cabinets are expensive and there is an alternative – to construct a purpose-made shower cubicle to fit the allocated space.

Proprietary shower enclosure

Choosing the site

When deciding upon the location of your shower, consider whether you can use the existing walls – or do you need new partitions to enclose the cubicle?

Freestanding

You can place the shower tray against a flat wall and either construct a stud partition on each side or surround the tray with a proprietary enclosure.

Corner site

If you position the tray in a corner of a room, then two sides of the cubicle are ready-made. Run a curtain around the tray or install a corner-entry enclosure with sliding doors. Alternatively, build a fixed side wall yourself and put either a door or a curtain across the entrance.

Built-in cupboards

To incorporate a shower cubicle unobtrusively in a bedroom, place it in a corner, as described above, then construct a built-in wardrobe between the shower and the opposite wall.

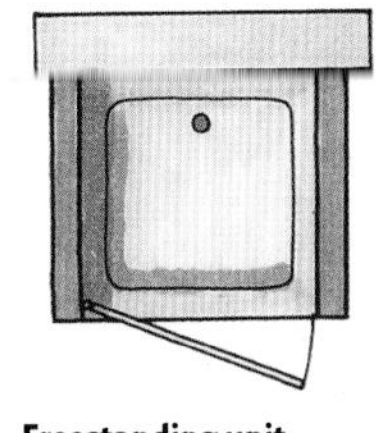

Freestanding unit
Two new partitions.

Freestanding unit
Proprietary enclosure.

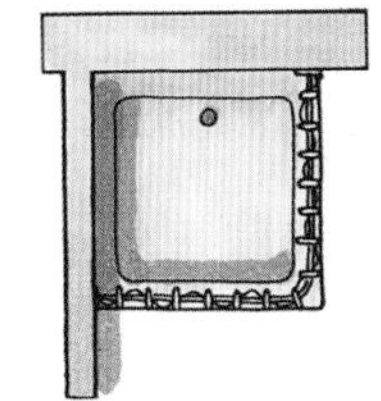

Corner site
Enclosed by a curtain.

Corner site
Partition and curtain.

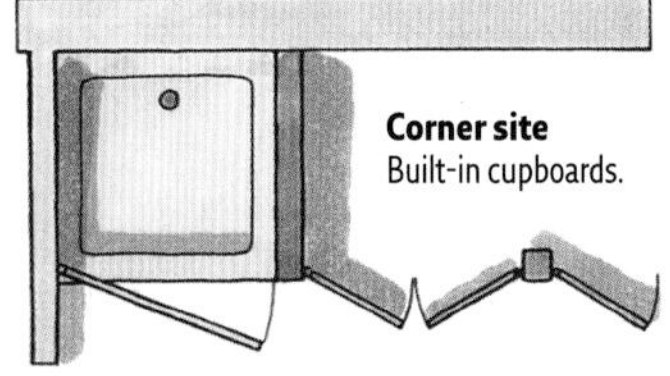

Corner site
Built-in cupboards.

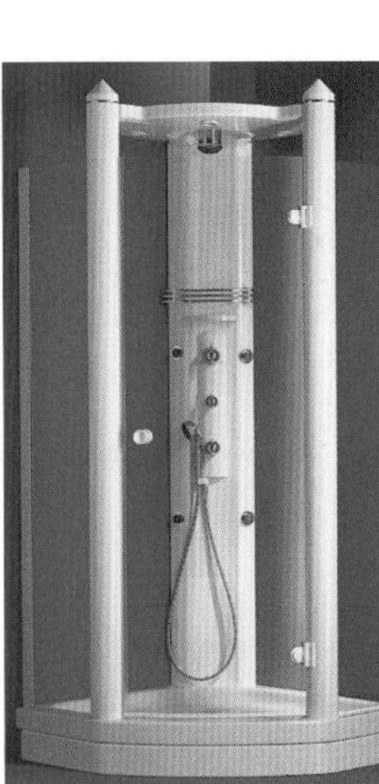

Proprietary unit
A typical kit includes a plastic corner pillar that conceals the plumbing. The kit comes complete with shower set, tray and enclosure.

Hiding the plumbing

One solution for concealing the pipes is to install a proprietary shower cubicle with a plastic pillar in the corner that is designed to hide the plumbing and house the mixer and adjustable sprayhead (see left).

If you erect a stud partition, then you can run the pipework between the studs. Screw exterior-grade plywood or cement-based wallboard on the inside of the frame for a tiled finish, or use prefinished uPVC bathroom wall panelling.

Mount the shower mixer and sprayhead. Finish the inside with ceramic tiles, then seal the shower tray joints with silicone sealant. It's easier to connect the plumbing to the shower mixer before you enclose the outside of the partition.

Cut decorative wall panelling to size, then fix using screws and the plastic corner profiles supplied. Finally, seal all joints with silicone sealant.

1 Ceramic tiles
2 Timber cover strip
3 Exterior-grade plywood, wallboard or wall panelling
4 Shower mixer
5 Pipework
6 Timber frame
7 Plasterboard
8 Shower tray

Running plumbing through a partition
Conceal pipework in a simple timber partition covered with ceramic tiles or panelling.

Shower trays

Shower trays are made from a variety of materials, but plastic trays are the most common. Lightweight ABS plastic trays tend to flex slightly in use, so it's particularly important to seal the edges carefully, using a good-quality silicone sealant (don't rely on grout). GRP trays are more substantial, while resin-bonded trays or ceramic trays are very solid.

The majority of shower trays are between 750 and 900mm (2ft 6in and 3ft) square. You can also buy trays that have a cut-off or rounded corner to save floor space. Larger rectangular trays provide more elbow room.

Most trays are designed to stand on a timber or masonry frame so that they lie about 150mm (6in) off the ground. Some have adjustable feet or a metal underframe helping to provide a fall for the waste pipe. Rigid types can be bedded in mortar. A plinth screwed across the front of the tray hides the underframe and plumbing, and provides access to the trap for servicing. Some shower trays are intended to be sunk, so that they are flush with the floor.

Enclosing a shower

A shower in a cubicle or over a bath needs to be provided with some means of preventing water spraying out onto the floor. Hanging a waterproof fabric curtain on curtain track or a tubular shower rail across the entrance is the simplest and cheapest method, but it is not really suitable for a power shower.

For a more satisfactory enclosure, use a metal-framed glass or plastic panelled unit. Hinged, sliding, or concertina doors operate within an adjustable frame fixed to the top edge of the tray and the side walls. Bed the lower track onto mastic to make a waterproof joint with the tray and, once you have completed the enclosure, run mastic between the framework and the surrounding walls.

SEE ALSO >Bathroom planning 14, Primers 40–41, Tiling 95–101, Glass-blocks 140, Stud partitions 151–3

Gravity-fed showers

Use the procedure below as a guide to the stage-by-stage installation of a cubicle and conventional gravity-fed shower. Check the instructions for your shower unit for any special requirements.

Ideally, you should run an independent cold supply from the storage tank; and for the hot supply, take a branch pipe directly from the vent pipe above the hot-water cylinder. Fit isolating gate valves in both supplies. Use the methods described earlier in this chapter for fitting plastic or copper supply pipes and drainage, in conjunction with the manufacturer's recommendations.

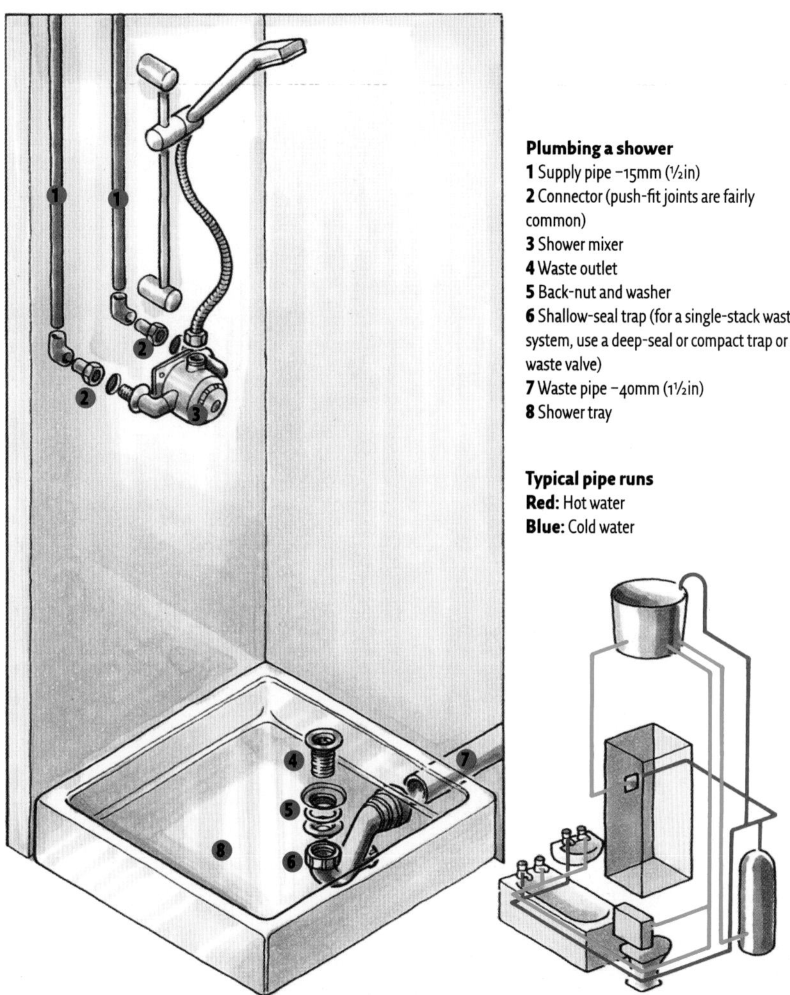

Plumbing a shower
1 Supply pipe –15mm (½in)
2 Connector (push-fit joints are fairly common)
3 Shower mixer
4 Waste outlet
5 Back-nut and washer
6 Shallow-seal trap (for a single-stack waste system, use a deep-seal or compact trap or a waste valve)
7 Waste pipe –40mm (1½in)
8 Shower tray

Typical pipe runs
Red: Hot water
Blue: Cold water

Fit the waste outlet in the shower tray and connect a shallow-seal trap, as for a bath. Alternatively, fit a compact trap that has a removable grill for easy cleaning.

Install the tray and run a 40mm (1½in) waste pipe to a hopper or soil stack. In the latter case, you must use a deep-seal trap or a suitable compact trap. Alternatively, you can fit a running trap or a waste valve. Check with your Building Control Officer.

To enclose a shower situated in a corner (see opposite), construct a stud partition on one side and line the inner surface with plywood or wallboard.

Cut a hole in the board for a flush-fitting shower mixer; or drill holes for the supply pipes to a surface-mounted model. Tile the inside of the cubicle with ceramic tiles, using waterproof adhesive and grout.

Fit the shower mixer and sprayhead to the tiled surface. Connect the pipework and run it back to the point of connection with the water supplies. Fit an isolating valve to each of the supply pipes, then turn off the water and make the connections.

Installing an electric shower

If you're installing an instantaneous shower in the cubicle, run both the 10mm² electrical supply cable and a single 15mm (½in) pipe from the rising main through the stud partition.

Fit a non-return valve and an isolating valve in the pipe. Drill two holes in the wall just behind the shower unit for the pipe and cable. Join a threaded or compression connector to the supply pipe, whichever is appropriate for the water inlet built into the shower unit.

Read the section in this book about wiring an instantaneous shower, especially the Building Regulations that relate to electrical wiring.

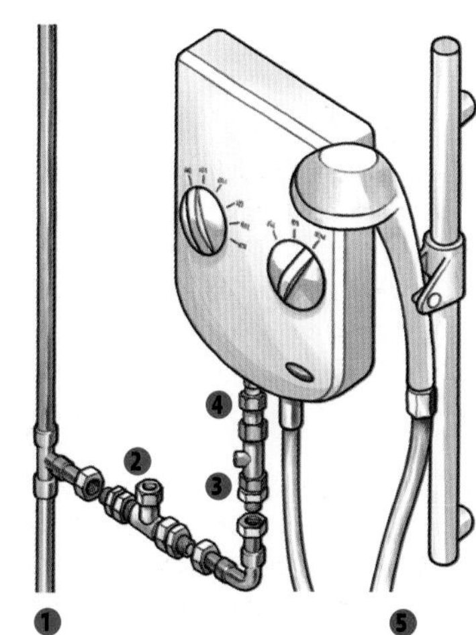

Plumbing an instantaneous shower
1 15mm (½in) pipe
2 Isolating valve
3 Non-return valve
4 Tap connector from rising main
5 Hose to sprayhead

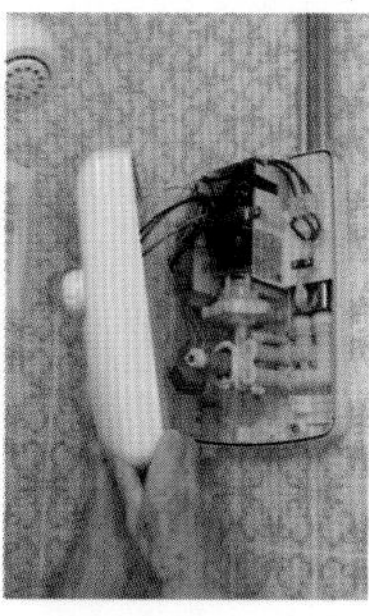

Fix the cover
Attach the cover to protect the inner workings

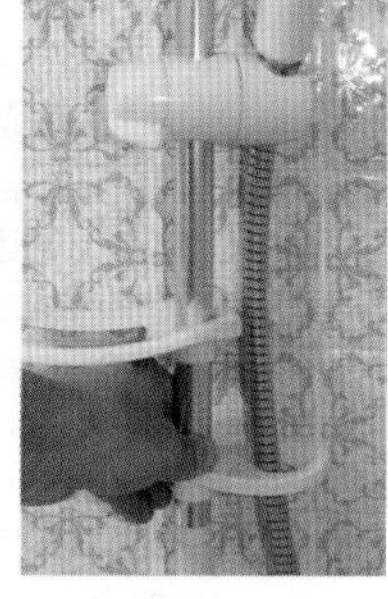

Hose restraint
A hose restraint stops the head from falling into the bath

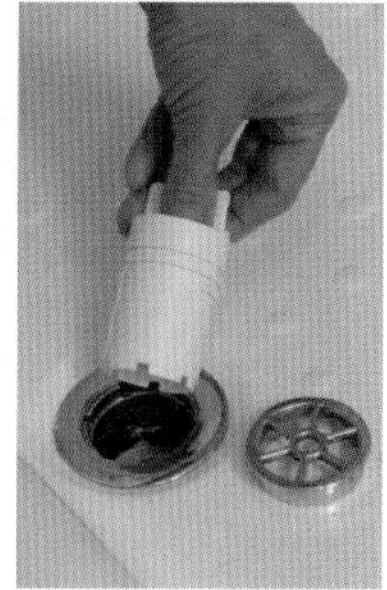

Cleaning compact traps
Compact shower traps have a dip tube for easy cleaning

SEE ALSO > Building Regulations on electrical wiring 284, Wiring electric showers 316, Turning off the water 348, Connecting pipes 361–2, 365

Installing power showers

If you're installing a brand-new power shower, it probably pays to opt for an all-in-one model with an integral pump. If you are merely unhappy with the performance of your existing shower, then it's much cheaper and more convenient to plumb in a separate pump.

Whichever system you choose, check that your cold-water storage tank is big enough - typically a minimum capacity of 115 litres (25 gallons). Some manufacturers also recommend a hot water cylinder with a minimum 161 litres (35 gallons) capacity.

Both types of shower need an electrical supply to drive the pump. The pump is wired to a ring main by means of a switched fused connection unit installed outside the bathroom, or you can fit a ceiling-mounted double-pole switch inside the bathroom. The shower pump switches on automatically as soon as the shower valve is operated.

Fitting an all-in-one shower

To plumb a shower with an integral pump, you can run dedicated hot and cold supplies to the shower, as when fitting a gravity-fed shower. Alternatively, you can connect the hot-water supply directly to the cylinder by using a cylinder flange. An Essex flange is connected to the side of the cylinder (**1**); but to avoid cutting into the cylinder wall, fit a Surrey flange that screws into the vent-pipe connection on top of the cylinder (**2**). Fit gate valves in the hot and cold pipes, so you're able to isolate them for servicing.

All-in-one showers are prone to vibration: on a timber-frame wall this can create considerable noise. Isolate the unit by mounting it on rubber tap washers slid over the fixing screws.

All tiling and grouting needs to be completed before mounting the shower on the wall.

Typical pipe runs
Red: Hot water
Blue: Cold water

Power shower with integral pump

Installing the shower

Drain the cold-water tank and drill a hole for a tank-connector fitting. Fit a gate valve close to the tank and run the pipe to the shower unit. Turn off the cold supply to the hot-water cylinder, and then open the hot taps in the bathroom to drain a small amount of water from the cylinder. Unscrew the vent-pipe connector (**3**) and catch any water left in the pipe with a towel.

Wrap PTFE tape around the threads of the Surrey flange, then screw it into the cylinder. Connect the original vent pipe to the top of the flange and run the hot supply for the shower from the side connection (**4**). Open the gate valves briefly to flush the pipes.

1 Essex flange

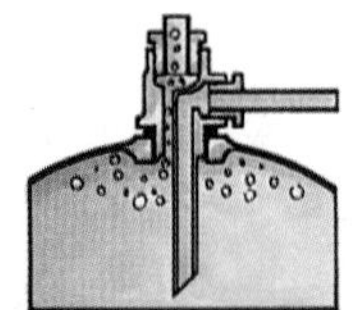

2 Surrey flange

3 Unscrew vent-pipe

4 Attach hot supply

Run the electrical cable to the shower, ready for connection. (See BUILDING REGULATIONS ON ELECTRICAL WIRING.)

Mount the shower unit, using the screws provided and taking care not to bore into pipes or cable.

Connect the pipes to the unit and connect up the electrical cable to the terminal block inside the unit. Metal pipes must be bonded to earth.

Installing a booster pump

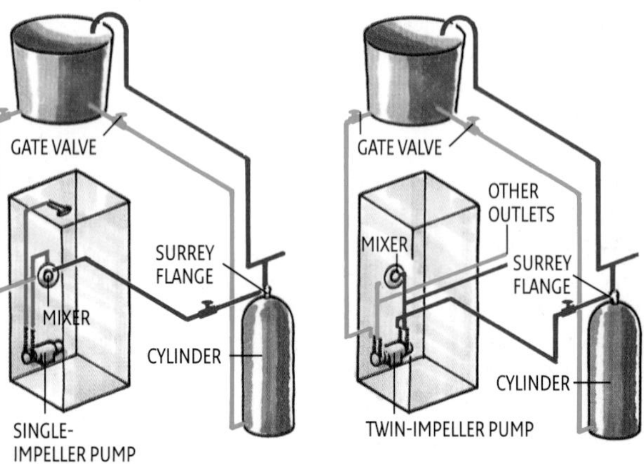

1 Single-impeller pump
Boosts ready-mixed water.

2 Twin-impeller pump
Can boost other outlets as well as a shower.

Fitting an electric pump can improve the performance of an existing shower. If you have access to the pipe running from the mixer to the sprayhead, you can install a single-impeller pump that boosts ready-mixed hot and cold water (**1**). If the pipework is embedded behind tiling, install a twin-impeller pump in the supply pipes before the mixer. The same twin-impeller pump can boost the supply to other outlets in the bathroom, too. (**2**).

Positioning the pump

Place the pump somewhere convenient for servicing, perhaps on the floor under the bath, behind a screw-fixed panel - but not where it will be splashed with water. Stand it on a foam mat or pads to reduce the noise from vibration, and don't screw it to the floor. Most pumps come with push-fit flexible connectors to join pipes to the pump and help to prevent vibration.

Connect up the pump to a switched fused connection unit (see top left). In use, the pump is activated automatically by flow switches.

The basic plumbing is identical to that described for installing an all-in-one shower. Flush the pipes before you switch on the pump.

SEE ALSO > Building Regulations on electrical wiring 284, Bathroom safety 286, Zones for bathrooms 287, Fused connection units 310, Turning off the water 348, Connecting pipes 361–2, 365, Storage tanks 391

Plumbing a bidet

A bidet is primarily for washing the genitals and lower body, though it can double as a footbath. Because of the stringent requirements of the Water Regulations, installing some types can be an expensive and time-consuming procedure. However, simpler versions are plumbed in just like a washbasin.

Rim-supply bidet

This type delivers warm water to the basin via a hollow rim, making it warmer to sit on. A douche spray provides the water for washing from the bottom of the basin. A device in the centre of the mixer tap diverts water from the rim to the sprayhead.

Because the sprayhead is submerged when the basin is full, it's possible that dirty water could flow back into the supply pipes. To prevent any risk of contamination, the Water Regulations lay down strict rules about how the bidet is plumbed in. There are several methods allowed, but in general the appliance must have a dedicated cold water supply running directly from the storage tank, with no other connections to it. The hot-water supply must be independent and connected to the vent pipe above the cylinder. It's essential to check with your water supplier before installing a bidet.

Over-rim-supply bidet

This type of bidet is simply a low-level basin. It is fitted with individual hot and cold taps or a basin mixer, and has a built-in overflow running to the waste outlet in the basin. The disadvantage of an over-rim bidet is that the rim is cold to sit on.

Installing the bidet

When plumbing an over-rim-supply bidet, use exactly the same procedures, pipes and connectors described for plumbing a washbasin. Fit the taps, waste outlet and trap, then use a spirit level to position the bidet before fixing it to the floor with non-corrosive screws and rubber washers. Supply the hot and cold taps with branch pipes from the existing bathroom plumbing, and take the waste pipe to the hopper or stack.

When attaching the bidet set and trap to a rim-supply appliance, follow the manufacturer's instructions. Screw the bidet to the floor before running 15mm (½in) supply pipes and a 32mm (1¼in) waste according to the Water Regulations (see below). Connect the cold supply to the tank at the same level as the existing supply pipe.

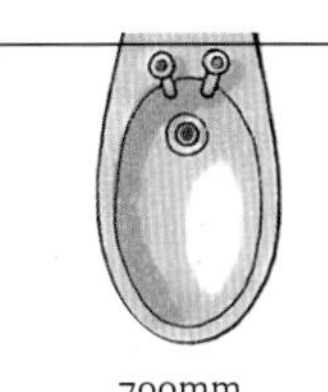

Space for a bidet
When planning the position of a bidet, allow sufficient knee room on each side – about 700mm (2ft 4in) overall.

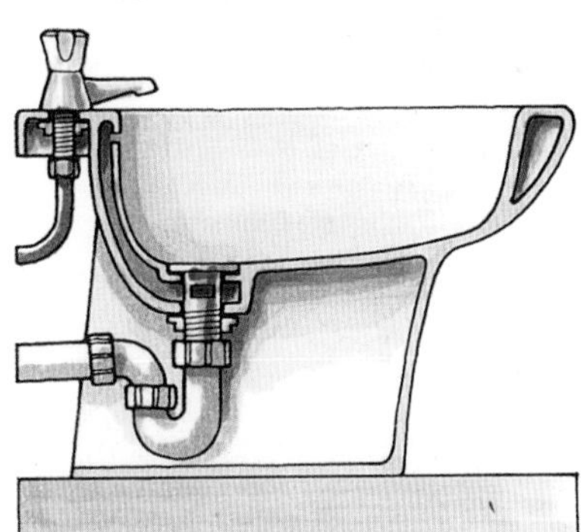

Over-rim-supply bidet
This type of bidet is simple to install. Follow the same procedure as for a washbasin.

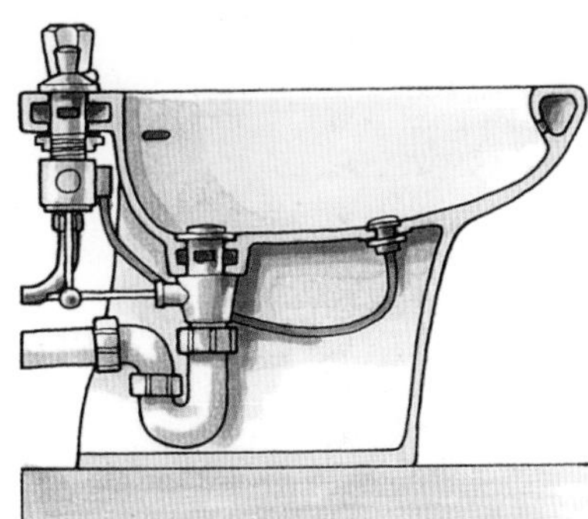

Rim-supply bidet
The installation of this type of bidet is complicated by the submerged douche spray. Independent plumbing is essential, as is a special mixer set to comply with the Water Regulations.

Plumbing an over-rim-supply bidet
1 Tap
2 Tap back-nut and washer
3 Tap connector
4 Supply pipe –15mm (½in)
5 Waste outlet
6 Waste back-nut and washer
7 Trap
8 Waste pipe –32mm (1¼in)

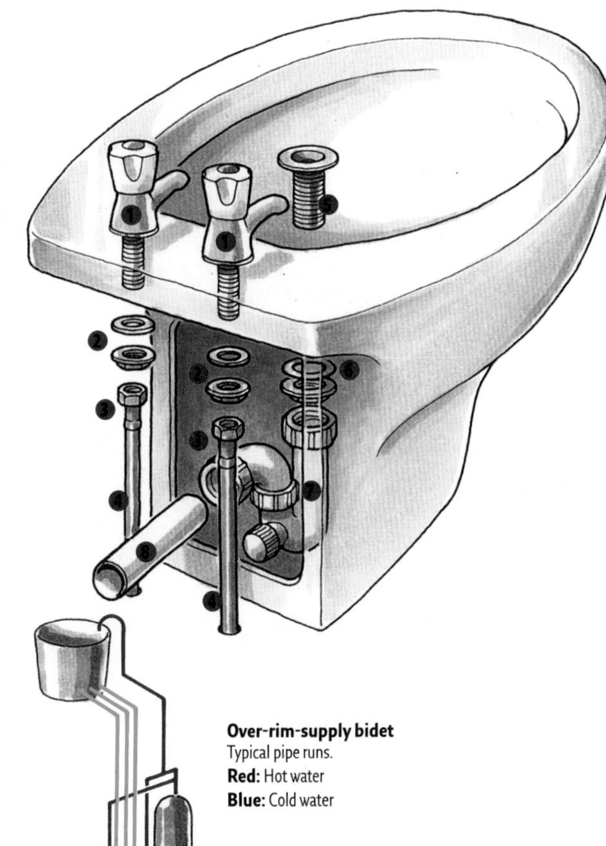

Over-rim-supply bidet
Typical pipe runs.
Red: Hot water
Blue: Cold water

SEE ALSO > Bathroom planning 14, Connecting pipes 361–2, 365, Washbasins 372–3, Taps 370–71, Tank supply 391

Kitchen sinks

If your ambition is to re-create a period-style kitchen, you may want a reproduction Butler or Belfast fire-clay sink with a separate teak or ceramic draining board. Alternatively, you could choose a stainless-steel sink top incorporating one or more bowls and drainer in a single pressing. You can match the colours in your kitchen with plastic, resin, ceramic, or one-piece moulded sink/worktop combinations in a wide variety of styles.

Choosing a kitchen sink

Choose the sink to make the best use of available space and to suit the style of your kitchen. If you don't have an automatic dishwasher, the kitchen sink must be large enough to cope with a considerable volume of washing-up (don't forget to allow for larger items, such as baking trays and oven racks). In addition, check that the bowl is deep enough to allow you to fill a bucket from the kitchen tap.

If space allows, select a unit with two bowls. If you plan to install a waste-disposal unit, one of the bowls will need to have a waste outlet of the appropriate size. Some sink units have a small bowl designed for waste disposal.

A double drainer is another useful feature; if there's no space, allow at least some room to the side of the bowl, to avoid mixing soiled and clean crockery.

One-piece sink tops are generally made to modular sizes to fit standard kitchen base units. However, many sinks are designed to be set into a continuous worktop – which offers greater flexibility in size, shape and, above all, positioning.

Inset stainless-steel sink
This one-and-a-half bowl unit has provision for a waste-disposal unit and is designed to be inset into a worktop.

Belfast or Butler sink
A period style still popular. Made of enamelled fireclay, it is deep and practical. Ceramic drainers are available to match.

Kitchen taps

Except for being somewhat taller, kitchen taps are comparable in style to those used for washbasins. They also incorporate similar mechanisms and are fitted using the same methods.

A kitchen mixer, however, has an additional feature: drinking water is supplied to it from the rising main, whereas the hot water usually comes from the same storage cylinder that supplies all the other hot taps in the house. A sink mixer should have separate waterways to isolate the one supply from the other until the water emerges from the spout; otherwise, you must have special check valves to prevent possible contamination of your drinking water.

If you are fitting a double-bowl sink, choose a mixer with a swivelling spout. Some sink mixers have a hot-rinse spray attachment for removing food scraps from crockery and saucepans.

Many mixer taps are supplied with small-bore copper or flexible tail pipes, which are joined to the supply pipes by a compression-joint or push-fit reducer.

Accessories for a kitchen sink

You can buy a variety of accessories to fit most kitchen sinks, including a hardwood or laminated-plastic chopping board that drops neatly into the rim of the bowl or drainer, and a selection of plastic-dipped wire baskets for rinsing vegetables or draining crockery.

Pump-action dispensers for soap and washing-up liquid rid the sink of plastic bottles and soap dishes.

Sink units and taps

There's a wide range of kitchen sinks and taps available for the domestic market. Steel, enamel, resin, ceramic, double, single, plain, coloured – a huge choice confronts you when you are planning your kitchen. A cross section of popular sinks, accessories and taps is shown below to assist you in making your decision.

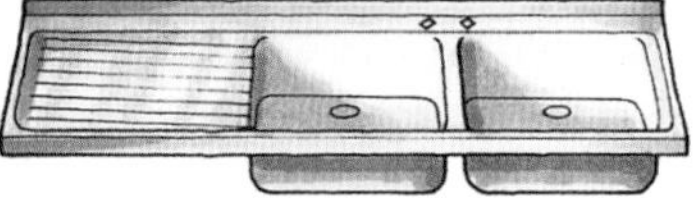

Double bowl with left-hand drainer

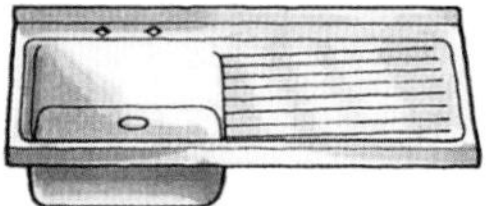

Single bowl with right-hand drainer

Inset double-bowl unit

Inset unit with waste-disposal bowl

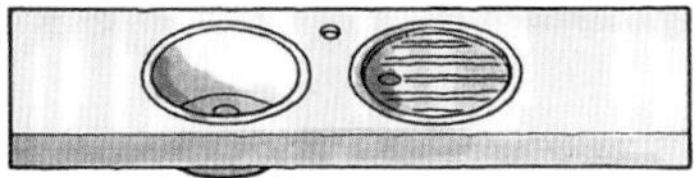

Individual sink and drainer

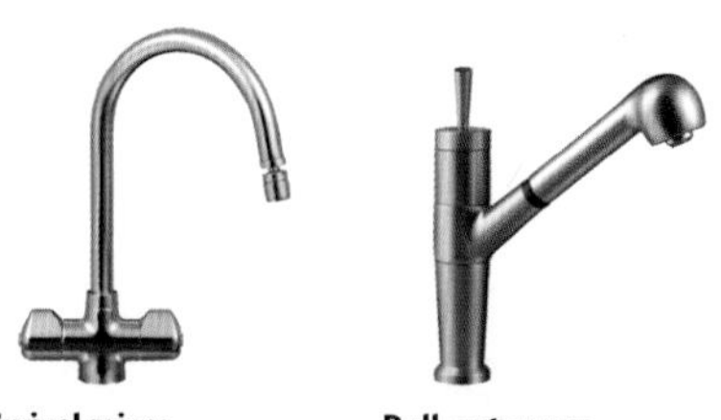

Swivel mixer **Pull-out spray**

Single-lever tap

Pot filler

SEE ALSO > Kitchen planning 15, Taps 370–71

Installing a sink

The trend for coloured sinks has given way to practical stainless steel. Another alternative is ceramic or Corian acrylic polymer, which incorporates the sink into a seamless worktop. This is favoured where hygiene is a critical issue since it does away with the crevices that can harbour bacteria.

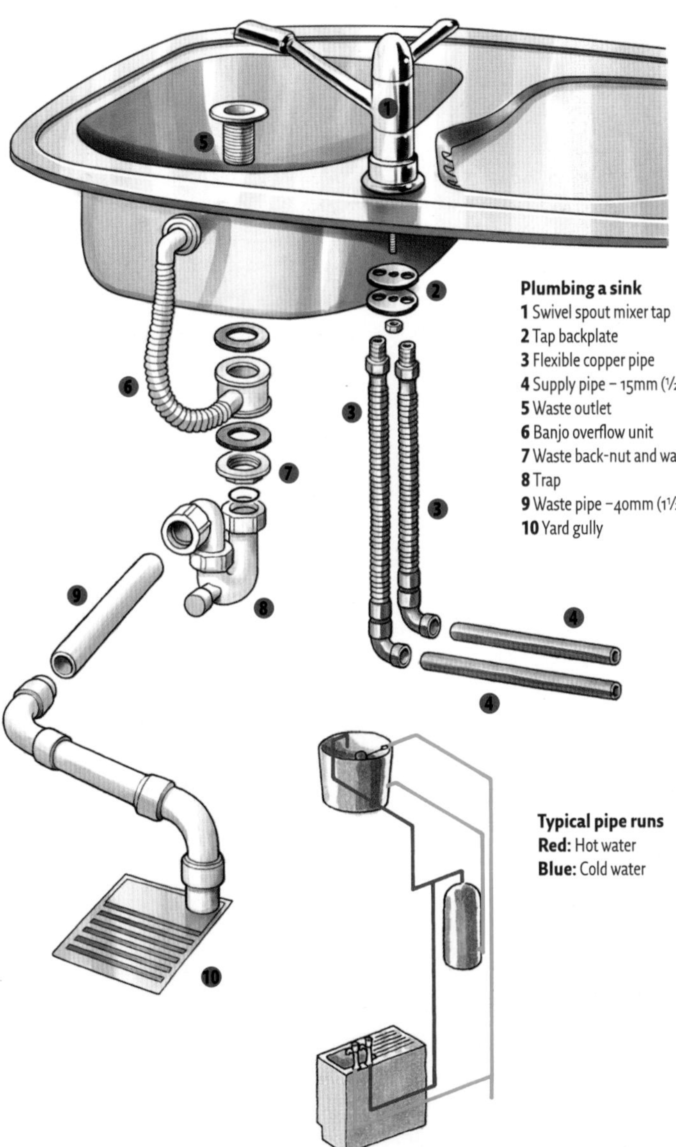

Plumbing a sink
1 Swivel spout mixer tap
2 Tap backplate
3 Flexible copper pipe
4 Supply pipe – 15mm (½in)
5 Waste outlet
6 Banjo overflow unit
7 Waste back-nut and washer
8 Trap
9 Waste pipe –40mm (1½in)
10 Yard gully

Typical pipe runs
Red: Hot water
Blue: Cold water

Plumbing the sink

Fit the taps and the overflow/waste outlet to the new sink before you place the sink in position.

Turn off the water supply to the taps, then remove the old sink by dismantling the plumbing. Remove the old pipework unless you plan to adapt it.

Install the new sink on its base unit or worktop, using the fittings provided; then, if needed, seal the rim of the sink. Run a 15mm (½in) cold-water supply pipe from the rising main, and a branch pipe of the same size from the nearest hot-water pipe. Fit miniature isolating valves in both of the supply pipes and connect them to the taps with flexible copper-tap connectors.

Fit the trap and run a 40mm (1½in) waste pipe through the wall behind the base unit to the yard gully. According to current Water Regulations, the pipe has to pass through the grid covering the gully (see left) but must stop short of the water in the gully trap. You can adapt an existing grid quite easily by cutting out one corner with a sharp hacksaw.

Anti-siphon trap
If your trap gurgles as the sink empties, you could replace it with an anti-siphon trap. This draws in air to break the vacuum in the waste pipe. You can also get T-fittings that do the same job – these are placed just downstream of the existing trap.

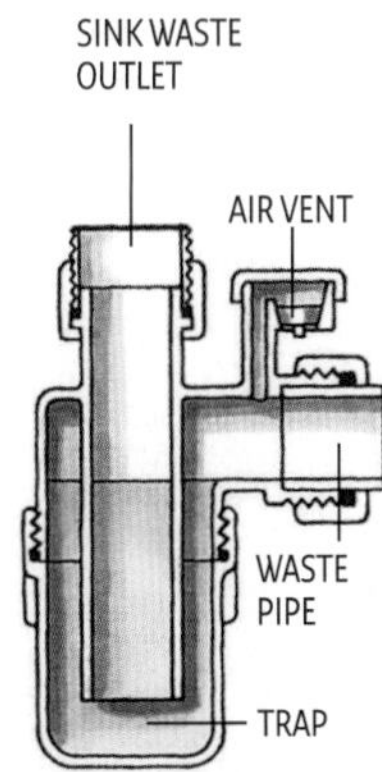

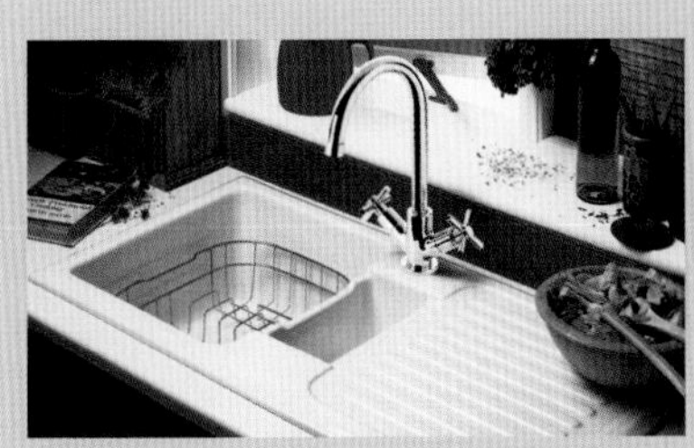

Plastic sinks are available in a wide range of styles and colours

Kitchen sink materials

Stainless steel is the most popular material for kitchen sinks as it resists heat and damage, wears well, is relatively cheap and can be formed into a wide variety of shapes. Being thin, it can be noisy in use, so sound-deadening pads are often applied to the underside.

Tough, heat-resistant plastic (encompassing a range of moulded materials) sinks come in a range of colours. The thick material is quiet in use. Sinks made from composite materials – often a mix of stone and resins – are becoming more popular for their looks and resilience, while there is still a place for traditional ceramic.

SEE ALSO > Miniature isolating valve 348, Tap connectors 360, Connecting pipes 361–2, 365, Overflow/waste 375

Washing machines

Washing machines and dishwashers are commonplace household appliances these days and they are pretty much identical in the way that they are plumbed in. They are attached by flexible hoses to a dedicated waste pipe or to the waste from the kitchen sink.

Waste-disposal units

A waste-disposal unit provides a hygienic method of dealing with soft food scraps – reserving the kitchen wastebin for dry refuse and bones.

The unit houses an electric motor that drives steel cutters or discs which grind up the food scraps into a fine slurry to be washed into the yard gully or soil stack. A continuous-feed model is operated by a manual, commonly pneumatic, switch: scraps are then fed into it while the cold tap is running. To prevent the unit being switched on accidentally, a batch-feed model cannot be operated until a removable plug is inserted in the sink waste outlet.

Waste-disposal units are generally designed to fit an 89mm (3½in) outlet in the base of the sink bowl.

With a sink waste outlet and seal in position, clamp a retaining collar to the outlet from under the sink and bolt or clip the unit housing to the collar.

The waste outlet from the unit itself fits a standard sink trap (not a bottle trap) and waste pipe. If the waste pipe runs to a yard gully, make sure it passes through the covering grid.

Wire the unit to a switched fused connection unit mounted above the worktop, out of the reach of children.

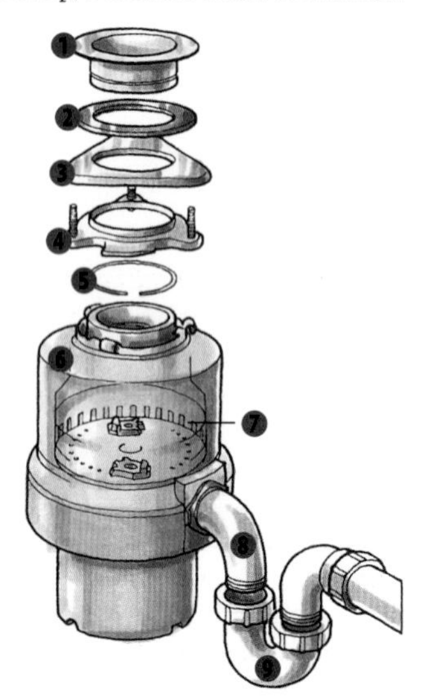

Waste-disposal unit
Units differ in detail, but the illustration shows the components typically used to clamp a waste-disposal unit to a sink.
1 Sink waste outlet
2 Gasket
3 Back-up ring
4 Collar
5 Snap ring
6 Unit housing
7 Cutters
8 Waste outlet
9 Trap

Many washing machines now have a cold fill only because lower wash temperatures mean that a hot fill is hardly ever required. Even if you have a hot and cold fill machine it can still be twinned into a single cold supply. This is often a more economical way of running the machine because you only heat the water required and do not have hot water standing in the supply pipes. In fact, a hot and cold fill machine might never get to use the hot water it draws because it fills from the water standing in the pipe, which is often cold. The water drawn from the heater or boiler is then simply sitting in the pipe going cold.

Water pressure

The machine's instructions should indicate what water pressure is required. If installed upstairs, make sure the drop from the storage tank to the machine is enough to provide the required pressure. Downstairs there is rarely any problem with pressure if you can take the cold water from the mains supply. However, check with your water supplier if you want to connect more than one machine.

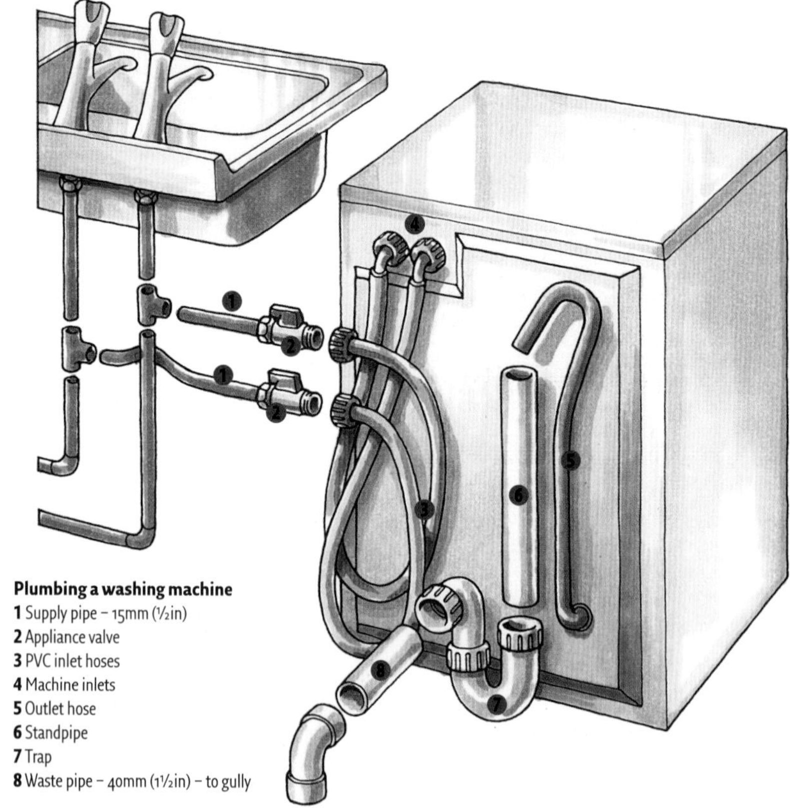

Plumbing a washing machine
1 Supply pipe – 15mm (½in)
2 Appliance valve
3 PVC inlet hoses
4 Machine inlets
5 Outlet hose
6 Standpipe
7 Trap
8 Waste pipe – 40mm (1½in) – to gully

Running the supply

Washing machines and dishwashers are supplied with PVC hoses to link the water inlets at the back of the appliance to service valves connected to the household plumbing. Using these valves, you can turn off the water when you need to service a machine, without having to disrupt the supply to the rest of the house. Select the type that provides the most practical method of connecting to the plumbing, depending on the location of the machine in relation to existing pipework.

SEE ALSO > Kitchen planning 15, Building Regulations on electrical wiring 284, Wiring kitchen appliances 311, Wiring a waste-disposal unit 311, Draining the system 348, Connecting pipes 361–2, 365, Storage tanks 391

Connecting to the supply

If you have to extend the plumbing to reach the machine, take branch pipes from the hot and cold pipes supplying the kitchen taps. Turn off the supply and drain down the pipe if possible, then cut through the existing pipes with a hacksaw (1) or pipe cutter, de-burr and clean the pipework, then insert a soldered or compression T-joint (2).

Add the branch pipes and terminate at a convenient position close to the machine. Then fit an appliance valve that has either a standard compression or push-fit joint for connecting to the pipework and a threaded outlet for the machine hose (3).

For branch pipes, use an in-line or elbow (right-angled) valve. A T-valve can be used where you have to break into an existing pipe running behind the machine. Self-cutting valves can also be used in this situation, but be aware that they may not provide enough flow for the appliance to function properly.

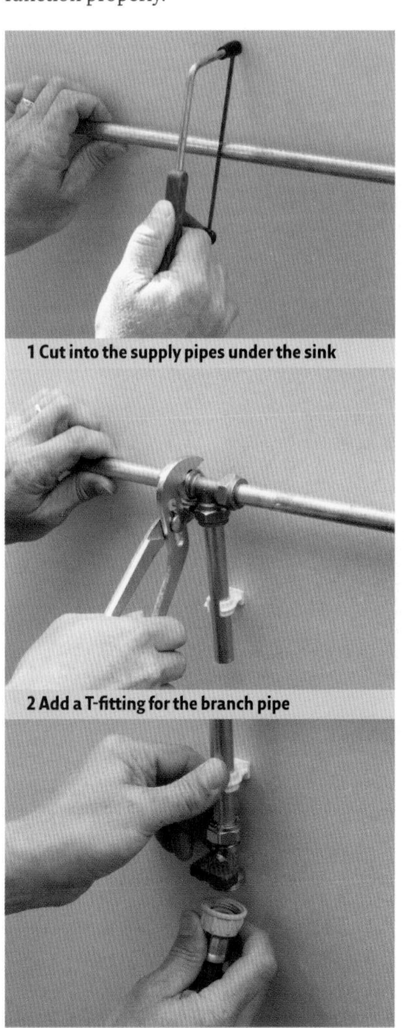

1 Cut into the supply pipes under the sink

2 Add a T-fitting for the branch pipe

3 Connect the hose to an appliance valve

Supplying drainage

The outlet hose from a dishwasher or washing machine must be connected to a waste system that will discharge the dirty water into either a yard gully or a single waste stack - not into a surface-water drain, where detergents could pollute rivers.

Standpipe and trap

The standard method, approved by all water suppliers, employs a vertical 40mm (1½in) plastic standpipe attached to a deep-seal trap (see opposite).

Most plumbing suppliers stock the standpipe, trap and wall fixings as a kit. The machine hose fits loosely into the open-ended pipe, so that dirty water won't be siphoned back into the machine. The machine manufacturer's instructions should tell you how to position the standpipe; in the absence of advice, ensure that the open end is at least 600mm (2ft) above the floor.

Cut a hole through the wall and run the waste pipe to a gully; or use a pipe boss to connect the waste to a drainage stack. Allow a minimum fall of 6mm (¼in) for every 300mm (1ft) of pipe run.

Draining to a sink trap

You can drain a washing machine to a sink trap that has a built-in spigot (1), but you should insert an in-line anti-siphon return valve in the machine's outlet hose. This is a small plastic device with a hose connector at each end (2). In order to drain a washing machine and dishwasher together, you will need a dual-spigot trap.

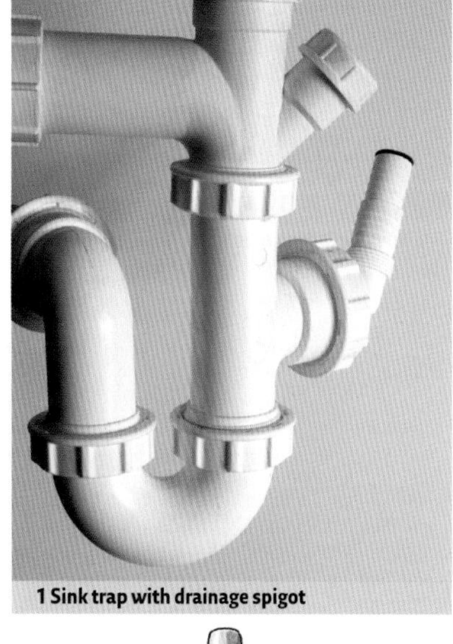

1 Sink trap with drainage spigot

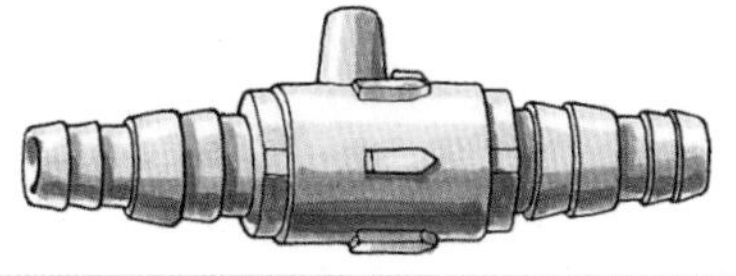

2 In-line anti-siphon hose valve

Appliance valves
Typical valves used to connect dishwashers and washing machines to the water supply.

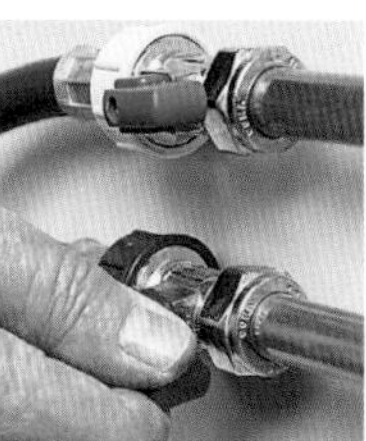

Preventing a flood

Overflowing dishwashers and washing machines can cause a great deal of damage in just a few minutes - particularly if the appliance is plumbed into an upstairs flat and water is able to find its way through the building.

Air-inlet valves

Most overflows occur simply because the water backs up the waste pipe and spills out over the standpipe or sink.

A sealed waste system succeeds in overcoming this problem - since it does away with the air gap that allows the water to overflow. The anti-vacuum function is formed, instead, by a fitting that incorporates a small air-inlet valve, which stops the waste pipe siphoning the machine. The discharge hose from the machine is connected to the nozzle of the vent fitting, and a length of 40mm (1½in) waste pipe is inserted between the fitting and the washing machine trap under the sink.

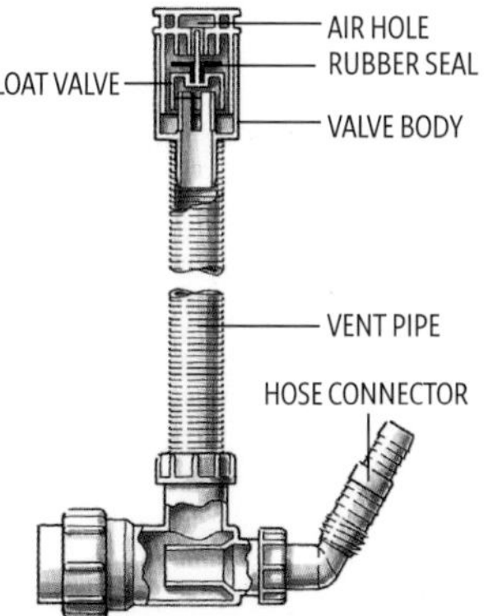

Anti-siphon devices

The standpipe-and-trap method of draining domestic appliances prevents back-siphonage by venting the pipe to the air, but there are other ways to deal with the problem. If an existing 32 or 40mm (1¼ or 1½in) waste pipe runs behind the machine, for example, you can attach a hose connector that incorporates a non-return valve to eliminate reverse flow. Connectors are available with short spigots (above), or can be attached to a standpipe.

Fitting an anti-siphon device

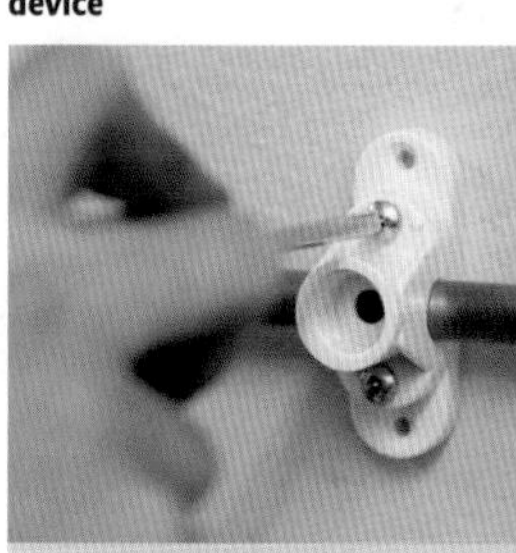

1 Clamp saddle over supply pipe

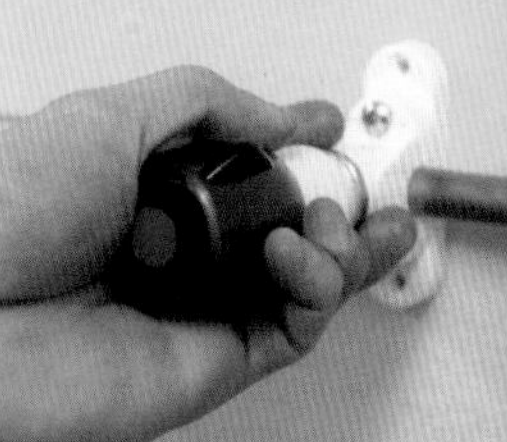

2 Screw the self-cutting valve in

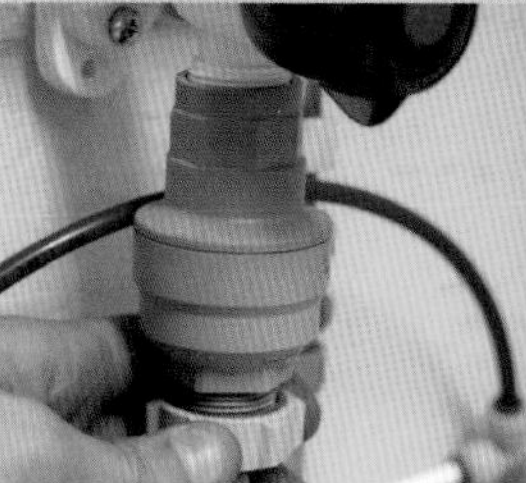

3 Attach device and machine hose

SEE ALSO > Cutting through a wall 369, Connecting pipes 361–2, 365

Water softeners

Harmful impurities are removed from the water supply, but the amount of minerals absorbed from the ground determines whether water is hard or soft. Rocky terrain gives rise to surface-run water, which is naturally soft – but where water runs through the ground, rather than over it, the higher mineral content produces hard water.

Installing a water softener

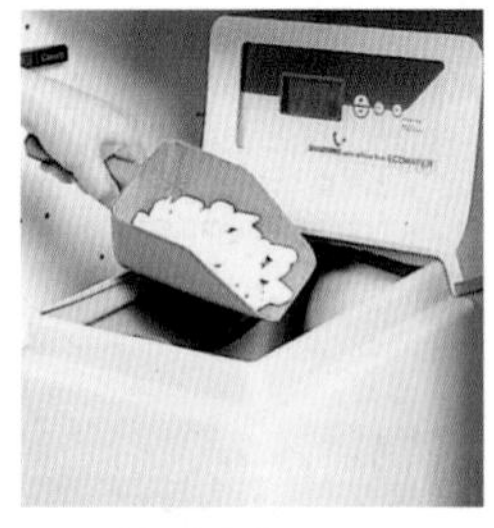

Water softener
A domestic unit, which fits neatly beneath the worktop, requires topping up with salt.

Installing a water softener may appear to be fairly complicated since it involves a great deal of joint making – both to fit the valves and branch pipes that supply and bypass the softener and to include the fittings that are necessary to comply with the Water Regulations.

The bypass assembly allows for the unit to be isolated for servicing while maintaining the supply of water to the rest of the house. In addition, you must install a branch pipe before the assembly, in order to supply unsoftened drinking water to the kitchen sink. Supply your garden tap from the same pipe – there's no need to waste softened water on the garden.

Install a non-return valve in the system, to prevent the reverse flow of salty water. A pressure-reducing valve may also be required (check with your water supplier). You will need a draincock, in order to empty the rising main. Some manufacturers supply an installation kit that includes all the necessary equipment. You will have to provide drainage in the form of a standpipe and trap, as for a washing machine.

Wire the water softener to a switched 3amp fused connection unit.

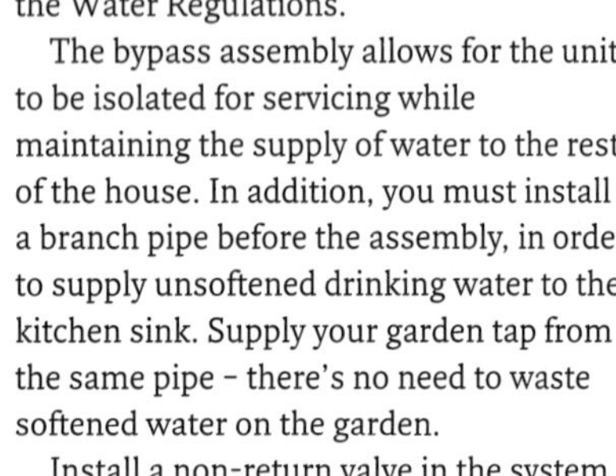

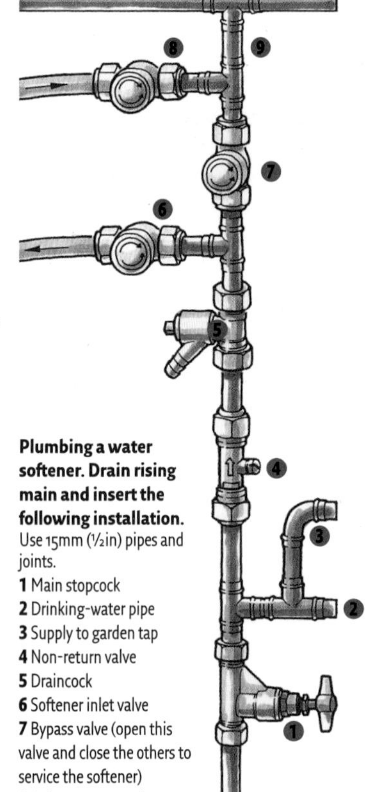

Plumbing a water softener. Drain rising main and insert the following installation.
Use 15mm (½in) pipes and joints.
1 Main stopcock
2 Drinking-water pipe
3 Supply to garden tap
4 Non-return valve
5 Draincock
6 Softener inlet valve
7 Bypass valve (open this valve and close the others to service the softener)
8 Softener return valve
9 Rising main

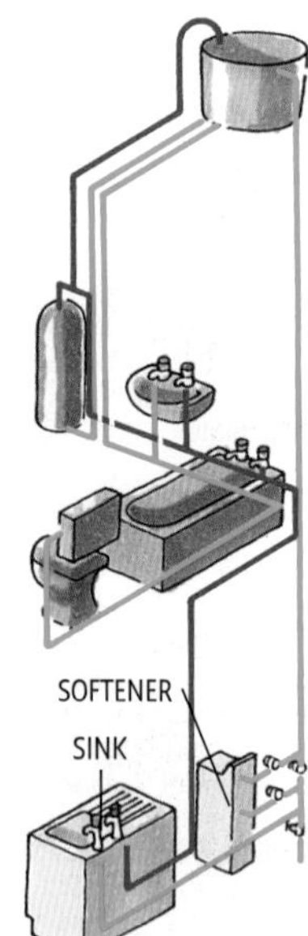

Typical pipe runs
A domestic system incorporating a softener.
Red: Hot water
Blue: Cold water

Domestic softeners

Water softeners work on the principle of ion exchange. The incoming water flows through a compartment containing a synthetic resin that absorbs scale-forming calcium and magnesium ions and releases sodium ions in their place.

After a period of about three or four days, the resin is unable to absorb any more mineral salts and the softener automatically flushes the compartment with a saline solution to regenerate the resin. Topping up with salt is required at intervals of perhaps two to three months. The softener is fitted with a timer so that you can programme regeneration when water consumption is at its lowest, usually during the early hours of the morning.

The unit must be connected to the rising main at the point where the water supply enters the house. For this reason, domestic softeners are usually designed to fit under a kitchen worktop.

Lime scale effects

The more obvious consequences of hard water are the discoloration of baths and basins, blocked sprayheads, blemished stainless-steel surfaces and furred-up kettles. Most people resign themselves to living with these effects – but they can be reduced, or even eliminated altogether, by installing a water softener.

Outside taps

A bib tap situated on an outside wall is convenient for attaching a hose for a lawn sprinkler or for washing the car. To comply with the Water Regulations, a double-seal non-return (check) valve must be incorporated in the plumbing, to prevent contaminated water being drawn back into the system. Provide a means of shutting off the water and draining the pipework during winter, and keep the outside pipe run as short as possible.

A self-cutting stoptap combining a non-return valve (below) simplifies the job.

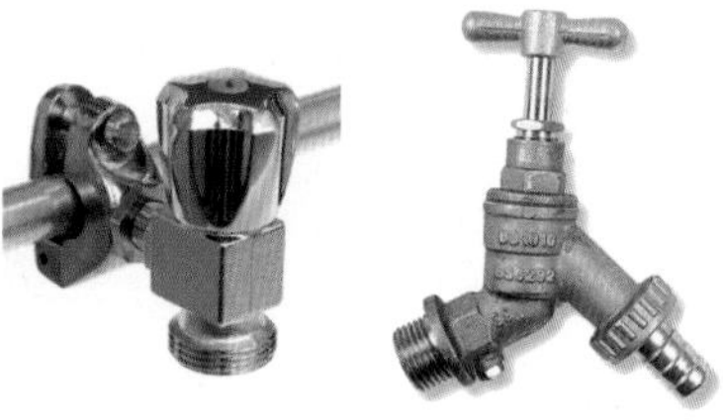

A self-cutting stoptap incorporating a non-return valve (left) can be used to feed a garden tap (right)

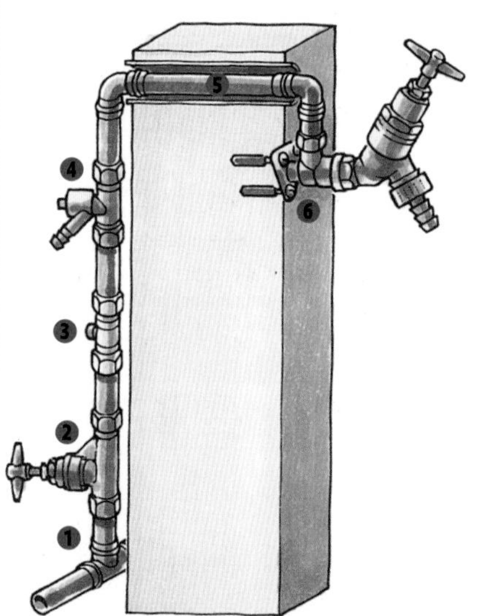

Pipes and fittings to supply a garden tap

Turn off and drain the mains supply. Fit a T-joint (1) to run the supply to the tap. Run a short length of pipe to a convenient position for another stopcock (2) or service valve, and for the non-return valve (3) if the tap doesn't include one, making sure that the arrows marked on both fittings point in the direction of flow. Fit a draincock (4) after this point. Run a pipe through the wall inside a length of plastic overflow (5), so that any leaks will be detected quickly and will not soak the masonry. Wrap PTFE tape around the bib-tap thread, then screw it into a wall plate attached to the masonry outside (6).

SEE ALSO > Building Regulations on electrical wiring 284, Fused connection units 310, Wiring kitchen appliances 311, Draining the system 348, Connecting pipes 361–2, 365, PTFE tape 362, Washing machines 388

Storage tanks

The cold-water storage tank, normally situated in the roof space, supplies the hot-water cylinder and all the cold taps in the house, other than the one in the kitchen that is used for drinking water. An old house may still have a galvanized-steel tank, which will eventually corrode, and, although it's possible to patch it, it makes sense to replace it before a serious leak develops. A circular 227 litre (50 gallon) polythene tank is a popular replacement, because it can be folded to pass through a narrow hatch to the loft.

Removing an old tank

Switch off all water-heating appliances, then close the stopcock on the rising main. Drain the storage tank by opening the cold taps in the bathroom.

Bail out the remaining water in the bottom of the tank, then use a spanner to dismantle the fittings connecting the float valve, distribution pipes and overflow to the tank. Use penetrating oil if the fittings are stiff with corrosion. Don't worry about damaging the old float valve as it's probably not worth using again.

The tank was probably put in the loft house before the roof structure was completed, so it almost certainly won't pass through the hatch. It would be too much of a job to cut it up, so just pull it to one side and leave it in the loft.

Prepare a firm base for the new tank by nailing stout planks across the joists, or lay a platform made from plywood 18mm (¾in) thick.

Plumbing a new tank

Once the new tank is in place, you can set about connecting the numerous pipes and fittings that are required.

Fitting the float valve

A float valve shuts off the flow of water from the rising main when the tank is full. Cut a hole for the float valve 75mm (3in) below the top of the tank. Slip a plastic washer onto the tail of the valve and pass it through the hole. Slide the reinforcing plate onto the tail, followed by another washer and a fixing nut, then tighten the fitting with the aid of two spanners.

Screw a tap connector onto the float valve, ready for connecting to the 15mm (½in) rising main.

Connecting the distribution pipes

The 22mm (¾in) pipes running to the cylinder and cold taps are attached by means of tank connectors – threaded inlets with a compression fitting for the pipework. Drill a hole for each tank connector, about 50mm (2in) above the bottom of the tank. Push the fittings through each hole, with one polythene washer on the inside. Wrap a couple of turns of PTFE tape around the threads, then fit the other washer. Screw the nut on, holding the tank connector to stop it turning. Don't overtighten the nut – or you will damage the washer, causing it to leak.

Take the opportunity to fit a gate valve to each distribution pipe, so you can cut off the supply of water without having to empty the tank.

Connecting the overflow

Drill a hole 25mm (1in) below the level of the float-valve inlet for the threaded connector of the overflow-pipe assembly. Pass the connector through the hole, fit a washer, and tighten its fixing nut on the inside of the tank. Fit the dip pipe and insect filter.

Attach a 22mm (¾in) plastic overflow pipe to the assembly. Run the pipe to the floor, then to the outside of the house, maintaining a continuous fall. The pipe must emerge in a conspicuous position, so that an overflow can be detected immediately. Clip the pipe to the roof timbers.

Modifying existing plumbing

Modify the rising main and distribution pipes to align with their fittings, then connect them with compression fittings. Don't use soldered joints near a plastic tank as there's a danger that heat could travel along the pipes and melt the tank. Clip all the pipework securely to the joists.

Open the main stopcock and check for leaks as the tank fills. Adjust the float arm to maintain a water level 25mm (1in) below the overflow outlet.

Adapt the vent pipe from the hot-water cylinder to pass through the hole in the lid. Finally, insulate the tank and pipework – but make sure there is no loft insulation under the cistern, as this will prevent warmth rising from below.

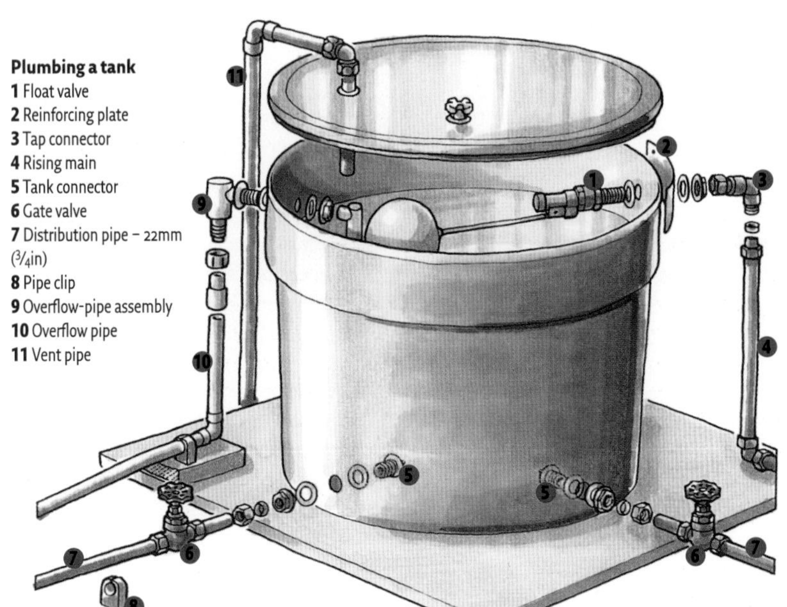

Plumbing a tank
1 Float valve
2 Reinforcing plate
3 Tap connector
4 Rising main
5 Tank connector
6 Gate valve
7 Distribution pipe – 22mm (¾in)
8 Pipe clip
9 Overflow-pipe assembly
10 Overflow pipe
11 Vent pipe

Tank cutters
Hire a tank cutter to bore holes in the tank for pipework. Some cutters are adjustable, so you can drill holes of different diameters. An alternative is to use a hole saw clamped to a drill bit.

Hole saw

Adjustable cutter

• **Bylaw 30 kits**
Make sure your new tank is supplied with a Bylaw 30 kit, to keep the water clean. This is a requirement of all water suppliers. The kit includes a close-fitting lid that excludes light and insects, and is fitted with a screened breather and a sleeved inlet for the vent pipe. In addition, there should be an overflow-pipe assembly that is screened to prevent insects crawling into the tank, a reinforcing plate to stiffen the cistern wall around the float valve, and an insulating jacket.

SEE ALSO > Insulation 362, Float valves 352–4, Adjusting a float arm 354, Gate valve 360, Tap connectors 360, Compression joints 362, Hot-water cylinders 392

Vented hot-water cylinders

In most houses, the hot water is heated and stored in a large copper cylinder situated in the airing cupboard. Cold water is fed to the base of the cylinder from the cold-water storage tank housed in the loft. As the water is heated, it rises to the top of the cylinder, where it is drawn off via a branch from the vent pipe to the hot taps. When the hot water is run off, it is replaced by cold water at the base of the cylinder, ready for heating.

Typical pipe runs
Red: Hot water
Blue: Cold water

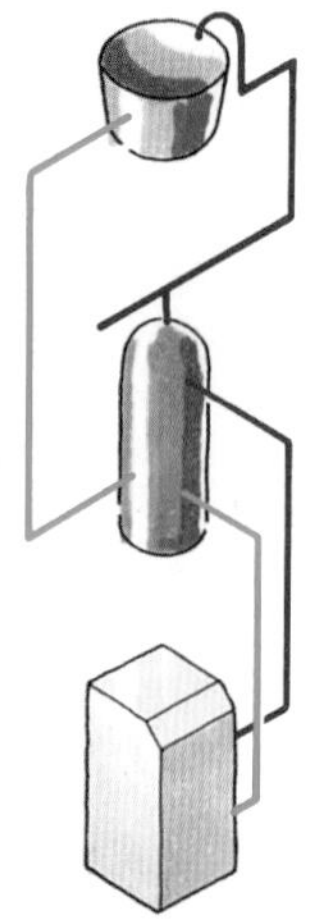

Direct water heating by means of a boiler

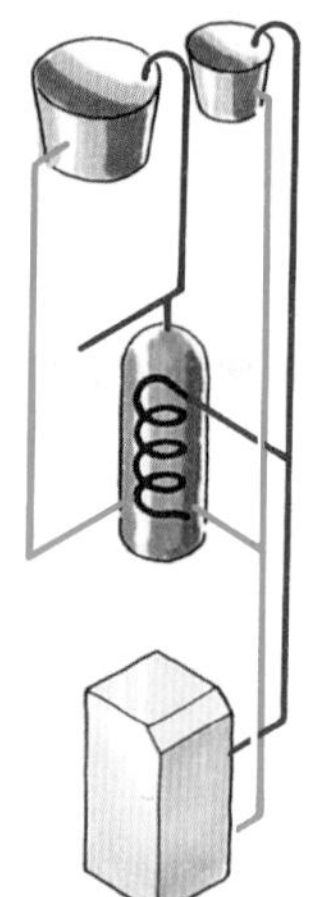

Indirect water heating employs the central-heating boiler

The vent pipe itself runs back to the loft, where it passes through the lid of the cold-water storage tank, with its open end just above the level of the water. The vent pipe provides a safe escape route for air bubbles and steam, should the system overheat.

When water is heated, it expands. The vent pipe accommodates some of this, but much of the water is forced back up the cold-feed pipe into the cold storage tank.

Methods of heating water

There are two different methods of heating the water in a vented hot-water cylinder: either directly - usually by means of electric immersion heaters - or indirectly, by a heat exchanger connected to the central-heating system.

Direct heating

Water heating can be accomplished solely by means of electric immersion heaters - either a single-element or double-element heater is fitted in the top of the cylinder, or there may be two individual side-entry heaters.

An alternative is for the water to be heated in a boiler, the sole purpose of which is to provide hot water for the cylinder. A cold-water pipe runs from the base of the cylinder to the boiler, where the water is heated; and it then returns to the top half of the cylinder.

Both methods are known as direct systems. In practice, a boiler-heated cylinder is generally fitted with an immersion heater as well, so that hot water can be supplied independently during the summer, when using the boiler would make the room where it is situated uncomfortably warm.

Indirect heating

When a house is centrally heated with radiators fed by a boiler, the water in the cylinder is usually heated indirectly by a heat exchanger.

Hot water from the boiler passes through the exchanger (a coiled tube within the cylinder), where the heat is transmitted to the stored water. The heat exchanger is part of a completely self-contained system, which has its own feed-and-expansion tank (a small storage tank in the loft) to top up the system. An open-ended vent pipe terminates over the same small tank.

The whole system is known as the primary circuit, and the pipes running from and back to the boiler are known as the primary flow and return. An indirect system is often supplemented with an immersion heater, to provide hot water during the summer months.

Direct cylinder
1 Vent pipe
2 Hot-water branch pipe
3 Lower immersion heater (provides hot water using cheaper night-rate electricity)
4 Upper immersion heater (used for daytime top-up heating only)
5 Cold-feed pipe
6 Draincock

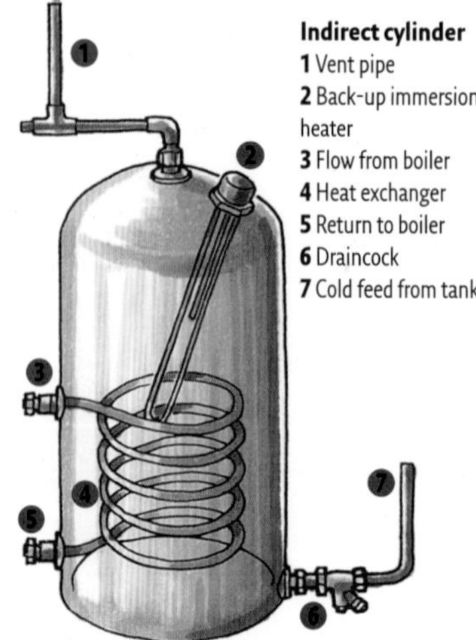

Indirect cylinder
1 Vent pipe
2 Back-up immersion heater
3 Flow from boiler
4 Heat exchanger
5 Return to boiler
6 Draincock
7 Cold feed from tank

Hot-water cylinders

The capacity of domestic cylinders normally ranges from about 114 litres (25 gallons) to 227 litres (50 gallons), although it is possible to obtain bigger cylinders. A cylinder with a capacity of between 182 and 227 litres (40 and 50 gallons) will store enough hot water to satisfy the needs of an average family for a whole day.

Some cylinders are made from thin, uninsulated copper and need to have a thick lagging jacket to reduce heat loss. However, for better performance use a Kite-marked factory-insulated cylinder that is precovered with a thick layer of foamed polyurethane.

Changing a cylinder

You may wish to replace an existing cylinder because it has sprung a leak, or because a larger one will allow you to take full advantage of cheap night-time electricity by storing more hot water. A simple replacement can sometimes be achieved without modifying the plumbing, but you'll have to adapt the pipework to fit a larger cylinder.

If you plan to install central heating at some point in the future, you can plumb in an indirect cylinder fitted with a double-element immersion heater and simply leave the heat-exchanging coil unconnected for the time being.

Place the new cylinder in position and check the existing pipework for alignment. Modify the pipes as need be, then make the connections, using PTFE tape to ensure that the threaded joints are watertight. Fit a draincock to the feed pipe from the tank, if there isn't one already installed. Fill the system and check for leaks before you heat the water and check again when the water is hot.

SEE ALSO > Lagging 257, Building Regulations on electrical wiring 284, Side-entry heaters 316, Replacing an element 317, Wiring immersion heaters 317, Draining the system 348, Connecting pipes 361–2, 365, Compression joints 362, PTFE tape 362

Unvented cylinders

An unvented cylinder supplies mains-pressure hot water throughout the house. This is achieved by connecting the cylinder directly to the rising main. Most manufacturers recommend a 22mm (3/4in) incoming pipe, but a 15mm (1/2in) main at high pressure is normally adequate. An unvented cylinder can be heated directly, using immersion heaters; or indirectly, provided you are not using a solid-fuel boiler.

Unvented cylinder

There are no storage tanks, feed-and-expansion tanks, or open-vent pipes associated with unvented cylinders. Instead, a diaphragm inside a pressure vessel mounted on top of the cylinder flexes to accommodate expanding water. If the vessel fails, an expansion-relief valve protects the system by releasing water via a discharge pipe.

There are several other safety devices associated with unvented cylinders. A normal thermostat should keep the temperature of the water in the cylinder below 65°C (150°F). If it reaches 90°C (195°F), then a second thermostat will either switch off the immersion heater or shut off the water supply from the boiler. Finally, if it should get as hot as 95°C (205°F), a temperature-relief valve opens and discharges water outside.

Bylaws and regulations

The installation of an unvented hot-water cylinder needs to comply with both the Water Regulations and the Building Regulations. It has to include all the necessary safety devices and be installed by a competent fitter, such as those registered with the Institute of Plumbing, the Construction Industry Training Board, or the Association of Installers of Unvented Hot Water Systems (Scotland and Northern Ireland). Have the installation serviced regularly by a similarly qualified fitter, to make sure all the equipment remains in good working order.

You must notify your water company and local Building Control Office if you intend to fit an unvented hot-water cylinder.

Thermal-store cylinder

A thermal-store cylinder reverses the indirect principle. Water heated by a central-heating boiler passes through the cylinder and transfers heat, via a highly efficient coiled heat exchanger, to mains-fed water supplying hot taps and showers. An integral feed-and-expansion tank is normally built on top of the cylinder.

When the system is working at maximum capacity, the mains-fed water is delivered at such a high temperature that cold water must be added via a thermostatic mixing valve plumbed into the outlet supplying taps and showers. As the cylinder is exhausted, less cold water is added. The thermal-store system provides mains-pressure hot water throughout the house, dispenses with the need for a cold-water storage tank in the loft, and increases the efficiency of the boiler.

A valve is needed to prevent the heat from the cylinder 'thermo-siphoning' (gravity circulating) around the central-heating system. This can be a motorized valve or a simple mechanical gravity-check (non-return) valve that is opened by the force of the central-heating pump.

As with all open-vented systems, the feed-and-expansion tank determines the head of water, and radiators must be lower than the tank in order to be filled with water. When the tank is combined with the cylinder, it needs to be situated on the top floor of the house in order to provide central heating throughout the building. If that is impossible, install a tankless thermal-store cylinder in your chosen location and fit a conventional feed-and-expansion tank in the loft.

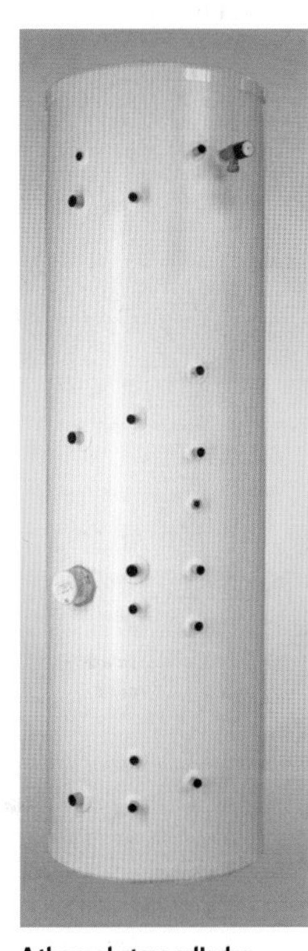

A thermal-store cylinder

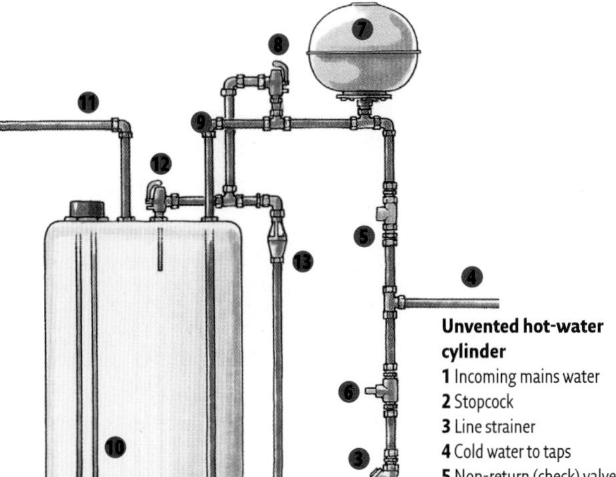

Unvented hot-water cylinder
1 Incoming mains water
2 Stopcock
3 Line strainer
4 Cold water to taps
5 Non-return (check) valve
6 Pressure limiter
7 Pressure vessel
8 Expansion-relief valve
9 Cold-water inlet
10 Immersion heater
11 Hot-water outlet
12 Temperature-relief valve
13 Air break (tundish)
14 Discharge pipe

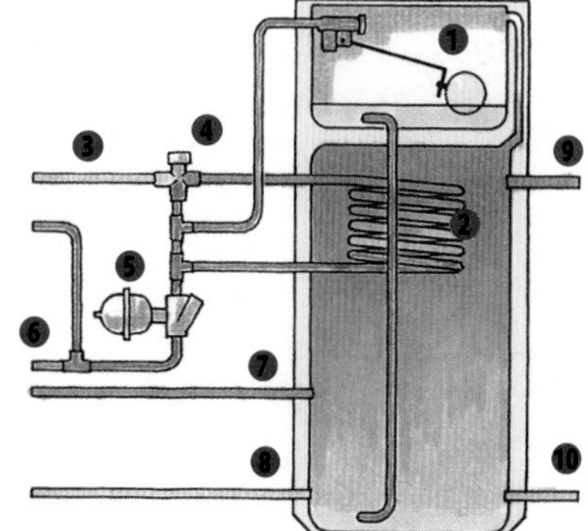

Thermal-store cylinder
1 Integral feed-and-expansion tank
2 Heat-exchanger
3 Supply pipe to hot taps/shower
4 Thermostatic mixing valve
5 Expansion vessel
6 Mains feed
7 Space-heating flow
8 Space-heating return
9 Boiler flow
10 Boiler return

Benefits of unvented systems

Thermal-store cylinders help to reduce boiler cycling and, because they heat water more quickly, can cut fuel usage by up to 15 per cent. Their capacities range from 80 to 210 litres (17½ to 46 gallons) and the systems can deliver flow rates of between 18 and 30L/min (31½ and 52½ pints). Unvented systems heat quickly and their high levels of insulation mean low heat losses. High flow rates in excess of 30L/min (52½ pints) are achievable.

SEE ALSO > Storage tanks 391, Wet central heating 405

Solar heating

Saving energy is a priority if we are to prevent further damage to our environment from the effects of carbon dioxide. The systems that have been developed to harness solar energy offer an effective alternative for heating domestic water. In contrast to the demand for space heating, which varies according to the season, hot water is required constantly throughout the year – and is well suited to heating with solar energy.

Using solar energy to heat water

Mount collectors on a south-facing roof

The idea of using the sun to provide free, non-polluting energy for heating water has always appealed to conservationists, but thanks to soaring energy costs and technological developments, solar power is becoming increasingly popular.

There are two main types of solar panel: solar collectors, which absorb energy from the sun and use it to heat water; and photovoltaic or solar electric panels, which convert solar radiation directly into electricity. Solar collectors are of most use in the home and there are two types: flat plate and evacuated tubes.

Flat plate collectors can be a simple sheet of metal painted black that absorbs the sun's energy. Water is fed through the panel in pipes attached to the metal sheet (a central heating radiator is often used in DIY panels) and picks up the heat in the metal. The metal sheet is embedded in an insulated box and covered with glass or clear plastic on the front.

The evacuated tube system is more expensive and uses a series of glass heat tubes grouped together. The tubes are highly insulated, due to a vacuum inside the glass. From the late spring through to early autumn, this type of system can produce a useful proportion of the household hot water. During the winter, the solar collectors provide useful 'preheat' that reduces the time it takes a boiler to heat water, thereby saving energy.

There are a number of companies that supply solar collectors for heating water, plus all the controls and pipework required to complete the job. If you carry out the plumbing yourself, the payback on the investment will be that much greater.

Ideally, a solar panel should be mounted on a south-facing roof at a 30° angle to the horizontal and out of reach of shadows from trees, buildings or chimneys.

A basic system

Most systems for supplying domestic hot water will require solar collectors that cover about 4sq m (4sq yd) of roof space. In order to trap maximum heat from the sun, the collectors should be mounted on a south-facing pitched roof. Collectors can be fitted, with minimal structural alterations, to almost any building, and planning approval is rarely required.

The most common way of utilizing solar energy to boost an existing water-heating system is to feed the hot water from the collectors to a second heat exchanger fitted inside your hot-water cylinder. This usually means replacing the cylinder with a dual-coil model.

An alternative technique is to plumb in a second well-insulated cylinder, which will 'preheat' the water before it is passed on to the main storage cylinder. This may involve raising the cold-water storage tank in order to feed the new preheat cylinder.

Controls

A pump is needed to circulate the water from the collectors to the cylinder coil and back to the collectors. A programmable thermostat, which operates the pump, senses when the panels are hotter than the water in the cylinder.

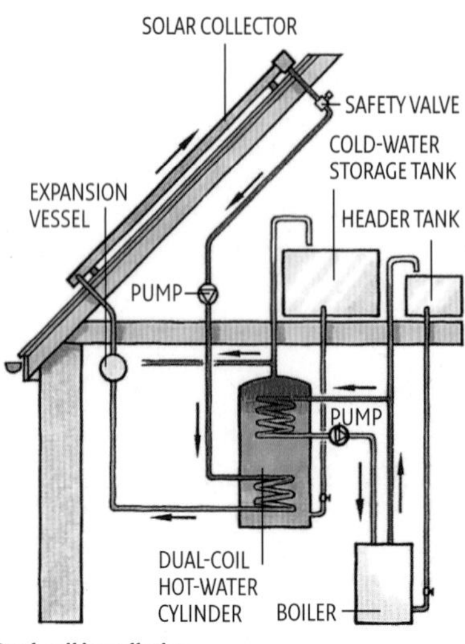

Dual-coil installation

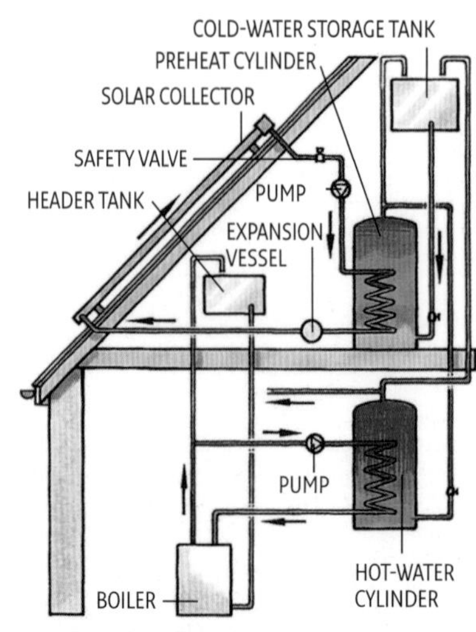

Two-cylinder installation

Point-of-use water heaters

Electric point-of-use water heaters are often designed to fit inside a cupboard or vanity unit beneath a sink or basin. You can install one of these heaters yourself, provided that it has a capacity of less than 9 litres (16 pints). Follow the manufacturer's instructions precisely, and fit a pressure-limiting valve and a filter (both of these are supplied as a kit). Also, make sure that the safety vent pipe discharges hot water to a place outside where it won't endanger anyone.

Cupboard-mounted water heater
1 Isolating valve
2 Cold supply to tap
3 Cold feed to heater
4 Hot supply from heater

SEE ALSO > Saving energy 28–9, Building Regulations on electrical wiring 284, Wiring instantaneous heaters 311, Connecting pipes 361–2, 365, Heat exchangers 280, Hot-water cylinders 392

Heating

Open fires

Even though most homes are now equipped with central heating, a great many living rooms still boast an open fireplace. The fireplace may contain a fuel-effect gas fire that provides the comforting aspects of a genuine fire without the inconvenience, but there are still many people who prefer to burn real fuel. Neither form of heating is particularly efficient or cost-effective compared with a glass-fronted room heater, for example; but for many the warm glow emanating from the hearth is justification enough.

Fitting a gas fire
All gas fires must be installed by a qualified fitter registered with CORGI (Council for Registered Gas Installers), who needs to check that the flue, hearth and ventilation are adequate. Always sweep the chimney before installing a fire of any sort. Use a smoke pellet to test the draw and to see if there is any leakage through to other flues.

How an open fire works

To burn properly, a fire needs a ready supply of oxygen (1) and an efficient means of escape for smoke and gases (2). If either of these is eliminated, the fire is stifled and eventually goes out.

A domestic fire is usually built on a barred grate (3), through which ash and debris fall into a removable tray. As the fuel burns, it gives off heated gases; these expand and become lighter than the surrounding air, so that they rise (4), sucking oxygen, in the form of fresh air, up through the base of the fire to maintain combustion. To prevent the smoke drifting out into the room, a flue above the fire provides an escape route, taking the smoke up above roof level to be discharged into the atmosphere.

A fire needs not only an effective chimney but also good ventilation in the room where it's burning, so that the air consumed by the fire is replenished continually. Sometimes the efficient draughtproofing of doors and windows can prevent a fire burning properly by denying it the constant supply of air that it needs. In such cases, ventilation must be provided, usually by means of an airbrick or a window vent; underfloor ventilation is another alternative.

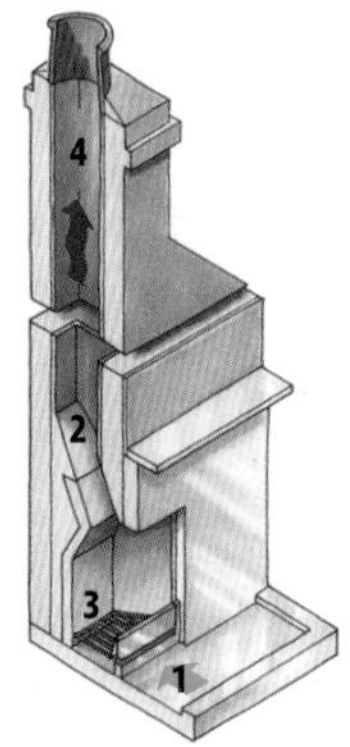

Oxygen in, smoke out
1 Air is sucked in as the smoke rises.
2 Smoke escapes up the narrow flue.
3 The grate lets air in and allows ash to drop into the tray below.
4 Smoke and gases are vented to the outside.

Mending a cracked fireback

Intense heat may eventually damage a fireback (see opposite). If the cracks are large, you will probably have to replace the fireback; fine cracks can be repaired.

Let the fireback cool for at least 48 hours, then brush away soot deposits. Rake the cracks out with a trowel point, undercutting their sides to make an inverted V-shape. Brush out the dust, and soak the area with water.

Using a trowel, work fire cement into the cracks; trowel away the surplus, and smooth the cement with a paintbrush dipped in water. Leave the cement to harden for a few days before lighting a fire.

Sweeping chimneys

Vacuum sweeping
You can have a chimney swept with a special vacuum cleaner. Its nozzle, inserted through a cover over the fire opening, sucks the soot out of the chimney. Although this is a relatively clean method, it may not remove heavy soot deposits or other obstructions.

Chemical cleaning
There are chemicals that will remove light deposits of soot and help prevent sooting in the future. In liquid or powder form, they are sprinkled onto a hot fire, producing a non-toxic gas that causes soot to crumble away from inside the chimney. They shouldn't be seen as a substitute for proper sweeping, however, as they won't remove anything like as much debris - or blockages such as birds' nests.

All solid fuels give off dust, ash, acids and tarry substances as they burn; and this combination of materials is carried up the chimney, where some of them are deposited as soot. If too much soot collects in a chimney, its size is effectively reduced internally, restricting the flow of gases and stopping the fire burning properly. A build-up of soot can even create a complete blockage, particularly at a bend in the chimney, and cause the more serious hazard of a chimney fire.

To prevent soot building up, have your chimney swept annually - if it is left unswept for too long, smoke begins to billow into the room and soot occasionally drops into the fire.

If you want to clean the chimney yourself, you can hire sets of brushes and canes for the purpose.

Remove any loose items from the hearth. If the room has a large rug or a carpet that isn't fitted, roll it back and cover it with a dust sheet for protection. Drape an old sheet or blanket over the fire surround, weighting it down along the mantle shelf and leaning something heavy against each side to form a seal with the edges of the surround.

Screw a brush head to the first cane and place it inside the flue above the fireplace, then gather the sheet around the cane and weight down its edges securely on the hearth. Now screw on the next cane and begin to push the brush up the flue.

Continue screwing on lengths of cane and pushing the brush upwards until you feel resistance cease as the brush emerges from the top of the chimney pot. If the pot is fitted with a cowl, try to anticipate when the brush will emerge, so you avoid pushing the cowl off the chimney.

If the brush meets an obstruction in the flue, pull it back slightly, then push upwards again, working it up and down until you clear the blockage. Don't twist the canes to and fro: this may unscrew a joint and leave the brush irretrievably stuck up the chimney.

Pull the brush back down, unscrewing the canes as they appear; then pull out the brush, and either shovel the heap of soot out of the grate or use a hired industrial vacuum cleaner.

There are other ways of dealing with the job than with a brush (see far left). However, given the potential for mess and possible damage to cowls, chimney sweeping is one job that may be best left to a professional sweep.

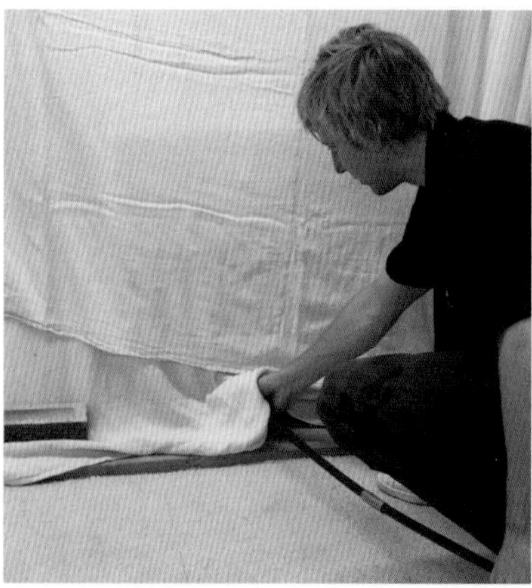

Sweeping a chimney
Seal off the fireplace with an old sheet and feed the canes up under it.

SEE ALSO > Treating stained chimneys 46, Ventilating fireplaces 273

Replacing a fireback

Some people abandon the possibility of using an existing fireplace simply because the cast fireback is damaged and looks unsightly. However, a functioning fireplace is such an asset that it is well worth removing a damaged fireback and replacing it.

Removing an old fireback

If you plan to replace a fireback, first measure the width across its mouth and order a new one of the same size. Standard sizes are 400 and 450mm (1ft 4in and 1ft 6in), although larger firebacks are available.

Before you remove the old fireback, cover the floor with a dust sheet and protect a tiled hearth with thick cardboard. Wear a mask and goggles when removing the grate and fireback.

The grate (1) may simply rest on the back hearth; or it may be screwed down and sealed to the fireback with asbestos rope and fire cement (2). If so, dampen the area with water, then take out the screws and chip away the cement with a hammer and cold chisel. Next, break out the old fireback (3) with a hammer and chisel, starting at one corner. Open up cracks until you can remove larger pieces.

Take care not to damage the fire surround when you are breaking the cement seal (4) between it and the fireback. Don't touch the asbestos-rope packing (5) between the surround and fireback unless it's in poor condition and needs replacing (see bottom right).

You will find heat-retaining rubble in the space behind the fireback (6). Dislodge this rubble with a hammer and chisel until you have cleared the opening completely.

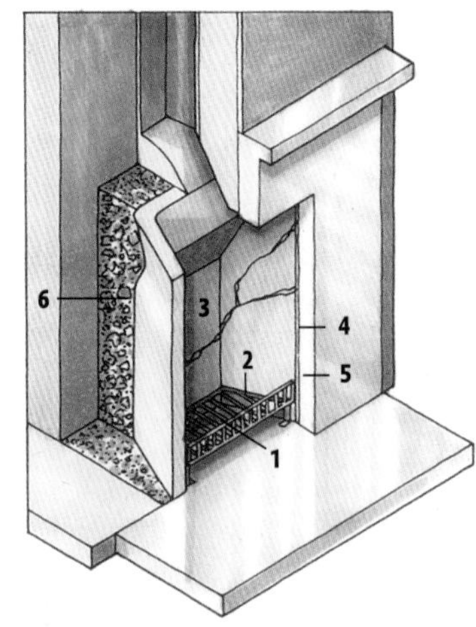

Taking out an old or damaged fireback
1 The grate may be fixed or freestanding.
2 The grate may be sealed with asbestos rope and fire cement.
3 The fireback will have to be broken out.
4 The surround is bonded to the fireback with fire cement.
5 Expansion-joint packing may need replacing.
6 You will need to clear rubble from the brick-lined opening.

Installing the new fireback

A new fireback is supplied in one piece ready for installing into a new opening. You'll probably have to cut it into two separate pieces in order to install it in an existing fireplace.

A recessed line runs horizontally across the fireback, indicating where the two halves must be separated. This can be done by tapping gently along the line with a bolster chisel and a hammer, or you could use an angle grinder. The two components can then be manoeuvred into position within the brick opening.

Mix a weak mortar, using 1 part lime : 6 parts builder's sand. Make a bed for the lower part of the fireback by trowelling a layer of mortar round the rear edge of the back hearth (1). Ease the lower fireback into position, at the same time pulling it forward so that it lightly compresses the rope packing at the edge of the fire surround. Check the fireback is upright.

Cut out two pieces of corrugated cardboard to the shape of the fireback's lower portion, then place them directly behind it (2). Fill the gap between the cardboard and the brickwork with a lightweight concrete mix of 6 parts vermiculite : 1 part cement (3). Alternatively, you can use 1 part lime : 2 parts sand : 4 parts broken brick (plus the old broken fireback) to bulk out the mix. Bring either filling up level with the top edge of the fireback's lower portion (4), tamping down the concrete with a piece of wood as you go.

Trowel a layer of fire cement (a ready-mixed heat-resistant cement, available in plastic pots or dispensing cartridges) along the top edge of the fireback's lower portion and set the upper portion in place on top of it (5), making sure that the two halves are lined up accurately. Trowel off surplus cement, and finish the joint by brushing it with clean water. Continue filling the space behind the fireback with the concrete mixture (or rubble), and tamp it down until the infill reaches the top.

Using the bedding-mortar mix, form a slope that runs from the top of the fireback up to the rear face of the chimney (6). This slope is called the 'flaunching', and it must be made parallel with the rear face of the loadbearing lintel that runs across the top of the fire opening (7). The two sloping surfaces form a 'throat', about 100mm (4in) wide, between them. This draws the smoke from the fire into the flue itself.

Trowel the flaunching smooth and, at each side, use mortar to fill in any gaps that might allow soot to collect.

Finally, seal the gap between the new fireback and the surround (8), using fire cement. Then replace the grate.

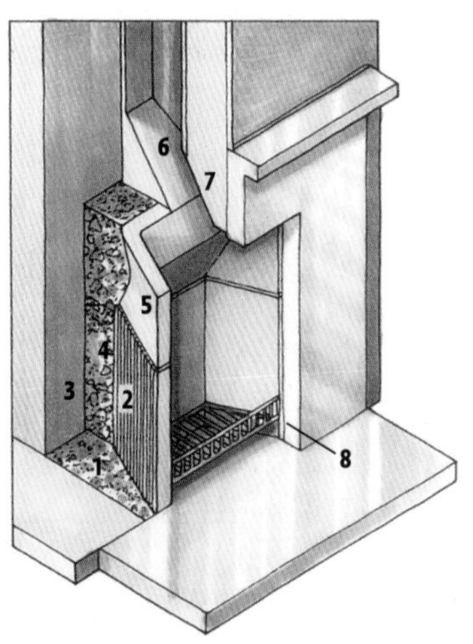

Installing a fireback
1 The back hearth supports the fireback.
2 Corrugated card leaves an expansion gap when it burns.
3 The rear space, to be filled with concrete or rubble.
4 Begin by infilling up to the edge of the lower part of fireback.
5 Upper section of fireback is set in place and infilled behind.
6 Mortar sloped to form flaunching.
7 Loadbearing lintel.
8 Fireback has to be sealed to the surround.

Sealing the fireback

The cement seal between the fireback and the surround must be renewed if cracked or broken, and when a new fireback is installed.

Wear a face mask. Repair the joint by chipping away the old cement with a hammer and cold chisel, then rake out the debris to uncover the expansion-joint packings. These are likely to be asbestos rope. If sound, leave them; if crumbling or broken, cover the floor with plastic sheet and spray the asbestos with water. Cut out the damp packing with a sharp knife and seal it in a labelled plastic bag. Carefully fold the sheeting for disposal and pick up any asbestos dust with a damp sponge (not with a vacuum cleaner). The local authority will advise on disposal. Repack with a fibreglass-rope seal, then brush the joint with clean water and trowel in fire cement to finish flush with the surround. Smooth off with a wet paintbrush.

SEE ALSO > Fitting a fire surround 400

Removing a fireplace

When restoring an old house, you may want to remove a fireplace in order to reinstate one with authentic period styling. Or perhaps you want to change the use of a room, and have decided to dispense with an unattractive fireplace altogether.

Half-round ridge tile

Commercial cowl

Capping the chimney
When you close off a fireplace opening, you need to cap the chimney to keep the rain out – while allowing enough of an outlet to draw air through the vent in the room below. Either replace the chimney pot with a half-round ridge tile bedded in cement (top), or fit a proprietary cowl or cap (above).

Saving a surround
Fire surrounds can be very heavy, especially stone, slate or marble ones. If you can lay your hands on an old mattress, place it in front of the surround before you pull it from the wall – so minimum damage will be done if it should fall.

Removing tiles
When restoring a tiled fire surround or hearth, it's possible to remove and replace damaged or broken tiles. Chop out at least one tile with a cold chisel, then prise the others off the surface by driving a bolster chisel behind them.

Taking out an old fire surround and superimposed hearth is easy enough, but it creates a lot of dust and debris. Start by sweeping the chimney, move all furniture away from the fireplace, roll back carpet, and cover everything with dust sheets.

Removing the hearth

Most superimposed hearths are laid after the fire surround has been fitted and so must come out first – but check beforehand that your surround has not been installed on top of the hearth.

Wearing safety goggles and heavy gloves, use a club hammer and bolster chisel to break the mortar seal between the superimposed hearth and the constructional hearth beneath it. Driving wooden wedges under the hearth will help to break the seal. Lever the hearth free with a crowbar or a garden spade and lift it clear.

Instead of a superimposed hearth, some fireplaces have a tiled constructional hearth that lies flush with the surrounding floorboards. You can leave the tiles in place and run the floorcovering over them.

Removing the surround

Most surrounds are fixed to the wall with screws driven through metal lugs, which are hidden by the plaster on the chimney breast. Chip away 25mm (1in) of plaster all round the surround to expose the lugs and take out the screws. If the screws are immovable, drill out the screwheads then, with the surround removed, grind off the remainder. The surround will be heavy, so get help when levering it from the wall (see left).

Brick and stone surrounds

A brick or stone surround can be taken out a piece at a time, using a bolster to break the mortar joints. There may also be metal ties holding it to the wall.

Marble surrounds

Marble surrounds are made in sections, so remove the shelf first, then the frieze or lintel, and lastly the side jambs.

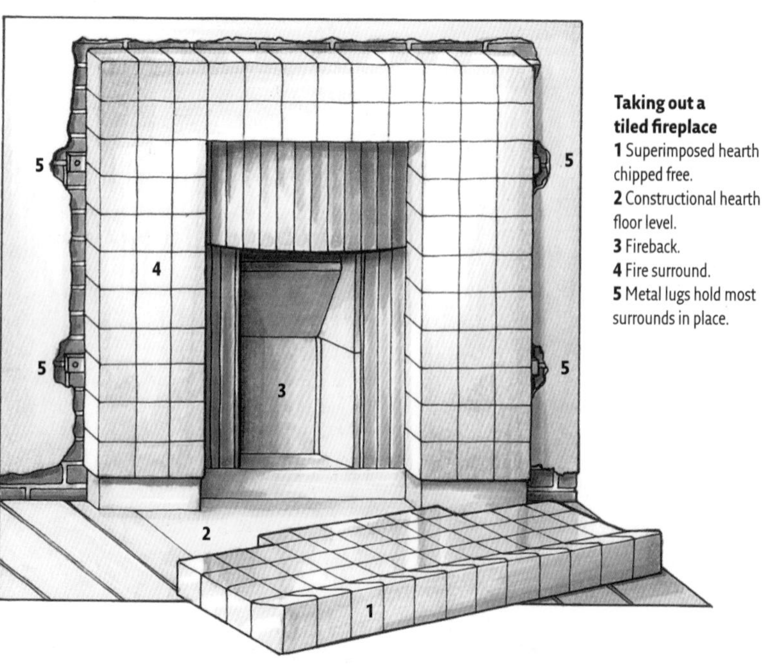

Taking out a tiled fireplace
1 Superimposed hearth chipped free.
2 Constructional hearth at floor level.
3 Fireback.
4 Fire surround.
5 Metal lugs hold most surrounds in place.

Stripping a fire surround

Stripping a cast-iron surround may uncover much of the detail that has been obscured under layers of old paint – but repaint it or treat with grate polish afterwards to stop the metal rusting.

Restoring a marble mantlepiece may well be worth the effort – but make sure the marble is genuine. A lot of old wooden and slate fireplaces were painted to resemble marble. Marble feels cold to the touch – so allow the surround to cool down, then compare it with an adjacent wooden skirting. Similarly, it was once common practice to paint cheap softwood surrounds to imitate better-quality woods; but if you look closely, you should be able to distinguish painted graining from real wood. You can have paint finishes such as marbling or graining restored by specialist decorators.

Mouldings on Adam-style surrounds are sometimes made of plaster. These are easily damaged by solvents and stripping tools, so take extra care when removing paint.

Some old fireplaces can be valuable and could be ruined by ill-advised stripping – check with an expert if you're in any doubt.

Stripping methods

Cast-iron and wooden fireplaces can be dipped in an industrial stripping tank, which is fast and effective – though it can dry out joints on wooden surrounds. Otherwise, use a gel or paste stripper, following the manufacturer's instructions.

Cast-iron fireplace
Strip thick paint to reveal the fine detail.

SEE ALSO > Chemical strippers 59, Sweeping a chimney 396, Hearth dimensions 400, Marble surrounds 400

Enclosing a fireplace

Having removed a fireplace, you can fill the opening with a thin panel on a wooden frame or by bricking it up. Panelling the opening will make it easier to reinstate the fireplace at some time in the future. In either case, it is necessary to fit a ventilator in the centre of the opening, just above skirting level. This provides a flow of air through the chimney to prevent condensation forming inside, which could eventually stain the wall.

Levelling the floor

Once you have removed the fireplace, use mortar or a self-levelling screed to make a solid constructional hearth, level with the floor. You could do the same with a boarded floor, if it's to be carpeted.

If you want exposed floorboards, chop back the concrete hearth with a hammer and cold chisel to make room for a new joist and floorboards.

A new joist for extending floorboards

Panelling the opening with plasterboard

Make a panel from 9mm (3/8in) plasterboard nailed to a 50 x 50mm (2 x 2in) sawn-timber frame fixed inside the fire opening. Nail the frame in the opening with masonry nails or nailable plugs, positioning the battens so that the plasterboard, when nailed on, will lie flush with the surrounding plaster. Set the battens back a further 3mm (1/8in) if a plaster skim is to be applied to the plaster-board. Cut an opening in the plasterboard for the ventilator, then plaster the wall and fit a new length of skirting to match the original. After decorating, fit a ventilator.

Panelling for a gas fire

If you want to mount a gas fire on the infill panelling, construct a similar frame from the type of metal studding that is used for building partition walls. Use asbestos-free fire-resistant insulation board for the panelling. Fix the panel to the frame, using countersunk self-tapping screws. Plaster over the panel to leave a flush finish.

The gas appliance must be fitted by a qualified gas installer, registered with CORGI. The installer can also cut the necessary opening in the panelling for the fire's flue outlet.

An inset frame to support plasterboard

An unused chimney must be ventilated

Installing a log-burning grate

To install a log-burning grate in a fireplace, you must first remove the old fireback and the rubble infill. You can leave the brickwork exposed, or line the opening with better-quality bricks, firebricks or stone.

Choose a grate that will leave a gap of 50 to 75mm (2 to 3in) at each side of the opening. The best grates have cast-iron firebacks to radiate heat into the room.

The original hearth may be suitable as a level surface for the grate; but if you have had to remove an old superimposed hearth, you will have to install a new one. This is normally at least 50mm (2in) thick and extends 300mm (1ft) in front of the grate. It must also extend at least 150mm (6in) on each side of the fire opening – or up to the width of any surround if this is greater.

The new superimposed hearth can be of brick, stone, or tiled concrete.

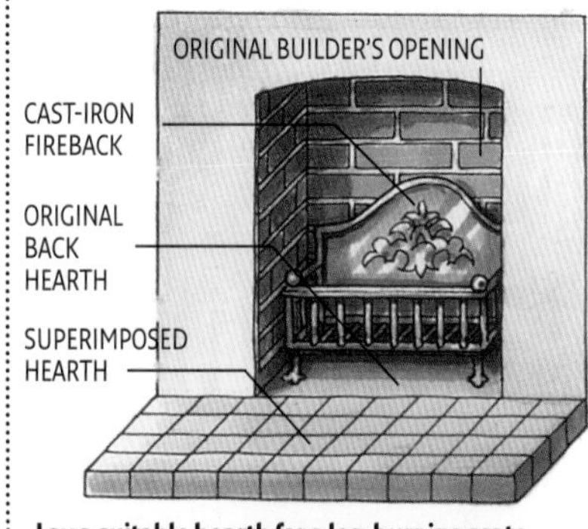

Lay a suitable hearth for a log-burning grate

Bricking up the opening

If you prefer to fill the opening with bricks, take out the existing bricks from alternate courses at the edges of the opening, so that the new brickwork can be 'toothed in'. Alternatively, fix lightweight concrete blocks to the brickwork on either side, using metal wall ties. Provide chimney ventilation by fitting an airbrick centrally in the masonry, just above skirting level. Plaster the masonry, and allow it to dry before fitting a length of skirting across the face of the chimney breast.

One of the bricks must be an airbrick

Change of use
Over the years, newly installed methods of heating have resulted in a variety of pots and cowls being used on this Victorian chimney stack.

SEE ALSO > Levelling concrete 47, Metal studding 155, Plasterboard 162, Laying floorboards 180, Fitting skirtings 218, Ventilating a fireplace 273, Airbricks 274, Removing a fireback 397, Laying bricks 444, Wall ties 448

Reinstating an old fireplace

Period fireplaces are now much sought after – both for the character they inject into a living room and for the improved resale value they bring to an older house. To reinstate a fireplace, you can either buy an original example from an architectural salvage company or choose a reproduction insert and surround. It's advisable to check that the fireplace opening, hearth and chimney are all in good condition and that your proposals comply with current Building Regulations. As a precaution, check with your Building Control Officer.

Fireplace styles
When reinstating a fireplace, choose one that suits the period style of your home.

Fitting an insert grate

Position the insert on the back hearth, placing it centrally in the fireplace opening. Check that it's plumb and square. If the opening is larger than the front plate of the insert, fill in the space at the sides with mortared bricks. If there's space above the insert, add a concrete lintel supported by the side brickwork. If the opening is not in the centre of the chimney breast, move the insert sideways.

Temporarily position the surround to see whether it fits snugly against the wall and grate. If necessary, pull the insert forward to butt up against the back of the surround. Now remove the surround and pack fibreglass rope behind the rim of the insert and seal the gap with fire cement. If the insert is made with fixing lugs, use them to fix it to the wall with brass screws and heat-resistant wallplugs.

Reduce the size of the opening if necessary

One-piece surround

One piece wooden and cast-iron types are usually fixed with screws through lugs or fixing plates at each side.

Hold the surround against the wall and centralize it on the grate. Check that the surround is level and plumb, then mark the positions of the fixings. Remove the surround, drill and plug the wall, and screw the surround in place.

Fill the void behind the insert with a lightweight concrete mix, and form a 'throat' (see REPLACING A FIREBACK). Fit a superimposed hearth.

Fill the void behind the insert with concrete

Fitting a marble surround

A marble surround is constructed from separate pieces – two hollow jambs, a frieze and a mantle shelf. Ideally, the frieze and jambs should overlap the edges of the insert grate. Lay the hearth before you erect the surround.

A metal loop on the inside of each jamb is wired to a screw driven into the wall. The loop, which is located near the top of the jamb, can be reached through the open top when the jamb is in place.

Bond the base of each jamb in a bed of plaster of Paris laid on the hearth. Working quickly before the plaster sets, bind the metal loops back to the wall with copper wire. Make sure each jamb is plumb, then apply dabs of plaster on the inside, to stick it to the wall.

The frieze is located in notches on the inside of the jambs. Apply plaster to the notches and stick the frieze in place. Lay the mantle shelf onto a thin bed of plaster spread along the frieze, and bond it back to the wall. Prop the front edge of the shelf until the plaster sets.

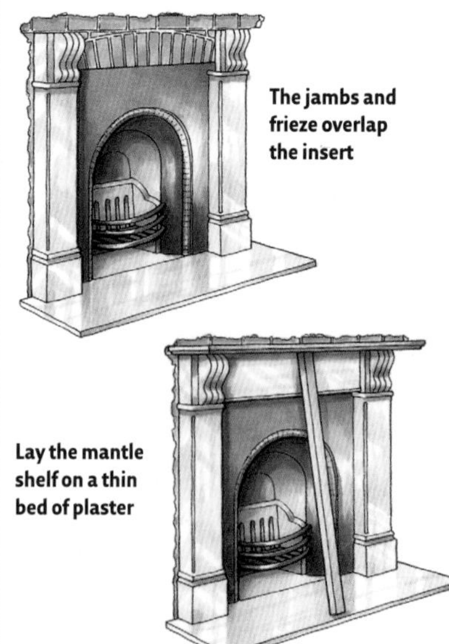

The jambs and frieze overlap the insert

Lay the mantle shelf on a thin bed of plaster

Reinstating a fireplace

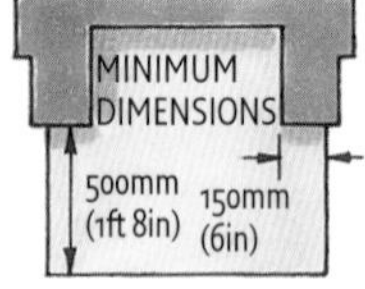

Constructional hearth
Before reinstating a fireplace, check that the constructional hearth complies with current Building Regulations.

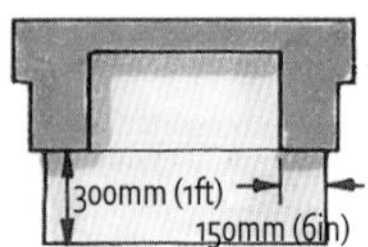

Superimposed hearth
Minimum dimensions for an open fire. The width of the hearth should not be less than the width of the fire surround.

SEE ALSO > Plastering 156–68, Fitting skirtings 218, Replacing a fireback 397, Fireplace lugs 398

Installing room heaters

Modern solid-fuel room heaters are highly efficient, and with the addition of a back boiler can provide domestic hot water and central heating. The toughened-glass doors give an attractive view of the glowing fire. Flame-effect gas-fired inset heaters are just as good to look at and easier to install.

Standing a heater on the hearth

Some room heaters are designed to stand on the hearth, just in front of the chimney breast. These radiate warmth from their casing, but their size can make them look obtrusive in a small room. Also, in order to accommodate a freestanding heater, you may have to extend your hearth (whether constructional or superimposed), since there has to be a space of at least 300mm (1ft) in front of the heater if it is open or has doors at the front, or 225mm (9in) if the front doesn't open.

This type of heater has a flue outlet at the rear, which must be connected to the chimney. This is normally achieved by passing the flue outlet through a metal backplate that closes off the fire opening. The projecting end of the outlet must stop short of the fireback by at least 100mm (4in) – if need be, remove the fireback to provide this clearance. If the void is very large, extend the outlet up into the main flue, with a seal all round, in order to create a satisfactory updraught.

The backplate should be of metal at least 1mm (18 gauge) thick. Fold its edges to form flanges through which fixing screws can be driven into heat-resistant wallplugs on each side of the fire opening. Seal the joint between the plate and the opening with fire cement and fibreglass-rope packing.

A backplate closes off the fire opening

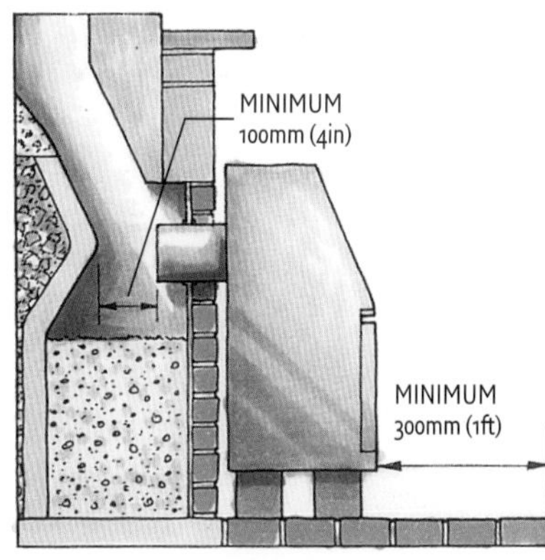

Important measurements for a room heater

Standing a heater in the fire opening

This type of heater has a vertical flue outlet, which must be connected to a closure plate set into the base of the chimney. The closure plate can be of metal or precast concrete. To fit the plate, remove some bricks from the chimney breast, just above the fire opening but below the loadbearing lintel.

If the plate is made from concrete, provide support by taking out a course of bricks at the bottom of the chimney and bed it in mortar. Insert a metal plate in a chased-out mortar joint. Bed a metal plate on fire cement, sealing the edges all round.

The heater's outlet should enter the chimney flue - seal the joint with fire cement and fibreglass-rope packing.

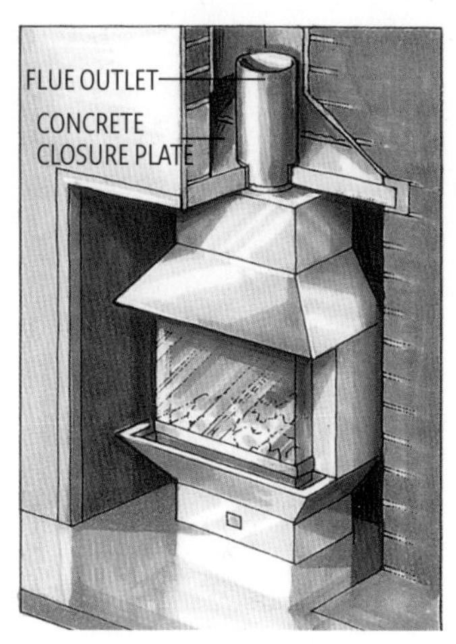

A horizontal plate seals off the chimney

An inset room heater

To install an inset (built-in) room heater, you must first take out the fireback and rubble infill. The heater has a flue outlet that passes through a closure plate into the chimney.

This type of appliance is designed to fill and seal the fire opening completely. To install one you may therefore have to modify your present fire surround or, if the opening is very large, build a new one. The heater's casing must fit snugly against the hearth and the wall or panel behind, so that you can make a perfect seal all round.

Most inset heaters are screwed down to the back hearth, and some types need a vermiculite-based infill behind the casing. This infill has to be in place before the chimney closure plate is fitted and the flue outlet connected. Some models are supplied with their own fire surround, complete with a drop-in closure plate designed for easy installation.

Flame-effect gas-fired inset heaters are available with realistic log or coal beds. They can use an existing lined flue or some have balanced flues, which make them very easy to install.

Inset gas heaters have very realistic fuel effects

- **Sweeping the chimney**
The flue above a solid-fuel heater can usually be swept by passing a brush up through the heater itself. If not, you will need a separate double-seal soot door, fitted in the closure plate or in the chimney breast (either on the inside or outside).

- **Hearth for a freestanding heater**
For a freestanding room heater, the constructional hearth has to be at least 840mm (2ft 9in) square and 125mm (5in) thick. It must extend not less than 300mm (1ft) in front of an open heater, and at least 225mm (9in) in front of a closed one.

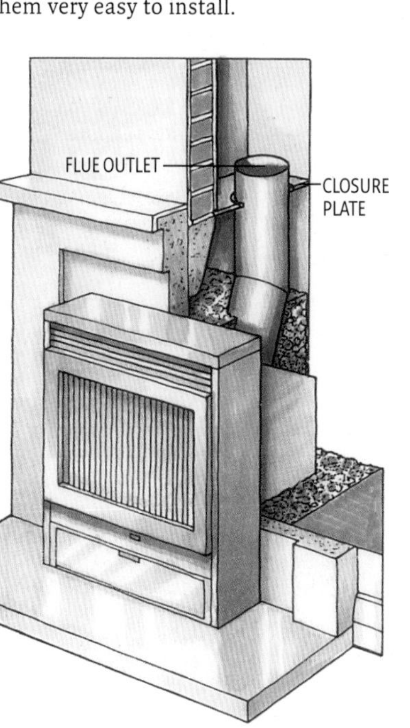

Inset room heater
The flue outlet connects to a horizontal closure plate in the base of the chimney. Some heaters require an infill behind the casing.

SEE ALSO > Lintels 139, Providing ventilation 273, Removing a fireback 397

Installing flue liners

If your house was built before 1965, there's a good chance that its chimneys are unlined. Either they are simple exposed-brick ducts or the insides are rendered with cement. Over the years, the corrosive elements in the smoke from the fire eat into the masonry, eroding it and allowing condensation to pass through to form damp patches on the chimney breast. In extreme cases, smoke can seep through, too.

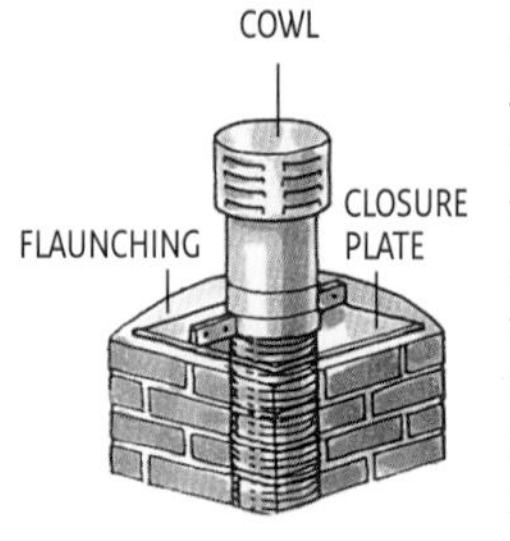

An approved cowl for a gas heater

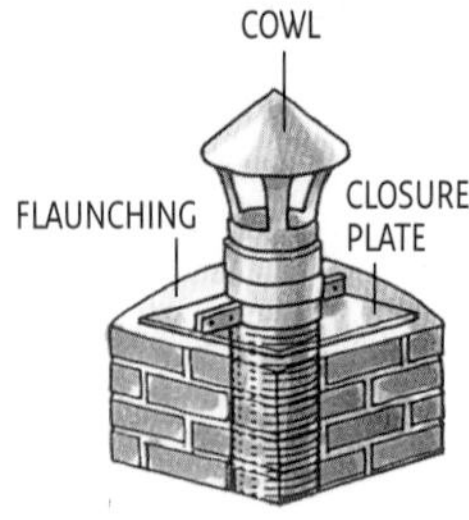

An approved cowl for oil-fired heaters

• **Casting a flue liner** Professional installers can cast a flue liner in situ. A deflated tube is lowered into the chimney. It is inflated, and a lightweight concrete infill is poured into the gap between the tube and the flue. When the infill has set, the tube is deflated and removed, leaving a smooth-bore flue liner.

Flexible flue liners

These problems can be dealt with by installing a flue liner, which protects the brickwork from the corrosive elements. A liner also reduces the 'bore' of the flue. This speeds up the flow of gases, preventing them from cooling and condensing, and the increased draught of air through the fire encourages more efficient combustion.

Liner types

Flue liners take the form of tubes, either one-piece or in sections, and are made of metal or some other rigid non-combustible material, such as pumice. A popular type of liner is a one-piece flexible corrugated tube of stainless steel that's fed into the flue. Thin-wall tubes are sufficient for gas appliances, but they burn through quickly if they are connected to solid-fuel or wood-burning stoves, so install a double-skinned liner with a smooth inner surface. Some installers recommend filling around the liner with lightweight insulation.

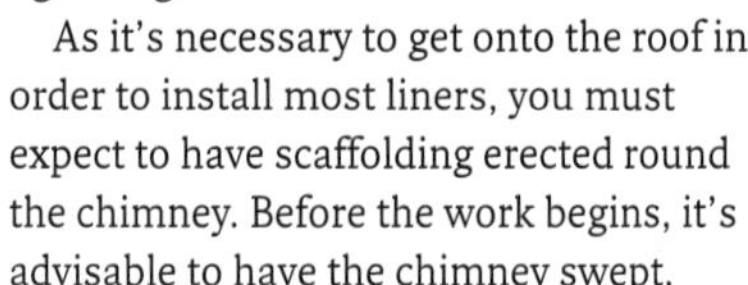

As it's necessary to get onto the roof in order to install most liners, you must expect to have scaffolding erected round the chimney. Before the work begins, it's advisable to have the chimney swept.

The installer will feed the liner into the chimney from the top. A weighted cord lowered down the chimney (**1**) is attached to the conical endpiece of the flue liner. An assistant pulls gently on the cord from below while the liner is fed down into the chimney (**2**). When the conical endpiece emerges in the fireplace, it is removed and either the liner is connected to a closure plate set across the base of the chimney or it is attached to the flue outlet of the heating appliance. Once the joint has been sealed with fire cement and fibreglass-rope packing, the chimney pot is replaced and mortared into place.

If the liner is connected to a gas or oil-fired appliance, a top closure plate is bedded on mortar laid on the top of the chimney and a cowl is fitted (**3**).

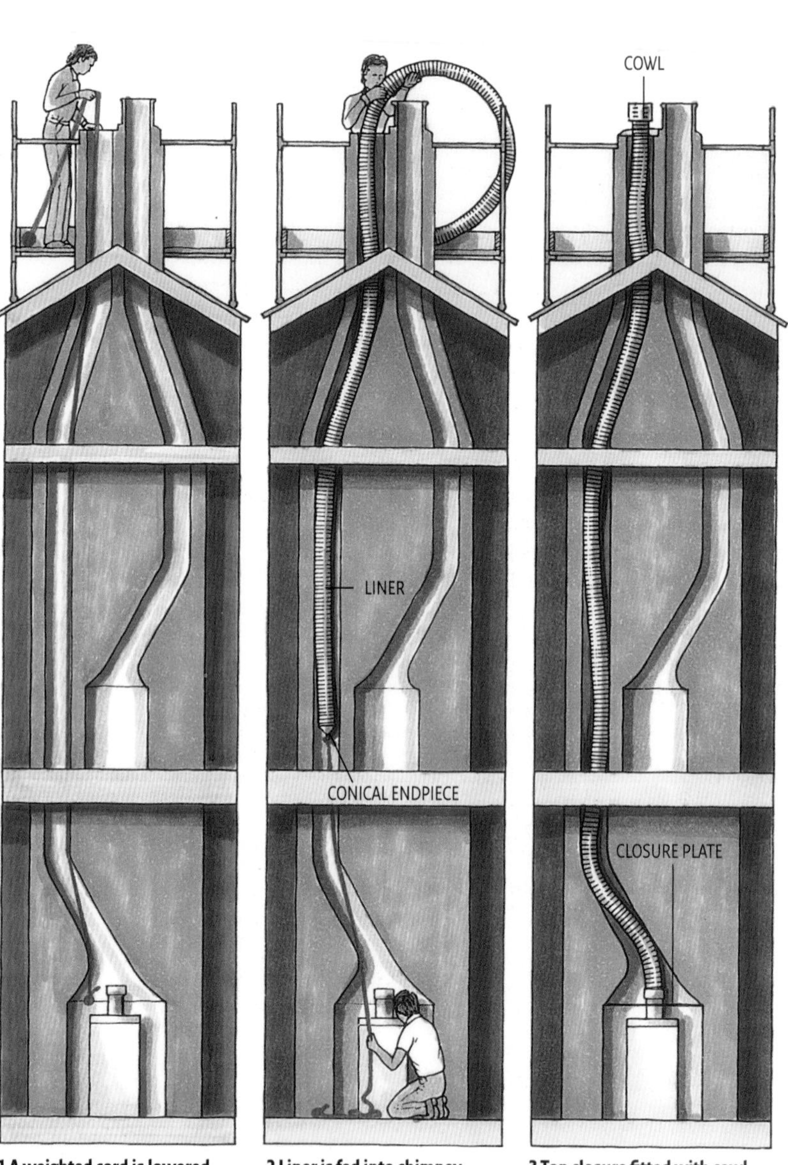

1 A weighted cord is lowered **2 Liner is fed into chimney** **3 Top closure fitted with cowl**

Safe access

Two units of scaffolding will make a half platform for a central or side chimney. Four units will provide an all-round platform. Use wooden pads to protect the roof covering from the scaffold supports.

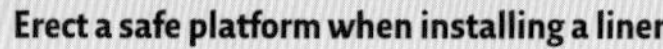

Erect a safe platform when installing a liner

SEE ALSO > Sweeping a chimney 396

Log-burning stoves

If you have ready access to plenty of cheap wood, one of the most economical ways to heat a room is with a modern slow-combustion log-burning stove. Like freestanding solid-fuel room heaters, these stoves can be stood on the hearth (when fitted with a rear flue outlet) or in the fireplace (when fitted with a top-mounted outlet).

A good wood-burning stove can burn all day or night with just one filling of logs. To get the full benefit of the heat that radiates from its casing, it's best to install the stove in front of the chimney breast.

You can stand it on your present superimposed hearth – provided that it projects the required minimum of 300mm (1ft) in front of the stove and at least 150mm (6in) on each side of it.

Otherwise, you will need to build a larger hearth. The hearth must be level and constructed from non-combustible materials such as stone, brick or tiles. Also, make sure your constructional hearth complies with current Building Regulations.

A log-burning stove is fitted with a flue pipe designed to pass through a horizontal plate that closes off the base of the chimney. The gap around the flue pipe is sealed with fire cement and fibreglass-rope packing. The closure plate must be fireproof.

Because burning wood produces heavy deposits of soot and tar, either the stove's flue pipe must be connected to a double-skinned stainless-steel liner or the flue itself has to be lined with lightweight concrete (see opposite).

Wood-burning stoves
Available in a range of traditional designs, wood-burning stoves epitomise country living.

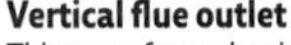

Vertical flue outlet
This type of stove has its flue sealed into the opening of a horizontal closure plate in the base of the chimney.

• Refinishing stoves
To renovate a dowdy stove, use an aerosol containing black satin-finish wood-stove paint. This special paint is heat-resistant and exceptionally durable. Before spraying, allow the stove to cool down and use a wire brush or sandpaper to remove old flaking paint.

Rear flue outlet
A rear flue outlet allows the stove to stand clear of the chimney breast.

Installing a sectional liner

A lightweight-concrete liner is very durable, and is suitable for any type of fuel. It's made in short sections, which are mortared together inside the flue. This type of liner is ideal for straight flues, although it can be adapted with standard elbow sections to fit offset flues. Most of these liners are made with interlocking joints, and some have locating collars, too.

The installer will have to remove the chimney pot, and may also need to make holes at key points in the chimney to gain access to the flue. A strong support is required at the bottom of the flue to support the liner and insulation.

The liner sections are lowered down the flue one at a time – with the top joint of each section being mortared to receive the next one. Once the liner is complete and any access openings have been rebuilt, the void around the liner is usually filled with lightweight concrete. However, that is not always considered necessary, since sectional liners possess excellent insulating properties (your installer will advise you about this).

Sectional flue liner
The pot and flaunching are removed to gain access to the chimney.

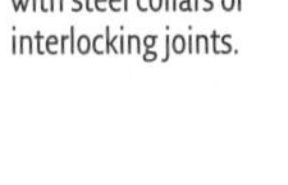

Sections may be joined with steel collars or interlocking joints.

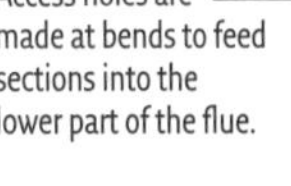

Access holes are made at bends to feed sections into the lower part of the flue.

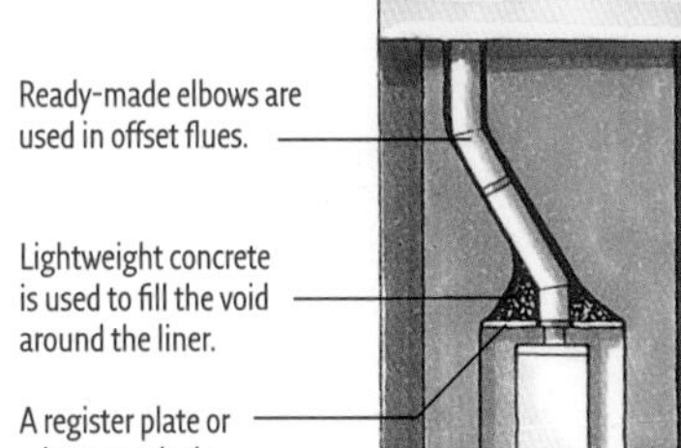

Ready-made elbows are used in offset flues.

Lightweight concrete is used to fill the void around the liner.

A register plate or adaptor seals the opening.

Cross-section of a typical installation

SEE ALSO > Removing a fireback 397, Hearth dimensions 400

Central heating

Of the various methods used over the years, central heating is the most energy-efficient, since it supplies heat from a single source (usually a boiler or furnace) to every room in the house, instead of the need for an individual heater or fireplace in each room. It is also relatively easy to maintain, because there is just the one heating appliance to control, clean and service.

Central-heating systems can be divided into two basic types: dry and wet systems. With the less-common dry system, heated air carries warmth to the rooms; with a wet system, the heat-carrying medium is water.

Dry central heating

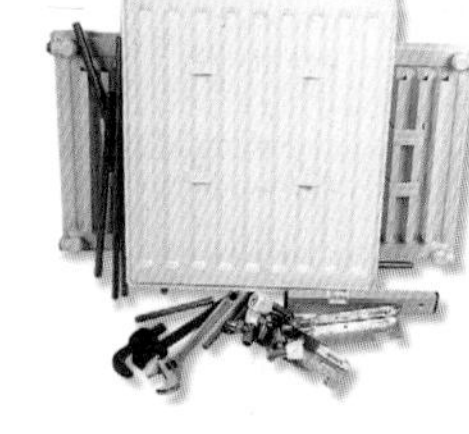

The heat source for the majority of warm-air central-heating systems is a large gas-fired furnace. Air is warmed by being passed relatively quickly over a metal heat exchanger containing hot gas fumes, which are eventually ducted to a flue. An integral fan blows the warmed air through ducts to the rooms being heated.

Each of these ducts ends in an adjustable damper, which is used to regulate the temperature in the room by controlling the amount of air that can flow through it. Ducting runs in this kind of system can be quite long and must be insulated for maximum efficiency.

There are also a number of electric systems that are regarded as forms of central heating. Among them are underfloor and ceiling heating systems. These use electric elements built into the structure of the floor or ceiling to warm their surfaces, which in turn radiate heat into the room.

A house kept warm with individual electric storage heaters is also usually classed as being centrally heated, even though each heater is a separate heat source. The individual heaters contain a number of heat-retaining firebricks, which are heated during the night by electric elements running on the low-cost Economy 7 electricity tariff. The units are individually controlled, so the bricks can give off the stored heat as required during the daytime - either by simple convection or with the aid of fans.

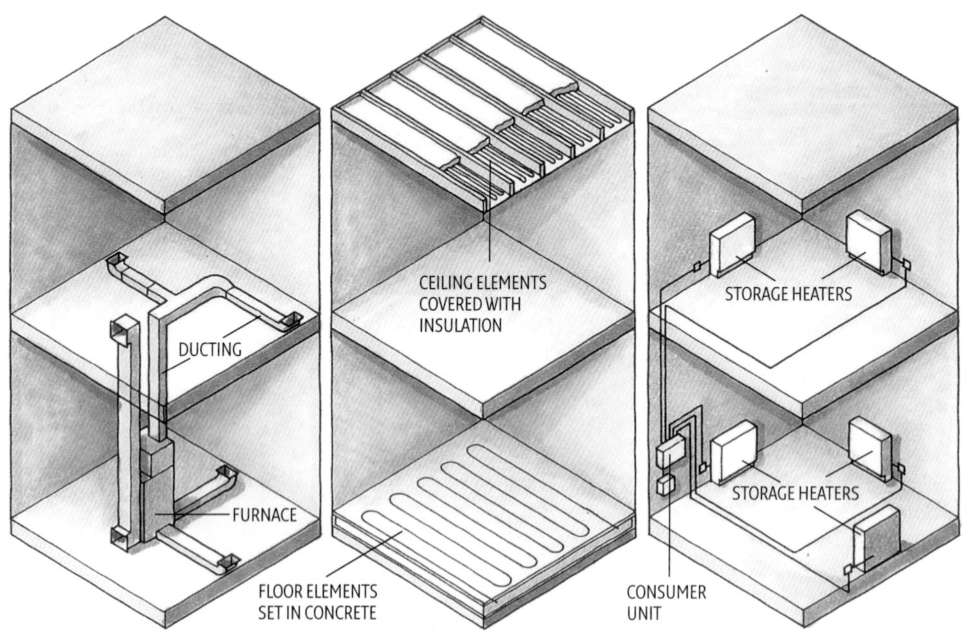

Warm-air systems
Heated air travels via ducts to the rooms, and then back to the furnace for reheating.

Floor and ceiling heating systems
Electric elements warm the floor or ceiling, and the heat is radiated into the room.

Storage heaters
These run on cheap electricity and have their own consumer unit, wiring and meter.

Choosing a system

Before you decide on a central-heating system, investigate which method is likely to work best for you - both in terms of installation and long-term benefit.

Dry central heating

Because of the amount of space and work required to run the ducts, a ducted warm-air system is not really practical unless incorporated into a house during its construction. Similarly, electric underfloor and ceiling systems for whole-house heating are best put in while a house is being built, since elements are installed in floors and ceilings.

Room storage heaters can be easily installed in an existing house, although they need a dedicated meter, consumer unit and wiring.

Wet central heating

Wet central-heating systems have proved to be economical, reliable and relatively easy to install. Their small-bore copper or plastic pipes can be run through floor and ceiling voids, clipped along skirting boards and up walls to supply hot water to panel radiators or low-profile skirting heaters.

Most systems use two 15mm (½in) copper pipes (see opposite, top); micro-bore heating uses smaller, 6 to 10mm (¼ to ⅜in), pipes and offers faster warm-up and less heat loss.

Underfloor systems are efficient and space-saving. They use concealed plastic pipes to emit heat.

Modern compact boilers are highly efficient and can be installed in a fireplace, utility room or in the kitchen.

Wet systems will prove to be the most economical, flexible choice for the vast majority of householders; the new generation of 'designer' fixtures means that radiators can make an eye-catching focal point, too.

SEE ALSO > Running cable 303–5, Copper plumbing 259, Radiators 407–8, Storage heaters 420, Underfloor heating 420

Wet central heating

Wet central heating is economic, efficient and reliable and by far the most common form of central heating. It offers relatively quick warm-up times and a variety of control options for flexibility and energy saving. Although it is prone to various problems, most of these are easily resolved in a well-designed system.

Open-vented systems

The most common form of wet central heating is the two-pipe open-vented system – in which water is heated by a boiler and pumped through small-bore pipes to radiators or convector heaters, where the heat from the water is released into the rooms. The water then circulates back to the boiler for reheating, using natural gas, bottled gas (propane), oil, electricity, or a solid fuel.

Thermostats and valves allow the output of the individual heat emitters to be adjusted automatically, and parts of the system can be shut down as required.

This type of system can be used to heat the domestic hot-water supply, as well as the house itself. Some older systems employ gravity circulation to heat the hot-water storage cylinder but incorporate an electric pump to force the water around the radiators. In most modern systems, a pump propels the water to the cylinder and radiators via diverter valves.

Sealed systems

A sealed system is an alternative to the traditional open-vented method. Water is fed into the system via a filling loop, which is temporarily connected to the mains. In place of a feed-and-expansion tank (see top right), a pressure vessel containing a flexible diaphragm accommodates the expansion of the water as the temperature rises. Should the system become overpressurized, a safety valve discharges some of the water.

There is less corrosion in a sealed system and, because it runs at a relatively high temperature, the radiators can be smaller. Because there's no feed-and-expansion tank installed in the loft, radiators can be placed anywhere in the house, including in the loft itself.

However, sealed systems must be completely watertight – since there is no automatic top up – and they have to be made with expensive, high-quality components to prevent pressure loss. A boiler with a high-temperature cutout is required, in case the ordinary thermostat fails. Also, radiators get very hot.

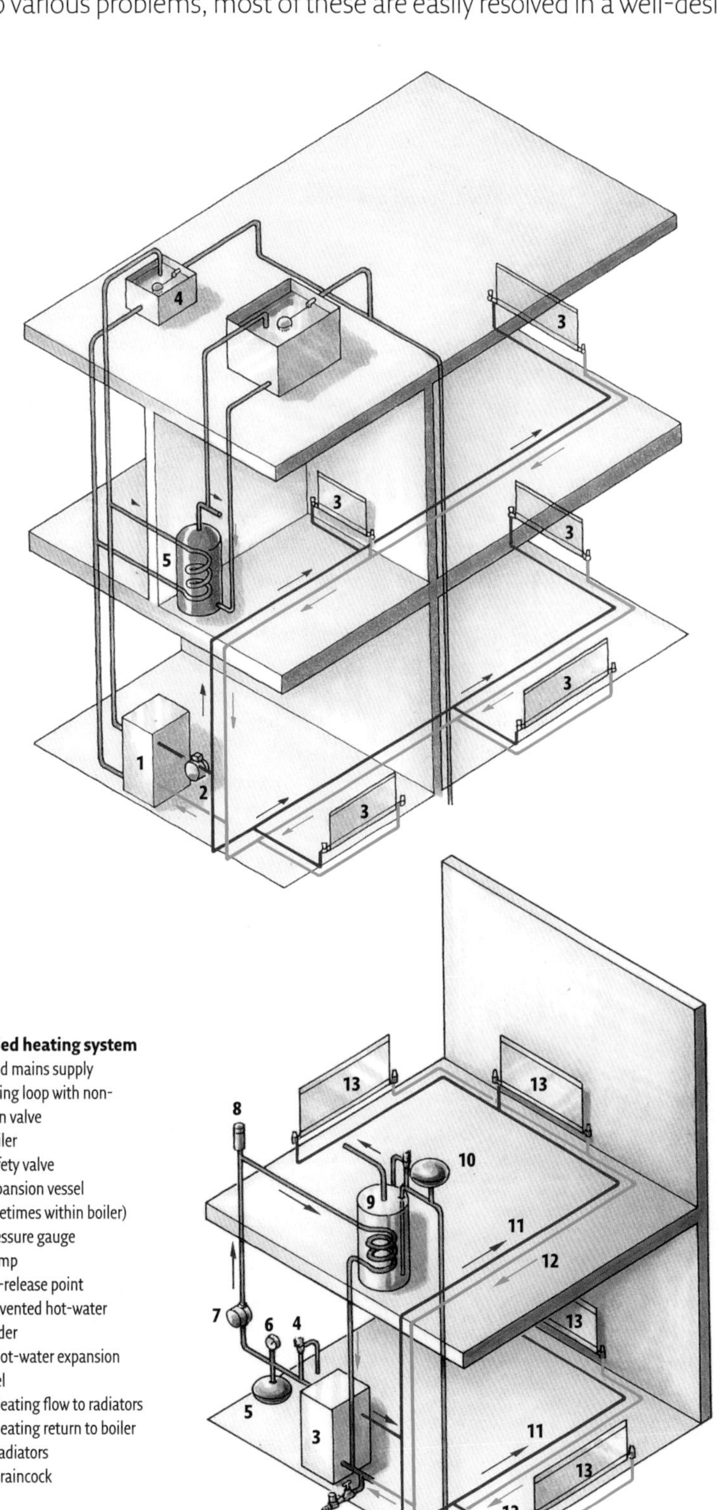

Open-vented system
The water heated by the boiler (**1**) is driven by a pump (**2**) through a two-pipe system to the radiators (**3**) or special convector heaters, which give off heat as the hot water flows through them, gradually warming the rooms to the required temperature; the water then returns to the boiler to be reheated. A feed-and-expansion tank (**4**), situated in the loft, keeps the system topped up and takes the excess of water created by the system overheating. The hot-water cylinder (**5**) is heated by gravity circulation. In the diagram, red indicates the flow of water from the pump and blue shows the return flow.

Sealed heating system
1 Cold mains supply
2 Filling loop with non-return valve
3 Boiler
4 Safety valve
5 Expansion vessel (sometimes within boiler)
6 Pressure gauge
7 Pump
8 Air-release point
9 Unvented hot-water cylinder
10 Hot-water expansion vessel
11 Heating flow to radiators
12 Heating return to boiler
13 Radiators
14 Draincock

• **One-pipe system**
In an outdated one-pipe system, heated water is pumped around the perimeter of the house through a single large-bore pipe that forms a loop. Flow and return pipes divert hot water to each radiator by means of gravity circulation. Larger radiators may be required at the end of the loop in order to compensate for heat loss. A one-pipe system incorporates a feed-and-expansion tank and a hot-water circuit similar to those used for conventional two-pipe systems.

SEE ALSO > Off-peak electricity 282, Hot-water cylinders 392–3

Central-heating boilers

Technological improvements have made it possible to produce central-heating boilers that are smaller and more efficient than their predecessors. Today, gas and oil are still the most popular fuels because, despite advances in solid-fuel technology, the dirt and inconvenience associated with solid fuels can't be ignored or overcome. Wood-burning boilers aren't really practical for suburban homes, though a wood-fired stove could be used to heat a room, perhaps with a small back boiler to provide hot water.

Condensing boilers

Condensing boilers extract more heat from the fuel than other types of boiler. This is achieved either by passing the water through a highly efficient heat exchanger or by having a secondary heat exchanger that uses heat from the flue to 'preheat' cool water returning from the radiators.

With a conventional boiler, the moisture within the exhaust gases passes through the flue as steam. In a condensing boiler, which extracts additional heat from the gases, the moisture condenses within the boiler and is drained through a pipe.

Building Regulations now require all new gas- and oil-fired boilers fitted in households to be of the condensing type, because of their low energy use, whether the installation is a new build or a replacement. More complex than a standard gas boiler, they are also more costly.

Strict rules apply on the location of the flue to avoid gases being vented across footpaths or under a neighbour's window, for instance. Your Building Control Officer will be able to advise.

• Gas installers
Gas boilers must be installed by competent fitters registered with CORGI (Council for Registered Gas Installers). Check, also, that your installer has the relevant public-liability insurance for working with gas.

• Boiler flues
All boilers need some means of expelling the combustion gases that result from burning fuel. Frequently this is effected by connecting the boiler to a conventional flue or chimney that takes the gases directly to the outside.

Alternatively, some boilers, known as room-sealed balanced-flue boilers, are mounted on an external wall and the flue gases are passed to the outside through a short horizontal duct. Balanced-flue ducts are divided into two passages – one for the outgoing flue gases, and the other for the incoming air needed for efficient combustion.

All boilers can be connected to a conventional flue, but gas and oil-fired boilers are also made for balanced-flue systems. If the boiler is fan-assisted, it can be mounted at some distance – typically 3 or 4m (10 or 12ft) – from the balanced-flue outlet.

Oil-fired boilers

Pressure-jet oil-fired boilers are fitted with controls similar to the ones for gas boilers described above. Oil boilers can be floor-standing or wall-mounted. Oil-fired heating requires a large external storage tank, with easy access for delivery tankers.

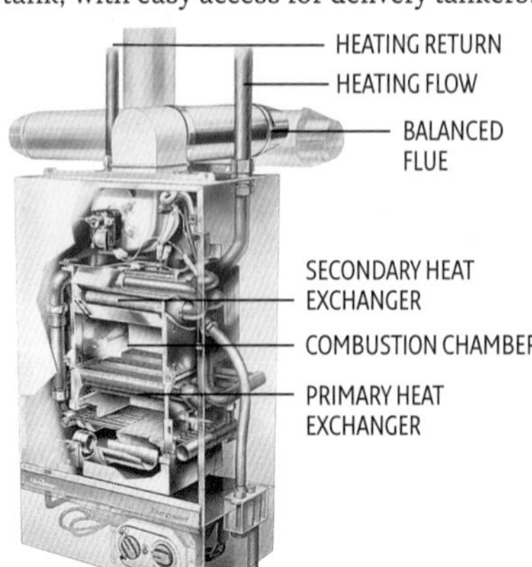

Condensing boiler

Gas-fired boilers

Older gas-fired boilers have pilot lights that burn constantly, in order to ignite the burners whenever heat is required. The burners may be operated manually or by a timer set to switch the heating on and off at selected times. The boiler can be linked to a room thermostat, so that the heating is switched on and off to keep temperatures at the required level throughout the house. Another thermostat inside the boiler prevents overheating.

An increasing number of boilers have energy -saving electronic ignition. The pilot is not lit until the room thermostat demands heat and cuts off once up to temperature.

Solid-fuel boilers

Solid-fuel boilers are invariably floor-standing and require a conventional flue. Back boilers are small enough to be built into a fireplace. The rate at which the fuel is burnt is controlled by a thermostatic damper or sometimes by a fan.

The system must have some means for the heat to escape in case of a circulation pump failure, or the water could boil, causing damage. This is usually in the form of a pipe that leads from the boiler and the heat exchanger in the domestic hot-water cylinder to a radiator situated in the bathroom, where the excess heat can be used to dry wet towels.

Some models have a hopper feed that tops them up automatically. You need a suitable place to store fuel for the boiler and the residual ash has to be removed regularly.

Combination boilers

Combination boilers provide both hot water to a sealed heating system and a separate supply of instant hot water directly to taps and showers. The advantages are ease of installation (no tanks or pipes in the loft), space-saving (no hot-water storage cylinder), economy (you heat only the water you use) and mains pressure at taps and shower heads. The main drawback is a fairly slow flow rate, so filling a bath can take a long time and it's not usually possible to use two hot taps at the same time. Combination boilers are therefore best suited to small households or flats. However, to overcome these problems, the newer generation of combination boilers incorporate a small hot-water storage tank.

Heating requirements

The capacity (heat output) of the boiler needed can be calculated by adding up the specified heat output of all the radiators, plus a 3kW allowance for a hot-water cylinder. Ten per cent is added to allow for very cold weather. The overall calculation is affected by the heat lost through the walls and ceiling, and also by the number of air changes caused by ventilation. Some plumbers' merchants will make the relevant calculations for you, if you provide them with the dimensions of each room. Alternatively, you can find calculators online.

The efficiency of a boiler is determined by its SEDBUK (Seasonal Efficiency of Domestic Boilers in the UK) rating from A to G. A-rated boilers are more than 90 per cent efficient.

SEE ALSO > Oil-storage regulations 25, Room heaters 401, Flue liners 402–3, Thermostats 409

Ventilating a boiler

A boiler that takes its combustion air from within the house and expels fumes through a conventional open flue (see opposite far left) must have access to a permanent ventilator fitted in an outside wall. The ventilator has to be of the correct size - as recommended by the boiler manufacturer - and must not contain a fly-screen mesh, which could become blocked. Refer to Building Regulations F1-1.8 for specific guidance. A boiler that is starved of air will create carbon monoxide - a lethal invisible gas that has no smell.

A cupboard that houses a balanced-flue room-sealed boiler must be fitted with ventilators at the top and bottom, to prevent the boiler overheating.

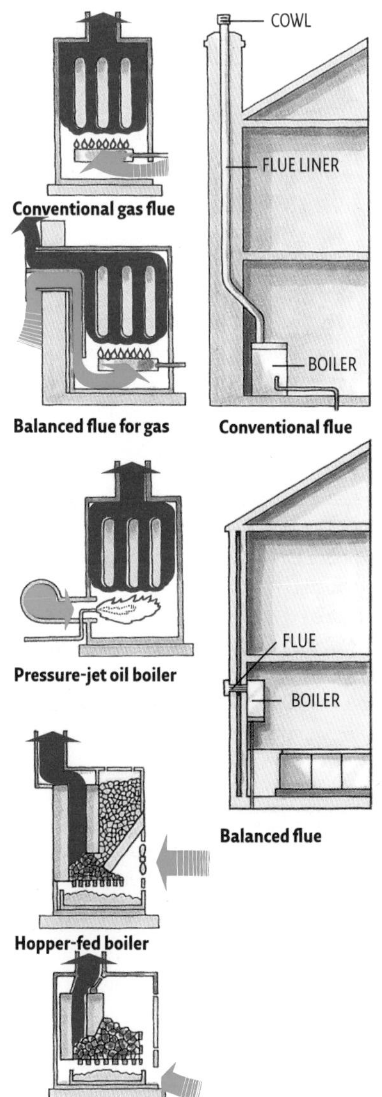

Conventional gas flue

Balanced flue for gas

Conventional flue

Pressure-jet oil boiler

Balanced flue

Hopper-fed boiler

Solid-fuel back boiler

Radiators

The hot water from a central-heating boiler is pumped along small-bore pipes connected to radiators, mounted at strategic points to heat individual rooms and hallways. The standard radiator is a double-skinned pressed-metal panel, which is heated by the hot water that flows through it.

Despite its name, a radiator emits only a fraction of its output as radiant heat - the rest being delivered by natural convection as the surrounding air comes into contact with the hot surfaces of the radiator. As the warmed air rises towards the ceiling, cooler air flows in around the radiator, and this air in turn is warmed and moves upwards. As a result, a very gentle circulation of air takes place in the room, and the temperature gradually rises to the optimum set on the room thermostat.

Panel radiators

Radiators are available in a wide range of sizes. The larger they are, the greater their heat output. Output for a given size can be increased further by using 'double radiators', which are made by joining two panels one behind the other. Most types of radiator have fins attached to their rear faces to induce convected heat.

The handwheel valve at one end of the radiator turns the flow of water on or off; the lockshield valve at the other end is set to balance the system, then left alone. An ordinary handwheel valve can be fitted at either end of a radiator, regardless of the direction of flow. However, thermostatic valves, which regulate the temperature of individual radiators, are marked with arrows to indicate the direction of flow and must be fitted accordingly.

A bleed valve is used to release air that can build up inside the radiator and prevent the panel from heating properly.

Decorative radiators
Radiators don't have to be white and flat. You could choose from modern takes on old-fashioned cast iron radiators, elegant vertical radiators in stainless steel, or curved, finned models designed for tight spaces or just to look good.

Double-panel radiator

Finned radiator

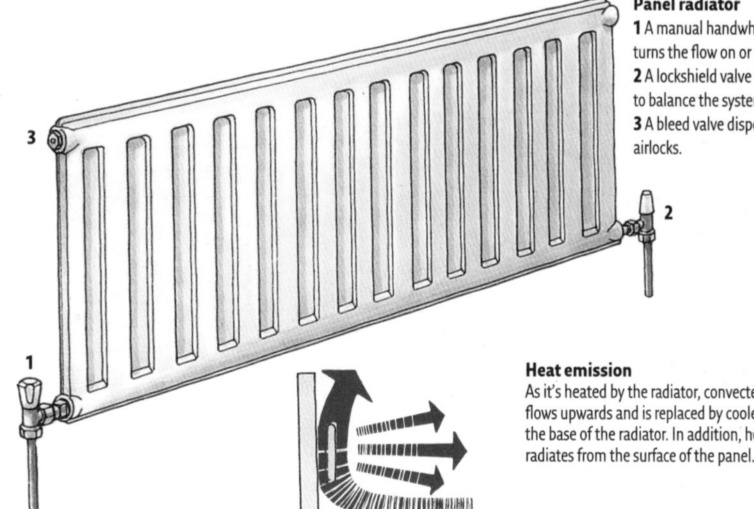

Panel radiator
1 A manual handwheel valve turns the flow on or off.
2 A lockshield valve is set to balance the system.
3 A bleed valve disperses airlocks.

Heat emission
As it's heated by the radiator, convected air flows upwards and is replaced by cooler air near the base of the radiator. In addition, heat radiates from the surface of the panel.

SEE ALSO > Reflective foil 257, Thermostatic valves 409, Bleeding radiators 413

Convectors and skirting radiators

Convectors and skirting radiators are a space-saving and more expensive alternative to panel radiators. Heat from hot water pumped through them is transferred to the air via fins or a panel, which replaces the skirting board in the room.

Rising warm air draws in cool air below

Fan-assisted convector This unit makes good use of the wasted space under a kitchen unit.

Convectors

Convector heaters can be used as part of a wet central-heating system. Some models are designed for inconspicuous fixing at skirting level.

Convectors emit none of their heat in the form of direct radiation. The hot water from the boiler passes through a finned pipe inside the heater, and the fins absorb the heat and transfer it to the air around them. The warmed air passes through a damper-controlled vent at the top of the heater, and at the same time cool air is drawn in through the open bottom to be warmed in turn.

With a fan-assisted convector heater, the airflow is accelerated over the fins in order to speed up room heating.

Positioning convectors and radiators

At one time, central-heating radiators and convector units were nearly always placed under windows, because the area around a window tends to be the coldest part of a room. However, if you've fitted double glazing to reduce heat loss and draughts, then it will be more efficient to place heaters elsewhere – especially if windows are hung with long curtains.

Finned radiators offer a greater heat output and more flexibility in their siting. The shape of a room can also affect the siting of radiators and, perhaps, the number. For example, it is difficult to heat a large L-shaped room with just a single radiator at one end. In situations like this it's probably best to consult a heating installer to help you decide upon the optimum number and position of heaters.

Wherever possible, avoid hanging curtains or standing furniture in front of a radiator or convector heater. Curtains and furniture absorb radiated heat – and curtains also trap convected heat.

The warm air rising from a radiator will eventually discolour the paint or wall-covering above it. Fitting a narrow shelf about 50mm (2in) above a radiator avoids staining, without inhibiting convection. Alternatively, enclose the radiator in a decorative cover – heat output is barely reduced, provided air is able to pass through the enclosure freely, especially at the top and bottom (see below).

Skirting radiators

A skirting radiator is a space-saving alternative to a conventional panel radiator and is designed for installation in place of a wooden skirting board.The twin copper-lined waterways and the outer casing are formed from a single aluminium extrusion (see below) and are clipped to the wall with a special bracket.

Made in various lengths up to 6m (19ft 6in) lengths and available in various finishes, skirting radiators are cut to length then joined at the corners of the room, using conventional soldered pipe joints. The pipework and valves are hidden from view, but are readily accessible for maintenance or repair.

Electric versions are also available.

Radiator covers

Fitting a cover around a radiator will turn it into a decorative feature. The cabinet must be ventilated to allow air into the bottom and for the convected warm air to exit from the top. A perforated panel is usually fitted across the front to dissipate the heat and add to the unit's appearance.

Cabinets are available in kit form to fit standard-size radiators. Alternatively, you can make your own from MDF board.

Making your own cabinet

A radiator cabinet can be designed to stand on the floor or to be hung on the wall at skirting height. A floor-standing version is described here.

Cut the shelf (1) and two end panels (2) from 18mm (3/4in) MDF. Make these components large enough to enclose the radiator and both valves.

Glue the panels to the shelf with dowel joints, and dowel a 50 x 25mm (2 x 1in) tie rail (3) between the sides at skirting level. Cut a new skirting moulding with a vent in the bottom edge (4) to fit along the base. Complete the box by applying a decorative moulding (5) around the edge of the shelf.

Cut a front panel (6) from either perforated hardboard, MDF, aluminium mesh or bamboo lattice, and mount it in a rebated MDF frame (7). Hold the frame in place with magnetic catches.

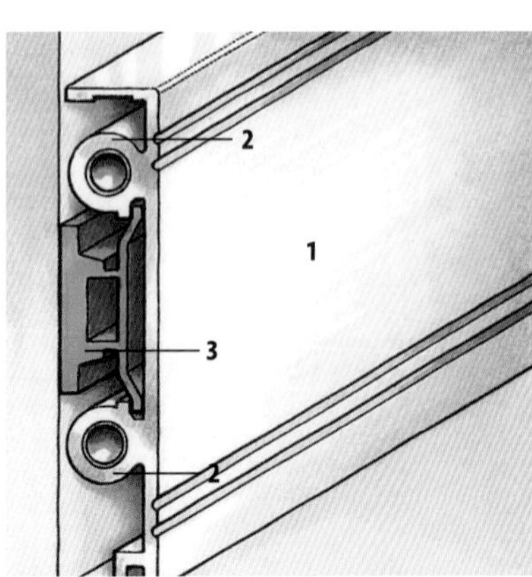

Skirting radiator
1 Aluminium extrusion
2 Copper-lined waterways
3 Mounting assembly

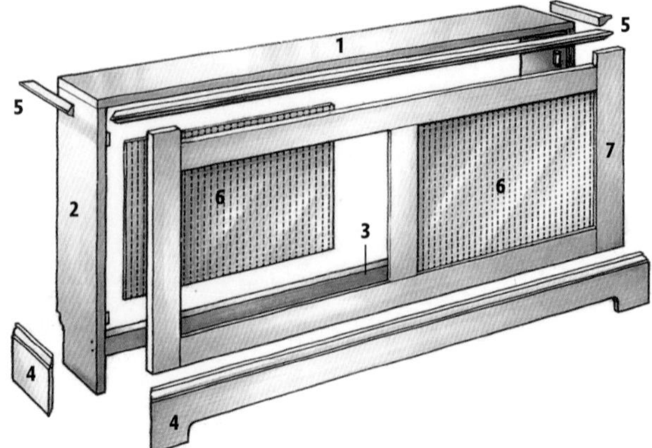

Floor-standing radiator cabinet
1 Shelf
2 End panel
3 Tie rail
4 Skirting
5 Moulding
6 Perforated panel
7 Frame

SEE ALSO > Reflective foil 257, Radiators 407

Controls for central heating

There are various automatic control systems and devices available for wet central heating that bring greater control and can help cut running costs by reducing wastage of heat to a minimum.

Automatic controllers can be divided into three basic types: temperature controllers (thermostats), automatic on-off switches (programmers and timers), and heating-circuit controllers (zone valves). These devices can be used, individually or in combination, to provide a very high level of control.

Thermostats

All boilers incorporate thermostats to prevent overheating. An oil-fired or gas boiler will have one that can be set to vary heat output by switching the unit on and off; and some models are also fitted with modulating burners, which adjust flame height to suit heating requirements. On a solid-fuel boiler, the thermostat opens and closes a damper that admits more or less air to the firebed to increase or reduce the rate of burning, as required.

A room thermostat - 'roomstat' for short - is often the only form of central-heating control fitted. It is placed in a room where the temperature usually remains fairly stable, and works on the assumption that any rise or drop in the temperature will be matched by similar variations throughout the house.

Roomstats control the temperature by means of simple on-off switching of the boiler - or the pump, if the boiler has to run constantly in order to provide hot water. The main drawback of a roomstat is that it can't sense temperature changes in other rooms - caused, for example, by the sun shining through a window or a separate heater being switched on.

More sophisticated temperature control is provided by a thermostatic valve, which can be fitted to a radiator instead of the standard manually operated valve. A temperature sensor opens and closes the valve, varying the heat output to maintain the desired temperature in the individual room. Thermostatic radiator valves need not be fitted in every room, but could reduce the heat in a kitchen or spare bedroom, for example, while a roomstat regulates the temperature in the rest of the house.

The most sophisticated thermostatic controller is a boiler-energy manager or 'optimizer', which collects data from sensors inside and outside the building in order to deduce the optimum running period so the boiler is not wastefully switched rapidly on and off.

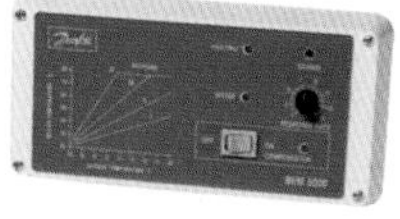

Boiler-energy manager

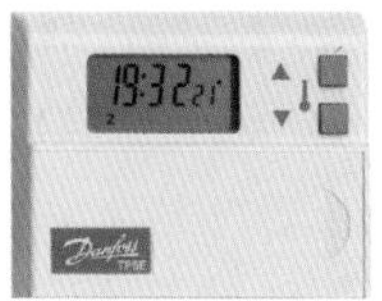

Room thermostat

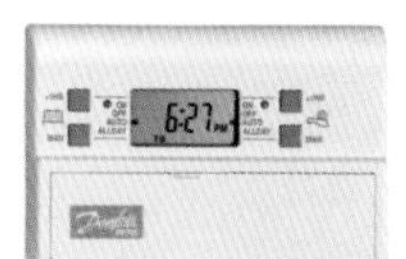

Programmer or timer

Thermostatic radiator valve

Zone-control valves

In most households the bedrooms are unoccupied for much of the day, so don't need heating continuously.

One way of avoiding such waste is to divide your central-heating system into circuits or 'zones' (upstairs and downstairs, for example) and to heat the whole house only when necessary. If you zone your house, make sure the unheated areas are adequately ventilated, to prevent condensation.

Control is via motorized valves linked to a timer or programmer that directs the heated water through selected pipes at predetermined times of the day. Alternatively, zone valves linked to individual thermostats can be used to provide separate temperature control for each zone.

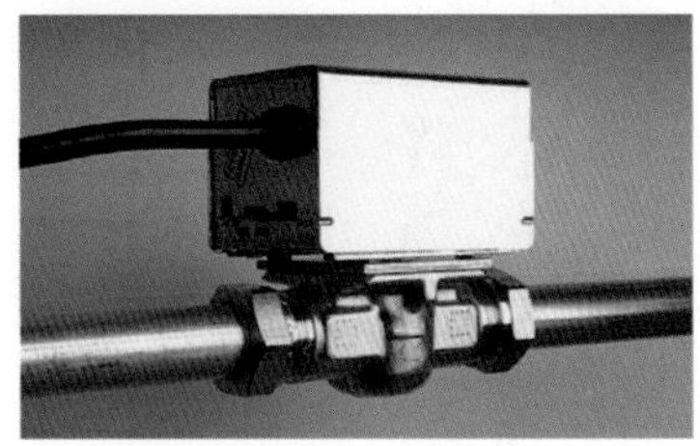

A motorized zone-control valve

Timers and programmers

You can cut fuel bills substantially by ensuring that the heating is not on while you are out or asleep. A timer can be set so that the system is switched on to warm the house before you get up and goes off just before you leave for work, then comes on again shortly before you return home and goes off at bedtime. The simpler timers provide two 'on' and two 'off' settings, which are normally repeated every day. A manual override enables you to alter the times for weekends and other changes in routine.

More sophisticated devices, known as programmers, offer a larger number of on-off programs - even a different one for each day of the week - as well as control of domestic hot water.

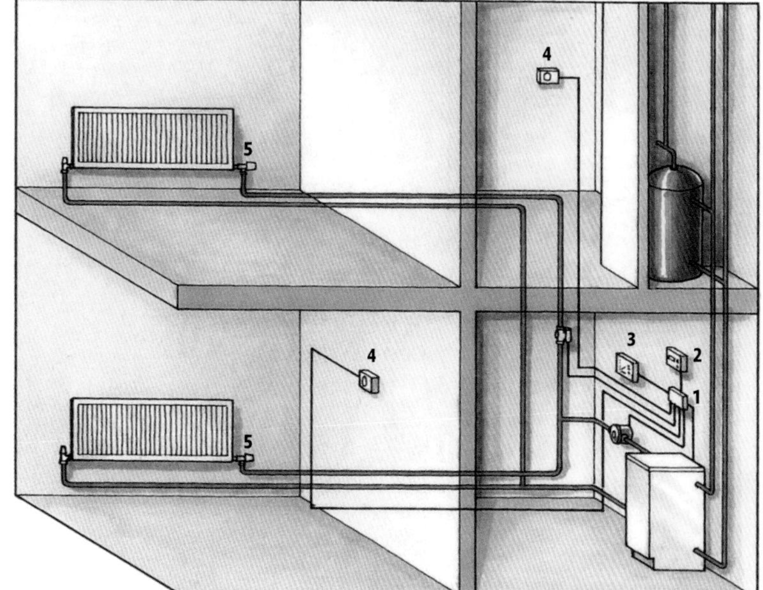

Heating controls
There are a number of ways to control heating:
1 A wiring centre connects the controls in the system.
2 A programmer/timer is used in conjunction with a zone valve to switch the boiler on or off at pre-set times, and run the heating and hot-water systems.
3 Optional boiler-energy manager controls the efficiency of the heating system.
4 Room thermostats are used to control the pump, or zone valves to regulate the overall temperature.
5 A non-electrical thermostatic radiator valve controls the temperature of an individual heater.

SEE ALSO > Radiators 407

Diagnosing heating problems

When heating systems fail to work properly, they can exhibit all sorts of symptoms, some of which can be difficult to diagnose without specialized knowledge and experience. However, it pays to check out the more common faults, summarized below, before calling out a heating engineer.

Hissing or banging sounds from boiler or heating pipes

This is caused by overheating due to:

- **Blocked chimney (if you have a solid-fuel boiler)** Sweep chimney to clear heavy soot.
- **Build-up of scale due to hard water** Shut down boiler and pump. Treat system with descaler. Drain, flush and refill system.
- **Faulty boiler thermostat** Shut down boiler. Leave pump working to circulate water, to cool system quickly. When it's cool, operate boiler thermostat control. If you don't hear a clicking sound, call in an engineer.
- **Lack of water in system** Shut down boiler. Check feed-and-expansion tank in loft. If empty, the valve may be stuck. Move float-valve arm up and down to restore flow and fill system. If this has no effect, check to see if mains water has been turned off by accident or (in winter) if supply pipe is frozen.
- **Pump not working (with a solid-fuel boiler)** Shut down boiler, then check that pump is switched on. If pump is not running, turn off power and check wired connections to it. If pump seems to be running but outlet pipe is cool, check for airlock by opening pump bleed screw. If pump is still not working, shut it down, drain system, remove pump and check for blockage. Clean pump or, if need be, replace it.

Radiators in one part of the house do not warm up

- **Timer or thermostat that controls relevant zone valve is not set properly or is faulty** Check timer or thermostat setting and reset if need be. If this has no effect, switch off power supply and check wired connections. If that makes no difference, replace unit.
- **Zone valve is faulty** Replace motor or drain system and replace entire valve.
- **Pump not working** *See above.*

All radiators remain cool, though boiler is operating normally

- **Pump not working** Check pump by listening or feeling for motor vibration. If pump is running, check for airlock by opening bleed valve. If this has no effect, the pump outlet may be blocked. Switch off boiler and pump, remove pump and clean or replace as necessary. If pump is not running, switch off and try to free spindle. Look for a large screw in the middle – removing or turning it will reveal the slotted end of the spindle. Turn this until the spindle feels free, then switch pump on again.
- **Pump thermostat or timer is set incorrectly or is faulty** Adjust thermostat or timer setting. If that has no effect, switch off power and check wiring connections. If they are in good order, call in an engineer.

Area at top of radiator stays cool

- **Airlock at top of radiator is preventing water circulating fully** Bleed radiator to release trapped air.

Single radiator doesn't warm up

- **Handwheel valve is closed** Open the valve.
- **Thermostatic radiator valve is set too low or is faulty** Adjust valve setting. If this has no effect, drain the system and replace the valve.
- **Lockshield valve not set properly** Remove lockshield cover and adjust valve setting until radiator seems as warm as those in other rooms. Have lockshield valve properly balanced when the system is next serviced.
- **Radiator valves blocked by corrosion** Close both radiator valves, remove radiator and flush out.

Cool patch in centre of radiator

- **Deposits of rust at bottom of radiator are restricting circulation of water** Close both radiator valves, remove radiator and flush out.

Boiler not working

- **Thermostat set too low** Check that roomstat and boiler thermostats are set correctly.
- **Programmer or timer not working** Check programmer or timer is switched on and set correctly. Replace if fault persists.
- **Gas boiler's pilot light goes out** Relight pilot following instructions supplied with boiler (these are usually printed on the back of the front panel). If pilot fails to ignite, have it replaced.

Continuous drip from overflow pipe of feed-and-expansion tank

- **Faulty float valve or leaking float, causing valve to stay open** Shut off mains water supply to feed-and-expansion tank and bale out to below level of float valve. Remove valve and fit new washer. Or, unscrew leaking float from arm and fit new one.
- **Leaking heat-exchanger coil in hot-water cylinder** Dripping from overflow will occur only if the feed-and-expansion tank is below the cold-water storage tank. Turn off boiler and mains water. Let system cool, then take dip-stick measurement in both tanks. Don't use water overnight – check again in morning. If water level has risen in the feed-and-expansion tank and dropped in the cold-water storage tank, replace hot water cylinder.

Water leaking from system

- **Loose pipe unions at joints, pump connections, boiler connections, etc.** Turn off boiler (or close down solid-fuel appliance) and switch off pump, then tighten leaking joints. If this has no effect, drain the system and remake joints.

SEE ALSO > Curing leaks 349, Float valves 452–4, Pipework 359–65, Plumbing joints 360–2, 364–5, Sweeping chimneys 396, Draining the system 411, Bleed valve 413, Removing a radiator 413, Replacing radiators 415

Draining and refilling

Although it's inadvisable to do so unnecessarily, there may be times when you have to drain your wet central-heating system completely and refill it. This could be for routine maintenance, when dealing with a fault, or because you have decided to extend the system or upgrade the boiler. The job can be done fairly easily if you follow the procedures outlined here.

Draining the system

Before draining your central-heating system, cool the water by shutting off the boiler and leaving the circulation pump running. The water in the system will cool quite quickly.

Switch off the pump and turn off the mains water supply to the feed-and-expansion tank in the loft either by closing the stopcock in the feed pipe or by laying a batten across the tank and tying the float arm to it.

The main draincock for the system will normally be in the return pipe near the boiler. Push one end of a garden hose onto its outlet and lead the other end of the hose to a gully or soakaway in the garden, then open the draincock. If you have no key for its square shank, use an adjustable spanner.

Most of the water will drain from the system, but some will be held in the radiators. To release the trapped water, start at the top of the house and carefully open the radiator bleed valves. Air will flow into the tops of the radiators, breaking the vacuum, and the water will drain out. Last of all, drain inverted pipe loops (see below).

Draining procedure
Turn off the mains supply to the tank at the feed-pipe stopcock (**1**). If there's no stopcock, tie the float-valve arm to a batten laid across the tank (**2**). With a hose pushed onto the main draincock (**3**) and its other end at a gully or soakaway outside, open the draincock and let the system empty. Release any water trapped in the radiators (**4**) by opening their bleed valves (**5**), starting at the top of the house. Be sure to close all draincocks before you refill the system.

Inverted pipe loops

Often when fitting a central-heating system in a house that has a solid ground floor, installers run the heating pipes from the boiler into the ceiling void and drop them down the walls to the individual radiators. These 'inverted pipe loops' have their own draincock and must be drained separately after the main system has been emptied.

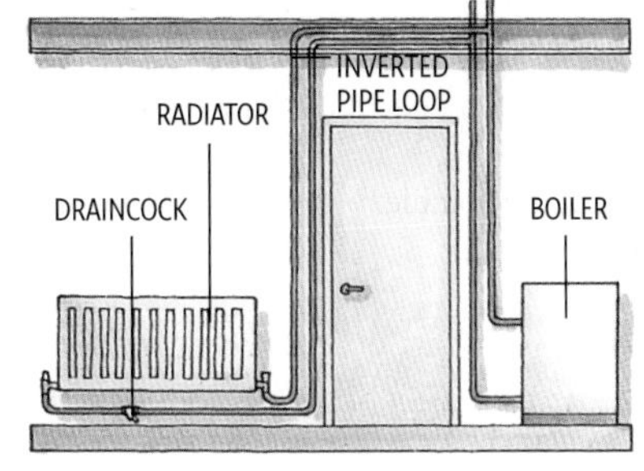

An inverted pipe loop has its own draincock

Refilling the system

Before refilling the system, check all the draincocks and bleed valves are closed.

Restore the water supply to the feed-and-expansion tank in the loft. Filling the system will trap air in the tops of the radiators – so when full, bleed all the radiators, starting at the bottom of the house. You may also have to bleed the circulating pump. Finally, check all the draincocks and bleed valves for leaks, and tighten them if necessary.

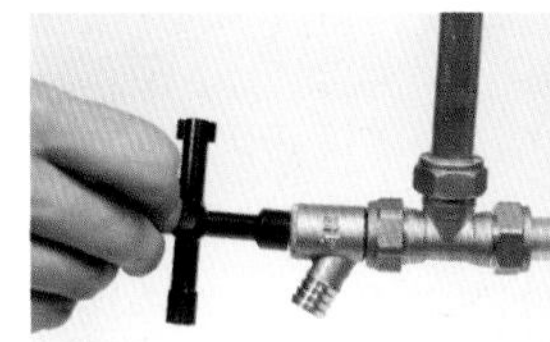
Draincock key
A special tool is available for operating draincocks.

Cleaning the system

After installing or modifying a central-heating system, flush the pipework to get rid of swarf and flux, which can induce corrosion and damage valves or the pump.

Turn the pump impeller with a screwdriver before running the system in order to make sure it's clear. If you can feel resistance, drain the system and remove the pump before cleaning and refitting.

Descaling

If your system is old or badly corroded, a harsh cleaner or descaler may expose minor leaks sealed by corrosion – so use a mild cleanser, introduced into the system via the feed-and-expansion tank or inject it into a radiator via the bleed valve. Manufacturers' instructions vary, but in general the cleanser is left in the system for a week, with the boiler set to a fairly high temperature.

Afterwards, turn off and drain the system, then refill and drain it several times – if possible, using a hose to run mains-pressure water through the system while draining it. Some cleansers must be neutralized before you can add a corrosion inhibitor.

If your boiler is making loud banging noises, treat it with a fairly powerful descaler, running the hot-water programme only.

• Power-flushing the system
After upgrading an older system, perhaps with a new boiler or radiators, you could flush the system yourself (see left), but it's advisable to have it cleansed thoroughly by a heating engineer, using a power-flushing unit. When it is connected, the unit pumps chemically-treated water through the system to flush out impurities.

SEE ALSO > Gully 347, Turning off the water 348, Bleeding radiators 413, Bleeding a pump 416

Maintaining your boiler

Oil-fired and gas boilers must be serviced annually to work efficiently and this work must be carried out by a qualified engineer. With either type of boiler, you can enter into a contract for regular maintenance with your fuel supplier or the original installer.

Servicing gas boilers
Any maintenance that involves dismantling any part of a gas boiler must be carried out by a CORGI-registered engineer, who should undertake all the necessary gas-safety checks as part of the service. There's no point in attempting to service the boiler yourself if you are not qualified and equipped to do so – it can also be dangerous, and you will be breaking the law.

Corrosion in the system

Modern boilers and radiators are made from fairly thin materials, and if you fail to take basic anti-corrosion measures, the life of the system can be reduced to 10 years or less. Corrosion may result either from hard-water deposits or from a chemical reaction between the water and the system's metal components.

Lime scale

Scale builds up quickly in hard-water areas of the country. Even a thin layer of lime scale on the inner wall of a boiler's heat exchanger reduces its efficiency and may cause banging and knocking within the system. In fact, the scale can insulate sections of the heat exchanger to such an extent that it produces 'hot spots', leading to premature failure of the component.

Rust

Rust corrodes steel components, most notably radiators. Most rusting occurs within weeks of filling the system; but if air is being sucked in constantly, then rusting is progressive. Having to bleed radiators regularly is a sure sign that air is being drawn into the system.

Sludge

Magnetite (black sludge) clogs the pump and builds up in the bottom of radiators, reducing their heat output.

Electrolytic action

Dissimilar metals, such as copper and aluminium, act like a battery in the acidic water that is present in some central-heating systems. This results in corrosion.

Locating gas boilers
Modern boilers fit snugly into standard kitchen cupboards.

Reducing corrosion

Drain about 600ml (1 pint) of water from the boiler or a radiator. Orange water denotes rusting, and black the presence of sludge. In either case, treat immediately with corrosion inhibitor (see below).

If there are no obvious signs of corrosion, test for inhibitor levels by dropping two plain steel nails into a jar containing some water from the system, and place two similar nails in a jar of clean tap water. After a few days the nails in the tap water should rust; but if the system contains sufficient corrosion inhibitor, the nails in the system water will remain bright – if they don't, your system needs topping up with inhibitor. It is important to use the same product that is already present in the system – if you don't know what that is, drain and flush the system, then refill with fresh water and inhibitor.

Adding corrosion inhibitor

You can slow down corrosion by adding a proprietary corrosion inhibitor to the water. This is best done when the system is first installed – but the inhibitor can be introduced into the system at any time, provided the boiler is descaled before doing so. If the system has been running for some time, it is better to flush it out first by draining and refilling it repeatedly until the water runs clean. Otherwise, drain off about 20 litres (4 gallons) of water – enough to empty the feed-and-expansion tank and a small amount of pipework – then pour the inhibitor into the tank and restore the water supply, which will carry the inhibitor into the pipes. About 5 litres (1 gallon) will be enough for most systems, but check the manufacturer's instructions. Finally, switch on the pump to distribute the inhibitor throughout the system.

Reducing scale

You can buy low-voltage coils to create a magnetic field that will prevent the heat exchanger of your boiler becoming coated with scale. However, unless you have soft water in your area, the only way to actually avoid hard water in the system is to install a water softener.

Before fitting any device to reduce scale, it is essential to seek the boiler manufacturer's advice.

Servicing schemes

It pays to have your central-heating system serviced regularly. Check the Yellow Pages for a suitable engineer, or ask the original installer of the system if they are willing to undertake the necessary servicing.

Gas installations

Gas suppliers offer a choice of servicing schemes for boilers, primarily provided to cover their own installations, but they will also service systems put in by other installers following a satisfactory inspection of the installation.

The simplest of the schemes provides for an annual check and adjustment of the boiler. If any repairs are found to be necessary, either at the time of the regular check or at other times during the year, then the labour and necessary parts are charged separately. But for an extra fee it is possible to have both free labour and free parts for boiler repairs at any time of year. The gas supplier will also extend the arrangement to include inspection of the whole heating system when the boiler is being checked, plus free parts and labour for repairs.

You may find that your installer or a local firm of CORGI heating engineers offers a similar choice of servicing and maintenance contracts.

Oil-fired installations

Installers of oil-fired central-heating systems and suppliers of fuel oil offer servicing and maintenance contracts similar to those outlined above for gas-fired systems. The choice of schemes available ranges from an annual check-up to complete cover for parts and labour whenever repairs are necessary.

As with the schemes for gas, it pays to shop around and make a comparison of the various services on offer and the charges that apply.

Solid-fuel systems

If you have a solid-fuel system, it is important to have the chimney and the flueway swept twice a year. The job is very similar to sweeping an open-fire chimney, access being either through the front of a room heater that has a back boiler or through a soot door in the flue pipe or chimney breast.

Once the chimney has been swept, clean out the boiler with a stiff brush, remove the dust and soot, lift out any broken fire bars and drop new ones in.

SEE ALSO > Water softeners 390, Sweeping chimneys 396, Flushing the system 411

System repairs and maintenance

Trapped air prevents radiators from heating up fully, and a regular intake of air can cause corrosion. If a radiator feels cooler at the top than at the bottom, it's likely that a pocket of air has formed inside it and is impeding full circulation of the water. Getting the air out of a radiator – 'bleeding' it – is a simple procedure.

Bleeding a radiator

First switch off the circulation pump, otherwise it may suck air into the radiator when a bleed valve is opened.

Each radiator has a bleed valve at one of its top corners, identifiable by a square-section shank in the centre of the round blanking plug. If you don't have a key, they are readily available from any DIY shop or ironmongers. Some valves are simply opened with a screwdriver.

Use the key to turn the valve's shank anticlockwise about a quarter of a turn. It shouldn't be necessary to turn it further – but have a small container handy to catch spurting water, in case you open the valve too far. You will probably also need a rag to mop up water that dribbles from the valve and it's wise to protect carpets in case of a spill. Don't try to speed up the process by opening the valve further than necessary to let the air out – that is likely to produce a deluge of water.

You will hear a hissing sound as the air escapes. Keep the key on the shank of the valve and when the hissing stops and the first dribble of water appears, close the valve tightly.

Blocked bleed valve

If no water or air comes out when you attempt to bleed a radiator, check whether the feed-and-expansion tank in the loft is empty. If the tank is full of water, then the bleed valve is probably blocked with paint.

Close the inlet and outlet valve at each end of the radiator, then remove the screw from the centre of the bleed valve. Clear the hole with a piece of wire, and reopen one of the radiator valves slightly to eject some water from the hole. Close the radiator valve again and refit the screw in the bleed valve. Open both radiator valves and test the bleed valve again.

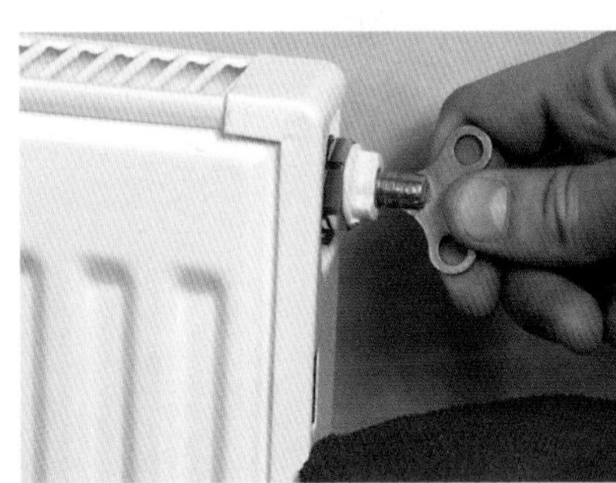

Dispersing an air pocket in a radiator

Fitting an air separator

If you are having to bleed a radiator or radiators frequently, a large quantity of air is entering the system, which can lead to serious corrosion.

Check that the feed-and-expansion tank in the loft is not acting like a radiator and warming up when you run the central heating or hot water. This indicates that hot water is being pumped through the vent pipe into the tank and taking air with it back into the system. Fit an air separator in the vent pipe, linked to the cold feed from the feed-and-expansion tank.

If the pump is fitted on the boiler return pipe, it may be sucking in air through the unions or through leaking valve spindles.

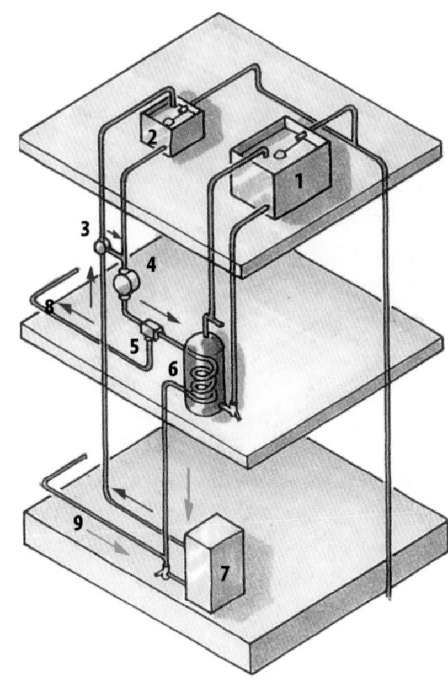

Heating system with air separator
1 Cold-water storage tank
2 Feed-and-expansion tank
3 Air separator
4 Pump
5 Motorized valve
6 Hot-water cylinder
7 Boiler
8 Radiator flow
9 Radiator return

Removing a radiator

There are a number of reasons why it may be necessary to remove a radiator – for example, to make decorating the wall behind it easier. You can remove individual radiators without having to drain the whole system.

Make sure you have plenty of rag to hand for mopping up spilled water, plus a jug and a large bowl. The water in the radiator may be very dirty – so roll back the floorcovering before you start.

Shut off both valves, turning the shank of the lockshield valve clockwise with a key or an adjustable spanner (**1**). Note the number of turns needed to close it, so that later you can reopen it by the same amount.

Unscrew the cap-nut that keeps the handwheel valve or lockshield valve attached to the adaptor in the end of the radiator (**2**). Hold the jug under the joint and open the bleed valve slowly to let the water drain out. Transfer the water from the jug to the bowl, and continue until no more water can be drained off.

Unscrew the cap-nut that keeps the other valve attached to the radiator, lift the radiator free from its wall brackets, and drain any remaining water into the bowl (**3**).

After replacing the radiator, tighten the cap-nuts on both valves. Close the bleed valve and reopen both valves (open the lockshield valve by the same number of turns you used when closing it). Last of all, bleed the air from the radiator.

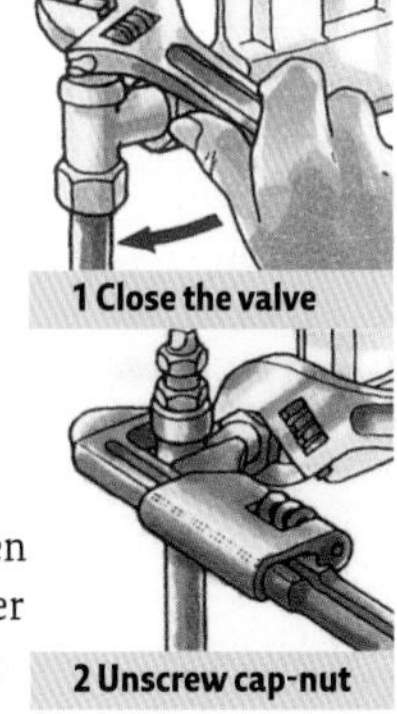

1 Close the valve

2 Unscrew cap-nut

3 Lift radiator from brackets and drain

SEE ALSO > Draining the system 411, Filling the system 411

Replacing radiator valves

Like taps, radiator valves can develop leaks, although they're usually relatively easy to cure. Occasionally, however, it's necessary to replace a faulty valve.

VALVE HEAD

SPINDLE

GLAND NUT

Leaking spindle
To stop a leak from a radiator-valve spindle, tighten the gland nut with a spanner. If the leak persists, undo the nut and wind a few turns of PTFE tape down into the spindle.

Curing a leaking radiator valve

Water leaking from a radiator valve is probably seeping from around the spindle (see left). However, when the water runs round and drips from the valve's cap-nut, it's the nut that often appears to be the source of the leak. Dry the valve, then hold a paper tissue against the various parts of the valve to ascertain exactly where the moisture is coming from. If the nut is leaking, tighten it gently; if that's unsuccessful, undo and reseal it (see right).

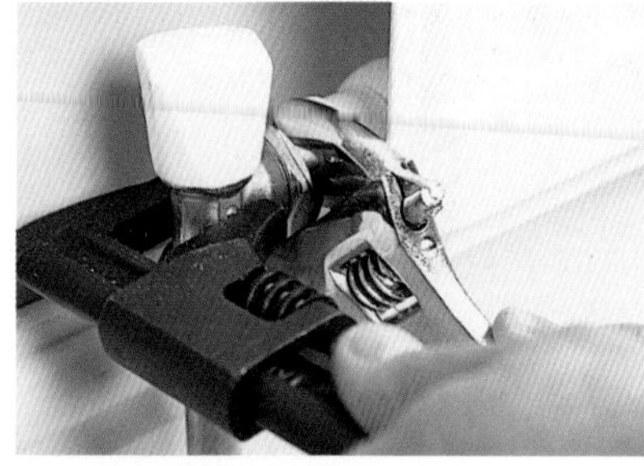

Grip leaky valve with wrench and tighten cap-nut

Replacing a worn or damaged valve

To replace a lockshield or thermostatic valve, drain the system, then lay rags under the valve to catch the dregs. Holding the body of the valve with a wrench (or water-pump pliers), use an adjustable spanner to unscrew the cap-nuts that hold the valve to the pipe (1) and also to the adaptor in the end of the radiator. Lift the valve from the end of the pipe (2); if you're replacing a lockshield valve, close it first – counting the turns, so you can open the new valve by the same number to balance the radiator.

Unscrew the valve adaptor from the radiator (3). You may be able to use an adjustable spanner, depending on the type of adaptor, or you may need a hexagonal radiator spanner.

Fitting the new valve

Ensure that the threads in the end of the radiator are clean. Drag the teeth of a hacksaw across the threads of the new adaptor to roughen them slightly, then wind PTFE tape four or five times around them. Screw the adaptor into the end of the radiator and tighten with a spanner.

Slide the valve cap-nut and a new olive over the end of the pipe and fit the valve (4) – but don't tighten the cap-nut yet. First, holding the valve body with a wrench, align it with the adaptor and tighten the cap-nut that holds them together (5). Then tighten the cap-nut that holds the valve to the water pipe and replace the valve head (6). Refill the system and check for leaks.

Replacing O-rings in a Belmont valve

The spindle of a Belmont valve is sealed with O-rings – which you can replace without having to drain the radiator. To find out which O-rings you need, take the plastic head of the valve to a plumbers' merchant before you begin work. On very old valves the rings are green, whereas the newer rings are red.

Undo the spindle (which has a left-hand thread). A small amount of water will leak out – but as you continue to remove the spindle, water pressure will seal the valve.

Prise off the O-rings, using a small screwdriver, and then lubricate the spindle with a smear of silicone grease. Slide on the new rings and replace the spindle.

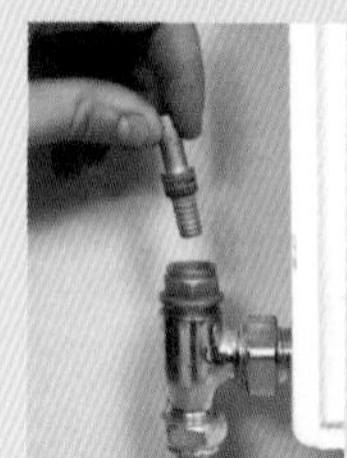

Replacing O-rings
O-rings are housed in grooves in the valve spindle. Water pressure will seal the valve as the spindle is removed.

• **Resealing a cap-nut**
Drain the system and undo the leaking nut. Smear the olive with silicone sealant and retighten the cap-nut. Don't overtighten the nut or you may damage the olive. As an alternative to sealant, wind two turns of PTFE tape around the olive (not around the threads).

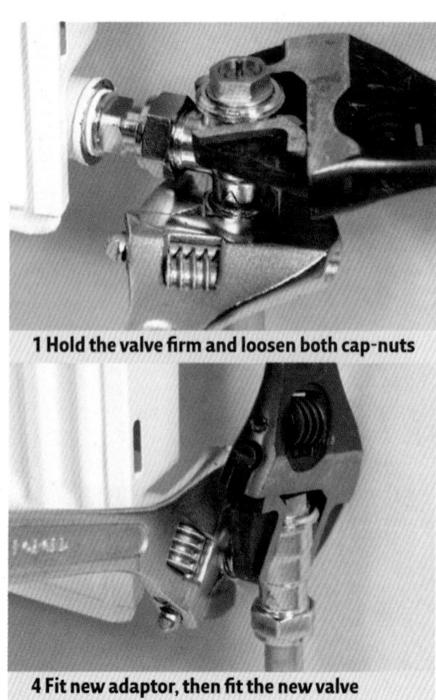

1 Hold the valve firm and loosen both cap-nuts

4 Fit new adaptor, then fit the new valve

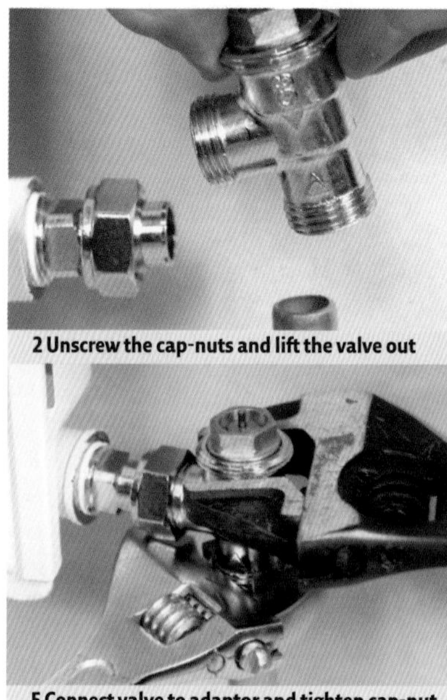

2 Unscrew the cap-nuts and lift the valve out

5 Connect valve to adaptor and tighten cap-nut

3 Remove the valve adaptor from the radiator

6 Replace the valve head

SEE ALSO > Draining the system 411, Spanners and wrenches 522

Replacing a radiator

Try to obtain a new radiator that is exactly the same size as the one you're planning to replace. This makes the job relatively easy and less disruptive, especially as the pipework may not have to be altered.

Simple replacement

Drain the old radiator and remove it from the wall. Unscrew the two valve adaptors at the bottom of the radiator, using an adjustable spanner or a hexagonal radiator spanner. Next, use a bleed key to unscrew the bleed valve; then remove both of the blanking plugs from the top of the radiator, using a radiator spanner (1).

Clean any corrosion or old PTFE tape from the threads of the adaptors and blanking plugs with wire wool (2), then wind four or five turns of new PTFE tape around the threads (3). Screw the plugs and adaptors into the new radiator, and then screw the bleed valve into its blanking plug.

Hang the new radiator on the wall brackets and connect the valves to their adaptors. Open the valves, then fill and bleed the radiator.

1 Remove the plugs, using a radiator spanner

2 Remove old PTFE tape and clean the threads

3 Tape the threads to make them watertight

Installing a different-pattern radiator

More work is involved in replacing a radiator if you can't get one to match the existing one. You may have to fit new wall brackets and alter the pipe runs.

Drain your central-heating system, then take the old brackets off the wall. Lay the new radiator face down on the floor and slide one of its brackets onto the hangers welded to the back of the radiator. Measure the position of the brackets (1) and transfer these measurements to the wall. You need to allow a clearance of 100 to 125mm (4 to 5in) below the radiator.

Line up the new radiator brackets with the pencil marks on the wall, mark the fixing-screw holes for them, drill and plug the holes, then screw on brackets (2).

Take up the floorboards below the radiator and sever the vertical portions of the feed and return pipes (either cap the old T-joints or replace them with straight joints). Connect the valves to the bottom of the radiator and hang it on its brackets.

Slip a new vertical pipe into each of the valves and, using either capillary or compression fittings, connect these pipes to the original pipework running under the floor (3). Tighten the nuts connecting the new pipes to the valves.

Finally, refill the system with water, and check all the new connections and joints for leaks.

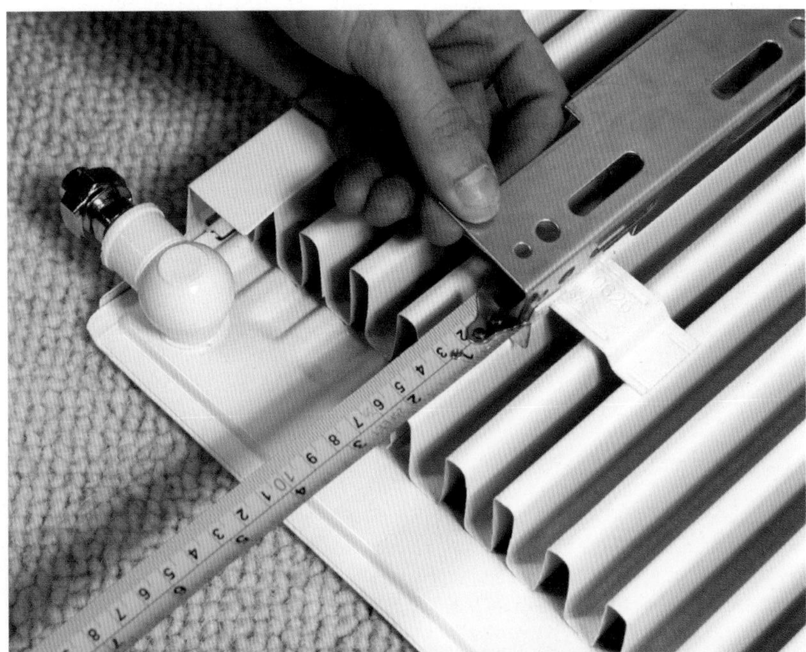

1 Measure the positions of the radiator brackets and transfer these dimensions to the wall

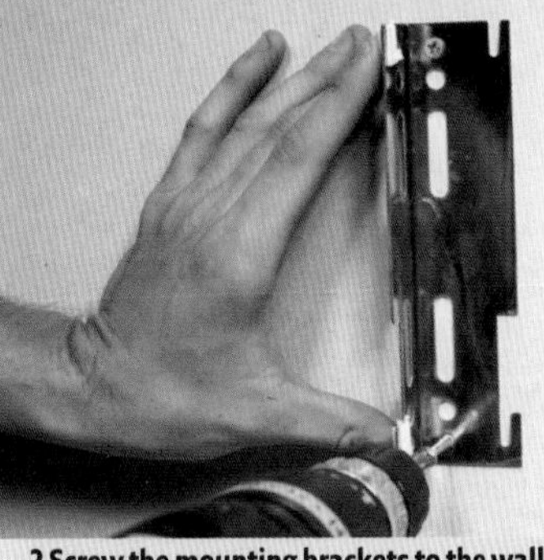

2 Screw the mounting brackets to the wall

3 Align vertical section of pipe with radiator valve

SEE ALSO > Connecting pipes 360–2, 364–5, Draining the system 411, Bleeding radiators 413, Removing radiators 413, Adjustable spanner 522

Servicing a pump

Wet central heating depends on a steady cycle of hot water being pumped from the boiler to the radiators and then back to the boiler for reheating. A faulty pump may result in poor circulation or none at all. Adjusting or bleeding the pump may be the answer; otherwise, it may need replacing.

Using a radiator thermometer
A pair of thermometers are used to measure the temperature drop across a radiator – one clipped to the feed and one to the supply pipes.

Bleeding the pump

If an airlock forms in the circulation pump, the impeller will spin ineffectually and the radiators and hot-water tank will fail to warm up properly. The cure is to bleed the air from the pump, a procedure similar to bleeding a radiator. Have a jar handy to catch any spilled water and watch that none can spill on any electrical devices.

Switch off the pump and look for a screw-in bleed valve in the pump's outer casing. It may be located behind a cover. Open the bleed valve slightly with a screwdriver or vent key until you hear air hissing out. When the hissing stops and a drop of water appears, close the bleed valve.

Open the bleed valve with a screwdriver

Adjusting the pump

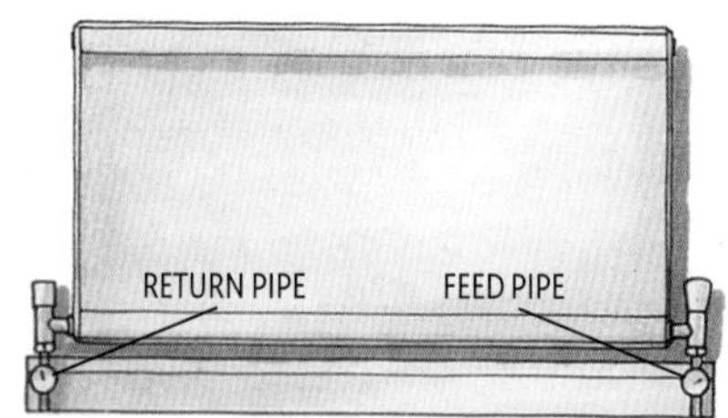

Clip thermometers to the radiator pipes

Adjust pump speed to alter the temperature

There are two basic types of central-heating pump: fixed-head and variable-head. Fixed-head pumps run at a single speed, while the speed of variable-head pumps is adjustable.

When fitting a variable-head pump, the installer balances the radiators, then adjusts the pump's speed to achieve an optimum temperature for every room. If you can't boost a room's temperature by opening the radiator's handwheel valve, try adjusting the pump speed. However, before adjusting the pump, you should check that all your radiators show the same temperature drop between their inlets and outlets. To test your radiators, you can obtain a pair of clip-on thermometers from a plumbers' merchant. Clip one of the thermometers to the feed pipe just below the radiator valve, and the other one to the return pipe, also below its valve. The difference between the temperatures registered by the thermometers should be about 11°C (20°F). If it's not, close the lockshield valve slightly to increase the difference in temperature; or open the valve to reduce it.

Having balanced all the radiators, you can now adjust the pump's speed by one increment at a time until the radiators are giving the overall temperatures you require. Depending on the make and model of pump, you may need to use a special tool, such as an Allen key, to make the adjustments. Switch off the pump before making each adjustment.

Replacing a worn pump

• **Bridging the gap**
Modern pumps are sometimes smaller than equivalent older models. If this proves to be the case, buy a converter designed to bridge the gap in the existing pipework.

If you have to replace a faulty pump, make sure the new one is of a similar specification. A good plumbers' merchant will be able to advise.

First, turn off the boiler and close the isolating valves situated on each side of the pump. If the pump lacks isolating valves, you will have to drain down the whole system.

At your consumer unit, identify the electrical circuit that supplies the pump and remove the relevant circuit fuse or MCB. Then take the coverplate off the pump (1) and disconnect its wiring.

With a bowl or bucket ready to catch the water from the pump, undo the nuts that hold the pump to the valves or pipework (2).

Having removed the old pump, install the new one (3), taking care to fit correctly any sealing washers that are provided. Tighten the connecting nuts.

Remove the coverplate from the new pump and feed in the flex. Connect the wires to the pump's terminals (4), then replace the coverplate. If the pump is of the variable-head type (see above), set the speed control to match the speed indicated on the old pump.

Open both isolating valves – or refill the system, if you had to drain it – then check the pump connections for leaks.

Open the pump's bleed valve to release any trapped air. Finally, replace the fuse or MCB in the consumer unit and test the pump.

1 Remove coverplate

2 Undo connecting nuts

3 Attach new pump

4 Connect power flex

SEE ALSO > Building Regulations on electrical wiring 284, Switching off the power 296, Removing a fuse 300, Draining the system 411, Filling the system 411

Replacing a control valve

Control valves add flexibility and control to central heating systems, but if they're worn or faulty, they can seriously impair the reliability of the system, and should be repaired or replaced promptly.

Two-port control valve
A two-port valve seals off a section of pipework when the water has reached the required temperature.

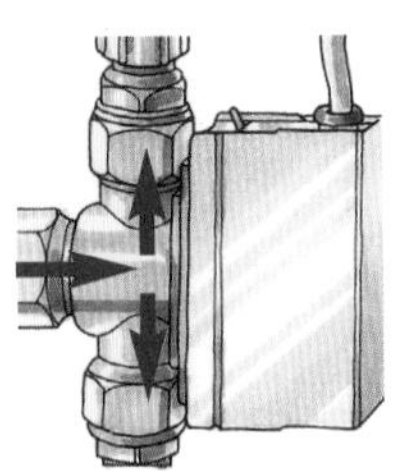

Three-port control valve
This type of valve can isolate the central heating from the hot-water circuit.

Replacing a faulty valve

When you buy a new valve, to avoid modifying pipework, make sure it is of the same pattern as the one you are replacing.

Drain the system. Then, at your consumer unit, remove the fuse or MCB for the circuit to which the central-heating controls are connected.

The flex from the valve will be wired to an adjacent junction box, which is also connected to the heating system's other controls. Take the cover off the box and disconnect the wiring for the valve – making a note of the terminals used, to make reconnection easier.

To remove the old valve, simply cut through the pipe on each side (1). When fitting the new valve, bridge the gap with short sections of pipe, complete with joints at each end (2). Spring the assembly into place and connect the joints to the old pipe, then tighten the valve cap-nuts (3). Connect the valve's flex to the junction box, then insert the circuit fuse or MCB.

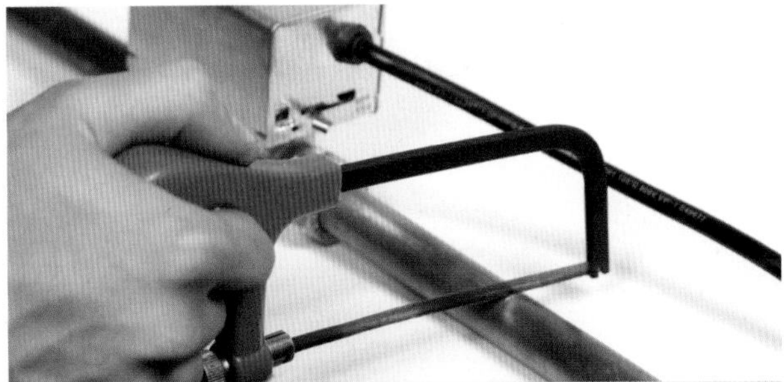

1 If you're unable to disconnect the valve, use a hacksaw to cut through the pipe on each side

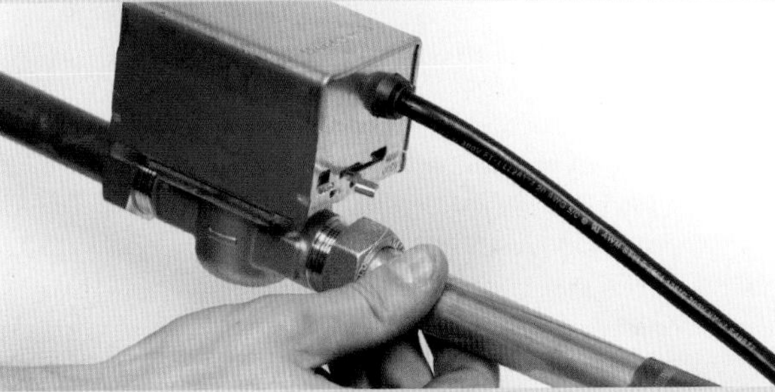

2 With the new valve connected to short sections of pipe, spring the assembly into the pipe run

3 Having connected the pipes, tighten the valve cap-nuts on each side, using a pair of adjustable spanners

Replacing the electric motor

If a motorized valve ceases to open, its electric motor may have failed. Before replacing the motor, use a mains tester to check whether it's receiving power. If it is, fit a new motor.

There is no need to drain the system. Switch off the electricity supply to the central-heating system – don't merely turn off the programmer, as motorized valves have a permanent live feed.

Once the power is off, remove the cover and undo the single screw that secures the motor (1). Open the valve, using the manual lever, and lift out the motor (2). Disconnect the two motor wires by cutting off the connectors.

Insert a new motor (available from a plumbers' merchant), then let the lever spring back to the closed position. Refit the retaining screw. Strip the ends and connect the wires, using the new connectors supplied (3). Replace the cover, and test the operation by turning on the power and running the system.

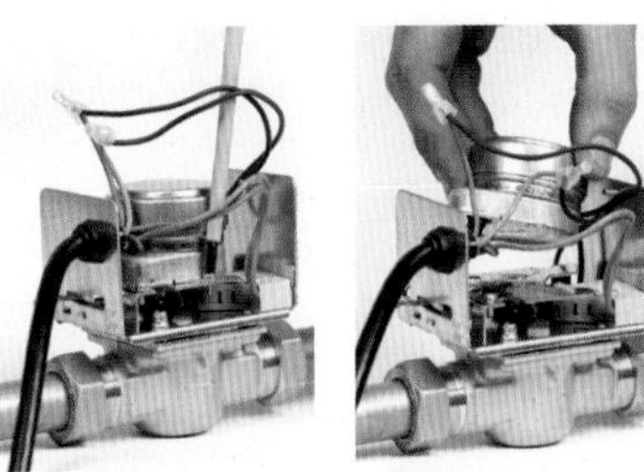

1 Remove cover and then retaining screw

2 Push lever to open valve; lift out motor

3 Join the wires, using the two connectors supplied

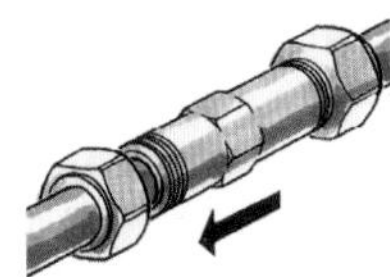

Compression coupling

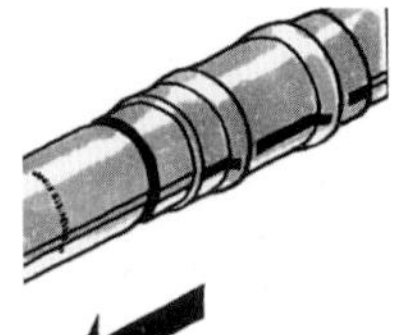

Soldered coupling

Slip couplings
It can sometimes be difficult to replace a valve using two conventional joints. If you can't spring the new assembly into place (see far left), use a slip coupling at one end. This coupling is free to slide along the pipe to bridge the gap.

SEE ALSO > Building Regulations on electrical wiring 284, Switching off the power 296, Removing a fuse 300, Junction box 309, Making pipe joints 360–2, 364–5, Heating controls 409, Draining the system 411

Underfloor heating

Thanks to flexible plastic plumbing, sophisticated controls and efficient insulation, underfloor heating is becoming a more popular and affordable form of central heating. Most systems are intalled as the house is being built, but specialist manufacturers have developed a range of warm-water heating systems to suit virtually any situation.

Underfloor-heating systems

Underfloor heating can be incorporated into any type of floor construction, including solid-concrete floors, boarded floating floors and suspended timber floors (see below). The heat emanates from a continuous length of plastic pipe that snakes across the floor – like an elongated radiator – across one or more rooms.

The entire floor area is divided into separate zones to provide the most efficient layout. Each zone is controlled by a roomstat and is connected to a thermostatically controlled multi-valve manifold that forms the heart of the system. The manifold controls the temperature of the water and the flow rate to the various zones. Once a room or zone reaches its required temperature, a valve automatically shuts off that part of the circuit. A flow meter for each of the zones allows the circuits to be balanced when setting up the system and subsequently monitors its performance.

The manifold, which is installed above floor level, is connected to the boiler via a conventional circulation pump.

• **Combining systems**
You can have radiators upstairs and underfloor heating downstairs. A mixing manifold will allow you to combine the two systems, using the same boiler. Any type of boiler is suitable for underfloor heating, but a condensing boiler is the most economical.

Benefits of underfloor heating

Although it's easier to incorporate underfloor heating while a house is being built, installing it in an existing building is possible, though you may have to raise floors to accommodate it. Underfloor heating can be made to work alongside a panel-radiator system and can provide the ideal solution for heating a new conservatory, for example.

Compared with panel radiators, an underfloor-heating system radiates heat more evenly and over a wider area. This has the effect of reducing hot and cold spots within the room and produces a more comfortable environment, where the air is warmest at floor level and cools as it rises towards the ceiling.

Underfloor heating is more energy-efficient and less costly to run than other central-heating systems because it operates at a lower temperature – and because there's a more even temperature throughout a room, the roomstat can be set a degree or two lower. With relatively cool water in the return cycle, a modern condensing boiler works even more efficiently.

Methods for installing underfloor heating

When underfloor heating is installed in a new building, the plastic tubes are usually set into a solid-concrete floor. Flooring insulation is laid over the base concrete, and rows of special pipe clips are fixed to the insulation; sometimes a metal mesh is used instead of the clips. The flexible heating tubes are then clipped into place at the required spacings (see opposite), and a concrete screed is poured on top.

With a boarded floating floor, a layer of grooved insulation is laid over the concrete base, and the pipes are set in aluminium 'diffusion' plates inserted in the grooves. The entire floor area is then covered with an edge-bonded chipboard or a similar decking material.

The heating pipes can be fastened with spacer clips to the underside of a suspended wooden floor. In this situation, clearance holes are drilled through the joists at strategic points to permit a continuous run of pipework. Reflective foil and thick blanket insulation is installed below the pipes.

It is possible to lay the pipes on top of a suspended floor, but this method raises the floor level by the thickness of the pipe assembly and the new decking.

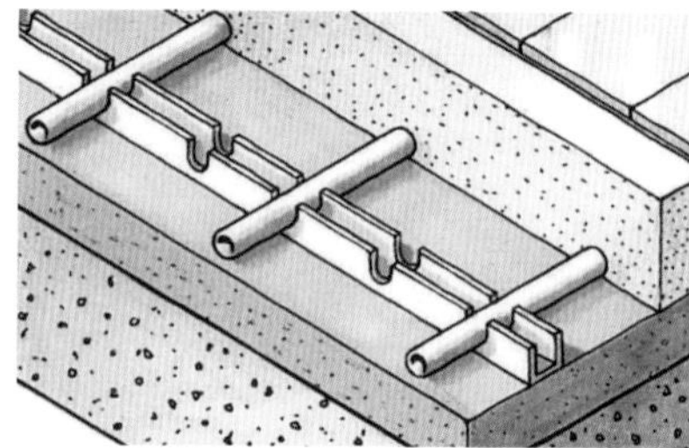

Screeded concrete floor

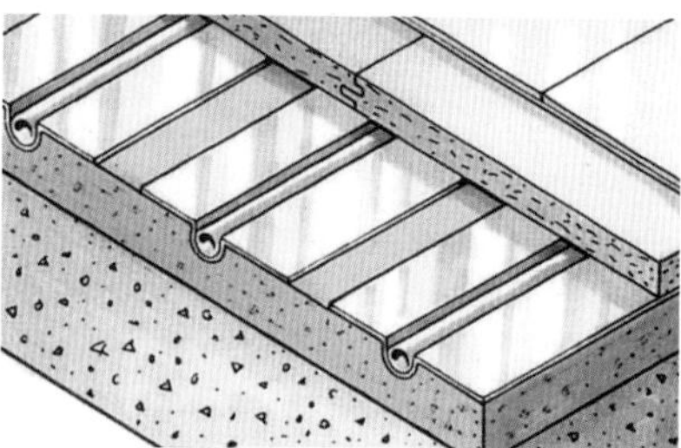

Boarded floating floor

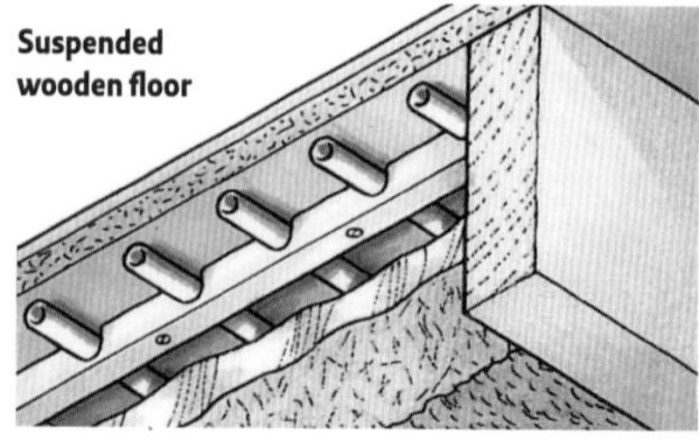

Suspended wooden floor

SEE ALSO > Floating floor 177, Panel radiators 4070, Thermostats 409

Installing underfloor heating

Underfloor heating is a good choice for heating a new conservatory. The large areas of glass in a conservatory present very few options for placing radiators, and the concrete slab that is typically used for conservatory floors provides an ideal base for this form of heating.

The basic plumbing system

Your supplier will suggest the best point to connect your new plumbing to the existing central-heating circuit. It can be at any convenient point, provided that the performance of your radiators will not be affected.

The pipework connecting the manifold for the underfloor heating to the radiator circuit can be metal or plastic, and it can be the same size as, but not larger than, the existing pipes. Again, your supplier will advise what to use.

The flow and return pipes from the manifold to the conservatory circuit (illustrated here, as an example) are connected to individual zone distributors, which in turn are connected to the flexible underfloor-heating tubes.

Basic system
1 Flow and return pipes from existing central-heating circuit.
2 Water-temperature mixing valve.
3 Pump
4 Manifold with zone valves.
5 Zone distributors.
6 Underfloor-heating tube.

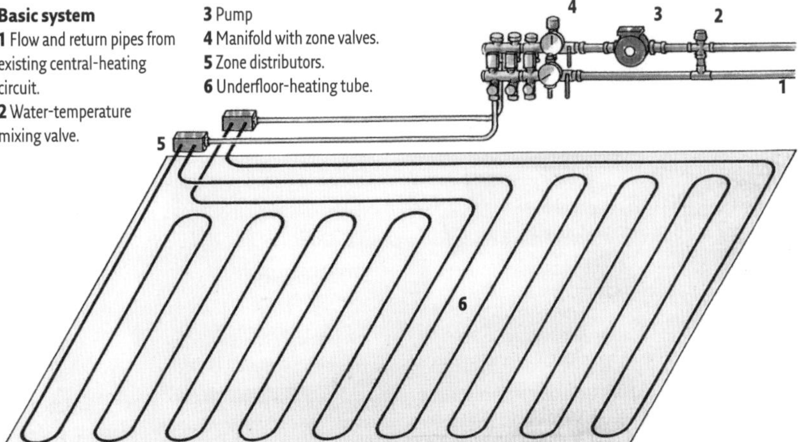

Where to start

Send details of your proposed extension to the underfloor-heating supplier. In order to be able to supply you with a well-planned scheme and quotation, the company will also need a scaled plan of your house and the basic details of your present central-heating system.

Floor construction
1 Blinded hardcore
2 DPM
3 Concrete base
4 Insulation
5 Edge insulation
6 Pipe clips and pipe
7 Screed
8 Floor tiles

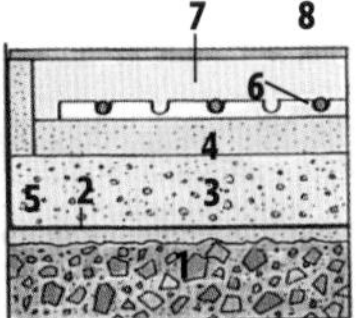

Your options

The simplest system will connect to the pipework of your existing radiator circuit. Heat for the extension will be available only when the existing central heating is running, although the temperature in the conservatory can be controlled independently by a roomstat connected to a motorized zone valve and the underfloor-heating pump.

For full control, the flow and return pipework to the underfloor system must be connected directly to the boiler, and the roomstat must be wired up to switch the boiler on and off and to control the temperature of the conservatory.

Constructing the floor

You will need to excavate the site and lay a concrete base as recommended by the conservatory manufacturer, a surveyor, or your local Building Control Officer. The base must include a damp-proof membrane.

Allow for a covering layer of floor insulation – a minimum of 50mm (2in) flooring-grade expanded polystyrene or 30mm (1¼in) extruded polyurethane (check with your Building Control Officer). The floor should be finished with a 65mm (2½in) sand-and-cement screed, plus the preferred floorcovering.

When laying the floor insulation slabs, you should install a strip of insulation, 25mm (1in) thick, all round the edges. This is to prevent cold bridging between the masonry walls and the floor screed.

Cut a hole through the house wall, ready for the new plumbing that will connect to the existing central-heating system.

Installing the system

Mount the manifold in a convenient place and connect the two distributor blocks below it – one for the flow, and the other for the return. Run the flow and return pipes back into the house, ready for connecting to the existing central-heating circuit. Install your new pump and a mixing valve in the flow and return pipes.

Following the layout supplied by the system's manufacturer, press the spikes of the pipe clips into the insulation at the prescribed spacing (**1**). Lay out the heating tubes for both coils, and clip them into place. Push the end of one of the coils into the flow distributor, and the other end of the same coil into the return distributor (**2**). Connect the other coil similarly.

Connect the flow and return pipes to the house's central-heating system – it pays to insert a pair of isolating valves at this point, so that you can shut off the new circuit for servicing. Fill, flush out and check the new system for leaks.

Apply the screed composed of 4 parts sharp sand : 1 part cement, with a plasticizer additive. Leave it to dry naturally for at least three weeks before laying your floorcovering.

Fit the roomstat at head height, out of direct sunlight, then make the electrical connections according to the instructions.

1 Press the pipe clips into place

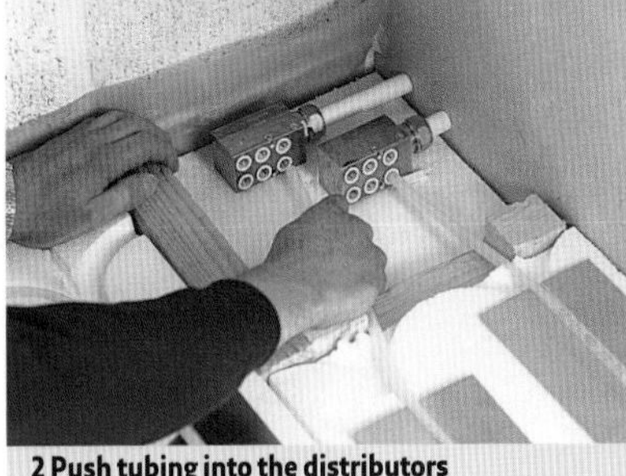

2 Push tubing into the distributors

SEE ALSO > Building Regulations on electrical wiring 284, Switching off the power 296. Pipe joints 360–2, 364–5, Heating controls 409, Draining the system 411

Electric heating

Electric heating is generally simple to install because it needs no pipes or chimneys. From a simple fan heater to centrally controlled storage heaters, there's a wide range of heating types to choose from – but unless you can run them on cheap night-time electricity, they will generally be more expensive to run than systems powered by other fuels.

Storage heating

Storage heaters contain a core of firebrick or similar material – when this is heated overnight it gradually releases the heat next day.

Early storage heaters were bulky and emitted heat at a set rate, so the user had no control over the output. The heat stored during the night could be adjusted – but this involved making an estimate of the next day's heating requirements, and a sudden change of weather could leave the user with too much or too little heat.

Current storage heaters are slimmer – as little as 150mm (6in) deep – and may be either wall-mounted or freestanding. They retain their heat more efficiently and enable greater control of heat output. Thermostatically controlled adjustable dampers and fans allow the units to be run at low levels in unoccupied rooms and then at a higher level when needed.

Some units retain a residue of stored heat, which reduces overnight charging and cuts costs further. Others monitor room temperatures at night, assess the next day's heating needs (a cold night is normally followed by a cold day) and adjust the heat charge accordingly.

Simple and unobtrusive storage heaters look at home in any interior

Electric storage heaters are best used in conjunction with cheap-rate night-time power available on the Economy 7 tariff – so called because of the seven hours of the night when the cheap rate is in force. To get the best from Economy 7 you need to be prepared to run appliances such as washing machines or dishwashers at night – and this may be inconvenient or distracting.

Heater considerations

Before considering storage heaters you need to think about whether or not they are suitable for your lifestyle. Because the heaters gradually lose heat over the day, they may not be the ideal choice for a busy family who are out for much of the day. Even though the units are very efficient at retaining heat, there may be less than is required by late evening. Any additional heat needed – or hot water, if an immersion heater is the only source of water heating – will be expensive because the daytime electricity tariff is more costly. Standing charges will be higher, too, because the tariff requires a special meter that records day and night consumption.

Like radiators, storage heaters should be placed below single-glazed windows to counteract draughts and balance the room temperature. With double glazing, they can go anywhere that's convenient and, if possible, should be positioned to give the best heat spread.

Storage heaters will need new wiring that connects to the Economy 7 meter.

Underfloor heating

Electric underfloor systems are less economical than their wet counterparts but, depending on the type chosen, are generally simpler to install.

Two main types are available: in-screed cables and heating mats. In-screed cables are installed in much the same way as the pipes in wet systems – a continuous single cable is snaked across the room and buried in the floor screed. This type is best for new builds, or projects where a new floor is being added.

Electric underfloor heating is simple to fix in a new floor or under tiles.

In heating mats, the cables are attached to a mesh and provide a quick method of covering regular-shaped areas. When laid under tiles the mat is embedded beneath the tile cement; otherwise the mat is buried in self-levelling compound.

In both cases there must be adequate insulation underneath the heating cables – if this is not present in the existing floor then it will be necessary to fit an insulated backing board to the floor first. By using this board it is possible to lay heating mats over existing wooden floors.

Electric radiators

Electric radiators look little different to those used in a wet system. They contain a liquid, usually oil, which is heated by an electric element, rather like a kettle. Electric radiators are commonly used in bathrooms, where they can be used independently of a wet central-heating system to dry towels or provide instant heat. Elsewhere in the house they can be independently operated or made to work like a wet central-heating system by wiring through a control box and roomstat.

A whole-house system would be quite expensive to run, but electric radiators are ideal in extensions, where it might be difficult to add to an existing central-heating system. They're also handy as top-up heat in large rooms. Wall-hung or floor-standing versions are available.

SEE ALSO > Off-peak rates 282, Building Regulations on electrical wiring 284

Working Outdoors

Planning a garden

Designing a garden is not an exact science. You may, for example, find that plants don't thrive, even though you have selected species that are recommended for your soil conditions. And trees don't always conform to the size specified in a catalogue. Nevertheless, forward planning can avert some of the more unfortunate mistakes, such as laying a patio where it will be in shade for most of the day, or digging a fish pond that's too small to create the required conditions for fish. Concentrate on planning the more permanent features first, taking into consideration how they will affect the planted areas of your garden.

Consider the details
Period-style cast ornaments that add character to a garden need not cost a fortune.

Juxtaposing textures
Create eye-catching focal points, using well-considered combinations of natural form and texture.

Getting inspired

There's no shortage of material from which you can draw inspiration – there are countless books, magazines and TV programmes devoted to garden planning. But, as no two gardens are alike, you probably won't find a plan that fits your plot exactly. However, you may be able to adapt a design to suit your needs or integrate some eye-catching details into your scheme.

Visiting real gardens is even better. Although large country estates and city parks are designed on a grand scale, you will be able to see how mature shrubs should look or how plants, stone and water can be used in a rockery or water garden.

Some towns and city boroughs host 'open days', when members of the public extend an invitation to anyone who wants to look around their gardens. Don't forget that friends and neighbours may have had to tackle problems similar to your own – and if nothing else, you may learn from their mistakes!

The approach

Before you put pencil to paper, think about the type of garden you want, and ask yourself whether it will sit happily with your house and its surroundings. Is it to be a formal garden, laid out in straight lines and geometric patterns – a style that often marries successfully with modern houses? Or do you prefer the more relaxed style of a rambling cottage garden? If you opt for the latter, remember that natural informality may not be as easy to achieve as you think, and your planting scheme will probably take years to mature into the garden you have in mind. Or maybe you're attracted to the idea of a Japanese-style garden – in effect a blend of both these styles, with every plant, stone and pool of water carefully positioned, so that the garden bears all the hallmarks of a man-made landscape and yet conveys a sense of natural harmony.

Planning on a small scale
Good garden design does not rely on having a large plot of land. Here, curvilinear shapes draw the eye through a delightful array of foliage and flowers planted around a beautifully manicured lawn and a small but perfectly balanced fish pond.

SEE ALSO > Building Regulations 22–7

Surveying the plot

In order to make the best use of your plot of land, you need to take fairly accurate measurements and check the prevailing conditions.

Measuring up

Make a note of the overall dimensions of your plot. At the same time, check the diagonal measurements - because your garden may not be the perfect rectangle or square it appears to be. The diagonals are especially important when plotting irregular shapes.

Slopes and gradients

Check how the ground slopes. You don't need an accurate survey, but at least jot down the direction of the slope and plot the points where the gradient begins and ends. You can get some idea of the differences in level by using a long straightedge and a spirit level. Place one end of the straightedge on the top of a bank, for example, and measure the vertical distance from the other end to the foot of the slope.

Keep any useful features

Plot the position of existing features, such as pathways, areas of lawn and established trees.

How about the weather?

Check the passage of the sun and the direction of prevailing winds. Don't forget that the angle of the sun will be higher in summer, and that a screen of deciduous trees will be less effective as a windbreak when the leaves drop.

Soil conditions

The type of soil you have in your garden is bound to influence your choice of plants, but you can easily adjust soil content by adding peat or fertilizers. Clay soil, which is greyish in colour, is heavy when wet and tends to crack when dry. A sandy soil feels gritty and loose in dry conditions. Acidic peat soil is dark brown and flaky. Pale-coloured chalky soil, which often contains flints, will not support acid-loving plants. Any soil that contains too many stones or too much gravel is unsuitable as topsoil.

Measuring a plot
To draw an accurate plan, note down the overall dimensions, including the diagonals.

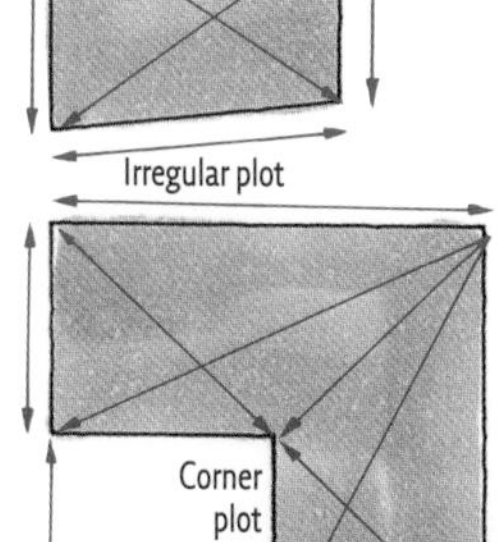

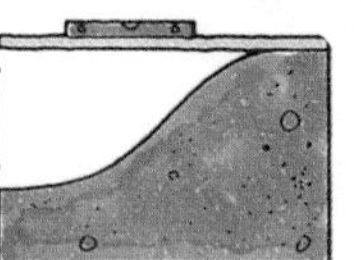

Gauging a slope
Use a straightedge and spirit level to measure the height of a bank.

Theme gardens
Deciding on a style or theme for your garden will help you with the overall planning right from the start. The very different themes shown here are examples of the seemingly random planting of a colourful cottage garden, the pleasing symmetry of formal layouts, and the 'natural' informality of a Japanese-style garden carefully constructed from selected rocks, pebbles and sculptural foliage.

SEE ALSO > Planning in more detail 424

Planning in more detail

Armed with all the measurements you've taken, make a simple drawing to try out your ideas. Then, to make sure your plan will work in reality, mark out the shapes and plot the important features in your garden.

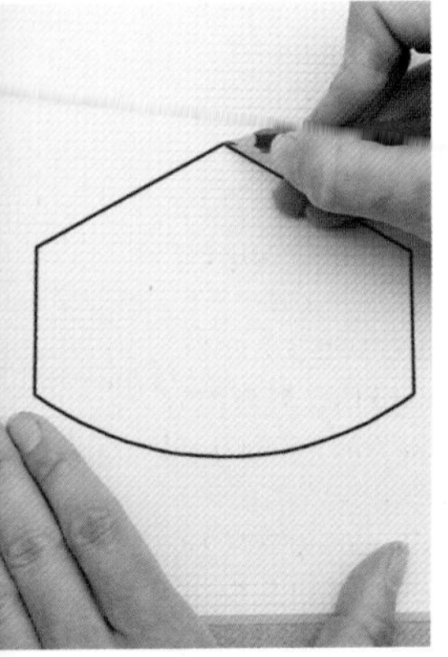

Drawing plans
Draw a garden plan on tracing paper laid over squared graph paper.

Drawing a plan on paper

Draw a plan of your garden on paper. It must be a properly scaled plan, or you are sure to make some gross errors – but it need not be professionally perfect. Use squared graph paper to plot the garden's dimensions and any relevant features – but do the actual drawing on tracing paper laid over the grid, so you can try out different ideas and makes alterations to your plan without having to redraw it each time.

Mark out straight lines with pegs and string

Plotting your design on the ground

Planning on paper is only the first stage. Gardens are rarely seen from above, so it is essential to plot the design on the ground to check your dimensions and view the features from different angles.

A pond or patio that seems enormous on paper may look pathetically small in reality. Other shortcomings, such as the way a tree will block the view from your proposed patio, become obvious once you lay out the plan full size.

Plot individual features – such as a patio or a raised flower bed – by driving pegs into the ground and stretching string lines between them.

Use a rope tied to a peg to scribe arcs on the ground, and mark the curved lines with stakes or a row of bricks.

A garden hose provides the ideal aid for marking out less regular curves. If you can scrape areas clear of weeds, that will define the shapes still further.

Use rope tied to a peg to scribe an arc

Practical experiments

When you have marked out your design, carry out a few experiments to check that it is practicable.

Will it be possible, for instance, for two people to pass each other on the garden path without having to step into the flowerbeds? Can you set down a wheelbarrow on the path without one of its legs slipping into the pond?

Try placing some furniture on the area you have marked out for your patio to make sure there is enough room to relax comfortably and sit down to a meal with visitors. Most people build a patio alongside the house, but if you have to put it elsewhere to find a sunny spot, will it become a chore to walk to and fro with drinks and snacks?

Siting a pond

Position a pond to avoid overhanging trees, and in an area where it will catch at least half a day's sunlight. Check that you can reach it with a hose and that you can run electrical cables to power a pump or lighting.

Common-sense safety

Don't make your garden an obstacle course. A narrow path alongside a pond, for example, may be hazardous or intimidating for an elderly relative; and low walls or planters near the edge of a patio could cause someone to trip.

Driveways and parking spaces

Allow a minimum width of 3m (9ft 9in) for a driveway, making sure there is enough room to open the doors of a car parked alongside a wall. And bear in mind that vehicles larger than your own might need to use the drive or parking space. If possible, allow room for the turning circle of your car; and make sure you will have a clear view of the traffic when you pull out into the road.

Try out irregular curves with a garden hose

Plotting curved features
Use rope tied to a peg to lay out circles and arcs on the ground.

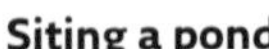

Don't neglect your neighbours

There are legal restrictions regarding what you can erect in your garden. However, even if you have a free hand, it's worth consulting your neighbours in case anything you're planning might inconvenience them. A wall or row of trees that throws shade across a neighbour's patio or blocks the light to their windows could be the source of a bitter dispute lasting for years.

Make sure two people can pass easily on a path

SEE ALSO > Official approval 23–7, Constructing ponds 472–8–00, Pumps and fountains 476

Growing climbers

There's a widely held belief that climbing plants, especially ivy, will damage any masonry wall.

If exterior rendering or the mortar between bricks or stonework is in poor condition, then a vigorous ivy plant will undoubtedly weaken the structure as its aerial roots attempt to extract moisture from the masonry. The roots will invade broken joints or rendering and, on finding a source of nourishment for the main plant, expand and burst the weakened material. This encourages damp to penetrate the wall.

Don't allow climbers to get out of control

However, when clinging to sound masonry, ivy can do no more than climb with the aid of training wires and its own sucker-like roots that do not provide nourishment but are for support only.

So long as the structure is sound and free from damp, there is even some benefit in allowing a plant to clothe a wall, since its close-growing mat of leaves, mostly with their drip tips pointing downwards, acts as insulation and provides some protection against the elements.

Climbers must be pruned regularly, so they don't penetrate between roof tiles or slates, or clog gutters and drainpipes. If a robust climber is allowed to grow unchecked, the weight of the mature plant may eventually topple a weakened wall.

Training wires
Climbing plants can be controlled by fixing horizontal wires at the required height.

Trees and foundations

When planning your garden, you will probably want to include some trees. However, you should think carefully about your choice of trees and their position – they could be potentially damaging to the structure of your house if planted too near to it.

Siting trees

Tree roots searching for moisture can do considerable harm to a drainage system, fracturing rigid pipework and penetrating joints, eventually blocking the drain.

Before planting a tree close to the house, find out how far its root system is likely to spread. Estimate its likely maximum height, and take this as a guide as to how far from the house you should plant the tree.

If you think an existing tree is likely to cause problems, don't be tempted to chop it down without first consulting your local planning department – some trees are protected by preservation orders and you could be fined if you cut down a protected tree without permission. A professional tree surgeon may be able to solve the problem by pruning its roots and branches.

Minor cracks in plaster and rendering are often the result of shrinkage as the structure dries out. Such cracks are not serious and can be repaired during normal maintenance, but more serious structural cracks are due to movement of the foundations. Trees planted too close to a building can add to the problem by removing moisture from the site, causing subsidence of the foundations as the supporting earth collapses. But tree felling can be just as damaging – the surrounding soil, which has stabilized over the years, swells as it takes up the moisture that was previously removed by the tree's root system. As a result, upward movement of the ground – known as heave – distorts the foundations, and cracks begin to appear.

Subsidence
A mature tree growing close to a house can draw so much water from the ground that the earth subsides, causing damage to the foundations.

Heave
When a mature tree is felled, the earth can absorb more water, causing it to swell until it displaces the foundations of the building.

SEE ALSO > Repairing cracks 44–5, Penetrating damp 247–9

Choosing fences

A fence is a popular form of boundary marker or garden screen, primarily because it is relatively inexpensive and takes very little time to erect. In the short term a fence is cheaper than a masonry wall, although one can argue that the cost of maintenance and replacement over a long period eventually cancels out the saving in cost. Wood has a comparatively short life, because it is susceptible to insect infestation and rot, but a fence can last for years if it's treated regularly with a preserver. And if you choose plastic or concrete components, then your fence will be virtually maintenance-free.

Natural-log fencing Construct your own informal fencing using split logs nailed to horizontal rails.

Talk to your neighbours

Discuss your plans with your neighbours, especially as you will require their permission if you want to work from both sides of the boundary when erecting the fence. Check the exact line of the boundary to make certain that you don't encroach upon your neighbour's land. The fence posts should run along the boundary or on your side of the line – and before you dismantle an old fence, make sure it is indeed yours to demolish.

If a neighbour is unwilling to replace an unsightly fence and won't even allow you to replace it at your expense, there is nothing to stop you erecting another fence alongside the original one – provided that it's on your property.

Although it is an unwritten law that a good neighbour erects a fence with the post and rails facing his or her own property, there are no legal restrictions that could force you to do so.

Chain-link fencing

Trellis fencing

Post-and-chain fencing

Planning permission

As a rule, you can build any fence up to 2m (6ft 6in) high without having to obtain planning permission. However, if your boundary adjoins a highway, you may not be allowed to erect any barrier higher than 1m (3ft 3in). In addition, there could be restrictions on fencing if the land surrounding your house has been designed as an open-plan area. Even so, many authorities will permit you to erect low boundary markers such as ranch-style or post-and-chain fencing.

You may be surprised by how much fencing you need to surround even a small garden – so it's worth considering the available options carefully, to make sure you invest your money in a fence that will meet your needs. Unless your priority is to keep neighbourhood children or animals out of your garden, privacy is most likely to be the prime consideration. There are a number of 'peep-proof' options, but you may have to compromise to some extent if you plan to erect a fence on a site exposed to strong prevailing winds. In this situation, you will need a fence that will act as a windbreak without offering so much resistance that the posts work loose within a couple of seasons.

Chain-link fencing

Consisting of wire netting stretched between posts, chain-link fencing is purely functional. It is made from strong galvanized or plastic-coated wire mesh that is suspended from a heavy-gauge cable, known as a straining wire, strung between the posts. Decorative wire fencing, which is available at many garden centres, is designed primarily for marking boundaries or supporting lightweight climbing plants. Except in a remote rural location, any chain-link fence will benefit from a screen of climbers or hedging plants.

SEE ALSO > Official approval 23–7, Infestation 242–3, Dry and wet rot 245, Preservers 246

Trellis fencing
Concertina-fold trellis constructed from thin softwood or from cedar laths is designed primarily to help plants climb a wall, but rigid panels made from softwood battens can be used in conjunction with fence posts to erect a substantial free-standing screen. Most garden centres stock a wide range of these decorative panels. A similar fence made from split rustic poles nailed to stout rails and posts forms a strong and attractive barrier.

Post-and-chain fencing
A post-and-chain fence is no more than a decorative feature intended to prevent people from inadvertently wandering off a path or pavement onto a lawn or flower-bed. This type of fencing is constructed by stringing lengths of painted metal or plastic chain between short posts sunk into the ground.

Closeboard fencing
A closeboard fence is made by nailing overlapping featherboard strips to horizontal rails. Featherboards are sawn planks that taper across their width, from 16mm (5/8in) at the thicker edge down to about 3mm (1/8in). The boards are usually 100mm (4in) or 150mm (6in) wide. The best-quality featherboards are made from cedar, but softwood is the usual choice in view of the amount of timber required to make a long closeboard fence. Although it is expensive, closeboard fencing forms a screen that is both strong and attractive. Being fixed vertically, the boards make a high fence quite difficult to climb from the outside – which makes them ideal for keeping intruders out.

Prefabricated panel fencing
Fences made from prefabricated panels nailed between timber posts are very popular, perhaps because they are so easy to erect. Standard fence panels are 1.8m (6ft) wide and range in height from 600mm (2ft) to 1.8m (6ft); they are supplied in 300mm (1ft) gradations.

Most prefabricated fence panels are made from interwoven or overlapping strips of wood sandwiched between a frame of sawn timber.

Overlapping-strip panels are usually designated as 'lap' or 'larchlap'. When the strips have a natural wavy edge, they are sometimes called 'rustic' or 'waney' lap.

Any panel fence tends to be good value for money and will provide durable screening – but if privacy is a consideration choose the lapped type, as interwoven strips can shrink in the summer, leaving gaps in the fence.

Interlap fencing
An interlap fence is made by nailing square-edged boards to horizontal rails, fixing the boards alternately on one side, then the other. Spacing is a matter of choice – you can overlap the edges of the boards for privacy, or space them apart to create a more decorative effect. This type of fencing is a sensible choice for a windy site. Although it's a sturdy screen, it permits a strong wind to pass through the gaps between the boards, reducing the amount of pressure exerted on the fence. Being equally attractive from either side, an interlap fence is perfect as boundary screening.

Picket fencing
The traditional low picket fence is still popular as a 'cottage-style' barrier at the front of the house, particularly where a high fence would look out of place. Narrow, vertical 'pales' with rounded or pointed tops are spaced at about 75 to 100mm (3 to 4in) centres. As they are laborious to build by hand, to keep down the cost most picket fences are sold as ready-made panels constructed from plastic or softwood.

Ranch-style fencing
Low-level fences made from simple horizontal rails fixed to short, stout posts are the modern counterpart of picket fencing. Used to divide up building plots in some housing developments, ranch-style fencing is often painted, although clear-finished or stained timber is just as attractive and much more durable. Softwood and some hardwoods are commonplace materials for this kind of fencing, but plastic ranch-style fences are also popular because of their clean, crisp appearance and also because there's no need to repaint them and there is very little maintenance.

Concrete fencing
A cast-concrete fence is maintenance-free, and it provides the same security and permanence as a wall built from brick or stone. Interlocking horizontal sections are built one upon the other, up to the required height. Each vertical stack is supported by grooves cast into the sides of purpose-made concrete fence posts. This relatively heavy fencing would be dangerous if the posts were not firmly embedded in concrete.

Closeboard fencing

Panel fence

Interlap fencing

Picket fencing

Ranch-style fence

Concrete fencing

SEE ALSO > Wood finishes 70–80, Preservers 246

Fence posts

Whatever type of fence you decide to erect, its strength and durability will rely on good-quality posts set solidly in the ground. Erecting the posts carefully and accurately is crucial to the longevity of the fence and may save you having to either re-erect or repair it in the future.

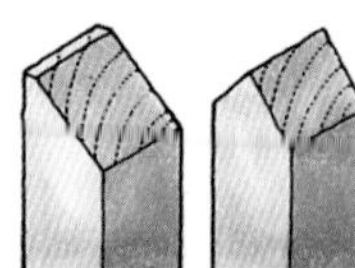

Capping fence posts
If you simply cut the end of a timber post square, the top of the post will rot relatively quickly. The solution is to cut a single or double bevel to shed the rainwater, or nail a cap made from wood or galvanized metal over the end of the post.

Choosing fence posts

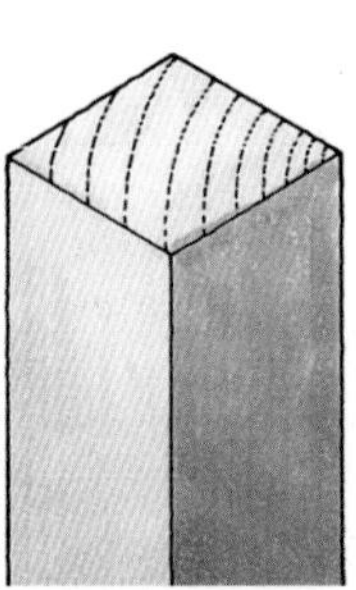

Square timber post

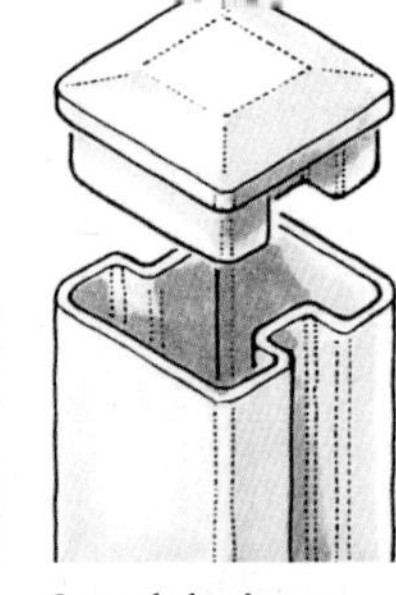

Capped plastic post

Angle-iron post

Tubular-steel post

Drilled concrete post

Mortised concrete post

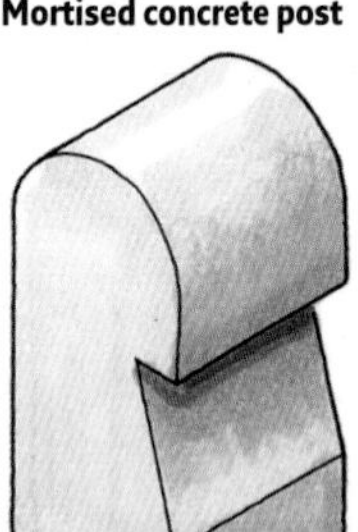

Grooved concrete post

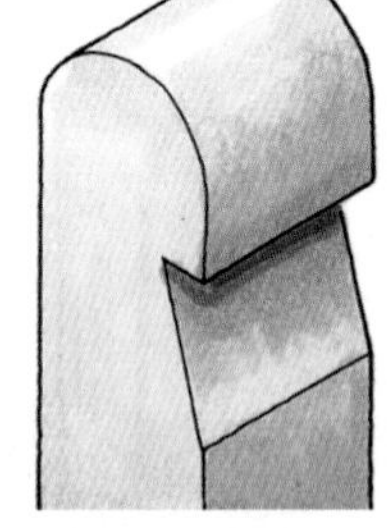

Notched end post

In some cases, the nature of the fencing will determine the choice of post. Concrete fencing, for example, has to be supported by compatible concrete posts. But in the main you can choose the material and style of post that suits the appearance of the fence.

Timber posts

Most fences are supported by square-section timber posts. Standard fence-post sizes are 75 or 100mm (3 or 4in) square, but gateposts 125, 150 and even 200mm (5, 6 and 8in) square are available. Unless you ask specifically for hardwood, most timber merchants will supply you with pretreated softwood posts.

Plastic posts

Extruded PVC posts are supplied with plastic fencing, together with moulded-plastic end caps and rail-fixing bolts and unions.

Metal posts

Angle-iron posts are made to support chain-link fences; and wrought-iron gates are often hung from plastic-coated tubular-steel posts. Angle-iron posts are very sturdy, but they do not make an attractive fence.

Concrete posts

A variety of reinforced-concrete posts, 100mm (4in) square, are produced to suit different styles of fence – drilled for chain-link fixings, mortised for rails, and recessed or grooved for panels. Special corner and end posts (see opposite) are notched to accommodate bracing struts for chain-link fencing.

Fixing to a wall

If a fence runs up to the house, fix the first post to the wall, using three expanding masonry bolts. Place a washer under each bolt head to stop the wood being crushed. Check that the post is vertical and, if need be, drive packing between the post and wall to make adjustments.

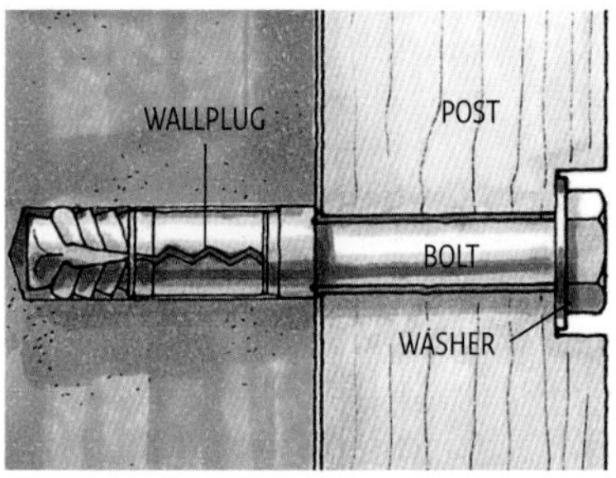

Bolting a post to a wall
If you are fitting a prefabricated panel against a wall-fixed post, counterbore the bolts so that the heads lie flush with the surface of the wood.

Removing old posts

If you are replacing a dilapidated fence, it may prove convenient to put the new posts in the same position as the old.

Begin by dismantling the featherboards and rails, or cut through the fixings so you can remove the fence panels. If any of the posts are bedded firmly or sunk into concrete, you will have to lever them out with a stout batten. Remove the topsoil from around each post to loosen it. Drive large nails into two opposite faces of the post, about 300mm (1ft) from the ground. Bind a length of rope around the post, just below the nails, and tie the ends to the tip of the batten. Build a pile of bricks close to the post, and use it as a fulcrum to lever the post out of the ground.

Preserving fence posts

Even when a timber fence post is pretreated to prevent rot, you can make doubly sure by soaking the base of each post in a bucket of chemical preserver overnight.

Untreated timber needs to be immersed for a similar period in a polythene-lined trough filled with preserver.

SEE ALSO > Preservers 246

Erecting fence posts

The type of fence you choose dictates whether you need to erect all the posts first or put them up one at a time, along with the other components. If you are building a prefabricated panel fence, for example, fix the posts as you erect the fence; but if you're putting up chain-link fencing, complete the run of posts first.

Marking out a row of fence posts

Drive a peg into the ground at each end of the fence run, and stretch a length of string between the pegs to align the row of posts. If possible, adjust the spacing to avoid obstructions such as large tree roots. If one or more posts have to be inserted across a paved patio, either lift enough slabs to allow you to dig the required holes or mark out the patio for bolt-down metal post sockets (see right).

Erecting the posts

Bury one quarter of each post. You can hire post-hole augers to remove the central core of earth. Twist the tool to drive it into the ground (**1**) and pull it out after every 150mm (6in) to remove the soil. When you have reached a sufficient depth, taper the sides of the hole slightly so that you can pack hardcore around the post.

Anchoring the post

Ram a layer of hardcore (broken bricks or small stones) into the bottom of the hole to support the base of the post and provide drainage. Get someone to hold the post upright while you brace it with battens nailed to the post and to stakes driven into the ground. Use guy ropes to support a concrete post. Check with a spirit level that the post is vertical (**2**).

Ram some more hardcore around the post, leaving a hole about 300mm (1ft) deep for filling with concrete. Top up with a fast-setting concrete mix made specially for erecting fence posts. Alternatively, mix some general-purpose concrete and tamp it into the hole with the end of a batten (**3**). Build the concrete just above the level of the soil and smooth it to slope away from the post. This will help shed rainwater and prevent rot.

Leave the concrete to harden before removing the struts. Support a panel fence temporarily, with struts wedged against the posts.

1 Dig the post hole

2 Brace the post

3 Tamp the concrete

Supporting end posts

Chain-link fence posts must resist the tension of the straining wires. Brace each end post (and some of the intermediate ones over a long run) with a strut made from a length of fence post. Shape the end of the strut to fit a notch cut into the post and nail it in place. You can order special precast concrete end posts and struts. Anchor the post in the ground and dig a trench 450mm (1ft 6in) deep alongside for the strut. Wedge a brick under the end of the strut, then ram hardcore around the post and strut. Fill the trench up to ground level with concrete. Support a corner post with two struts at right angles.

Braced end post

Using metal sockets

Instead of digging holes for your fence posts, you can plug the base of each post into a square socket attached to a metal spike that is driven into firm ground. Similar sockets can be bolted to existing paving or set in fresh concrete.

Use 600mm (2ft) spikes for fences up to 1.2m (4ft) high, and 750mm (2ft 6in) spikes for a 1.8m (6ft) fence. Place a proprietary driving tool into the socket to protect the metal and then drive the spike partly into the ground with a sledgehammer.

Hold a spirit level against the socket to make certain the spike is upright (**1**), then hammer the spike into the ground until only the socket is visible. Insert the post and, depending on the type of spike, secure it by screwing through the side of the socket or by tightening clamping bolts (**2**). If you're putting up a panel fence, use the edge of a fixed panel to position the next spike.

1 Use a level to check the spike is vertical

2 Tighten the bolts to clamp the post

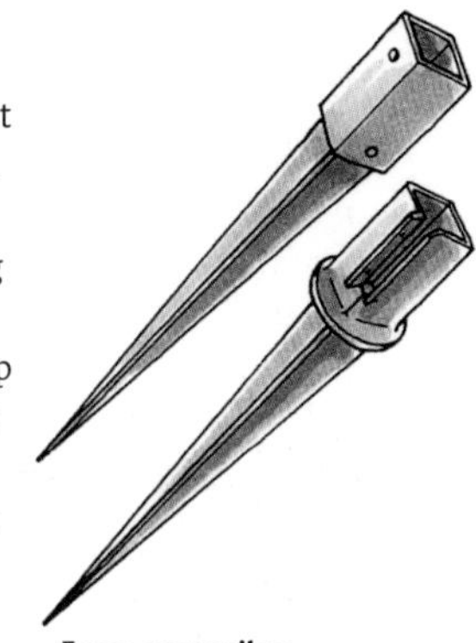
Fence-post spikes

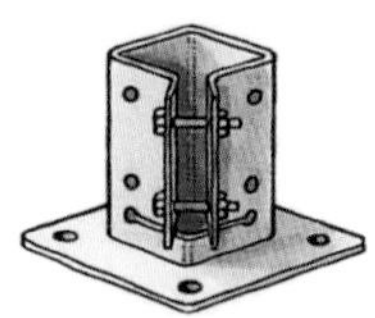
Bolted sockets
Bolt this type of socket to existing patios and concrete driveways.

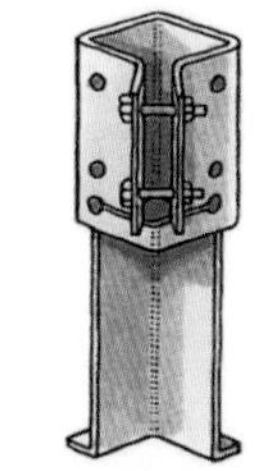
Embedded sockets
Embed this type of socket in wet concrete.

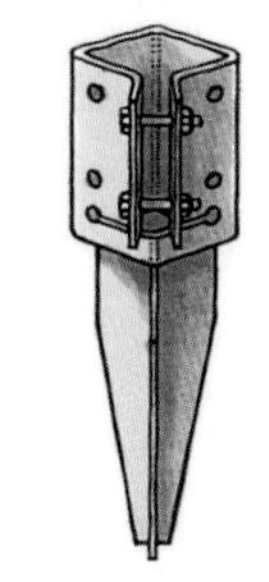
Repair socket
Allows replacement of rotten or broken posts set in concrete. Cut off the old post flush with the concrete and then drive the spike into the centre of the stump.

SEE ALSO > Chain-link fencing 426, Intermediate posts 430, Straining wires 430, Erecting a panel fence 432, Mixing concrete 455

Putting up chain-link fencing

To support chain-link fencing, set out a row of timber, concrete or angle-iron posts, spacing them no more than 3m (10ft) apart. Brace the end posts with struts to resist the pull exerted by the straining wires. A long run needs a braced intermediate post every 70m (225ft) or so.

Using timber posts

Using a turnbuckle
Apply tension by turning the turnbuckle with a metal bar.

Support chain-link fencing on straining wires. Since it's impossible to tension the heavy-gauge wire by hand, large straining bolts are used to stretch it between the posts – one to coincide with the top of the fencing, one about 150mm (6in) from the ground, and a third one midway between.

Drill 10mm (3/8in) diameter holes through the posts. Insert a bolt into each hole and fit a washer and nut (**1**), leaving enough thread to provide about 50mm (2in) movement once you begin to apply tension to the wire.

Pass the end of the wire through the eye of a bolt, then twist it around itself with pliers (**2**). Stretch the wire along the run of fencing, stapling it to each post and strut (**3**), but leave enough slack for the wire to move when tensioned.

Cut the wire to length and twist it through the bolt at the other end of the fence. Tension the wire from both ends by turning the nuts with a spanner (**4**).

Standard straining bolts provide enough tension for the average garden fence, but over a long run of fencing – 70m (225ft) or more – use a turnbuckle for each wire, applying tension with a metal bar (see left).

Cleat and stretcher bar

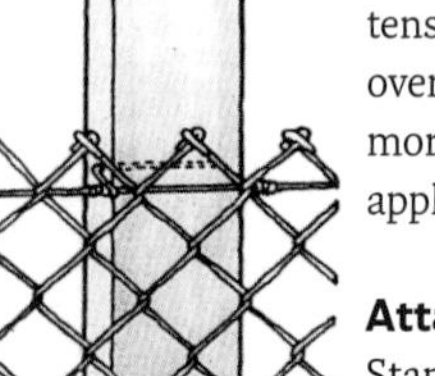

Wire tied to post

Attaching the mesh

Staple each end link to the post (**5**). Unroll the mesh and pull it taut. Tie it to straining wires every 300mm (1ft) with galvanized wire (**6**). Fix to the post at the far end.

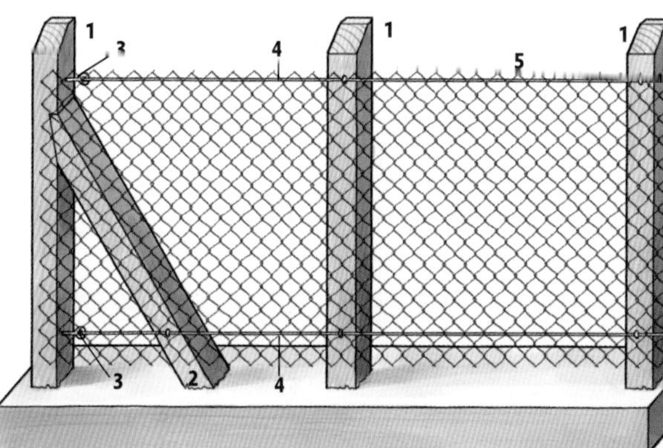

Chain-link fencing
1 Post
2 Strut
3 Straining bolt
4 Straining wire
5 Wire mesh

1 Insert a straining bolt in the end post

3 Staple the wire to each post and strut

5 Staple mesh to post

2 Attach a straining wire to the bolt

4 Tension the bolt at the far end of the fence

6 Tie with wire loops

Using concrete posts

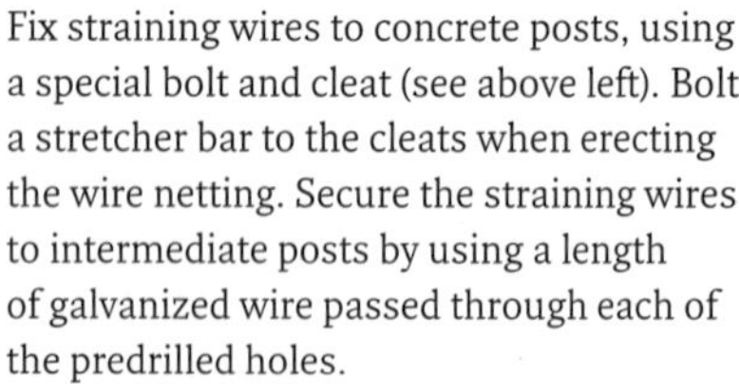

Fix straining wires to concrete posts, using a special bolt and cleat (see above left). Bolt a stretcher bar to the cleats when erecting the wire netting. Secure the straining wires to intermediate posts by using a length of galvanized wire passed through each of the predrilled holes.

Winding bracket

Using angle-iron posts

Stretcher bars with winding brackets for applying tension to straining wires are supplied with angle-iron fence posts (see left). Pass the straining wire through the hole in every intermediate post.

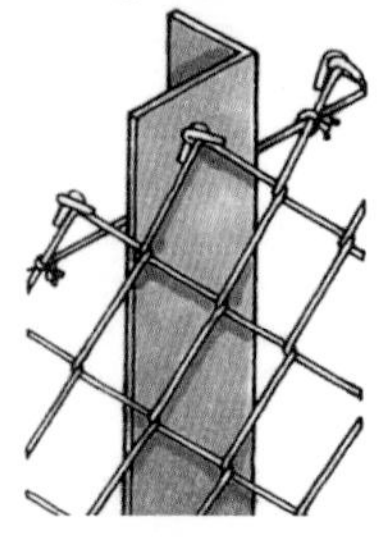

Wire goes through post

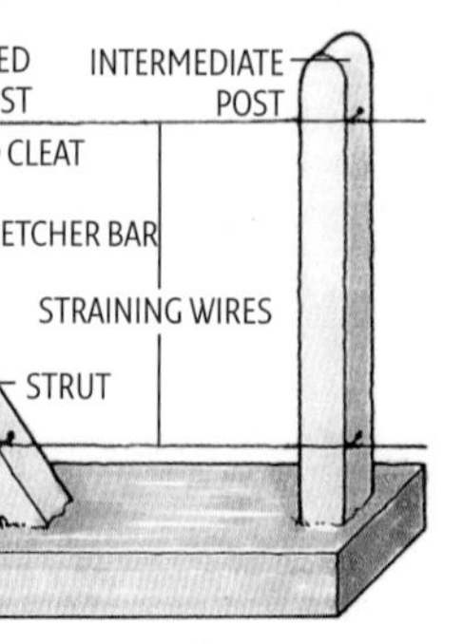

Concrete fence posts

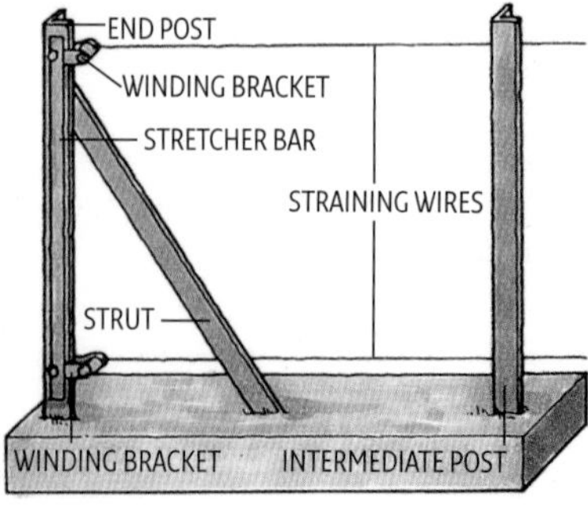

Angle-iron posts

SEE ALSO > Fence posts 428–9, Bracing struts 429

Erecting closeboard fences

The featherboards used to panel a closeboard fence are nailed to triangular-section arris rails mortised into the fence posts. Concrete posts – and some wooden ones – are supplied ready-mortised, but if you buy standard timber posts you'll either have to cut the mortises yourself or use end brackets (see below right) instead. Space fence posts no more than 3m (10ft) apart. Fix horizontal gravel boards at the foot of the fence. Nail capping strips across the tops of the boards.

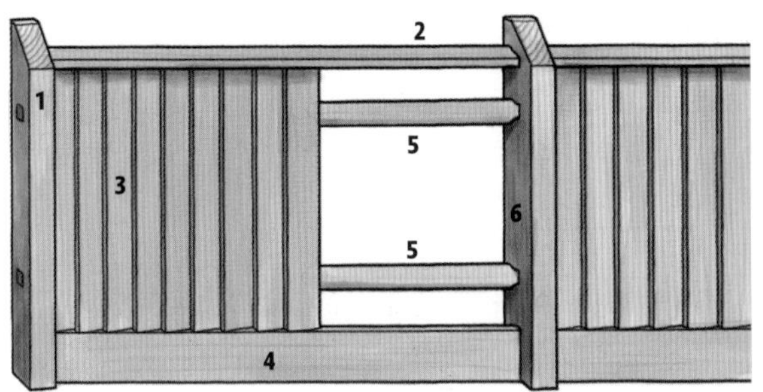

Closeboard fencing
1 End post
2 Capping strip
3 Featherboards
4 Gravel board
5 Arris rail
6 Intermediate post

Erecting the framework

When using plain wooden posts, mark and cut 50 x 22mm (2 x ⅞in) mortises for the arris rails, about 150mm (6in) above and below the ends of the fixed featherboards. For fencing more than 1.2m (4ft) high, cut mortises for a third rail midway between the others. Position the mortises 25mm (1in) from the front face of each post (the face on the featherboarded side of the fence).

As you erect the fence, cut the rails to length and shape a tenon on each end, using a coarse rasp or Surform file (**1**). Paint preserver onto the shaped ends and into the mortises before you assemble the rails.

Erect the first fence post and pack hardcore around its base. Get someone to hold the post steady while you fit the arris rails and erect the next post, tapping it onto the ends of the rails with a mallet (**2**). Check that the rails are horizontal and the posts vertical before packing hardcore around the second post. Construct the entire run of posts and rails in the same way. If you can't manoeuvre the last post onto the tenoned rails, cut the rails square and fix them to the post with metal end brackets.

Check the whole run once more to ensure that the rails are bedded firmly in their mortises and that the framework is true, then secure each rail by driving a nail through the post into the tenon (**3**) or by drilling a hole and inserting a wooden dowel. Pack concrete around each post and leave it to set.

Fitting the boards

Gravel boards

Some concrete posts are mortised to take gravel boards; fit the boards at the same time as the arris rails. If concrete posts are not mortised, bed treated wooden cleats into the concrete filling at the base of each post and screw the gravel board to the cleat when the concrete has set.

To fit gravel boards to wooden posts, skew-nail cleats to the foot of each post, then nail the boards to the cleats (**4**). Some metal post sockets are made with brackets for attaching gravel boards.

Featherboards

Cut the featherboards to length and treat the end grain with preservative. Stand the first featherboard on the gravel board, butting its thicker edge against the post. Nail the board to the arris rails with galvanized nails, about 18mm (¾in) from the thick edge. Place the next featherboard in position, overlapping the thin edge of the fixed board by 12mm (½in). Check that it's vertical, then nail it in the same way. Don't drive a nail through both boards, or they may split should the wood shrink. To space the other boards equally, make a spacer block from a scrap of wood (**5**).

Plane the last board to fit against the next post and fix it, this time with two nails per rail. Finally, nail capping strips along the tops of the featherboards, then cut the posts to length and cap them.

1 Shape the arris rails to fit the mortises

2 Tap post onto the rails

3 Nail rails in place

4 Nail gravel boards to the cleats

5 Use a spacer block to position featherboards

End brackets
Instead of cutting mortise-and-tenon joints, you can use special metal brackets to join arris rails to fence posts.

Capping the fence
Nail a wooden capping strip to the ends of the featherboards to shed rainwater.

SEE ALSO > Preservers 246, Capping posts 428, Erecting posts 429, Fence-post sockets 429, Surform file 492, Skew-nailing 505, Cutting a mortise 509

Erecting panel fencing

To prevent a prefabricated panel rotting, either fit gravel boards – as on a closeboard fence – or leave a gap at the bottom by supporting a panel temporarily on two bricks while you fix it to the fence posts.

Using timber posts

Pack the first post into its hole with hardcore. Then get someone to hold a panel against the post while you skew-nail through the frame into the post. If you can work from both sides, drive three nails from each side of the fence. If the wood used for the frame is likely to split, blunt the nails by tapping their points with a hammer. Alternatively, use rust-proofed metal angle brackets to secure the panels. Construct the entire fence by erecting panels and posts alternately.

Fit pressure-treated gravel boards; and nail capping strips along the panels, if they have not already been fitted by the manufacturer. Finally, cut each post to length and cap it.

Wedge struts made from scrap timber against each post to keep it vertical, then top up the holes with concrete. If you're unable to work from both sides, you will have to fill each hole as you build the fence.

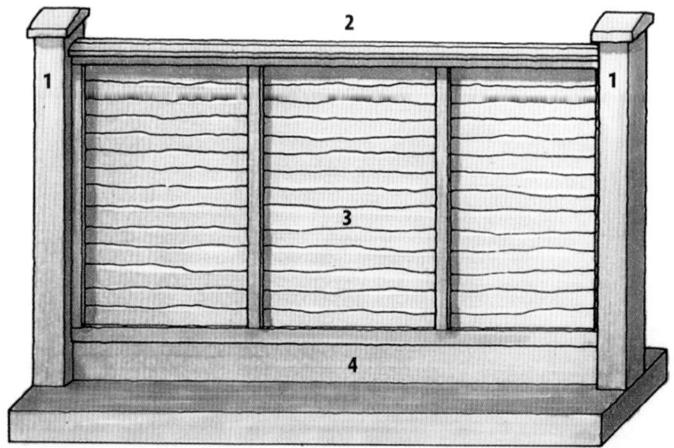

Panel fence
1 Fence posts
2 Capping strip
3 Prefabricated panel
4 Gravel board

Nail the panel through its frame

Or use angle brackets to fix panels to posts

Concrete post grooved to take panels

Using concrete posts

Grooved concrete fence posts will support prefabricated panels without the need for additional fixings.

Building a panel fence
Support a panel on bricks and get a helper to push it against the post while you nail it.

SEE ALSO > Skew-nailing 505, Preservers 246, Capping posts 428, Erecting posts 429, Concrete 454–61

Post-and-rail fences

A simple ranch-style fence is no more than a series of horizontal rails fixed to short posts concreted into the ground. A picket fence is constructed similarly, but with vertical pales fixed to the rails.

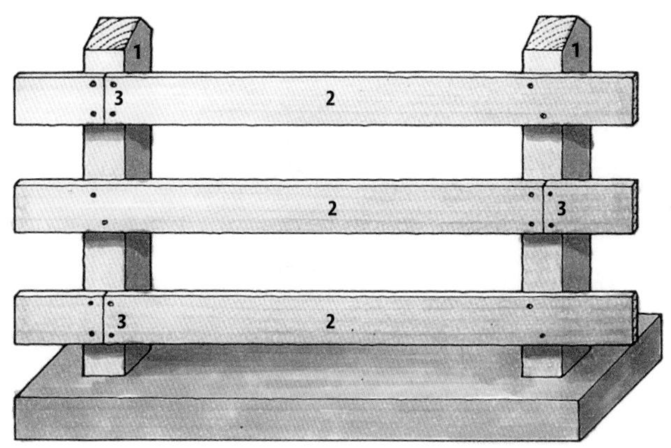

Ranch-style fence
1 Short posts
2 Horizontal rails
3 Rail joints

Fixing horizontal rails

You can screw the rails directly to the posts, but the fence is likely to last longer if you cut a shallow notch in the post to locate each rail before fixing it permanently in place.

Join two horizontal rails by butting them over a fence post. Arrange to stagger such joints so that you don't end up with all the rails butted on the same posts.

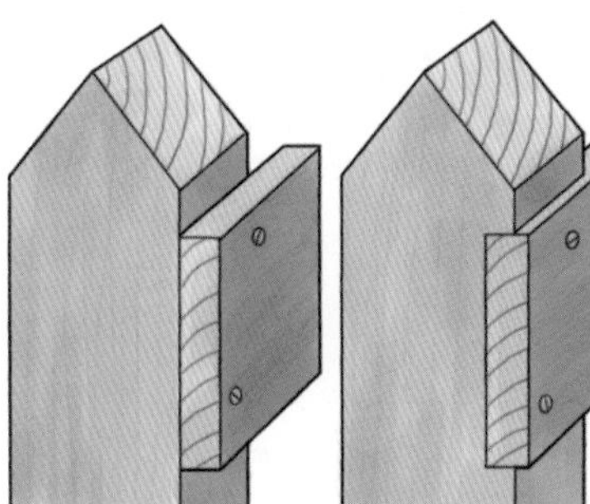

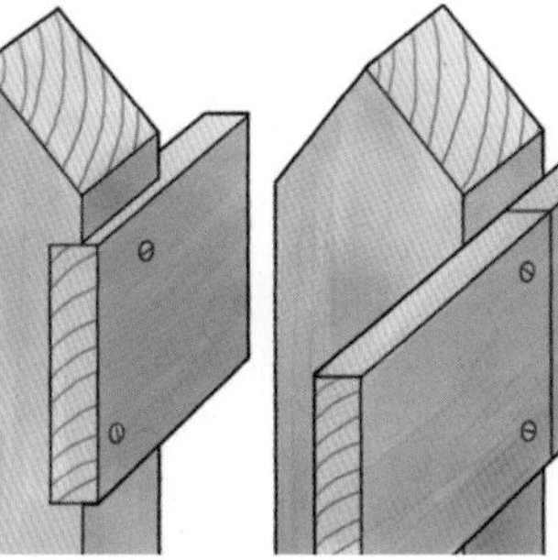

Building plastic ranch-style fencing
The basic construction of a plastic ranch-style fence is similar to one built from timber – but follow the manufacturer's instructions concerning the method for joining the rails to the posts.

Screw rail to post **Or notch the post first** **Butt rails on posts**

Fixing picket panels

When constructing a low picket fence from ready-made panels – which are designed to fit between the posts – it is best to either buy or make metal brackets for attaching a pair of panels to each post. Be sure to prime and paint home-made steel brackets to prevent the metal corroding.

Use metal brackets to fix picket-fence panels

Erecting fences on sloping ground

Slope running across

If a slope runs across your garden so that a neighbour's garden is higher than your own, either build brick retaining walls between the posts or set paving slabs in concrete to hold back the soil.

Downhill slope

The posts need to be set vertically, even when you are erecting a fence on a sloping site. Chain-link fencing or ranch-style rails can follow the slope of the land if you wish; but fence panels should be stepped and the triangular gaps beneath them filled with gravel boards or retaining walls.

Retaining wall for a crossways slope

Step fence panels to allow for a downhill slope

Supporting a rotted post

Buried timber posts often rot below ground level, leaving a perfectly sound section above. To save buying a whole new post, you can make a passable repair by bracing the upper section with a short concrete spur.

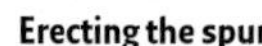

Erecting the spur
First, dig the soil from around the rotted stump and remove it. Insert the spur and pack hardcore around it (1), then fill with concrete (2). Drill pilot holes in the wooden post for coach screws – woodscrews with hexagonal heads (3). Insert the screws, using a spanner to draw the post tightly against the spur.

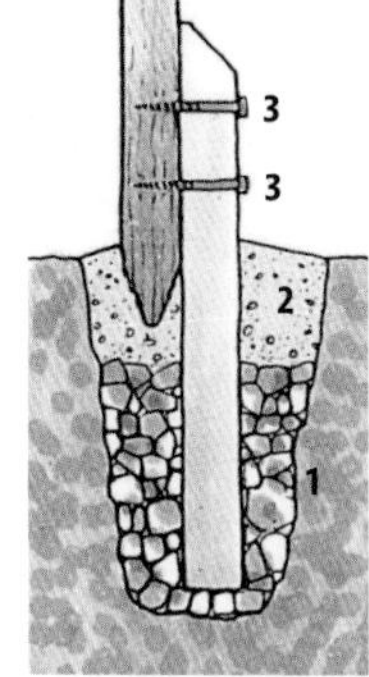

SEE ALSO > Erecting posts 429, Building walls 442–51

Choosing a gate

Browsing through suppliers' catalogues, you will find that gates are grouped according to their intended location – because it's where a gate is hung that has the greatest influence on its design and style. When choosing a gate, give due consideration to the character of the house and its surroundings. Buy a gate that matches the style of fence or complements the wall from which it is hung. If in doubt, aim for simplicity.

Side gates

An unprotected side entrance is an open invitation for intruders to slip in unnoticed and gain access to the back of your house. Side gates are designed to deter burglars while affording easy access for tradesmen. These gates are invariably 2m (6ft 6in) high and are made either from wrought iron or from stout sections of timber. Wooden gates are heavy and are therefore braced with strong diagonal members to keep them rigid. With security in mind, choose a closeboarded or tongued and grooved gate – as their vertical boards are difficult to climb. Fit strong bolts top and bottom.

Entrance gates

An entrance gate is designed as much for its appearance as its function, but it must be sturdy enough to withstand frequent use. For this reason, wooden gates are often braced with a diagonal strut running from the top of the latch stile down to the bottom of the hanging or hinge stile. Don't hang a gate with the strut running the other way, or the bracing will have no effect whatsoever.

Common fence styles are reflected in the type of entrance gates you can buy. Picket, closeboard and ranch-style gates are all available, and there are simple frame-and-panel gates made with solid timber or exterior-grade plywood panels that serve to keep the frame rigid. If the tops of both the stiles (uprights) are cut at an angle, they will tend to shed rainwater, reducing the likelihood of wet rot.

Decorative iron gates are often used for entrances, but make sure the style is appropriate for the building and its location. An ostentatious gate may look out of place in front of a simple modern house or a country cottage.

Drive gates

First, decide whether hanging a gate across your drive is a good idea. Stepping out of your car into the road in order to open the gate can be dangerous unless there's plenty of room to park the vehicle temporarily in front of the gate. Drive gates invariably open into the property; so if the drive slopes up from the road, make sure there's adequate ground clearance for a wide gate. Alternatively, hang a pair of smaller gates that meet in the centre.

Gateposts and piers

Gateposts and masonry piers need to be anchored securely to the ground, to take the leverage exerted by a heavy gate. This is especially important for relatively wide drive gates.

Choose hardwood posts whenever possible, and select the size according to the weight of the gate. Posts 100mm (4in) square are adequate for entrance gates, but use 125mm (5in) posts for gates that are 2m (6ft 6in) high. For a gate across a drive, choose posts 150mm (6in) or even 200mm (8in) square.

If you opt for concrete gateposts, look for posts predrilled to accept hinges and a catch. Otherwise, you'll have to screw these fittings to a strip of timber bolted securely to the post.

Square or cylindrical tubular-steel posts are available with hinge pins, gatestops and catches welded in place. Unless they are plastic-coated, metal posts need to be painted to protect them from rust.

A pair of masonry piers is another possibility. Each pier should be at least 328mm (1ft 1½in) square and built on a firm concrete footing. For heavy gates, the hinge pier should be reinforced with a metal rod buried in the footing and running centrally through the pier.

SEE ALSO > Painting metal 82–3, Ledged-and-braced doors 183. Wet rot 245, Footings 443, Building piers 448–9

Hardware for gates

A range of specialized hardware has been developed for hanging heavy garden gates, to cope with the strain on their fixings.

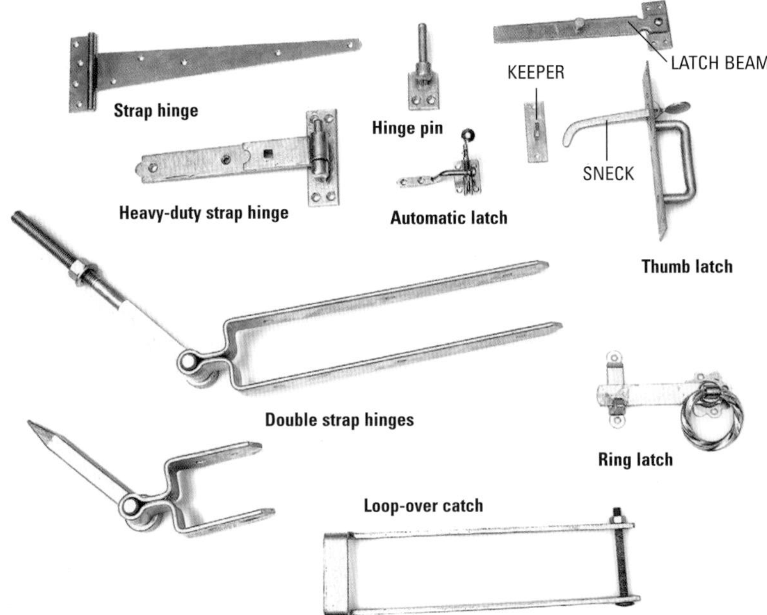

Hinges

Strap hinges

Most side and entrance gates are hung on strap hinges. Screw the longer flap to the gate rail, and the vertical flap to the face of the post. Heavy gates require a hinge that's bolted through the top rail.

Wide drive gates are best hung from double strap hinges, made with long flaps bolted on each side of the top rail.

Hinge pins

Collars welded to metal gates drop over hinge pins attached to the gateposts. To prevent a gate being lifted off its hinges, drill a hole through the top pin and fit a split pin and washer.

Latches and catches

Automatic latches

Simple wooden gates are usually fitted with a latch that operates automatically as the gate is closed.

Thumb latches

Pass the sneck (lifter bar) of a thumb latch through a slot cut in the gate, then screw the handle to the front. Screw the latch beam to the inner face, where the sneck can lift the beam from the hooked keeper fixed to the gatepost.

Ring latches

A ring latch works in a similar way to a thumb latch but is usually operated, from inside only, by twisting the ring handle to lift the latch beam.

Loop-over catches

When hanging a pair of wide gates, one is fixed with a bolt that locates in a socket concreted into the ground. A U-shape metal catch on the other gate drops over the stile of the fixed gate.

Materials for gates

Although wooden gates are often made from relatively cheap softwood, a wood such as cedar or oak will last longer. Most so-called 'wrought-iron' gates are made from mild-steel bar, which must be primed and painted.

Gateposts

Gateposts are set in concrete, but the post holes should be linked by a concrete bridge to provide extra support.

Erecting gateposts

Lay the gate on the ground with a post on each side. Check that the posts are parallel and that they are the required distance apart to accommodate hinges and catch. Nail two battens from post to post and another diagonally to keep the posts in line while you erect them (**1**).

Dig a trench across the entrance, making it 300mm (1ft) wide and long enough to take both posts. It need be no deeper than 300mm (1ft) in the centre, but dig a post hole at each end – 450mm (1ft 6in) deep for a low entrance gate, 600mm (2ft) deep for a tall side gate.

Set the battened gateposts in the holes with hardcore and concrete, using temporary battens to hold them upright until the concrete has set (**2**).

Drive gateposts
Hang wide farm-style gates on posts set in holes 900mm (3ft) deep. Erect the latch post in concrete, like any fence post, but bolt a stout piece of timber across the base of the hinge post before anchoring it in concrete.

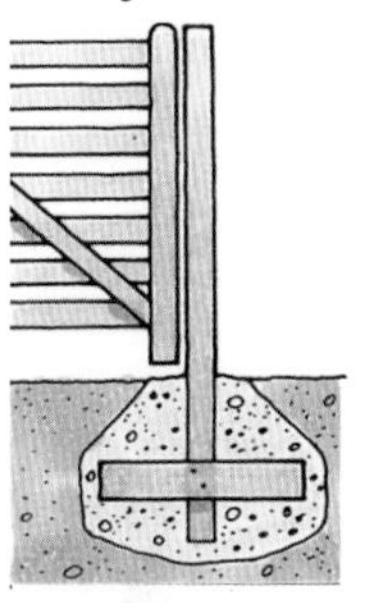

Supporting wide gates
Bolt a balk of timber to the hinge post to help support the weight of a wide gate.

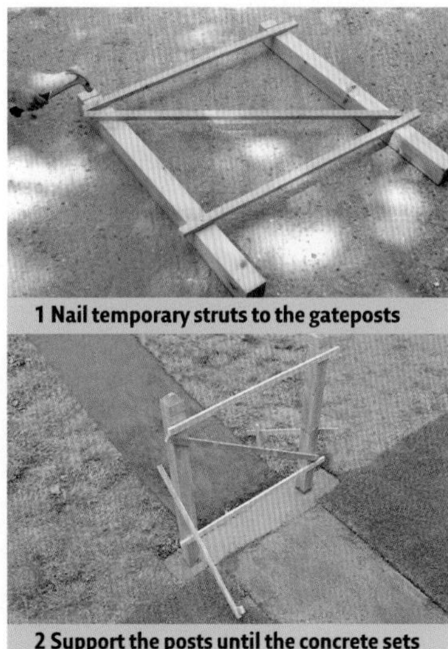

1 Nail temporary struts to the gateposts

2 Support the posts until the concrete sets

Hanging a gate
Stand the gate between the posts and prop it up on a pair or bricks or wooden blocks to hold it at the required height off the ground. Tap in pairs of wedges on each side of the gate until it is held securely. Then mark the positions of the hinges and catch.

SEE ALSO > Priming and painting metal 60–61, 82–3, Preservers 246, Erecting posts 429

Building walls

Whatever kind of masonry structure you are building, the basic techniques are broadly similar. However, it's well worth hiring a professional builder or bricklayer when the structure is complicated or extensive, especially if it will have to bear considerable loads or stress.

Compressive strength of bricks
The compressive strength of bricks is specified in Newtons per square millimetre (N/mm²). Average-strength facings will generally be rated about 20N/mm². Class A engineering bricks have a compressive strength of not less than 70N/mm², Class B a strength of not less than 50N/mm².

Walls for different locations

Retaining walls

A retaining wall is designed to hold back a bank of earth when terracing a sloping site. Raised planting beds often serve a similar purpose.

Provided it's not excessively high, a retaining wall is quite easy to build, although strictly speaking it should slope back into the bank to resist the weight of the earth. You must also allow for drainage, in order to reduce water pressure behind the wall.

Retaining walls can be constructed with bricks, concrete blocks or stone. Sometimes they are dry-laid, with earth packed into the crevices between stones in order to accommodate plants.

Boundary walls

A brick or stone wall that surrounds your property provides security and privacy while creating an attractive background for trees and shrubs.

New bricks complement a formal garden or a modern setting, while second-hand materials or undressed stone blend well with an old, established garden. If you aren't able to match existing masonry exactly, disguise the difference in colour by brushing liquid fertilizer onto the wall to encourage lichen to grow. Alternatively, hide the junction with a climbing plant. You need local-authority approval to build a wall higher than 1m (3ft 3in) if it adjoins a highway, or one that is over 2m (6ft 6in) high elsewhere.

Dividing walls

Many gardeners like to divide up a plot with walls in order to add interest to an otherwise featureless site. For example, you can build a wall to form a visual break between a patio and an area of grass, or perhaps to define the edge of a pathway. This type of dividing wall is often no more than 600 to 750mm (2ft to 2ft 6in) high.

Use simple concrete-block or brick walls to create separate areas inside a workshop or garage.

Screen walls

Screens are dividing walls that provide a degree of privacy without completely masking the garden beyond. They are usually built with decorative pierced blocks, sometimes combined with brick or solid-block bases and piers.

Amateur bricklayers

It is difficult to suggest which aspects of bricklaying are likely to overstretch the capabilities of an amateur builder, as this differs from one individual to another and also depends on the nature of the job. Clearly, it would be foolhardy for anyone to try to build a two-storey house without having had a great deal of experience, augmented by professional tuition. And even building a high boundary wall, which is simple in terms of technique, may be arduous if the wall is a very long one or if you have to allow for changes in gradient.

The simple answer is to practise with relatively low retaining walls, decorative screens or dividing walls until you have mastered the skills of laying bricks and concrete blocks solidly one upon another, and have developed the ability to build a wall that is straight and absolutely vertical. At that point, you may wish to move on to more demanding bricklaying projects.

Stone-built retaining wall

Decorative pierced-block screen

Boundary wall of yellow brick

Artificial-stone blocks make attractive dividing walls

SEE ALSO > Official approval 23–7, Cavity walls 138, Damp-proof course 247

Choosing bricks

At one time, bricks were named after their district of origin, where a particular clay imparted a distinctive colour. Nowadays names are often chosen by manufacturers to suggest the continuation of that tradition. Typical examples are London stocks, Leicester reds, Blue Staffs and so on. The colour and texture are of interest when trying to match existing masonry, but of equal importance are the variety, durability and type of brick.

Types of brick

Solid bricks

The majority of bricks are solid throughout and are either flat on all surfaces or have a depression known as a 'frog' on one face. When filled with mortar, the frog keys the bricks.

Cored or perforated bricks

Cored bricks have holes through them, performing the same function as the frog. A wall made with cored bricks must be finished with a solid-brick or slab coping.

Special shapes

Specially shaped bricks are made for decorative brickwork. Master bricklayers draw upon the full range when building structures such as arches and chamfered or rounded corners. Shaped bricks are made for coping walls.

Double-cant coping

Standard cored brick

Bullnose brick

Standard brick with frog

Squint for shaped corner

Half-round coping

Varieties of brick

Facings

Facings are made as much for their appearance as their structural qualities and, as such, are available in a wide range of colours and textures. Facings are used for exposed brickwork.

Commons

Commons are cheap general-purpose bricks used primarily for plastered or rendered brickwork, the inner leaf of cavity walls and foundations. They are not colour-matched as carefully as facings, but the mottled effect of a wall built with commons is not unattractive. Concrete building blocks have now all but replaced commons for cavity walling and internal partition walls.

Engineering bricks

Engineering bricks are exceptionally dense and strong. You are unlikely to need them for the average wall, but because they are impervious to water they are sometimes used to construct damp-proof courses.

Storing bricks
When your bricks are delivered, stack them carefully on a flat, dry base and cover them with polythene sheet or a tarpaulin. This prevents them becoming saturated, which could cause staining as well as an increased risk of frost damage to the mortar and the bricks themselves.

Seconds
The term 'seconds' denotes second-hand, rather than second-rate, bricks. They should be cheaper than new bricks, but demand can inflate prices. Using seconds might be the only way you can match the colour of weathered brickwork.

Durability of bricks

Frost resistance

Freezing causes moisture within a brick to expand, which sometimes causes the surface of the brick to spall (flake). Bricks are made with different degrees of frost resistance.

F2-category bricks are totally frost-resistant, even when a saturated wall is exposed to freezing. They are especially suitable for walls in coastal regions. These bricks were previously designated as 'special quality'.

F1-category bricks (previously known as 'ordinary quality') are moderately frost-resistant. Though suitable for most external uses, these bricks may suffer if they are subjected to extreme weathering or if used for a retaining wall that holds back poorly drained soil.

Fo-category bricks (previously designated as 'internal quality') are likely to be damaged by frost and should be used for building internal walls only. Make sure these bricks are stored under cover.

Soluble-salt content

The materials from which bricks are manufactured contain impurities, such as soluble salts, that can attack cement mortar and cause efflorescence to form on the surface of a wall.

For general-purpose brickwork, use S1-category bricks. So-category bricks should be used in completely dry locations only. Bricks designated S2 are intended for use in locations subjected to prolonged saturation – such as foundations and retaining walls.

Buying bricks

The dimensions of a standard brick are 215 x 102.5 x 65mm (8½ x 4 x 2½in), but these sometimes vary by a few millimetres – even within the same batch of bricks. Brick manufacturers normally specify a nominal size, which includes an additional 10mm (⅜in) on each of the dimensions in order to allow for the mortar joint.

To calculate how many bricks you will need, allow approximately 60 bricks for every square metre (50 bricks per square yard) of single-skin walling. Add an extra 5 per cent for cutting and breakages. Bricks are normally cheaper if you order them in sufficient quantity direct from the manufacturer.

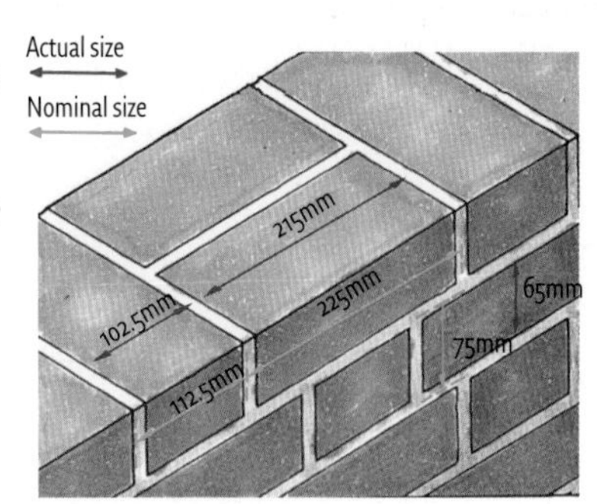

SEE ALSO > Efflorescence 42, Coloured and textured bricks 438, Laying bricks 444–9, Coping a wall 446

Brick colour and texture

The popularity of brick as a building material is derived largely from its range of subtle colours and textures, which actually improve with weathering. Weathered brick can be difficult to match by using a manufacturer's catalogue, so try to borrow samples from your supplier's stock – or if you have spare bricks, take one to the supplier to compare it with new bricks.

Decorative combination of coloured bricks

Colour

The colour of bricks is largely determined by the type of clay used for their manufacture, although their colour may be modified by the addition of certain minerals and by the temperature of firing. Large manufacturers supply a wide variety of colours; and you can also buy brindled (multicoloured or mottled) bricks, which are useful for blending with existing masonry.

Texture

Texture is as important to the appearance of a brick wall as colour. Simple rough or smooth textures are created by the choice of materials. Others are imposed upon the clay by scratching, rolling, brushing, and so on. A brick may be textured all over, or on the sides and ends only.

Brick colours and textures
A small selection from the wide range of colours and textures available.
1 Smooth blended
2 Handmade
3 Sandfaced yellow
4 Smooth blue engineering
5 Sandfaced grey
6 Smooth red stock
7 Wirecut brindle
8 Textured buff multi
9 London stock (second)
10 Wirecut blue
11 Red common
12 Coarse fletton
13 Moulded fletton
14 Dragfaced red multi

Pattern formed by projecting headers

Look out for second-hand moulded bricks

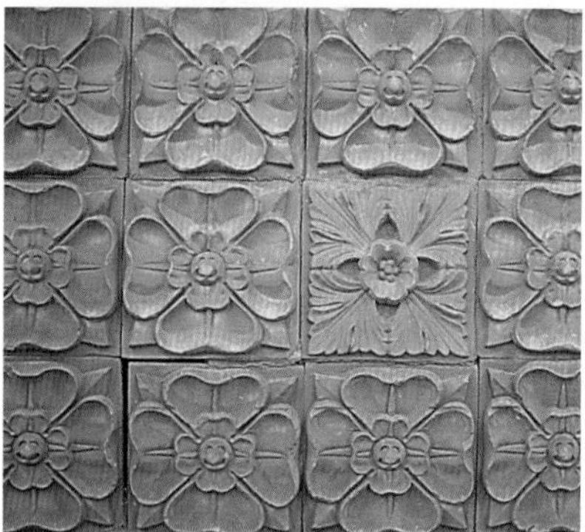

Sometimes whole panels are available

Weathered antique bricks are much sought after

SEE ALSO > Choosing bricks 437, Laying bricks 444–9

Choosing concrete blocks

Cast-concrete blocks were introduced as a cheap substitute for bricks that were to be covered with plaster or render, but they are now used in a variety of situations – from foundations to soundproof internal partitions. Indeed, modern concrete blocks are superior to clay bricks in terms of acoustic and thermal insulation.

Density

Lightweight-concrete blocks
Made from aerated or foamed concrete, these blocks can be carried easily in one hand, which enables bricklayers to build walls quickly and safely. Aerated blocks can be drilled, cut to shape and chased for electric cables, using handtools or power tools. They are used extensively in the building trade for the construction of both internal and external walls.

Dense-concrete blocks
Made from relatively heavy concrete, these are also known as dense-aggregate blocks or medium-density blocks.

Nowadays, because of the availability of lightweight loadbearing blocks, dense-concrete blocks are used less frequently, even though they are slightly cheaper than equivalent building blocks made of aerated concrete.

Varieties of block

Construction
The majority of building blocks are simple rectangular blocks of cement-grey or white concrete. The larger ones, especially if they are made from dense concrete, are available in the form of hollow blocks with enclosed supporting ribs between the outer skins. Including voids not only reduces the weight of the blocks, but allows for metal rods to be inserted in order to reinforce retaining walls. With cellular blocks, the voids are open at the bottom only.

Grades
Standard-grade blocks have no aesthetic qualities whatsoever. They are used for the structural core of a wall that is going to be either rendered or plastered, and so are usually made with zigzag 'keying' on both faces.

Fair-face building blocks, which are intended to be visible, usually have smooth faces. However, some fair-face blocks are shot-blasted in order to create a hard-wearing finely textured surface finish.

Paint-quality concrete blocks are ideal for a wall that is to be decorated directly with masonry paint.

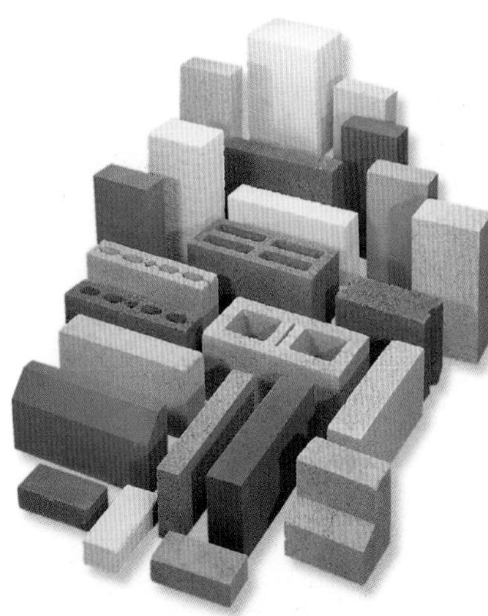

Qualities

Loadbearing
Lightweight and dense-concrete blocks are produced for non-loadbearing and load-bearing applications, but dense-concrete blocks are made in a greater range of high compressive strengths. Even so, it's possible to buy lightweight blocks that are perfectly suited to building loadbearing foundations and multistorey dwellings.

Insulating
Aerated blocks greatly reduce the transmission of heat and sound. Blocks with superior acoustic-insulation properties are made specifically for partitions and party walls. Those that have a high degree of thermal insulation reduce the need for secondary insulation.

Moisture and frost resistance
Most concrete blocks are generally weatherproof. Totally frost-resistant and moisture-proof blocks are made for foundations and walling below ground.

Buying blocks

When the blocks are delivered, have them unloaded as near as possible to the construction site. Stack them on a flat, dry base and protect them from rain and frost with a polythene sheet.

Available sizes
The average concrete block measures 450 x 225mm (1ft 6in x 9in) and ranges in thickness from 75 to 230mm (3 to 9in). Specials – such as foundation blocks – may be similar in length and height but may differ in thickness. Brick-size concrete blocks, known as coursing bricks, are made for infilling above door and window lintels.

The dimensions given above are actual sizes, but some manufacturers may specify nominal sizes (also known as 'coordinating sizes'), which include a 10mm (3/8in) allowance for mortar on the length and height. Since block walls are often constructed with just one skin of masonry, the thickness of a block is normally given as the actual size.

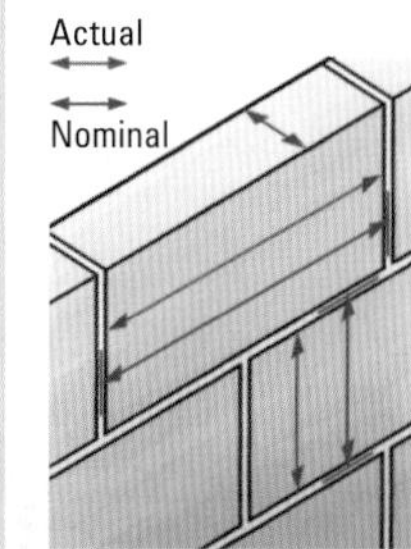

Sizes of structural blocks
The nominal size of a block refers to the length and height only. The thickness is always specified as the actual size.

Screen blocks

Pierced concrete blocks are used for building decorative screens in the garden. The blocks are not bonded like brickwork or structural blocks and therefore require supporting brick piers. Matching coping slabs and pier caps are available for finishing the top of the screen.

Screen blocks should not be used to build loadbearing walls, but they can support a lightweight structure.

Standard sizes
Decorative screen blocks are invariably 300mm (1ft) square and 90mm (about 3½in) thick.

SEE ALSO > Compressive strength 436, Laying bricks 444–9, Coping a wall 446

Stone: natural and artificial

Artificial-stone blocks, made from poured concrete, can look very convincing once they have weathered. Depending on where you live, these blocks may be easier to obtain than natural building stone, and are probably cheaper. Aesthetically, however, nothing can surpass quarried stone, such as granite or sandstone.

Natural stone
Whether it be roughly hewn or finely dressed, natural stone is durable and weathers superbly.

Natural stone

Limestone, sandstone and granite are all suitable materials for building walls. Flint and slate are laid using specialized methods, and both are frequently used in combination with other materials.

Stone bought in its natural state is classed as random rubble (undressed); it is a perfect choice for dry-stone walling in an informal garden setting. For more regular masonry, ask for squared rubble (semi-dressed) stone, which is cut into reasonably uniform blocks but with uneven surfaces. Ashlar is fully dressed stone with machine-cut faces. The cost of stone increases in proportion to the degree of preparation required.

Semi-dressed natural-stone blocks

Dry-stone retaining wall

Split-stone walling

Knapped-flint boundary wall

Artificial-stone walling
(below left)
Cast-concrete blocks that simulate real stonework are used to construct attractive walling and planters.

Slate-effect walling
(below right)
Good-quality concrete walling is difficult to distinguish from real slate once it has weathered. What looks like narrow sections of slate are actually cast as large interlocking blocks that can be laid quickly.

Obtaining stone

In practical terms, the type of stone you can use for walling depends almost entirely on where you live. In some parts of the country there are restrictions governing the choice of building materials – and, in any case, a structure built from indigenous stone is more likely to blend into its surroundings. Buying stone from a local quarry also makes economical sense. Most quarries sell stone by the tonne, and will be able to give you advice on quantity and price.

If you live in a town or city, obtaining natural stone can be a problem. You may be prepared to buy a few small boulders for a rockery from a local garden centre, but the cost of buying enough stone for even a short run of walling is likely to be prohibitive. If you don't want to use artificial stone made from cast concrete, your only alternative is to hire a truck and drive to a quarry out of town.

Another source of materials, and possibly the cheapest way to obtain dressed stone, is to visit a demolition site. Prices vary considerably, but the cost of transport may be less than a trip to a quarry.

Artificial-stone blocks

The stretcher faces of concrete blocks made specifically for garden walling are textured to resemble natural stone. Single blocks are laid in mortar and bonded like real stonework; and there are larger blocks that look like two or three courses of squared rubble or dressed stone.

SEE ALSO > Choosing concrete blocks 439, Laying blocks 450, Building with stone 451, Building retaining walls 452

Mortar for building walls

Mortar is employed to bind together bricks, concrete blocks or stones. The durability of the wall depends to a certain extent upon the quality of the mortar used in its construction. If it's mixed correctly, mortar is strong yet flexible – but if the ingredients are in the wrong proportions, the mortar is likely to be weak or, conversely, so hard that it is prone to cracking. If too much water is added to the mix, the mortar will be squeezed out of the joints by the weight of the masonry. If the mortar is too dry, then adhesion will be poor.

Correct consistency
The mortar mix should be firm enough to hold its shape when you make a depression in the mix.

Lime mortar
Much old brickwork was built using lime mortar. When cement-based mortar is used to repoint soft brickwork there's an increased risk of spalling and cracked pointing. You can buy powdered hydraulic lime to mix with sand and water: 1 part lime to 2.5 parts sand. Mix to the consistency of cottage cheese. Wear gloves and goggles when handling lime.

The ingredients of mortar

General-purpose mortar is made from cement, hydrated lime and sand, mixed together with enough water to make a workable paste.

Cement is the hardening agent that binds the other ingredients together. The lime slows down the drying process and prevents the mortar setting too quickly. It also makes the mix flow well, so that it fills gaps in the masonry and adheres to the texture of blocks or bricks. Sand acts as an aggregate, adding body to the mortar, and reduces the possibility of shrinkage.

For general-purpose mortar, fine builder's sand is ideal – but if you want a pale mortar for bonding white screen blocks, use silver sand instead.

Plasticizers

If you're laying masonry in a period of cold weather, substitute a proprietary plasticizer for the lime. The plasticizer produces an aerated mortar in which the tiny air bubbles allow water to expand in freezing conditions, thus reducing the risk of cracking. Premixed masonry cement, which has an aerating agent, is ready for mixing with sand.

Ready-mixed mortar

This type of mortar contains all the essential ingredients mixed to the correct proportions – you simply add water.

Mixing mortar

Mortar should be discarded if it isn't used within 2 hours of being mixed – so make only as much as you can use within that time. An average of about 2 minutes for laying each brick is a reasonable estimate.

Choose a flat site upon which to mix the materials – a sheet of plywood will do – and dampen it slightly, in order to prevent it absorbing water from the mortar. Make a pile of half the amount of sand that is to be used, then add the other ingredients. Put the rest of the sand on top, and mix the dry materials thoroughly.

Scoop a depression in the pile and add clean tap water – never use contaminated or salty water. Push the dry mix from around the edge of the pile into the water until it has absorbed enough for you to blend the mix with a shovel, using a chopping action. Add more water, little by little, until the mortar has a butter-like consistency – slipping easily from the shovel, but firm enough to hold its shape if you make a hollow in the mix. If the sides of the hollow collapse, add more dry ingredients until the mortar firms up. Make sure the mortar is sufficiently moist – since dry mortar won't form a strong bond with the masonry. If the mortar stiffens up while you are working, add just enough water to restore the consistency.

Bricklayers' terms

Bricklayers use a number of specialized terms to describe their craft and materials. Those used frequently are listed below, others are described as they occur.

BRICK FACES (the surfaces of a brick)
Stretcher faces – the long sides of a brick
Header faces – the short ends of a brick
Bedding faces – the top and bottom surfaces
Frog – the depression in one bedding face

COURSE (horizontal row of bricks)
Stretcher course – a single course with stretcher faces visible
Header course – a single course with header faces visible
Coping – the top course designed to protect the wall from rainwater
Bond – the pattern produced by staggering alternate courses so that vertical joints are not aligned one above the other
Stretcher – a single brick from a stretcher course
Header – a single brick from a header course
Closure brick – the last brick laid in a course

CUT BRICKS (bricks cut to even up the bond)
Bat – a brick cut across its width (e.g. half bat, three-quarter bat)
Queen closer – a brick cut along its length

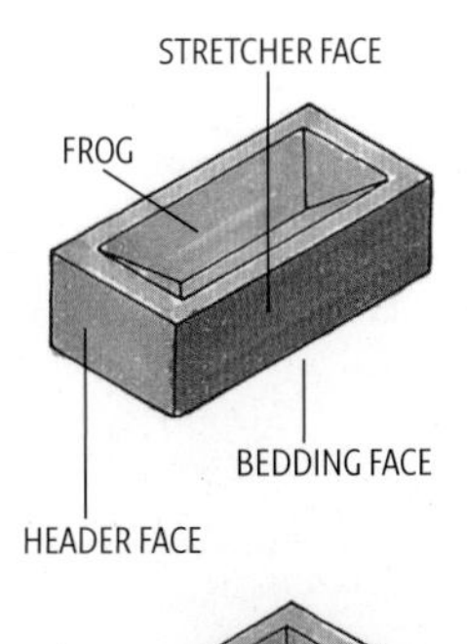

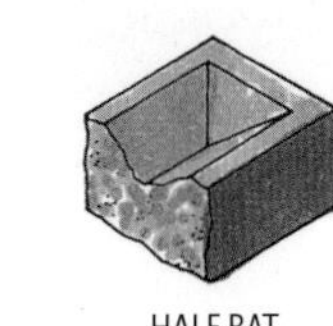

HALF BAT

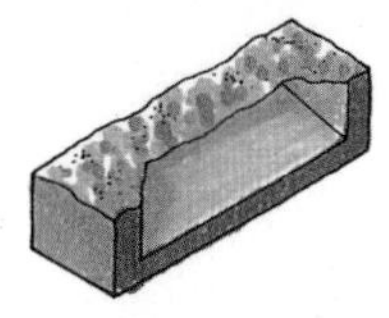

QUEEN CLOSER

Proportions for masonry mixes

Mix the ingredients according to the prevailing conditions at the building site. Use a general-purpose mortar for moderate conditions where the wall is reasonably sheltered. A stronger mix is required for severe conditions where the wall will be exposed to wind and driving rain, or if the site is elevated or near the coast. If you're using plasticizer rather than lime, follow the manufacturer's instructions regarding the quantity you should add to the sand.

Estimating quantity
When building a single-skin wall, allow approximately 1cu m (1⅓ cu yd) of sand (other ingredients in proportion) to lay either 3364 bricks, 1946 average concrete blocks, or 1639 decorative screen blocks.

Masonry cement
This is a ready-mixed cement that's used without adding lime or plasticizer.

MORTAR-MIXING PROPORTIONS	Cement/lime mortar	Plasticized mortar	Masonry cement
General-purpose mortar (moderate conditions)	1 part cement 1 part lime 6 parts sand	1 part cement 6 parts sand/plasticizer	1 part masonry cement 5 parts sand
Strong mortar (severe conditions)	1 part cement ½ part lime 4 parts sand	1 part cement 4 parts sand/plasticizer	1 part masonry cement 3 parts sand

SEE ALSO > Cutting bricks 444

Bonding brickwork

Although mortar is extremely strong under compression, its tensile strength is relatively weak. If bricks were stacked one upon the other, so that the vertical joints were continuous, any movement within the wall would pull the joints apart. Bonding the brickwork staggers the vertical joints, transmitting the load along the entire length of the wall.

Stretcher bond

Flemish bond

Honeycomb bond

Stretcher bond

The stretcher bond is used for single-thickness walls – including the two leaves of a cavity wall employed in the construction of modern buildings. Half bats are used to complete the bond at the end of a straight wall, while a corner is formed by alternating headers and stretchers.

English bond

If you were to build a wall 215mm (8½in) thick by laying courses of stretcher-bonded bricks side by side, there would be a weak vertical joint running centrally down the wall. An English bond strengthens the wall by using alternate courses of headers. Staggered joints are maintained at the end of the wall and at right-angle corners by inserting a queen closer before the last header.

Flemish bond

The Flemish bond is another method used for building a solid wall 215mm (8½in) thick. Every course is laid with alternate headers and stretchers. Stagger the joint at the end of a course and at corners by laying a queen closer before the header.

Decorative bonds

Stretcher, English and Flemish bonds are designed to construct strong walls; decorative qualities are incidental. Other bonds, used primarily for their visual effect, are suitable for low non-loadbearing walls only. They need to be supported by a conventionally bonded base and piers.

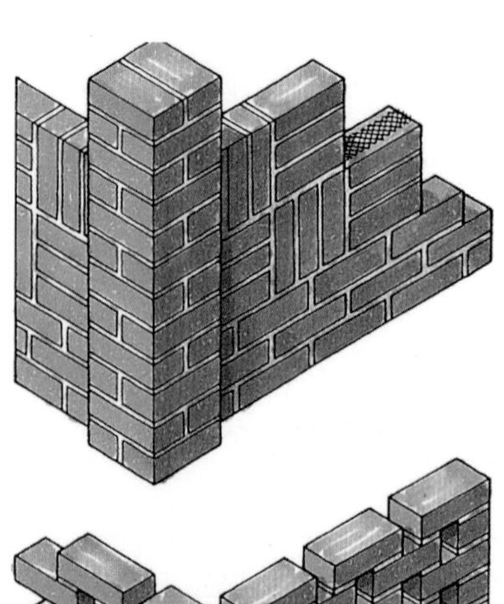

Stack bonding

Laying bricks in groups of three creates a basket-weave effect. Strengthen the continuous vertical joints with wall ties.

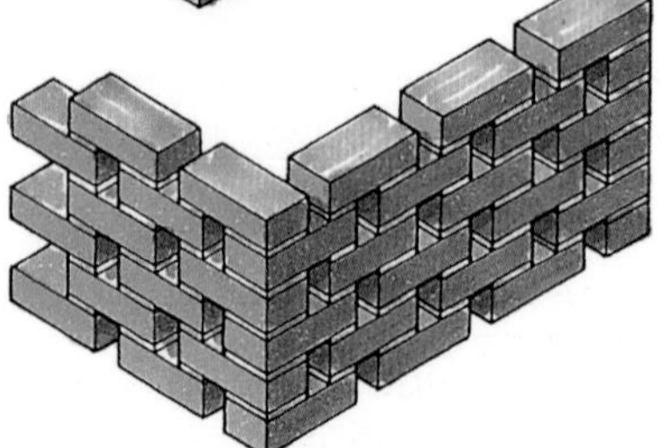

Honeycomb bond

You can build an open decorative screen by using a stretcher-like bond with a quarter-bat-size space between each brick. This type of screen has to be built with care, in order to keep the bond regular. Cut quarter bats to fill the gaps in the top course.

Strength and stability

It is easy enough to appreciate the loads and stresses imposed upon the walls of a house or outbuilding – and hence the need for solid foundations with adequate methods of reinforcement and protection to prevent them collapsing. But it is not so obvious that even simple garden walling requires similar measures to ensure its stability. It's merely irritating if a low dividing wall or planter falls apart, but a serious injury could result from the collapse of a heavy boundary wall.

The basic structure of a wall

Unless you design and build a wall in the correct manner, it will not be strong and stable.

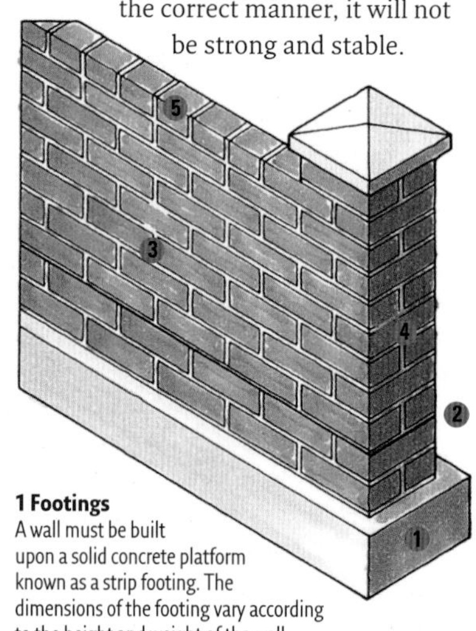

1 Footings
A wall must be built upon a solid concrete platform known as a strip footing. The dimensions of the footing vary according to the height and weight of the wall.

2 Damp-proof course
A layer of waterproof material 150mm (6in) above ground level stops water rising from the soil. It is not required for most garden walling unless the wall abuts a building with a similar DPC.

3 Bonding
The staggered pattern of the bricks is not merely decorative. It's designed primarily to spread the static load along the wall and to tie the individual bricks together.

4 Piers
Straight walls that exceed a certain height and length must be buttressed at regular intervals with thick columns of brickwork, known as piers.

5 Coping
The coping prevents frost damage by shedding rainwater, which could seep into the upper brick joints.

SEE ALSO > Damp-proof course 247, Bricks 437–8, Copings 446, Wall ties 448, Building piers 448–9

Footings for garden walls

The Building Regulations govern the size and reinforcement of the footings required to support high walls, especially loadbearing walls. However, the majority of garden walls can be built upon concrete footings laid in a straight-sided trench.

Size of footings

The footing needs to be sufficiently substantial to support the weight of the wall. The surrounding soil must be firm and well drained, to avoid possible subsidence. It is unwise to set footings in ground that has been infilled recently, such as a new building site. Take care also to avoid tree roots and drainpipes. If the trench begins to fill with water as you are digging, seek professional advice before proceeding.

Dig the trench deeper than the footing itself, so that the first one or two courses of brick are below ground level. This will allow for an adequate depth of soil for planting right up to the wall.

If the soil is not firmly packed when you reach the required depth, dig deeper until you reach a firm level; then fill the bottom of the trench with compacted hardcore up to the lowest level of the proposed footing.

RECOMMENDED DIMENSIONS FOR FOOTINGS

Type of wall	Height of wall	Thickness of footing	Width of footing
One brick thick	Up to 1m (3ft 3in)	150mm (6in)	300mm (1ft)
Two bricks thick	Up to 1m (3ft 3in)	225 to 300mm (9in to 1ft)	450mm (1ft 6in)
Two bricks thick	Over 1m (3ft 3in) up to 2m (6ft 6in)	375 to 450mm (1ft 3in to 1ft 6in)	450 to 600mm (1ft 6in to 2ft)
Retaining wall	Up to 1m (3ft 3in)	150 to 300mm (6in to 1ft)	375 to 450mm (1ft 3in to 1ft 6in)

Sloping sites

If the ground slopes gently, simply ignore the gradient and make footings perfectly level. If the site slopes noticeably, make a stepped footing by placing plywood shuttering across the trench at regular intervals. Calculate the height and length of the steps, using multiples of normal brick size.

Support plywood shuttering with stakes

Setting out the footings

For a straight footing, set up two profile boards (see right) made from timber 25mm (1in) thick nailed to stakes that are driven into the ground at each end of the proposed trench, but well outside the work area.

Drive nails into the top edge of each board and stretch lines between them to mark the front and back edges of the wall. Then drive nails into the boards on each side of the wall line to indicate the width of the footing, and stretch other lines between these nails (**1**). Next, remove the lines marking the wall - but leave the nails in place, so that you can replace the lines when you lay the bricks.

Place a spirit level against the remaining lines to mark the edge of the footing on the ground (**2**). Mark the ends of the footing, which should extend beyond the end of the wall by half the wall's thickness. Before you remove the lines, mark out each edge of the trench on the ground, using a spade. Leave the profile boards in place.

Turning corners

If your wall is going to have a right-angled corner, set up two sets of profile boards. Check carefully that the lines form a true right angle, using the 3 : 4 : 5 principle (**3**).

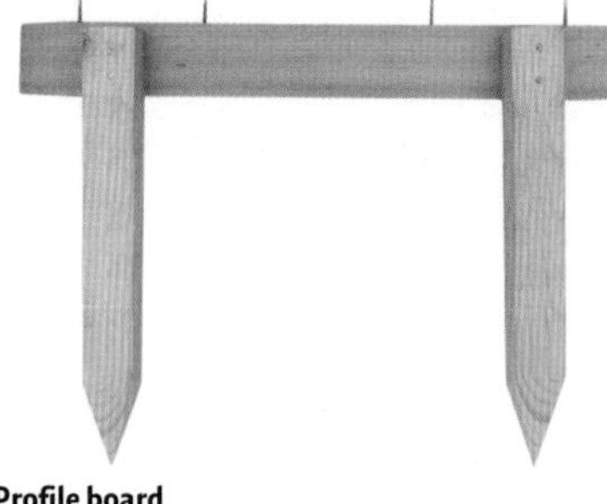
Profile board

Digging the trench

Excavate the trench, keeping the sides vertical; and check that the bottom is level, using a long straight piece of wood and a spirit level. Drive a stake into the bottom of the trench, near one end, until the top of the stake represents the depth of the footing. Drive in more stakes at about 1m (3ft) intervals and check that the tops are level (**4**).

Filling the trench

Pour a foundation mix of concrete (see MIXING CONCRETE BY VOLUME) into the trench, then tamp it down firmly with a stout piece of timber until it is exactly level with the top of the stakes. Leave the stakes in place, and allow the footing to harden thoroughly before building the wall.

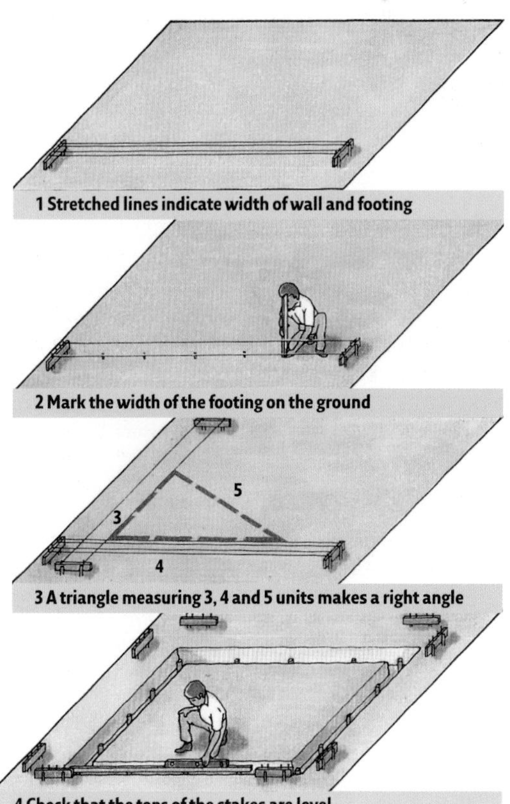

1 Stretched lines indicate width of wall and footing

2 Mark the width of the footing on the ground

3 A triangle measuring 3, 4 and 5 units makes a right angle

4 Check that the tops of the stakes are level

SEE ALSO > The 3:4:5 principle 106, Mixing concrete 455–7

Laying bricks

Spreading a bed of mortar ('throwing a line') requires practice before you can do it at speed – so at first concentrate on laying bricks accurately. Using mortar of exactly the right consistency helps to keep the visible faces of the bricks clean. In hot, dry weather dampen the footings and bricks before you begin, but let any surface water evaporate before you lay the bricks.

Tools for basic bricklaying
Although you can improvise a number of builder's tools, you will have to buy some of the more specialized tools that are used by bricklayers.

• **Brick cleaner**
Wash mortar off your tools as soon as the job is finished. If need be, use an acidic brick cleaner to remove hardened mortar. Follow manufacturers' instructions carefully, and wear PVC gloves and goggles.

Basic bricklaying techniques

Hold the trowel with your thumb in line with the handle and pointing towards the tip of the blade (**1**).

Scoop a measure of mortar out of the pile and shape it roughly to match the dimensions of the trowel blade. Pick up the mortar by sliding the blade under the pile, settling the mortar onto the trowel with a slight jerk of the wrist (**2**).

Spread the mortar along the top course by aligning the edge of the trowel with the centre line of the bricks (**3**). As you tip the blade to deposit the mortar, draw the trowel back towards you to stretch the bed over two to three bricks. Furrow the mortar by pressing the point of the trowel along the centre of the bed (**4**).

Pick up a brick with your other hand (**5**), but don't extend your thumb too far onto the stretcher face or it will disturb the bricklayer's line (see opposite) as you place the brick in position. Press the brick into the bed, picking up excess mortar squeezed from the joint by sliding the edge of the trowel along the face of the wall (**6**).

Spread mortar onto the header of the next brick, making a neat 10mm (3/8in) bed for the header joint (**7**). Press the brick against its neighbour, scooping off excess mortar with the trowel.

Having laid three bricks, use a spirit level to check that they are horizontal. Make any adjustments by tapping them down with the trowel handle (**8**).

Hold the spirit level along the outer edge of the bricks to check that they are in line. To move a brick sideways, tap the upper edge with the trowel at about 45 degrees (**9**).

Cutting bricks
To cut bricks, use a bolster chisel to mark the line on all faces by tapping gently with a hammer. Realign the blade on the visible stretcher face and strike the chisel firmly.

1 The correct way to hold a brick trowel

2 Scoop a measure of mortar onto the trowel

3 Stretch the bed of mortar along the course

4 Furrow the mortar with the point of the trowel

5 Pick up a brick with your thumb on the edge

6 Push the brick down and remove excess mortar

7 Spread mortar onto the head of the next brick

8 Level the bricks with the trowel handle

9 Tap the bricks sideways to align them

SEE ALSO > Bricks 437–8, Mixing mortar 441, Building tools 510–13

Building a stretcher-bonded wall

Over a certain height, a single-width brick wall is structurally weak unless it is either supported with piers or changes direction by forming right-angle corners. The ability to construct accurate right-angle corners is a requirement for building most structures, even simple garden planters.

1 Mark the face of the wall on the footing

Setting out the corners

Mark out the footings and the face of the wall by stretching string lines between profile boards (see SETTING OUT THE FOOTINGS).

When the footings have been filled and the concrete has set, either use a plumb line or hold a spirit level lightly against the lines to mark the corners and the face of the wall on the footing (**1**). Join up the marks on the concrete, using a pencil and a straight batten, then check the accuracy of the corners with a builder's square.

Finally, check that the alignment is straight by stretching a string line between the corner marks.

Building corners

Construct the corners first as a series of steps or 'leads'. Throw a bed of mortar on the footing, and then lay three bricks in both directions against the marked line. Using a spirit level, make sure the bricks are level in all directions, including across the diagonal (**2**).

Build the leads to a height of five stepped courses, using a marked-out gauge stick to measure the height of each course as you proceed (**3**). Use alternate headers and stretchers to form the actual point of the corner.

Plumb the corner, and check the alignment of the stepped bricks by holding a spirit level against them (**4**).

Protecting a wall
To protect the brickwork from rain or frost, cover newly built walls overnight with sheets of polythene or a tarpaulin. Weight the edges of the covers with bricks.

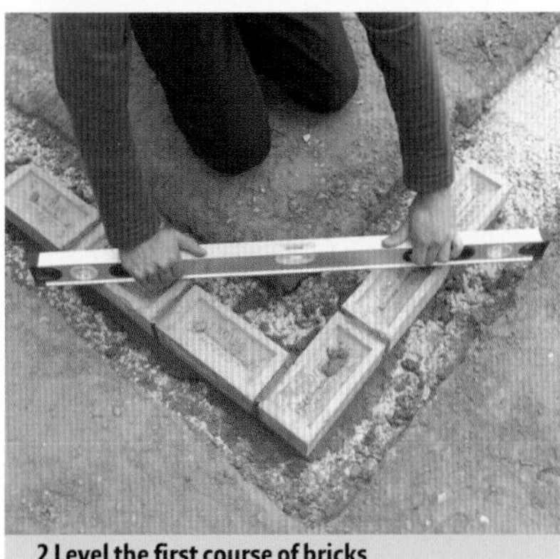

2 Level the first course of bricks

3 Check the height with a gauge stick

4 Check that the steps are in line

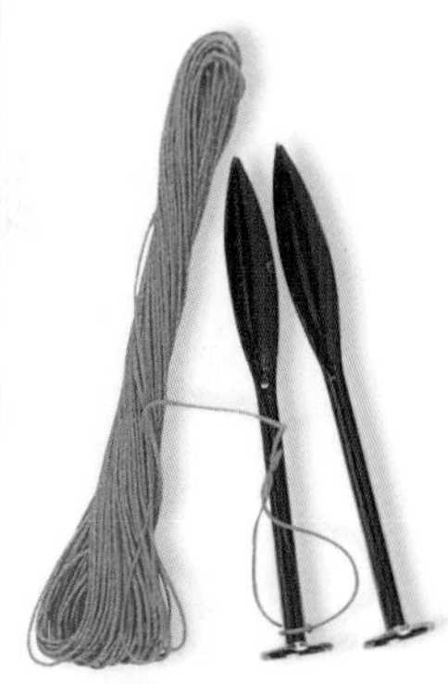

Bricklayer's line
Bricklayers use a nylon line as a guide for keeping bricks level. The line is stretched between two flat-bladed pins that are driven into vertical joints at each end of the wall.

Building the straight sections

Stretch a bricklayer's line between the corners so that it aligns perfectly with the top of the first course (**5**).

Lay the first straight course of bricks from both ends towards the middle. As you near the middle point, lay the last few bricks dry to make certain they will fit. If necessary, cut the central or 'closure' brick to fit. Mortar the bricks in place, and finish by spreading mortar onto both ends of the closure brick and onto the header faces of the bricks on each side (**6**). Scoop off excess mortar with the trowel. Lay subsequent courses between the leads in the same way, raising the bricklayer's line each time.

To build the wall higher, raise the corners first, by constructing leads to the required height, and then fill in between with bricks.

5 Stretch a bricklayer's line for the first course

6 Lay the last, or 'closure', brick carefully

SEE ALSO > Bricks 437–8, Bonding bricks 442, Footings 443, Profile boards 443, Copings 446, Building piers 449, Gauge stick 511

Pointing brickwork

Pointing the mortar between the bricks makes for packed, watertight joints as well as enhancing the appearance of the wall. Well-struck joints and clean brickwork are essential if the wall is to look professionally built. For best results, the mortar must be shaped when it has just the right consistency.

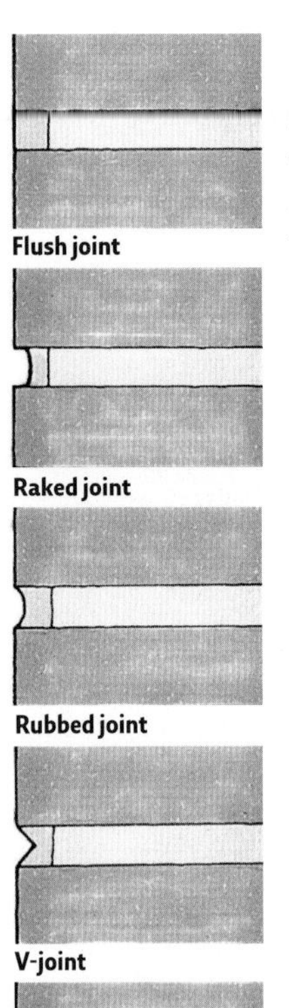

Flush joint

Raked joint

Rubbed joint

V-joint

Weatherstruck joint

Brushing the brickwork
Let the shaped joints harden a little before cleaning scraps of mortar from the face of the wall with a medium-soft banister brush. Sweep the brush lightly across the joints to avoid damaging the mortar.

Consistency of the mortar

If the mortar is still too wet, the joint will not be crisp and you may drag mortar out from between the bricks. On the other hand, if it's left to harden too long, pointing will be hard work and you may leave dark marks on the joint.

Test the consistency of the mortar by pressing your thumb into a joint. If it holds a clear impression without sticking to your thumb, the mortar is just right for pointing. Because it's important to start shaping the joints at exactly the right moment, you may have to point the work in stages before you can complete the wall. Shape the joints to match existing brickwork, or choose a profile that is suitable for the prevailing weather conditions.

Shaping the mortar joints

Flush joint

After using the edge of your trowel to scrape the mortar flush, stipple the joints with a stiff-bristle brush to expose the sand aggregate.

Raked joint

Use a piece of wood or metal to rake out the joints to a depth of about 6mm (¼in), then compress them again by smoothing the mortar lightly with a piece of rounded dowel rod. Raked joints do not shed water, so they are not suitable for exposed work.

Rubbed (concave) joint

Buy a shaped jointing tool to make a rubbed joint, or improvise with a length of bent tubing. Scrape the mortar flush first, then drag the tool along the joints. Finish the vertical joints, then shape the horizontal ones. This is a utilitarian joint, ideal for a wall built with second-hand bricks that are not good enough to take a crisp joint.

Shape the mortar with a jointing tool

V-joint

Produced in a similar way to the rubbed joint, the V-joint gives a smart finish to new brickwork and sheds rainwater well.

Weatherstruck joint

The angled weatherstruck joint will withstand harsh conditions. Use a small pointing trowel to shape the vertical joints (**1**) – they can slope to the left or right, but be consistent.

Shape the horizontal joints, allowing the mortar to spill out slightly at the base of each joint. Finish the joint by cutting off excess mortar with a tool called a Frenchman, which is rather like a table knife with its tip bent at 90 degrees. You can improvise one by bending a strip of metal. Make a neat, straight edge to the mortar, using a batten aligned with the bottom of each joint to guide the Frenchman (**2**); nail two scraps of wood to the batten to hold it away from the wall.

1 Shape a weatherstruck joint with a trowel

2 Remove excess mortar with a Frenchman

Coping brick walls

The coping – which forms the top course of the wall – protects the brickwork from weathering and gives the wall a finished appearance.

Integral coping
You could finish the wall by laying the last course frog downwards – but a coping of half bats laid on end looks more professional.

Brick coping
Specially shaped coping bricks are designed to shed rainwater.

Slab coping
Choose a stone or concrete slab that is wider than the wall.

Tile-and-brick coping
Lay roof tiles or special creasing tiles beneath a coping of bricks.

Technically, a coping that is flush with both faces of the wall is called a capping. A true coping projects from the face, so that water drips clear.

You can finish a wall with a coping of matching bricks or create a pleasing contrast with engineering bricks, which also offer superior water resistance. Alternatively, buy special coping bricks designed to shed rainwater.

Stone or cast-concrete slabs are popular for coping garden walls. Both are quick to lay and are usually wide enough to form low bench-type seating.

On an exposed site, consider installing a bituminous-felt DPC under the coping to reduce the risk of frost attack; or lay two courses of plain roof tiles with staggered joints and a brick coping above. Let the tiles project from the face of the wall, but run a sloping mortar joint along the top of the projection to shed water.

SEE ALSO > Damp-proof course 247, Engineering bricks 437

Building intersecting walls

When building new garden walls that intersect at right angles, either join them by bonding the brickwork (see below) or take the easier option and link them with wall ties at every third course. If the intersecting wall is more than 2m (6ft 6in) in length, make the junction a control joint by using straight metal strips as wall ties.

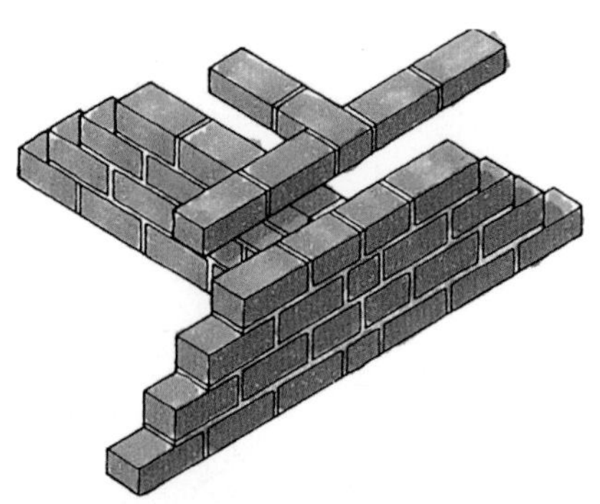
Stretcher bond

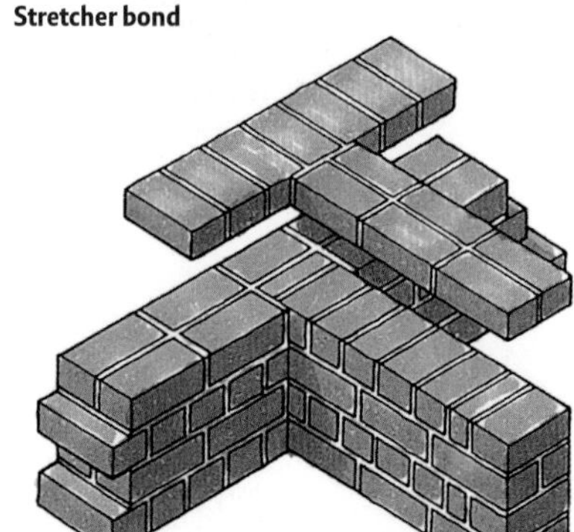
English bond

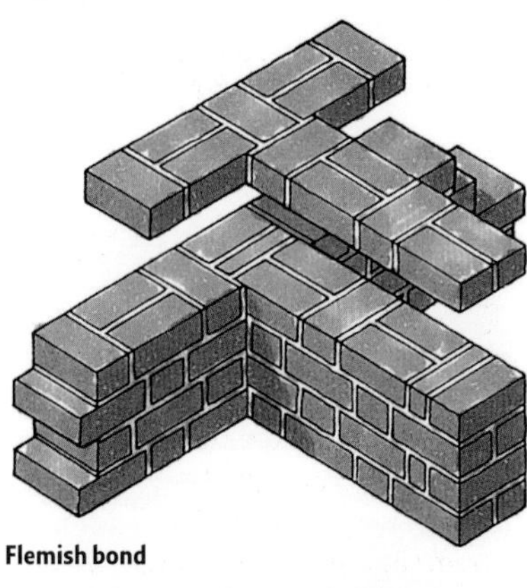
Flemish bond

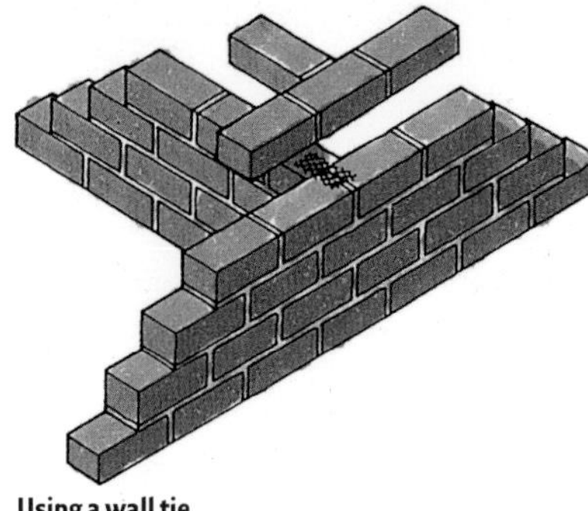
Using a wall tie

Building up to a wall

When building a new wall to intersect with an existing wall of a house, you must include a damp-proof course in order to prevent water bridging the house's DPC via the new masonry. You must also make a positive joint between the walls.

Inserting a DPC

The Building Regulations require a damp-proof course to be installed in all habitable buildings. This consists of a layer of impervious material built into the mortar bed 150mm (6in) above ground level. When you build a new wall, its DPC must coincide with the DPC in the existing structure. Use a roll of bituminous felt, chosen to match the thickness of the new wall.

Locate the house's DPC and build the first few courses of the new wall up to that level. Spread a thin bed of mortar on the bricks, and lay the DPC upon it with the end of the roll turned up against the existing wall. The next course of bricks will trap the DPC between the header joint and the wall. Lay more mortar on top of the DPC to produce a standard 10mm (3/8in) joint, ready for laying the next course in the normal way. If you have to join rolls of DPC, overlap the ends by 150mm (6in).

Tying-in the new wall

The traditional method for linking a new wall with an existing structure involves chopping recesses in the brickwork at every fourth course. End bricks of the new wall are set into the recesses, bonding the two structures together. However, a simpler method is to bolt to the wall a stainless-metal connector designed to anchor bricks or concrete blocks, using special wall ties. Standard connectors will accommodate walls from 100 to 250mm (4 to 10in) thick.

Bolt a connector to the old wall, just above the DPC (1), using expanding bolts or stainless-steel coach screws and wallplugs. Mortar the end of a brick before laying it against the connector (2). At every third course, hook a wall tie into one of the lugs in the connector and bed each tie in the mortar joint (3).

Lap the existing DPC with the new roll

DPC on a sloping site
When the site slopes noticeably, the wall footing is stepped to keep the top of the wall level. If you include a DPC in the wall, that too must follow the line of the steps to keep it the required height above ground level.

1 Bolt the stainless-steel connector to the wall

2 Lay the bricks against the connector

3 Bed a special wall tie in the mortar joint

You can tooth a wall into the brickwork

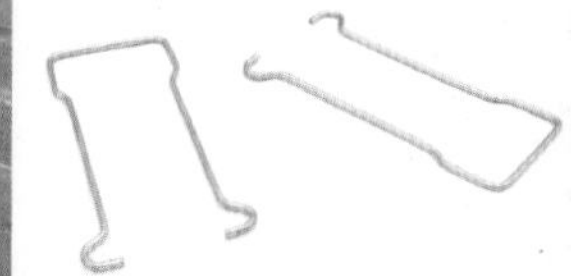
Wall ties for attaching to the connector

SEE ALSO > Damproof course 247, Bricks 437–8, Stepped footings 443, Bricklaying techniques 444, Wall ties 448, Control joints 449

Brick piers

A pier is a freestanding column of masonry that may be used, for example, as a support for a porch or a pergola or to form an individual gatepost. When a column is built as part of a wall, it is more accurately termed a pilaster. In practice, however, the word column is often used to mean either structure. To avoid confusion, any supporting brick column will be described here as a pier.

Structural considerations

Over a certain length and height (see below), a freestanding wall must be buttressed at regular intervals by piers. The wall's straight sections have to be tied to the piers, either by a brick bond or by inserting metal wall ties in every third course of bricks.

Whatever its height, any single-width brick wall would benefit from supporting piers at each end and at gateways, where it is most vulnerable. Piers also serve to improve the appearance of this type of wall.

Piers that are more than 1m (3ft 3in) high, especially those supporting gates, should be built around steel reinforcing rods set in the concrete footings.

Whether reinforcement is included or not, allow for the size of the piers when you are designing the footings.

Wall ties
If you prefer the appearance of bonded-brick piers, construct them as shown below. It is easier, however, to use wall ties to reinforce continuous vertical joints in the brickwork, especially when you are building a wall centred on piers.

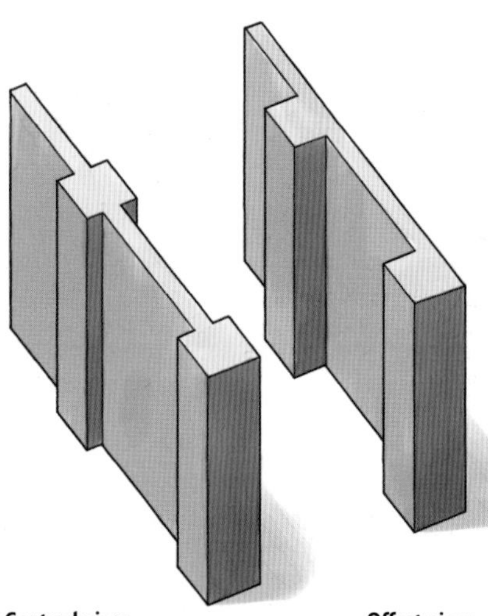

Centred piers

Offset piers

Designing the piers

Piers should be placed no more than 3m (9ft 9in) apart in walls over a certain height (see chart below). The wall itself can be flush with one face of each pier, but the structure is stronger if the wall is centred on the piers.

Piers should be a minimum of twice the thickness of a wall that is 102.5mm (4in) thick, but you need to build piers 328mm (1ft 1½in) square to buttress a wall 215mm (8½in) thick or when reinforcement is required – for gateways, for example.

INCORPORATING PIERS IN A BRICK WALL

Thickness of wall	Maximum height without piers	Maximum pier spacing
102.5mm (4in)	450mm (1ft 6in)	3m (9ft 9in)
215mm (8½in)	1.35m (4ft 6in)	3m (9ft 9in)

Bonding piers
Although it's simpler to tie a wall to a pier with wall ties (see above), it is relatively easy to bond a pier into a wall that is of single-brick width.

Colour key
You will have to cut certain bricks to bond a pier into a straight wall. Whole bricks are coloured with a light tone; three-quarter bats with a medium tone; and half bats with a dark tone.

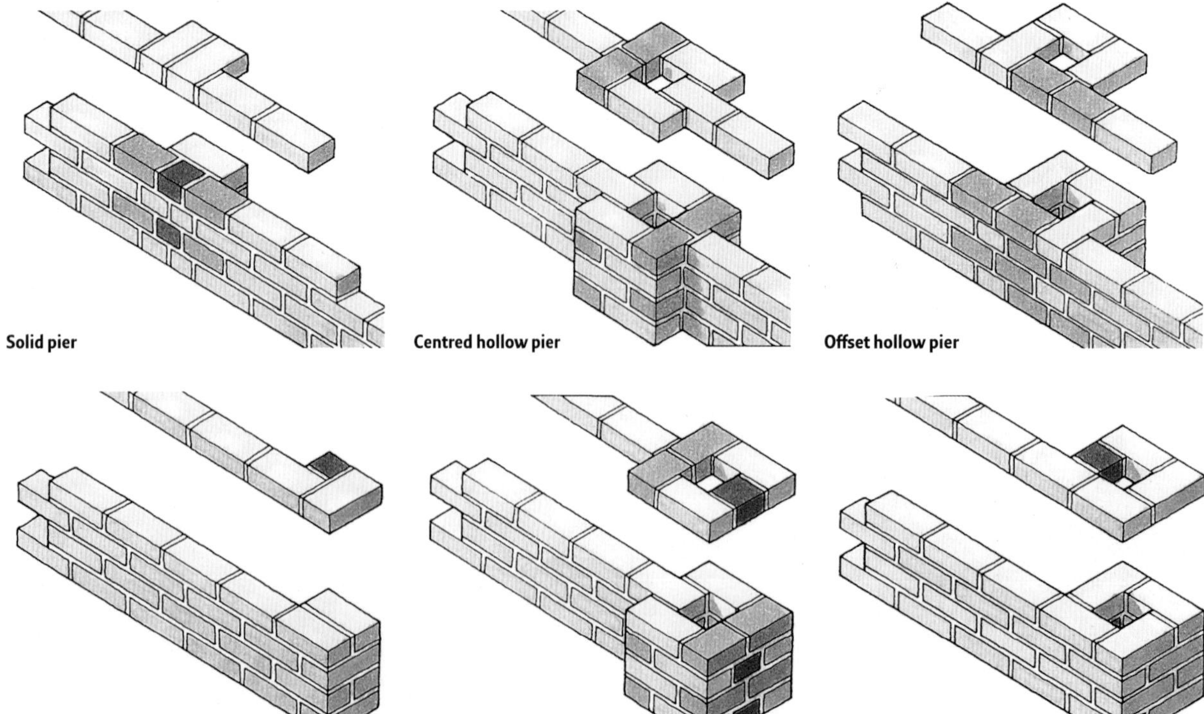

Solid pier

Centred hollow pier

Offset hollow pier

Solid end pier

Centred hollow end pier

Offset hollow end pier

SEE ALSO > Bricks 437–8, Footings 443, Laying bricks 444–7

Building brick piers

Accurately mark out the positions of the piers on the concrete footing and then, between them, mark out the face of the wall itself.

Lay the first course of bricks for the piers, using a bricklayer's line stretched between two stakes to align them (**1**). Adjust the position of the line if necessary, and fill in between with the first straight course, working from both ends towards the middle (**2**). Build alternate pier and wall courses, checking that the bricks are laid level and the faces and corners of the piers are vertical. At every third course, push metal wall ties into the mortar bed to span the joints between the wall and piers (**3**). Continue in the same way to the required height of the wall, then raise the piers by at least one extra course (**4**). Lay a coping along the wall, and cap the piers with concrete or stone slabs (**5**).

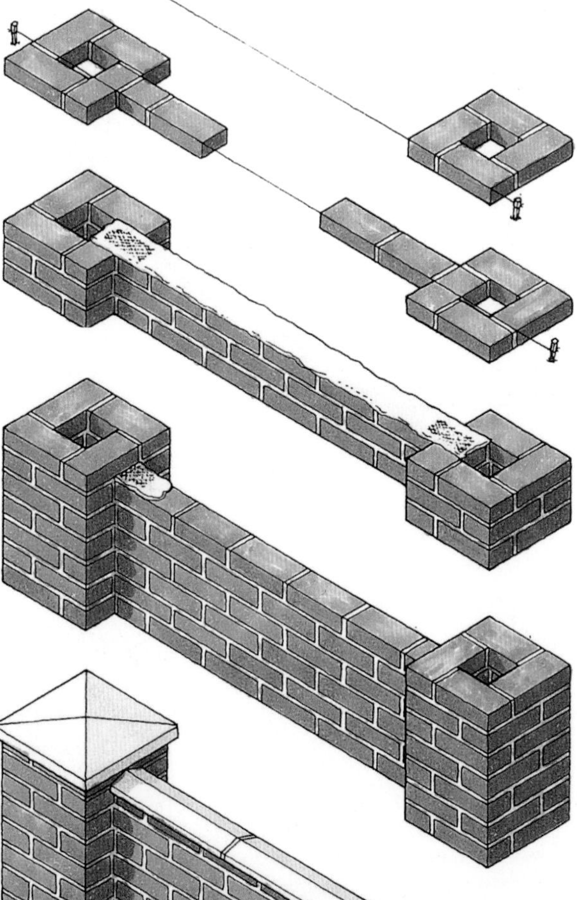

1 Lay pier bases
Stretch a bricklayer's line to position the bases of the piers.

2 Lay first wall course
Use the line to ensure the first course of bricks is built perfectly straight.

3 Lay pier ties
Join the piers to the wall by inserting wall ties into every third course. Put a tie into alternate courses for a gate-supporting pier.

4 Raise the piers
Build the piers higher than the wall to allow for a decorative coping along the top course.

5 Lay the coping
Lay coping slabs and cap the piers.

Positioning piers
This brick-built pier has been strategically placed to support the wall and disguise the junction where the ground level changes.

Control joints

A brick wall moves from time to time as a result of the expansion and contraction of the materials. Over short distances the movement has hardly any effect, but in a long wall it can crack the structure.

To compensate for this movement, build continuous unmortared vertical joints into the wall at intervals of about 6m (19ft 6in). Although these control joints can be placed in a straight section of walling, it is more convenient to place them where the wall meets a pier. Build the pier and wall as normal – but omit the mortar from the header joints of the wall. Instead of inserting standard wall ties, embed a galvanized strip, 3mm (⅛in) thick, in the mortar bed. Lightly grease one half of the strip with petroleum jelly – so that it can slide lengthwise to allow for movement and yet still key the wall and pier together. When the wall is complete, fill the joint from both sides with mastic.

Control joint

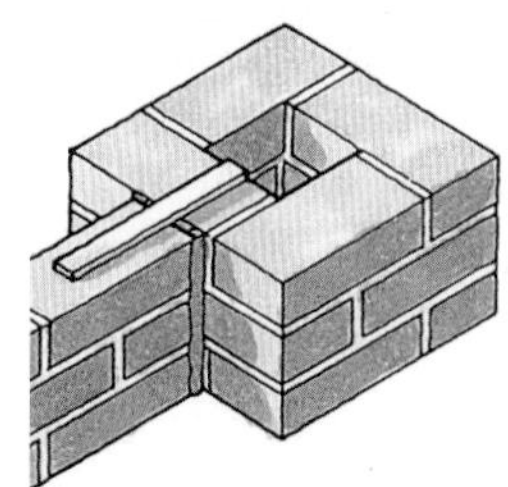

Making a control joint
When making a control joint, tie the pier to the wall with galvanized-metal strips (shown here before the bed of mortar is laid). Mastic is squeezed into the vertical joint between the wall and the pier.

Reinforcing a pier

Use 16mm (⅝in) steel reinforcing bars to strengthen brick piers. If the pier is less than 1m (3ft 3in) in height, use a single continuous length of bar; for taller piers, embed a bent 'starter' bar in the footing, projecting a minimum of 500mm (1ft 8in) above the level of the concrete. As the work proceeds, use galvanized wire to bind extension bars to the projection of the starter bar, up to within 50mm (2in) of the top of the pier. Fill in around the bar with concrete as you build the pier, packing it carefully to avoid disturbing the brickwork.

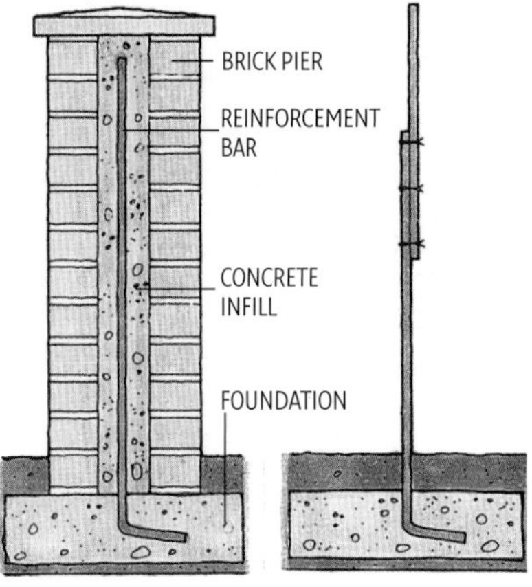

A reinforced pier **Extended starter bar**

SEE ALSO > Bricks 437–8, Bricklaying techniques 444, Bricklayers' line 445, Setting out 445

Building with concrete blocks

Don't dampen concrete blocks before you lay them – since wet blocks may shrink and crack the mortar joints as the wall dries out. Block walls need the same type of concrete footings and mortar mixes as brickwork. Because concrete blocks are made in a greater variety of sizes, you can build a wall of any thickness, using a simple stretcher bond. Make the mortar joints flush with the surface of a wall that is to be rendered or plastered. For painted or exposed blockwork, point the joints using a style that is appropriate to the location and to enhance the appearance of the wall.

Colourful block walls
Paint-quality blocks decorated with smooth masonry paint make a welcome change from the usual monotonous grey concrete.

• **Building piers**
High freestanding garden walls constructed from blocks must be supported by piers at 3m (9ft 9in) intervals.

Building a partition wall

It is usual to divide up large interior spaces with non-loadbearing stud partitions; but if your house is built on a concrete pad, a practical alternative is to use concrete blocks. If you're going to install a doorway in the partition, plan its position to avoid cutting too many blocks. Allow for the wooden doorframe and lining, as well as a precast lintel to support the masonry above the opening. Fill the space above the lintel with concrete coursing bricks.

Bolt metal connectors to the existing structure in order to support each end of the new partition wall. Plumb the connectors accurately to make sure the new wall is built perfectly upright.

Lay the first course of blocks without mortar, across the room, to check their spacing and to determine the position of a doorway. Mark the positions of the blocks before building stepped leads at each end, as for brickwork. Check for accuracy with a spirit level, and then fill in between the leads with blocks.

Build another three courses, anchoring the end blocks to the connectors with wall ties in every joint. Leave the mortar to harden overnight before you continue.

Cutting blocks

Cut a block by scoring a line right round it, using a bolster chisel and straightedge. Deepen the line into a groove by striking the chisel sharply with a club hammer, working your way round the block until it fractures along the chiselled groove.

Cutting a concrete block

Building a partition

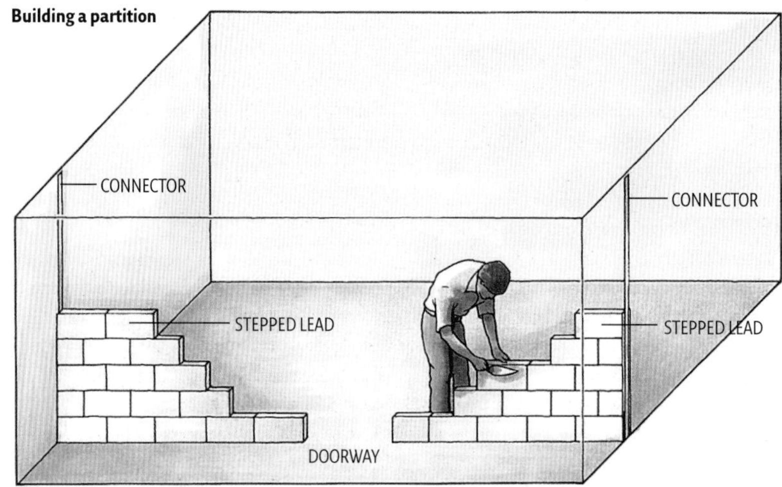

Building intersecting garden walls

Butt intersecting garden walls together with a continuous vertical joint between them, but anchor the structure as for brickwork with wire-mesh wall ties. If you build a wall with heavyweight hollow blocks, use stout metal tie bars with a bend at each end. Fill the block voids with mortar to embed the ends of the bars. Install a tie in every course.

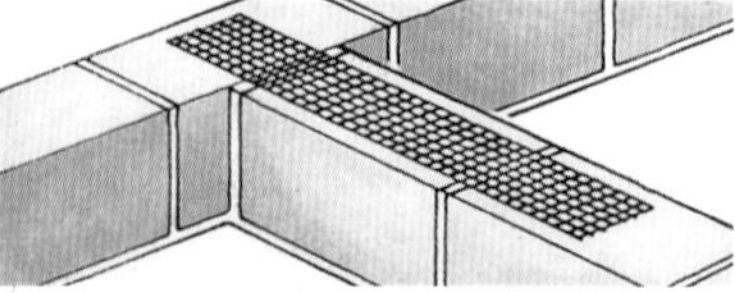

Wire-mesh wall ties for solid blocks

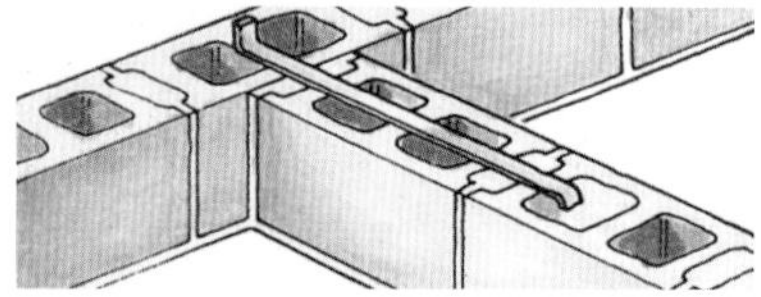

Metal tie bar for hollow blocks

Control joints

Walls more than 6m (19ft 6in) long should be built with a continuous vertical control joint to allow for expansion. Place an unmortared joint in a straight section of wall or against a pier and bridge the gap with galvanized-metal strips, as for brickwork. Fill the vertical joint with flexible mastic.

If you need to insert a control joint in a partition wall, it's convenient to form the joint at a door opening – take it round one end of the lintel and then vertically to the ceiling. Having filled the joint with mortar in the normal way, rake it out to a depth of 18mm (¾in) on both sides of the wall, then fill flush with mastic.

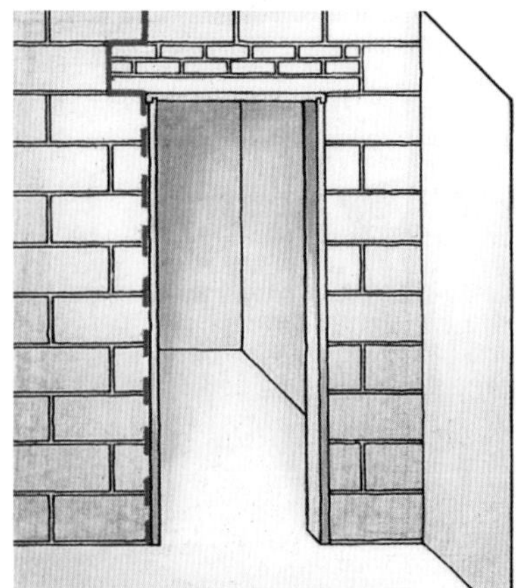

Forming a control joint next to a door opening
On both sides of the wall, take the joint around the lintel and up to the ceiling.

SEE ALSO > Stud partitions 151–3, Blocks 439, Mixing mortar 441, Stretcher bond 442, Bricklaying techniques 444, Stepped leads 445, Pointing 446, Intersecting walls 447, Wall connectors 447, Control joints 449

Building with stone

Constructing garden walling with natural stone requires a different approach to building with bricks or concrete blocks. A stone wall has to be as stable as any other masonry wall, but its visual appeal relies on the coursing being less regular – indeed, there is no real coursing when a wall is built with undressed stone.

Designing the wall

A dry-stone wall must be 'battered' – in other words, it has to have a wide base and the sides must slope inwards. For a wall about 1m (3ft 3in) in height – it's dangerous to build a dry-stone wall any higher – the base should be no less than 450mm (1ft 6in) wide; and you need to provide a minimum slope of 25mm (1in) for every 600mm (2ft) of height.

Traditionally, the base of this type of wall rests on a bed of sand 100mm (4in) deep, laid on compacted soil at the bottom of a shallow trench. For a more reliable foundation, lay a 100mm (4in) concrete footing, making it about 100mm (4in) wider than the wall on each side.

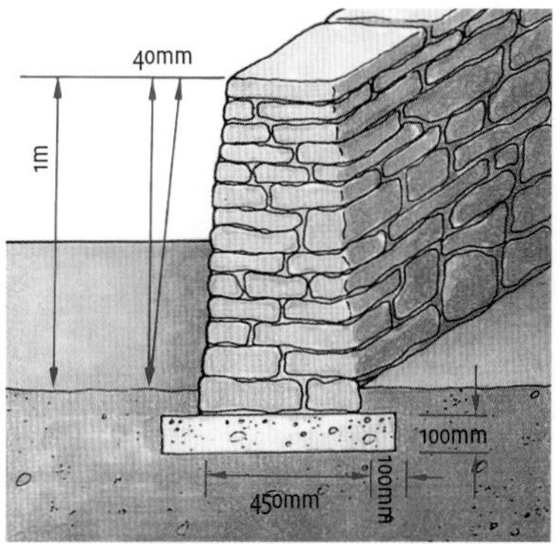

Proportions of a stone wall

Structural considerations

Not all stone walls are built with mortar, although it is often used with dressed or semi-dressed stone in order to provide additional stability.

Instead, many walls are tapered – with heavy flat stones laid at the base of the wall, followed by proportionally smaller stones as the height increases. This traditional form of construction was developed to prevent walls made with unmortared stones toppling sideways when subjected to high winds or the weight of farm animals.

Far from detracting from its appearance, the informality of this type of construction suits a country-style garden perfectly.

Building a dry-stone wall

A true dry-stone wall relies on a selective choice of stones and careful placement to provide stability. However, there's no reason why you can't introduce mortar, particularly within the core of the wall, and still maintain the appearance of dry-stone walling.

Another way to help stabilize a wall is to bed the stones in soil, packing it firmly into the crevices as you lay each course. This enables you to plant alpines or other rockery plants in the wall, even during construction.

When you are selecting the masonry, look out for flat stones in a variety of sizes and make sure you have some that are large enough to run the full width of the wall, especially at the base of the structure. Placed at regular intervals, these 'bonding' stones are important components, as they tie the loose rubble into a cohesive structure.

Constructing the wall

Assuming you're using soil as your jointing material, spread a 25mm (1in) layer over the footing and then place a substantial bonding stone across the width to form the bed of the first course (**1**). Lay other stones, about the same height as the bonding stone, along each side of the wall, pressing them down into the soil to make a firm base. It's worth stretching a bricklayer's line along each side of the wall to help you make a reasonably straight base.

Lay smaller stones between to fill out the base of the wall (**2**), then pack more soil into all the crevices.

Spread another layer of soil on top of the base and lay a second course of stones, bridging the joints between the stones below (**3**). Press the stones down firmly, so they lean inwards towards the centre of the wall. As you proceed, check by eye that the coursing is about level and remember to include bonding stones at regular intervals.

You can introduce plants into the larger crevices or hammer smaller stones into the chinks to lock large stones in place.

At the top of the wall, either fill the core with soil for plants or lay large, flat coping stones, balancing them with packed soil. Finally, brush loose soil from the wall faces.

Dry-stone wall
Traditional dry-stone walling is stable without having to fill the joints with mortar.

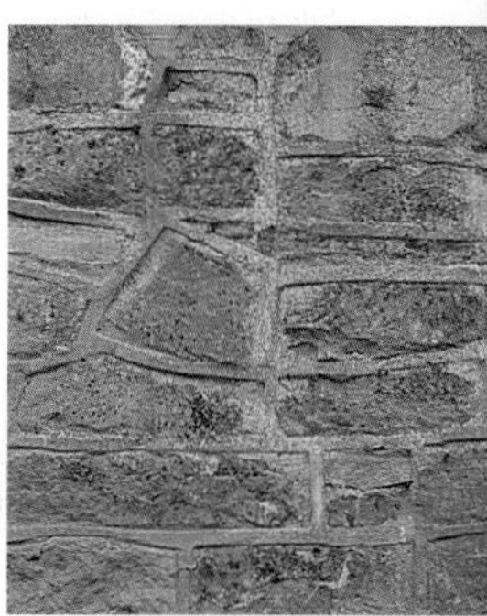

Pointed stonework
Mortar is required for buildings and substantial freestanding walls constructed from dressed or semi-dressed stone.

Reinforcing the wall
Hammer small stones into the gaps between the larger stones to lock them in place.

1 Lay a bonding stone across the end of the wall

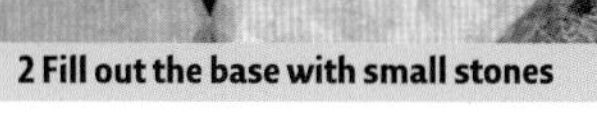

2 Fill out the base with small stones

3 Lay a second course of stones

SEE ALSO > Natural stone 440, Footings 443, Bricklayer's line 445

Building low retaining walls

Retaining walls are designed to hold back a bank of earth, but don't attempt to cut into a steep bank and restrain it with a single high wall. Apart from the obvious dangers of the wall collapsing, terracing the slope with a series of low walls is a more attractive solution, as it offers opportunities for imaginative planting.

Choosing your materials

Both bricks and concrete blocks make sturdy retaining walls, provided that they are reinforced with metal bars buried in a sound concrete footing. Either run the bars through hollow concrete blocks or build a double skin of brickwork, rather like a miniature cavity wall, using wall ties to bind each skin together.

The mass and weight of natural stone make it ideal for retaining walls. A stone wall should be battered (see BUILDING WITH STONE) to an angle of 50mm (2in) for every 300mm (1ft) of height, to provide support for the bank. For safety, don't build higher than 1m (3ft 3in).

A skilful professional builder could construct a perfectly safe dry-stone retaining wall – but unless you have had sufficient experience, it is advisable to use mortar for additional rigidity.

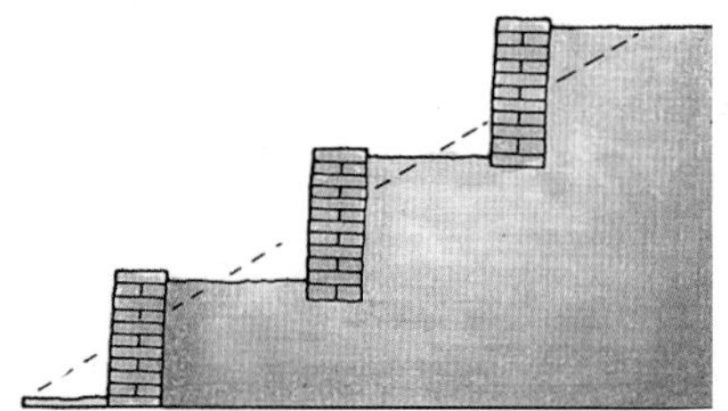

Terracing with retaining walls

Retaining wall of hollow concrete blocks

Use two skins of brick tied together

Stone wall retaining a bank of earth

Constructing the wall

Excavate the soil to provide enough room to dig the footing and construct the wall. If the bank is loosely packed, restrain it temporarily with sheets of scrap plywood or corrugated iron. Drive metal pegs into the bank to hold the sheets in place (1). Lay the footing at the base of the bank, and allow it to set before you begin building the wall.

Use conventional techniques to build a block or brick wall. Lay uncut stones as if you were building a dry-stone wall, but set each course on mortar. If you use regular stone blocks, stagger the joints and select stones of different proportions to add variety to the wall. Bed the stones in mortar.

You must allow for drainage behind the wall, or the soil will become waterlogged. So when you lay the second course of stones, embed 22mm (¾in) plastic pipes in the mortar bed, sloping them slightly downwards away from the bank. Lay the pipes about 1m (3ft) apart, making sure that they pass right through the wall and project a little from the face (2).

1 Hold back the earth with scrap boards

2 Set plastic pipes in the wall for drainage

Finishing a stone wall

When the wall is complete, rake out the joints so that it looks like a genuine dry-stone wall. An old paintbrush is a useful tool for smoothing the mortar in deep crevices, in order to make firm watertight joints. It is best to point regular stones with concave rubbed joints.

Allow the mortar to set hard before filling behind the wall. Lay hardcore at the base to cover the drainage pipes, and pack shingle against the wall as you replace the soil.

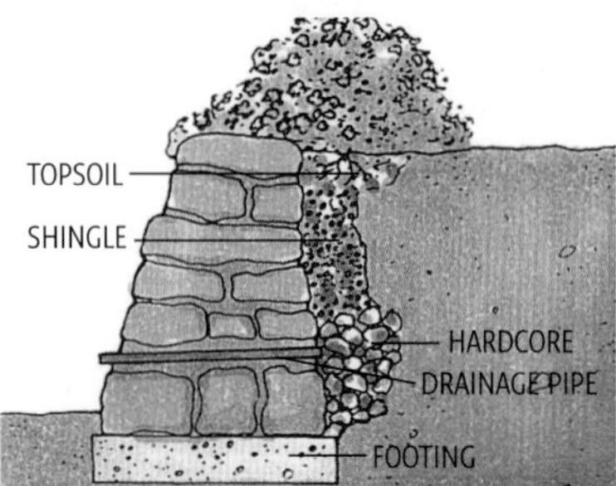

Filling behind a stone wall

SEE ALSO > Footings 443, Laying bricks 444–9, Pointing 446, Reinforcing bars 449

Paths, drives and patios

For many people, paving of any kind is associated with the old 'back yard' environment, devoid of plants, trees and grass. But in reality, introducing paving into a garden provides an opportunity to create contrasts of colour and texture, which are intensified by sunlight and deep shade.

The marriage of different materials offers numerous possibilities. It may be convenient to define areas of paving as paths, drives or patios, but they are only names to describe the function of particular spaces in the garden. There's no reason why you cannot blend one area into another by using the same material throughout, or by employing similar colours to link one type of paving with another. On the other hand, you could take a completely different approach and deliberately juxtapose coarse and smooth textures or pale and dark tones to make one space stand out from the next.

Paved patio
A paved area that's surrounded by walls built from stone or brick makes a perfect suntrap.

Sometimes a hard and unyielding surface can be softened by the addition of foliage. And plants that otherwise recede into a background of soil and grass are seen to advantage against stone and gravel.

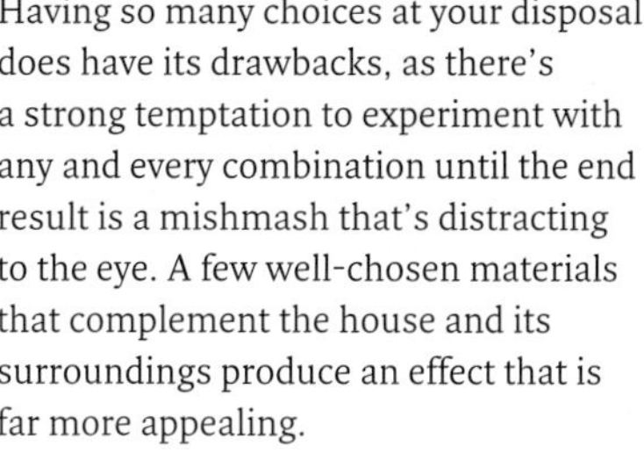

Having so many choices at your disposal does have its drawbacks, as there's a strong temptation to experiment with any and every combination until the end result is a mishmash that's distracting to the eye. A few well-chosen materials that complement the house and its surroundings produce an effect that is far more appealing.

SEE ALSO > Concrete mixes 457, Finishing concrete 461, Paving slabs 462

Working with concrete

Concrete is more versatile than some people imagine. It may appear to be a rather drab, utilitarian material for the garden, but you can add texture and colour to ordinary concrete or make good use of one of the many types of cast-concrete slabs and bricks made for paving patios, paths and driveways.

Storing materials

If you buy sand and aggregate in sacks, use as much as you require for the job and keep the rest bagged up until you need it again. Loose ingredients should be piled separately on a hard surface or on thick polythene sheets. Cover the piles with weighted sheets of plastic.

Storing cement is more critical. It's usually sold in paper sacks, which will absorb moisture from the ground - so pile them on a board propped up on battens. It's best to keep cement in a dry shed or garage; but if you have to store it outdoors, cover the bags with sheets of plastic weighted down with bricks.

Once a bag is opened, cement will absorb moisture from the air, so keep a partly used bag in a sealed plastic sack.

Storing ingredients
Use a plank of wood to separate piles of sand and aggregate. Keep bags of cement under cover.

Ingredients of concrete

In its simplest form, concrete consists of cement and fine particles of stone (sand and pebbles) known as aggregate. The dry ingredients are mixed with water to create a chemical reaction with the cement, which binds the aggregate into a hard, dense material.

The initial hardening process takes place quite quickly. But although the mix becomes unworkable after a couple of hours, depending on the temperature and humidity, the concrete has no real strength for 3 to 7 days.

The hardening process continues for up to a month, or as long as there is moisture still present within the concrete. Moisture is essential to the reaction; consequently, concrete must not be allowed to dry out too quickly during the first few days.

Cement

Standard Portland cement, sold in 50kg (110lb) bags, is used in the manufacture of concrete. In its dry condition, it is a fine grey powder.

In some areas of the country, the soil contains soluble sulphates that are harmful to concrete (your local Building Control Officer can advise you about this). If necessary, use special sulphate-resisting Portland cement.

Sand

Sharp sand - a rather coarse and gritty material - constitutes part of the aggregate of a concrete mix. Don't buy fine builder's sand (used for mortar); and avoid unwashed or beach sand, both of which contain impurities that can affect the quality of the concrete.

Builders' merchants sell sharp sand loose by the cubic metre (or cubic yard). However, it is often more convenient to buy it packed in large plastic bags if you have to transport it by car or van.

Coarse aggregate

Coarse aggregate is gravel or crushed stone composed of particles large enough to be retained by a 5mm (¼in) sieve, up to a maximum size of 20mm (¾in) for normal use. Once again, it can be bought loose by the cubic metre (cubic yard) or in smaller quantities packed in plastic sacks.

Pigments

Special pigments can be added to a concrete mix in order to colour it, but it's difficult to guarantee an even colour from one batch to another.

Combined aggregate

Naturally occurring sand-and-gravel mix - known as ballast - is sold as a combined aggregate for concreting. The proportion of sand to gravel is not guaranteed unless the ballast has been reconstituted to adjust the mix, so you may need to do this yourself. In any case, make sure the ballast has been washed thoroughly to remove any impurities.

Dry-packed concrete

You can buy dry cement mixed with sand and aggregate in the required proportions for making concrete. Choose the proportion that best suits the job you have in mind. Fast-setting concrete for erecting fence posts is one typical ready-mixed product.

Concrete mix is sold in various-size bags up to 50kg (110lb). Available from the usual outlets, this is a more expensive way of buying concrete ingredients, but it's a simple and convenient method of ordering exactly the amount you need. Before you add water, make sure the ingredients are mixed thoroughly.

Water

Use ordinary tap water. Impurities and salt contained in river or sea water are detrimental to concrete.

PVA admixture

You can buy a PVA admixture from builders' merchants to make a smoother concrete mix that is less susceptible to frost damage. Follow the manufacturers' instructions for its use.

SEE ALSO > Calculating quantities 457, Cleaning equipment 459, Laying concrete 458–61

Mixing concrete

Hire a small mixing machine if you need to prepare a large volume of concrete, but for the average job it's perhaps more convenient to mix it by hand. It isn't necessary to weigh the ingredients – simply mix them by volume, choosing the proportions that suit the job in hand.

Mixing by hand

Use two large buckets to measure the ingredients, one for the cement and – in order to keep the cement perfectly dry – another, identical, bucket for the sand and coarse aggregate. Using two shovels is also a good idea.

Measure the materials accurately, levelling them with the rim of the bucket. Tap the side of the bucket with the shovel as you load it with sand or cement, so that the loose particles are shaken down.

Mix the sand and coarse aggregate first, on a hard, flat surface. Scoop a depression in the pile for the measure of cement, and mix all the ingredients until they form an even colour.

Form another depression and add some water from a watering can. Push the dry ingredients into the water from around the edge (1) until the surface water has been absorbed, then mix the batch by chopping the concrete with the shovel. Add more water, then turn the concrete from the bottom of the pile and chop it as before until the whole batch has an even consistency.

To test the workability of the mix, form a series of ridges by dragging the back of the shovel across the pile (2). The surface of the concrete should be flat and even in texture, and the ridges should hold their shape without slumping.

1 Push the dry ingredients into the water

2 Make ridges with the shovel

Mixing by machine

Make sure you set up the concrete mixer on a hard, level surface and that the drum is upright before you start the motor. Use a bucket to pour half the measure of coarse aggregate into the drum and add water. Add the sand and cement alternately in small batches, plus the rest of the aggregate. Keep on adding water little by little along with the other ingredients.

Let the batch mix for a few minutes. Then tilt the drum of the mixer while it is still rotating and turn out some of the concrete into a wheelbarrow, so you can test its consistency (see above). If necessary, return the concrete to the mixer to adjust it.

Machine safety

When you hire a concrete mixer, take time to read the safety advice that's supplied with the machine.

- Make sure you understand the operating instructions before you turn the machine on.
- Prop the mixer with blocks of woods until it is level and stable.
- Never put your hands or shovel into the drum while the mixer is running.
- Don't lean over a rotating drum to inspect the contents.
- It is advisable to wear goggles when mixing concrete.

Ready-mixed concrete

If you need a lot of concrete for a driveway or large patio, it may be worth ordering a delivery of ready-mixed concrete from a local supplier.

Always contact the supplier well in advance to discuss your particular requirements. Specify the proportions of the ingredients, and say whether you require a retarding agent to slow down the setting time. (Once a normal mix of concrete is delivered, you will have about 2 hours in which to finish the job. A retarding agent can add a couple of hours to the setting time.) Tell the supplier exactly what you need the concrete for, and accept his advice. For quantities of less than 6cu m (8cu yd), you may find you have to shop around for a supplier who is willing to deliver without making an additional charge.

In order to avoid moving the concrete too far by wheelbarrow, you will want it discharged as close to the site as possible, if not directly into place. However, the chute on a delivery truck can reach only so far, and if the vehicle is too large or heavy to drive onto your property you will need several helpers to move the concrete while it is still workable. A single cubic metre of concrete will fill 25 to 30 large wheelbarrows. If it takes longer than 30 to 40 minutes to discharge the load, you may have to pay extra.

Professional mixing

There are companies who will deliver concrete ingredients and mix them to your specifications on the spot. All you have to do is barrow the concrete and pour it into place. There's no waste, as you pay only for the concrete you use. Telephone a local company for details on price and minimum quantity.

Ready-mixed concrete can be delivered directly to your home

SEE ALSO > Calculating quantities 457, Cleaning equipment 459, Laying concrete 458–61

Designing concrete paving

The notion of having to design simple concrete pads and pathways may seem odd, but there are important factors to consider if the concrete is to be durable. At the least, you will have to decide on the thickness of the concrete that is needed to support the weight of traffic, and the angle of slope required to drain off surface water.

When an area of concrete is large or if it's a complicated shape, you need to incorporate control joints to allow the material to expand and contract. If a pad is for a habitable building, then it must include a damp-proof membrane to prevent moisture rising from the ground. Even the proportions of sand, cement and aggregate used in the mix have to be considered carefully.

Deciding on the slope

A freestanding pad can be laid perfectly level, especially when it's supporting a small outbuilding – but a very slight slope or fall will prevent water collecting in puddles if you have failed to get the concrete absolutely flat. If a pad is laid directly against a house, it must have a definite fall away from the building; and any parking area or drive must shed water to provide adequate traction for vehicles and to minimize the formation of ice. When concrete is laid against a building, it must be at least 150mm (6in) below the existing damp-proof course.

Sloping floors
Although you can build upon a perfectly flat base, it is a good idea to slope the floor towards the door of a garage or outbuilding that is to be scrubbed out from time to time. Alternatively, slope a floor in two directions towards the middle to form a shallow drain that runs to the door.

USE OF PAVING	ANGLE OF FALL
Pathways	Not required.
Drive	1 in 40 (25mm per metre, 1in per yard)
Patio Parking space	1 in 60 away from the building (16mm per metre, 5/8in per yard)
Pads for garages and outbuildings	1 in 80 towards the door (12.5mm per metre, 1/2in per yard)

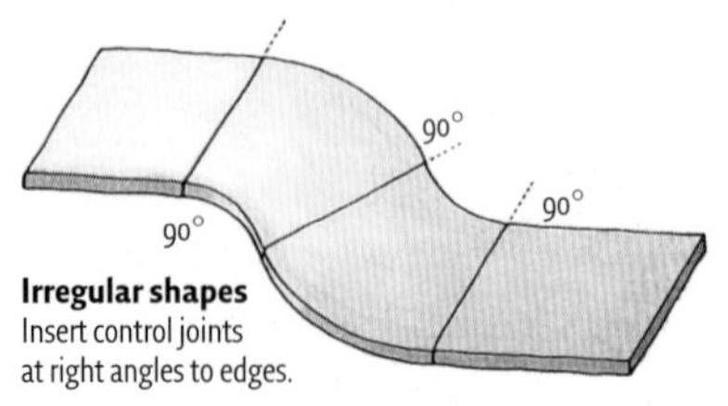

Irregular shapes
Insert control joints at right angles to edges.

Recommended thicknesses for concrete

The normal thicknesses recommended for concrete paving assume it will be laid on a firm subsoil. If the soil is clay or peat, increase the thickness by about 50 per cent. The same applies to a new site, where the soil may not be compacted.

Unless the concrete is for pedestrian traffic only, lay a subbase of compacted hardcore below the paving. This will absorb ground movement without affecting the concrete itself. A subbase is not essential for a very lightweight structure, such as a small wooden shed; but in case you want to increase the weight at some time in the future, it is wisest to install a subbase at the outset.

Pathways
For pedestrian traffic only:
Concrete: 75mm (3in)
Subbase: Not required

Patios
Any extensive area of concrete for pedestrian traffic:
Concrete: 100mm (4in)
Subbase: 100mm (4in)

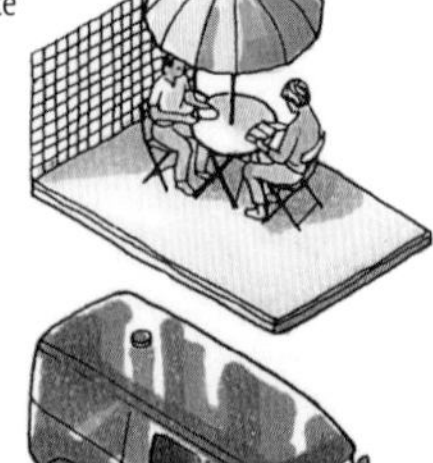
Driveways
Drive used for an average family car only:
Concrete: 125mm (5in)
Subbase: 150mm (6in)
For heavier vehicles, such as delivery trucks:
Concrete: 150mm (6in)
Subbase: 150mm (6in)

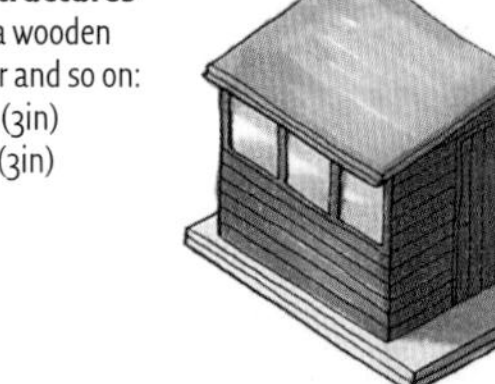
Lightweight structures
Support pad for a wooden shed, coal bunker and so on:
Concrete: 75mm (3in)
Subbase: 75mm (3in)

Parking space
Exposed paving for parking family car:
Concrete: 125mm (5in)
Subbase: 150mm (6in)

Garage
Thicken up the edges of a garage pad to support the weight of the walls:
Concrete:
Floor: 125mm (5in)
Edges: 200mm (8in)
Subbase:
Minimum 150mm (6in)

Allowing for expansion

Changes in temperature cause concrete to expand and contract. If this movement is allowed to happen at random, then a pad or pathway will crack at the weakest or most vulnerable point.

Control joints composed of a compressible material will either absorb the movement or concentrate the force in predetermined areas where it will do little harm. The joints should meet the sides of a concrete area at more or less 90 degrees. Always place a control joint between concrete and a wall, and around inspection chambers.

Positioning control joints

The exact position of the control joints will depend on the area and shape of the concrete pad, path or driveway.

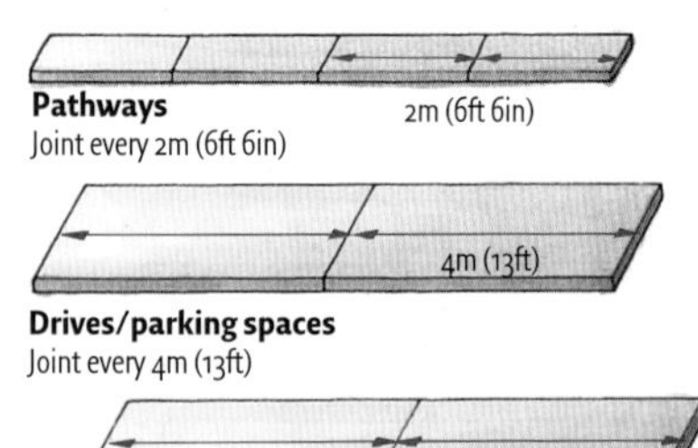

Pathways
Joint every 2m (6ft 6in)

Drives/parking spaces
Joint every 4m (13ft)

Concrete pads
Joints no more than 4m (13ft) apart and around inspection chambers

Divide a pad into equal bays if:
- the length is more than twice the width
- the longest dimension is more than 40 times the thickness
- the longest dimension exceeds 4m (13ft)

SEE ALSO > Damp-proof membrane 176–7, Laying subbase 459, Control joints 460

Calculating quantities

To estimate the amount of materials that will be required, you need to calculate the volume of concrete in the finished pad, path or drive. Measure the surface area of the site, and multiply that figure by the thickness of the concrete.

Estimating quantities of concrete

Use the gridded diagram below to estimate the volume of concrete you will need.

Read off the area of the site in square metres (square yards) and trace it across horizontally to meet the angled line indicating the thickness of the concrete. Trace the line up to find the volume in cubic metres (cubic yards).

VOLUME OF CONCRETE REQUIRED
Cu yd 1 2 3 4 5 6
Cu m 1 2 3 4 5
AREA TO BE CONCRETED
Sq yd 5 10 15 20 25 30 35
Sq m 5 10 15 20 25 30
THICKNESS
Garage-pad edges: 200mm (8in)
Heavy-vehicle drives: 150mm (6in)
Car-parking drives and garage floors: 125mm (5in)
Patios: 100mm (4in)
Pathways and light structures: 75mm (3in)

Estimating quantities of ingredients

Use the bar chart below to estimate the quantities of cement, sand and aggregate you will require to mix the volume of concrete arrived at by using the chart above.

The figures are based on the quantity of ingredients required to mix one cubic metre of concrete for a particular type of mix, plus about 10 per cent to allow for wastage.

	CUBIC METRES OF CONCRETE									
		1.00	1.50	2.00	2.50	3.00	3.50	4.00	4.50	5.00
GENERAL-PURPOSE MIX										
	Cement (50kg bags)	7.00	10.50	14.00	17.50	21.00	24.50	28.00	31.50	35.00
plus	Sand (cubic metres)	0.50	0.75	1.00	1.25	1.50	1.75	2.00	2.25	2.50
	Aggregate (cubic metres)	0.75	1.15	1.50	1.90	2.25	2.65	3.00	3.40	3.75
or	Ballast (cubic metres)	0.90	1.35	1.80	2.25	2.70	3.15	3.60	4.05	4.50
FOUNDATION MIX										
	Cement (50kg bags)	6.00	9.00	12.00	15.00	18.00	21.00	24.00	27.00	30.00
plus	Sand (cubic metres)	0.55	0.80	1.10	1.40	1.65	1.95	2.20	2.50	2.75
	Aggregate (cubic metres)	0.75	1.15	1.50	1.90	2.25	2.65	3.00	3.40	3.75
or	Ballast (cubic metres)	1.00	1.50	2.00	2.50	3.00	3.50	4.00	4.50	5.00
PAVING MIX										
	Cement (50kg bags)	9.00	13.50	18.00	22.50	27.00	31.50	36.00	40.50	45.00
plus	Sand (cubic metres)	0.45	0.70	0.90	1.15	1.35	1.60	1.80	2.00	2.25
	Aggregate (cubic metres)	0.75	1.15	1.50	1.90	2.25	2.65	3.00	3.40	3.75
or	Ballast (cubic metres)	1.00	1.50	2.00	2.50	3.00	3.50	4.00	4.50	5.00

Calculating areas

Squares and rectangles

Calculate the area of rectangular paving by multiplying width by length.

Example:
2m x 3m = 6sq m
78in x 117in = 9126sq in or 7sq yd

Circles

Use the formula πr^2 to calculate the area of a circle (π = 3.14, r = radius of the circle).

Example:
3.14 x 2sq m = 3.14 x 4 = 12.56sq m
3.14 x 78sq in = 3.14 x 6084 = 19104sq in or 14.75sq yd

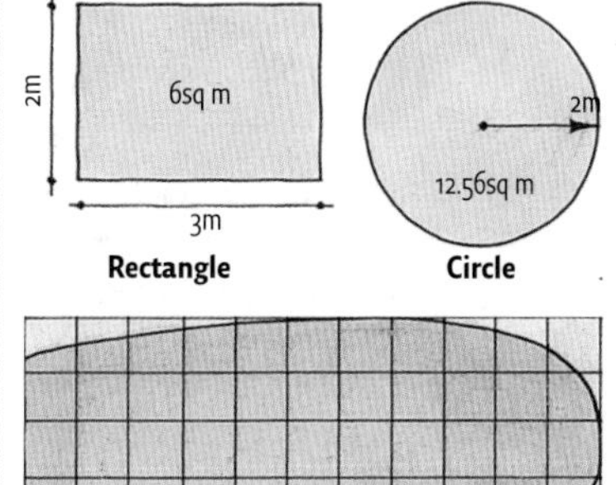

Irregular shapes
Draw an irregular area of paving on squared paper. To find the approximate area, count the whole squares and average out the portions.

SEE ALSO > Ingredients of concrete 454, Mixing concrete 455

Laying a concrete pad

Laying a simple pad as a base for a small shed or similar structure involves all the basic principles of concreting – including building a retaining formwork, as well as pouring, levelling and finishing the concrete. Provided that the base is less than 2m (6ft 6in) square, there's no need to include control joints.

Mixing concrete by volume

Whatever container you use to measure out the ingredients (shovel bucket or wheelbarrow), the proportions remain the same.

MIXING CONCRETE BY VOLUME			
Type of mix		Proportions	For 1cu m concrete
GENERAL PURPOSE			
Use in most situations including covered pads other than garage floors.		1 part cement	6.4 bags (50kg)
	plus	2 parts sand	0.448cu m
		3 parts aggregate	0.672cu m
	or	4 parts ballast	0.896cu m
FOUNDATION			
Use for footings at the base of masonry walls.		1 part cement	5.6 bags (50kg)
	plus	2½ parts sand	0.49cu m
		3½ parts aggregate	0.686cu m
	or	5 parts ballast	0.98cu m
PAVING			
Use for parking areas, drives, pathways, and garage floors.		1 part cement	8 bags (50kg)
	plus	1½ parts sand	0.42cu m
		2½ parts aggregate	0.7cu m
	or	3½ parts ballast	0.98cu m

Excavating the site

First, mark out the area of the concrete pad with string lines attached to pegs driven into the ground outside the work area (**1**). Then remove the lines to excavate the site, but replace them afterwards to help position the formwork that will hold the concrete in place.

Remove the topsoil and all vegetable matter within the site down to a level that allows for the combined thickness of concrete and subbase. Extend the area of excavation about 150mm (6in) outside the space allowed for the pad. Cut back any roots you encounter and, if there's any turf, put it aside to cover the infill surrounding the completed pad. Finally, level the bottom of the excavation by dragging a board across it and compact the soil with a garden roller.

Erecting the formwork

Until the concrete sets hard, it must be supported all round by formwork. For a straightforward rectangular pad, construct the formwork from softwood planks, 25mm (1in) thick, set on edge. The planks, which must be as wide as the finished depth of concrete, need to be held in place temporarily with stout 50 x 50mm (2 x 2in) wooden stakes. Second-hand or sawn timber is quite adequate. If it is slightly thinner than 25mm (1in), just use more stakes to brace it. If you have to join planks, butt them end to end, nailing a cleat on the outside.

Using the string lines as a guide, erect one board at the 'high' end of the pad and drive stakes behind it at about 1m (3ft) intervals or less, with one for each corner. The tops of the stakes and board must be level and need to correspond to the proposed surface of the pad exactly. Nail the board to the stakes (**2**).

Set up another board opposite the first one – but before you nail it to the stakes, establish the crossfall with a spirit level and straightedge. Work out the difference in level from one side of the pad to the other. For example, a pad that is 2m (6ft 6in) wide should drop 25mm (1in) over that distance. Tape a shim of timber to one end of the straightedge and, with the shim resting on the 'low' stakes, place the other end on the opposite board (**3**). Drive home each low stake until the spirit level reads horizontal, and then nail the board flush with the tops of the stakes.

Erect the ends of the formwork. Allowing the boards to overshoot at the corners will make it easier to dismantle them when the concrete has set (**4**). Use the straightedge, this time without the shim, to level the boards across the formwork.

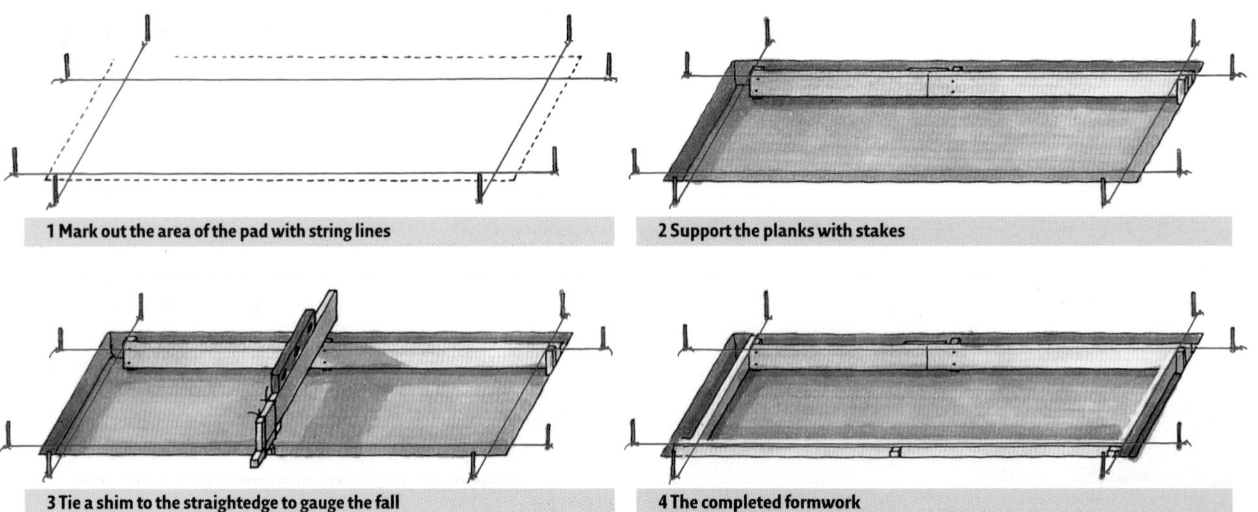

1 Mark out the area of the pad with string lines

2 Support the planks with stakes

3 Tie a shim to the straightedge to gauge the fall

4 The completed formwork

SEE ALSO >Ingredients of concrete 454, Control joints 460, Deciding on the slope 456, Pad thickness 456, Finishing concrete 461,

Laying the subbase

Hoggin, a natural mixture of gravel and sand, is an ideal material for a subbase - but you can use crushed stone or brick, provided you throw out any plaster, scrap metal or similar rubbish. Also remove large lumps of masonry, as they will not compact well. Pour hardcore into the formwork and rake it fairly level before tamping it down with a heavy balk of timber (5). If there are any stubborn lumps, break them up with a heavy hammer. Fill in low spots with more hardcore or sharp sand until the subbase comes up to the underside of the formwork boards.

Filling with concrete

Mix the concrete as near to the site as is practicable and transport the fresh mix to the formwork in a wheelbarrow. Set up firm runways of scaffold boards if the ground is soft, especially around the perimeter of the formwork.

Dampen the subbase and formwork with a fine spray, and let surface water evaporate before tipping the concrete in place. Start filling from one end of the site and push the concrete firmly into the corners (**6**). Rake it level until the concrete stands about 18mm (¾in) above the level of the boards.

Tamp down the concrete with the edge of a plank, 50mm (2in) thick, that is long enough to reach across the formwork. Starting at one end of the site, compact the concrete with steady blows of the plank, moving it along by about half its thickness each time. Cover the whole area twice and then remove excess concrete, using the plank with a sawing action (7). Fill any low spots, then compact and level the concrete once more.

To retain the moisture, cover the pad with sheets of polythene, taped at the joints and weighted down with bricks around the edge. Alternatively, use wet sacking and keep it damp for 3 days, using a fine spray. Try to avoid laying concrete in very cold weather; but if that's unavoidable, spread a layer of earth or sand on top of the sheeting to insulate the concrete from frost.

It's perfectly safe to walk on the concrete after 3 days, but leave it for about a week before removing the formwork and erecting a shed or similar outbuilding.

Finishing the edges

If any of the edges of a concrete pad are exposed, the sharp corners could cause a painful injury - so radius the corners with an edging float. Run the float along the formwork as you finish the surface of the concrete.

This type of float is not expensive, but if you have difficulty obtaining one, you can make a float from thin sheet metal. Bend the piece of metal over a rod or tube, 18mm (¾in) in diameter, and then screw a wood batten to form a handle in the centre.

Radius the corner, using an edging float

5 Level the hardcore base with a heavy balk of timber

6 Pour the concrete, starting in one corner

7 Use a sawing action to remove excess concrete

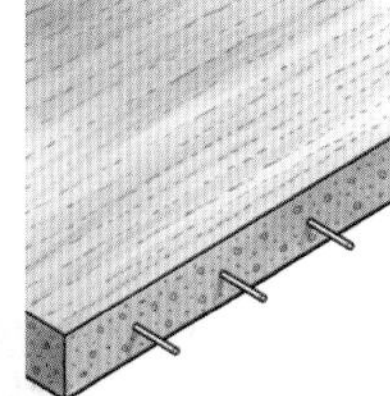

Extending a pad
If you want to enlarge your patio, simply butt a new section of concrete against the existing pad. The butt joint will in itself serve as a control joint. To add a narrow strip to a pad (so that you can erect a larger shed, for example), drill holes in the edge of the pad and use epoxy adhesive to glue in short reinforcing rods before pouring the fresh concrete.

Cleaning tools and machinery

At the end of a working day wash all traces of concrete from your tools and wheelbarrow. When you have finished using a concrete mixer, add a few shovels of coarse aggregate and a little water, then run the machine for a couple of minutes to scour the inside of the drum. Dump the aggregate, then hose out the drum with clean water.

Shovel unused concrete into sacks, ready for disposal at a refuse dump, and wash the mixing area with a stiff broom. Never hose concrete or any of the separate ingredients into a drain.

SEE ALSO > Mixing concrete 455

Laying paths and drives

Paths and drives are laid and compacted in the same way as rectangular pads, using similar formwork to contain the concrete. However, the proportions of most paths and drives make the inclusion of control joints essential, to allow for expansion and contraction. You will have to install a subbase beneath a drive, but a pathway can be laid on compacted soil levelled with sharp sand. Establish a slight fall across the site to shed rainwater.

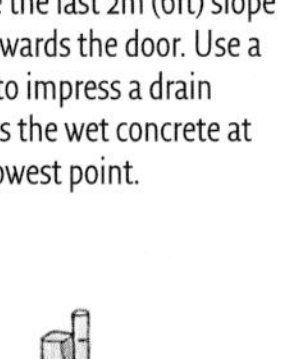

A sloping drive
If you build a drive on a sloping site, make the transition from level ground as gentle as possible. If the drive runs towards a garage, make the last 2m (6ft) slope up towards the door. Use a pole to impress a drain across the wet concrete at the lowest point.

Setting out paths and drives

Excavate the site, allowing for the thickness of the subbase and concrete. Level the bottom of the excavation, using a board to scrape the surface flat.

Drive accurately levelled pegs into the ground along the site, to act as datum points for the formwork. Space them about 2m (6ft 6in) apart along the centre of the pathway. Drive in the first peg until its top corresponds exactly to the proposed surface of the concrete. Use either a water level or a long straightedge and spirit level to position every other peg.

To make a water level, push a short length of transparent plastic tubing into each end of an ordinary garden hose. Holding both ends together, fill the hose with water until it appears in the tube at both ends. Then mark the level on both tubes. As long as the ends remain open, the water level at each end is constant – enabling you to establish a level over any distance, even around corners. When you move the hose, cork each end to retain the water.

Tie one end of the hose to the first datum peg, ensuring that the marked level aligns with the top of the peg. Use the other end to establish the level of every other peg along the pathway. To set a fall with a water level, make a mark on one tube below the surface of the water and use that as a gauge for the top of the peg.

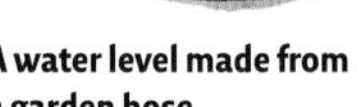

A water level made from a garden hose

Erecting formwork

Construct formwork from planks 25mm (1in) thick, as for a concrete pad. To check for level, rest a straightedge on the nearest datum peg (**1**).

If the drive or path is very long, it may be cheaper to hire metal 'road forms'. Straight-sided formwork is made from rigid units, but flexible sections are available to form curves. If you want to bend wooden formwork, make a series of closely spaced, parallel sawcuts across the width of the plank in the area of the curve.

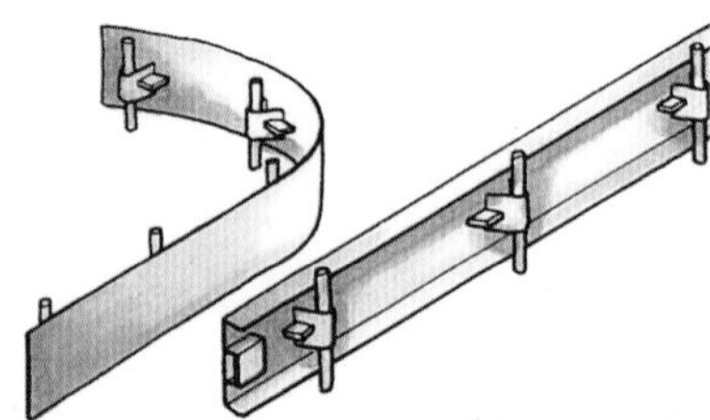

Curved and straight road forms

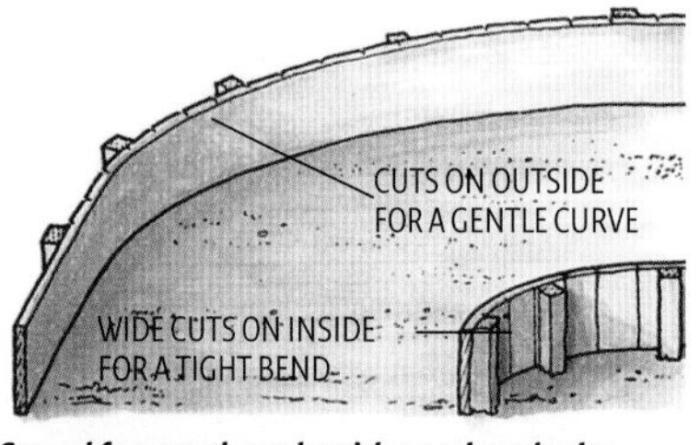

Curved formwork made with wooden planks

Installing control joints

Install a permanent expansion joint every 2m (6ft 6in) for a pathway, and every 4m (13ft) along a drive. For a patio, you can install similar joints or use alternate-bay construction (see opposite).

Cut strips of either rot-proofed hardboard or softwood 12mm (½in) thick to fit exactly between the formwork and to match the depth of the concrete. Before pouring, hold the control joints in place with mounds of concrete and nails driven into the formwork on each side of the board (**2**).

As you fill the formwork, pack more concrete on both sides of each joint and tamp towards each joint from both sides, so that it is not dislodged.

On a narrow path, to prevent the concrete cracking between joints, cut grooves 18mm (¾in) deep across the compacted concrete to form dummy joints alternating with the physical ones. The simplest method is to cut a length of T-section metal to fit between the formwork boards. Place the strip on the surface of the wet concrete and tap it down with a mallet (**3**). Carefully lift the strip out of the concrete to leave a neat impression. If the concrete should move, a crack will develop unnoticed at the bottom of the groove.

Place strips of thick bituminous felt between concrete and an adjoining wall to absorb expansion. Hold the felt in place with mounds of concrete (as described above) before pouring the full amount of concrete into the site.

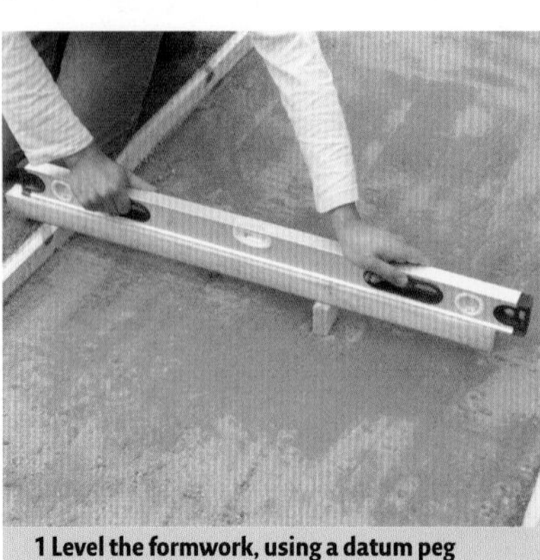

1 Level the formwork, using a datum peg

2 Support board with concrete and nails

3 Make a dummy joint with T-section metal

SEE ALSO > Preservers 246, Control joints 456, Crossfall 456, Pad thickness 456, Formwork 458, Tamping concrete 459

Alternate-bay method

It is not always possible to lay all the concrete in a single operation – in which case, it's easier to divide the formwork crosswise with additional planks, known as 'stop ends', to create equal-size bays.

By filling alternate bays with concrete, you have plenty of time to compact and level each section and more room in which to manoeuvre. It is a convenient way to lay a large patio, for example, and it is the only method you can use for drives or paths that butt against a wall. Alternate-bay construction is also frequently used for building a drive on a steep slope, to prevent the heavy wet concrete from slumping downhill.

There is no need to install control joints when using bay construction, but you may want to form dummy joints for a neat appearance (see opposite).

Laying concrete next to a wall

Stand in the empty bays so you can compact concrete laid against a wall. When the first bays have set hard, remove the stop ends and fill the gaps, using the surface of the firm concrete as a level. Don't drive or park a vehicle on a concrete drive for 10 days after laying.

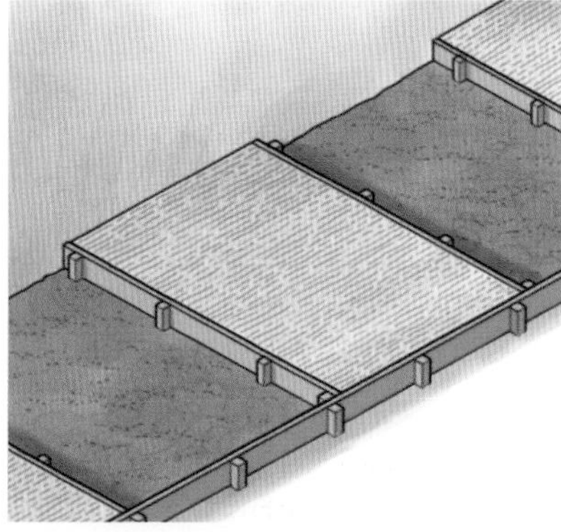

Construct bays when laying concrete next to a wall

Inspection chambers

Guard against expansion damaging an inspection chamber by surrounding it with control joints. Place formwork around the chamber and fill with concrete. When it's set, remove the boards and place either felt strips or preserver-treated softwood boards on all sides.

Surround an inspection chamber with formwork

Surface finishes

The surface finishes produced by tamping or striking off with a sawing action are perfectly adequate for a workmanlike skid-proof surface for a pad, drive or pathway – but you can produce a range of other finishes once you have compacted and levelled the concrete.

Float finishes

You can smooth the tamped concrete by sweeping a wooden float across the surface, or make an even finer texture by finishing with a plasterer's trowel (steel float). Let the concrete dry out a little before using a float, or you will bring water to the top and weaken it – which will eventually result in a dusty residue on the hardened concrete. Bridge the formwork with a stout plank so that you can reach the centre, or hire a skip float with a long handle for large pads.

Brush finishes

To produce a finely textured surface, you can draw a yard broom across the setting concrete. Flatten the concrete initially with a wooden float and then make parallel passes with the broom, held at a low angle in order to avoid 'tearing' the surface.

Exposed-aggregate finish

Embedding small stones or pebbles in the surface makes a very attractive and practical finish, although you will need a little practice in order to do it successfully.

Scatter dampened pebbles onto the freshly laid concrete, and tamp them firmly with a block of timber till they are flush with the surface (1). Place a plank across the formwork and apply your full weight to make sure the surface is even. Leave it to harden for a while until all the surface water has evaporated, then use a very fine spray and a brush to wash away the cement from around the pebbles until they protrude (2). Cover the concrete for about 24 hours, then lightly wash the surface again to clean any sediment off the pebbles. Cover the concrete again, and leave it to harden thoroughly.

1 Tamp pebbles into fresh concrete

2 Wash the cement from around the pebbles

Removing oil stains
Oil and fuel spills can spoil the appearance of concrete drives and parking spaces. Using a stiff-bristle brush, scrub individual stains with a proprietary drive cleaner; and then 20 minutes later wash the concrete with a diluted solution of the same cleaner. Finally, hose the drive or parking space with clean water.

SEE ALSO > Preservers 246, Control joints 456, Tamping concrete 459

Paving slabs

Paving slabs are made either by hydraulic pressing or by casting in moulds to create the desired finish. Pigments and selected aggregates added to the concrete mix are used to create the illusion of a range of muted colours or natural stone. Combining two or more colours or textures within the same area of paving can be very striking.

Regular or informal paving
Constructing a simple grid from square slabs (left) is relatively easy. Although mixed paving (below) is more difficult to lay, it is richer in texture, colour and shape.

Shapes and sizes

Although some manufacturers offer a wider choice than others, there's a fairly standard range of shapes and modular sizes. It is usually possible to carry the largest slabs without help, but it's a good idea to get an assistant to help manoeuvre them carefully into place.

Square and rectangular

A single size and shape can be employed to make grid-like patterns or, when staggered, to create a bonded-brickwork effect. Use rectangular slabs to form a basket-weave or herringbone pattern. Alternatively, combine different sizes so as to create the impression of random paving, or mix slabs with a different type of paving to create a colourful contrast. Mixing slabs in this way requires a degree of restraint to prevent a paved area looking uncoordinated – but if you get it right, the result can be a feast for the eye.

Hexagonal slabs
Hexagonal slabs form honeycomb patterns. You can use half slabs to edge areas that are paved in straight lines.

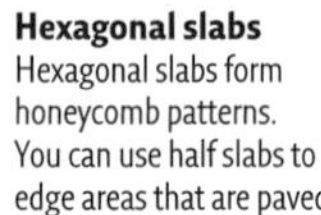

Half-hexagonal slabs

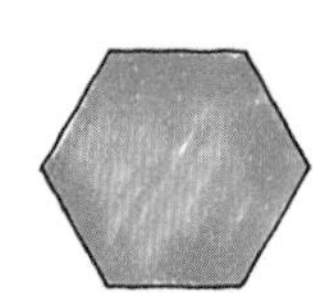

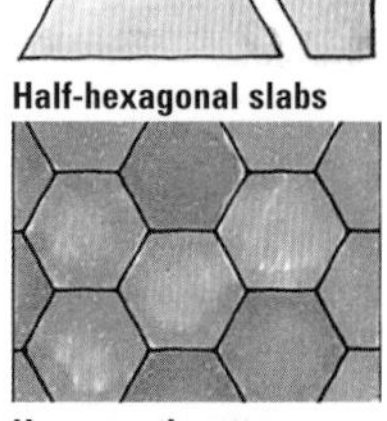

Honeycomb pattern

Tapered slabs
Use tapered slabs to edge ponds and for encircling trees or making curved steps. Progressively larger slabs can be used for laying circular areas of paving.

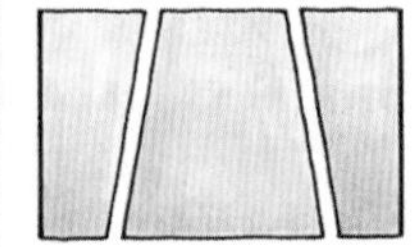

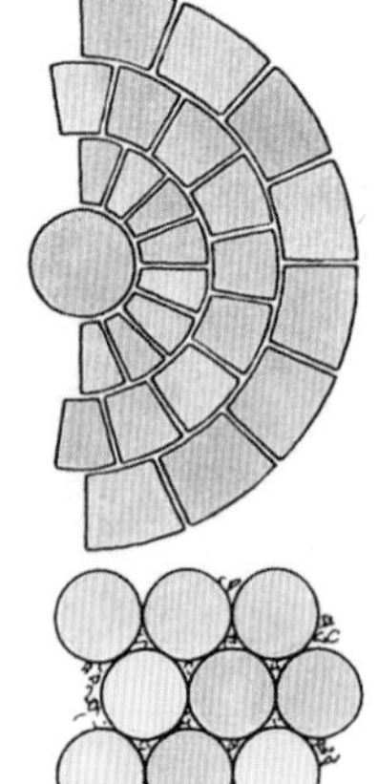

Circular slabs
Circular slabs make perfect individual stepping stones across a lawn or flower bed, but for a wide area fill the spaces between with cobbles or gravel.

Butted circular slabs

SEE ALSO > Brick pavers 467

Laying paving slabs

Although laying paving slabs involves a good deal of physical labour, in terms of technique it's no more complicated than tiling a wall. Accurate setting out and careful laying, especially during the early stages, will help you achieve perfect results.

Setting out the area of paving

Wherever feasible, plan an area of paving so that it can be laid with whole slabs only. This eliminates the arduous task of cutting units to fit. Use pegs and string to mark out the perimeter of the paved area, and check the measurements before you excavate.

You can use a straight wall as a datum line and measure away from the wall. Or if the location dictates that you have to lay slabs near the house, allow for a 100 to 150mm (4 to 6in) margin of gravel between the paving and wall. A gravel margin not only saves time and money by using fewer slabs, but also provides an area for planting climbers and for adequate drainage to keep the wall dry.

Even so, establish a slope of 16mm per metre (5/8in per yard) across the paving, so that most of the surface water will drain into the garden. Any paving must be 150mm (6in) below a damp-proof course, in order to protect the building.

As paving slabs are made to fairly precise dimensions, marking out an area simply involves accurate measurement, allowing for a 6 to 10mm (¼ to 3/8in) gap between the slabs. Some slabs are cast with sloping edges to provide a tapered joint and should be butted edge to edge.

Preparing a base for the paving

Paving slabs must be laid upon a firm, level base, but the depth and substance of that base depend on the type of soil and the proposed use of the paving.

For straightforward patios and paths, remove vegetable matter and topsoil to allow for the thickness of the slabs, plus a 35mm (1½in) layer of sharp sand and an extra 18mm (¾in) – so the paving will be below the level of surrounding turf, in order to prevent damage to your lawn mower. Compact the soil with a garden roller, and then spread the sand with a rake and level it by scraping and tamping with a length of timber.

To support heavier loads, or if the soil is composed of clay or peat, lay a subbase of firmly compacted hardcore – broken bricks or crushed stone – to a depth of 75 to 100mm (3 to 4in) before spreading the sand to level the surface. If you plan to park vehicles on the paving, increase the depth of hardcore to 150mm (6in).

Cutting paving slabs

It is often necessary to trim concrete paving slabs to size in order to fit narrow margins.

Mark a line across a slab with chalk or a soft pencil. Place the slab on a bed of sand and, wearing plastic goggles, use a bolster and hammer to chisel a groove about 3mm (1/8in) deep along the line.

Turn the slab face down and, with the hammer, tap firmly along the groove until the slab splits. If need be, clean up the edge with a bolster.

To obtain a perfect cut, hire an angle grinder fitted with a stone-cutting disc.

Using an angle grinder
An angle grinder makes short work of a concrete paving slab. Wear protective gloves, goggles and a face mask.

Level the sand base with a piece of wood

Laying and levelling the slabs

1 Lay five blobs of mortar under each slab

3 Check the fall with a spirit level

2 Level the slab with a block and hammer

4 Fill the joints with a dry mortar mix

Lay the edging slabs on the sand, working in both directions from a corner. When you are satisfied with their positions, lift the slabs one at a time, so you can set them on a bed of mortar (1 part cement : 4 parts sand). Lay a large blob of mortar under each corner, and one more to support the centre of the slab (**1**). If you intend to drive vehicles across the slabs, lay a continuous bed of mortar about 50mm (2in) thick. Wet the back of each slab just before you lay it on top of the mortar. Level each slab by tapping with a heavy hammer, using a block of wood to protect the surface (**2**). Add mortar to fill flush any gaps under the the slabs.

Lay three slabs at a time, inserting spacers between, then check the alignment. To gauge the slope across the paving, drive datum pegs along the high side, with the top of each peg corresponding to the finished surface of the paving, and then use a straightedge with a packing piece under one end to check the fall on the slabs (**3**). Lay the other slabs, each time working outwards from the corner in order to keep the joints square. Remove the spacers before the mortar sets, but don't walk on the paving for 2 to 3 days.

To fill the gaps between the paving slabs, brush a dry mortar mix of 1 part cement : 3 parts sand into the open joints (**4**), then sprinkle the area with a very fine spray of water to consolidate the mortar.

SEE ALSO > Mixing mortar 441, Crossfall 456, Subbase 457, 459

Timber decking

Decking – an offshoot of the American love of outdoor leisure and entertaining – has become extremely popular in this country. Timber is warm to the touch and creates a homely atmosphere that's difficult to achieve with concrete or brick paving. Building a deck can make good use of an area where grass won't grow, or provide a way of covering an unsightly old patio. Being relatively lightweight, wooden decking is ideal for roof gardens, too.

Decking screws
Special plated decking screws are designed to be driven straight into the wood, using a power tool. The longer ones are for building the framework (plated coach screws are a suitable alternative), while the smaller ones are for fixing deck boards to the joists.

Designing your deck

One of the advantages of building in wood is that you can construct a deck to fit a site of almost any shape and size. And you don't have to be a skilled carpenter. However, if you plan to build a raised deck more than 600mm (2ft) from the ground, you should get professional help or advice.

When deciding on the best place for your deck, think about whether you want it to be in the sun most of the time. Or would it be better in a shady spot during the hottest part of the day? It is always worth modifying your design to accommodate trees: just build round them, making sure they have enough room to grow and move with the wind. You may want to take advantage of the view from your garden – but you need to respect your neighbours' privacy, too.

If the best place for your deck is next to the house, incorporate removable panels to gain access to manhole covers and drains – and make sure you don't compromise the damp-proof course or cover airbricks.

Decking materials

Some people like to use reclaimed timber from a salvage yard, or incorporate a variety of materials into their design. However, most of the DIY outlets now stock ready-machined and sanded decking components, which make construction easier.

If you are prepared to pay relatively high prices, you can buy hardwood decking; but softwood is cheaper and perfectly suitable, provided it is tanalized (pressure-treated with preservative) and guaranteed against rot for 15 or 20 years.

Decking materials
Typical components available from DIY outlets:
1 Joists come in various sizes for constructing the underlying framework.
2 Deck boards – plain or ribbed surface.
3 Notched bearer for simple ground-level decks.
4 Newel post for balustrades. The same timber can be used for deck-support posts and corner bracing.
5 Ready-cut stringer for making steps up to a raised deck.
6 Balusters – there's a wide variety of styles.
7 Standard panels or 'tiles' that drop into a framework constructed from notched bearers.
8 Polypropylene sheeting that suppresses weed growth while allowing rainwater to drain away.
9 Fixings – plated decking screws and coach bolts.

SEE ALSO > Damp-proof course 247, Airbricks 274, Planning a garden 422–4

Laying ground-level decks

Ground-level decking is simple to construct and ideal for a deck accessed directly from the house. It is also the best option for a roof garden. You can buy factory-made bearers and panels, or make the supporting framework from joists and cover it with smooth or ribbed deck boards.

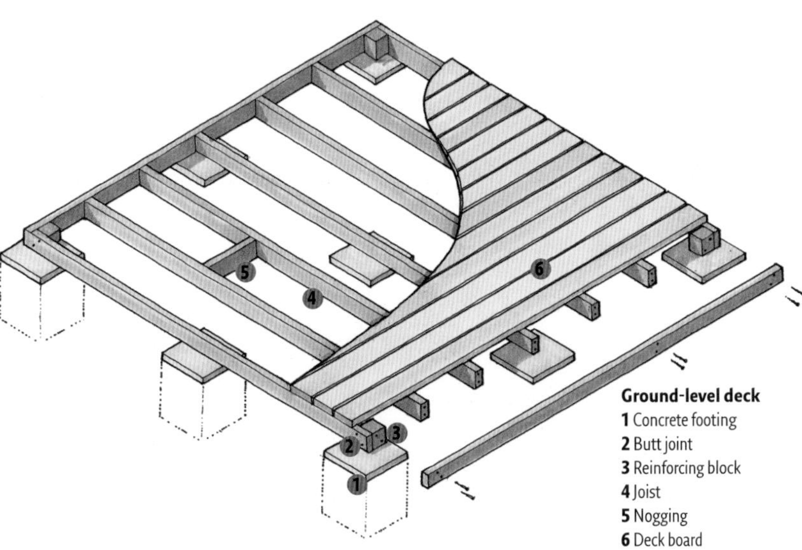

Ground-level deck
1 Concrete footing
2 Butt joint
3 Reinforcing block
4 Joist
5 Nogging
6 Deck board

Constructing the deck

Preparing the ground

Unless you are building onto an existing concrete base, remove any turf and level the ground – ideally adding a shallow layer of gravel topped with sharp sand. Before constructing the deck, lay down a sheet of polypropylene to prevent weed growth.

An even better solution, especially for a garden with poor drainage, is to place your deck on concrete footings (1) laid every 1200mm (4ft) across the site. For the footings, dig holes approximately 300mm (1ft) square and 300mm (1ft) deep and fill them with concrete, using a straight beam and a spirit level to check that their top surfaces are all level with one another. Just before the concrete sets hard, shape the exposed edges of the footings with a trowel. For additional protection, place offcuts of bituminous felt (DPC) between the decking and the concrete. Lay polypropylene sheeting between the footings.

Building the framework

Construct the outer frame from joists, butt-jointed at the corners (2) and reinforced with blocks cut from 95mm (4in) square posts (3). Whenever you cut tanalized timber, you must coat the cut surfaces with a chemical preserver. Screw each joist to the corner blocks, using 80mm (3in) deck-construction screws. Alternatively, you can use plated coach screws, but will need to drill pilot and clearance holes before inserting them. Whichever you use, stagger the screws to ensure there is sufficient clearance inside the reinforcing block.

Access may be restricted if you are erecting the deck in a corner of the garden – in which case, start by making the internal corner joint first and work outwards from there.

Having constructed the outer frame, cut joists (4) to fit snugly inside the frame. Fix them at 400mm (1ft 4in) centres, driving two 145mm (5¾in) deck-construction screws through the framework into each end of every joist; if you are planning to lay the deck boards diagonally, fix the joists at 300mm (1ft) centres. If you can't drive in screws from outside the framework, skew-screw the joists to the frame from the inside using shorter deck-construction screws. Straighten any slightly bowed joists by nailing noggings between them (5).

Laying the deck boards

Cut deck boards (6) to length and lay them at right angles to the joists. Drive two decking screws through the boards into each joist. Leave a 3 to 6mm (⅛ to ¼in) gap between the boards to provide adequate rainwater runoff.

Bearers and panels

Another method of constructing a ground-level deck is to lay proprietary notched bearers on polypropylene sheeting laid over levelled ground.

If necessary, drive a decking screw into each of the frame joints to make sure the top surfaces of the bearers are flush. Then lay a ready-made panel or deck tile over each square within the framework and secure each panel with decking screws.

Alternatively, cover the framework with deck boards, as described left.

Laying notched bearers
Bearers come with joints already cut to make assembly easier.

Cover the deck bearers with ready-made panels

Fix the first board
Lay the first deck board flush with the frame or allow it to overhang slightly.

Using spacers
As you fix the other boards in place, use a convenient spacer to keep the gaps even.

SEE ALSO > Noggings 152, Preservers 246, Felt DPC 447, Mixing concrete 000, Concrete mixes 455, Pilots holes 502, Skew-nailing 505

Building a raised deck

Support a raised deck on short posts, making allowance for a sloping site. Create interesting changes of level by combining ground-level and raised decks. Don't build a deck higher than 600mm (2ft) without professional help.

Decking oil
Timber tends to weather naturally to an attractive silver-grey. However, if you want to revive the colour of the wood, coat it with decking oil.

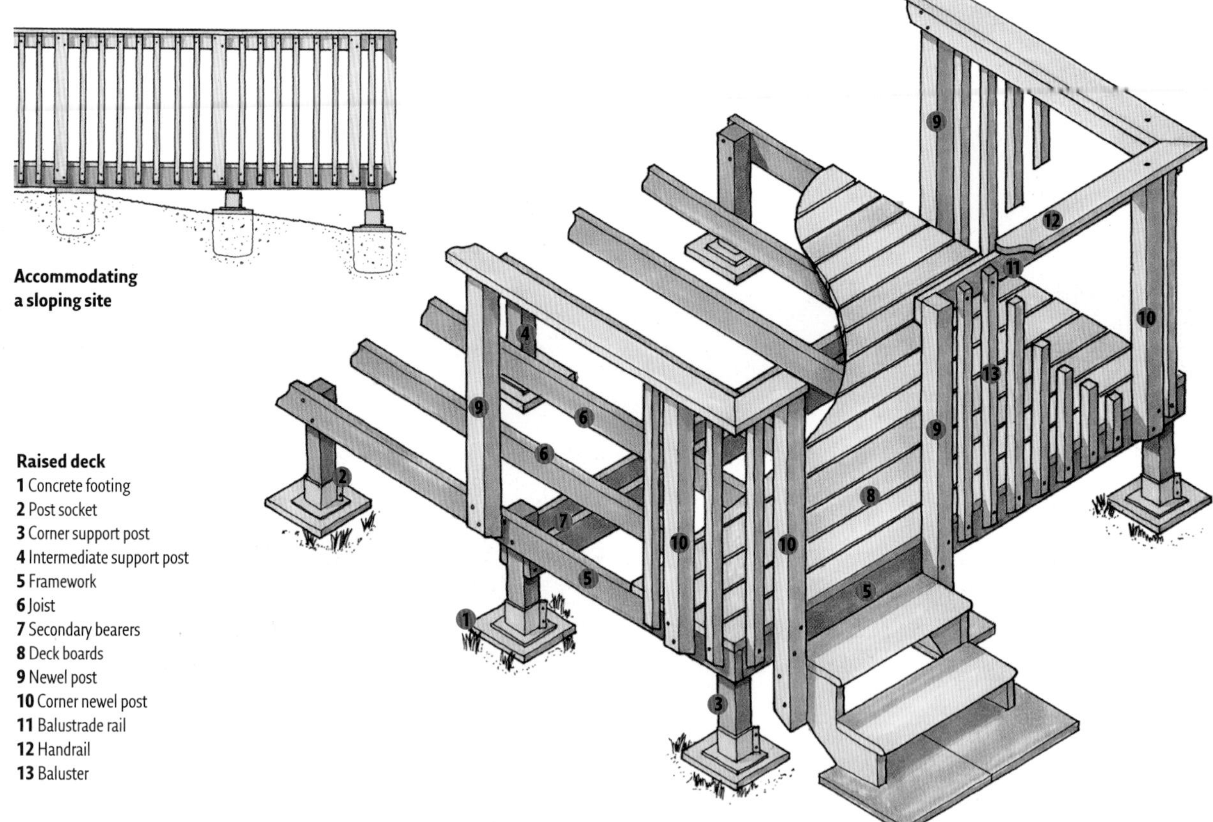

Accommodating a sloping site

Raised deck
1 Concrete footing
2 Post socket
3 Corner support post
4 Intermediate support post
5 Framework
6 Joist
7 Secondary bearers
8 Deck boards
9 Newel post
10 Corner newel post
11 Balustrade rail
12 Handrail
13 Baluster

Constructing the deck

Lay concrete footings (**1**) as for a ground-level deck. Support the deck on 95 x 95mm (4 x 4in) posts, held vertically in metal post sockets (**2**) fixed to each footing with expansion bolts. Support posts are also used to reinforce the outer frame at each corner (**3**) and are placed at 1200mm (4ft) centres across the entire area of the deck (**4**). Construct the outer frame from 140 x 47mm (6 x 2in) joists, screwed to the support posts at each corner (**5**) as for a ground-level deck.

Screw similar-size joists (**6**) between the outer frame members. Fix the joists at 400mm (1ft 4in) centres, driving two 145mm (5¾in) deck-construction screws through the framework into each end of every joist. If you cannot insert the screws from outside the frame, hang the joists from joist hangers attached to the inside of the frame.

Provide additional support for the joists by screwing a pair of 140 x 47mm (6 x 2in) secondary bearers to every second row of support posts (**7**). Fix the deck boards (**8**) in place, as described for a ground-level deck.

Bolt each socket to its footing

Tighten the bolts to clamp the post

Making the balustrade

For safety, every raised deck needs to have a balustrade. Decking manufacturers offer a wide variety of styles. Shown here is a simple balustrade, 1m (3ft 3in) high, constructed from readily available components.

Bolt newel posts, 95 x 95mm (4 x 4in) square, to the outside of the framework (**9**), using two coach bolts per post. Shape the bottom end of each post by cutting a bevel, and saw the top end square. The newel posts should be no more than 1200mm (4ft) apart. Bolt a pair at each corner (**10**), placing each of them 150mm (6in) from the corner of the deck.

Join the newel posts together with a narrow deck board (**11**) screwed to the inside of each row of posts. Butt-joint and screw these rails at the corners.

Screw another deck board to the top edge of the horizontal rail to form a flat handrail (**12**). Mitre the handrails where they meet at the corners, and secure

SEE ALSO > Joist hangers 174, Post sockets 429, Ground-level decks 465, Expansion bolts 535

each joint with a single screw driven through the edge.

Screw proprietary balusters (**13**), no more than 100mm (4in) apart, to the horizontal rail and the framework of the deck. Square-section balusters may come with a bevel at each end. If you have to saw the balusters to length, cut a similar bevel to match.

Bolt newel posts to the framework

Building steps

Decking manufacturers supply ready-made components for simple wooden steps. Cut the components to length and screw them together. Then either screw the completed steps to the decking framework or, as shown here, bolt the steps to slightly longer newel posts bolted on each side of the steps. Support the base of the steps on levelled paving slabs.

An accumulation of dirt and algae can make the wood slippery. Scrub your deck boards and steps at least once a year with a proprietary decking cleaner.

Adding a skirting

To prevent litter being blown under a raised deck, fit skirting below the framework. You can buy proprietary slatted panels and cut them to fit your deck.

Bolt the steps in place

Paving with bricks

Bricks make charming paths. The wide variety of textures and colours available offers endless possibilities of pattern – but choose the type of brick carefully, bearing in mind the sort of use your paving can expect.

Brick paving

Ordinary housebricks are often used for paths and small patios, even though there is the risk of spalling in freezing conditions – unless they happen to be engineering bricks. Their slightly uneven texture and colour are the very reasons why second-hand bricks are so much in demand for garden paving – so a little frost damage is usually acceptable.

However, housebricks are not really suitable if the paved area is to be a parking space or driveway, especially if it's going to be used by heavy vehicles. For a surface that will be durable even under severe conditions, use concrete bricks instead. These are generally slightly smaller than standard housebricks, being something like 200 x 100 x 65mm (8 x 4 x 2½in), but there are many variations in size and also in shape and colour, making possible a wide range of paving – from regular tiled effects to less formal cobbled surfaces.

Brick pavers
Cast-concrete pavers are available in a variety of colours, styles and shapes. Textured setts are ideal for non-slip garden pathways. Brindle concrete blocks are often used for drives and parking areas.

Interlocking concrete pavers

SEE ALSO > Brick patterns 468

Laying brick paving

Laying bricks over a wide area is very time-consuming, and it helps if at least two people can work together, dividing up the various tasks between them. Also, it's well worth the extra expense of hiring tools that will make the work faster and more efficient.

Brick patterns

Unlike brick walls, which must be bonded in a certain way for stability, brick paths, patios and car-parking areas can be laid to any pattern that appeals to you. Try out your ideas on gridded paper, using the examples shown below for inspiration.

Concrete bricks, which have one finished surface, are often chamfered all round to define their shape and emphasize whatever pattern you choose. Many bricks have spacers moulded into the sides to help form accurate joints. Housebricks can be laid on edge or face down, showing the wide face normally unseen in a wall.

Brick-paved drive and parking space

Herringbone pattern with straight edging

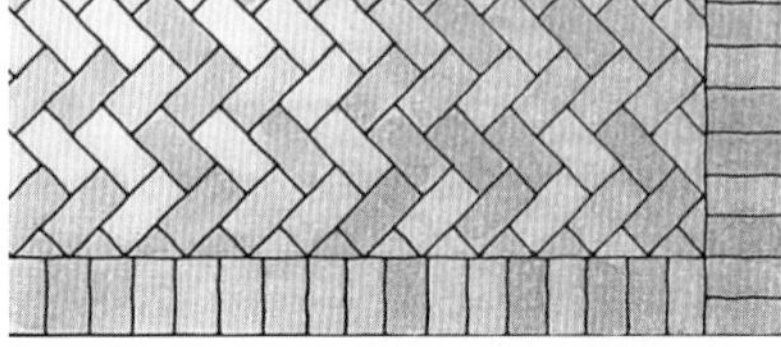

Angled herringbone with straight edging

Whole bricks surrounding coloured half bats

Stretcher-bond brickwork

Cane-weave pattern

Mottled-brick garden path

Concrete-sett path edged with flush pavers

Providing a base for brick paving

Lay brick pathways and patios on a 75mm (3in) hardcore base, covered with a 50mm (2in) layer of compacted slightly damp sharp sand. When laying concrete bricks for a drive, you need to increase the depth of hardcore to 150mm (6in). Fully compact the hardcore and fill all voids, so that sand from the bedding course is not lost to the sub-base. Provide a crossfall on patios and drives, as for concrete. Make sure that the surface of the paving is not less than 150mm (6in) below a DPC protecting a building.

Retaining edges

Unless the brick path is laid against a wall or some similar structure, the edges of the paving must be contained by a permanent restraint. Timber treated with chemical preserver is one solution, constructed like the formwork for concrete. The edging boards should be flush with the surface of the path, but drive the stakes below ground so that they can be covered by soil or turf.

Concrete paving, in particular, needs a more substantial edging of bricks set in concrete. Dig a trench that is deep and wide enough to take a row of bricks on end plus a 100mm (4in) concrete 'foundation'. Lay the bricks while the concrete is still wet – holding them in place temporarily with a staked board while you pack more concrete behind the edging. Once the concrete has set, remove the board and lay hardcore and sand in the excavation.

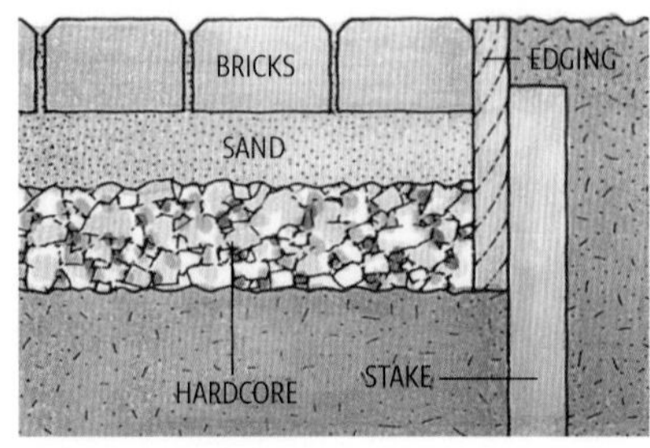

Wooden retaining edge

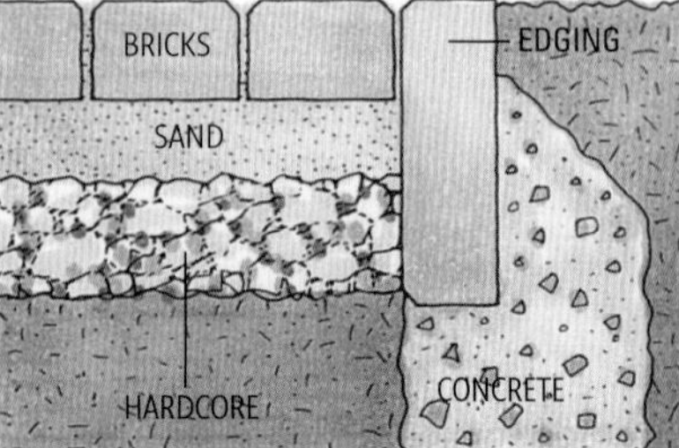

Brick retaining edge

SEE ALSO > Preservers 246, Engineering bricks 437, Brick bonding 442, Mixing concrete 455, Fall for patios and drives 456, Erecting formwork 458, Laying hardcore 459

Compacting and levelling the sand

When the bricks are first laid on the sand they should project 10mm (3/8in) above the edging restraints, to allow for bedding them in at a later stage.

Spread sand to about two-thirds of its finished thickness across the area to be paved and then compact it, using a hired vibrating plate.

Spread more sand on top and level it with a notched spreader that spans the edging (**1**).

If the paving is too wide for a spreader, lay levelling battens on the hardcore base and scrape the sand to the required depth using a straightedge (**2**). Then remove the battens and fill the voids carefully with sand.

Vibrating plate
Use a petrol-driven vibrating plate for levelling and bedding in concrete pavers.

1 Level the sand with a notched spreader

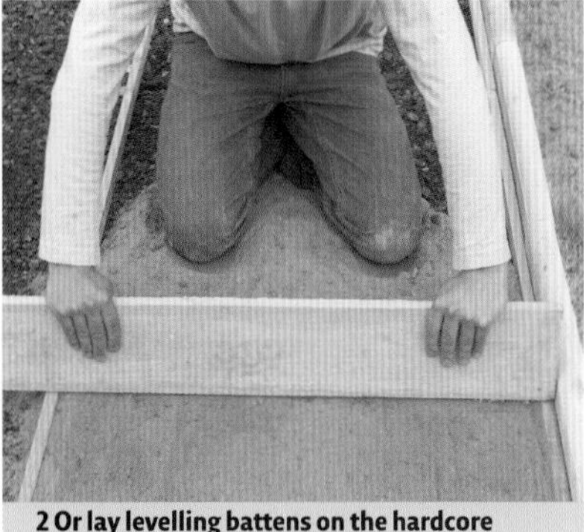

2 Or lay levelling battens on the hardcore

Bedding in the bricks

Lay the bricks on the sand to your chosen pattern. Work from one end of the site, kneeling on a board placed across the bricks (**3**). Never stand on the bed of sand. Lay whole bricks only, leaving any gaps at the edges to be filled with cut bricks after you have laid an area of approximately 1 to 2sq m (1 to 2½sq yd). Concrete bricks have fixed spacers, so butt them together tightly.

Fill any of the remaining spaces with bricks cut with a bolster and club hammer. If you are paving a large area, it's worth hiring a purpose-made guillotine.

When the area of paving is complete, run the vibrating plate over the surface two or three times, until it has worked the bricks down into the sand and flush with the outer edging (**4**).

Vibrating the bricks will work some sand up between them; complete the job by brushing more kiln-dried joint-filling sand across the finished paving and vibrating it into the open joints.

Brick guillotine
Hire a guillotine to cut concrete paving bricks.

3 Lay the bricks to your chosen pattern

4 A vibrating plate levels brick paving perfectly

Drainage accessories

An existing manhole cover often spoils the appearance of paving. The solution is to replace the cover with a special hollow version that is designed to be filled with concrete bricks and merges into the surrounding paving.

Draining rainwater from a large flat area of paving can be a problem. One solution is to include one or more linear drainage channels running to a soakaway.

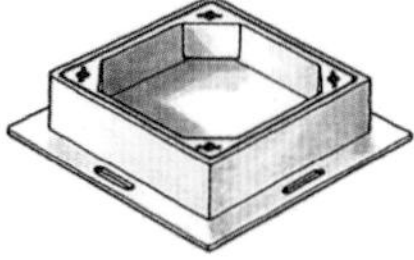

Manhole cover

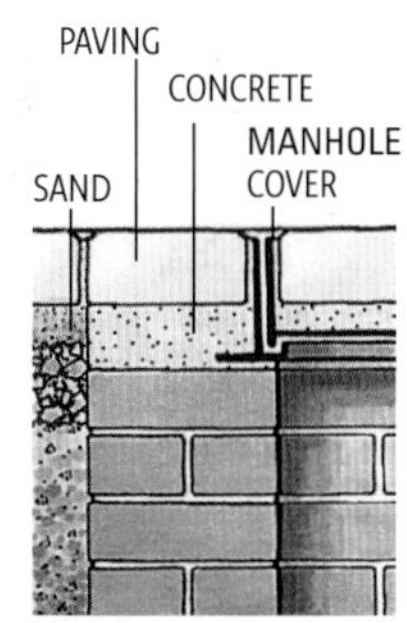

Frame bedded in concrete

Inset manhole cover

The metal frame of an inset manhole cover should be bedded in concrete, which is then overlaid with paving that runs right up to the rim of the access hole. Make sure the rim is just below the finished surface of the paving.

Linear drainage channel

Plastic U-section drainage channels linked end to end are bedded in a 100mm (4in) concrete base, which is haunched (built up on both sides) to hold the channel in place. The first row of bricks on each side of the channel is bedded in the concrete, and should finish 3 to 6mm (1/8 to ¼in) above the level of the plastic or metal grating used to cover the channel.

A special end cap is available for connecting to a main drain, or you can drain the water into a soakaway about 1m (4ft) square and at least 1m (4ft) deep. Fill the soakaway with coarse rubble, up to the level of the hardcore base laid for the paving.

Cutting the channel
Use a panel saw to cut a plastic drainage channel to length.

SEE ALSO > Cutting bricks 444

Building garden steps

Designing a garden for a sloping site offers plenty of possibilities for creating attractive changes of level – by terracing areas of paving or having planting beds held in place by retaining walls. However, so people are able to move from one level to another safely, at least one flight of steps will be required.

Designing steps

If you have a large garden where the slope is very gradual, a series of steps with wide treads and low risers can make an impressive feature.

If the slope is steep, to avoid a staircase appearance construct a flight of steps composed of a few treads interposed with wide flat landings – where the flight can change direction to add further interest and offer a different view of the garden. In fact, a shallow flight can be virtually a series of landings, perhaps circular in plan, sweeping up the slope in a curve.

For steps to be both comfortable and safe to use, the proportion of tread (the part you stand on) to riser (the vertical part of the step) is important. As a rough guide, construct steps so that the depth of the tread (from front to back) plus twice the height of the riser equals 650mm (2ft 2in). For example, match 300mm (1ft) treads with 175mm (7in) risers; 350mm (1ft 2in) treads with 150mm (6in) risers; and so on. Never make treads less than 300mm (1ft) deep, or risers higher than 175mm (7in).

• **Slippery steps**
Steps can become slippery if algae is allowed to grow on the treads. Brush affected steps with a solution of 1 part household bleach to 4 parts water. After 48 hours, wash them with clean water and repeat the treatment. You can also treat the steps with a proprietary fungicidal solution.

Paved steps built with natural-stone risers

Using concrete slabs

Paving slabs in their various forms are ideal for making firm, flat treads for garden steps. Construct the risers from concrete blocks or bricks, allowing the treads to overhang by 25 to 50mm (1 to 2in) in order to cast a shadow line to define the edge of the step.

So you can gauge the number of steps required, measure the difference in height from the top of the slope to the bottom. Next, mark the position of the risers with pegs and roughly shape the steps in the soil.

Either lay concrete slabs, bedded in sand, flush with the ground at the foot of the slope or dig a trench for hardcore and a 100 to 150mm (4 to 6in) concrete base to support the first riser (**1**). When the concrete has set, construct the riser from two courses of mortared bricks, checking the alignment with a spirit level (**2**). Fill behind the riser with compacted hardcore until it is level, then lay the tread on a bed of mortar (**3**). Using a spirit level as a guide, tap down the tread until it slopes very slightly towards its front edge, in order to shed rainwater and so prevent ice forming.

Measure from the front edge of the tread to mark the position of the next riser on the slabs (**4**), then construct the next step in the same way.

Landscaping each side

It is usually possible to landscape the slope at each side of a flight of steps and to turf or plant it to prevent the soil washing down onto the steps. Another solution is to retain the soil with large stones, perhaps extending into a rockery on one or both sides.

1 Dig the footing for the first riser

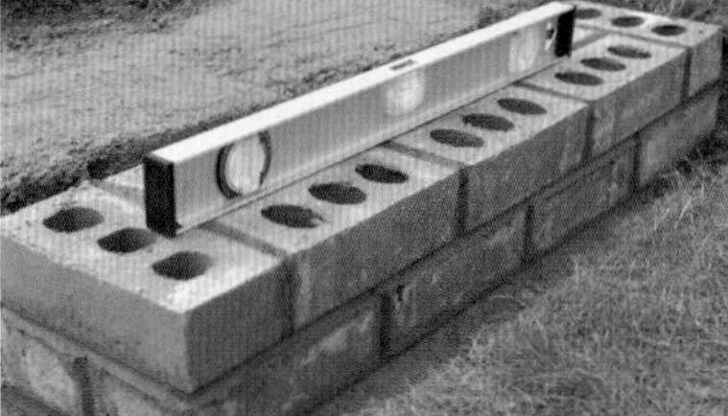

2 Build a brick riser and level it

3 Lay the tread on mortar

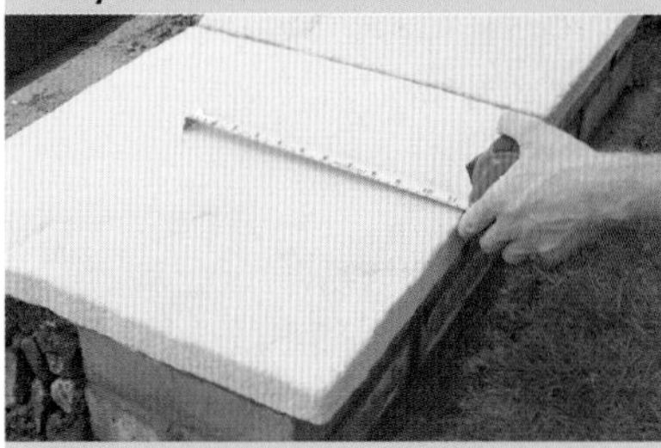

4 Mark the position of the next riser

Paving-slab steps
A section through a simple flight of garden steps built with brick risers and paving slabs.
1 Concrete footing
2 Brick-built riser
3 Hardcore infill
4 Paving-slab tread

SEE ALSO > Mixing mortar 441, Footings 443, Bricklaying techniques 444, Retaining walls 452, Paving slabs 462

Repairing concrete steps

Casting new steps in concrete requires such complicated formwork that the end result hardly justifies the effort involved, especially when it's possible to construct better-looking steps from cast-concrete slabs and blocks. Nevertheless, if you have a flight of concrete steps in your garden, you will want to keep them in good condition.

Like other forms of masonry, concrete suffers from 'spalling' – frost breaks down the surface of the material and fragments flake off. Spalling frequently occurs along the front edges of steps where foot traffic adds to the problem. Repair broken edges as soon as you can – since, as well as being unattractive, damaged steps can be dangerous.

Building up broken edges

Wearing safety goggles, chip away some of the concrete around the damaged area to provide a good grip for fresh concrete. Cut a board to the height of the riser and prop it against the step (1).

Mix a small batch of general-purpose concrete, adding a little PVA bonding agent to help it adhere to the step. Dilute some bonding agent with water (say, 3 parts water : 1 part bonding agent) and brush it onto the damaged area, stippling it into the crevices. When the surface becomes tacky, fill the hole with concrete mix flush with the edge of the board (2). Radius the front edge slightly with an edging float, running it against the board.

1 Prop a board against the riser

2 Fill the front edge with concrete

Building log steps

You can use sawn lengths of timber to build attractive steps that suit an informal garden. As it's not always possible to obtain uniform logs, you may have to make up the height of the riser with two or more slimmer logs. Alternatively, buy purpose-made pressure-treated logs, machined with a flat surface on two faces. Soak your own timber in chemical preserver.

Remove any turf and cut a regular slope in the earth bank, then compact the soil by treading it down. Sharpen stakes cut from logs 75mm (3in) in diameter and drive them into the ground, one at each end of a step (1).

Place a heavy log behind the stakes, bedding it down in the soil until it is level (2), and pack broken-brick hardcore behind it to construct the tread of the step (3). To finish the step, shovel a layer of gravel on top of the hardcore, then rake the gravel level with the top of the log riser.

If you're unable to obtain large logs, you can build a step from two or three straight slimmer logs, holding them against the stakes with hardcore as you construct the riser (4).

Finish by laying a gravel path at the top and bottom of the flight of steps.

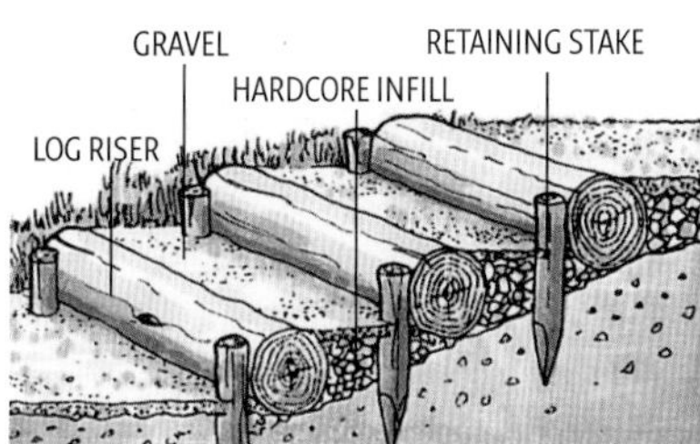

Log steps

Making curved steps

To build a series of curved steps, choose materials that will make construction as easy as possible. One option is to use tapered concrete slabs for the treads, designing the circumference of the steps to suit the proportions of the slabs. Alternatively, use bricks laid flat or on edge to build the risers. Set the bricks to radiate from the centre of the curve, and fill the slightly tapered joints with mortar. Use a length of string attached to a peg driven into the ground as an improvised compass to mark out the curve of each step.

After roughly shaping the soil, lay a concrete foundation for the bottom riser. Build the risers and treads as for regular paving-slab steps (see opposite), using the improvised string compass as a guide.

1 Drive a stake at each end of a step

2 Place a log behind the stakes

3 Fill behind the log with hardcore

4 Make up a riser with two slim logs

Curved steps made entirely from bricks

Log steps

Paved circular landing

SEE ALSO > Preservers 246, Footings 443, Concrete mixes 457, Edging float, 459, Laying hardcore 459, Tapered slabs 462

Creating water gardens

There is nothing like still or running water to enliven a garden. Waterfalls and fountains have an almost mesmerizing fascination, and the sound of trickling water has a delightfully soothing effect. Even a small area of still water will support all manner of interesting pond life and plants – with the additional bonus of the images of trees, rocks and sky reflected in its placid surface.

Well worth it
A healthy pond requires careful construction to begin with and regular maintenance thereafter. However, the effort will be amply repaid – especially if you include some form of running water to add sound and sparkling light to the scene.

SEE ALSO > Installing pond liners 474–5, Building a cascade 477

Pond liners

It's not by chance that the number of garden ponds has greatly increased in recent years. Their popularity is largely due to the fact that easily installed rigid and flexible pond liners are now readily available, which make it possible to create a water garden by putting in just a few days' work.

In the past it was necessary to line a pond with concrete. While it is true that concrete is a very versatile material, there is always the possibility of a leak developing through cracks caused by ground movement or the force of expanding ice. There are no such worries with flexible liners or those made from rigid plastic. Building formers for a concrete pond involves both labour and expense, and when the pond is finished it has to be left to season for about a month – during which time it needs to be emptied and refilled a number of times to ensure that the water will be safe for fish and plant life. In contrast, you can introduce plants into a pool lined with plastic or rubber as soon as the water itself has matured, which takes no more than a few days.

Ordering a flexible liner

Use a simple formula to calculate the size of the liner you will need. Disregarding any complicated shapes and planting shelves and so on, simply take the overall length and width of the pond and add twice the maximum depth to each dimension to arrive at the size of the liner. If possible, adapt your design to fall within the nearest stock liner size – or you will have to pay extra for a special order.

POND DIMENSIONS	
Length – 3m	9ft 9in
Width – 2m	6ft 6in
Depth – 450mm	1ft 6in
SIZE OF LINER	
3m + 0.900m = 3.9m	9ft 9in + 3ft = 12ft 9in
2m + 0.900m = 2.9m	6ft 6in + 3ft = 9ft 6in

Choosing a pond liner

The advantages of proprietary pond liners over concrete are fairly obvious, but there are a number of options to choose from – depending on the size and shape of the pond you wish to create and how much you are planning to spend.

Pond under construction
This ambitious project uses a flexible liner in the construction of a water garden.

Rigid plastic liners

Regular visitors to garden centres will be familiar with the range of preformed plastic pond liners. A rigid liner is in effect a ready-made one-piece pond – including planting shelves and, in some cases, recessed troughs to accommodate marsh or bog gardens.

The best pond liners are those made from rigid glass-reinforced plastic (fibreglass), which is very strong and is also resistant to the effects of frost or ice. Almost as good – and more economical – are liners made from vacuum-formed plastic. Provided they are handled with a reasonable degree of care and installed correctly, rigid plastic pond liners are practically leak-proof. A very acceptable water garden can be created with a carefully selected series of pond liners linked together by watercourses.

Flexible liners

For complete freedom of design, choose a flexible-sheet liner that will hug the contours of a pond of virtually any shape and size.

For a relatively inexpensive flexible pond liner, choose a polyvinyl acetate (PVC) sheet in the region of 0.35 mm thick. More durable PVC liners are available in thicknesses of about 0.5mm. Plastic liners are guaranteed for many years of normal use – but if you want your pond to last for 50 years or more, choose a thicker membrane made from synthetic rubber.

Black rubber liners are made in a wide range of stock sizes, up to about 10 x 15m (32 x 50ft). The thicker the liner, the more likely it is to crease as you fill the pond with water. However, creases are hardly noticeable once the pond has matured.

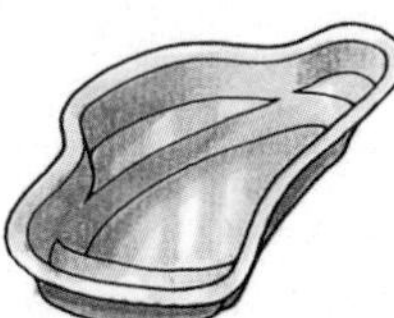

Rigid pond liner
Rigid liners are moulded from plastic.

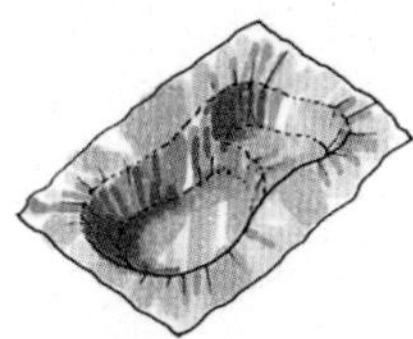

Flexible liner
The best-quality flexible liners are made from butyl.

SEE ALSO > Installing pond liners 474–5, Building a cascade 477

Constructing ponds

A pond must be sited correctly if it is to have any chance of maturing into an attractive, clear stretch of water. Don't place a pond under deciduous trees: falling leaves will pollute the water as they decay, causing fish to become ill or die. Laburnum trees are especially poisonous.

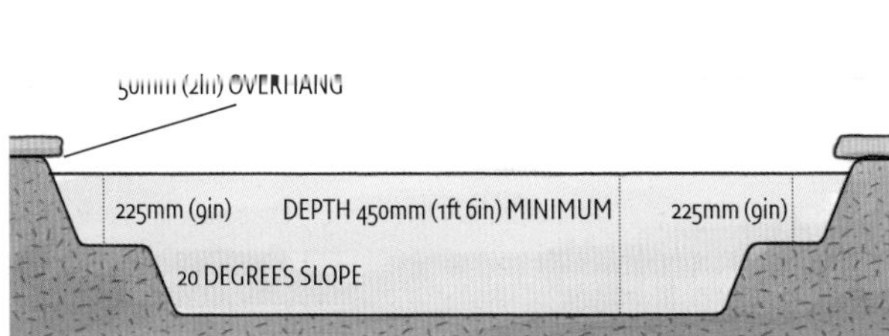

Important dimensions for a garden pond

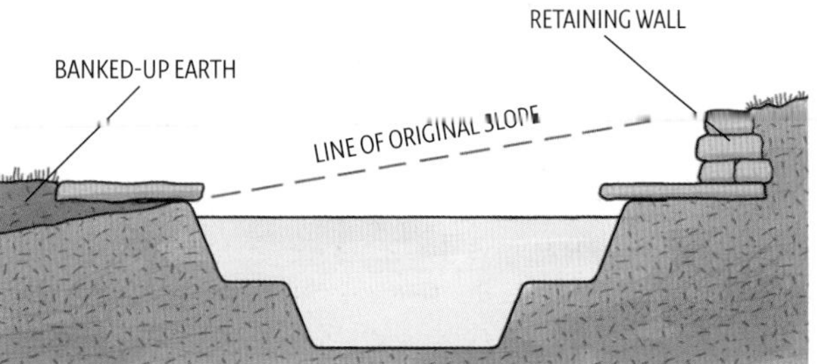

Accommodating a sloping site

The need for sunlight

Although sunlight promotes the growth of algae – which causes ponds to turn a pea-green colour – it is also necessary to encourage the growth of water plants. An abundance of oxygenating plants will compete with the algae for mineral salts and, aided by the shade that is cast by floating and marginal plants, they will help to keep the water clear.

Volume of water

The pond's dimensions are important in creating harmony between plants and fish. It is difficult to maintain the right conditions for clear water in a pond that is less than 3.75sq m (40sq ft) in surface area – but the volume of water is even more vital. A pond up to about 9sq m (100sq ft) in area needs to be 450mm (1ft 6in) deep. As the area increases you will have to dig deeper, to about 600mm (2ft) or more, although it's hardly ever necessary to dig deeper than 750mm (2ft 6in).

1 Mark the perimeter of the liner

2 Measure the depth of the excavation

3 Make sure the liner stands level

4 Infill with sifted soil or sand

Designing the shape of your pond

Although there's a huge variety of rigid plastic liners available, you are limited to the shapes selected by the manufacturers. There are no such limitations if you use a flexible pond liner, although curved shapes take up the slack better than straight-sided pools do.

The profile of the pond must be designed to fulfil certain requirements. To grow marginal plants, you will need a shelf 225mm (9in) wide around the edge of the pond, 225mm (9in) below the surface of the water. This will take a standard 150mm (6in) planting crate, with ample water above, and you can always raise the crate on bricks or pieces of paving. The sides of the pond should slope at about 20 degrees, to prevent the collapse of soil during construction and to allow the liner to stretch without promoting too many creases. It will also allow a sheet of ice to float upwards without damaging the liner. Judge the angle by measuring 75mm (3in) inwards for every 225mm (9in) of depth. If the soil is very sandy, increase the angle of slope slightly.

Installing a rigid liner

Stand a rigid pond liner in position and prop it up with cardboard boxes, both to check its orientation and to mark its perimeter on the ground.

Use a spirit level to plot key points on the ground (**1**) and mark them with small pegs. You will need to dig outside this line, so absolute accuracy is not required.

Lay a straightedge across the top and measure the depth of the excavation (**2**), including marginal shelves. Keep the excavation as close as possible to the shape of the liner, but extend it by 150mm (6in) on all sides. Compact the base and cover it with a layer of sharp sand 25mm (1in) deep. Lower the liner and bed it down firmly into the sand. Check that the pool stands level (**3**) and wedge it temporarily but firmly with wooden battens until the backfill of soil or sand can hold it.

Start to fill the liner with water from a hose and, at the same time, pour sifted soil or dry sand behind the liner (**4**). There's no need to hurry, as it will take some time to fill the pond. Reach into the excavation and pack soil under the marginal shelves with your hands.

When the liner is firmly bedded in the soil, either finish the edge with stones as for a flexible liner (see opposite) or re-lay turf to cover the rim of the liner.

SEE ALSO > Rigid liners 473, Building a rockery 477

Installing a flexible liner

Mark out the shape of the pond on the ground – a garden hose is useful for trying out curves. Before you start excavating the soil, look down from an upstairs window at the shape you have plotted, to make sure you are happy with the proportions of your pond.

Excavating and lining the pond

Excavate the pond to the level of the planting shelf, then mark and dig out the deeper sections (**1**). Remove sharp stones and roots from the sides and bottom of the excavation.

The slabs surrounding the pond need to be 18mm (¾in) below the turf. Cut back the turf to allow for the stones, and then every metre (3ft) or so drive wooden datum pegs into the exposed surround. Level the tops of all the pegs, and use a straightedge (**2**) to check the level across the pond as well. Remove or pack earth around the pegs to bring the surrounding soil to a consistent level.

When the surround is level, remove the pegs and, to cushion the liner, spread a 12 to 25mm (½ to 1in) layer of slightly damp sand over the base and sides of the excavation (**3**). Alternatively, cover the excavation with a proprietary pond-liner underlay.

Installing the liner

Drape the liner across the excavation with an even overlap all round. Hold it in place with bricks while you introduce water from a hose (**4**). Filling a large pond will take several hours, but check the liner regularly, moving the bricks as it stretches. A few creases are inevitable, but you can lose most of them if you keep the liner fairly taut and ease it into shape as the water rises.

When the level reaches 50mm (2in) below the edge of the liner, turn off the water. Cut off surplus liner with scissors, leaving a 150mm (6in) overlap all round (**5**). Push long nails through the overlap into the soil, so the liner can't slip.

Laying the surround

Select flat stones that follow the shape of the pond, with a reasonably close fit between them. Let the stones project over the water by about 50mm (2in).

Wearing goggles, use a bolster chisel to cut stones to fit the gaps behind the larger edging stones. Lift the stones one or two at a time and bed them on two or three strategically placed mounds of mortar, composed of 1 part cement : 3 parts soft sand (**6**).

Tap the stones level with a mallet and fill the joints with a trowel – use a paintbrush to smooth the joints. Don't drop mortar into the water, or you will have to refill the pond before introducing fish or plants.

Stopping your pond overflowing

Every garden pond needs topping up from time to time – and, as many gardeners know to their cost, it is all too easy to forget to turn off the water and flood the garden when the pond overflows. As a precaution, build a simple drain beneath the pond's edging stones to allow excess water to escape. This also provides a means of running electric flex into the pond to power a pump or lighting.

Cut corrugated-plastic sheet to make two strips, about 150mm (6in) wide and long enough to run under the edging stones. Pop-rivet the strips together to make a channel about 25mm (1in) deep.

Scrape earth and sand from beneath the liner to make a shallow recess that will accommodate the channel laid on top of the liner; then lay edging stones on top to hold the channel in place. Dig a small soakaway behind the channel and fill it up to the level of the stones with rubble topped with turf or fine gravel.

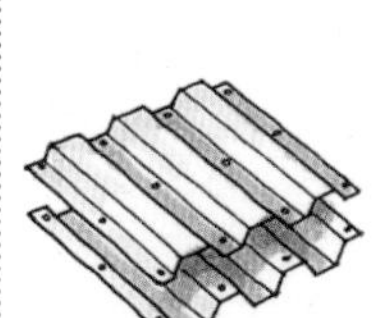

Drain components

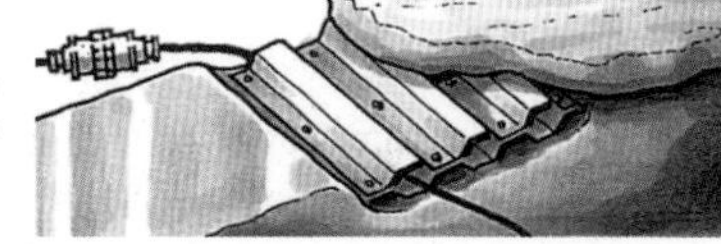

Place the drain beneath the edging stones

1 Dig the excavation as accurately as possible

4 Stretch the liner by filling the pond

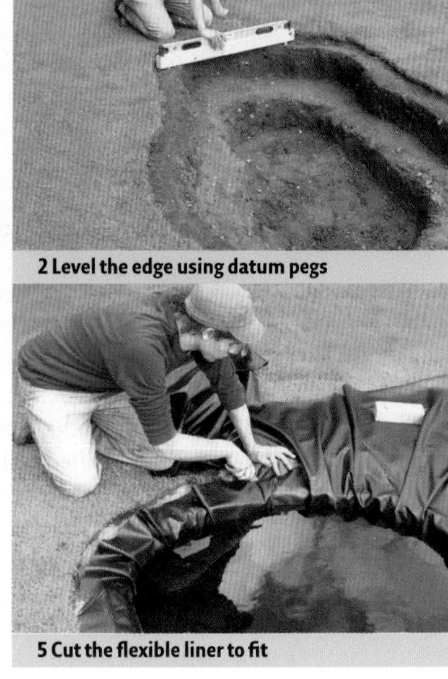

2 Level the edge using datum pegs

5 Cut the flexible liner to fit

3 Line the excavation with damp sand

6 Lay edging stones to complete the pond

SEE ALSO > Flexible liners 473, Cutting slabs 463, Pumps 476

Raised-edged ponds

If you want a more formal pond, you can build a raised edge using bricks or concrete blocks. A surround about 450mm (1ft 6in) high serves as a deterrent for small children while also providing seating. If you prefer a lower wall, say 225mm (9in) high, create planting shelves at ground level, digging the pond deeper in the centre. Place planting crates on blocks around the edge of a deep raised pond.

Building the edging

Lay 100 to 150mm (4 to 6in) concrete footings to support walls constructed from two skins of masonry set apart to match the width of flat coping stones. Allow for an overhang of 50mm (2in) over the water's edge, and lap the outer wall by 12 to 18mm (½ to ¾in). To save money, you may prefer to use cheap common bricks or plain concrete blocks for the inner skin, while reserving more expensive decorative bricks or facing blocks for the outer skin of the wall.

You can either line a raised pond with a standard flexible liner or order a prefabricated fitted liner to reduce the amount of creasing at the corners. Trap the edge of the liner underneath the coping stones.

Raised-edge pond
A beautifully designed water feature, built from artificial-stone blocks and coping slabs. The small cascade is powered by a submersible pump.

Partly excavated pond

Fully raised pond built with a cavity wall

Alternative pond edging

An edging of flat stones is useful for tending water plants and fish, but often a more natural setting is required. Incorporate a shelf around the pond – as for marginal plants, though this time it is for an edging of rocks. If you place them carefully, there is no need to mortar them in. Arrange rocks behind the edging to cover the liner.

In order to create a shallow beach-like edging, slope the soil at a very shallow angle and lay large pebbles or flat rocks upon the liner. You can merge them with a rockery, or let them form a natural water line.

To discourage cats poaching fish from the pond, create an edging of trailing plants – without a firm foothold, a cat will feel uncomfortable reaching into water. Bed a strip of soft wire netting in the mortar below the edging stones, and cut the strip to overhang the water by about 150mm (6in) as a support for the plants. Once established, the plants, will disguise the edge of the liner.

Rock-edged pond

Pebble-strewn shelf

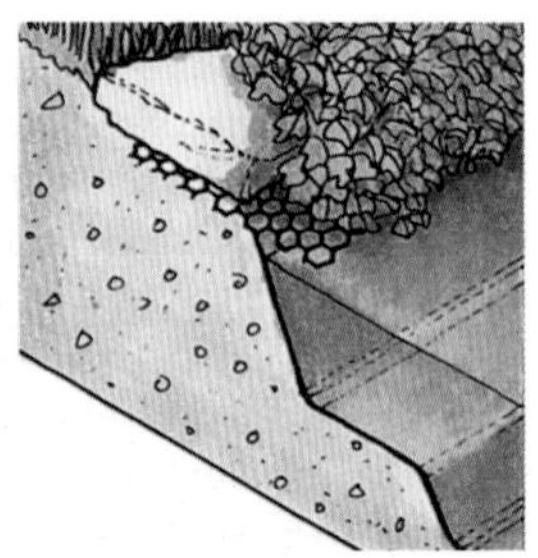

A wire edge supports plants

Pumps and fountains

Submersible pumps for fountains and cascades are operated either directly from the mains electrical supply or via a transformer that reduces the voltage. Get a qualified electrician to help you install the necessary equipment.

An extra-low-voltage pump is perfectly safe, and can be installed and wired simply. Place the pump in the water and run its cable beneath the edging stones, to a waterproof connector attached to the extension lead of a transformer installed inside the house. With this system, you can remove the pump for servicing without disturbing the extension cable or transformer. Run the pump regularly, to keep it in good working order.

Place a submersible cascade pump close to the edge of the pond, so that you can disconnect the hose running to the cascade when you need to service the pump. Stand a fountain unit on a flat stone, so the jet of water is vertical. Plant water lilies some distance away from a fountain, as falling water will encourage the flowers to close up.

Combination pump and filter

For efficient filtration of the pond water, install a separate filter tank, which you can bury beside the pond or hide with planting (see opposite). However, for small ponds with low fish stocks, you can buy a submersible pump with its own built-in filtration system and ultra-violet clarifier that will prevent the water turning green due to the presence of algae. Some units include a fountain head and an outlet to deliver water to a cascade.

SEE ALSO > Building Regulations 284, Using electricity outdoors 336, Garden lighting and pumps 341, Pond drain 341, Bricks 437–8, Concrete blocks 439, Footings 443, Laying bricks 444–9, Flexible liners 473

Building a rockery and cascade

A cascade running through a tastefully planted rockery adds a further dimension to a water garden. The technique for building a series of watercourses is not as complicated as you might expect – and at the same time you can cover much of the groundwork needed to create the rockery. Providing running water is also an ideal way of filtering your pond.

You will be surprised at the amount of soil produced by excavating a pond. To avoid waste and the trouble of transporting it to a local dump, use it to create a poolside rockery. If you include a filter and a small reservoir on the higher ground, you can pump water from the main pond through the filter into the reservoir and return it via the trickling cascade.

If you order them from a garden centre, buying a large enough number of natural stones to give the impression of a real rocky outcrop can work out extremely expensive. A cheaper way is to use cast reproduction rocks, which will eventually weather in quite well. However, your best option is to purchase natural stone direct from a local quarry. Rocks can be very heavy, so get the quarry to deliver as close to the site as possible; and hire a strong trolley to move individual stones about the garden.

A rockery and cascade are built as one operation, but for the sake of clarity they are described separately here.

Lifting large stones
Use a rope to lift and position large rocks.

Creating a cascade

Rigid-liner manufacturers make moulded cascade kits for embedding in rockeries – you simply cover the edges with stones, soil and trailing plants. Alternatively, you may prefer to create your own custom-made watercourse, using offcuts of flexible liner.

Installing the liner

So that the cascade can discharge directly into the main pond, form a small inlet at the side of the pond by leaving a large flap of flexible liner (**1**). Build shallow banks at each side of the inlet and line it with stones. Create a stepped watercourse ascending in stages to the reservoir. Line the watercourse with flexible liner, overlapping the offcuts on the face of each cascade. Tuck the edge of each lower piece of liner under the edge of the piece above, and hold the pieces in place with stones.

To retain water in small pools along the watercourse, cut each step with a slope towards the rear (**2**) and place stones along the lip for the desired effect (**3**). A flat stone will produce a sheet of water; a layer of pebbles will create a rippling cascade. As the construction work progresses, test the watercourse by running water from a garden hose.

Bury the flexible hose from the cascade pump in the rockery – making sure there are no sharp bends, which would restrict the flow of water. Attach the hose to the filter tank at the top of the watercourse (**4**). Conceal the tank behind rocks at the back of the rockery, where it can discharge filtered water into the reservoir.

A rigid plastic reservoir will have a lip moulded in one edge, which allows water to escape down the watercourse. If you use flexible liner to construct a reservoir (**5**), you will need to shape the edge to form a low point (**6**) and support a flat stone over the opening in order to hide the liner.

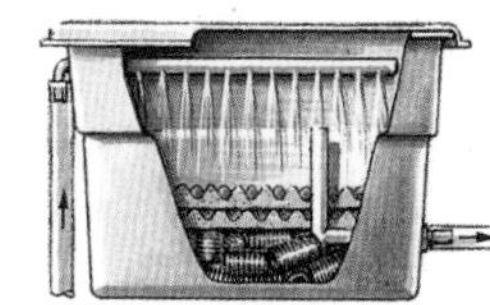

Filter tanks
Pumps usually have built-in foam filters, but these are not sufficient to keep the water in a sizeable pond clear and healthy enough for fish. It is preferable to install a plastic tank containing a combination of foam filters that will remove debris, plus a layer of biological filter medium to take out pollutants created by rotting vegetation and fish excreta.

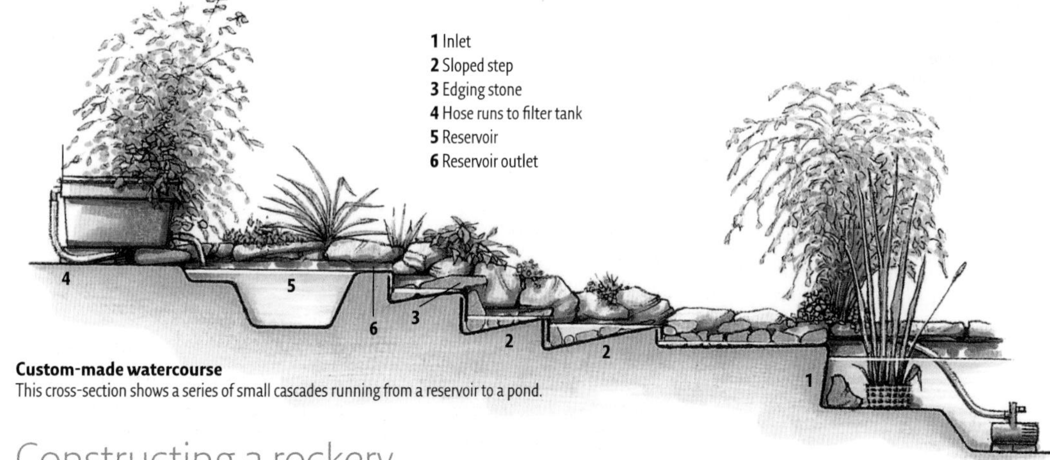

Custom-made watercourse
This cross-section shows a series of small cascades running from a reservoir to a pond.

Constructing a rockery

To create an illusion of layers of rock, select and place each stone in a rockery carefully. Stones placed haphazardly at odd angles tend to resemble a spoil heap rather than a natural outcrop. Take care not to strain yourself when lifting rocks. Keep your feet together and use your leg muscles to do the work, keeping your back as straight as possible. To move a particularly heavy rock, slip a rope around it.

Lay large flat rocks to form the front edge of the rockery, placing soil behind and between them to form a level platform. Compact the soil to anchor the rocks.

Lay subsequent layers of rock set back from the first, but not in a regular pattern. Place some to create steep embankments, others to form a gradual slope of wide steps. As the work progresses, brush soil off the rocks into the crevices.

SEE ALSO > Pond liners 473

Creating a pebble pool

One of the pleasures of a secluded garden is to be able to appreciate the sounds of birdsong and rustling trees and the rippling tones of running water. Given the right location, nature provides the wind and the birds – but in most cases we have to supply the running water ourselves.

Given sufficient space, most people opt for a fountain or a small cascade trickling into a garden pond. But what if you only have a small garden or patio? A space-saving water feature is the ideal solution. All you need is a submersible recirculating pump placed in a miniature moulded-plastic pool set in the ground and covered with decorative pebbles. This type of water feature can be situated close to the house – within earshot of the windows and conveniently placed for wiring into your power supply.

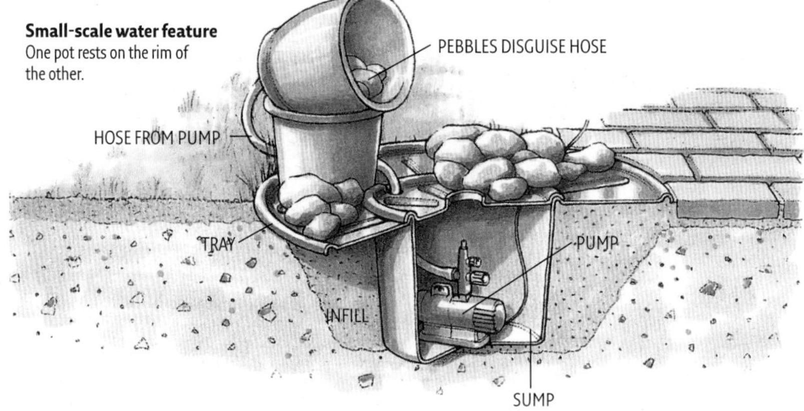

Small-scale water feature
One pot rests on the rim of the other.

Installing a moulded pool

Moulded-plastic pools take the form of shallow round or square trays with a deep bucket-like centre section or sump. A perforated or moulded lid is provided to cover the sump and to support the layer of pebbles that are used to disguise the feature once it has been installed.

Excavating the pool

Start by digging a hole slightly larger than the size of the tray. Make the hole deep enough to set the edge of the tray level with or just below the surface of the patio. You also need to allow for a layer of sand – to be placed on the compacted base of the excavated hole – on which to bed the sump. Set the sump in place and partially fill it with water to help keep it steady. Carefully backfill the sides with earth or sand; build up the infill until the sump and tray are well supported and level.

Fitting the pump

Following the manufacturer's instructions, connect the pump's cable to your power supply – which must include a residual current device (RCD), in order to protect the circuit. Ask an electrician to help with the installation.

Drill a discreet hole in a convenient door or window frame for the pump's cable, and seal the gap around the cable with silicone sealant.

Connect a length of hose to the pump's water outlet and then place the pump in the sump, which you can now fill with water. Test that the pump is working. Lead the hose to one side and fit the lid in place. It may be necessary to trim the edge of the lid in order to accommodate the hose.

Making the cascade

Two ceramic plant pots can make a simple cascade. Balance one of the pots at an angle on the rim of the other one and stand them on the tray. Feed the end of the hose into the drain hole in the bottom of the angled pot and then seal the hole with silicone sealant. You may find this is easier to do if you disconnect the hose from the pump once the hose has been cut to length.

With the pots in position, place some random-size pebbles around them to cover the sump tray. Put a few pebbles inside the angled pot, to weigh it down and conceal the end of the hose. Arrange potted plants to help disguise the hose at the rear. Run the pump, and try various arrangements of pebbles in and around the pots to create an attractive surround.

Routine maintenance

Top up the buried sump occasionally to make up for natural evaporation.

At the end of the season, remove the pump and clean the filter. This will mean rearranging the pebbles, which provides an opportunity to remove leaf litter and to clean up generally.

Water-feature pump
For a patio water feature, choose a small cascade-type pump. If you're in doubt about the performance of a particular unit, check the manufacturer's literature or, if need be, consult your supplier.

SEE ALSO > RCDs 297, Pumps and fountains 476

Tools and Skills

Your personal tool kit

If you talk to people who make a living using tools, you will find that they guard them jealously: they are loath to lend their tools, and even less likely to borrow them. The way a person uses or sharpens a tool – and even his or her working stance – will shape and modify it until it works better for its owner than in other hands.

Buying tools

When it comes to building up a kit, the choice of tools is equally personal. No two professionals' tool kits are identical, and each might select different tools to do the same job. The tools shown and described on the following pages will enable you to tackle all but the more specialized tasks involved in repairing, decorating, extending and maintaining your home and garden, although the final choice is yours.

No one buys a complete kit of tools all at once. Apart from the considerable cost, it makes more sense to buy tools as you need them. However, it's worth buying the best you can afford, as top-quality tools are always a wise investment. Not only will they perform well, but they will also last longer, provided they are used, stored and maintained properly.

We have listed the essential tools for each 'trade' under specific headings – plumber's tool kit, decorator's tool kit, and so on. But a great many tools are common to all trades, and you will find that you will gradually add to your tool kit as you tackle a growing range of activities. Start with the basic kit described below and gradually add to it as the need arises.

Basic starter kit

This basic kit will enable you to carry out essential repairs and maintenance, but you will need to extend the range to carry out most of the work described in this manual. Later in this chapter you will find detailed descriptions of each tool and how to use it.

- **Steel tape measure**
- **Spirit level**
- **Plumb line**
- **Universal panel saw**
- **Junior hacksaw**
- **Block plane**
- **Set of wood chisels** up to 25mm (1in) wide
- **Sharpening stone**
- **Claw hammer**
- **Pin hammer**
- **Club hammer**
- **Cold chisel**
- **Bolster chisel**
- **Pincers**
- **Flat-tip and cross-head screwdrivers** including small terminal screwdrivers for fitting electrical plugs
- **Craft knife**
- **Pliers**
- **Wire strippers**
- **Wallpaper scraper**
- **Filling knife**
- **Set of flat paintbrushes** up to 50mm (2in) wide
- **Paint roller and tray**
- **Sink plunger**
- **Open-ended spanners**
- **Medium-size adjustable spanner**
- **Radiator key**
- **Wire brush**
- **Power jigsaw**
- **Finishing sander**
- **Power drill**
- **Twist drills**
- **Masonry drills**
- **Stepladder**
- **Portable bench**

SEE ALSO > Woodworking tools 487–504, Building tools 510–13, Ladders 514–16, Plumbing tools 517–25, Electrical tools 526

Decorating tools

Most home owners collect a fairly extensive kit of tools for decorating their houses or flats. Although traditionalists will want to stick to tried-and-tested tools and to materials of proven reliability, others may prefer to try recent innovations aimed at making the work easier and faster for the home decorator.

• **Masking tape**
Low-tack self-adhesive tape is used to mask paintwork or glass in order to keep them free of paint when you are decorating adjacent surfaces. Wide tape, up to 150mm (6in) in width, is used to protect fitted carpets while you are painting the skirting boards.

• **Abrasives**
Wet-and-dry abrasive paper is used for smoothing new paintwork or varnish before applying the final coat. It consists of silicon-carbide particles glued to a waterproof backing paper. Alternatively, use a nylon-fibre pad impregnated with abrasive material.

Tools for preparation

Whether you're tiling, painting or papering, make sure the surface to which the materials will be applied is sound and clean.

Wallpaper and paint scrapers

The wide stiff blade of a scraper is for removing softened paint or soaked paper. A scraper with a blade 100 to 125mm (4 to 5in) wide is best for stripping wallpaper, while a narrow one, no more than 25mm (1in) wide, is better for removing paint from window frames and doorframes.

A serrated scraper will score impervious wallcoverings so that water or stripping solution can penetrate faster.

Shavehook

This is a special scraper for removing old paint and varnish. A straight-sided triangular shavehook is fine for scraping flat surfaces, but one with a combination blade can be used on concave and convex mouldings too.

Hot-air stripper

An electric hot-air stripper softens old paint prior to removing it with a scraper. With most strippers, you can adjust the temperature. Interchangeable nozzles are designed to concentrate the heated air or direct it away from window panes.

Wire brushes

You can use a handbrush with steel-wire 'bristles' to remove flaking paint and particles of rust from metalwork before repainting it. However, the job becomes easier if you use a rotary wire cup brush fitted into the chuck of an electric drill. Whatever method you adopt, wear goggles or safety glasses to protect your eyes.

Vinyl gloves

Most people wear ordinary household 'rubber' gloves as protection for their hands when washing down or preparing paintwork - but tough PVC work gloves are more hardwearing and will protect your skin against many harmful chemicals.

Wallpaper scorer

Running a scorer across a wall punches minute perforations through the paper so that water or steam can penetrate faster.

Filling knife

A filling knife looks like a paint scraper, but has a flexible blade for forcing filler into cracks in timber or plaster. Patch large areas of damaged wall with a plasterer's trowel.

Mastic guns

Flexible mastic is used to seal joints between materials with different rates of expansion, which would eventually eject a rigid filler. Mastic is usually applied from a cartridge clipped into a spring-loaded gun.

Steam stripper

To remove wallpaper quickly, either buy or hire an electric steam-generating stripper. All steam strippers work on similar principles - but follow any specific safety instructions that come with the machine.

Fill the stripper's reservoir with water and plug the tool into a socket outlet. Hold the steaming plate against the wallpaper until it is soft enough to be removed with a scraper.

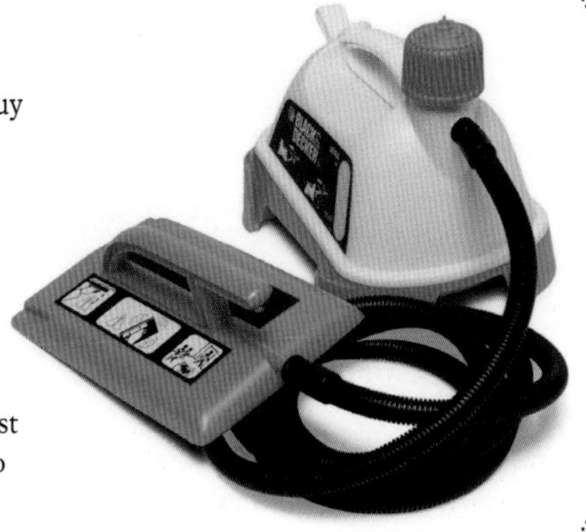

SEE ALSO > Stripping paper 51, Stripping wood 58–9

Paintbrushes

Some paintbrushes are made from natural animal hair. Hog bristle is the best, but it is often mixed with inferior horse hair or ox hair to reduce cost. Synthetic-bristle brushes are generally the least expensive, and are quite adequate for the home decorator.

Banister brush
A household banister brush gives excellent results when used for painting rough or rendered walls.

Paint kettle
To carry paint to a work site, decant a little into a cheap, lightweight plastic paint kettle.

Paint shield and scraper
There are various plastic and metal shields for protecting glass when you are painting window frames and glazing bars. If the glass does get spattered, it can be cleaned with a blade clipped into a special holder.

Flat paintbrushes

The filling is set in rubber, pitch or resin, and is bound to the wooden or plastic handle with a pressed-metal ferrule. You will need several sizes, up to 62mm (2½in), for painting, varnishing and staining woodwork.

Cutting-in brush

The filling of a cutting-in brush, or 'bevelled sash tool', is cut at an angle so that you can paint moulded glazing bars right up into the corners and against the glass. Most painters make do with a 12mm (½in) flat brush.

Radiator brush

Unless you take a radiator off the wall for decorating, you will need a special brush to paint the back of it and the wall behind.

There are two types of radiator brush. One has a standard flat paintbrush head at right angles to a long wire handle. The other is like an ordinary paintbrush but has an angled plastic handle.

Wall brush

When applying emulsion paint with a brush, use a flat 150mm (6in) wall brush designed for the purpose.

Choosing a brush

The bristles of a good brush – the 'filling' – are densely packed. When you fan them with your fingers, they should spring back into shape immediately. Flex the tip of the brush against your hand to see if any bristles work loose. Even a good brush will shed a few bristles at first, but never clumps of bristles. The ferrule should be fixed firmly to the handle.

Bristle types

Bristle is ideal for paintbrushes, since each hair tapers naturally and splits at the tip into even finer filaments that hold paint well. Bristle is also tough and resilient.

Synthetic 'bristle' (usually made of nylon) is designed to resemble the characteristics of real bristle, and a good-quality nylon brush will serve most painters as well as a bristle one.

Cleaning paintbrushes

Water-based paints

As soon as you finish working, wash the bristles with warm soapy water, flexing them between your fingers to work the paint out of the roots. Then rinse the brush in clean water and shake out the excess. Smooth the bristles and slip an elastic band round their tips to hold the shape of the filling while it is drying.

Solvent-based paints

If you're using solvent-based paints, you can suspend the brush overnight in enough water to cover the bristles, then blot it with kitchen paper before you resume painting.

When you have finished painting, brush out excess paint onto newspaper, then flex the bristles in a bowl of thinners. Some finishes need special thinners – so check for this on the container. Otherwise, use white spirit or a chemical brush cleaner. Wash the dirty thinners from the bristles with hot soapy water, then rinse the brush.

Hardened paint

If paint has hardened on a brush, soften it by soaking the bristles in brush cleaner. It will then become water-soluble and will wash out easily with hot water. If the old paint is very stubborn, dip the bristles in some paint stripper.

Soak the bristles in brush cleaner

Bind the bristles together until the brush dries

SEE ALSO > Paint stripper 59, Using brushes 66, 68, Painting wood 71–3, Using a paint shield 73, Painting radiators 83

Pads and rollers

A paint roller is the ideal tool for painting a large area of wall or ceiling quickly. Paint pads help inexperienced decorators to apply paints and wood dyes quickly and evenly; although they aren't universally popular, no one would dispute their usefulness for painting large flat areas. Paint pads are unlikely to drip paint provided they are loaded properly.

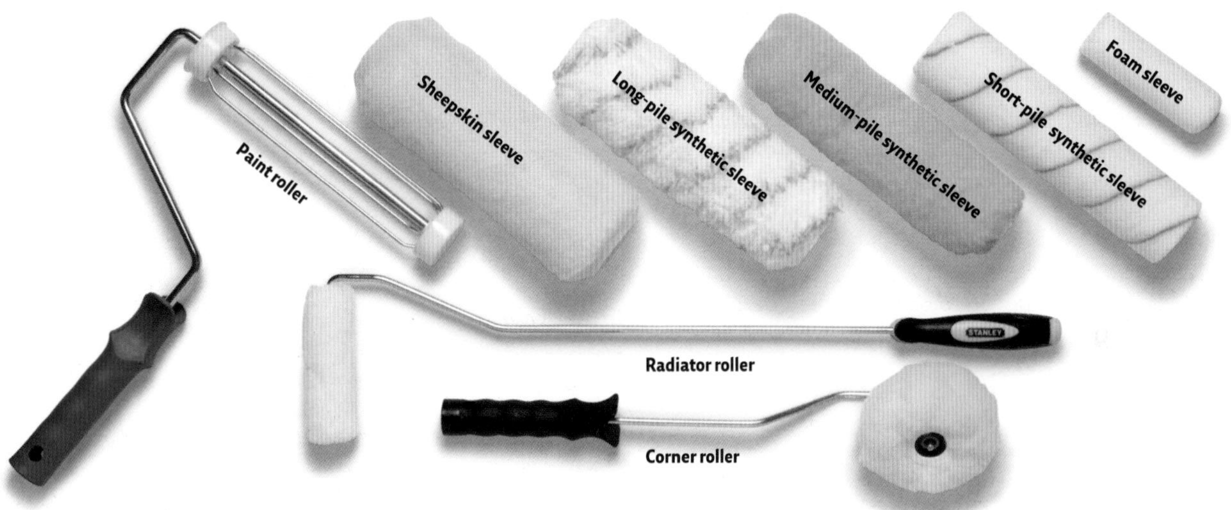

Paint pads

Standard pads

There is a range of rectangular paint pads for decorating walls, ceilings and flat woodwork. These standard pads have a short mohair pile on their painting surfaces and most have detachable handles.

Corner pad

A mohair-covered pad wrapped around a triangular applicator spreads paint simultaneously onto both sides of an internal corner. Paint into the corner first, then pick up the wet edges and continue with a standard pad.

Sash pad

A sash pad has a small mohair sole for painting the glazing bars of sash windows. Most sash pads incorporate plastic guides to stop them straying onto the glass.

Pad tray

Pads and trays are normally sold as sets. The trays have a loading roller or ribbed shelf that distributes paint evenly onto the sole of a pad drawn across it.

Paint rollers

The cylindrical sleeves that apply the paint are interchangeable and slide onto a roller attached to the cranked handle of the tool. The sleeves are very easy to swap or to remove for washing.

Sizes of roller sleeves

Sleeves for standard rollers are 175mm (7in) or 225mm (9in) long, but it is also possible to buy other sizes.

Types of roller sleeve

You can buy roller sleeves of various materials to suit different surface textures and kinds of paint. Most sleeves are made of sheepskin or synthetic fibres, cropped to different lengths. A sheepskin sleeve can hold more paint than one that is made from synthetic fibre, although it costs about 25 per cent more.

Choose a long-pile sleeve for emulsion or masonry paint on rough or textured surfaces. A medium-pile sleeve is best for emulsion or satin-finish oil paints on smooth surfaces. For gloss paints, use a short-pile sleeve.

Inexpensive plastic-foam sleeves are unsatisfactory for applying oil paints or emulsions. They leave air bubbles in the painted surface, and the foam often distorts as it dries after washing. But they are cheap enough to be thrown away after use with finishes, such as bituminous paint, that would be difficult to remove even from a short-pile sleeve.

Use a coarse expanded-foam sleeve for applying textured paints and coatings.

Corner roller

You can't paint into a corner with a standard roller. So unless there are to be different adjacent colours, paint the corner first with a shaped corner roller.

Radiator roller

This is a thin roller on a long wire handle for painting behind radiators and pipes.

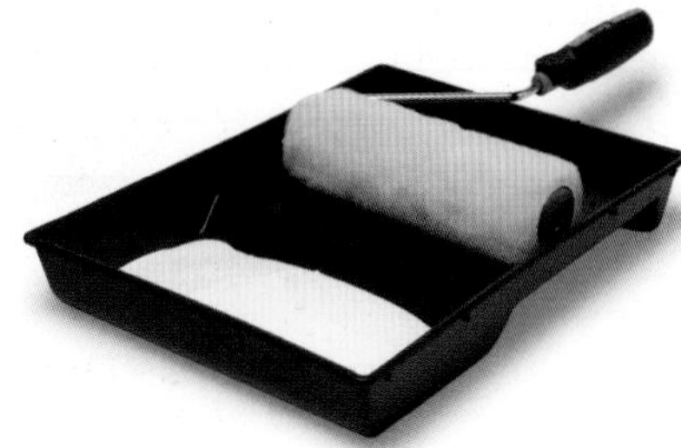

Roller tray

A paint roller is loaded from a sloping plastic or metal tray, the deep end of which acts as a paint reservoir. Load the roller by rolling paint from the deep end up and down the tray's ribbed slope once or twice, to get even distribution on the sleeve.

SEE ALSO > Using a paint pad 69, Using a roller 69, Cleaning pads and rollers 484

Cleaning paint pads

Before dipping a new pad into paint for the first time, brush it with a clothes brush to remove any loose filaments.

When you have finished painting, blot the pad on old newspaper then wash it in the appropriate solvent - water, white spirit or brush cleaner, or any special thinner recommended by the paint manufacturer. Squeeze the foam and rub the pile with gloved fingertips, then wash the pad in hot soapy water and rinse it.

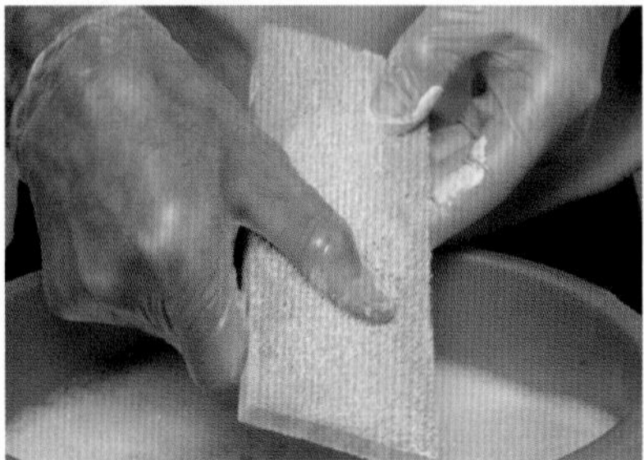

Rub solvent into the pile with gloved hands

Cleaning a paint roller

Remove most of the excess paint by running the roller backwards and forwards across some old newspapers. If you are planning to use the roller next day, apply a few drops of the appropriate thinner to the sleeve and then wrap it in plastic. Otherwise, clean, wash and rinse the sleeve before the paint has time to dry.

Water-based paints

If you've been using emulsion or acrylic paint, flush most of it out under running water then massage a little liquid detergent into the pile of the sleeve and flush it again.

Solvent-based paints

To remove solvent-based paints, pour some thinner into the roller tray and slowly roll the sleeve back and forth in it. Squeeze the roller and agitate the pile with gloved hands. When the paint has dissolved, wash the sleeve in hot soapy water.

Run the roller over newspaper to remove paint

Paint-spraying equipment

Spraying is worth considering when you are planning to paint the outside walls of a building. Spraying equipment is readily available, even from large DIY stores, and you can hire it. It's possible to spray most exterior paints and finishes if they are thinned properly, but tell the hire company which paint you intend to use, so they can supply the right spray gun with the correct nozzle. Get goggles and a respirator at the same time.

Compressor-operated spray

With this equipment, the paint is mixed with compressed air to emerge as a fine spray. Some compressors deliver air to an intermediate tank and top it up as the air is drawn off by the spray gun, but most hired compressors supply air directly to the gun.

The trigger opens a valve to admit air, and at the same time opens the paint outlet at the nozzle. The paint is drawn from a container, usually mounted below the gun, and mixes with air at the tip. Most guns have air-delivery horns at the sides of the nozzle in order to produce a fan-shaped spray.

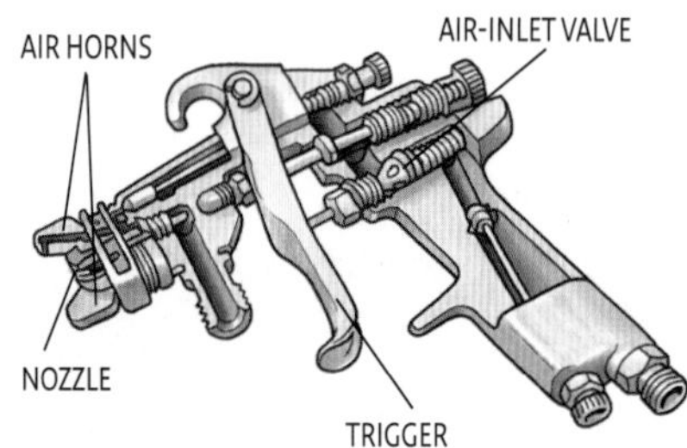

Components of a spray gun

Spray gun and compressor

Airless sprayer

In an airless sprayer, an electric pump delivers the paint itself at high pressure to the spray gun. The paint is picked up through a plastic tube inserted in the paint container, and the pump forces it through a high-pressure hose to a filter and pressure regulator, which you adjust to produce the required spray pattern. The paint leaves the nozzle at such high pressure that it can penetrate skin. Most spray guns of this kind therefore have safety shields on their nozzles.

Preparation

As far as possible, plan to work on a dry and windless day. Also, allow time to mask off windows, doors and pipework.

Follow the setting-up and handling instructions supplied with the equipment. Unless you are an experienced sprayer, practise beforehand on an inconspicuous section of wall.

SEE ALSO > Using a spray gun 66

Using sprayers safely

Follow safety recommendations supplied with the sprayer, and take the following precautions:

- Wear goggles and a respirator when spraying.
- Don't spray indoors without proper extraction equipment.
- Atomized oil paint is highly flammable, so extinguish any naked lights and never smoke when you are spraying paint.
- Don't leave spraying equipment unattended, especially where there are children or pets.
- If the spray gun has a safety lock, engage it whenever you are not actually spraying.
- Unplug the equipment and release the pressure in the hose before trying to clear a blocked nozzle.
- Never aim the gun, even when it is empty, at yourself or anyone else.

Spraying faults

Streaked paintwork
An uneven, streaked finish will result if you do not overlap the passes of the gun.

Patchy paintwork
Coverage won't be consistent if you move the gun in an arc. Point it directly at the wall and move parallel to it.

Orange-peel texture
A wrinkled paint film resembling the texture of orange peel is usually caused by spraying paint that is too thick.

Alternatively, if the paint seems to be the right consistency, you may be moving the gun too slowly.

Paint runs
Runs will occur if you apply too much paint – probably by holding the gun too close to the surface you are spraying.

Powdery finish
This is caused by paint drying before it reaches the wall. The remedy is to hold the gun a little closer to the wall's surface.

Spattering
If the pressure is too high, the finish will look speckled. To avoid spattering, lower the pressure till the finish is satisfactory.

Paperhanging tools

You can improvise some of the tools needed for paperhanging. However, even purpose-made equipment is inexpensive, so it's worth having a decent kit.

Tape measure
A retractable steel tape is best for measuring walls and ceilings in order to estimate the amount of wallcovering you will need.

Plumb line
Any small weight suspended on fine string can be used to mark the position of one edge of a strip of wallpaper. Hold the end of the line close to the ceiling, allow the weight to come to rest, and then mark the wall at points down the length of the line.

A purpose-made plumb line has a pointed metal weight called a plumb bob. The more expensive versions have a string that retracts into a hollow plumb bob containing coloured chalk, so the string is coated with chalk every time it is withdrawn. With the string stretched taut, snap it like a bowstring to leave a chalk line on the wall or ceiling.

Paste brush
Use either a wide wall brush or a short-pile roller to apply paste to the back of wallcoverings.

Paperhanger's brush
This is used for smoothing wallcoverings onto a wall or ceiling. Its bristles should be soft, so as not to damage delicate paper, but springy enough to provide the pressure to squeeze out air bubbles and excess paste.

Seam roller
Use a hardwood or plastic seam roller to press down the seams between strips of wallpaper – but don't use one on delicate or embossed wallcoverings.

Paperhanger's scissors
Any fairly large scissors can be used for trimming wallpaper to length, but special paperhanger's scissors have extra-long blades to achieve a straight cut.

Craft knife
Use a knife to trim paper round light fittings and switches, and to achieve perfect butt joints by cutting through overlapping edges of paper. The knife must be extremely sharp to avoid tearing the paper, so use one with disposable blades that you can change as soon as one gets blunt. Some craft knives have short double-ended blades clamped in a metal or plastic handle. Others have long retractable blades that are snapped off in short sections to leave a new sharp point.

Pasting table
You can paste wallcoverings on any flat surface, but a purpose-made pasting table provides a much more convenient working surface. It stands higher than the average dining table – but is only 25mm (1in) wider than a standard roll of wallpaper, which makes it easier to spread paste without getting it onto the worktop.

SEE ALSO > Pasting wallcoverings 87, Hanging wallcoverings 88–94

Tiling tools

Most of the tools in a tiler's kit are for applying ceramic wall and floor tiles. Different tools are required for laying soft tiles and vinyl sheeting.

Spirit level
You will need a spirit level for setting up temporary battens in order to align a field of tiles both horizontally and vertically.

Profile gauge
A profile gauge is used for copying the shape of door mouldings or pipework to provide a pattern so you can fit soft floorcoverings. As you press the steel pins of the profile gauge against the object you wish to copy, they slide back, replicating the shape.

Serrated trowel
Make a ridged bed for tiles by drawing the toothed edge of a plastic spreader or steel tiler's trowel through the adhesive.

Tile cutter
Most tilers use a lever-action jig fitted with a steel wheel (similar to a glass cutter's) for scoring the glazed surface of ceramic tiles. The tile snaps cleanly along the scored line (see below right).

Tile saw
A tile saw has a bent-metal frame that holds a thin wire rod under tension. The rod is coated with particles of tungsten carbide, which are hard enough to cut through ceramic tiles. As the rod is circular in section, it will cut in any direction, making it possible to saw along curved lines.

Grout spreader or rubber float
The spreader has a hard-rubber blade mounted in a plastic handle. The float looks similar to a wooden float but has a rubber sole. Both tools are used for spreading grout into the gaps between ceramic tiles.

Nibblers
It is impossible to snap a very narrow strip off a ceramic tile. Instead, score the line with a tile cutter then break off the waste little by little with tile nibblers. These resemble pincers but have sharper jaws, made of tungsten-carbide, that open automatically when you relax your grip on the spring-loaded handles.

Tile files
To smooth a cut edge, use either an inexpensive abrasive-mesh file or an abrasive-coated file fitted with a handle.

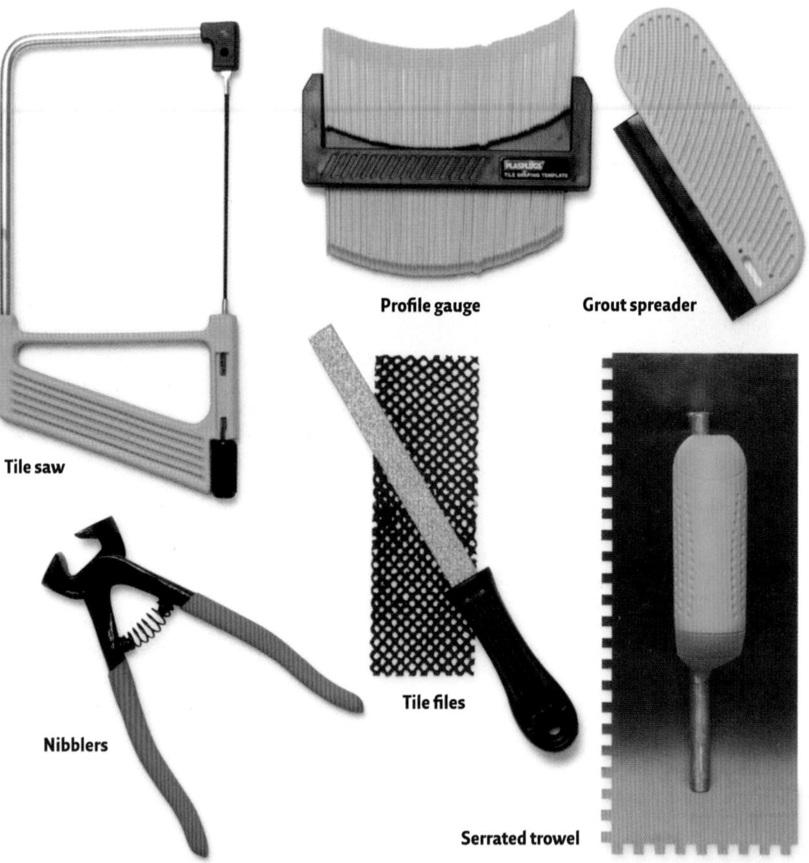

Cutting tiles

Lever-action jig
A jig makes it easy to cut and fit tiles for the margins around a field of tiles. If you need to cut a lot of tiles, especially thick floor or wall tiles, buy a sturdy lever-action jig. After pushing the cutting wheel across the tile's glazed surface, press down on the lever to snap the tile.

Press down on the lever to snap the tile

Powered wet saw
If you need to cut thick unglazed tiles, hire a powered wet saw with a diamond-coated blade. The same tool is ideal for cutting corners out of ceramic tiles that have to be fitted around an electrical socket or switch.

Feed the tile at a steady pace into the blade

SEE ALSO >Tiling walls 98–101, Tiling floors 103–7

Woodworking tools

A full woodworking tool kit is enormous, but for general home maintenance you can make do with a fairly limited selection of handtools and a few basic power tools.

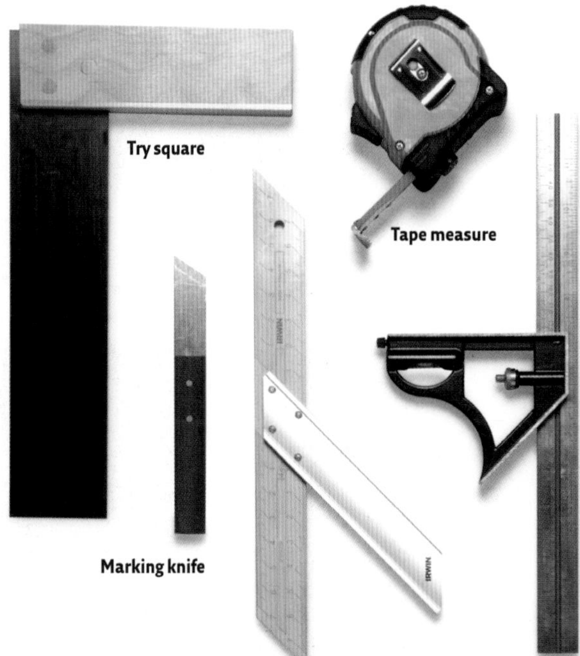

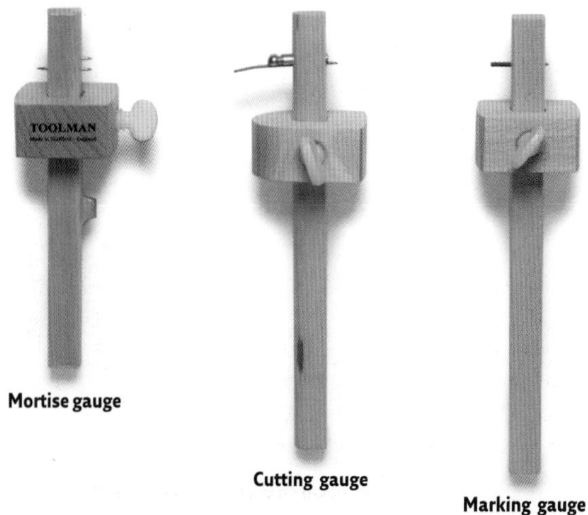

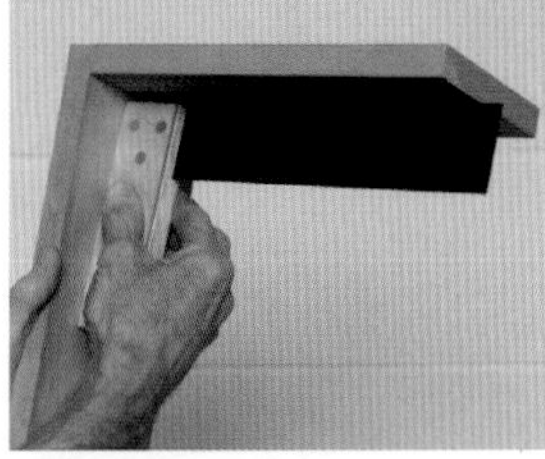

Checking for square
Check an internal angle with a try square.

Checking planed timber
View the work against the light to check you are planing square.

Tools for measuring and marking

Take care of your measuring and marking tools. If they are thrown carelessly into a tool box, try squares can be knocked out of true and gauges will become blunt and inaccurate.

Tape measure and folding rule

Although a folding boxwood rule is the traditional cabinet-maker's tool, a modern retractable steel tape measure is more versatile. Choose a tape that is about 5m (16ft) long and which can be locked open at any point, so that even a large workpiece can be measured single-handedly. Don't let the spring-loaded tape snap back into its case, or the hook riveted to the end of the tape will eventually work loose.

Try square

A try square is used for checking the accuracy of jointed corners and planed timber, and also for marking out work-pieces that are to be cut 'square'. Some try squares are made with the top of the stock cut at 45 degrees for marking out mitre joints.

It's worth buying the largest square you can afford: they are available with blades up to 300mm (1ft) long.

Mitre square

This is used like a try square, but for marking out 45-degree mitre joints.

Combination square

A combination square is a very versatile tool. Essentially it is a try square, but instead of a fixed blade it has a calibrated rule that slides in the stock to make a blade of any length up to 250mm (10in). This serves as a useful depth gauge. The head has an angled face for marking mitres and incorporates a small spirit level for checking vertical and horizontal surfaces.

Marking knife

Before sawing timber, mark the cutting line with a knife – this is more accurate than marking with a pencil and prevents the fibres of the wood breaking out when you saw across the grain. The blade of a marking knife is ground on one side only; run the flat face against the square or bevel.

Marking gauge

With a marking gauge, you can score a line parallel to an edge. Slide the stock along the beam until it is the required distance from the pin. Press the face of the stock against the edge of the timber and, with the pin touching the wood's surface, push the tool away from you to scribe the line.

Cutting gauge

If you try to score a line across the grain with a marking gauge, the pin will tear the surface – whereas a cutting gauge, which has a small sharp blade, is ideal for the purpose. The blade is held in place by a removable wedge.

Mortise gauge

This type of gauge has two pins, one fixed and the other movable, for marking the parallel sides of mortise-and-tenon joints. First set the points to match the width of the mortise chisel and then adjust the stock to place the mortise the required distance from the edge of the wood. Mark the limits of the mortise, using a try square (**1**), then score the two lines with the gauge (**2**). With the same setting, mark the tenon on the rail.

1 Mark the joint ends

2 Score the lines

SEE ALSO > Woodworking joints 505–9

Hand-held saws

Although power tools take much of the hard work out of sawing timber, for a simple job it's often easier to reach for a simple hand-held saw rather than set up a circular saw or a powered jigsaw.

Handsaws

Handsaws, with their flexible unsupported blades, are used to convert solid timber and man-made boards.

Ripsaw
The ripsaw is designed for sawing solid timber along its length. Each of its teeth is like a tiny chisel that slices the timber along its grain. Alternate teeth are 'set' – bent outward in opposite directions – so that the 'kerf' (the groove cut in the timber) is slightly wider than the thickness of the blade. If saws were not set, they would jam in the kerf.

Crosscut saw
Unlike ripsaw teeth, which are filed square with the face of the blade, crosscutting teeth are filed at an angle to form points that score lines along both sides of the kerf before the wood in between is removed. This allows the saw to cut across the grain of solid timber without tearing the fibres.

Panel and universal saws
The teeth of a panel saw are set and shaped like those of a crosscut saw but, being smaller and closer together, they cut a finer kerf. The saw is used mainly for cutting man-made boards.

With teeth similar in shape to those of a crosscut saw, a universal saw is designed to cut both with and across the grain.

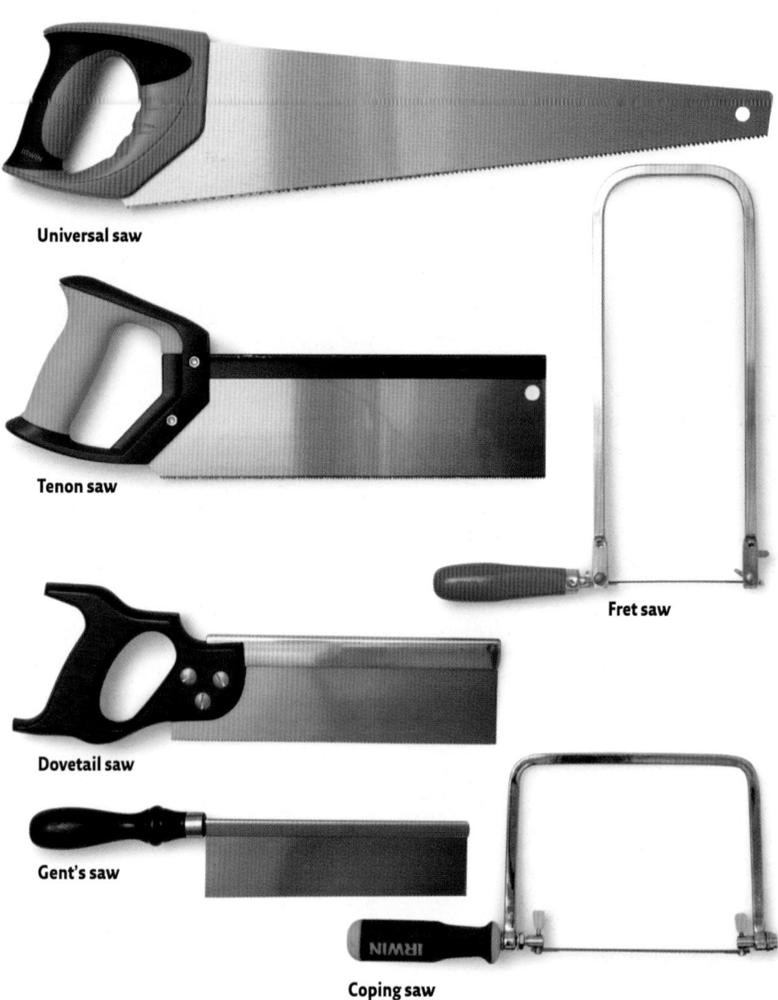

Universal saw

Tenon saw

Fret saw

Dovetail saw

Gent's saw

Coping saw

Backsaws

The blade of a backsaw is stiffened with a heavy metal strip folded over its top edge. The relatively fine teeth make it ideal for cutting joints.

Tenon saw
A tenon saw has small teeth shaped and set like those of a crosscut saw. It is the perfect saw for general-purpose woodworking and joinery.

Dovetail saw
Use a dovetail saw for fine cabinet-making.

Gent's saw
This cheap alternative to a dovetail saw has a straight handle.

Storing saws

Glue dowel pegs into a stout batten and screw it to the wall, then hang your saws from the pegs.

SEE ALSO > Sharpening saws 490, Power saws 491

Frame saws

A frame saw is fitted with a very slim blade for cutting curves. So it doesn't bend, the blade is held taut by the strong metal frame.

Fret saw

A fret-saw blade is so fine that the spring of the frame is able to keep it under tension. The blade is held at each end in a clamp tightened by a thumbscrew or wing nut, with the teeth of the blade pointing towards the handle.

Coping saw

A coping saw has teeth that are coarse enough to cut fairly thick timber as well as relatively thin man-made boards.

A coping saw's blade has to be replaced if it breaks or when it gets blunt. Loosen the handle with a few anticlockwise turns. Hook the new blade into the pin furthest from the handle, then press the frame down on your workbench and locate the other end of the blade. Tension the blade by turning the handle clockwise. Make sure the teeth point away from the handle and that the two pins are aligned so the blade isn't twisted.

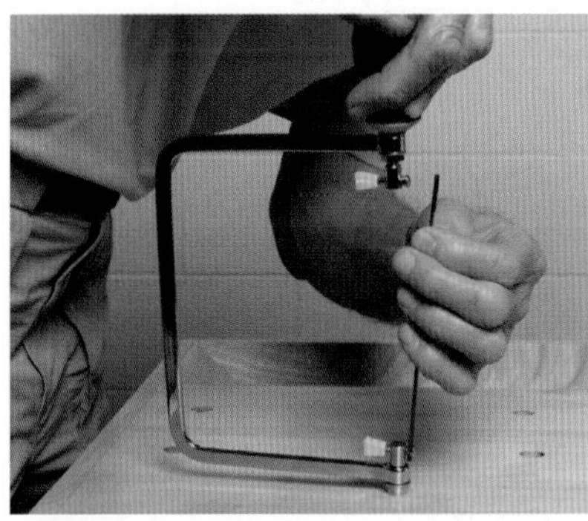

Fitting a coping-saw blade

Using saws

Hold a handsaw or backsaw with your forefinger extended towards the tip of the blade. This keeps the blade in line with your forearm and helps you to make a straight cut.

When ripsawing, support the board on sawhorses. Start at one end using short backward strokes only, steadying the saw blade with the tip of your thumb against its flat face. Lengthen your stroke once you have established the kerf, and continue cutting with slow regular strokes, using the full length of the blade. Whenever necessary, move the sawhorses to provide a clear path for the blade. As you approach the end of the board, turn it round and start a fresh cut from that end, sawing back to meet the original kerf.

When crosscutting, support the offcut with your free hand and finish the cut with slow gentle strokes to avoid breaking off the last few wood fibres.

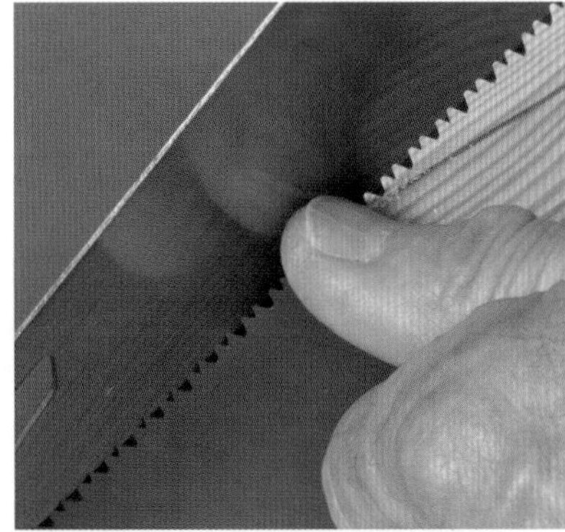

Steady the blade with the tip of your thumb

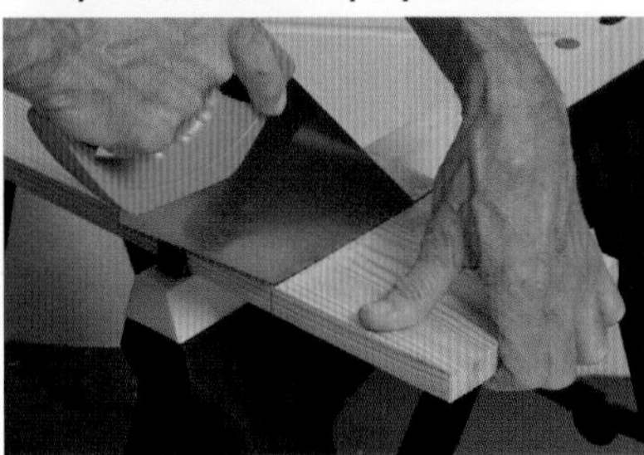

Support the offcut with your free hand

Cutting with a back saw

Support the work in a vice or on a bench hook, and hold the saw at a shallow angle to establish the kerf. As the cut progresses, gradually level the blade until you are sawing parallel to the face of the wood.

A bench hook is a simple jig, used when crosscutting narrow sections of wood with a backsaw. Steady the 'hook' against the front edge of the bench, then hold the work firmly against the top block with one hand.

Hold a backsaw at a shallow angle to start the cut

Support the work on a bench hook

Using a coping saw

The blade is held between pins that swivel so you can turn it in the direction of the cut, swinging the frame out of the way.

Use a coping saw to cut a large hole in a piece of wood. Having marked out the hole, drill a small one inside the outline. Pass the blade through the small hole and then connect it to the saw frame. Cut out the hole, adjusting the angle of the blade to the frame as required, then dismantle the saw to free the blade.

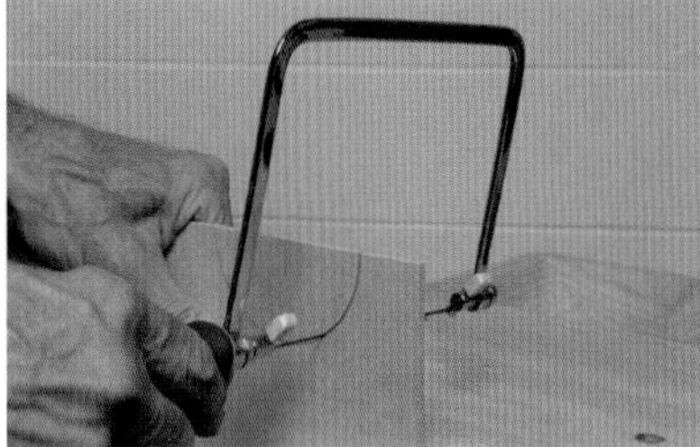

Adjust the blade of a coping saw to clear the work

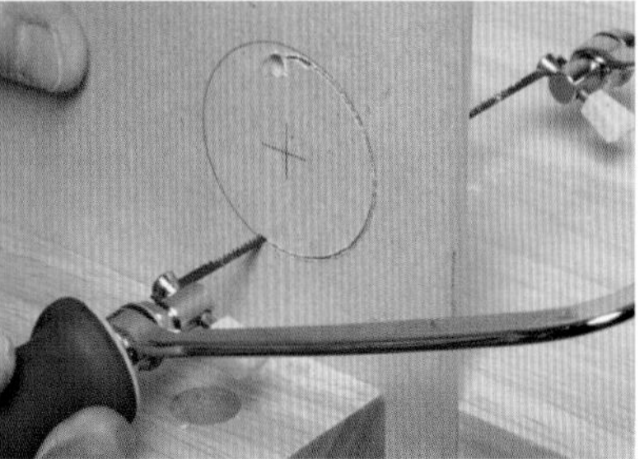

Cutting a hole with a coping saw

Using a fret saw

Hold the wood over the edge of the workbench so you can saw with the blade upright, pulling on it from below.

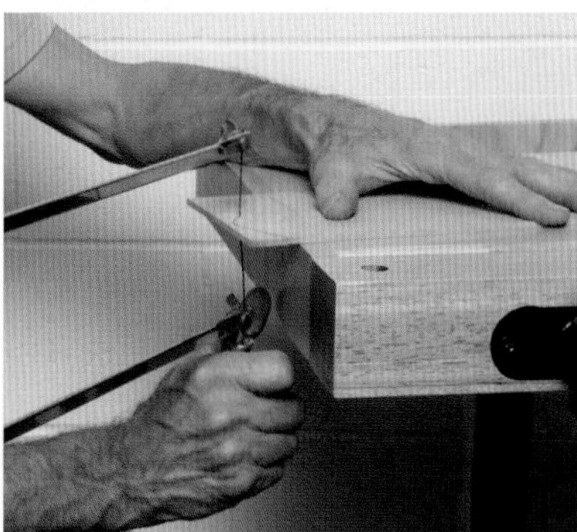

Keep the blade of a fret saw upright

Using a mitre box
A mitre box has slots set at 45 degrees to guide the saw blade when you are cutting mitre joints. There are also slots set at 90 degrees to guide the blade when cutting square butt joints.

Padsaw or keyhole saw

A padsaw is for cutting holes in panels. Having a blade that is wider than a coping saw's, it's easier to use on straight cuts. As there's no frame to restrict its movement, a padsaw can be used for jobs such as cutting the slot for a letter box.

SEE ALSO > Sharpening saws 490, Jigsaws 491, Hole saws 491

Sharpening saws

In order to cut properly, saws must be sharpened carefully with special tools – so you may prefer to have them sharpened professionally, especially any that are finer than a tenon saw. If you want to keep them in tip-top condition yourself, you will need to buy a saw file for sharpening the teeth and a saw set for bending the teeth.

Saw-sharpening tools

A saw file is triangular in section. In theory, its length should relate precisely to the spacing of the saw's teeth, but in practice you can use one file about 150mm (6in) long for handsaws and another, 100mm (4in) long, for a tenon saw. You can also buy a file guide, which locates over the saw's teeth and keeps the file at a constant angle.

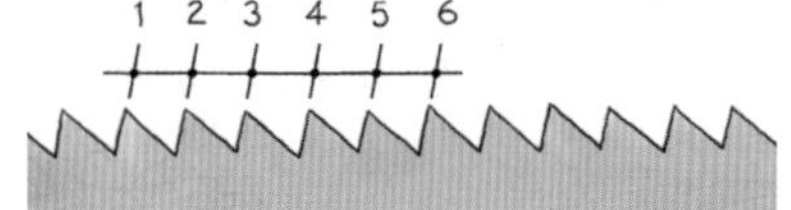

Count the number of points per 25mm (1in)

Closing the handles of a saw set squeezes the saw tooth between a plunger and an angled anvil, which you set first to correspond with the number of tooth points per 25mm (1in) on the saw blade. To set the anvil, close the handles and release the locking screw at the end of the tool. Turn the anvil till the required setting number on its edge aligns with the plunger, then tighten the locking screw.

Topping a saw

1 Mount a file in a hardwood block

Topping restores all of a saw's teeth to the same height. It is not essential every time a saw is sharpened, but a light topping will produce a spot of bright metal on each point that helps you to sharpen the teeth evenly.

Near the bottom edge of a block of hardwood, cut a groove that will grip a smooth hand file (**1**). Clamp the saw, teeth uppermost, between two battens held in a vice and, with the wood block held against the flat of the blade, pass the file two or three times along the tops of the teeth (**2**).

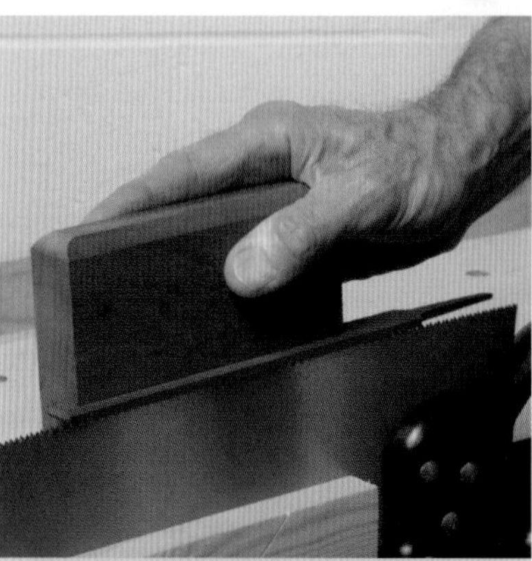

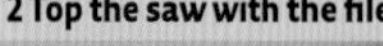

2 Top the saw with the file

Setting the teeth

Adjust the saw set to the right number of points (see above) and, starting at one end of the saw, place the set over the first tooth facing away from you. Align the plunger with the centre of the tooth. Hold the set steady and squeeze the handles together (**3**). Set every other tooth – those facing away from you – then turn the saw round and set those in between.

3 Set the saw teeth

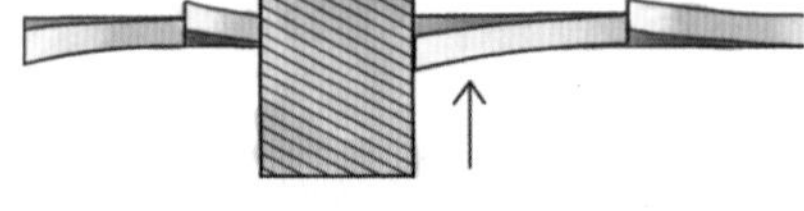

Sharpening a ripsaw

Clamp the blade between two battens with its teeth projecting just above the edges of the wood. Starting near the toe of the saw, place the saw file on the first tooth bent away from you and against the leading edge of the tooth next to it. Holding the file square to the blade, make two or three strokes until the edge of the tooth is shiny right up to its point and half of the bright topping spot has disappeared. Working towards the handle, file alternate teeth in this way; then turn the saw round and sharpen the teeth in between until the bright spots are completely removed.

Sharpening a crosscut saw

Use a similar method, but hold the file at an angle of 65 degrees to the blade, with the tip of the file pointing in the direction of the saw handle.

SEE ALSO > Handsaws 488, Backsaws 488, Hand file 524

Power saws

Power saws are invaluable for cutting heavy structural timbers and large man-made boards. Cordless saws are especially convenient when working outdoors or when you need to turn off mains electricity.

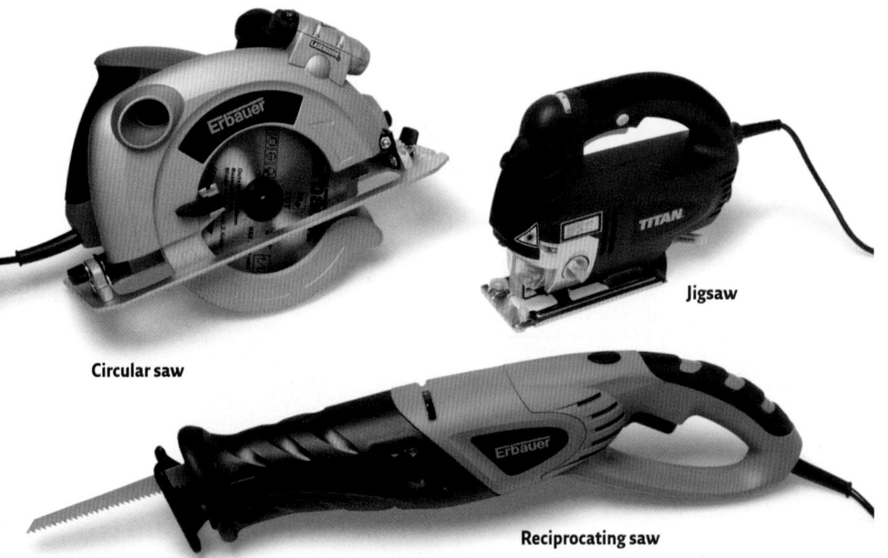
Jigsaw

Circular saw

Reciprocating saw

Portable circular saws

When you buy or hire a circular saw, choose one with a blade no smaller than 190mm (7½in) in diameter. Its motor will be powerful enough to give a blade speed able to cut thick timber and man-made boards without straining the saw or scorching the work.

You can buy blades designed specifically for ripping or crosscutting, but a chisel-tooth blade can perform both functions reasonably well. The best-quality blades have carbide-tipped teeth. There are also special blades and abrasive discs for cutting metal and stone.

On most circular saws, you can adjust the angle of the blade for cutting bevels.

Reciprocating saws

These saws are especially useful for jobs such as cutting openings in stud partitions.

Power jigsaws

Mains-powered and cordless jigsaws are primarily for making curved cuts in timber and man-made boards. Although they invariably have guide fences for straight cutting, the fences are rarely sturdy enough to stop the blade wandering.

Discard jigsaw blades when they become blunt. As jigsaw blades are fairly cheap, it's worth buying some of the special blades for cutting plastics, metal, plasterboard and ceramics.

Circular-saw safety

- Always unplug a circular saw before you adjust or change the blade.
- Fit new blades with the teeth at the bottom of the blade facing in the direction of the cut.
- Circular saws must have a fixed blade guard and a lower guard that swings back as the cut proceeds. Never use the saw without these guards in place, and always make sure that the lower guard closes automatically when the blade clears the work.
- The work must be securely held, either on sawhorses or a workbench.
- Never have the electrical flex in front of the saw blade.
- Don't force the blade into the wood. If it jams in the kerf, back off a little until it returns to full speed.
- Make sure the blade has stopped spinning before you put down a circular saw.
- Don't wear loose clothing, a necktie or necklace, as any of these could become entangled in the machine.

Using a circular saw

When accuracy of cut isn't too important, you can use a circular saw freehand, employing the notch in the sole plate as a sight to guide the blade along a marked line. Place the tip of the sole plate on the work and align the notch with the line. Switch on and let the blade run up to speed, then advance the saw steadily.

Hole saws
You can buy a set of hole saws for cutting perfectly round holes of different diameters. These are attached to a special twist drill that fits into the chuck of a power drill.

Making straight cuts

Circular saws have removable and adjustable fences to guide the blade parallel to the edge of the work. When necessary, you can extend the fence by screwing a narrow batten to it.

Alternatively, clamp a strip of wood onto the work to guide the edge of the saw's sole plate.

Clamping the strip at different angles across the wood allows you to make mitres and other bevelled cuts.

Using a jigsaw

Rest the front of the sole plate on the edge of the work, squeeze the trigger, and then advance the blade into the work. Don't force or twist the blade, or it will break. Having switched off, let the blade come to rest before you put the saw down.

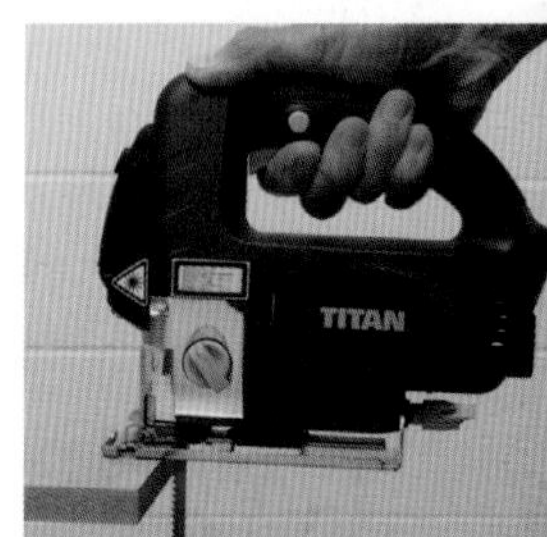

Starting a straight cut

Cutting holes with a jigsaw

The simplest way to cut a large hole in a panel is first to drill a starter hole into which you can insert the jigsaw blade, but you can start by 'plunge cutting'. Tilt the jigsaw onto the front edge of its sole plate, with the tip of the blade just above the surface of the work, then switch on the saw and gradually lower the blade into the wood until it is upright and the sole plate is flat on the surface.

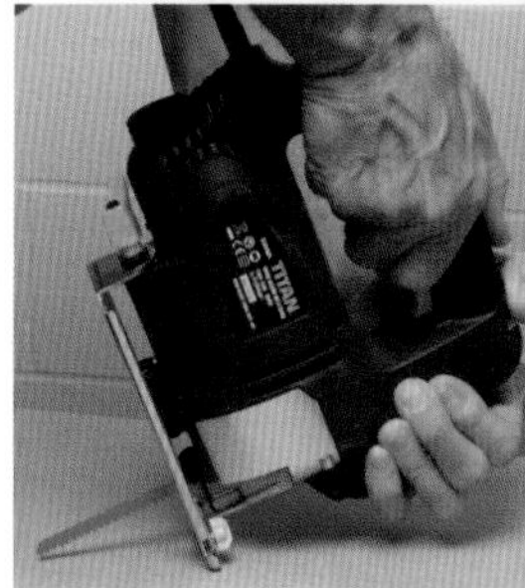
Plunge cutting

SEE ALSO > Crosscut saw 488, Ripsaw 488, Frame saws 488–9

Hand planes

There are a great many planes for shaping and smoothing wood, but unless you intend to take up woodwork seriously, you need only a few basic tools.

Bench planes

Bench planes are general-purpose tools for smoothing wood to make joints between boards or to level the surface of several boards glued together. Bench planes are all similar in design, differing only in the length of the sole.

Smoothing plane

Jack plane

Jointer plane

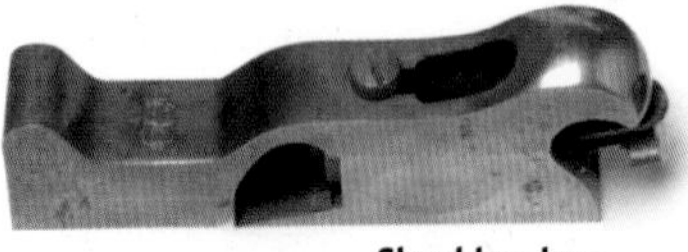

Shoulder plane

Block plane

Surform tools
These tools have disposable blades made with small regularly spaced teeth with sharp cutting edges, facing forwards. There are Surform planes and files, all used primarily for shaping curved components.

Jointer plane

This is the longest bench plane, with a sole as much as 600mm (2ft) long. The jointer is designed for truing up the long edges of boards that are to be butted and glued together. It is also useful for levelling large flat panels, since the long sole bridges minor irregularities until the blade shaves them down – whereas a plane with a shorter sole would simply follow the uneven surface.

Jack plane

A jack plane 350 to 375mm (1ft 2in to 1ft 3in) long is a good all-purpose tool. If you can afford only one bench plane, choose a jack plane.

Smoothing plane

A finely set smoothing plane is used for putting the final surface on a piece of timber after it has been reduced to size with a jack plane or jointer.

Block plane

The blade of a block plane is mounted at a shallow angle so that its edge can slice smoothly through the end grain of timber. Since it is small and lightweight (you can hold the tool in the palm of one hand), a block plane is also ideal for all kinds of fine trimming and shaping.

Shoulder plane

A shoulder plane is not a tool you need every day – but, because its blade spans the whole width of its squarely machined body, it is ideal for trimming the square shoulders of large joints and rebates. With the body removed, the exposed blade can trim a rebate right up to a stopped end.

Replaceable-blade plane

This type of bench plane is equipped with short disposable blades that are discarded as soon as they become blunt.

Storing planes

It is good practice never to place a plane sole-down on the bench while you are working – always lay it on its side.

Similarly, a plane should be stored on its side, and with the blade withdrawn to preserve its cutting edge.

For long-term storage, dismantle and clean the plane, then wipe all bare metal parts with an oily rag to prevent rusting.

Oil a plane prior to long-term storage

Adjusting a plane

Before you use a bench plane, adjust the angle and depth of the blade. Check the angle by 'sighting' down the sole of the plane from the toe, and use the lateral-adjustment lever behind the blade to set the cutting edge so that it projects an equal amount across the width of the sole.

Use the knurled adjusting nut in front of the handle to set the depth to take off a fine shaving.

Use the lever to set the angle of the blade

SEE ALSO > Sharpening planes 494

Planing flat and square

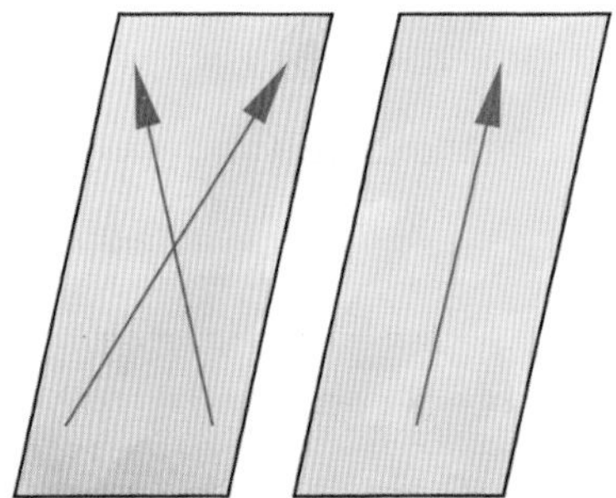

Planing a wide flat surface
To plane a wide surface as flat as possible, first work across it diagonally in two directions, following the general direction of the grain. Check that the work is flat by holding a steel straightedge against the surface, then finish by planing parallel with the grain, taking very fine shavings.

Planing a square edge
Keep the plane flat on the edge of the work by holding the toe down with the thumb of your free hand. Press the fingers of the same hand against the side of the wood, to guide the tool on a straight course.

Trimming end grain

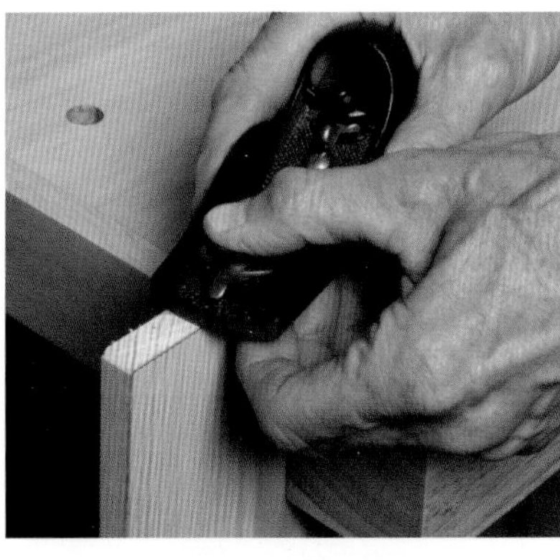

Trimming with a block plane
Cut a line all round the work with a marking knife, then set the workpiece vertically in a vice. To prevent the wood splitting, form a chamfer down to the line on one edge by planing towards the centre. Plane the end square, working from the other edge down to the marked line until you have removed the chamfer.

Using a shooting board
You can also trim end grain using a bench plane on its side, running it on a jig known as a shooting board. The blade must be sharp and finely set. Holding the work against the jig's stop prevents the wood splitting.

Power planers

A power planer is particularly useful for smoothing and shaping large structural timbers, and perfect for trimming the bottom edge of a door in order to accommodate a new carpet. When the tool is fitted with a guide fence, its revolving cutter block can be used for planing rebates.

Most power planes can be fixed upside down in a bench-mounted frame so that you can pass timber across the cutters, using both hands.

Blunt planer blades are not designed to be sharpened – simply replace them with a new pair.

Spokeshaves

A spokeshave is a miniature plane for shaping curved edges.

Use one that has a flat base to shape convex curves, and one with a bellied base when shaping concave curves. When using either tool, shape the curve from two directions so as to work with the grain at all times. Sharpen a spokeshave cutter as you would the blade of a plane.

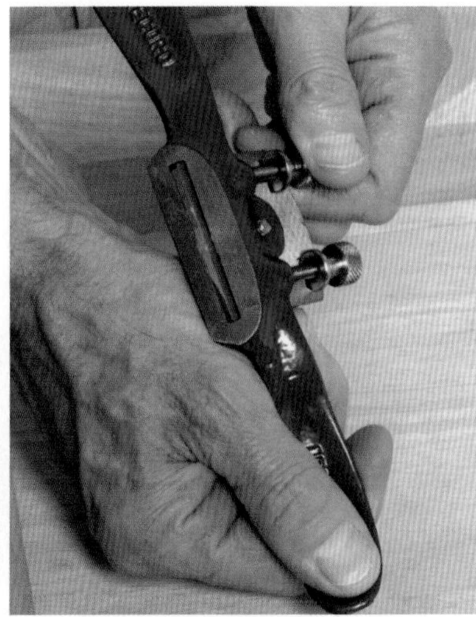

Adjusting the cutter
Use the two adjusting screws to produce a fine setting, then turn the central locking screw to 'fix' the spokeshave's cutter.

Using a spokeshave
With your thumbs on the back edges of the handles, push the spokeshave away from you. Rock the tool backwards or forwards as you work, to produce a continuous shaving.

SEE ALSO > Marking knife 487

Sharpening planes

To keep its sharp cutting edge, a plane blade must be honed on a flat oilstone. Choose one with a medium grit on one side – to remove metal quickly – and fine grit on the other side for the final honing of the edge.

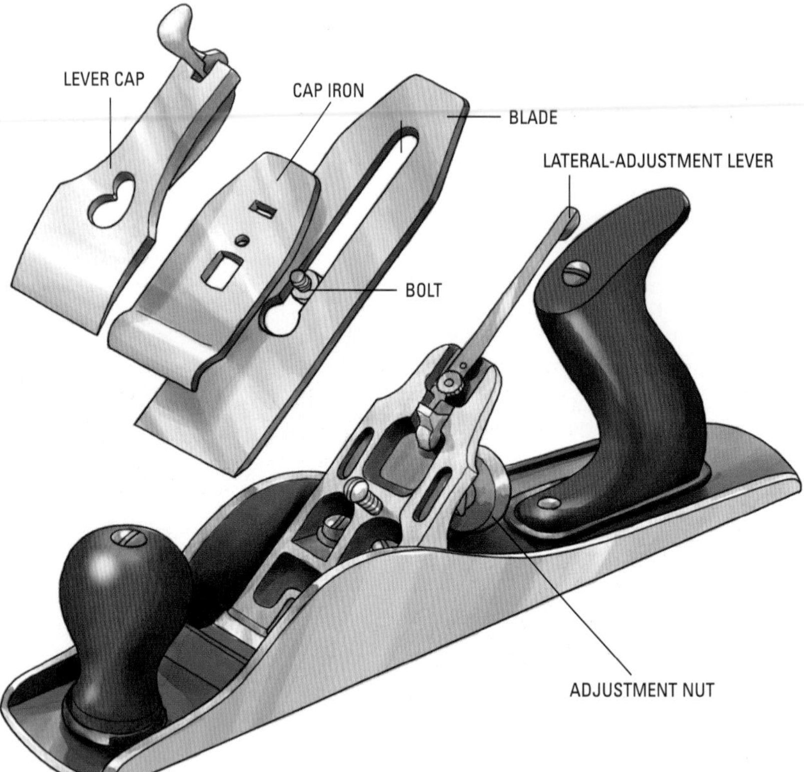

Removing and replacing a blade

The blade of a bench or block plane is clamped in place by a metal lever cap. Slacken the lever to remove the cap and lift the blade out of the plane. The blade of a bench plane has a cap iron bolted to it to break and curl the shavings as they are trimmed from the wood. Undo the fixing bolt with a screwdriver and remove the cap iron before you sharpen the blade.

When you replace the cap iron, place it across the blade (**1**) then swivel it until they are aligned (**2**), making sure you don't drag the cap iron across the cutting edge in the process. Now slide the iron to within 1mm (1⁄16in) of the cutting edge (**3**).

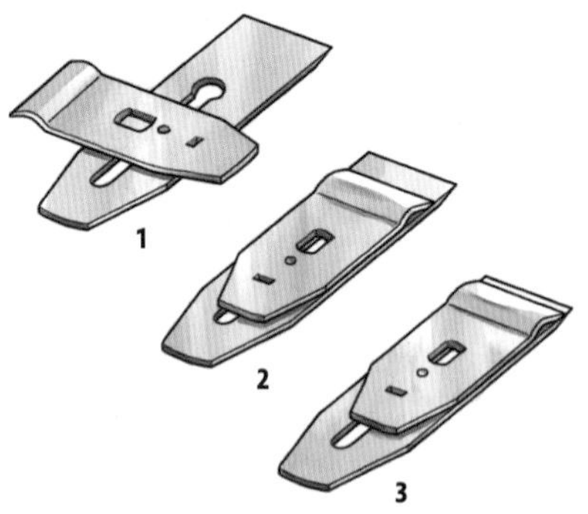

Honing a blade

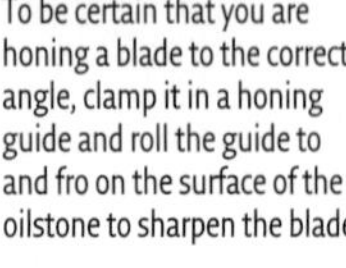

Using a honing guide
To be certain that you are honing a blade to the correct angle, clamp it in a honing guide and roll the guide to and fro on the surface of the oilstone to sharpen the blade.

The cutting edge of a plane blade will have been ground to an angle of about 25 degrees. The object of sharpening it on an oilstone is to hone the leading edge only to about 30 degrees.

Hold the blade against the stone at the correct angle and rub it to and fro to produce a sharp edge. A wide blade must be held at an angle across the stone so that the whole edge is in contact with the surface (**1**). Keep the stone lubricated with a little oil while you work.

Honing creates a burr along the cutting edge. Remove it by laying the back face of the blade flat on the stone (**2**) and making several passes along the surface.

1 Hone the cutting edge on an oilstone

2 Then remove the burr

Grinding blades

If you chip the cutting edge of a plane blade (against a nail, for example), regrind it on a bench grinder. Hold the blade against the tool rest and move the cutting edge from side to side against the revolving wheel until it is straight and clean. Use only light pressure and dip the blade into water regularly to cool it. Finally, sharpen the ground edge by honing it on an oilstone.

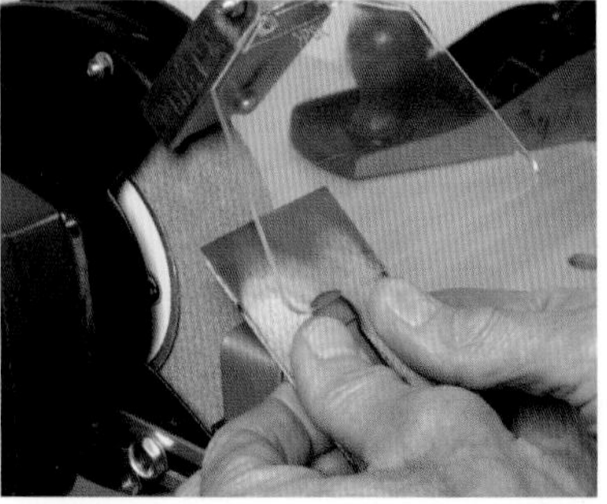

Move the blade slowly from side to side

SEE ALSO > Bench planes 492

Power routers

A power router is a sophisticated tool that cuts grooves, housings and rebates and a wide range of mouldings. A router cutter revolves so fast that it produces as clean a cut across the grain as with it.

When using a power router, always let the bit run up to full speed before you allow it to come into contact with the work; and lift it clear of the groove or moulding before you switch off.

Because the bit revolves clockwise, you have to feed the machine against the rotation when moulding an edge - so the cutter pulls itself into the wood.

Router cutters and bits

Router cutters are fitted into a collet at the base of the tool and are locked in place by tightening a nut. Pressing down on the handles plunges the cutter through a hole in the base plate and into the wood. A straight grooving cutter must be used in conjunction with a fence or guide. The cylindrical pilot tip of a moulding or rebating cutter runs against the edge of the work to prevent the cutter biting too deeply.

Although it is possible to grind and hone power-router bits yourself, they must be perfectly symmetrical. It is therefore generally better to have them sharpened professionally.

Routing edge mouldings

Rest the baseplate of the router on the upper surface of the work, and when the cutter has run up to full speed feed it against and along the edge of the timber.

If you need to mould all four edges of a rectangular piece of wood, shape the end grain first and then run the router along each side of the workpiece.

Cutting an edge moulding

Cutting grooves and housings

To cut a groove parallel to an edge, fit and set the adjustable guide fence or run the edge of the router baseplate against a batten clamped to the work.

To cut a wide groove, use two parallel battens to guide the bit along both sides of the groove, then remove the waste from the centre.

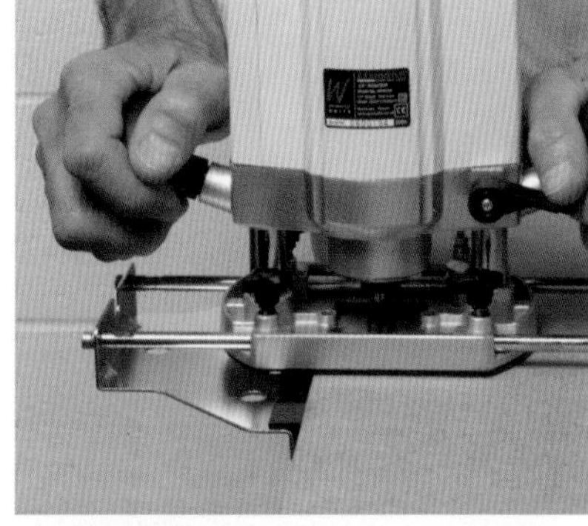

Use the fence to guide a cutter on a straight path

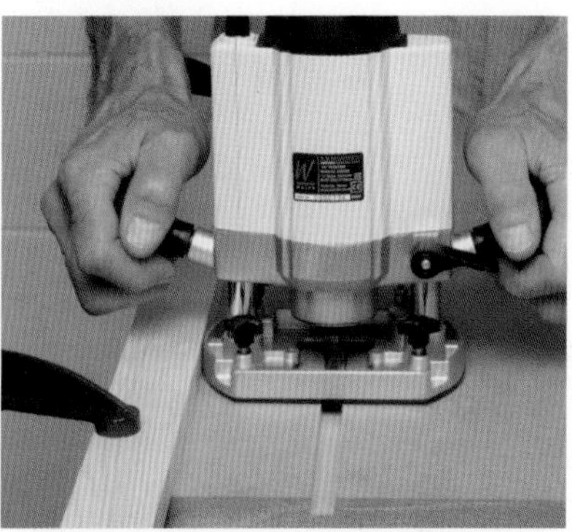

Or run the baseplate against a clamped batten

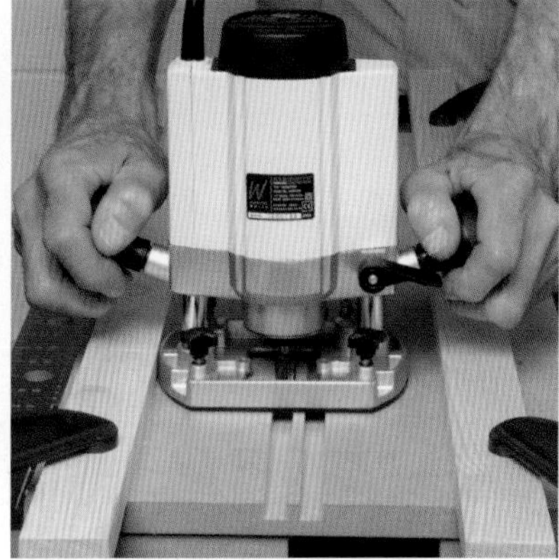

Use two guide battens when cutting a wide groove

SEE ALSO > G-cramps 503

Chisels and gouges

Chisels are general-purpose woodcutting tools, but are mostly used to remove the waste from joints or to pare and trim them to size. Gouges are similar to wood chisels, but their blades are curved in cross section for work such as cutting the shoulders of a joint to fit against a turned leg or scooping out the waste from a 'finger pull' on a drawer front or sliding cupboard door. Wood chisels and gouges have handles made of boxwood or impact-resistant plastic.

Chisel sizes
The size of a chisel refers to the width of its cutting edge. Although chisels range in width from 3mm (1/16in) to 50mm (2in), a selection of sizes up to 25mm (1in) should be sufficient for most woodworking purposes.

Firmer chisel

A firmer chisel has a strong, flat rectangular-section blade. Designed for chopping out waste wood, it is strong enough to be driven with a mallet or hammer – though you should never use a hammer on a wooden handle.

Bevel-edge chisel

A bevel-edge chisel is used for paring – especially for trimming undercuts such as dovetail joints or housings. The bevels enable you to work the blade in spaces that would be inaccessible to a firmer chisel. However, a bevel-edge chisel is not as strong as a firmer chisel and may break if used for heavy work. If a little extra force is needed to drive the chisel forward, use the ball of your hand or push down on the handle with your shoulder.

Gouges

The cutting edge of an in-cannel gouge is formed by grinding the inside of the curved blade. This type of gouge is used for trimming rounded shoulders.

An out-cannel gouge is ground on the outside, so that the blade will not be driven into the wood when it is being used to scoop out shallow recesses.

Bevel-edge chisel

Firmer chisel

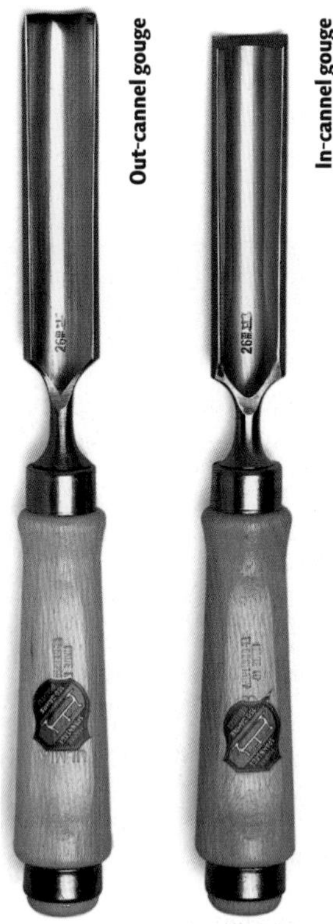

Storing chisels

You can make a rack for chisels and gouges by gluing spacer blocks between two strips of plywood, leaving a slot for the blades. Screw the rack to the wall behind your workbench, so the tools are within easy reach.

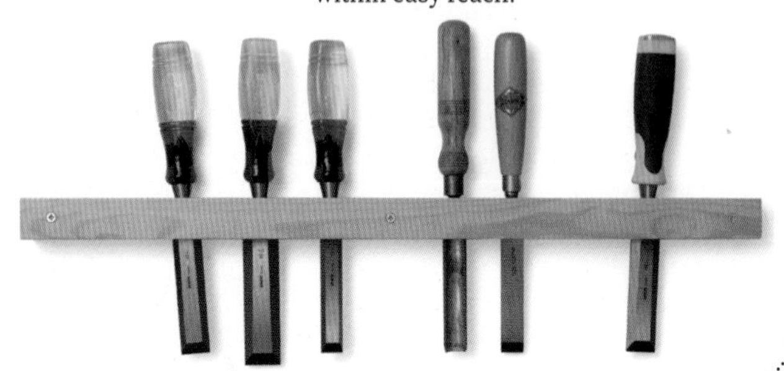

Removing waste wood

Don't chop out too much waste in one go – the wood will split or the chisel will be driven over the line of the joint, resulting in a poor fit. Remove the waste a little at a time, working back to the marked line. Use a mallet at first, but finish off by hand.

Chop out the waste a little at a time

Paring with a chisel

Finish a joint by paring away very thin shavings, using a bevel-edge chisel. Control the blade with finger and thumb, steadying your hand against the work, while applying pressure to the tip of the handle with your other hand.

Hold the blade between finger and thumb

SEE ALSO > Carpenter's mallet 501

Sharpening chisels and gouges

Sharpen a chisel as you would a plane blade – but hone it across the whole surface of the oilstone in a figure-of-eight pattern to avoid uneven wear on the stone.

Honing an out-cannel gouge

Stand to the side of the oilstone and rub the bevel of the gouge along the stone from end to end in a figure-of-eight pattern (1). At the same time, rock the blade from side to side to hone the curved edge evenly. Remove the burr from the inside of the cutting edge with a slipstone (2) – a small oilstone shaped to fit a variety of gouge sizes.

1 Honing the gouge

2 Removing the burr

Honing an in-cannel gouge

Sharpen the bevel on the inside of an in-cannel gouge by honing with a slipstone (1). Then remove the burr by holding the back of the blade flat on an oilstone and rocking it from side to side while sliding it up and down the stone (2).

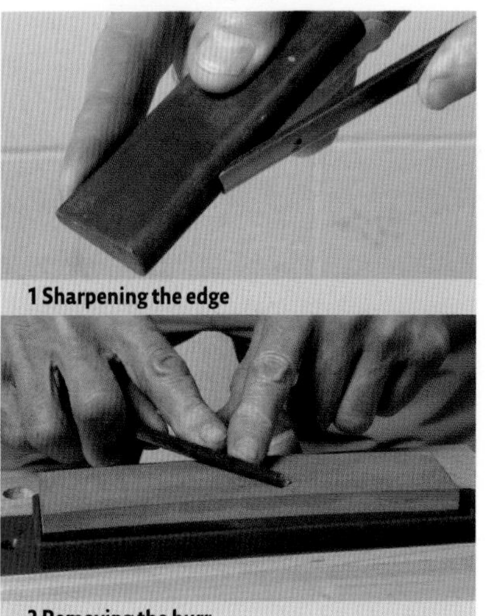

1 Sharpening the edge

2 Removing the burr

Abrasives and scrapers

Abrasive papers are used for putting a smooth finish on wood. Sand in the direction of the grain – tiny scratches made by cross-grain sanding may not appear until the work has been polished or varnished. Flat surfaces are sanded smooth, but you can get a better finish with a cabinet scraper.

Abrasive papers

Still widely referred to as 'sandpaper', abrasive papers are graded by the size and spacing of the grit. There are coarse, medium and fine grits – also designated by number (the higher the number, the finer the grit). On 'open-coat' papers the particles are spaced wide apart to reduce clogging. The more tightly packed 'closed-coat' papers produce a finer finish.

Glasspaper is inexpensive and relatively soft. Use it for the first stages of sanding, especially on softwoods. Garnet paper is harder and produces a better finish. Reddish in colour, it is used for sanding softwoods and hardwoods. Silicon-carbide paper – usually known as wet-and-dry paper – is most commonly used for smoothing paint-work, but you can also use it dry to produce an extra-smooth finish on hardwoods.

Using abrasive papers

Fold the sheet of paper over the edge of a bench and tear it into convenient strips. To smooth flat surfaces or square edges, wrap a strip of paper round a cork sanding block; on curves, use your fingertips to apply the paper. To sand mouldings, wrap abrasive paper round a dowel or shaped block.

As the work proceeds, use progressively finer grades of paper. Before the final sanding, dampen the wood with water to raise the grain. When the wood is dry, sand it with a very fine abrasive.

To sand end grain, first rub the grain with your fingers: the wood feels rougher in one direction than the other. Sand the grain in the smoother direction only, not to and fro.

Use a shaped block when sanding a moulding

Wood scrapers

Scrapers produce an extremely smooth surface finish on wood. Whereas abrasive papers leave minute scratches on the surface, scrapers remove fine shavings.

Cabinet scraper

This is a simple rectangle of thin steel used for scraping flat surfaces. Curved-edge versions are used for working mouldings and carved wood.

Hook scraper

A hook scraper's disposable blade slides into a clip at the end of a wooden handle. Simply pull the scraper towards you along the grain of the wood, applying light pressure.

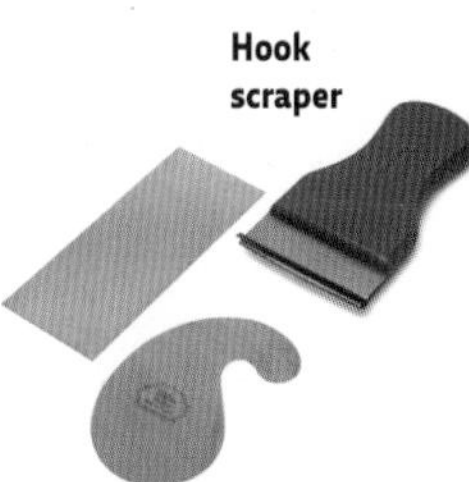

Hook scraper

Cabinet scrapers

Using a cabinet scraper

Hold the scraper in both hands, pressing it into a slightly curved shape with your thumbs. Tilt the scraper away from you and work diagonally across the surface in two directions to scrape the wood flat. Finally, scrape lightly in the direction of the grain.

Slightly tilt a scraper

Sharpening a scraper

A cabinet scraper is sharpened by raising a burr along its edge. Straight and curved scrapers are both sharpened in a similar way, although it's harder to turn an even burr along a curved edge.

First, draw-file the edge of the scraper and hone it perfectly square on an oilstone (1). To raise the burr, hold the scraper flat on a workbench then stroke the edge firmly several times with the curved back of a gouge (2). This stretches the metal along the edge of the scraper, which produces the burr. Turn the burr to project from the face of the scraper by holding the scraper upright on the bench and stroking the burred corner with the gouge held at an angle to the face (3).

Keep the gouge's cutting edge well away from your fingers when sharpening a cabinet scraper.

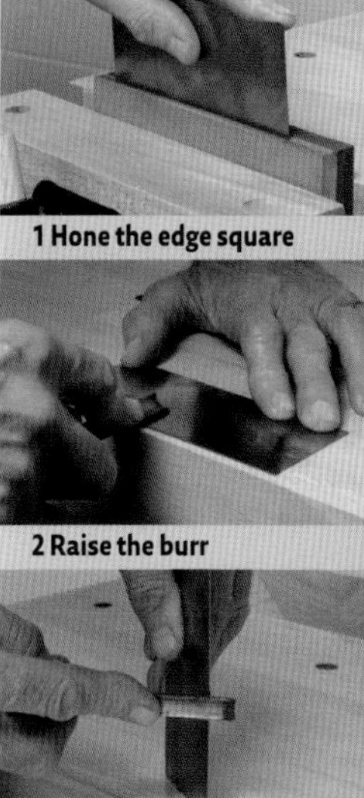

1 Hone the edge square

2 Raise the burr

3 Turn the burr over

SEE ALSO > Preparing woodwork 52–9, Sharpening planes 494, Power sanders 498, Draw-filing 525

Power sanders

Power sanders ease the chore of sanding large surfaces, but rarely produce a surface good enough for a clear finish – so a final sanding by hand is usually required.

Belt sander

A belt sander has a continuous loop of abrasive paper passing round a revolving drum at each end. A flat plate between the two drums presses the moving abrasive against the wood.

Finishing sanders

A finishing sander produces a surface that needs only a light sanding by hand before you apply a clear polish. On this type of sander, a strip of abrasive paper is stretched across a flat rubber pad that is moved by the motor in a tight, rapid orbital pattern. A cordless finishing sander is convenient for working outdoors.

Specialized orbital sanders (Delta sanders) with small triangular plates are designed for sanding in tight corners.

Orbital disc sander

This power tool – sometimes called a random orbital sander – has a sanding disc that moves eccentrically and simultaneously rotates, leaving the surface of the wood virtually scratch-free. The flexible backing pad copes with curved surfaces.

Foam drum sander
This flexible plastic-foam drum covered by an abrasive-paper band is driven by a central shaft that fits into the chuck of a power drill. The drum deforms against irregularly curved workpieces.

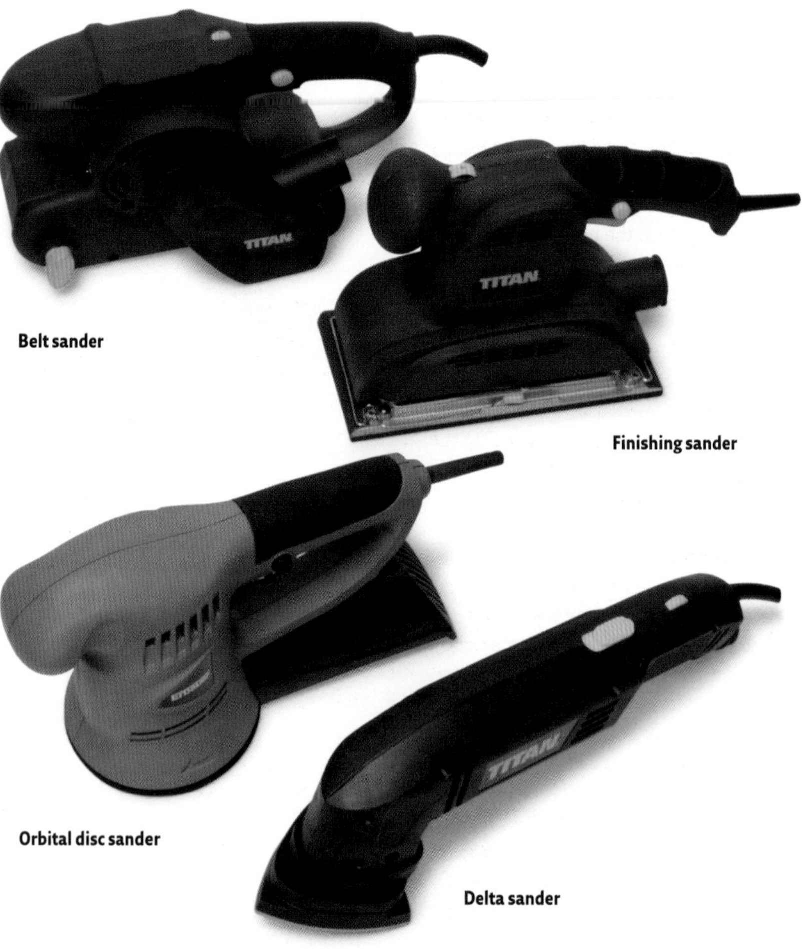

Belt sander

Finishing sander

Orbital disc sander

Delta sander

Using a belt sander

Switch on the machine and lower it gently onto the work, then make forward and backward passes with the sander, holding it parallel to the grain. The weight of the machine provides enough pressure to do the work, especially when the abrasive band is fresh. Cover the surface with overlapping passes, but don't let the sander ride over the edges of the work or it will round them over. Lift the sander from the surface before you switch it off, and don't put the tool aside before the belt comes to a stop. Following the manufacturer's instructions, change to a finer-grade belt to remove the marks left by the previous sanding.

Disc sanders

The simplest disc sander is a flexible rubber pad with a central shaft that is gripped in the chuck of a power drill. An abrasive-paper disc is bolted to the face of the pad. This type of sander is not suitable for fine woodwork, since it inevitably leaves swirling scratch marks that have to be removed with a finishing sander or cabinet scraper before a clear finish can be applied. However, it is a handy tool for cleaning up old floorboards.

Using a rubber-disc sander

With the drill running, flex the edge of the rubber disc against the wood. Keep the sander moving along the work to avoid deep scratching.

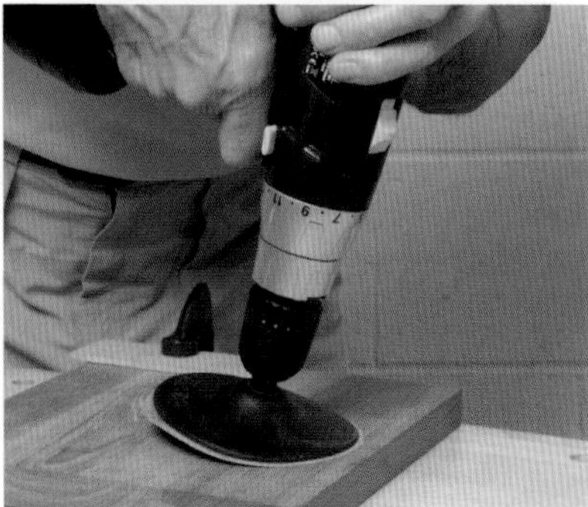

SEE ALSO > Preparing woodwork 52–9, Sanding a wooden floor 54–6, Abrasives and scrapers 497

Drills and braces

The availability of power drills – especially the improved range of cordless tools – has reduced the need for hand-operated drills and ratchet braces. However, electric tools have not completely eradicated the demand for these tools, which are very convenient and also inexpensive.

Brace

A brace is designed for boring holes that have a relatively large diameter. The bit is driven into the wood by the turning force of the handle, plus pressure on the head of the tool. A good-quality brace has a ratchet so you can turn the bit in one direction only when working in confined spaces where a full turn of the handle isn't possible.

Hand drill

For small-diameter holes use a hand drill (sometimes called a wheelbrace). Some models have a cast body enclosing the drive mechanism to keep gear wheels and pinions free from dust.

Brace bits

Brace bits have a square-section tang that fits into the jaws of the tool's chuck.

An auger bit has helical twists along its shank that remove the waste as the bit bores into the wood. Being the same diameter as the cutting tip, the twisted shank keeps the bit straight when you are boring deep holes. A tapered lead screw helps to draw the bit into the timber, and knife-edge spurs cut the perimeter of the hole before the bit enters the wood.

An expansive bit has an adjustable spurred cutter for boring holes of up to 75mm (3in) in diameter.

A centre bit is fast-cutting because it has no helical twists to create friction, but it tends to wander off line. It's best for drilling man-made boards, in which the holes are never very deep.

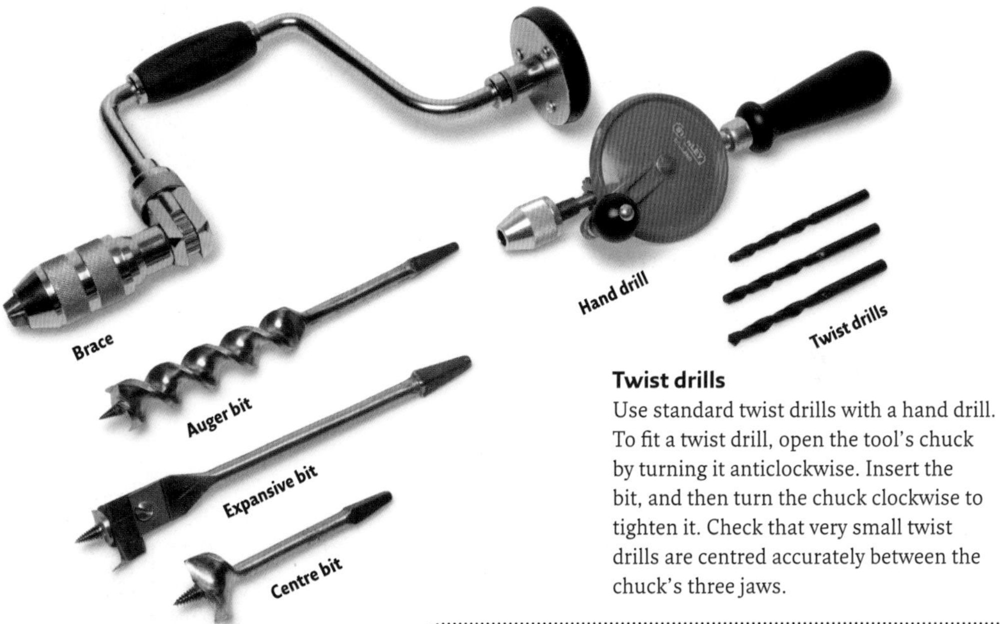

Twist drills

Use standard twist drills with a hand drill. To fit a twist drill, open the tool's chuck by turning it anticlockwise. Insert the bit, and then turn the chuck clockwise to tighten it. Check that very small twist drills are centred accurately between the chuck's three jaws.

Using drills and braces

When using a brace, don't let the bit burst through the back of the work and split the wood. As soon as the lead screw emerges, turn the work over and complete the hole from the other side.

Using a hand drill

Centre the drill bit on the work. This will be easier if the centre for the hole has been marked with a bradawl puncture. Give the bit a start by moving the handle to and fro until the bit bites into the wood, then crank the handle to drive the bit clockwise.

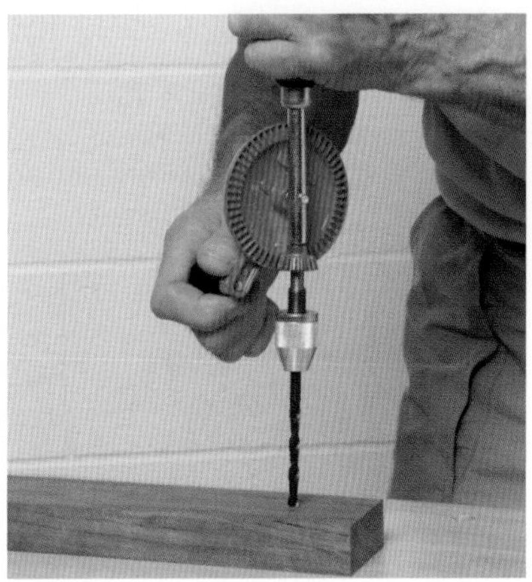

Rotate the handle back and forth until the bit bites

Sharpening drill bits

Brace bits are sharpened with fine needle files. Put an edge on a spur by stroking its inside face with a flat file (1), then rest the point of the bit on a bench and sharpen the cutting edge with a triangular file (2).

It's possible to sharpen a blunt twist drill on a bench grinder, but it takes practice to centre the point. An electric sharpening jig centres the drill point automatically. Insert the tip of the drill in the top of the jig and switch on for a few seconds to grind one cutting edge; then rotate the drill one half turn and repeat the process.

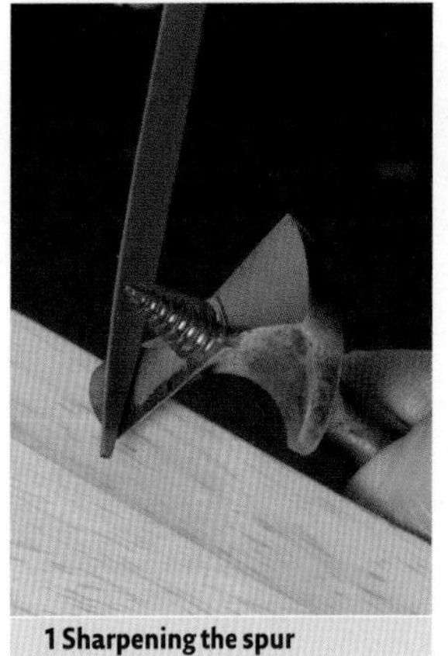

1 Sharpening the spur

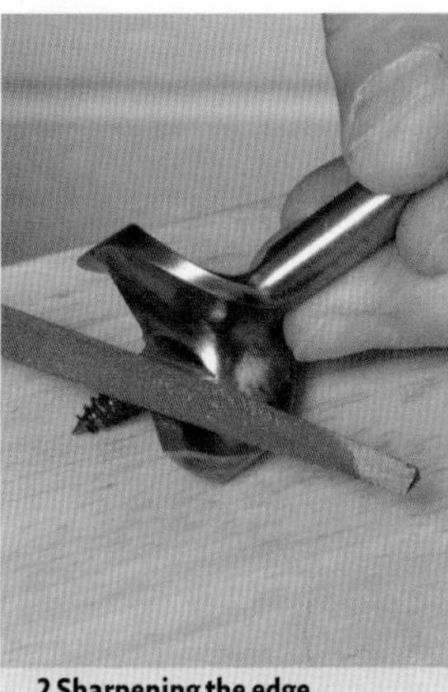

2 Sharpening the edge

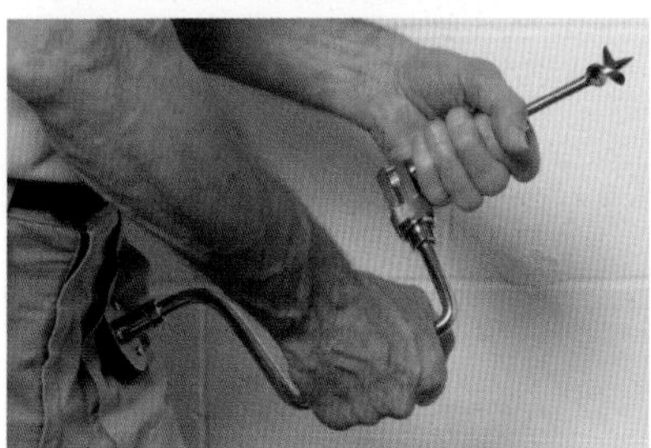

Fitting a brace bit

Grip the chuck in one hand and turn the handle of the brace clockwise to open the jaws. Drop the bit into the chuck, then tighten the chuck on the bit by turning the handle in the anticlockwise direction.

SEE ALSO > Power drills 500, Needle files 524

Power drills

The electric drill is the most widely sold and used power tool on the market. Manufacturers try to satisfy this huge demand by producing an immense range of drills, from cheap almost throwaway tools to sophisticated professional models. Most households are equipped with a mains-powered drill and often also have a cordless drill, which avoids the inconvenience and dangers of trailing flex.

Using a drill stand
In order to bore holes that are absolutely square to the face of the work, mount your power drill in a vertical drill stand.

Dowelling jig
A dowelling jig ensures alignment of dowel holes and also keeps the drill bit perpendicular to the work.

Power drill

Modern drills sold for the DIY market are now as sophisticated as those once made for professional use. It is worth buying a drill with a powerful motor that can cope with a wide range of jobs.

Cordless power drill

Drills powered by rechargeable batteries do away with the need for an extension lead when working in a remote work site. Choose a cordless drill that has a variable-speed facility for inserting woodscrews and a hammer action for drilling into masonry. It is convenient to have a spare battery, so you are able to continue working while recharging a flat battery.

Power-drill bits

A variety of bits can be used in a power drill, depending on the kind of hole you want to bore.

You can use standard twist drills of any size up to the maximum opening of the chuck. To bore larger holes, use reduced-shank twist drills

With spade bits you can drill holes up to 38mm (1½in) in diameter. Place the sharp lead point of the bit on the centre of the hole before squeezing the trigger of the drill.

With slotted-head or cross-head screwdriver bits, you can use your electric drill as a power screwdriver.

To sink the head of a countersunk woodscrew so that it's flush with the surface of the work, make a tapered recess in the top of the clearance hole with a countersink bit.

A drill-and-countersink bit makes the pilot hole, clearance hole and countersink recess for a woodscrew in a single operation. As it is matched to one specific screw size, it is only worth purchasing when you are planning to use a fair number of identical screws.

A plug cutter is used to make cylindrical plugs of wood for concealing the heads of screws sunk below the surface of the work.

A dowel bit is a twist drill with a sharp lead point and cutting spurs that help keep it on line when you are boring holes for dowel joints.

Useful features

Before you buy a power drill, make sure it has all the features that you are likely to require.

Chuck size

The chuck size refers to the maximum diameter of bit shank that the drill's chuck can accommodate. A 10 or 13mm (⅜in or ½in) chuck is adequate for most purposes. You can drill holes of a diameter greater than the chuck size by using spade bits with cutters that are larger than their shanks.

Some chucks are tightened with a special toothed key, but many drills are made with keyless chucks that take a firm grip on the bit simply by turning a cylindrical collar that surrounds the mechanism.

Variable speed

With a variable-speed drill, you are able to select the ideal speed for drilling different materials. A slow speed uses the drill's power to produce more torque (turning force) for drilling into masonry or metal; a high speed produces a clean cut when drilling wood. You can select a maximum speed with a dial, or run the tool at any convenient speed by varying the pressure on the trigger. A variable-speed facility is essential if you want to use a power drill for driving screws.

Reverse rotation

If you want to use a screwdriver bit with your power drill, make sure its rotation can be reversed - so you can take screws out as well as being able to insert them.

Percussion or hammer action

Operating a switch converts an electric drill from smooth rotation to a hammer action that delivers several hundred blows per second to the revolving chuck. This action is only used when drilling into brick or stone. The hammer vibration helps by breaking up hard particles ahead of specially toughened masonry bits.

SEE ALSO > Brace 499, Hand drill 499, Power screwdriver 502

Hammers and mallets

Driving in a nail is so simple that one hammer would seem to be as effective as another, but using one that is the right shape and weight for the job makes for easier, trouble-free work. A mallet has its own specific uses and should not be used for hammering nails.

Claw hammer

This is a heavy general-purpose hammer and probably the most useful one to have in a basic tool kit. The claw at the back of the head is for levering out nails. In order to cope with the leverage, the hammer head has to be fixed firmly to a strong shaft.

The traditional adze-eye head has a deep, square socket driven and wedged onto a tough but flexible hickory shaft. However, an all-metal claw hammer is an even better tool. Its steel shaft won't bend or break; the head can't work loose; and the rubber grip is both comfortable and shock-absorbing.

Cross-peen hammer

For tasks that are too delicate for a heavy claw hammer, use a medium-weight cross-peen hammer. Its wedge-shaped peen is for setting (starting) a nail held between finger and thumb.

Pin hammer

A small, lightweight pin hammer is the perfect tool for tapping in small panel pins and tacks.

Carpenter's mallet

A carpenter's mallet is for driving a chisel or gouge into wood. Its striking faces are angled so as to deliver square blows to the end of the chisel or gouge.

Soft mallet

Although you can use a carpenter's mallet to knock joints together or apart, a softer rubber or plastic mallet is less likely to mark the wood.

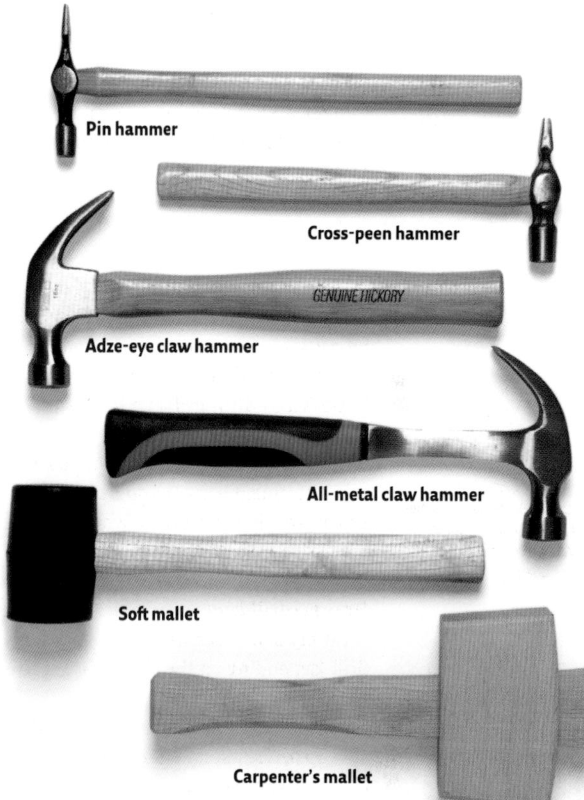

Carpenter's mallet

Using hammers

Set a nail in wood with one or two taps of the hammer until it stands upright without support, then drive it home with firm steady blows, keeping your wrist straight and the hammer face square to the nailhead.

Using a nail set

A nail set is a punch with a hollow-ground tip used for sinking nails below the surface of the wood. Nail sets are made in several sizes, for use with large and small nails. Having driven the nail almost flush, hold the nail set upright between thumb and fingertips and place its tip on the protruding nailhead, then tap the set with your hammer. With a heavy hammer very little force is needed to sink the nail.

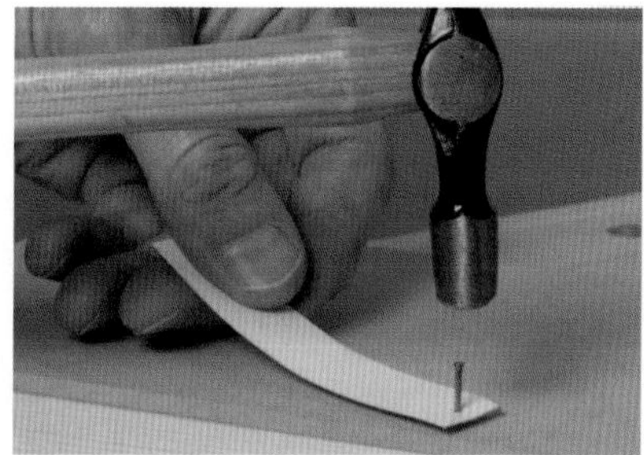

Hammering small nails

If the nail is very small, either set it with the hammer peen or push it through a piece of thin card to steady it. Before you tap the nail flush with the wood, tear the card away.

Blind nailing

To hide a nail fixing, lift a flap of wood with a gouge, sink the nail with a nail set, and then glue the flap and cramp it flat.

Removing a bent nail

If you bend a nail while driving it in with a claw hammer, lever it out by sliding the claw under the nailhead and pulling back on the end of the shaft of the hammer. The hammer's curved head will roll on the wood without doing too much damage, but you can protect the work by placing a piece of thick card or hardboard under the hammer head. A thick packing of this kind will also give you extra leverage for removing a long nail.

If a nailhead is too small to catch in a claw hammer, lever it out with carpenter's pincers. Grip the nail with the jaws resting on the wood, then squeeze the handles together and roll the pincers away from you. As with a claw hammer, cardboard or hardboard packing will protect the wood.

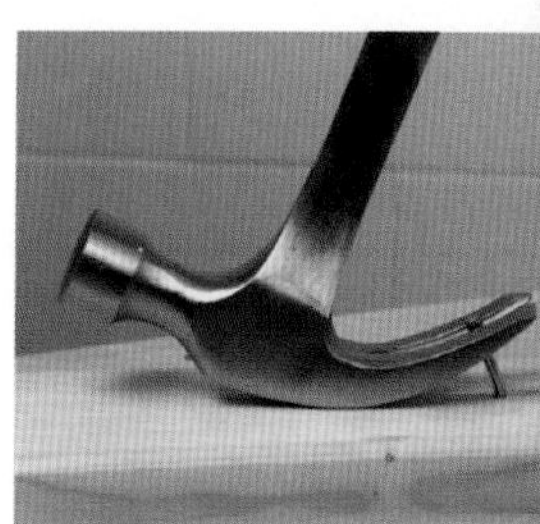

Use a claw hammer to remove a bent nail

Extract small nails with a pair of pincers

Sanding a hammer head

You are more likely to bend nails if your hammer head is greasy. To provide a better grip, rub the hammer's face on fine abrasive paper.

SEE ALSO > Chisels and gouges 496, Nails 532–3

Screwdrivers

A woodworker's tool kit needs to include a number of screwdrivers because it is important to match the size of the driver to the screw. If you use a screwdriver with a tip that is slightly too big or too small, it is likely to slip out of the slot as you turn it, damaging both the screw and the surrounding wood.

Bradawl
Use a bradawl to cut a starter hole for small woodscrews.

Cabinet screwdriver

A cabinet screwdriver has a shaft that is ground on two sides to produce a flat, square tip. It may have a hardwood handle, strengthened with a metal ferrule, or a plastic handle moulded onto the shaft.

Cross-head screwdriver

Use a matching cross-head screwdriver to drive screws that have cruciform slots. Using a flat-tip driver to turn a cross-head screw invariably damages the screw's head.

Ratchet screwdriver

Using a ratchet screwdriver, you can insert and remove screws without having to adjust your grip on the handle of the driver. You can select clockwise or anticlockwise rotation, or lock the ratchet and use the tool like an ordinary fixed screwdriver. Some ratchet screwdrivers come with a range of interchangeable bits.

Cabinet screwdriver

Cross-head screwdriver

Ratchet screwdriver

Power screwdriver

Power screwdriver

A cordless electric screwdriver that takes interchangeable bits is especially convenient for working in confined spaces. It invariably has a spindle lock so you can set the tool manually to put the final turn on a screw or loosen it before you apply power. If the screwdriver is fitted with torque control, you have the option of a low setting to stop you overtightening small screws and a higher setting for large fittings.

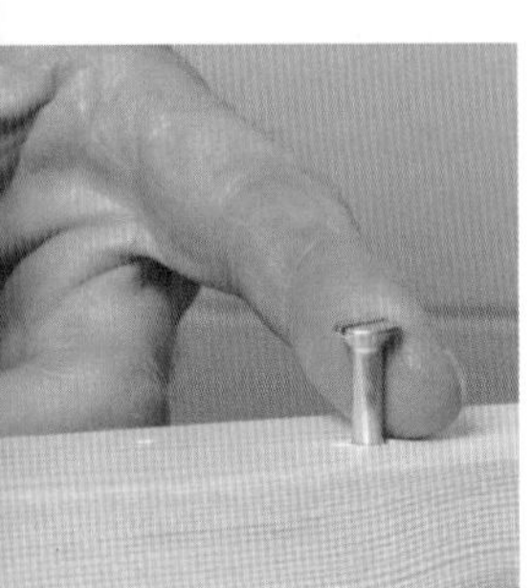

Easing a tight screw
If a screw is a tight fit in the hole you have drilled for it, withdraw it slightly and put a little grease on its shank.

Reshaping a flat tip

A screwdriver tip that is worn tends to slip out of the slot and damage the workpiece. Regrind each side of a straight-tip screwdriver, then grind the tip square.

Repair a damaged tip on a grindstone

Inserting woodscrews

You may split the wood if you drive in a conventional screw without boring a hole for it first. To make a starter hole for a small screw, place the flat tip of a bradawl across the grain of the wood, then press it in and twist.

To guide a large screw, drill a pilot hole, followed by a clearance hole for the shank. For the pilot hole, use a drill bit slightly narrower than the thread of the screw, but drill the clearance hole fractionally larger than the screw's shank. Use a countersink bit to make recesses to accommodate the heads of countersunk screws.

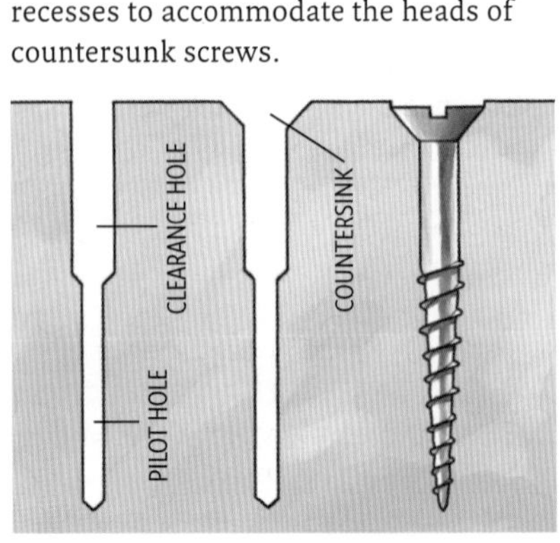

Bore pilot and clearance holes for large screws

Extracting old screws

Before attempting to extract a painted-over screw, scrape the paint from the slot with the end of a hacksaw blade – or, for the best results, place a corner of the screwdriver tip in the slot and tap it sideways until it fits snugly. Without disturbing the tip, turn the screwdriver to break the seal and extract the screw.

When a screw's slot has been stripped completely, remove the head with a power drill. Mark the centre of the head with a centre punch, then use progressively larger drill bits to remove the metal in stages. Extracting the shaft and screw thread is all but impossible.

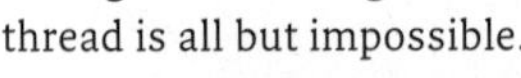

Drive the tip of a screwdriver across a painted slot

SEE ALSO > Cordless drill 500, Centre punch 517, Screws 533–5

Wood cramps

Cramps are for holding glued joints together while the adhesive sets. They are also used to assemble temporarily structures constructed from wood and man-made boards to see if they work or fit, and for holding small workpieces on a bench while you are working on them.

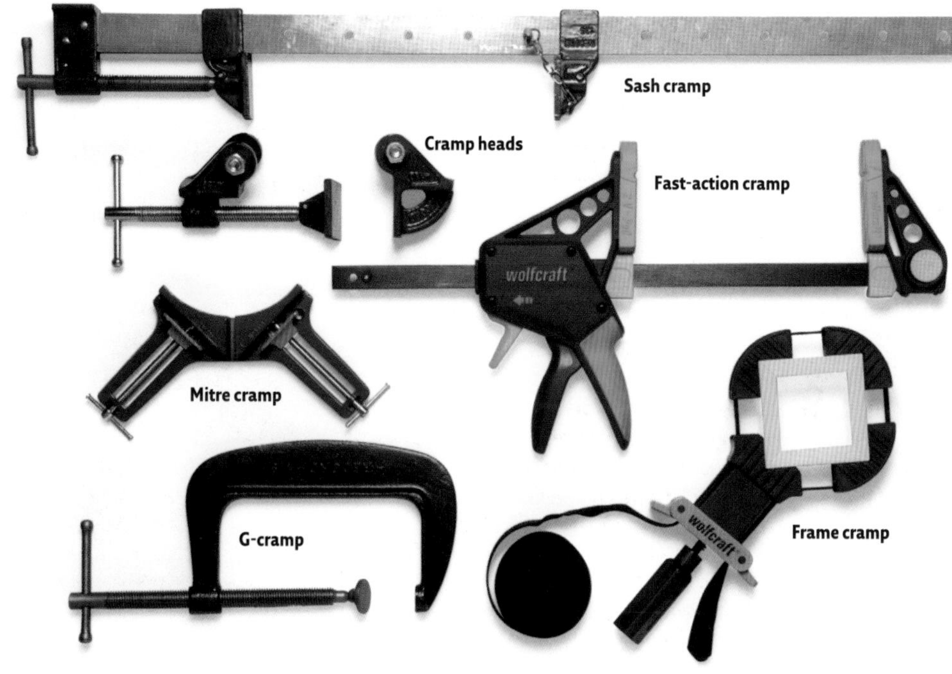

Sash cramp

A sash cramp is a long metal bar with a screw-adjustable jaw at one end. Another jaw, known as the tail slide, is free to move along the bar, but can be fixed at any convenient point by inserting a metal peg in one of a series of holes along the cramp. Sash cramps are for clamping large glued frames, and it's worth having a couple of medium-size ones in your tool kit.

Cramp heads

If you need an extra-long sash cramp, hire a pair of cramp heads. Use a 75 x 25mm (3 x 1in) softwood rail as a cramp bar, locating the heads on it by plugging their pegs into holes drilled through the wood.

G-cramp

A screw-adjusted G-cramp grips the work between the adjustable shoe and the cast-metal frame. You're will need at least one 150mm (6in) and one 300mm (1ft) G-cramp.

Fast-action cramp

This type of cramp can be operated very quickly - especially useful when glue is setting rapidly.

Frame and mitre cramps

The four plastic corner blocks of a simple frame cramp hold the glued corners of a mitred frame while a strap is pulled taut around the blocks in order to apply equal pressure to all four joints.

A mitre cramp holds one joint at a time. Made of cast metal, it clamps the two mitred members against a right-angle fence.

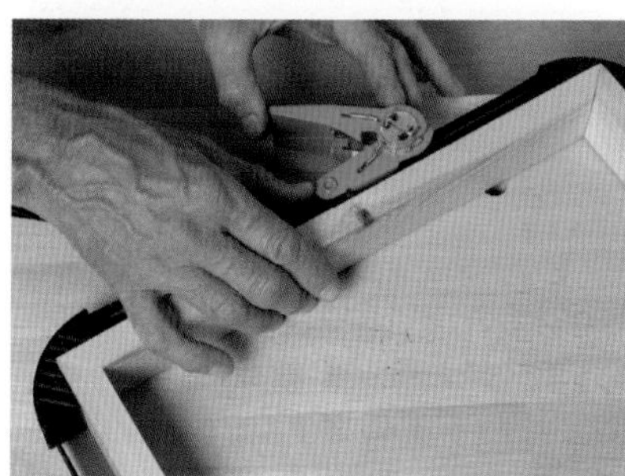

Web cramp

A web cramp acts like a frame cramp. The nylon webbing is tensioned by adjusting a ratchet mechanism.

Clamping boards edge to edge

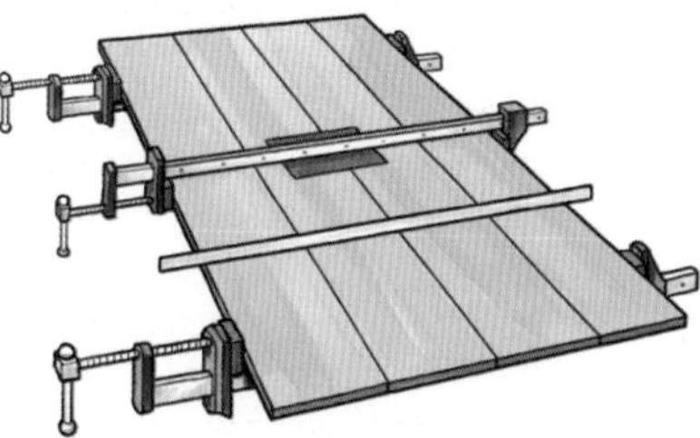

To clamp several glued boards edge to edge, use at least three sash cramps. Place one of the cramps on top of the assembly to prevent the boards bowing under pressure from the other two. A long sash cramp will bend as you tighten it, so protect the wood by inserting strips of hardboard packing between the sash bars and the work.

Lay a straightedge across the clamped boards to check that the panel is flat. If the panel isn't flat, correct the distortion by slackening or tightening the cramps as need be.

If a board is misaligned, tap it back into position by placing a softwood block across the joint and striking the block firmly with a heavy hammer.

Clamping a jointed frame

Prepare and adjust your sash cramps before you glue and assemble a jointed frame. If you have to waste time adjusting them after the joints are glued, the adhesive may begin to stiffen before you can close the joints properly.

Set the tail slides to accommodate the frame and make sure that the adjustable jaws will have enough movement to tighten the joints. Place the cramps in line with the joints, using softwood packing strips to protect the work from the metal jaws.

Apply pressure gradually, first with one cramp and then the other, until the joints are tightly closed (1).

Check that the frame is square by measuring both diagonals. If they aren't equal, set the cramps at a slight angle to the frame so as to pull it square by squeezing the long diagonal (2).

Use a damp cloth to remove excess glue squeezed from the joints. After about 10 minutes, tighten each cramp very slightly to take up the slack that sometimes results from air and glue escaping under pressure from the joints.

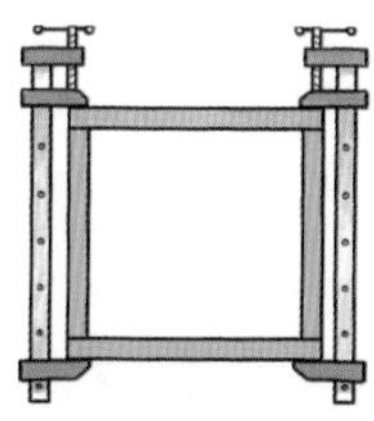

1 Sash cramps square to a jointed frame

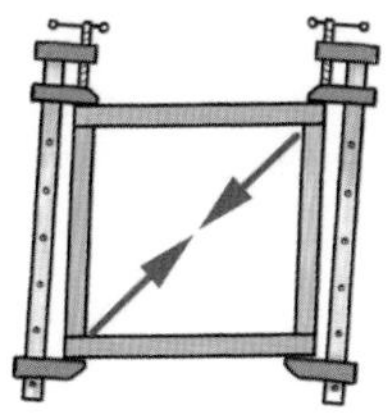

2 Sash cramps set at an angle to the frame

SEE ALSO > Woodworking joints 505–9

Benches and vices

A woodworking bench must be strong and rigid. Working with heavy timbers and man-made boards puts a considerable strain on a bench, and the stress imposed by sawing and hammering will eventually weaken a poorly constructed one.

Woodworker's bench

The hardwood underframe of a woodworker's bench is constructed with strong joints to prevent the frame flexing. The underframe can usually be dismantled or the worktop removed to make it easier to move a heavy bench.

The thick hardwood worktop is normally made from short-grain beech. A storage recess or tool well keeps the worktop free from tools, so you can lay large boards on it.

Better-quality benches have an end vice, built onto one end of the worktop, for clamping long sections of timber between metal pegs called bench stops.

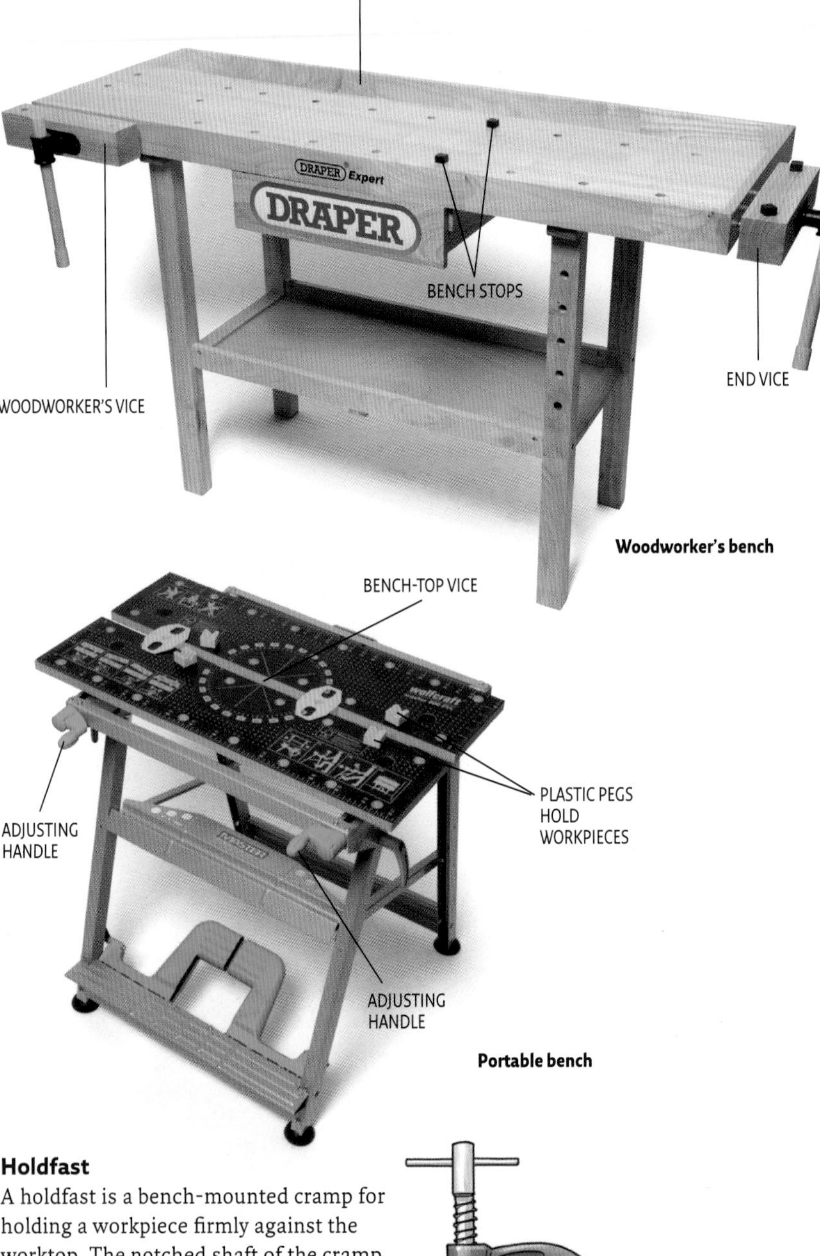

Woodworker's bench

Portable bench

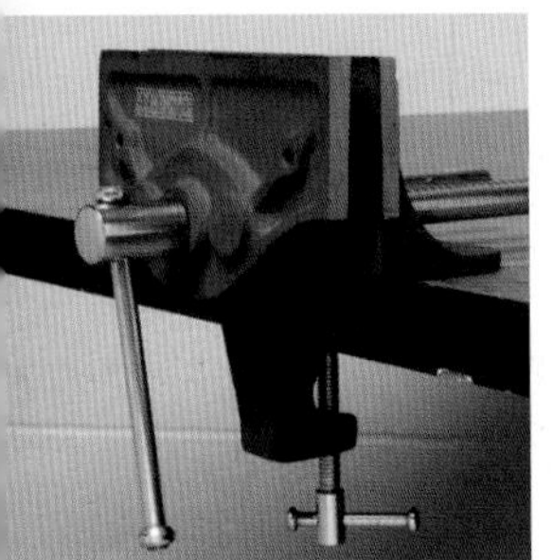

Clamp-on vice
A lightweight vice can be clamped temporarily to the edge of any worktop. Although not as good as a proper woodworker's vice, it is a lot cheaper.

Portable bench

A portable workbench can be folded away between jobs. The two halves of the thick worktop are in effect vice jaws, operated by adjusting handles at the ends of the bench. Because the handles work independently, the jaws can hold tapered workpieces. Plastic pegs fit into holes in the worktop to hold work laid flat on it, and can be arranged to hold irregular shapes.

Woodworker's vice

A feature of most benches is a large woodworker's vice. This is normally fixed to the worktop, close to one leg, so the top will not flex when you are working on wood held in the vice. If you have a metal vice, wooden linings (pads) must be fixed inside the jaws to protect the work from the metal edges.

A quick-release lever on the front of some vices allows you to open and shut the jaws quickly, turning the handle only for final adjustments.

Holdfast

A holdfast is a bench-mounted cramp for holding a workpiece firmly against the worktop. The notched shaft of the cramp is slipped into a metal collar that is let into the bench.

When pressure is applied with the cramp's tommy bar, the shaft rocks over to lock in the collar and the shoe at the end of the pivoting arm bears down on the workpiece. A pair of holdfasts, one at each end of the bench, is ideal for clamping long boards.

A holdfast clamps the work firmly to the bench top

SEE ALSO > Bench hook 489, Mitre box 489

Woodworking joints

Craftsmen have invented countless ingenious ways of joining pieces of timber together. Some are as decorative as they are practical, but for general joinery and home maintenance only a few basic woodworking joints are needed.

Butt joints

When you cut a piece of wood square and butt it against its neighbour you need some kind of mechanical fixing to hold the joint together, as the end grain doesn't glue strongly enough for adhesive alone to be used.

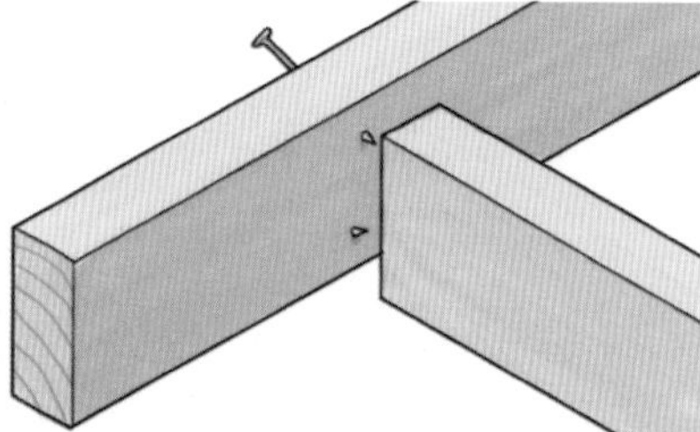

Nailed butt joints
The grip between the nails and the wood is usually enough to hold the joint together, but for stronger fixings drive the nails in at an angle. When angled nails fix wood onto the end grain of another member, the technique is called dovetail-nailing; when they pass through the side of a section it is known as skew-nailing.

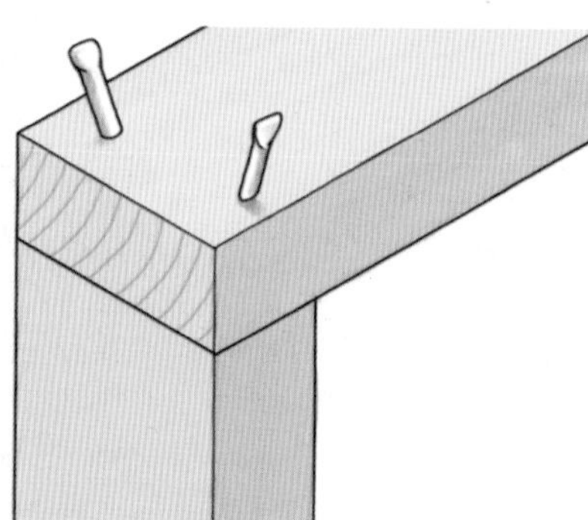

Dovetail-nailed butt joint

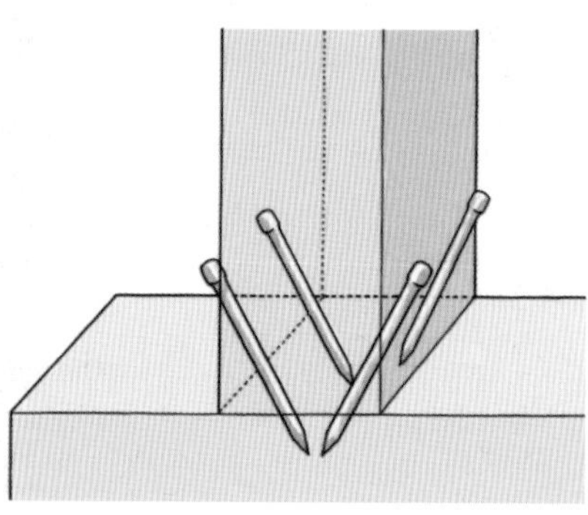

Skew-nailed butt joint

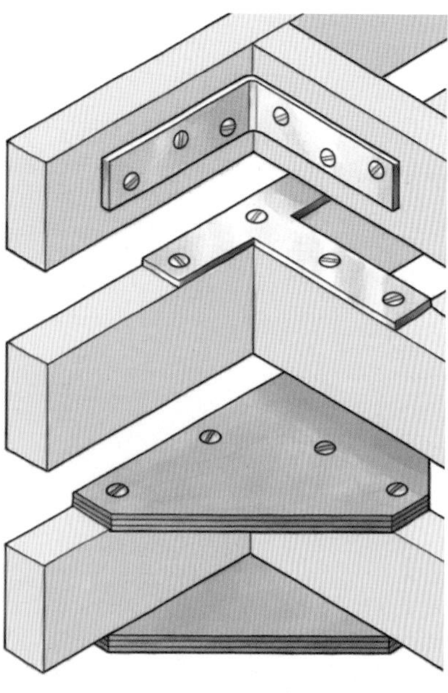

Bracket and plate fixings
A screwed-on metal right-angle bracket or T-bracket makes a strong, though not very attractive, butt joint. Similarly, you can reinforce a butt joint by nailing or screwing a plywood plate across it.

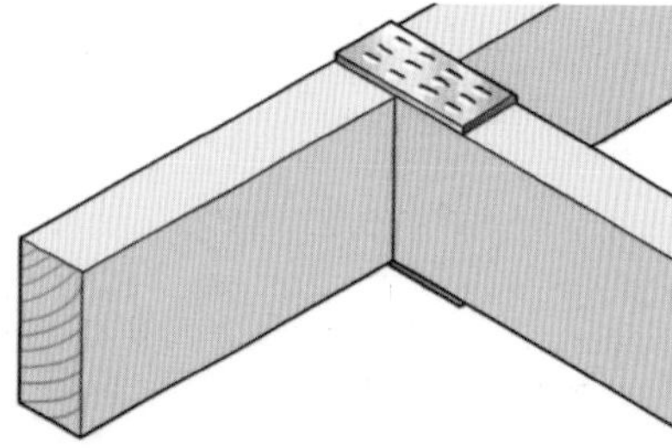

Timber connectors
The sharp pointed teeth of metal timber connectors grip like a bed of nails.

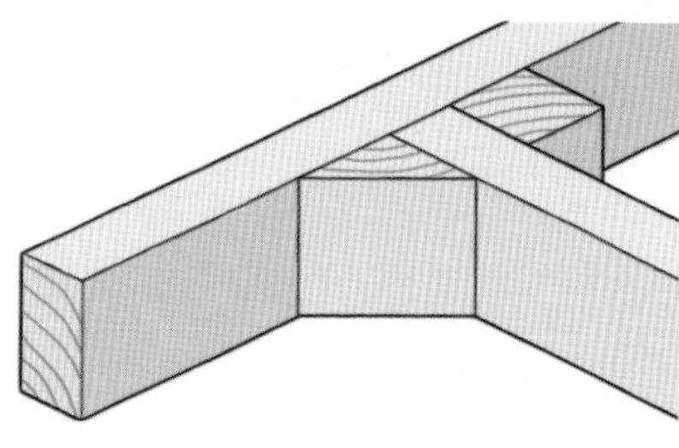

Corner blocks
Either pin and glue or screw a square or triangular block of wood in the angle between two components.

Halving joints

Halving joints can be adapted to join lengths of wood at a corner or T-joint, or where components cross one another.

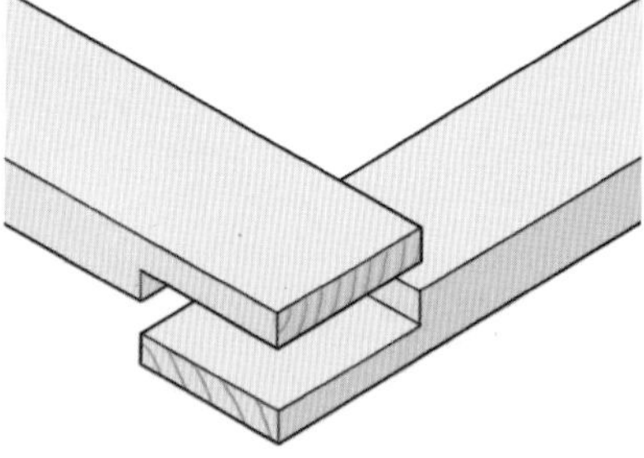

Cutting a corner halving joint
To join two pieces of wood at a corner, cut an identical tongue in the end of each component – as for a T-halving joint, but clamp the components side by side and cut the shoulders simultaneously (1). Reinforce the glued joint with screws (2).

1 Cut both shoulders simultaneously

2 Reinforce the glued joint

SEE ALSO > Marking gauge 487, Marking knife 487, Try square 487, Tenon saw 488, Bench hook 489, Paring wood 496, Cramps 503, Cutting a T-halving joint 506, Nails 532–3

Cutting a T-halving joint

Lay the crossrail on the side rail and mark the width of the housing on it with a marking knife (1), extending the lines halfway down each edge of the rail.

With a marking gauge set to exactly half the thickness of the rails, score the centre lines on both rails (2). Mark the shoulder of the tongue on the crossrail (3), allowing for a tongue slightly longer than the width of the side rail. Hold the crossrail at an angle in a vice (4) and saw down to the shoulder on one edge, keeping to the waste side of the line.

Then turn the rail round and saw down to the shoulder on the opposite edge. Finally, saw down square to the shoulder line (5) and remove the waste by sawing across the shoulder line (6).

To cut the housing in the side rail, saw down both the shoulder lines to the halfway mark, then make several sawcuts across the waste (7). Pare out the waste with a chisel down to the marked lines, working from both sides (8).

Glue and assemble the joint; and when it has set, plane the end of the tongue flush with the side rail.

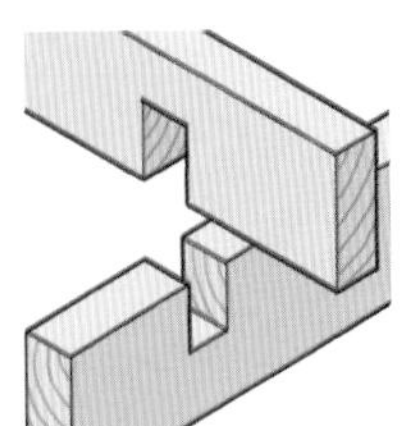

Edge-to-edge cross halving joint
Clamp the two parts together, then mark and saw both halves of the joint. Remove the clamps and chisel out the waste.

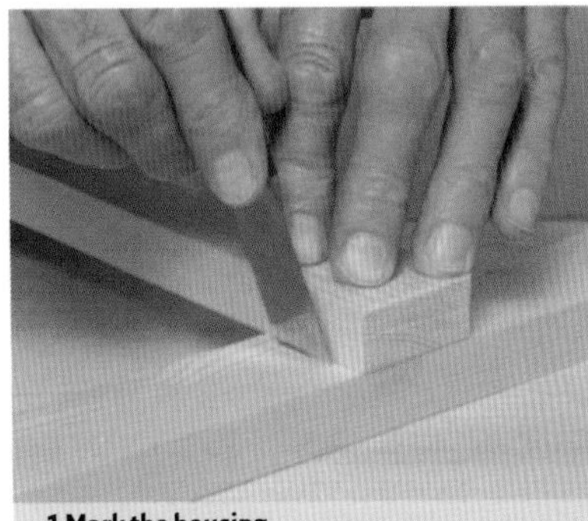

1 Mark the housing

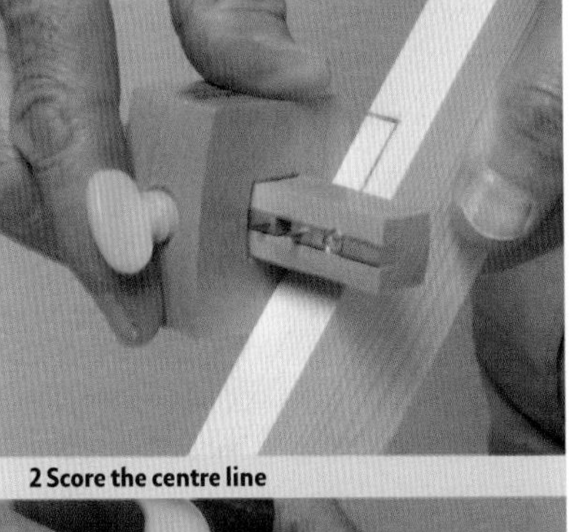

2 Score the centre line

3 Mark the shoulder

4 Saw with the rail held at an angle

5 Saw square with the shoulder

6 Saw across the shoulder line

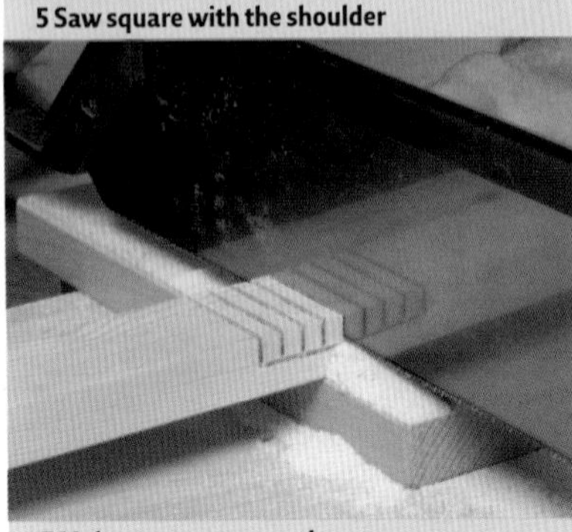

7 Make sawcuts across the waste

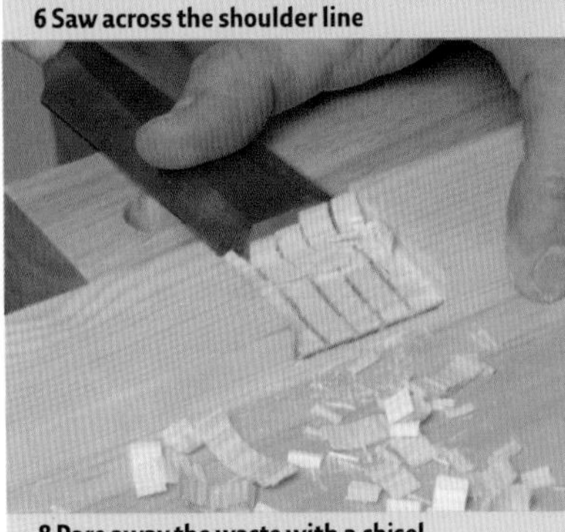

8 Pare away the waste with a chisel

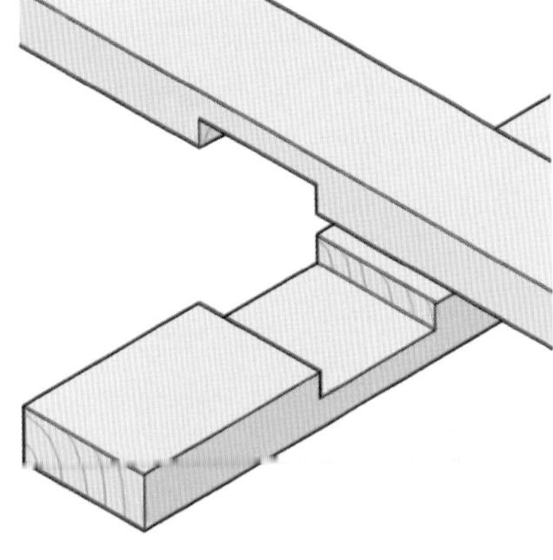

Cutting a cross halving joint

To make a cross halving joint, hold the two components together, side by side, and mark both joints simultaneously. Then separate the components and saw across the shoulder lines and remove the waste with a chisel (as described above left).

Overlap joint

You can make a simple overlap joint by laying one square-cut board across another and fixing them with nails or screws.

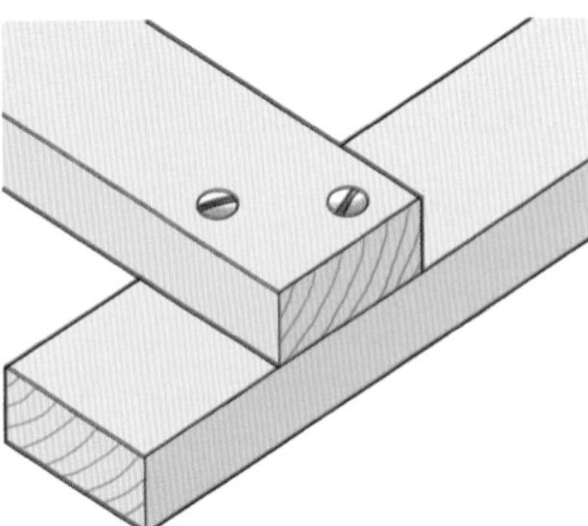

Making an overlap joint

Clamp the components together accurately with a G-cramp, and drill pilot and clearance holes for the screws. Remove the cramp, apply glue, and then screw the components together.

Drill pilot holes for the screws

SEE ALSO > Marking gauge 487, Marking knife 487, Try square 487, Tenon saw 488, Bench hook 489, Paring wood 496, Cramps 503

Lap joints

This is a simple joint for joining two wide boards at a corner.

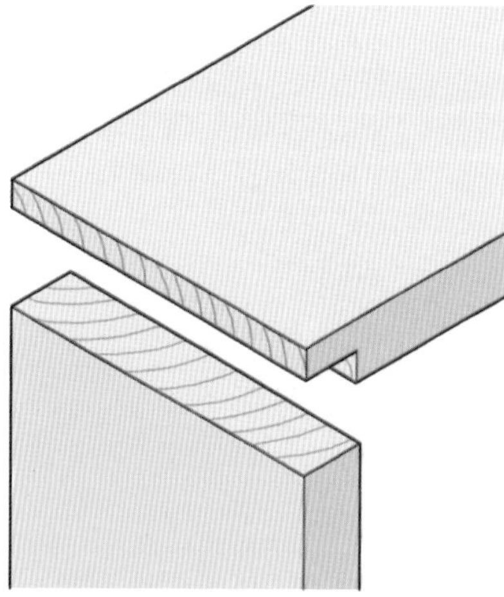

Cutting a lap joint

Cut the square-ended board first and use it to mark out the width of the rebate on the other board (1). Scribe the line with a marking knife.

Set a marking gauge to about half the timber's thickness and mark the tongue on the end grain (2). Cut out the rebate with a tenon saw, then glue and dovetail-nail the joint (see NAILED BUTT JOINTS).

1 Mark the width of the rebate

2 Mark out the tongue

Bridle joints

A bridle joint is used for making strong joints for a frame.

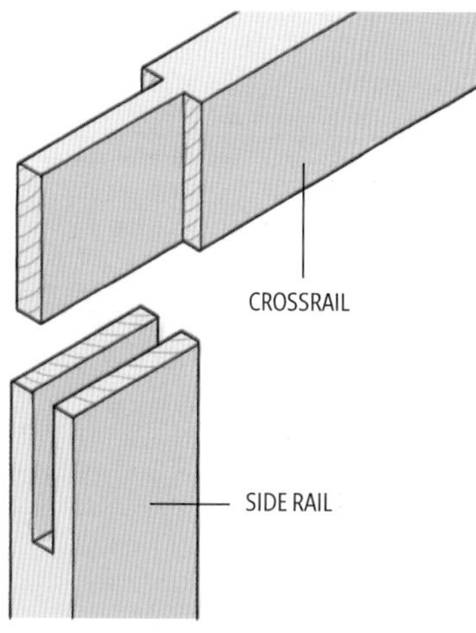

Cutting a corner bridle joint

To make a corner bridle joint, cut equal-size tongues – two on the side rail and one centred on the crossrail. Mark them out with a mortise gauge, making all three slightly longer than the width of the rails. Cut the waste away from both sides of the crossrail tongue with a tenon saw, as described for a T-halving joint (see opposite).

To form the side-rail tongues, saw down to the shoulder on both sides, keeping to the waste side of the two marked lines, then chop out the waste with a narrow firmer chisel or mortise chisel.

Glue and assemble the joint and, when the glue has set, plane the ends of the over-long tongues flush with the rails.

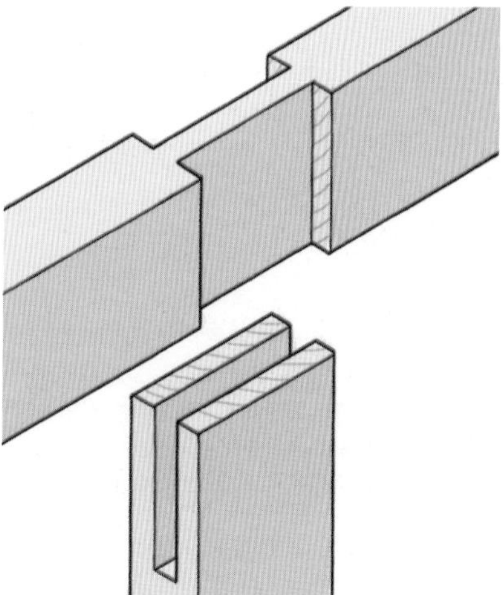

T-bridle joint

When a crossrail joins an upright rail or leg, cut two tongues on the upright (as for a corner bridle joint) and cut a housing on each side of the crossrail, as for a T-halving joint. The depth of the housings must, of course, be equal to the thickness of the tongues.

Housing joints

Housing joints are often used for shelves and similar structures. A through housing can be seen from both sides of the structure, whereas a stopped housing is not visible from the front.

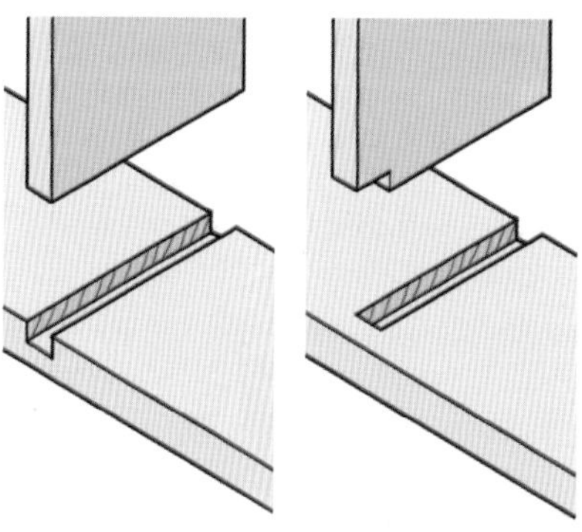

Through housing **Stopped housing**

Cutting a stopped housing

Using the other half of the joint as a guide, mark out the the width of the housing, but stop about 18mm (¾in) short of the front edge. Then with a marking gauge set to about a third of the board's thickness, mark the housing depth on the edge of the board. To give the saw clearance, remove about 38mm (1½in) of the housing at the stopped end, first with a drill and then with a chisel (1). Saw down both sides of the housing and pare out the waste to leave a level bottom.

In the front corner of the other board, cut a notch (2) to fit the stopped housing, so that the two front edges lie flush when the joint is assembled.

1 Chop out a clearance for the saw

2 Cut a notch from the front corner

SEE ALSO > Marking gauge 487, Marking knife 487, Mortise gauge 487, Try square 487, Tenon saw 488, Power routers 495, Drill stand 500, Nailed butt joints 505

Cutting a through housing

Square the end of one board and use it to mark out the width of the housing on the other board (**1**); then, with a marking gauge set to about a third of the board's thickness, mark the depth of the housing on both edges (**2**). Saw along both sides of the housing (**3**), keeping just on the waste side of the two lines. Chisel out the waste, working from both edges of the board (**4**), and then pare it flat with the chisel.

1 Mark the side of the housing

2 Mark the depth of the housing

3 Saw along each side of the housing

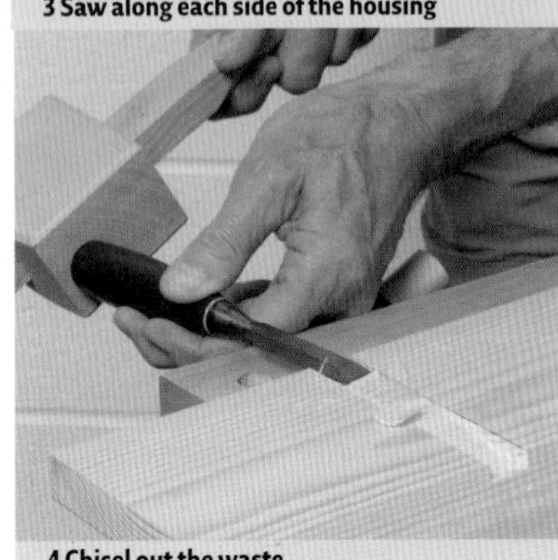

4 Chisel out the waste

Dowel joints

Dowel joints are strong and versatile. They can secure butt-jointed rails, mitred frames and long boards butted edge to edge. Use dowels that are about one-third the thickness of the wood.

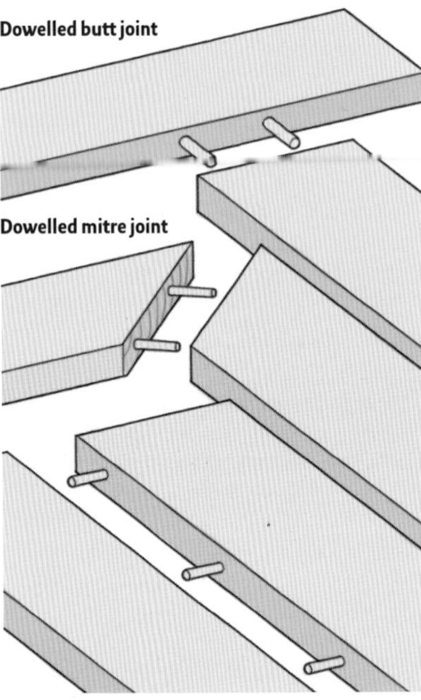

Cutting a dowel joint

When joining boards edge to edge, cut the dowels about 38mm (1½in) long; otherwise, saw the dowels to a length equal to two-thirds the width of the rails. File chamfers on both ends of each dowel and saw a groove along each one (**1**), so air and surplus glue can escape when the joint is assembled. To save time, you can buy ready-cut and chamfered dowels that are grooved all round.

If you are using a dowelling jig, then you won't need to mark the centres of the dowel holes. Otherwise, set a marking gauge to the centre line on both rails (**2**) and drive panel pins into the edge of the side rail to mark dowel-hole centres, then cut them to short sharp points with diagonal cutters (**3**). Line up the rails and push them together for the metal points to mark the end grain of the crossrail (**4**), then pull out the cut panel pins.

Using a power drill, with the appropriate dowel bit, bore the holes to a depth just over half the length of the dowels, then glue and assemble the joint. You will find that drilling accurate dowel holes is much easier if you use a purpose-made dowel bit and have the drill mounted in a vertical drill stand.

1 Saw a slot for the glue to escape

2 Score centre lines on each component

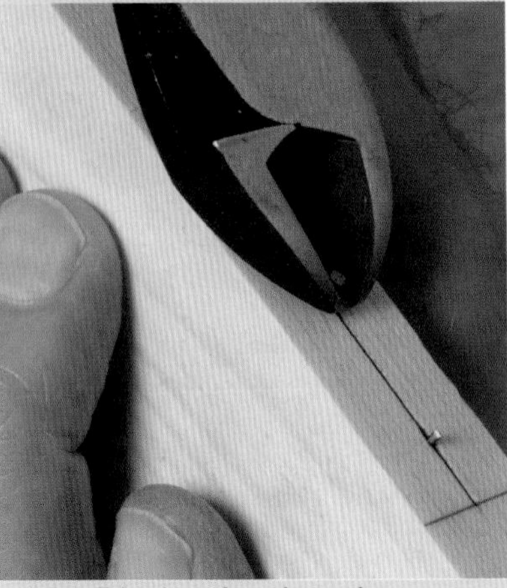

3 Cut off the pins to form sharp points

4 Mark the hole centres on the crossrail

SEE ALSO > Marking gauge 487, Marking knife 487, Try square 487, Tenon saw 488, Power routers 495, Dowel bits 500, Power drills 500, Diagonal cutters 526

Mortise-and-tenon joints

A mortise and tenon is a strong joint for narrow components - and essential for chair and table frames. A through tenon can be wedged for extra strength, but a stopped tenon is neater.

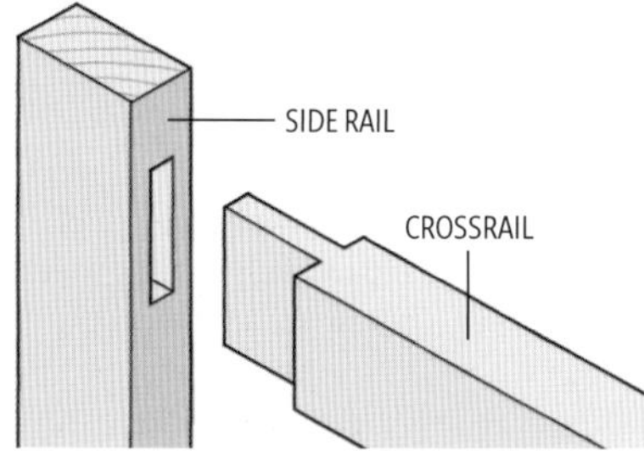

Cutting a mortise and tenon

Mark the width of the mortise, using the crossrail as a guide (1), and mark the shoulder of the tenon all round the crossrail (2). Set a mortise gauge to one-third of the crossrail's thickness and mark both the mortise and the tenon (3). Cut the tenon the same way as the tongue of a T-halving joint. Remove the waste from the mortise with an electric drill (preferably mounted in a drill stand), then square up its ends and sides with a chisel. Glue and assemble the joint.

1 Mark the width of the mortise

2 Mark the tenon shoulder

3 Mark the thickness of the joint

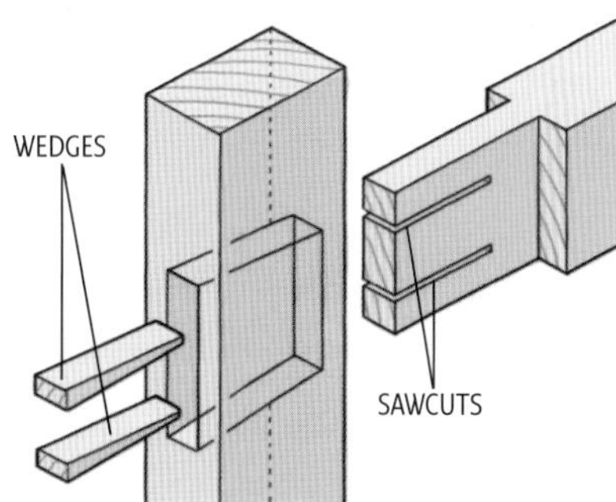

Cutting a through tenon

When a tenon is to pass right through a side rail, cut it slightly longer than the width of the rail and saw two slots through it. Glue and assemble the joint, then drive glued hardwood wedges into the sawcuts to expand the tenon in the mortise. When the glue has set, plane the wedges and the tenon flush with the rail.

Mitre joints

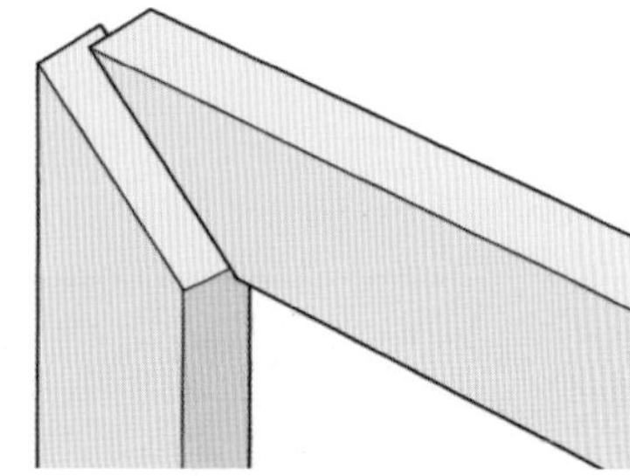

Cutting a mitre joint

A right-angled mitre joint is made by sawing the ends of two rails to 45 degrees in a mitre box, then butting them together. Trim the mitres with a finely set plane on a shooting board, and assemble the glued joint in a mitre cramp. If the meeting faces of the rails are fairly large, glue alone will hold them together; but you can reinforce a mitre joint by sawing two slots across the corner and gluing strips of veneer into them. Plane the veneers flush with the rails after the glue has set.

Reinforce a mitre joint with strips of veneer

Scarf joints

A scarf joint is used for joining two lengths of timber end to end.

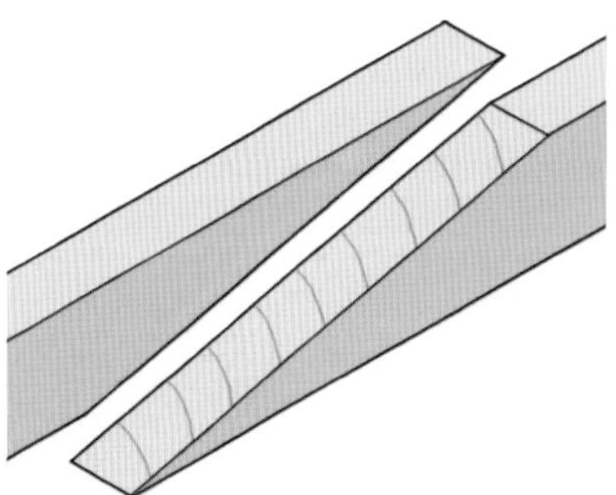

Making a scarf joint

Clamp the two lengths side by side, with their ends flush, and mark out the angled cut. The span of a scarf joint should be four times the width of the timber (1).

Saw and plane both lengths down to the marked line simultaneously, then unclamp them. Glue the two angled faces together, securing them with battens and G-cramps while the glue sets (2).

If the scarf joint is likely to be subjected to a great deal of stress, you can reinforce it with plywood plates screwed to both sides of the rails.

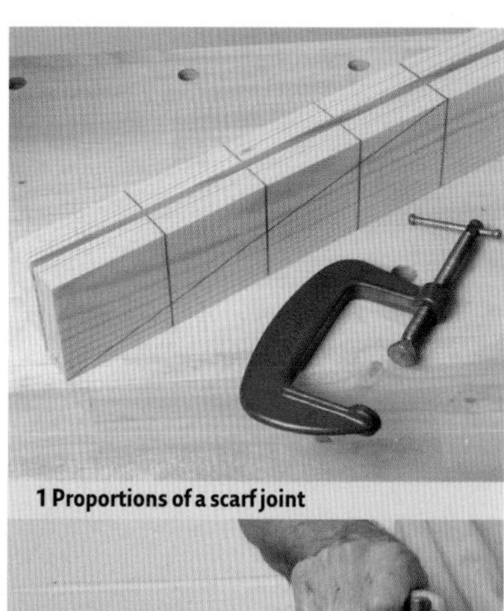
1 Proportions of a scarf joint

2 Clamp the joint between G-cramps

SEE ALSO > Marking gauge 487, Marking knife 487, Mortise gauge 487, Try square 487, Tenon saw 488, Mitre box 489, Drill stand 500, Cramps 503, T-halving joint 506

Building tools

A specialist such as a plasterer, joiner or bricklayer needs only a limited set of tools, whereas the amateur is more like a one-man general builder – who has to be able to tackle all kinds of construction and repair work and therefore requires a much wider range of tools. The tool kit suggested here is for making repairs and improvements to your home and for tasks such as erecting garden structures and laying paving.

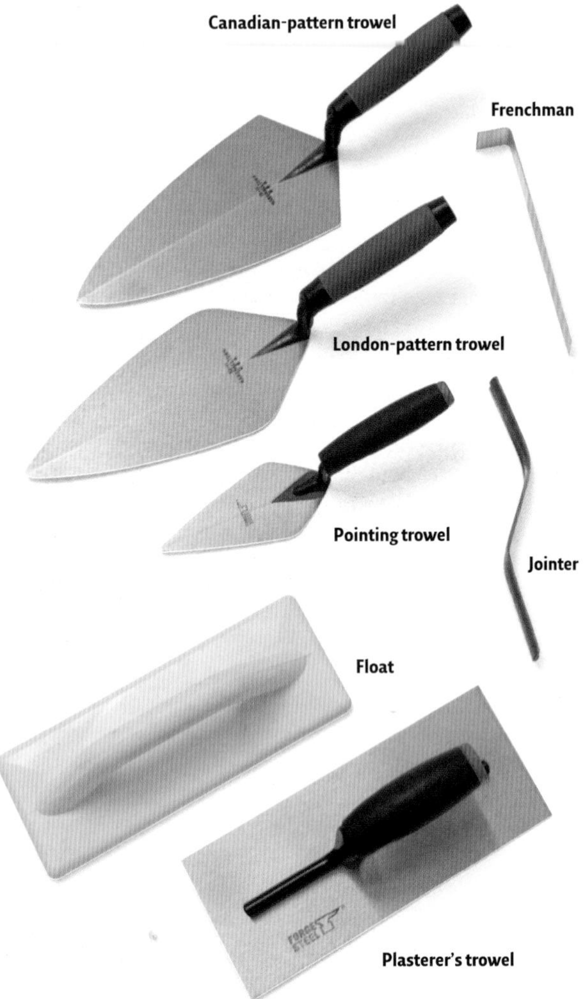

Floats and trowels

For a professional builder, floats and trowels have their specific uses – but in home maintenance a repointing trowel may often be the ideal tool for patching small areas of plaster, or a plasterer's trowel for smoothing concrete.

Brick trowels

A brick trowel is for handling and placing mortar when laying bricks or concrete blocks. A professional might use one with a blade as long as 300mm (1ft) – but such a trowel is too heavy and unwieldy for the amateur, so buy a good-quality brick trowel with a fairly short blade.

The blade of a London-pattern trowel has one curved edge for cutting bricks, a skill that takes practice to perfect. The blade's other edge is straight, for picking up mortar. You can buy left-handed versions of this trowel, or opt for a similar trowel with two straight edges.

A Canadian-pattern trowel (sometimes called a Philadelphia brick trowel) is also symmetrical, having a wide blade with two curved edges.

Pointing trowel

A pointing trowel is designed for repairing and shaping mortar joints between bricks. The blade is only about 100mm (4in) long.

Jointer

Use a jointer to shape concave mortar joints between bricks. The tool's narrow blade is dragged along the horizontal and vertical joints, shaping the mortar into shallow depressions.

Frenchman

A Frenchman is a specialized tool for scraping off excess mortar from brickwork jointing. You can make one by heating and bending an old table knife or a metal strip.

Wooden or plastic float

A wooden builder's float is for applying and smoothing cement renderings and concrete to a fine, attractive texture. The more expensive ones have detachable handles, so their wooden blades can be replaced when they wear. Similar floats made from plastic are also available.

Plasterer's trowel

A plasterer's trowel is a steel float for applying plaster and cement renderings to walls. Dampened, it is also used for 'polishing' – smoothing the surface of the material when it has firmed up. Some builders prefer to apply rendering with a heavy trowel and finish it with a more flexible blade, but you need to be quite skilled to exploit such subtle differences.

Boards for carrying mortar or plaster

Any convenient-sized sheet of 12 or 18mm (½ or ¾in) exterior-grade plywood can be used as a mixing board for plaster or mortar. A panel about 1m (3ft) square makes an ideal mixing board, while a smaller spot board, about 600mm (2ft) square, is convenient for carrying the material to the work site. Screw some battens to the underside of either board to make it easier to lift and carry. You will also need a lightweight hawk for carrying pointing mortar or plaster.

A home-made hawk
Make a hawk by nailing a block of wood underneath a plywood board, so you can plug a handle into it.

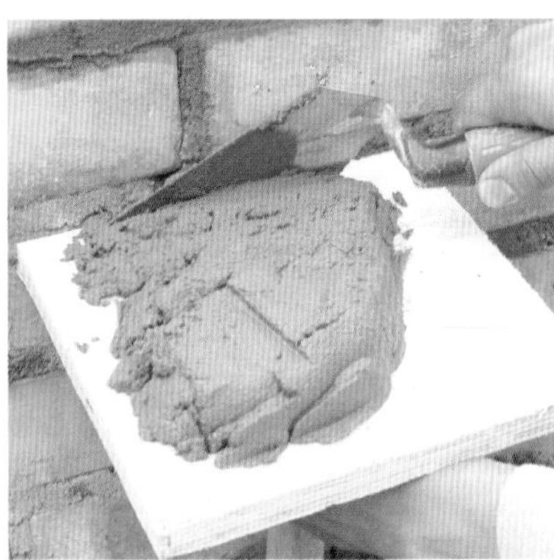

Using a pointing hawk
A pointing hawk makes the filling of mortar joints very easy. Place the lip of the hawk just under a horizontal joint and scrape the mortar into place with a small trowel or jointer.

SEE ALSO > Plastering 157–61, Mortar 441, Bricklaying 444–9

Tools for levelling and measuring

Tape measure
An ordinary retractable steel tape measure is adequate for most purposes. But if you need to measure a large plot, buy or hire a wind-up tape, which can be up to 30m (100ft) in length.

Builder's square
A large set square is useful when setting out brick or concrete-block corners. The best squares are stamped out of sheet metal, but you can make a serviceable one by cutting out a right-angled triangle from thick plywood with a hypotenuse of about 750mm (2ft 6in). Cut out the centre of the triangle to reduce the weight.

Spirit level
A spirit level is a machine-made straightedge incorporating special glass tubes or vials that contain a liquid. In each vial an air bubble floats. When a bubble rests exactly between two lines marked on the glass, that indicates that the structure on which the level is held is properly horizontal or vertical, depending on the orientation of the vial.

Buy a wooden or lightweight aluminium level 600 to 900mm (2 to 3ft) long. A well-made one is very strong, but treat it with care and always clean mortar or plaster from it before they set.

Try square
Use a large try square for marking out square cuts or joints on timber. The same tool is used to check that wood is planed square and to make sure an internal corner forms a right angle.

Plumb line
A small, heavy weight hung on a length of fine string is used for judging whether a structure or surface is vertical.

Bricklayer's line
This is a nylon line used as a guide for laying bricks or blocks level. It is stretched between two flat-bladed pins - which are driven into vertical joints at the ends of a wall - or between line blocks that hook over the bricks at the ends of a course. As a substitute, you can stretch string between two stakes driven into the ground outside the line of the wall.

Steel pins and line
You can buy special flat-bladed pins, or make your own by hammering flats on 100mm (4in) nails.

Line blocks
The blocks grip the corners of the bricks at the end of a course, and the line passes through their slots.

Plasterer's rule
This is simply a straight length of wood that is used for scraping plaster and rendering undercoats level.

Straightedge
Any length of straight rigid timber can be used to check whether a surface is flat or, in conjunction with a spirit level, to see whether two points are at the same height.

Gauge stick
For gauging the height of brick courses, calibrate a softwood batten by making sawcuts across it at 75mm (3in) intervals - which is the thickness of a brick plus its mortar joint.

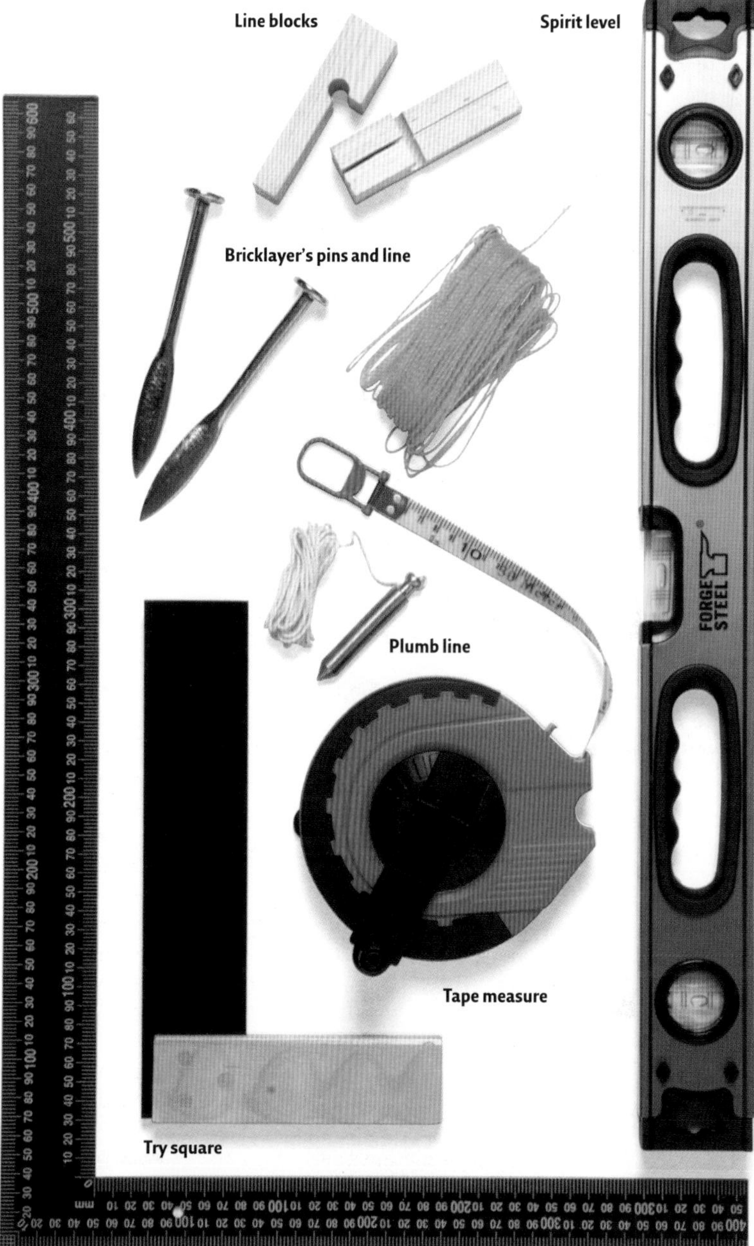

Using a water level

A water level comprises a flexible hose full of water with a short transparent gauge at each end. Since water level remains constant, the levels in the gauges are always identical and so can be used for marking identical heights, even over long distances and round obstacles and bends.

If you don't want to buy a water level, make one by plugging short lengths of transparent plastic tubing into the ends of a garden hose. Then fill the hose with water until it appears in both tubes.

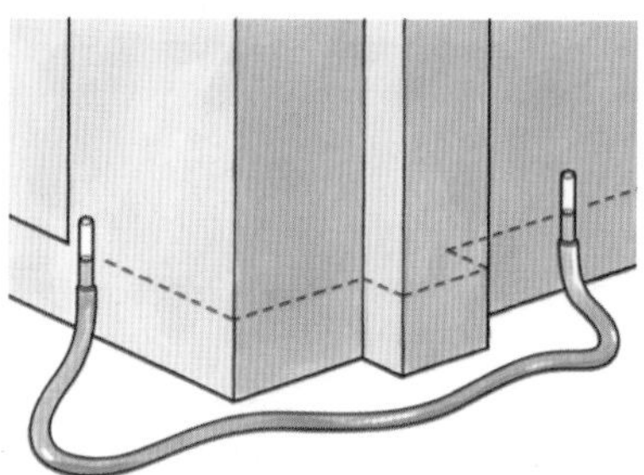

Measuring around a corner
One distinct advantage of using a water level is being able to take measurements around a corner.

SEE ALSO > Bricklaying 444–9

Hammers

Several types of hammer are useful on a building site.

Claw hammer

Choose a strong claw hammer for building stud partitions, making doorframes and window frames, nailing floorboards and putting up garden fencing.

Club hammer

A heavy club hammer is used for driving cold chisels and for a variety of demolition jobs. It is also useful for driving large masonry nails into walls.

Sledgehammer

Hire a sledgehammer if you have to break up hardcore or paving. It's also the best tool for driving stakes or fence posts into the ground, though you can make do with a club hammer if the ground is not too hard.

Sledgehammer and club hammer

Mallet

A wooden carpenter's mallet is the proper tool for driving a wood chisel. But you can use a metal hammer instead if the chisel has an impact-resistant plastic handle.

Drills

A powerful electric drill is invaluable to a builder. A cordless version is useful when you have to bore holes outdoors or in lofts and cellars that lack convenient electric sockets.

Drilling masonry for inserting wallplugs
Set the drill to hammer action and low speed. Wrap tape round the bit to mark the depth to be drilled, allowing for slightly more depth than the length of the plug. Drill the hole in stages, partly withdrawing the bit at times in order to clear the debris. To catch falling dust, tape an envelope or paper bag just below the position of the hole before starting to drill.

Power drill

Buy a good-quality power drill, plus a range of twist drills and spade bits for drilling timber. Make sure the drill has a percussion or hammer action for drilling walls.

When drilling into masonry you need to use special drill bits tipped with tungsten carbide. The smaller ones are matched to the size of standard wall-plugs; and there are also much larger ones with reduced shanks that fit into a standard power-drill chuck. As the larger bits are expensive, it pays to hire them. Percussion bits are even tougher than standard masonry bits and have shatter-proof tips.

Brace

A brace is the ideal handtool for drilling large holes in timber. In addition, when fitted with a screwdriver bit, it provides the necessary leverage for inserting or extracting large woodscrews.

Saws

Every builder needs a range of saws, including an electric circular saw or a reciprocating saw for cutting heavy structural timbers. There are also some specialized saws for cutting metal and even for sawing through masonry.

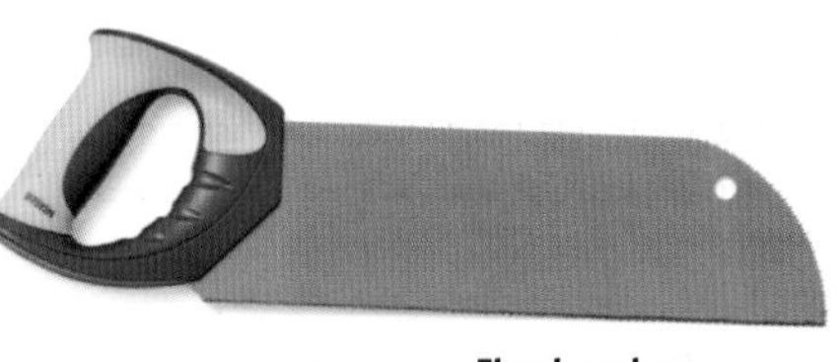

Floorboard saw

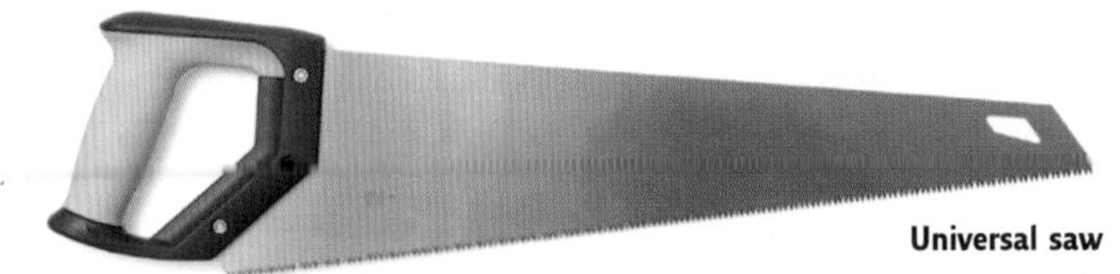

Universal saw

Masonry saw

Universal saw

A single handsaw that can be used equally well for ripping solid planks lengthwise and crosscutting them to size is a useful tool to have on a building site. A saw with hardened teeth is also an asset.

Masonry saw

Masonry saws closely resemble the hand-saws used for wood, but their hardened or tungsten-carbide teeth are designed to cut brick, concrete and stone.

Floorboard saw

If you prise a floorboard above its neigh-bours, you will be able to cut across it with an ordinary tenon saw – but the curved cutting edge of a floorboard saw makes it easier to avoid damaging the boards on either side.

Hacksaw

The hardened-steel blades of a hacksaw have fine teeth for cutting metal. Use one to cut steel concrete-reinforcing rods or small pieces of sheet metal.

All-purpose saw

An all-purpose saw is able to cut wood, metal, plastics and building boards. This type of saw is especially useful for cutting secondhand timber, which may contain nails or screws that would blunt the blade of an ordinary woodsaw.

Glazier's tools

There's little point in trying to cut glass yourself when replacing a broken window. It is better to have it cut by a professional glazier, then fit the new pane using the tools described below.

Hacking knife

Clipped-point putty knife

Straight putty knife

Hacking knife

A hacking knife has a heavy steel blade for chipping old putty out of window rebates in order to remove the glass. Place the point between the putty and the frame, then tap the back of the blade with a hammer.

Putty knife

The blunt blade of a putty knife is used for shaping and smoothing fresh putty. You can choose between clipped-point and straight blades, according to your personal preference.

SEE ALSO > Repairing broken glass 196, Brace 499, Power drills 500, Hammers and mallets 501, Hacksaws 518

Builder's chisels

As well as chisels for cutting and paring wood joints, you'll need some special ones when you are working on masonry.

Cold chisel

Cold chisels are made from solid-steel hexagonal-section rod. They are primarily for cutting metal bars and chopping the heads off rivets, but a builder will use one for cutting chases in plaster and brickwork or for chopping out old brick pointing.

Plugging chisel

A plugging chisel has a narrow, flat 'bit' (tip) for cutting out old or eroded pointing. It's worth having one when you need to repoint a large area of brickwork .

Bolster chisel

The wide 'bit' of a bolster chisel is designed for cutting bricks and concrete blocks. It is also useful for levering up floorboards.

Slip a plastic safety sleeve over a chisel to guard your hand against a misplaced blow from a club hammer.

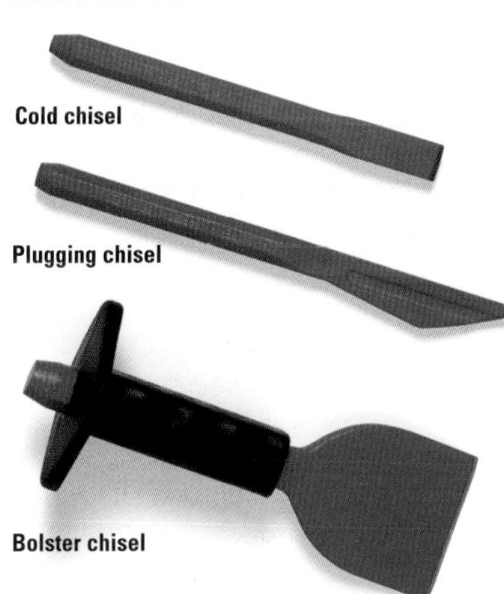

Work gloves

For safety, wear strong work gloves whenever you're carrying paving slabs, concrete blocks or rough timber. The best work gloves have leather palms and fingers, although you may prefer a pair with ventilated backs for comfort in hot weather.

Digging tools

Much building work requires some kind of digging – for laying strip foundations and concrete pads, sinking rows of post holes, and so on. You probably have the basic tools in your garden shed; the others you can hire.

Pickaxe

Use a medium-weight pickaxe to break up heavily compacted soil – especially if it contains a lot of buried rubble.

Mattock

The wide blade of a mattock is ideal for breaking up heavy clay soil, and it's better than an ordinary pickaxe for ground that is riddled with tree roots.

Spade

Buy a good-quality spade for excavating soil and mixing concrete. One with a stainless-steel blade is best, but alloy steel lasts reasonably well. Choose a strong hardwood shaft split to form a D-shaped handle that is riveted with metal plates to its crosspiece. Make sure the hollow shaft socket and blade are forged in one piece.

Although square spade blades seem to be more popular, many builders prefer a round-mouth or pointed spade with a long pole handle for digging deep holes and trenches.

Shovel

You can use a spade for mixing and placing concrete or mortar, but the raised edges of a shovel retain it better.

Garden rake

Use an ordinary garden rake for spreading gravel or levelling wet concrete. Be sure to wash your rake before concrete sets on it.

Wheelbarrow

Most garden wheelbarrows aren't strong enough to cope with serious building work, which generally involves carting heavy loads of rubble and wet concrete.

Unless the tubular underframe of the wheelbarrow is rigidly strutted, you may well find that the barrow's thin metal body will distort and spill its load as you are crossing rough ground.

Check, too, that the axle is fixed securely – a cheap barrow can lose its wheel as you are tipping a load of hardcore, concrete or earth into an excavation.

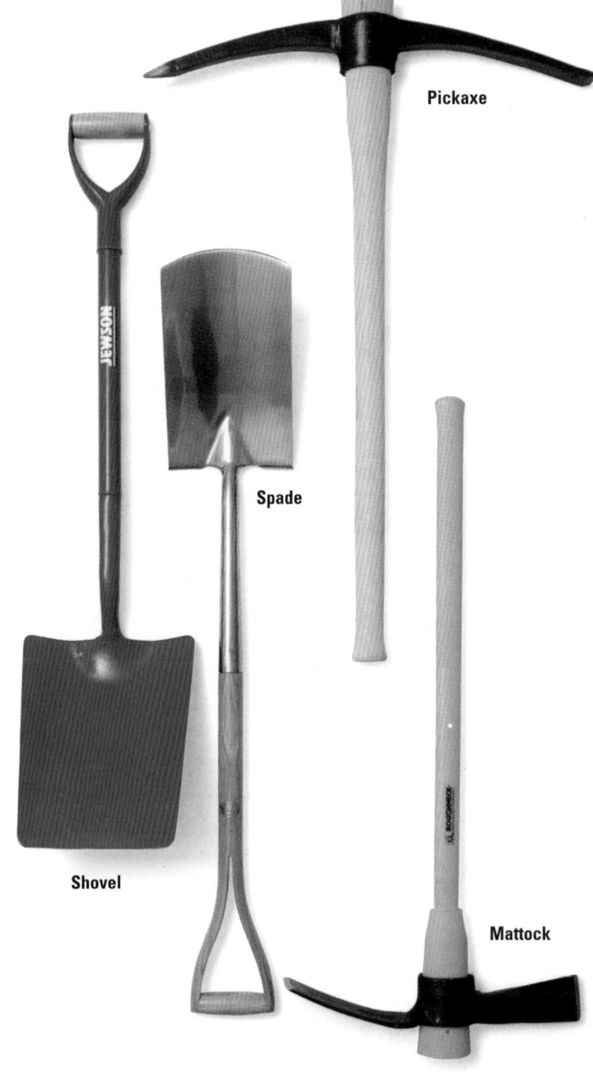

Crowbar

A crowbar, or wrecking bar, is used for demolishing timber framework. Force the flat tip between the components and use the leverage of the long shaft to prise them apart. Choose a crowbar that has a claw at one end for removing large nails.

Slater's ripper

To replace individual slates you must cut their fixing nails without disturbing the slates overlapping them, and for this you need a slater's ripper. Pass the long hooked blade up between the slates, locate one of the hooks over the fixing nail, and pull down sharply to cut it.

- **Screwdrivers**
Most people gradually acquire an assortment of flat-tip and cross-head screwdrivers over a period of time. Alternatively, you can purchase a power screwdriver with a range of bits or buy screwdriver bits for your power drill.
- **Planes**
Most household joinery needs only skimming to leave a fairly smooth finish. A jack plane, which is a medium-size bench plane, is the most versatile general-purpose tool.

SEE ALSO > Replacing roof slates 126, Cutting a chase 303, Erecting fence posts 429, Bench planes 492, Screwdrivers 502

Ladders and scaffolding

Whether you need to reach guttering or require a simple step-up to paint the living-room ceiling, it is essential to use strong and stable equipment. Even for small jobs that don't justify the cost of buying ladders or scaffolding, it's advisable to hire them rather than make do. For a small outlay, you can buy accessories that make working on a ladder safer and more comfortable.

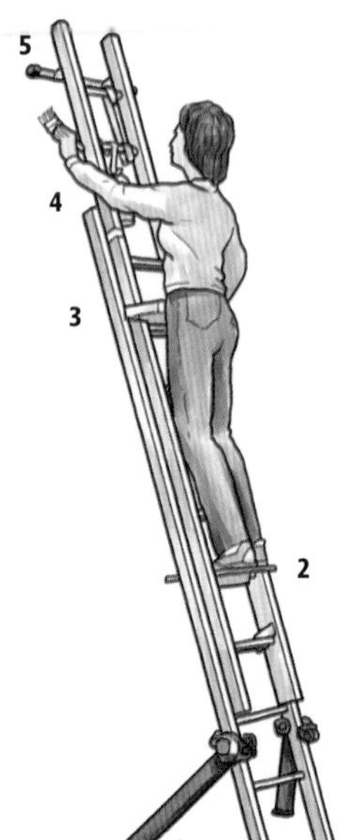

Ladder accessories
This ladder has stabilizers (1) for uneven ground, a foot rest (2), a tool tray (3), a paint-can hook (4), and a stay (5) to hold the top away from eaves.

Ladder accessories

Ladder stay

A stay holds the ladder away from the wall. It is an essential piece of equipment when painting overhanging eaves and gutters – otherwise you would be forced to lean back, risking overbalancing.

Tool tray and paint-can hook

You should always support yourself with one hand on a ladder, so use a wire or bent-metal hook to hang a paint can or bucket from a rung. A clip-on tray is ideal for holding a small selection of tools.

Clip-on platform

A wide flat board that clamps onto the rungs provides a comfortable platform to stand on while working for long periods.

Stabilizers

These are bolt-on accessories that prevent the ladder from slipping and compensate for uneven ground.

Ladders and towers

Lightweight metal stepladders are essential when decorating indoors. It's worth having at least one that stands about 2m (6ft 6in) high, so you can reach a ceiling without having to stand on the top step. A shorter second ladder may be more convenient for other jobs, and you can use both with scaffold boards to build a platform.

Outdoors, you will need ladders that reach up to the eaves. Double and triple extension ladders can be heavy. Some of the longer extending ladders are operated by a rope and pulley, which makes them easier to extend single-handed.

To estimate the length of ladder you are going to need, add together the ceiling heights of your house and then add at least 1m (3ft 3in) to the length – to allow for leaning the ladder at an angle and for safe access to a platform.

There are dual-purpose or even multi-purpose ladders designed to convert from stepladder to straight ladder, and some fold to make a work platform. This type of versatile ladder is a good compromise.

Sectional scaffold frames can be hired and built up to form towers at any height for decorating inside and outside. Broad feet prevent the scaffold sinking into the ground, and adjustable versions allow you to level it. Some models have locking castors that enable you to move the tower.

Towers are ideal for painting a large expanse of wall outdoors. Indoors, smaller platforms made from the same scaffold components bring high ceilings within easy reach.

Alloy stepladder **Dual-purpose ladder** **Scaffold tower** **Extending ladder**

SEE ALSO > Work platforms 516

Ladder safety

More accidents are caused by using ladders unwisely than by faulty equipment. Erect the ladder safely before you climb it – and move it when work is out of reach. Never lean to the side, or you will overbalance. Follow these simple, commonsense rules:

Safety aloft

Never climb higher than four rungs from the top of the ladder, or you won't be able to balance properly and there will be no handholds within reach. Keep both your feet on a rung, and your hips centred between the uprights. Avoid slippery footholds by placing a sack or doormat at the foot of the ladder, so you can dry your boots before you ascend.

Securing the ladder

If the ground is soft, place a wide board under the feet of a ladder; screw a batten across the board to hold the ladder in place. On hard ground, make sure the ladder has anti-slip end caps, and lay a sandbag (or a tough polythene bag filled with earth) at the base. Secure the stiles with rope tied to stakes driven into the ground at each side and just behind the ladder.

When you extend a ladder, the sections should overlap by at least a quarter of their length. Don't lean the top of the ladder against gutters, soil pipes or drainpipes, as they may give way – and especially not against glass.

It's a good idea to fix ring bolts at regular intervals into the masonry just below the fascia board. This is an excellent way to secure the top of a ladder, as you will have equally good anchor points wherever you choose to position it. Alternatively, fix large screw eyes to the masonry or a sound fascia board and attach the ladder to them.

Staking a ladder
Secure the base of a ladder by lashing it to stakes driven into the ground.

Features to look for

When you buy or hire a ladder, bear in mind that:

- Adjustability is a prime consideration. Choose a ladder that will enable you to gain access to various parts of the building and will convert to a compact unit for storage.
- End caps or foot pads are an advantage, to prevent the ladder from slipping on hard ground.
- The rungs of overlapping sections of an extension ladder should align, or the gap between the rungs might be too small to secure a good foothold.
- Choose an extension ladder with an automatic latch that locks the extension to its rung.
- Check that you can buy or hire a range of accessories (see opposite) to fit your make of ladder.
- Choose a stepladder with a platform at the top to take paint cans and trays.
- Treads should be comfortable to stand on. Stepladders with wide, flat treads are the best choice.
- Stepladders with extended stiles give you a handhold at the top of the steps.

How to handle a ladder

Ladders can be heavy and unwieldy, so handle them properly to avoid damaging property and to make sure you don't injure yourself or anyone else.

Carry a ladder upright, not slung across your shoulder. Hold the ladder vertically, and bend your knees slightly, then rock the ladder back against your shoulder. Grip one rung lower down while you support the ladder at head height with your other hand, then straighten your knees.

To erect a ladder, lay it on the ground with its feet against the wall. Gradually raise it to vertical as you walk towards the wall. Pull the feet out from the wall so that the ladder is resting at an angle of about 70 degrees – if the ladder extends to 8m (26ft), for example, its feet should be 2m (6ft 6in), or a quarter of its height, from the wall.

Hold an extending ladder upright while raising it to the required height. If it is a heavy ladder, get someone to hold it while you operate the mechanism.

Carrying a ladder
Carry the ladder upright, leaning it back against your shoulder. Grip one rung low down and the stile at head height.

Erecting a ladder
When the ladder is erected, its base should be a quarter of its height away from the wall, so that it is correctly balanced.

SEE ALSO > Work platforms 516

Erecting work platforms

Some decorators move a ladder little by little as the work progresses. However, constantly moving ladders becomes tedious, and may lead to an accident as you try to reach just a bit further before having to move along. It is safer to build a work platform that allows you to tackle a large area without moving the structure.

Improvised platform
A simple yet safe platform made from stepladders and a scaffold board.

Work platforms

You can hire a pair of decorators' trestles and bridge them with a scaffold board, or make a similar structure using two step-ladders. Clamp or tie the board to the rungs and use two boards - one on top of the other - if two people need to use the platform at once. Alternatively, you can buy a foldable work platform.

Another solution is to use scaffold-tower components to make a mobile platform. One with locking castors is ideal for painting or papering ceilings.

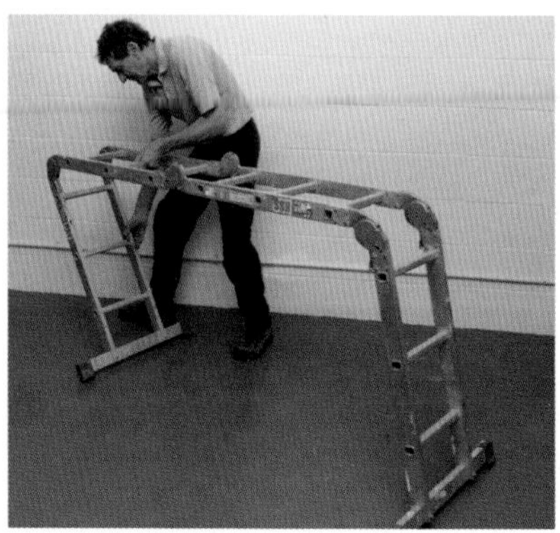

Some ladders fold to make a sturdy work platform

Decorating in a stairwell

It's not always easy to build a platform that is safe and convenient for decorating in a stairwell. The simplest method is to use a dual-purpose ladder, which can be adjusted to stand evenly on a flight of stairs. Anchor the steps with rope through a couple of large screw eyes fixed to the stair risers. When the stairs are carpeted, the holes will be concealed.

Rest a scaffold board between the ladder and the landing to form a bridge. Screw the board to the landing and tie the other end to the ladder.

Alternatively, construct a tailor-made platform from ladders and boards to suit your staircase. Make sure the boards and ladders are clamped, screwed or lashed together securely, and that the ladders cannot slip on the stair treads. If need be, screw wooden battens to the stairs and landings in order to prevent the feet of ladders moving.

Scaffold towers

It is best to erect scaffolding when you are decorating outside. Towers made from slot-together frames are available for hire, and heights up to about 9m (30ft) are possible. The taller towers have supporting 'outriggers' to prevent them toppling.

Build the lower section of the frame first and level it with adjustable feet before you erect the tower itself. Build a platform at the top with toe boards all round to prevent tools being knocked off. Extend the framework to provide handrails all round. Secure the tower to the house by tying it to ring bolts fixed into the masonry.

Some towers incorporate a staircase inside the scaffold frame; floors with trap doors enable you to ascend to the top of the tower. If you cannot hire such a tower, the safest alternative is to use a ladder, but make sure it extends at least 1m (3ft 3in) above the staging.

Using a ladder, it is difficult to reach windows and walls above an extension. With a scaffold tower, however, you can construct a cantilevered section that rests on the roof of the extension.

Stair scaffold
Erect a platform with scaffold frames to compensate for the slope of a staircase.

Dual-purpose ladder
Use this type of ladder to straddle the stairs, and a scaffold board to create a level platform.

Tailor-made platform
Build a sturdy platform made from scaffold boards, ladders and boxes to suit the layout of your stairwell.

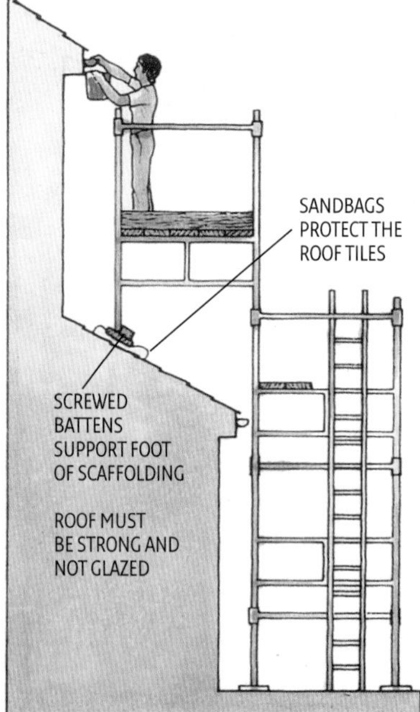

Erecting a cantilevered platform
To spread the load, rest a cantilevered section of scaffolding on a board made from two battens screwed together.

SEE ALSO > Papering stairwells 91, Ladders 514–15

Plumbing tools

Although plastics have been used for drainage for some time, the advent of ones suitable for mains-pressure and hot water has affected the plumbing trade more radically. However, brass fittings and pipework made from copper and other metals are still extensively used for domestic plumbing, so the plumber's tool kit is still basically for working metal.

Equipment for removing blockages

You don't have to get a plumber to clear blocked appliances and pipes or even main drains. All the necessary equipment can be bought or hired.

Sink plunger

This is a simple but effective tool for clearing a blockage from a sink, washbasin or bath trap. A pumping action on the flexible cup forces air and water along the pipe to disperse the blockage.

Hydraulic pump

A blocked waste pipe can be cleared with a hand-operated hydraulic pump. A downward stroke creates a powerful jet of water that should push the obstruction clear. If, however, the blockage is lodged firmly, an upward stroke may create enough suction to pull the obstruction out of place.

WC auger

The short coiled-wire WC auger designed for clearing WC and gully traps is rotated by a handle in a rigid hollow shaft.

Drain auger

A flexible coiled-wire drain auger will pass through small-diameter waste pipes to clear blockages. Pass the corkscrew-like head into the waste pipe until it reaches the blockage and clamp the cranked handle onto the other end, then turn it to rotate the head and engage the blockage. Push and pull the auger until the pipe is clear.

Drain rods

You can hire a complete set of rods and fittings for clearing main drains and inspection chambers. The rods come in 1m (3ft 3in) lengths of polypropylene with threaded brass connectors. The clearing heads comprise a double-worm corkscrew fitting and a rubber plunger. You can hire a hinged scraper for clearing the open channels in inspection chambers.

Drain rods

Drain auger

WC auger

Hydraulic pump

Sink plunger

Measuring and marking

Tools for measuring and marking metal are similar to those used for wood, but they are made and calibrated for greater accuracy because metal parts must fit with precision.

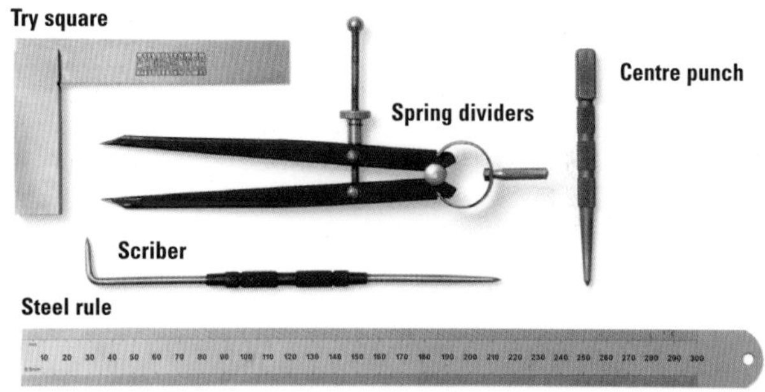

Scriber

For precise work, use a pointed hardened-steel scriber to mark lines and hole centres on metal. Use a pencil to mark the centre of a bend, as a scored line made with a scriber may open up when the metal is stretched on the outside of the bend.

Spring dividers

Spring dividers are similar to a pencil compass, but both legs have steel points. These are adjusted to the required spacing by a knurled nut on a threaded rod that links the legs.

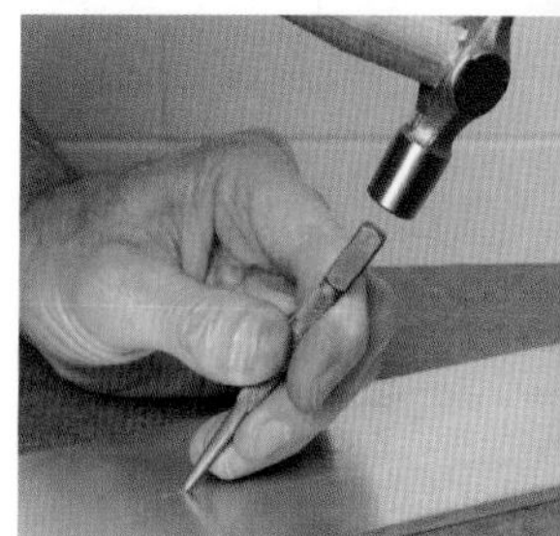

Correcting a misplaced centre mark
If the mark is not accurate, angle the punch towards the true centre, tap it to extend the mark in that direction, and then mark the centre again.

Centre punch

A centre punch is an inexpensive tool for marking the centres of holes to be drilled. With its point on dead centre, strike the punch with a hammer.

Steel rule

You will need a long tape measure for estimating pipe runs and positioning appliances, but use a steel rule for marking out small components.

Try square

You can use a woodworker's try square to mark out or check right angles; however, an all-metal engineer's try square is precision-made for metalwork. For general-purpose work, choose a 150mm (6in) try square.

SEE ALSO > Clearing a sink 356, Clearing a WC 3570, Clearing drains 358

Metal-cutting tools

You can cut solid bar, sheet and tubular metal with an ordinary hacksaw, but there are tools specifically designed for cutting sheet metal and pipes.

Hacksaws

General-purpose hacksaw

A modern hacksaw has a tubular-steel frame with a light cast-metal handle. The frame is adjustable to accommodate replaceable blades of different lengths, which are tensioned by tightening a wing nut at one end of the saw.

Junior hacksaw

Use a junior hacksaw for cutting small-bore tubing and thin metal rod. The simplest ones have a solid spring-steel frame that holds the blade under tension. Others have a tensioning device similar to the one on larger hacksaws.

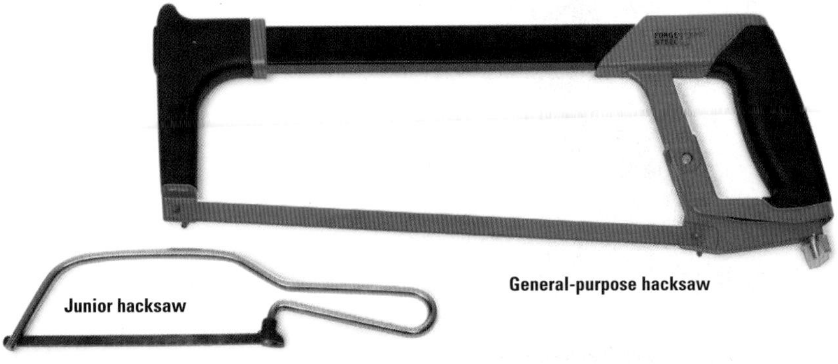

Junior hacksaw

General-purpose hacksaw

Using hacksaws

Sawing metal bar or square tube

Hold the work in an engineer's vice, with the marked cutting line as close to the jaws as possible in order to prevent the metal vibrating as you saw.

Start the cut just on the waste side of the line with short strokes until the kerf (sawcut) is about 1mm (1/16in) deep. Then turn the metal 90 degrees in the vice, so that the kerf faces away from you, and cut a similar kerf in the new face.

Continue in this way until the kerf runs right round the bar or tube. Continue to cut through a bar with long steady strokes. Steady the end of the saw with your free hand; and if necessary, put a little light oil on the blade.

Engineer's vice
A large engineer's or metal-worker's vice has to be bolted to the workbench, but smaller ones can be clamped on. Slip soft fibre liners over the jaws to protect workpieces held in the vice.

Sawing rod or pipe

As you cut a cylindrical rod or hollow tube, rotate it away from you till the kerf runs right round the rod or tube before you sever the metal.

Sawing sheet metal

To saw a small piece of sheet metal, sandwich it between two strips of wood clamped in a vice. Adjust the metal to place the cutting line close to the strips, then saw down the waste side of the line with steady strokes and with the blade held at a slight angle to the work.

To cut a thin sheet of metal, clamp it between two pieces of MDF and cut through all three layers simultaneously.

Turn a square tube or bar through 90 degrees

Rotate a cylindrical rod away from you

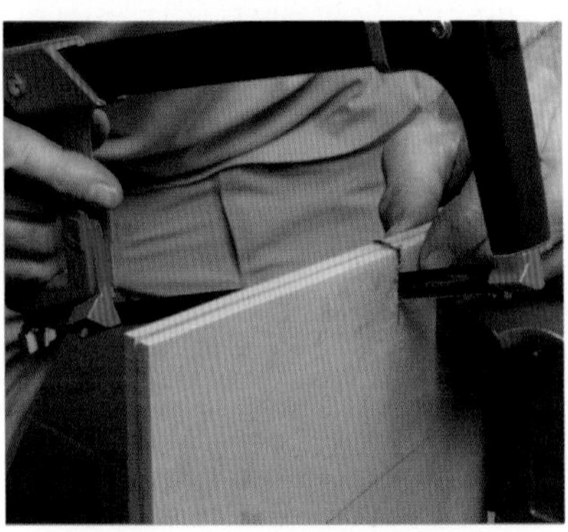

Sandwich thin sheet metal between MDF

Hacksaw blades

You can buy 200, 250 and 300mm (8, 10 and 12in) hacksaw blades. Try the different lengths till you find the one that suits you best. Choose the hardness and size of teeth according to the type of metal you are planning to cut.

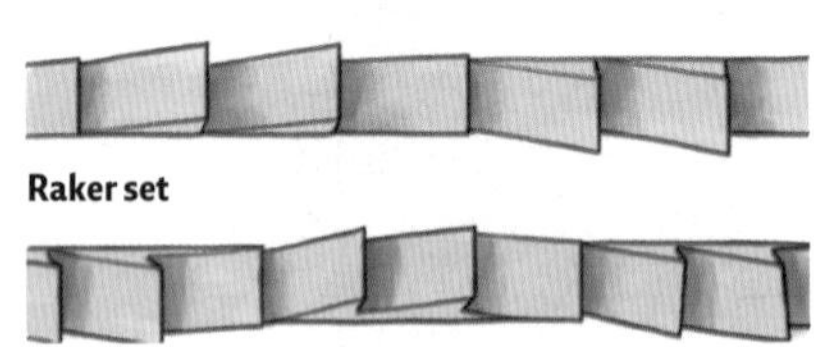

Raker set

Wavy set

Size and set of teeth

A coarse hacksaw blade has 14 to 18 teeth per 25mm (1in); a fine one has 24 to 32. The teeth are set (bent sideways) to make a cut wider than the blade's thickness, to prevent it jamming in the work. Coarse teeth are 'raker set' – with pairs of teeth bent to opposite sides and separated by a tooth left in line with the blade to clear metal waste from the kerf. Fine teeth are too small to be raker set, and the whole row is 'wavy set'. Use a coarse blade for cutting soft metals like brass and aluminium, which would clog fine teeth, and a fine blade for thin sheet and the harder metals.

Hardness

A hacksaw blade must be harder than the metal it is cutting, or its teeth will quickly blunt. A flexible blade with hardened teeth will cut most metals, but there are fully hardened blades that stay sharp longer and are less prone to losing teeth. However, being rigid and brittle, they break easily. Blades of high-speed steel are expensive and even more brittle than the fully hardened ones, but they will cut very hard alloys.

SEE ALSO > Metal scriber 517, Try square 517

Fitting hacksaw blades

It is impossible to sharpen hacksaw blades, so insert a new blade when the old one breaks or becomes blunt.

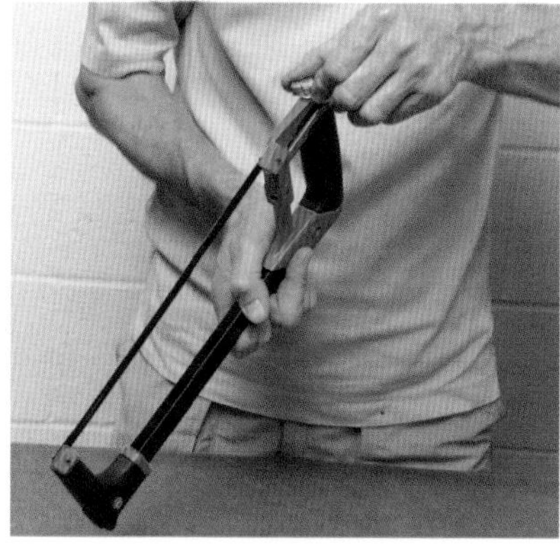

Fitting a standard hacksaw blade
With its teeth pointing away from the handle, slip a new blade onto the pins at each end of the hacksaw frame. Apply tension with the wing nut. If the new blade tends to wander off line as you cut, tighten the wing nut.

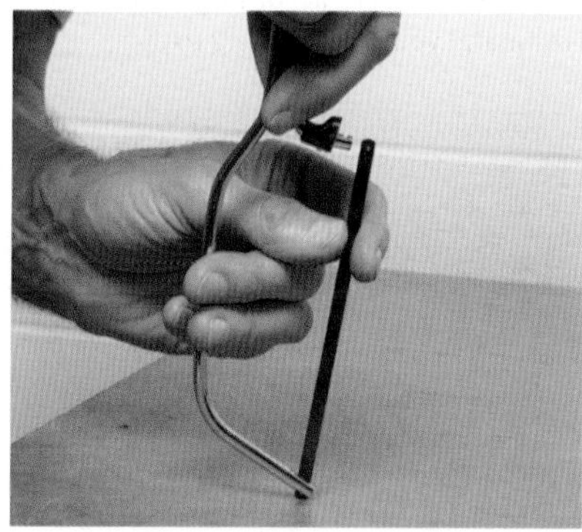

Fitting a blade to a junior hacksaw
To fit a blade, locate it in the slot at the front of the frame and bow the frame against a workbench until the blade fits into the rear slot.

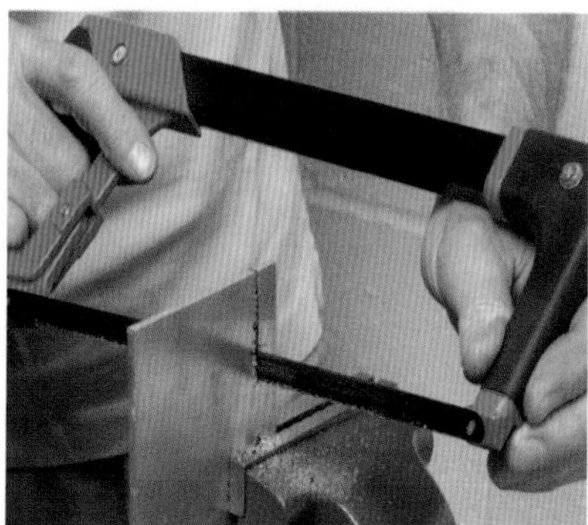

Turning a blade
Sometimes it's easier to work with the blade turned at an angle to the frame. To do so, reassemble the saw with the blade located on the angled pins.

Straight tinsnips

Universal tinsnips

Tinsnips

Tinsnips are used for cutting sheet metal. Straight snips have wide blades for cutting straight edges. If you try to cut curves with them, the waste usually gets caught against the blades; but it is possible to cut a convex curve by progressively removing small straight pieces of waste down to the marked line. Universal snips have thick narrow blades that cut a curve in one pass and will also make straight cuts.

Using tinsnips
As you cut along the marked line, let the waste curl away from the sheet. To cut thick sheet metal, clamp one handle of the snips in a vice, so you can apply your full weight to the other one.

Try not to close the jaws completely every time, as that can cause a jagged edge on the metal. Wear thick gloves when cutting sheet metal.

Sharpening tinsnips
Clamp one handle in a vice and sharpen the cutting edge with a smooth file. File the other edge and finish by removing the burrs from the backs of the blades on an oiled slipstone.

Tube cutters

A tube cutter slices the ends off pipes at exactly 90 degrees to their length. The pipe is clamped between the cutting wheel and an adjustable slide with two rollers, and is cut as the tool is moved round it. The adjusting screw is tightened between each revolution.

A pipe slice, which works like a tube cutter, can be operated in confined spaces.

Clamp one handle of the snips in a vice

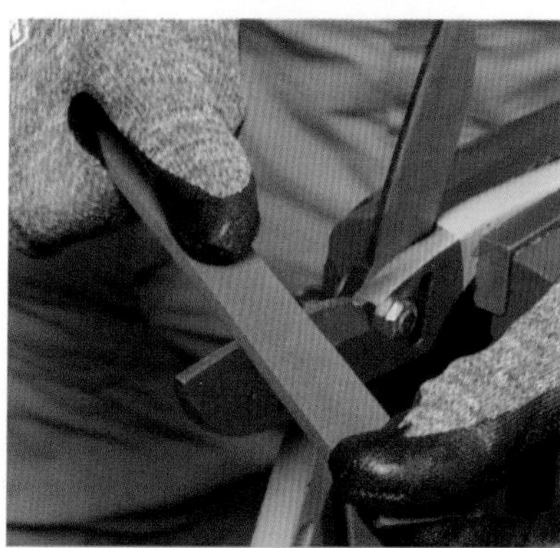

Sharpen the cutting edge with a smooth file

Tube cutter

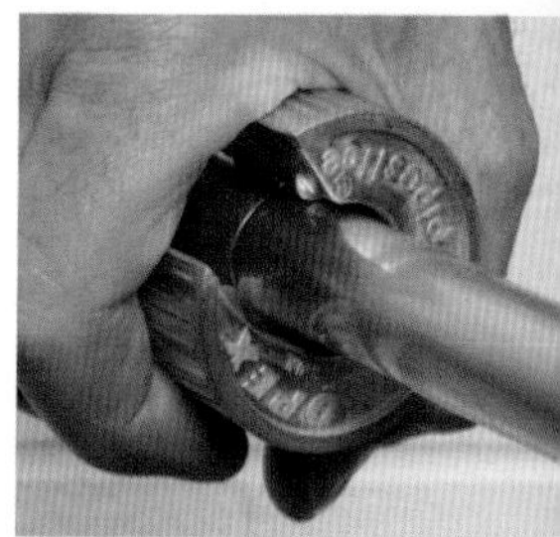

Pipe slice
Rotate the tool around a pipe to sever the metal.

SEE ALSO > Cutting pipe 361, Slipstone 497

Tools for joining metal

You can make permanent watertight joints with solder, a molten alloy that acts like a glue when it cools and solidifies. Mechanical fixings such as compression joints, rivets, and nuts and bolts are also used for joining metal.

Soldering irons

For successful soldering, the work has to become hot enough for the solder to melt and flow – otherwise it solidifies before it can completely penetrate the joint.

Use a low-powered pencil-point iron to apply the necessary heat when soldering electrical connections. To bring sheet metal up to working temperature, use a larger iron with a tapered tip.

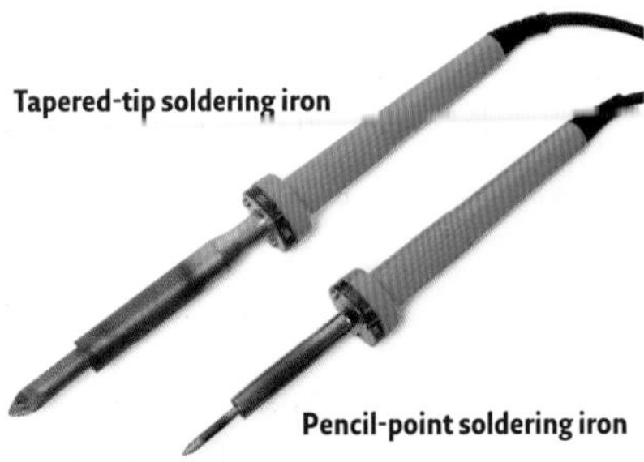

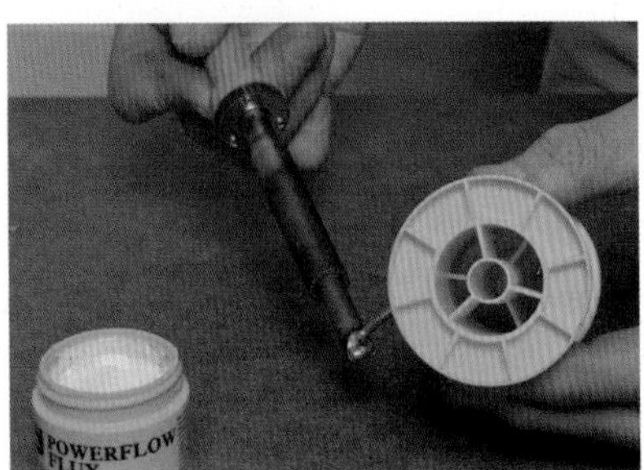

Tinning a soldering iron

The tip of a soldering iron has to be 'tinned' to keep it oxide-free. Clean the cool tip with a file; then heat it to working temperature, dip it in flux, and apply a stick of solder to coat it evenly.

Using a soldering iron

Clean the mating surfaces of the joint to a bright finish. Coat them with flux and then tin the mating surfaces as described left. Apply the hot iron along the joint to heat the metal thoroughly, causing the solder to reflow and join the two pieces of metal.

Metal riveters

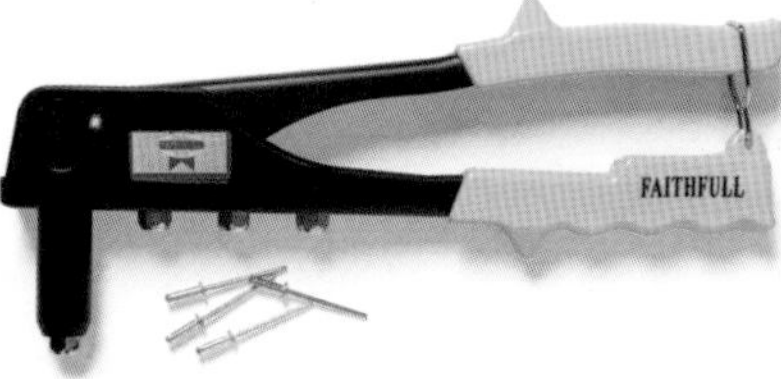

Join thin sheet metal with a blind riveter, a hand-operated tool with plier-like handles. It uses special rivets with long shanks that break off, leaving slightly raised heads on both sides of the work.

Using a riveter

Clamp the two sheets together and drill holes right through the metal, matching the diameter of the rivets. Open the handles of the riveter and insert the rivet shank in the head (1). Push the rivet through a hole in the workpiece and, while pressing the tool hard against the metal, squeeze the handles to compress the rivet head on the far side (2). When the rivet is fully expanded, the shank will snap off in the tool.

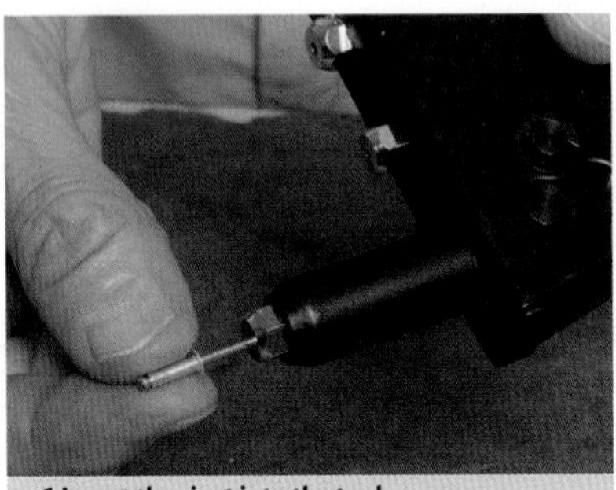

1 Insert the rivet into the tool

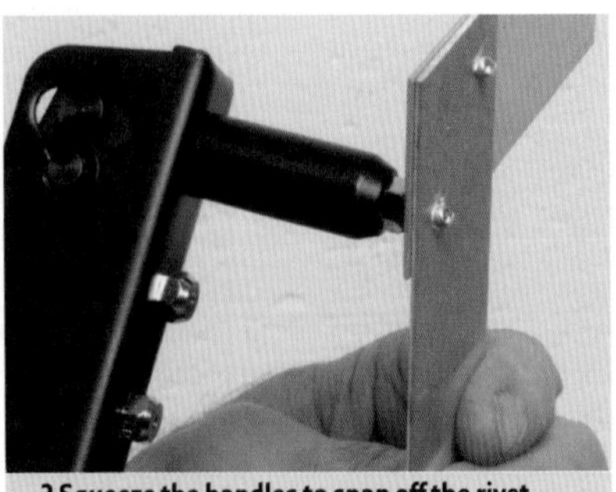

2 Squeeze the handles to snap off the rivet

Solder and flux

Solders

Solders are designed to melt at relatively low temperatures, but they will not work in the presence of water.

When working on hot-water and cold-water plumbing, use a lead-free solder. It has a slightly higher melting point than the old lead solder and makes stronger joints.

Flux

To be soldered successfully, a joint has to be perfectly clean and free from oxides. Even after the metal has been cleaned with wire wool or emery, oxides form immediately, making a positive bond between the solder and metal impossible. Flux is therefore used to form a chemical barrier against oxidation.

Corrosive or 'active' flux, applied with a brush, dissolves oxides but must be washed from the surface with water as soon as the solder solidifies, or it will go on corroding the metal.

A 'passive' flux, in paste form, is used where it is impossible to wash the joint thoroughly. Although it does not dissolve oxides, it excludes them adequately for soldering copper plumbing joints and electrical connections.

Another alternative is to use wire solder that contains flux inside its hollow core. The flux flows just before the solder melts.

To flush flux from a central-heating system, fill it with water and let it heat up, then switch off and drain the system. This should be repeated a couple of times.

SEE ALSO > Twist drills 523, Drill stand 500

Gas torch

Even a large soldering iron can't heat thick metal fast enough to compensate for heat loss from the joint, and this is very much the situation when you solder pipework. Although the copper unions have very thin walls, the pipe on each side dissipates so much heat that a soldering iron cannot get the joint itself hot enough to form a watertight soldered seal. You therefore need to use a gas torch with an intensely hot flame to heat the work quickly. The torch runs on liquid gas contained under pressure in a disposable metal canister that screws onto the gas inlet. More sophisticated torches are refuelled from a can of butane. With a basic torch, open the control valve and light the gas released from the nozzle, then adjust the valve until the flame roars and is bright blue. Some torches have an electronic ignition switch.

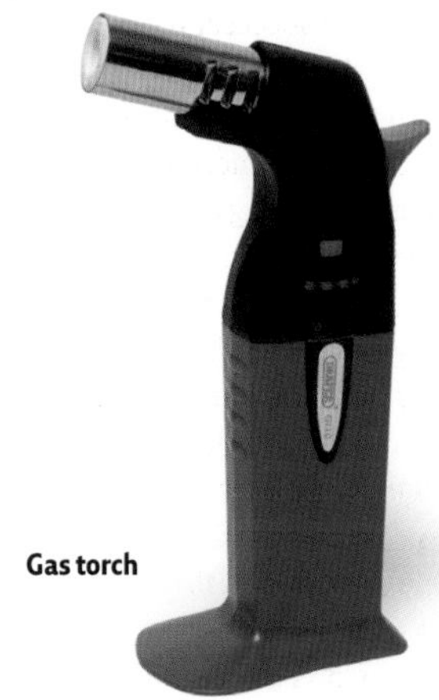

Gas torch

Fireproof mat

Buy a fireproof mat from a plumber's merchant to protect flammable surfaces from the heat of a gas torch.

Soldering plumbing joints

Having cleaned and assembled a copper end-feed joint, heat the entire joint evenly. When the flux begins to bubble, remove the flame and touch the tip of the solder wire to two or three points around the mouth of each sleeve. The joint is full of solder when a bright ring appears around each sleeve. Allow the joint to cool.

Metal benders

Thick or hard metal must be heated before it can be bent successfully, but soft copper piping and sheet metal can be bent while cold.

Bending springs

You can bend small-diameter copper pipes over your knee – but their walls must be supported with a coiled spring to prevent them buckling.

Push an internal spring inside the pipe, or slide an external one over it. Either type of spring must fit the pipe exactly.

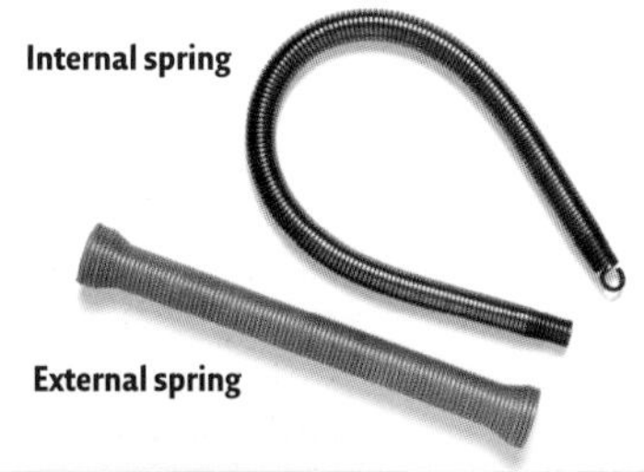

Internal spring

External spring

Tube bender

With a tube bender, a pipe is bent over one of two fixed curved formers that are designed to give the optimum radii for plumbing and support the walls of the pipe during bending. Each has a matching straight former, which is placed between the pipe and a steel roller on a movable lever. Operating this lever bends the pipe over the curved former.

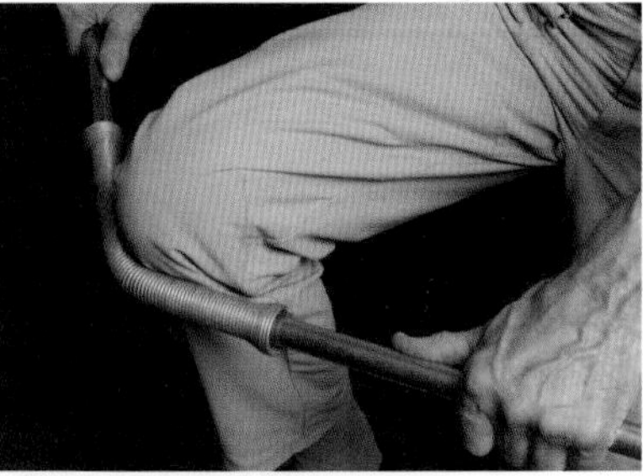

Support the bend with your knee

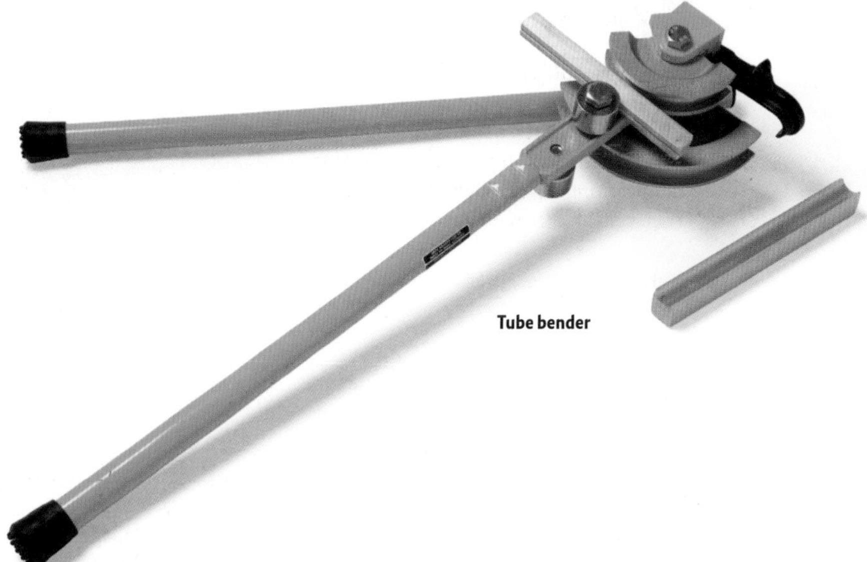

Tube bender

Soft mallet

Soft mallets have a head made of hard rubber or plastic. They are used in bending strip or sheet metal, which would be damaged by a metal hammer.

To bend sheet metal at a right angle, clamp it between stout battens along the bending line. Start at one end and bend the metal over one of the battens by tapping it with the mallet. Don't attempt the full bend at once, but work along the sheet, increasing the angle gradually and keeping it constant along the length until the metal lies flat on the batten. Tap out any kinks.

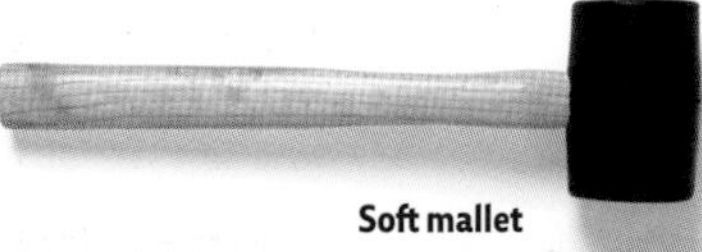

Soft mallet

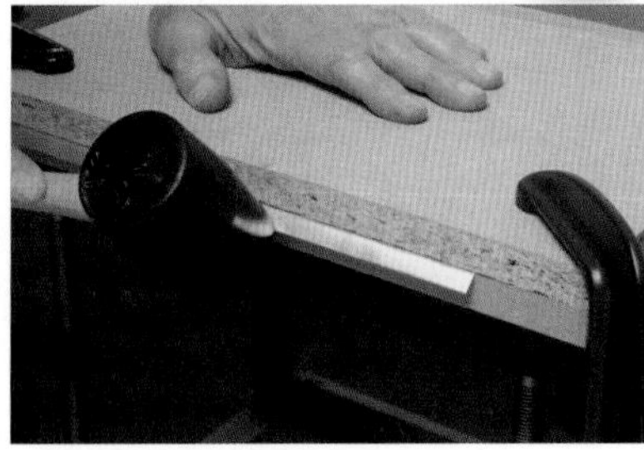

Work along the sheet, gradually increasing the angle

SEE ALSO > Joining pipe 361, Bending pipe 363

Spanners and wrenches

A professional plumber uses a great variety of spanners and wrenches on a wide range of fittings and fixings. However, there is no need to buy them all, as you can hire ones that you need only occasionally.

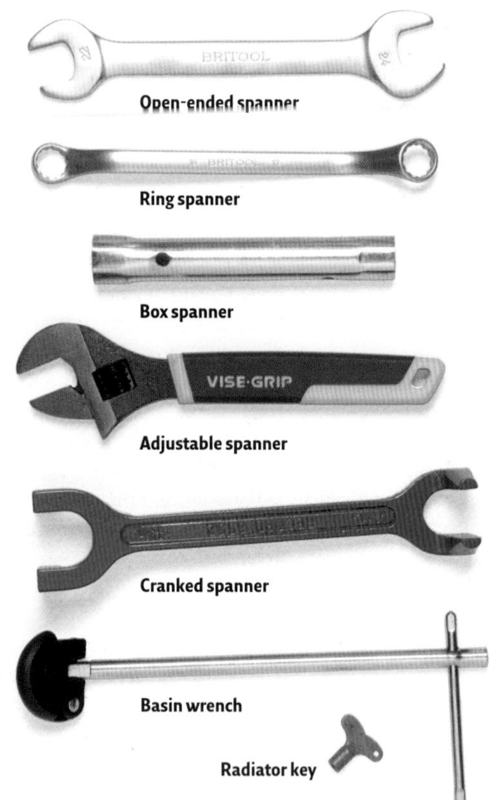

Open-ended spanner
Ring spanner
Box spanner
Adjustable spanner
Cranked spanner
Basin wrench
Radiator key

Open-ended spanner
A set of open-ended spanners is essential for a plumber or metalworker. Pipes generally run into a fitting or accessory, and the only tool you can use is a spanner with open jaws.

The spanners are usually double-ended (perhaps in a combination of metric and imperial sizes), and the sizes are duplicated within a set to enable you to manipulate two identical nuts simultaneously – on a compression joint, for example.

Ring spanner
Being a closed circle, the head of a ring spanner is stronger and fits better than that of an open-ended one. It is specially handy for loosening a corroded nut, provided you are able to slip the spanner over it.

Box spanner
A box spanner is a steel tube with hexagonal ends. The turning force is applied with a tommy bar slipped through holes drilled in the tube.

Don't use a very long bar – too much leverage may strip the thread of the fitting or distort the walls of the spanner.

Adjustable spanner
Having a movable jaw, an adjustable spanner is not as strong as an open-ended or ring spanner, but is often the only tool that will fit a large nut or one that's coated with paint.

Make sure the spanner fits the nut snugly, by rocking it slightly as you tighten the jaws, and grip the nut with the roots of the jaws. If you use just the tips, they can spring apart slightly under force and the spanner will slip.

Cranked spanner
A cranked spanner is a special double-ended wrench for reaching tap connectors in confined spaces.

Basin wrench
A basin wrench (for the same job) has a pivoting jaw that can be set for either tightening or loosening a fitting.

Radiator key
A small 'key' is used to open and close the air vent (bleed valve) at the top of a central-heating radiator that needs to be 'bled'.

Plier wrench
A plier wrench locks onto the work. It grips round stock or damaged nuts, and is often used as a small cramp.

Stillson wrench
The adjustable toothed jaws of a Stillson wrench are for gripping pipework. As force is applied to the handle, the jaws tighten on the work.

Chain wrench
A chain wrench does the same job as a Stillson wrench, but can be used on pipework and fittings with a very large diameter. Wrap the chain tightly round the work and engage it with the hook at the end of the wrench, then lever the handle towards the toothed jaw to apply turning force.

Strap wrench
With a strap wrench you can disconnect chromed pipework without damaging its surface. Wrap the smooth strap round the pipe, then pass its end through the slot in the head of the tool and pull it tight. Levering on the handle rotates the pipe.

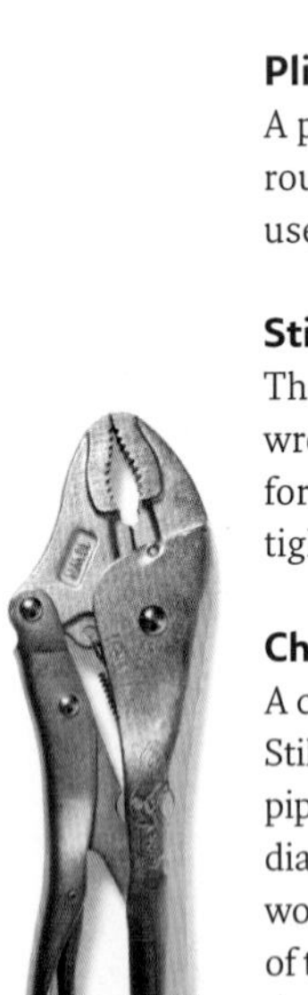
Plier wrench

Stillson wrench
Chain wrench
Strap wrench

SEE ALSO > Replacing taps 371, Bleeding a radiator 413

Using spanners and wrenches

Choose a 12-point ring spanner. It is fast to use and will fit both square and hexagonal nuts. You can buy combination spanners with a ring at one end and an open jaw at the other.

Whichever spanner you choose, make sure it is a snug fit on the nut or bolt.

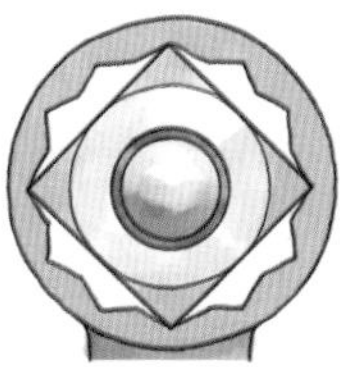

Square nut

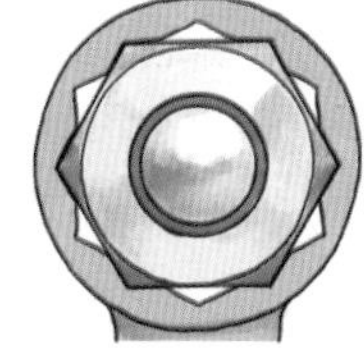

Hexagonal nut

Achieving a tight fit

A spanner must be a good fit, or it will round the corners of the nut. You can pack out the jaws with a thin 'shim' of metal if a snug fit is not possible.

Insert a thin shim to avoid rounding-over the nut

Using a plier wrench

To close the jaws, squeeze the handles while slowly turning the adjusting screw clockwise (1). Eventually the jaws will snap together, gripping the work securely. To release the tool's grip on the work, pull the release lever (2).

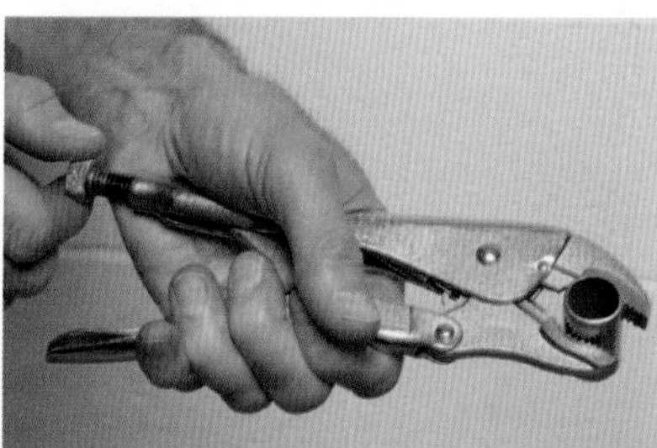

1 Squeeze the handles and adjust the wrench

2 Pull on the lever to release the wrench

Metal drills

Special-quality steel bits are made for drilling holes in metal. Cut large holes in sheet metal with a cone drill.

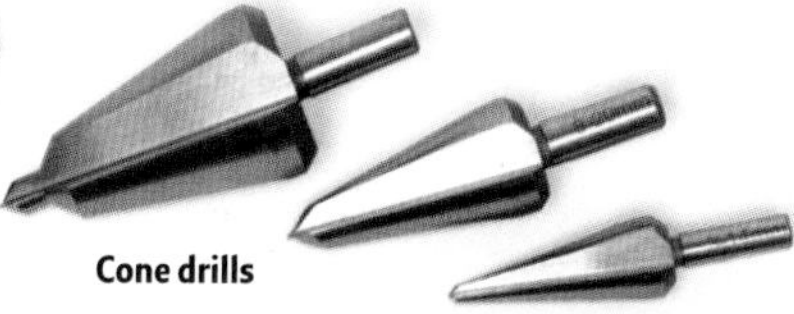

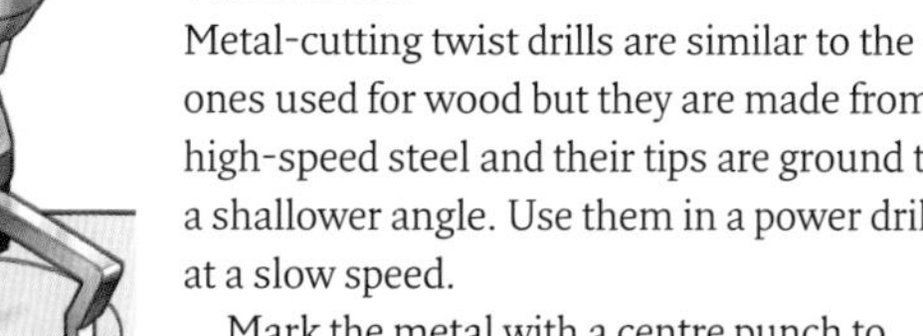

Tank cutter
Use a tank cutter to cut large-diameter holes.

Masonry core drills
These are heavy-duty versions of the woodworking hole saw. Masonry core drills cut holes up to 150mm (6in) diameter in brick or stone walls for running new waste pipes to the outside.

Twist drills

Metal-cutting twist drills are similar to the ones used for wood but they are made from high-speed steel and their tips are ground to a shallower angle. Use them in a power drill at a slow speed.

Mark the metal with a centre punch to locate the drill point, and clamp the work in a vice or to the bed of a vertical drill stand. Drill slowly and steadily, and keep the bit oiled. To drill a large hole, make a small hole first to guide the larger drill bit.

When drilling sheet metal, the bit can jam and produce a ragged hole as it exits on the far side of the workpiece. As a precaution, clamp the work between pieces of plywood and drill through all three layers.

Cone drills

Large twist drills tend to distort thin sheet metal, often leaving a ragged-edge to the hole. To bore relatively large holes in sheet metal, use a tapered cone drill that cuts progressively larger holes up to a maximum diameter. The largest cone drill will bore holes from 16 to 30mm (5/8 to 1 1/8in) in diameter. These drills will also bore holes in plastic sheet.

Use a power drill mounted in a drill stand, and select a low speed when boring holes with cone drills.

Tank cutter

Use a tank cutter to make holes for pipework in plastic or metal cold-water storage tanks.

Pipe-freezing equipment

To work on plumbing without having to drain the system, you can form temporary ice plugs in the pipework. The water in the system has to be cold and not flowing.

Using freezing equipment

You can buy a kit containing a canister of liquid freezing gas, plus two or more 'jackets' to wrap round the pipework at the points where you want the water to freeze. Bind each jacket securely to the pipe (1); then attach the flexible tube to the nozzle on the jacket and to the canister. Inject the recommended amount of gas, which is determined by the changing weight of the canister (2). It takes a few minutes for the ice plug to form in a metal pipe. If the job takes more than half an hour to complete, you may have to inject more gas.

Alternatively, you can hire an electric freezer connected to two blocks that you clamp over the pipework. An electric freezer will keep the water frozen until you finish the job and switch off.

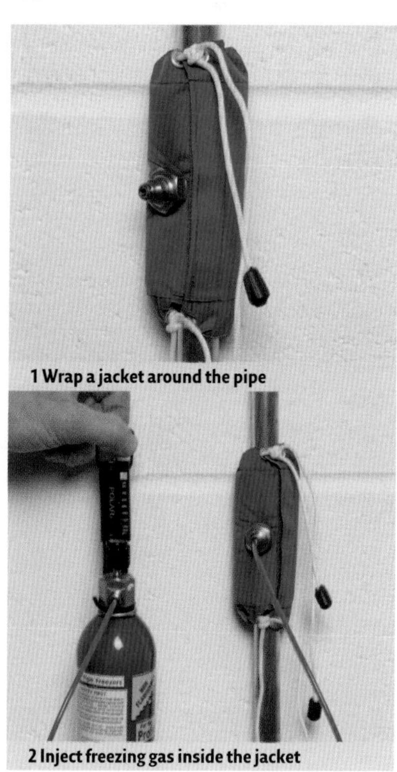

1 Wrap a jacket around the pipe

2 Inject freezing gas inside the jacket

SEE ALSO > Thawing frozen pipes 349, Insulating pipes 257, Water-storage tanks 391, Drill stand 500, Centre punch 517

Metal files

Files are used for shaping and smoothing metal components and removing sharp edges. They are relatively inexpensive, so you can afford to have a good selection in your tool kit.

Classifying files

The working faces of a file are composed of parallel ridges – or 'teeth' – set at about 70 degrees to its edges. A file is classified according to the size and spacing of its teeth and whether it has one or two sets of teeth.

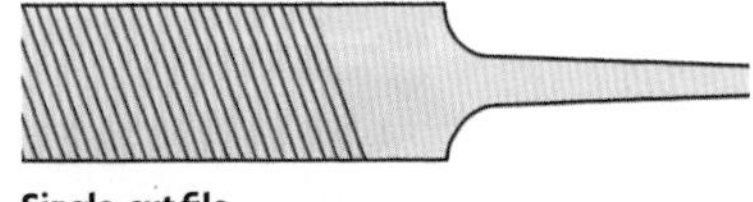

Single-cut file

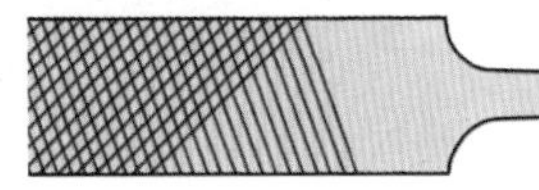

Double-cut file

A single-cut file has one set of teeth, which virtually cover each of its faces. A double-cut file has a second set of identical teeth crossing the first at a 45-degree angle. Some files are single-cut on one side and double-cut on the other.

The spacing of teeth relates directly to their size: the finer the teeth, the more closely packed they are. Degrees of coarseness are expressed as number of teeth per 25mm (1in).

Use progressively finer files to remove marks left by coarser ones.

Needle files

FILE CLASSIFICATION

Bastard file – coarse grade (26 teeth per 25mm), used for initial shaping.

Second-cut file – medium grade (36 teeth per 25mm), used for preliminary smoothing.

Smooth file – fine grade (47 teeth per 25mm), used for final smoothing.

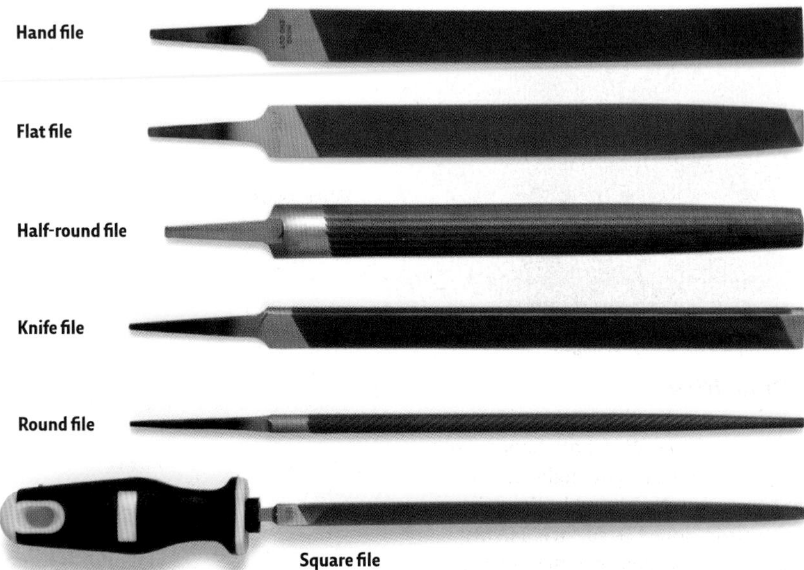

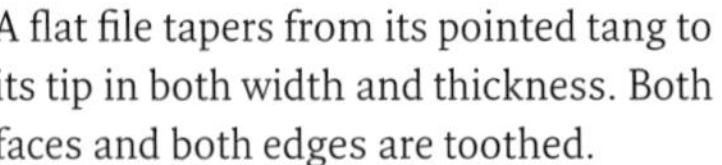

Flat file

A flat file tapers from its pointed tang to its tip in both width and thickness. Both faces and both edges are toothed.

Hand file

Hand files are parallel-sided but tapered in their thickness. Most of them have one smooth edge for filing up to a corner without damaging it.

Half-round file

This tool has one rounded face for shaping inside curves.

Round file

A round file is for shaping tight curves and enlarging holes.

Square file

Square files are used for cutting narrow slots and smoothing the edges of small rectangular holes.

Knife file

A file with one slim 'knife-blade' edge is designed for accurately shaping and smoothing undercut apertures of less than 90 degrees. Alternatively, use a triangular file, similar to those used for sharpening wood saws.

Needle files

These are miniature versions of standard files and are all made in extra-fine grades. Needle files are used for precise work and to sharpen brace bits.

File safety

Always fit a wooden or plastic handle on the tang of a file before you use it. If an unprotected file catches on the work, then the tang could be driven into the palm of your hand. Having fitted a handle, tap its end on a bench to tighten its grip.

To remove a handle, hold the blade of the file in one hand and strike the ferrule away from you with a block of wood.

Knock an old handle from the tang

Tap the new file handle on the bench

SEE ALSO > Saw file 490

Using files

When using any file, keep it flat on the work and avoid rocking it during forward strokes. Hold it steady, with the fingers of one hand resting on its tip, and make slow firm strokes with the full length of the file.

To avoid vibration, hold the work low in the jaws of a vice or clamp it between two battens.

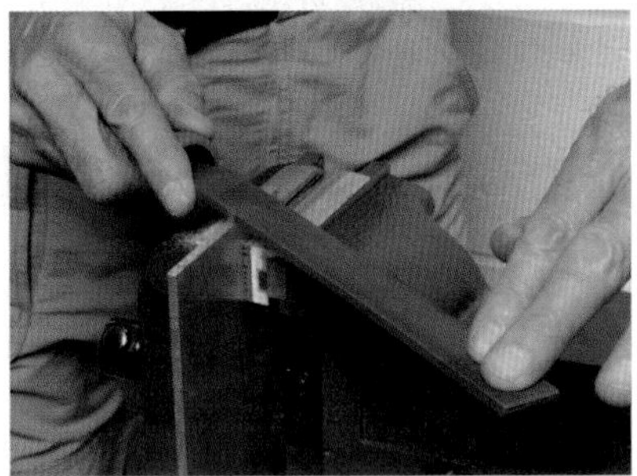

Steady the file with your fingers

Draw-filing

You can give metal a smooth finish by draw-filing. With both hands, hold a smooth file at right angles to the work and slide the tool backwards and forwards along the surface. Finally, polish the workpiece with emery cloth wrapped round the file.

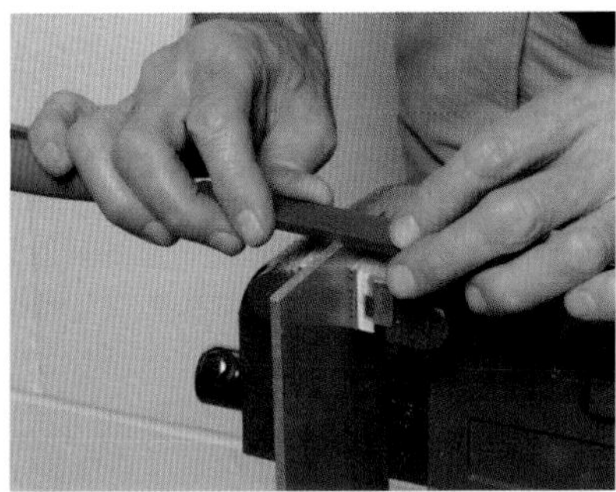

Slide the file backwards and forwards

Cleaning a file

Soft metal tends to clog file teeth. When a file stops cutting efficiently, brush along the teeth with a fine wire brush; and then rub chalk on the file to help reduce clogging in future.

Clean out clogged file teeth with a wire brush

Finishing metal

Before painting or soldering metal, you should always make sure it is clean and free from rust.

Wire brush

Use a steel-wire handbrush to clean rusty or corroded metal.

Wire wool

Wire wool is a mass of very thin steel filaments. It is used to remove file marks and to clean oxides and dirt from metals.

Emery cloth and paper

Emery is a natural black grit which, when backed with paper or cloth, is ideal for polishing metals. There is a range of grades from coarse to fine. For the best finish, use progressively finer abrasives as the work proceeds.

Using emery cloth and paper

To avoid rounding the crisp edges of a flat component, glue a sheet of emery paper to a board and rub the metal on the abrasive.

To finish round stock or pipes, loop a strip of emery cloth over the work and pull alternately on each end.

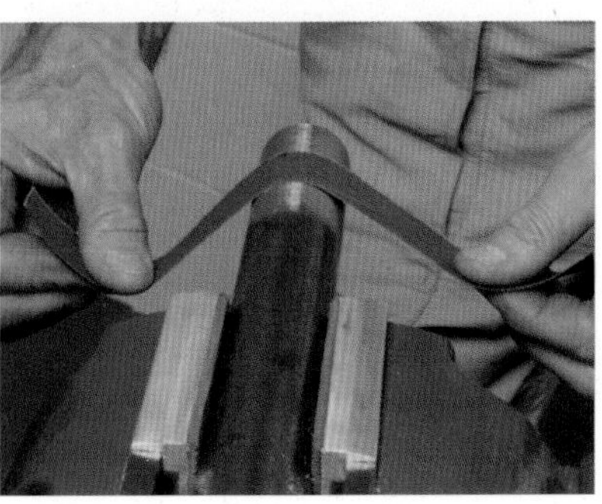

Clean a metal tube with emery cloth

Buffing mop

Metals can be brought to a shine by hand, using a liquid metal polish and a soft cloth - but for a really high gloss, use a buffing mop in a bench-mounted power drill or grinder.

Using a buffing mop

After applying a stick of buffing compound (a fine abrasive with wax) to the revolving mop, move the work from side to side against the lower half, keeping any edges facing downwards.

Woodworking tools
A plumber needs a set of basic woodworking tools in order to lift floorboards, notch joists for pipe runs, and attach pipe clips.

Pliers

Pliers are for improving your grip on small components and for bending and shaping metal rod and wire. With their side cutters, they can also be used to crop wire.

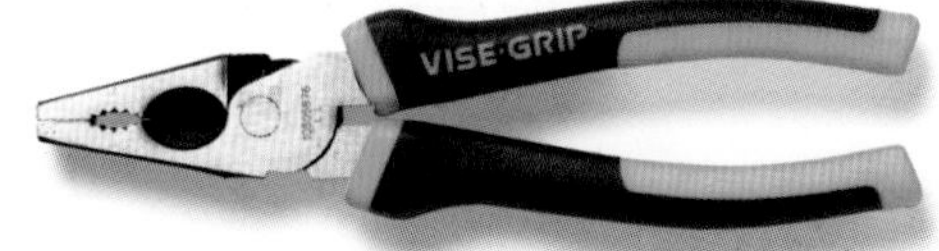

Engineer's pliers

For general-purpose work, buy a sturdy pair of engineer's pliers. The toothed jaws have a curved section for gripping round stock and also have side cutters for cropping wire.

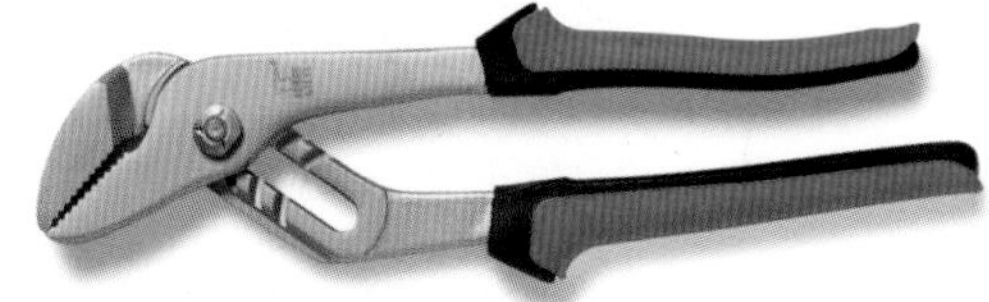

Slip-joint or water-pump pliers

The special feature of slip-joint pliers is a movable pivot for enlarging the jaw spacing. The extra-long handles give a good grip on pipes and other fittings. Use smooth-jaw pliers to grip chromed fittings.

SEE ALSO > Preparing metals 60–61

Electrical tools

You need only a limited range of tools to make electrical connections, but an extensive general-purpose tool kit is required for making cable runs and mounting electrical accessories.

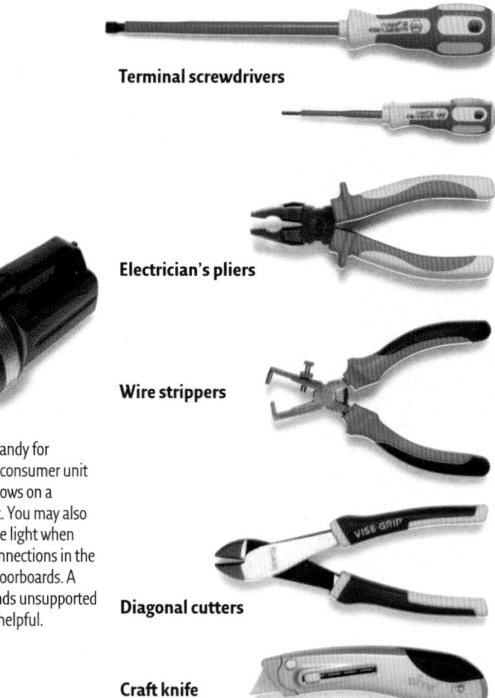

Terminal screwdrivers

Electrician's pliers

Wire strippers

Diagonal cutters

Craft knife

Torch
Keep a torch handy for checking your consumer unit when a fuse blows on a lighting circuit. You may also need to provide light when working on connections in the loft or below floorboards. A torch that stands unsupported is particularly helpful.

Terminal screwdrivers

A terminal screwdriver has a long, slim cylindrical shaft that is ground to a flat tip.

For turning screw terminals in sockets and larger appliances, buy a screwdriver with a plastic handle and a plastic insulating sleeve on its shaft. Use a smaller screwdriver with a very slim shaft to work on ceiling roses or to tighten plastic terminal blocks in small fittings.

Buy only good-quality screwdrivers - the soft tips on cheap ones soon twist out of shape.

Electrician's pliers

These are engineer's pliers with insulating sleeves shrunk onto their handles. You can use pliers to crop circuit conductors.

Diagonal cutters

Diagonal cutters will crop thick conductors more effectively than electrician's pliers, but you may need a junior hacksaw to cut meter leads.

Wire strippers

To remove the insulation from cable and flex, use a pair of wire strippers with jaws shaped to cut through the covering without damaging the wire core. There is a multi-purpose version that can both strip the insulation and crop conductors to length.

Craft knife

A knife with sharp disposable blades is best for slitting and peeling the sheathing encasing cable and flex.

Power drill

A cordless power drill is ideal for boring cable holes through timbers and for making wallplug fixings. As well as standard masonry bits for wall fixings, you will need a much longer bit for boring through brick walls and clearing access channels behind skirting boards.

If you shorten the shaft of a wide-tipped spade bit, you can use it in a power drill between floor joists.

Testers

You can buy reliable testers without having to spend a great deal of money. Most good DIY outlets stock a range of them.

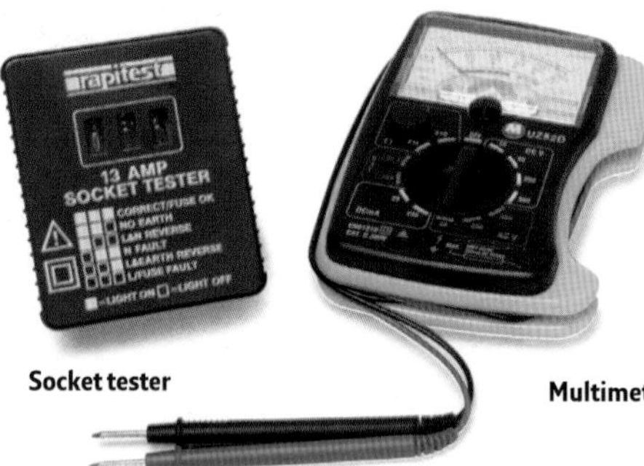

Socket tester

Multimeter

Mains-voltage tester

Mains-voltage tester

Mains testers are designed to tell you whether a circuit is completely 'dead' after you have turned off the power at the consumer unit. Be sure to buy a tester that's intended for use with mains voltage - similar devices are sold in auto shops for testing 12V car wiring only.

Multimeter

An electrician needs a multimeter, for measuring insulation resistance and continuity. There are digital instruments that give readings on an LCD screen, and there are analogue ones with a needle that moves across a scale on a dial. With some meters, you can select an audible signal to tell you when there is continuity.

Socket tester

A simple plug-in device can be used to test the connections inside a 13amp socket outlet without having to turn off the power or expose internal wiring.

General-purpose tools

Every electrician needs tools for lifting floorboards, cutting cables and fitting mounting boxes.

- Claw hammer - for nailing cable clips to walls and timbers.
- Club hammer and cold chisel - for cutting channels in plaster and brickwork in order to bury cables or mounting boxes.
- Cabinet screwdriver - for fixing mounting boxes to walls.
- Spirit level - for checking that mounting boxes are fixed horizontally.
- Plasterer's trowel or filling knife - for covering concealed cable with plaster or other kinds of filler.
- Bolster chisel - for levering up floorboards.
- Wood chisels - for notching floor joists.
- Padsaw or power jigsaw - for cutting through floorboards close to skirtings.
- A floorboard saw is the best tool for cutting through tongued and grooved floorboards.
- A small spanner is needed for making some earth connections.

SEE ALSO > Building Regulations 284, Testing 288–9, Jigsaws 491, Wood chisels 496, Cordless drills 500, Hammers 501, 512, Screwdrivers 502, Plasterer's trowel 510, Spirit level 511, Floorboard saw 512, Bolster chisel 513, Cold chisel 513, Spanners 522

Reference

Timber and man-made boards

Timber is classified into two main groups, softwood and hardwood, according to the type of tree it comes from. Softwoods are from coniferous evergreen trees such as firs and pines, whereas hardwoods are from broad-leaved deciduous trees. Some hardwoods, particularly from tropical rainforests, are now endangered species – so look at the product labelling or check with the supplier to make sure the timber comes from a sustainable source.

Softwoods

Most of the wood you see in a timberyard is softwood. It is cheaper than hardwoods and is more widely used for structural house timbers, floorboards, stairs and cheap domestic furniture. Softwoods may be referred to as whitewood, pine, or redwood.

Buying softwood

Most softwood is available in rough and smooth versions known as 'sawn' and 'planed'. The rough unplaned surface of sawn timber means that it is suitable only for jobs where it will be out of sight.

Wherever appearance is important, you need planed wood. Having been through a planing machine, this will be relatively smooth. But here a confusion can arise. Planed timber – or PAR (planed all round) – is always slightly thinner and narrower than its nominal dimensions. Machine planing takes about 4 to 6mm (5/32 to ¼in) off the width and thickness of the wood, but the loss is not uniform, so PAR is generally referred to in terms of its nominal size (the size before planing). You usually need to take this into account when planning jobs involving planed wood – however, prepacked planed wood sold in DIY stores is now sometimes labelled in finished sizes.

Timberyards use the metric system, but most assistants are experts at instant conversion and will advise you if you think and work with imperial dimensions.

Choosing softwood

A number of defects are found in softwood, which can mar the appearance or weaken the wood. These should be avoided, if possible. It is best to pick out the wood yourself, especially when appearance is important.

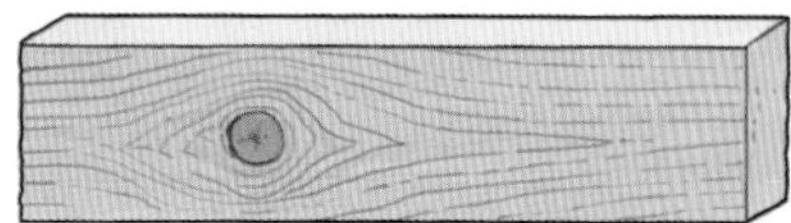

Knots

Knots can look attractive in pine boards, but they must be 'live' knots – the glossy brown ones. The black 'dead' knots will shrink and may drop out, leaving unsightly holes that invariably weaken the wood.

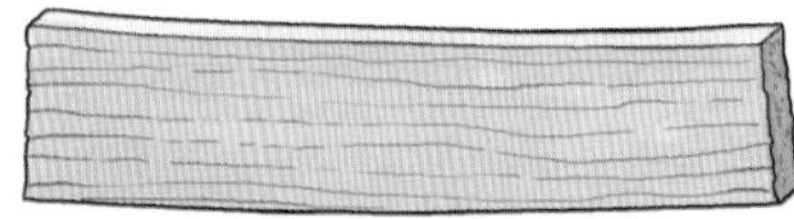

Warping

Distorted wood is another common problem. Look along the edges of each board you buy to check that it is not bowed or twisted.

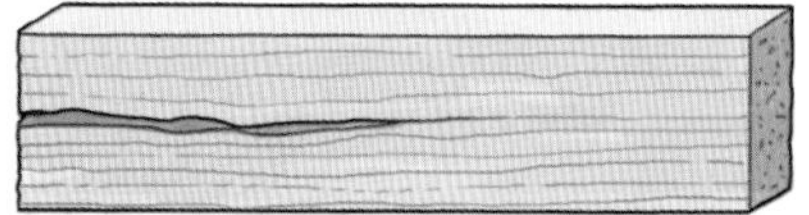

End shakes

These are splits at the ends of boards caused by rapid drying. Such sections of timber should be regarded as waste, for which there is no charge.

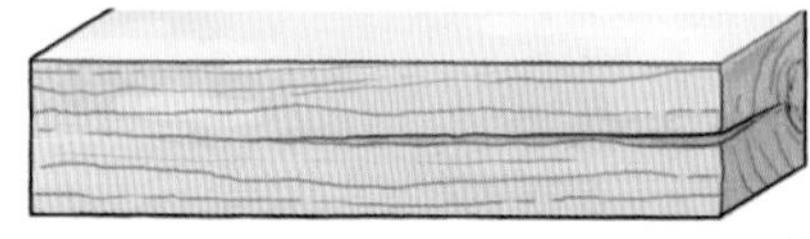

Heart shakes

These are splits that occur along radial lines in the log. When they are combined at the centre of the tree, they are known as star shakes.

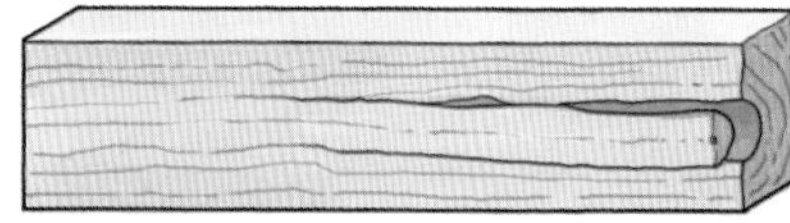

Cup shakes

These occur parallel to the tree's annual 'rings' – the layers of new wood that grow each year. Typically, a board cut from the centre of the tree may have the central ring split away from the other ones along its length.

Surface checking

This is fine cracking on the surface of timber. Very fine cracks may be removed by planing, or filled if the work is to be painted. Wood with wider cracks should be rejected.

Other defects

Watch out for irregularities such as strips of bark adhering to the wood, damage from rough handling in the yard and dark water staining.

Sizes and sections

Planed softwood comes in a variety of standard thicknesses and widths, from sections of a nominal 12 x 25mm (½ x 1in) to 75 x 225mm (3 x 9in) planks.

You can purchase planed softwood tongued and grooved for flooring or matchboarding, and it is also available machined in a variety of sectional shapes (mouldings) for such uses as skirting boards, architraves, glazing bars, dadoes and picture rails.

Cutting to size

Timberyards will generally cut a plank to approximately the length you want – unless that would leave an offcut too small to be sold, in which case you'll have to buy the whole plank.

At a cost, a timberyard that has woodworking machinery will cut wood to size for you. However, most yards use a handsaw to cut standard sawn or planed stock to length. To be sure of obtaining the exact size you require, buy the wood slightly overlength and carefully cut off the waste yourself.

Seasoning softwood

When a tree is converted into usable sections of wood, it contains a high level of moisture. To make the wood stable and workable, the wood is dried or 'seasoned' to a set moisture content. Softwood is usually seasoned by kiln-drying; but as it is often exposed to damp in the timberyard, the moisture level can rise again. It's therefore best to let the wood dry out and stabilize indoors for a week or so – preferably in the room where it is to be used and lying flat, not propped against a wall.

SEE ALSO > Mouldings 530

Hardwoods

Hardwoods are more expensive than softwoods, and usually have to be bought from specialist timber merchants.

Ordering hardwoods

Some hardwoods - for example, oak and meranti - are typically stocked by timber-yards, but a wider range is available from specialist suppliers.

Like softwoods, commonly stocked hardwoods are listed in nominal sizes. Specialist timber merchants will machine the wood to a finished size; or sell you whole planks as cut from the log, ready seasoned for you to convert into smaller sizes with the necessary machinery.

Hardwoods are relatively knot-free, but can suffer from warping, shakes and checks. The figure and colour of the wood may vary from tree to tree of the same species, and also depend on the way the wood is cut from the log.

If you need to match a hardwood with one already used in your home, check it carefully - as woods are not always what they appear to be. Wood dyes are often used to improve the colour of the timber or change its appearance to resemble another species.

Working with hardwoods

In order to work hardwoods - which, as their name suggests, are generally somewhat harder than softwoods - your tools need to be sharpened more frequently and honed to a fine cutting edge.

Screw fixings require drilled pilot holes. If you are screwing into oak, use brass or plated screws; because of the acidic nature of the wood, steel screws will stain it black.

The dust that's created when machining hardwoods can be unpleasant if inhaled. It is therefore advisable to wear a suitable face mask or respirator when working with these woods.

Hardwoods such as teak are naturally oily - and so to give best results joints need to be glued with a synthetic-resin adhesive.

Hardwood veneers

Veneers are thin slices of wood cut from the log in various ways. For centuries, expensive hardwoods have been used in veneer form to cover cheaper timber. Today a wide range of veneers is available for laying onto man-made boards in order to create a luxurious-looking material that is far more stable than solid wood.

Veneers can be bought either as single leaves or in bundles. Preveneered boards are also available.

Man-made boards

Five types of man-made board are widely used - plywood, chipboard, blockboard, hardboard and fibreboard.

Plywood

Plywood is a sheet material made by bonding a number of thin wood veneers, or plies, together under high pressure. These may be of the same thickness throughout, or the core veneers may be thicker than the face veneers.

Typically, to maintain stability, the plies are laid in an odd number with their grain direction alternating. Special flexible plywood, made with the grain of all the plies running in the same direction, can be bent to take up relatively tight curves.

Most types of plywood are made entirely from pine, birch or gaboon, but you can also buy plywood boards faced with quality hardwoods or melamine.

The type of glue used to manufacture it determines whether plywood is suitable for interior or exterior use.

Chipboard

Chipboard is a relatively cheap material manufactured by gluing small softwood chips together under pressure. There are several grades, including moisture-resistant types for flooring and roofing. Standard chipboard, which is sanded smooth on both sides, can be filled and primed for painting. It also makes a good substrate for veneer. Chipboard faced with timber or melamine veneers is also available. Thick melamine-faced boards are made for kitchen worktops.

Blockboard

Blockboard consists of a core of rectangular-section wood battens sandwiched between two double layers of pressure-bonded veneer. It is used where structural strength and stability are needed: for an unsupported span of worktop, for example, or shelving that has to bear a heavy load.

Blockboard is an excellent material for veneering - but where appearance is important, exposed edges need to be covered with strips of solid wood known as lipping. Lipping may be applied before or after veneering.

Hardboard

Hardboard is a dense sheet material made from compressed softwood pulp. Structurally it is not as strong as other man-made boards, but it is cheap and very stable.

Standard hardboard is brown in colour and 3.2mm (⅛in) thick, with one smooth side and one textured. Other types include:

Duo-faced hardboard - having a smooth surface on both sides.

Prefinished hardboard - with a white finish or printed wood-grain effect.

Textured hardboard - with a decorative moulded surface.

Flame-retardant hardboard - more resistant to fire.

Oil-tempered hardboard - resistant to moisture.

Perforated hardboard - pierced with holes.

Fibreboards

Fibreboards are made from compressed wood fibre in various densities. Soft types are used for insulation, pinboard and wall sheathing. Medium-density fibreboard (MDF) is a dense material with fine smooth surfaces on both sides. Its edges machine well, so are easy to finish with paint or veneer. A grooved board, 6mm (¼in) thick, is made for bending into curved shapes.

• Coloured MDF
Dyed right through to the core, ready-coloured MDF is ideal for making children's toys and furniture.

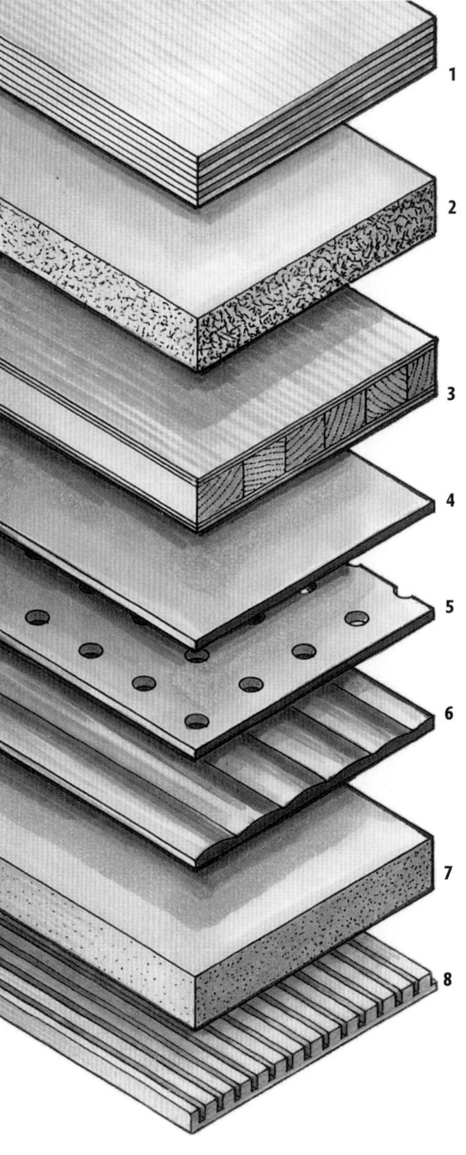

Man-made boards
1 Plywood
2 Chipboard
3 Blockboard
4 Standard hardboard
5 Perforated hardboard
6 Textured hardboard
7 Medium-density fibreboard (MDF)
8 Flexible MDF

SEE ALSO > Preparing man-made boards 53

Mouldings

Cheap softwoods are generally used for the larger joinery mouldings such as skirtings and architraves, although some are made in hardwood. Smaller sections, for dowelling, picture-framing and decorative cover mouldings, are usually made from hardwoods.

Period-style mouldings are generally more ornate than modern ones.

If you need to replace a wooden moulding but aren't able to find the right profile to match, you can have the shape machined by a specialist firm. Simply supply them with a pattern or sample piece.

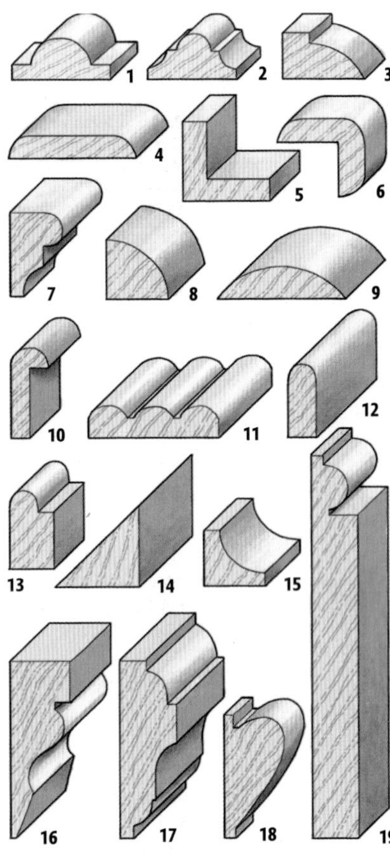

Moulding sections
1 Astragal
2 Double astragal
3 Glass bead
4 'D' shape
5 Flat corner
6 Cushion corner
7 Broken ogee
8 Quadrant
9 Half round
10 Hockey stick
11 Reeded
12 Parting bead
13 Staff bead
14 Triangle
15 Scotia
16 Architrave
17 Dado
18 Picture rail
19 Skirting

Adhesives

Modern adhesives are greatly superior to the old glues they have supplanted. Although there is no true 'universal glue' that will stick anything to anything, you can bond most materials if you use the appropriate adhesive.

Woodworking adhesives

To glue wood and man-made boards for use indoors, apply a polyvinyl (PVA) woodworking glue to one or both of the mating surfaces. Clamp or weight the work, and wipe off any excess glue squeezed from the joint with a damp cloth. The joint can be handled within 30 minutes, and the bond will be complete in 24 hours.

Outdoors, use a waterproof exterior PVA glue or a polyurethane glue or a powdered synthetic-resin glue that you mix with water. Alternatively, you can use a two-part resorcinol or urea adhesive. The two parts – a resin and a hardener – are either mixed or applied separately to the faces being glued; in the latter case, the adhesive begins to set only when the faces are brought together. All these glues require the work to be clamped during the setting period.

Contact adhesives

These adhesives were developed for fixing melamine laminates to man-made boards. Originally they stuck instantly on contact, but most modern versions have what is called 'slidability' – which allows some repositioning of a laminate that has not been placed accurately.

Apply the adhesive to both surfaces. Let it become touch-dry and then press them firmly together. For larger panels, place a layer of waxed paper or polythene sheet between the bonding surfaces and, working from one edge, gradually withdraw the paper or plastic as you press the laminate down onto the board.

Adhesives for floorcoverings

Flooring adhesives need to be versatile enough to fix a wide range of coverings – cork, vinyl, linoleum and many others – to such surfaces as floorboards, concrete, cement screed and hardboard underlays. They must also be able to withstand regular floor-washing and the spillage of various liquids. Such multi-purpose flooring adhesives are made from synthetic resin or latex. They will stick almost any covering to any floor surface. They are semi-flexible and will not crack or fail due to slight movement of the covering.

Ceramic-tile adhesive

Ceramic wall tiles are fixed in place with adhesive that is available ready-mixed or in powder form. Some are dual-purpose, for use as an adhesive and grout. Ordinary 'thin-bed' adhesives are for tiling on fairly flat surfaces; and there are 'thick-bed' ones for use on rough and uneven surfaces.

Use a water-resistant version for kitchens and bathrooms. Epoxy-based grouts resist mould growth and help keep kitchens and bathrooms germ-free.

Ceramic floor tiles are usually laid with a cement-based tile adhesive. Thick quarry tiles are sometimes laid on a sand-and-cement mortar, to which a special builder's adhesive – PVA bonding agent – can be added to improve adhesion.

Gluing metals

Metals can be glued with epoxy-resin adhesives, which produce a powerful bond. The adhesives come in two parts, a resin and a hardener, which are supplied in separate tubes or a special twin dispenser. Both parts are mixed together, then used within a prescribed time after mixing.

Epoxy-resin adhesives are also generally suitable for joining glass, ceramics, glass fibre and rigid plastic. However, some products will not join all of these materials, so make sure you get the right adhesive for the job.

Cyanoacrylates

The cyanoacrylates, or 'superglues', come close to being universal adhesives that will stick anything. They rapidly bond a great many materials, including human skin – so take great care when handling them.

Usually supplied in tubes with fine nozzles, superglues must be used sparingly. Most are thin liquids, but a gel type is also available. They are commonly used for joining small objects made of metal, glass, ceramic, glass fibre or rigid plastic.

Acrylic polymer adhesive

This solvent-free adhesive, sold in cartridges, is used in place of mechanical fixings, such as nails and screws, to secure wooden mouldings and boards.

SEE ALSO > Architectural mouldings 216, Fitting architraves 217, Replacing skirtings 218

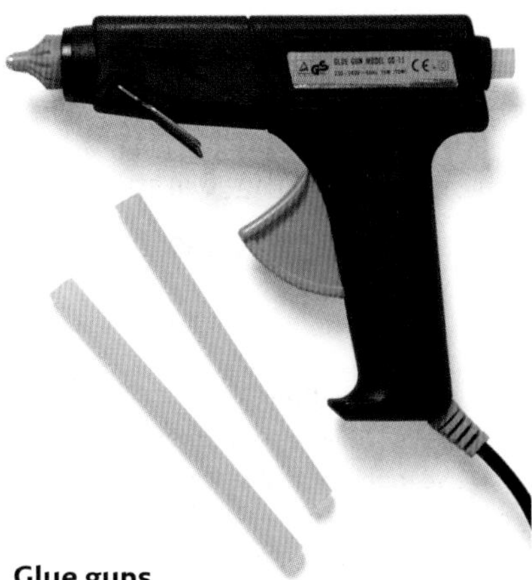

Glue guns

An electric 'hot-melt' glue gun is loaded with a rod of solid glue that melts under heat; the glue is discharged as a liquid onto the work when the gun is activated. The components are pressed or clamped together and the glue bonds as it cools. Glue guns are useful for accurate spot-gluing, and there is a choice of glue rods for use with various materials. The glues cool and set within 20 to 90 seconds.

Adhesive solvents

When using an adhesive, you will inevitably put some where you don't want it. So have the right solvent handy for the glue in question and use it promptly. The more the glue has set, the harder it is to remove; and once the glue has set hard, it may be impossible to dissolve it.

ADHESIVE	SOLVENT
PVA woodworking glue	Water
Synthetic resin	Water
Rubber-based contact glue	Acetone
Rubber resin	Petrol
Synthetic latex	Water
Epoxy resin	Methylated spirit or acetone. If hard, liquid paint stripper (not on skin).
Cyanoacrylates (superglues)	Special manufacturer's solvent
Acrylic adhesive	Water
Polyurethane foam	Special manufacturer's solvent

Brand-name guide to adhesives

Unless a manufacturer prints the type of glue on its container, it can be difficult to identify the adhesive you need. The brand names listed below are intended to help you recognize a type of glue. This is not necessarily a list of recommended products.

WOODWORKING ADHESIVES

- Aerolite (Synthetic resin)
- Antel One Shot (Synthetic resin)
- Evo-stik Wood Adhesive (PVA)
- Evo-stik Weatherproof Adhesive (PVA)
- Evo-stik Polyurethane Wood Glue
- Humbrol Extramite (Synthetic resin)
- Humbrol Extraphen (Synthetic resin)
- Joiners Mate Mitre Bond (Synthetic resin)
- No Nonsense PVA Wood Glue
- No Nonsense Polyurethane Wood Glue
- Titebond Polyurethane Glue

CONTACT ADHESIVES

- Bostik Contact
- Dunlop Thixofix
- Everbuild Spray Contact Adhesive
- Evo-stik Impact
- Evo-stik Timebond
- Evo-stik Trade Contact Adhesive
- No Nonsense Liquid Contact Adhesive

FLOORING ADHESIVES

- Bostik Instant-PRO Sheet Vinyl Adhesive
- Bostik Instant-PRO Carpet and Cork Tile Adhesive
- Evo-stik Flooring Adhesive
- L80 Multibond Gold
- Roberts Acrylic Sheet Vinyl Adhesive
- Roberts Water Based Rubber Tile Adhesive

CYANOACRYLATES

- Araldite Superglue
- Bostik Blits Stik
- Everbuild Superglue
- Evo-stik Repair Adhesive
- Loctite Super Glue Brushable
- Loctite Super Glue Gel
- UniBond Repair Adhesive

GENERAL-PURPOSE BUILDING ADHESIVES

- Everbuild Stixall
- Evo-stik Liquid Nails
- Evo-stik Serious Stuff
- Geocel Crystal Clear
- Geocel Fixer Mate
- No Nonsense Grab Adhesive
- Pinkgrip
- UniBond No More Nails
- UniBond Mega Grip

WALL-TILE ADHESIVES

- BAL Blue Star
- BAL Tile & Grout
- Dunlop Fix-N-Grip
- Dunlop Waterproof
- Dunlop Anti Mould
- Evo-Stik Tile and Grout
- Evo-stik Waterproof Adhesive and Grout
- UniBond Wall Tile Adhesive and Grout
- UniBond Waterproof Wall Tile Adhesive

FLOOR-TILE ADHESIVES

- Dunlop Tile On Wood
- Evo-stik Tile A Floor
- Evo-stik Concrete Floors
- UniBond Tiling Concrete Floors
- UniBond Tile On Walls
- UniBond Tiling Wooden Floors
- UniBond Tile On Floors

METALWORKING ADHESIVES

- Araldite (Epoxy resin)
- Evo-Stik Liquid Metal
- Metolux Metostick

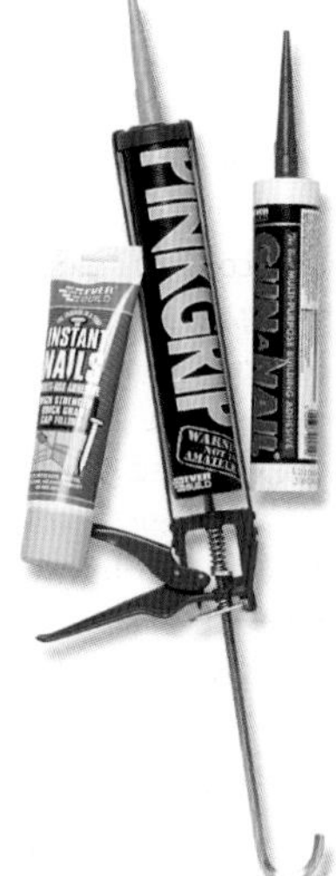

Building adhesives
There is a vast range of general-purpose building adhesives for gluing anything from roof tiles to carpet gripper strips. Similar glues are used for bonding wooden mouldings and skirting boards to the wall.

KEY TO TYPES OF ADHESIVE

1 PVA woodworking adhesive
2 Synthetic-resin/Resorcinol and urea
3 Rubber-based contact
4 Epoxy-resin
5 Rubber-resin
6 Synthetic-latex
7 Cyanoacrylates
8 Acrylic polymer
9 PVA/Acrylic tile adhesive
10 Polyurethane foam

Use this chart as a guide for gluing the materials listed below to those across the top.	WOOD AND MAN-MADE BOARDS	MASONRY	PLASTER	METAL	STONE	GLASS	CERAMIC	RIGID PLASTIC/ FIBRE GLASS
WOOD/MAN-MADE BOARDS	1,2,3,6,9	6,9	6,9	5,9	6,9	5,9	5,9	5,9
METAL	5,9			5,8,9	5,8,9	5,8,9	5,8,9	4,8,9
SYNTHETIC LAMINATES	4	4	4		4			4
FLOORCOVERINGS	6,7	6,7			6,7		6,7	
CEILING TILES/PANELS	7,10	7,10	7,10		7,10			
CERAMIC	5,9,10	10	10	5,9	10	5,8,9	5,8,9	5,9
STONE	5,9	5,9	9	5,9	5,9	5,9		
GLASS	4,5	5	5	5,8,9	5	5,8,9	5,8,9	5,9
RIGID PLASTICS/GLASS FIBRE	4,8,10			4,7,8	8,10	4,8	4,8	4,7,8

SEE ALSO > Replacing skirtings 218, Man-made boards 529

Fixings

A crucial aspect of any assembly or construction is choosing the right method of fixing. In addition to the time-honoured variety of nails and screws for woodwork and nuts, bolts and rivets for metalwork, nowadays there are a number of patent devices that speed and simplify many jobs.

Nails

• Avoiding split wood
If wood seems likely to split, blunt the point of a nail with a light hammer blow. A blunt nail punches its way through timber, instead of forcing the fibres apart.

• Removing a dent from wood
If you dent wood with a misplaced hammer blow, put a few drops of hot water on the dent and let the wood swell. When it is dry, smooth the wood with abrasive paper.

Nails afford a cheap, simple method of fixing for a variety of timber structures. They're useful for holding glued joints together, and can be applied decoratively to upholstery. There are many types of nail both for general use and for specific purposes.

Round plain-head wire nail
Rough general carpentry.
Bright steel or galvanized.
20 to 150mm (3/4 to 6in).

Round lost-head wire nail
Joinery. Head can be punched in and concealed.
Bright steel.
40 to 75mm (1½ to 3in).

Lath nail
For fixing laths and thin battens.
Galvanized.
25 to 40mm (1 to 1½in).

Annular nail
For extra-secure fixings.
Bright or stainless steel.
20 to 100mm (3/4 to 4in).

Oval wire nail
Carpentry. Can be punched in and concealed. Less likely to split the wood than round wire nails.
Bright steel.
25 to 150mm (1 to 6in).

Cut clasp nail
Carpentry, and for fixing wood to masonry.
Black iron or galvanized.
25 to 200mm (1 to 8in).

Cut floor nail
For nailing floorboards to joists.
Black iron or galvanized.
40 to 75mm (1½ to 3in).

Square twisted nail
General-purpose. Twisted shank gives extra grip.
Bright steel or sherardized.
20 to 100mm (3/4 to 4in).

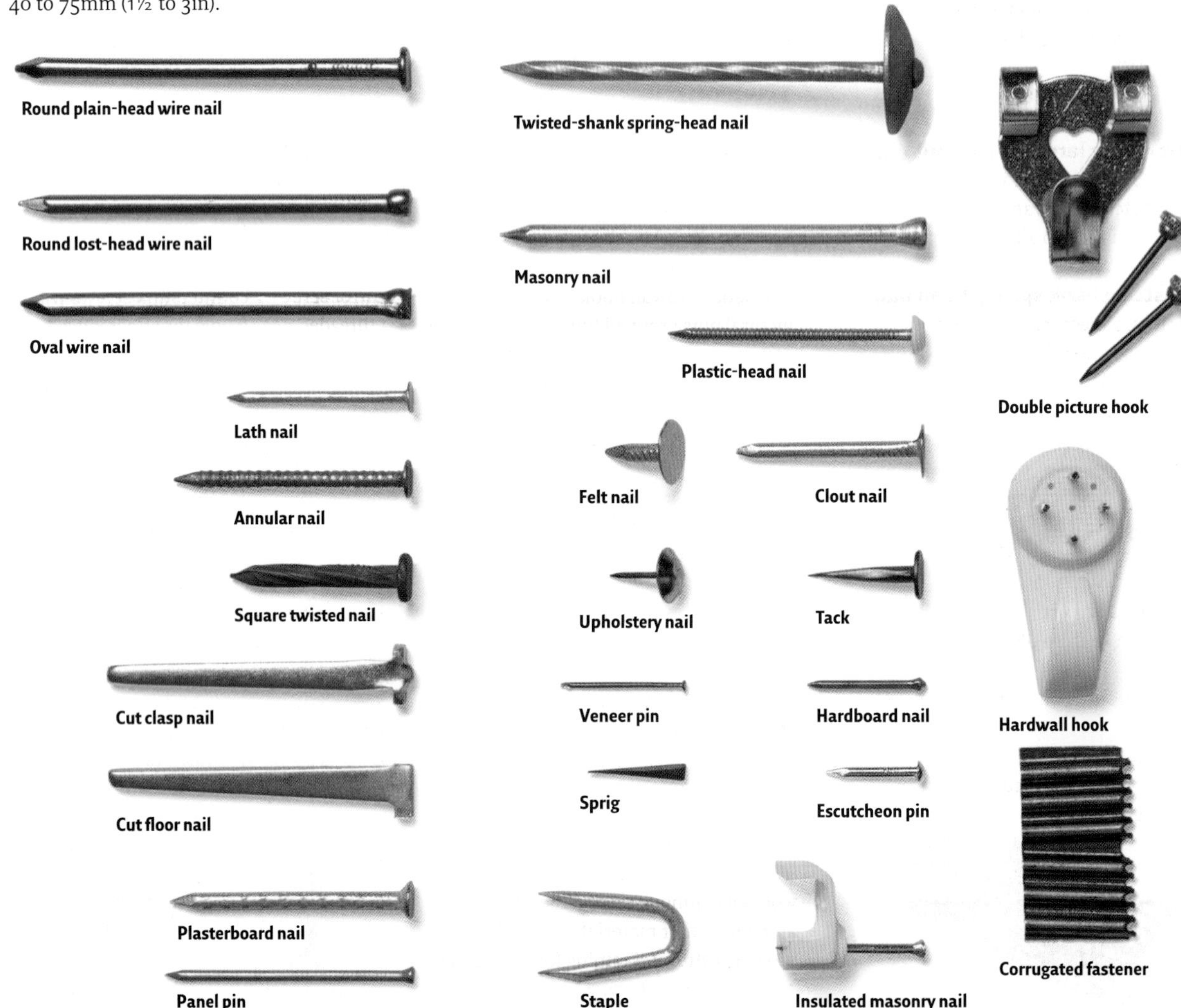
Round plain-head wire nail
Round lost-head wire nail
Oval wire nail
Lath nail
Annular nail
Square twisted nail
Cut clasp nail
Cut floor nail
Plasterboard nail
Panel pin
Twisted-shank spring-head nail
Masonry nail
Plastic-head nail
Felt nail
Clout nail
Upholstery nail
Tack
Veneer pin
Hardboard nail
Sprig
Escutcheon pin
Staple
Insulated masonry nail
Double picture hook
Hardwall hook
Corrugated fastener

SEE ALSO > Hammers 501, Nailing techniques 501, Removing nails 501, Nailing joints 505

Plasterboard nail
For fixing plasterboard to battens. Jagged shank gives good grip.
Bright steel, sherardized or galvanized.
30 to 40mm (1¼ to 1½in).

Panel pin
Cabinet-making and fine joinery.
Bright steel.
15 to 50mm (⅝ to 2in).

Veneer pin (moulding pin)
For applying veneers and small mouldings.
Bright steel.
15 to 50mm (⅝ to 2in).

Hardboard nail
For fixing hardboard and light plywood. Diamond-shaped head is driven in flush with board.
Coppered.
20 to 40mm (¾ to 1½in).

Corrugated fastener
For making rough butted or mitre framing joints.

Clout (slate) nail
For fixing slates and roofing materials.
Galvanized or bright steel, aluminium or copper.
20 to 100mm (¾ to 4in).

Felt nail or large-head clout nail
For attaching roofing felt, webbing etc.
Bright steel or galvanized.
12 to 50mm (½ to 2in).

Twisted-shank spring-head nail
For fixing sheet materials and man-made boards.
Galvanized.
65mm (2½in).

Masonry nail
For fixing wood to masonry.
Hard bright steel.
23 to 85mm (⅞ to 3⅜in).

Escutcheon pin
For fixing keyhole plates etc.
Brass.
15 or 20mm (⅝ or ¾in).

Timber connector
For making rough butted or mitre wood joints.

Sprig
For holding window glazing in the frame.
Black iron.
12 to 20mm (½ to ¾in).

Staple
Rough carpentry, and for fixing fencing wire.
Bright steel or galvanized.
10 to 40mm (⅜ to 1½in).

Upholstery nail
For upholstering furniture. Domed decorative head.
Brass, bronze, chromed or antique.
3 to 12mm (⅛ to ½in).

Tack
For carpeting, and attaching fabric to wood.
Blued, coppered or galvanized.
6 to 30mm (¼ to 1¼in).

Plastic-head nail
Stainless-steel nail with ringed shank and shatter-proof plastic head. For fixing plastic cladding.
30 to 65mm (1¼ to 2½in).

Insulated masonry nail
For securing electric cable and microbore pipe to masonry. The nail is driven through a plastic cable clip. Available in a variety of sizes

Picture hooks
Brass hooks for hanging pictures on a wall are held in place by hardened-steel pins.

Plastic hardwall hooks have short integral pins grouped together. These pins can be driven into very dense materials without bending.

Screws

Screws are manufactured with a small range of head shapes, suited to various purposes, and in a choice of materials and finishes. They are usually made of mild steel, but hardened steel is also used.

Solid-brass and stainless-steel screws do not rust. Steel screws are sometimes plated with zinc, chromium or brass to make them corrosion-resistant. There are also bronzed, sherardized and japanned screws.

Screw fixing
For anything other than rough work, use screws in preference to nails when joining wooden components together or for attaching other materials to wood. Screws provide a strong clamping force, and they can be taken out to allow components to be removed or adjusted without damage to the parts. When combined with glue, they can be used to clamp joints tight without the need for cramps.

Screw threads
Traditional woodscrews have a plain 'full' shank below the head that acts as a dowel. The shank is about one-third the length of the screw, the remainder being threaded and ending with a gimlet point.

More modern screws have a modified thread that may be single or double. They have a sharp point that makes starting easier, and a shank that's smaller in diameter than the thread - so that the smaller screws, at least, don't require a pilot hole to be drilled. Some screws are threaded along their entire length and so can be driven in quickly using a power screwdriver with little risk of splitting the wood.

Screwheads
There are six basic head shapes:
Countersunk head, for work where the screw must be recessed, either flush with the surface or below it.

Roundhead (sometimes called domed) - usually used with sheet material that is too thin for countersinking.

Raised head - a combination of domed and countersunk, often used for attaching metal items, such as door furniture, to wood.

Mirror screws - countersunk screws with a threaded centre hole for attaching a decorative dome are used for fixing wall mirrors and the like in place.

Pan head and flange head - similar to roundhead screws but mainly found on self-tapping screws used for joining sheet metal.

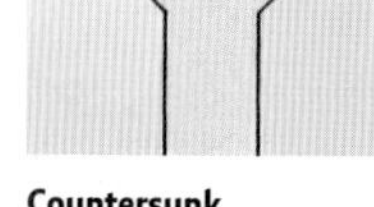
Countersunk

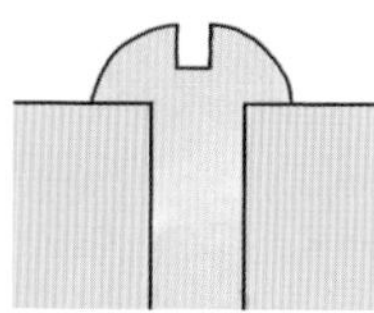
Roundhead

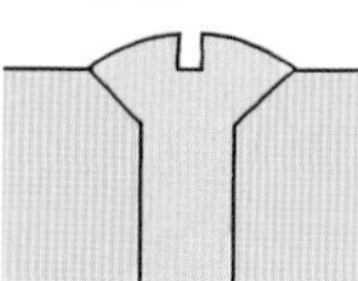
Raised head

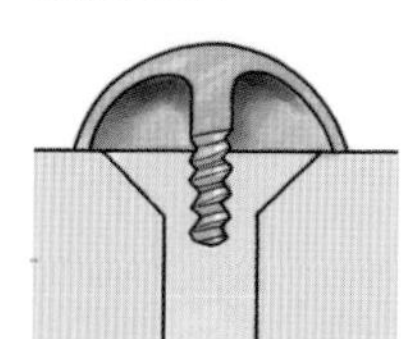
Mirror screw

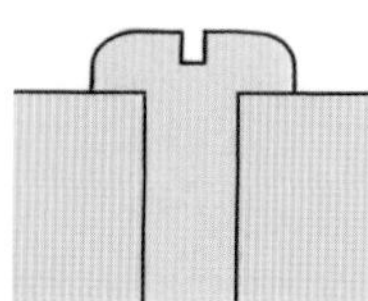
Pan head

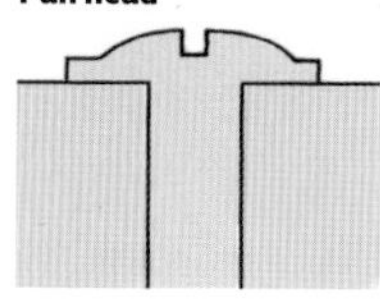
Flange head

Slotted and cross-slotted heads
A further subdivision of all these screws is between those with slotted heads and those with cross-slotted heads, which need cross-head screwdrivers. Cross-slotted heads provide a better grip and are ideal for use with power screwdrivers.

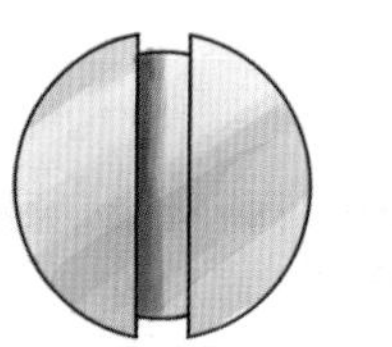
Slotted head

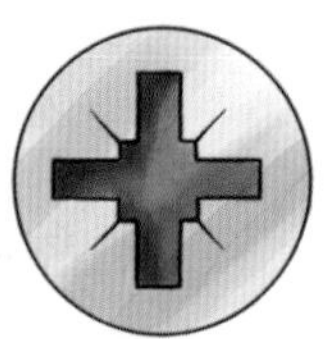
Cross-head

SEE ALSO > Fitting carpets 114, Roof slates/tiles 123, Roofing felt 128, Fixing plasterboard 163, Replacing broken glass 196, Screwdrivers 502, Nailing joints 505

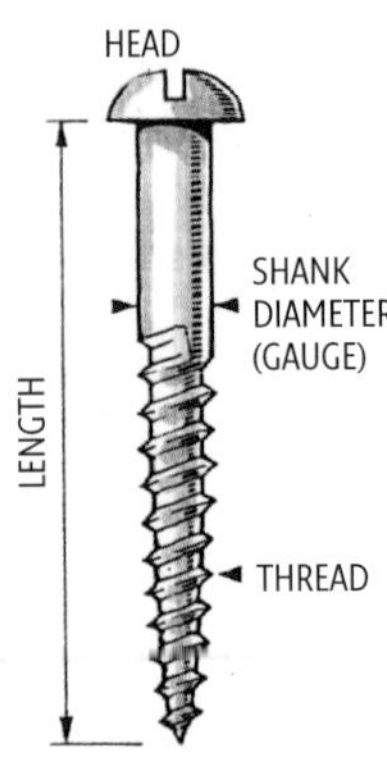

Parts of a screw
When ordering screws, it helps avoid confusion if you use the accepted terminology.

Screw sizes and gauges

All screws are described in terms of their length (given in millimetres or inches) and their gauge (swg) – shank diameter – which is expressed as a simple number from 1 to 20. The thicker the screw, the higher its gauge number. The gauges in most general use are 4, 6, 8 and 10. Some are now given in metric sizes only.

The length of a screw is the distance between its pointed tip and the part of the head that lies flush with the work surface. Woodscrews are made in lengths ranging from 6 to 150mm (¼ to 6in) – but not every combination of length, head shape and material is available, let alone stocked, in every gauge. The widest choice is generally to be found within gauges 6 to 12.

MDF screws
Made with sharp twin-thread spiral points, these screws are designed to penetrate the hard surface of MDF without the need for a pilot hole.

Cups, sockets and caps

Countersunk and raised-head screws can be used with metal screw cups, which improve their clamping force and also make for a neat appearance.

Plastic sockets with snap-on caps are available to conceal the heads of screws. Also, there are simple semi-domed plastic caps that plug into flush-mounted cross-head screwheads.

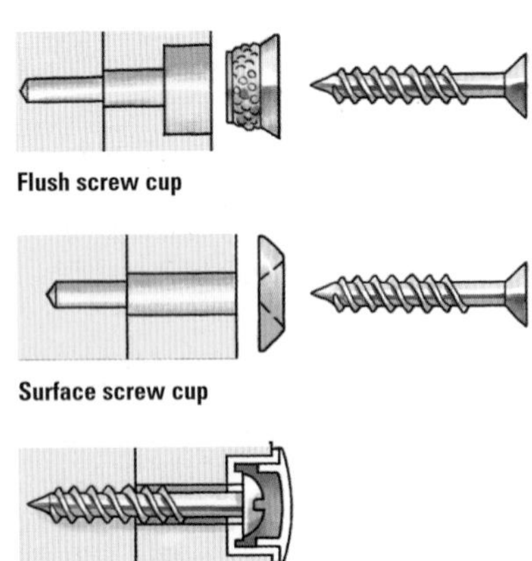

Flush screw cup

Surface screw cup

Plastic socket and cap

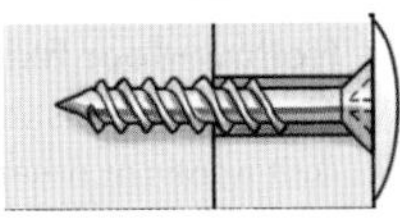

Plastic cap

Types of screw

Machine-made gimlet-point woodscrews have changed little since the nineteenth century. However, since the introduction of man-made boards and electric screwdrivers manufacturers have produced screws with new thread and head forms.

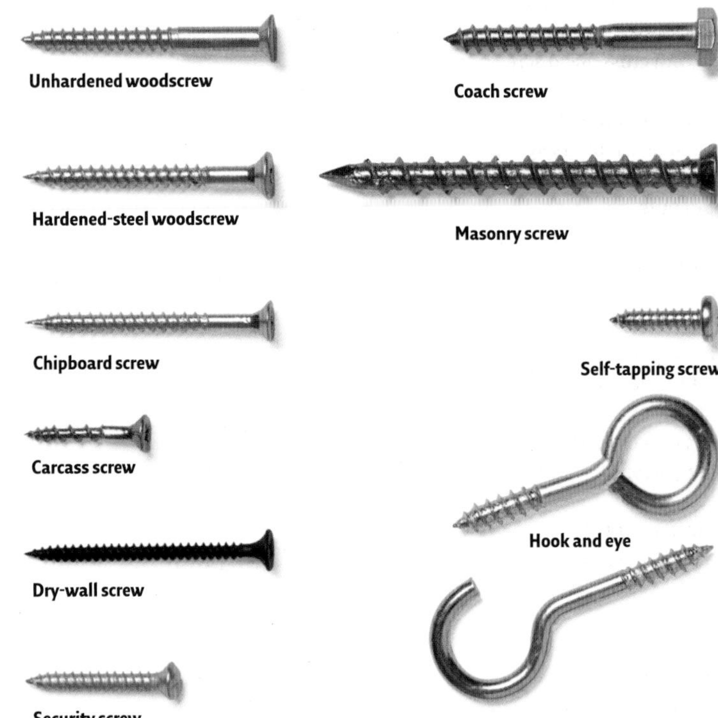

Unhardened woodscrew

Hardened-steel woodscrew

Chipboard screw

Carcass screw

Dry-wall screw

Security screw

Coach screw

Masonry screw

Self-tapping screw

Hook and eye

Unhardened woodscrews

The traditional woodscrew, with its single-helix thread, is made in a wide range of sizes, head types and materials. It is suitable for most woods and is particularly suited for fixing metal fittings such as hinges, locks and catches. This type of screw requires a pilot hole and shank-clearance hole to be drilled prior to insertion.

Length: 9 to 150mm (⅜ to 6in).
Diameter/gauge: 2 to 18swg.

Hardened-steel woodscrews

Countersunk or roundhead screws are available with twin steep-pitch threads for fast insertion. They can be used with all types of solid wood and man-made boards. The hardened metal makes it possible to drive these screws into a range of relatively soft materials without the need for pilot holes.

Length: 12 to 100mm (½ to 4in).
Diameter/gauge: 3 to 12swg.

Chipboard screw

These hardened-steel screws are primarily used for chipboard, but are also suitable as general-purpose woodscrews. Made with countersunk heads only, they have a single-helix thread. Although pilot holes are required for most materials, you can drive small-diameter screws directly into softwoods or low-density man-made boards.

Length: 12 to 100mm (½ to 4in).
Diameter/gauge: 3 to 6mm (⅛ to ¼in).

Carcass screws

These hardened-steel screws with a coarse single-helix thread are designed to be driven into the edge of chipboard without splitting it. Although not always necessary, drilling a pilot hole makes for easy insertion.

Length: 45mm (1¾in).
Diameter/gauge: 8swg.

Dry-wall screws

A special range of hardened screws with twin threads are made for fixing plasterboard or fibreboard to wooden or metal furring strips or studs. Each screw has a sharp point for drilling its own hole and a bugle-shaped countersunk head that enables it to bed down into the board material.

Length: 25 to 75mm (1 to 3in).
Diameter/gauge: 3.5 and 4.2mm (¼ and 5/32in).

SEE ALSO > Countersink bits 500, Inserting woodscrews 502, Screwdrivers 502

Security screws
The heads of these countersunk screws have special slots that permit the screw to be driven into the work – but reject the tip of the screwdriver when the action is reversed in an attempt to remove the screw. The latest type has twin threads and is for use with cross-head screwdrivers.

Length: 18 to 50mm (¾ to 2in).
Diameter/gauge: 6 to 12swg.

Coach screws
Coach screws are made from unhardened steel and are used for heavy-duty applications such as building a workbench. They have a square head and are driven into the work with a spanner. Use a large washer to prevent the head cutting into the timber.

Length: 25 to 150mm (1 to 6in).
Diameter/gauge: 6 to 12mm (¼ to ½in).

Self-tapping screws
Self-tapping screws are designed to cut their own thread in materials such as plastics and thin sheet metal. They are made from case-hardened steel and are normally available in four head forms – countersunk, raised head, pan head and flange head – either slotted or cross-head. Hexagonal-head screws are available for insertion using a spanner.

Length: 6 to 63mm (¼ to 2½in).
Diameter/gauge: 4 to 14swg.

Masonry screws
These extra-hard screws with a special dual thread can be driven directly into all types of masonry without the need for wallplugs.

Length: 57 to 100mm (2¼ to 4in).
Diameter/gauge: 4.8 and 6.4mm (3/16 and ¼in).

Screw hooks and eyes
Made of steel, screw hooks and eyes have a conventional woodscrew thread for fixing to a wall or panel. Plain or shouldered screw hooks are made in a variety of sizes and with round or square-shaped hooks, either bright-plated or plastic-coated. The hooks provide fixing points for cords, chains and so on.

Wall fixings

To make secure fixings to anything other than solid wood or man-made boards involves the use of fixing aids. These range from simple plugs that take a woodscrew in a hole drilled in brick or masonry to elaborate heavy-duty devices complete with bolts. There are also special products for making fixings to hollow walls.

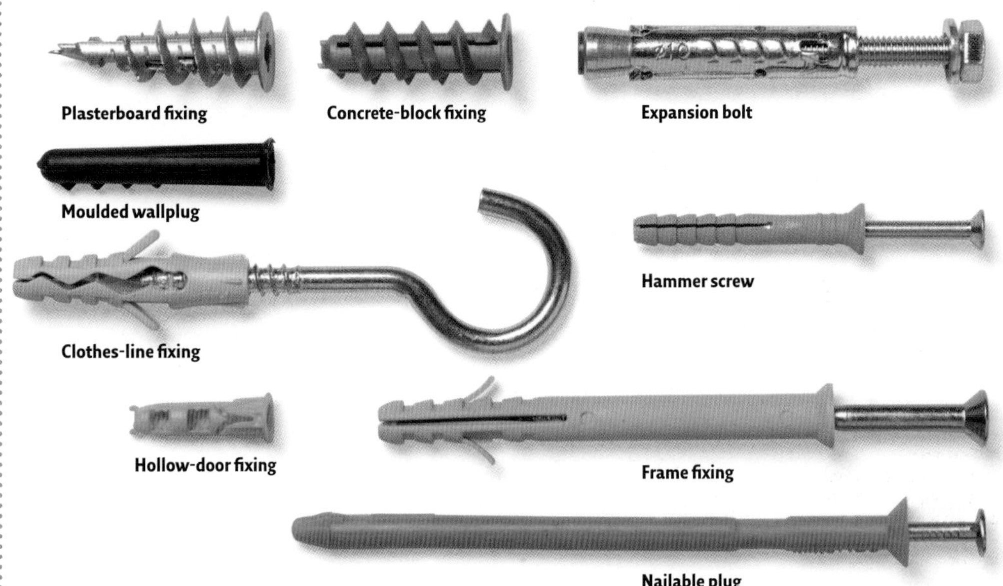

Resin fixings
There is a range of fixings designed for setting in resin that is injected into holes drilled into masonry. Resin-injecting kits are available from DIY stores and mail-order outlets.

Wallplugs
These relatively simple fixings anchor a variety of screws. There are moulded-plastic wallplugs that take a range of standard-gauge woodscrews, generally from No 4 to No 14. Some plugs are colour-coded for easy recognition. A wallplug is pushed into a drilled hole and then the screw is driven into the plug, which expands to grip the sides of the hole tightly.

There are also metal or plastic plugs with a coarse thread and a sharp point that cuts its own hole in a plasterboard wall. A similar fitting makes permanent fixings in lightweight concrete blockwork.

Some nylon or metal wallplugs come complete with coach screws or with screw hooks – for use as clothesline attachments or scaffolding anchors, for example.

Expansion bolts
There are various designs, but all work on the same basic principle: a bolt is screwed into a segmental metal or plastic shell and engages the thread of an expander. As the bolt is tightened, the expander forces the segments apart to grip the sides of the hole. Hooks and eyes that employ a similar principle are also available.

Nailable plugs
These can be used in place of wallplugs and screws. There are two types. The one comprises a flanged expansion sleeve with a masonry nail; the other consists of a ready-assembled wallplug and 'hammer screw'. Both types are hammered into a drilled hole; but only the hammer screw can be removed, using a screwdriver. These plugs are often used for fixing frames, battens, wall linings and skirting boards.

Frame fixings
These are designed to speed up screw fixings in wood, plastic or metal door and window frames by eliminating the need to mark out and predrill the fixing holes. Supplied with a plated screw or bolt, these long fittings are available with plastic plugs.

The item to be fixed is first placed in position and a clearance hole drilled through it into the wall. The frame fixing is then fitted and the screw tightened.

Hollow-door fixing
This special plastic plug is for attaching coat hooks or other items to thin-skinned hollow doors.

SEE ALSO > Drilling masonry 512, Masonry bits 512

Fixings for hollow walls

There are all sorts of devices for making fixings to hollow walls composed of plasterboard on studs, or lath and plaster, and so on. Most of them operate on the principle of opening out behind the panel and gripping it in some way.

Special wallplugs, plastic toggles and collapsible anchors all have segments that open out or fold up against the inside face of the wallboard or panel.

Rubber-sleeve anchor
A rubber-sleeve anchor has a steel bolt which, when tightened, draws up an internal nut that makes the rubber sleeve bulge out behind the panel.

Gravity toggles and spring toggles
These fittings have arms that open out inside the cavity. A gravity toggle has a single arm, pivoted near one end so that its own weight causes it to drop. A spring toggle has two spring-loaded arms that fly open when they are clear of the hole and a bolt that draws them tight up against the panel.

Some types of anchor remain in the hole if the screw has to be removed. Others, such as nylon anchors and spring toggles, will be lost in the cavity. A rubber anchor can be removed and then used again.

None of these devices should be used for fixings meant to take a heavy load. Instead, locate the timber wall studs and fix directly into them. On lath-and-plaster walls, even for moderate loads, use the larger spring and gravity toggles, rather than plug-type fixing devices.

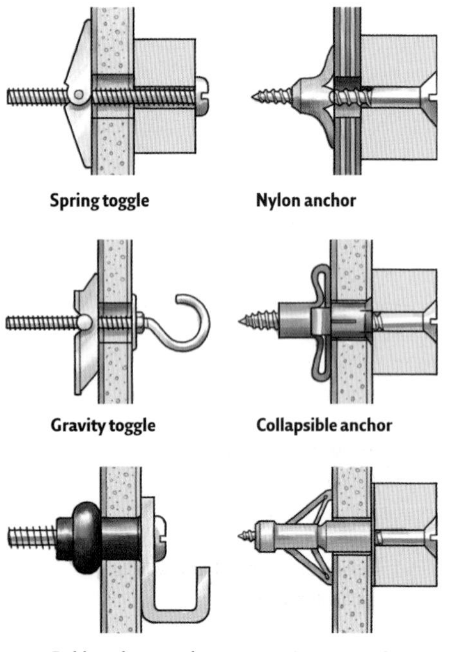

Knock-down fittings

Woodscrews in their various forms serve as simple and effective fasteners for all manner of assemblies. However, there are times when the material may require reinforcement or even an alternative mechanical fitting in order to hold the parts together. Knock-down fittings allow components to be easily put together and easily taken apart.

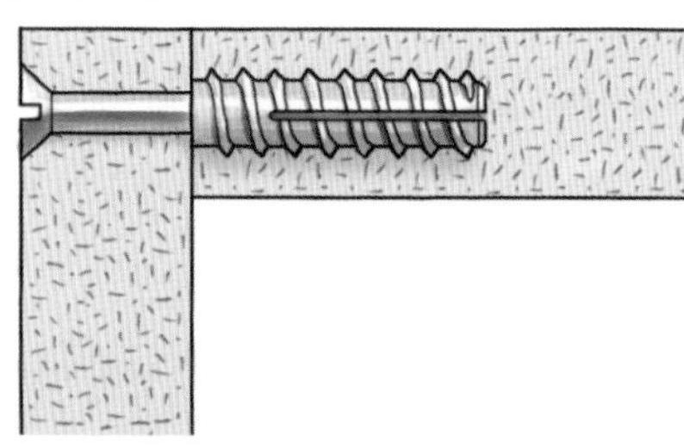

Chipboard fastener
This fitting has a nylon insert with an external thread that is driven into a hole in the face or edge of chipboard to provide a secure fixing for woodscrews.

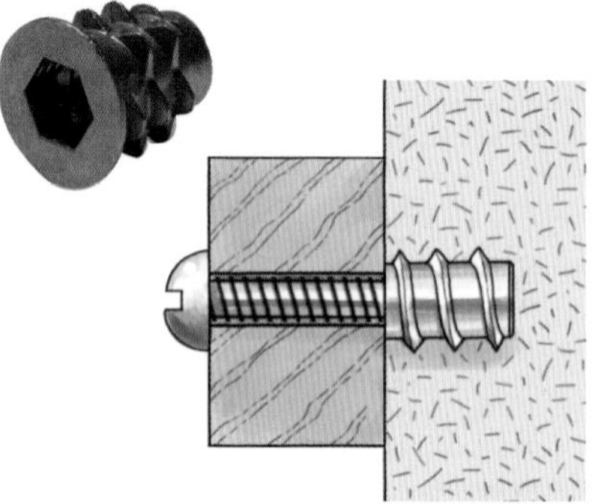

Screw socket
This is a metal insert that is threaded internally to receive a bolt. A screw socket makes a neat concealed fixing.

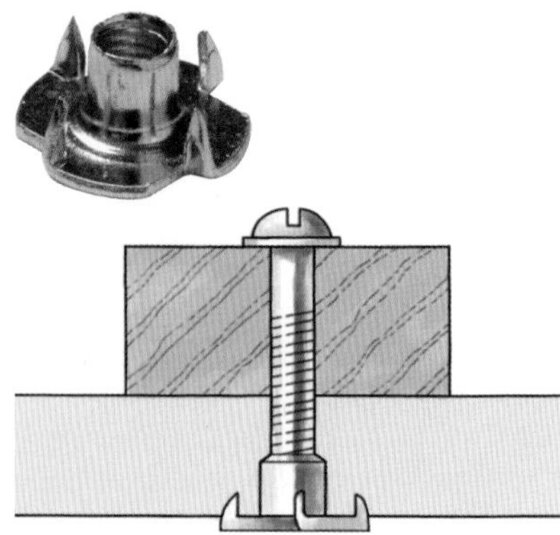

Tee nut
This is employed to make a strong bolt fastening in wood. When the metal nut is pressed into the back of a hole drilled in the component, the projecting prongs bite into the wood.

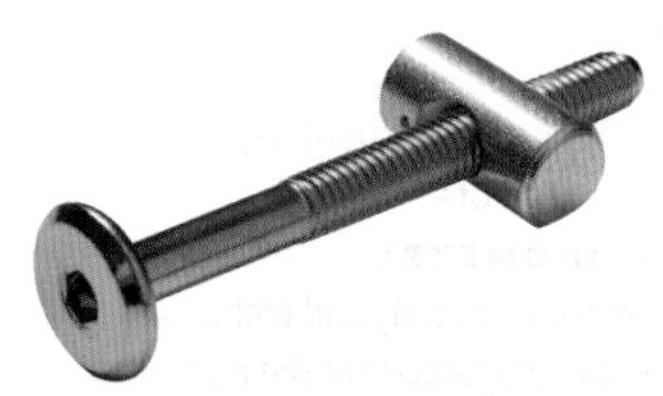

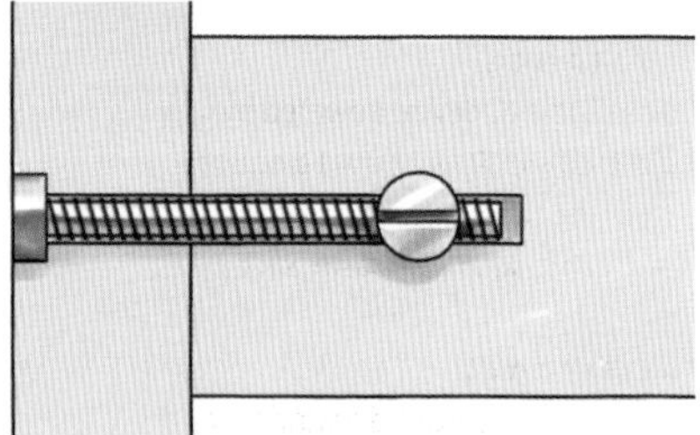

Cross dowel
A steel cross dowel is a strong fixing for joining the ends of rails to side panels or frames. The dowel is housed in a stopped hole drilled in the underside of the rail. A threaded hole through the side of the dowel receives a bolt. A clearance hole for the bolt is drilled in the end of the rail.

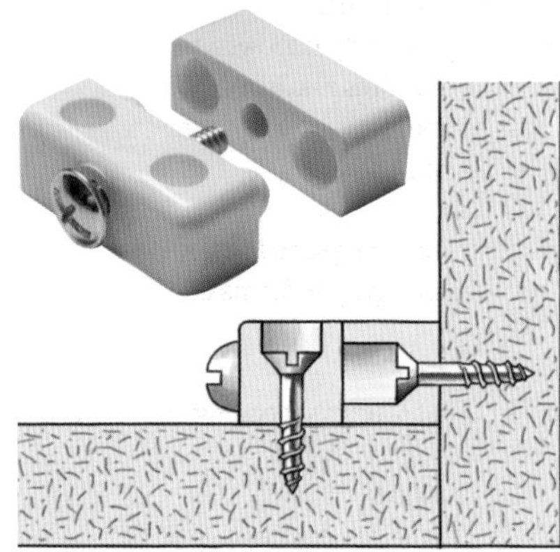

Block joint
Block joints are used to join panels at right angles to one another. Made in various patterns, they are basically plastic blocks made in two halves that are screwed to the panels and bolted together. Moulded dowels in one half locate in holes in the other for accurate alignment.

SEE ALSO > Inserting woodscrews 502, Drilling masonry 512

Glossary

ACCESSORY
An electrical component permanently connected to a circuit – a switch, socket outlet, fused connection unit etc.

AGGREGATE
Particles of sand or stone mixed with cement and water to make concrete, or added to paint to make a textured finish.

AIRLOCK
A blockage in a pipe caused by a trapped bubble of air.

ANTHROPOMETRY
The comparative study and technique of sizes and proportions of the human body.

APPLIANCE
A machine or device powered by electricity. *or* A functional piece of equipment connected to the plumbing, such as a basin, sink, bath etc.

ARCHITRAVE
The moulding around a window or door.

ARRIS
The sharp edge at the meeting of two surfaces.

BACK-SIPHONING
The siphoning of part of a plumbing system caused by the failure of mains water pressure.

BALANCED FLUE
A ducting system that allows a heating appliance, such as a boiler, to draw fresh air from and discharge gases to the outside of a building.

BALLAST
Naturally occurring sand and gravel mix used as aggregate for making concrete.

BALUSTER
One of a set of posts supporting a stair handrail.

BALUSTRADE
The protective barrier alongside a staircase or landing.

BANISTERS
See Balustrade.

BASECOAT
A flat coat of paint over which a decorative glaze is applied.

BATT
A short cut length of glass-fibre or mineral-fibre insulant.

BATTEN
A narrow strip of wood.

BATTER
The slope of the face of a wall that leans backwards or tapers from bottom to top.

BLIND
To cover with sand.

BLOWN
Broken away, as when a layer of cement rendering has parted from a wall.

BORE
The hollow part of a pipe or tube. *or* To drill a hole.

BURR
The rough raised edge left on a workpiece after cutting or filing.

BUTTERCOAT
The top layer of cement render.

CAME
The grooved strip of lead that holds the glass in a leaded light or stained-glass window.

CAP-NUT
The nut used to tighten a fitting onto pipework.

CASING
The timber lining of a door or window opening.

CATENARY WIRE
A length of wire cable suspended horizontally between two points.

CAVITY WALL
A wall made of two separate, parallel masonry skins with an air space between them.

CHAMFER
A narrow flat surface along the edge of a workpiece – normally at an angle of 45 degrees to adjacent surfaces. *or* To plane the angled surface.

CHASE
A groove cut in masonry or plaster to accept pipework or an electrical cable. *or* To cut or channel such grooves.

CIRCUIT
A complete path through which an electric current can flow.

CONCAVE
Curving inwards.

CONDUCTOR
A component, usually a length of wire, along which an electric current will pass.

CONVEX
Curving outwards.

CORNICE
Continuous horizontal moulding between the walls and ceiling of a room.

COUNTERBORE
To cut a hole that allows the head of a bolt or screw to lie below a surface. *or* Such a hole.

COUNTERSINK
To cut a tapered recess that allows the head of a screw to lie flush with a surface. *or* The tapered recess itself.

COVING
A prefabricated moulding used to make a cornice.

CUP
To bend as a result of shrinkage, specifically across the width of a piece of wood.

DADO
The lower part of an interior wall – usually defined by a moulded wooden rail at about waist height (the dado rail).

DAMP-PROOF COURSE
A layer of impervious material that prevents moisture rising from the ground into the walls of a building.

DAMP-PROOF MEMBRANE
A layer of impervious material that prevents moisture rising through a concrete floor.

DATUM POINT
The point from which measurements are taken.

DPC
See Damp-proof course.

DPM
See Damp-proof membrane.

DRIP GROOVE
A groove cut or moulded in the underside of a windowsill to prevent rainwater running back to the wall.

DROP
A strip of wallpaper measured and cut to length ready for pasting to a wall.

EARTH
A connection between an electrical circuit and the earth (ground). *or* A terminal to which the connection is made.

EAVES
The edges of a roof that project beyond the walls.

EFFLORESCENCE
A white powdery deposit caused by soluble salts migrating to the surface of a wall or ceiling.

END GRAIN
The surface of wood exposed after cutting across the fibres.

EXTENSION
A room or rooms added to an existing building.

EXTENSION LEAD
A length of electrical flex for temporarily connecting the short permanent flex of an appliance to a wall socket.

FACE EDGE
In woodworking, the surface planed square to the face side.

FACE SIDE
In woodworking, the flat planed surface from which other dimensions and angles are measured and worked.

FALL
A downward slope.

FASCIA
A strip of wood that covers the ends of rafters and to which external guttering is fixed.

FEATHER
To wear away or smooth an edge until it is undetectable.

FENCE
An adjustable guide to keep the cutting edge of a tool a set distance from the edge of a workpiece.

FLASHING
A weatherproof junction between a roof and a wall or chimney, or between one roof and another.

FLAUNCHING
A mortared slope at the top of a fireback or round a chimney pot.

FLUTE
A rounded concave groove.

FOOTING
A narrow concrete foundation for a wall.

FRASS
Powdered wood produced by the activity of woodworm.

FROG
The angled depression in one face of some housebricks.

FURRING BATTENS
See Furring strips.

FURRING STRIPS
Parallel strips of wood fixed to a wall or ceiling to provide a framework for attaching panels.

FUSE BOARD
Where the main electrical service cable is connected to the house circuitry. *or* The accumulation of consumer unit, meter etc.

GALVANIZED
Covered with a protective coating of zinc.

GEL
A substance with a thick jelly-like consistency.

GLAZE
A liquid finish, usually colourless, to which paint or pigments are added. Once applied to a surface, the glaze is worked with various tools and brushes to create decorative effects. *or* To put glass or clear plastic into a frame.

GOING
The horizontal measurement between the top and bottom risers of a stair or the depth of one tread.

GRAIN
The general direction of wood fibres. *or* The pattern produced on the surface of timber by cutting through the fibres. See also End grain and Short grain.

GROMMET
A ring of rubber or plastic used to line a hole to protect electrical cable from chafing. A blind grommet incorporates a thin web of plastic or rubber that seals the hole until the web is cut to provide access for a cable.

GROOVE
A long narrow channel cut in plaster or wood in the general direction of the grain. *or* To cut such channels.

GROUNDS
Strips of wood fixed to a wall to provide nail-fixing points for skirting boards, door casings etc. See also Pallets.

GULLET
The notch formed between two saw teeth.

HARDCORE
Broken bricks or stones used to form a sub-base below paving, foundations etc.

HARDWOOD
Timber from deciduous trees.

HEAD
The height of the surface of water above a specific point, used as a measurement of pressure – for example, a head of 2m (6ft). *or* The top horizontal member of a wooden frame.

HEAD PLATE
The top horizontal member of a stud partition.

HEAVE
An upward swelling of ground caused by excessive moisture.

HELICAL
Spiral shaped.

HOGGIN
A fine ballast, usually with a clay content, used to form a sub-base for concrete pads or paving.

HONE
To sharpen a cutting edge.

HORNS
Extended door or window stiles, designed to protect the corners from damage while in storage.

HOUSING
A long narrow channel cut across the general direction of wood grain to form part of a joint.

INSULATION
Materials used to reduce the transmission of heat or sound.*or* Nonconductive material surrounding electrical wires or connections to prevent the passage of electricity.

JAMB
The vertical side member of a doorframe or window frame.

JOIST
A horizontal wooden or metal beam (such as an RSJ) used to support a structure such as a floor, ceiling or wall.

KERF
The groove cut by a saw.

KEY
To abrade or incise a surface in order to provide a better grip when gluing something to it.

KNOTTING
Sealer, made from shellac, that prevents wood resin bleeding through a surface finish.

KNURLED
Impressed with a series of fine grooves designed to improve the grip, for instance a knurled knob or handle.

LATH AND PLASTER
A method of finishing a timber-frame wall or ceiling. Narrow strips of wood are nailed to the studs or joists to provide a supporting framework for plaster or tiles.

LEAD
A stepped section of brickwork or blockwork built at each end of a wall to act as a guide to the height of the intermediate coursing.

LINTEL
A horizontal beam used to support the wall over a door or window opening.

MARBLING
Simulating real marble with coloured glazes. *or* The finished effect.

MARINE PLYWOOD
Exterior-grade plywood.

MASTIC
A nonsetting compound used to seal joints.

MICROPOROUS
See Moisture-vapour permeable.

MITRE
A joint formed between two pieces of wood by cutting bevels of equal angle at the ends of each piece. *or* To cut the joint.

MOISTURE-VAPOUR PERMEABLE
Used to describe a finish that allows moisture to escape from timber, allowing it to dry out, while protecting the wood from rainwater or damp. The same term is used to describe a paint that can be applied over new plaster without sealing in the moisture.

MONO-PITCH ROOF
A roof that slopes in one direction only.

MORTISE
A rectangular recess cut in timber to receive a matching tongue or tenon.

MOUSE
A small weight used to help pass a line through a narrow vertical space.

MULLION
A vertical dividing member of a window frame.

MUNTIN
A central vertical member of a panel door.

NEEDLE
A stout wooden beam used with props to support the section of a wall above an opening prior to the installation of an RSJ or lintel.

NEUTRAL
The section of an electrical circuit that carries the flow of current back to source. *or* A terminal to which the connection is made. *or* A colour composed mainly of black and white.

NEWEL
The post at the top or bottom of a flight of stairs, which supports the handrail.

NOGGING
A short horizontal wooden member between studs.

NOSING
The front edge of a stair tread.

OUTER STRING
See String.

OXIDIZE
To form a layer of metal oxide, as in rusting.

PALLET
A wooden plug built into masonry to provide a fixing point for a door casing.

PARE
To remove fine shavings from wood with a chisel.

PARGETING
The internal render of a chimney.

PARTY WALL
The wall between two houses over which each of the adjoining owners has equal rights in law.

PENETRATING OIL
A thin lubricant that will seep between corroded components and ease them apart.

PHASE
The part of an electrical circuit that carries the flow of current to an appliance or accessory. Also known as live.

PILE
Raised fibres that stand out from a backing material, for instance in a carpet.

PILOT HOLE
A small-diameter hole drilled prior to the insertion of a woodscrew to act as a guide for its thread.

PINCH ROD
A wooden batten used to gauge the width of a frame or opening.

PME
See Protective multiple earth.

POINT LOAD
The concentration of forces on a very small area.

PRIMER
The first coat of a paint system applied to protect wood or metal. A wood primer reduces the absorption of subsequent undercoats and top coats. A metal primer prevents corrosion.

PROFILE
The outline or contour of an object.

PROTECTIVE MULTIPLE EARTH
A system of electrical wiring in which the neutral part of the circuit is used to take earth-leakage current to earth.

PTFE
Polytetrafluorethylene – a material used to make tape for sealing threaded plumbing fittings.

PURLIN
A horizontal beam that provides intermediate support for rafters or sheet roofing.

RAFTER
One of a set of parallel sloping beams that form the main structural element of a roof.

RATCHET
A device that permits movement in one direction only by restricting the reversal of a toothed wheel or rack.

RCD
See Residual current device.

REBATE
A stepped rectangular recess along the edge of a workpiece, usually forming part of a joint. *or* To cut such recesses.

RENDER
A thin layer of cement-based mortar applied to exterior walls to provide a protective finish. Sometimes fine stone aggregate is embedded in the mortar. *or* To apply such mortar.

RESIDUAL CURRENT DEVICE
A device that monitors the flow of electrical current through the live and neutral wires of a circuit. When an RCD detects an imbalance caused by earth leakage, it cuts off the supply of electricity as a safety precaution.

REVEAL
The vertical side of an opening in a wall.

RISER
The vertical part of a step.

RISING MAIN
The pipe that supplies water under mains pressure, usually to a storage tank in the roof.

ROLLED STEEL JOIST (RSJ)
A steel beam, usually with a cross section in the form of a capital letter I.

RSJ
See Rolled steel joist.

RUB JOINT
Glued wood rubbed together and held by suction until it sets.

RUBBER
A pad of cotton wool wrapped in soft cloth used to apply stain, shellac polish etc.

SASH
The openable part of a window.

SCORE
To scratch a line with a pointed tool. See also Scribe.

SCRATCHCOAT
The bottom layer of cement.

SCREED
A thin layer of mortar applied to give a smooth surface to concrete etc. *or* A shortened name for screed batten.

SCREED BATTEN
A thin strip of wood fixed to a surface to act as a guide to the thickness of an application of plaster or render.

SCRIBE
To copy the profile of a surface on the edge of sheet material that is to be butted against it. *or* To mark a line with a pointed tool. See also Score.

SETT
A small rectangular paving block.

SHEATHING
The outer layer of insulation surrounding an electrical cable or flex.

SHORT CIRCUIT
The accidental rerouting of electricity to earth, which increases the flow of current and blows a fuse.

SHORT GRAIN
When the general direction of wood fibres lies across a narrow section of timber.

SILL
The lowest horizontal member of a frame that surrounds a door or window. *or* The lowest horizontal member of a stud partition.

SLEEPER WALL
A low masonry wall that serves as an intermediate support for ground-floor joists.

SOAKAWAY
A pit filled with rubble or gravel into which water is drained.

SOFFIT
The underside of part of a building such as an archway or the eaves etc.

SOFTWOOD
Timber from coniferous trees.

SOLE PLATE
Another term for a stud-partition sill. *or* A wooden member used as a base to level a loadbearing timber-frame wall.

SPALLING
Flaking of the outer face of masonry caused by expanding moisture in icy conditions.

SPANDREL
The triangular infill below the outer string of a staircase.

STAFF BEAD
The innermost strip of timber holding a sliding sash in a window frame.

STILE
A vertical side member of a door or window sash.

STOPPER
A wood filler made in colours to match various kinds of timber.

STRING
A board running from one floor to another into which staircase treads and risers are jointed. The one on the open side of a staircase is known as the outer string; the one against the wall is called the wall string.

STUD PARTITION
A timber-frame interior dividing wall.

STUDS
The vertical members of a timber-frame wall.

SUBSIDENCE
A sinking of the ground caused by the shrinkage of excessively dry soil.

SUPPLEMENTARY BONDING
The connecting to earth of electrical appliances and exposed metal pipework in a bathroom or kitchen.

TAMP
To pack down firmly with repeated blows.

TEMPLATE
A cut-out pattern made from paper, wood, metal etc to help shape a workpiece accurately.

TENON
A projecting tongue on the end of a piece of wood that fits into a corresponding mortise.

TERMINAL
A connection to which the bared ends of electrical cable or flex are attached.

THINNER
A solvent, such as turpentine, used to dilute paint or varnish.

THIXOTROPIC
Term used to describe paints that have a jelly-like consistency until stirred or applied, at which point they become liquefied.

TOP COAT
The outer layer of a paint system.

TORQUE
A rotational force.

TRANSOM
A horizontal dividing member of a window frame.

TRAP
A bent section of pipe below a bath, sink etc. It contains standing water to prevent the passage of gases.

TREAD
The horizontal part of a step.

UNDERCOAT
A layer or layers of paint used to obliterate the colour of a primer and build a protective body of paint before applying a top coat.

VAPOUR BARRIER
A layer of impervious material that prevents the passage of moisture-laden air.

VAPOUR CHECK
See Vapour barrier.

WALL PLATE
A horizontal timber member placed along the top of a wall to support the ends of joists and spread their load.

WALL STRING
See String.

WALL TIE
A strip of metal or bent wire used to bind sections of masonry together.

WANEY EDGE
A natural wavy edge on a plank. It may still be covered by bark.

WATER HAMMER
Vibration in plumbing caused by fluctuating water pressure.

WEATHERED
Showing signs of exposure to the weather. *or* Sloped so as to shed rainwater.

WEEP HOLE
A small hole at the base of a cavity wall that allows absorbed water to drain to the outside.

WORKPIECE
An object in the process of being shaped, produced or otherwise worked on. Sometimes referred to simply as the 'work'.

Index

Picture Credits

Special photography as follows:

PLANNING AHEAD
Colin Bowling

DECORATING
Airedale/David Murphy

REPAIRS & IMPROVEMENTS
Colin Bowling
Airedale/David Murphy

HOME SECURITY
Colin Bowling

INFESTATION, ROT & DAMP
Airedale/David Murphy

INSULATION & VENTILATION
Airedale/David Murphy

ELECTRICITY
Colin Bowling

PLUMBING
Focus Publishing
Colin Bowling

HEATING
Focus Publishing
Colin Bowling

WORKING OUTDOORS
Airedale/David Murphy

TOOLS & SKILLS
Colin Bowling

Other images by Paul Chave, Peter Higgins, Ben Jennings and Neil Waving.

Key to photographic credits
L = Left, R = Right, T = Top, TL = Top left, TC = Top centre, TR = Top right, C = Centre, UC = Upper centre, UCL = Upper centre left, UCR = Upper centre right, CL = Centre left, CR = Centre right, LCL = Lower centre left, LC = Lower centre, LCR = Lower centre right, B = Bottom, BL = Bottom left, BC = Bottom centre, BR = Bottom right

Picture sources

The authors and producers wish to thank the following companies and individuals who supplied photographs.

10, Rentokil Ltd BL; Inklink CL; Ann Kelley/Elizabeth Whiting Associates CR
11, Fired Earth BR; Marshalls Mono Ltd TR
16, RICS (Royal Institution of Chartered Surveyors) CL; IStructE (Institution of Structural Engineers) LCL
17, RIBA (Royal Institute of British Architects) TL; RTPI (Royal Town Planning Institute) CL
18, Edward Bock/Corbis TL; FMB (Federation of Master Builders) CL
23, The Velux Company TL; Friedhelm Thomas/Elizabeth Whiting Associates BC; Pixland/Corbis TR; Inklink BR
28, Fernando Bengoechea/Beateworks/Corbis
29, Evergreener TR; Honeywell CR
30, Albert Jackson
33, Oscar Paisley/Red Cover C; Di Lewis/ Elizabeth Whiting Associates BL; Elliott Kaufman/Beateworks/Corbis BR
34, David Gless/Elizabeth Whiting Associates BR
35, Heuga - Interface Europe Ltd T
36, Fired Earth BR; Ikea BL
37, Lu Jeffrey/Elizabeth Whiting Associates BL
39, Ideal (UK) Standard Ltd T; Andreas von Einsiedel/Elizabeth Whiting Associates B
42, Simon Gilham BR; Inklink CL, LCL, BL
44, Simon Gilham CL, C
46, Blue Circle Industries BL; Inklink BR; Simon Gilham CL, LCL
47, Blue Circle Industries TR
54, Hire Technicians Group Ltd TL
55, Ian Parry/Traditional Homes Magazine TR
58, Simon Gilham BL, BR; Inklink BC
60, Simon Gilham BL, BC, BR
64, Simon Jennings
67, Fired Earth TL
75, Good Wood Finishes R
76, Sadolin
77, Inklink TR
80, Langlow Products Ltd CL
82, Hammerite
83, Simon Gilham BR
88, Spike Powell/Elizabeth Whiting Associates TL
89, Sanderson BR
90, Sanderson TR
91, Shona Wood
92, Shona Wood
96, Stonell Ltd TL; Bonar and Flotex Ltd BR
97, The Rubber Flooring Company TR
101, Topps Tiles TR
102, Judge Ceiling Systems TL
103, Amtico TR
104, Di Lewis/Elizabeth Whiting Associates TC
105, Wicanders TL
106, Fired Earth TL
107, Topps Tiles TR
109, Topps Tiles TR
112, Topps Tiles CR
115, Tim Street-Porter/Elizabeth Whiting Associates TC
120, Mclean Homes/Martine Hamilton Knight/Arcaid
122, photos.com TC; Velux LCL; John Shepherd/istockphoto BL; David Moore/Timber Repair Systems BR
125, Sandtoft TL; Inklink CL; Dreadnought Tiles BL
126, Inklink TL
134, Shona Wood TL
147, Bruce Hemming/Elizabeth Whiting Associates TR
148, G E Fabbri C, CR, B, BR; Inklink TL
172, Philip Wegener/Beateworks/Corbis
173, Edina van der Wyck/Media10 Images
183, David Giles/Elizabeth Whiting Associates TR
185, Inklink LCR
190, Hörmann (UK) Ltd TR; Inklink TL
191, John Carr Sales Ltd C, Magnet CR
192, Simon Jennings
193, Inklink TC; Edifice TR; Simon Jennings CR; Quentin Harriot/Elizabeth Whiting Associates BC
197, Shona Wood
199, Simon Jennings
200, G E Fabbri
204, Velux
205, Shona Wood TL, Plantation Shutters BL, BC
206, Rosebys BL
209, Shona Wood BC; Richard Burbidge BL; Fired Earth R
213, Shona Wood
215, Richard Burbidge
219, Mark Luscombe-Whyte/Elizabeth Whiting Associates
222, Ken Kirkwood BC; Spur Shelving Ltd BR
223, Inklink
224, G E Fabbri
225, G E Fabbri
226, Spur Shelving Ltd TL; G E Fabbri
227, G E Fabbri
230, Ladderstore.com
233, Inklink TR, BL
238, Ian Parry/Elizabeth Whiting Associates BL; Tommy Candler/Elizabeth Whiting Associates TR
240, Kidde Safety Europe Ltd CL
242, Rentokil Ltd BL
244, Sorex Ltd BR, BL; Abatis BC
245, Simon Jennings LR; David Cropp, Rentokil UK Ltd BL, BC
248, Environment Agency BL; Ronseal Ltd TL
249, Ronseal Ltd TR
250, Simon Jennings BR
252, Dampcoursing Ltd TR
260, The Original Box Sash Window Company Ltd BL, G E Fabbri C
264, Own Label Products TL
265, Ciga
266, Thermawrap TR
283, DEFRA
319, Graham Dixon
322, Ikea L
326, Ring Lighting TL, UCL, CL; Ikea LCL
334, Ikea BR
341, Rodney Hyett/Elizabeth Whiting Associates CR; Oase Living Water
352, Opella Ltd CL
353, Screwfix TR
362, Cuprofit/IBP Group BR
370, Ideal Standard
372, Ideal Standard C, LCL, LC, BC, BL
374, Ideal Standard
378, Saniflo Ltd
379, Ideal Standard C, CR; Aqualisa Products Ltd BR
380, Ideal Standard TL
381, Mira Showers BL
382, Ideal Standard TL; Hans Grohe Ltd CL
386, Franke UK Ltd CL, C, LCR, LR; Rangemaster BCR, BR
387, Rangemaster BL
392, Albion Water Heaters Ltd
393, Rayotec Ltd
394, Solartwin
396, Stovax Ltd TL
398, Inklink BR
399, Simon Jennings BR; Stovax Ltd TR
400, Inklink TL; Burley Appliances TC
410, Burley Appliances
403, Charnwood UK
408, Myson
420, Vent-Axia TC; Devi Electroheat Ltd BL
422, John Glover/The Garden Picture Library CR; Simon Jennings TL, CL, BL
423, Henk Dijkman/The Garden Picture Library C; Simon Jennings R; Clay Perry/The Garden Picture Library T; Ron Sutherland/The Garden Picture Library B
424, Marshalls Mono Ltd L
425, Simon Jennings TL, R; Alan Marshall BL
426, Simon Jennings
427, Simon Jennings
433, Simon Jennings
434, Simon Jennings
435, Simon Jennings
436, Simon Jennings
447, Simon Jennings
438, Simon Jennings
440, Bradstone, Aggregate Industries Ltd BC, BR; Simon Jennings TL, UCL, UCR; Albert Jackson LCL, LCR; Marshalls Mono Ltd BL
442, Simon Jennings
449, Simon Jennings
450, Simon Jennings TL
451, Simon Jennings UR, CR;
452, Simon Jennings
453, Rodney Hyett/Elizabeth Whiting Associates CL; Simon Jennings BC; Marshalls Mono Ltd TR
455, Mixamate BL
459, Wickes Building Supplies Ltd, BR
461, Ronseal Ltd TR; Cement and Concrete Association TC, BCL
462, Barlow Tyrie Ltd TL; Marshalls Mono Ltd BL
464, Forest Garden Plc C; Simon Jennings L; Marshalls Mono Ltd B
465, Forest Garden Plc UCR; Marshalls Mono Ltd TR
466, Liberon Ltd TL
467, Marshalls Mono Ltd CR; Simon Jenning BR
468, Marshalls Mono Ltd TL
470, Lotus Water Gardens TL, BL
471, Simon Jennings
472, Stapeley Gardens CR; Albert Jackson R
473, Stapeley Gardens L
476, Marshalls Mono Ltd
478, David Day

Every effort has been made to trace copyright holders. We apologize in advance for any unintentional omissions and would be pleased to insert the appropriate acknowledgement in any subsequent edition.

Acknowledgements

The authors and publishers would like to thank the many people and organisations who helped in the creation of this book.

For their generous support in contributing tools and products for photography:

CAPEL MANOR
www.capel.ac.uk

DRAPER TOOLS
www.draper.co.uk

L.G HARRIS & CO. LTD
www.lgharris.co.uk

IRWIN TOOLS
www.irwin.co.uk

MONUMENT TOOLS
www.monument-tools.com

PLASPLUGS
www.plasplugs.com

SAINT GOBAIN ADHESIVES
www.saint-gobain.co.uk

SCREWFIX
www.screwfix.com

WOLFCRAFT
www.wolfcraft.co.uk

For supplying images and products for artist's reference and photography:

Amtico www.amtico.com
Aqualisa Products Ltd www.aqualisa.co.uk
Armstrong World Industries Ltd www.armstrong-ceilings.co.uk
Arthur Sanderson and Sons Ltd
AVS Fencing www.avsfencing.co.uk
Axminster Carpets Ltd www.axminster-carpets.co.uk
Axminster Power Tool Centre www.axminster.co.uk
BASF Construction Chemicals Ltd www.basf-cc.co.uk
Brandon Hire www.brandonhire.plc.uk
Brintons Ltd www.brintons.net
British Gypsum Ltd
Burley Appliances www.burley.co.uk
C. Brewer & Sons Ltd
Charnwood www.charnwood.com
Chemical Building Products www.chemicalbuildingproducts.co.uk
Ciga www.ciga.co.uk
City Sound www.secondaryglazing.org.uk
Crown Paint www.crownpaint.co.uk
Crucial Trading www.crucial-trading.com
Cuprinol www.cuprinol.co.uk
Dampcoursing Ltd www.dampcoursing.com
DEVI Electroheat Ltd www.devi.co.uk
Devimat www.devi.co.uk
Drakes Plumbing Supplies www.drakes.biz
Dreadnought Tiles www.dreadnought-tiles.co.uk
Eliza Tinsley Ltd www.elizatinsley.co.uk
Energy Saving Trust www.energysavingtrust.org.uk

ERA products www.era-security.com
Evergreener www.evergreener.com
Expamet www.expamet.co.uk
Fired Earth www.firedearth.com
Flotex www.flotex.co.uk
Forbo Flooring www.forbo-flooring.co.uk
Franke UK Ltd www.franke.co.uk
Glidevale www.glidevale.com
Green Tiles
Hammerite www.hammerite.com
Hepworth Plumbing Products Ltd
Hewden www.hewden.co.uk
Honeywell www.honeywell.com
Hozelock www.hozelock.co.uk
Hunter Plastics Ltd
IBP Conex Ltd www.ibpgroup.com
Ideal Standard www.ideal-standard.co.uk
Ikea www.ikea.com
International Paints
www.international-paints.co.uk
Jeld Wen www.jeldwen.co.uk
Jewson Ltd www.jewson.co.uk
Johnson Tiles www.johnson-tiles.com
Judge Ceiling Systems
www.judge-ceilings.co.uk
Kidde Safety Europe Ltd
www.kiddesafetyeurope.co.uk
Knauf www.knaufinsulation.com
Ladderstore.com www.ladderstore.com
Marley Floors Ltd
Marshalls Plc www.marshalls.co.uk
Meshdirect www.meshdirect.co.uk
Metpost www.metpost.co.uk
Mira Showers www.mirashowers.com
Mixamate www.mixamate.co.uk
Myson www.myson.co.uk
New Career Skills Ltd
www.newcareerskills.co.uk
Oase www.oase-livingwater.com
The Original Box Sash Window Company
www.boxsash.com
OutlandStone www.outlandstone.co.uk
Own Label Products www.o-l-p.com
The Plumb Center www.plumbcenter.co.uk
Radiating Style www.radiatingstyle.com
Rangemaster www.rangemaster.co.uk
Rayotec Ltd www.rayotec.com
Response Electronics Plc
Ring Ltd www.ring.ltd.uk
Rolawn www.rolawn.co.uk
Ronseal www.ronseal.co.uk
Rosebys www.rosebys.co.uk
The Rubber Tile Flooring Company
www.therubberflooringcompany.co.uk
Ruberoid www.ruberoid.co.uk
Rustins Ltd
Ryalux www.ryalux.com
Sadolin www.sadolin.co.uk
Sanderson www.sanderson-online.co.uk
Sandtoft www.sandtoft.co.uk
Solartwin www.solartwin.com
Sorex Ltd www.sorex.com
SoundStop www.soundstop.co.uk
Stanley Europe
Stapeley Water Gardens www.stapeleywg.com
Thermawrap www.thermawrap.co.uk
Timber Repair Systems www.timber-repair.co.uk
Topps Tiles www.toppstiles.co.uk
Touchwood Products www.sashwindows.info
Velux www.velux.co.uk
Vent-Axia www.vent-axia.com

For their time, creative input and generous assistance:

Andrew Adams
at Airedale: Ruth Prentice, David Murphy, Amanda Jensen, Anthony Cairns and Murdo Culver
John Armstrong
Ryan Beecroft
Bill and Daphne Bees
Brian Bowling
Doug and Mary Bridle
Matthew Brown
at Capel Manor: Julie Ryan, Roger Sygrave, Ian, Terry, Jim and Chris
Rachel Carr
Simon Chapman
Martin Clancy
John Collier
Andrew Cross
Roger and Louise Etherington
Andrew Gillman
Neal Hancock
Nick Harris
Martin and Jill Herman
Joanna Holmes
Mike Jackson
Maureen Jackson
Michael and Valerie Judge
Gawaine Lewis
Meriam Mohammed
Siobhan Moynihan
Simon Osbourne
Doreen Pope
James Prentice
Clive Richardson
Amanda Smith
Andrew Smith
Anna Stanley
Michelle Thompson
Stephen White
Mark Whiting
Lorraine Willis

For their general assistance:

151 Products Ltd www.151.co.uk
3M United Kingdom Plc www.3m.com/uk
AEI Security & Communications Ltd
www.aeisecurity.com
Akzo Nobel Specialist Coatings
www.akzonobel.uk.com
Allen Concrete www.alleconcrete.co.uk
Ardex UK Ltd www.ardex.co.uk
Aristocast Originals Ltd www.plasterware.net
Aritech UK
Armitage Shanks Ltd www.armitage-shanks.co.uk
Armstrong World Industries Ltd
www.armstrong.com
Blue Circle Cement
Bonar and Flotex Ltd www.bonarfloors.com
Bondaglass-Voss Ltd
Border Stone www.borderstone.co.uk
Bostik Ltd www.bostik.com
Bradstone, Aggregate Industries UK Ltd www.bradstone.com
C. Brewer & Sons Ltd www.brewers.co.uk
The Brick Development Association
www.brick.org.uk
British Cement Association
www.cementindustry.co.uk
British Coal Corporation
British Flue and Chimney Manufacturers' Association ww.feta.co.uk/bfcma/index.htm
British Gas www.britishgas.co.uk
British Gypsum Ltd
www.british-gypsum.bpb.com
British Red Cross Society www.redcross.org.uk
Building Research Establishment
www.bre.co.uk
Richard Burbidge Decorative Timber
www.richardburbidge.co.uk
Caradon Catnic Ltd
Caradon Everest Ltd
Caradon Mira Ltd
Caradon Plumbing Ltd
The Carpet Bureau
Carvall Group Ceramics Ltd
www.carvallgroup.com
Castle Care Tech Ltd
www.castle-caretech.com
Castle Nails
Cavity Insulation Guarantee Agency
www.ciga.co.uk
Celcon Ltd www.celcon.co.uk
Celotex Ltd www.celotex.co.uk
Cementone Beaver Ltd
A. W. Champion Ltd www.championtimber.com
Creda www.creda.co.uk
Crittall Steel Windows
www.crittall-windows.co.uk
Custom Audio Designs
www.customaudiodesigns.co.uk
Daryl Showers
www.daryl-showers.co.uk
Detection Systems (UK)
Dixon Group Wallcoverings Ltd
Dow Construction Products
www.dow.com/styrofoam/europe
Draught Proofing Advisory Association Ltd
www.dpaa-association.org.uk
Eco Deck UK Ltd www.ecodeckuk.com
Ecomax Accoustics Ltd
Energy Efficiency Office
English Abrasives & Chemicals Ltd
Environment Agency
www.environment-agency.gov.uk
Eswa Ltd www.eswa.co.uk
Everbuild Building Products Ltd
www.everbuild.co.uk
Evode Ltd
Excel Industries Ltd www.excelfibre.com
External Wall Insulation Association
Federation of Master Builders www.fmb.org.uk
Fire Protection Association www.thefpa.co.uk
Artur Fischer (UK) Ltd www.fischer.co.uk
Forest Garden Plc www.forestgarden.co.uk
Furnell Abrasives Ltd
www.national-abrasives.com
GardTec Ltd
GET Plc www.getplc.com
Glass and Glazing Federation www.ggf.co.uk
Greenbrook Electrical Plc
www.greenbrook.co.uk
Hans Grohe Ltd
Hanson Brick www.hansonbrick.com
Henkel Ltd
Hepworth Building Products
www.hepworth.co.uk
Hepworth Heating Ltd
Hire Technicians Group Ltd www.hiretech.biz
Home Office Communication Directorate
www.homeoffice.gov.uk/about-us/organisation/directorate-search/cd
Humbrol Ltd
Hunter Plastics Ltd www.hunterplastics.co.uk
ICI Paints www.icipaints.com
Heuga – Interface Europe Ltd
www.interfaceflooring.com
Institution of Structural Engineers
www.istructe.org.uk
IPPEC Heating Systems www.ippec.co.uk
Kalon Decorative Products
www.sigmakalon.co.uk
Langlow Products Division
Laserfix Ltd
Lectros International Ltd www.lectros.com
Liberon Ltd www.liberon.co.uk
LightGraphix Ltd www.lightgraphix.co.uk
London Fire and Emergency Planning Authority
www.london-fire.gov.uk/lfepa/lfepa.asp
London & Lancashire Rubber Co. Ltd
www.londonandlancs.com
Lovesee Glazing
Marley Eternit www.marleyeternit.co.uk
Marley Extrusions Ltd
www.marleyplumbinganddrainage.com
Marley Floors Ltd www.marleyfloors.com
McAlpine & Co Ltd
www.mcalpineplumbing.com
Micromark www.micromark.co.uk
MK Electric Ltd www.mkelectric.co.uk
Moseley-Stone
Mykal Industries Ltd www.mykal.co.uk
John Myland Ltd www.mylands.co.uk
National Approval Council for Security Systems
www.nsi.org.uk
National Association of Loft Insulation Contractors
http://dubois.vital.co.uk/database/ceed/loft.html
National Cavity Insulation Association
http://dubois.vital.co.uk/database/ceed/cavity.html
Nettlefolds Ltd www.nettlefolds.com
Oase (UK) Ltd
www.oase-livingwater.com
Oracstar Ltd
Packaged Electrical Products Ltd www.o-l-p.com
Palace Chemicals Ltd
www.palacechemicals.co.uk
Pickwick Papers www.pickwickpapers.co.uk
Pilkington Glass Ltd www.pilkington.com
Plasti-Kote Ltd
www.plasti-kote.co.uk
Polycell Products Ltd www.polycell.co.uk
Protech Direct www.protechdirect.co.uk
Quickbond Ltd www.quickbond.co.uk
The Rawlplug Co. Ltd www.rawlplug.co.uk
Redland Roofing Systems Ltd
www.redland.co.uk
Rentokil Products
www.rentokil-initial.com
Response Electronics Plc
www.responseelectronics.com
Rockwool Ltd www.rockwool.co.uk
Royal Institute of British Architects
www.riba.org; www.architecture.com
Royal Institute of Chartered Surveyors
www.rics.org
Royal Town Planning Institute www.rtpi.org.uk
Rustins Ltd www.rustins.co.uk
SEAC Ltd www.seac.uk.com
Sound Solution Ltd www.soundstop.co.uk
Spur Shelving Ltd www.spurshelving.co.uk
Steinel (UK) Ltd www.steinel.de
StoneFlair Ltd www.stoneflair.com
Stovax Ltd www.stovax.com
STV International Ltd www.stvpestcontrol.com
Tetrosyl (Building Products) Ltd
www.tetrosyl.com
Tor Coatings Ltd
www.tor-coatings.com
TRADA www.trada.co.uk
Trevi Showers www.trevishowers.co.uk
Triton Plc www.tritonshowers.co.uk
Wickes Building Supplies Ltd www.wickes.co.uk
Willan Building Services Ltd www.willan.co.uk
Winther Browne www.wintherbrowne.co.uk
Xpelair Ltd
www.applied-energy.com/en/xpelair
Yale Security Products www.yalelock.com